CURRENT ISSUES
AND
ENDURING QUESTIONS
A Guide to
Critical Thinking and Argument,
with Readings

CURRENT ISSUES
AND
ENDURING QUESTIONS
A Guide to
Critical Thinking and Argument,
with Readings

SIXTH EDITION

SYLVAN BARNET
Professor of English, Tufts University

HUGO BEDAU
Professor of Philosophy, Tufts University

Bedford/St. Martin's   BOSTON   ◆   NEW YORK

For Bedford/St. Martin's

Developmental Editor: Maura E. Shea
Production Editor: Deborah Baker
Senior Production Supervisor: Catherine Hetmansky
Marketing Manager: Brian Wheel
Editorial Assistant: Emily Goodall
Copyeditor: Rosemary Winfield
Text Design: Sandra Rigney
Cover Design: Donna Lee Dennison
Composition: Pine Tree Composition, Inc.
Printing and Binding: Haddon Craftsmen, Inc.

President: Charles H. Christensen
Editorial Director: Joan E. Feinberg
Editor in Chief: Karen S. Henry
Director of Marketing: Karen Melton
Director of Editing, Design, and Production: Marcia Cohen
Managing Editor: Elizabeth M. Schaaf

Library of Congress Control Number: 2001087438

Manufactured in the United States of America.

6 5 4 3 2 1
f e d c b a

For information, write: Bedford/St. Martin's, 75 Arlington Street, Boston, MA 02116 (617-399-4000)

ISBN: 0–312–39013–0

Acknowledgments

Floyd Abrams, "Save Free Speech" from the *New York Times,* November 23, 1993. Copyright © 1993 by the New York Times Company. Reprinted with the permission of the *New York Times.*

"Affirmative Action Means Justice." © Scott Braley, IMPACT VISUALS.

Anonymous, "Labor 101" from the *Wall Street Journal,* May 12, 2000. Copyright © 2000 by Dow Jones & Company, Inc. Reprinted by permission of the *Wall Street Journal.* All rights reserved.

W. H. Auden, "The Unknown Citizen" from *W. H. Auden: Collected Poems,* edited by Edward Mendelson. Copyright © 1940 and renewed © 1968 by W. H. Auden. Reprinted with the permission of Random House, Inc.

Preface

This book is a text—a book about reading other people's arguments and writing your own arguments—and it is also an anthology—a collection of more than a hundred selections, ranging from Plato to the present, with a strong emphasis on contemporary arguments. In a moment we will be a little more specific about what sorts of essays we include, but first we want to mention our chief assumptions about the aims of a course that might use *Current Issues and Enduring Questions: A Guide to Critical Thinking and Argument, with Readings.*

Probably most students and instructors would agree that, *as critical readers,* students should be able to

- Summarize accurately an argument they have read;
- Locate the thesis of an argument;
- Locate the assumptions, stated and unstated;
- Analyze and evaluate the strength of the evidence and the soundness of the reasoning offered in support of the thesis; and
- Analyze, evaluate, and account for discrepancies among various readings on a topic (for example, explain why certain facts are used, why others are ignored, or why two sources might interpret the same facts differently).

Probably, too, students and instructors would agree that, *as thoughtful writers,* students should be able to

- Imagine an audience and write effectively for it (for instance, by using the appropriate tone and providing the appropriate amount of detail);
- Present information in an orderly and coherent way;
- Be aware of their own assumptions;
- Locate sources and incorporate them into their own writing, not simply by quoting extensively or by paraphrasing but also by having digested material so that they can present it in their own words;
- Properly document all borrowings—not merely quotations and paraphrases but also borrowed ideas; and

- Do all these things in the course of developing a thoughtful argument of their own.

In the first edition of this book we quoted Edmund Burke and John Stuart Mill. Burke said, "He that wrestles with us strengthens our nerves, and sharpens our skill. Our antagonist is our helper." Mill said, "He who knows only his own side of the cause knows little." These two quotations continue to reflect the view of argument that underlies this text: In writing an essay one is engaging in a serious effort to know what one's own ideas are and, having found them, to contribute to a multisided conversation. One is not setting out to trounce an opponent, and that is partly why such terms as *marshaling evidence, attacking an opponent,* and *defending a thesis* are misleading. True, in television talk shows we see people who have made up their minds and who are concerned only with pushing their own views and brushing aside all other views. But we learn by listening to others and also by listening to ourselves. We draft a response to something we have read, and in the very act of drafting we may find—if we think critically about the words we are putting down on paper—we are changing (perhaps slightly, perhaps radically) our own position. Even if we do not drastically change our views, we and our readers at least come to understand why we hold the views we do.

FEATURES

The Text

Parts One and Two   Part One, Critical Thinking and Reading (Chapters 1–3), and Part Two, Critical Writing (Chapters 4–6), together offer a short course in methods of thinking about and in writing arguments. By "thinking" we mean serious analytic thought, including analysis of one's own assumptions (Chapter 1); by "writing" we mean the use of effective, respectable techniques, not gimmicks (such as the notorious note a politician scribbled in the margin of the text of his speech: "Argument weak; shout here"). For a delightfully wry account of the use of gimmicks, we recommend that you consult "The Art of Controversy" in *The Will to Live* by the nineteenth-century German philosopher Arthur Schopenhauer. Schopenhauer reminds readers that a Greek or Latin quotation (however irrelevant) can be impressive to the uninformed and that one can knock down almost any proposition by loftily saying, "That's all very well in theory, but it won't do in practice."

We offer lots of advice about how to set forth an argument, but we do not offer instruction in one-upmanship. Rather, we discuss responsible ways of arguing persuasively. We know, however, that before one can write a persuasive argument, one must clarify one's own ideas—a process that includes arguing with oneself—to find out what one really thinks about a problem. Therefore, we devote Chapter 1 to critical thinking, Chapters 2 and 3 to critical reading, and Chapters 4, 5, and 6 to critical writing. Parts One and Two together contain thirty readings (six are student papers) for analysis and discussion. Moreover, each of the three chapters in Part One contains a casebook—a group of closely related readings. For instance, in Chapter 1, the casebook on testing consists of three essays: The first, by Paul Goodman, urges that grades be abolished; the second, Leon Botstein's op-ed piece arguing that standardized tests get in the way of learning, is accompanied by four letters of response; the third is Diane Ravitch's "In Defense of Testing."

All of the essays in the book are accompanied by questions.[1] This is not surprising, given the emphasis we place on asking questions in order to come up with ideas for writing. Among the chief questions that writers should ask, we suggest, are "What is X?" and "What is the value of X?" (pp. 190–95). By asking such questions—for instance (to look only at these two types of questions), "Is the fetus a person?" or "Is Arthur Miller a better playwright than Tennessee Williams?"—a writer probably will find ideas coming, at least after a few moments of head-scratching. The device of developing an argument by identifying issues is, of course, nothing new. Indeed, it goes back to an ancient method of argument used by classical rhetoricians, who identified a *stasis* (an issue) and then asked questions about it: Did X do such-and-such? If so, was the action bad? If bad, how bad? (Finding an issue or *stasis*—a position where one stands—by asking questions is discussed in Chapter 5.)

In keeping with our emphasis on writing as well as reading, we raise issues not only of what can roughly be called the "content" of the essays but also of what can (equally roughly) be called the "style"—that is, the ways in which the arguments are set forth. Content and style, of course, cannot finally be kept apart. As Cardinal Newman said, "Thought and meaning are inseparable from each other.... *Style is thinking out into language.*" In our questions we sometimes ask the student to evaluate the effectiveness of an essay's opening paragraph, to explain a shift in tone from one paragraph to the next, or to characterize the persona of the author as revealed in the whole essay. In short, the book is not designed as an introduction to some powerful ideas (though in fact it is that, too); it is designed as an aid to writing thoughtful, effective arguments on important political, social, scientific, ethical, and religious issues.

The essays reprinted in this book also illustrate different styles of argument that arise, at least in part, from the different disciplinary backgrounds of the various authors. Essays by journalists, lawyers, judges, social scientists, policy analysts, philosophers, critics, activists, and other writers—including undergraduates—will be found in these pages. The authors develop and present their views in arguments that have distinctive features reflecting their special training and concerns. The differences in argumentative styles found in these essays foreshadow the differences students will

---

[1]With a few exceptions, the paragraphs in the essays are, for ease of reference, numbered in increments of five (5, 10, 15, and so forth). The exceptions involve essays in which paragraphs are uncommonly long; in such cases, every paragraph is numbered.

encounter in the readings assigned in many of their other courses. (Part Three, which offers a philosopher's view, a logician's view, a moralist's view, a psychologist's view, a lawyer's view, and a literary critic's view, also reveals differences in argumentative styles.)

Parts One and Two, then, are a preliminary (but we hope substantial) discussion of such topics as *identifying assumptions, getting ideas by means of invention strategies, using printed and electronic sources, interpreting visual sources, evaluating kinds of evidence,* and *organizing material,* as well as an introduction to some ways of thinking.

Part Three   Part Three, Further Views on Argument, consists of Chapters 7–12. The first of these, Chapter 7, A Philosopher's View: The Toulmin Model, is a summary of the philosopher Stephen Toulmin's method for analyzing arguments. This summary will assist those who wish to apply Toulmin's methods to some of the readings in our book. The next chapter, A Logician's View: Deduction, Induction, Fallacies, offers a more rigorous analysis of these topics than is usually found in composition courses and reexamines from a logician's point of view material already treated briefly in Chapter 3. Chapter 9, A Moralist's View: Ways of Thinking Ethically (new to this edition), consists of a discussion of amoral, immoral, and moral reasoning, A Checklist for Moral Reasoning, and three challenging essays. Chapter 10, A Lawyer's View: Steps toward Civic Literacy, introduces students to some basic legal concepts such as the distinction between civil and criminal cases, and then gives majority and minority opinions in three cases: burning the flag, searching students for drugs, and establishing the right to an abortion. We accompany these judicial opinions with questions that invite the student to participate in these exercises in democracy. Chapter 11, A Psychologist's View: Rogerian Argument, with an essay by psychotherapist Carl R. Rogers, complements the discussion of audience, organization, and tone in Chapter 5. Finally, Chapter 12, A Literary Critic's View: Arguing about Literature, should help students to see the things literary critics argue about and *how* they argue. Students can apply what they learn not only to the literary readings that appear in the chapter (poems by Robert Frost and Andrew Marvell and stories by Kate Chopin) but also to the readings that appear in Part Six, Enduring Questions, where we include eleven poems, two stories, and a play.

The Anthology

Part Four   Part Four, Current Issues: Occasions for Debate (Chapters 13–18), begins with A Checklist for Analyzing a Debate and then offers six pairs of arguments — on abortion, affirmative action, gay marriage, gun control, sex education, and women in the military — all of which are accompanied by topics for critical thinking that widen the student's view of the issues. Here, as in Part Five, many of the selections (drawn from such sources as the *National Review* and the *New York Times*) are very short—scarcely longer than the 500-word essays that students are often asked to write.

Part Five   Part Five, Current Issues: Casebooks (Chapters 19–26), gives the student eight casebooks—that is, several voices discussing an issue. For example, a casebook on business ethics (Chapter 19) begins with Nobel Prize–winner Milton Friedman's classic essay, "The Social Responsibility of Business Is to Increase Its Profits," follows it with three letters responding to Friedman, and then gives an essay by the chief executive officer of Levi Strauss & Co., who argues that because ethical considerations pay off, businesses must be environmentally conscious. This casebook concludes with a cluster of materials on Nike's moral responsibilities, including a statement by Nike's founder and CEO, letters of response to the statement, and three articles from business publications. The casebook on privacy (Chapter 24) includes several e-mail postings.

Part Six   Part Six, Enduring Questions: Essays, Stories, Poems, and a Play (Chapters 27–29), extends the arguments to three topics: Chapter 27, What Is the Ideal Society? (the nine voices here range from Thomas More, Thomas Jefferson, and Martin Luther King Jr., to literary figures W. H. Auden, Langston Hughes, and Ursula K. Le Guin); Chapter 28, How Free Is the Will of the Individual within Society? (among the ten authors are Plato, Susan Glaspell, George Orwell, and Stanley Milgram); and Chapter 29, What Are the Grounds of Religious Faith? (among the ten selections are writings by Paul, Bertrand Russell, Emily Dickinson, and Judith Ortiz Cofer).

Instructor's Edition

The Instructor's Edition includes an appendix, Resources for Teaching, with detailed suggestions about ways to approach the essays and with many additional suggestions for writing.

A Shorter Edition

For instructors who do not require a text with a large number of essays, a shorter edition of this book, *Critical Thinking, Reading, and Writing: A Brief Guide to Argument,* Fourth Edition, is also available. The shorter version contains Parts One, Two, and Three (Chapters 1–12) of the present book as well as its own Casebook on the State and the Individual, drawn from readings in the longer edition.

WHAT'S NEW TO THE SIXTH EDITION

We have made some significant changes in the sixth edition that we believe enrich the book:

- **Fresh and timely new readings**   Forty-six of the readings (40 percent) are new, as are fourteen topics of current interest. New topics include standardized tests, women in the military, business ethics, juvenile crime and punishment, and privacy.

- **Coverage of Visual Rhetoric: Images as Arguments**   This discusson (in Chapter 3) helps students to analyze a variety of images, including advertisements, cartoons, documentary photographs, and public monuments. Some thirty images are integrated throughout the book.

- **Unique coverage of moral reasoning**   Because moral reasoning underlies most arguments on controversial issues, a new chapter called A Moralist's View: Ways of Thinking Ethically (Chapter 9) explains the differences between amoral, immoral, and moral reasoning and presents three readings that employ moral reasoning.

- **Updated and expanded research features**   Chapter 6, Using Sources, has been revised to provide the latest information on finding, evaluating, and documenting electronic and other sources. A new student essay documented in APA style now complements the student essay in MLA style.

- **More student writing**   The book now includes six essays on current issues by student writers, as well as two student literary analysis essays, and several letters written by students in response to newspaper op-ed pieces. These essays serve not only as models but also as arguments for analysis.

- **New companion Web site**   The companion Web site at <www.bedfordstmartins.com/barnetbedau> offers students and instructors an extensive set of annotated links on argument and on the controversial topics in the book. Brain-teasers allow students to test their understanding of logic and analysis, and instructors can share assignments and ideas for syllabi with colleagues across the nation.

In preparing the sixth edition we were greatly aided by suggestions from instructors who were using the fifth edition. In line with their recommendations, in Part One, Critical Thinking and Reading, nine of the eighteen readings are new — and some are accompanied by letters of response. New casebooks in Part One are devoted to tests (Chapter 1) and to the use of computers in college (Chapter 3). Also new in Chapter 3 is a discussion entitled Visual Rhetoric: Images as Arguments, which includes eleven illustrations ranging from Maya Lin's Vietnam Veterans Memorial to a cover from the *Utne Reader* showing Mr. Spock from television's *Star Trek*. This discussion will help students to analyze the twenty-odd images that appear elsewhere in the book.

Part Two, Critical Writing, includes four new essays (one of them is a student's research paper) and an amplified discussion of electronic sources.

In Part Three we have added Chapter 9, A Moralist's View; we accompany our discussion of amoral reasoning, immoral reasoning, and moral reasoning with three new readings, one of which is Garrett Hardin's classic essay, "Lifeboat Ethics: The Case against Helping the Poor."

In Part Four, Current Issues: Occasions for Debate, and Part Five, Current Issues: Casebooks, we have changed some of the readings in the issues that we retained, and we have introduced new issues—women in the military, business ethics, juvenile crime, and privacy.

Part Six, Enduring Questions: Essays, Stories, Poems, and a Play, now includes in Chapter 27, What Is the Ideal Society?, a substantial passage from Edward Bellamy's *Looking Backward.*

There can be no doubt about the urgency of the topics that we have added or about the need to develop civic literacy, but there can be lots of arguments about the merits of the positions offered in the selections. That's where the users of the book—students and instructors—come in.

ACKNOWLEDGMENTS

Finally, it is our pleasant duty to thank those who have strengthened the book by their advice: Alan Ainsworth, Houston Community College; Roy M. Anker, Calvin College; Jim Arlandson, California Baptist College; Robert Baird, University of Illinois; Janet Barnwell, Louisiana State University; Claudia Basha, Victor Valley College; Mark Bedau; Frank Beesley, University of Nebraska at Lincoln; Donavin Bennes, University of North Dakota; Jack A. Bennett, Sinclair Community College; Laurie J. Bergamini, State University of New York at Plattsburgh; Jeffrey Berger, Community College of Philadelphia; B. J. Bowman, Radford University; Anthony Boyle, Fairleigh Dickinson University; Moana Boyle, Ricks College; Beverly M. Braud, Southwest Texas State University; Sally J. Bright, Tulsa Community College; Edward Brooks, Bergen Community College; Duane Bruce, University of Hartford; Jacintha Burke, King's College; Jim Butterfield, Western Michigan University; Jenna Call, Cape Fear Community College; Mary Cantrell, Tulsa Community College; Janet Carter, Bridgewater State College; Brandon Cesmat, Palomar College; Claire Chantell, University of Illinois at Urbana–Champaign; Jo Chern, University of Wisconsin at Green Bay; Barbara G. Clark, Adams State College; Denise Clark, Santa Clara University; Elsie Clark, Durham Technical Community College; James Clarke, Washington State University; Lorna Clymer, University of California at Santa Barbara; Sherill Cobb, Collin County Community College; Bobbie Cohen, Florida University; Paul Cohen, Southwest Texas

State University; Daniel F. Collins, Cape Fear Community College; Minnie A. Collins, Seattle Central Community College; Neil Connelly, Cape Fear Community College; Marie Conte, California State University–Dominguez Hills; Genevieve Coogan, Houston Northwest Community College; Dr. Michael E. Cooley, Berry College; Marcia Corcoran, Evergreen Valley College; Susan Carolyn Cowan, University of Southern California; Jody Cross-Hansen, Hofstra University; Linda Daigle, Houston Central Community College; Susan Dalton, Almanace Community College; Anne D'Arcy, California State University–Hayward; Fara Darland, Scottsdale Community College; James M. Decker, Olive–Harvey College; Robert Denham, Roanoke College; Kent R. DeVault, Central Washington University; Allen DiWederburg, Clackamas Community College; Carl Dockery, Tri-County Community College; Paula Doctor, Muskegon Community College; Mary Lee Donahue, Rowan University; Alberta M. Dougan, Southeast Missouri State University; Elizabeth Elclepp, Rancho Santiago Community College; Diane El-Rouaiheb, University of Louisville; Hal Enger, San Diego Mesa College; R. Scott Evans, University of the Pacific; Lynn H. Ezzell, Cape Fear Community College; Dianne Fallon, State University of New York at Binghamton; Amy Farmer, University of Illinois; Sandra Feldman, Sonoma State University; Sister Isabella Ferrell, Cardinal Stritch College; John Finnegan, West Liberty State College; Jane Fischer, Southwest State University; Robert H. Fleeson, New Hampshire College; Anne Marie Frank, Elmhurst College; Amy Freed, Virginia Polytechnic Institute; George Freund, Santa Rose Junior College; Tamara Fritze, Utah Valley State College; Stephen Fullmer, Utah Valley State College; Michael J. Galgano, James Madison University; Joseph E. Geist, Central Methodist College; David Glaub, University of Wisconsin–Parkside; Sheryl Gobble, San Diego City College; Stuart Goodman, Duke University; Nathanael Gough, Forsyth Technical Community College; Mary Anne F. Grabarek, Durham Technical Community College; Tim Gracyk, Santa Clara University; Becky C. Graham, Livingston University; Rebecca Graham, University of Minnesota–Morris; Richard Grande, Pennsylvania State University; Mark A. Graves, Bowling Green State University; Kate Gray, Clackamas Community College; Dr. Laura Gray-Rosendale, Northern Arizona University; Monika E. Gross, Bowie State University; Verge Hagopian, Orange Coast College; Dennis R. Hall, University of Louisville; William M. Hamlin, Idaho State University; William Hampl, Bridgewater State College; Donald Heidt, College of the Canyons; Charles Heimler, California State University at Hayward; Janet Ruth Heller, Grand Valley State University; John C. Herold, Elon College; Edwin L. Hetfield Jr., Onondaga Community College; Katherine Hoffman, Roanoke College; Pau-San Hoh, Marist College; Susan Honeyman, Lawrence Technological University; Cathy Hope, Tarleton State University; Diane W. Howard, Valdosta State University; Rosemary T. Hunkeler, University of Wisconsin–Parkside; Barbara Hunter, Wright College; Joan Hutchison, Oakland Community

College; Dr. Brian D. Ingraffia, Biola University; Shelly Jaffray, Rancho Santiago Community College; Carol A. Jagielnik, University of Wisconsin–Parkside; Bonita Nahoum Jaros, Rancho Santiago College; Alison Jasper, California Polytechnic State University; Heather Bryant Jordan, Harvard University; Janet Juhnke, Kansas Wesleyan University; Diane M. Kammeyer, Anoka-Ramsey Community College; Priscilla Kelly, Slippery Rock University; Michael Kent, San Bernardino Valley College; Mary Jane Kinnebrew, San Jacinto College Central; Geoffrey Klinger, University of Iowa; Bobbie Knable, Tufts University; Prudence Kohl, Baldwin–Wallace College; Catherine W. Kroll, Sonoma State University; Elaine W. Kromhout, Indian River Community College; Lita A. Kurth, Santa Clara University; Dr. Ivonne Lamazares, Miami-Dade Community College–North; Brother Christopher Lambert, Quincy College; Richard L. Larson, Lehman College; John Lawing, Regent University; Erin Lebofsky, Temple University; J. N. Lee, Portland State University; Charles Lefcourt, State University of New York at Buffalo; Cynthia Lehman-Budd, Baldwin–Wallace College; Mary Lenard, University of Wisconsin–Parkside; Elizabeth Lewis, Manhattanville College; L. M. Lewis, University of Texas at Brownsville; Alex Liddie, Trenton State College; Miriam Lilley, College of the Canyons; John Little, James Madison University; Martin Litz, Raymond Walters College; Warren H. Loveless, Indiana State University; Christopher Lukasik, University of Washington; Tom Lynch, California State University at Hayward; Carter Lyons, James Madison University; Nelly McFeely, California State University and Merritt College; Ted McFerrin, Collin County Community College; Natalie McKnight, Boston University; Marcia MacLennan, Kansas Wesleyan University; Kelli Maloy, West Virginia University; Ruth E. Manson, South Dakota State University; Alan P. Marks, University of Maine; Diane Marlett, University of Wisconsin at Green Bay; Brian Massey, Winthrop College; Alice Maudsley, Cleveland State University; James May, Pennsylvania State University; Carl E. Meacham, State University of New York–Oneonta; Dan C. Miller, University of Northern Colorado; Peggy A. Moore, College of Siskiyous; Richard Moore, Delgado Community College; Linda Morante, College of the Desert; Robin Morris, Cape Fear Community College; Mary Munsil, University of Southern California; Cris Newport, New Hampshire Technical Institute; Melanie Ohler; Leonard Orr, Washington State University; Roswell Park, State University of New York at Buffalo; Scott Payne, University of Louisville; Robert Peltier, Trinity College; Nancy P. Pope, Washington University; Constance Putnam; Jan Rainbird, California State University at Fullerton; Sally Lynn Raines, West Virginia University; Carol Redmore, Highland Community College; Elaine Reed, Kutztown University; M. Resnick, State University of New York at Farmingdale; Dan Richards; Susan Roberson, Auburn University; Helen M. Robinette, Glassboro State College; Linda Rosekraus, State University of New York, College at Cortland; Barbara E. Roshak, Monmouth University; Jennifer

O. Rosti, Roanoke College; Julie H. Rubio, University of Southern California at Long Beach; Rebecca Sabounchi, University of Texas; Christine Sauer, The University of Findlay; Suzette Schlapkohl, Scottsdale Community College; Henry Schwarzschild; Brad Scott, American River College of Golden Gate University; Harsh Sharma, Buffalo State College; Hassell B. Sledd, Slippery Rock University; Sydney J. Slobodnik, University of Illinois at Urbana–Champaign; Andrew J. Smyth, St. Louis University; Daniel R. Snyder, Sagwan Valley University; Lynn Steiner, Cuesta College; Skaidrite Stelzer, University of Toledo; Elisabeth Stephens, University of North Carolina at Greensboro; Ed Stieve, Nova College; Barbara W. Stewart, Long Beach City College; Steven Strang, Massachusetts Institute of Technology; Suba Subbarao, Oakland Community College; Catherine Sutton, University of Louisville; Richard C. Taylor, East Carolina University; Diane Thompson, Harrisburg Area Community College; Eve Thompson, College of the Siskiyous; Linda Toonen, University of Wisconsin at Green Bay; David Tumpleman, Monroe Community College; Pauline Uchmanowicz, University of Rhode Island; Lynn A. Walkiewicz, Cazenovia College; Kathleen Walsh, Central Oregon Community College; Nancy Weingart, John Carrol University; Stephen White; Phyllis C. Whitesoll, Franklin and Marshall College; Allen D. Widerburg, Clackamas Community College; Marilyn Wienk, Elmira College; Stephen Wilhoit, University of Dayton; Josie Williams, Durham Technical Community College; Joseph Wilson, Anna Maria College; James Yard, Delaware Valley College; Michelle L. Zath, Berry College; Bruce D. Zessin, University of Wisconsin at Waukesha.

We would like especially to thank Janet E. Gardner of the University of Massachusetts, Dartmouth, who revised the research chapter to encompass the latest advice and information on using electronic sources and who helped prepare the new section on analyzing images. We would also like to thank Martha Friedman and Virginia Creeden who adeptly managed art research and text permissions respectively.

We are also indebted to the people at Bedford/St. Martin's, especially to our editor Maura Shea, who is wise, patient, supportive, and unfailingly helpful. Steve Scipione, our editor for all of the preceding editions, has left a lasting impression on us and on the book; without his work on the first five editions, there probably would not be a sixth. Others at Bedford/St. Martin's to whom we are deeply indebted include Charles H. Christensen, Joan E. Feinberg, Elizabeth Schaaf, Deborah Baker, Catherine Hetmansky, and Emily Goodall, all of whom have offered countless valuable (and invaluable) suggestions. Intelligent, informed, firm yet courteous, persuasive—all of these folk know how to think and how to argue.

Brief Contents

Contents

MAX SHULMAN, Love Is a Fallacy   329

*A short story about the limits of logic: "Can you give me one logical reason
why you should go steady with Petey Bellows?"*

9 A Moralist's View: Ways of Thinking Ethically   338

AMORAL REASONING   339

IMMORAL REASONING   341

MORAL REASONING: A CLOSER LOOK   343

CRITERIA FOR MORAL RULES   345

A CHECKLIST FOR MORAL REASONING   346

United States v. Holmes   348

*Who ought to survive when all cannot? Here is the decision a judge reached
in a case that involved throwing some passengers out of an overcrowded
lifeboat.*

PETER SINGER, Famine, Affluence, and Morality   356

*A moral philosopher argues that it is the responsibility of affluent nations,
such as the United States, to assist poor nations in which people are starving
to death.*

GARRETT HARDIN, Lifeboat Ethics: The Case against Helping
the Poor   368

*A professor of human ecology argues that a prosperous country is like a
lifeboat that is nearly full; taking on additional passengers—helping the
desperately needy of poor countries—will, he says, swamp the lifeboat.*

10 A Lawyer's View: Steps toward Civic Literacy   379

CIVIL AND CRIMINAL CASES   380

TRIAL AND APPEAL   381

DECISION AND OPINION   381

MAJORITY, CONCURRING, AND DISSENTING
OPINIONS   382

FACTS AND LAW   383

Part Four

Part One

CRITICAL THINKING AND READING

1

Critical Thinking

The comedian Jack Benny cultivated the stage personality of a penny-pincher. In one of his skits a stickup man thrusts a gun into Benny's ribs and says, "Your money or your life." Utter silence. The robber, getting no response, and completely baffled, repeats, "Your money or your life." Short pause, followed by Benny's exasperated reply: "I'm *thinking*, I'm *thinking*!"

Without making too much of this gag, we want to point out that Benny is using the word *thinking* in the sense that we use it in *critical thinking*. *Thinking*, by itself, can mean almost any sort of mental activity, from idle daydreaming ("During the chemistry lecture I kept thinking about how I'd like to go camping") to careful analysis ("I'm thinking about whether I can afford more than one week — say two weeks — of camping in the Rockies," or even "I'm thinking about *why* Benny's comment strikes me as funny," or, "I'm thinking about why you find Benny's comment funny and I don't").

In short, when we add the adjective *critical* to the noun *thinking*, we pretty much eliminate reveries, just as we also eliminate snap judgments. We are talking about searching for hidden assumptions, noticing various facets, unraveling different strands, and evaluating what is most significant. (The word *critical* comes from a Greek word, *krinein*, meaning "to separate," "to choose"; it implies conscious, deliberate inquiry.)

THINKING ABOUT DRIVER'S LICENSES
AND SCHOOL ATTENDANCE:
IMAGINATION, ANALYSIS, EVALUATION

By way of illustration let's think critically about a law passed in West Virginia in 1989. The law provides that although students may drop out of school at the age of sixteen, no dropout younger than eighteen can hold a driver's license.

What ought we to think of such a law?

• Is it fair?
• What is its purpose?
• Is it likely to accomplish its purpose?
• Might it unintentionally do some harm?
• If so, can we weigh the potential harm against the potential good?

Suppose you had been a member of the West Virginia state legislature in 1989: How would you have voted?

In thinking critically about a topic, we try to see it from all sides before we come to our conclusion. We conduct an argument with ourselves, advancing and then questioning opinions.

• What can be said *for* the proposition, and
• What can be said *against* it?

Our first reaction may be quite uncritical, quite unthinking: "What a good idea!" or "That's outrageous!" But critical thinking requires us to reflect further, trying to support our position *and also* trying to see the other side. One can almost say that the heart of critical thinking is a *willingness to face objections to one's own beliefs,* a willingness to adopt a skeptical attitude not only toward authority and toward views opposed to our own but also toward common sense—that is, toward the views that seem obviously right to us. If we assume we have a monopoly on the truth and we dismiss as bigots those who oppose us, or if we say our opponents are acting merely out of self-interest, and we do not in fact analyze their views, we are being critical but we are not engaged in critical thinking.

Critical thinking requires us to use our *imagination,* seeing things from perspectives other than our own and envisioning the likely consequences of our position. (This sort of imaginative thinking—grasping a perspective other than our own and considering the possible consequences of positions—is, as we have said, very different from daydreaming, an activity of unchecked fantasy.)

Thinking critically involves, along with imagination (so that we can see our own beliefs from another point of view), a twofold activity:

analysis, finding the parts of the problem and then separating them, trying to see how things fit together; and

evaluation, judging the merit of our claims and assumptions and the weight of the evidence in their favor.

If we engage in imaginative, analytic, and evaluative thought, we will have second and third ideas; almost to our surprise we may find ourselves adopting a position that we initially couldn't imagine we would hold. As we think about the West Virginia law, we might find ourselves coming up with a fairly wide variety of ideas, each triggered by the preceding idea but not necessarily carrying it a step further. For instance, we may think *X* and then immediately think, "No, that's not quite right. In fact, come to think of it, the opposite of *X* is probably true." We haven't carried *X* further, but we have progressed in our thinking.

WRITING AS A WAY OF THINKING

"To learn to write," Robert Frost said, "is to learn to have ideas." But how do we get ideas? One way, practiced by the ancient Greeks and Romans and still regarded as among the best ways, is to consider what the ancients called **topics,** from the Greek word *topos,* meaning "place," as in our word *topography* (a description or representation of a place). For the ancients, certain topics, put into the form of questions, were in effect places where one went to find ideas. Among the classical *topics* were

- Definition (What is it?);
- Comparison (What is it like or unlike?);
- Relationship (What caused it, and what will it cause?);
- Testimony (What is said about it, for instance by experts?).

All of these topics or idea-generating places will be treated in detail in later chapters, but here we can touch briefly on a few of them.

If we are talking about the West Virginia law, it's true that we won't get ideas by asking questions concerning definition, but we may generate ideas by asking ourselves if this law is like any other (and, if so, how well did the corresponding law work) and by asking what caused this law and what it may in turn cause. Similarly, if we go to the topic of testimony, we may want to find out what some students, teachers, parents, police officers, and lawmakers have to say.

If you think you are at a loss for ideas when confronted with an issue (and when confronted with an assignment to write about it), you probably will find ideas coming to you if you turn to the relevant classical topics and begin jotting down your responses. (In classical terminology, you are engaged in the process of **invention,** from the Latin *invenire,* "to come upon," "to find.") Seeing your ideas on paper—even in the briefest form—will help bring other ideas to mind and will also help you to evaluate them. For instance, after jotting down ideas as they come and responses to them,

1. You might go on to organize them into two lists, pro and con;
2. Next, you might delete ideas that, when you come to think about them, strike you as simply wrong or irrelevant; and
3. Then you might develop those ideas that strike you as pretty good.

You probably won't know where you stand until you have gone through some such process. It would be nice if we could make a quick decision, immediately justify it with three excellent reasons, and then give three further reasons showing why the opposing view is inadequate. In fact, however, we almost never can come to a reasoned decision without a good deal of preliminary thinking.

Consider again the West Virginia law. Here is a kind of inner dialogue that you might engage in as you think critically about it:

> The purpose is to give students an incentive to stay in school by making them pay a price if they choose to drop out.
>
> Adolescents will get the message that education really is important.
>
> But come to think of it, *will* they? Maybe they will see this as just another example of adults bullying young people.
>
> According to a newspaper article, the dropout rate in West Virginia decreased by 30 percent in the year after the bill was passed.
>
> Well, that sounds good, but is there any reason to think that kids who are pressured into staying really learn anything? The *assumption* behind the bill is that if would-be dropouts stay in school, they—and society—will gain. But is the assumption sound? Maybe such students will become resentful, will not learn anything, and may even be so disruptive that they will interfere with the learning of other students.

Notice how part of the job is *analytic,* recognizing the elements or complexities of the whole, and part is *evaluative,* judging the adequacy of all of these ideas, one by one. Both tasks require *imagination.*

So far we have jotted down a few thoughts and then immediately given some second thoughts contrary to the first. Of course, the counterthoughts might not immediately come to mind. For instance, they might not occur until we reread the jottings, or try to explain the law to a friend, or until we sit down and begin drafting an essay aimed at supporting or undermining the law. Most likely, in fact, some good ideas won't occur until a second or third or fourth draft.

Here are some further thoughts on the West Virginia law. We list them more or less as they arose and as we typed them into a word processor— not sorted out neatly into two groups, pro and con, or evaluated as you would want to do in further critical thinking of your own. And of course, a later step would be to organize the material into some useful pattern. As you read, you might jot down your own responses in the margin.

```
Education is not optional, something left for the indi-
vidual to take or not to take--like going to a concert,
jogging, getting annual health checkups, or getting
eight hours of sleep each night. Society has determined
that it is for the public good that citizens have a sub-
stantial education, so we require education up to a cer-
tain age.
```

Come to think about it, maybe the criterion of age doesn't make much sense. If we want an educated citizenry, it would make more sense to require people to attend school until they demonstrated competence in certain matters rather than until they reached a certain age. Exceptions, of course, would be made for mentally retarded persons and perhaps for certain other groups.

What is needed is not legal pressure to keep teenagers in school but schools that hold the interest of teenagers.

A sixteen-year-old usually is not mature enough to make a decision of this importance.

Still, a sixteen-year-old who finds school unsatisfying and who therefore drops out may become a perfectly useful citizen.

Denying a sixteen-year-old a driver's license may work in West Virginia, but it would scarcely work in a state with great urban areas, where most high school students rely on public transportation.

We earn a driver's license by demonstrating certain skills. The state has no right to take away such a license unless we have demonstrated that we are unsafe drivers.

To prevent a person of sixteen from having a driver's license prevents that person from holding certain kinds of jobs, and that's unfair.

A law of this sort deceives adults into thinking that they have really done something constructive for teenage education, but it may work against improving the schools. If we are really serious about educating youngsters, we have to examine the curriculum and the quality of our teachers.

Doubtless there is much that we haven't said, on both sides, but we hope you will agree that the issue deserves thought. In fact, eighteen states now revoke the driver's license of a teenager who drops out of school, and four of these states go even further and revoke the licenses of students whose academic work does not reach a given standard. On the other hand, Louisiana, which for a while had a law like West Virginia's, dropped it in 1997.

If you were a member of a state legislature voting on this proposal, you would *have* to think about the issue. But just as a thought experiment, try to put into writing your tentative views.

One other point about this issue. If you had to think about the matter *today,* you might also want to know whether the West Virginia legislation of 1989 is considered a success and on what basis. That is, you would want to get answers to such questions as the following:

- What sort of evidence tends to support the law or tends to suggest that the law is a poor idea?
- Did the reduction in the dropout rate continue, or did the reduction occur only in the first year following the passage of the law?
- If indeed students who wanted to drop out did not, was their presence in school a good thing, both for them and for their classmates?
- Have some people emerged as authorities on this topic? What makes them authorities, and what do they have to say?
- Has the constitutionality of the bill been tested? With what results?

Some of these questions require you to do **research** on the topic. The questions raise issues of fact, and some relevant evidence probably is available. If you are to arrive at a conclusion in which you can have confidence, you will have to do some research to find out what the facts are.

Even without doing any research, however, you might want to look over the ideas, pro and con, perhaps adding some totally new thoughts or perhaps modifying or even rejecting (for reasons that you can specify) some of those already given. If you do think a bit further about this issue, and we hope that you will, notice an interesting point about *your own* thinking: It probably is not *linear* (moving in a straight line from *A* to *B* to *C*) but *recursive,* moving from *A* to *C* and back to *B* or starting over

---

A CHECKLIST FOR CRITICAL THINKING

Attitudes

✓ Does my thinking show imaginative open-mindedness and intellectual curiosity?

  ✓ Am I willing to examine my assumptions?

  ✓ Am I willing to entertain new ideas—both those that I encounter while reading and those that come to mind while writing?

✓ Am I willing to exert myself—for instance, to do research—to acquire information and to evaluate evidence?

Skills

✓ Can I summarize an argument accurately?

✓ Can I evaluate assumptions, evidence, and inferences?

✓ Can I present my ideas effectively—for instance, by organizing and by writing in a manner appropriate to my imagined audience?

at *C* and then back to *A* and *B*. By zigging and zagging almost despite yourself, you'll get to a conclusion that may finally seem correct. In retrospect it seems obvious; *now* you can chart a nice line from *A* to *B* to *C*—but that was not at all evident to you at the start.

EXAMINING ASSUMPTIONS

In Chapter 3 we will discuss **assumptions** (normally, unexamined beliefs) in some detail, but here we want to emphasize the importance of *examining* assumptions, both those that you encounter when you read and those that underlie your own essays.

Let's think a bit further about the West Virginia driver's license law. What assumptions did the legislature make in enacting this statute? We earlier mentioned one such assumption: If the law helped to keep teenagers from dropping out of school, then that was a good thing for them and for society in general. Perhaps the legislature made this assumption *explicit,* and its advocates defended it on this ground. Perhaps not; maybe the legislature just took this point for granted, leaving this assumption *implicit* (or *tacit*) and unargued, believing that everyone *shared* the assumption. But of course, everyone didn't share it, in particular many teenagers who wanted to drop out of school at sixteen and get their driver's license immediately.

Consider, for instance, a newspaper article concerning antisocial activities on campus, ranging from boisterous behavior (including, say, the shouting of racial epithets) to vandalism, theft, and physical violence (perhaps stimulated by excessive drinking), including rape. Until thirty or so years ago, many colleges assumed that they stood *in loco parentis,* "in the place of a parent." What did this mean? Parents would be unlikely to turn over to the police a youngster who struck a sibling or who dipped into the family cookie jar that contained loose change but rather would handle the matter within the family; in a similar manner, college administrators would seek to educate offenders, perhaps by reprimands, perhaps by probation or suspension, or in the most severe cases by expulsion. But the assumption that colleges ought to engage in this sort of quasi-judicial activity when students are alleged to break the law on campus can be questioned. Should colleges be in the business of judging crimes? Or should they let the courts take care of the offenders?

On May 5 and May 6, 1996, the *New York Times* ran a two-part story on the topic of campus discipline. Newspaper stories of this sort are supposed to report the facts, but inevitably they stimulate responses; people want to offer their views on what they have been reading. They may want to argue that the newspaper report was inaccurate, that it was accurate so far as it went but missed the big issue, or—and here is our point—that it is not enough simply to report such things: "Something must be done!" One reader of the *Times* story was John Silber, who at that time was president of Boston University. He wrote the following op-ed piece (an essay of opinion, printed opposite the editorial page).

As you read Silber's piece, note his assumptions. Does he make any assumptions that you do not share? If so, what are they?

John Silber

Students Should Not Be above the Law

In medieval Europe, there were two parallel court systems: the church's and the king's. The big difference between them was that the church courts did not resort to capital punishment.

In an age when all felonies were capital crimes, the church court was, from the defendants' point of view, considerably more attractive.

Although in theory these courts were limited to clergymen, in practice one proved clerical status by being able to read. And this skill was indulgently tested. One had to read a verse of one's own choosing from the Bible. Hence, the foresighted felon memorized his verse. It assured him of what was known as "benefit of clergy."

This system now seems quaint. But today colleges and universities increasingly tend to circumvent the courts and bury serious criminal cases in their own judicial systems. For instance, a young man at Miami University in Oxford, Ohio, is being allowed to graduate this year even though he was put on "student conduct probation" after he was accused of sexually assaulting an eighteen-year-old freshman who was sleeping.

Colleges have a right to establish judicial codes to assure civility in the classroom, on the campus, and in residences. But the administration of these codes should not give criminals sanctuary from the law.

Yet in many cases administrators successfully press students not to bring criminal behavior to the attention of the police and instead use campus disciplinary proceedings to judge charges of rape, arson, and assault.

No campus court can impose a fine or imprison anyone for a single day. The most serious sanction is expulsion. The penalty for criminal assault is often not much worse than being tossed out of a club.

College judicial systems were originally intended to deal with infractions that were neither felonies nor misdemeanors, perhaps not even torts. And most disciplinary proceedings don't have the basics required for a fair trial: a professional and independent judiciary, enforceable rules of procedure, effective and fairly applied sanctions.

But this is not the most serious problem. Once again, students are receiving special treatment. This treatment was the great scandal of the Vietnam War: The ability to gain entry to and finance college provided a "benefit of clergy" to middle-class young adults who avoided the draft.

Many administrators recoil from the idea that they should 10 operate a collegiate criminal justice system. One can understand why. Outside of law school faculties, few academics have an interest in prosecution.

There is, of course, a simple way for administrators to avoid this entanglement. They can refer all criminal cases to the real criminal justice system. This is their obligation, not merely as administrators but as citizens. (Indeed, there is a name for a citizen who becomes aware of a crime and does not report it: an accessory after the fact.)

Students, predictably, don't like this idea. But in my twenty-five years as a college president, I have heard again and again that students wish to be treated as adults. But I have also heard their repeated demands that they be exempted from the laws of Boston, of Massachusetts, and of the United States.

These two demands are contradictory. Legally, college students are adults. There is, of course, a difference between legal adulthood and substantive adulthood. Some people achieve substantive adulthood at twelve; others never do. But except for the anomaly of the drinking age, everyone can claim legal adulthood at eighteen. And that includes the obligation to be held accountable for criminal behavior—not in juvenile courts or in the even more lenient courts of the academy but in the adult courts.

When colleges and universities usurp the role of the courts, they deny justice to victims. But they also do a terrible wrong to perpetrators, for they deny them entrance into the adult world of responsible action. And in this they fail utterly as educators.

Silber opens his essay by informing the reader about the medieval system of criminal justice, which exempted clerics from the risk of punishments handed out by the criminal courts. By the fourth paragraph we can see the point of this opening; it was to draw a parallel between the assumed unfairness of that medieval practice and (what Silber regards as) the unfair student disciplinary procedures in use by our colleges and universities. Thus, Silber in effect opens his essay on the basis of this crucial assumption:

> It was unfair to give advantages in medieval times to clerics when accused of crimes, and it is no less unfair to give advantages to college students today when they are accused of crimes.

Silber does not argue for this proposition; he does not even assert it explicitly. But he presupposes it as the launching pad for his criticism of today's college disciplinary practices.

In a similar manner, Silber closes his essay with another important assumption:

> College students who are legally adults (eighteen or over) ought to be given the same treatment when accused of crimes as other adults are.

Clearly, college faculty and administrators charged with the responsibility of coping with student misbehavior on campus do not accept this assumption; if they did, the problem that agitates Silber would never have arisen in the first place.

In other places he makes assumptions of no great importance — for instance, this one in paragraph 10:

> Law school faculties have an interest in prosecution.

Whether or not this proposition is true makes little difference to Silber's overall argument; its role is the minor one of reinforcing Silber's claim (no doubt true) that college and university faculty and administrators are typically very uncomfortable when it comes to disciplinary sanctions for students guilty of serious wrongdoing.

In paragraph 8, Silber draws a contrast between the rough-and-ready disciplinary practices on campus and the strict by-the-rules procedures of the criminal courts. This position might stimulate the reader to wonder whether Silber assumes the following:

> College disciplinary practices would be much better if they incorporated the basic procedures that the criminal law requires for a fair trial.

However, by the time the reader reaches paragraph 11 (if not before) it becomes clear that Silber has no interest in this alternative; instead, this is what he assumes:

> There are only two alternatives: Either college authorities continue down the current unfair path, or they wash their hands of any attempt to deal with students accused of criminal behavior by turning them over to the mercies of the criminal courts.

The third alternative — tightening up college disciplinary procedures — is never considered.

In other cases it is not entirely clear just what Silber assumes. He obviously assumes the following:

> College disciplinary practices usurp the role of the courts in the criminal justice system.

But does he also assume that this usurpation occurs only occasionally, or does he think that it happens quite often? Silber gives no statistical data to qualify his assumption, and so his readers are left uncertain whether they are worrying about a major problem affecting hundreds of college students every year or whether Silber is riled up over events of no great frequency.

Do you agree with Silber's assertions that

- It is wrong for college officials in some circumstances to "press students not to bring criminal behavior to the attention of the police and instead use campus disciplinary proceedings to judge charges of rape, arson, and assault" (para. 6)?
- Administrators have an "obligation" to "refer all criminal cases to the real criminal justice system" and their failure to do so makes them "an accessory after the fact" (para. 11)?
- "When colleges and universities usurp the role of the courts, . . . they also do a terrible wrong to perpetrators, for they deny them entrance into the adult world of responsible action" (para. 14)?

You may agree or disagree, in whole or in part, with Silber's argument; but it is important in either case for you to realize that he makes certain assumptions and to think about their implications. For instance, if you agree that administrators who fail to report actions that may later prove to be criminal behavior are "accessories after the fact" (persons who screen or assist felons), are you willing to concede that campus rape crisis centers and other counseling activities may find it impossible to function?

Consider, too, if assumptions allegedly founded on facts are indeed based on facts. Thus, Silber asserts in paragraph 6 that "in many cases administrators successfully press students not to bring criminal behavior to the attention of the police." "Many cases" indicates that he assumes the practice is widespread. If this assumption were questioned, and Silber offered as evidence solely his long experience as a college administrator, would you think that you had to accept the assumption? On the other hand, could you just brush off his assumption as merely the view of one person?

An op-ed piece such as Silber's is likely to set readers thinking — not merely thinking about direct replies or refutations but about related issues. For instance, it might stimulate a reader to respond with a letter to the editor, suggesting that

- College faculty and administrators have a duty to assist young people in understanding what it means to act responsibly and that this duty is not effectively fulfilled by handing them over to the police in borderline cases;
- Alcohol is the chief cause of most fraternity-related violence and crime and that colleges need to do more to educate students about drinking; or
- The real problem is that the *accused* may not get justice because college judicial boards are not restricted to the rules of evidence used by lawyers and judges in court.

One letter-writer was moved by Silber's essay to write about an aspect of the issue that she thought was important and that he had neglected. We reprint this letter here.

Judith H. Christie
What about the Faculty?

To the Editor:

Conspicuously absent from John Silber's argument that colleges not "usurp the role of courts" in dealing with student criminal behavior (Op-Ed, May 9) is any criticism of the manner in which college administrators routinely deal with student complaints of faculty misconduct.

With few exceptions, it has long been the practice of colleges to ignore female students' charges of sexual harassment by male faculty members or to deal with such accusations behind closed doors.

In the rare instances where faculty members are dismissed for sexual harassment, their records do not reflect the reason; that these teachers are free to seek positions at other institutions keeps academia's "dirty little secret" secret.

Faculty members, like students, should be held accountable for their behavior; they, too, are adults and have long enjoyed the "benefit of clergy" exemption Mr. Silber rightly deplores.

- Do you agree that Silber does not raise the point Christie makes?
- Do you think that Christie makes a good point?
- If you do agree that he does not raise her point and that her point is a good one, do you think the omission is a weakness in Silber's essay? Why, or why not?

A CHECKLIST FOR EXAMINING ASSUMPTIONS

✓ What assumptions does the writer's argument presuppose?
✓ Are these assumptions explicit or implicit?
✓ Are these assumptions important to the author's argument or only incidental?
✓ Does the author give any evidence of being aware of the hidden assumptions in her or his argument?
✓ Would a critic be likely to share these assumptions, or are they exactly what a critic would challenge?

> ✓ What sort of evidence would be relevant to supporting or rejecting these assumptions?
> ✓ Are you willing to grant the author's assumptions?
>   ✓ If not, why not?

Remember, also, to ask these questions (except the last two) when you are reading your own drafts. And remember to ask yourself why some people may *not* grant your assumptions.

A CASEBOOK ON EXAMINING ASSUMPTIONS: What Values Do Tests Have?

Now let's turn to a second issue that is very much a part of a student's daily life—tests and grades. We begin with an essay by Paul Goodman, who proposes a sort of test of his own, a "test" not in the sense of an examination but in the sense of an experiment. Goodman suggests that if half a dozen prestigious colleges abolished grading, the education of students might improve—and not only at those colleges. (When you read his essay, locate the assumption beneath this view.) We follow Goodman's essay with an essay by Leon Botstein, first published in the *New York Times* on May 28, 2000, also arguing that testing interferes with learning. Botstein's essay provoked responses from readers of the newspaper, and we reprint these letters after we offer a brief bit of advice, "A Checklist for Evaluating Letters of Response." Finally, we end the chapter with an essay by Diane Ravitch, "In Defense of Testing," from *Time* (September 11, 2000).

Paul Goodman

Paul Goodman (1911–1972) did his undergraduate work at the City College of New York and his graduate work—he held a Ph.D.—at the University of Chicago. He taught in several colleges and universities, where he was highly popular even in the 1960s, a period when students tended to distrust anyone over thirty. Perhaps some of his popularity was due to his often expressed view that students were exploited by a corrupt society. "A Proposal to Abolish Grading" (the title is ours) is an extract from Goodman's Compulsory Miseducation and the Community of Scholars *(1966).*

A Proposal to Abolish Grading

Let half a dozen of the prestigious Universities—Chicago, Stanford, the Ivy League—abolish grading, and use testing only and entirely for pedagogic purposes as teachers see fit.

Anyone who knows the frantic temper of the present schools will understand the transvaluation of values that would be effected by this modest innovation. For most of the students, the competitive grade has come to be the essence. The naive teacher points to the beauty of the subject and the ingenuity of the research; the shrewd student asks if he is responsible for that on the final exam.

Let me at once dispose of an objection whose unanimity is quite fascinating. I think that the great majority of professors agree that grading hinders teaching and creates a bad spirit, going as far as cheating and plagiarizing. I have before me the collection of essays, *Examining in Harvard College,* and this is the consensus. It is uniformly asserted, however, that the grading is inevitable; for how else will the graduate schools, the foundations, the corporations *know* whom to accept, reward, hire? How will the talent scouts know whom to tap?

By testing the applicants, of course, according to the specific task-requirements of the inducting institution, just as applicants for the Civil Service or for licenses in medicine, law, and architecture are tested. Why should Harvard professors do the testing *for* corporations and graduate schools?

The objection is ludicrous. Dean Whitla, of the Harvard Office of Tests, points out that the scholastic-aptitude and achievement tests used for *admission* to Harvard are a super-excellent index for all-around Harvard performance, better than high-school grades or particular Harvard course-grades. Presumably, these college-entrance tests are tailored for what Harvard and similar institutions want. By the same logic, would not an employer do far better to apply his own job-aptitude test rather than to rely on the vagaries of Harvard sectionmen. Indeed, I doubt that many employers bother to look at such grades; they are more likely to be interested merely in the fact of a Harvard diploma, whatever that connotes to them. The grades have most of their weight with the graduate schools—here, as elsewhere, the system runs mainly for its own sake.

It is really necessary to remind our academics of the ancient history of Examination. In the medieval university, the whole point of the gruelling trial of the candidate was whether or not to accept him as a peer. His disputation and lecture for the Master's was just that, a masterpiece to enter the guild. It was not to make comparative evaluations. It was not to weed out and select for an extra-mural licensor or employer. It was certainly not to pit one young fellow against another in an ugly competition. My philosophic impression is that the medievals thought they knew what a good job of work was and that we are competitive because we do not know. But the more status is achieved by largely irrelevant competitive evaluation, the less will we ever know.

(Of course, our American examinations never did have this purely guild orientation, just as our faculties have rarely had absolute autonomy; the examining was to satisfy Overseers, Elders, distant Regents — and they as paternal superiors have always doted on giving grades, rather than accepting peers. But I submit that this set-up itself makes it impossible for the student to *become* a master, to *have* grown up, and to commence on his own. He will always be making A or B for some overseer. And in the present atmosphere, he will always be climbing on his friend's neck.)

Perhaps the chief objectors to abolishing grading would be the students and their parents. The parents should be simply disregarded; their anxiety has done enough damage already. For the students, it seems to me that a primary duty of the university is to deprive them of their props, their dependence on extrinsic valuation and motivation, and to force them to confront the difficult enterprise itself and finally lose themselves in it.

A miserable effect of grading is to nullify the various uses of testing. Testing, for both student and teacher, is a means of structuring, and also of finding out what is blank or wrong and what has been assimilated and can be taken for granted. Review — including high-pressure review — is a means of bringing together the fragments, so that there are flashes of synoptic insight.

There are several good reasons for testing, and kinds of test. But if 10 the aim is to discover weakness, what is the point of down-grading and punishing it, and thereby inviting the student to conceal his weakness, by faking and bulling, if not cheating? The natural conclusion of synthesis is the insight itself, not a grade for having had it. For the important purpose of placement, if one can establish in the student the belief that one is testing *not* to grade and make invidious comparisons but for his own advantage, the student should normally seek his own level, where he is challenged and yet capable, rather than trying to get by. If the student dares to accept himself as he is, a teacher's grade is a crude instrument compared with a student's self-awareness. But it is rare in our universities that students are encouraged to notice objectively their vast confusion. Unlike Socrates, our teachers rely on power-drives rather than shame and ingenuous idealism.

Many students are lazy, so teachers try to goad or threaten them by grading. In the long run this must do more harm than good. Laziness is a character-defense. It may be a way of avoiding learning, in order to protect the conceit that one is already perfect (deeper, the despair that one *never* can). It may be a way of avoiding just the risk of failing and being down-graded. Sometimes it is a way of politely saying, "I won't." But since it is the authoritarian grown-up demands that have created such attitudes in the first place, why repeat the trauma? There comes a time when we must treat people as adult, laziness and all. It is one thing courageously to fire a do-nothing out of your class; it is quite another thing to evaluate him with a lordly F.

Most important of all, it is often obvious that balking in doing the work, especially among bright young people who get to great universities, means exactly what it says: The work does not suit me, not this subject, or not at this time, or not in this school, or not in school altogether. The student might not be bookish; he might be school-tired; perhaps his development ought now to take another direction. Yet unfortunately, if such a student is intelligent and is not sure of himself, he *can* be bullied into passing, and this obscures everything. My hunch is that I am describing a common situation. What a grim waste of young life and teacherly effort! Such a student will retain nothing of what he has "passed" in. Sometimes he must get mononucleosis to tell his story and be believed.

And ironically, the converse is also probably commonly true. A student flunks and is mechanically weeded out, who is really ready and eager to learn in a scholastic setting, but he has not quite caught on. A good teacher can recognize the situation, but the computer wreaks its will.

Topics for Critical Thinking and Writing

1. Consider Goodman's opening paragraph. What is he assuming when he proposes that "prestigious Universities . . . abolish grading"? Do you agree with the assumption? Why, or why not?

2. In paragraph 3, Goodman says that "the great majority of professors agree that grading hinders teaching." What evidence does he offer to support this claim? What arguments might be made that grading assists teaching? Should Goodman have made them and perhaps then shown their weakness?

3. Goodman proposes that business, industry, and government do their own testing (para. 4). Can you think of a sensible reply in defense of the status quo? If so, set it forth in 500 words.

4. Goodman relies on (but never defends) a strong correlation between testing and the competition for grades he thinks is characteristic even of the best colleges. Write a 250-word essay on this topic: "Does Testing Lead to Competition for Grades?"

5. Suppose the faculty of your college voted to continue grading as usual but not to divulge the grades to students, except at graduation and for students who are failing or on the verge of failure. Would such practice mitigate, aggravate, or leave untouched the complaints Goodman voices against grades?

6. As a student, have grades helped you to learn, or have grades hindered you? Drawing on your own experience, argue for or against grades in an essay of 500 words.

7. If you have been a student in an ungraded course, describe the course, and evaluate the experience.

8. Read the essay by Diane Ravitch (p. 24). Where, if at all, does she agree with Goodman about the role of testing in higher education?

Leon Botstein

Leon Botstein, president of Bard College, is the author of Jefferson's Children: Education and the Promise of American Culture *(1997). The following essay originally appeared in the* New York Times *on May 28, 2000 — that is, at a time when the presidential candidates Al Gore and George W. Bush were talking a good deal about improving education in the United States.*

A Tyranny of Standardized Tests

The good news about education has become obvious: The quality of public schools is now on center stage in national politics. From George W. Bush and Al Gore down to aspirants for state and local office, all politicians have embraced the cause of standards and excellence. The bad news is that the remedy everyone but teachers and pupils wants to prescribe is more testing.

The mistrust of schools and teachers has become so widespread that the only politically viable solution seems to be to impose more standardized tests. Forty-nine states have now adopted curriculum standards that explicitly require testing in order to measure the performance of pupils, teachers, principals, and superintendents; by 2003, 26 states will have mandatory statewide tests for high school graduation. As a nation, we now administer at least 500,000 different kinds of standardized tests a year.

Testing has also become big business. We spend more than $200 million a year on it. The market for standardized tests is growing faster than that for textbooks. Unfortunately, the two go together all too neatly; three publishing companies dominate the market for tests and textbooks alike.

The tyranny of testing has become so intense that teachers may find themselves spending more than half the year teaching specifically for tests; their jobs and the standing of their schools are on the line. Not surprisingly, some teachers in New York and Maryland have been accused of cheating to improve their pupils' test scores.

The problem is that our mode of testing is primitive and out of date. 5 We still adhere to the so-called objective, machine-readable examinations pioneered in the mid-1950s. In the case of the Regents examination in New York, the questions themselves are often confusing or deliberately obscure and sometimes even embody errors.

Who, after all, is writing our English and mathematics tests? Not our leading writers, scholars, and mathematicians. Furthermore, we still confuse speed with competence. Knowledge and understanding are not about rapid reflexes; learning is not a sport. Quickness of recall does not indicate depth of understanding.

Nor do all pupils know the right answer in the same manner or get the wrong answer or fail to grasp something the same way. Knowledge and skills are always approximations. A pupil who confuses World War I with World War II knows something more than one who mistakes World War I for the American Revolution. Today's testing instruments do not effectively account for how and what pupils know.

Even worse, they are not designed to measure the rate of change in each test taker. When we go for a medical checkup, we are evaluated not only in terms of an objective standard of health but on the progress or deterioration in our own particular bodies since the last examination.

The most egregious aspect of our mania for testing is that pupils never find out what they got wrong and why they got it wrong. High school students taking the Regents exams in New York do not get their tests back; neither do the vast majority of millions of children taking Iowa and Stanford tests or statewide reading exams. Most often, even the teachers don't get the results back in time to help them in their teaching.

What is the use of test results that are released months later, mea- 10 suring a classroom, a school, a district, or a state in terms of aggregate test scores? Would we tolerate a system in sports where the calls of umpires and linesmen remained a secret until the next season and the hits and errors of particular players were never revealed or justified?

In Texas, studies have shown that weeks after taking the Texas Assessment of Academic Skills test created in the 1990s, pupils fail to show the apparent mastery of knowledge registered when they first took the tests.

Testing can and must be linked to learning. A mistake (and right answers) must be analyzed and corrected immediately for each pupil individually, just the way we respond when we teach sports and music. As it stands today, testing is little more than an adult political obsession that just results in more tests and profits for test makers.

Yet we now possess the means to change testing fundamentally. Rapid advances in computers and declining costs make powerful new technologies, once reserved for government and industry, accessible: technology involving complex computer simulation, as in pilot training, and manipulation of data. We can design tests that are interactive in a way that both helps learning and raises the standards of education. Even for young children, it would be possible to throw away the No. 2 pencils and machine-scanned answer sheets and have the student tested at the computer itself.

There needs to be an initiative between government and the software industry to develop a new generation of tests. Programs can be written that inform the test taker immediately why the answer was right or wrong and that lead the pupil through the logic of the question to confirm understanding or correct ignorance. Politicians and school boards can still get their treasured measurements of timed test scores; as players are timed in a chess game, the clock for each test taker can stop and start as the individual goes through every question, discovering how and why he or she arrived at answers.

Computers also make it possible to measure the rate of change for each   15 pupil—indicating not only the student's progress but the teacher's effectiveness. Diagnostic tests at the beginning of each year can be designed that reveal what a pupil can and cannot do or does and does not know, establishing a baseline. If in the same classroom one fifth grader reads only at a second-grade level and another on an eighth-grade level, a teacher should be evaluated by what is learned by each of them over the course of a year.

Connecting testing to learning could also free teachers from forced adherence to bland state-approved textbooks. They would be given the opportunity to select and choose materials that meet the needs of each pupil. They would be able to justify the sort of differentiated, case-by-case decisions for which true professionals should be trained.

Reforming testing practices to make all this happen, however, will not be easy. Because software companies and the entrenched testing and textbook industry respond to short-term profit motives, public investment will be required for the longer-term work of adapting computer technologies to a new kind of testing.

Without a radical reform in the way we test, there will be no improvement in learning and educational standards. We can bridge the gap between those who are passionate about measuring standards and those who are ideologically opposed to testing as discriminatory and unfair.

What our politicians are offering us now is more of the same: a misguided reliance on a monopoly in a pseudoscience of testing that defines teaching and depresses learning.

Topics for Critical Thinking and Writing

1. When Botstein asserts that "teachers may find themselves spending more than half the year teaching specifically for tests" (para. 4), is he assuming that this is undesirable? If so, what's wrong with that? If not, why does he mention the point?

2. Botstein clearly disapproves of classroom teaching based on "forced adherence to bland state-approved textbooks" (para. 16). In making this complaint, do you think he is assuming that *all, most,* or only *some* classroom teaching suffers from this fault? Based on your own high school experience, which assumption seems most plausible? Explain.

3. Botstein refers to "the tyranny of testing" (para. 4). What does he mean by this phrase (is he exaggerating, for example)?

4. Consider the two arguments by analogy that Botstein uses in paragraphs 8 and 10. Do you find them persuasive? Why, or why not?

5. By the time Botstein has reached paragraph 13, he has ceased to be (as he appeared to be) an opponent of all testing; instead, he has become an advocate of new kinds of testing. Do you think he is being inconsistent?

6. How might Botstein reply to the complaint that he never tells the reader what the point of testing is — what advantages it has over an educational regime with no testing whatsoever?

A CHECKLIST FOR
EVALUATING LETTERS OF RESPONSE

After reading the letters responding to an editorial or to a previous letter, go back and read each letter with the following questions in mind:

✓ What assumption(s) does the letter writer make? Do you share the assumption(s)?

✓ What is the writer's claim?

✓ What evidence, if any, does the writer offer to support the claim?

✓ Is there anything about the style of the letter — the distinctive use of language, the tone — that makes the letter especially engaging or especially annoying?

With these questions in mind — and others of your own invention — read the following four letters of response to Botstein that the *New York Times* printed.

Letters of Response to Leon Botstein from Janet Rudolph, Jerome Henkin, Batya Lewton, and Sidney Wilson

To the Editor:

Re "A Tyranny of Standardized Tests," by Leon Botstein (op-ed, May 28):

As the parent of three, I've learned that testing measures only a small portion of a child's intellectual reservoir as well as his special talents and gifts. And yet standardized testing is often used as the method of choice to pigeonhole students, guiding important choices like college placement and future employment.

Tests, by their nature, stress some values over others. They do not, as a rule, measure creativity, music and artistic ability, ethics, human relationships, or independent thinking.

Tests may have value as a tool in education, but they are a very poor, even destructive measure of a person.

Janet Rudolph
Woodmere, N.Y., May 28, 2000

To the Editor:

Leon Botstein (op-ed, May 28) suggests that computer programs that measure learning progress for each student also be used to evaluate teacher effectiveness. But learning is far more complex than comparing before and after tests.

A much more accurate, although subjective, gauge of teacher effectiveness is change in a child's conception of himself as a learner. I have a student in my eleventh-grade American literature class who has been failing. Last week, she kept writing notes and passing them to other students while I led the class in analyzing several modern poems.

My annoyance turned to delight when I discovered that she had written a poem in class and was making copies for her friends. This girl had created a poem and shared it with her friends. No one can take that accomplishment away from her; no computerized test can measure her pride and joy.

Jerome Henkin
Yonkers, May 28, 2000

To the Editor:

Leon Botstein (op-ed, May 28) writes, "We still confuse speed with competence." That statement pinpoints a key problem with all standardized testing. Timed tests do not truly determine a student's competence. I taught many students (1956–1971) in the New York City school system whose test scores belied their true abilities.

Diagnostic tests in math used to be given in New York City schools during the first week of school. In 1956, elementary school students were given a simple six-page diagnostic math test by their classroom teachers to determine which skills they had learned in their previous grade and which skills had to be retaught or reinforced. The teacher marked the tests and grouped the students according to their needs in math.

It is time to return to simple diagnostic tests, untimed and marked by the classroom teacher.

Batya Lewton
New York, May 28, 2000

To the Editor:

While Leon Botstein's suggestion about improving the quality of testing through modern technology is valid (op-ed, May 28), it tends to reinforce the idea that this avenue is what educational progress requires.

What is more important is the environment in which education occurs. A teaching philosophy that fires a student with the objective of the social good and a passion for the truth is what drives the educational engine.

The most constructive direction, therefore, is to attract those who are most capable of directing the classroom activity. Experience at times when better pay made teaching more attractive compared with other occupations suggests that raising teacher salaries is the best way to accomplish this.

Sidney Wilson
New City, N.Y., May 30, 2000

Topics for Critical Thinking and Writing

1. Take one of the preceding letters, and set forth the assumption(s) that the writer makes. Do you think all reasonable people would agree with the assumption(s)? If not, why not?

2. Write (but do not mail) a short letter to one of the letter writers, supporting or modifying the view expressed in the writer's letter.

3. If you were the editor of the newspaper and could print only one of these letters, which one would you print? Why?

Diane Ravitch

Diane Ravitch has taught history and education at Teachers College, Columbia University, and has served as Assistant Secretary of Education. Her latest book is Left Back: A Century of Failed School Reforms *(2000). The following essay was originally published in* Time *(September 11, 2000).*

In Defense of Testing

No one wants to be tested. We would all like to get a driver's license without answering questions about right of way or showing that we can parallel park a car. Many future lawyers and doctors probably wish they could join their profession without taking an exam.

But tests and standards are a necessary fact of life. They protect us—most of the time—from inept drivers, hazardous products, and shoddy professionals. In schools too, exams play a constructive role. They tell public officials whether new school programs are making a difference and where new investments are likely to pay off. They tell teachers what their students have learned—and have not. They tell parents how their children are doing compared with others their age. They encourage students to exert more effort.

It is important to recall that for most of this century, educators used intelligence tests to decide which children should get a high-quality education. The point of IQ testing was to find out how much children were capable of learning rather than to test what they had actually learned. Based on IQ scores, millions of children were assigned to dumbed-down programs instead of solid courses in science, math, history, literature, and foreign languages.

This history reminds us that tests should be used to improve education, not ration it. Every child should have access to a high-quality education. Students should have full opportunity to learn what will be tested; otherwise their test scores will merely reflect whether they come from an educated family.

In the past few years, we have seen the enormous benefits that flow   5
to disadvantaged students because of the information provided by state tests. Those who fall behind are now getting extra instruction in after-school classes and summer programs. In their efforts to improve student performance, states are increasing teachers' salaries, testing new teachers, and insisting on better teacher education.

Good tests should include a mix of essay, problem-solving, short-answer, and even some multiple-choice questions. On math quizzes, students should be able to show how they arrived at their answer. The tests widely used today often rely too much on multiple-choice questions, which encourage guessing rather than thinking. Also, they frequently ignore the importance of knowledge. Today's history tests, for example, seldom expect the student to know any history—sometimes derided as "mere facts"—but only to be able to read charts, graphs, and cartoons.

Performance in education means the mastery of both knowledge and skills. This is why it is reasonable to test teachers to make sure they know their subject matter, as well as how to teach it to young children. And this is why it is reasonable to assess whether students are ready to advance to the next grade or graduate from high school. To promote students who cannot read or do math is no favor to them. It is like pushing them into a deep pool before they have learned to swim. If students need extra time and help, they should get it, but they won't unless we first carefully assess what they have learned.

Topics for Critical Thinking and Writing

1. Ravitch asserts that "Every child should have access to a high-quality education" (para. 4). On what assumptions do you think this assertion rests?

2. State in one sentence the thesis of Ravitch's essay; which of the seven paragraphs in her essay do you rely on?

3. Ravitch (para. 2) claims that tests "encourage students to exert more effort." She does not say to what they devote this extra effort. What do you think?

4. Ravitch claims that "Performance in education means the mastery of both knowledge and skills" (para. 7). Explain the difference between knowledge and skills. Are the studies you are taking (or took) in your freshman year in college devoted more to acquiring knowledge or to acquiring skills?

5. Ravitch believes that graduation from high school ought to be based on some standard of performance, even if it means holding back some

students so that they cannot graduate with their classmates (para. 7). Can you think of a case from your own experience where an obviously unqualified classmate (a) was promoted with the rest of the class or (b) was held back to repeat a year's work? What is your evaluation of the results from either a or b?

Exercises

1. Think further about the 1989 West Virginia law that prohibits high school dropouts younger than eighteen from holding a driver's license. Jot down pros and cons, and then write a balanced dialogue between two imagined speakers who hold opposing views on the merits of the law. You'll doubtless have to revise your dialogue several times, and in revising your drafts you will find that further ideas come to you. Present *both* sides as strongly as possible. (You may want to give the two speakers distinct characters; for instance, one may be a student who has dropped out and the other a concerned teacher, or one a parent—who perhaps argues that he or she needs the youngster to work full-time driving a delivery truck—and one a legislator. But do not write as if the speakers must present the arguments they might be expected to hold. A student might argue *for* the law, and a teacher *against* it.)

2. Take one of the following topics, and jot down all the pro and con arguments you can think of in, say, ten minutes. Then, at least an hour or two later, return to your jottings and see whether you can add to them. Finally, as in Exercise 1, write a balanced dialogue, presenting each idea as strongly as possible. (If none of these topics interests you, talk with your instructor about the possibility of choosing a topic of your own.) Suggested topics:

   a. Colleges should not award athletic scholarships.
   b. Bicyclists and motorcyclists should be required by law to wear helmets.
   c. High school teachers should have the right to search students for drugs on school grounds.
   d. Smoking should be prohibited in all parts of all college buildings.
   e. College administrators should take no punitive action against students who use racist language or language that offends any minority.
   f. Students should have the right to drop out of school at any age.
   g. In rape trials the names of the alleged victims should not be released to the public.

2

Critical Reading: Getting Started

Some books are to be tasted, others to be chewed, and some few to be chewed and digested. —FRANCIS BACON

ACTIVE READING

In the passage that we quote at the top of the page, Bacon makes at least two good points. One is that books are of varying worth; the second is that a taste of some books may be enough.

But even a book (or an essay) that you will chew and digest is one that you first may want to taste. How can you get a taste—that is, how can you get some sense of a piece of writing *before* you sit down to read it carefully?

Previewing

Even before you read the work, you may have some ideas about it, perhaps because you already know something about the **author.** You know, for example, that a work by Martin Luther King Jr. will probably deal with civil rights. You know, too, that it will be serious and eloquent. On the other hand, if you pick up an essay by Woody Allen, you will probably expect it to be amusing. It may be serious—Allen has written earnestly about many topics, especially those concerned with the media—but it's your hunch that the essay will be at least somewhat entertaining and probably will not be terribly difficult. In short, a reader who has some knowledge of the author probably has some idea of what the writing will be like, and so the reader reads it in a certain mood. Admittedly, most of the authors represented in this book are not widely known, but we give biographical notes that may provide you with some sense of what to expect.

The **place of publication** may also tell you something about the essay. For instance, the *National Review* (formerly edited by William F.

Buckley Jr.) is a conservative journal. If you notice that an essay on affirmative action was published in the *National Review,* you are probably safe in tentatively assuming that the essay will not endorse affirmative action. On the other hand, *Ms.* is a liberal magazine for women, and an essay on affirmative action published in *Ms.* will probably be an endorsement.

The **title** of an essay, too, may give you an idea of what to expect. Of course, a title may announce only the subject and not the author's thesis or point of view ("On Gun Control," "Should Drugs Be Legal?"), but fairly often it will indicate the thesis too, as in "Give Children the Vote" and "Gay Marriages: Make Them Legal." Knowing more or less what to expect, you can probably take in some of the major points even on a quick reading.

Skimming: Finding the Thesis

Although most of the material in this book is too closely argued to be fully understood by merely skimming, still, skimming can tell you a good deal. Read the first paragraph of an essay carefully because it may announce the author's **thesis** (chief point, major claim), and it may give you some sense of how the argument for that thesis will be conducted. (What we call the thesis can also be called the main idea, the point, or even the argument, but in this book we use *argument* to refer not only to the thesis statement but also to the entire development of the thesis in the essay.) Run your eye over the rest, looking for key expressions that indicate the author's conclusions, such as "It follows, then, that . . ." Passages of this sort often occur as the first or last sentence in a paragraph. And of course, pay attention to any headings within the text. Finally, pay special attention to the last paragraph because it probably will offer a summary and a brief restatement of the writer's thesis.

Having skimmed the work, you probably know the author's thesis, and you may detect the author's methods—for instance, whether the author supports the thesis chiefly by personal experience, by statistics, or by ridiculing the opposition. You also have a clear idea of the length and some idea of the difficulty of the piece. You know, then, whether you can read it carefully now before dinner or whether you had better put off a careful reading until you have more time.

Reading with a Pencil: Underlining, Highlighting, Annotating

Once you have a general idea of the work—not only an idea of its topic and thesis but also a sense of the way in which the thesis is argued—you can then go back and start reading it carefully.

As you read, **underline** or **highlight** key passages, and make **annotations** in the margins (but not in library books, please). Because you are reading actively, or interacting with the text, you will not simply let your eye rove across the page. You will underline or highlight what seem to be the chief points, so that later when you review the essay you can easily locate the main passages. But don't overdo a good thing. If you find yourself underlining or highlighting most of a page, you are probably not thinking carefully enough about what the key points are. Similarly, your marginal annotations should be brief and selective. Probably they will consist of hints or clues, things like "really?," "doesn't follow," "!!!," "???," "good," "compare with Jones," and "check this." In short, in a paragraph you might underline or highlight a key definition, and in the margin you might write "good" or, on the other hand, "?," if you think the definition is fuzzy or wrong. You are interacting with the text and laying the groundwork for eventually writing your own essay on what you have read.

What you annotate will depend largely on your **purpose.** If you are reading an essay in order to see the ways in which the writer organizes an argument, you will annotate one sort of thing. If you are reading in order to challenge the thesis, you will annotate other things. Here is a passage from an essay entitled "On Racist Speech," with a student's rather skeptical, even aggressive annotations. But notice that at least one of the annotations—"Definition of 'fighting words'"—apparently was made chiefly in order to remind the reader of where an important term appears in the essay. The essay, printed in full on page 46, is by Charles R. Lawrence III, a professor of law at Stanford University. It originally appeared in the *Chronicle of Higher Education* (October 25, 1989), a publication read chiefly by college and university faculty members and administrators.

Example of such a policy?

University officials who have formulated underlined{policies} to respond to incidents of racial harassment have been characterized in the press as "thought police," but such policies generally do nothing more than impose (sanctions) against intentional face-to-face insults. When racist speech takes the form of face-to-face insults, catcalls, or other assaultive speech aimed at an individual or small group of persons, it falls directly within the "fighting words" exception to First Amendment protection. The Supreme Court has held that words which "by their very utterance inflict injury or tend to incite an immediate breach of the peace" are not protected by the First Amendment.

What about sexist speech?

Definition of "fighting words"

?

Example?

If the purpose of the First Amendment is to foster the greatest amount of speech, racial insults disserve that purpose. Assaultive racist speech functions as a preemptive strike. The invective is experienced as a blow, not as a proffered idea, and once the blow is struck, it is unlikely that a dialogue will follow. Racial insults are particularly undeserving of First Amendment protection because the perpetrator's intention is not to discover truth or initiate dialogue but to injure the victim. In most situations, members of minority groups realize that they are likely to lose if they respond to epithets by fighting and are forced to remain silent and submissive.

Really? Probably depends on the individual.

How does he know?

y must ech ays k "to cover th"?

"This, Therefore That"

To arrive at a coherent thought or a coherent series of thoughts that will lead to a reasonable conclusion, a writer has to go through a good deal of preliminary effort; and if the writer is to convince the reader that the conclusion is sound, the reasoning that led to the conclusion must be set forth in detail, with a good deal of "This, therefore that," and "If this, then that." The arguments in this book require more comment than President Calvin Coolidge provided when his wife, who hadn't been able to go to church on a Sunday, asked him what the preacher's sermon was about. "Sin," he said. His wife persisted: "What did the preacher say about it?" Coolidge's response: "He was against it."

But, again, when we say that most of the arguments in this book are presented at length and require careful reading, we do not mean that they are obscure; we mean, rather, that the reader has to take the sentences one by one. And speaking of one by one, we are reminded of an episode in Lewis Carroll's *Through the Looking-Glass:*

> "Can you do Addition?" the White Queen asked. "What's one and one and one and one and one and one and one and one and one and one?"
> "I don't know," said Alice. "I lost count."
> "She can't do Addition," the Red Queen said.

It's easy enough to add one and one and one and so on, and Alice can, of course, do addition, but not at the pace that the White Queen sets. Fortunately, you can set your own pace in reading the cumulative thinking set forth in the essays we reprint. Skimming won't work, but slow reading—and thinking about what you are reading—will.

When you first pick up an essay, you may indeed want to skim it, for some of the reasons mentioned on page 28, but sooner or later you have to settle down to read it and to think about it. The effort will be worthwhile. John Locke, the seventeenth-century English philosopher, said,

> *Reading* furnishes the mind with materials of knowledge; it is *thinking* [that] makes what we read ours. We are of the ruminating kind, and it is not enough to cram ourselves with a great load of collections; unless we chew them over again they will not give us strength and nourishment.

First, Second, and Third Thoughts

Suppose you are reading an argument about pornographic pictures. For the present purpose, it doesn't matter whether the argument favors or opposes censorship. As you read the argument, ask yourself whether *pornography* has been adequately defined. Has the writer taken the trouble to make sure that the reader and the writer are thinking about the same thing? If not, the very topic under discussion has not been adequately fixed, and therefore further debate over the issue may well be so unclear as to be futile. How, then, ought a topic such as this be fixed for effective critical thinking?

It goes without saying that pornography can't be defined simply as pictures of nude figures or even of nude figures copulating, for such a definition would include not only photographs taken for medical, sociological, and scientific purposes but also some of the world's great art. Nobody seriously thinks pornography includes such things.

Is it enough, then, to say that pornography "stirs lustful thoughts" or "appeals to prurient interests"? No, because pictures of shoes probably stir lustful thoughts in shoe fetishists, and pictures of children in ads for underwear probably stir lustful thoughts in pedophiles. Perhaps, then, the definition must be amended to "material that stirs lustful thoughts in the average person." But will this restatement do? First, it may be hard to agree on the characteristics of "the average person." True, in other matters the law often assumes that there is such a creature as "the reasonable person," and most people would agree that in a given situation there might be a reasonable response—for almost everyone. But we cannot be so sure that the same is true about the emotional responses of this "average person." In any case, far from stimulating sexual impulses, sadomasochistic pictures of booted men wielding whips on naked women probably turn off "the average person," yet this is the sort of material that most people would agree is pornographic.

Something must be wrong, then, with the definition that pornography is material that "stirs lustful thoughts in the average person." We began with a definition that was too broad ("pictures of nude figures"), but now we have a definition that is too narrow. We must go back to the drawing board. This is not nitpicking. The label "average person" was found to be inadequate in a pornography case argued before the Supreme Court; because the materials in question were aimed at a homosexual audience, it was agreed that the average person would not find them sexually stimulating.

One difficulty has been that pornography is often defined according to its effect on the viewer ("genital commotion," Father Harold Gardiner, S.J., called it, in *Catholic Viewpoint on Censorship*), but different people, we know, may respond differently. In the first half of the twentieth century, in an effort to distinguish between pornography and art—after all, most people don't want to regard Botticelli's *Venus* or Michelangelo's *David* as "dirty"—it was commonly said that a true work of art does not stimulate in the spectator ideas or desires that the real object might stimulate. But in 1956 Kenneth Clark, probably the most influential English-speaking art critic of our time, changed all that; in a book called *The Nude* he announced that "no nude, however abstract, should fail to arouse in the spectator some vestige of erotic feeling."

SUMMARIZING AND
PARAPHRASING

Perhaps the best thing to do with a fairly difficult essay is, after a first reading, to reread it and simultaneously to take notes on a sheet of paper, perhaps summarizing each paragraph in a sentence or two. Writing a summary will help you to

- Understand the contents and
- See the strengths and weaknesses of the piece.

Don't confuse a summary with a paraphrase; a **paraphrase** is a word-by-word or phrase-by-phrase rewording of a text, a sort of translation of the author's language into your own. A paraphrase is therefore as long as the original or even longer; a **summary** is much shorter. Paraphrasing can be useful in helping you to grasp difficult passages; summarizing is useful in helping you to get the gist of the entire essay. (Caution: Do *not* incorporate a summary or a paraphrase into your own essay without acknowledging your source and stating that you are summarizing or paraphrasing.)

Let's further examine the distinction between summary and paraphrase in connection with the opening paragraph of an essay called "Being Asynchronous" (1995), written by Nicholas Negroponte, a professor at the Massachusetts Institute of Technology. Here is the paragraph:

> A face-to-face or telephone conversation is real time and synchronous. Telephone tag is a game played to find the opportunity to be synchronous. Ironically, this is often done for exchanges, which themselves require no synchrony whatsoever and could just as well be handled by non-real-time message passing. Historically, asynchronous communication, like letter writing, has tended to be more formal and less off-the-cuff exchanges. This is changing with voice mail and answering machines.

It's our guess that you found these sentences a bit hard to follow. After all, words like *synchronous, synchrony, asynchronous,* and even *real time* may be puzzling. If you were going to write about this paragraph, you might want to paraphrase it first of all in an effort to help yourself to understand it. That is, you might want to reword the passage, *not in an effort to make it briefer but in an effort to make it clearer.* Here is our paraphrase of the first two sentences:

> When we speak to a person face-to-face or on the telephone, the two of us are speaking within the same period of time (synchronous time). But when we leave a telephone message asking someone to call us, that person later does so, we are not there to answer, and the person leaves

a message for us, we are engaging in asynchronous communication—
that is, we are communicating but not within the same period.

This is what we make of Negroponte's first two sentences. We originally
paraphrased them to clarify them in our minds, and if we were writing
an essay about Negroponte's essay, we might want to include the paraphrase to help our readers understand his sentences.

Here is Negroponte's entire essay.

Being Asynchronous

A face-to-face or telephone conversation is real time and synchronous. Telephone tag is a game played to find the opportunity to be synchronous. Ironically, this is often done for exchanges, which themselves
require no synchrony whatsoever and could just as well be handled by
non-real-time message passing. Historically, asynchronous communication, like letter writing, has tended to be more formal and less off-
the-cuff exchanges. This is changing with voice mail and answering machines.

I have met people who claim they cannot understand how they (and
we all) lived without answering machines at home and voice mail at the
office. The advantage is less about voice and more about off-line processing and time shifting. It is about leaving messages versus engaging somebody needlessly in online discussion. In fact, answering machines are
designed slightly backward. They should not only activate when you are
not there or don't want to be there, but they should *always* answer the
telephone and give the caller the opportunity to simply leave a message.

One of the enormous attractions of e-mail is that it is not interrup-
tive like a telephone. You can process it at your leisure, and for this reason you may reply to messages that would not stand a chance in hell of
getting through the secretarial defenses of corporate, telephonic life.

E-mail is exploding in popularity because it is *both* an asynchronous
and a computer-readable medium. The latter is particularly important,
because interface agents will use those bits to prioritize and deliver messages differently. Who sent the message and what it is about could determine the order in which you see it—no different from the current
secretarial screening that allows a call from your six-year-old daughter to
go right through, while the CEO of the XYZ Corporation is put on hold.
Even on a busy workday, personal e-mail messages might drift to the top
of the heap.

Not nearly as much of our communications need to be contempora-   5
neous or in real time. We are constantly interrupted or forced into being
punctual for things that truly do not merit such immediacy or prompt-
ness. We are forced into regular rhythms, not because we finished eating
at 8:59 P.M., but because the TV program is about to start in one minute.

Our great-grandchildren will understand our going to the theater at a given hour to benefit from the collective presence of human actors, but they will not understand the synchronous experiencing of television signals in the privacy of our home—until they look at the bizarre economic model behind it.

We won't go on to paraphrase the entire essay—our paraphrase would be at least as long as the original—but now we will offer a summary of the entire essay, a sense of the gist of the whole:

> Negroponte argues that far more conversation takes place with the two speakers face-to-face or talking on the phone ("synchronous" or "contemporaneous" or "real" time) than is necessary or desirable. E-mail and answering machines, which allow for a sort of conversation in which each speaker participates at a convenient time, have the great advantage of letting us work at our own rhythm without interruptions.

Summarizing each paragraph or each group of closely related paragraphs will help you to follow the thread of the discourse and, when you are finished, will provide you with a useful map of the essay. Then, when you reread the essay yet again, you may want to underline passages that you now understand are the author's key ideas—for instance, definitions, generalizations, summaries—and you may want to jot notes in the margins, questioning the logic, expressing your uncertainty, or calling attention to other writers who see the matter differently.

Here is a paragraph from a 1973 decision of the U.S. Supreme Court, written by Chief Justice Warren Burger, setting forth reasons that the government may censor obscene material. We follow it with a sample summary.

> If we accept the unprovable assumption that a complete education requires the reading of certain books, and the well-nigh universal belief that good books, plays, and art lift the spirit, improve the mind, enrich the human personality, and develop character, can we then say that a state legislature may not act on the corollary assumption that commerce in obscene books, or public exhibitions focused on obscene conduct, have a tendency to exert a corrupting and debasing impact leading to antisocial behavior? The sum of experience, including that of the past two decades, affords an ample basis for legislatures to conclude that a sensitive, key relationship of human existence, central to family life, community welfare, and the development of human personality, can be debased and distorted by crass commercial exploitation of sex. Nothing in the Constitution prohibits a State from reaching such a conclusion and acting on it legislatively simply because there is no conclusive empirical data.

Now for a student's summary. Notice that the summary does *not* include the reader's evaluation or any other sort of comment on the original; it is simply an attempt to condense the original. Notice too that, because its purpose is merely to assist the reader to grasp the ideas of the original by focusing on them, it is written in a sort of shorthand (not every sentence is a complete sentence), though, of course, if this summary were being presented in an essay, it would have to be grammatical.

```
        Unprovable but acceptable assumption that good
    books etc. shape character, so that legislature can as-
    sume obscene works debase character. Experience lets
    one conclude that exploitation of sex debases the indi-
    vidual, family, and community. Though no conclusive ev-
    idence for this view, Constitution lets states act on
    it legislatively.
```

The first sentence of the original, some eighty words, is reduced in the summary to nineteen words. Of course the summary loses much of the detail and flavor of the original: "Good books etc." is not the same as "good books, plays, and art"; and "shape character" is not the same as "lift the spirit, improve the mind, enrich the human personality, and develop character." But the statement in the summary will do as a rough approximation, useful for a quick review. More important, the act of writing a summary forces the reader to go slowly and to think about each sentence of the original. Such thinking may help the reader-writer to see the complexity—or the hollowness—of the original.

The sample summary in the preceding paragraph was just that, a summary; but when writing your summaries, you will often find it useful to inject your own thoughts ("seems far-fetched," "strong point," "I don't get it"), enclosing them within square brackets, [ ], or in some other way keeping these responses distinct from your summary of the writer's argument. Remember, however, that if your instructor asks you to hand in a summary,

- It should not contain ideas other than those found in the original piece.
- You can rearrange these, add transitions as needed, and so forth, but
- The summary should give the reader nothing but a sense of the original piece.

We don't want to nag you, but we do want to emphasize the need to read with a pencil in hand. If you read slowly and take notes, you will find that what you read will give you the strength and nourishment that Locke spoke of.

Having insisted that although skimming is a useful early step and that the essays in this book need to be read slowly because the writers build one reason on another, we will now seem to contradict ourselves by presenting an essay that can *almost* be skimmed. Susan Jacoby's essay originally appeared in the *New York Times,* a thoroughly respectable newspaper but not one that requires its readers to linger over every sentence. Still, compared with most of the news accounts, Jacoby's essay requires close reading. When you read the essay, you will notice that it zigs and zags, not because Jacoby is careless or wants to befuddle her readers but because she wants to build a strong case to support her point of view and must therefore look at some widely held views that she does *not* accept; she must set these forth and then give her reasons for rejecting them.

Susan Jacoby

Susan Jacoby (b. 1946), a journalist since the age of seventeen, is well known for her feminist writings. "A First Amendment Junkie" (our title) appeared in a "Hers" column in the New York Times *in 1978.*

A First Amendment Junkie

It is no news that many women are defecting from the ranks of civil libertarians on the issue of obscenity. The conviction of Larry Flynt, publisher of *Hustler* magazine — before his metamorphosis into a born-again Christian — was greeted with unabashed feminist approval. Harry Reems, the unknown actor who was convicted by a Memphis jury for conspiring to distribute the movie *Deep Throat,* has carried on his legal battles with almost no support from women who ordinarily regard themselves as supporters of the First Amendment. Feminist writers and scholars have even discussed the possibility of making common cause against pornography with adversaries of the women's movement — including opponents of the equal rights amendment and "right-to-life" forces.

All of this is deeply disturbing to a woman writer who believes, as I always have and still do, in an absolute interpretation of the First Amendment. Nothing in Larry Flynt's garbage convinces me that the late Justice Hugo L. Black was wrong in his opinion that "the Federal Government is without any power whatsoever under the Constitution to put any type of burden on free speech and expression of ideas of any kind (as distinguished from conduct)." Many women I like and respect tell me I am wrong; I cannot remember having become involved in so many heated discussions of a public issue since the end of the Vietnam War. A feminist writer described my views as those of a "First Amendment junkie."

Many feminist arguments for controls on pornography carry the implicit conviction that porn books, magazines, and movies pose a greater threat to women than similarly repulsive exercises of free speech pose to other offended groups. This conviction has, of course, been shared by everyone— regardless of race, creed, or sex—who has ever argued in favor of abridging the First Amendment. It is the argument used by some Jews who have withdrawn their support from the American Civil Liberties Union because it has defended the right of American Nazis to march through a community inhabited by survivors of Hitler's concentration camps.

If feminists want to argue that the protection of the Constitution should not be extended to *any* particularly odious or threatening form of speech, they have a reasonable argument (although I don't agree with it). But it is ridiculous to suggest that the porn shops on 42nd Street are more disgusting to women than a march of neo-Nazis is to survivors of the extermination camps.

The arguments over pornography also blur the vital distinction between expression of ideas and conduct. When I say I believe unreservedly in the First Amendment, someone always comes back at me with the issue of "kiddie porn." But kiddie porn is not a First Amendment issue. It is an issue of the abuse of power—the power adults have over children—and not of obscenity. Parents and promoters have no more right to use their children to make porn movies than they do to send them to work in coal mines. The responsible adults should be prosecuted, just as adults who use children for back-breaking farm labor should be prosecuted.

Susan Brownmiller, in *Against Our Will: Men, Women and Rape,* has described pornography as "the undiluted essence of antifemale propaganda." I think this is a fair description of some types of pornography, especially of the brutish subspecies that equates sex with death and portrays women primarily as objects of violence.

The equation of sex and violence, personified by some glossy rock record album covers as well as by *Hustler,* has fed the illusion that censorship of pornography can be conducted on a more rational basis than other types of censorship. Are all pictures of naked women obscene? Clearly not, says a friend. A Renoir nude is art, she says, and *Hustler* is trash. "Any reasonable person" knows that.

But what about something between art and trash—something, say, along the lines of *Playboy* or *Penthouse* magazines? I asked five women for their reactions to one picture in *Penthouse* and got responses that ranged from "lovely" and "sensuous" to "revolting" and "demeaning." Feminists, like everyone else, seldom have rational reasons for their preferences in erotica. Like members of juries, they tend to disagree when confronted with something that falls short of 100 percent vulgarity.

In any case, feminists will not be the arbiters of good taste if it becomes easier to harass, prosecute, and convict people on obscenity charges. Most of the people who want to censor girlie magazines are equally opposed to open discussion of issues that are of vital concern to women: rape, abortion, menstruation, contraception, lesbianism — in fact, the entire range of sexual experience from a women's viewpoint.

Feminist writers and editors and filmmakers have limited financial 10 resources: Confronted by a determined prosecutor, Hugh Hefner[1] will fare better than Susan Brownmiller. Would the Memphis jurors who convicted Harry Reems for his role in *Deep Throat* be inclined to take a more positive view of paintings of the female genitalia done by sensitive feminist artists? *Ms.* magazine has printed color reproductions of some of those art works; *Ms.* is already banned from a number of high school libraries because someone considers it threatening and/or obscene.

Feminists who want to censor what they regard as harmful pornography have essentially the same motivation as other would-be censors: They want to use the power of the state to accomplish what they have been unable to achieve in the marketplace of ideas and images. The impulse to censor places no faith in the possibilities of democratic persuasion.

It isn't easy to persuade certain men that they have better uses for $1.95 each month than to spend it on a copy of *Hustler?* Well, then, give the men no choice in the matter.

I believe there is also a connection between the impulse toward censorship on the part of people who used to consider themselves civil libertarians and a more general desire to shift responsibility from individuals to institutions. When I saw the movie *Looking for Mr. Goodbar,* I was stunned by its series of visual images equating sex and violence, coupled with what seems to me the mindless message (a distortion of the fine Judith Rossner novel) that casual sex equals death. When I came out of the movie, I was even more shocked to see parents standing in line with children between the ages of ten and fourteen.

I simply don't know why a parent would take a child to see such a movie, any more than I understand why people feel they can't turn off a television set their child is watching. Whenever I say that, my friends tell me I don't know how it is because I don't have children. True, but I do have parents. When I was a child, they did turn off the TV. They didn't expect the Federal Communications Commission to do their job for them.

I am a First Amendment junkie. You can't OD on the First Amend- 15 ment, because free speech is its own best antidote.

Suppose we want to make a rough summary, more or less paragraph by paragraph, of Jacoby's essay. Such a summary might look something like this (the numbers refer to Jacoby's paragraphs):

[1]**Hugh Hefner** Founder and longtime publisher of *Playboy* magazine. [Editors' note.]

1. Although feminists usually support the First Amendment, when it comes to pornography, many feminists take pretty much the position of those who oppose ERA and abortion and other causes of the women's movement.

2. Larry Flynt produces garbage, but I think his conviction represents an unconstitutional limitation of freedom of speech.

3, 4. Feminists who want to control (censor) pornography argue that it poses a greater threat to women than similar repulsive speech poses to other groups. If feminists want to say that all offensive speech should be restricted, they can make a case, but it is absurd to say that pornography is a "greater threat" to women than a march of neo-Nazis is to survivors of concentration camps.

5. Trust in the First Amendment is not refuted by kiddie porn; kiddie porn is not a First Amendment issue but an issue of child abuse.

6, 7, 8. Some feminists think censorship of pornography can be more "rational" than other kinds of censorship, but a picture of a nude woman strikes some women as base and others as "lovely." There is no unanimity.

9, 10. If feminists censor girlie magazines, they will find that they are unwittingly helping opponents of the women's movement to censor discussions of rape, abortion, and so on. Some of the art in the feminist magazine *Ms.* would doubtless be censored.

11, 12. Like other would-be censors, feminists want to use the power of the state to achieve what they have not achieved in "the marketplace of ideas." They display a lack of faith in "democratic persuasion."

13, 14. This attempt at censorship reveals a desire to "shift responsibility from individuals to institutions." The responsibility--for instance, to keep young people from equating sex with violence--is properly the parents'.

15. We can't have too much of the First Amendment.

Jacoby's **thesis,** or major claim, or chief proposition—that any form of censorship of pornography is wrong—is clear enough, even as early as the end of her first paragraph, but it gets its life or its force from the **reasons** offered throughout the essay. If we want to reduce our summary even further, we might say that Jacoby supports her thesis by arguing several subsidiary points. We will merely assert them briefly, but Jacoby **argues** them—that is, she gives reasons:

    a. Pornography can scarcely be thought of as more offensive than Nazism.

    b. Women disagree about which pictures are pornographic.

    c. Feminists who want to censor pornography will find that they help antifeminists to censor discussions of issues advocated by the women's movement.

    d. Feminist who favor censorship are in effect turning to the government to achieve what they haven't achieved in the free marketplace.

    e. One sees this abdication of responsibility in the fact that parents allow their children to watch unsuitable movies and television programs.

If we want to present a brief summary in the form of one coherent paragraph—perhaps as part of our own essay to show the view we are arguing in behalf of or against—we might write something like this summary. (The summary would, of course, be prefaced by a **lead-in** along these lines: "Susan Jacoby, writing in the *New York Times,* offered a forceful argument against censorship of pornography. Jacoby's view, briefly, is . . .".)

When it comes to censorship of pornography, some feminists take a position shared by opponents of the feminist movement. They argue that pornography poses a greater threat to women than other forms of offensive speech offer to other groups, but this interpretation is simply a mistake. Pointing to kiddie porn is also a mistake, for kiddie porn is an issue involving not the First Amendment but child abuse. Feminists who support censorship of pornography will inadvertently aid those who wish to censor discussions of abortion and rape or censor art that is published in magazines such as Ms. The solution is not for individuals to turn to institu-

tions (that is, for the government to limit the First
Amendment) but for individuals to accept the responsibility for teaching young people not to equate sex with
violence.

Whether we agree or disagree with Jacoby's thesis, we must admit that the reasons she sets forth to support it are worth thinking about. Only a reader who closely follows the reasoning with which Jacoby buttresses her thesis is in a position to accept or reject it.

Topics for Critical Thinking and Writing

1. What does Jacoby mean when she says she is a "First Amendment junkie"?

2. The essay is primarily an argument against the desire of some feminists to try to censor pornography of the sort that appeals to some heterosexual adult males, but the next-to-last paragraph is about television and children. Is the paragraph connected to Jacoby's overall argument? If so, how?

3. Evaluate the final paragraph as a final paragraph. (Effective final paragraphs are not, of course, all of one sort. Some, for example, round off the essay by echoing something from the opening; others suggest that the reader, having now seen the problem, should think further about it or even act on it. But a good final paragraph, whatever else it does, should make the reader feel that the essay has come to an end, not just broken off.)

4. This essay originally appeared in the *New York Times*. If you are unfamiliar with this newspaper, consult an issue or two in your library. Next, in a paragraph, try to characterize the readers of the paper—that is, Jacoby's audience.

5. Jacoby claims in paragraph 2 that she "believes . . . in an absolute interpretation of the First Amendment." What does such an interpretation involve? Would it permit shouting "Fire!" in a crowded theater even though the shouter knows there is no fire? Would it permit shouting racist insults at blacks or immigrant Vietnamese? Spreading untruths about someone's past? If the "absolutist" interpretation of the First Amendment does permit these statements, does that argument show that nothing is morally wrong with uttering them? (*Does* the First Amendment, as actually interpreted by the Supreme Court today, permit any or all of these claims? Consult your reference librarian for help in answering this question.)

6. Jacoby implies that permitting prosecution of persons on obscenity charges will lead eventually to censorship of "open discussion" of important issues such as "rape, abortion, menstruation, contraception, lesbianism" (para. 9). Do you find her fears convincing? Does she give any evidence to support her claim?

A CHECKLIST FOR GETTING STARTED

✓ Have I adequately previewed the work?
✓ Can I state the thesis?
✓ If I have jotted down a summary,
  ✓ Is the summary accurate?
  ✓ Does the summary mention all the chief points?
  ✓ If there are inconsistencies, are they in the summary or the original selection?
  ✓ Will the summary be clear and helpful?

A CASEBOOK FOR CRITICAL READING: Should Some Kinds of Speech Be Censored?

Now we present a series of essays that we think are somewhat more difficult than Jacoby's but that address in more detail some of the issues of free speech that she raises. We suggest you read each one through to get its gist and then read it a second time, jotting down after each paragraph a sentence or two summarizing the paragraph. Keep in mind the First Amendment to the Constitution, which reads, in its entirety,

> Congress shall make no law respecting an establishment of religion, or prohibiting the free exercise thereof; or abridging the freedom of speech, or of the press; or the right of the people peaceably to assemble, and to petition the government for a redress of grievances.

See the companion Web site **www.bedfordstmartins.com/ barnetbedau** for links related to free speech.

Susan Brownmiller

Susan Brownmiller (b. 1935), a graduate of Cornell University, is the founder of Women against Pornography and the author of several books, including Against Our Will: Men, Women, and Rape *(1975). The essay reprinted here is from* Take Back the Night *(1980), a collection of essays edited by Laura Lederer. The book has been called "the manifesto of antipornography feminism."*

Let's Put Pornography Back in the Closet

Free speech is one of the great foundations on which our democracy rests. I am old enough to remember the Hollywood Ten, the screenwriters who went to jail in the late 1940s because they refused to testify before a congressional committee about their political affiliations. They tried to use the First Amendment as a defense, but they went to jail because in those days there were few civil liberties lawyers around who cared to champion the First Amendment right to free speech, when the speech concerned the Communist party.

The Hollywood Ten were correct in claiming the First Amendment. Its high purpose is the protection of unpopular ideas and political dissent. In the dark, cold days of the 1950s, few civil libertarians were willing to declare themselves First Amendment absolutists. But in the brighter, though frantic, days of the 1960s, the principle of protecting unpopular political speech was gradually strengthened.

It is fair to say now that the battle has largely been won. Even the American Nazi party has found itself the beneficiary of the dedicated, tireless work of the American Civil Liberties Union. But—and please notice the quotation marks coming up—"To equate the free and robust exchange of ideas and political debate with commercial exploitation of obscene material demeans the grand conception of the First Amendment and its high purposes in the historic struggle for freedom. It is a misuse of the great guarantees of free speech and free press."

I didn't say that, although I wish I had, for I think the words are thrilling. Chief Justice Warren Burger said it in 1973, in the United States Supreme Court's majority opinion in *Miller v. California*. During the same decades that the right to political free speech was being strengthened in the courts, the nation's obscenity laws also were undergoing extensive revision.

It's amazing to recall that in 1934 the question of whether James   5
Joyce's *Ulysses* should be banned as pornographic actually went before the Court. The battle to protect *Ulysses* as a work of literature with redeeming social value was won. In later decades, Henry Miller's *Tropic* books, *Lady Chatterley's Lover,* and the *Memoirs of Fanny Hill* also were adjudged not obscene. These decisions have been important to me. As the author of *Against Our Will,* a study of the history of rape that does contain explicit sexual material, I shudder to think how my book would have fared if James Joyce, D. H. Lawrence, and Henry Miller hadn't gone before me.

I am not a fan of *Chatterley* or the *Tropic* books, I should quickly mention. They are not to my literary taste, nor do I think they represent female sexuality with any degree of accuracy. But I would hardly suggest that we ban them. Such a suggestion wouldn't get very far anyway. The battle to protect these books is ancient history. Time does march on, quite methodically. What, then, is unlawfully obscene, and what does the First Amendment have to do with it?

In the *Miller* case of 1973 (not Henry Miller, by the way, but a porn distributor who sent unsolicited stuff through the mails), the Court came up with new guidelines that it hoped would strengthen obscenity laws by giving more power to the states. What it did in actuality was throw everything into confusion. It set up a three-part test by which materials can be adjudged obscene. The materials are obscene if they depict patently offensive, hard-core sexual conduct; lack serious scientific, literary, artistic, or political value; and appeal to the prurient interest of an average person—as measured by contemporary community standards.

"Patently offensive," "prurient interest," and "hard-core" are indeed words to conjure with. "Contemporary community standards" are what we're trying to redefine. The feminist objection to pornography is not based on prurience, which the dictionary defines as lustful, itching desire. We are not opposed to sex and desire, with or without the itch, and we certainly believe that explicit sexual material has its place in literature, art, science, and education. Here we part company rather swiftly with old-line conservatives who don't want sex education in the high schools, for example.

No, the feminist objection to pornography is based on our belief that pornography represents hatred of women, that pornography's intent is to humiliate, degrade, and dehumanize the female body for the purpose of erotic stimulation and pleasure. We are unalterably opposed to the presentation of the female body being stripped, bound, raped, tortured, mutilated, and murdered in the name of commercial entertainment and free speech.

These images, which are standard pornographic fare, have nothing to   10
do with the hallowed right of political dissent. They have everything to do with the creation of a cultural climate in which a rapist feels he is merely giving in to a normal urge and a woman is encouraged to believe that sexual masochism is healthy, liberated fun. Justice Potter Stewart once said about hard-core pornography, "You know it when you see it," and that certainly used to be true. In the good old days, pornography looked awful. It was cheap and sleazy, and there was no mistaking it for art.

Nowadays, since the porn industry has become a multimillion dollar business, visual technology has been employed in its service. Pornographic movies are skillfully filmed and edited, pornographic still shots using the newest tenets of good design artfully grace the covers of *Hustler, Penthouse,* and *Playboy,* and the public—and the courts—are sadly confused.

The Supreme Court neglected to define "hard-core" in the *Miller* decision. This was a mistake. If "hard-core" refers only to explicit sexual intercourse, then that isn't good enough. When women or children or men—no matter how artfully—are shown tortured or terrorized in the service of sex, that's obscene. And "patently offensive," I would hope, to our "contemporary community standards."

Justice William O. Douglas wrote in his dissent to the *Miller* case that no one is "compelled to look." This is hardly true. To buy a paper at the corner newsstand is to subject oneself to a forcible immersion in pornography, to be demeaned by an array of dehumanized, chopped-up parts of the female anatomy, packaged like cuts of meat at the supermarket. I happen to like my body and I work hard at the gym to keep it in good shape, but I am embarrassed for my body and for the bodies of all women when I see the fragmented parts of us so frivolously, and so flagrantly, displayed.

Some constitutional theorists (Justice Douglas was one) have maintained that any obscenity law is a serious abridgement of free speech. Others (and Justice Earl Warren was one) have maintained that the First Amendment was never intended to protect obscenity. We live quite compatibly with a host of free-speech abridgements. There are restraints against false and misleading advertising or statements — shouting "fire" without cause in a crowded movie theater, etc. — that do not threaten, but strengthen, our societal values. Restrictions on the public display of pornography belong in this category.

The distinction between permission to publish and permission to dis-   15
play publicly is an essential one and one which I think consonant with First Amendment principles. Justice Burger's words which I quoted above support this without question. We are not saying "Smash the presses" or "Ban the bad ones," but simply "Get the stuff out of our sight." Let the legislatures decide — using realistic and humane contemporary community standards — what can be displayed and what cannot. The courts, after all, will be the final arbiters.

Topics for Critical Thinking and Writing

1. Objecting to Justice Douglas's remark that no one is "'compelled to look'" (para. 13), Brownmiller says, "This is hardly true. To buy a paper at the corner newsstand is to subject oneself to a forcible immersion in pornography, to be demeaned by an array of dehumanized, chopped-up parts of the female anatomy, packaged like cuts of meat at the supermarket." Is this true at your local newsstand, or are the sex magazines kept in one place, relatively remote from the newspapers?

2. When Brownmiller attempts to restate the "three-part test" for obscenity established by the Supreme Court in *Miller v. California,* she writes (para. 7): "The materials are obscene if they depict . . ." and so on. She should have written: "The materials are obscene if and only if they depict . . ." and so on. Explain what is wrong here with her "if," and why "if and only if" is needed.

3. In her next-to-last paragraph, Brownmiller reminds us that we already live quite comfortably with some "free-speech abridgements." The examples she gives are that we may not falsely shout "fire" in a crowded theater and may not issue misleading advertisements. Do you think that

these widely accepted restrictions are valid evidence in arguing on behalf of limiting the display of what Brownmiller considers pornography?
Why, or why not?

4. Brownmiller insists that defenders of the First Amendment, who will
surely oppose laws that interfere with the freedom to publish, need not
go on to condemn laws that regulate the freedom to "display publicly"
pornographic publications. Do you agree? Suppose a publisher insists
that he cannot sell his product at a profit unless he is permitted to display it to advantage and that restriction on the latter amounts to interference with his freedom to publish. How might Brownmiller reply?

5. In her last paragraph Brownmiller says that "contemporary community
standards" should be decisive. Can it be argued that because standards
vary from one community to another and from time to time even in the
same place, her recommendation subjects the rights of a minority to the
whims of a majority? The Bill of Rights, after all, was supposed to safeguard constitutional rights from the possible tyranny of the majority.

6. When Brownmiller accuses "the public . . . and the courts" of being
"sadly confused" (para. 11), what does she think they are confused
about? The definition of *pornography* or *obscenity*? The effects of such literature on men and women? Or is it something else?

Charles R. Lawrence III

*Charles R. Lawrence III (b. 1943), author of numerous articles in law jour-
nals and coauthor of* The Bakke Case: The Politics of Inequality *(1979),
teaches law at Stanford University. This essay originally appeared in the*
Chronicle of Higher Education *(October 25, 1989), a publication read
chiefly by faculty and administrators at colleges and universities. An amplified version of the essay appeared in* Duke Law Journal *(February 1990).*

On Racist Speech

I have spent the better part of my life as a dissenter. As a high school
student, I was threatened with suspension for my refusal to participate
in a civil defense drill, and I have been a conspicuous consumer of my
First Amendment liberties ever since. There are very strong reasons for
protecting even racist speech. Perhaps the most important of these is that
such protection reinforces our society's commitment to tolerance as a
value, and that by protecting bad speech from government regulation,
we will be forced to combat it as a community.

But I also have a deeply felt apprehension about the resurgence of
racial violence and the corresponding rise in the incidence of verbal and
symbolic assault and harassment to which blacks and other traditionally
subjugated and excluded groups are subjected. I am troubled by the way
the debate has been framed in response to the recent surge of racist inci-

dents on college and university campuses and in response to some universities' attempts to regulate harassing speech. The problem has been framed as one in which the liberty of free speech is in conflict with the elimination of racism. I believe this has placed the bigot on the moral high ground and fanned the rising flames of racism.

Above all, I am troubled that we have not listened to the real victims, that we have shown so little understanding of their injury, and that we have abandoned those whose race, gender, or sexual preference continues to make them second-class citizens. It seems to me a very sad irony that the first instinct of civil libertarians has been to challenge even the smallest, most narrowly framed efforts by universities to provide black and other minority students with the protection the Constitution guarantees them.

The landmark case of *Brown v. Board of Education* is not a case that we normally think of as a case about speech. But *Brown* can be broadly read as articulating the principle of equal citizenship. *Brown* held that segregated schools were inherently unequal because of the *message* that segregation conveyed—that black children were an untouchable caste, unfit to go to school with white children. If we understand the necessity of eliminating the system of signs and symbols that signal the inferiority of blacks, then we should hesitate before proclaiming that all racist speech that stops short of physical violence must be defended.

University officials who have formulated policies to respond to incidents of racial harassment have been characterized in the press as "thought police," but such policies generally do nothing more than impose sanctions against intentional face-to-face insults. When racist speech takes the form of face-to-face insults, catcalls, or other assaultive speech aimed at an individual or small group of persons, it falls directly within the "fighting words" exception to First Amendment protection. The Supreme Court has held that words which "by their very utterance inflict injury or tend to incite an immediate breach of the peace" are not protected by the First Amendment. 5

If the purpose of the First Amendment is to foster the greatest amount of speech, racial insults disserve that purpose. Assaultive racist speech functions as a preemptive strike. The invective is experienced as a blow, not as a proffered idea, and once the blow is struck, it is unlikely that a dialogue will follow. Racial insults are particularly undeserving of First Amendment protection because the perpetrator's intention is not to discover truth or initiate dialogue but to injure the victim. In most situations, members of minority groups realize that they are likely to lose if they respond to epithets by fighting and are forced to remain silent and submissive.

Courts have held that offensive speech may not be regulated in public forums such as streets where the listener may avoid the speech by moving on, but the regulation of otherwise protected speech has been permitted when the speech invades the privacy of the unwilling listener's home or when the unwilling listener cannot avoid the speech.

Racist posters, fliers, and graffiti in dormitories, bathrooms, and other common living spaces would seem to clearly fall within the reasoning of these cases. Minority students should not be required to remain in their rooms in order to avoid racial assault. Minimally, they should find a safe haven in their dorms and in all other common rooms that are a part of their daily routine.

I would also argue that the university's responsibility for ensuring that these students receive an equal educational opportunity provides a compelling justification for regulations that ensure them safe passage in all common areas. A minority student should not have to risk becoming the target of racially assaulting speech every time he or she chooses to walk across campus. Regulating vilifying speech that cannot be antici- pated or avoided would not preclude announced speeches and rallies — situations that would give minority-group members and their allies the chance to organize counterdemonstrations or avoid the speech altogether.

The most commonly advanced argument against the regulation of racist speech proceeds something like this: We recognize that minority groups suffer pain and injury as the result of racist speech, but we must allow this hate mongering for the benefit of society as a whole. Freedom of speech is the lifeblood of our democratic system. It is especially impor- tant for minorities because often it is their only vehicle for rallying sup- port for the redress of their grievances. It will be impossible to formulate a prohibition so precise that it will prevent the racist speech you want to suppress without catching in the same net all kinds of speech that it would be unconscionable for a democratic society to suppress.

Whenever we make such arguments, we are striking a balance on 10 the one hand between our concern for the continued free flow of ideas and the democratic process dependent on that flow, and, on the other, our desire to further the cause of equality. There can be no meaningful discussion of how we should reconcile our commitment to equality and our commitment to free speech until it is acknowledged that there is real harm inflicted by racist speech and that this harm is far from trivial.

To engage in a debate about the First Amendment and racist speech without a full understanding of the nature and extent of that harm is to risk making the First Amendment an instrument of domination rather than a vehicle of liberation. We have not known the experience of victim- ization by racist, misogynist, and homophobic speech, nor do we equally share the burden of the societal harm it inflicts. We are often quick to say that we have heard the cry of the victims when we have not.

The *Brown* case is again instructive because it speaks directly to the psychic injury inflicted by racist speech by noting that the symbolic mes- sage of segregation affected "the hearts and minds" of Negro children "in a way unlikely ever to be undone." Racial epithets and harassment often cause deep emotional scarring and feelings of anxiety and fear that pervade every aspect of a victim's life.

Brown also recognized that black children did not have an equal opportunity to learn and participate in the school community if they bore the additional burden of being subjected to the humiliation and psychic assault contained in the message of segregation. University students bear an analogous burden when they are forced to live and work in an environment where at any moment they may be subjected to denigrating verbal harassment and assault. The same injury was addressed by the Supreme Court when it held that sexual harassment that creates a hostile or abusive work environment violates the ban on sex discrimination in employment of Title VII of the Civil Rights Act of 1964.

Carefully drafted university regulations would bar the use of words as assault weapons and leave unregulated even the most heinous of ideas when those ideas are presented at times and places and in manners that provide an opportunity for reasoned rebuttal or escape from immediate injury. The history of the development of the right to free speech has been one of carefully evaluating the importance of free expression and its effects on other important societal interests. We have drawn the line between protected and unprotected speech before without dire results. (Courts have, for example, exempted from the protection of the First Amendment obscene speech and speech that disseminates official secrets, that defames or libels another person, or that is used to form a conspiracy or monopoly.)

Blacks and other people of color are skeptical about the argument 15 that even the most injurious speech must remain unregulated because, in an unregulated marketplace of ideas, the best ones will rise to the top and gain acceptance. Our experience tells us quite the opposite. We have seen too many good liberal politicians shy away from the issues that might brand them as being too closely allied with us.

Whenever we decide that racist speech must be tolerated because of the importance of maintaining societal tolerance for all unpopular speech, we are asking blacks and other subordinated groups to bear the burden for the good of all. We must be careful that the ease with which we strike the balance against the regulation of racist speech is in no way influenced by the fact that the cost will be borne by others. We must be certain that those who will pay that price are fairly represented in our deliberations and that they are heard.

At the core of the argument that we should resist all government regulation of speech is the ideal that the best cure for bad speech is good, that ideas that affirm equality and the worth of all individuals will ultimately prevail. This is an empty ideal unless those of us who would fight racism are vigilant and unequivocal in that fight. We must look for ways to offer assistance and support to students whose speech and political participation are chilled in a climate of racial harassment.

Civil rights lawyers might consider suing on behalf of blacks whose right to an equal education is denied by a university's failure to ensure a nondiscriminatory educational climate or conditions of employment. We must embark upon the development of a First Amendment jurisprudence grounded in the reality of our history and our contemporary experience. We must think hard about how best to launch legal attacks against the most indefensible forms of hate speech. Good lawyers can create exceptions and narrow interpretations that limit the harm of hate speech without opening the floodgates of censorship.

Everyone concerned with these issues must find ways to engage actively in actions that resist and counter the racist ideas that we would have the First Amendment protect. If we fail in this, the victims of hate speech must rightly assume that we are on the oppressors' side.

Topics for Critical Thinking and Writing

1. Summarize Lawrence's essay in a paragraph. (You may find it useful first to summarize each paragraph in a sentence and then to revise these summary sentences into a paragraph.)

2. In a sentence state Lawrence's thesis (his main point).

3. Why do you suppose Lawrence included his first paragraph? What does it contribute to his argument?

4. Paragraph 7 argues that "minority students" should not have to endure "racist posters, fliers, and graffiti in dormitories, bathrooms, and other common living spaces." Do you think that Lawrence would also argue that straight white men should not have to endure posters, fliers, or graffiti that speak of "honkies" or "rednecks"? On what do you base your answer?

5. In paragraph 8 Lawrence speaks of "racially assaulting speech" and of "vilifying speech." It is easy to think of words that fit these descriptions, but what about other words? Is *Uncle Tom,* used by an African American about another African American who is eager to please whites, an example? Or take the word *gay.* Surely this word is acceptable because it is widely used by homosexuals, but what about *queer* (used by some homosexuals but usually derogatory when used by heterosexuals)? A third example: There can be little doubt that women are demeaned when males speak of them as *chicks* or *babes,* but are these terms "assaulting" and "vilifying"?

6. Find out if your college or university has a code governing hate speech. If it does, evaluate it. If your college has no such code, imagine that you are Lawrence, and draft one of about 250 words. (See especially his paras. 5, 7, and 14.)

Derek Bok

Derek Bok was born in 1930 in Bryn Mawr, Pennsylvania, and educated at Stanford University and Harvard University, where he received a law degree. From 1971 to 1991 he served as president of Harvard University. The following essay, first published in the Boston Globe *in 1991, was prompted by the display of Confederate flags hung from a window of a Harvard dormitory.*

Protecting Freedom of Expression on the Campus

For several years, universities have been struggling with the problem of trying to reconcile the rights of free speech with the desire to avoid racial tension. In recent weeks, such a controversy has sprung up at Harvard. Two students hung Confederate flags in public view, upsetting students who equate the Confederacy with slavery. A third student tried to protest the flags by displaying a swastika.

These incidents have provoked much discussion and disagreement. Some students have urged that Harvard require the removal of symbols that offend many members of the community. Others reply that such symbols are a form of free speech and should be protected.

Different universities have resolved similar conflicts in different ways. Some have enacted codes to protect their communities from forms of speech that are deemed to be insensitive to the feelings of other groups. Some have refused to impose such restrictions.

It is important to distinguish between the appropriateness of such communications and their status under the First Amendment. The fact that speech is protected by the First Amendment does not necessarily mean that it is right, proper, or civil. I am sure that the vast majority of Harvard students believe that hanging a Confederate flag in public view — or displaying a swastika in response — is insensitive and unwise because any satisfaction it gives to the students who display these symbols is far outweighed by the discomfort it causes to many others.

I share this view and regret that the students involved saw fit to be-   5
have in this fashion. Whether or not they merely wished to manifest their pride in the South — or to demonstrate the insensitivity of hanging Confederate flags, by mounting another offensive symbol in return — they must have known that they would upset many fellow students and ignore the decent regard for the feelings of others so essential to building and preserving a strong and harmonious community.

To disapprove of a particular form of communication, however, is not enough to justify prohibiting it. We are faced with a clear example of the conflict between our commitment to free speech and our desire to foster a community founded on mutual respect. Our society has wrestled with this problem for many years. Interpreting the First Amendment, the Supreme Court has clearly struck the balance in favor of free speech.

While communities do have the right to regulate speech in order to uphold aesthetic standards (avoiding defacement of buildings) or to protect the public from disturbing noise, rules of this kind must be applied across the board and cannot be enforced selectively to prohibit certain kinds of messages but not others.

Under the Supreme Court's rulings, as I read them, the display of swastikas or Confederate flags clearly falls within the protection of the free-speech clause of the First Amendment and cannot be forbidden simply because it offends the feelings of many members of the community. These rulings apply to all agencies of government, including public universities.

Although it is unclear to what extent the First Amendment is enforceable against private institutions, I have difficulty understanding why a university such as Harvard should have less free speech than the surrounding society—or than a public university.

One reason why the power of censorship is so dangerous is that it is   10 extremely difficult to decide when a particular communication is offensive enough to warrant prohibition or to weigh the degree of offensiveness against the potential value of the communication. If we begin to forbid flags, it is only a short step to prohibiting offensive speakers.

I suspect that no community will become humane and caring by restricting what its members can say. The worst offenders will simply find other ways to irritate and insult.

In addition, once we start to declare certain things "offensive," with all the excitement and attention that will follow, I fear that much ingenuity will be exerted trying to test the limits, much time will be expended trying to draw tenuous distinctions, and the resulting publicity will eventually attract more attention to the offensive material than would ever have occurred otherwise.

Rather than prohibit such communications, with all the resulting risks, it would be better to ignore them, since students would then have little reason to create such displays and would soon abandon them. If this response is not possible—and one can understand why—the wisest course is to speak with those who perform insensitive acts and try to help them understand the effects of their actions on others.

Appropriate officials and faculty members should take the lead, as the Harvard House Masters have already done in this case. In talking with students, they should seek to educate and persuade, rather than resort to ridicule or intimidation, recognizing that only persuasion is likely to produce a lasting, beneficial effect. Through such effects, I believe that we act in the manner most consistent with our ideals as an educational institution and most calculated to help us create a truly understanding, supportive community.

Topics for Critical Thinking and Writing

1. Bok sketches the following argument (paras. 8 and 9): The First Amendment protects free speech in public universities and colleges; Harvard is

not a public university; therefore, Harvard does not enjoy the protection of the First Amendment. This argument is plainly invalid. Bok clearly rejects the conclusion ("I have difficulty understanding why . . . Harvard should have less free speech . . . than a public university"). What would need to be revised in the premises to make the argument valid? Do you think Bok would accept or reject such a revision?

2. Bok objects to censorship that simply prevents students from being "offended." He would not object to the campus police preventing students from being harmed. In an essay of 100 words, explain the difference between conduct that is *harmful* and conduct that is (merely?) *offensive*.

3. Bok advises campus officials (and students) simply to "ignore" offensive words, flags, and so forth (para. 13). Do you agree with this advice? Or do you favor a different kind of response? Write a 250-word essay on the theme "How We Ought to Respond to the Offensive Misconduct of Others."

Jean Kilbourne

A graduate of Wellesley College, Jean Kilbourne is now a visiting scholar at Wellesley. She is the author of Deadly Persuasion: Why Women and Girls Must Fight the Addictive Power of Advertising *(1999), issued in paperback as* Can't Buy My Love: How Advertising Changes the Way We Think and Feel *(2000). In her book she argues that advertising contributes to health problems—not only those traced to cigarette smoking but also eating disorders and alcoholism. In the following extract from her book, Kilbourne argues that it is immoral for advertisers to target children. The title of the extract is the editors', and the notes have been renumbered.*

"Own This Child"

Some [Web] sites offer prizes to lure children into giving up the e-mail addresses of their friends too.[1] Online advertising targets children as young as four in an attempt to develop "brand loyalty" as early as possible. Companies unrelated to children's products have Web sites for children, such as Chevron's site, which features games, toys, and videos touting the importance of—surprise!—the oil industry.[2] In this way, companies can create an image early on and can also gather marketing data. As one ad says to advertisers, "Beginning this August, Kidstar will be able to reach every kid on the planet. And you can, too."

The United States is one of the few industrialized nations in the world that thinks that children are legitimate targets for advertisers. Belgium, Denmark, Norway, and the Canadian province of Quebec ban all advertising to children on television and radio,[3] and Sweden and Greece are pushing for an end to all advertising aimed at children throughout the European Union.[4] An effort to pass similar legislation in the United States in the 1970s was squelched by a coalition of food and toy companies, broadcasters, and ad agencies. Children in America appear to have value primarily as new consumers. As an ad for juvenile and infant bedding and home accessories says, "Having children is so rewarding. You get to buy childish stuff and pretend it's for them." Our public policy — or lack thereof — on every children's issue, from education to drugs to teen suicide to child abuse, leaves many to conclude that we are a nation that hates its children.

However, the media care about them. The Turner Cartoon Network tells advertisers, "Today's kids influence over $130 billion of their parent's spending annually. Kids also spend $8 billion of their own money. That makes these little consumers big business."[5] Not only are children influencing a lot of spending in the present, they are developing brand loyalty and the beginnings of an addiction to consumption that will serve corporations well in the future. According to Mike Searles, president of Kids 'Я' Us, "If you own this child at an early age, you can own this child for years to come. Companies are saying, 'Hey, I want to own the kid younger and younger.'"[6] No wonder Levi Strauss & Co. finds it worthwhile to send a direct mailing to seven- to twelve-year-old girls to learn about them when they are starting to form brand opinions.[7] According to the senior advertising manager, "This is more of a long-term relationship that we're trying to explore." There may not seem much harm in this until we consider that the tobacco and alcohol industries are also interested in long-term relationships beginning in childhood — and are selling products that can indeed end up "owning" people.

Advertisers are willing to spend a great deal on psychological research that will help them target children more effectively. Nintendo U.S. has a research center which interviews at least fifteen hundred children every week.[8] Kid Connection, a unit of the advertising agency Saatchi & Saatchi, has commissioned what the company calls "psycho-cultural youth research" studies from cultural anthropologists and clinical psychologists.[9] In a recent study, psychologists interviewed young people between the ages of six and twenty and then analyzed their dreams, drawings, and reactions to symbols. Meanwhile, the anthropologists spent over five hundred hours watching other children use the Internet.

Children are easily influenced. Most little children can't tell the difference between the shows and the commercials (which basically means they are smarter than the rest of us). The toys sold during children's programs are often based on characters in the programs. Recently the Center for Media Education asked the Federal Trade Commission to examine "kidola," a television marketing strategy in which toy companies promise to buy blocks of commercial time if a local broadcast station airs programs associated with their toys.[10]

One company has initiated a program for advertisers to distribute samples, coupons, and promotional materials to a network of twenty-two thousand day care centers and 2 million preschool children.[11] The editor-in-chief of *KidStyle,* a kids' fashion magazine that made its debut in 1997, said, "It's not going to be another parenting magazine. This will be a pictorial magazine focusing on products."[12]

Perhaps most troubling, advertising is increasingly showing up in our schools, where ads are emblazoned on school buses, scoreboards, and book covers, where corporations provide "free" material for teachers, and where many children are a captive audience for the commercials on Channel One, a marketing program that gives video equipment to desperate schools in exchange for the right to broadcast a "news" program studded with commercials to all students every morning. Channel One is hardly free, however—it is estimated that it costs taxpayers $1.8 billion in lost classroom time.[13] But it certainly is profitable for the owners who promise advertisers "the largest teen audience around" and "the undivided attention of millions of teenagers for twelve minutes a day." Another ad for Channel One boasts, "Our relationship with 8.1 million teenagers lasts for six years [rather remarkable considering most of theirs last for . . . like six days]."[14] Imagine the public outcry if a political or religious group offered schools an information package with ten minutes of news and two minutes of political or religious persuasion.[15] Yet we tend to think of commercial persuasion as somehow neutral, although it certainly promotes beliefs and behavior that have significant and sometimes harmful effects on the individual, the family, the society, and the environment.

"Reach him at the office," says an ad featuring a small boy in a business suit, which continues, "His first day job is kindergarten. Modern can put your sponsored educational materials in the lesson plan." Advertisers are reaching nearly 8 million public-school students each day.[16]

Cash-strapped and underfunded schools accept this dance with the devil. And they are not alone. As many people become less and less willing to pay taxes to support public schools and other institutions and services, corporations are only too eager to pick up the slack—in exchange for a captive audience, of course. As one good corporate citizen, head of an outdoor advertising agency, suggested, "Perhaps fewer libraries would be closing their doors or reducing their services if they wrapped their buildings in tastefully done outdoor ads."[17]

According to the Council for Aid to Education, the total amount corporations spend on "educational" programs from kindergarten through high school has increased from $5 million in 1965 to about $500 million today.[18] The Seattle School Board recently voted to aggressively pursue advertising and corporate sponsorship.[19] "There can be a Nike concert series and a Boeing valedictorian," said the head of the task force. We already have market-driven educational materials in our schools,[20] such as Exxon's documentary on the beauty of the Alaskan coastline or the McDonald's Nutrition Chart and a kindergarten curriculum that teaches children to "Learn to Read through Recognizing Corporate Logos."[21]

No wonder so many people fell for a "news item" in *Adbusters* (a Canadian magazine that critiques advertising and commercialism) about a new program called "Tattoo You Too!", which pays schools a fee in exchange for students willing to be tattooed with famous corporate logos, such as the Nike "swoosh" and the Guess question mark. Although the item was a spoof, it was believable enough to be picked up by some major media. I guess nothing about advertising seems unbelievable these days.

There are penalties for young people who resist this commercialization. In the spring of 1998 Mike Cameron, a senior at Greenbrier High School in Evans, Georgia, was suspended from school.[22] Why? Did he bring a gun to school? Was he smoking in the boys' room? Did he assault a teacher? No. He wore a Pepsi shirt on a school-sponsored Coke day, an entire school day dedicated to an attempt to win ten thousand dollars in a national contest run by Coca-Cola.

Coke has several "partnerships" with schools around the country in which the company gives several million dollars to the school in exchange for a long-term contract giving Coke exclusive rights to school vending machines.[23] John Bushey, an area superintendent for thirteen schools in Colorado Springs who signs his correspondence "The Coke Dude," urged school officials to "get next year's volume up to 70,000 cases" and suggested letting students buy Coke throughout the day and putting vending machines "where they are accessible all day." Twenty years ago, teens drank almost twice as much milk as soda. Today they drink twice as much soda as milk. Some data suggest this contributes to broken bones while they are still teenagers and to osteoporosis in later life.

NOTES

1. F. Rich, "howdydoody.com," *New York Times* 8 June 1997: E15.
2. I. Austen, "But First, Another Word from Our Sponsors," *New York Times* 18 Feb. 1999: E1, E8.
3. M. F. Jacobson and L. A. Mazur, "Marketing Madness: A Survival Guide for a Consumer Society," *Westview Press* 1995: 28. Also J. Weber, "Selling to Kids: At What Price?" *Boston Globe* 18 May 1997: F4.
4. J. Koranteng, "Sweden Presses EU for Further Ad Restrictions," *Advertising Age International* 12 April 1999: 2.
5. Ad, *New York Times* (Calif. ed.) 8 Feb. 1993: C7.
6. R. Harris, "Children Who Dress for Excess: Today's Youngsters Have Become Fixated with Fashion," *Los Angeles Times* 12 Nov. 1989: A1.
7. C. Krol, "Levi's Reach Girls as They Develop Their Opinions on Brands," *Advertising Age* 20 April 1998: 29.
8. Stephen Kline, author of *Out of the Garden: Toys and Children's Culture in the Age of TV Marketing*, interview with McLaren, "The Babysitter's Club," *Stay Free!* Spring 1997: 10.
9. I. Austen, "But First, Another Word from Our Sponsors," *New York Times* 18 Feb. 1999: E1, E8.
10. Center for Media Education, 1511 K Street N.W., Suite 518, Washington, D.C. 20005, 202-628-2620.
11. J. Carroll, "Adventures into New Territory," *Boston Globe* 24 Nov. 1996: D5.
12. A. M. Kerwin, "'KidStyle' Crafts Customized Ad Opportunities," *Advertising Age* 28 April 1997: 46.
13. "Reading, Writing . . . and TV Commercials," *Enough!* Spring 1999: 10.

14. "Our Relationship with 8.1 Million Teenagers . . . ," *Advertising Age* 29 June 1998: S27.

15. H. Rank, "Channel One: Misconceptions Three," *English Journal* 81.4 (April 1992): 31–32.

16. Some corporations sponsor contests and incentive programs, such as an essay-writing contest sponsored by Reebok shoes, which then uses the information to fine-tune the appeal of its advertisements to youth (*Not for Sale!* [Center for Commercial-Free Public Education, Oakland, CA: Spring 1997]: 1), and a Kellogg's contest which had kids make sculptures out of Rice Krispies and melted marshmallows (N. Labi, "Classrooms for Sale," *Time* 19 April 1999: 44). Schools can earn points for every Campbell's soup label or AT&T long-distance phone call, which can then be redeemed for athletic and educational equipment. And a math textbook introduces a decimal division problem as follows: "Will is saving his allowance to buy a pair of Nike shoes that cost $68.25. If Will earns $3.25 per week, how many weeks will Will need to save?" Beside the text is a full-color picture of Nikes (C. L. Hays, "Math Book Salted with Brand Names Raises New Alarm," *New York Times* 21 March 1999: 1).

17. B. Wilkins, "Moving from Blight to Blessing," *Advertising Age* 2 June 1997: 32.

18. K. Zernike, "Let's Make a Deal: Business Seek Classroom Access," *Boston Globe* 2 Feb. 1997: A1, B6.

19. *Not for Sale!* (Center for Commercial-Free Public Education, Oakland, CA) Spring 1997: 1.

20. J. Carroll, "Adventures into New Territory," *Boston Globe* 24 Nov. 1996: D1, D5.

21. *Not for Sale!* (Center for Commercial-Free Public Education, Oakland, CA) Winter 1999: 1.

22. Associated Press, "Pepsi Prank Goes Flat," *Boston Globe* 26 March 1998: A3.

23. J. Foreman, "Sugar's 'Empty Calories' Pile Up," *Boston Globe* 1 March 1999: C1, C4.

Topics for Critical Thinking and Writing

1. In her second paragraph, Kilbourne tells us that some countries "ban all advertising to children on television and radio." Do you favor such a law? Why, or why not?

2. In her third paragraph, Kilbourne indicates her distress that children "are developing brand loyalty and the beginnings of an addiction to consumption." Are you loyal to certain brands? If so, do you think this loyalty is a bad thing? Explain. And are you addicted to consumption? (*Addicted*, of course, implies a loss of self-control. Elsewhere in her book Kilbourne argues, perhaps rightly, that most of us are more deeply influenced by advertising than we are willing to grant or than we are aware.)

3. Beginning in paragraph 7, Kilbourne calls our attention to the practice of allowing companies to donate materials to schools in exchange for ads. The schools accept these materials—with the ads—because they cannot afford to buy the materials. Should such a practice be forbidden? For instance, should a school reject funds that are offered on behalf of "a Nike concert series" (para. 10)? If you are aware that your secondary school accepted material, along with the accompanying advertisements, do you think the ads influenced your behavior? Explain.

4. Do you think Mike Cameron ought to have been suspended for wearing a Pepsi shirt on a Coke day (para. 12)? Should he have been reprimanded by the school authorities? Would it make any difference if (a) he didn't know it was a Coke day, (b) he knew it was a Coke day and refused to go along because he strongly opposed commercial sponsorship of this sort, or (c) he knew it was a Coke day but thought it would be amusing to be the only holdout?

5. Is there really such a thing as an "addiction to consumption" (para. 3)? Write a 500-word essay on the theme "Excessive Juvenile Consumption, Yes; Addiction to Consumption, No."

6. In her final paragraph, Kilbourne expresses her unhappiness that young people today drink more soda than milk. Are you convinced that they should drink more milk than soda? If so, where did you get the idea that milk is more healthful than soda?

3

Critical Reading: Getting Deeper into Arguments

He that wrestles with us strengthens our nerves, and sharpens our skill.
Our antagonist is our helper. —EDMUND BURKE

PERSUASION, ARGUMENT, DISPUTE

When we think seriously about an argument (not name calling or mere rationalization), not only do we hear ideas that may be unfamiliar, but we are also forced to examine closely our own cherished opinions, and perhaps for the first time we really come to see the strengths and weaknesses of what we believe. As John Stuart Mill put it, "He who knows only his own side of the case knows little."

It is customary, and useful, to distinguish between persuasion and argument. **Persuasion** has the broader meaning. To persuade is to win over—whether by giving reasons (that is, by argument), by appealing to the emotions, or, for that matter, by using torture. **Argument,** one form of persuasion, relies on reason; it offers statements as reasons for other statements. Rhetoricians often use the Greek word **logos,** which merely means "word" or "reason," to denote this aspect of persuasive writing—the appeal to reason. (The appeal to the emotions is known as **pathos.** Strictly speaking, *pathos* is Greek for "suffering," but it now covers all sorts of emotional appeal—for instance, to one's sense of pity or one's sense of patriotism.)

Notice that an argument, in the sense of statements that are offered as reasons for other statements, does not require two speakers or writers who represent opposed positions. The Declaration of Independence is an argument, setting forth the colonists' reasons for declaring their independence. In practice, of course, someone's argument usually advances reasons in opposition to someone else's position or belief. But even if one is writing only for oneself, trying to clarify one's thinking by setting forth reasons, the result is an argument. In a **dispute,** however, two or more people express views that are at odds.

59

Most of this book is about argument in the sense of the presentation of reasons, but of course, reason is not the whole story. If an argument is to be effective, it must be presented persuasively. For instance, the writer's **tone** (attitude toward self, topic, and audience) must be appropriate if the discourse is to persuade the reader. The careful presentation of the self is not something disreputable, nor is it something that publicity agents or advertising agencies invented. Aristotle (384–322 B.C.) emphasized the importance of impressing on the audience that the speaker is a person of good sense and high moral character. (He called this aspect of persuasion **ethos,** the Greek word for "character," as opposed to *logos,* which we have noted is the word for persuasion by appealing to reason.) We talk at length about tone, along with other matters such as the organization of an argument, in Chapter 5, but here we deal with some of the chief devices used in reasoning, and we glance at emotional appeals.

We should note at once, however, that an argument presupposes a fixed **topic.** Suppose we are arguing about Jefferson's assertion, in the Declaration of Independence, that "all men are created equal." Jones subscribes to this statement, but Smith says it is nonsense and argues that one has only to look around to see that some people are brighter than others, or healthier, or better coordinated, or whatever. Jones and Smith, if they intend to argue the point, will do well to examine what Jefferson actually wrote:

> We hold these truths to be self-evident, that all men are created equal: that they are endowed by their Creator with certain unalienable rights; and that among these are life, liberty, and the pursuit of happiness.

There is room for debate over what Jefferson really meant and about whether he is right, but clearly he was talking about *equality of rights,* and if Smith and Jones wish to argue about Jefferson's view of equality— that is, if they wish to offer their reasons for accepting, rejecting, or modifying it—they will do well first to agree on what Jefferson said or what he probably meant to say. Jones and Smith may still hold different views; they may continue to disagree on whether Jefferson was right and proceed to offer arguments and counterarguments to settle the point. But only if they can agree on *what* they disagree about will their dispute get somewhere.

REASON VERSUS RATIONALIZATION

Reason may not be our only way of finding the truth, but it is a way we often rely on. The subway ran yesterday at 6:00 A.M. and the day before at 6:00 A.M. and the day before, and so I infer from this evidence that it is also running today at 6:00 A.M. (a form of reasoning known as **induction**). Or: Bus drivers require would-be passengers to present the exact change; I do not have the exact change; therefore, I infer I cannot ride on the bus (**deduction**). (The terms *induction* and *deduction* will be discussed shortly.)

We also know that, if we set our minds to a problem, we can often find reasons (not necessarily sound ones but reasons nevertheless) for almost anything we want to justify. Here is an entertaining example from Benjamin Franklin's *Autobiography:*

> I believe I have omitted mentioning that in my first voyage from Boston, being becalmed off Block Island, our people set about catching cod and hauled up a great many. Hitherto I had stuck to my resolution of not eating animal food, and on this occasion, I considered with my master Tryon the taking of every fish as a kind of unprovoked murder, since none of them had or ever could do us any injury that might justify the slaughter. All this seemed very reasonable. But I had formerly been a great lover of fish, and when this came hot out of the frying pan, it smelt admirably well. I balanced some time between principle and inclination, till I recollected that when the fish were opened I saw smaller fish taken out of their stomachs. Then thought I, if you eat one another, I don't see why we mayn't eat you. So I dined upon cod very heartily and continued to eat with other people, returning only now and then occasionally to a vegetable diet. So convenient a thing it is to be a *reasonable creature,* since it enables one to find or make a reason for everything one has a mind to do.

Franklin, of course, is being playful; he is *not* engaging in critical thinking. He tells us that he loved fish, that this fish "smelt admirably well," and so we are prepared for him to find a reason (here one as weak as "Fish eat fish, so people may eat fish") to abandon his vegetarianism. (But think: Fish also eat their own young. May we therefore eat ours?) Still, Franklin touches on a truth: If necessary, we can find reasons to justify whatever we want. That is, instead of reasoning we may *rationalize* (devise a self-serving but dishonest reason), like the fox in Aesop's fables who, finding the grapes he desired were out of his reach, consoled himself with the thought they were probably sour.

Probably we can never be certain that we are not rationalizing, but—except when, like Franklin, we are being playful—we can seek to think critically about our own beliefs, scrutinizing our assumptions, looking for counterevidence, and wondering if different conclusions can reasonably be drawn.

SOME PROCEDURES IN ARGUMENT

Definition

Definition, we mentioned in our first chapter, is one of the classical *topics*, a "place" to which one goes with questions; in answering the questions, one finds ideas. When we define, we are answering the question

"What is it?," and in answering this question as precisely as we can, we will find, clarify, and develop ideas.

We have already glanced at an argument over the proposition that "all men are created equal," and we saw that the words needed clarification. *Equal* meant, in the context, not physically or mentally equal but something like "equal in rights," equal politically and legally. (And of course, "men" meant "men and women.") Words do not always mean exactly what they seem to: There is no lead in a lead pencil, and a standard 2-by-4 is 1⅝ inches in thickness and 3⅜ inches in width.

Definition by Synonym   Let's return, for a moment, to *pornography*, a word that, we saw, is not easily defined. One way to define a word is to offer a **synonym.** Thus, pornography can be defined, at least roughly, as "obscenity" (something indecent). But definition by synonym is usually only a start because we find that we will have to define the synonym and, besides, that very few words have exact synonyms. (In fact, *pornography* and *obscenity* are not exact synonyms.)

Definition by Example   A second way to define something is to point to an example (this is often called **ostensive definition,** from the Latin *ostendere,* "to show"). This method can be very helpful, ensuring that both writer and reader are talking about the same thing, but it also has its limitations. A few decades ago many people pointed to James Joyce's *Ulysses* and D. H. Lawrence's *Lady Chatterley's Lover* as examples of obscene novels, but today these books are regarded as literary masterpieces. Possibly they can be obscene and also be literary masterpieces. (Joyce's wife is reported to have said of her husband, "He may have been a great writer, but . . . he had a very dirty mind.")

One of the difficulties of using an example, however, is that the example is richer, more complex than the term it is being used to define, and this richness and complexity get in the way of achieving a clear definition. Thus, if one cites Lawrence's *Lady Chatterley's Lover* as an example of pornography, a listener may erroneously think that pornography has something to do with British novels or with heterosexual relationships outside of marriage. Yet neither of these ideas is part of the concept of pornography.

We are not trying here to formulate a satisfactory definition of *pornography;* our object is to say that an argument will be most fruitful if the participants first agree on what they are talking about and that one way to secure such agreement is to define the topic ostensively. Choosing the right example, one that has all the central or typical characteristics, can make a topic not only clear but vivid.

Definition by Stipulation   In arguing, you can legitimately offer a **stipulative definition,** saying, perhaps, that by *Native American* you mean any person with any Native American blood; or you might say,

"For the purpose of the present discussion, I mean by a *Native American* any person who has at least one grandparent of pure Native American blood." A stipulative definition is appropriate where

- No fixed or standard definition is available, and
- Some arbitrary specification is necessary to fix the meaning of a key term in the argument.

Not everyone may be willing to accept your stipulative definition, and alternatives can probably be defended. In any case, when you stipulate a definition, your audience knows what *you* mean by the term thus defined.

Of course, it would *not* be reasonable to stipulate that by *Native American* you mean anyone with a deep interest in North American aborigines. That's just too idiosyncratic to be useful. Similarly, an essay on Jews in America will have to rely on some definition of the key idea. Perhaps the writer will stipulate the definition used in Israel: A Jew is a person who has a Jewish mother or, if not born of a Jewish mother, a person who has formally adopted the Jewish faith. Or perhaps the writer will stipulate another meaning: Jews are people who consider themselves to be Jews. Some sort of reasonable definition must be offered.

To stipulate, however, that by *Jews* you mean "persons who believe that the area formerly called Palestine rightfully belongs to the Jews" would hopelessly confuse matters. Remember the old riddle and the answer: If you call a dog's tail a leg, how many legs does a dog have? Answer: Four. Calling a tail a leg doesn't make it a leg.

Suppose someone says she means by a *Communist* "anyone who opposes the president, does not go to church, and favors a more nearly equal distribution of wealth and property." A dictionary or encyclopedia will tell us that a person is a Communist who accepts the main doctrines of Karl Marx (or perhaps of Marxism-Leninism). For many purposes, we may think of Communists as persons who belong to some Communist political party, by analogy with Democrats and Republicans. Or we may even think of a Communist as someone who supports what is common to the constitutions and governments currently in power in China and Cuba. But what is the point of the misleading stipulative definition of *Communist* given at the beginning of this paragraph, except to cast disapproval on everyone whose views bring them within the definition?

There is no good reason for offering this definition, and there are two goods reasons against it. The first is that we already have perfectly adequate definitions of *Communist,* and one should learn them and rely on them until the need to revise and improve them occurs. The second reason for refraining from using a misleading stipulative definition is that it is unfair to tar with a dirty and sticky brush nonchurchgoers and the rest by calling them derogatory names they do not deserve. Even if it is true that Communists favor more egalitarian distribution of wealth and property, the converse is *not* true: Not all egalitarians are Communists. Furthermore, if something is economically unsound or morally objectionable about such egalitarianism, the only responsible way to make that point is to argue against it.

A stipulation may be helpful and legitimate. Here is the opening paragraph of an essay by Richard B. Brandt titled "The Morality and Rationality of Suicide" (from *A Handbook for the Study of Suicide,* edited by Seymour Perlin). Notice that

- The author first stipulates a definition, and
- Then, aware that the definition may strike some readers as too broad and therefore unreasonable or odd, he offers a reason on behalf of his definition:

> "Suicide" is conveniently defined, for our purposes, as doing something which results in one's death, either from the intention of ending one's life or the intention to bring about some other state of affairs (such as relief from pain) which one thinks it certain or highly probable can be achieved only by means of death or will produce death. It may seem odd to classify an act of heroic self-sacrifice on the part of a soldier as suicide. It is simpler, however, not to try to define "suicide" so that an act of suicide is always irrational or immoral in some way; if we adopt a neutral definition like the above we can still proceed to ask when an act of suicide in that sense is rational, morally justifiable, and so on, so that all evaluations anyone might wish to make can still be made.

Sometimes a definition that at first seems extremely odd can be made acceptable, if strong reasons are offered in its support. Sometimes, in fact, an odd definition marks a great intellectual step forward. For instance, recently the Supreme Court recognized that *speech* includes symbolic nonverbal expression such as protesting against a war by wearing armbands or by flying the American flag upside down. Such actions, because they express ideas or emotions, are now protected by the First Amendment. Few people today would disagree that *speech* should include symbolic gestures. (We include an example of controversy over precisely this issue, in Derek Bok's "Protecting Freedom of Expression on the Campus," in Chapter 2.)

An example that seems notably eccentric to many readers and thus far has not gained much support is from page 94 of Peter Singer's *Practical Ethics,* in which the author suggests that a nonhuman being can be a *person.* He admits that "it sounds odd to call an animal a person" but says that it seems so only because of our bad habit of sharply separating ourselves from other species. For Singer, *persons* are "rational and self-conscious beings, aware of themselves as distinct entities with a past and a future." Thus, although a newborn infant is a human being, it is not a person; on the other hand, an adult chimpanzee is not a human being but probably is a person. You don't have to agree with Singer to know exactly what he means and where he stands. Moreover, if you read his essay, you may even find that his reasons are plausible and that by means of his unusual definition he has enlarged your thinking.

The Importance of Definitions   Trying to decide on the best way to define a key idea or a central concept is often difficult as well as controversial. *Death,* for example, has been redefined in recent years. Traditionally, a person was dead when there was no longer any heartbeat. But with advancing medical technology, the medical profession has persuaded legislatures to redefine *death* by reference to cessation of cerebral and cortical functions—so-called brain death. Recently, some scholars have hoped to bring clarity into the abortion debate by redefining *life.*

Traditionally, human life begins at birth or perhaps at viability (the capacity of a fetus to live independently of the uterine environment). Now, however, some are proposing a "brain birth" definition, in the hope of resolving the abortion controversy. A *New York Times* story of November 8, 1990, reported that these thinkers want abortion to be prohibited by law at the point where "integrated brain functioning begins to emerge—about seventy days after conception." Whatever the merits of such a redefinition, the debate is convincing evidence of just how important the definition of certain terms can be.

Last Words about Definition   Since Plato's time, in the fourth century B.C., it has often been argued that the best way to give a definition is to state the *essence* of the thing being defined. Thus, the classic example defines *man* as "a rational animal." (Today, to avoid sexist implications, instead of *man* we would say *human being* or *person.*) That is, the property of *rational animality* is taken to be the essence of every human creature, and so it must be mentioned in the definition of *man.* This statement guarantees that the definition is neither too broad nor too narrow. But philosophers have long criticized this alleged ideal type of definition, on several grounds, one of which is that no one can propose such definitions without assuming that the thing being defined has an essence in the first place—an assumption that is not necessary. Thus, we may want to define *causality,* or *explanation,* or even *definition* itself, but it is doubtful whether it is sound to assume that any of these things has an essence.

A much better way to provide a definition is to offer a set of **sufficient and necessary conditions.** Suppose we want to define the word *circle* and are conscious of the need to keep circles distinct from other geometrical figures such as rectangles and spheres. We might express our definition by citing sufficient and necessary conditions as follows: "Anything is a circle *if and only if* it is a closed plane figure, all points on the circumference of which are equidistant from the center." Using the connective "if and only if" (called the *biconditional*) between the definition and what is being defined helps to force into our consciousness the need to make the definition neither too exclusive (too narrow) nor too inclusive (too broad). Of course, for most ordinary purposes we don't require such a formally precise and explicit definition. Nevertheless, perhaps the best criterion to keep in mind when assessing a proposed definition is whether it can be stated in the "if and only if" form, and whether, if it is so stated, it is true; that is, if it truly specifies *all and only* the things covered by the word being defined.

Thus, to summarize, definitions can be given by

- Synonym,
- Example,
- Stipulation,
- Mention of the essence, and
- Statement of necessary and sufficient conditions.

Assumptions

In Chapter 1 we discussed the **assumptions** made by the authors of two essays on campus discipline. But we have more to say about assumptions. We have already said that in the form of discourse known as argument certain statements are offered as reasons for other statements. But even the longest and most complex chain of reasoning or proof is fastened to assumptions, one or more *unexamined beliefs*. (Even if such a belief is shared by writer and reader, it is no less an assumption.) Benjamin Franklin argued against paying salaries to the holders of executive offices in the federal government on the grounds that men are moved by ambition and by avarice (love of power and of money) and that powerful positions conferring wealth incite men to do their worst. These assumptions he stated, though he felt no need to argue them at length because he assumed that his readers shared them.

An assumption may be unstated. For example, John Silber in his essay on whether students should be above the law (p. 10) assumes that just as it was unfair in medieval times to give advantages to clerics accused of crimes, it is likewise unfair to give advantages to college students today when they are accused of crimes. He doesn't argue for this proposition, he doesn't even assert it. But it underlies much of his criticism of current college disciplinary procedures. A writer, painstakingly arguing specific points, may choose to keep one or more of the assumptions tacit. Or the writer may be as unaware of some underlying assumption as of the surrounding air. For example, Franklin didn't even bother to state another assumption. He must have assumed that persons of wealth who accept an unpaying job (after all, only persons of wealth could afford to hold unpaid government jobs) will have at heart the interests of all classes of people, not only the interests of their own class. Probably Franklin did not state this assumption because he thought it was perfectly obvious, but if you think critically about the assumption, you may find reasons to doubt it. Surely one reason we pay our legislators is to make certain that the legislature does not consist only of people whose incomes may give them an inadequate view of the needs of others.

An Example: Assumptions in the Argument Permitting Abortion

1. Ours is a pluralistic society, in which we believe that the religious beliefs of one group should not be imposed on others.
2. Personal privacy is a right, and a woman's body is hers, not to be violated by laws that tell her she may not do certain things to her body.

But these (and other) arguments *assume* that a fetus is not—or not yet—a person and therefore is not entitled to the same protection against assaults that we are. Virtually all of us assume that it is usually wrong to kill a human being. Granted, we may find instances in which we believe it is acceptable to take a human life, such as self-defense against a would-be murderer. But even here we find a shared assumption that persons are ordinarily entitled not to be killed.

The argument about abortion, then, usually depends on opposed assumptions: For one group, the fetus is a human being and a potential person—and this potentiality is decisive. But for the other group it is not. Persons arguing one side or the other of the abortion issue ought to be aware that opponents may not share their assumptions.

Premises and Syllogisms

Premises are stated assumptions used as reasons in an argument. (The word comes from a Latin word meaning "to send before" or "to set in front.") A premise thus is a statement set down—assumed—before the argument is begun. The joining of two premises—two statements taken to be true—to produce a conclusion, a third statement, is called a **syllogism** (Greek for "a reckoning together"). The classic example is this:

Major premise: All human beings are mortal.

Minor premise: Socrates is a human being.

Conclusion: Socrates is mortal.

Deduction

The mental process of moving from one statement ("All human beings are mortal") through another ("Socrates is a human being") to yet a further statement ("Socrates is mortal") is called **deduction,** from Latin for "lead down from." In this sense, deductive reasoning does not give us any new knowledge, although it is easy to construct examples that have so many premises, or premises that are so complex, that the conclusion really does come as news to most who examine the argument. Thus, the great detective Sherlock Holmes was credited by his admiring colleague, Dr. Watson, with unusual powers of deduction. Watson meant in part that Holmes could see the logical consequences of apparently disconnected reasons, the number and complexity of which left others at a loss. What is common in all cases of deduction is that the reasons or premises offered are supposed to contain within themselves, so to speak, the conclusion extracted from them.

Often a syllogism is abbreviated. Martin Luther King Jr., defending a protest march, wrote in "Letter from Birmingham Jail":

> You assert that our actions, even though peaceful, must be condemned because they precipitate violence.

Fully expressed, the argument that King attributes to his critics would be stated thus:

> Society must condemn actions (even if peaceful) that precipitate violence.
>
> This action (though peaceful) will precipitate violence.
>
> Therefore, society must condemn this action.

An incomplete or abbreviated syllogism in which one of the premises is left unstated, of the sort found in King's original quotation, is called an **enthymeme** (Greek for "in the mind").

Here is another, more whimsical example of an enthymeme, in which both a premise and the conclusion are left implicit. Henry David Thoreau remarked that "Circumstantial evidence can be very strong, as when you find a trout in the milk." The joke, perhaps intelligible only to people born before 1930 or so, depends on the fact that milk used to be sold "in bulk" — that is, ladled out of a big can directly to the customer by the farmer or grocer. This practice was finally prohibited in the 1930s because for centuries the sellers, in order to increase their profit, were known to dilute the milk with water. Thoreau's enthymeme can be fully expressed thus:

> Trout live only in water.
>
> This milk has a trout in it.
>
> Therefore, this milk has water in it.

These enthymemes have three important properties: Their premises are *true*, the form of their argument is *valid*, and they leave *implicit* either the conclusion or one of the premises.

Sound Arguments

The purpose of a syllogism is to present reasons that establish its conclusion. This is done by making sure that the argument satisfies both of two independent criteria:

- First, all of the premises must be *true.*
- Second, the syllogism must be *valid.*

Once these criteria are satisfied, the conclusion of the syllogism is guaranteed. Any such argument is said to establish or to prove its conclusion or, to use another term, is said to be **sound.** Here's an example of a sound argument, a syllogism that proves its conclusion:

No city in Nevada has a population over 200,000.

Denver has a population over 200,000.

Therefore, Denver is not a city in Nevada.

Each premise is **true,** and the syllogism is **valid,** so it establishes its conclusion.

But how do we tell in any given case that an argument is sound? We perform two different tests, one for the truth of each of the premises and another for the validity of the argument.

The basic test for the **truth** of a premise is to determine whether what it asserts corresponds with reality; if it does, then it is true, and if it doesn't, then it is false. Everything depends on the content of the premise — what it asserts — and the evidence for it. (In the preceding syllogism, the truth of the premises can be tested by checking population statistics in a recent almanac.)

The test for **validity** is quite different. We define a valid argument as one in which the conclusion follows from the premises, so that if all the premises are true then the conclusion *must* be true, too. The general test for validity, then, is this: If one grants the premises, one must also grant the conclusion. Or to put it another way, if one grants the premises but denies the conclusion, is one caught in a self-contradiction? If so, the argument is valid; if not, the argument is invalid.

The preceding syllogism obviously passes this test. If you grant the population information given in the premises but deny the conclusion, you have contradicted yourself. Even if the population information were in error, the conclusion in this syllogism would still follow from the premises — the hallmark of a valid argument! The conclusion follows because the validity of an argument is a purely formal matter concerning the *relation* between premises and conclusion given what they mean.

One can see this relationship more clearly by examining an argument that is valid but that, because one or both of the premises are false, does *not* establish its conclusion. Here is an example of such a syllogism:

The whale is a large fish.

All large fish have scales.

Therefore, whales have scales.

We know that the premises and the conclusion are false: Whales are mammals, not fish, and not all large fish have scales (sharks have no scales, for instance). But where the issue is the validity of the argument, the truth of the premises and the conclusion is beside the point. Just a little reflection assures us that *if* both of these premises were true, then the conclusion would have to be true as well. That is, anyone who grants the premises of this syllogism and yet denies the conclusion has contradicted herself. So the validity of an argument does not in any way depend on the truth of the premises or the conclusion.

A sound argument, as we said, is an argument that passes both the test of true premises and the test of valid inference. To put it another way, a sound argument is one that passes the test of *content* (the premises are true, as a matter of fact) and the test of *form* (its premises and conclusion, by virtue of their very meanings, are so related that it is impossible for the premises to be true and the conclusion false).

Accordingly, an unsound argument, an argument that fails to prove its conclusion, suffers from one or both of two defects. First, not all of the premises are true. Second, the argument is invalid. Usually it is one or both of these defects that we have in mind when we object to someone's argument as "illogical." In evaluating someone's deductive argument, therefore, you must always ask: Is it vulnerable to criticism on the ground that one (or more) of its premises is false? Or is the inference itself vulnerable because whether or not all the premises are all true, even if they were the conclusion still wouldn't follow?

A deductive argument *proves* its conclusion if and only if *two conditions* are satisfied: (1) All the premises are *true,* and (2) it would be *inconsistent to assert the premises and deny the conclusions.*

A Word about False Premises   Suppose that one or more of the premises of a syllogism is false but the syllogism itself is valid. What does that tell us about the truth of the conclusion? Consider this example:

All Americans prefer vanilla ice cream to other flavors.

Tiger Woods is an American.

Therefore, Tiger Woods prefers vanilla ice cream to other flavors.

The first (or major) premise in this syllogism is false. Yet the argument passes our formal test for validity; it is clear that if one grants both premises, one must accept the conclusion. So we can say that the conclusion *follows from* its premises, even though the premises *do not prove* the conclusion. This is not as paradoxical as it may sound. For all we know, the conclusion of this argument may in fact be true; Tiger Woods may indeed prefer vanilla ice cream, and the odds are that he does because consumption statistics show that a majority of Americans prefer vanilla. Nevertheless, if the conclusion in this syllogism is true, it is not because this argument proved it.

A Word about Invalid Syllogisms   Usually, one can detect a false premise in an argument, especially when the suspect premise appears in someone else's argument. A trickier business is the invalid syllogism. Consider this argument:

All crows are black.

This bird is black.

Therefore, this bird is a crow.

Let's assume that both of the premises are true. This tells us nothing about the truth of the conclusion because the argument is invalid. The *form* of the reasoning, the structure of the argument, is such that its premises (whether true or false) do not guarantee the conclusion. Even if both the premises were true, the conclusion might still be false.

In the preceding syllogism, the conclusion may well be true. It could be that the bird referred to in the second (minor) premise is a crow. But the conclusion might be false because not only crows are black; ravens and blackbirds are also black. If the minor premise is asserted on the strength of observing a blackbird, then the conclusion surely is false: *This* bird is *not* a crow. So the argument is invalid, since as it stands it would lead us from true premises to accept a false conclusion.

How do we tell, in general and in particular cases, whether a syllogism is valid? As you know, chemists use litmus paper to enable them to tell instantly whether the liquid in a test tube is an acid or a base. Unfortunately, logic has no litmus test to tell us instantly whether an argument is valid or invalid. Logicians beginning with Aristotle have developed techniques that enable them to test any given argument, no matter how complex or subtle, to determine its validity. But the results of their labors cannot be expressed in a paragraph or even a few pages; not for nothing are semester-long courses devoted to teaching formal deductive logic. Apart from advising you to consult Chapter 8, A Logician's View: Deduction, Induction, Fallacies, all we can do here is repeat two basic points.

First, validity of deductive arguments is a matter of their *form* or *structure*. Even syllogisms like the one on Denver on page 69 come in a large variety of forms (256 different ones, to be precise), and only some of these forms are valid. Second, all valid deductive arguments (and only such arguments) pass this test: If one accepts all the premises, then one must accept the conclusion as well. Hence, if it is possible to accept the premises but reject the conclusion (without self-contradiction, of course), then the argument is invalid.

Let us exit from further discussion of this important but difficult subject on a lighter note. Many illogical arguments masquerade as logical. Consider this example: If it takes a horse and carriage four hours to go from Pinsk to Chelm, does it follow that if you have a carriage with two horses you will get there in two hours? In Chapter 8, we discuss at some length other kinds of deductive arguments, as well as **fallacies,** which are kinds of invalid reasoning.

Induction

Whereas the purpose of deduction is to extract the hidden consequences of our beliefs and assumptions, the purpose of **induction** is to use information about observed cases in order to reach a conclusion about unobserved cases. (The word comes from the Latin *in ducere,* "to lead into," or "to lead up to.") If we observe that the bite of a certain snake is poisonous, we may conclude on this evidence that another snake of the same general type is also poisonous. Our inference might be even broader. If we observe that snake after snake of a certain type has a poisonous bite and that these snakes are all rattlesnakes, we are tempted to **generalize** that all rattlesnakes are poisonous.

By far the most common way to test the adequacy of a generalization is to confront it with one or more **counterexamples.** If the counterexamples are genuine and reliable, then the generalization must be false. For example, Ronald Takaki's essay on the "myth" of Asian racial superiority (p. 102) is full of examples that contradict the alleged superiority of Asians; they are counterexamples to that thesis and they help to expose it as a "myth." What is true of Takaki's reasoning is true generally in argumentative writing. We are constantly testing our generalizations against actual or possible counterexamples.

Unlike deduction, induction gives us conclusions that go beyond the information contained in the premises used in their support. Not surprisingly, the conclusions of inductive reasoning are not always true, even when all the premises are true. On page 60 we gave as an example the belief that the subway runs at 6:00 A.M. every day, based on our observation that on previous days it ran at 6:00 A.M. Suppose, following this reasoning, one arrives at the subway platform just before 6:00 A.M. on a given day only to discover after an hour of waiting that there still is no train. What inference should we draw to explain this? Possibly today is Sunday, and the subway doesn't run before 7:00 A.M. Or possibly there was a breakdown earlier this morning. Whatever the explanation, we relied on a sample that was not large enough (a larger sample might have included some early morning breakdowns) or not representative enough (a more representative sample would have included the later starts on holidays).

A Word about Samples   When we reason inductively, much depends on the size and the quality of the sample. We may interview five members of Alpha Tau Omega and find that all five are Republicans, yet we cannot legitimately conclude that all members of ATO are Republicans. The problem is not always one of failing to interview large numbers. A poll of ten thousand college students tells us very little about "college students" if all ten thousand are white males at the University of Texas. Such a sample, because it leaves out women and minority males, obviously is not sufficiently *representative* of "college students" as a group. Further, though not all of the students at the University of Texas are from Texas or even from the Southwest, it is quite likely that the student body is not fully representative (for instance, in race and in income) of American college students. If this conjecture is correct, even a truly representative sample of University of Texas students would not allow one to draw firm conclusions about American college students.

In short: An argument that uses samples ought to tell the reader how the samples were chosen. If it does not provide this information, the argument may rightly be treated with suspicion.

Evidence

Experimentation   Induction is obviously of use in arguing. If, for example, one is arguing that handguns should be controlled, one will point to specific cases in which handguns caused accidents or were used to commit crimes. If one is arguing that abortion has a traumatic effect on women, one will point to women who testify to that effect. Each instance constitutes **evidence** for the relevant generalization.

In a courtroom, evidence bearing on the guilt of the accused is introduced by the prosecution, and evidence to the contrary is introduced by the defense. Not all evidence is admissible (hearsay, for one, is not, even if it is true), and the law of evidence is a highly developed subject in jurisprudence. In the forum of daily life, the sources of evidence are less disciplined. Daily experience, a particularly memorable observation, an unusual event we witnessed—any or all of these may be used as evidence for (or against) some belief, theory, hypothesis, or explanation. The systematic study of what experience can yield is what science does, and one of the most distinctive features of the evidence that scientists can marshal on behalf of their claims is that it is the result of **experimentation.** Experiments are deliberately contrived situations, often quite complex in their technology, and designed to yield particular observations. What the ordinary person does with unaided eye and ear, the scientist does, much more carefully and thoroughly, with the help of laboratory instruments.

The variety, extent, and reliability of the evidence obtained in daily life and in the laboratory are quite different. It is hardly a surprise that in our civilization much more weight is attached to the "findings" of scientists than to the corroborative (much less the contrary) experiences of the ordinary person. No one today would seriously argue that the sun really does go around the earth just because it looks that way; nor would we argue that because viruses are invisible to the naked eye they cannot cause symptoms such as swellings and fevers, which are quite plainly visible.

Examples   One form of evidence is the **example.** Suppose that we argue that a candidate is untrustworthy and should not be elected to public office. We point to episodes in his career — his misuse of funds in 1994 and the false charges he made against an opponent in 1997 — as examples of his untrustworthiness. Or if we are arguing that President Truman ordered the atom bomb dropped to save American (and, for that matter, Japanese) lives that otherwise would have been lost in a hard-fought invasion of Japan, we point to the stubbornness of the Japanese defenders in battles on the islands of Saipan, Iwo Jima, and Okinawa, where Japanese soldiers fought to the death rather than surrender.

These examples, we say, show us that the Japanese defenders of the main islands would have fought to the end, even though they knew they would be defeated. Or if we take a different view of Truman's action and argue that the war in effect was already won and that Truman had no justification for dropping the bomb, we can cite examples of the Japanese willingness to end the war, such as secret negotiations in which they sent out peace feelers.

An example is a sample; the two words come from the same Old French word, *essample,* from the Latin *exemplum,* which means "something taken out" — that is, a selection from the group. A Yiddish proverb shrewdly says that "'For example' is no proof," but the evidence of well-chosen examples can go a long way toward helping a writer to convince an audience.

In arguments, three sorts of examples are especially common:

• Real events,
• Invented instances (artificial or hypothetical cases), and
• Analogies.

We will treat each of these briefly.

REAL EVENTS   In referring to Truman's decision to drop the atom bomb, we have already touched on examples drawn from real events, the battles at Saipan and elsewhere. And we have also seen Ben Franklin pointing to an allegedly real happening, a fish that had consumed a smaller fish. The advantage of an example drawn from real life, whether a great historical event or a local incident, is that its reality gives it weight. It can't simply be brushed off.

On the other hand, an example drawn from reality may not provide as clear-cut an instance as could be wished for. Suppose, for instance, that someone cites the Japanese army's behavior on Saipan and on Iwo

Jima as evidence that the Japanese later would have fought to the death in an American invasion of Japan and would therefore have inflicted terrible losses on themselves and on the Americans. This example is open to the response that in August 1945, when Truman authorized dropping the bomb, the situation was very different. In June and July 1945, Japanese diplomats had already sent out secret peace feelers; Emperor Hirohito probably wanted peace by then; and so on.

Similarly, in support of the argument that nations will not resort to atomic weapons, some people have offered as evidence the fact that since World War I the great powers have not used poison gas. But the argument needs more support than this fact provides. Poison gas was not decisive or even highly effective in World War I. Moreover, the invention of gas masks made it obsolete.

In short, any *real* event is, so to speak, so entangled in its historical circumstances that one may question whether indeed it is adequate or even relevant evidence in the case being argued. In using a real event as an example (and real events certainly can be used), the writer ordinarily must demonstrate that the event can be taken out of its historical context and be used in the new context of argument. Thus, in an argument against any further use in warfare of atomic weapons, one might point to the example of the many deaths and horrible injuries inflicted on the Japanese at Hiroshima and Nagasaki, in the confident belief that these effects of nuclear weapons will invariably occur and did not depend on any special circumstances of their use in Japan in 1945.

INVENTED INSTANCES   **Artificial** or **hypothetical cases, invented instances,** have the great advantage of being protected from objections of the sort just given. Recall Thoreau's trout in the milk; that was a colorful hypothetical case that nicely illustrated his point. An invented instance ("Let's assume that a burglar promises not to shoot a householder if the householder swears not to identify him. Is the householder bound by the oath?") is something like a drawing of a flower in a botany textbook or a diagram of the folds of a mountain in a geology textbook. It is admittedly false, but by virtue of its simplifications it sets forth the relevant details very clearly. Thus, in a discussion of rights, the philosopher Charles Frankel says,

> Strictly speaking, when we assert a right for X, we assert that Y has a duty. Strictly speaking, that Y has such a duty presupposes that Y has the capacity to perform this duty. It would be nonsense to say, for example, that a nonswimmer has a moral duty to swim to the help of a drowning man.

This invented example is admirably clear, and it is immune to charges that might muddy the issue if Frankel, instead of referring to a wholly abstract person, Y, talked about some real person, Jones, who did not rescue a drowning man. For then he would get bogged down over arguing about whether Jones *really* couldn't swim well enough to help, and so on.

Yet invented cases have their drawbacks. First and foremost, they cannot be used as evidence. A purely hypothetical example can illustrate a point or provoke reconsideration of a generalization, but it cannot substitute for actual events as evidence supporting an inductive inference. Sometimes such examples are so fanciful, so remote from life that they fail to carry conviction with the reader. Thus the philosopher Judith Jarvis Thomson, in the course of an argument entitled "A Defense of Abortion," asks us to imagine that we wake up one day and find that against our will a celebrated violinist whose body is not adequately functioning has been hooked up into our body, for life-support. Do we have the right to unplug the violinist? Readers of the essays in this book will have to decide for themselves whether the invented cases proposed by various authors are helpful or whether they are so remote that they hinder thought. Readers will have to decide, too, about when they can use invented cases to advance their own arguments.

But we add one point: Even a highly fanciful invented case can have the valuable effect of forcing us to see where we stand. We may say that we are, in all circumstances, against vivisection. But what would we say if we thought that an experiment on one mouse would save the life of someone we love? Or conversely, if one approves of vivisection, would one also approve of sacrificing the last giant panda to save the life of a senile stranger, a person who in any case probably would not live longer than another year? Artificial cases of this sort can help us to see that, well, no, we didn't really mean to say such-and-such when we said so-and-so.

ANALOGIES   The third sort of example, **analogy,** is a kind of comparison. Strictly, an analogy is an extended comparison in which different things are shown to be similar in several ways. Thus, if one wants to argue that a head of state should have extraordinary power during wartime, one can argue that the state at such a time is like a ship in a storm: The crew is needed to lend its help, but the decisions are best left to the captain. (Notice that an analogy compares things that are relatively *un*like. Comparing the plight of one ship to another or of one government to another is not an analogy; it is an inductive inference from one case of the same sort to another such case.) Or take another analogy: We have already glanced at Judith Thomson's hypothetical case in which the reader wakes up to find himself or herself hooked up to a violinist. Thomson uses this situation as an analogy in an argument about abortion. The reader stands for the mother, the violinist for the unwanted fetus. Whether this analogy is close enough to pregnancy to help illuminate our thinking about abortion is something that you may want to think about.

The problem with argument by analogy is this: Two admittedly different things are agreed to be similar in several ways, and the arguer goes on to assert or imply that they are also similar in the point that is being argued. (That is why Thomson argues that if something is true of the reader-hooked-up-to-a-violinist, it is also true of the pregnant mother-hooked-up-to-a-fetus.) But of course, despite some similarities, the two things that are said to be analogous and that are indeed similar in characteristics *A, B,* and *C* are also different—let's say in characteristics *D* and *E.* As Bishop Butler said, about two hundred fifty years ago, "Everything is what it is, and not another thing."

Analogies can be convincing, especially because they can make complex issues simple. "Don't change horses in midstream," of course, is not a statement about riding horses across a river but about choosing leaders in critical times. Still, in the end, analogies can prove nothing. What may be true about riding horses across a stream need not be true about choosing leaders in troubled times or not true about a given change of leadership. Riding horses across a stream and choosing leaders are, at bottom, different things, and however much these activities may be said to resemble one another, they remain different, and what is true for one need not be true for the other.

Analogies can be helpful in developing our thoughts. It is sometimes argued, for instance—on the analogy of the doctor-patient or the lawyer-client or the priest-penitent relationship—that newspaper and television reporters should not be required to reveal their confidential sources. That is worth thinking about: Do the similarities run deep enough, or are there fundamental differences? Or take another example: Some writers who support abortion argue that the fetus is not a person any more than the acorn is an oak. That is also worth thinking about. But one should also think about this response: A fetus is not a person, just as an acorn is not an oak, but an acorn is a potential oak, and a fetus is a potential person, a potential adult human being. Children, even newborn infants, have rights, and one way to explain this claim is to call attention to their potentiality to become mature adults. And so some people argue that the fetus, by analogy, has the rights of an infant, for the fetus, like the infant, is a potential adult.

While we're on this subject let's consider a very brief comparison made by Jill Knight, a member of the British Parliament, speaking about abortion:

> Babies are not like bad teeth, to be jerked out because they cause suffering.

Her point is effectively put; it remains for the reader to decide whether or not fetuses are *babies* and if a fetus is not a baby, *why* it can or can't be treated like a bad tooth. And yet a further bit of analogical reasoning, again about abortion: Thomas Sowell, an economist at the Hoover Institute, grants that women have a legal right to abortion, but he objects to the government's paying for abortions:

> Because the courts have ruled that women have a legal right to an abortion, some people have jumped to the conclusion that the government has to pay for it. You have a constitutional right to privacy, but the government has no obligation to pay for your window shades. (*Pink and Brown People*, p. 57)

We leave it to the reader to decide if the analogy is compelling — that is, if the points of resemblance are sufficiently significant to allow one to conclude that what is true of people wanting window shades should be true of people wanting abortions.

Authoritative Testimony   Another form of evidence is **testimony,** the citation or quotation of authorities. In daily life we rely heavily on authorities of all sorts: We get a doctor's opinion about our health, we read a book because an intelligent friend recommends it, we see a movie because a critic gave it a good review, and we pay at least a little attention to the weather forecaster.

In setting forth an argument, one often tries to show that one's view is supported by notable figures, perhaps Jefferson, Lincoln, and Martin Luther King Jr., or scientists who won the Nobel Prize. You may recall that in the second chapter, in talking about definitions of pornography, we referred to Kenneth Clark. To make certain that you were impressed by his testimony even if you had never heard of him, we described him as "probably the most influential English-speaking art critic of our time." But heed some words of caution:

- Be sure that the authority, however notable, is an authority on the topic in question (a well-known biologist on vitamins, yes, but not on the justice of a war).

- Be sure the authority is not biased. A chemist employed by the tobacco industry isn't likely to admit that smoking may be harmful, and a "director of publications" (that means a press agent) for a hockey team isn't likely to admit that watching or even playing ice hockey stimulates violence.

- Beware of nameless authorities: "a thousand doctors," "leading educators," "researchers at a major medical school."

- Be careful in using authorities who indeed were great authorities in their day but who now may be out of date (Adam Smith on economics, Julius Caesar on the art of war, Louis Pasteur on medicine).

- Cite authorities whose opinions your readers will value. William F. Buckley Jr.'s opinion means a good deal to readers of the *National*

Review but not to most feminists. Gloria Steinem's opinion carries weight with many feminists but not much with persons who support traditional family values. If you are writing for the general reader, your usual audience, cite authorities who are likely to be accepted by the general reader.

One other point: *You* may be an authority. You probably aren't nationally known, but on some topics you perhaps can speak with authority, the authority of personal experience. You may have been injured on a motorcycle while riding without wearing a helmet, or you may have escaped injury because you wore a helmet; you may have dropped out of school and then returned; you may have tutored a student whose native language is not English, or you may be such a student and you may have received tutoring. You may have attended a school with a bilingual education program. Your personal testimony on topics relating to these issues may be invaluable, and a reader will probably consider it seriously.

Statistics   The last sort of evidence we discuss here is quantitative or statistical. The maxim "More is better" captures a basic idea of quantitative evidence. Because we know that 90 percent is greater than 75 percent, we are usually ready to grant that any claim supported by experience in 90 percent of the cases is more likely to be true than an alternative claim supported by experience only 75 percent of the time. The greater the difference, the greater our confidence. Consider an example. Honors at graduation from college are often computed on a student's cumulative grade-point average (GPA). The undisputed assumption is that the nearer a student's GPA is to a perfect record (4.0), the better scholar he or she is, and therefore the more deserving of highest honors. Consequently, a student with a GPA of 3.9 at the end of her senior year is a stronger candidate for graduating summa cum laude than another student with a GPA of 3.6. When faculty members on the honors committee argue over the relative academic merits of graduating seniors, we know that these quantitative, statistical differences in student GPAs will be the basic (even if not the only) kind of evidence under discussion.

GRAPHS, TABLES, NUMBERS   Statistical information can be marshaled and presented in many forms, but it tends to fall into two main types: the graphic and the numerical. Graphs, tables, and pie charts are familiar ways of presenting quantitative data in an eye-catching manner. To prepare the graphics, however, one first has to get the numbers themselves under control, and for many purposes (such as writing argumentative essays) it is probably more convenient simply to stick with the numbers themselves.

But should the numbers be presented in percentages or in fractions? Should one report, say, that the federal budget underwent a twofold increase over the decade, that it increased by 100 percent, that it doubled, or that the budget at the beginning of the decade was one-half what it was at the end? Taken strictly, these are equivalent ways of saying the same thing. Choice among them, therefore, in an example like this perhaps will rest on whether one's aim is to dramatize the increase (a 100 percent increase looks larger than a doubling) or to play down the size of the increase.

THINKING ABOUT STATISTICAL EVIDENCE   Statistics often get a bad name because it is so easy to misuse them, unintentionally or not, and so difficult to be sure that they have been correctly gathered in the first place. (We remind you of the old saw "There are lies, damned lies, and statistics.") Every branch of social science and natural science needs statistical information, and countless decisions in public and private life are based on quantitative data in statistical form. It is important, therefore, to be sensitive to the sources and reliability of the statistics and to develop a healthy skepticism when confronted with statistics whose parentage is not fully explained.

Consider, for instance, statistics that kept popping up during the baseball strike of 1994. The owners of the clubs said that the average salary of a major-league player was $1.2 million. (The **average** in this case is the result of dividing the total number of salary dollars by the number of players.) The players' union, however, did not talk about the average; rather, the union talked about the **median**, which was less than half of the average, a mere $500,000. (The *median* is the middle value in a distribution. Thus, of the 746 players, 363 earned less than $500,000, 361 earned more, and 22 earned exactly $500,000.) The union said, correctly, that *most* players earned a good deal less than the $1.2 million figure that the owners kept citing; but the $1.2 million average sounded more impressive to the general public, and that is the figure that the guy in the street mentioned when asked for an opinion about the strike.

Here is a more complicated example of the difficulty of interpreting statistics. Violent crime increased in the 1960s and early 1970s, then leveled off, and began to decline in 1981. Did America become more violent for a while and then become more law-abiding? Bruce Jackson in *Law and Disorder* suggests that much of the rise in the 1960s was due to the baby boom of 1948 to 1952. Whereas in 1960 the United States had only about 11 million people aged twenty to twenty-four, by 1972 it had almost 18 million of them, and it is people in this age group who are most likely to commit violent crimes. The decline in the rate of violent crime in the 1980s was accompanied by a decline in the proportion of the population in this age group—though, of course, some politicians and law enforcement officers took credit for the reduction in violent crime.

One other example may help to indicate the difficulties of interpreting statistics. According to the San Francisco police department, in 1990 the city received 1,074 citizen complaints against the police. Los Angeles received only half as many complaints in the same period, and Los Angeles has five times the population of San Francisco. Does this mean that the police of San Francisco are much rougher than the police of Los Angeles? Possibly. But some specialists who have studied the statistics not only for these two cities but also for many other cities have concluded that a department with proportionately more complaints against it is not necessarily more abusive than a department with fewer complaints. According to these experts, the more confidence that the citizens have in their police force, the more the citizens will complain about police misconduct. The relatively small number of complaints against the Los Angeles police department thus may indicate that the citizens of Los Angeles are so intimidated and have so little confidence in the system that they do not bother to complain.

If it is sometimes difficult to interpret statistics, it is often at least equally difficult to establish accurate statistics. Consider this example:

> Advertisements are the most prevalent and toxic of the mental pollutants. From the moment your radio alarm sounds in the morning to the wee hours of late-night TV, microjolts of commercial pollution flood into your brain at the rate of about three thousand marketing messages per day. (Kalle Lasn, *Culture Jam,* 18–19)

Lasn's book includes endnotes as documentation, so, curious about the statistics, we turn to the appropriate page and we find this information concerning the source of his data:

> "three thousand marketing messages per day." Mark Landler, Walecia Konrad, Zachary Schiller, and Lois Therrien, "What Happened to Advertising?" *BusinessWeek,* September 23, 1991, page 66. Leslie Savan in *The Sponsored Life* (Temple University Press, 1994), page 1, estimated that "16,000 ads flicker across an individual's consciousness daily." I did an informal survey in March 1995 and found the number to be closer to 1,500 (this included all marketing messages, corporate images, logos, ads, brand names, on TV, radio, billboards, buildings, signs, clothing, appliances, in cyberspace, etc., over a typical twenty-four hour period in my life). (219)

Well, this endnote is odd. In the earlier passage, you will recall, the author asserted that "about three thousand marketing messages per day" flood into a person's brain. Now, in the documentation, he helpfully cites a source for that statistic, from *BusinessWeek*—though we have not the faintest idea of how the authors of the article in *BusinessWeek* came up with that figure. Oddly, he goes on to offer a very different figure (16,000 ads), and then, to our utter confusion, he offers yet a third figure, 1,500, based on his own "informal survey." Probably the one thing we can safely say about all three figures is that none of them means very much. Even if the compilers of the statistics told us exactly how they counted—let's say that among countless other criteria they assumed that the average person reads one magazine per day and that the average magazine contains 124 advertisements—it would be hard to take them seriously. After all, in leafing through a magazine, some people may read many ads, some may read none. Some people may read some ads carefully—but perhaps to enjoy their absurdity. Our point: Although the author in his text said, without implying any uncertainty, that "about three thousand marketing messages per day" reach an individual, it is evident (if one checks the endnote) that even he is confused about the figure he gives.

We are not suggesting, of course, that everyone who uses statistics is trying to deceive or even that many who use statistics are unconsciously deceived by them. We mean only to suggest that statistics are open to widely different interpretations and that often those columns of numbers, so precise with their decimal points, are in fact imprecise and possibly even worthless because they may be based on insufficient or biased samples.

A CHECKLIST FOR EVALUATING STATISTICAL EVIDENCE

Regard statistical evidence (like all other evidence) cautiously, and don't accept it until you have thought about these questions:

✓ Was it compiled by a disinterested source? Of course, the name of the source does not always reveal its particular angle (for example, People for the American Way), but sometimes the name lets you know what to expect (National Rifle Association, American Civil Liberties Union).

✓ Is it based on an adequate sample? (A study pointed out that criminals have an average IQ of 91 to 93, whereas the general population has an IQ of 100. The conclusion drawn was that criminals have a lower IQ than the general population. This reading may be accurate, but some doubts have been expressed. For instance, because the entire sample of criminals consisted only of *convicted* criminals, this sample may be biased; possibly the criminals with higher IQs have enough intelligence not to get caught. Or if they are caught, perhaps they are smart enough to hire better lawyers.)

✓ Is the statistical evidence recent enough to be relevant?

✓ How many of the factors likely to be relevant were identified and measured?

✓ Are the figures open to a different and equally plausible interpretation? (Remember the decline in violent crime, for which law enforcement officers took credit.)

Quiz

What is wrong with the following statistical proof that children do not have time for school?

One-third of the time they are sleeping (about 122 days);

One-eighth of the time they are eating (three hours a day, totaling 45 days);

One-fourth of the time is taken up by summer and other vacations (91 days);

Two-sevenths of the year is weekends (104 days).

Total: 362 days—so how can a kid have time for school?

NONRATIONAL APPEALS

Satire, Irony, Sarcasm

In talking about definition, deduction, and evidence, we have been talking about means of rational persuasion. But as mentioned earlier, there are also other means of persuasion. Take force, for example. If *X* kicks *Y*, threatens to destroy *Y*'s means of livelihood, or threatens *Y*'s life, *X* may persuade *Y* to cooperate. As Al Capone noted, "You can get more out of people with a gun and a kind word than with just a kind word." One form of irrational but sometimes highly effective persuasion is **satire**—that is, witty ridicule. A cartoonist may persuade viewers that a politician's views are unsound by caricaturing (and thus ridiculing) the politician's appearance or by presenting a grotesquely distorted (funny, but unfair) picture of the issue.

Satiric artists often use caricature; satiric writers, also seeking to persuade by means of ridicule, often use **verbal irony.** In irony of this sort there is a contrast between what is said and what is meant. For instance, words of praise may be meant to imply blame (when Shakespeare's Cassius says, "Brutus is an honorable man," he means his hearers to think that Brutus is dishonorable), and words of modesty may be meant to imply superiority ("Of course, I'm too dumb to understand this problem"). Such language, when heavy-handed, is called **sarcasm** ("You're a great guy," said to someone who will not lend the speaker ten dollars). If it is witty—if the jeering is in some degree clever—it is called irony rather than sarcasm.

Although ridicule is not a form of argument (because it is not a form of reasoning), passages of ridicule, especially verbal irony, sometimes appear in essays that are arguments. These passages, like reasons, or for that matter like appeals to the emotions, are efforts to persuade the hearer to accept the speaker's point of view. For example, in Judy Brady's essay "I Want a Wife" (p. 120), the writer, a woman, does not really mean that she wants a wife. The pretense that she wants a wife gives the essay a playful, joking quality; her words must mean something other than what they seem to mean. But that she is not merely joking (satire has been defined as "joking in earnest") is evident; she is seeking to persuade. She has a point, and she could argue it straight, but that would produce a very different sort of essay.

Emotional Appeals

It is sometimes said that good argumentative writing appeals only to reason, never to emotion, and that any sort of emotional appeal is illegitimate, irrelevant. Logic textbooks may even stigmatize with Latin labels the various sorts of emotional appeal — for instance, *argumentum ad populam* (appeal to the prejudices of the mob, as in "Come on, we all know that schools don't teach anything anymore") and *argumentum ad misericordiam* (appeal to pity, as in "No one ought to blame this poor kid for stabbing a classmate because his mother was often institutionalized for alcoholism and his father beat him").

True, appeals to emotion may get in the way of the facts of the case; they may blind the audience by, in effect, throwing dust in its eyes or by stimulating tears. A classic example is found in Shakespeare's *Julius Caesar*, when Marc Antony addresses the Roman populace after Brutus, Cassius, and others have assassinated Caesar. The real issue is whether Caesar was becoming tyrannical (as the assassins claim) and would therefore curtail the freedom of the people. Antony turns from the evidence and stirs the mob against the assassins by appealing to its emotions. In the ancient Roman biographical writing that Shakespeare drew on, Sir Thomas North's translation of Plutarch's *Lives of the Noble Grecians and Romans*, Plutarch says that Antony,

> perceiving that his words moved the common people to compassion, . . . framed his eloquence to make their hearts yearn [that is, grieve] the more, and, taking Caesar's gown all bloody in his hand, he laid it open to the sight of them all, showing what a number of cuts and holes it had upon it. Therewithal the people fell presently into such a rage and mutiny that there was no more order kept.

Here are a few extracts from Antony's speeches in Shakespeare's play. Antony begins by asserting that he will speak only briefly:

> Friends, Romans, countrymen, lend me your ears;
> I come to bury Caesar, not to praise him.

After briefly offering some rather insubstantial evidence that Caesar gave no signs of behaving tyrannically (for example, "When that the poor have cried, Caesar hath wept"), Antony begins to play directly on the emotions of his hearers. Descending from the platform so that he may be in closer contact with his audience (like a modern politician, he wants to work the crowd), he calls attention to Caesar's bloody toga:

> If you have tears, prepare to shed them now.
> You all do know this mantle; I remember

The first time ever Caesar put it on:
'Twas on a summer's evening, in his tent,
That day he overcame the Nervii.
Look, in this place ran Cassius' dagger through;
See what a rent the envious Casca made;
Through this, the well-belovèd Brutus stabbed. . . .

In these few lines Antony first prepares the audience by suggesting to them how they should respond ("If you have tears, prepare to shed them now"), then flatters them by implying that they, like Antony, were intimates of Caesar (he credits them with being familiar with Caesar's garment), then evokes a personal memory of a specific time ("a summer's evening")—not just any old specific time but a very important one, the day that Caesar won a battle against the Nervii (a particularly fierce tribe in what is now France). In fact, Antony was *not* at the battle, and he did not join Caesar until three years later, but Antony does not mind being free with the facts. His point here is not to set the record straight; rather, it is to stir the mob against the assassins. He goes on, daringly but successfully, to identify one particular slit in the garment with Cassius's dagger, another with Casca's, and a third with Brutus's. Antony, of course, cannot know which slit was made by which dagger, but his rhetorical trick works. Notice, too, that he arranges the three assassins in climactic order, since Brutus (Antony claims) was especially beloved by Caesar:

Judge, O you gods, how dearly Caesar loved him!
This was the most unkindest cut of all;
For when the noble Caesar saw him stab,
Ingratitude, more strong than traitor's arms,
Quite vanquished him. Then burst his mighty heart. . . . (3.2.75–188)

Nice. According to Antony, the noble-minded Caesar—Antony's words have erased all thought of the tyrannical Caesar—died not from the wounds inflicted by daggers but from the heartbreaking perception of Brutus's ingratitude. Doubtless there was not a dry eye in the house. We can all hope that if we are ever put on trial, we have a lawyer as skilled in evoking sympathy as Antony.

The oration is obviously successful in the play and apparently was successful in real life, but it is the sort of speech that prompts logicians to write disapprovingly of attempts to stir feeling in an audience. (As mentioned earlier in this chapter, the evocation of emotion in an audience is called **pathos,** from the Greek word for "emotion" or "suffering.") There is nothing inherently wrong in stimulating our audience's emotions, but when an emotional appeal confuses the issue that is being argued about or shifts the attention away from the facts of the issue, we can reasonably speak of the fallacy of emotional appeal.

No fallacy is involved, however, when an emotional appeal heightens the facts, bringing them home to the audience rather than masking them. If we are talking about legislation that would govern police actions, it is legitimate to show a photograph of the battered, bloodied face of an alleged victim of police brutality. Of course, such a photograph cannot tell the whole truth; it cannot tell us if the subject threatened the officer with a gun or repeatedly resisted an order to surrender. But it can tell us that the victim was severely beaten and (like a comparable description in words) evoke in us emotions that may properly enter into our decision about the permissible use of police evidence. Similarly, an animal rights activist who is arguing that calves are cruelly confined might reasonably tell us about the size of the pen in which the beast — unable to turn around or even to lie down — is kept. Others may argue that calves don't much care about turning around or have no right to turn around, but the verbal description, which unquestionably makes an emotional appeal, can hardly be called fallacious or irrelevant.

In appealing to emotions then, the important things are

- Not to falsify (especially by oversimplifying) the issue and
- Not to distract attention from the facts of the case.

A CHECKLIST FOR ANALYZING AN ARGUMENT

✓ What is the writer's thesis? Ask yourself:
  ✓ What claim is being asserted?
  ✓ What assumptions are being made — and are they acceptable?
  ✓ Are important terms satisfactorily defined?
✓ What support is offered on behalf of the claim? Ask yourself:
  ✓ Are the examples relevant, and are they convincing?
  ✓ Are the statistics (if any) relevant, accurate, and complete? Do they allow only the interpretation that is offered in the argument?
  ✓ If authorities are cited, are they indeed authorities on this topic, and can they be regarded as impartial?
  ✓ Is the logic — deductive and inductive — valid?
  ✓ If there is an appeal to emotion — for instance, if satire is used to ridicule the opposing view — is this appeal acceptable?
✓ Does the writer seem to you to be fair? Ask yourself:
  ✓ Are counterarguments adequately considered?
  ✓ Is there any evidence of dishonesty or of a discreditable attempt to manipulate the reader?

Focus on the facts and concentrate on offering reasons (essentially, statements linked with "because"), but you may also legitimately bring the facts home to your readers by seeking to induce in them the appropriate emotions. Your words will be fallacious only if you stimulate emotions that are not rightly connected with the facts of the case.

DOES ALL WRITING CONTAIN ARGUMENTS?

Our answer to the question we have just posed is no—but probably *most* writing *does* contain an argument of sorts. Or put it this way: The writer wants to persuade the reader to see things the way the writer sees them— at least until the end of the essay. After all, even a recipe for a cherry pie in a food magazine—a piece of writing that is primarily expository (how to do it) rather than argumentative (how a reasonable person ought to think about this topic)—probably includes, near the beginning, a sentence with a hint of an argument in it, such as "*Because* [a sign that a *reason* will be offered] this pie can be made quickly and with ingredients (canned cherries) that are always available, give it a try, and it will surely become one of your favorites." Clearly, such a statement cannot stand as a formal argument— a discussion that takes account of possible counterarguments, that relies chiefly on logic and little if at all on emotional appeal, and that draws a conclusion that seems irrefutable. Still, it is something of an argument on behalf of making a pie with canned cherries. In this case, a claim is made (the pie will become a favorite), and two *reasons* are offered in support of this claim:

- It can be made quickly, and
- The chief ingredient—because it is canned—can always be at hand.

The underlying *assumptions* are

- You don't have a great deal of time to waste in the kitchen, and
- Canned cherries are just as tasty as fresh cherries—and even if they aren't, well, you wouldn't know the difference.

When we read a lead-in to a recipe, then, we won't find a formal argument, but we probably will get a few words that seek to persuade us to keep reading. And most writing does contain such material—sentences that give us a reason to keep reading, that engage our interests, and that make us want to stay with the writer for at least a little longer. If the recipe happens to be difficult and time-consuming, the lead-in may say, "Although this recipe for a cherry pie, using fresh cherries that you will have to pit, is a bit more time-consuming than the usual recipe that calls for canned cherries, once you have tasted it you will never go back to canned cherries." Again, although the logic is scarcely compelling, the persuasive element is evident. The assumption here is that you have a discriminating palate; once you have tasted a pie made with fresh cherries, you will never again enjoy the canned stuff. The writer is not giving us a formal argument, with abundant evidence and with a detailed refutation of counterarguments, but we do know where the writer stands and how the writer wishes us to respond.

VISUAL RHETORIC: IMAGES AS ARGUMENTS

In January 2000, a fierce debate raged in Columbia, South Carolina. At issue was whether the state legislature should take down the Confederate battle flag, which had flown over the state capitol for nearly forty years. African American groups and other opponents of the flag claimed that the symbol glorified a racist past and continued to promote bigotry and intolerance. Supporters, mostly whites, insisted that there were no racial overtones in the display of an icon that, they said, was a part of the South's cultural heritage and that honored those who had fought for freedom from domination by the more powerful North. The battle flag eventually came down in July 2000, but not before its presence had caused several influential groups to punish South Carolina economically by a boycott. A great deal of bad blood was created on both sides. The issue even made its presence felt in the presidential race later in the year, when candidate George W. Bush, claiming neutrality, said the issue should be decided by the state; his opponent Al Gore, on the other hand, said the flag should come down, and he accused Bush of insensitivity to the feelings of black Americans.

The flag itself — a visual symbol that sparked much debate and fury — was seen on both sides not merely as the cause of argument but as part of the argument. American courts have recognized that certain forms of nonverbal expression are considered "speech." On page 387 we give the U.S. Supreme Court's ruling that a person who protests a war by burning an American flag is engaging in a form of "speech" protected by the Constitution. Similarly, the Confederate flag flying above the capitol "said" (so to speak) that certain values were to be honored; those who opposed flying the flag argued that it said something else. "Visual language" requires "visual literacy"; we have to learn how to read the nonverbal signs that are all around us.

Take, for instance, the visual images that all of us offer daily by means of the clothing that we wear. Uniforms tell the passerby that someone is a police officer, a nurse, a boy scout, but uniforms of another sort — the ordinary kinds of clothing that most of us wear — also tell the passerby that we are a banker, lawyer, or businessman (dark suit and necktie), a bodybuilder (form-fitting T-shirt), a tourist (provide your own description), or a student (again, you can provide your own description). We may say that we wear anything that comes to hand, but the truth is that there are certain kinds of clothing—even certain brands of jeans—we wouldn't be caught dead in. Further, the clothes students and faculty wear to class are probably not the clothes they wear at a wedding or a job interview. When looking for a job, we wear a certain kind of clothing—that is, we adorn our body with certain symbols—that will send the visual message that our inside, our self, is someone who is highly responsible. Of course, each of us has many selves—the student, the responsible member of a family, the trusted employee, and so on—and we have a variety of wardrobes that allow us to signify these various selves, or, more precisely, we send visual messages to people who can be expected to read them correctly.

You have no doubt heard that a picture is worth a thousand words. An index of how closely we associate the visual and the verbal might be found in the language we use when we are trying to persuade someone. *"Look* at this from another angle," we say, or, "Do you *see* what I mean?" We talk about our *perspective,* and we *illustrate* our points with examples. The concept of visual language and its importance in persuasion is built into the very idiom of English. We've already made passing reference to such nonverbal persuasive language as graphs and tables or schematic drawings in textbooks. Yet "reading" visual language is, of course, different from reading and analyzing traditional verbal arguments, and it deserves some special attention here.

Visual Persuasion:
(1) Reading the Human-Made Landscape

It has been suggested—with some justice—that we live in an increasingly visual age, bombarded as we are by billboards, posters, advertisements, movies and television, and the now-ubiquitous World Wide Web. But the idea of visual persuasion is hardly new. At his trial in 399 B.C. Socrates refused to participate in the common but, in his mind, demeaning practice of calling forth his weeping family and friends to present a spectacle that would stir the judges to mercy. In the Middle Ages elaborate church art, including statuary and stained glass windows, helped teach Bible stories—and their associated Christian values—to a largely illiterate populace. Indeed, the churches themselves, with their flying buttresses and spires and ornate carvings, spoke volumes about the culture's attitudes toward the power and glory of God. It could be argued that the beautiful rose window of Chartres cathedral is every bit as much a piece of persuasive language as is an editorial in your local paper. And a baron's massive castle very clearly told his rivals that his power was not to be disputed.

Buildings, especially public buildings, still send us messages. Reading our buildings and monuments can tell us a great deal about the people who created them and who pay reverence to them. The J. Edgar Hoover Building in Washington, D.C., with its masses of precast concrete, looks like a fortress, uninviting, impregnable—the very image of the Federal Bureau of Investigation. Or consider the materials of some college and university buildings. Adobe works well at the University of New Mexico, but would it be right for the Air Force Academy in Colorado? (The Academy uses different materials to send its message—notably aluminum, steel, and glass.) Similarly, the Neo-gothic style that was used for many colleges and universities in the late nineteenth century and the first half of the twentieth, with the suggestion of otherworldliness, can hardly be used for, say, a modern business school.

Consider the Tomb of the Unknowns (1931) in Arlington National Cemetery. Many of the monument's architectural details, some of which may be seen in the accompanying photographs, can be read and analyzed in much the same manner that we might read a traditional printed text. The white marble sarcophagus—white is associated with purity, marble with dignity—is built atop the grave of an unidentified soldier killed in World War I, and beside it are three additional white marble slabs, honoring soldiers who died in World War II, Korea, and Vietnam. The stark whiteness and the clean, neoclassical lines of the monument give it a simple yet solemn appearance, an impression heightened in the first photograph by the dress uniform and rigid posture of the soldier who serves as an honor guard. The second photograph, of the far side of the monument, shows three Greek figures: Peace holds a dove, Victory holds an olive branch, and Valor holds a broken sword. The focus, then, is not on the grittiness and courage of soldiers, as it is in the Marine Corps Memorial (1954) nearby, which shows marines struggling to raise the flag at the summit of Mt. Suribachi on Iwo Jima. Rather, the Tomb of the Unknowns speaks (through its whiteness, its marble, its severe geometry, its classical figures) of the antiquity and thus by implication the nobility of the ideals for which they died. Even the location of the tomb, on a hill, is symbolic because the classical gods were thought to dwell in lofty places.

By way of contrast to the Tomb of the Unknowns and to the Marine Corps Memorial, consider the Vietnam Veterans Memorial (1982). Here, a pair of 200-foot polished black granite walls join to make a broad V, embracing a gently sloping plot of ground. On the walls, which rise from ground level to a height of about 10 feet at the vertex, are inscribed the names of the 57,939 Americans who died in the Vietnam War. Unlike the tomb at Arlington (p. 92, top), which has images of peace, victory, and valor, the Vietnam memorial says nothing—visually or verbally— about the values that the soldiers died for; and unlike the Marine Corps

Memorial (p. 92, bottom), which depicts active soldiers, it says nothing about their appearance, the difficulty of their struggle, or their courage. The Vietnam War was highly contested at home, but the Vietnam Veterans Memorial says nothing of this either. Rather, it says only—by naming names—that these people died. It provides a site for reflection— literally, since visitors to the wall see their own images reflected among the names carved in the polished granite. Further, as visitors approach the wall, perhaps to read or even to touch some of the names, the inclined ground causes them to step downward—a step into the grave— and then, after their close encounter with the wall, they move upward. Its success as a monument is undisputed; the Vietnam Veterans Memorial is the most-visited memorial in all of Washington.

These memorials, of course, do not offer arguments in the way that written arguments about wars and patriotism might do. Visuals on their own rarely, if ever, offer sound arguments—they cannot be subjected to tests for truth or validity—but they are often very persuasive

nonetheless, and they are often used as evidence in larger arguments. Premises and assumptions tend to remain unstated in visual persuasion; deciphering them requires highly active reading.

Sometimes words do accompany the visual elements of monuments. For instance, the Tomb of the Unknowns bears this inscription: HERE RESTS IN HONORED GLORY AN AMERICAN SOLDIER KNOWN BUT TO GOD. The inscription, combined with the other elements of the tomb, performs a number of functions. The phrase "honored glory" leaves no room for doubt as to the attitude a visitor should assume toward these fallen soldiers, and the reference to God connects patriotism to a higher power. We are reminded by the text that we do not know the identity of the soldier, but we know all we need to: The soldier is an American, he died for a worthy cause, and he is known to God. For these reasons, he is to be honored. Here, as in many other instances, the visual and the verbal prove a powerful combination, but most of the persuasive work is done by the white marble, the classical images, the presence of a sentry, and the site on a hill.

Visual Persuasion:
(2) Reading Advertisements

Advertising is one of the most common forms of visual persuasion we encounter in everyday life. None of us is so unsophisticated these days as to believe everything we see in an ad, yet the influence of advertising in our culture is pervasive and subtle. Consider, for example, a much-reproduced poster sponsored by Gatorade, featuring Michael Jordan. Such an image costs an enormous amount to produce and disseminate, and nothing in it is left to chance. The photograph of Jordan is typical, his attitude simultaneously strained and graceful, his face exultant, as he performs the feat for which he is so well known and about which most of us could only dream. We are aware of a crowd watching him, but the people in this crowd appear tiny, blurred, and indistinct compared to the huge image in the foreground; the photograph, like the crowd, focuses solely on Jordan. He is a legend, an icon of American culture. He is dressed not in his Chicago Bulls uniform but in a USA jersey, connecting his act of gravity-defying athleticism with the entire nation and with our sense of patriotism. The red, white, and blue of the uniform strengthens this impression in the original color photograph of the advertisement.

What do we make of the verbal message boldly written along the left-hand margin of the poster, "Be like Mike"? We are certainly not foolish enough to believe that drinking Gatorade will enable us to perform like Michael Jordan on the basketball court. But who among us wouldn't like to "Be like Mike" in some small way, to enjoy even a glancing association with his athletic grace and power — to say nothing of his fame, wealth, and sex appeal? Though the makers of Gatorade surely know we will not all rush out to buy their drink to improve our game, they are banking on the expectation that the association of their name with Jordan, and our memory of their logo in association with Jordan's picture, will create a positive impression of their product. If Mike drinks Gatorade — well, why shouldn't I give it a try? The good feelings and impressions created by the ad will, the advertisers hope, travel with us the next time we consider buying a sports drink.

As we discuss the power of advertising, it is appropriate to say a few words about the corporate logos that appear everywhere these days — on billboards, in newspapers and magazines, on television, and on tee shirts. It is useful to think of a logo as a sort of advertisement in shorthand. A logo is a single, usually simple, image that carries with it a whole world of associations and impressions. (The makers of Gatorade would certainly hope that we will be reminded of Michael Jordan and his slam dunk when we see their product name superimposed over the orange lightning bolt.)

Photography and Truth

Photographs have historically been considered especially powerful as tools of persuasion, in part because a photo, unlike, say, a drawing or a graph, is generally believed to show real people and events rather than an artist's or statistician's conception of the truth. "The camera doesn't lie." Of course, this common saying is at best an oversimplification. We will leave aside for the moment the fact that photographs can be tampered with (and with increasing ease using the new digital technologies). Even an unretouched photograph is far from a pure or unmediated look at the truth. A skilled photographer, like any other artist, makes many significant choices that effect the final image we see. Decisions about what to include within the frame — and what to exclude — as well as the precise moment to take the picture, are most obvious. Additionally, though, such elements as depth of field, color balance, length of exposure, light and shadow, and dozens of other considerations make a huge difference in the impact of the photograph on a viewer. A gritty, grainy black-and-white photo of a bombed building is likely to be more effective than a color photograph of the same building because the color itself may help to make the photo attractive, sensuous, appealing.

One of the most memorable images of the Vietnam War for many Americans is Huynh Cong (Nick) Ut's 1972 photograph of children fleeing a napalm strike (p. 96). If you have seen this picture before, you almost certainly remember the young girl near the center of the frame. Both the composition of the photo and the emotional resonance of the image draw our eyes to her form. Her facial expression suggests both pain and terror, an impression heightened by the awkward position in which she holds her body as she runs. She appears, however, to be uninjured — though in fact her back was badly burned. The startling fact of her nakedness and her thin, frail-looking body increase her aspect of vulnerability. We are left to wonder what has happened to this child, why she is naked, what she is fleeing from, and toward what she is running.

As we continue to look at the photograph, we become aware of additional aspects. The other children tell us that this is not merely an individual tragedy but one with wider-ranging implications. The billowing smoke that ominously fills the entire background simultaneously reinforces the sense of enormity and increases the mystery by hiding the scene from which the children flee. And the seemingly casual attitude of the soldiers behind the children is deeply disturbing. Is it possible these men have seen so much suffering that they are unmoved by the scene before them? Or that moments earlier they were shooting the villagers?

Ut's picture was widely reproduced in the United States and in 1973 earned him a Pulitzer Prize. Although it would be false to suggest that a single image changed the course of the war, this widely circulated photograph surely had an immense impact on the attitudes of many Americans. It increased awareness of the human cost of the conflict and reminded newspaper readers that not only soldiers or "the enemy" were victims. The picture contributed to the discourse of the antiwar effort; public pressure to end the war greatly increased after the publication of this photograph.

A Note on Using Visuals in Your Own Paper

Every paper uses some degree of visual persuasion, merely in its appearance: perhaps a title page, certainly margins (ample — but not so wide that they tell the reader that the writer is unable to write a paper of the assigned length), double-spacing for the convenience of the reader, paragraphing (again for the convenience of the reader), and so on. But you may also want to use images — for example, pictures, graphs, or pie charts. Keep a few guidelines in mind as you begin to work with images, "writing" visuals into your own argument with at least as much care as you would read them in others':

- Never include an image merely because you like the way it looks or because it is generally related to your topic.

- Consider carefully the needs and prejudices of your audience, and select the type of visuals—graphs, drawings, photographs—likely to be most persuasive to that audience.

- Consider the effect of color, composition, and placement within your document. Because images are most effective when they appear near the text that supplements them, do not group all of your images at the end of the paper.

Remember especially that a visual is almost never self-supporting or self-explanatory. It may be evidence for your argument, but it is not an argument unto itself. (As evidence, however, it can be very compelling: Witness Ut's photograph of napalm victims.) Be sure to fully explain each visual you use, integrating it into the verbal text that provides the logic and principal support of your thesis. No matter how attractive or professional-looking a picture may be, it may puzzle and distract your reader if its relevance is not explained. At worst, it will be a source of annoyance and weaken your case rather than strengthen it. Used well, though, visual elements have an important place in the language of argument.

A CHECKLIST FOR ANALYZING IMAGES (ESPECIALLY ADVERTISEMENTS)

✓ What about the image immediately gets your attention? Size? Position on the page? Beauty of the image? Grotesqueness of the image? Humor?

✓ Does the image appeal to the emotions? Examples: Images of starving children or maltreated animals appeal to our sense of pity; images of military valor may appeal to our patriotism; images of luxury may appeal to our envy; images of sexually attractive people may appeal to our desire to be like them; images of violence or of extraordinary ugliness (as, for instance, in some ads showing a human fetus being destroyed) may seek to shock us.

✓ Does the image make an ethical appeal—that is, does it appeal to our character as a good human being? Ads by charitable organizations often appeal to our sense of decency, fairness, and pity, but ads that appeal to our sense of prudence (ads for insurance companies or for investment houses) also essentially are making an ethical appeal.

✓ What is the relation of print to image? Does the image do most of the work, or does it serve to attract us and to lead us on to read the text?

IMAGES FOR ANALYSIS

In 1936, photographer Dorothea Lange (1895–1965) took a series of pictures, including the two below, of a migrant mother and her children. Widely reprinted in the nation's newspapers, these photographs helped to dramatize for the American public the poverty of displaced workers during the Great Depression.

Topics for Critical Thinking and Writing

1. Lange drew increasingly near to her subject as she took this series of pictures. Make a list of details gained and lost by framing the mother and children more closely. The final shot in the series (above, right) became the most famous and most widely reprinted. Do you find it more effective than the other? Why, or why not?

2. Note the expression on the mother's face, the position of her body, and the way she interacts with her children. What sorts of relationships are implied? Why is it significant that she does not look at her children or at the camera? How is the effect of the photographs altered based on how much we can see of the children's faces?

3. As we mentioned earlier in this chapter, these photographs constitute a sort of persuasive "speech." Of what, exactly, might the photographer be trying to persuade her viewers? Try to state the purpose of this photograph by completing this sentence, "Lange would like the viewers of her photographers to . . ." Write a brief essay (250 words) making the same case. Compare your written argument to Lange's visual one. Which form of persuasion do you find more effective? Why?

4. Whom do you think Lange had in mind as her original audience? What assumptions does she make about that audience? What sorts of evidence does she use to reach them?

During World War II, the United States government produced a series of posters bearing the legend "This is the enemy." These posters depicted racially stereotyped images of both German and Japanese soldiers, generally engaged in acts of violence.

Topics for Critical Thinking and Writing

1. It has been claimed that one role of propaganda is to dehumanize "the enemy" so that (a) soldiers will feel less remorse about the killing in which they might engage and (b) civilians will continue to support the war effort. What specific features of this poster contribute to this propaganda function?

2. Some would claim that such a racially provocative image should never be used because it is potentially harmful to all Asians, including patriotic Asian Americans. (Consisting solely of Japanese American volunteers, the 442nd Regimental Combat Team was by war's end the most decorated unit in U. S. military history for its size and length of service.) Others believe that the ordinary rules do not apply in times of national crisis and that, as the old saying has it, "All's fair in love and war." In an essay of 500 words, argue one or the other of these propositions. Refer to this poster as one piece of your evidence.

Billing itself as "the best of the alternative media," the left-leaning Utne Reader *focuses on issues of social change, politics, the environment, gender, and community. It publishes original articles and reprints of works from other small magazines and journals. Daniel Craig painted this cover for the magazine in 1998.*

Topics for Critical Thinking and Writing

1. This picture of Mr. Spock from television's *Star Trek* parodies a type of portraiture popular in Renaissance Europe, exemplified by this portrait of Giuliano de' Medici, thought to be a copy of a lost portrait by Raphael (1483–1520). Which aspects of this portraiture style does Craig adopt in his parody? Is the parody funny? In addition to amusement, what other purposes might it have?

2. For this parody to be effective, a viewer must have some familiarity with two cultural traditions—European Renaissance portraiture and the *Star Trek* television series. What assumptions does the *Utne Reader* make about its readership? After looking closely at both the visual and verbal elements of the magazine cover, what guesses would you make about the readership's demographics, education, and interests?

3. The word *renaissance* literally means "rebirth." What associations does the word conjure for you? What might be the meaning here of *new renaissance?*

4. How recognizable an icon is Mr. Spock? What does he represent? The *Utne Reader*'s cover copy claims, "High tech may rule today, but tomorrow belongs to the human spirit." There is a certain irony, then, that the character of Mr. Spock continually proclaims his nonhuman heritage and his knowledge of science and technology. How appropriate is he as a representation of this "new renaissance"? Explain.

Topics for Critical Thinking and Writing

Gather some of the graphical materials used to promote and reflect your college or university—including a screen shot of its World Wide Web site, the college catalog, and the brochures and other materials sent to prospective students.

1. How effectively are visuals used in these materials? Note the use of color and composition and the way the visual elements interact with the printed texts. What appears in the photographs? What is left out? How are logos and other icons used, and what do they suggest?

2. What is the purpose of each document? Can you tell who is the intended audience for these materials? Does the style of the visuals change when addressing different purposes or audiences?

3. What is the dominant image that your college or university administration seems to be putting forth? Are there different, maybe even competing, images of your school at work? How accurate a story do these materials tell about your campus? Write an essay (250 words) in which you explain to prospective students the ways in which the promotional materials capture, or fail to capture, the true spirit of your campus.

4. Compare the Web site of your institution to one or two from very different institutions—perhaps a community college, a large state university, or an elite private college. How do you account for the similarities and differences among the sites?

ARGUMENTS FOR ANALYSIS

Ronald Takaki

Ronald Takaki, the grandson of agricultural laborers who had come from Japan, is professor of ethnic studies at the University of California at Berkeley. He is the editor of From Different Shores: Perspectives on Race and Ethnicity in America *(1987) and the author of (among other writings)* Strangers from a Different Shore: A History of Asian-Americans

(1989). The essay that we reprint appeared originally in the New York Times *on June 16, 1990.*

The Harmful Myth of Asian Superiority

Asian Americans have increasingly come to be viewed as a "model minority." But arc thcy as successful as claimed? And for whom are they supposed to be a model?

Asian Americans have been described in the media as "excessively, even provocatively" successful in gaining admission to universities. Asian American shopkeepers have been congratulated, as well as criticized, for their ubiquity and entrepreneurial effectiveness.

If Asian Americans can make it, many politicians and pundits ask, why can't African Americans? Such comparisons pit minorities against each other and generate African American resentment toward Asian Americans. The victims are blamed for their plight, rather than racism and an economy that has made many young African American workers superfluous.

The celebration of Asian Americans has obscured reality. For example, figures on the high earnings of Asian Americans relative to Caucasians are misleading. Most Asian Americans live in California, Hawaii, and New York—states with higher incomes and higher costs of living than the national average.

Even Japanese Americans, often touted for their upward mobility, have not reached equality. While Japanese American men in California earned an average income comparable to Caucasian men in 1980, they did so only by acquiring more education and working more hours.   5

Comparing family incomes is even more deceptive. Some Asian Amcrican groups do have higher family incomes than Caucasians. But they have more workers per family.

The "model minority" image homogenizes Asian Americans and hides their differences. For example, while thousands of Vietnamese American young people attend universities, others are on the streets. They live in motels and hang out in pool halls in places like East Los Angeles; some join gangs.

Twenty-five percent of the people in New York City's Chinatown lived below the poverty level in 1980, compared with 17 percent of the city's population. Some 60 percent of the workers in the Chinatowns of Los Angeles and San Francisco are crowded into low-paying jobs in garment factories and restaurants.

"Most immigrants coming into Chinatown with a language barrier cannot go outside this confined area into the mainstream of American industry," a Chinese immigrant said. "Before, I was a painter in Hong Kong, but I can't do it here. I got no license, no education. I want a living; so it's dishwasher, janitor, or cook."

Hmong and Mien refugees from Laos have unemployment rates that 10
reach as high as 80 percent. A 1987 California study showed that three
out of ten Southeast Asian refugee families had been on welfare for four
to ten years.

Although college-educated Asian Americans are entering the professions and earning good salaries, many hit the "glass ceiling" — the barrier
through which high management positions can be seen but not reached.
In 1988, only 8 percent of Asian Americans were "officials" and "managers," compared with 12 percent for all groups.

Finally, the triumph of Korean immigrants has been exaggerated. In
1988, Koreans in the New York metropolitan area earned only 68 percent of the median income of non-Asians. More than three-quarters of
Korean greengrocers, those so-called paragons of bootstrap entrepre-
neurialism, came to America with a college education. Engineers, teachers, or administrators while in Korea, they became shopkeepers after
their arrival. For many of them, the greengrocery represents dashed
dreams, a step downward in status.

For all their hard work and long hours, most Korean shopkeepers do
not actually earn very much: $17,000 to $35,000 a year, usually representing the income from the labor of an entire family.

But most Korean immigrants do not become shopkeepers. Instead,
many find themselves trapped as clerks in grocery stores, service workers
in restaurants, seamstresses in garment factories, and janitors in hotels.

Most Asian Americans know their "success" is largely a myth. They 15
also see how the celebration of Asian Americans as a "model minority"
perpetuates their inequality and exacerbates relations between them and
African Americans.

Topics for Critical Thinking and Writing

1. What is the thesis of Takaki's essay? What is the evidence he offers for
   its truth? Do you find his argument convincing? Explain your answers
   to these questions in an essay of 500 words.

2. Takaki several times uses statistics to make a point. Do some of the statistics seem more convincing than others? Explain.

3. Consider Takaki's title. To what group(s) is the myth of Asian superiority harmful?

4. Suppose you believed that Asian Americans are economically more successful in America today, relative to white Americans, than African
   Americans are. Does Takaki agree or disagree with you? What evidence,
   if any, does he cite to support or reject the belief?

5. Takaki attacks the "myth" of Asian American "success" and thus rejects
   the idea that they are a "model minority" (recall the opening and closing
   paragraphs). What do you think a genuine model minority would be like?
   Can you think of any racial or ethnic minority in the United States that
   can serve as a model? Explain why or why not in an essay of 500 words.

James Q. Wilson

James Q. Wilson is Collins Professor of Management and Public Policy at the University of California at Los Angeles. Among his books are Thinking about Crime *(1975),* Bureaucracy *(1989),* The Moral Sense *(1993), and* Moral Judgment *(1997). The essay that we reprint appeared originally in the* New York Times Magazine *on March 20, 1994.*

Just Take Away Their Guns

The president wants still tougher gun control legislation and thinks it will work. The public supports more gun control laws but suspects they won't work. The public is right.

Legal restraints on the lawful purchase of guns will have little effect on the illegal use of guns. There are some 200 million guns in private ownership, about one-third of them handguns. Only about 2 percent of the latter are employed to commit crimes. It would take a Draconian, and politically impossible, confiscation of legally purchased guns to make much of a difference in the number used by criminals. Moreover, only about one-sixth of the handguns used by serious criminals are purchased from a gun shop or pawnshop. Most of these handguns are stolen, borrowed, or obtained through private purchases that wouldn't be affected by gun laws.

What is worse, any successful effort to shrink the stock of legally purchased guns (or of ammunition) would reduce the capacity of law-abiding people to defend themselves. Gun control advocates scoff at the importance of self-defense, but they are wrong to do so. Based on a household survey, Gary Kleck, a criminologist at Florida State University, has estimated that every year, guns are used — that is, displayed or fired — for defensive purposes more than a million times, not counting their use by the police. If his estimate is correct, this means that the number of people who defend themselves with a gun exceeds the number of arrests for violent crimes and burglaries.

Our goal should not be the disarming of law-abiding citizens. It should be to reduce the number of people who carry guns unlawfully, especially in places — on streets, in taverns — where the mere presence of a gun can increase the hazards we all face. The most effective way to reduce illegal gun-carrying is to encourage the police to take guns away from people who carry them without a permit. This means encouraging the police to make street frisks.

The Fourth Amendment to the Constitution bans "unreasonable   5 searches and seizures." In 1968 the Supreme Court decided (*Terry v. Ohio*) that a frisk — patting down a person's outer clothing — is proper if the officer has a "reasonable suspicion" that the person is armed and dangerous. If a pat-down reveals an object that might be a gun, the officer can enter the suspect's pocket to remove it. If the gun is being carried illegally, the suspect can be arrested.

The reasonable-suspicion test is much less stringent than the probable-cause standard the police must meet in order to make an arrest. A reasonable suspicion, however, is more than just a hunch; it must be supported by specific facts. The courts have held, not always consistently, that these facts include someone acting in a way that leads an experienced officer to conclude criminal activity may be afoot; someone fleeing at the approach of an officer; a person who fits a drug courier profile; a motorist stopped for a traffic violation who has a suspicious bulge in his pocket; a suspect identified by a reliable informant as carrying a gun. The Supreme Court has also upheld frisking people on probation or parole.

Some police departments frisk a lot of people, but usually the police frisk rather few, at least for the purpose of detecting illegal guns. In 1992 the police arrested about 240,000 people for illegally possessing or carrying a weapon. This is only about one-fourth as many as were arrested for public drunkenness. The average police officer will make *no* weapons arrests and confiscate *no* guns during any given year. Mark Moore, a professor of public policy at Harvard University, found that most weapons arrests were made because a citizen complained, not because the police were out looking for guns.

It is easy to see why. Many cities suffer from a shortage of officers, and even those with ample law-enforcement personnel worry about having their cases thrown out for constitutional reasons or being accused of police harassment. But the risk of violating the Constitution or engaging in actual, as opposed to perceived, harassment can be substantially reduced.

Each patrol officer can be given a list of people on probation or parole who live on that officer's beat and be rewarded for making frequent stops to insure that they are not carrying guns. Officers can be trained to recognize the kinds of actions that the Court will accept as providing the "reasonable suspicion" necessary for a stop and frisk. Membership in a gang known for assaults and drug dealing could be made the basis, by statute or Court precedent, for gun frisks.

The available evidence supports the claim that self-defense is a legitimate form of deterrence. People who report to the National Crime Survey that they defended themselves with a weapon were less likely to lose property in a robbery or be injured in an assault than those who did not defend themselves. Statistics have shown that would-be burglars are threatened by gun-wielding victims about as many times a year as they are arrested (and much more often than they are sent to prison) and that the chances of a burglar being shot are about the same as his chances of going to jail. Criminals know these facts even if gun control advocates do not and so are less likely to burgle occupied homes in America than occupied ones in Europe, where the residents rarely have guns.

Some gun control advocates may concede these points but rejoin that the cost of self-defense is self-injury: Handgun owners are more likely to shoot themselves or their loved ones than a criminal. Not quite. Most gun accidents involve rifles and shotguns, not handguns. Moreover, the rate of fatal gun accidents has been declining while the level of gun ownership has been rising. There are fatal gun accidents just as there are fatal car accidents, but in fewer than 2 percent of the gun fatalities was the victim someone mistaken for an intruder.

Those who urge us to forbid or severely restrict the sale of guns ignore these facts. Worse, they adopt a position that is politically absurd. In effect, they say, "Your government, having failed to protect your person and your property from criminal assault, now intends to deprive you of the opportunity to protect yourself."

Opponents of gun control make a different mistake. The National Rifle Association and its allies tell us that "guns don't kill, people kill" and urge the Government to punish more severely people who use guns to commit crimes. Locking up criminals does protect society from future crimes, and the prospect of being locked up may deter criminals. But our experience with meting out tougher sentences is mixed. The tougher the prospective sentence the less likely it is to be imposed, or at least to be imposed swiftly. If the Legislature adds on time for crimes committed with a gun, prosecutors often bargain away the add-ons; even when they do not, the judges in many states are reluctant to impose add-ons.

Worse, the presence of a gun can contribute to the magnitude of the crime even on the part of those who worry about serving a long prison sentence. Many criminals carry guns not to rob stores but to protect themselves from other armed criminals. Gang violence has become more threatening to bystanders as gang members have begun to arm themselves. People may commit crimes, but guns make some crimes worse. Guns often convert spontaneous outbursts of anger into fatal encounters. When some people carry them on the streets, others will want to carry them to protect themselves, and an urban arms race will be underway.

And modern science can be enlisted to help. Metal detectors at airports have reduced the number of airplane bombings and skyjackings to nearly zero. But these detectors only work at very close range. What is needed is a device that will enable the police to detect the presence of a large lump of metal in someone's pocket from a distance of ten or fifteen feet. Receiving such a signal could supply the officer with reasonable grounds for a pat-down. Underemployed nuclear physicists and electronics engineers in the post-cold-war era surely have the talents for designing a better gun detector.

Even if we do all these things, there will still be complaints. Innocent people will be stopped. Young black and Hispanic men will probably be stopped more often than older white Anglo males or women of any race. But if we are serious about reducing drive-by shootings, fatal gang wars and lethal quarrels in public places, we must get illegal guns off the street. We cannot do this by multiplying the forms one fills out at gun shops or by pretending that guns are not a problem until a criminal uses one.

Topics for Critical Thinking and Writing

1. If you had to single out one sentence in Wilson's essay as coming close to stating his thesis, what sentence would that be? Why do you think it states, better than any other sentence, the thesis of the essay?

2. In his third paragraph Wilson reviews some research by a criminologist purporting to show that guns are important for self-defense in American households. Does the research as reported show that displaying or firing guns in self-defense actually prevented crimes? Or wounded aggressors? Suppose you were also told that in households where guns may be used defensively, thousands of innocent people are injured, and hundreds are killed—for instance, children who find a loaded gun and play with it. Would you regard these injuries and deaths as a fair tradeoff? Explain. What does the research presented by Wilson really show?

3. In paragraph 12 Wilson says that people who want to severely restrict the ownership of guns are in effect saying, "'Your government, having failed to protect your person and your property from criminal assault, now intends to deprive you of the opportunity to protect yourself.'" What reply might an advocate of severe restrictions make? (Even if you strongly believe Wilson's summary is accurate, try to put yourself in the shoes of an advocate of gun control, and come up with the best reply that you can.)

4. Wilson reports in paragraph 7 that the police arrest four times as many drunks on the streets as they do people carrying unlicensed firearms. Does this strike you as absurd, reasonable, or mysterious? Does Wilson explain it to your satisfaction?

5. In his final paragraph Wilson grants that his proposal entails a difficulty: "Innocent people will be stopped. Young black and Hispanic men will probably be stopped more often than older white Anglo males or women of any race." Assuming that his predictions are accurate, is Wilson's proposal therefore fatally flawed and worth no further thought, or (to take the other extreme view) do you think that innocent people who fall into certain classifications will just have to put up with frisking, for the public good?

6. In an essay of no more than 100 words, explain the difference between the "reasonable-suspicion test" and the "probable-cause standard" that the courts use in deciding whether a street frisk is lawful. (You may want to organize your essay into two paragraphs, one on each topic, or perhaps into three if you want to use a brief introductory paragraph.)

7. Wilson criticizes both gun control advocates and the National Rifle Association for their ill-advised views. In an essay of 500 words, state his criticisms of each side, and explain whether and to what extent you agree.

Nora Ephron

Nora Ephron, born in 1941, attended Wellesley College. She worked as a reporter for the New York Post, *then took a job as a columnist with* Esquire, *and soon became a senior editor there. Ephron has written screenplays and directed films, including* Sleepless in Seattle *(1993), and has continued to write essays on a wide variety of topics. "The Boston Photographs" is from her collection* Scribble, Scribble: Notes on the Media *(1978).*

The Boston Photographs

"I made all kinds of pictures because I thought it would be a good rescue shot over the ladder . . . never dreamed it would be anything

else. . . . I kept having to move around because of the light set. The sky was bright and they were in deep shadow. I was making pictures with a motor drive and he, the fire fighter, was reaching up and, I don't know, everything started falling. I followed the girl down taking pictures. . . . I made three or four frames. I realized what was going on and I completely turned around, because I didn't want to see her hit."

You probably saw the photographs. In most newspapers, there were three of them. The first showed some people on a fire escape—a fireman, a woman, and a child. The fireman had a nice strong jaw and looked very brave. The woman was holding the child. Smoke was pouring from the building behind them. A rescue ladder was approaching, just a few feet away, and the fireman had one arm around the woman and one arm reaching out toward the ladder. The second picture showed the fire escape slipping off the building. The child had fallen on the escape and seemed about to slide off the edge. The woman was grasping desperately at the legs of the fireman, who had managed to grab the ladder. The third picture showed the woman and child in midair, falling to the ground. Their arms and legs were outstretched, horribly distended. A potted plant was falling too. The caption said that the woman, Diana Bryant, nineteen, died in the fall. The child landed on the woman's body and lived.

The pictures were taken by Stanley Forman, thirty, of the *Boston Herald American.* He used a motor-driven Nikon F set at 1/250, f5.6-S. Because of the motor, the camera can click off three frames a second. More than four hundred newspapers in the United States alone carried the photographs: The tear sheets from overseas are still coming in. The *New York Times* ran them on the first page of its second section; a paper in south Georgia gave them nineteen columns; the *Chicago Tribune,* the *Washington Post* and the *Washington Star* filled almost half their front pages, the *Star* under a somewhat redundant headline that read: SENSATIONAL PHOTOS OF RESCUE ATTEMPT THAT FAILED.

The photographs are indeed sensational. They are pictures of death in action, of that split second when luck runs out, and it is impossible to look at them without feeling their extraordinary impact and remembering, in an almost subconscious way, the morbid fantasy of falling, falling off a building, falling to one's death. Beyond that, the pictures are classics, old-fashioned but perfect examples of photojournalism at its most spectacular. They're throwbacks, really, fire pictures, 1930s tabloid shots; at the same time they're technically superb and thoroughly modern — the sequence could not have been taken at all until the development of the motor-driven camera some sixteen years ago.

Most newspaper editors anticipate some reader reaction to photo-   5
tographs like Forman's; even so, the response around the country was enormous, and almost all of it was negative. I have read hundreds of the letters that were printed in letters-to-the-editor sections, and they repeat the same points. "Invading the privacy of death." "Cheap sensationalism." "I thought I was reading the *National Enquirer.*" "Assigning the agony of a human being in terror of imminent death to the status of a side-show act." "A tawdry way to sell newspapers." The *Seattle Times* received sixty letters and calls; its managing editor even got a couple of them at home. A reader wrote the *Philadelphia Inquirer:* "*Jaws* and *Towering Inferno* are playing downtown; don't take business away from people who pay good money to advertise in your own paper." Another reader wrote the *Chicago Sun-Times:* "I shall try to hide my disappointment that Miss Bryant wasn't wearing a skirt when she fell to her death. You could have had some award-winning photographs of her underpants as her

skirt billowed over her head, you voyeurs." Several newspaper editors wrote columns defending the pictures: Thomas Keevil of the *Costa Mesa* (California) *Daily Pilot* printed a ballot for readers to vote on whether they would have printed the pictures; Marshall L. Stone of Maine's *Bangor Daily News*, which refused to print the famous assassination picture of the Vietcong prisoner in Saigon, claimed that the Boston pictures showed the dangers of fire escapes and raised questions about slumlords. (The burning building was a five-story brick apartment house on Marlborough Street in the Back Bay section of Boston.)

For the last five years, the *Washington Post* has employed various journalists as ombudsmen, whose job is to monitor the paper on behalf of the public. The *Post's* current ombudsman is Charles Seib, former managing editor of the *Washington Star;* the day the Boston photographs appeared, the paper received over seventy calls in protest. As Seib later wrote in a column about the pictures, it was "the largest reaction to a published item that I have experienced in eight months as the *Post's* ombudsman. . . .

"In the *Post's* newsroom, on the other hand, I found no doubts, no second thoughts . . . the question was not whether they should be printed but how they should be displayed. When I talked to editors . . . they used words like 'interesting' and 'riveting' and 'gripping' to describe them. The pictures told of something about life in the ghetto, they said (although the neighborhood where the tragedy occurred is not a ghetto, I am told). They dramatized the need to check on the safety of fire escapes. They dramatically conveyed something that had happened, and that is the business we're in. They were news. . . .

"Was publication of that [third] picture a bow to the same taste for the morbidly sensational that makes gold mines of disaster movies? Most papers will not print the picture of a dead body except in the most unusual circumstances. Does the fact that the final picture was taken a millisecond before the young woman died make a difference? Most papers will not print a picture of a bare female breast. Is that a more inappropriate subject for display than the picture of a human being's last agonized instant of life?" Seib offered no answers to the questions he raised, but he went on to say that although as an editor he would probably have run the pictures, as a reader he was revolted by them.

In conclusion, Seib wrote: "Any editor who decided to print those pictures without giving at least a moment's thought to what purpose they served and what their effect was likely to be on the reader should ask another question: Have I become so preoccupied with manufacturing a product according to professional traditions and standards that I have forgotten about the consumer, the reader?"

It should be clear that the phone calls and letters and Seib's own re-   10
action were occasioned by one factor alone: the death of the woman. Obviously, had she survived the fall, no one would have protested; the pictures would have had a completely different impact. Equally obvi-

ously, had the child died as well—or instead—Seib would undoubtedly have received ten times the phone calls he did. In each case, the pictures would have been exactly the same—only the captions, and thus the responses, would have been different.

But the questions Seib raises are worth discussing—though not exactly for the reasons he mentions. For it may be that the real lesson of the Boston photographs is not the danger that editors will be forgetful of reader reaction, but that they will continue to censor pictures of death precisely because of that reaction. The protests Seib fielded were really a variation on an old theme—and we saw plenty of it during the Nixon-Agnew years—the "Why doesn't the press print the good news?" argument. In this case, of course, the objections were all dressed up and cleverly disguised as righteous indignation about the privacy of death. This is a form of puritanism that is often justifiable; just as often it is merely puritanical.

Seib takes it for granted that the widespread though fairly recent newspaper policy against printing pictures of dead bodies is a sound one; I don't know that it makes any sense at all. I recognize that printing pictures of corpses raises all sorts of problems about taste and titillation and sensationalism; the fact is, however, that people die. Death happens to be one of life's main events. And it is irresponsible—and more than that, inaccurate—for newspapers to fail to show it, or to show it only when an astonishing set of photos comes in over the Associated Press wire. Most papers covering fatal automobile accidents will print pictures of mangled cars. But the significance of fatal automobile accidents is not

that a great deal of steel is twisted but that people die. Why not show it? That's what accidents are about. Throughout the Vietnam war, editors were reluctant to print atrocity pictures. Why *not* print them? That's what that was about. Murder victims are almost never photographed; they are granted their privacy. But their relatives are relentlessly pictured on their way in and out of hospitals and morgues and funerals.

I'm not advocating that newspapers print these things in order to teach their readers a lesson. The *Post* editors justified their printing of the Boston pictures with several arguments in that direction; every one of them is irrelevant. The pictures don't show anything about slum life; the incident could have happened anywhere, and it did. It is extremely unlikely that anyone who saw them rushed out and had his fire escape strengthened. And the pictures were not news—at least they were not national news. It is not news in Washington, or New York, or Los Angeles that a woman was killed in a Boston fire. The only newsworthy thing about the pictures is that they were taken. They deserve to be printed because they are great pictures, breathtaking pictures of something that happened. That they disturb readers is exactly as it should be: that's why photojournalism is often more powerful than written journalism.

Topics for Critical Thinking and Writing

1. In paragraph 5 Ephron refers to "the famous assassination picture of the Vietcong prisoner in Saigon." The photo shows the face of a prisoner who has been shot in the head at close range, just a moment before the photo was taken. Jot down the reasons why you would or would not approve of printing it in a newspaper. Think, too, about this: If the photo were not about a war—if it did not include the soldiers and the burning village in the rear—but showed children fleeing from an abusive parent or from an abusive sibling, would you approve of printing it in a newspaper?

2. In paragraph 9 Ephron quotes a newspaperman as saying that before printing Forman's pictures of the woman and the child falling from the fire escape, editors should have asked themselves "what purpose they served and what their effect was likely to be on the reader." If you were an editor, what would your answers be? By the way, the pictures were *not* taken in a ghetto, and they did *not* expose slum conditions.

3. In fifty words or so, write a precise description of what you see in the third of the Boston photographs. Do you think readers of your description would be "revolted" by the picture (para. 8), as were many viewers, the *Washington Post's* ombudsman among them? Why, or why not?

4. Ephron thinks it would be a good thing if more photographs of death and dying were published by newspapers (paras. 11–13). In an essay of 500 words, state her reasons and your evaluation of them.

Michael Levin

Michael Levin, educated at Michigan State University and Columbia University, has taught philosophy at Columbia and now at City College of the City University of New York. Levin has written numerous papers for professional journals and a book entitled Metaphysics and the Mind-Body Problem *(1979). The following essay is intended for a general audience.*

The Case for Torture

It is generally assumed that torture is impermissible, a throwback to a more brutal age. Enlightened societies reject it outright, and regimes suspected of using it risk the wrath of the United States.

I believe this attitude is unwise. There are situations in which torture is not merely permissible but morally mandatory. Moreover, these situations are moving from the realm of imagination to fact.

Death: Suppose a terrorist has hidden an atomic bomb on Manhattan Island which will detonate at noon on July 4 unless . . . (here follow the usual demands for money and release of his friends from jail). Suppose, further, that he is caught at 10 A.M. of the fateful day, but—preferring death to failure—won't disclose where the bomb is. What do we do? If we follow due process—wait for his lawyer, arraign him—millions of people will die. If the only way to save those lives is to subject the terrorist to the most excruciating possible pain, what grounds can there be for not doing so? I suggest there are none. In any case, I ask you to face the question with an open mind.

Torturing the terrorist is unconstitutional? Probably. But millions of lives surely outweigh constitutionality. Torture is barbaric? Mass murder is far more barbaric. Indeed, letting millions of innocents die in deference to one who flaunts his guilt is moral cowardice, an unwillingness to dirty one's hands. If *you* caught the terrorist, could you sleep nights knowing that millions died because you couldn't bring yourself to apply the electrodes?

Once you concede that torture is justified in extreme cases, you have 5 admitted that the decision to use torture is a matter of balancing innocent lives against the means needed to save them. You must now face more realistic cases involving more modest numbers. Someone plants a bomb on a jumbo jet. He alone can disarm it, and his demands cannot be met (or if they can, we refuse to set a precedent by yielding to his threats). Surely we can, we must, do anything to the extortionist to save the passengers. How can we tell 300, or 100, or 10 people who never asked to be put in danger, "I'm sorry, you'll have to die in agony, we just couldn't bring ourselves to . . ."

Here are the results of an informal poll about a third, hypothetical, case. Suppose a terrorist group kidnapped a newborn baby from a hospital. I asked four mothers if they would approve of torturing kidnappers if that were necessary to get their own newborns back. All said yes, the most "liberal" adding that she would like to administer it herself.

I am not advocating torture as punishment. Punishment is addressed to deeds irrevocably past. Rather, I am advocating torture as an acceptable measure for preventing future evils. So understood, it is far less objectionable than many extant punishments. Opponents of the death penalty, for example, are forever insisting that executing a murderer will not bring back his victim (as if the purpose of capital punishment were supposed to be resurrection, not deterrence or retribution). But torture, in the cases described, is intended not to bring anyone back but to keep innocents from being dispatched. The most powerful argument against using torture as a punishment or to secure confessions is that such practices disregard the rights of the individual. Well, if the individual is all that important—and he is—it is correspondingly important to protect the rights of individuals threatened by terrorists. If life is so valuable that it must never be taken, the lives of the innocents must be saved even at the price of hurting the one who endangers them.

Better precedents for torture are assassination and pre-emptive attack. No Allied leader would have flinched at assassinating Hitler, had that been possible. (The Allies did assassinate Heydrich.) Americans would be angered to learn that Roosevelt could have had Hitler killed in 1943—thereby shortening the war and saving millions of lives—but refused on moral grounds. Similarly, if nation A learns that nation B is about to launch an unprovoked attack, A has a right to save itself by destroying B's military capability first. In the same way, if the police can by torture save those who would otherwise die at the hands of kidnappers or terrorists, they must.

Idealism: There is an important difference between terrorists and their victims that should mute talk of the terrorists' "rights." The terrorist's victims are at risk unintentionally, not having asked to be endangered. But the terrorist knowingly initiated his actions. Unlike his victims, he volunteered for the risks of his deed. By threatening to kill for profit or idealism, he renounces civilized standards, and he can have no complaint if civilization tries to thwart him by whatever means necessary.

Just as torture is justified only to save lives (not extort confessions or   10 recantations) it is justifiably administered only to those *known* to hold innocent lives in their hands. Ah, but how can the authorities ever be sure they have the right malefactor? Isn't there a danger of error and abuse? Won't We turn into Them?

Questions like these are disingenuous in a world in which terrorists proclaim themselves and perform for television. The name of their game is public recognition. After all, you can't very well intimidate a government into releasing your freedom fighters unless you announce that it is your group that has seized its embassy. "Clear guilt" is difficult to define, but when 40 million people see a group of masked gunmen seize an airplane on the evening news, there is not much question about who the perpetrators are. There will be hard cases where the situation is murkier. Nonetheless, a line demarcating the legitimate use of torture can be drawn. Torture only the obviously guilty, and only for the sake of saving innocents, and the line between Us and Them will remain clear.

There is little danger that the Western democracies will lose their way if they choose to inflict pain as one way of preserving order. Paralysis in the face of evil is the greater danger. Some day soon a terrorist will threaten tens of thousands of lives, and torture will be the only way to save them. We had better start thinking about this.

Topics for Critical Thinking and Writing

1. In his first four paragraphs, Levin uses hypothetical cases (these are also commonly called *invented instances*), and he pretty much assumes you agree in these cases that torture is acceptable. (For this presumed agreement, see the first sentence in para. 5.) Do you agree? If not, why?

2. In paragraph 11 Levin asserts that although "There will be hard cases" where the situation is murky, "Nonetheless, a line demarcating the legitimate use of torture can be drawn." He then draws the line: "Torture only the obviously guilty, and only for the sake of saving innocents, and the line between Us and Them will remain clear." His essay is built on hypothetical cases. Can you invent a hypothetical case where the line between Us and Them is *not* clear?

3. Levin ends his essay by saying, "Some day soon a terrorist will threaten tens of thousands of lives, and torture will be the only way to save them." Given the fact that he wrote this essay in 1982, can we say that time has refuted this argument?

4. Is it reasonable to reply to Levin that we never know that the accused both is really guilty and will break under torture and therefore that torture is never justified? Why, or why not?

5. Let's look now at some matters of style. Evaluate Levin's title and his first two paragraphs. Notice that the first paragraph ends with a relatively long sentence and the second paragraph begins with a relatively short sentence. What is the effect of this sequence?

6. In paragraph 7, Levin says that "Opponents of the death penalty, for example, are forever insisting that executing a murderer will not bring back his victim." Suppose instead of "are forever insisting" he had said "sometimes argue." What would be the difference in tone—the difference in the speaker's voice and therefore in your sense of what sort of person the speaker is? What does Levin gain or lose by writing the sentence as he does?

Anna Lisa Raya

Daughter of a second-generation Mexican American father and a Puerto Rican mother, Anna Lisa Raya grew up in Los Angeles. While an undergraduate at Columbia University in New York, she wrote and published this essay on identity.

It's Hard Enough Being Me

[Student Essay]

When I entered college, I *discovered* I was Latina. Until then, I had never questioned who I was or where I was from: My father is a second-generation Mexican-American, born and raised in Los Angeles, and my mother was born in Puerto Rico and raised in Compton, Calif. My home is El Sereno, a predominantly Mexican neighborhood in L.A. Every close friend I have back home is Mexican. So I was always just Mexican. Though sometimes I was just Puerto Rican—like when we would visit Mamo (my grandma) or hang out with my Aunt Titi.

Upon arriving in New York as a first-year student, 3000 miles from home, I not only experienced extreme culture shock, but for the first time I had to define myself according to the broad term "Latina." Although culture shock and identity crisis are common for the newly minted collegian who goes away to school, my experience as a newly minted Latina was, and still is, even more complicating. In El Sereno, I felt like I was part of a majority, whereas at the College I am a minority.

I've discovered that many Latinos like myself have undergone similar experiences. We face discrimination for being a minority in this country while also facing criticism for being "whitewashed" or "sellouts" in the countries of our heritage. But as an ethnic group in college, we are forced to define ourselves according to some vague, generalized Latino experience. This requires us to know our history, our language, our music, and our religion. I can't even be a content "Puerto Mexican" because I have to be a politically-and-socially-aware-Latina-with-a-chip-on-my-shoulder-because-of-how-repressed-I-am-in-this-country.

I am none of the above. I am the quintessential imperfect Latina. I can't dance salsa to save my life, I learned about Montezuma and the Aztecs in sixth grade, and I haven't prayed to the *Virgen de Guadalupe* in years.

Apparently I don't even look Latina. I can't count how many times 5 people have just assumed that I'm white or asked me if I'm Asian. True, my friends back home call me *güera* ("whitey") because I have green eyes and pale skin, but that was as bad as it got. I never thought I would wish my skin were a darker shade or my hair a curlier texture, but since I've been in college, I have—many times.

Another thing: my Spanish is terrible. Every time I call home, I berate my mama for not teaching me Spanish when I was a child. In fact, not knowing how to speak the language of my home countries is the biggest problem that I have encountered, as have many Latinos. In Mexico there is a term, *pocha*, which is used by native Mexicans to ridicule Mexican-Americans. It expresses a deep-rooted antagonism and dislike for those of us who were raised on the other side of the border. Our failed attempts to speak pure, Mexican Spanish are largely responsible for the dislike. Other Latin American natives have this same attitude. No matter how well a Latino speaks Spanish, it can never be good enough.

Yet Latinos can't even speak Spanish in the U.S. without running the risk of being called "spic" or "wetback." That is precisely why my mother refused to teach me Spanish when I was a child. The fact that she spoke Spanish was constantly used against her: It prevented her from getting good jobs, and it would have placed me in bilingual education—a construct of the Los Angeles public school system that has proved to be more of a hindrance to intellectual development than a help.

To be fully Latina in college, however, I *must* know Spanish. I must satisfy the equation: Latina [equals] Spanish-speaking.

So I'm stuck in this black hole of an identity crisis, and college isn't making my life any easier, as I thought it would. In high school, I was being prepared for an adulthood in which I would be an individual, in which I wouldn't have to wear a Catholic school uniform anymore. But though I led an anonymous adolescence, I knew who I was. I knew I was different from white, black, or Asian people. I knew there was a language other than English that I could call my own if I only knew how to speak it better. I knew there were historical reasons why I was in this country, distinct reasons that make my existence here easier or more difficult than other people's existence. Ultimately, I was content.

Now I feel pushed into a corner, always defining, defending, and 10 proving myself to classmates, professors, or employers. Trying to understand who and why I am, while understanding Plato or Homer, is a lot to ask of myself.

A month ago, I heard three Nuyorican (Puerto Ricans born and raised in New York) writers discuss how New York City has influenced their writing. One problem I have faced as a young writer is finding a voice that is true to my community. I was surprised and reassured to discover that as Latinos, these writers had faced similar pressures and conflicts as myself; some weren't even taught Spanish in childhood. I will never forget the advice that one of them gave me that evening: She said that I need to be true to myself. "Because people will always complain about what you are doing—you're a 'gringa' or a 'spic' no matter what," she explained. "So you might as well do things for yourself and not for them."

I don't know why it has taken 20 years to hear this advice, but I'm going to give it a try. *Soy yo* and no one else. *Punto.*[1]

Topics for Critical Thinking and Writing

1. When Raya says she "discovered" she was Latina, to what kind of event is she referring? Was she coerced or persuaded to declare herself as Latina, or did it come about in some other way?

2. Is Raya on balance glad or sorry that she did not learn Spanish as a child? What evidence can you point to in her essay one way or the other?

3. What is an "identity crisis" (para. 9)? Does everyone go through such a crisis about the time one enters college? Did you? Or is this an experience that only racial minorities in predominantly white American colleges undergo?

Judy Brady

Born in San Francisco in 1937, Judy Brady married in 1960 and two years later earned a bachelor's degree in painting at the University of Iowa. Active in the women's movement and in other political causes, she has worked as an author, an editor, and a secretary. The essay reprinted here, written before she and her husband separated, appeared originally in the first issue of Ms. *in 1971.*

I Want a Wife

I belong to that classification of people known as wives. I am A Wife. And, not altogether incidentally, I am a mother.

Not too long ago a male friend of mine appeared on the scene fresh from a recent divorce. He had one child, who is, of course, with his ex-wife. He is looking for another wife. As I thought about him while I was ironing one evening, it suddenly occurred to me that I, too, would like to have a wife. Why do I want a wife?

I would like to go back to school so that I can become economically independent, support myself, and, if need be, support those dependent upon me. I want a wife who will work and send me to school. And while I am going to school I want a wife to take care of my children. I want a wife to keep track of the children's doctor and dentist appointments. And to keep track of mine, too. I want a wife to make sure my children eat properly and are kept clean. I want a wife who will wash the children's clothes and keep them mended. I want a wife who is a

---

[1] *Soy yo . . . Punto.* I'm me . . . Period. [Editors' note.]

good nurturant attendant to my children, who arranges for their schooling, makes sure that they have an adequate social life with their peers,
takes them to the park, the zoo, etc. I want a wife who takes care of the
children when they are sick, a wife who arranges to be around when
the children need special care, because, of course, I cannot miss classes
at school. My wife must arrange to lose time at work and not lose the
job. It may mean a small cut in my wife's income from time to time, but
I guess I can tolerate that. Needless to say, my wife will arrange and pay
for the care of the children while my wife is working.

I want a wife who will take care of *my* physical needs. I want a wife
who will keep my house clean. A wife who will pick up after my children, a wife who will pick up after me. I want a wife who will keep my
clothes clean, ironed, mended, replaced when need be, and who will see
to it that my personal things are kept in their proper place so that I can
find what I need the minute I need it. I want a wife who cooks the
meals, a wife who is a *good* cook. I want a wife who will plan the menus,
do the necessary grocery shopping, prepare the meals, serve them pleasantly, and then do the cleaning up while I do my studying. I want a wife
who will care for me when I am sick and sympathize with my pain and
loss of time from school. I want a wife to go along when our family takes
a vacation so that someone can continue to care for me and my children
when I need a rest and change of scene.

I want a wife who will not bother me with rambling complaints   5
about a wife's duties. But I want a wife who will listen to me when I feel
the need to explain a rather difficult point I have come across in my
course of studies. And I want a wife who will type my papers for me
when I have written them.

I want a wife who will take care of the details of my social life. When
my wife and I are invited out by my friends, I want a wife who will take
care of the babysitting arrangements. When I meet people at school that
I like and want to entertain, I want a wife who will have the house
clean, will prepare a special meal, serve it to me and my friends, and not
interrupt when I talk about things that interest me and my friends. I
want a wife who will have arranged that the children are fed and ready
for bed before my guests arrive so that the children do not bother us. I
want a wife who takes care of the needs of my guests so that they feel
comfortable, who makes sure that they have an ashtray, that they are
passed the hors d'oeuvres, that they are offered a second helping of the
food, that their wine glasses are replenished when necessary, that their
coffee is served to them as they like it. And I want a wife who knows
that sometimes I need a night out by myself.

I want a wife who is sensitive to my sexual needs, a wife who makes
love passionately and eagerly when I feel like it, a wife who makes sure
that I am satisfied. And, of course, I want a wife who will not demand
sexual attention when I am not in the mood for it. I want a wife who assumes the complete responsibility for birth control, because I do not

want more children. I want a wife who will remain sexually faithful to me so that I do not have to clutter up my intellectual life with jealousies. And I want a wife who understands that *my* sexual needs may entail more than strict adherence to monogamy. I must, after all, be able to relate to people as fully as possible.

If, by chance, I find another person more suitable as a wife than the wife I already have, I want the liberty to replace my present wife with another one. Naturally, I will expect a fresh, new life; my wife will take the children and be solely responsible for them so that I am left free.

When I am through with school and have a job, I want my wife to quit working and remain at home so that my wife can more fully and completely take care of a wife's duties.

My God, who *wouldn't* want a wife?   10

Topics for Critical Thinking and Writing

1. If one were to summarize Brady's first paragraph, one might say it adds up to "I am a wife and a mother." But analyze it closely. Exactly what does the second sentence add to the first? And what does "not altogether incidentally" add to the third sentence?

2. Brady uses the word *wife* in sentences where one ordinarily would use *she* or *her*. Why? And why does she begin paragraphs 4, 5, 6, and 7 with the same words, "I want a wife"?

3. In her second paragraph Brady says that the child of her divorced male friend "is, of course, with his ex-wife." In the context of the entire essay, what does this sentence mean?

4. Complete the following sentence by offering a definition: "According to Judy Brady, a wife is. . . ."

5. Try to state the essential argument of Brady's essay in a simple syllogism. (*Hint:* Start by identifying the thesis or conclusion you think she is trying to establish, and then try to formulate two premises, based on what she has written, that would establish the conclusion.)

6. Drawing on your experience as observer of the world around you (and perhaps as husband, wife, or former spouse), do you think Brady's picture of a wife's role is grossly exaggerated? Or is it (allowing for some serious playfulness) fairly accurate, even though it was written in 1971? If grossly exaggerated, is the essay therefore meaningless? If fairly accurate, what attitudes and practices does it encourage you to support? Explain.

7. Whether or not you agree with Brady's vision of marriage in our society, write an essay (500 words) titled "I Want a Husband," imitating her style and approach. Write the best possible essay, and then decide which of the two essays—yours or hers—makes a fairer comment on current society. Or if you believe Brady is utterly misleading, write an essay titled "I Want a Wife," seeing the matter in a different light.

8. If you feel that you have been pressed into an unappreciated, unreasonable role—built-in babysitter, listening post, or girl (or boy or man or woman) Friday—write an essay of 500 words that will help the reader to see both your plight and the injustice of the system. (*Hint:* A little humor will help to keep your essay from seeming to be a prolonged whine.)

A CASEBOOK:
How Valuable Are
Computers in College?

Nate Stulman

Nate Stulman published this short essay in the New York Times *in March 1999, when he was a sophomore at Swarthmore College. The essay evoked several letters of response that the newspaper printed and that we reprint.*

The Great Campus Goof-Off Machine

[Student Essay]

Conventional wisdom says that computers are a necessary tool for higher education. Many colleges and universities these days require students to have personal computers, and some factor the cost of one into tuition. A number of colleges have put high-speed Internet connections in every dorm room. But there are good reasons to question the wisdom of this preoccupation with computers and the Internet.

Take a walk through the residence halls of any college in the country and you'll find students seated at their desks, eyes transfixed on their computer monitors. What are they doing with their top-of-the-line PC's and high-speed T-1 Internet connections?

They are playing Tomb Raider instead of going to chemistry class, tweaking the configurations of their machines instead of writing the paper due tomorrow, collecting mostly useless information from the World Wide Web instead of doing a math problem set—a host of other activity that has little or nothing to do with traditional academic work.

I have friends who have spent whole weekends doing nothing but playing Quake or Warcraft or other interactive computer games. One friend sometimes spends entire evenings—six to eight hours—scouring the Web for images and modifying them just to have a new background on his computer desktop.

And many others I know have amassed overwhelming collections of   5
music on their computers. It's the searching and finding that they seem

to enjoy: Some of them have more music files on their computers than they could play in months.

Several people who live in my hall routinely stay awake all night chatting with dormmates online. Why walk 10 feet down the hall to have a conversation when you can chat on the computer—even if it takes three times as long?

You might expect that personal computers in dorm rooms would be used for nonacademic purposes, but the problem is not confined to residence halls. The other day I walked into the library's reference department, and five or six students were grouped around a computer—not conducting research but playing Tetris. Every time I walk past the library's so-called research computers, it seems that at least half are being used to play games, chat or surf the Internet aimlessly.

Colleges and universities should be wary of placing such an emphasis on the use of computers and the Internet. The Web may be useful for finding simple facts, but serious research still means a trip to the library.

For most students, having a computer in the dorm is more of a distraction than a learning tool. Other than computer science or mathematics majors, few students need more than a word processing program and access to e -mail in their rooms.

It is true, of course, that students have always procrastinated and wasted time. But when students spend four, five, even ten hours a day on computers and the Internet, a more troubling picture emerges—a picture all the more disturbing because colleges themselves have helped create the problem.

Topics for Critical Thinking and Writing

1. Do you believe that high-speed Internet connections are "a necessary tool for higher education" (para. 1)? Why, or why not?

2. Stulman claims that a walk through a dormitory or even the reference room in the library reveals that many students are playing computer games instead of going to class or writing papers. Does your experience confirm his assertion? Even if this is so, what is the relevance of this fact (if it is a fact) to his assertion that "few students need more than a word processing program and access to e-mail in their rooms" (para. 9)?

3. Stulman concedes that "students have always procrastinated and wasted time" (para. 10). When the editors of this book were in college, leisure time (and time stolen from classrooms and study halls) was devoted to cards—poker, hearts, bridge, pinochle. Is there any reason to think that today's undergraduates are devoting (or should we say wasting?) even more time to surfing the Web?

4. In his final paragraph, Stulman says that "colleges themselves have helped create the problem." If you think there is some (or much) truth

in Stulman's essay, what do you think colleges can do to diminish or eliminate the problem?

5. What remedy, if any, does Stulman propose? Is he, for instance, in favor of censorship? Denying access to the Net on student-owned computers? Is there any remedy for what worries Stulman?

6. Try to design an experiment (hypothetical, of course) that would enable us to tell, on balance, whether current uses of the computer facilitate, handicap, or make no discernible difference in helping students perform in their college courses.

7. Stulman is writing about Swarthmore, a small, elite liberal arts college. Are things worse or better or about the same in your college? Write a 500-word paper on the topic "How My Friends and I Waste Time." (Your essay may—but need not—implicitly argue that what appears to be a waste of time is a necessary period of relaxation or perhaps a period when social skills are developed.)

Stulman's essay predictably evoked letters from readers of the *New York Times*. In our first chapter (page 22), we offered a checklist that can be used in reading such letters. For convenience we reprint it here.

✓ What assumption(s) does the letter writer make? Do you share the assumption(s)?

✓ What is the writer's claim?

✓ What evidence, if any, does the writer offer to support the claim?

✓ Is there anything about the style of the letter—the distinctive use of language, the tone—that makes the letter especially engaging or especially annoying?

With these questions in mind—and others of your own invention— read the letters of response to Stulman that the *New York Times* printed.

Letters of Response to Nate Stulman
from Mark Cassell, Paul Hogarth,
David Schwartz, Chris Toulouse, Jo Manning,
Robert Kubey, and Kenneth R. Jolls

To the Editor:

Nate Stulman (op-ed, March 15) inserts a healthy "byte" of caution into the discussion of classroom technology. New technologies clearly offer great opportunities for learning and research. In my introductory courses, for example, I suggest Web-based resources to help with researching and writing papers.

The problem is that while offering a great time-saving resource for collecting information, the new technologies do not easily teach students how to search in a discriminating manner or how to think critically about the information they download.

Our enthusiasm for cyber-pedagogy should not prevent us from at least recognizing its potential negative impact on students who are far more likely to have surfed the Web than to have visited a library before they enter college.

Mark Cassell

Kent, Ohio, March 15, 1999

The writer is an assistant professor of political science at Kent State University.

To the Editor:

As an undergraduate I understand Nate Stulman's point that our fellow students spend way too much time on the computer ("The Great Campus Goof-Off Machine," op-ed, March 15). But Mr. Stulman's notion that universities are doing a disservice by providing Internet access—which will revolutionize the way we live—is downright foolish. High school and college students get in car accidents all the time; does that mean they shouldn't drive?

The bottom line is that college life is a learning experience, a time in which students learn to live independently and to acquire self-discipline. I spend a lot of time on the Internet, and maybe I should be doing my schoolwork instead. But I have also learned to limit my surfing time, spend hours studying, and learn to enjoy life.

Paul Hogarth

Berkeley, Calif., March 15, 1999

To the Editor:

The Internet is not merely a tool for "finding simple facts," as opposed to one for doing serious research, as Nate Stulman claims, but the ultimate tool for fact-finding ("The Great Campus Goof-Off Machine," op-ed, March 15).

Through the World Wide Web services my university subscribes to, I can read the thousands of different journals that are online, covering AIDS research to international policy theory. The academic applications of the information available are endless.

Contrary to Mr. Stulman, computer science or math majors are not the only students who need computers other than for e-mail and word processing.

The Internet has changed the way that research can be done in any field.

David Schwartz
Medford, Mass., March 15, 1999

To the Editor:

Nate Stulman's "Great Campus Goof-Off Machine" (op-ed, March 15) sounds off-key to those of us who are trying to teach Internet literacy to college students.

While there are some power users on campus, their presence is a rarity among the rest of the student population. And even among power users, students with scant sense of the differences between conservatives and liberals are regularly fooled by Web sites produced by political extremists (try "affirmative action" in any major search engine).

That the Internet is now so woven into the lives of college students should caution us against shrugging off its importance. Just because one of the major uses of computers is to play games does not mean that colleges can afford to treat them like toys.

Chris Toulouse
Hempstead, N.Y., March 16, 1999
The writer is an assistant professor of sociology at Hofstra University.

To the Editor:

I share Nate Stulman's concerns for the Internet generation, but students in all disciplines are well served by the World Wide Web (op-ed, March 15). I don't know what our freshman English students would do without the Modern Language Association's database or the business students without access to Lexis-Nexis.

Computer games will always be with us, and there will always be students who would rather fritter away their four years in front of a flashing screen. But it can't be denied that valid Web-based research tools are being used by serious students.

Jo Manning
Coral Gables, Fla., March 17, 1999
The writer is a reference librarian, University of Miami.

To the Editor:

The academic performance of some undergraduates may indeed suffer by virtue of extensive time spent on the Internet (op-ed, March 15). About 5 percent to 10 percent of students, typically males and more frequently first- and second-year students, report staying up late at night using chat lines and e-mail and then feeling tired the next day in class or missing class altogether. Alfred University reported in 1996 that there was an increase that year in students dismissed for academic failure and that half of them listed excessive Internet use as one of their problems.

College administrators are beginning to recognize that the computers and Internet services they laud and support also permit uses that are not in the best interests of new students.

Robert Kubey
Highland Park, N.J., March 15, 1999
The writer is an associate professor of journalism and media studies,
Rutgers University.

To the Editor:

As a means for increasing the scope of learning, the potential of computers remains unequaled (op-ed, March 15). But computer-assisted instruction is still heavy on promise and light on delivery.

Educational applications are rarely developed by our best scholars and are often lacking in the excitement that attracts students to the games and other diversions that Nate Stulman mentions. Educational software development is not a must-do for innovative young academics chasing the tenure carrot.

Buying the technology to give to students is far easier than finding creative ways for them to learn with it. If writing software to teach chemistry, for instance, became as important as doing the research to advance it, progress could be made.

Kenneth R. Jolls
Ames, Iowa, March 16, 1999
The writer is a professor of chemical engineering, Iowa State University.

Topics for Critical Thinking and Writing

1. Professor Cassell suggests that students who use the Internet do not know "how to search in a discriminating manner or how to think critically about the information they download." Might the same be said about students who used periodicals and books in the library? Or are there substantial differences between printed sources and Internet sources and between the ways in which one thinks about these sources?

2. Write (but do not mail) a letter of two or three paragraphs to Paul Hogarth, responding to his letter. By the way, how effective is his analogy comparing Internet abuse with car accidents ("High school and college students get in car accidents all the time; does that mean they shouldn't drive"?)?

3. David Schwartz argues that the Internet is of great value to the serious researcher. Have you used it for serious research, and, if so, have you found it of great value? In any case, write a response (500 words) to Stulman's essay, focusing on the Net's value or lack of value for research.

4. Reread Professor Toulouse's letter, and then write a paragraph that (a) begins "Professor Toulouse's main point can be summarized thus" and (b) includes the words "his evidence is . . ."

5. Jo Manning says that the Modern Language Association's database is essential for "freshman English students" and Lexis-Nexis is essential for "business students." If you belong to one of these categories, in 500 words evaluate the assertion, based on your experience. If you have not taken a freshman English course and are not a business student but believe the Internet is invaluable for some of your own academic work, in 500 words set forth your position.

Part Two

CRITICAL WRITING

4

Writing an Analysis
of an Argument

ANALYZING AN ARGUMENT

Examining the Author's Thesis

Most of your writing in other courses will require you to write an analysis of someone else's writing. In a course in political science you may have to analyze, say, an essay first published in *Foreign Affairs*, perhaps reprinted in your textbook, that argues against raising tariff barriers to foreign trade; or a course in sociology may require you to analyze a report on the correlation between fatal accidents and drunk drivers under the age of twenty-one. Much of your writing, in short, will set forth reasoned responses to your reading, as preparation for making an argument of your own.

Obviously you must understand an essay before you can analyze it thoughtfully. You must read it several times—not just skim it—and (the hard part) you must think about it. Again, you'll find that your thinking is stimulated if you take notes and if you ask yourself questions about the material. Notes will help you to keep track of the writer's thoughts and also of your own responses to the writer's thesis. The writer probably *does* have a thesis, a point, and if so, you must try to locate it. Perhaps the thesis is explicitly stated in the title or in a sentence or two near the beginning of the essay or in a concluding paragraph, but perhaps you will have to infer it from the essay as a whole.

Notice that we said the writer *probably* has a thesis. Much of what you read will indeed be primarily an argument; the writer explicitly or implicitly is trying to support some thesis and to convince you to agree with it. But some of what you read will be relatively neutral, with the argument just faintly discernible—or even with no argument at all. A work may, for instance, chiefly be a report: Here are the data, or here is what *X, Y,* and *Z* said; make of it what you will. A report might simply state how various ethnic groups voted in an election. In a report of this sort, of course, the writer hopes to persuade readers that the facts are correct, but no thesis is advanced, at least not explicitly or perhaps even consciously; the writer is not evidently arguing a point and trying to change our minds. Such a document differs greatly from an essay by a political analyst who presents similar findings in order to persuade a candidate to sacrifice the votes of this ethnic bloc in order to get more votes from other blocs.

Examining the Author's Purpose

While reading an argument, try to form a clear idea of the author's **purpose.** Judging from the essay or the book, was the purpose to persuade, or was it to report? An analysis of a pure report (a work apparently without a thesis or argumentative angle) on ethnic voting will deal chiefly with the accuracy of the report. It will, for example, consider whether the sample poll was representative.

Much material that poses as a report really has a thesis built into it, consciously or unconsciously. The best evidence that the prose you are reading is argumentative is the presence of two kinds of key terms:

- **Transitions that imply the drawing of a conclusion:** *therefore, because, for the reason that, consequently;*
- **Verbs that imply proof:** *confirms, verifies, accounts for, implies, proves, disproves, is (in)consistent with, refutes, it follows that.*

Keep your eye out for such terms, and scrutinize their precise role whenever they appear. If the essay does not advance a thesis, think of a thesis (a hypothesis) that it might support or some conventional belief that it might undermine.

Examining the Author's Methods

If the essay advances a thesis, you will want to analyze the strategies or methods of argument that allegedly support the thesis.

- Does the writer quote authorities? Are these authorities really competent in this field? Are equally competent authorities who take a different view ignored?
- Does the writer use statistics? If so, are they appropriate to the point being argued? Can they be interpreted differently?
- Does the writer build the argument by using examples, or analogies? Are they satisfactory?
- Are the writer's assumptions acceptable?
- Does the writer consider all relevant factors? Has he or she omitted some points that you think should be discussed? For instance,

should the author recognize certain opposing positions, and perhaps concede something to them?

- Does the writer seek to persuade by means of ridicule? If so, is the
ridicule fair: Is it supported also by rational argument?

In writing your analysis, you will want to tell your reader something
about the author's purpose and something about the author's **methods.**
It is usually a good idea at the start of your analysis—if not in the first
paragraph then in the second or third—to let the reader know the purpose (and thesis, if there is one) of the work you are analyzing and then
to summarize the work briefly.

Next you will probably find it useful (your reader will certainly find
it helpful) to write out *your* thesis (your evaluation or judgment). You
might say, for instance, that the essay is impressive but not conclusive, or
is undermined by convincing contrary evidence, or relies too much on
unsupported generalizations, or is wholly admirable, or whatever. Remember, because your paper is itself an argument, it needs its own thesis.

And then, of course, comes the job of setting forth your analysis and
the support for your thesis. There is no one way of going about this
work. If, say, your author gives four arguments (for example: an appeal
to common sense, the testimony of authorities, the evidence of comparisons, an appeal to self-interest),

- You may want to take up these four arguments in sequence.
- Or you may want to begin by discussing the simplest of the four
and then go on to the more difficult ones.
- Or you may want first to discuss the author's two arguments that
you think are sound and then turn to the two that you think are
not. Or perhaps the reverse.
- And as you warm to your thesis, you may want to clinch your case
by constructing a fifth argument, absent from the work under
scrutiny but in your view highly important.

In short, the organization of your analysis may or may not follow the organization of the work you are analyzing.

Examining the Author's Persona

You will probably also want to analyze something a bit more elusive
than the author's explicit arguments: the author's self-presentation.
Does the author seek to persuade readers partly by presenting himself or
herself as conscientious, friendly, self-effacing, authoritative, tentative,
or in some other light? Most writers do two things:

- They present evidence, and
- They present themselves (or, more precisely, they present the
image of themselves that they wish us to behold).

In some persuasive writing this **persona** or **voice** or presentation of the self may be no less important than the presentation of evidence.

In establishing a persona, writers adopt various rhetorical strategies, ranging from the use of characteristic words to the use of a particular form of organization. For instance, the writer who speaks of an opponent's "gimmicks" instead of "strategy" is trying to downgrade the opponent and also to convey the self-image of a streetwise person. On a larger scale, consider the way in which evidence is presented and the kind of evidence offered. One writer may first bombard the reader with facts and then spend relatively little time drawing conclusions. Another may rely chiefly on generalizations, waiting until the end of the essay to bring the thesis home with a few details. Another may begin with a few facts and spend most of the space reflecting on these. One writer may seem professorial or pedantic, offering examples of an academic sort; another, whose examples are drawn from ordinary life, may seem like a regular guy. All such devices deserve comment in your analysis.

The writer's persona, then, may color the thesis and help it develop in a distinctive way. If we accept the thesis, it is partly because the writer has won our goodwill by persuading us of his good character (*ethos*, in Aristotle's terms). Later we will talk more about the appeal to the character of the speaker — the so-called *ethical appeal*.

The author of an essay may, for example, seem fair minded and open minded, treating the opposition with great courtesy and expressing interest in hearing other views. Such a tactic is, of course, itself a persuasive device. Or take an author who appears to rely on hard evidence such as statistics. This reliance on seemingly objective truths is itself a way of seeking to persuade — a rational way, to be sure, but a mode of persuasion nonetheless.

Especially in analyzing a work in which the author's persona and ideas are blended, you will want to spend some time commenting on the persona. Whether you discuss it near the beginning of your analysis or near the end will depend on your own sense of how you want to construct your essay, and this decision will partly depend on the work you are analyzing. For example, if the author's persona is kept in the background and is thus relatively invisible, you may want to make that point fairly early to get it out of the way and then concentrate on more interesting matters. If, however, the persona is interesting — and perhaps seductive, whether because it seems so scrupulously objective or so engagingly subjective — you may want to hint at this quality early in your essay, and then develop the point while you consider the arguments.

Summary

In the last few pages we have tried to persuade you that, in writing an analysis of your reading, you must do the following:

- Read and reread thoughtfully. Writing notes will help you to think about what you are reading.
- Be aware of the purpose of the material to which you are responding.

We have also tried to point out these facts:

- Most of the nonliterary material that you will read is designed to argue, to report, or to do both.
- Most of this material also presents the writer's personality, or voice, and this voice usually merits attention in an analysis. An essay on, say, nuclear war, in a journal devoted to political science, may include a voice that moves from an objective tone to a mildly ironic tone to a hortatory tone, and this voice is worth commenting on.

Possibly all this explanation is obvious. There is yet another point, though, equally obvious but often neglected by students who begin by writing an analysis and end up by writing only a summary, a shortened version of the work they have read:

- Although your essay is an analysis of someone else's writing, and you may have to include a summary of the work you are writing about, your essay is *your* essay. The thesis, the organization, and the tone are yours. Your thesis, for example, may be that although the author is convinced she has presented a strong case, her case is far from proved. The organization of your paper may be deeply indebted to the work you are analyzing, but it need not be. The author may have begun with specific examples and then gone on to make generalizations and to draw conclusions, but you may begin with the conclusions. Similarly, your tone may resemble your subject's (let's say the voice is courteous academic), but it will nevertheless have its own ring, its own tone of (say) urgency, or caution, or coolness.

AN ARGUMENT, ITS ELEMENTS, AND A STUDENT'S ANALYSIS OF THE ARGUMENT

Stanley S. Scott

Stanley S. Scott (1933–1992) was vice president and director of corporate affairs of Philip Morris Companies Inc. This essay originally appeared on December 29, 1984, in the op-ed page of the New York Times.

Smokers Get a Raw Deal

The Civil Rights Act, the Voting Rights Act, and a host of antidiscrimination laws notwithstanding, millions of Americans are still forced to sit in the back of planes, trains, and buses. Many more are subject to segregation in public places. Some are even denied housing and employment: victims of an alarming—yet socially acceptable—public hostility.

This new form of discrimination is based on smoking behavior.

If you happen to enjoy a cigarette, you are the potential target of violent antismokers and overzealous public enforcers determined to force their beliefs on the rest of society.

Ever since people began smoking, smokers and nonsmokers have been able to live with one another using common courtesy and common sense. Not anymore. Today, smokers must put up with virtually unenforceable laws regulating when and where they can smoke—laws intended as much to discourage smoking itself as to protect the rights of nonsmokers. Much worse, supposedly responsible organizations devoted to the "public interest" are encouraging the harassment of those who smoke.

This year, for example, the American Cancer Society is promoting 5 programs that encourage people to attack smokers with canisters of gas, to blast them with horns, to squirt them with oversized water guns, and burn them in effigy.

Harmless fun? Not quite. Consider the incidents that are appearing on police blotters across America:

> In a New York restaurant, a young man celebrating with friends was zapped in the face by a man with an aerosol spray can. His offense: lighting a cigarette. The aggressor was the head of a militant antismoker organization whose goal is to mobilize an army of two million zealots to spray smokers in the face.

> In a suburban Seattle drugstore, a man puffing on a cigarette while he waited for a prescription to be filled was ordered to stop by an elderly customer who pulled a gun on him.

> A twenty-three-year-old lit up a cigarette on a Los Angeles bus. A passenger objected. When the smoker objected to the objection, he was fatally stabbed.

> A transit policeman, using his reserve gun, shot and fatally wounded a man on a subway train in the Bronx in a shootout over smoking a cigarette.

The basic freedoms of more than 50 million American smokers are at risk today. Tomorrow, who knows what personal behavior will become socially unacceptable, subject to restrictive laws and public ridicule? Could travel by private car make the social engineers' hit list because it is less safe than public transit? Could ice cream, cake, and cookies become socially unacceptable because their consumption causes obesity? What about sky diving, mountain climbing, skiing, and contact sports? How far will we allow this to spread?

The question all Americans must ask themselves is: Can a nation that has struggled so valiantly to eliminate bias based on race, religion, and sex afford to allow a fresh set of categories to encourage new forms of hostility between large groups of citizens?

After all, discrimination is discrimination, no matter what it is based on.

Let's examine Scott's essay with an eye to identifying those elements we mentioned earlier in this chapter (pp. 133–36) that deserve notice when examining *any* argument: the author's *thesis, purpose, methods,* and *persona.* And while we're at it, let's also notice some other features of Scott's essay that will help us appreciate its effects and evaluate its strengths and weaknesses. All this will put us in a better position to write an evaluation or to write an argument of our own confirming, extending, or rebutting Scott's argument.

Title   Scott starts off with a bang: No one likes a "raw deal," and if that's what smokers are getting, then they probably deserve better. So already in his title, Scott has made a plea for the reader's sympathy. He has also indicated something about his *topic,* his *thesis,* and (in the words "raw deal") something of his *persona:* He is a regular guy, someone who does not use fancy language but who calls a spade a spade.

Thesis   What is the basic *thesis* Scott is arguing? By the end of the second paragraph his readers have a good idea, and surely by paragraph 7, they can state his thesis explicitly, perhaps in these words: Smokers today are victims of unfair discrimination. Writers need not announce their thesis in so many words, but they ought to have a thesis, a point they want to make, and they ought to make it evident fairly soon — as Scott does.

Purpose   There's really no doubt that Scott's *purpose* in this essay is to *persuade* the reader to adopt his view of the plight of today's smokers. This amounts to trying to persuade us that his thesis (stated above) is *true.* Scott, however, does not show that his essay is argumentative or persuasive by using any of the key terms that normally mark argumentative prose. He doesn't call anything his "conclusion," none of his statements is labeled "my reasons" or "my premises," and he doesn't connect any clauses or sentences with a "therefore" or a "because."

But this doesn't matter. The argumentative nature of his essay is revealed by the *judgment* he states in paragraph 2: Smokers are experiencing undeserved discrimination. This is, after all, his thesis in brief form. Any author who has a thesis as obvious as Scott does is likely to want to persuade his readers to agree with it. To do that, he needs to try to *support* it; accordingly, the bulk of the rest of Scott's essay constitutes just such support.

Method   Scott's principal method of argument is to cite a series of *examples* (introduced by para. 6) in which the reader can see what Scott believes is actual discrimination against smokers. This is his *evidence* in support of his thesis. (Ought we to trust him here? He cites no sources for the events he reports. On the other hand, these examples sound plausible, and so we probably shouldn't demand documentation for them.) The nature of his thesis doesn't require experimental research or support from recognized authorities. All it requires is some *reported instances* that can properly be described as "harassment" (para. 4, end). Scott, of course, is relying here on an *assumption:* Harassment is unfair discrimination—but few would quarrel with that assumption.

Notice the *language* in which Scott characterizes the actions of the American Cancer Society ("blast," "squirt," "burn"—all in para. 5). He chose these verbs deliberately, to convey his disapproval of these actions and subtly persuade the reader to disapprove of them, too.

Another distinctive feature of Scott's method of argument is found in paragraph 7, after the examples. Here, he drives his point home by using the argumentative technique known as *the thin end of the wedge.* (We discuss it later on p. 324. The gist of the idea is that just as the thin end of the wedge makes a small opening that will turn into a larger one, so a small step may lead to a large step. The idea is also expressed in the familiar phrase, "Give him an inch and he'll take a mile.") Scott here argues that tolerating discrimination today against a vulnerable minority (smokers) could lead to tolerating widespread discrimination against other minorities (mountain climbers) tomorrow—perhaps even a minority that includes the reader. (Does he exaggerate by overstating his case? Or are his examples well chosen and plausible?)

Notice, finally, the role that *rhetorical questions* play in Scott's argument. (A **rhetorical question,** such as Scott's "How far will we allow this to spread?" in para. 7, is a question to which no answer is expected because only one answer can reasonably be made.) Writers who use a rhetorical question save themselves the trouble of offering further evidence to support their claims; the person asking the rhetorical question assumes the reader understands and agrees with the questioner's unstated answer.

Persona   Scott presents himself as a no-nonsense defender of the rights of a beleaguered minority. This may add little or nothing to the soundness of his argument, but it surely adds to its persuasive effect. By presenting himself as he does—plain-speaking but righteously indignant—Scott effectively jars the reader's complacency (surely, all the good guys *oppose* smoking—or do they?), and he cultivates at least the reader's grudging respect (we all like to see people stand up for their rights, and the more unpopular the cause the more we are likely to respect the sincere advocate).

Closing Paragraph   Scott ends with one of those seeming platitudes that tolerates no disagreement—"discrimination is discrimination," thus making one last effort to enlist the reader on his side. We say "seeming platitudes" because, when you come to think about it, of course not all discrimination is morally objectionable. After all, what's unfair with "discriminating" against criminals by punishing them?

Consider a parallel case, that popular maxim "Business is business." What is it, really, but a disguised claim to the effect that *in business, unfair practices must be tolerated or even admired.* But as soon as this sentiment is reformulated by removing its disguise as a tautology, its controversial character is immediately evident. So with Scott's "discrimination is discrimination"; it is designed to numb the reader into believing that all discrimination is *objectionable* discrimination. The critic might reply to Scott in the same vein: There is discrimination, and there is discrimination.

Let's turn now to a student's analysis of Scott's essay—and then to our analysis of the student's analysis.

Tom Wu

English 2B

Professor McCabe

March 13, 2001

                    Is All Discrimination Unfair?

        Stanley S. Scott's "Smokers Get a Raw

Deal," though a poor argument, is an extremely

clever piece of writing. Scott writes clearly,

and he holds a reader's attention. Take his

opening paragraph, which evokes the bad old days

of Jim Crow segregation, when blacks were forced

to ride at the back of the bus. Scott tells us,

to our surprise, that there still are Americans

who are forced to ride at the back of the bus.

Who, we wonder, are the people who are treated

so unfairly--or we would wonder, if the title of

the essay hadn't let us make an easy guess. They

are smokers. Of course, most Americans detest

segregation, and Scott thus hopes to tap our

feelings of decency and fair play so that we

will recognize that smokers are people too and

ought not to be subjected to the same evil that

African Americans were subjected to. He returns

to this motif at the end of his essay, when he

says, "After all, discrimination is discrimina-

tion, no matter what it is based on." Scott is,

so it seems, on the side of fair play.

        But discrimination has two meanings. One

is the ability to make accurate distinctions,

as in "She can discriminate between instant

coffee and freshly ground coffee." The second

meaning is quite different: an act based on

prejudice, as in "She does not discriminate

against the handicapped," and this is Scott's

meaning. Blacks were the victims of discrimination in this second sense when they were forced
to sit at the back of the bus simply because
they were black, not because they engaged in
any action that might reasonably be perceived
as offensive or harmful to others. That sort of
segregation was the result of prejudice; it
held people accountable for something (their
color) over which they had no control. But
smokers voluntarily engage in an action that
can be annoying to others (like playing loud
music on a radio at midnight with the windows
open) and that may have effects that can injure
others. In pursuing their "right," smokers thus
can interfere with the rights of others. In
short, the "segregation" and "discrimination"
against smokers is in no way comparable to the
earlier treatment of blacks. Scott illegiti-
mately--one might say outrageously--suggests
that segregating smokers is as unjust and as
blindly prejudiced as was the segregating of
African Americans.

Between his opening and his closing paragraphs, which present smokers as victims of
"discrimination," he cites several instances of
smokers who were subjected to violence, including two smokers who were killed. His point is,
again, to show that smokers are being treated
as blacks once were and are in effect subjected to lynch law. The instances of violence
that he cites are deplorable, but they scarcely
prove that it is wrong to insist that people do
not have the unrestricted right to smoke in

public places. It is clearly wrong to assault
smokers, but surely these assaults do not
therefore make it right for smokers to subject
others to smoke that annoys and may harm.

    Scott's third chief argument, set forth in
the third paragraph from the end, is to claim
that if today we infringe on "the basic freedoms of more than 50 million American smokers,"
we will perhaps tomorrow infringe on the freedom of yet other Americans. Here Scott makes an
appeal to patriotism ("basic freedoms," "American") and at the same time warns the reader
that the reader's innocent pleasures, such as
eating ice cream or cake, are threatened. But
this extension is preposterous: Smoking undoubtedly is greatly bothersome to many nonsmokers and may even be unhealthy for them;
eating ice cream cannot affect onlookers. If it
was deceptive to classify smokers with blacks,
it is equally deceptive to classify smoking
with eating ice cream. Scott is trying to tell
us that if we allow smokers to be isolated, we
will wake up and find that we are the next who
will be isolated by those who don't happen to
like our habits, however innocent. The nation,
he says, in his next-to-last paragraph, has
"struggled so valiantly [we are to pat ourselves on the back] to eliminate bias based on
race, religion, and sex." Can we, he asks, afford to let a new bias divide us? The answer,
of course, is that indeed we should discriminate, not in Scott's sense but in the sense of
making distinctions. We discriminate, entirely

Wu 4

properly, between the selling of pure food and
of tainted food, between law-abiding citizens
and criminals, between licensed doctors and unlicensed ones, and so on. If smokers are a serious nuisance and a potential health hazard,
it is scarcely un-American to protect the innocent from them. That's not discrimination (in
Scott's sense) but is simply fair play.

AN ANALYSIS OF THE STUDENT'S ANALYSIS

Tom Wu's essay seems to us to be excellent, doubtless the product of a good deal of thoughtful revision. Of course, he does not cover every possible aspect of Scott's essay— he concentrates on Scott's reasoning and says very little about Scott's style—but we think that, given the limits of 500 to 750 words, he does a good job. What makes the student's essay effective? We can list the chief reasons:

- The essay has a title that is of at least a little interest, giving a hint of what is to follow. A title such as "An Analysis of an Argument" or "Scott on Smoking" would be acceptable, certainly better than no title at all, but in general it is a good idea to try to construct a more informative or a more interesting title that (like this one) arouses interest, perhaps by stirring the reader's curiosity.
- The author identifies his subject (he names the writer and the title of his essay) early.
- He reveals his thesis early. His topic is Scott's essay; his thesis or point is that it is clever but wrongheaded. Notice, by the way, that he looks closely at Scott's use of the word *discrimination* and that he defines this word carefully. Defining terms is often essential in argumentative essays. Of course, Scott did *not* define the word, probably because he hoped his misuse of it would be overlooked.
- He takes up all of Scott's main points.

- He uses a few brief quotations to let us hear Scott's voice and to assure us that he is staying close to Scott, but he does not pad his essay with long quotations.

- The essay has a sensible organization. The student begins with the beginning of Scott's essay and then, because Scott uses the opening motif again at the end, touches on the end. The writer is not skipping around; he is taking a single point (a "new discrimination" is on us) and following it through.

- He turns to Scott's next argument—that smokers are subjected to violence. He doesn't try to touch on each of Scott's four examples—he hasn't room, in an essay of 500 to 750 words—but he treats their gist fairly.

- He touches on Scott's next point—that no one will be safe from other forms of discrimination—and shows that it is both a gross exaggeration and, because it equates utterly unlike forms of behavior, a piece of faulty thinking.

- He concludes (without the stiffness of saying "in conclusion") with some general comments on discrimination, thus picking up a motif he introduced early in his essay. His essay, like Scott's, uses a sort of frame, or, changing the figure, it finishes off by tying a knot that was begun at the start. He even repeats the words "fair play," which he used at the end of his first paragraph, and neatly turns them to his advantage.

- Notice, finally, that he sticks closely to Scott's essay. He does not go off on a tangent and talk about the harm that smokers do to themselves. Because the assignment was to analyze Scott's essay (rather

---

A CHECKLIST FOR AN ESSAY ANALYZING AN ARGUMENT

✓ In your opening paragraph (or opening paragraphs), do you give the reader a good idea of what your essay will be doing? Do you identify the essay you will discuss, and introduce your subject?

✓ Is your essay fair? Does it face all of the strengths (and weaknesses) of the argument under discussion?

✓ Have you used occasional quotations to let your reader hear the tone of the author and to ensure fairness and accuracy?

✓ Is your analysis effectively organized? Probably you can't move through the original essay paragraph by paragraph, but have you created a coherent structure for your own essay?

✓ If the original essay relies partly on the writer's tone, have you sufficiently discussed this matter?

✓ Is your own tone appropriate?

than to offer his own views on smoking), he confines himself to analyzing the essay.

Query: Good though this essay is, would it be better if Tom Wu in his first paragraph had briefly summarized Scott's essay?

Exercise

Take one of the essays not yet discussed in class or an essay assigned now by your instructor, and in an essay of 500 words analyze and evaluate it.

ARGUMENTS FOR ANALYSIS

Elizabeth Joseph

Elizabeth Joseph is an attorney and lives in Utah. This essay appeared in the New York Times *in 1991.*

My Husband's Nine Wives

I married a married man. In fact, he had six wives when I married him seventeen years ago. Today, he has nine.

In March, the Utah Supreme Court struck down a trial court's ruling that a polygamist couple could not adopt a child because of their marital style. Last month, the national board of the American Civil Liberties Union, in response to a request from its Utah chapter, adopted a new policy calling for the legalization of polygamy.

Polygamy, or plural marriage, as practiced by my family is a paradox. At first blush, it sounds like the ideal situation for the man and an oppressive one for the women. For me, the opposite is true. While polygamists believe that the Old Testament mandates the practice of plural marriage, compelling social reasons make the life style attractive to the modern career woman.

Pick up any women's magazine and you will find article after article about the problems of successfully juggling career, motherhood, and marriage. It is a complex act that many women struggle to manage daily; their frustrations fill up the pages of those magazines and consume the hours of afternoon talk shows.

In a monogamous context, the only solutions are compromises. The kids need to learn to fix their own breakfast, your husband needs to get used to occasional microwave dinners, you need to divert more of your income to ensure that your preschooler is in a good day care environment.   5

I am sure that in the challenge of working through these compromises, satisfaction and success can be realized. But why must women only embrace a marital arrangement that requires so many tradeoffs?

When I leave for the sixty-mile commute to court at 7 A.M., my two-year-old daughter, London, is happily asleep in the bed of my husband's wife, Diane. London adores Diane. When London awakes, about the time I'm arriving at the courthouse, she is surrounded by family members who are as familiar to her as the toys in her nursery.

My husband Alex, who writes at night, gets up much later. While most of his wives are already at work, pursuing their careers, he can almost always find one who's willing to chat over coffee.

I share a home with Delinda, another wife, who works in town government. Most nights, we agree we'll just have a simple dinner with our three kids. We'd rather relax and commiserate over the pressures of our work day than chew up our energy cooking and doing a ton of dishes.

Mondays, however, are different. That's the night Alex eats with us. 10 The kids, excited that their father is coming to dinner, are on their best behavior. We often invite another wife or one of his children. It's a special event because it only happens once a week.

Tuesday night, it's back to simplicity for us. But for Alex and the household he's dining with that night, it's their special time.

The same system with some variation governs our private time with him. While spontaneity is by no means ruled out, we basically use an appointment system. If I want to spend Friday evening at his house, I make an appointment. If he's already "booked," I either request another night or if my schedule is inflexible, I talk to the other wife and we work out an arrangement. One thing we've all learned is that there's always another night.

Most evenings, with the demands of career and the literal chasing after the needs of a toddler, all I want to do is collapse into bed and sleep. But there is also the longing for intimacy and comfort that only he can provide, and when those feelings surface, I ask to be with him.

Plural marriage is not for everyone. But it is the life style for me. It offers men the chance to escape from the traditional, confining roles that often isolate them from the surrounding world. More important, it enables women, who live in a society full of obstacles, to fully meet their career, mothering, and marriage obligations. Polygamy provides a whole solution. I believe American women would have invented it if it didn't already exist.

Topics for Critical Thinking and Writing

1. In her third paragraph Joseph suggests that "compelling social reasons" make polygamy "the life style attractive to the modern career woman." How does she support this assertion? Do you think that she adequately supports it? Why, or why not?

2. Try to imagine advantages that Joseph does not discuss for women in polygamy—for example, for women who are divorced or widowed. Whether or not you support polygamy, make the strongest arguments for these advantages that you can (and then, if you wish, answer them).

3. Joseph does not suggest or discuss any problems in polygamous marriages. What problems occur to you? Why should she or should she not have discussed them?

4. Many societies have practiced (and continue to practice) plural marriage, but it is illegal in the United States. Do you think that plural marriage should be a legal option? Why, or why not?

5. Does Joseph's article provide an answer to Brady's "I Want a Wife"? Read the essay (pages 120–22), imagine you are Brady, and answer this question. Or imitating Joseph, write an article supporting polyandry (the practice of having more than one husband at a time).

6. Which would a feminist be more likely to think about Joseph after reading her essay: (a) She is a pathetic figure, obviously brainwashed into believing she has a fully satisfying and autonomous life. (b) She obviously approves of her domestic situation, so who are we to judge otherwise? (c) You provide a better alternative if you can think of one.

7. Ask your mother to read Joseph's essay, discuss it with her, and then write a 500-word essay on the theme: What My Mother Thinks about Polygamy.

Jeff Jacoby

Jeff Jacoby is a columnist for the Boston Globe, *where this essay was originally published on February 20, 1997.*

Bring Back Flogging

Boston's Puritan forefathers did not indulge miscreants lightly.

For selling arms and gunpowder to Indians in 1632, Richard Hopkins was sentenced to be "whipt, & branded with a hott iron on one of his cheekes." Joseph Gatchell, convicted of blasphemy in 1684, was ordered "to stand in pillory, have his head and hand put in & have his toung drawne forth out of his mouth, & peirct through with a hott iron." When Hannah Newell pleaded guilty to adultery in 1694, the court ordered "fifteen stripes Severally to be laid on upon her naked back at the Common Whipping post." Her consort, the aptly named Lambert Despair, fared worse: He was sentenced to 25 lashes "and that on the next Thursday Immediately after Lecture he stand upon the Pillory for . . . a full hower with Adultery in Capitall letters written upon his brest."

Corporal punishment for criminals did not vanish with the Puritans—Delaware didn't get around to repealing it until 1972—but for all relevant purposes, it has been out of fashion for at least 150 years. The day is long past when the stocks had an honored place on the Boston Common, or when offenders were publicly flogged. Now we practice a more enlightened, more humane way of disciplining wrong-doers: We lock them up in cages.

Imprisonment has become our penalty of choice for almost every of-fense in the criminal code. Commit murder; go to prison. Sell cocaine; go to prison. Kite checks; go to prison. It is an all-purpose punishment, suitable—or so it would seem—for crimes violent and nonviolent, mo-tivated by hate or by greed, plotted coldly or committed in a fit of pas-sion. If anything, our preference for incarceration is deepening—behold the slew of mandatory minimum sentences for drug crimes and "three-strikes-you're-out" life terms for recidivists. Some 1.6 million Americans are behind bars today. That represents a 250 percent increase since 1980, and the number is climbing.

We cage criminals at a rate unsurpassed in the free world, yet few of   5 us believe that the criminal justice system is a success. Crime is out of control, despite the deluded happy talk by some politicians about how "safe" cities have become. For most wrongdoers, the odds of being ar-rested, prosecuted, convicted, and incarcerated are reassuringly long. Fifty-eight percent of all murders do *not* result in a prison term. Likewise 98 percent of all burglaries.

Many states have gone on prison-building sprees, yet the penal sys-tem is choked to bursting. To ease the pressure, nearly all convicted felons are released early—or not locked up at all. "About three of every four convicted criminals," says John DiIulio, a noted Princeton criminol-ogist, "are on the streets without meaningful probation or parole super-vision." And while everyone knows that amateur thugs should be deterred before they become career criminals, it is almost unheard of for judges to send first- or second-time offenders to prison.

Meanwhile, the price of keeping criminals in cages is appalling—a common estimate is $30,000 per inmate per year. (To be sure, the cost to society of turning many inmates loose would be even higher.) For tens of thousands of convicts, prison is a graduate school of criminal studies: They emerge more ruthless and savvy than when they entered. And for many offenders, there is even a certain cachet to doing time—a stint in prison becomes a sign of manhood, a status symbol.

But there would be no cachet in chaining a criminal to an outdoor post and flogging him. If young punks were horsewhipped in public after their first conviction, fewer of them would harden into lifelong felons. A humiliating and painful paddling can be applied to the rear end of a crook for a lot less than $30,000—and prove a lot more educational than ten years' worth of prison meals and lockdowns.

Are we quite certain the Puritans have nothing to teach us about dealing with criminals?

Of course, their crimes are not our crimes: We do not arrest blasphe- 10
mers or adulterers, and only gun control fanatics would criminalize the
sale of weapons to Indians. (They would criminalize the sale of weapons
to anybody.) Nor would the ordeal suffered by poor Joseph Gatchell—
the tongue "peirct through" with a hot poker—be regarded today as
anything less than torture.

But what is the objection to corporal punishment that doesn't maim
or mutilate? Instead of a prison term, why not sentence at least some
criminals—say, thieves and drunk drivers—to a public whipping?

"Too degrading," some will say. "Too brutal." But where is it written
that being whipped is more degrading than being caged? Why is it more
brutal to flog a wrongdoer than to throw him in prison—where the risk
of being beaten, raped, or murdered is terrifyingly high?

The *Globe* reported in 1994 that more than two hundred thousand
prison inmates are raped each year, usually to the indifference of the
guards. "The horrors experienced by many young inmates, particularly
those who . . . are convicted of nonviolent offenses," former Supreme
Court Justice Harry Blackmun has written, "border on the unimaginable." Are those horrors preferable to the short, sharp shame of corporal punishment?

Perhaps the Puritans were more enlightened than we think, at least
on the subject of punishment. Their sanctions were humiliating and
painful, but quick and cheap. Maybe we should readopt a few.

Topics for Critical Thinking and Writing

1. When Jacoby says (para. 3) that today we are more "enlightened" than
   our Puritan forefathers because where they used flogging, "We lock
   them up in cages," is he being ironic? Explain.

2. Suppose you agree with Jacoby. Explain precisely (a) what you mean by
   flogging (does Jacoby explain what he means?) and (b) how much flogging is appropriate for the crimes of housebreaking, rape, robbery, and
   murder.

3. In an essay of 250 words, explain why you think that flogging would be
   more (or less) degrading and brutal than imprisonment.

4. At the end of his essay Jacoby draws to our attention the terrible risk of
   being raped in prison as an argument in favor of replacing imprisonment with flogging. Do you think he mentions this point at the end because he believes it is the strongest or most pervasive of all those he
   mentions? Why, or why not?

5. It is often said that corporal punishment does not have any effect or, if it
   does, the effect is the negative one of telling the recipient that violence is
   an acceptable form of behavior. But suppose it were demonstrated that

the infliction of physical pain reduced at least certain kinds of crimes, perhaps shoplifting or unarmed robbery. Should we adopt the practice?

6. Jacoby draws the line (para. 11) at punishment that would "maim or mutilate." Why draw the line here? Some societies punish thieves by amputating a hand. Suppose we knew that this practice really did seriously reduce theft. Should we adopt it? How about adopting castration (surgical or chemical) for rapists? For child molesters?

Katha Pollitt

Katha Pollitt (b. 1949) often writes essays on literary, political, and social topics for The Nation, *a liberal journal that on January 30, 1995, published the essay that we reprint here. Some of Pollitt's essays have been collected and published in a volume called* Reasonable Creatures *(1994). Pollitt is also widely known as a poet; her first collection of poems,* Antarctic Traveller *(1982), won the National Book Critics Circle award for poetry.*

It Takes Two: A Modest Proposal for Holding Fathers Equally Accountable

"You start out with the philosophy that you can have as many babies as you want . . . if you don't ask the government to take care of them. But when you start asking the government to take care of them, the government ought to have some control over you. I would say, for people like that, if they want the government to take care of their children I would be for something like Norplant, mandatory Norplant."

What well-known politician made the above remarks? Newt Gingrich? Jesse Helms? Dan Quayle? No, it was Marion Barry, newly installed Democratic mayor of our nation's capital, speaking last November to Sally Quinn of the *Washington Post.* The same Marion Barry whose swearing-in on January 2 featured a poetry reading by Maya Angelou, who, according to the *New York Times,* "drew thunderous applause when she pointed at Mr. Barry and crooned: 'Me and my baby, we gonna shine, shine!'" Ms. Angelou sure knows how to pick them.

One of my neighbors told me in the laundry room that it wasn't very nice of me to have mentioned Arianna Huffington's millions when we "debated" spirituality and school prayer on *Crossfire* the other day. So I won't belabor Mayor Barry's personal history[1] here. After all, the great thing about Christianity, of which Mayor Barry told Ms. Quinn he is now a fervent devotee, is that you can always declare yourself reformed, reborn, and redeemed. So maybe Mayor ("Bitch set me up") Barry really

---

[1]**Mayor Barry's personal history** Marion Barry served six months in prison for possessing drugs. [Editors' note.]

is the man to "bring integrity back into government," as he is promising to do.

But isn't it interesting that the male politicians who go all out for family values — the deadbeat dads, multiple divorcers, convicted felons, gropers, and philanderers who rule the land — always focus on women's behavior and always in a punitive way? You could, after all, see the plethora of women and children in poverty as the fruits of male feckless-ness, callousness, selfishness, and sexual vanity. We hear an awful lot about pregnant teens, but what about the fact that 30 percent of fathers of babies born to girls under sixteen are men in their twenties or older? What about the fact that the condom is the only cheap, easy-to-use, ef-fective, side-effectless nonprescription method of contraception — and it is the male partner who must choose to use it? What about the 50 per-cent of welfare mothers who are on the rolls because of divorce — i.e., the failure of judges to order, or husbands to pay, adequate child support?

Marion Barry's views on welfare are shared by millions: Women   5 have babies by parthenogenesis or cloning, and then perversely demand that the government "take care of them." Last time I looked, taking care of children meant feeding, bathing, and singing the Barney song, and mothers, not government bureaucrats, were performing those tasks. It is not the mother's care that welfare replaces, but the father's cash. Newt Gingrich's Personal Responsibility Act is directed against unmarried moms, but these women are actually assuming a responsibility that their babies' fathers have shirked. It's all very well to talk about orphanages, but what would happen to children if mothers abandoned them at the rate fathers do? A woman who leaves her newborn in the hospital and never returns for it still makes headlines. You'd need a list as thick as the New York City phone book to name the men who have no idea where or how or who their children are.

My point is not to demonize men, but fair's fair. If we've come so far down the road that we're talking about mandatory Norplant, about starving women into giving up their kids to orphanages (Republican ver-sion) or forcing young mothers to live in group homes (Democratic ver-sion); if *The Bell Curve* coauthor Charles Murray elicits barely a peep when he suggests releasing men from financial obligations to out-of-wedlock children; and if divorced moms have to hire private detectives to get their exes to pay court-awarded child support, then it's time to en-sure that the Personal Responsibility Act applies equally to both sexes. For example:

1. A man who fathers a child out of wedlock must pay $10,000 a year or 20 percent of his income, whichever is greater, in child support until the child reaches twenty-one. If he is unable to pay, the government will, in which case the father will be given a workfare (no wage) job and a dorm residence comparable to those

provided homeless women and children—i.e., curfews, no visitors, and compulsory group-therapy sessions in which, along with other unwed fathers, he can learn to identify the patterns of irresponsibility that led him to impregnate a woman so thoughtlessly.

2. A man who fathers a second child out of wedlock must pay child support equal to that for the first; if he can't, or is already on workfare, he must have a vasectomy. A sample of his sperm will be preserved so he can father more children if he becomes able to support the ones he already has.

3. Married men who father children out of wedlock or in sequential marriages have the same obligations to all their children, whose living standards must be as close to equal as is humanly possible. This means that some older men will be financially unable to provide their much-younger trophy wives with the babies those women often crave. Too bad!

4. Given the important role played by fathers in everything from   10
upping their children's test scores to teaching them the meaning of terms like "wide receiver" and "throw weight," divorced or unwed fathers will be legally compelled to spend time with their children or face criminal charges of child neglect. Absentee dads, not overburdened single moms, will be legally liable for the crimes and misdemeanors of their minor children, and their paychecks will be docked if the kids are truant.

5. In view of the fact that men can father children unknowingly, all men will pay a special annual tax to provide support for children whose paternity is unknown. Men wishing to avoid the tax can undergo a vasectomy at state expense, with sperm to be frozen at personal expense (Republican version) or by government subsidy (Democratic version).

As I was saying, fair's fair.

Topics for Critical Thinking and Writing

1. In paragraph 5 Pollitt sums up what she says is a common view of welfare: "Women have babies by parthenogenesis or cloning, and then perversely demand that the government 'take care of them.'" What absurdity is she calling to our attention?

2. In paragraph 4 Pollitt cites three important facts for her argument pointing to "male . . . selfishness" as a chief cause of women on welfare. Consult some reliable source—a word with the reference librarian will probably help guide you to the right place—and verify at least one of these facts.

3. In paragraph 5 Pollitt mentions "Newt Gingrich's Personal Responsibility Act." With the assistance of your college's librarian, locate the text,

or at least a summary, of this proposed law. Then look up the Republicans' *Contract with America,* edited by Ed Gillespie and Bob Schellhas (1994), and check out what is described there as the Family Reinforcement Act. How do these two proposed laws differ?

4. Reread the first five paragraphs. Do you think that Pollitt has helped you to think about a problem? Or has she muddied the waters? Explain.

5. Pollitt declares not only once but twice (paras. 6 and 12) that "fair's fair." People also sometimes say "business is business." Both expressions look like more tautologies (needless repetitions), explaining or justifying nothing—yet they aren't really tautologies at all. What do you think is the rhetorical or persuasive function of such expressions?

6. Do you think that any of Pollitt's five proposals might become law? If not, why not, and, further, what *is* her purpose in offering them?

7. If you have read Jonathan Swift's "A Modest Proposal" (p. 179), explain why Pollitt echoes Swift's title in her own title.

David Cole

David Cole, a professor at Georgetown University Law Center, is a volunteer staff attorney for the Center for Constitutional Rights. This essay originally appeared in The Nation *on October 17, 1994.*

Five Myths about Immigration

For a brief period in the mid-nineteenth century, a new political movement captured the passions of the American public. Fittingly labeled the "Know-Nothings," their unifying theme was nativism. They liked to call themselves "Native Americans," although they had no sympathy for people we call Native Americans today. And they pinned every problem in American society on immigrants. As one Know-Nothing wrote in 1856: "Four-fifths of the beggary and three-fifths of the crime spring from our foreign population; more than half the public charities, more than half the prisons and almshouses, more than half the police and the cost of administering criminal justice are for foreigners."

At the time, the greatest influx of immigrants was from Ireland, where the potato famine had struck, and Germany, which was in political and economic turmoil. Anti-alien and anti-Catholic sentiments were the order of the day, especially in New York and Massachusetts, which received the brunt of the wave of immigrants, many of whom were dirt-poor and uneducated. Politicians were quick to exploit the sentiment: There's nothing like a scapegoat to forge an alliance.

I am especially sensitive to this history: My forebears were among those dirt-poor Irish Catholics who arrived in the 1860s. Fortunately for them, and me, the Know-Nothing movement fizzled within fifteen years. But its pilot light kept burning, and is turned up whenever the American public begins to feel vulnerable and in need of an enemy.

Although they go by different names today, the Know-Nothings have returned. As in the 1850s, the movement is strongest where immigrants are most concentrated: California and Florida. The objects of prejudice are of course no longer Irish Catholics and Germans; 140 years later, "they" have become "us." The new "they"—because it seems "we" must always have a "they"—are Latin Americans (most recently, Cubans), Haitians, and Arab Americans, among others.

But just as in the 1850s, passion, misinformation and shortsighted   5
fear often substitute for reason, fairness, and human dignity in today's immigration debates. In the interest of advancing beyond know-nothingism, let's look at five current myths that distort public debate and government policy relating to immigrants.

America is being overrun with immigrants. In one sense, of course, this is true, but in that sense it has been true since Christopher Columbus arrived. Except for the real Native Americans, we are a nation of immigrants.

It is not true, however, that the first-generation immigrant share of our population is growing. As of 1990, foreign-born people made up only 8 percent of the population, as compared with a figure of about 15 percent from 1870 to 1920. Between 70 and 80 percent of those who immigrate every year are refugees or immediate relatives of U.S. citizens.

Much of the anti-immigrant fervor is directed against the undocumented, but they make up only 13 percent of all immigrants residing in the United States, and only 1 percent of the American population. Contrary to popular belief, most such aliens do not cross the border illegally but enter legally and remain after their student or visitor visa expires. Thus, building a wall at the border, no matter how high, will not solve the problem.

Immigrants take jobs from U.S. citizens. There is virtually no evidence to support this view, probably the most widespread misunderstanding about immigrants. As documented by a 1994 A.C.L.U. Immigrants' Rights Project report, numerous studies have found that immigrants actually *create* more jobs than they fill. The jobs immigrants take are of course easier to see, but immigrants are often highly productive, run their own businesses, and employ both immigrants and citizens. One study found that Mexican immigration to Los Angeles County between 1970 and 1980 was responsible for 78,000 new jobs. Governor Mario Cuomo reports that immigrants own more than 40,000 companies in New York, which provide thousands of jobs and $3.5 billion to the state's economy every year.

Immigrants are a drain on society's resources. This claim fuels many of   10
the recent efforts to cut off government benefits to immigrants. However, most studies have found that immigrants are a net benefit to the economy because, as a 1994 Urban Institute report concludes, "immi-

grants generate significantly more in taxes paid than they cost in services received." The Council of Economic Advisers similarly found in 1986 that "immigrants have a favorable effect on the overall standard of living."

Anti-immigrant advocates often cite studies purportedly showing the contrary, but these generally focus only on taxes and services at the local or state level. What they fail to explain is that because most taxes go to the federal government, such studies would also show a net loss when applied to U.S. citizens. At most, such figures suggest that some redistribution of federal and state monies may be appropriate; they say nothing unique about the costs of immigrants.

Some subgroups of immigrants plainly impose a net cost in the short run, principally those who have most recently arrived and have not yet "made it." California, for example, bears substantial costs for its disproportionately large undocumented population, largely because it has on average the poorest and least educated immigrants. But that has been true of every wave of immigrants that has ever reached our shores; it was as true of the Irish in the 1850s, for example, as it is of Salvadorans today. From a long-term perspective, the economic advantages of immigration are undeniable.

Some have suggested that we might save money and diminish incentives to immigrate illegally if we denied undocumented aliens public services. In fact, undocumented immigrants are already ineligible for most social programs, with the exception of education for schoolchildren, which is constitutionally required, and benefits directly related to health and safety, such as emergency medical care and nutritional assistance to poor women, infants, and children. To deny such basic care to people in need, apart from being inhumanly callous, would probably cost us more in the long run by exacerbating health problems that we would eventually have to address.

Aliens refuse to assimilate, and are depriving us of our cultural and political unity. This claim has been made about every new group of immigrants to arrive on U.S. shores. Supreme Court Justice Stephen Field wrote in 1884 that the Chinese "have remained among us a separate people, retaining their original peculiarities of dress, manners, habits, and modes of living, which are as marked as their complexion and language." Five years later, he upheld the racially based exclusion of Chinese immigrants. Similar claims have been made over different periods of our history about Catholics, Jews, Italians, Eastern Europeans, and Latin Americans.

In most instances, such claims are simply not true; "American culture" has been created, defined, and revised by persons who for the most part are descended from immigrants once seen as anti-assimilationist. Descendants of the Irish Catholics, for example, a group once decried as separatist and alien, have become presidents, senators, and representatives (and all of these in one family, in the case of the Kennedys). Our society exerts tremendous pressure to conform, and cultural separatism rarely survives a generation. But more important, even if this claim were true, is this a legitimate rationale for limiting immigration in a society built on the values of pluralism and tolerance?

Noncitizen immigrants are not entitled to constitutional rights. Our government has long declined to treat immigrants as full human beings, and nowhere is that more clear than in the realm of constitutional rights. Although the Constitution literally extends the fundamental protections in the Bill of Rights to all people, limiting to citizens only the right to vote and run for federal office, the federal government acts as if this were not the case.

In 1893 the executive branch successfully defended a statute that required Chinese laborers to establish their prior residence here by the testimony of "at least one credible white witness." The Supreme Court ruled that this law was constitutional because it was reasonable for Congress to presume that nonwhite witnesses could not be trusted.

The federal government is not much more enlightened today. In a pending case I'm handling in the Court of Appeals for the Ninth Circuit, the Clinton Administration has argued that permanent resident aliens lawfully living here should be extended no more First Amendment rights than aliens applying for first-time admission from abroad—that is, none. Under this view, students at a public university who are citizens may express themselves freely, but students who are not citizens can be deported for saying exactly what their classmates are constitutionally entitled to say.

Growing up, I was always taught that we will be judged by how we treat others. If we are collectively judged by how we have treated immigrants—those who would appear today to be "other" but will in a generation be "us"—we are not in very good shape.

Topics for Critical Thinking and Writing

1. What are the "five current myths" about immigration that Cole identifies? Why does he describe them as "myths" (rather than "errors," "mistakes," or "falsehoods")?

2. In an encyclopedia or other reference work in your college library, look up the Know-Nothings. What, if anything, of interest do you learn about the movement that is not mentioned by Cole in his opening paragraphs (1–4)?

3. Cole attempts to show how insignificant the immigrant population really is (in paras. 7 and 13) because it is such a small fraction (8 percent in 1990) of the total population. Suppose someone said to him, "That's all very well, but 8 percent of the population is still 20 million people—far more than the 15 percent of the population during the years from 1870 to 1920." How might he reply?

4. Suppose Cole is right, that most illegal immigration results from over-staying visitor and student visas (para. 8). Why not pass laws prohibiting foreign students from studying here, since so many abuse the privilege? Why not pass other laws forbidding foreign visitors?

5. Cole cites a study (para. 9) showing that "Mexican immigration to Los Angeles County between 1970 and 1980 was responsible for 78,000 new jobs." Suppose it were also true that this immigration was responsible for 78,000 other Mexican immigrants who joined criminal gangs or were otherwise not legally employed. How might Cole respond?

6. Cole admits (para. 12) that in California, the large population of undocumented immigrants imposes "substantial costs" on taxpayers. Does Cole offer any remedy for this problem? Should the federal government bear some or all of these extra costs that fall on California?

7. Cole thinks that "cultural separatism" among immigrants "rarely survives a generation" (para. 15). His evidence? Look at the Irish Catholics. But suppose someone argued that this is weak evidence: Today's immigrants are not Europeans, they are Asian and Hispanic; they will never assimilate to the degree that European immigrants did—their race, culture, religion, language, and the trend toward "multiculturalism" all block the way. How might Cole reply?

8. Do you think that immigrants who are not citizens and not applying for citizenship ought to be allowed to vote in state and local elections (the Constitution forbids them to vote in federal elections, as Cole points out in para. 16)? Why, or why not? How about illegal immigrants?

Stuart Taylor Jr.

Stuart Taylor Jr., a senior writer for National Journal *magazine, published this essay in* NJ *on July 15, 2000, in his regular column, "Opening Argument."*

School Prayer: When Constitutional Principles Clash

It may now be unconstitutional for a public school teacher or student leader to recite the Pledge of Allegiance in class. Or at a football game. Or at a graduation. Or to recite the Declaration of Independence. Or to sing the national anthem.

At least, this is a plausible reading of the Supreme Court's 6–3 decision on June 19 that struck down a Texas high school's policy of allowing an elected student leader to pray over the public address system at football games. It seems most unlikely, of course, that the Justices would actually take the radical step of banishing the pledge from school ceremonies anytime soon—if only because it would be all too obvious that if the law says that, then the law is an ass. But the more-liberal Justices might have to strain to avoid carrying their logic that far. And the three dissenters had reason to complain that "the tone of the Court's opinion . . . bristles with hostility to all things religious in public life."

To be sure, the Texas school may have crossed the line into unconstitutional sponsorship of religion. Justice John Paul Stevens properly stressed in his opinion for the majority that various detailed provisions of the school's recently adopted policy—which authorized election of a single student leader for the entire season to deliver "a brief invocation and/or message" before each home game—rendered it "simply . . . a continuation" of the school's long-standing practice of sponsoring official prayers. That inference was enhanced by allegations that school officials had "chastis[ed] children who held minority religious beliefs" and had "distribut[ed] Gideon Bibles on school premises."

But Stevens did not stop there. He also implied strongly that the Court would strike down as an act of the state *any* prayer initiated by a majority vote of students, even at a school whose administrators have always eschewed endorsing any form of religion and have made it clear that nonreligious and religious messages are equally welcome. "The majoritarian process implemented by the district guarantees, by definition, that minority candidates will never prevail and that their views will be effectively silenced," Stevens asserted, leaving them "at the mercy of the majority" and feeling a "sense of isolation and affront."

Really? One Ben Marcus recalled in *Time* that far from "'isolation and affront' . . . I sometimes found an unexpected degree of the opposite: inclusion and camaraderie with my teammates after taking part in the pregame prayers, a solemn connection that I wanted to scoff at but, because it moved me, could not." 5

The kind of prayer that Marcus found so benign is apparently too redolent of the Spanish Inquisition for the Supreme Court's taste: "Students . . . feel immense social pressure . . . to be involved in . . . high school football," Stevens explained, and thus "to risk facing a personally offensive religious ritual. . . . [So] the delivery of a pregame prayer has the improper effect of coercing those present to participate in an act of religious worship." Wow.

Here we have two untenable propositions: that even though those present are free to sit or stand silently, turn their backs, or leave, any vote by a student majority to have prayers amounts to (1) "coercion" of nonbelievers and religious minorities to (2) *participate* in an act of religious worship."

And that brings us to the Pledge of Allegiance. The most obvious problem is the phrase "under God," which was inserted in 1954 between "one nation" and "indivisible." Under the Court's reasoning, those two words alone would seem to make the thousands of teachers who regularly lead their students in the pledge into serial violators of the establishment clause. (The same could also be said of teachers who lead students in singing the national anthem. The last verse includes: "And this be our motto: 'In God is our trust.'") Well, we can fix that little problem by stripping "under God" out of the pledge, can't we? Nope. Not if we superimpose the logic of the June 19 Stevens opinion upon that of the famous 1943 decision striking down a West Virginia law that had compelled all students—on pain of expulsion and prosecution of their parents—to join in saluting and pledging allegiance to the flag.

Ruling that Jehovah's Witnesses had a right to refuse to salute or to recite the pledge (which did not then refer to God), Justice Robert H. Jackson penned some of the most stirring words in all of constitutional law: "If there is any fixed star in our constitutional constellation, it is that no official, high or petty, can prescribe what shall be orthodox in politics, nationalism, religion, or other matters of opinion or force citizens to confess by word or act their faith therein." It violates the freedom of *speech*, Jackson held, to compel anybody to join in a public statement on *any* "matter of opinion" over his or her objection—whether or not religion is a factor.

"The refusal of these persons to participate in the ceremony," Jack-   10
son added, "does not interfere with or deny rights of others to do so." But now comes the June 19 Stevens opinion, which deems it "coercing those present to participate" when a student majority votes for a ceremony (at least a religious one) to which any student objects.

It's hard to see why a patriotic ceremony would be any less coercive than a religious one. So it might be logical (if dumb) to extend to patriotic ceremonies Stevens's assertion that "school sponsorship of a religious message is impermissible because it sends the ancillary message to members of the audience who are nonadherents that they are outsiders, not full members of the political community."

Suppose that the child of a Symbionese Liberation Army veteran, or of a Chinese diplomat, objects on political grounds to hearing the pledge recited at school. Under the 1943 decision, the child clearly could not be compelled to join in, and rightly so. But would Stevens also bar the school from allowing *anyone* to recite the pledge, with or without "under God," lest it send a message that those who object are "outsiders, not full members of the political community"?

A similar argument could be made for barring a recital of the Declaration of Independence if any student objects to the idea that "all men are created equal"—not to mention the neo-theocratic stuff that Thomas Jefferson threw in about being "endowed by their Creator with certain inalienable rights."

Far-fetched? Sure. But it's unclear how and where the Court can stop sliding down this slope. And "if the speech of the majority may be restricted to avoid giving offense to the minority," as Jeffrey Rosen suggests in the *New Republic*, some evangelical Christians might raise equally plausible objections to evolution being taught in their presence, "on the grounds that it offends their belief in creationism."

Speaking of which, consider another vote by the same 6–3 majority, 15 also on June 19, involving a Louisiana school board's policy on teaching evolution. The policy did not bar such teaching, or require the teaching of creationism. It simply said that whenever "the scientific theory of evolution is to be presented," teachers should tell students three things: that it is "not intended to influence or dissuade the biblical version of Creation or any other concept"; that each student has "the basic right and privilege . . . to form his/her own opinion or maintain beliefs taught by parents on this very important matter of the origin of life and matter"; and that "students are urged to exercise critical thinking and gather all information possible and closely examine each alternative toward forming an opinion."

That's it. Seems pretty innocuous—indeed, enlightened—to me. Yet six Justices voted without comment to let stand a federal appellate decision striking down the policy as yet another establishment of religion. The dissent, by Justice Antonin Scalia, seems persuasive: "Far from advancing religion . . . the [effect of the] disclaimer . . . is merely to advance freedom of thought . . . [by an] acknowledgment of beliefs widely held among the people of this country."

Yes, there really are a lot of people in the hinterland who still believe such stuff. Not many of them went to Ivy League schools, or hang out with Supreme Court Justices. Nor do their traditions and beliefs get much consideration in such sophisticated quarters. So now we have come, in Scalia's words, to "bar[ring] a school district from even suggesting to students that other theories besides evolution—including, but not limited to, the Biblical theory of creation—are worthy of their consideration."

Small wonder that some conservative Christians are starting to ask, as did an Illinois woman quoted last month by the *New York Times,* "How long it will be before they tell us we can't pray in public places"?

Topics for Critical Thinking and Writing

1. Why does Taylor say that if the Supreme Court were to bar saying the Pledge of Allegiance in a public high school, "the law [would be] an ass" (para. 2)?

2. Our country is famous worldwide for its sharp constitutional line separating church from state. Do you think this separation is important or not? Explain.

3. Do you think that vigorous opposition to school-sponsored prayers implies "hostility to all things religious in public life" (para. 2)? Explain.

4. In paragraph 5 Taylor cites the testimony of a man named Ben Marcus. Why do you think Taylor cites Ben Marcus rather than, say, someone

named Chris Jackson? How much weight do you give to the evidence that Marcus offers?

5. Why does Taylor describe as "untenable" the two propositions he mentions in paragraph 7? Are they untenable because no one, literally, could hold both? Or by "untenable" does he mean something else? If so, what?

6. Taylor thinks the Supreme Court's decision of June 19, 2000, may have put the Court onto a slippery slope (para. 14). Where does Taylor think that slope ends?

M. Scott Peck

Dr. Peck, born in 1936 in New York City, was trained as a psychiatrist but now devotes his time chiefly to lecturing and writing. We reprint an essay that originally appeared in Newsweek *in 1997; the ideas in this essay are developed at length in Peck's subsequent book,* Denial of the Soul: Spiritual and Medical Perspectives on Euthanasia *(1997).*

Living Is the Mystery

The current debate over euthanasia is often simplistic. The subject is complex. We don't even have a generally agreed-upon definition of the word. Is euthanasia solely an act committed by someone—a physician or family member—on someone else who is ill or dying? Or can the term also be used for someone who is ill or dying who kills himself without the assistance of another? Does euthanasia require the patient's consent? The family's consent? Is it separable from other forms of suicide or homicide? How does it differ from simply "pulling the plug"? If one type of euthanasia consists of refraining from the use of "heroic measures" to prolong life, how does one distinguish between those measures that are heroic and those that are standard treatment? What is the relationship between euthanasia and pain? Is there a distinction to be made between physical pain and emotional pain? How does one assess degrees of suffering? Above all, why are ethical issues involved, and what might they be?

I believe that all patients deserve fully adequate medical relief from physical pain. Emotional pain may be another matter. It is very difficult to say no to emotional demands of those suffering severe physical disease, but that doesn't mean it shouldn't be done. I have always resonated to two quotations: "Life is not a problem to be solved but a mystery to be lived" and "Life is what happens to us while we are making other plans." I find I need to remind myself of these quotations on a daily basis. Among other things, they point out to me that the loss of control, the irrationality, the mystery, and the insecurity inherent in dying are also inherent to living. The emotional suffering involved in dealing with these realities strikes me as a very important segment of what I call existential suffering. It seems to me that "true euthanasia" patients suffer not so much from a problem of death as from a problem of life. I think they have a lot to learn from being assisted to face this problem rather than being assisted to kill themselves in order to avoid it.

More than anything else, our differing beliefs about the existence or nonexistence of the human soul make euthanasia a subject for passionate ethical and moral debate. I am of a position that dictates against a laissez-faire attitude toward euthanasia, or what could be termed "euthanasia on demand." While I am passionate about this position forged out of complexity, I am also profoundly aware that I do not know personally what it is like to be totally and permanently incapacitated or to live under a death sentence as a result of a very specific disease with a rapidly deteriorating course. In other words, I have not been there. All that I write here, therefore, should be taken with at least that much of a grain of salt.

If I were a jurist, my judgment would be to keep physician-assisted suicide illegal. This would be my decision for three reasons:

1. The other extreme—making assisted suicide so fully legal that it   5
is considered a right—has, I believe, profound negative implications for society as a whole. My concern is not simply, as another author has put it, that "euthanasia breeds euthanasia" or that the floodgates would be opened. My primary concern is the message that would be given to society. It would be yet another secular message that we need not wrestle with God, another message denying the soul and telling us that this is solely our life to do with as we please. It would be a most discouraging message. It would not encourage us to face the natural existential suffering of life to learn how to overcome it, to learn how to face emotional hardship—the kind of hardship that calls forth our courage. Instead, it would be a message that we are entitled to take the easy way out. It would be a message pushing our society further along the worst of the directions it has already been taking.

2. A decision for the middle ground legalizing assisted suicide under certain circumstances and not others would lead us into a legal quagmire. Despite their enormous expense and frustration, such quagmires might be all to the good if we were prepared to wallow in them. I do not believe that we are currently so prepared.

3. As a society, we are not yet ready to grapple with the euthanasia issue in a meaningful way. There are just too many even more important issues that need to be decided first: the right to physical pain relief, the right to hospice comfort care, the right to public education that is not wholly secular, the right to free discourse about the soul and human meaning, the right to education about the nature of existential suffering, the right to medical care in general, and the right to quasi-euthanasia for the chronically but not fatally ill. Only when we are clear about these matters, among others, will we be in a position to tackle the issue of legalizing physician-assisted suicide for the terminally ill.

I submit that the answer to the problem of assisted suicide lies not in more euthanasia but in more hospice care. The first order of business should be to establish that dying patients have a constitutional right to competent hospice care. Only *after* this right has been established does it make sense for the courts to turn their attention to the question of whether terminally ill patients should have an additional constitutional right to physician-assisted euthanasia.

I am not for rushing to resolve the euthanasia debate but for enlarging and heating it up. If we can do this, it is conceivable to me that historians of the future will mark the debate as a turning point in U.S. history, on a par with the Declaration of Independence. They will see it as a watershed time when a possibly moribund society almost magically became revitalized. It is both my experience and that of others that whenever we are willing to engage ourselves fully in the mystery of death, the experience is usually enlivening. I believe that the euthanasia debate, besides requiring that we confront certain societal problems, offers the greatest hope in forcing us to encounter our own souls — often for the first time.

Topics for Critical Thinking and Writing

1. What's the difference between a debate that's simple and a debate that's "simplistic" (para. 1)?

2. Examine carefully the list of a dozen or so questions with which Peck opens his essay (para. 1). By the time he's finished, has he answered each of these questions? To your satisfaction? Pick one of these questions and his answer to it, and write a 250-word essay explaining whether you agree or disagree with him.

3. What is "existential suffering" (paras. 2 and 5)? How do you think it differs from ordinary physical pain and mental suffering?

4. What is the "laissez-faire attitude toward euthanasia" (para. 3) that Peck deplores? In a word, how would you characterize his attitude?

5. Consider the three reasons Peck offers in favor of keeping physician-assisted suicide illegal (paras. 5, 6, and 7). Which strikes you as the best, and which the least convincing? Explain why in an essay of 500 words.

6. Peck lists half a dozen or so "rights" that he thinks take priority over any alleged right of physician-assisted suicide (para. 7). Do you agree that we have these rights? How would you argue with someone who insisted that we have no such rights? Choose one of the rights that Peck mentions, and write a 500-word essay supporting or criticizing the idea that we have this right.

7. In his next-to-last paragraph, Peck favors "more hospice care." What is a hospice, and what kind of care does it provide?

Peter Singer

Peter Singer is the Ira W. DeCamp Professor of Bioethics at Princeton University. A native of Australia, he is a graduate of the University of Melbourne and Oxford University and the author or editor of more than two dozen books, including Animal Liberation *(1975),* Practical Ethics *(1979), and* Rethinking Life and Death *(1995). He has written on a variety of ethical issues, but he is especially known for caring about the welfare of animals.*

This essay originally appeared in the New York Review of Books *(April 5, 1973), as a review of* Animals, Men and Morals, *edited by Stanley and Roslind Godlovitch and John Harris.*

Animal Liberation

I

We are familiar with Black Liberation, Gay Liberation, and a variety of other movements. With Women's Liberation some thought we had come to the end of the road. Discrimination on the basis of sex, it has been said, is the last form of discrimination that is universally accepted and practiced without pretense, even in those liberal circles which have long prided themselves on their freedom from racial discrimination. But one should always be wary of talking of "the last remaining form of discrimination." If we have learned anything from the liberation movements, we should have learned how difficult it is to be aware of the ways in which we discriminate until they are forcefully pointed out to us. A liberation movement demands an expansion of our moral horizons, so that practices that were previously regarded as natural and inevitable are now seen as intolerable.

Animals, Men and Morals is a manifesto for an Animal Liberation movement. The contributors to the book may not all see the issue this way. They are a varied group. Philosophers, ranging from professors to graduate students, make up the largest contingent. There are five of them, including the three editors, and there is also an extract from the unjustly neglected German philosopher with an English name, Leonard Nelson, who died in 1927. There are essays by two novelist/critics, Brigid Brophy and Maureen Duffy, and another by Muriel the Lady Dowding, widow of Dowding of Battle of Britain fame and the founder of "Beauty without Cruelty," a movement that campaigns against the use of animals for furs and cosmetics. The other pieces are by a psychologist, a botanist, a sociologist, and Ruth Harrison, who is probably best described as a professional campaigner for animal welfare.

Whether or not these people, as individuals, would all agree that they are launching a liberation movement for animals, the book as a whole amounts to no less. It is a demand for a complete change in our attitudes to nonhumans. It is a demand that we cease to regard the exploitation of other species as natural and inevitable, and that, instead, we see it as a continuing moral outrage. Patrick Corbett, Professor of Philosophy at Sussex University, captures the spirit of the book in his closing words:

> We require now to extend the great principles of liberty, equality, and fraternity over the lives of animals. Let animal slavery join human slavery in the graveyard of the past.

The reader is likely to be skeptical. "Animal Liberation" sounds more like a parody of liberation movements than a serious objective. The reader may think: We support the claims of blacks and women for equality because blacks and women really are equal to whites and males — equal in intelligence and in abilities, capacity for leadership, rationality, and so on. Humans and nonhumans obviously are not equal in these respects. Since justice demands only that we treat equals equally, unequal treatment of humans and nonhumans cannot be an injustice.

This is a tempting reply, but a dangerous one. It commits the non-   5
racist and nonsexist to a dogmatic belief that blacks and women really are just as intelligent, able, etc., as whites and males — and no more. Quite possibly this happens to be the case. Certainly attempts to prove that racial or sexual differences in these respects have a genetic origin have not been conclusive. But do we really want to stake our demand for equality on the assumption that there are no genetic differences of this kind between the different races or sexes? Surely the appropriate response to those who claim to have found evidence for such genetic differences is not to stick to the belief that there are no differences, whatever the evidence to the contrary; rather one should be clear that the claim to equality does not depend on IQ. Moral equality is distinct from factual equality. Otherwise it would be nonsense to talk to the equality of human beings, since humans, as individuals, obviously differ in intelligence and almost any ability one cares to name. If possessing greater intelligence does not entitle one human to exploit another, why should it entitle humans to exploit nonhumans?

Jeremy Bentham expressed the essential basis of equality in his famous formula: "Each to count for one and none for more than one." In other words, the interests of every being that has interests are to be taken into account and treated equally with the like interests of any other being. Other moral philosophers, before and after Bentham, have made the same point in different ways. Our concern for others must not depend on whether they possess certain characteristics, though just what that concern involves may, of course, vary according to such characteristics.

Bentham, incidentally, was well aware that the logic of the demand for racial equality did not stop at the equality of humans. He wrote:

> The day *may* come when the rest of the animal creation may acquire those rights which never could have been withholden from them but by

the hand of tyranny. The French have already discovered that the blackness of the skin is no reason why a human being should be abandoned without redress to the caprice of a tormentor. It may one day come to be recognized that the number of the legs, the villosity of the skin, or the termination of the *os sacrum,* are reasons equally insufficient for abandoning a sensitive being to the same fate. What else is it that should trace the insuperable line? Is it the faculty of reason, or perhaps the faculty of discourse? But a full-grown horse or dog is beyond comparison a more rational, as well as a more conversable animal, than an infant of a day, or a week, or even a month, old. But suppose they were otherwise, what would it avail? The question is not, Can they *reason?* nor Can they *talk?* but, Can they *suffer?*[1]

Surely Bentham was right. If a being suffers, there can be no moral justification for refusing to take that suffering into consideration, and, indeed, to count it equally with the like suffering (if rough comparisons can be made) of any other being.

So the only question is: Do animals other than man suffer? Most people agree unhesitatingly that animals like cats and dogs can and do suffer, and this seems also to be assumed by those laws that prohibit wanton cruelty to such animals. Personally, I have no doubt at all about this and find it hard to take seriously the doubts that a few people apparently do have. The editors and contributors of *Animals, Men and Morals* seem to feel the same way, for although the question is raised more than once, doubts are quickly dismissed each time. Nevertheless, because this is such a fundamental point, it is worth asking what grounds we have for attributing suffering to other animals.

It is best to begin by asking what grounds any individual human has for supposing that other humans feel pain. Since pain is a state of consciousness, a "mental event," it can never be directly observed. No observations, whether behavioral signs such as writhing or screaming or physiological or neurological recordings, are observations of pain itself. Pain is something one feels, and one can only infer that others are feeling it from various external indications. The fact that only philosophers are ever skeptical about whether other humans feel pain shows that we regard such inference as justifiable in the case of humans.

Is there any reason why the same inference should be unjustifiable for other animals? Nearly all the external signs which lead us to infer pain in other humans can be seen in other species, especially "higher" animals such as mammals and birds. Behavioral signs — writhing, yelping, or other forms of calling, attempts to avoid the source of pain, and many others — are present. We know, too, that these animals are biologically similar in the relevant respects, having nervous systems like ours which can be observed to function as ours do.

[1] *The Principles of Morals and Legislation,* ch. XVII, sec. 1, footnote to paragraph 4. [All notes are the author's unless otherwise specified.]

So the grounds for inferring that these animals can feel pain are nearly as good as the grounds for inferring other humans do. Only nearly, for there is one behavioral sign that humans have but nonhumans, with the exception of one or two specially raised chimpanzees, do not have. This, of course, is a developed language. As the quotation from Bentham indicates, this has long been regarded as an important distinction between man and other animals. Other animals may communicate with each other, but not in the way we do. Following Chomsky,[2] many people now mark this distinction by saying that only humans communicate in a form that is governed by rules of syntax. (For the purposes of this argument, linguists allow those chimpanzees who have learned a syntactic sign language to rank as honorary humans.) Nevertheless, as Bentham pointed out, this distinction is not relevant to the question of how animals ought to be treated, unless it can be linked to the issue of whether animals suffer.

This link may be attempted in two ways. First, there is a hazy line of philosophical thought, stemming perhaps from some doctrines associated with Wittgenstein, which maintains that we cannot meaningfully attribute states of consciousness to beings without language. I have not seen this argument made explicit in print, though I have come across it in conversation. This position seems to me very implausible, and I doubt that it would be held at all if it were not thought to be a consequence of a broader view of the significance of language. It may be that the use of a public, rule-governed language is a precondition of conceptual thought. It may even be, although personally I doubt it, that we cannot meaningfully speak of a creature having an intention unless that creature can use a language. But states like pain, surely, are more primitive than either of these, and seem to have nothing to do with language.

Indeed, as Jane Goodall points out in her study of chimpanzees, when it comes to the expression of feelings and emotions, humans tend to fall back on nonlinguistic modes of communication which are often found among apes, such as a cheering pat on the back, an exuberant embrace, a clasp of hands, and so on.[3] Michael Peters makes a similar point in his contribution to *Animals, Men and Morals* when he notes that the basic signals we use to convey pain, fear, sexual arousal, and so on are not specific to our species. So there seems to be no reason at all to believe that a creature without language cannot suffer.

The second, and more easily appreciated way of linking language and the existence of pain is to say that the best evidence that we can have that another creature is in pain is when he tells us that he is. This is a distinct line of argument, for it is not being denied that a non-language-user conceivably could suffer, but only that we could know

---

[2]**Chomsky** Noam Chomsky (b. 1928), a professor of linguistics and the author of (among other books) *Language and Mind* (1972). [Editors' note.]
[3]Jane van Lawick-Goodall, *In the Shadow of Man* (Houghton Mifflin, 1971), p. 225.

that he is suffering. Still, this line of argument seems to me to fail, and for reasons similar to those just given. "I am in pain" is not the best possible evidence that the speaker is in pain (he might be lying) and it is certainly not the only possible evidence. Behavioral signs and knowledge of the animal's biological similarity to ourselves together provide adequate evidence that animals do suffer. After all, we would not accept linguistic evidence if it contradicted the rest of the evidence. If a man was severely burned, and behaved as if he were in pain, writhing, groaning, being very careful not to let his burned skin touch anything, and so on, but later said he had not been in pain at all, we would be more likely to conclude that he was lying or suffering from amnesia than that he had not been in pain.

Even if there were stronger grounds for refusing to attribute pain to   15
those who do not have a language, the consequences of this refusal might lead us to examine these grounds unusually critically. Human infants, as well as some adults, are unable to use language. Are we to deny that a year-old infant can suffer? If not, how can language be crucial? Of course, most parents can understand the responses of even very young infants better than they understand the responses of other animals, and sometimes infant responses can be understood in the light of later development.

This, however, is just a fact about the relative knowledge we have of our own species and other species, and most of this knowledge is simply derived from closer contact. Those who have studied the behavior of other animals soon learn to understand their responses at least as well as we understand those of an infant. (I am not referring to Jane Goodall's and other well-known studies of apes. Consider, for example, the degree of understanding achieved by Tinbergen from watching herring gulls.[4]) Just as we can understand infant human behavior in the light of adult human behavior, so we can understand the behavior of other species in the light of our own behavior (and sometimes we can understand our own behavior better in the light of the behavior of other species).

The grounds we have for believing that other mammals and birds suffer are, then, closely analogous to the grounds we have for believing that other humans suffer. It remains to consider how far down the evolutionary scale this analogy holds. Obviously it becomes poorer when we get further away from man. To be more precise would require a detailed examination of all that we know about other forms of life. With fish, reptiles, and other vertebrates the analogy still seems strong, with molluscs like oysters it is much weaker. Insects are more difficult, and it may be that in our present state of knowledge we must be agnostic about whether they are capable of suffering.

If there is no moral justification for ignoring suffering when it occurs, and it does occur in other species, what are we to say of our atti-

[4]N. Tinbergen, *The Herring Gull's World* (Basic Books, 1961).

tudes toward these other species? Richard Ryder, one of the contributors to *Animals, Men and Morals,* uses the term "speciesism" to describe the belief that we are entitled to treat members of other species in a way in which it would be wrong to treat members of our own species. The term is not euphonious, but it neatly makes the analogy with racism. The nonracist would do well to bear the analogy in mind when he is inclined to defend human behavior toward nonhumans. "Shouldn't we worry about improving the lot of our own species before we concern ourselves with other species?" he may ask. If we substitute "race" for "species" we shall see that the question is better not asked. "Is a vegetarian diet nutritionally adequate?" resembles the slaveowner's claim that he and the whole economy of the South would be ruined without slave labor. There is even a parallel with skeptical doubts about whether animals suffer, for some defenders of slavery professed to doubt whether blacks really suffer in the way whites do.

I do not want to give the impression, however, that the case for Animal Liberation is based on the analogy with racism and no more. On the contrary, *Animals, Men and Morals* describes the various ways in which humans exploit nonhumans, and several contributors consider the defenses that have been offered, including the defense of meat-eating mentioned in the last paragraph. Sometimes the rebuttals are scornfully dismissive, rather than carefully designed to convince the detached critic. This may be a fault, but it is a fault that is inevitable, given the kind of book this is. The issue is not one on which one can remain detached. As the editors state in their Introduction:

> Once the full force of moral assessment has been made explicit there can be no rational excuse left for killing animals, be they killed for food, science, or sheer personal indulgence. We have not assembled this book to provide the reader with yet another manual on how to make brutalities less brutal. Compromise, in the traditional sense of the term, is simple unthinking weakness when one considers the actual reasons for our crude relationships with the other animals.

The point is that on this issue there are few critics who are genuinely 20
detached. People who eat pieces of slaughtered nonhumans every day find it hard to believe that they are doing wrong; and they also find it hard to imagine what else they could eat. So for those who do not place nonhumans beyond the pale of morality, there comes a stage when further argument seems pointless, a stage at which one can only accuse one's opponent of hypocrisy and reach for the sort of sociological account of our practices and the way we defend them that is attempted by David Wood in his contribution to his book. On the other hand, to those unconvinced by the arguments, and unable to accept that they are merely rationalizing their dietary preferences and their fear of being thought peculiar, such sociological explanations can only seem insultingly arrogant.

II

The logic of speciesism is most apparent in the practice of experimenting on nonhumans in order to benefit humans. This is because the issue is rarely obscured by allegations that nonhumans are so different from humans that we cannot know anything about whether they suffer. The defender of vivisection cannot use this argument because he needs to stress the similarities between man and other animals in order to justify the usefulness to the former of experiments on the latter. The researcher who makes rats choose between starvation and electric shocks to see if they develop ulcers (they do) does so because he knows that the rat has a nervous system very similar to man's, and presumably feels an electric shock in a similar way.

Richard Ryder's restrained account of experiments on animals made me angrier with my fellow men than anything else in this book. Ryder, a clinical psychologist by profession, himself experimented on animals before he came to hold the view he puts forward in his essay. Experimenting on animals is now a large industry, both academic and commercial. In 1969, more than 5 million experiments were performed in Britain, the vast majority without anesthetic (though how many of these involved pain is not known). There are no accurate U.S. figures, since there is no federal law on the subject, and in many cases no state law either. Estimates vary from 20 million to 200 million. Ryder suggests that 80 million may be the best guess. We tend to think that this is all for vital medical research, but of course it is not. Huge numbers of animals are used in university departments from Forestry to Psychology, and even more are used for commercial purposes, to test whether cosmetics can cause skin damage, or shampoos eye damage, or to test food additives or laxatives or sleeping pills or anything else.

A standard test for foodstuffs is the "LD50." The object of this test is to find the dosage level at which 50 percent of the test animals will die. This means that nearly all of them will become very sick before finally succumbing or surviving. When the substance is a harmless one, it may be necessary to force huge doses down the animals, until in some cases sheer volume or concentration causes death.

Ryder gives a selection of experiments, taken from recent scientific journals. I will quote two, not for the sake of indulging in gory details, but in order to give an idea of what normal researchers think they may legitimately do to other species. The point is not that the individual researchers are cruel men, but that they are behaving in a way that is allowed by our speciesist attitudes. As Ryder points out, even if only 1 percent of the experiments involve severe pain, that is 50,000 experiments in Britain each year, or nearly 150 every day (and about fifteen times as many in the United States, if Ryder's guess is right). Here then are two experiments:

O. S. Ray and R. J. Barrett of Pittsburgh gave electric shocks to the feet of 1,042 mice. They then caused convulsions by giving more intense shocks through cup-shaped electrodes applied to the animals' eyes or through pressure spring clips attached to their ears. Unfortunately some of the mice who "successfully completed Day One training were found sick or dead prior to testing on Day Two." [*Journal of Comparative and Physiological Psychology*, 1969, vol. 67, pp. 110–116]

At the National Institute for Medical Research, Mill Hill, London, W. Feldberg and S. L. Sherwood injected chemicals into the brains of cats—"with a number of widely different substances, recurrent patterns of reaction were obtained. Retching, vomiting, defecation, increased salivation and greatly accelerated respiration leading to panting were common features." . . .

The injection into the brain of a large dose of Tubocuraine caused the cat to jump "from the table to the floor and then straight into its cage, where it started calling more and more noisily whilst moving about restlessly and jerkily . . . finally the cat fell with legs and neck flexed, jerking in rapid clonic movements, the condition being that of a major [epileptic] convulsion . . . within a few seconds the cat got up, ran for a few yards at high speed, and fell in another fit. The whole process was repeated several times within the next ten minutes, during which the cat lost faeces and foamed at the mouth."

This animal finally died thirty-five minutes after the brain injection. [*Journal of Physiology*, 1954, vol. 123, pp. 148–167]

There is nothing secret about these experiments. One has only to 25 open any recent volume of a learned journal, such as the *Journal of Comparative and Physiological Psychology*, to find full descriptions of experiments of this sort, together with the results obtained—results that are frequently trivial and obvious. The experiments are often supported by public funds.

It is a significant indication of the level of acceptability of these practices that, although these experiments are taking place at this moment on university campuses throughout the country, there has, so far as I know, not been the slightest protest from the student movement. Students have been rightly concerned that their universities should not discriminate on grounds of race or sex, and that they should not serve the purposes of the military or big business. Speciesism continues undisturbed, and many students participate in it. There may be a few qualms at first, but since everyone regards it as normal, and it may even be a required part of a course, the student soon becomes hardened and, dismissing his earlier feelings as "mere sentiment," comes to regard animals as statistics rather than sentient beings with interests that warrant consideration.

Argument about vivisection has often missed the point because it has been put in absolutist terms: Would the abolitionist be prepared to let thousands die if they could be saved by experimenting on a single animal? The way to reply to this purely hypothetical question is to pose another: Would the experimenter be prepared to experiment on a human orphan under six months old, if it were the only way to save many lives? (I say "orphan" to avoid the complication of parental feelings, although in doing so I am being overfair to the experimenter, since the nonhuman subjects of experiments are not orphans.) A negative answer to this question indicates that the experimenter's readiness to use nonhumans is simple discrimination, for adult apes, cats, mice, and other mammals are more conscious of what is happening to them, more self-directing, and, so far as we can tell, just as sensitive to pain as a human infant. There is no characteristic that human infants possess that adult mammals do not have to the same or a higher degree.

(It might be possible to hold that what makes it wrong to experiment on a human infant is that the infant will in time develop into more than the nonhuman, but one would then, to be consistent, have to oppose abortion, and perhaps contraception, too, for the fetus and the egg and sperm have the same potential as the infant. Moreover, one would still have no reason for experimenting on a nonhuman rather than a human with brain damage severe enough to make it impossible for him to rise above infant level.)

The experimenter, then, shows a bias for his own species whenever he carries out an experiment on a nonhuman for a purpose that he would not think justified him in using a human being at an equal or lower level of sentience, awareness, ability to be self-directing, etc. No one familiar with the kind of results yielded by these experiments can have the slightest doubt that if this bias were eliminated the number of experiments performed would be zero or very close to it.

III

If it is vivisection that shows the logic of speciesism most clearly, it is 30 the use of other species for food that is at the heart of our attitudes toward them. Most of *Animals, Men and Morals* is an attack on meat eating—an attack which is based solely on concern for nonhumans, without reference to arguments derived from consideration of ecology, macrobiotics, health, or religion.

The idea that nonhumans are utilities, means to our ends, pervades our thought. Even conservationists who are concerned about the slaughter of wildfowl but not about the vastly greater slaughter of chickens for our tables are thinking in this way—they are worried about what we would lose if there were less wildlife. Stanley Godlovitch, pursuing the Marxist idea that our thinking is formed by the activities we undertake in satisfying our needs, suggests that man's first classification of his environment was into Edibles and Inedibles. Most animals came into the first category, and there they have remained.

Man may always have killed other species for food, but he has never exploited them so ruthlessly as he does today. Farming has succumbed to business methods, the objective being to get the highest possible ratio of output (meat, eggs, milk) to input (fodder, labor costs, etc.). Ruth Harrison's essay "On Factory Farming" gives an account of some aspects of modern methods, and of the unsuccessful British campaigns for effective controls, a campaign which was sparked off by her *Animal Machines* (London: Stuart, 1964).

Her article is in no way a substitute for her earlier book. This is a pity since, as she says, "Farm produce is still associated with mental pictures of animals browsing in the fields . . . of hens having a last forage before going to roost. . . ." Yet neither in her article nor elsewhere in *Animals, Men and Morals* is this false image replaced by a clear idea of the nature and extent of factory farming. We learn of this only indirectly, when we hear of the code of reform proposed by an advisory committee set up by the British government.

Among the proposals, which the government refused to implement on the grounds that they were too idealistic, were: *"Any animal should at least have room to turn around freely."*

Factory farm animals need liberation in the most literal sense. Veal calves are kept in stalls 5 feet by 2 feet. They are usually slaughtered when about four months old, and have been too big to turn in their stalls for at least a month. Intensive beef herds, kept in stalls only proportionately larger for much longer periods, account for a growing percentage of beef production. Sows are often similarly confined when pregnant, which, because of artificial methods of increasing fertility, can be most of the time. Animals confined in this way do not waste food by exercising, nor do they develop unpalatable muscle.

"A dry bedded area should be provided for all stock." Intensively kept animals usually have to stand and sleep in slatted floors without straw, because this makes cleaning easier.

"Palatable roughage must be readily available to all calves after one week of age." In order to produce the pale veal housewives are said to prefer, calves are fed on an all-liquid diet until slaughter, even though they are long past the age at which they would normally eat grass. They develop a craving for roughage, evidenced by attempts to gnaw wood from their stalls. (For the same reason, their diet is deficient in iron.)

"Battery cages for poultry should be large enough for a bird to be able to stretch one wing at a time." Under current British practice, a cage for four or five laying hens has a floor area of 20 inches by 18 inches, scarcely larger than a double page of the *New York Review of Books*. In this space, on a sloping wire floor (sloping so the eggs roll down, wire so the dung drips through) the birds live for a year or eighteen months while artificial lighting and temperature conditions combine with drugs in their food to squeeze the maximum number of eggs out of them. Table birds are also sometimes kept in cages. More often they are reared in sheds, no less crowded. Under these conditions all the birds' natural activities are frustrated, and they develop "vices" such as

pecking each other to death. To prevent this, beaks are often cut off, and the sheds kept dark.

How many of those who support factory farming by buying its produce know anything about the way it is produced? How many have heard something about it, but are reluctant to check up for fear that it will make them uncomfortable? To nonspeciesists, the typical consumer's mixture of ignorance, reluctance to find out the truth, and vague belief that nothing really bad could be allowed seems analogous to the attitudes of "decent Germans" to the death camps.

There are, of course, some defenders of factory farming. Their arguments are considered, though again rather sketchily, by John Harris. Among the most common: "Since they have never known anything else, they don't suffer." This argument will not be put by anyone who knows anything about animal behavior, since he will know that not all behavior has to be learned. Chickens attempt to stretch wings, walk around, scratch, and even dustbathe or build a nest, even though they have never lived under conditions that allowed these activities. Calves can suffer from maternal deprivation no matter at what age they were taken from their mothers. "We need these intensive methods to provide protein for a growing population." As ecologists and famine relief organizations know, we can produce far more protein per acre if we grow the right vegetable crop, soy beans for instance, than if we use the land to grow crops to be converted into protein by animals who use nearly 90 percent of the protein themselves, even when unable to exercise.

There will be many readers of this book who will agree that factory farming involves an unjustifiable degree of exploitation of sentient creatures, and yet will want to say that there is nothing wrong with rearing animals for food, provided it is done "humanely." These people are saying, in effect, that although we should not cause animals to suffer, there is nothing wrong with killing them.

There are two possible replies to this view. One is to attempt to show that this combination of attitudes is absurd. Roslind Godlovitch takes this course in her essay, which is an examination of some common attitudes to animals. She argues that from the combination of "animal suffering is to be avoided" and "there is nothing wrong with killing animals" it follows that all animal life ought to be exterminated (since all sentient creatures will suffer to some degree at some point in their lives). Euthanasia is a contentious issue only because we place some value on living. If we did not, the least amount of suffering would justify it. Accordingly, if we deny that we have a duty to exterminate all animal life, we must concede that we are placing some value on animal life.

This argument seems to me valid, although one could still reply that the value of animal life is to be derived from the pleasures that life can have for them, so that, provided their lives have a balance of pleasure over pain, we are justified in rearing them. But this would imply that we ought to produce animals and let them live as pleasantly as possible, without suffering.

At this point, one can make the second of the two possible replies to the view that rearing and killing animals for food is all right so long as it is done humanely. This second reply is that so long as we think that a nonhuman may be killed simply so that a human can satisfy his taste for meat, we are still thinking of nonhumans as means rather than as ends in themselves. The factory farm is nothing more than the application of technology to this concept. Even traditional methods involve castration, the separation of mothers and their young, the breaking up of herds, branding or earpunching, and of course transportation to the abattoirs and the final moments of terror when the animal smells blood and senses danger. If we were to try rearing animals so that they lived and died without suffering, we should find that to do so on anything like the scale of today's meat industry would be a sheer impossibility. Meat would become the prerogative of the rich.

I have been able to discuss only some of the contributions to this 45 book, saying nothing about, for instance, the essays on killing for furs and for sport. Nor have I considered all the detailed questions that need to be asked once we start thinking about other species in the radically different way presented by this book. What, for instance, are we to do about genuine conflicts of interest like rats biting slum children? I am not sure of the answer, but the essential point is just that we *do* see this as a conflict of interests, that we recognize that rats have interests too. Then we may begin to think about other ways of resolving the conflict — perhaps by leaving out rat baits that sterilize the rats instead of killing them.

I have not discussed such problems because they are side issues compared with the exploitation of other species for food and for experimental purposes. On these central matters, I hope that I have said enough to show that this book, despite its flaws, is a challenge to every human to recognize his attitudes to nonhumans as a form of prejudice no less objectionable than racism or sexism. It is a challenge that demands not just a change of attitudes, but a change in our way of life, for it requires us to become vegetarians.

Can a purely moral demand of this kind succeed? The odds are certainly against it. The book holds out no inducements. It does not tell us that we will become healthier, or enjoy life more, if we cease exploiting animals. Animal Liberation will require greater altruism on the part of mankind than any other liberation movement, since animals are incapable of demanding it for themselves, or of protesting against their exploitation by votes, demonstrations, or bombs. Is man capable of such genuine altruism? Who knows? If this book does have a significant effect, however, it will be a vindication of all those who have believed that man has within himself the potential for more than cruelty and selfishness.

Topics for Critical Thinking and Writing

1. In his fourth paragraph Singer formulates an argument on behalf of the skeptical reader. Examine that argument closely, restate it in your own words, and evaluate it. Which of its premises is most vulnerable to criticism? Why?

2. Singer quotes with approval (para. 7) Bentham's comment, "The question is not, Can they *reason?* nor Can they *talk?* but, Can they *suffer?*" Do you find this argument persuasive? Can you think of any effective challenge to it?

3. Singer allows that although developed linguistic capacity is not necessary for a creature to have pain, perhaps such a capacity is necessary for "having an intention" (para. 12). Do you think this concession is correct? Have you ever seen animal behavior that you would be willing to describe or explain as evidence that the animal has an intention to do something, despite knowing that the animal cannot talk?

4. Singer thinks that the readiness to experiment on animals argues against believing that animals don't suffer pain (see para. 21). Do you agree with this reasoning?

5. Singer confesses (para. 22) to being made especially angry "with my fellow men" after reading the accounts of animal experimentation. What is it that aroused his anger? Do such feelings, and the acknowledgment that one has them, have any place in a sober discussion about the merits of animal experimentation? Why, or why not?

6. What is "factory farming" (paras. 32–40)? Why is Singer opposed to it?

7. To the claim that there is nothing wrong with "rearing and killing animals for food," provided it is done "humanely," Singer offers two replies (paras. 42–44). In an essay of 250 words summarize them briefly and then indicate whether either persuades you, and why or why not.

8. Suppose someone were to say to Singer: "You claim that capacity to suffer is the relevant factor in deciding whether a creature deserves to be treated as my moral equal. But you're wrong—the relevant factor is whether the creature is *alive.* Being alive is what matters, not being capable of feeling pain." In one or two paragraphs declare what you think would be Singer's reply.

9. Do you think it is worse to kill an animal for its fur than to kill, cook, and eat an animal? Is it worse to kill an animal for sport than to kill it for medical experimentation? What is Singer's view? Explain your view, making use of Singer's if you wish, in an essay of 500 words.

10. Are there any arguments, in your opinion, that show the immorality of eating human flesh (cannibalism) but that do not show a similar objection to eating animal flesh? Write a 500-word essay in which you discuss the issue.

Jonathan Swift

Jonathan Swift (1667–1745) was born in Ireland of English stock. An Anglican clergyman, he became Dean of St. Patrick's in Dublin in 1723, but the post he really wanted, one of high office in England, was never given to him. A prolific pamphleteer on religious and political issues, Swift today is known not as a churchman but as a satirist. His best known works are Gulliver's Travels *(1726, a serious satire but now popularly thought of as a children's book) and "A Modest Proposal" (1729). In "A Modest Proposal," which was published anonymously, Swift addresses the great suffering that the Irish endured under the British.*

A Modest Proposal

For Preventing the Children of Poor People in Ireland from Being a Burden to Their Parents or Country, and for Making Them Beneficial to the Public

It is a melancholy object to those who walk through this great town or travel in the country, when they see the streets, the roads, and cabin doors, crowded with beggars of the female sex, followed by three, four, or six children, all in rags and importuning every passenger for an alms. These mothers, instead of being able to work for their honest livelihood, are forced to employ all their time in strolling to beg sustenance for their helpless infants: who as they grow up either turn thieves for want of work, or leave their dear native country to fight for the Pretender in Spain, or sell themselves to the Barbadoes.

I think it is agreed by all parties that this prodigious number of children in the arms, or on the backs, or at the heels of their mothers, and frequently of their fathers, is in the present deplorable state of the kingdom a very great additional grievance; and, therefore, whoever could find out a fair, cheap, and easy method of making these children sound, useful members of the commonwealth, would deserve so well of the public as to have his statue set up for a preserver of the nation.

But my intention is very far from being confined to provide only for the children of professed beggars; it is of a much greater extent, and shall take in the whole number of infants at a certain age who are born of parents in effect as little able to support them as those who demand our charity in the streets.

As to my own part, having turned my thoughts for many years upon this important subject, and maturely weighed the several schemes of our projectors,[1] I have always found them grossly mistaken in their computation. It is true, a child just dropped from its dam may be supported by

---

[1] **projectors** Persons who devise plans. [All notes are the editors'.]

her milk for a solar year, with little other nourishment; at most not above the value of 2s.,[2] which the mother may certainly get, or the value in scraps, by her lawful occupation of begging; and it is exactly at one year old that I propose to provide for them in such a manner as instead of being a charge upon their parents or the parish, or wanting food and raiment for the rest of their lives, they shall on the contrary contribute to the feeding, and partly to the clothing, of many thousands.

There is likewise another great advantage in my scheme, that it will prevent those voluntary abortions, and that horrid practice of women murdering their bastard children, alas! too frequent among us! sacrificing the poor innocent babes I doubt more to avoid the expense than the shame, which would move tears and pity in the most savage and inhuman breast.

The number of souls in this kingdom being usually reckoned one million and a half, of these I calculate there may be about 200,000 couple whose wives are breeders; from which number I subtract 30,000 couple who are able to maintain their own children (although I apprehend there cannot be so many, under the present distress of the kingdom); but this being granted, there will remain 170,000 breeders. I again subtract 50,000 for those women who miscarry, or whose children die by accident or disease within the year. There only remain 120,000 children of poor parents annually born. The question therefore is, how this number shall be reared and provided for? which, as I have already said, under the present situation of affairs, is utterly impossible by all the methods hitherto proposed. For we can neither employ them in handicraft or agriculture; we neither build houses (I mean in the country) nor cultivate land; they can very seldom pick up a livelihood by stealing, till they arrive at six years old, except where they are of towardly parts; although I confess they learn the rudiments much earlier; during which time they can, however, be properly looked upon only as probationers; as I have been informed by a principal gentleman in the county of Cavan, who protested to me that he never knew above one or two instances under the age of six, even in a part of the kingdom so renowned for the quickest proficiency in that art.

I am assured by our merchants, that a boy or a girl before twelve years old is no salable commodity; and even when they come to this age they will not yield above 3£. or 3£. 2s. 6d.[3] at most on the exchange; which cannot turn to account either to the parents or kingdom, the charge of nutriment and rags having been at least four times that value.

I shall now therefore humbly propose my own thoughts, which I hope will not be liable to the least objection.

I have been assured by a very knowing American of my acquaintance in London, that a young healthy child well nursed is at a year old a most delicious, nourishing, and wholesome food, whether stewed,

[2]**2s.** Two shillings.
[3]**£. . . . d.** £ is an abbreviation for "pound sterling," and *d.* for "pence."

roasted, baked, or broiled; and I make no doubt that it will equally serve in a fricassee or a ragout.

I do therefore humbly offer it to public consideration that of the 120,000 children already computed, 20,000 may be reserved for breed, whereof only one-fourth part to be males; which is more than we allow to sheep, black cattle, or swine; and my reason is, that these children are seldom the fruits of marriage, a circumstance not much regarded by our savages; therefore one male will be sufficient to serve four females. That the remaining 100,000 may, at a year old, be offered in sale to the persons of quality and fortune through the kingdom; always advising the mother to let them suck plentifully in the last month, so as to render them plump and fat for a good table. A child will make two dishes at an entertainment for friends; and when the family dines alone, the fore or hind quarter will make a reasonable dish, and seasoned with a little pepper or salt will be very good boiled on the fourth day, especially in winter.

I have reckoned upon a medium that a child just born will weigh twelve pounds, and in a solar year, if tolerably nursed, will increase to twenty-eight pounds.

I grant this food will be somewhat dear, and therefore very proper for landlords, who, as they have already devoured most of the parents, seem to have the best title to the children.

Infant's flesh will be in season throughout the year, but more plentiful in March, and a little before and after: for we are told by a grave author, an eminent French physician, that fish being a prolific diet, there are more children born in Roman Catholic countries about nine months after Lent than at any other season; therefore, reckoning a year after Lent, the markets will be more glutted than usual, because the number of popish infants is at least three to one in this kingdom: and therefore it will have one other collateral advantage, by lessening the number of papists among us.

I have already computed the charge of nursing a beggar's child (in which list I reckon all cottagers, laborers, and four-fifths of the farmers) to be about 2s. per annum, rags included; and I believe no gentleman would repine to give 10s. for the carcass of a good fat child, which, as I have said, will make four dishes of excellent nutritive meat, when he has only some particular friend or his own family to dine with him. Thus the squire will learn to be a good landlord, and grow popular among the tenants; the mother will have 8s. net profit, and be fit for work till she produces another child.

Those who are more thrifty (as I must confess the times require) may flay the carcass; the skin of which artificially dressed will make admirable gloves for ladies, and summer boots for fine gentlemen.

As to our city of Dublin, shambles[4] may be appointed for this purpose in the most convenient parts of it, and butchers we may be assured will not be wanting: although I rather recommend buying the children alive, and dressing them hot from the knife as we do roasting pigs.

4shambles Slaughterhouses.

A very worthy person, a true lover of his country, and whose virtues I highly esteem, was lately pleased in discoursing on this matter to offer a refinement upon my scheme. He said that many gentlemen of this kingdom, having of late destroyed their deer, he conceived that the want of venison might be well supplied by the bodies of young lads and maidens, not exceeding fourteen years of age nor under twelve; so great a number of both sexes in every country being now ready to starve for want of work and service; and these to be disposed of by their parents, if alive, or otherwise by their nearest relations. But with due deference to so excellent a friend and so deserving a patriot, I cannot be altogether in his sentiments; for as to the males, my American acquaintance assured me from frequent experience that their flesh was generally tough and lean, like that of our schoolboys by continual exercise, and their taste disagreeable; and to fatten them would not answer the charge. Then as to the females, it would, I think, with humble submission be a loss to the public, because they soon would become breeders themselves: and besides, it is not improbable that some scrupulous people might be apt to censure such a practice (although indeed very unjustly), as a little bordering upon cruelty; which, I confess, has always been with me the strongest objection against any project, how well soever intended.

But in order to justify my friend, he confessed that this expedient was put into his head by the famous Psalmanazar[5] a native of the island Formosa, who came from thence to London about twenty years ago: and in conversation told my friend, that in his country when any young person happened to be put to death, the executioner sold the carcass to persons of quality as a prime dainty; and that in his time the body of a plump girl of fifteen, who was crucified for an attempt to poison the emperor, was sold to his imperial majesty's prime minister of state, and other great mandarins of the court, in joints from the gibbet, at 400 crowns. Neither indeed can I deny, that if the same use were made of several plump young girls in this town, who without one single groat to their fortunes cannot stir abroad without a chair, and appear at the playhouse and assemblies in foreign fineries which they never will pay for, the kingdom would not be the worse.

Some persons of a depending spirit are in great concern about the vast number of poor people, who are aged, diseased, or maimed, and I have been desired to employ my thoughts what course may be taken to ease the nation of so grievous an encumbrance. But I am not in the least pain upon that matter, because it is very well known that they are every day dying and rotting by cold and famine, and filth and vermin, as fast as can be reasonably expected. And as to the young laborers, they are now in as hopeful a condition: They cannot get work, and consequently pine

---

[5]**Psalmanazar** George Psalmanazar (c. 1679–1763), a Frenchman who claimed to be from Formosa (now Taiwan); he wrote *An Historical and Geographical Description of Formosa* (1704). The hoax was exposed soon after publication.

away for want of nourishment, to a degree that if at any time they are accidentally hired to common labor, they have not strength to perform it; and thus the country and themselves are happily delivered from the evils to come.

I have too long digressed, and therefore shall return to my subject. I think the advantages by the proposal which I have made are obvious and many, as well as of the highest importance. 20

For first, as I have already observed, it would greatly lessen the number of papists, with whom we are yearly overrun, being the principal breeders of the nation as well as our most dangerous enemies; and who stay at home on purpose to deliver the kingdom to the Pretender, hoping to take their advantage by the absence of so many good Protestants, who have chosen rather to leave their country than stay at home and pay tithes against their conscience to an Episcopal curate.

Secondly, The poor tenants will have something valuable of their own, which by law may be made liable to distress and help to pay their landlord's rent, their corn and cattle being already seized, and money a thing unknown.

Thirdly, Whereas the maintenance of 100,000 children from two years old and upward, cannot be computed at less than 10s. apiece per annum, the nation's stock will be thereby increased £50,000 per annum, beside the profit of a new dish introduced to the tables of all gentlemen of fortune in the kingdom who have any refinement in taste. And the money will circulate among ourselves, the goods being entirely of our own growth and manufacture.

Fourthly, The constant breeders beside the gain of 8s. sterling per annum by the sale of their children, will be rid of the charge of maintaining them after the first year.

Fifthly, This food would likewise bring great custom to taverns, where the vintners will certainly be so prudent as to procure the best receipts for dressing it to perfection, and consequently have their houses frequented by all the fine gentlemen, who justly value themselves upon their knowledge in good eating; and a skilful cook who understands how to oblige his guests, will contrive to make it as expensive as they please. 25

Sixthly, This would be a great inducement to marriage, which all wise nations have either encouraged by rewards or enforced by laws and penalties. It would increase the care and tenderness of mothers toward their children, when they were sure of a settlement for life to the poor babes, provided in some sort by the public, to their annual profit instead of expense. We should see an honest emulation among the married women, which of them would bring the fattest child to the market. Men would become as fond of their wives during the time of their pregnancy as they are now of their mares in foal, their cows in calf, their sows when they are ready to farrow; nor offer to beat or kick them (as is too frequent a practice) for fear of a miscarriage.

Many other advantages might be enumerated. For instance, the addition of some thousand carcasses in our exportation of barreled beef, the propagation of swine's flesh, and improvement in the art of making good bacon, so much wanted among us by the great destruction of pigs, too frequent at our table; which are no way comparable in taste or magnificence to a well-grown, fat, yearling child, which roasted whole will make a considerable figure at a lord mayor's feast or any other public entertainment. But this and many others I omit, being studious of brevity.

Supposing that 1,000 families in this city would be constant customers for infants' flesh, besides others who might have it at merrymeetings, particularly at weddings and christenings, I compute that Dublin would take off annually about 20,000 carcasses; and the rest of the kingdom (where probably they will be sold somewhat cheaper) the remaining 80,000.

I can think of no one objection that will possibly be raised against this proposal, unless it should be urged that the number of people will be thereby much lessened in the kingdom. This I freely own, and it was indeed one principal design in offering it to the world. I desire the reader will observe, that I calculate my remedy for this one individual kingdom of Ireland and for no other that ever was, is, or I think ever can be upon earth. Therefore let no man talk to me of other expedients: of taxing our absentees at 5s. a pound; of using neither clothes nor household furniture except what is of our own growth and manufacture; of utterly rejecting the materials and instruments that promote foreign luxury; of curing the expensiveness of pride, vanity, idleness, and gaming in our women; of introducing a vein of parsimony, prudence, and temperance; of learning to love our country, in the want of which we differ even from Laplanders and the inhabitants of Topinamboo; of quitting our animosities and factions, nor acting any longer like the Jews, who were murdering one another at the very moment their city was taken; of being a little cautious not to sell our country and conscience for nothing; of teaching landlords to have at least one degree of mercy toward their tenants; lastly, of putting a spirit of honesty, industry, and skill into our shopkeepers; who, if a resolution could now be taken to buy only our native goods, would immediately unite to cheat and exact upon us in the price the measure, and the goodness, nor could ever yet be brought to make one fair proposal of just dealing, though often and earnestly invited to it.

Therefore I repeat, let no man talk to me of these and the like expedients, till he has at least some glimpse of hope that there will be ever some hearty and sincere attempt to put them in practice. 30

But as to myself, having been wearied out for many years with offering vain, idle, visionary thoughts, and at length utterly despairing of success, I fortunately fell upon this proposal; which, as it is wholly new, so it has something solid and real, of no expense and little trouble, full in our own power, and whereby we can incur no danger in disobliging England. For this kind of commodity will not bear exportation, the flesh being of too tender a consistence to admit a long continuance in salt, although perhaps I could name a country which would be glad to eat up our whole nation without it.

After all, I am not so violently bent upon my own opinion as to reject any offer proposed by wise men, which shall be found equally innocent, cheap, easy, and effectual. But before something of that kind shall be advanced in contradiction to my scheme, and offering a better, I desire the author or authors will be pleased maturely to consider two points. First, as things now stand, how they will be able to find food and raiment for 100,000 useless mouths and backs. And secondly, there being a round million of creatures in human figure throughout this kingdom, whose subsistence put into a common stock would leave them in debt 2,000,000£. sterling, adding those who are beggars by profession to the bulk of farmers, cottagers, and laborers, with the wives and children who are beggars in effect; I desire those politicians who dislike my overture, and may perhaps be so bold as to attempt an answer, that they will first ask the parents of these mortals, whether they would not at this day think it a great happiness to have been sold for food at a year old in the manner I prescribe, and thereby have avoided such a perpetual scene of misfortunes as they have since gone through by the oppression of landlords, the impossibility of paying rent without money or trade, the want of common sustenance, with neither house nor clothes to cover them from the inclemencies of the weather, and the most inevitable prospect of entailing the like or greater miseries upon their breed for ever.

I profess, in the sincerity of my heart, that I have not the least personal interest in endeavoring to promote this necessary work, having no other motive than the public good of my country, by advancing our trade, providing for infants, relieving the poor, and giving some pleasure to the rich. I have no children by which I can propose to get a single penny; the youngest being nine years old, and my wife past childbearing.

Topics for Critical Thinking and Writing

1. In paragraph 4 the speaker of the essay mentions proposals set forth by "projectors" — that is, by advocates of other proposals or projects. On the basis of the first two paragraphs of "A Modest Proposal," how would you characterize *this* projector, the speaker of the essay? Write your characterization in one paragraph. Then, in a second paragraph, characterize the projector as you understand him, having read the entire essay. In your second paragraph, indicate what *he thinks he is* and also what the reader sees he really is.

2. The speaker or persona of "A Modest Proposal" is confident that selling children "for a good table" (para. 10) is a better idea than any of the then current methods of disposing of unwanted children, including

abortion and infanticide. Can you think of any argument that might favor abortion or infanticide for parents in dire straits, rather than the projector's scheme?

3. In paragraph 29 the speaker considers, but dismisses out of hand, several other solutions to the wretched plight of the Irish poor. Write a 500-word essay in which you explain each of these ideas and their combined merits as an alternative to the solution he favors.

4. What does the projector imply are the causes of the Irish poverty he deplores? Are there possible causes he has omitted? If so, what are they?

5. Imagine yourself as one of the poor parents to whom Swift refers, and write a 250-word essay explaining why you prefer not to sell your infant to the local butcher.

6. The modern version of the problem to which the proposal is addressed is called "population policy." How would you describe our nation's current population policy? Do we have a population policy, in fact? If not, what would you propose? If we do have one, would you propose any changes in it? Why, or why not?

7. It is sometimes suggested that just as persons need to get a license to drive a car, to hunt with a gun, or to marry, a husband and wife ought to be required to get a license to have a child. Would you favor this idea, assuming that it applied to you as a possible parent? Would Swift? Explain your answers in an essay of 500 words.

8. Consider the six arguments advanced in paragraphs 21 to 26, and write a 1,000-word essay criticizing all of them. Or if you find that one or more of the arguments is really unanswerable, explain why you find it so compelling.

9. Write your own "modest proposal," ironically suggesting a solution to a problem. Possible topics: health care or schooling for the children of illegal immigrants, overcrowded jails, children who have committed a serious crime, homeless people.

5

Developing an Argument
of Your Own

PLANNING, DRAFTING, AND
REVISING AN ARGUMENT

First, hear the wisdom of Mark Twain: "When the Lord finished the world, He pronounced it good. That is what I said about my first work, too. But Time, I tell you, Time takes the confidence out of these incautious early opinions."

All of us, teachers and students, have our moments of confidence, but for the most part we know that it takes an effort to write clear, thoughtful prose. In a conversation we can cover ourselves with such expressions as "Well, I don't know, but I sort of think . . . ," and we can always revise our position ("Oh, well, I didn't mean it that way"), but once we have handed in the final version of our writing we are helpless. We are (putting it strongly) naked to our enemies.

Getting Ideas

In Chapter 1 we quoted Robert Frost, "To learn to write is to learn to have ideas," and we offered suggestions about getting ideas, a process traditionally called **invention.** A moment ago we said that we often improve our ideas when we try to explain them to someone else. Partly, of course, we are responding to questions or objections raised by our companion in the conversation, but partly we are responding to ourselves; almost as soon as we hear what we have to say, we may find that it won't do, and, if we are lucky, we may find a better idea surfacing. One of the best ways of getting ideas is to talk things over.

The process of talking things over usually begins with the text that you are reading: Your marginal notes, your summary, and your queries

parenthetically incorporated within your summary are a kind of dialogue between you and the author you are reading. More obviously,
when you talk with friends about your topic, you are trying out and developing ideas. Finally, after reading, taking notes, and talking, you may
feel that you now have clear ideas and you need only put them into
writing. And so you take a sheet of blank paper, and perhaps a paralyzing thought suddenly strikes: "I have ideas but just can't put them into
words."

Despite what many people believe,

- Writing is not only a matter of putting one's ideas into words.

- Just as talking with others is a way of getting ideas, *writing is a way
  of getting and developing ideas.*

Writing, in short, can be an important part of critical thinking. If fear of
putting ourselves on record is one big reason we have trouble writing,
another big reason is our fear that we have no ideas worth putting
down. But by jotting down notes—or even free associations—and by
writing a draft, however weak, we can help ourselves to think our way
toward good ideas.

Freewriting   Writing for five or six minutes, nonstop, without censoring what you produce is one way of getting words down on paper
that will help to lead to improved thoughts. Some people who write on a
computer find it useful to dim the screen so they won't be tempted to
look up and fiddle too soon with what they have just written. Later they
illuminate the screen, scroll back, and notice some keywords or passages
that can be used later in drafting a paper.

Listing   Jotting down items, just as you do when you make a shopping list, is another way of getting ideas. When you make a shopping list,
you write *ketchup,* and the act of writing it reminds you that you also
need hamburger rolls—and *that* in turn reminds you (who knows how
or why?) that you also need a can of tuna fish. Similarly, when you prepare a list of ideas for a paper, jotting down one item will generate another. Of course, when you look over the list you will probably drop
some of these ideas—the dinner menu will change—but you are making progress.

Diagramming   Sketching some sort of visual representation of an
essay is a kind of listing. Three methods of diagramming are especially
common.

- **Clustering**   Write, in the middle of a sheet of paper, a word or
  phrase summarizing your topic (for instance, *health care;* see diagram), circle it, and then write down and circle a related word (for
  example, *gov't-provided*). Perhaps this leads you to write *higher*

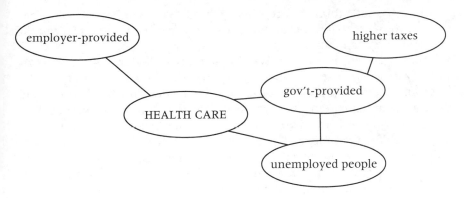

taxes, and you then circle this phrase and connect it to *gov't-provided.* The next thing that occurs to you is *employer-provided* — and so you write this down and circle it. You will not connect this to *higher taxes,* but you will connect it to *health care* because it is a sort of parallel to *gov't-provided.* The next thing that occurs to you is *unemployed people.* This category does not connect easily with *employer-provided,* so you won't connect these two terms with a line, but you probably will connect *unemployed people* with *health care* and maybe also with *gov't-provided.* Keep going, jotting down ideas, and making connections where possible, indicating relationships.

- **Branching**   Some writers find it useful to build a tree, moving from the central topic to the main branches (chief ideas) and then to the twigs (aspects of the chief ideas).

- **Comparing in columns**   Draw a line down the middle of the page, and then set up oppositions. For instance, if you are concerned with health care, you might head one column *gov't-provided* and the other *employer-provided,* and you might then, under the first column, write *covers unemployed* and under the second column, write *omits unemployed.* You might go on to write, under the first column, *higher taxes,* and under the second, *higher prices* — or whatever else relevant comes to mind.

All of these methods can, of course, be executed with pen and paper, but if you write on a computer, you may also be able to use them, depending on the capabilities of your program.

Whether you are using a computer or a pen, you put down some words and almost immediately see that they need improvement, not simply a little polishing but a substantial overhaul. You write, "Truman was justified in dropping the atom bomb for two reasons," and as soon as you write these words, a third reason comes to mind. Or perhaps one of those "two reasons" no longer seems very good. As the little girl shrewdly replied when an adult told her to think before she spoke, "How do I know what I think before I hear what I say?" We have to see what we say, we have to get something down on paper, before we realize that we need to make it better.

Writing, then, is really **rewriting**—that is, **revising**—and a revision is a *re-vision*, a second look. The paper that you hand in should be clear and may even seem effortless to the reader, but in all likelihood the clarity and apparent ease are the result of a struggle with yourself, a struggle during which you greatly improved your first thoughts. You begin by putting down your ideas, such as they are, perhaps even in the random order in which they occurred, but sooner or later comes the job of looking at them critically, developing what is useful in them and chucking out what is not. If you follow this procedure you will be in the company of Picasso, who said that he "advanced by means of destruction."

Whether you advance bit by bit (writing a sentence, revising it, writing the next, and so on) or whether you write an entire first draft and then revise it and revise it again and again is chiefly a matter of temperament. Probably most people combine both approaches, backing up occasionally but trying to get to the end fairly soon so that they can see rather quickly what they know, or think they know, and can then start the real work of thinking, of converting their initial ideas into something substantial.

Getting Ideas by Asking Questions   Getting ideas, we said when we talked about **topics** and **invention** strategies in Chapter 1 (pp. 3–6) is mostly a matter of asking (and then thinking about) questions. We append questions to the end of each argumentative essay in this book, not to torment you but to help you to think about the arguments—for instance, to turn your attention to especially important matters. If your instructor asks you to write an answer to one of these questions, you are lucky: Examining the question will stimulate your mind to work in a definite direction.

If a topic is not assigned, and you are asked to write an argument, you will find that some ideas (possibly poor ones, at this stage, but that doesn't matter because you will soon revise) will come to mind if you ask yourself questions. You can begin finding where you stand on an issue (**stasis**) by asking the following five basic questions:

1. What is *X?*
2. What is the value of *X?*
3. What are the causes (or the consequences) of *X?*
4. What should (or ought or must) we do about *X?*
5. What is the evidence for my claims about *X?*

Let's spend a moment looking at each of these questions.

1. **What is *X?*** We can hardly argue about the number of people sentenced to death in the United States in 2000—a glance at the appro-

priate government report will give the answer—but we can argue about whether or not capital punishment as administered in the United States is discriminatory. Does the evidence, we can ask, support the view that in the United States the death penalty is unfair? Similarly, we can ask whether a human fetus is a human being (in saying what something is, must we take account of its potentiality?), and, even if we agree that a fetus is a human being, we can further ask about whether it is a *person*. In *Roe v. Wade* the U.S. Supreme Court ruled that even the "viable" unborn human fetus is not a "person" as that term is used in the Fifth and Fourteenth Amendments. Here the question is this: Is the essential fact about the fetus that it is a person?

An argument of this sort makes a claim—that is, it takes a stand—but notice that it does not also have to argue for an action. Thus, it may argue that the death penalty is administered unfairly—that's a big enough issue—but it need not therefore go on to argue that the death penalty should be abolished. After all, another possibility is that the death penalty should be administered fairly. The writer of the essay may be doing enough if he or she establishes the truth of the claim and leaves to others the possible courses of action.

2. **What is the value of *X*?** No one can argue with you if you say you *prefer* the plays of Tennessee Williams to those of Arthur Miller. But as soon as you say that Williams is a *better* playwright than Miller, you have based your preference on implicit standards, and it is incumbent on you to support your preference by giving evidence about the relative skill, insight, and accomplishments of Williams and of Miller. Your argument is an evaluation. The question now at issue is the merits of the two authors and the standards appropriate for such an appraisal. (For a discussion of literary evaluations, see pp. 426–430.)

In short, an essay offering an evaluation normally has two purposes: (1) to set forth an assessment and (2) to convince the reader that the assessment is reasonable. In writing an evaluation you will have to establish criteria, and these will vary depending on your topic. For instance, if you are comparing the artistic merit of the plays by Williams and by Miller, you may want to talk about the quality of the characterization, the significance of the theme, and so on. But if the topic is, Which playwright is more suitable to be taught in high school?, other criteria may be appropriate, such as the difficulty of the language, the presence of obscenity, and so on.

3. **What are the causes (or the consequences) of *X*?** Why did the rate of auto theft increase during a specific period? If we abolish the death penalty, will that cause the rate of murder to increase? Notice, by the way, that such problems may be complex. The phenomena that people usually argue about—say, such things as inflation, war, suicide, crime—have many causes, and it is therefore often a mistake to speak of *the* cause of *X*. A writer in *Time* mentioned that the life expectancy of an average American male is about sixty-seven years, a figure that compares

unfavorably with the life expectancy of males in Japan and Israel. The *Time* writer suggested that an important cause of the relatively short life span is "the pressure to perform well in business." Perhaps. But the life expectancy of plumbers is no greater than that of managers and executives. Nutrition authority Jean Mayer, in an article in *Life*, attributed the relatively poor longevity of American males to a diet that is "rich in fat and poor in nutrients." Doubtless other authorities propose other causes, and in all likelihood no one cause accounts for the phenomenon.

4. **What should (or ought or must) we do about *X*?** Must we always obey the law? Should the law allow eighteen-year-olds to drink alcohol? Should eighteen-year-olds be drafted to do one year of social service? Should pornography be censored? Should steroid use by athletes be banned? Ought there to be Good Samaritan laws, making it a legal duty to intervene to save a person from death or great bodily harm, when one might do so with little or no risk to oneself? These questions involve conduct and policy; how we answer them will reveal our values and principles.

An essay answering questions of this sort usually begins by explaining what the issue is—and why the reader should care about it—and then offers the proposal, paying attention to the counterarguments.

5. **What is the evidence for my claims about *X*?** Critical reading, writing, and thinking depend essentially on identifying and evaluating the evidence for and against the claims one makes and encounters in the writings of others. It is not enough to have an *opinion* or belief one way or the other; you need to be able to support your opinions—the bare fact of your sincere belief in what you say or write is not itself any *evidence* that what you believe is true.

So what are good reasons for opinions, adequate evidence for one's beliefs? The answer, of course, depends on what kind of belief or opinion, assertion or hypothesis, claim or principle, you want to assert. For example, there is good evidence that President John F. Kennedy was assassinated on November 22, 1963, because this is the date for his death reported in standard almanacs. You could further substantiate the date by checking the back issues of the *New York Times*. But a different kind of evidence is needed to support the proposition that the chemical composition of water is H_2O; and you will need still other kinds of evidence to support your beliefs about the likelihood of rain tomorrow, the probability that the Red Sox will win the pennant this year, the twelfth digit in the decimal expansion of pi, the average cumulative grades of the graduating seniors over the past three years in your college, the relative merits of *Hamlet* and *Death of a Salesman*, and the moral dimensions of sexual harassment. None of these issues is merely a matter of opinion; yet on some of them, educated and informed people may disagree over the reasons and the evidence and what they show. Your job as a critical thinker is to be alert to the relevant reasons and evidence, and to make the most of them as you present your views.

Again, an argument may take in two or more of these five issues. Someone who argues that pornography should (or should not) be censored will have to mark out the territory of the discussion by defining pornography (our first issue: What is *X?*). The argument probably will also need to examine the consequences of adopting the preferred policy (our third issue) and may even have to argue about its value—our second issue. (Some people maintain that pornography produces crime, but others maintain that it provides a harmless outlet for impulses that otherwise might vent themselves in criminal behavior.) Further, someone arguing about the wisdom of censoring pornography might have to face the objection that censorship, however desirable on account of some of its consequences, may be unconstitutional and that even if censorship were constitutional, it would (or might) have undesirable side effects, such as repressing freedom of political opinion. And one will always have to keep asking oneself the fifth question, What is the evidence for my claims?

Thinking about one or more of these questions may get you going. For instance, thinking about the first question, What is *X?*, will require you to produce a definition, and as you work at producing a satisfactory definition, you may find new ideas arising. If a question seems relevant, start writing, even if you write only a fragmentary sentence. You'll probably find that one word leads to another and that ideas begin to appear. Even if these ideas seem weak as you write them, don't be discouraged; you have put something on paper, and returning to these words, perhaps in five minutes or perhaps the next day, you will probably find that some are not at all bad and that others will stimulate you to better ones.

It may be useful to record your ideas in a special notebook reserved for the purpose. Such a **journal** can be a valuable resource when it comes time to write your paper. Many students find it easier to focus their thoughts on writing if during the period of gestation they have been jotting down relevant ideas on something more substantial than slips of paper or loose sheets. The very act of designating a notebook as your journal for a course can be the first step in focusing your attention on the eventual need to write a paper.

If what we have just said does not sound convincing, and you know from experience that you often have trouble getting started with your writing, don't despair; first aid is at hand in a sure-fire method that we will now explain.

The Thesis

Let's assume that you are writing an argumentative essay—perhaps an evaluation of an argument in this book—and you have what seems to be a pretty good draft or at least a bunch of notes that are the result of hard thinking. You really do have ideas now, and you want to present them effectively. How will you organize your essay? No one formula works best for every essayist and for every essay, but it is usually advisable to formulate a basic **thesis,** a central point, a chief position, and to state it early. Every essay that is any good, even a book-length one, has a thesis, a main point, which can be stated briefly. Remember Coolidge's remark on the preacher's sermon on sin: "He was against it." Don't confuse the **topic** (sin) with the thesis (opposition to sin). The thesis is the argumentative theme, the author's primary claim or contention, the proposition that the rest of the essay will explain and defend. Of course, the thesis may sound commonplace, but the book or essay or sermon ought to develop it interestingly and convincingly.

Here are some sample theses:

- Smoking should be prohibited in all enclosed public places.
- Smoking should be limited to specific parts of enclosed public places and entirely prohibited in small spaces, such as elevators.
- Proprietors of public places such as restaurants and sports arenas should be free to determine whether they wish to prohibit, limit, or impose no limitations on smokers.

Imagining an Audience

Of course, the questions that you ask yourself to stimulate your thoughts will depend primarily on what you are writing about, but additional questions are always relevant:

- Who are my readers?
- What do they believe?
- What common ground do we share?
- What do I want my readers to believe?
- What do they need to know?

These questions require a little comment. The literal answer to the first probably is "the teacher," but (unless you are given instructions to the contrary) you should not write specifically for the teacher; instead, you should write for an audience that is, generally speaking, like your classmates. In short, your imagined audience is literate, intelligent, and moderately well informed, but it does not know everything that you know, and it does not know your response to the problem that you are addressing.

The essays in this book are from many different sources, each with its own audience. An essay from the *New York Times* is addressed to the educated general reader; an essay from *Ms.* is addressed to readers sympathetic to the feminist movement. An essay from *Commonweal,* a Roman Catholic publication addressed to the nonspecialist, is likely to differ in point of view or tone from one in *Time,* even though both articles may advance approximately the same position. The writer of the article in

Commonweal may, for example, effectively cite church fathers and distinguished Roman Catholic writers as authorities, whereas the writer of an article addressed largely to non-Catholic readers probably will cite few or even none of these figures because the audience might be unfamiliar with them or, even if familiar, might be unimpressed by their views.

The tone as well as the gist of the argument is in some degree shaped by the audience. For instance, popular journals, such as the *National Review* and *Ms.*, are more likely to use ridicule than are journals chiefly addressed to, say, an academic audience.

The Audience as Collaborator

If you imagine an audience and keep asking yourself what this audience needs to be told and what it doesn't need to be told, you will find that material comes to mind, just as it comes to mind when a friend asks you what a film you saw was about, who was in it, and how you liked it.

Your readers do not have to be told that Thomas Jefferson was an American statesman in the early years of this country's history, but they do have to be told that Thomas Huxley was a late-nineteenth-century English advocate of Darwinism. Why? You would identify Huxley because it's your hunch that your classmates never heard of him, or even if they may have heard the name, they can't quite identify it. But what if your class has been assigned an essay by Huxley? In that case your imagined reader knows Huxley's name and knows at least a little about him, so you don't have to identify Huxley as an Englishman of the nineteenth century. But you do still have to remind your reader about relevant aspects of his essay, and you do have to tell your reader about your responses to them.

After all, even if the instructor has assigned an essay by Huxley, you cannot assume that your classmates know the essay inside out. Obviously, you can't say, "Huxley's third reason is also unconvincing," without reminding the reader, by means of a brief summary, of his third reason. Again,

- Think of your classmates as your imagined readers; put yourself in their shoes, and
- Be sure that your essay does not make unreasonable demands.

If you ask yourself, "What do my readers need to know?" (and "What do I want them to believe?"), you will find some answers arising, and you will start writing.

We have said that you should imagine your audience as your classmates. But this is not the whole truth. In a sense, your argument is addressed not simply to your classmates but to the world interested in ideas. Even if you can reasonably assume that your classmates have read only one work by Huxley, you will not begin your essay by writing "Huxley's essay is deceptively easy." You will have to name the work; it is possible that a reader has read some other work by Huxley. And by precisely identifying your subject you help to ease the reader into your essay.

Similarly, you won't begin by writing,

```
The majority opinion in Walker v. City of Birmingham
was that . . .
```

Rather, you'll write something like this:

```
In Walker v. City of Birmingham, the U.S. Supreme Court
ruled in 1966 that city authorities acted lawfully when
they jailed Martin Luther King Jr. and other clergymen
in 1963 for marching in Birmingham without a permit.
Justice Potter Stewart delivered the majority opinion,
which held that . . .
```

By the way, if you think you suffer from a writing block, the mere act of writing out such obvious truths will help you to get started. You will find that putting a few words down on paper, perhaps merely copying the essay's title or an interesting quotation from the essay, will stimulate you to jot down thoughts that you didn't know you had in you.

Here, again, are the questions about audience. If you write with a word processor, consider putting these questions into a file. For each assignment, copy (with the Copy command) the questions into the file you are currently working on, and then, as a way of generating ideas, *enter your responses, indented, under each question.*

- Who are my readers?
- What do they believe?
- What common ground do we share?
- What do I want my readers to believe?
- What do they need to know?

Thinking about your audience can help you to put some words on paper; even more important, it can help you to get ideas. Our second and third questions about the audience ("What do they believe?" and "How much common ground do we share?") will usually help you get ideas flowing. Presumably your imagined audience does not share your views, or at least does not fully share them. But why? How can these readers hold a position that to you seems unreasonable? If you try to put yourself into your readers' shoes, and if you think about what your audience knows or thinks it knows, you will find yourself getting ideas.

You do not believe (let's assume) that people should be allowed to smoke in enclosed public places, but you know that some people hold a different view. Why do they hold it? Try to state their view *in a way that would be satisfactory to them*. Having done so, you may come to perceive that your conclusions and theirs differ because they are based on different premises, perhaps different ideas about human rights. Examine the opposition's premises carefully, and explain, first to yourself and ultimately to your readers, why you find some premises unacceptable.

Possibly some facts are in dispute, such as whether nonsmokers may be harmed by exposure to tobacco. The thing to do, then, is to check the facts. If you find that harm to nonsmokers has not been proved, but you nevertheless believe that smoking should be prohibited in enclosed public places, of course you can't premise your argument on the wrongfulness of harming the innocent (in this case, the nonsmokers). You will have to develop arguments that take account of the facts, whatever they are.

Among the relevant facts there surely are some that your audience or your opponent will not dispute. The same is true of the values relevant to the discussion; the two of you are very likely to agree, if only you stop to think about it, that you share belief in some of the same values (such as the principle mentioned above, that it is wrong to harm the innocent). These areas of shared agreement are crucial to effective persuasion in argument. If you wish to persuade, you'll have to begin by finding *premises you can share with your audience.* Try to identify and isolate these areas of agreement. There are two good reasons for doing so:

- There is no point in disputing facts or values on which you and your readers really agree.
- It usually helps to establish goodwill between you and your opponent when you can point to beliefs, assumptions, facts, and values that the two of you share.

In a few moments we will return to the need to share some of the opposition's ideas.

Recall that in writing college papers it is usually best to write for a general audience, an audience rather like your classmates but without the specific knowledge that they all share as students enrolled in one course. If the topic is smoking in public places, the audience presumably consists of smokers and nonsmokers. Thinking about our fifth question on page 194 — What do the readers need to know? — may prompt you to give statistics about the harmful effects of smoking. Or if you are arguing on behalf of smokers, it may prompt you to cite studies claiming that no evidence conclusively demonstrates that cigarette smoking is harmful to nonsmokers. If indeed you are writing for a general audience, and you are not advancing a highly unfamiliar view, our second question (What does the audience believe?) is less important here, but if the audience is specialized, such as an antismoking group, a group of restaurant owners who fear that antismoking regulations will interfere with their business, or a group of civil libertarians, an effective essay will have to address their special beliefs.

In addressing their beliefs (let's assume that you do not share them or do not share them fully), you must try to establish some common ground. If you advocate requiring restaurants to provide nonsmoking areas, you should at least recognize the possibility that this arrangement will result in inconvenience for the proprietor. But perhaps (the good news) the restaurant will regain some lost customers or will attract some new customers. This thought should prompt you to think of kinds of evidence, perhaps testimony or statistics.

When one formulates a thesis and asks questions about it, such as who the readers are, what do they believe, what do they know, and what do they need to know, one begins to get ideas about how to organize the material, or at least one begins to see that some sort of organization will have to be worked out. The thesis may be clear and simple, but the reasons (the argument) may take many pages. The thesis is the point; the argument sets forth the evidence that is offered to support the thesis.

The Title

It's not a bad idea to announce your thesis in your **title.** If you scan the table of contents of this book, you will notice that a fair number of essayists use the title to let the readers know, at least in a very general way, what position will be advocated. Here are a few examples:

Gay Marriages: Make Them Legal

Students Should Not Be above the Law

Why Handguns Must Be Outlawed

True, these titles are not especially engaging, but the reader welcomes them because they give some information about the writer's thesis.

Some titles do not announce the thesis but they at least announce the topic:

Is All Discrimination Unfair?

On Racist Speech

Why Make Divorce Easy?

Although not clever or witty, these titles are informative.

Some titles seek to attract attention or to stimulate the imagination:

A First Amendment Junkie

A Crime of Compassion

Addicted to Health

All of these are effective, but a word of caution is appropriate here. In your effort to engage your reader's attention, be careful not to sound like a wise guy. You want to engage your readers, not turn them off.

Finally, be prepared to rethink your title *after* you have finished the last draft of your paper. A title somewhat different from your working title may be an improvement because the emphasis of your finished paper may have turned out to be rather different from what you expected when you first thought of a title.

The Opening Paragraphs

A good introduction arouses the reader's interest and helps prepare the reader for the rest of the paper. How? Opening paragraphs usually do at least one (and often all) of the following:

- Attract the reader's interest (often with a bold statement of the thesis, or with an interesting statistic, quotation, or anecdote),
- Prepare the reader's mind by giving some idea of the topic and often of the thesis,
- Give the reader an idea of how the essay is organized, and
- Define a key term.

You may not wish to announce your thesis in your title, but if you don't announce it there, you should set it forth very early in the argument, in your introductory paragraph or paragraphs. In her title "Human Rights and Foreign Policy," Jeanne J. Kirkpatrick merely announces her topic (subject) as opposed to her thesis (point), but she begins to hint at the thesis in her first paragraph, by deprecating President Jimmy Carter's policy:

> In this paper I deal with three broad subjects: first, the content and consequences of the Carter administration's human rights policy; second, the prerequisites of a more adequate theory of human rights; and third, some characteristics of a more successful human rights policy.

Or consider this opening paragraph from Peter Singer's "Animal Liberation" (p. 166):

> We are familiar with Black Liberation, Gay Liberation, and a variety of other movements. With Women's Liberation some thought we had come to the end of the road. Discrimination on the basis of sex, it has been said, is the last form of discrimination that is universally accepted and practiced without pretense, even in those liberal circles which have long prided themselves on their freedom from racial discrimination. But one should always be wary of talking of "the last remaining form of discrimination." If we have learned anything from the liberation movements, we should have learned how difficult it is to be aware of the ways in which we discriminate until they are forcefully pointed out to

us. A liberation movement demands an expansion of our moral horizons, so that practices that were previously regarded as natural and inevitable are now seen as intolerable.

Although Singer's introductory paragraph nowhere mentions animal liberation, in conjunction with its title it gives us a good idea of what Singer is up to and where he is going. Singer knows that his audience will be skeptical, so he reminds them that many of us in previous years were skeptical of reforms that we now take for granted. He adopts a strategy used fairly often by writers who advance highly unconventional theses: Rather than beginning with a bold announcement of a thesis that may turn off some of his readers because it sounds offensive or absurd, Singer warms his audience up, gaining their interest by cautioning them politely that although they may at first be skeptical of animal liberation, if they stay with his essay they may come to feel that they have expanded their horizons.

Notice, too, that Singer begins by establishing common ground with his readers; he assumes, probably correctly, that they share his view that other forms of discrimination (now seen to be unjust) were once widely practiced and were assumed to be acceptable and natural. In this paragraph, then, Singer is not only showing himself to be fair-minded but is also letting us know that he will advance a daring idea. His opening wins our attention and our goodwill. A writer can hardly hope to do more. (In a few pages we will talk a little more about winning the audience.)

In your introductory paragraphs

- You may have to give some background informing or reminding your readers of material that they will need to keep in mind if they are to follow your essay.
- You may wish to define some terms, if the terms are unfamiliar or if you are using familiar terms in an unusual sense.

In writing, or at least in revising these paragraphs, remember to keep in mind this question: What do my readers need to know? Remember, your aim throughout is to write *reader-friendly* prose, and keeping the needs and interests of your audience constantly in mind will help you achieve this goal.

After announcing the topic, giving the necessary background, and stating your position (and perhaps the opposition's) in as engaging a manner as possible, it is usually a good idea to give the reader an idea of *how* you will proceed—that is, what the organization will be. Look on the preceding page at Kirkpatrick's opening paragraph, for an obvious illustration. She tells us she will deal with three subjects, and she names them. Her approach in the paragraph is concise, obvious, and effective.

Similarly, you may, for instance, want to announce fairly early that there are four common objections to your thesis and that you will take them up one by one, beginning with the weakest (or most widely held, or whatever) and moving to the strongest (or least familiar), after which you will advance your own view in greater detail. Not every argument begins with refuting the other side, though many arguments do. The point to remember is that you usually ought to tell your readers where you will be taking them and by what route.

Organizing and Revising the Body of the Essay

Most argumentative essays more or less follow this organization:

1. Statement of the problem
2. Statement of the structure of the essay
3. Statement of alternative solutions
4. Arguments in support of the proposed solution
5. Arguments answering possible objections
6. A summary, resolution, or conclusion

Let's look at each of these six steps.

1. **Statement of the problem**   Whether the problem is stated briefly or at length depends on the nature of the problem and the writer's audience. If you haven't already defined unfamiliar terms or terms you use in a special way, probably now is the time to do so. In any case, it is advisable here to state the problem objectively (thereby gaining the trust of the reader) and to indicate why the reader should care about the issue.
2. **Statement of the structure of the essay**   After stating the problem at the appropriate length, the writer often briefly indicates the structure of the rest of the essay. The commonest structure is suggested below, in points 3 and 4.
3. **Statement of alternative solutions**   In addition to stating the alternatives fairly, the writer probably conveys willingness to recognize not only the integrity of the proposers but also the (partial) merit of at least some of the alternative solutions.

The point made in the previous sentence is important and worth amplifying. Because it is important to convey your goodwill—your sense of fairness—to the reader, it is advisable to let your reader see that you are familiar with the opposition and that you recognize the integrity of those who hold that view. This you do by granting its merits as far as you can. (For more about this approach, see the essay by Carl R. Rogers on p. 416.)

The next stage, which constitutes most of the body of the essay, usually is this:

4. **Arguments in support of the proposed solution**   The evidence offered will, of course, depend on the nature of the problem. Relevant statistics, authorities, examples, or analogies may come to mind or be available. This is usually the longest part of the essay.

5. **Arguments answering possible objections** These arguments may suggest that
   a. The proposal won't work (perhaps it is alleged to be too expensive, or to make unrealistic demands on human nature, or to fail to get to the heart of the problem);
   b. The proposed solution will create problems greater than the difficulty to be resolved. (A good example of a proposal that produced dreadful unexpected results is the law mandating a prison term for anyone over eighteen in possession of an illegal drug. Heroin dealers then began to use children as runners, and cocaine importers followed the practice.)
6. **A summary, resolution, or conclusion** Here the writer may seek to accommodate the views of the opposition as far as possible but clearly suggests that the writer's own position makes good sense. A conclusion—the word comes from the Latin *claudere*, "to shut"—ought to provide a sense of closure, but it can be much more than a restatement of the writer's thesis. It can, for instance, make a quiet emotional appeal by suggesting that the issue is important and that the ball is now in the reader's court.

Of course not every essay will follow this six-step pattern, but let's assume that in the introductory paragraphs you have sketched the topic (and have shown or nicely said, or implied, that the reader doubtless is interested in it) and have fairly and courteously set forth the opposition's view, recognizing its merits and indicating the degree to which you can share part of that view. You now want to set forth your arguments explaining why you differ on some essentials.

In setting forth your own position, you can begin either with your strongest reasons or your weakest. Each method of organization has advantages and disadvantages. If you begin with your strongest, the essay may seem to peter out; if you begin with the weakest, you build to a climax, but your readers may not still be with you because they may have felt at the start that the essay was frivolous. The solution to this last possibility is to make sure that even your weakest argument is an argument of some strength. You can, moreover, assure your readers that stronger points will soon be offered and you offer this point first only because you want to show that you are aware of it and that, slight though it is, it deserves some attention. The body of the essay, then, is devoted to arguing a position, which means offering not only supporting reasons but also refutations of possible objections to these reasons.

Doubtless you will sometimes be uncertain, as you draft your essay, whether to present a given point before or after another point. When you write, and certainly when you revise, try to put yourself into your reader's shoes: Which point do you think the reader needs to know first? Which point *leads to* which further point? Your argument should not be a mere list of points, of course; rather, it should clearly integrate one point with another in order to develop an idea. But in all likelihood you won't have a strong sense of the best organization until you have written a draft and have reread it. You are likely to find that the organization needs some revising in order to make your argument clear to a reader.

Checking Paragraphs   When you revise your draft, watch out also for short paragraphs. Although a paragraph of only two or three sentences (like some in this chapter) may occasionally be helpful as a transition between complicated points, most short paragraphs are undeveloped paragraphs. (Newspaper editors favor very short paragraphs because they can be read rapidly when printed in the narrow columns typical of newspapers. Many of the essays reprinted in this book originally were published in newspapers, hence they consist of very short paragraphs. There is no reason for you to imitate this style in the argumentative essays you will be writing.)

In revising, when you find a paragraph of only a sentence or two or three, check first to see if it should be joined to the paragraph that precedes or follows. Second, if on rereading you are certain that a given paragraph should not be tied to what comes before or after, think about amplifying the paragraph with supporting detail (this is not the same as mere padding).

Checking Transitions   Make sure, too, in revising, that the reader can move easily from the beginning of a paragraph to the end and from one paragraph to the next. Transitions help the reader to perceive the connections between the units of the argument. For example (that's a transition, of course, indicating that an illustration will follow), they may

- **Illustrate:** *for example, for instance, consider this case;*
- **Establish a sequence:** *a more important objection, a stronger example, the best reason;*
- **Connect logically:** *thus, as a result, therefore, so, it follows;*
- **Compare:** *similarly, in like manner, just as, analogously;*
- **Contrast:** *on the other hand, in contrast, however, but;*
- **Summarize:** *in short, briefly.*

Expressions such as these serve as guideposts that enable your reader to move easily through your essay.

When writers revise an early draft, they chiefly

- **Unify** the essay by eliminating irrelevancies;
- **Organize** the essay by keeping in mind an imagined audience;
- **Clarify** the essay by fleshing out thin paragraphs, by making certain that the transitions are adequate, and by making certain that

generalizations are adequately supported by concrete details and examples.

We are not talking about polish or elegance; we are talking about fundamental matters. Be especially careful not to abuse the logical connectives (*thus, as a result,* and so on). If you write several sentences followed by *therefore* or a similar word or phrase, be sure that what you write after the *therefore* really *does follow* from what has gone before. Logical connectives are not mere transitional devices used to link disconnected bits of prose. They are supposed to mark a real movement of thought — the essence of an argument.

The Ending

What about concluding paragraphs, in which you try to summarize the main points and reaffirm your position? If you can look back over your essay and can add something that enriches it and at the same time wraps it up, fine, but don't feel compelled to say, "Thus, in conclusion, I have argued X, Y, and Z, and I have refuted Jones." After all, *conclusion* can have two meanings: (1) ending, or finish, as the ending of a joke or a novel, or (2) judgment or decision reached after deliberation. Your essay should finish effectively (the first sense), but it need not announce a judgment (the second).

If the essay is fairly short, so that a reader can more or less keep the whole thing in mind, you may not need to restate your view. Just make sure that you have covered the ground and that your last sentence is a good one. Notice that the student essay printed later in this chapter (p. 214) does not end with a formal conclusion, though it ends conclusively, with a note of finality.

By a note of finality we do *not* mean a triumphant crowing. It's usually far better to end with the suggestion that you hope you have by now indicated why those who hold a different view may want to modify it and accept yours.

If you study the essays in this book, or, for that matter, the editorials and op-ed pieces in a newspaper, you will notice that writers often provide a sense of closure by using one of the following devices:

- A return to something in the introduction,
- A glance at the wider implications of the issue (for example, if smoking is restricted, other liberties are threatened),
- An anecdote that engagingly illustrates the thesis, or
- A brief summary (but this sort of ending may seem unnecessary and even tedious, especially if the paper is short and if the summary merely repeats what has already been said).

Two Uses of an Outline

The Outline as a Preliminary Guide   Some writers find it useful to sketch an **outline** as soon as they think they know what they want to say, even before they write a first draft. This procedure can be helpful in planning a tentative organization, but remember that in revising a draft new ideas will arise, and the outline may have to be modified. A preliminary outline is chiefly useful as a means of getting going, not as a guide to the final essay.

The Outline as a Way of Checking a Draft   Whether or not you use a preliminary outline, we suggest that after you have written what you hope is your last draft, you make an outline of it; there is no better way of finding out whether the essay is well organized.

Go through the draft and jot down the chief points in the order in which you make them. That is, prepare a table of contents—perhaps a phrase for each paragraph. Next, examine your jottings to see what kind of sequence they reveal in your paper:

1. Is the sequence reasonable? Can it be improved?
2. Are any passages irrelevant?
3. Does something important seem to be missing?

If no coherent structure or reasonable sequence clearly appears in the outline, then the full prose version of your argument probably doesn't have any, either. Therefore, produce another draft, moving things around, adding or subtracting paragraphs—cutting and pasting into a new sequence, with transitions as needed—and then make another outline to see if the sequence now is satisfactory.

You are probably familiar with the structure known as a **formal outline.** A major point is indicated by I, and points within this major point are indicated by A, B, C, and so on. Divisions within A, B, C, are indicated by 1, 2, 3, and so on, thus:

I. Arguments for opening all Olympic sports to professionals
   A. Fairness
      1. Some Olympic sports are already open to professionals.
      2. Some athletes who really are not professionals are classified as professionals.
   B. Quality (achievements would be higher)

You may want to outline your draft according to this principle, or it may be enough if you simply jot down a phrase for each paragraph and indent the subdivisions. But keep these points in mind:

- It is not enough for the parts to be ordered reasonably;
- The order must be made clear to the reader, probably by means of transitions such as *for instance, on the other hand, we can now turn to an opposing view,* and so on.

Tone and the Writer's Persona

Although this book is chiefly about argument in the sense of rational discourse—the presentation of reasons in support of a thesis or conclusion—the appeal to reason is only one form of persuasion. Another form is the appeal to emotion—to pity, for example. Aristotle saw, in addition to the appeal to reason and the appeal to emotion, a third form of persuasion, the appeal to the character of the speaker. He called it the **ethical appeal** (the Greek word for this kind of appeal is **ethos,** "character"). The idea is that effective speakers convey the suggestion that they are

- Informed,
- Intelligent,
- Benevolent, and
- Honest.

Because they are perceived as trustworthy, their words inspire confidence in their listeners. It is, of course, a fact that when we read an argument we are often aware of the *person* or *voice* behind the words, and our assent to the argument depends partly on the extent to which we can share the speaker's assumptions, look at the matter from the speaker's point of view—in short, *identify* with this speaker.

How can a writer inspire the confidence that lets readers identify themselves with the writer? To begin with, the writer should possess the virtues Aristotle specified: intelligence or good sense, honesty, and benevolence or goodwill. As the Roman proverb puts it, "No one gives what he does not have." Still, possession of these qualities is not a guarantee that you will convey them in your writing. Like all other writers, you will have to revise your drafts so that these qualities become apparent, or, stated more moderately, you will have to revise so that nothing in the essay causes a reader to doubt your intelligence, honesty, and goodwill. A blunder in logic, a misleading quotation, a snide remark—all such slips can cause readers to withdraw their sympathy from the writer.

But of course all good argumentative essays do not sound exactly alike; they do not all reveal the same speaker. Each writer develops his or her own voice or (as literary critics and teachers call it) **persona.** In fact, one writer will have several voices or personae, depending on the topic and the audience. The president of the United States delivering an address on the State of the Union has one persona; chatting with a reporter at his summer home he has another. This change is not a matter of hypocrisy. Different circumstances call for different language. As a French writer put it, there is a time to speak of "Paris" and a time to speak of "the capital of the nation." When Lincoln spoke at Gettysburg, he didn't say "Eighty-seven years ago," but "Four score and seven years ago." We might say that just as some occasions required him to be the folksy Honest Abe, the occasion of the dedication of hallowed ground required him to be formal and solemn, and so the president of the United States appropriately used biblical language. The election campaigns called for one persona, and this occasion called for a different persona.

When we talk about a writer's persona, we mean the way in which the writer presents his or her attitudes

- Toward *the self,*
- Toward *the audience,* and
- Toward *the subject.*

Thus, if a writer says,

> I have thought long and hard about this subject, and I can say with assurance that . . .

we may feel that we are listening to a self-satisfied ass who probably is simply mouthing other people's opinions. Certainly he is mouthing other people's clichés: "long and hard," "say with assurance."

Let's look at a slightly subtler example of an utterance that reveals an attitude. When we read that

> President Nixon was hounded out of office by journalists,

we hear a respectful attitude toward Nixon ("President Nixon") and a hostile attitude toward the press (they are beasts, curs who "hounded" our elected leader). If the writer's attitudes were reversed, she might have said something like this:

> The press turned the searchlight on Tricky Dick's criminal shenanigans.

"Tricky Dick" and "criminal" are obvious enough, but notice that "shenanigans" also implies the writer's contempt for Nixon, and of course, "turned the searchlight" suggests that the press is a source of illumination, a source of truth. The original version and the opposite version both say that the press was responsible for Nixon's resignation, but the original version ("President Nixon was hounded") conveys indignation toward journalists, whereas the revision conveys contempt for Nixon.

These two versions suggest two speakers who differ not only in their view of Nixon but also in their manner, including the seriousness with which they take themselves. Although the passage is very short, it seems to us that the first speaker conveys righteous indignation ("hounded"), whereas the second conveys amused contempt ("shenanigans"). To our ears the tone, as well as the point, differs in the two versions.

We are talking about **loaded words,** words that convey the writer's attitude and that by their connotations are meant to win the reader to the writer's side. Compare *freedom fighter* with *terrorist*, *pro-choice* with *pro-abortion*, or *pro-life* with *anti-choice*. *Freedom fighter, pro-choice*, and *pro-life* sound like good things; speakers who use these words are seeking to establish themselves as virtuous people who are supporting worthy causes. The **connotations** (associations, overtones) of these pairs of words differ, even though the **denotations** (explicit meanings, dictionary definitions) are the same, just as the connotations of *mother* and *female parent* differ, although the denotations are the same. Similarly, although Lincoln's "four score and seven" and "eighty-seven" both denote "thirteen less than one hundred," they differ in connotation.

Tone is not only a matter of connotations (*hounded out of office*, versus, let's say, *compelled to resign*, or *pro-choice* versus *pro-abortion*); it is also a matter of such things as the selection and type of examples. A writer who offers many examples, especially ones drawn from ordinary life, conveys a persona different from that of a writer who offers no examples or only an occasional invented instance. The first of these probably is, one might say, friendlier, more down-to-earth.

Last Words on Tone   On the whole, in writing an argument it is advisable to be courteous, respectful of your topic, of your audience, and of people who hold views you are arguing against. It is rarely good for one's own intellectual development to regard as villains or fools persons who hold views different from one's own, especially if some of them are in the audience. Keep in mind the story of the two strangers on a train who, striking up a conversation, found that both were clergymen, though of different faiths. Then one said to the other, "Well, why shouldn't we be friends? After all, we both serve God, you in your way and I in His."

Complacency is all right when telling a joke but not when offering an argument:

- Recognize opposing views,
- Assume they are held in good faith,
- State them fairly (if you don't, you do a disservice not only to the opposition but to your own position because the perceptive reader will not take you seriously), and
- Be temperate in arguing your own position: "If I understand their view correctly . . ."; "It seems reasonable to conclude that . . ."; "Perhaps, then, we can agree that. . . ."

We, One, or I?

The use of *we* in the last sentence brings us to another point: May the first-person pronouns *I* and *we* be used? In this book, because two of us are writing, we often use *we* to mean the two authors. And we sometimes use *we* to mean the authors and the readers, as in phrases like the one that ends the previous paragraph. This shifting use of one word can be troublesome, but we hope (clearly the *we* here refers only to the authors) that we have avoided any ambiguity. But can, or should, or must, an individual use *we* instead of *I*? The short answer is no.

If you are simply speaking for yourself, use *I*. Attempts to avoid the first person singular by saying things like "This writer thinks . . . ," and "It is thought that . . . ," and "One thinks that . . . ," are far more irritating (and wordy) than the use of *I*. The so-called editorial *we* is as odd sounding in a student's argument as is the royal *we*. Mark Twain said that the only ones who can appropriately say *we* are kings, editors, and people with a tapeworm. And because one *one* leads to another, making the sentence sound (James Thurber's words) "like a trombone solo," it's best to admit that you are the author, and to use *I*. But of course, there is no need to preface every sentence with "I think." The reader knows that the essay is yours; just write it, using *I* when you must, but not needlessly.

Avoiding Sexist Language

Courtesy (as well as common sense) requires that you respect the feelings of your readers. Many people today find offensive the implicit sexism in the use of male pronouns to denote not only men but also women ("As the reader follows the argument, he will find . . ."). And sometimes the use of the male pronoun to denote all people is ridiculous: "An individual, no matter what his sex, . . ."

In most contexts there is no need to use gender-specific nouns or pronouns. One way to avoid using *he* when you mean any person is to use *he or she* (or *she or he*) instead of *he*, but the result is sometimes a bit cumbersome — although it is superior to the overly conspicuous *he/she* and to *s/he*.

Here are two simple ways to solve the problem:

- *Use the plural* ("As readers follow the argument, they will find . . ."), or
- *Recast the sentence* so that no pronoun is required ("Readers following the argument will find . . .").

Because *man* and *mankind* strike many readers as sexist when used in such expressions as "Man is a rational animal" and "Mankind has not yet solved this problem," consider using such words as *human being, person, people, humanity,* and *we*. (*Examples:* "Human beings are rational animals"; "We have not yet solved this problem.")

PEER REVIEW

Your instructor may suggest—or may even require—that you submit an early draft of your essay to a fellow student or small group of students for comment. Such a procedure benefits both author and readers: You get the responses of a reader and the student-reader gets experience in

---

A PEER REVIEW CHECKLIST FOR
A DRAFT OF AN ARGUMENT

Read the draft through, quickly. Then read it again, with the following questions in mind.

✓ Does the draft show promise of fulfilling the assignment?

✓ Looking at the essay as a whole, what thesis (main idea) is advanced?

✓ Are the needs of the audience kept in mind? For instance, do some words need to be defined? Is the evidence (for instance, the examples, and the testimony of authorities) clear and effective?

✓ Can you accept the assumptions? If not, why not?

✓ Is any obvious evidence (or counterevidence) overlooked?

✓ Is the writer proposing a solution? If so,
  ✓ Are other equally attractive solutions adequately examined?
  ✓ Has the writer overlooked some unattractive effects of the proposed solution?

✓ Looking at each paragraph separately,
  ✓ What is the basic point?
  ✓ How does each paragraph relate to the essay's main idea or to the previous paragraph?
  ✓ Should some paragraphs be deleted? Be divided into two or more paragraphs? Be combined? Be put elsewhere? (If you outline the essay by jotting down the gist of each paragraph, you will get help in answering these questions.)
  ✓ Is each sentence clearly related to the sentence that precedes and to the sentence that follows?
  ✓ Is each paragraph adequately developed? Are there sufficient details, perhaps brief supporting quotations from the text?
  ✓ Are the introductory and concluding paragraphs effective?

✓ What are the paper's chief strengths?

✓ Make at least two specific suggestions that you think will assist the author to improve the paper.

thinking about the problems of developing an argument, especially in thinking about such matters as the degree of detail that a writer needs to offer to a reader and the importance of keeping the organization evident to a reader.

A STUDENT'S ESSAY, FROM ROUGH NOTES TO FINAL VERSION

While we were revising this textbook, we asked the students in one of our classes to write a short essay (500–750 words) on some ethical problem that concerned them. Because this assignment was the first writing assignment in the course, we explained that a good way to get ideas is to ask oneself some questions, jot down responses, question those responses, and write freely for ten minutes or so, not worrying about contradictions. We invited our students to hand in their initial jottings along with the finished essay, so that we could get a sense of how they proceeded as writers. Not all of them chose to hand in their jottings, but we were greatly encouraged by those who did. What was encouraging was the confirmation of an old belief, the belief—we call it a fact—that students will hand in a thoughtful essay if before they prepare a final version they nag themselves, ask themselves *why* they think this or that, jot down their responses, and are not afraid to change their minds as they proceed.

Here are the first jottings of a student, Emily Andrews, who elected to write about whether to give money to street beggars. She simply put down ideas, one after the other.

Help the poor? Why do I (sometimes) do it?

I feel guilty, and think I should help them: poor, cold, hungry (but also some of them are thirsty for liquor, and will spend the money on liquor, not on food).

I also feel annoyed by them--most of them:

Where does the expression "the deserving poor" come from?

And "poor but honest"? Actually, that sounds a bit odd. Wouldn't "rich but honest" make more sense?

Why don't they work? Fellow with red beard, always by bus stop in front of florist's shop, always wants a handout. He is a regular, there all day every day, so I guess he is in a way "reliable," so why doesn't he put the same time in on a job?

Or why don't they get help? Don't they know they need it? They <u>must</u> know they need it.

Maybe that guy with the beard is just a con artist.
Maybe he makes more money by panhandling than he would
by working, and it's a lot easier!

Kinds of poor--how to classify??
    drunks, druggies, etc.
    mentally ill (maybe drunks belong here too)
    decent people who have had terrible luck

Why private charity?

Doesn't it make sense to say we (fortunate individuals)
should give something--an occasional handout--to people
who have had terrible luck? (I suppose some people
might say that there is no need for any of us to give
anything--the government takes care of the truly
needy--but I do believe in giving charity. A month ago
a friend of the family passed away, and the woman's
children suggested that people might want to make a donation in her name, to a shelter for battered women. I
know my parents made a donation.)

BUT how can I tell who is who, which are which? Which
of these people asking for "spare change" really need
(deserve???) help, and which are phonies? Impossible to
tell.

Possibilities:
    Give to no one
    Give to no one but make an annual donation, maybe to
    United Way
    Give a dollar to each person who asks. This would
    probably not cost me even a dollar a day
    Occasionally do without something--maybe a CD--or a
    meal in a restaurant--and give the money I save to
    people who seem worthy.

WORTHY? What am I saying? How can I, or anyone, tell?
The neat-looking guy who says he just lost his job may
be a phony, and the dirty bum--probably a drunk--may
desperately need food. (OK, so what if he spends the
money on liquor instead of food? At least he'll get a
little pleasure in life. No! It's not all right if he
spends it on drink.)

Other possibilities:
    Do some volunteer work?
    To tell the truth, I don't want to put in the time. I
    don't feel that guilty.

So what's the problem?

Is it, How I can help the very poor (handouts, or through an organization)? or

How I can feel less guilty about being lucky enough to be able to go to college, and to have a supportive family?

I can't quite bring myself to believe I should help every beggar who approaches, but I also can't bring myself to believe that I should do nothing, on the grounds that:
    a. it's probably their fault
    b. if they are deserving, they can get gov't help.
       No, I just can't believe that. Maybe some are too proud to look for government help, or don't know that they are entitled to it.

What to do?

On balance, it seems best to
    a. give to United Way
    b. maybe also give to an occasional individual, if I happen to be moved, without worrying about whether he or she is "deserving" (since it's probably impossible to know).

A day after making these notes Emily reviewed them, added a few points, and then made a very brief selection from them to serve as an outline for her first draft:

Opening para.: "poor but honest"? Deserve "spare change"?

Charity: private or through organizations?
        pros and cons
        guy at bus
        it wouldn't cost me much, but . . . better to give through organizations

Concluding para.: still feel guilty?
        maybe mention guy at bus again?

After writing and revising a draft, Emily Andrews submitted her essay to a fellow student for peer review. She then revised her work in light of the suggestions she received and in light of her own further thinking.

On the next page we give the final essay. If after reading the final version you reread the early jottings, you will notice that some of the jottings never made it into the final version. But without the jottings, the essay probably could not have been as interesting as it is. When the writer made the jottings, she was not so much putting down her ideas as *finding* ideas by the process of writing.

Emily Andrews
Professor Barnet
English 102
January 16, 2001

              Why I Don't Spare "Spare Change"

     "Poor but honest." "The deserving poor." I
don't know the origin of these quotations, but
they always come to mind when I think of "the
poor." But I also think of people who, perhaps
through alcohol or drugs, have ruined not only
their own lives but also the lives of others in
order to indulge in their own pleasure. Perhaps
alcoholism and drug addiction really are "diseases," as many people say, but my own feeling--
based, of course, not on any serious study--is
that most alcoholics and drug addicts can be
classified with the "undeserving poor." And that
is largely why I don't distribute spare change
to panhandlers.

     But surely among the street people there
are also some who can rightly be called "deserving." Deserving what? My spare change? Or simply
the government's assistance? It happens that I
have been brought up to believe that it is appropriate to make contributions to charity--
let's say a shelter for battered women--but if I
give some change to a panhandler, am I making a
contribution to charity and thereby helping
someone, or, on the contrary, am I perhaps simply encouraging someone not to get help? Or
maybe even worse, am I supporting a con artist?

     If one believes in the value of private
charity, one can give either to needy individu-

als or to charitable organizations. In giving
to a panhandler one may indeed be helping a
person who badly needs help, but one cannot be
certain that one is giving to a needy individual. In giving to an organization such as the
United Way, on the other hand, one can feel
that one's money is likely to be used wisely.
True, confronted by a beggar one may feel that
this particular unfortunate individual needs
help at this moment--a cup of coffee or a sand-
wich--and the need will not be met unless I put
my hand in my pocket right now. But I have come
to think that the beggars whom I encounter can
get along without my spare change, and indeed
perhaps they are actually better off for not
having money to buy liquor or drugs.

It happens that in my neighborhood I encounter few panhandlers. There is one fellow
who is always by the bus stop where I catch the
bus to the college, and I never give him anything precisely because he is always there. He
is such a regular that, I think, he ought to be
able to hold a regular job. Putting him aside,
I probably don't encounter more than three or
four beggars in a week. (I'm not counting
street musicians. These people seem quite able
to work for a living. If they see their "work"
as playing or singing, let persons who enjoy
their performances pay them. I do not consider
myself among their audience.) The truth of the
matter is that, since I meet so few beggars, I
could give each one a dollar and hardly feel
the loss. At most, I might go without seeing a

movie some week. But I know nothing about these people, and it's my impression--admittedly based on almost no evidence--that they simply prefer begging to working. I am not generalizing about street people, and certainly I am not talking about street people in the big urban centers. I am talking only about the people whom I actually encounter.

That's why I usually do not give "spare change," and I don't think I will in the future. These people will get along without me. Someone else will come up with money for their coffee or their liquor, or, at worst, they will just have to do without. I will continue to contribute occasionally to a charitable organization, not simply (I hope) to salve my conscience but because I believe that these organizations actually do good work. But I will not attempt to be a mini-charitable organization, distributing (probably to the unworthy) spare change.

Finally, here are a few comments about the essay:

- *The title is informative,* alerting the reader to the topic and the author's position. (By the way, the student told us that in her next-to-last draft the title was "Is It Right to Spare 'Spare Change'?" This title, like the revision, introduces the topic but not the author's position. The revised version seems to us to be more striking.)

- *The opening paragraph holds a reader's interest,* partly by alluding to the familiar phrase "the deserving poor" and partly by introducing the *un*familiar phrase "the *un*deserving poor." Notice, too, that this opening paragraph ends by clearly asserting the author's thesis. Of course, writers need not always announce their thesis early, but it is usually advisable to do so. Readers like to know where they are going.

- *The second paragraph* begins by voicing what probably is the reader's somewhat uneasy—perhaps even negative—response to the first paragraph. That is, *the writer has a sense of her audience;* she knows how her reader feels, and she takes account of the feeling.

- *The third paragraph clearly sets forth the alternatives.* A reader may disagree with the writer's attitude, but the alternatives seem to be stated fairly.

- *The last two paragraphs are more personal* than the earlier paragraphs. The writer, more or less having stated what she takes to be the facts, now is entitled to offer a highly personal response to them.

- *The final paragraph nicely wraps things up* by means of the words "spare change," which go back to the title and to the end of the first paragraph. The reader thus experiences a sensation of completeness. The essayist, of course, has not solved the problem for all of us for all time, but she presents a thoughtful argument and ends the essay effectively.

Exercise

In an essay of 500 words, state a claim and support it with evidence. Choose an issue in which you are genuinely interested and about which you already know something. You may want to interview a few experts and do some reading, but don't try to write a highly researched paper. Sample topics:

1. Students in laboratory courses should not be required to participate in the dissection of animals.
2. Washington, D.C., should be granted statehood.
3. Puerto Rico should be granted statehood.
4. Women should, in wartime, be exempted from serving in combat.
5. The annual Miss America contest is an insult to women.
6. The government should not offer financial support to the arts.
7. The chief fault of the curriculum in high school was . . .
8. Grades should be abolished in college and university courses.
9. No specific courses should be required in colleges or universities.

6

Using Sources

WHY USE SOURCES?

We have pointed out that one gets ideas by writing. In the exercise of writing a draft, ideas begin to form, and these ideas stimulate further ideas, especially when one questions—when one *thinks* about—what one has written. But of course in writing about complex, serious questions, nobody is expected to invent all the answers. On the contrary, a writer is expected to be familiar with the chief answers already produced by others and to make use of them through selective incorporation and criticism. In short, writers are not expected to reinvent the wheel; rather, they are expected to make good use of it and perhaps round it off a bit or replace a defective spoke. In order to think out your own views in writing, you are expected to do some preliminary research into the views of others.

We use the word *research* broadly. It need not require taking copious notes on everything written on your topic; rather, it can involve no more than familiarizing yourself with at least some of the chief responses to your topic. In one way or another, almost everyone does some research. If we are going to buy a car, we may read an issue or two of a magazine or visit a Web site that rates cars, or we may talk to a few people who own models that we are thinking of buying, and then we visit a couple of dealers to find out who is offering the best price.

Research, in short, is not an activity conducted only by college professors or by students who visit the library in order to write research papers. It is an activity that all of us engage in to some degree. In writing a research paper, you will engage in it to a great degree. But doing research is not the whole of a research paper. The reader expects the writer to have *thought* about the research and to develop an argument based on the findings. Many businesses today devote an entire section to research and development. That's what is needed in writing, too. The reader wants not only a lot of facts but also a developed idea, a point to which the facts lead. Don't let your reader say of your paper what Gertrude Stein said of Oakland, California: "When you get there, there isn't any there there."

Consider arguments about whether athletes should be permitted to take anabolic steroids, drugs that supposedly build up muscle, restore energy, and enhance aggressiveness. A thoughtful argument on this subject will have to take account of information that the writer can gather only by doing some research. Do steroids really have the effects commonly attributed to them? And are they dangerous? If they are dangerous, how dangerous are they? (After all, competitive sports are inherently dangerous, some of them highly so. Many boxers, jockeys, and football players have suffered severe injury, even death, from competing. Does anyone believe that anabolic steroids are more dangerous than the contests themselves?) Obviously, again, a respectable argument about steroids will have to show awareness of what is known about them.

Or take this question: Why did President Truman order that atomic bombs be dropped on Hiroshima and Nagasaki? The most obvious answer is to end the war, but some historians believe he had a very different purpose. In their view, Japan's defeat was ensured before the bombs were dropped, and the Japanese were ready to surrender; the bombs were dropped not to save American (or Japanese) lives but to show Russia that we were not to be pushed around. Scholars who hold this view, such as Gar Alperovitz in *Atomic Diplomacy,* argue that Japanese civilians in Hiroshima and Nagasaki were incinerated not to save the lives of American soldiers who otherwise would have died in an invasion of Japan but to teach Stalin a lesson. Dropping the bombs, it is argued, marked not the end of the Pacific War but the beginning of the Cold War.

One must ask: What evidence supports this argument or claim or thesis, which assumes that Truman could not have thought the bomb was needed to defeat the Japanese because the Japanese knew they were defeated and would soon surrender without a hard-fought defense that would cost hundreds of thousands of lives? What about the momentum that had built up to use the bomb? After all, years of effort and $2 billion had been expended to produce a weapon with the intention of using it to end the war against Germany. But Germany had been defeated without the use of the bomb. Meanwhile, the war in the Pacific continued unabated. If the argument we are considering is correct, all this background counted for little or nothing in Truman's decision, a decision purely diplomatic and coolly indifferent to human life. The task for the writer is to evaluate the evidence available and then to argue for or against the view that Truman's purpose in dropping the bomb was to impress the Soviet government.

A student writing on the topic will certainly want to read the chief books on the subject (Alperovitz's, cited above, Martin Sherwin's *A World Destroyed,* and John Toland's *The Rising Sun*) and perhaps reviews of them, especially the reviews in journals devoted to political science. (Reading a searching review of a serious scholarly book is a good way to identify quickly some of the book's main contributions and controversial claims.) Truman's letters and statements and books and articles about Truman are also clearly relevant, and doubtless important articles are to be found in recent issues of scholarly journals and electronic sources. In fact, even an essay on such a topic as whether Truman was morally justified in using the atomic bomb for *any* purpose will be a stronger essay if it is well informed about such matters as the estimated loss of life that an invasion would have cost, the international rules governing weapons, and Truman's own statements about the issue.

How does one go about finding the material needed to write a well-informed argument? We will provide help, but first we want to offer a few words about choosing a topic.

CHOOSING A TOPIC

We will be brief. If a topic is not assigned, choose one that

- Interests you and
- Can be researched with reasonable thoroughness in the allotted time.

Topics such as censorship, the environment, and sexual harassment obviously impinge on our lives, and it may well be that one such topic is of especial interest to you. But the scope of these topics makes researching them potentially overwhelming. Type the word *censorship* into an **Internet** search engine, and you will be referred to thousands of information sources.

This brings us to our second point—a compassable topic. Any of the topics above would need to be narrowed substantially before you could begin searching in earnest. Similarly, a topic such as the causes of World War II can hardly be mastered in a few weeks or argued in a ten-page paper. It is simply too big.

You can, however, write a solid paper analyzing, evaluating, and arguing for or against General Eisenhower's views on atomic warfare. What were they, and when did he hold them? (In his books of 1948 and 1963 Eisenhower says that he opposed the use of the bomb before Hiroshima and that he argued with Secretary of War Henry Stimson against dropping it, but what evidence supports these claims? Was Eisenhower attempting to rewrite history in his books?) Eisenhower's own writings and books and other information sources on Eisenhower will, of course, be the major sources for a paper on this topic, but you will also want to look at books and articles about Stimson and at publications that contain information about the views of other generals, so that, for instance, you can compare Eisenhower's view with Marshall's or MacArthur's.

Your instructor understands that you are not going to spend a year writing a 200-page book, but you should understand that you must do more than consult a single Web site on Eisenhower and the article on atomic energy in an encyclopedia.

FINDING MATERIAL

Your sources will, of course, depend on your topic. Some topics will require no more than a trip to the library or an afternoon spent at your personal computer, but others may require interviews. If you are writing about some aspect of AIDS, for instance, you probably will find it useful to consult your college or community health center.

For facts, you ought to try to consult experts—for instance, members of the faculty or other local authorities on art, business, law, and so forth; for opinions and attitudes, you will usually consult interested laypersons. Remember, however, that experts have their biases and that "ordinary" people may have knowledge that experts lack. When interviewing experts, keep in mind Picasso's comment: "You musn't always believe what I say. Questions tempt you to tell lies, particularly when there is no answer."

INTERVIEWING PEERS
AND LOCAL AUTHORITIES

If you are interviewing your peers, you will probably want to make an effort to get a representative sample. Of course, even within a group not all members share a single view—many African Americans favor affirmative action but not all do, and many gays favor legalizing gay marriage but, again, some don't. Make an effort to talk to a range of people who might be expected to offer varied opinions. You may learn some unexpected things.

Here we will concentrate, however, on interviews with experts.

1. **Finding subjects for interviews**   If you are looking for expert opinions, you may want to start with a faculty member on your campus. You may already know the instructor, or you may have to scan the catalog to see who teaches courses relevant to your topic. Department secretaries and college Web sites are good sources of information about the special interests of the faculty and also about lecturers who will be visiting the campus.

2. **Doing preliminary homework** (1) Know something about the person whom you will be interviewing. Biographical reference works such as *Who's Who in America, Who's Who among Black Americans, Who's Who of American Women,* and *Directory of American Scholars* may include your interviewee, or, again, a departmental secretary may be able to provide a vita for a faculty member. (2) In requesting the interview, make evident your interest in the topic and in the person. (If you know something about the person, you will be able to indicate why you are asking him or her.) (3) Request the interview, preferably in writing, a week in advance, and ask for ample time — probably half an hour to an hour. Indicate whether or not the material will be confidential, and (if you want to use a recorder) ask if you may record the interview. (4) If the person accepts the invitation, ask if he or she recommends any preliminary reading, and establish a time and a suitable place, preferably not the cafeteria during lunchtime.

3. **Preparing thoroughly** (1) If your interviewee recommended any reading or has written on the topic, read the material. (2) Tentatively formulate some questions, keeping in mind that (unless you are simply gathering material for a survey of opinions) you want more than yes or no answers. Questions beginning with *Why* and *How* will usually require the interviewee to go beyond yes and no.

Even if your subject has consented to let you bring a recorder, be prepared to take notes on points that strike you as especially significant; without written notes, you will have nothing if the recorder has malfunctioned. Further, by taking occasional notes you will give the interviewee some time to think and perhaps to rephrase or to amplify a remark.

4. **Conducting the interview** (1) Begin by engaging in brief conversation, without taking notes. If the interviewee has agreed to let you use a recorder, settle on the place where you will put it. (2) Come prepared with an opening question or two, but as the interview proceeds, don't hesitate to ask questions that you had not anticipated asking. (3) Near the end — you and your subject have probably agreed on the length of the interview — ask the subject if he or she wishes to add anything, perhaps by way of clarifying some earlier comment. (4) Conclude by thanking the interviewee and by offering to provide a copy of the final version of your paper.

5. **Writing up the interview** (1) As soon as possible — certainly within twenty-four hours after the interview — review your notes and clarify them. At this stage, you can still remember the meaning of your abbreviated notes and shorthand devices (maybe you have been using *n* to stand for *nurses* in clinics where abortions are performed), but if you wait even a whole day you may be puzzled by your own notes. If you have recorded the interview, you may want to transcribe all of it — the laboriousness of this task is one good reason why many interviewers do not use recorders — and you may then want to scan the whole and mark the parts that now strike you as especially significant. If you have

taken notes by hand, type them up, along with your own observations, for example, "Jones was very tentative on this matter, but she said she was inclined to believe that. . . ." (2) Be especially careful to indicate which words are direct quotations. If in doubt, check with the interviewee.

USING THE LIBRARY

Most topics, as we have said, will require research in the library. Notice that we have spoken of a topic, not of a thesis or even of a *hypothesis* (tentative thesis). Advanced students, because they are familiar with the rudiments of a subject (say, the origins of the Cold War) usually have not only a topic but also a hypothesis or even a thesis in mind. Less experienced students are not always in this happy position: Before they can offer a hypothesis, they have to find a problem. Some instructors assign topics; others rely on students to find their own topics, based on readings in the course or in other courses.

When you have a *topic* ("Eisenhower and the atomic bomb") and perhaps a *thesis* (an attitude toward the topic, a claim that you want to argue, such as "Eisenhower's disapproval of the bomb was the product of the gentleman-soldier code that he had learned at West Point"), it is often useful to scan a relevant book. You may already know of a relevant book, and it is likely in turn to cite others. If, however, you don't know of any book, you can find one by consulting the catalog in the library, which lists books not only by author and by title but also by subject. There are many computerized cataloguing systems; your librarian can teach you how to use the one in your college or university library.

If there are many books on the topic, how do you choose just one? Choose first a fairly thin one, of fairly recent date, published by a reputable publisher. You may even want to jot down two or three titles and then check reviews of these books before choosing one book to skim. Your college or university library may subscribe to *Books in Print with Reviews,* an electronic database that contains citations and the full text of book reviews from several reliable journals and magazines. Many other more specialized databases exist for scholarly book reviews, or you might find one of these print indexes helpful:

Book Review Digest (1905–)

Book Review Index (1965–)

Humanities Index (1974–)

Index to Book Reviews in the Humanities (1960–)

Social Sciences Index (1974–)

Book Review Digest includes brief extracts from the reviews, and so look there first, but its coverage is not as broad as the other indexes.

Skimming a recent academic book is a good way to get an overview of a topic, and it may help you to form a tentative thesis and focus your research further. But because the publication process takes a year or more, even a book with a publication date of this year may have been written at least a year earlier (and on some issues—for instance, regulations concerning cloning or censorship of the Internet—some of the information in the source may be outdated). Articles in academic journals, too, usually are written many months before they are published, but magazines and newspapers or their electronic equivalents can provide you with up-to-date information. Articles, whether in academic journals or in current magazines, have the further advantage of being short, so they are likely to be more focused than a book; they therefore may speak more directly to your tentative thesis.

To find articles in periodicals, begin with the computerized search tools that now are available in most college and university libraries. Two of the most popular search tools are *InfoTrac* and the *Readers' Guide to Periodical Literature*. Your library probably has at least one of these CD-ROM systems, each of which indexes hundreds of popular and semipopular magazines (like *Time* and *Scientific American*) and well-respected newspapers (like the *New York Times* and the *Washington Post*). If your topic is one in which there is wide public interest, these **databases** will point you toward many potential research sources. Using these systems is simply a matter of launching the appropriate software, typing in one or two keywords related to your topic, and perhaps narrowing the search with additional words if the database turns up more than a few references to the terms you enter.

Even better than *InfoTrac* and the *Readers' Guide*, however, are the many specialized academic indexes now available on CD-ROM. These indexes, which list scholarly books and articles in specialized academic journals, are up-to-date and therefore are among the most valued tools. To find articles in journals, consult the *Humanities Index* and the *MLA International Bibliography* for topics in the humanities; for topics in psychology and other social sciences, consult *PsycLit* and the *Social Science Index*. Your college librarian can guide you to indexes for engineering and hard sciences, business and industry, education, the arts, or whatever field you are working in. Some of these indexes (such as the popular education index *ERIC* and the *Newspaper Abstracts*) not only provide bibliographic information but also include abstracts, or short summaries, of the articles they index or even the full text of the printed article. Which search tools you use will depend both on your topic and on what is available in your library. All of the major systems are designed to be easy to use, but if you experience difficulty, don't hesitate to ask the librarian for advice about which system to use and how to use it.

Annual print versions of many of these bibliographies and indexes also exist. If you prefer to use a print document or if your library doesn't have the CD-ROM database you need, ask your librarian for advice about using a more traditional search method.

FINDING INFORMATION ONLINE

If you have an Internet connection, you don't have to go any further than your personal computer to access a wealth of information for your research paper. This information may come from a number of online sources, including text archives, listservs (e-mail discussion groups), and Usenet newsgroups. But unless you already know of a particular source for your paper, the best place to begin an Internet search is with the **World Wide Web**. In addition, a good Web site will often, along with providing information, point to other on- and offline sources of related interest.

Dozens of search engines are available to help you start your research, some of the most popular being AltaVista, Lycos, Yahoo!, and Excite. If you do not already have a favorite, ask teachers, a librarian, or friends about their preferences, and experiment with several of them to find one you like. Most search engines give you two options for how to find relevant documents and information. The first is a keyword search in which you type in a word or phrase and the engine scans the Net for documents containing that word or phrase. If your topic is highly focused and you have very specific search terms in mind, a keyword search may work well for you, but entering a broad topic like *affirmative action* or *euthanasia* will result in thousands of hits, many of them of little value to you. The other type of search is topic based. This allows you to select from a menu of broad topic areas, such as *government* or *entertainment,* and narrow the topic through a series of menus until you reach a more specific topic, like *divorce law* or *television violence.* Many search engines select the references that appear under their topic searches, filtering out those whose content is particularly suspect.

We have two words of caution if you plan to use the Internet for serious research. First, the early stages of your research may take longer than planned. The Net is huge, fast-changing, and chaotic, and navigating it is not easy. Computer systems crash, Web pages move or disappear altogether, and the discourse surrounding a controversial topic like censorship or abortion can change overnight. Second, remember that the Net is highly democratic; anyone who can get online can express an opinion. The advantage is that knowledgeable people can offer information quickly, but the disadvantage is that careless scholars, blowhards, and liars can shed misinformation. It is always important for researchers to evaluate their sources, but evaluation is especially important when the source is online.

EVALUATING SOURCES

Finding a source of information related to your topic is not sufficient; you must be sure that the source is both valid and appropriate for your purposes. A quick evaluation of your sources before you begin carefully reading and taking notes on them may save you an enormous amount of time and frustration. Skim each source quickly, and keep the following in mind as you skim.

A recent book or article is usually preferable to an older one. Not only should your information be as up-to-date as possible, but recent works often effectively summarize previous research. (An exception to the rule "newer is better" would be if you have chosen an older work for a specific purpose, such as to compare it to more recent work to demonstrate changing attitudes.) In the case of Internet sources, sites will often indicate when they were last updated; if the one you use doesn't, you have no way of knowing reliably how fresh the information is.

As far as possible, try to determine the credibility of the author. The

---

A CHECKLIST FOR EVALUATING SOURCES

For Books (also useful for CD-ROMs and published databases):

✓ Is the book recent? If not, is the information you will be using from it likely or unlikely to change over time?

✓ How credible is the author?

✓ Is the book published by a respectable press?

✓ Is the book broad enough in its focus and written in a style you can understand?

✓ Does the book relate directly to your tentative thesis, or is it of only tangential interest?

✓ Do the arguments in the book seem sound, based on what you have learned about skillful critical reading and writing?

For Articles from Periodicals:

✓ Is the periodical recent?

✓ Is the author's name given? Does he or she seem a credible source?

✓ Is the periodical respectable and serious?

✓ How directly does the article speak to your topic and tentative thesis?

✓ If the article is from a scholarly journal, are you sure you understand it?

For Internet Sources:

✓ How up-to-date is the site?

✓ Is there an author listed for the site or document?

✓ Is the information associated with a reliable host site?

✓ Does the site rely on substance—or on flash alone?

author's credentials are often briefly described on the book jacket or at the back of the book; these may reveal if the author is indeed an expert in the field, and even his or her possible biases about the topic. But what if the work is anonymous, as many newspaper articles and Internet sources are? Anonymous articles are not necessarily bad sources, but approach them with a bit of caution; why might an author not have put his or her name on a piece?

You will also want to determine the credibility of the publisher (especially in the case of anonymous works). Though publisher credibility may be difficult for you to judge, you can usually trust large, nationally recognized companies and presses associated with universities more than smaller, less well-known publishers. (If you have doubts, ask your instructor or librarian about a particular publisher.) Remember that academic journals tend to be more respectable than popular magazines and that among magazines a hierarchy exists; an article from *Newsweek* usually is more credible than one from *People*. A similar hierarchy exists for newspapers: the *Washington Post* is powerfully credible, while tabloids such as the *Midnight Globe* are not. With online sources you often can tell, either from the document itself or from a close look at the Internet address, if a Web site, archive, or other source is associated with a reliable institution, such as a university, library, or government agency. While this does not guarantee accuracy, it does help to establish the credibility of the information. A final word about Internet sources: Don't let a flashy, expensive-looking Web site distract you from thinking critically about the site's content. While graphics, fancy fonts, audio and video clips, and the like can enhance a good site, a reliable source must offer more than a good show.

If you were researching a paper on reform of divorce law, for instance, how would you evaluate the Web site on page 228? Both the text and graphics for this Web site suggest immediately that it is not a scholarly source but the Internet equivalent of a popular magazine. The colors are bright, and there are ads for matchmaking services and links to "professionals and products." It is, in short, a commercial venture, designed to provide people in the process of divorce with advice and support while, not incidentally, making some money for the advertisers and sponsors of the site.

Does this mean the site is unreliable and will be useless for your paper? Not necessarily. There may well be hidden nuggets here that could enrich your paper, perhaps recent statistics on numbers of divorces or a pertinent quotation from someone engaged in the process of divorce. It does, however, mean that you must exercise caution if you choose to cite this information. At the very least, your paper will need to acknowledge the nature of your information source, so that your readers will know up front the potential bias of the site. Certainly you would want the paper to include information from some more scholarly sources as well.

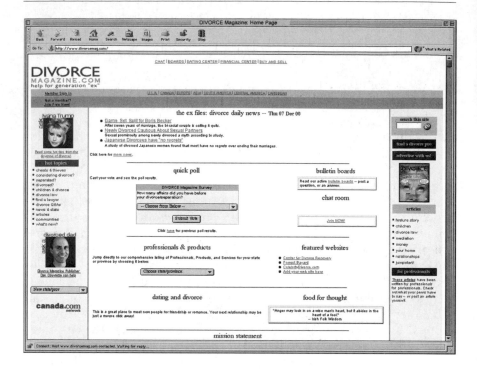

TAKING NOTES

When it comes to taking notes, all researchers have their own habits that they swear by, and they can't imagine any other way of working. We still prefer to take notes on four- by six-inch index cards, while others use a notebook or a computer for note-taking. Whatever method you use, the following techniques should help you maintain consistency and keep organized during the research process:

1. If you use a notebook or cards, write in ink (pencil gets smudgy), and write on only one side of the card or paper. (Notes on the backs of cards tend to get lost, and writing on the back of paper will prevent you from later cutting up and rearranging your notes.)
2. Put only one idea in each notebook or computer entry or on each card (though an idea may include several facts).
3. Put a brief heading on each entry or card, such as "Truman's last words on A-bomb."
4. Summarize, for the most part, rather than quote at length.
5. Quote only passages in which the writing is especially effective, or passages that are in some way crucial.
6. Make sure that all quotations are exact. Enclose quoted words within quotation marks, indicate omissions by ellipses (three

spaced periods: . . .), and enclose within square brackets ([ ]) any insertions or other additions you make.

7. *Never* copy a passage, changing an occasional word. *Either* copy it word for word, with punctuation intact, and enclose it within quotation marks, *or* summarize it drastically. If you copy a passage but change a word here and there, you may later make the mistake of using your note verbatim in your essay, and you will be guilty of plagiarism.

8. Give the page number of your source, whether you summarize or quote. If a quotation you have copied runs in the original from the bottom of page 210 to the top of page 211, in your notes put a diagonal line (/) after the last word on page 210, so that later, if in your paper you quote only the material from page 210, you will know that you must cite 210 and not 210–11.

9. Indicate the source. The author's last name is enough if you have consulted only one work by the author; but if you consult more than one work by an author, you need further identification, such as the author's name and a short title.

10. Add your own comments about the substance of what you are recording. Such comments as "but contrast with Sherwin" or "seems illogical" or "evidence?" will ensure that you are thinking as well as writing and will be of value when you come to transform your notes into a draft. Be sure, however, to enclose such notes within double diagonals (//), or to mark them in some other way, so that later you will know they are yours and not your source's. If you use a computer for note taking, you may wish to write your comments in italics or in a different font.

11. In a separate computer file or notebook page or on separate index cards, write a bibliographic entry for each source. The information in each entry will vary, depending on whether the source is a book, a periodical, an electronic document, and so forth. The kind of information (for example, author and title) needed for each type of source can be found in the sections on MLA Format: The List of Works Cited (p. 244) or APA Format: The List of References (p. 255).

A WORD ABOUT PLAGIARISM

Plagiarism is the unacknowledged use of someone else's work. The word comes from a Latin word for "kidnapping," and plagiarism is indeed the stealing of something engendered by someone else. We won't deliver a sermon on the dishonesty (and folly) of plagiarism; we intend only to help you understand exactly what plagiarism is. The first thing to say is that plagiarism is not limited to the unacknowledged quotation of words.

A *paraphrase* is a sort of word-by-word or phrase-by-phrase translation of the author's language into your language. True, if you paraphrase you are using your own words, but you are also using someone else's ideas, and, equally important, you are using this other person's sequence of thoughts. Even if you change every third word in your source, and you do not give the author credit, you are plagiarizing. Here is an example of this sort of plagiarism, based on the previous sentence:

> Even if you alter every third or fourth word from your source, and you fail to give credit to the author, you will be guilty of plagiarism.

Even if the writer of this paraphrase had cited a source after it, the writer would still be guilty of plagiarism because the passage borrows not only the idea but the shape of the presentation, the sentence structure. The writer of this passage hasn't really written anything; he or she has only adapted something. What the writer needs to do is to write something like this:

> Changing an occasional word does not free the writer from the obligation to cite a source.

And the source would still need to be cited, if the central idea were not a commonplace one.

You are plagiarizing if without giving credit you use someone else's ideas—even if you put these ideas entirely into your own words. When you use another's ideas, you must indicate your indebtedness by saying something like "Alperovitz points out that . . ." or "Secretary of War Stimson, as Martin Sherwin notes, never expressed himself on this point." Alperovitz and Sherwin pointed out something that you had not thought of, and so you must give them credit if you want to use their findings.

Again, even if after a paraphrase you cite your source, you are plagiarizing. How, you may wonder, can you be guilty of plagiarism if you cite a source? Easy. A reader assumes that the citation refers to information or an opinion, *not* to the presentation or development of the idea; and of course, in a paraphrase you are not presenting or developing the material in your own way.

Now consider this question: *Why* paraphrase? Often there is no good answer. Since a paraphrase is as long as the original, you may as well quote the original, if you think that a passage of that length is worth quoting. Probably it is *not* worth quoting in full; probably you should *not* paraphrase but rather should drastically *summarize* most of it, and perhaps quote a particularly effective phrase or two. As we explained on pages 32–34, the chief reason to paraphrase a passage is to clarify it—that is, to make certain that you and your readers understand a passage that— perhaps because it is badly written—is obscure.

Generally what you should do is to take the idea and put it entirely into your own words, perhaps reducing a paragraph of a hundred words to a sentence of ten words, but you must still give credit for the idea. If you believe that the original hundred words are so perfectly put that they cannot be transformed without great loss, you'll have to quote them and cite your source. But clearly there is no point in paraphrasing the author's hundred words into a hundred of your own. Either quote or summarize, but cite the source.

Keep in mind, too, that almost all generalizations about human nature, no matter how common and familiar (for instance, "males are innately more aggressive than females") are not indisputable facts; they are at best hypotheses on which people differ and therefore should either not be asserted at all or should be supported by some cited source or authority. Similarly, because nearly all statistics (whether on the intelligence of criminals or the accuracy of lie detectors) are the result of some particular research and may well have been superseded or challenged by other investigators, it is advisable to cite a source for any statistics you use unless you are convinced they are indisputable, such as the number of registered voters in Memphis in 1988.

On the other hand, there is something called **common knowledge,** and the sources for such information need not be cited. The term does not, however, mean exactly what it seems to. It is common knowledge, of course, that Ronald Reagan was an American president (so you don't cite a source when you make that statement), and under the conventional interpretation of this doctrine, it is also common knowledge that he was born in 1911. In fact, of course, few people other than Reagan's wife and children know this date. Still, information that can be found in many places and that is indisputable belongs to all of us; therefore, a writer need not cite her source when she says that Reagan was born in 1911. Probably she checked a dictionary or an encyclopedia for the date, but the source doesn't matter. Dozens of sources will give exactly the same information, and in fact, no reader wants to be bothered with a citation on such a point.

Some students have a little trouble developing a sense of what is and what is not common knowledge. Although, as we have just said, readers don't want to hear about the sources for information that is indisputable and can be documented in many places, if you are in doubt about whether to cite a source, cite it. Better risk boring the reader a bit than risk being accused of plagiarism.

COMPILING AN
ANNOTATED BIBLIOGRAPHY

When several sources have been identified and gathered, many researchers prepare an annotated bibliography. This is a list providing all

relevant bibliographic information (just as it will appear in your Works
Cited list or References list) as well as a brief descriptive and evaluative
summary of each source—perhaps one to three sentences. Your instructor may ask you to provide an annotated bibliography for your research
project.

An annotated bibliography serves three main purposes. First, constructing such a document helps you to master the material contained in
any given source. To find the heart of the argument presented in an article or book, phrase it briefly, and comment on it, you must understand
it fully. Second, creating an annotated bibliography helps you to think
about how each portion of your research fits into the whole of your
project, how you will use it, and how it relates to your topic and thesis.
Finally, in constructing an annotated bibliography at this early stage, you
will get some hands-on practice at bibliographic format, thereby easing
the job of creating your final bibliography (the Works Cited list or References list for your paper).

Below are two examples of entries for an annotated bibliography in
MLA (Modern Language Association) format for a project on the effect
of violence in the media. The first is for a book, the second for an article
from a periodical. Notice that each

- Begins with a bibliographic entry—author (last name first), title,
  and so forth—and then
- Provides information about the content of the work under consideration, suggesting how each may be of use to the final research
  paper.

Clover, Carol J. Men, Women, and Chain Saws: Gender in
    the Modern Horror Film. Princeton: Princeton UP,
    1992. The author focuses on Hollywood horror
    movies of the 1970s and 1980s. She studies repre-
    sentations of women and girls in these movies and
    the responses of male viewers to female charac-
    ters, suggesting that this relationship is more
    complex and less exploitative than the common wis-
    dom claims.

Winerip, Michael. "Looking for an Eleven O'Clock Fix."
    New York Times Magazine 11 Jan. 1998: 30-40. The
    article focuses on the rising levels of violence
    on local television news and highlights a station
    in Orlando, Florida, that tried to reduce its de-
    pictions of violence and lost viewers as a result.
    Winerip suggests that people only claim to be

against media violence, while their actions prove
otherwise.

WRITING THE PAPER

Organizing Your Notes

If you have read thoughtfully, taken careful (and, again, thoughtful) notes on your reading, and then (yet again) thought about these notes, you are well on the way to writing a good paper. You have, in fact, already written some of it, in your notes. By now you should clearly have in mind the thesis you intend to argue. But you still have to organize the material, and, doubtless, even as you set about organizing it, you will find points that will require you to do some additional research and much additional thinking.

Divide your notes into clusters, each devoted to one theme or point (for instance, one cluster on the extent of use of steroids, another on evidence that steroids are harmful, yet another on arguments that even if harmful they should be permitted). If your notes are in a computer file, use your word processor's cut and paste features to rearrange the notes into appropriate clusters. If you use index cards, simply sort them into packets. If you take notes in a notebook, either mark each note with a number or name indicating the cluster to which it belongs, or cut the notes apart and arrange them as you would cards. Put aside all notes that—however interesting—you now see are irrelevant to your paper.

Next, arrange the clusters or packets into a tentative sequence. In effect, you are preparing a **working outline.** At its simplest, say, you will give three arguments on behalf of *X* and then three counterarguments. (Or you might decide that it is better to alternate material from the two sets of three clusters each, following each argument with an objection. At this stage, you can't be sure of the organization you will finally use, but make a tentative decision.)

The First Draft

Draft the essay, without worrying much about an elegant opening paragraph. Just write some sort of adequate opening that states the topic and your thesis. When you revise the whole later, you can put some effort into developing an effective opening. (Most experienced writers find that the opening paragraph in the final version is almost the last thing they write.)

If your notes are on cards or notebook paper, carefully copy into the draft all quotations that you plan to use. If your notes are in a computer, you may simply cut and paste them from one file to another. Do keep in mind, however, that rewriting or retyping quotations will make you think carefully about them and may result in a more focused and thoughtful paper. (In the next section of this chapter we will talk briefly about leading into quotations and about the form of quotations.) Be sure to include citations in your drafts so that if you must check a reference later it will be easy to do so.

Later Drafts

Give the draft, and yourself, a rest—perhaps for a day or two—and then go back to it. Read it over, make necessary revisions, and then **outline** it. That is, on a sheet of paper chart the organization and development, perhaps by jotting down a sentence summarizing each paragraph or each group of closely related paragraphs. Your outline or map may now show you that the paper obviously suffers from poor organization. For instance, it may reveal that you neglected to respond to one argument or that one point is needlessly treated in two places. It may also help you to see that if you gave three arguments and then three counterarguments, you probably should instead have followed each argument with its rebuttal. On the other hand, if you alternated arguments and objections, it may now seem better to use two main groups, all the arguments and then all the criticisms.

No one formula is always right. Much will depend on the complexity of the material. If the arguments are highly complex, it is better to respond to them one by one than to expect a reader to hold three complex arguments in mind before you get around to responding. If, however, the arguments can be stated briefly and clearly, it is effective to state all three and then to go on to the responses. If you write on a word processor, you will find it easy, even fun, to move passages of text around. Even so, you will probably want to print out a hard copy from time to time to review the structure of your paper. Allow enough time to produce several drafts.

A few more words about organization: There is a difference between

- A paper that *has* an organization and
- A paper that helpfully lets the reader know what the organization is.

Write papers of the second sort, but (there is always a "but") take care not to belabor the obvious. Inexperienced writers sometimes either hide the organization so thoroughly that a reader cannot find it, or, on the other hand, they so ploddingly lay out the structure ("Eighth, I will show . . .") that the reader becomes impatient. Yet it is better to be overly explicit than to be obscure.

The ideal, of course, is the middle route. Make the overall strategy of your organization evident by occasional explicit signs at the beginning of a paragraph ("We have seen . . . ," "It is time to consider the objections. . . ," "By far the most important . . ."); elsewhere make certain that the implicit structure is evident to the reader. When you reread your draft, if you try to imagine that you are one of your classmates, you will probably be able to sense exactly where explicit signs are needed and where they are not needed. Better still, exchange drafts with a classmate in order to exchange (tactful) advice.

Choosing a Tentative Title

By now a couple of tentative titles for your essay should have crossed your mind. If possible, choose a title that is both interesting and informative. Consider these three titles:

```
Are Steroids Harmful?
The Fuss over Steroids
Steroids: A Dangerous Game
```

"Are Steroids Harmful?" is faintly interesting, and it lets the reader know the gist of the subject, but it gives no clue about the writer's thesis, the writer's contention or argument. "The Fuss over Steroids" is somewhat better, for it gives information about the writer's position. "Steroids: A Dangerous Game" is still better; it announces the subject ("steroids") and the thesis ("dangerous"), and it also displays a touch of wit because "game" glances at the world of athletics.

Don't try too hard, however; better a simple, direct, informative title than a strained, puzzling, or overly cute one. And remember to make sure that everything in your essay is relevant to your title. In fact, your title should help you to organize the essay and to delete irrelevant material.

The Final Draft

When at last you have a draft that is for the most part satisfactory, check to make sure that **transitions** from sentence to sentence and from paragraph to paragraph are clear ("Further evidence," "On the other hand," "A weakness, however, is apparent"), and then worry about your opening and your closing paragraphs. Your **opening paragraph** should be clear, interesting, and focused; if neither the title nor the first paragraph announces your thesis, the second paragraph probably should do so.

The **final paragraph** need not say, "In conclusion, I have shown that. . . ." It should effectively end the essay, but it need not summarize your conclusions. We have already offered a few words about final paragraphs (p. 204), but the best way to learn how to write such paragraphs is to study the endings of some of the essays in this book and to adopt the strategies that appeal to you.

Be sure that all indebtedness is properly acknowledged. We have talked about plagiarism; now we will turn to the business of introducing quotations effectively.

QUOTING FROM SOURCES

The Use and Abuse of Quotations

When is it necessary, or appropriate, to quote? Sometimes the reader must see the exact words of your source; the gist won't do. If you are arguing that Z's definition of *rights* is too inclusive, your readers have to know exactly how Z defined *rights*. Your brief summary of the definition may be unfair to Z; in fact, you want to convince your readers that you are being fair, and so you quote Z's definition, word for word. Moreover, if the passage is only a sentence or two long, or even if it runs to a paragraph, it may be so compactly stated that it defies summary. And to attempt to paraphrase it—substituting *natural* for *inalienable*, and so forth—saves no space and only introduces imprecision. There is nothing to do but to quote it, word for word.

Second, you may want to quote a passage that could be summarized but that is so effectively stated that you want your readers to have the pleasure of reading the original. Of course, readers will not give you credit for writing these words, but they will give you credit for your taste and for your effort to make especially pleasant the business of reading your paper.

In short, use (but don't overuse) quotations. Speaking roughly, quotations should occupy no more than 10 or 15 percent of your paper, and they may occupy much less. Most of your paper should set forth your ideas, not other people's ideas.

How to Quote

Long and Short Quotations   **Long quotations** (five or more lines of typed prose or three or more lines of poetry) are set off from your text. To set off material, start on a new line, indent one inch from the left margin, and type the quotation double-spaced. Do not enclose quotations within quotation marks if you are setting them off.

Short quotations are treated differently. They are embedded within the text; they are enclosed within quotation marks, but otherwise they do not stand out.

All quotations, whether set off or embedded, must be exact. If you omit any words, you must indicate the ellipsis by substituting three spaced periods for the omission; if you insert any words or punctuation, you must indicate the addition by enclosing it within square brackets, not to be confused with parentheses.

Leading into a Quotation   Now for a less mechanical matter, the way in which a quotation is introduced. To say that it is "introduced" implies that one leads into it, though on rare occasions a quotation appears without an introduction, perhaps immediately after the title. Normally one leads into a quotation by giving the name of the author and (no less important) clues about the content of the quotation and the purpose it serves in the present essay. For example:

> William James provides a clear answer to Huxley when he says that ". . ."

The writer has been writing about Huxley and now is signaling readers that they will be getting James's reply. The writer is also signaling (in "a clear answer") that the reply is satisfactory. If the writer believed that James's answer was not really acceptable, the lead-in might have run thus:

> William James attempts to answer Huxley, but his response does not really meet the difficulty Huxley calls attention to. James writes, ". . ."

or thus:

> William James provided what he took to be an answer to Huxley when he said that ". . ."

In this last example, clearly the words "what he took to be an answer" imply that the essayist will show, after the quotation from James, that the answer is in some degree inadequate. Or the essayist may wish to suggest the inadequacy even more strongly:

> William James provided what he took to be an answer to Huxley, but he used the word <u>religion</u> in a way that Huxley would not have allowed. James argues that ". . ."

If after reading something by Huxley the writer had merely given us "William James says . . . ," we wouldn't know whether we were getting confirmation, refutation, or something else. The essayist would have put a needless burden on the readers. Generally speaking, the more difficult the quotation, the more important is the introductory or explanatory lead-in, but even the simplest quotation profits from some sort of brief lead-in, such as "James reaffirms this point when he says . . ."

DOCUMENTATION

In the course of your essay, you will probably quote or summarize material derived from a source. You must give credit, and although there is no one form of documentation to which all scholarly fields subscribe, you will probably be asked to use one of two. One, established by the Modern Language Association (MLA), is used chiefly in the humanities;

the other, established by the American Psychological Association (APA), is used chiefly in the social sciences.

We include two papers that use sources. "Why Trials Should Not Be Televised" (p. 260) uses the MLA format. "The Role of Spirituality and Religion in Mental Health" (p. 277) follows the APA format. (You may notice that various styles are illustrated in other selections we have included.)

A Note on Footnotes (and Endnotes)

Before we discuss these two formats, a few words about footnotes are in order. Before the MLA and the APA developed their rules of style, citations commonly were given in footnotes. Although today footnotes are not so frequently used to give citations, they still may be useful for another purpose. (The MLA suggests endnotes rather than footnotes, but all readers know that, in fact, footnotes are preferable to endnotes. After all, who wants to keep shifting from a page of text to a page of notes at the rear?) If you want to include some material that may seem intrusive in the body of the paper, you may relegate it to a footnote. For example, in a footnote you might translate a quotation given in a foreign language, or you might demote from text to footnote a paragraph explaining why you are not taking account of such-and-such a point. By putting the matter in a footnote you are signaling the reader that it is dispensable; it is something relevant but not essential, something extra that you are, so to speak, tossing in. Don't make a habit of writing this sort of note, but there are times when it is appropriate.

MLA Format:
Citations within the Text

Brief citations within the body of the essay give credit, in a highly abbreviated way, to the sources for material you quote, summarize, or make use of in any other way. These *in-text citations* are made clear by a list of sources, titled Works Cited, appended to the essay. Thus, in your essay you may say something like this:

```
Commenting on the relative costs of capital punishment
and life imprisonment, Ernest van den Haag says that he
doubts "that capital punishment really is more expen-
sive" (33).
```

The **citation,** the number 33 in parentheses, means that the quoted words come from page 33 of a source (listed in the Works Cited) written by van den Haag. Without a Works Cited, a reader would have no way of knowing that you are quoting from page 33 of an article that appeared in the February 8, 1985, issue of the *National Review.*

Usually the parenthetic citation appears at the end of a sentence, as in the example just given, but it can appear elsewhere; its position will depend chiefly on your ear, your eye, and the context. You might, for example, write the sentence thus:

```
Ernest van den Haag doubts that "capital punishment
really is more expensive" than life imprisonment (33),
but other writers have presented figures that contra-
dict him.
```

Five points must be made about these examples:

1. **Quotation marks** The closing quotation mark appears after the last word of the quotation, *not* after the parenthetic citation. Since the citation is not part of the quotation, the citation is not included within the quotation marks.

2. **Omission of words (ellipsis)** If you are quoting a complete sentence or only a phrase, as in the examples given, you do not need to indicate (by three spaced periods) that you are omitting material before or after the quotation. But if for some reason you want to omit an interior part of the quotation, you must indicate the omission by inserting an *ellipsis,* the three spaced dots, enclosed in square brackets. To take a simple example, if you omit the word "really" from van den Haag's phrase, you must alert the reader to the omission:

```
Ernest van den Haag doubts that "capital punishment
[. . .] is more expensive" than life imprisonment (33).
```

Suppose you are quoting a sentence but wish to omit material from the end of the sentence. Suppose, also, that the quotation forms the end of your sentence. Write a lead-in phrase, quote what you need from your source, then type the bracketed ellipses for the omission, close the quotation, give the parenthetic citation, and finally type a fourth period to indicate the end of your sentence.

Here's an example. Suppose you want to quote the first part of a sentence that runs, "We could insist that the cost of capital punishment be reduced so as to diminish the differences." Your sentence would incorporate the desired extract as follows:

```
Van den Haag says, "We could insist that the cost of
capital punishment be reduced [. . .]" (33).
```

3. **Punctuation with parenthetic citations** In the preceding examples, the punctuation (a period or a comma in the examples) *follows* the citation. If, however, the quotation ends with a question mark, include the question mark *within* the quotation, since it is part of the quotation, and put a period *after* the citation:

```
Van den Haag asks, "Isn't it better--more just and
more useful--that criminals, if they do not have the
certainty of punishment, at least run the risk of suf-
fering it?" (35).
```

But if the question mark is your own and not in the source, put it after
the citation, thus:

```
What answer can be given to van den Haag's doubt that
"capital punishment really is more expensive" (33)?
```

4. **Two or more works by an author**   If your list of Works Cited
includes two or more works by an author, you cannot, in your essay,
simply cite a page number because the reader will not know which of
the works you are referring to. You must give additional information.
You can give it in your lead-in, thus:

```
In "New Arguments against Capital Punishment," van den
Haag expresses doubt "that capital punishment really is
more expensive" than life imprisonment (33).
```

Or you can give the title, in a shortened form, within the citation:

```
Van den Haag expresses doubt that "capital punishment
really is more expensive" than life imprisonment ("New
Arguments" 33).
```

5. **Citing even when you do not quote**   Even if you don't quote
a source directly, but use its point in a paraphrase or a summary, you
will give a citation:

```
Van den Haag thinks that life imprisonment costs more
than capital punishment (33).
```

Note that in all of the previous examples, the author's name is given in
the text (rather than within the parenthetic citation). But there are several other ways of giving the citation, and we shall look at them now.
(We have already seen, in the example given under paragraph 4, that
the title and the page number can be given within the citation.)

AUTHOR AND PAGE NUMBER IN PARENTHESES

```
It has been argued that life imprisonment is more
costly than capital punishment (van den Haag 33).
```

AUTHOR, TITLE, AND PAGE NUMBER IN PARENTHESES

We have seen that if the Works Cited list includes two or more
works by an author, you will have to give the title of the work on which

you are drawing, either in your lead-in phrase or within the parenthetic citation. Similarly, if you are citing someone who is listed more than once in the Works Cited, and for some reason you do not mention the name of the author or the work in your lead-in, you must add the information in your citation:

> Doubt has been expressed that capital punishment is as costly as life imprisonment (van den Haag, "New Arguments" 33).

A GOVERNMENT DOCUMENT OR A WORK OF CORPORATE AUTHORSHIP

Treat the issuing body as the author. Thus, you will write something like this:

> The Commission on Food Control, in Food Resources Today, concludes that there is no danger (37-38).

A WORK BY TWO OR MORE AUTHORS

If a work is by *two or three authors,* give the names of all authors, either in the parenthetic citation (the first example below) or in a lead-in (the second example below):

> There is not a single example of the phenomenon (Smith, Dale, and Jones 182-83).

> Smith, Dale, and Jones insist there is not a single example of the phenomenon (182-83).

If there are *more than three authors,* give the last name of the first author, followed by *et al.* (an abbreviation for *et alii,* Latin for "and others"), thus:

> Gittleman et al. argue (43) that . . .

or

> On average, the cost is even higher (Gittleman et al. 43).

PARENTHETIC CITATION OF AN INDIRECT SOURCE (CITATION OF MATERIAL THAT ITSELF WAS QUOTED OR SUMMARIZED IN YOUR SOURCE)

Suppose you are reading a book by Jones in which she quotes Smith and you wish to use Smith's material. Your citation must refer the reader to Jones—the source you are using—but of course, you cannot attribute the words to Jones. You will have to make it clear that you are quoting

Smith, and so after a lead-in phrase like "Smith says," followed by the quotation, you will give a parenthetic citation along these lines:

```
(qtd. in Jones 324-25).
```

PARENTHETIC CITATION OF TWO OR MORE WORKS

```
The costs are simply too high (Smith 301; Jones 28).
```

Notice that a semicolon, followed by a space, separates the two sources.

A WORK IN MORE THAN ONE VOLUME

This is a bit tricky. If you have used only one volume, in the Works Cited you will specify the volume, and so in the parenthetic in-text citation you will not need to specify the volume. All that you need to include in the citation is a page number, as illustrated by most of the examples that we have given.

If you have used more than one volume, your parenthetic citation will have to specify the volume as well as the page, thus:

```
Jackson points out that fewer than one hundred fifty
people fit this description (2: 351).
```

The reference is to page 351 in volume 2 of a work by Jackson.

If, however, you are citing not a page but an entire volume—let's say volume 2—your parenthetic citation will look like this:

```
Jackson exhaustively studies this problem (vol. 2).
```

or

```
Jackson (vol. 2) exhaustively studies this problem.
```

Notice the following points:

- In citing a volume and page, the volume number, like the page number, is given in arabic (not roman) numerals, even if the original used roman numerals to indicate the volume number.
- The volume number is followed by a colon, then a space, then the page number.
- If you cite a volume number without a page number, as in the last example quoted, the abbreviation is *vol.* Otherwise do *not* use such abbreviations as *vol.* and *p.* and *pg.*

AN ANONYMOUS WORK

For an anonymous work, give the title in your lead-in, or give it in a shortened form in your parenthetic citation:

A Prisoner's View of Killing includes a poll taken of
the inmates on death row (32).

or

A poll is available (Prisoner's View 32).

AN INTERVIEW

Probably you won't need a parenthetic citation because you'll say something like

Vivian Berger, in an interview, said . . .

or

According to Vivian Berger, in an interview . . .

and when your reader turns to the Works Cited, he or she will see that Berger is listed, along with the date of the interview. But if you do not mention the source's name in the lead-in, you will have to give it in the parentheses, thus:

Contrary to popular belief, the death penalty is not
reserved for serial killers and depraved murderers
(Berger).

AN ELECTRONIC SOURCE

Electronic sources, such as those found on CD-ROMs or the Internet, are generally not divided into pages. Therefore, the in-text citation for such sources cite the author's name (or, if a work is anonymous, the title) only:

According to the World Wide Web site for the American
Civil Liberties Union . . .

If the source does use pages or breaks down further into paragraphs or screens, insert the appropriate identifier or abbreviation (*p.* or *pp.* for page or pages; *par.* or *pars.* for paragraph or paragraphs; *screen* or *screens*) before the relevant number:

The growth of day care has been called "a crime against
posterity" by a spokesman for the Institute for the
American Family (Terwilliger, screens 1-2).

MLA Format:
The List of Works Cited

As the previous pages explain, parenthetic documentation consists of references that become clear when the reader consults the list titled Works Cited given at the end of an essay.

The list of Works Cited continues the pagination of the essay; if the last page of text is 10, then the Works Cited begins on its own page, in this case page 11. Type the page number in the upper right corner, a half inch from the top of the sheet and flush with the right margin. Next, type the heading Works Cited (*not* enclosed within quotation marks and not italic), centered, one inch from the top, and then double-space and type the first entry.

An Overview   Here are some general guidelines.

FORM ON THE PAGE

- Begin each entry flush with the left margin, but if an entry runs to more than one line, indent a half inch, for each succeeding line of the entry. This is known as a hanging indent, and most word processing programs can achieve this effect easily.
- Double-space each entry, and double-space between entries.
- Underline titles of works published independently—for instance, books, pamphlets, and journals. Enclose within quotation marks a work not published independently—for instance, an article in a journal, or a short story.
- If you are citing a book that includes the title of another book, underline the main title, but do *not* underline the title mentioned. Example:

    A Study of Mill's On Liberty

- In the sample entries below, pay attention to the use of commas, colons, and the space after punctuation.

ALPHABETIC ORDER

- Arrange the list alphabetically by author, with the author's last name first.
- For information about anonymous works, works with more than one author, and two or more works by one author, see below.

A Closer Look   Here is more detailed advice.

THE AUTHOR'S NAME

Notice that the last name is given first, but otherwise the name is given as on the title page. Do not substitute initials for names written out on the title page.

If your list includes two or more works by an author, do not repeat the author's name for the second title but represent it by three hyphens followed by a period. The sequence of the works is determined by the alphabetic order of the titles. Thus, Smith's book titled *Poverty* would be listed ahead of her book *Welfare*. See the example on page 246, listing two works by Roger Brown.

Anonymous works are listed under the first word of the title or the second word if the first is *A, An,* or *The* or a foreign equivalent. We discuss books by more than one author, government documents, and works of corporate authorship on pages 246–47.

THE TITLE

After the period following the author's name, allow one space and then give the title. Take the title from the title page, not from the cover or the spine, but disregard any unusual typography such as the use of all capital letters or the use of the ampersand (*&*) for *and*. Underline the title and subtitle (separate them by a colon) with one continuous underline to indicate italics, but do not underline the period that concludes this part of the entry.

- Capitalize the first word and the last word.
- Capitalize all nouns, pronouns, verbs, adjectives, adverbs, and subordinating conjunctions (for example, *although, if, because*).
- Do not capitalize (unless it's the first or last word of the title or the first word of the subtitle) articles (*a, an, the*), prepositions (for instance, *in, on, toward, under*), coordinating conjunctions (for instance, *and, but, or, for*), or the *to* in infinitives.

Examples:

The Death Penalty: A New View

On the Death Penalty: Toward a New View

On the Penalty of Death in a Democracy

PLACE OF PUBLICATION, PUBLISHER, AND DATE

For the place of publication, provide the name of the city; you can usually find it either on the title page or on the reverse of the title page. If a number of cities are listed, provide only the first. If the city is not likely to be known, or if it may be confused with another city of the same name (as is Oxford, Mississippi, with Oxford, England), add the name of the state, abbreviated using the two-letter postal code.

The name of the publisher is abbreviated. Usually the first word is enough (*Random House* becomes *Random*), but if the first word is a first name, such as in *Alfred A. Knopf*, the surname (*Knopf*) is used instead. University presses are abbreviated thus: *Yale UP, U of Chicago P, State U of New York P.*

The date of publication of a book is given when known; if no date appears on the book, write *n.d.* to indicate "no date."

SAMPLE ENTRIES   Here are some examples, illustrating the points we have covered thus far:

Brown, Roger. Social Psychology. New York: Free, 1965.

---. Words and Things. Glencoe, IL: Free, 1958.

Douglas, Ann. The Feminization of American Culture. New
     York: Knopf, 1977.

Hartman, Chester. The Transformation of San Francisco.
     Totowa: Rowman, 1984.

Kellerman, Barbara. The Political Presidency: Practice
     of Leadership from Kennedy through Reagan. New
     York: Oxford UP, 1984.

Notice that a period follows the author's name and another period follows the title. If a subtitle is given, as it is for Kellerman's book, it is separated from the title by a colon and a space. A colon follows the place of publication, a comma follows the publisher, and a period follows the date.

A BOOK BY MORE THAN ONE AUTHOR

The book is alphabetized under the last name of the first author named on the title page. If there are *two or three authors,* the names of these are given (after the first author's name) in the normal order, *first name first:*

Gilbert, Sandra M., and Susan Gubar. The Madwoman in
     the Attic: The Woman Writer and the Nineteenth-
     Century Literary Imagination. New Haven: Yale UP,
     1979.

Notice, again, that although the first author's name is given *last name first,* the second author's name is given in the normal order, first name first. Notice, too, that a comma is put after the first name of the first author, separating the authors.

If there are *more than three authors,* give the name only of the first and then add (but *not* enclosed within quotation marks and not italic) *et al.* (Latin for "and others").

Altshuler, Alan, et al. The Future of the Automobile.
     Cambridge: MIT P, 1984.

GOVERNMENT DOCUMENTS

If the writer is not known, treat the government and the agency as the author. Most federal documents are issued by the Government Printing Office (abbreviated to *GPO*) in Washington, D.C.

> United States Congress. Office of Technology Assess-
>   ment. Computerized Manufacturing Automation:
>   Employment, Education, and the Workplace. Washing-
>   ton, D.C.: GPO, 1984.

WORKS OF CORPORATE AUTHORSHIP

Begin the citation with the corporate author, even if the same body is also the publisher, as in the first example:

> American Psychiatric Association. Psychiatric Glossary.
>   Washington: American Psychiatric Association,
>   1984.

> Carnegie Council on Policy Studies in Higher Education.
>   Giving Youth a Better Chance: Options for Educa-
>   tion, Work, and Service. San Francisco: Jossey,
>   1980.

A REPRINT, FOR INSTANCE A PAPERBACK VERSION
OF AN OLDER CLOTHBOUND BOOK

After the title, give the date of original publication (it can usually be found on the reverse of the title page of the reprint you are using), then a period, and then the place, publisher, and date of the edition you are using. The example indicates that Gray's book was originally published in 1970 and that the student is using the Vintage reprint of 1971.

> Gray, Francine du Plessix. Divine Disobedience: Pro-
>   files in Catholic Radicalism. 1970. New York: Vin-
>   tage, 1971.

A BOOK IN SEVERAL VOLUMES

If you have used more than one volume, in a citation within your essay you will (as explained on p. 242) indicate a reference to, say, page 250 of volume 3 thus: (3: 250).

If, however, you have used only one volume of the set—let's say volume 3—in your entry in the Works Cited, specify which volume you used, as in the next example:

> Friedel, Frank. Franklin D. Roosevelt. Vol. 3. Boston:
>   Little, 1973. 4 vols.

With such an entry in the Works Cited, the parenthetic citation within your essay would be to the page only, not to the volume and page, because a reader who consults the Works Cited will understand that you used only volume 3. In the Works Cited, you may specify volume 3 and not give the total number of volumes, or you may add the total number of volumes, as in the example above.

ONE BOOK WITH A SEPARATE TITLE IN A SET OF VOLUMES

Sometimes a set with a title makes use also of a separate title for each book in the set. If you are listing such a book, use the following form:

> Churchill, Winston. The Age of Revolution. New York:
>   Dodd, 1957. Vol. 3 of History of the English-
>   Speaking Peoples. 4 vols. 1956–58.

A BOOK WITH AN AUTHOR AND AN EDITOR

> Churchill, Winston, and Franklin D. Roosevelt. The Com-
>   plete Correspondence. Ed. Warren F. Kimball. 3
>   vols. Princeton: Princeton UP, 1985.

> Kant, Immanuel. The Philosophy of Kant: Immanuel Kant's
>   Moral and Political Writings. Ed. Carl J.
>   Friedrich. New York: Modern, 1949.

If the book has one editor, the abbreviation is *ed.;* if two or more editors, *eds.*

If you are making use of the editor's introduction or other editorial material rather than of the author's work, list the book under the name of the editor rather than of the author, as shown below under An Introduction, Foreword, or Afterword on page 249.

A REVISED EDITION OF A BOOK

> Arendt, Hannah. Eichmann in Jerusalem. Rev. and en-
>   larged ed. New York: Viking, 1965.

> Honour, Hugh, and John Fleming. The Visual Arts: A His-
>   tory. 2nd ed. Englewood Cliffs: Prentice, 1986.

A TRANSLATED BOOK

> Franqui, Carlos. Family Portrait with Fidel: A Memoir.
>   Trans. Alfred MacAdam. New York: Random, 1984.

AN INTRODUCTION, FOREWORD, OR AFTERWORD

```
Goldberg, Arthur J. Foreword. An Eye for an Eye? The
     Morality of Punishing by Death. By Stephen
     Nathanson. Totowa: Rowman, 1987. v-vi.
```

Usually an introduction or comparable material is listed under the name of the author of the book (here Nathanson) rather than under the name of the writer of the foreword (here Goldberg), but if you are referring to the apparatus rather than to the book itself, use the form just given. The words *Introduction, Preface, Foreword,* and *Afterword* are neither enclosed within quotation marks nor underlined.

A BOOK WITH AN EDITOR BUT NO AUTHOR

Let's assume that you have used a book of essays written by various people but collected by an editor (or editors), whose name(s) appears on the collection.

```
LaValley, Albert J., ed. Focus on Hitchcock. Englewood
     Cliffs: Prentice, 1972.
```

A WORK WITHIN A VOLUME OF WORKS BY ONE AUTHOR

The following entry indicates that a short work by Susan Sontag, an essay called "The Aesthetics of Silence," appears in a book by Sontag titled *Styles of Radical Will.* Notice that the inclusive page numbers of the short work are cited, not merely page numbers that you may happen to refer to but the page numbers of the entire piece.

```
Sontag, Susan. "The Aesthetics of Silence." Styles of
     Radical Will. New York: Farrar, 1969. 3-34.
```

A BOOK REVIEW

Here is an example, citing Gerstein's review of Walker's book. Gerstein's review was published in a journal called *Ethics.*

```
Gerstein, Robert S. Rev. of Punishment, Danger and
     Stigma: The Morality of Criminal Justice, by Nigel
     Walker. Ethics 93 (1983): 408-10.
```

If the review has a title, give the title between the period following the reviewer's name and *Rev.*

If a review is anonymous, list it under the first word of the title, or under the second word if the first is *A, An,* or *The.* If an anonymous review has no title, begin the entry with *Rev. of,* and then give the title of the work reviewed; alphabetize the entry under the title of the work reviewed.

AN ARTICLE OR ESSAY—NOT A REPRINT—
IN A COLLECTION

A book may consist of a collection (edited by one or more persons) of new essays by several authors. Here is a reference to one essay in such a book. (The essay by Balmforth occupies pages 19 to 35 in a collection edited by Bevan.)

```
Balmforth, Henry. "Science and Religion." Steps to
    Christian Understanding. Ed. R. J. W. Bevan. Lon-
    don: Oxford UP, 1958. 19-35.
```

AN ARTICLE OR ESSAY REPRINTED IN A COLLECTION

The previous example (Balmforth's essay in Bevan's collection) was for an essay written for a collection. But some collections reprint earlier material, such as essays from journals or chapters from books. The following example cites an essay that was originally printed in a book called *The Cinema of Alfred Hitchcock*. This essay has been reprinted in a later collection of essays on Hitchcock, edited by Albert J. LaValley, and it was LaValley's collection that the student used.

```
Bogdanovich, Peter. "Interviews with Alfred Hitchcock."
    The Cinema of Alfred Hitchcock. New York: Museum
    of Modern Art, 1963. 15-18. Rpt. in Focus on
    Hitchcock. Ed. Albert J. LaValley. Englewood
    Cliffs: Prentice, 1972. 28-31.
```

The student has read Bogdanovich's essay or chapter, but not in Bogdanovich's book, where it occupied pages 15 to 18. The material was actually read on pages 28 to 31 in a collection of writings on Hitchcock, edited by LaValley. Details of the original publication—title, date, page numbers, and so forth—were found in LaValley's collection. Almost all editors will include this information, either on the copyright page or at the foot of the reprinted essay, but sometimes they do not give the original page numbers. In such a case, you need not include the original numbers in your entry.

Notice that the entry begins with the author and the title of the work you are citing (here, Bogdanovich's interviews), not with the name of the editor of the collection or the title of the collection.

AN ENCYCLOPEDIA OR OTHER ALPHABETICALLY
ARRANGED REFERENCE WORK

The publisher, place of publication, volume number, and page number do *not* have to be given. For such works, list only the edition (if it is given) and the date.

For a *signed* article, begin with the author's last name. (If the article is signed with initials, check elsewhere in the volume for a list of abbreviations, which will inform you who the initials stand for, and use the following form.)

> Williams, Donald C. "Free Will and Determinism." Ency-
> clopedia Americana. 1987 ed.

For an *unsigned article,* begin with the title of the article:

> "Automation." The Business Reference Book. 1977 ed.

> "Tobacco." Encyclopaedia Britannica: Macropaedia. 1988
> ed.

A TELEVISION OR RADIO PROGRAM

Be sure to include the title of the episode or segment (in quotation marks), the title of the show (underlined), the network, the call letters and city of the station, and the date of broadcast. Other information, such as performers, narrator, and so forth, may be included if pertinent.

> "Back to My Lai." Narr. Mike Wallace. 60 Minutes. CBS.
> 29 Mar. 1998.

> "Juvenile Justice." Narr. Ray Suarez. Talk of the Na-
> tion. National Public Radio. WBUR, Boston. 15 Apr.
> 1998.

AN ARTICLE IN A SCHOLARLY JOURNAL   The title of the article is enclosed within quotation marks, and the title of the journal is underlined to indicate italics.

Some journals are paginated consecutively; the pagination of the second issue begins where the first issue leaves off. Other journals begin each issue with page 1. The forms of the citations differ slightly.

A JOURNAL THAT IS PAGINATED CONSECUTIVELY

> Vilas, Carlos M. "Popular Insurgency and Social Revolu-
> tion in Central America." Latin American Perspec-
> tives 15 (1988): 55-77.

Vilas's article occupies pages 55 to 77 in volume 15, which was published in 1988. (Notice that the volume number is followed by a space, then by the year in parentheses, and then by a colon, a space, and the page numbers of the entire article.) Because the journal is paginated consecutively, the issue number does *not* need to be specified.

A JOURNAL THAT BEGINS EACH ISSUE WITH PAGE 1

If the journal is, for instance, a quarterly, there will be four page 1's each year, so the issue number must be given. After the volume number, type a period and (without hitting the space bar) the issue number, as in the next example:

```
Greenberg, Jack. "Civil Rights Enforcement Activity of
        the Department of Justice." Black Law Journal 8.1
        (1983): 60-67.
```

Greenberg's article appeared in the first issue of volume 8 of the *Black Law Journal*.

AN ARTICLE IN A WEEKLY, BIWEEKLY, MONTHLY, OR BIMONTHLY PUBLICATION

Do not include volume or issue numbers, even if given.

```
Lamar, Jacob V. "The Immigration Mess." Time 27 Feb.
        1989: 14-15.
```

```
Markowitz, Laura. "A Different Kind of Queer Marriage."
        Utne Reader Sept.-Oct. 2000: 24-26.
```

AN ARTICLE IN A NEWSPAPER

Because a newspaper usually consists of several sections, a section number or a capital letter may precede the page number. The example indicates that an article begins on page 1 of section 2 and is continued on a later page.

```
Chu, Harry. "Art Thief Defends Action." New York Times
        8 Feb. 1989, sec. 2: 1+.
```

AN UNSIGNED EDITORIAL

```
"The Religious Tyranny Amendment." Editorial. New York
        Times 15 Mar. 1998, sec. 4: 16.
```

A LETTER TO THE EDITOR

```
Lasken, Douglas. "Teachers Reject Bilingual Education."
        Letter. New York Times 15 Mar. 1998, sec. 4: 16.
```

A PUBLISHED OR BROADCAST INTERVIEW

Give the name of the interview subject and the interviewer, followed by the relevant publication or broadcast information, in the following format:

```
Green, Al. Interview with Terry Gross. Fresh Air.
        National Public Radio. WFCR, Amherst, MA. 16 Oct.
        2000.
```

AN INTERVIEW YOU CONDUCT

Jevgrafovs, Alexandre L. Personal [or Telephone] inter-
      view. 14 Dec. 1997.

PERSONAL CORRESPONDENCE

Raso, Robert. Letter [or E-mail] to the author. 6 Jan.
      1998.

CD-ROM

CD-ROMs are cited very much like their printed counterparts. To the
usual print citation information, add (1) the title of the database, underlined; (2) the medium (*CD-ROM*); (3) the vendor's name; and (4) the
date of electronic publication.

Louisberg, Margaret. <u>Charlie Brown Meets Godzilla: What
      Are Our Children Watching?</u> Urbana: ERIC Clearing-
      house on Elementary and Early Childhood Education,
      1990. <u>ERIC</u>. CD-ROM. SilverPlatter. May 1997.

"Pornography." <u>The Oxford English Dictionary</u>. 2nd ed.
      CD-ROM. Oxford: Oxford UP, 1992.

A PERSONAL OR PROFESSIONAL WEB SITE

Include the following elements, separated by periods: the name of
the person who created the site (omit if not given, as in the example
below), site title (underlined), name of any sponsoring institution or organization, date of access, and electronic address.

<u>School for Marine Science and Technology</u>. U of Massachu-
      setts Dartmouth. 10 Oct. 2000. <http://www.cmast
      .umassd.edu/>.

AN ARTICLE IN AN ONLINE PERIODICAL

Give the same information as you would for a print article, plus the
date of access and electronic address.

Trammell, George W. "Cirque du O. J." <u>Court Technology
      Bulletin</u>. July-Aug. 1995. 12 Sept. 1996. <http://
      www.ncsc.dni.us/ncsc/bulletin/v07n04.htm>.

AN ONLINE POSTING

Citation includes the author's name, subject line of posting, description *Online posting,* date material was posted, name of the forum, date of
access, and address.

```
Ricci, Paul. "Global Warming." Online posting. 10 June
    1996. Global Electronic Science Conference. 22
    Sept. 1997. <http://www.science.envir/earth>.
```

A DATABASE SOURCE

Treat material obtained from a computer service, such as Bibliographies Retrieval Service (BRS), like other printed material, but at the end of the entry add (if available) the title of the database (underlined), publication medium (*Online*), name of the computer service, and date of access.

```
Jackson, Morton. "A Look at Profits." Harvard Business
    Review 40 (1962): 106-13. Online. BRS. 23 Dec.
    1995.
```

Caution: Although we have covered the most usual kinds of sources, it is entirely possible that you will come across a source that does not fit any of the categories that we have discussed. For approximately two hundred pages of explanations of these matters, covering the proper way to cite all sorts of troublesome and unbelievable (but real) sources, see Joseph Gibaldi, *MLA Handbook for Writers of Research Papers,* Fifth Edition (New York: Modern Language Association of America, 1999).

APA Format:
Citations within the Text

Your paper will conclude with a separate page headed References, in which you list all of your sources. If the last page of your essay is numbered 10, number the first page of the References 11.

The APA style emphasizes the date of publication; the date appears not only in the list of references at the end of the paper but also in the paper itself, when you give a brief parenthetic citation of a source that you have quoted or summarized or in any other way used. Here is an example:

```
Statistics are readily available (Smith, 1989, p. 20).
```

The title of Smith's book or article will be given at the end of your paper, in the list titled References. We discuss the form of the material listed in the References after we look at some typical citations within the text of a student's essay.

A SUMMARY OF AN ENTIRE WORK

```
Smith (1988) holds the same view.
```

or

```
Similar views are held widely (Smith, 1988; Jones &
Metz, 1990).
```

A REFERENCE TO A PAGE OR TO PAGES

```
Smith (1988) argues that "the death penalty is a lot-
tery, and blacks usually are the losers" (p. 17).
```

**A REFERENCE TO AN AUTHOR WHO IN THE
LIST OF REFERENCES IS REPRESENTED BY
MORE THAN ONE WORK**

If in the References you list two or more works that an author published in the same year, the works are listed in alphabetic order, by the first letter of the title. The first work is labeled *a,* the second *b,* and so on. Here is a reference to the second work that Smith published in 1989:

```
Florida presents "a fair example" of how the death
penalty is administered (Smith, 1989b, p. 18).
```

APA Format:
The List of References

Your brief parenthetic citations are made clear when the reader consults the list you give in the References. Type this list on a separate page, continuing the pagination of your essay.

An Overview   Here are some general guidelines.

FORM ON THE PAGE
- Begin each entry flush with the left margin, but if an entry runs to more than one line, indent five spaces for each succeeding line of the entry.
- Double-space each entry, and double-space between entries.

ALPHABETIC ORDER
- Arrange the list alphabetically by author.
- Give the author's last name first and then the initial of the first name and of the middle name (if any).
- If there is more than one author, name all of the authors, again inverting the name (last name first) and giving only initials for first and middle names. (But do not invert the editor's name when the entry begins with the name of an author who has written an article in an edited book.) When there are two or more authors, use an ampersand (*&*) before the name of the last author. Example (here, of an article in the tenth volume of a journal called *Developmental Psychology*):

```
Drabman, R. S., & Thomas, M. H. (1974). Does media vio-
     lence increase children's tolerance of real-life
     aggression? Developmental Psychology, 10, 418-421.
```

• If you list more than one work by an author, do so in the order of publication, the earliest first. If two works by an author were published in the same year, give them in alphabetic order by the first letter of the title, disregarding *A, An,* or *The,* and their foreign equivalent. Designate the first work as *a,* the second as *b.* Repeat the author's name at the start of each entry.

Donnerstein, E. (1980a). Aggressive erotica and vio-
    lence against women. Journal of Personality and
    Social Psychology, 39, 269–277.

Donnerstein, E. (1980b). Pornography and violence
    against women. Annals of the New York Academy of
    Sciences, 347, 227–288.

Donnerstein, E. (1983). Erotica and human aggression.
    In R. Green and E. Donnerstein (Eds.), Aggression:
    Theoretical and empirical reviews (pp. 87–103).
    New York: Academic Press.

FORM OF TITLE
• In references to books, capitalize only the first letter of the first word of the title (and of the subtitle, if any) and capitalize proper nouns. Underline the complete title (but not the period at the end).
• In references to articles in periodicals or in edited books, capitalize only the first letter of the first word of the article's title (and subtitle, if any) and all proper nouns. Do not put the title within quotation marks. Type a period after the title of the article. For the title of the journal and the volume and page numbers, see the next instruction.
• In references to periodicals, give the volume number in arabic numerals, and underline it. Do *not* use *vol.* before the number, and do not use *p.* or *pg.* before the page numbers.

Sample References   Here are some samples to follow.

A BOOK BY ONE AUTHOR

Pavlov, I. P. (1927). Conditioned reflexes (G. V.
    Anrep, Trans.). London: Oxford University Press.

A BOOK BY MORE THAN ONE AUTHOR

Belenky, M. F., Clinchy, B. M., Goldberger, N. R., &
    Torule, J. M. (1986). Women's ways of knowing: The

development of self, voice, and mind. New York:
Basic Books.

A COLLECTION OF ESSAYS

Christ, C. P., & Plaskow, J. (Eds.). (1979). Woman-
    spirit rising: A feminist reader in religion. New
    York: Harper & Row.

A WORK IN A COLLECTION OF ESSAYS

Fiorenza, E. (1979). Women in the early Christian move-
    ment. In C. P. Christ & J. Plaskow (Eds.), Woman-
    spirit rising: A feminist reader in religion (pp.
    84-92). New York: Harper & Row.

GOVERNMENT DOCUMENTS

If the writer is not known, treat the government and the agency as
the author. Most federal documents are issued by the U.S. Government
Printing Office in Washington, D.C. If a document number has been assigned, insert that number in parentheses between the title and the following period.

United States Congress. Office of Technology Assess-
    ment. (1984). Computerized manufacturing automa-
    tion: Employment, education, and the workplace.
    Washington, D.C.: U.S. Government Printing Office.

AN ARTICLE IN A JOURNAL WITH CONTINUOUS PAGINATION

Tversky, A., & Kahneman, D. (1981). The framing of de-
    cisions and the psychology of choice. Science,
    211, 453-458.

AN ARTICLE IN A JOURNAL THAT PAGINATES
EACH ISSUE SEPARATELY

Foot, R. J. (1988-89). Nuclear coercion and the ending
    of the Korean conflict. International Security,
    13(4), 92-112.

The reference informs us that the article appeared in issue number 4 of
volume 13.

AN ARTICLE FROM A MONTHLY OR WEEKLY MAGAZINE

Greenwald, J. (1989, February 27). Gimme shelter. Time,
    133, 50-51.

Maran, S. P. (1988, April). In our backyard, a star ex-
    plodes. Smithsonian, 19, 46-57.

AN ARTICLE IN A NEWSPAPER

Connell, R. (1989, February 6). Career concerns at
    heart of 1980s' campus protests. Los Angeles
    Times, pp. 1, 3.

(*Note:* If no author is given, simply begin with the title followed by the
date in parentheses.)

A BOOK REVIEW

Daniels, N. (1984). Understanding physician power [Re-
    view of the book, The social transformation of
    American medicine]. Philosophy and Public Affairs,
    13, 347-356.

Daniels is the reviewer, not the author of the book. The book under review is called *The Social Transformation of American Medicine,* but the review, published in volume 13 of *Philosophy and Public Affairs,* had its own
title, "Understanding Physician Power."
    If the review does not have a title, retain the square brackets, and
use the material within as the title. Proceed as in the example just given.

A WEB SITE

American Psychological Association. (1995). Lesbian and
    gay parenting. Retrieved 12 June 2000 from the
    World Wide Web: http://www.apa.org/pi/parent/html.

AN ARTICLE IN AN ONLINE PERIODICAL

Carpenter, S. (2000, October). Biology and social envi-
    ronments jointly influence gender development.
    Monitor on Psychology 31. Retrieved 20 Sept. 2000
    from: http://www.apa.org/monitor/oct00/maccoby
    .html.

For a full account of the APA method of dealing with all sorts of unusual citations, see the fourth edition (1994) of the APA manual, *Publication Manual of the American Psychological Association.*

A CHECKLIST FOR PAPERS USING SOURCES

✓ All borrowed words and ideas credited?

✓ Quotations and summaries not too long?

✓ Quotations accurate?

✓ Quotations provided with helpful lead-ins?

✓ Documentation in proper form?

And of course, you will also ask yourself the questions that you would ask of a paper that did not use sources, such as:

✓ Topic sufficiently narrowed?

✓ Thesis (to be advanced or refuted) stated early and clearly, perhaps even in title?

✓ Audience kept in mind? Opposing views stated fairly and as sympathetically as possible? Controversial terms defined?

✓ Assumptions likely to be shared by readers? If not, are they argued rather than merely asserted?

✓ Focus clear (evaluation, recommendation of policy)?

✓ Evidence (examples, testimony, statistics) adequate and sound?

✓ Inferences valid?

✓ Organization clear (effective opening, coherent sequence of arguments, unpretentious ending)?

✓ All worthy opposition faced?

✓ Tone appropriate?

✓ Has the paper been carefully proofread?

✓ Is the title effective?

✓ Is the opening paragraph effective?

✓ Is the structure reader-friendly?

✓ Is the closing paragraph effective?

AN ANNOTATED STUDENT RESEARCH PAPER IN MLA FORMAT

The following argument makes good use of sources. Early in the semester the students were asked to choose one topic from a list of ten, and to write a documented argument of 750 to 1,250 words (three to five pages of double-spaced typing). The completed paper was due two weeks after the topics were distributed. The assignment, a prelude to working on a research paper of 2,500 to 3,000 words, was in part designed to give students practice in finding and in using sources. Citations are given in the MLA form.

The *MLA Handbook* does not insist on a title page and outline, but many instructors prefer them.

Title one-third down page

Why Trials Should Not Be Televised
By
Theresa Washington

All lines centered

Professor Wilson
English 102
December 12, 2001

Washington i

Outline

Thesis: The televising of trials is a bad idea
because it has several negative effects
on the First Amendment: it gives viewers
a deceptive view of particular trials
and of the judicial system in general,
and it degrades the quality of media reporting outside the courtroom.

I. Introduction
   A. Trend toward increasing trial coverage
   B. First Amendment versus Sixth Amendment
II. Effect of televising trials on First
    Amendment
   A. Provides deceptive version of truth
      1. Confidence in verdicts misplaced
         a. William Smith trial
         b. Rodney King trial
      2. Nature of TV as a medium
         a. Distortion in sound bites
         b. Stereotyping trial participants
         c. Misleading camera angles
         d. Commentators and commercials
   B. Confuses viewers about judicial system
      1. Contradicts basic concept "innocent
         until proven guilty"
      2. Can't explain legal complexities
   C. Contributes to media circus outside of
      court
      1. Blurs truth and fiction
      2. Affects print media in negative ways
      3. Media makes itself the story
      4. Distracts viewers from other issues
III. Conclusion

Small roman numerals for page with outline

Roman numerals for chief units (I, II, etc.); capital letters for chief units within these largest units; for smaller and smaller units, arabic numerals and lowercase letters

Why Trials Should Not Be Televised

Although trials have been televised on and off since the 1950s,[1] in the last few years the availability of trials for a national audience has increased dramatically.[2] Media critics, legal scholars, social scientists, and journalists continue to debate the merits of this trend.

Proponents of cameras in the courtroom argue, falsely, I believe, that confidence in the fairness of our institutions, including the judicial system, depends on a free press, guaranteed by the First Amendment. Keeping trials off television is a form of censorship, they say. It limits the public's ability to understand (1) what is happening in particular trials and (2) how the judicial system operates, which is often confusing to laypeople. Opponents claim that televising trials threatens the defendant's Sixth Amendment rights to a fair trial because it can alter the behavior of the trial participants, including the jury ("Tale"; Thaler).

Regardless of its impact on due process of law,[3] TV in court does not serve the First Amendment well. Consider the first claim, that particular trials are easier to understand when televised. But does watching trials on television really allow the viewer to "see it like it is," to get the full scope and breadth of a trial? Steven Brill, founder of Court TV, would like us to believe so. He points out that most high-profile defendants in televised trials

Title is focused and announces the thesis.

Double-space between title and first paragraph— and throughout the essay.

1" margin on each side and at bottom

Summary of opposing positions

Parenthetic reference to an anonymous source and also to a source with a named author

Superscript numerals indicate endnotes.

Washington 2

have been acquitted; he names William Kennedy
Smith, Jimmy Hoffa, John Connally, and John
Delorean as examples (Clark 821). "Imagine if
[Smith's trial] had not been shown and he got
off. Millions of people would have said the
Kennedys fixed the case" (Brill qtd. in "Tale"
29). Polls taken after the trial seem to confirm this claim, since they showed the public
by and large agreed with the jury's decision to
acquit (Quindlen).

However, Thaler points out that the public
can just as easily disagree with the verdict as
agree, and when this happens, the effects can
be catastrophic. One example is the Rodney King
case. Four white Los Angeles police officers
were charged in 1991 with severely beating
African American Rodney King, who, according to
the officers, had been resisting arrest. At
their first trial, all four officers were acquitted. This verdict outraged many African
Americans throughout the country; they felt the
evidence from watching the trial overwhelmingly
showed the defendants to be guilty. The black
community of south-central Los Angeles expressed its feelings by rioting for days
(Thaler 50-51).

Clearly the black community did not experience the trial the same way the white community and the white jury did. Why? Marty
Rosenbaum, an attorney with the New York State
Defenders Association, points out that viewers
cannot experience a trial the same way trial
participants do. "What you see at home 'is not

Parenthetic
reference to
author and page

Parenthetic
reference to an
indirect source (a
borrowed quo-
tation)

what jurors see'" (qtd. in Thaler 70). The
trial process is slow, linear, and methodical,
as the defense and prosecution each builds its
case, one piece of information at a time
(Thaler 11). The process is intended to be
thoughtful and reflective, with the jury weighing all the evidence in light of the whole
trial (Altheide 299-301). And it emphasizes
words--both spoken and written--rather than images (Thaler 11).

In contrast, TV's general strength is in
handling visual images that entertain or that
provoke strong feelings. News editors and reporters choose footage for its assumed visual
and emotional impact on viewers. Words are made
to fit the images, not the other way around, and
they tend to be short catchy phrases, easy to
understand (Thaler 4, 7). As a result, the fif-
teen- to thirty-second "sound bites" in nightly
newscasts often present trial events out of context, emphasizing moments of drama rather than
of legal importance (Thaler 7; Zoglin 62).

Furthermore, this emphasis on emotional
visuals leads to stereotyping the participants,
making larger-than-life symbols out of them,
especially regarding social issues (Thaler 9):
abused children (the Menendez brothers), the
battered wife (Hedda Nussbaum), the abusing
husband (Joel Steinberg, O. J. Simpson), the
jealous lover (Amy Fisher), the serial killer
(Jeffrey Dahmer), and date rapist (William
Smith). It becomes difficult for viewers to see
defendants as ordinary human beings.

Although no words are quoted, the idea is borrowed, and so the source is cited.

Clear transition ("In contrast")

Parenthetic citation of two sources

Washington 4

One can argue, as Brill has done, that gavel-to-gavel coverage of trials counteracts the distortions in sound-bite journalism (Clark 821). Yet even here a number of editorial assumptions and decisions affect what viewers see. Camera angles and movements reinforce in the viewer differing degrees of intimacy with the trial participant; close-ups are often used for sympathetic witnesses, three-quarter shots for lawyers, and profile shots for defendants (Entner 73-75).[4]

On-air commentators also shape the viewers' experience. Several media critics have noted how much commentators' remarks often have the play-by-play tone of sportscasters informing viewers of what each side (the defense and the prosecution) needs to win (Cole 245; Thaler 71, 151). Continual interruptions for commercials add to the impression of watching a spectacle. "The CNN coverage [of the Smith trial] isn't so much gavel-to-gavel, actually, as gavel-to-commercial-to-gavel, with former CNN Gulf War correspondent Charles Jaco acting more as ringleader than reporter" (Bianculli 60). This encourages a sensationalistic tone to the proceedings that the jury does not experience. In addition, breaking for ads frequently occurs at important points in the trial (Thaler 48).

In-court proponents also believe that watching televised trials will help viewers understand the legal aspects of the judicial system. In June 1991, a month before Court TV went on the air, Vincent Blasi, a law professor at

Summary of an opposing view countered with a clear transition ("Yet")

Author lets reader hear the opposition by means of a brief quotation

Omitted material indicated by three periods, with a fourth to mark the end of a sentence

Columbia University, told <u>Time</u> magazine, "Today
most of us learn about judicial proceedings
from lawyers' sound bites and artists'
sketches [. . .]. Televised proceedings [such
as Court TV] ought to dispel some of the myth
and mystery that shroud our legal system" (qtd.
in Zoglin 62).

    But after several years of Court TV and
CNN, we can now see this is not so. As a
medium, TV is not good at educating the general
public, either about concepts fundamental to
our judicial system or about the complexities
in particular cases.

    For example, one basic concept--"innocent
until proven guilty"--is contradicted in televised trials in numerous subtle ways: Commentators sometimes make remarks about (or omit
comment on) actions of the defense or prosecution that show a bias against the defendant.

    Media critic Lewis Cole, watching the trial
of Lorena Bobbitt on Court TV in 1994, observed:

Quotation of more than four lines, indented 1″ from left margin (ten spaces), double-spaced, parenthetic reference set off from quotation

> Court TV commentators rarely chal-
> lenged the state's characterization
> of what it was doing, repeating with-
> out comment, for instance, the prose-
> cution's claims about protecting the
> reputation of Lorena Bobbitt and con-
> centrating on the prosecution deci-
> sion to pursue both cases as a
> tactical matter, rather than inquir-
> ing how the prosecution's view of the
> incident as a "barroom brawl" had
> limited its approach to and under-
> standing of the case. (245)

Washington 6

Camera angles play a role also: Watching the defendant day after day in profile, which makes him or her seem either vulnerable or remote, tends to reinforce his or her guilt (Entner 158).

Thaler points out that these editorial effects arise because the goals of the media (print as well as electronic) differ from the goals of the judicial system. His argument runs as follows: The court is interested in determining only whether the defendant broke the law. The media (especially TV) focus on acts to reinforce social values, whether they're codified into law or not. This can lead viewers to conclude that a defendant is guilty because pretrial publicity or courtroom testimony reveals he or she has transgressed against the community's moral code, even when the legal system later acquits. This happened in the case of Claus von Bulow, who between 1982 and 1985 was tried and acquitted twice for attempting to murder his wife and who clearly had behaved in reprehensible ways in the eyes of the public (35). It also happened in the case of Joel Steinberg, who was charged with murdering his daughter. Extended televised testimony by his former partner, Hedda Nussbaum, helped paint a portrait of "a monster" in the eyes of the public (140-42). Yet the jury chose to convict him on the lesser charge of manslaughter. When many viewers wrote to the prosecutor, Peter Casolaro, asking why the verdict was not first-degree murder, he had to conclude that TV does

Argument supported by specific examples

Washington 7

not effectively teach about due process of law
(176).

In addition to being poor at handling
basic judicial concepts, television has difficulty conveying more complex and technical aspects of the law. Sometimes the legal nature of
the case makes for a poor translation to the
screen. Brill admitted that, despite attempts
at hourly summaries, Court TV was unable to
convey to its viewers any meaningful understanding of the case of Manuel Noriega (Thaler
61), the Panamanian leader who was convicted by
the United States in 1992 of drug trafficking
and money laundering ("Former"). In other
cases, like the Smith trial, the "civics lesson" gets swamped by its sensational aspects
(Thaler 45). In most cases print media are better at exploring and explaining legal issues
than is TV (Thaler 4).

In addition to shaping the viewer's perceptions of trial reality directly, in-court TV
also negatively affects the quality of trial
coverage outside of court, which in turn limits
the public's "right to know." Brill likes to
claim that Court TV helps to counteract the
sensationalism of such tabloid TV shows as A
Current Affair and Hard Copy, which pay trial
participants to tell their stories and publish
leaks from the prosecution and defense. "I
think cameras in the courtroom is [sic] the
best antidote to that garbage" (Brill qtd. in
Clark 821). However, as founder and editor of
Court TV, he obviously has a vested interest in

Transition briefly
summarizes and
then moves to
a new point.

The author uses
"[*sic*]" (Latin for
"thus") to indicate
that the oddity is
in the source and
is not by the au-
thor of the paper.

Washington 8

affirming his network's social and legal worth.
There are several ways that in-court TV, rather
than supplying a sobering contrast, helps to
feed the media circus surrounding high-profile
trials (Thaler 43).

One way is by helping to blur the line between reality and fiction. This is an increasing trend among all media but is especially
true of TV, whose footage can be combined and
recombined in so many ways. An excellent example of this is the trial of Amy Fisher, who
pleaded guilty in September 1992 to shooting
her lover's wife and whose sentencing was televised by Court TV (Thaler 83). Three TV movies
about this love triangle appeared on network TV
in the same week, just one month after she had
been sentenced to five to fifteen years of jail
(Thaler 82). Then Geraldo Rivera, the syndicated TV talk-show host, held a mock grand jury
trial of her lover, Jocy Buttafuoco; even
though Buttafuoco had not at that point been
charged with a crime, Geraldo felt many viewers
thought he ought to have been (Thaler 83). Then
A Current Affair had a series that "tried"
Fisher for events and behaviors that never got
resolved in the actual trial. The announcer on
the program said, "When Ms. Fisher copped a
plea and went to jail, she robbed the public of
a trial, leaving behind many unanswered questions. Tonight we will try to [. . .] complete
the unwritten chapter" ("Trial"). Buttafuoco's
lawyer from the trial served as a consultant on
this program (Thaler 84). This is also a good

Washington 9

Useful analysis of
effect of TV

example of how tabloid TV reinforces people's
beliefs and plays on people's feelings. Had her
trial not been televised, the excitement surrounding her case would not have been so high.
Tabloid TV played off the audience's expectation for what a televised trial should and
could reveal. Thus in-court television becomes
one more ingredient in the mix of docudramas,
mock trials, talk shows, and tabloid journalism. This limits the public's "right to know"
by making it difficult to keep fact separate
from storytelling.

Square brackets
indicate that the
author has altered
text from a capital
to a lowercase
letter.

In-court TV also affects the quality of
print journalism. Proponents like to claim that
"[f]rom the standpoint of the public's right to
know, there is no good reason why TV journalists should be barred from trials while print
reporters are not" (Zoglin 62). But when TV is
present, there is no level playing field among
the media. Because it provides images, sound,
movement, and a greater sense of speed and
immediacy, TV can easily outcompete other media
for audience attention and thus for advertising
dollars. In attempts to keep pace, newspapers
and magazines offer more and more of the kinds
of stories that once were beneath their standards, such as elaborate focus both on sensational aspects of the case and on
"personalities, analysis, and prediction"
rather than news (Thaler 45). While these attributes have always been part of TV and the
tabloid print press, this trend is increasingly
apparent in supposedly reputable papers like

Washington 10

the New York Times. During the Smith trial, for
example, the Times violated previously accepted
boundaries of propriety by not only identifying
the rape victim but also giving lots of intimate details about her past (Thaler 45).

Because the media are, for the most part,
commercial, slow periods--and all trials have
them--must always be filled with some "story."
One such story is increasingly the media self-
consciously watching and analyzing itself, to
see how it is handling (or mishandling) coverage of the trial (Thaler 43). At the Smith
trial, for example, one group of reporters was
covering the trial while another group covered
the other reporters (Thaler 44).[5] As bizarre as
this "media watching" is, there would be no
"story" if the trial itself had not been televised.

Last but not least, televising trials dis-
tracts viewers from other important issues.
Some of these are abstract and thus hard to understand (like the savings-and-loan scandal in
the mid-1980s or the causes of lingering unemployment in the 1990s), while others are
painful to contemplate (like overseas wars and
famines). Yet we have to stay aware of these
issues if we are to function as active citizens
in a democracy.

Altogether, televising trials is a bad
idea. Not only does it provide deceptive impressions about what's happening in particular
trials; it also doesn't reveal much about our
judicial system. In addition, televising trials

No citation is
needed for a point
that can be
considered
common
knowledge, but
the second
sentence *is*
documented.

Useful summary
of main points

Washington 11

helps to lower the quality of trial coverage
outside of court, thus increasingly depriving
the public of neutral, fact-based reporting. A
healthy free press depends on balance and knowing when to accept limits. Saturating viewers
with extended media coverage of sensational
trials oversteps those limits. In this case,
more is not better.

Yet it is unlikely that TV coverage will
be legally removed from the courtroom, now that
it is here. Only one state (New York) has ever
legislated a return to nontelevised trials (in
1991), and even it changed its mind in 1992
(Thaler 78). Perhaps the best we can do is to
educate ourselves about the pitfalls of televising the judicial system, as we struggle to
do so with the televised electoral process.

Realistic appraisal
of the current
situation and a
suggestion of what
the reader can do

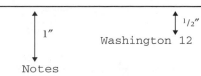

1/2″

1″

Washington 12

Double-space between heading and notes and throughout notes.

Notes

[1] Useful discussions of this history can be found in Clark (829-32) and Thaler (19-31).

Superscript number followed by one space

[2] Cable networks have been showing trial footage to national audiences since at least 1982, when Cable News Network (CNN) covered the trial of Claus von Bulow (Thaler 33). It continues to show trials. In the first week of February 1995, four to five million homes accounted for the top fifteen most-watched shows on cable TV; all were CNN segments of the O. J. Simpson trial ("Cable TV"). In July 1991, Steven Brill founded the Courtroom Television Network, or "Court TV" (Clark 821). Like CNN, it broadcasts around the clock, showing gavel-to-gavel coverage. It now claims over fourteen million cable subscribers (Clark 821) and, as of January 1994, had televised over 280 trials ("In Camera" 27).

[3] Thaler's study The Watchful Eye is a thoughtful examination of the subtle ways in which TV in court can affect trial participants, inhibiting witnesses from coming forward, provoking grandstanding in attorneys and judges, and pressuring juries to come up with verdicts acceptable to a national audience.

Each note begins with 1/2″ indent (five typewriter spaces), but subsequent lines of each note are flush left.

[4] Sometimes legal restrictions determine camera angles. For example, in the Steinberg trial (1988), the audience and the jury were not allowed to be televised by New York state law. This required placing the camera so that the judge and witnesses were seen in "full frontal view" (generally a more neutral or

Washington 13

positive stance). The lawyers could be seen
only from the rear when questioning witnesses,
and the defendant was shot in profile (Thaler
110-11). These camera angles, though not chosen
for dramatic effect, still resulted in emotionally laden viewpoints not experienced by the
jury. George W. Trammell, a Los Angeles Superior Court Judge, has written on how technology
can interfere with the fairness of the trial
system. He claims that "Technology, well managed, can be a great benefit. Technology poorly
managed benefits no one."

5 At the Smith trial a journalist from one
German newspaper inadvertently filmed another
German reporter from a competing newspaper
watching the Smith trial in the pressroom outside the courtroom (Thaler 44).

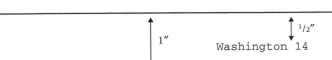

Washington 14

Works Cited

Altheide, David. "TV News and the Social Construction of Justice." Justice and the Media: Issues and Research. Ed. Ray Surette. Springfield, IL: Thomas, 1984. 292–304.

Alphabetical by author's last name

Bianculli, David. "Shame on You, CNN." New York Post 11 Dec. 1992: 60.

Hanging indent ¹/₂″

"Cable TV Squeezes High Numbers and Aces Competition." All Things Considered. National Public Radio. 9 Feb. 1994. Unedited transcript. Segment 12. NPR Audience Services. Washington.

Transcript of radio program

Clark, Charles S. "Courts and the Media." CQ Researcher 23 Sept. 1994: 817–40.

Cole, Lewis. "Court TV." Nation 21 Feb. 1994: 243–45.

Entner, Roberta. "Encoding the Image of the American Judiciary Institution: A Semiotic Analysis of Broadcast Trials to Ascertain Its Definition of the Court System." Diss. New York U, 1993.

The title of an unpublished work is not italicized but is enclosed within quotation marks.

"Former Panamanian Leader Noriega Sentenced." Facts on File 16 July 1992: 526. InfoTrac: Magazine Index Plus 1992–Feb. 1995. CD-ROM. Information Access. Feb. 1995.

CD-ROM source

"In Camera with Court TV." New Yorker 24 Jan. 1994: 27–28.

Quindlen, Anna. "The Glass Eye." New York Times 18 Dec. 1991: A29.

"A Tale of a Rug." Economist 15 Jan. 1994: 28–29.

Anonymous source alphabetized under first word (or second if first is A, An, or The)

Washington 15

Thaler, Paul. The Watchful Eye: American Jus-
    tice in the Age of the Television Trial.
    Westport: Praeger, 1994.

Television pro-
gram "The Trial That Had to Happen: The People ver-
    sus Amy Fisher." A Current Affair. Fox.
    WFXT, Boston. 1-4 Feb. 1993.

No page reference
for this in-text
Internet citation
Trammell, George W. "Cirque du O. J." Court
    Technology Bulletin July/Aug. 1995. World
    Wide Web. 12 Sept. 1995 <http://
    www.ncsc.dni.us/ncsc/bulletin/v07n04.htm>.

Zoglin, Richard. "Justice Faces a Screen Test."
    Time 17 June 1991: 62.

AN ANNOTATED
STUDENT RESEARCH PAPER
IN APA FORMAT

The following paper is an example of a student paper that uses APA
format.

The Role of Spirituality and Religion
in Mental Health

Laura DeVeau

English 102
Professor Gardner
April 12, 2001

The APA-style cover page gives title, author, and course information.

278USING SOURCES

Short form of title
and page number
as running head

Citation of mul-
tiple works from
references

Acknowledgment
of opposing view-
points

Religion in Mental Health 1

The Role of Spirituality and Religion
in Mental Health

It has been called "a vestige of the
childhood of mankind," "the feeling of something true, total and absolute," "an otherworldly answer as regards the meaning of life"
(Jones, 1991, p. 1; Amaro, 2000; Kristeva,
1987, p. 27). It has been compared to medicine,
described as a psychological cure for mental
illness, and also referred to as the cause of a
dangerous fanaticism. With so many differing
opinions on the impact of religion in people's
lives, where would one begin a search for the
truth? Who has the answer: Christians, humanists, objectivists, atheists, psychoanalysts,
Buddhists, philosophers, cults? This was my
dilemma at the advent of my research into how
religion and spirituality affect the mental
health of society as a whole.

In this paper, I explore the claims,
widely accepted by professionals in the field
of psychology, that religious and spiritual
practices have a negative impact on mental
health. In addition, though, I cannot help but
reflect on how this exploration has changed my
beliefs as well. Religion is such a personal
experience that one cannot be dispassionate in
reporting it. One can, however, subject the evidence provided by those who have studied the
issue to critical scrutiny. Having done so, I
find myself in disagreement with those who
claim religious feelings are incompatible with
sound mental health. There is a nearly limit-

Religion in Mental Health 2

less number of beliefs regarding spirituality. Some are organized and involve rituals like mass or worship. Many are centered around the existence of a higher being, while others focus on the self. I have attempted to uncover the perfect set of values that lead to a better lifestyle, but my research has pointed me in an entirely different direction, where no single belief seems to be adequate but where spiritual belief in general should be valued more highly than it is currently in mental health circles.

Thesis explicitly introduced

I grew up in a moderately devout Catholic family. Like many young people raised in a household where one religion is practiced by both parents, it never occurred to me to question those beliefs. I went through a spiritual cycle, which I believe much of Western society also experiences. I attended religious services because I had to. I possessed a blind, unquestioning acceptance of what I was being taught because the adults I trusted said it was so. Like many adolescents and young adults, though, I stopped going to church when I was old enough to decide because I thought I had better things to do. At this stage, we reach a point when we begin searching for a meaning to our existence. For some, this search is brought on by a major crisis or a feeling of emptiness in their daily lives, while for others it is simply a part of growing up. This is where we begin to make personal choices, but with the barrage of options, where do we turn?

Beginning with the holistic health movement in the eighties, there has been a mass shift from traditional religions to less structured

Religion in Mental Health 3

spiritual practice such as meditation, yoga, the Cabala, and mysticism (Beyerman, 1989). They venture beyond the realm of conventional dogmatism and into the new wave of spirituality. Many of these practices are based on the notion that health of the mind and spirit equals health of the body. Associated with this movement is a proliferation of retreats offering a chance to get in touch with the beauty and silence of nature and seminars where we can take "a break from our everyday environment where our brains are bustling and our bodies are exhausting themselves" ("Psychological benefits," 1999). A major concept of the spiritual new wave is that it focuses inward toward the individual psyche, rather than outward toward another being like a god. Practitioners do not deny the existence of this being, but they believe that to fully love another, we must first understand ourselves. Many find this a preferable alternative to religions where the individual is seen as a walking dispenser of sin who is very fortunate to have a forgiving creator. It is also a relief from the scare tactics like damnation used by traditional religions to make people behave. Many, therefore, praise the potential psychological benefits of such spirituality.

While I believe strongly in the benefits of the new wave, I am not willing to do away with structured religion, for I found that it also has its benefits. Without the existence of churches and temples, it would be harder to expose the public to values beneficial to mental stability. It is much more difficult to hand a

Author and date cited for summary or paraphrase

Anonymous source cited by title and date

Clear transition refers to previous paragraph

Religion in Mental Health 4

child a copy of the Cabala and say "Read this, and then get back to me on it" than it is to bring a child to a service where the ideas are represented with concrete examples. My religious upbringing presented me with a set of useful morals and values, and it does the same for millions of others who are brought up in this manner. Many people, including some followers of the new wave, are bitter toward Christianity because of events in history like the Crusades, the Inquisition, the Salem witch trials, and countless other horrific acts supposedly committed in the name of God. But these events were not based on biblical teachings but on purely human greed and lust for power. We should not reject the benevolent possibilities of organized religion on the basis of historical atrocities any more than we should abandon public education because a few teachers are known to mistreat children.

Another factor contributing to the reluctance concerning religion is the existence of cults that seduce people into following their extreme teachings. The victims are often at vulnerable times in their lives, and the leaders are usually very charming, charismatic, and sometimes also psychotic or otherwise mentally unstable. Many argue that if we acknowledge these groups as dangerous cults, then we must do the same for traditional religions such as Christianity and Islam, which are likewise founded on the teachings of charismatic leaders. Again, though, critics are too quick to conflate all religious and spiritual practice; we must distinguish between those who pray and attend

Religion in Mental Health 5

services and those who commit group suicide because they think that aliens are coming to take
over the world. Cults have provided many psychologists, who are eager to discount religion
as a factor in improving mental health, with an
easy target. Ellis (1993), the founder of
rational-emotive therapy, cites many extreme
examples of religious commitment, such as cults
and antiabortion killings, to show that commitment is hazardous to one's sanity. Anomalies
like these should not be used to speak of religion as a whole, though. Religion is clearly
the least of these people's mental problems.

Besides Ellis, there are many others in
the field of psychology who do not recognize
religion as a potential aid for improving the
condition of the psyche. Actually, fewer than
45 percent of the members of the American Psychiatric Association even believe in God. The
general American public has more than twice
that percentage of religious devotees (Larson,
1998). Going back to the days of Freud, many
psychologists have held atheist views. The father of psychoanalysis himself called religion
a "universal obsessional neurosis." Psychologists have long rejected research that demonstrates the benefits of spirituality by saying
that this research is biased. They claim that
such studies are out to prove that religion
helps because the conductors are religious
people who need to justify their beliefs.

While this may be true in some instances,
there is also some quite empirical research
available to support the claims of those who
promote religion and spirituality. The Journal

When the author's name appears in text, only the date is cited in paren- theses.

Religion in Mental Health 6

for the Scientific Study of Religion has conducted many studies examining the effects of religion on individuals and groups. In one
example, the relationship between religious coping methods and positive recovery after major
stressful events was observed. The results indicated not only that spirituality was not harmful
to the mind but that "the positive religious
coping pattern was tied to benevolent outcomes,
including fewer symptoms of psychological
distress, [and] reports of psychological and
spiritual growth as a result of the stressor"
(Pargament et al., 1998, p. 721). Clearly, the
benefits of piety can, in fact, be examined em-
pirically, and in some cases the results point
to a positive correlation between religion and
mental health.

Bracketed word in
quotation not in
original source

Author, date, and
page number are
cited for a direct
quotation.

        But let us get away from statistics and
studies. If religion is both useless and dangerous, as so many psychologists claim, we must ask
why has it remained so vital a part of humanity
for so long. Even if it can be reduced to a mere
coping method that humans use to justify their
existence and explain incomprehensible events,
is it futile? I would suggest that this alone
represents a clear benefit to society. Should
religion, if it cannot be proven as "true," be
eliminated and life based on scientific fact
alone? Surely many would find this a pointless
existence. With all the conflicting knowledge I
have gained about spirituality during my personal journey and my research, one idea is
clear. It is not the depth of devotion, the time
of life when one turns to religion, or even the
particular beliefs or combination of beliefs one

chooses to adopt that will improve the quality
of life. There is no right or wrong answer when
it comes to self-fulfillment. It is whatever
works for the individual, even if that means
holding no religious or spiritual beliefs at
all. But clearly there are benefits to be
gained, at least for some individuals, and mental health professionals need to begin acknowledging this fact in their daily practice.

Conclusion
restates and
strengthens thesis

Religion in Mental Health 8

References

Amaro, J. (2000). Psychology, psychoanalysis and religious faith. Nielsen's psychology of religion pages. Retrieved March 6, 2000 from the World Wide Web: http://www.psy www.com/psyrelig/amaro.html

Beyerman A. K. (1989). The holistic health movement. Tuscaloosa: Alabama University Press.

Ellis, A. (1993). Dogmatic devotion doesn't help, it hurts. In B. Slife (Ed.), Taking sides: Clashing views on controversial psychological issues (pp. 297-301). New York: Scribner.

Jones, J. W. (1991). Contemporary psychoanalysis and religion: Transference and transcendence. New Haven: Yale University Press.

Kristeva, J. (1987). In the beginning was love: Psychoanalysis and faith. New York: Columbia University Press.

Larson, D. (1998). Does religious commitment improve mental health? In B. Slife (Ed.), Taking sides: Clashing views on controversial psychological issues (pp. 292-296). New York: Scribner.

Pargament, K. I., Smith, B. W., Koening, H. G., Perez, L. (1998). Patterns of positive and negative religious coping with major life stressors. Journal for the Scientific Study of Religion, 37, 710-724.

"Psychological benefits." (1999). Walking the labyrinth. Retrieved April 3, 2000 from the World Wide Web: http://www.labyrinthway.com, html/benefits.html

References begin on a new page.

A World Wide Web source

A book

An article or chapter in a book

An article in a journal

Anonymous source alphabetized by title

Part Three

FURTHER VIEWS ON ARGUMENT

7

A Philosopher's View: The Toulmin Model

In Chapter 3, we explained the contrast between *deductive* and *inductive* arguments to focus on the two main ways in which we reason, either

- Making explicit something concealed in what we already accept (**deduction**) or
- Using what we have observed as a basis for asserting or proposing something new (**induction**).

Both types of reasoning share some structural features, as we also noticed. Thus, all reasoning is aimed at establishing some **thesis** (or conclusion) and does so by means of some **reasons**. These are two basic characteristics that any argument contains.

After a little scrutiny we can in fact point to several features shared by all arguments, deductive and inductive, good and bad alike. We use the vocabulary popularized by Stephen Toulmin in his book *An Introduction to Reasoning* (1979; second edition 1984) to explore the various elements of argument.

THE CLAIM

Every argument has a purpose, goal, or aim—namely, to establish a **claim** (*conclusion* or *thesis*). Suppose you were arguing in favor of equal rights for women. You might state your thesis or claim as follows:

    Men and women ought to have equal rights.

A more precise formulation of the claim might be

    Men and women ought to have equal legal rights.

A still more precise formulation might be

    Equal legal rights for men and women ought to be pro-
    tected by our Constitution.

The third version of this claim states what the controversy in the 1970s over the Equal Rights Amendment was all about.

Consequently, in reading or analyzing someone else's argument, your first question should naturally be: What is the argument intended to prove or establish? *What claim is it making?* Has this claim been clearly and precisely formulated, so that it unambiguously asserts what its advocate wants to assert?

GROUNDS

Once we have the argument's purpose or point clearly in mind and thus know what the arguer is claiming to establish, then we can ask for the evidence, reasons, support—in short, for the **grounds**—on which that claim is based. In a deductive argument these grounds are the premises from which the claim is deduced; in an inductive argument the grounds are the evidence—a sample, an observation, or an experiment—that makes the claim plausible or probable.

Not every kind of claim can be supported by every kind of ground, and conversely, not every kind of ground gives equally good support for every kind of claim. Suppose I claim that half the students in the classroom are women. I can ground this claim in any of several ways.

1. I can count all the women and all the men. Suppose the total equals fifty. If the number of women is twenty-five, and the number of men is twenty-five, I have vindicated my claim.
2. I can count a sample of, say, ten students and find that in the sample five of the students are women and thus have inductive—plausible but not conclusive—grounds for my claim.
3. I can point out that the students in the college divide equally into men and women and claim that this class is a representative sample of the whole college.

Obviously, ground 1 is stronger than ground 2, and 2 is far stronger than ground 3.

So far we have merely restated points about premises and conclusions covered in Chapter 3. But now we want to consider four additional features of arguments.

WARRANTS

Once we have the claim or the point of an argument fixed in mind and the evidence or reasons offered in its support, the next question to ask is *why* these reasons support this conclusion. What is the **warrant**, or guarantee, that the reasons proffered do support the claim or lead to the conclusion? In simple deductive arguments, the warrant takes different forms, as we shall see. In the simplest cases, we can point to the way in which the *meanings* of the key terms are really equivalent. Thus, if John is taller than Bill, then Bill must be shorter than John because of the meaning in English of "is shorter than" and "is taller than." In this case, the warrant is something we can state quite literally and explicitly.

In other cases, we may need to be more resourceful. A reliable tactic is to think up a simple *parallel argument*—that is, an argument exactly parallel in form and structure to the argument we are trying to defend. We then point out that if we are ready to accept the simpler argument, then we must accept the more complex argument because both arguments have exactly the same structure. For example, in her much-discussed essay of 1972 on the abortion controversy, "A Defense of Abortion," philosopher Judith Thomson argues that a pregnant woman has the right to an abortion to save her life, even if it involves the death of her unborn child. She anticipates that some readers may balk at her reasoning, and so she offers this parallel argument: Suppose you were locked in a tiny room with another human being, which through no fault of its own is growing uncontrollably, with the result that it is slowly crushing you to death. Of course, it would be morally permissible to kill the other person to save your own life. With the reader's presumed agreement on that conclusion, the parallel argument concerning the abortion situation—so Thomson hopes—is obvious and convincing.

In simple inductive arguments, we are likely to point to the way in which observations or sets of data constitute a *representative sample* of a whole (unexamined) population. Here, the warrant is the representativeness of the sample. For instance, in projecting a line on a graph through a set of points, we defend one projection over alternatives on the ground that it makes the smoothest fit through most of the points. In this case, the warrant is *simplicity* and *inclusiveness*. Or in defending one explanation against competing explanations of a phenomenon, we appeal to the way in which the preferred explanation can be seen as a *special case* of generally accepted physical laws. Examples of such warrants for inductive reasoning will be offered in following pages (see Chapter 8, A Logician's View: Deduction, Induction, Fallacies, p. 298).

Establishing the warrants for our reasoning—that is, explaining why our grounds really support our claims—can quickly become a highly technical and exacting procedure that goes far beyond what we can hope to explain in this book. Only a solid course or two in formal deductive logic and statistical methods can do justice to our current state of knowledge about these warrants. Developing a "feel" for why reasons or grounds are or are not relevant to what they are alleged to support is the most we can hope to do here without recourse to more rigorous techniques.

Even without formal training, however, one can sense that something is wrong with many bad arguments. Here is an example. British professor C. E. M. Joad found himself standing on a station platform, annoyed because he had just missed his train, when another train, making an unscheduled stop, pulled up to the platform in front of him. He decided to jump aboard, only to hear the porter say "I'm afraid you'll have to get off, sir. This train doesn't stop here." "In that case," replied Joad, "don't worry. I'm not on it."

BACKING

The kinds of reasons appropriate to support an amendment to the Constitution are completely different from the kinds appropriate to settle the question of what caused the defeat of Napoleon's invasion of Russia. Arguments for the amendment might be rooted in an appeal to fairness, whereas arguments about the military defeat might be rooted in letters and other documents in the French and Russian archives. The canons of good argument in each case derive from the ways in which the scholarly communities in law and history, respectively, have developed over the years to support, defend, challenge, and undermine a given kind of argument. Thus, the support or **backing** appropriate for one kind of argument might be quite inappropriate for another kind of argument.

Another way of stating this point is to recognize that once you have given reasons for a claim, you are then likely to be challenged to explain why these reasons are good reasons—why, that is, one should believe these reasons rather than regard them skeptically. Why (a simple example) should we accept the testimony of Dr. X when Dr. Y, equally renowned, supports the opposite side? Or why is it safe to rest a prediction on a small though admittedly carefully selected sample? Or why is it legitimate to argue that (1) if I dream I am the King of France, then I must exist, whereas it is illegitimate to argue that (2) if I dream I am the King of France, then the King of France must exist? To answer these kinds of challenges is to *back up* one's reasoning, and no argument is any better than its backing.

MODAL QUALIFIERS

As we have seen, all arguments are made up of assertions or propositions, which can be sorted into four categories:

- The *claim* (conclusion, thesis to be established),
- The *grounds* (explicit reasons advanced),
- The *warrant* (the principle that connects the ground to the claim), and
- The *backing* (implicit assumptions).

All these kinds of propositions have an explicit or tacit **modality** in which they are asserted, indicating the scope and character with which they are believed to hold true. Is the claim, for instance, believed to be *necessary*—or only *probable*? Is the claim believed to be *plausible*—or only *possible*? Of two reasons for a claim, both may be *good*, but one may be *better* than the other. Indicating the modality with which an assertion is advanced is crucial to any argument for or against it.

Empirical generalizations are typically *contingent* on various factors, and it is important to indicate such contingencies to protect the generalization against obvious counterexamples. Thus, consider this empirical generalization:

Students do best on final examinations if they study hard for them.

Are we really to believe that students who study regularly throughout the whole course and so do not need to cram for the final will do less well than students who neglect regular work in favor of several all-nighters at the last minute? Probably not; what is really meant is that *all other things being equal* (in Latin, *ceteris paribus*), concentrated study just before an exam will yield good results. Alluding to the contingencies in this way shows that the writer is aware of possible exceptions and that they are conceded right from the start.

Assertions also have varying **scope,** and indicating their scope is equally crucial to the role that an assertion plays in argument. Thus, suppose you are arguing against smoking, and the ground for your claim is this:

Heavy smokers cut short their life span.

Such an assertion will be clearer, as well as more likely to be true, if it is explicitly **quantified.** Here, there are three obvious alternative quantifications to choose among: *all* smokers cut short their life span, *most* do, or only *some* do. Until the assertion is quantified in one of these ways, we really do not know what is being asserted—and so we do not know what degree and kind of evidence and counterevidence is relevant. Other quantifiers include *few, rarely, many, often, sometimes, perhaps, usually, more or less, regularly, occasionally.*

In sum, sensitivity to the quantifiers and qualifiers appropriate for each of our assertions, whatever their role in an argument, will help prevent you from asserting exaggerations and other misguided generalizations.

REBUTTALS

Very few arguments of any interest are beyond dispute, conclusively knockdown affairs in which the claim of the argument is so rigidly tied to its grounds, warrants, and backing and its quantifiers and qualifiers so precisely orchestrated that it really proves its conclusion beyond any possibility of doubt. On the contrary, most arguments have many counterarguments, and sometimes one of these counterarguments is the most convincing.

Suppose one has taken a sample that appears to be random: An interviewer on your campus accosts the first ten students she encounters, and seven of them happen to be fraternity or sorority members. She is now ready to argue that seven-tenths of enrolled students belong to Greek organizations.

You believe, however, that the Greeks are in the minority and point out that she happens to have conducted her interview around the corner from the Panhellenic Society's office just off Sorority Row. Her random sample is anything but. The ball is now back in her court as you await her response to your rebuttal.

As this example illustrates, it is safe to say that we do not understand our own arguments very well until we have tried to get a grip on the places in which they are vulnerable to criticism, counterattack, or refutation. Edmund Burke (quoted in Chapter 3 but worth repeating) said, "He that wrestles with us strengthens our nerves, and sharpens our skill. Our antagonist is our helper." Therefore, cultivating alertness to such weak spots, girding one's loins to defend at these places, always helps strengthen one's position.

A MODEL ANALYSIS USING THE TOULMIN METHOD

To see how the Toulmin method can be used, let's apply it to an argument in this book, Susan Jacoby's "A First Amendment Junkie," on page 36.

The Claim   Jacoby's central thesis or claim is this: Any form of *censorship* — including feminist censorship of pornography in particular — *is wrong.*

Grounds   Jacoby offers six main reasons or grounds for her claim, roughly in this sequence (but arguably not in this order of importance).

First, feminists exaggerate the harm caused by pornography because they confuse expression of offensive ideas with harmful conduct.

Second, letting the government censor the expression of ideas and attitudes is the wrong response to the failure of parents to control the printed materials that get into the hands of their children.

Third, there is no unanimity even among feminists over what is pornography and what isn't.

Fourth, permitting censorship of pornography to please feminists could well lead to censorship on many issues of concern to feminists ("rape, abortion, menstruation, contraception, lesbianism").

Fifth, censorship under law shows a lack of confidence in the democratic process.

Finally, censorship of words and pictures is suppression of self-expression, and that violates the First Amendment.

Warrants   Each of these six grounds needs its own warrant, and the warrants vary considerably in their complexity. Jacoby (like most writers) is not so didactic as to make these warrants explicit. Taking them in order, this is what they look like.

First, since the First Amendment protects speech in the broadest sense, the censorship that the feminist attack on pornography advocates is *inconsistent* with the First Amendment.

Second, if feminists want to be consistent, then they must advocate censorship of *all* offensive self-expression, but such a radical interference with free speech (amounting virtually to repeal of the First Amendment) is indefensible.

Third, if feminists can't agree over what is pornographic, the censorship of pornography they propose is bound to be arbitrary.

Fourth, feminists ought to see that *they risk losing more than they can hope to gain* if they succeed in censoring pornography.

Fifth, the democratic process can be trusted to weed out harmful utterances.

Sixth, if feminists have a legal right to censor pornography, anti-feminists will claim the same right on other issues.

Backing   Why should the reader agree with Jacoby's grounds? She does not appeal to expert authority, the results of experimental tests or other statistical data, or the support of popular opinion. Instead, she relies principally on two things—but without saying so explicitly.

First, she assumes that the reader accepts the propositions that *freedom of self-expression is valuable* and that *censoring self-expression requires the strongest of reasons*. If there is no fundamental agreement on these propositions, several of her reasons cease to support her claim.

Second, she relies on the reader's open-mindedness and willingness to evaluate common sense (untechnical, ordinary, familiar) considerations at each step of the way. She relies also on the reader having had some personal experience with erotica, pornography, and art. Without that open-mindedness and experience, a reader is not likely to be persuaded by her rejection of the feminist demand for censorship.

Modal Qualifiers   Jacoby defends what she calls an "absolute interpretation" of the First Amendment—that is, the view that *all* censorship of words, pictures, and ideas is not only inconsistent with the First Amendment but is also politically unwise and morally objectionable. She allows that *some* pornography is highly offensive (it offends her, she insists); she allows that *some* pornography ("kiddie porn") may even be harmful to *some* viewers. But she also insists that *more* harm than good would result from the censorship of pornography. She points out that *some* paintings of nude women are art, not pornography; she implies that it is *impossible* to draw a sharp line between permissible erotic pornography and impermissible offensive pornography. She clearly believes that *all* Americans ought to understand and defend the First Amendment under the "absolute interpretation" she favors.

Rebuttals   Jacoby mentions several objections to her views, and perhaps the most effective aspect of her entire argument is her skill in identifying possible objections and meeting them effectively. (Notice the diversity of the objections and the various ways in which she replies.)

Objection: Some of her women friends tell her she is wrong.

Rebuttal: She admits she's a "First Amendment junkie," and she doesn't apologize for it.

Objection: "Kiddie porn" is harmful and deserves censorship.

Rebuttal: Such material is *not* protected by the First Amendment because it is an "abuse of power" of adults over children.

Objection: Pornography is a form of violence against women, and therefore it is especially harmful.

Rebuttal: (1) No, it really isn't harmful, but it is disgusting and offensive. (2) In any case, it's surely not as harmful as allowing American neo-Nazis to parade in Jewish neighborhoods. (Jacoby is referring to the march in Skokie, Illinois, in 1977, upheld by the courts as permissible political expression under the First Amendment despite its offensiveness to survivors of the Nazi concentration camps.)

Objection: Censoring pornography advances public respect for women.

Rebuttal: Censoring *Ms.* magazine, which antifeminists have already done, undermines women's freedom and self-expression.

Objection: Reasonable people can tell pornography when they see it, so censoring it poses no problems.

Rebuttal: Yes, there are clear cases of gross pornography; but there are lots of borderline cases, as women themselves prove when they disagree over whether a photo in *Penthouse* is offensively erotic or "lovely" and "sensuous."

A CHECKLIST FOR
USING THE TOULMIN METHOD

✓ What claim does the argument make?

✓ What grounds are offered for the claim?

✓ What warrants the inferences from the grounds to the claim?

✓ What backing supports the claim?

✓ With what modalities are the claim and grounds asserted?

✓ To what rebuttals are the claim, grounds, and backing vulnerable?

See the companion Web site **www.bedfordstmartins .com/barnetbedau** for links related to the Toulmin model.

8

A Logician's View:
Deduction, Induction,
Fallacies

In Chapter 3 we introduced these terms. Here we discuss them in greater detail.

DEDUCTION

The basic aim of deductive reasoning is to start with some assumption or premise and extract from it a conclusion—a logical consequence—that is concealed but implicit in it. Thus, taking the simplest case, if I assert as a premise

    1a. The cat is on the mat.

it is a matter of simple deduction to infer the conclusion that

    1b. The mat is under the cat.

Anyone who understands English would grant that 1b follows 1a—or equivalently, that 1b can be validly deduced from 1a—because whatever two objects, *A* and *B*, you choose, if *A* is *on B*, then *B* must be *under A*.

Thus, in this and all other cases of valid deductive reasoning, we can say not only that we are entitled to *infer* the conclusion from the premise—in this case, infer 1b from 1a—but that the premise *implies* the conclusion. Remember, too, the conclusion that the mat is under the cat 1b, inferred or deduced from the statement that the cat is on the mat 1a, does not depend on the truth of the statement that the cat is on the mat. The cat may in fact be hiding under the mat, but if the speaker (falsely) asserts that the cat is *on* the mat, the hearer validly (that is to say, logically) concludes that the mat is under the cat, 1b. Thus, 1b follows from

1a whether or not 1a is true; consequently, if 1a is true then so is 1b; but if 1a is false then 1b must be false also.

Let's take another example—more interesting but comparably simple:

2a. President Truman was underrated by his critics.

Given 2a, a claim amply verified by events of the 1950s, one is entitled to infer

2b. The critics underrated President Truman.

On what basis can we argue that 2a implies 2b? The two propositions are equivalent because a rule of English grammar assures us that we can convert the position of subject and predicate phrases in a sentence by shifting from the passive to the active voice (or vice versa) without any change in the conditions that make the proposition true (or false).

Both pairs of examples illustrate that in deductive reasoning, our aim is to transform, reformulate, or restate in our conclusion some (or, as in the two examples above, all) of the information contained in our premises.

Remember, even though a proposition or statement follows from a previous proposition or statement, the statements need not be true. We can see why if we consider another example. Suppose someone asserts or claims that

3a. The Hudson River is longer than the Mississippi.

As every student of American geography knows, 3a is false. But false or not, we can validly deduce from it

3b. The Mississippi is shorter than the Hudson.

This inference is valid (even though the conclusion is untrue) because the conclusion follows logically (more precisely, deductively) from 3a: In English, as we know, the meaning of "*A* is shorter than *B*," which appears in 3b, is simply the converse of "*B* is longer than *A*," which appears in 3a.

The deductive relation between 3a and 3b reminds us again that the idea of *validity*, which is so crucial to deduction, is not the same as the idea of *truth*. False propositions have implications—logical consequences—too, every bit as precisely as do true propositions.

In the three pairs of examples so far, what can we point to as the *warrant* for our claims? Well, look at the reasoning in each case; the arguments rely on rules of ordinary English, on the accepted meanings of words like *on*, *under*, and *underrated*.

In many cases, of course, the deductive inference or pattern of reasoning is much more complex than that which we have seen in the examples so far. When we introduced the idea of deduction in Chapter 3, we gave as our primary example the *syllogism*. Here is another example:

4. Texas is larger than California; California is larger than Arizona; therefore, Texas is larger than Arizona.

The conclusion in this syllogism is derivable from the two premises; that is, anyone who asserts the two premises is committed to accepting the conclusion as well, whether or not one thinks of it.

Notice again that the *truth* of the conclusion is not established merely by validity of the inference. The conclusion in this syllogism happens to be true. And the premises of this syllogism imply the conclusion. But the argument establishes the conclusion only because both of the premises on which the conclusion depends are true. Even a Californian admits that Texas is larger than California, which in turn is larger than Arizona. In other words, argument 4 is a *sound* argument because (as we explained in Chapter 3) it is valid and all its premises are true. All—and only—arguments that *prove* their conclusions have these two traits.

How might we present the warrant for the argument in 4? Short of a crash course in formal logic, either of two strategies might suffice. One is to argue from the fact that the validity of the inference depends on the meaning of a key concept, *being larger than*. This concept has the property of *transitivity*, a property that many concepts share (for example, *is equal to, is to the right of, is smarter than*—all are transitive concepts). Consequently, whatever A, B, and C are, if A is larger than B, and B is larger than C, then A will be larger than C. The final step is to substitute "Texas," "California," and "Arizona" for A, B, and C, respectively.

A second strategy, less abstract and more graphic, is to think of representing Texas, California, and Arizona by nested circles. Thus, the first premise in argument 4 would look like this:

The second premise would look like this:

The conclusion would look like this:

We can see that this conclusion follows from the premises because it amounts to nothing more than what one gets by superimposing the two premises on each other. Thus, the whole argument can be represented like this:

The so-called middle term in the argument—California—disappears from the conclusion; its role is confined to be the link between the other two terms, Texas and Arizona, in the premises. (This is an adaptation of the technique used in elementary formal logic known as Venn diagrams.) In this manner one can give graphic display to the important fact that the conclusion follows from the premises because one can literally *see* the conclusion represented by nothing more than a representation of the premises.

Both of these strategies bring out the fact that validity of deductive inference is a purely *formal* property of argument. Each strategy abstracts the form from the content of the propositions involved to show how the concepts in the premises are related to the concepts in the conclusion.

Not all deductive reasoning occurs in syllogisms, however, or at least not in syllogisms like the one in 4. (The term *syllogism* is sometimes used to refer to any deductive argument of whatever form, provided only that it has two premises.) In fact, syllogisms such as 4 are not the commonest form of our deductive reasoning at all. Nor are they the simplest (and of course, not the most complex). For an argument that is even simpler, consider this:

> 5. If the horses are loose, then the barn door was left unlocked. The horses are loose. Therefore, the barn door was left unlocked.

Here the pattern of reasoning is called **modus ponens,** which means positing or laying down the minor premise ("the horses are loose"). It is also called **hypothetical syllogism** because its major premise ("if the horses are loose, then the barn door was left unlocked") is a hypothetical or conditional proposition. The argument has the form: If *A* then *B*; *A*; therefore, *B*. Notice that the content of the assertions represented by *A* and *B* do not matter; any set of expressions having the same form or structure will do equally well, including assertions built out of meaningless terms, as in this example:

> 6. If the slithy toves, then the gyres gimble. The slithy toves. Therefore, the gyres gimble.

Argument 6 has exactly the same form as argument 5, and as a piece of deductive inference it is every bit as good. Unlike 5, however, 6 is of no interest to us because none of its assertions make any sense (unless you are a reader of Lewis Carroll's "Jabberwocky," and even then the sense of 6 is doubtful). You cannot, in short, use a valid deductive argument to prove anything unless the premises and the conclusion are *true,* but they can't be true unless they *mean* something in the first place.

This parallel between arguments 5 and 6 shows once again that deductive validity in an argument rests on the *form* or structure of the argument, and not on its content or meaning. If all one can say about an argument is that it is valid—that is, its conclusion follows from the premises—one has not given a sufficient reason for accepting the argument's conclusion. It has been said that the Devil can quote Scripture; similarly, an argument can be deductively valid and of no further interest or value whatever because valid (but false) conclusions can be drawn from false or even meaningless assumptions. For example,

> All spiders have six legs.
>
> All six-legged insects are poisonous.
>
> Therefore, all spiders are poisonous.

Here, the conclusion follows validly from the premises, even though all three propositions are false. Nevertheless, although validity by itself is not enough, it is a necessary condition of any deductive argument that purports to establish its conclusion.

Now let us consider another argument with the same form as 5 and 6, only more interesting.

> 7. If President Truman knew the Japanese were about to surrender, then it was immoral of him to order that atom bombs be dropped on Hiroshima and Nagasaki. Truman knew the Japanese were about to surrender. Therefore, it was immoral of him to order dropping those bombs.

As in the two previous examples, anyone who assents to the premises in argument 7 must assent to the conclusion; the form of arguments 5, 6, and 7 is identical. But do the premises of argument 7 *prove* the conclusion? That depends on whether both premises are true. Well, are they? This turns on a number of considerations, and it is worthwhile pausing to examine this argument closely to illustrate the kinds of things that are involved in answering this question.

Let us begin by examining the second (minor) premise. Its truth is controversial even to this day. Autobiography, memoranda, other documentary evidence—all are needed to assemble the evidence to back up the grounds for the thesis or claim made in the conclusion of this valid argument. Evaluating this material effectively will probably involve not only further deductions, but inductive reasoning as well.

Now consider the first (major) premise in argument 7. Its truth doesn't depend on what history shows but on the moral principles one accepts. The major premise has the form of a hypothetical proposition ("if . . . then . . .") and asserts a connection between two very different kinds of things. The antecedent of the hypothetical (the clause following "if") mentions facts about Truman's *knowledge,* and the consequent of the hypothetical (the clause following "then") mentions facts about the *morality* of his conduct in light of such knowledge. The major premise as a whole can thus be seen as expressing *a principle of moral responsibility.*

Such principles can, of course, be controversial. In this case, for instance, is the principle peculiarly relevant to the knowledge and conduct of a president of the United States? Probably not; it is far more likely that this principle is merely a special case of a more general proposition about anyone's moral responsibility. (After all, we know a great deal more about the conditions of our own moral responsibility than we do about those of high government officials.) We might express this more general principle in this way: If we have knowledge that would make our violent conduct unnecessary, then we are immoral if we deliberately act violently anyway. Thus, accepting this general principle can serve as a basis for defending the major premise of argument 7.

We have examined this argument in some detail because it illustrates the kinds of considerations needed to test whether a given argument is not only valid but whether its premises are true—that is, whether its premises really prove the conclusion.

The great value of the form of argument known as hypothetical syllogism, exemplified by arguments 5, 6, and 7, is that the structure of the argument is so simple and so universally applicable in reasoning that it is often both easy and worthwhile to formulate one's claims so that they can be grounded by an argument of this sort.

Before leaving the subject of deductive inference, consider three other forms of argument, each of which can be found in actual use elsewhere in the readings in this volume. The simplest of these is **disjunctive syllogism,** so called because, again, it has two premises, and its major premise is a **disjunction.** That is, a disjunctive syllogism is a complex assertion built from two or more alternatives joined by the conjunction *or;* each of these alternatives is called a **disjunct.** For example,

8. Either censorship of television shows is overdue, or our society is indifferent to the education of its youth. Our society is not indifferent to the education of its youth. Therefore, censorship of television is overdue.

Notice, by the way, that the validity of an argument, as in this case, does not turn on pedantic repetition of every word or phrase as the argument moves along; nonessential elements can be dropped, or equivalent expressions substituted for variety without adverse effect on the reasoning. Thus, in conversation or in writing, the argument in 8 might actually be presented like this:

9. Either censorship of television is overdue, or our society is indifferent to the education of its youth. But, of course, we aren't indifferent; it's censorship that's overdue.

The key feature of disjunctive syllogism, as example 9 suggests, is that the conclusion is whichever of the disjuncts is left over after the others have been negated in the minor premise. Thus, we could easily have a very complex disjunctive syllogism, with a dozen disjuncts in the major premise, and seven of them denied in the minor premise, leaving a conclusion of the remaining five. Usually, however, a disjunctive argument is formulated in this manner: Assert a disjunction with two or more disjuncts in the major premise; then *deny all but one* in the minor premise; and infer validly the remaining disjunct as the conclusion. That was the form of argument 9.

Another type of argument, especially favored by orators and rhetoricians, is the **dilemma.** Ordinarily we use the term *dilemma* in the sense of an awkward predicament, as when we say, "His dilemma was that he didn't have enough money to pay the waiter." But when logicians refer to a dilemma, they mean a forced choice between two or more equally unattractive alternatives. For example, the predicament of the U.S. government during the mid-1980s as it faced the crisis brought on by terrorist attacks on American civilian targets, which were believed, during that time, to be inspired and supported by the Libyan government, can be formulated in a dilemma:

10. If the United States bombs targets in Libya, innocent people will be killed and the Arab world will be angered. If the United States doesn't bomb Libyan targets, then terrorists will go unpunished and the United States will lose respect among other governments. Either the United States bombs Libyan targets or it doesn't. Therefore, in either case unattractive consequences will follow: The innocent will be killed, or terrorists will go unpunished.

Notice first the structure of the argument: two conditional propositions asserted as premises, followed by another premise that states a **necessary truth.** (The premise, "Either we bomb the Libyans or we don't," is a disjunction; since its two alternatives are exhaustive, one of the two alternatives must be true. Such a statement is often called analytically true, or a *tautology.*) No doubt the conclusion of this dilemma follows from its premises.

But does the argument prove, as it purports to do, that whatever the U.S. government does, it will suffer "unattractive consequences"? It is customary to speak of "the horns of the dilemma," as though the challenge posed by the dilemma were like a bull ready to gore you whichever direction you turn. But if the two conditional premises failed to exhaust the possibilities, then one can escape from the dilemma by going "between the horns"; that is, by finding a third alternative. If (as in this case) that is not possible, one can still ask whether both of the main premises are true. (In this argument, it should be clear that neither of these main premises spells out all or even most of the consequences that could be foreseen.) Even so, in cases where both these conditional premises are true, it may be that the consequences of one alternative are nowhere nearly so bad as those of the other. If that is true, but our reasoning stops before evaluating that fact, we may be guilty of failing to distinguish between the greater and the lesser of two admitted evils. The logic of the dilemma itself cannot decide this choice for us. Instead, we must bring to bear empirical inquiry and imagination to the evaluation of the grounds of the dilemma itself.

Writers commonly use the term *dilemma* without explicitly formulating the dilemma to which they refer, leaving it for the readers to do. And sometimes, what is called a dilemma really isn't one. (Remember the dog's tail? Calling it a leg doesn't make it one.) As an example, consider the plight of Seaman Holmes in the case of *United States v. Holmes* (p. 347). Either Holmes decides to throw some passengers overboard to keep the rowboat afloat, or he doesn't. If he does throw some overboard, he may be guilty of murder. If he doesn't throw them overboard, the rowboat may sink and all the passengers and crew in it drown. Neither the defense nor prosecuting attorney nor the judge actually formulates Holmes's predicament in the language of a dilemma, as we have, but it is plain to see that this is exactly how we ought to view Holmes's problem: Which of the horns of the dilemma should he embrace, and why? Or is there a third way for him to act, allowing him to go between those horns?

Finally, one of the most powerful and dramatic forms of argument is **reductio ad absurdum** (from the Latin, meaning "reduction to absurdity"). The idea of a reductio argument is to disprove a proposition by showing the absurdity of its inevitable conclusion. It is used, of course, to refute your opponent's position and prove your own. For example, in Plato's *Republic,* Socrates asks an old gentleman, Cephalus, to define what right conduct is. Cephalus says that it is paying your debts and keeping your word. Socrates rejects this answer by showing that it leads to a contradiction. He argues that Cephalus cannot have given the correct answer because if we assume that he did, we will be quickly led into contradictions; in some cases when you keep your word you will nonetheless be doing the wrong thing. For suppose, says Socrates, that you borrowed a weapon from a man, promising to return it when he asks for it. One day he comes to your door, demanding his weapon and swearing angrily that he intends to murder a neighbor. Keeping your word under those circumstances is absurd, Socrates implies, and the reader of the dialogue is left to infer that Cephalus's definition, which led to this result, is refuted.

Let's take a closer look at another example. Suppose you are opposed to any form of gun control, whereas I am in favor of gun control. I might try to refute your position by attacking it with a reductio argument. To do that, I start out by assuming the very opposite of what I believe or favor and try to establish a contradiction that results from following out the consequences of this initial assumption. My argument might look like this:

11. Let's assume your position—namely, that there ought to be no legal restrictions whatever on the sale and ownership of guns. That means that you'd permit having every neighborhood hardware store sell pistols and rifles to whoever walks in the door. But that's not all. You apparently also would permit selling machine guns to children, antitank weapons to lunatics, small-bore cannons to the near-sighted, as well as guns and the ammunition to go with them to anyone with a criminal record. But this is utterly preposterous. No one could favor such a dangerous policy. So the only question worth debating is what kind of gun control is necessary.

Now in this example, my reductio of your position on gun control is not based on claiming to show that you have strictly contradicted yourself, for there is no purely logical contradiction in opposing all forms of gun control. Instead, what I have tried to do is to show that there is a contradiction between what you profess—no gun controls whatever—and what you probably really believe, if only you will stop to think about it—no lunatic should be allowed to buy a loaded machine gun.

My refutation of your position rests on whether I succeed in establishing an inconsistency among your own beliefs. If it turns out that you really believe lunatics should be free to purchase guns and ammunition, then my attempted refutation fails.

In explaining reductio ad absurdum, we have had to rely on another idea fundamental to logic, that of **contradiction,** or inconsistency. (We used this idea, remember, to define validity in Chapter 3. A deductive argument is valid if and only if affirming the premises and denying the conclusion results in a contradiction.) The opposite of contradiction is **consistency,** a notion of hardly less importance to good reasoning than validity. These concepts deserve a few words of further explanation and illustration. Consider this pair of assertions:

12. Abortion is homicide.
13. Racism is unfair.

No one would plausibly claim that we can infer or deduce 13 from 12, or, for that matter, 12 from 13. This almost goes without saying, because there is no evident connection between these two assertions. They are unrelated assertions; logically speaking, they are *independent* of each other. In such cases the two assertions are mutually *consistent;* that is, both could be true—or both could be false. But now consider another proposition:

14. Euthanasia is not murder.

Could a person assert 12 *Abortion is homicide* and also assert 14 *Euthanasia is not murder*, and be consistent? This question is equivalent to asking whether one could assert the **conjunction** of these two propositions—namely,

15. Abortion is homicide and euthanasia is not murder.

It is not so easy to say whether 15 is consistent or inconsistent. The kinds of moral scruples that might lead a person to assert one of these conjuncts (that is, one of the two initial propositions, *Abortion is homicide* and *Euthanasia is not murder*) might lead to the belief that the other one must be false and thus to the conclusion that 15 is inconsistent. (Notice that if 12 were the assertion that *Abortion is murder*, instead of *Abortion is homicide*, the problem of asserting consistently both 12 and 14 would be more acute.) Yet if we think again, we might imagine someone being convinced that there is no inconsistency in asserting that *Abortion is homicide*, say, and that *Euthanasia is not murder*, or even the reverse. (For instance, suppose you believed that the unborn deserve a chance to live and that putting elderly persons to death in a painless manner and with their consent confers a benefit on them.)

Let us generalize: We can say of any set of propositions that they are *consistent* if and only if *all could be true together*. (Notice that it follows from this definition that propositions that mutually imply each other, as do *The cat is on the mat* and *The mat is under the cat*, are consistent.) Remember that, once again, the truth of the assertions in question does not matter. Two propositions can be consistent or not, quite apart from whether they are true. Not so with falsehood: It follows from our definition of consistency that an *inconsistent* proposition must be *false*. (We have relied on this idea in explaining how a reductio ad absurdum works.)

Assertions or claims that are not consistent can take either of two forms. Suppose you assert proposition 12, that abortion is homicide, early in an essay you are writing, but later on you assert

16. Abortion is harmless.

You have now asserted a position on abortion that is strictly contrary to the one with which you began; contrary in the sense that both assertions 12 and 16 cannot be true. It is simply not true that if an abortion involves killing a human being (which is what *homicide* strictly means), then it causes no one any harm (killing a person always causes harm—even if it is excusable, justifiable, not wrong, the best thing to do in the circumstances, and so on). Notice that although 12 and 16 cannot both be true, they can both be false. In fact, many people who are perplexed about the morality of abortion believe precisely this. They concede that abortion does harm the fetus, so 16 must be false; but they also believe that abortion doesn't kill a person, so 12 must also be false.

Or consider another, simpler case. If you describe the glass as half empty and I describe it as half full, both of us can be right; the two assertions are consistent, even though they sound vaguely incompatible. (This is the reason that disputing over whether the glass is half full or half empty has become the popular paradigm of a futile, purely *verbal disagreement.*) But if I describe the glass as half empty whereas you insist that it is two-thirds empty, then we have a real disagreement; your description and mine are strictly contrary, in that both cannot be true—although both can be false. (Both are false if the glass is only one-quarter full.)

This, by the way, enables us to define the difference between a pair of **contradictory** propositions and a pair of **contrary** propositions. Two propositions are contrary if and only if both cannot be true (though both can be false); two propositions are contradictory if and only if they are such that if one is true the other must be false, and vice versa. Thus, if Jack says that Alice Walker's *The Color Purple* is a better novel than Mark Twain's *Huckleberry Finn*, and Jill says, "No, *Huckleberry Finn* is better than *The Color Purple*," she is contradicting Jack. If what either one of them says is true, then what the other says must be false.

A more subtle case of contradiction arises when two or more of one's own beliefs implicitly contradict each other. We may find ourselves saying "Travel is broadening," and saying an hour later, "People don't really change." Just beneath the surface of these two beliefs lies a self-contradiction: How can travel broaden us unless it influences—and changes—our beliefs, values, and outlook? But if we can't really change ourselves, then traveling to new places won't change us, either. (Indeed, there is a Roman saying to the effect that travelers change the skies above them, not their hearts.) "Travel is broadening" and "People don't change" collide with each other; something has to give.

Our point, of course, is not that you must never say today something that contradicts something you said yesterday. Far from it; if you think you were mistaken yesterday, of course you will take a different position today. But what you want to avoid is what George Orwell called *doublethink* in his novel *1984*: "*Doublethink* means the power of holding two contradictory beliefs in one's mind simultaneously, and accepting them both."

Genuine contradiction, and not merely contrary assertion, is the situation we should expect to find in some disputes. Someone advances a thesis—such as the assertion in 12, *Abortion is homicide*—and someone else flatly contradicts it by the simple expedient of negating it, thus:

17. Abortion is not homicide.

If we can trust public opinion polls, many of us are not sure whether to agree with 12 or with 17. But we should agree that whichever is true, *both* cannot be true, and *both* cannot be false. The two assertions, between them, exclude all other possibilities; they pose a forced choice for our belief. (Again, we have met this idea, too, in a reductio ad absurdum.)

Now it is one thing for Jack and Jill in a dispute or argument to contradict each other. It is quite another matter for Jack to contradict himself. One wants (or should want) to avoid self-contradiction because of the embarrassing position in which one then finds oneself. Once I have contradicted myself, what are others to believe I really believe? What, indeed, *do* I believe, for that matter?

It may be, as Emerson observed, that a "foolish consistency is the hobgoblin of little minds"—that is, it may be shortsighted to purchase a consistency in one's beliefs at the expense of flying in the face of common sense. But making an effort to avoid a foolish inconsistency is the hallmark of serious thinking.

While we are speaking of inconsistency, we should spend a moment on **paradox.** The word refers to two different things:

- An assertion that is essentially self-contradictory and therefore cannot be true and
- A seemingly contradictory assertion that nevertheless may be true.

An example of the first might be, "Evaluations concerning quality in literature are all a matter of personal judgment, but Shakespeare is the world's greatest writer." It is hard to make any sense out of this assertion. Contrast it with a paradox of the second sort, a *seeming* contradiction that may make sense, such as "The longest way round is the shortest way home," or "Work is more fun than fun," or "The best way to find happiness is not to look for it." Here we have assertions that are striking because as soon as we hear them we realize that although they seem inconsistent and self-defeating, they contain (or may contain) profound truths. Paradoxes of this second sort are especially common in religious texts, where they may imply a mysterious reality concealed by a world of contradictory appearances. Examples are "Some who are last shall be first, and some who are first shall be last" (Jesus, quoted in Luke 13:30), and "Death, thou shalt die" (the poet John Donne, alluding to the idea that the person who has faith in Jesus dies to this world but lives eternally). If you use the word *paradox* in your own writing—for instance, to characterize an argument that you are reading—be sure that your reader will understand in which sense you are using the word. (And, of course, you will not want to write paradoxes of the first, self-contradictory sort.)

INDUCTION

Deduction involves logical thinking that applies to any assertion or claim whatever—because every possible statement, true or false, has its deductive logical consequences. Induction is relevant to one kind of assertion only; namely, to **empirical** or *factual* claims. Other kinds of assertions (such as definitions, mathematical equations, and moral or legal norms) simply are not the product of inductive reasoning and cannot serve as a basis for further inductive thinking.

And so, in studying the methods of induction, we are exploring tactics and strategies useful in gathering and then using **evidence**—empirical, observational, experimental—in support of a belief as its ground. Modern scientific knowledge is the product of these methods, and they differ somewhat from one science to another because they depend on the theories and technology appropriate to each of the sciences. Here, all we can do is discuss generally the more abstract features common to inductive inquiry generally. For fuller details, you must eventually consult your local physicist, chemist, geologist, or their colleagues and counterparts in other scientific fields.

Observation and Inference

Let us begin with a simple example. Suppose we have evidence (actually we don't, but that will not matter for our purposes) in support of the claim that

1. In a sample of 500 smokers 230 persons observed have cardiovascular disease.

The basis for asserting 1—the evidence or ground—would be, presumably, straightforward physical examination of the 500 persons in the sample, one by one.

With this claim in hand, we can think of the purpose and methods of induction as being pointed in both of two opposite directions: toward establishing the basis or ground of the very empirical proposition with which we start (in this example the observation stated in 1) or toward understanding what that observation indicates or suggests as a more general, inclusive, or fundamental fact of nature.

In each case, we start from something we *do* know (or take for granted and treat as a sound starting point)—some fact of nature, perhaps a striking or commonplace event that we have observed and recorded—and then go on to something we do *not* fully know and perhaps cannot directly observe. In example 1, only the second of these two orientations is of any interest, and so let us concentrate exclusively on it. Let us also generously treat as a *method* of induction any regular pattern or style of nondeductive reasoning that we could use to support a claim such as that in 1.

Anyone truly interested in the observed fact that *230 of 500 smokers have cardiovascular disease* is likely to start speculating about, and thus be interested in finding out, whether any or all of several other propositions are also true. For example, one might wonder whether

2. *All* smokers have cardiovascular disease or will develop it during their lifetimes.

This claim is a straightforward generalization of the original observation as reported in claim 1. When we think inductively about the linkage between 1 and 2, we are reasoning from an observed sample (some smokers—that is, 230 of the 500 *observed*) to the entire membership of a more inclusive class (*all* smokers, whether observed or not). The fundamental question raised by reasoning from the narrower claim 1 to the broader claim 2 is whether we have any ground for believing that what is true of *some* members of a class is true of them *all*. So the difference between 1 and 2 is that of *quantity* or scope.

We can also think inductively about the *relation* between the factors mentioned in 1. Having observed data as reported in 1, we may be tempted to assert a different and profounder kind of claim:

   3. Smoking *causes* cardiovascular disease.

Here our interest is not merely in generalizing from a sample to a whole class; it is the far more important one of *explaining* the observation with which we began in claim 1. Certainly the preferred, even if not the only, mode of explanation for a natural phenomenon is a *causal* explanation. In proposition 3, we propose to explain the presence of one phenomenon (cardiovascular disease) by the prior occurrence of an independent phenomenon (smoking). The observation reported in 1 is now being used as evidence or support for this new conjecture stated in 3.

Our original claim in 1 asserted no causal relation between anything and anything else; whatever the cause of cardiovascular disease may be, that cause is not observed, mentioned, or assumed in assertion 1. Similarly, the observation asserted in claim 1 is consistent with many explanations. For example, the explanation of 1 might not be 3, but some other, undetected, carcinogenic factor unrelated to smoking—for instance, exposure to high levels of radon. The question one now faces is what can be added to 1, or teased out of it, to produce an adequate ground for claiming 3. (We shall return to this example for closer scrutiny.)

But there is a third way to go beyond 1. Instead of a straightforward generalization, as we had in 2, or a pronouncement on the cause of a phenomenon, as in 3, we might have a somewhat more complex and cautious further claim in mind, such as this:

   4. Smoking is a factor in the causation of cardiovascular disease in
      some persons.

This proposition, like 3, advances a claim about causation. But 4 is obviously a weaker claim than 3. That is, other observations, theories, or evidence that would require us to reject 3 might be consistent with 4; evidence that would support 4 could easily fail to be enough to support 3. Consequently, it is even possible that 4 is true although 3 is false, because 4 allows for other (unmentioned) factors in the causation of cardiovascular disease (genetic or dietary factors, for example) which may not be found in all smokers.

Propositions 2, 3, and 4 differ from proposition 1 in an important respect. We began by assuming that 1 states an empirical fact based on direct observation, whereas these others do not. Instead, they state empirical *hypotheses* or conjectures—tentative generalizations not fully confirmed—each of which goes beyond the observed facts asserted in 1. Each of 2, 3, and 4 can be regarded as an *inductive inference* from 1. We can also say that 2, 3, and 4 are hypotheses relative to 1, even if relative to some other starting point (such as all the information that scientists today really have about smoking and cardiovascular disease) they are not.

Probability

Another way of formulating the last point is to say that whereas proposition 1, a statement of observed fact (*230 out of 500 smokers have cardiovascular disease*), has a **probability** of 1.0—that is, it is absolutely certain—the probability of each of the hypotheses stated in 2, 3, and 4, *relative* to 1 is smaller than 1.0. (We need not worry here about how much smaller than 1.0 the probabilities are, nor about how to calculate these probabilities precisely.) Relative to some starting point other than 1, however, the probability of these same three hypotheses might be quite different. Of course, it still would not be 1.0, absolute certainty. But it takes only a moment's reflection to realize that, whatever may be the probability of 2 or 3 or 4 relative to 1, those probabilities in each case will be quite different relative to different information, such as this:

5. Ten persons observed in a sample of 500 smokers have cardiovascular disease.

The idea that a *given proposition can have different probabilities* relative to different bases is fundamental to all inductive reasoning. It can be convincingly illustrated by the following example. Suppose we want to consider the probability of this proposition being true:

6. Susanne Smith will live to be eighty.

Taken as an abstract question of fact, we cannot even guess what the probability is with any assurance. But we can do better than guess; we can in fact even calculate the answer, if we are given some further information. Thus, suppose we are told that

7. Susanne Smith is seventy-nine.

Our original question then becomes one of determining the probability that 6 is true given 7; that is, relative to the evidence contained in proposition 7. No doubt, if Susanne Smith really is seventy-nine, then the probability that she will live to be eighty is greater than if we know only that

8. Susanne Smith is more than nine years old.

Obviously, a lot can happen to Susanne in the seventy years between nine and seventy-nine that is not very likely to happen to her in the one year between seventy-nine and eighty. And so, proposition 6 is more probable relative to proposition 7 than it is relative to proposition 8.

Let us disregard 7 and instead further suppose for the sake of the argument that the following is true:

9. Ninety percent of the women alive at seventy-nine live to be eighty.

Given this additional information, we now have a basis for answering our original question about proposition 6 with some precision. But suppose, in addition to 8, we are also told that

10. Susanne Smith is suffering from inoperable cancer.

and also that

11. The survival rate for women suffering from inoperable cancer is 0.6 years (that is, the average life span for women after a diagnosis of inoperable cancer is about seven months).

With this new information, the probability that 6 will be true has dropped significantly, all because we can now estimate the probability in relation to a new body of evidence.

The probability of an event, thus, is not a fixed number but one that varies because it is always relative to some evidence—and given different evidence, one and the same event can have different probabilities. In other words, the probability of any event is always relative to how much is known (assumed, believed), and because different persons may know different things about a given event, or the same person may know different things at different times, one and the same event can have two or more probabilities. This conclusion is not a paradox but a logical consequence of the concept of what it is for an event to have (that is, to be assigned) a probability.

If we shift to the *calculation* of probabilities, we find that generally we have two ways to calculate them. One way to proceed is by the method of **a priori** or **equal probabilities**—that is, by reference to the relevant possibilities taken abstractly and apart from any other information. Thus, in an election contest with only two candidates, Smith and Jones, each of the candidates has a fifty-fifty chance of winning (whereas in a three-candidate race, each candidate would have one chance in three of winning). Therefore, the probability that Smith will win is 0.5, and the probability that Jones will win is also 0.5. (The sum of the probabilities of all possible independent outcomes must always equal 1.0, which is obvious enough if you think about it.)

But in politics the probabilities are not reasonably calculated so abstractly. We know that many empirical factors affect the outcome of an election and that a calculation of probabilities in ignorance of those factors is likely to be drastically misleading. In our example of the two-candidate election, suppose Smith has strong party support and is the incumbent, whereas Jones represents a party long out of power and is further handicapped by being relatively unknown. No one who knows anything about electoral politics would give Jones the same chance of winning as Smith. The two events are not equiprobable in relation to all the information available.

Not only that, a given event can have more than one probability. This happens whenever we calculate a probability by relying on different bodies of data that report how often the event in question has been observed to happen. Probabilities calculated in this way are **relative frequencies.** Our earlier hypothetical example of Susanne Smith provides an illustration. If she is a smoker and we have observed that 100 out of a random set of 500 smokers are observed to have cardiovascular disease, we have a basis for claiming that she has a probability of 100 in 500, or 0.2 (one-fifth), of having this disease. However, if we had other data showing that 250 out of 500 women smokers aged eighty or older have cardiovascular disease, we have a basis for believing that there is a probability of 250 in 500, or 0.5 (one-half), that she has this disease. Notice, of course, that in both calculations we assume that Susanne Smith is not among the persons we have examined. In both cases we infer the probability with which she has this disease from observing its frequency in populations that exclude her.

Both methods of calculating probabilities are legitimate; in each case the calculation is relative to observed circumstances. But as the examples show, it is most reasonable to have recourse to the method of equiprobabilities only when few or no other factors affecting possible outcomes are known.

Mill's Methods

Let us return to our earlier discussion of smoking and cardiovascular disease and consider in greater detail the question of a causal connection between the two phenomena. We began thus:

1. In a sample of 500 smokers 230 persons observed have cardiovascular disease.

We regarded 1 as an observed fact, though in truth, of course, it is mere supposition. Our question now is, how might we augment this information so as to strengthen our confidence that

3. Smoking *causes* cardiovascular disease.

or at least

4. Smoking is a factor in the causation of cardiovascular disease in some persons.

Suppose further examination showed that

12. In the sample of 230 smokers with cardiovascular disease, no other suspected factor (such as genetic predisposition, lack of physical exercise, age over fifty) was also observed.

Such an observation would encourage us to believe 3 or 4 is true. Why? We are encouraged to believe it because we are inclined to believe also that whatever the cause of a phenomenon is, it must *always* be present when its effect is present. Thus, the inference from 1 to 3 or 4 is supported by 12, using **Mill's Method of Agreement,** named after the British philosopher, John Stuart Mill (1806–1873), who first formulated it. It is called a method of agreement because of the way in which the inference relies on *agreement* among the observed phenomena where a presumed cause is thought to be *present.*

Let us now suppose that in our search for evidence to support 3 or 4 we conduct additional research and discover that

13. In a sample of 500 nonsmokers, selected to be representative of both sexes, different ages, dietary habits, exercise patterns, and so on, none is observed to have cardiovascular disease.

This observation would further encourage us to believe that we had obtained significant additional confirmation of 3 or 4. Why? Because we now know that factors present (such as male sex, lack of exercise, family history of cardiovascular disease) in cases where the effect is absent (no cardiovascular disease observed) cannot be the cause. This is an example of **Mill's Method of Difference,** so called because the cause or causal factor of an effect must be *different* from whatever the factors are that are present when the effect is *absent.*

Suppose now that, increasingly confident we have found the cause of cardiovascular disease, we study our first sample of 230 smokers ill with the disease, and discover this:

14. Those who smoke two or more packs of cigarettes daily for ten or more years have cardiovascular disease either much younger or much more severely than those who smoke less.

This is an application of **Mill's Method of Concomitant Variation,** perhaps the most convincing of the three methods. Here we deal not merely with the presence of the conjectured cause (smoking) or the absence of the effect we are studying (cardiovascular disease), as we were previously, but with the more interesting and subtler matter of the *degree and regularity of the correlation* of the supposed cause and effect. According to the observations reported in 14, it strongly appears that the more we have of the "cause" (smoking), the sooner or the more intense the onset of the "effect" (cardiovascular disease).

Notice, however, what happens to our confirmation of 3 and 4 if, instead of the observation reported in 14, we had observed

15. In a representative sample of 500 nonsmokers, cardiovascular disease was observed in 34 cases.

(Let us not pause here to explain what makes a sample more or less representative of a population, although the representativeness of samples is vital to all statistical reasoning.) Such an observation would lead us almost immediately to suspect some other or additional causal factor: Smoking might indeed be *a* factor in causing cardiovascular disease, but it can hardly be *the* cause because (using Mill's Method of Difference) we cannot have the effect, as we do in the observed sample reported in 15, unless we also have the cause.

An observation such as the one in 15, however, is likely to lead us to think our hypothesis that *smoking causes cardiovascular disease* has been disconfirmed. But we have a fallback position ready; we can still defend a weaker hypothesis, namely 4, *Smoking is a factor in the causation of cardiovascular disease in some persons.* Even if 3 stumbles over the evidence in 15, 4 does not. It is still quite possible that smoking is a factor in causing this disease, even if it is not the *only* factor—and if it is, then 4 is true.

Confirmation, Mechanism, and Theory

Notice that in the discussion so far, we have spoken of the *confirmation* of a hypothesis, such as our causal claim in 4, but not of its *verification*. (Similarly, we have imagined very different evidence, such as that stated in 15, leading us to speak of the *dis*confirmation of 3, though not of its *falsi*fication.) Confirmation (getting some evidence for) is weaker than verification (getting sufficient evidence to regard as true); and our (imaginary) evidence so far in favor of 4 falls well short of conclusive support. Further research—the study of more representative or much larger samples, for example—might yield very different observations. It might lead us to conclude that although initial research had confirmed our hypothesis about smoking as the cause of cardiovascular disease, the additional information obtained subsequently disconfirmed the hypothesis. For most interesting hypotheses, both in detective stories and in modern science, there is both confirming and disconfirming evidence simultaneously. The challenge is to evaluate the hypothesis by considering such conflicting evidence.

As long as we confine our observations to *correlations* of the sort reported in our several (imaginary) observations, such as proposition 1, *230 smokers in a group of 500 have cardiovascular disease,* or 12, *230 smokers with the disease share no other suspected factors,* such as lack of exercise, any defense of a *causal* hypothesis such as claim 3, *Smoking causes cardiovascular disease,* or claim 4, *Smoking is a factor in causing the disease,* is not likely to convince the skeptic or lead those with beliefs alternative to 3 and 4 to abandon them and agree with us. Why is that? It is because a causal hypothesis without any account of the *underlying mechanism* by means of which the (alleged) cause produces the effect will seem superficial. Only when we can specify in detail *how* the (alleged) cause produces the effect will the causal hypothesis be convincing.

In other cases, in which no mechanism can be found, we seek instead to embed the causal hypothesis in a larger *theory,* one that rules out as incompatible any causal hypothesis except the favored one. (That is, we appeal to the test of consistency and thereby bring deductive reasoning to bear on our problem.) Thus, perhaps we cannot specify any mechanism—any underlying structure that generates a regular sequence of events, one of which is the effect we are studying—to explain why, for example, the gravitational mass of a body causes it to attract other bodies. But we can embed this claim in a larger body of physical theory that rules out as inconsistent any alternative causal explanation. To do that convincingly in regard to any given causal hypothesis, as this example suggests, requires detailed knowledge of the current state of the relevant body of scientific theory, something far beyond our aim or need to consider in further detail here.

FALLACIES

The straight road on which sound reasoning proceeds gives little latitude for cruising about. Irrationality, carelessness, passionate attachment to one's unexamined beliefs, and the sheer complexity of some issues, not to mention Original Sin, occasionally spoil the reasoning of even the best of us. Although in this book we reprint many varied voices and arguments, we hope we have reprinted no readings that exhibit the most flagrant errors or commit the graver abuses against the canons of good reasoning. Nevertheless, an inventory of those abuses and their close examination can be an instructive (as well as an amusing) exercise—instructive because the diagnosis and repair of error helps to fix more clearly the principles of sound reasoning on which such remedial labors depend; amusing because we are so constituted that our perception of the nonsense of others can stimulate our mind, warm our heart, and give us comforting feelings of superiority.

The discussion that follows, then, is a quick tour through the twisting lanes, mudflats, forests, and quicksands of the faults that one sometimes encounters in reading arguments that stray from the highway of clear thinking.

We can and do apply the term *fallacy* to many types of errors, mistakes, and confusions in oral and written discourse, in which our reasoning has gone awry. For convenience, we can group the fallacies by referring to the six aspects of reasoning identified in the Toulmin Method, described earlier (p. 289). Let us take up first those fallacies that spoil our *claims* or our *grounds* for them. These are errors in the meaning, clarity, or sense of a sentence or of some word or phrase in a sentence being used in the role of a claim or ground. They are thus not so much errors of *reasoning* as they are errors in *reasons* or in the *claims* that our reasons are intended to support or criticize.

Many Questions

The old saw, "When did you stop beating your wife?" illustrates the **fallacy of many questions.** This question, as one can readily see, is unanswerable unless all three of its implicit presuppositions are true. The questioner presupposes that (1) the addressee has or had a wife, (2) he has beaten her, and (3) he has stopped beating her. If any of these presuppositions is false, then the question is pointless; it cannot be answered strictly and simply with a date.

Ambiguity

Near the center of the town of Concord, Massachusetts, is an empty field with a sign reading "Old Calf Pasture." Hmm. A pasture in former times in which calves grazed? A pasture now in use for old calves? An erstwhile pasture for old calves? These alternative readings arise because of **ambiguity;** brevity in the sign has produced a group of words that give rise to more than one possible interpretation, confusing the reader and (presumably) frustrating the sign-writer's intentions.

Consider a more complex example. Suppose someone asserts *People have equal rights* and also *Everyone has a right to property.* Many people believe both these claims, but their combination involves an ambiguity. On one interpretation, the two claims entail that everyone has an *equal right* to property. (That is, you and I each have an equal right to whatever property we have.) But the two claims can also be interpreted to mean that everyone has a *right to equal property.* (That is, whatever property you have a right to, I have a right to the same, or at least equivalent, property.) The latter interpretation is radically revolutionary, whereas the former is not. Arguments over equal rights often involve this ambiguity.

Death by a Thousand Qualifications

In a letter of recommendation, sent in support of an applicant for a job on your newspaper, you find this sentence: "Young Smith was the best student I've ever taught in an English course." Pretty strong endorsement, you think, except that you do not know, because you have not been told, the letter writer is a very junior faculty member, has been teaching for only two years, is an instructor in the history department, taught a section of freshman English as a courtesy for a sick colleague, and had only eight students enrolled in the course. Thanks to these implicit qualifications, the letter writer did not lie or exaggerate in his praise; but the effect of his sentence on you, the unwitting reader, is quite misleading. The explicit claim in the letter, and its impact on you, is quite different from the tacitly qualified claim in the mind of the writer.

Death by a thousand qualifications gets its name from the ancient torture of death by a thousand small cuts. Thus, a bold assertion can be virtually killed, its true content reduced to nothing, bit by bit, as all the appropriate or necessary qualifications are added to it. Consider another example. Suppose you hear a politician describing another country (let's call it Ruritania so as not to offend anyone) as a "democracy"—except it turns out that Ruritania doesn't have regular elections, lacks a written constitution, has no independent judiciary, prohibits religious worship except of the state-designated deity, and so forth. So what is left of the original claim that Ruritania is a democracy is little or nothing. The qualifications have taken all the content out of the original description.

Oversimplification

"Poverty causes crime," "Taxation is unfair," "Truth is stranger than fiction"—these are examples of generalizations that exaggerate and therefore oversimplify the truth. Poverty as such can't be the sole cause of crime because many poor people do not break the law. Some taxes may be unfairly high, others unfairly low—but there is no reason to believe that *every* tax is unfair to all those who have to pay it. Some true stories do amaze us as much or more than some fictional stories, but the reverse is true, too. (In the language of the Toulmin Method, **oversimplification** is the result of a failure to use suitable modal qualifiers in formulating one's claims or grounds or backing.)

False Dichotomy

Sometimes oversimplification takes a more complex form, in which contrary possibilities are wrongly presented as though they were exhaustive and exclusive. "Either we get tough with drug users, or we must surrender and legalize all drugs." Really? What about doing neither and instead offering education and counseling, detoxification programs, and incentives to "Say no"? A favorite of debaters, **either/or** reasoning always runs the risk of ignoring a third (or fourth) possibility. Some disjunctions are indeed exhaustive: "Either we get tough with drug users, or we do not." This proposition, though vague (what does "get tough" really mean?), is a tautology; it cannot be false, and there is no third alternative. But most disjunctions do not express a pair of *contradictory* alternatives: They offer only a pair of *contrary* alternatives, and mere contraries do not exhaust the possibilities (recall our discussion of contraries versus contradictories on pp. 306–09).

An example of **false dichotomy** can be found in the essay by Jeff Jacoby on flogging (p. 149). His entire discussion is built on the relative superiority of whipping over imprisonment, as though there was no alternative punishment worth considering. But of course, there is, notably community service (especially for white-collar offenders, juveniles, and many first offenders).

Hasty Generalization

From a logical point of view, **hasty generalization** is the precipitous move from true assertions about *one* or a *few* instances to dubious or even false assertions about *all*. For example, while it may be true, based on your personal experience, that the only native Hungarians you personally know do not speak English very well, that is no basis for asserting that Hungarians do not speak English very well. Or if the clothes you recently ordered by mail turn out not to fit very well, it doesn't follow that *all* mail-order clothes turn out to be too large or too small. A hasty generalization usually lies behind a **stereotype**—that is, a person or event treated as typical of a whole class. Thus, in 1914, after the German invasion of Belgium, during which some atrocities were committed by the invaders, the German troops were quickly stereotyped by the Allies as brutal savages who skewered helpless babies on their bayonets.

Equivocation

In a delightful passage in Lewis Carroll's *Through the Looking Glass*, the king asks his messenger, "Who did you pass on the road?" and the messenger replies, "Nobody." This prompts the king to observe, "Of course, Nobody walks slower than you," provoking the messenger's sullen response: "I do my best. I'm sure nobody walks much faster than I do." At this the king remarks with surprise, "He can't do that or else he'd have been here first!" (This, by the way, is the classic predecessor of the famous comic dialogue "Who's on First?" between the comedians Bud Abbott and Lou Costello.) The king and the messenger are equivocating on the term *nobody*. The messenger uses it in the normal way as an indefinite pronoun equivalent to "not anyone." But the king uses the word as though it were a proper noun, *Nobody*, the rather odd name of some person. No wonder the king and the messenger talk right past each other.

Equivocation (from the Latin for "equal voice"— that is, giving utterance to two meanings at the same time in one word or phrase) can ruin otherwise good reasoning, as in this example: *Euthanasia is a good death; one dies a good death when one dies peacefully in old age; therefore, euthanasia is dying peacefully in old age.* The etymology of *euthanasia* is literally "a good death," and so the first premise is true. And the second premise is certainly plausible. But the conclusion of this syllogism is false. Euthanasia cannot be defined as a peaceful death in one's old age, for two reasons. First, euthanasia requires the intervention of another person who kills someone (or lets the person die); second, even a very young person can be given euthanasia. The problem arises because "a good death" is used in the second premise in a manner that does not apply to euthanasia. Both meanings of "a good death" are legitimate, but when used together, they constitute an equivocation that spoils the argument.

The fallacy of equivocation takes us from the discussion of confusions in individual claims or grounds to the more troublesome fallacies that infect the linkages between the claims we make and the grounds (or reasons) for them. These are the fallacies that occur in statements that, following the vocabulary of the Toulmin Method, are called the *warrant* of reasoning. Each fallacy is an example of reasoning that involves a **non sequitur** (Latin for "It does not follow"). That is, the *claim* (the conclusion) does not follow from the *grounds* (the premises).

For a start, here is an obvious non sequitur: "He went to the movies on three consecutive nights, so he must love movies." Why doesn't the claim ("he must love movies") follow from the grounds ("He went to the movies on three consecutive nights")? Perhaps the person was just fulfilling an assignment in a film course (maybe he even hated movies so much that he had postponed three assignments to see films and now had to see them all in quick succession), or maybe he went with a girlfriend who was a movie buff, or maybe . . . —well, one can think of any number of other possible reasons.

Composition

Could an all-star team of professional basketball players beat the Boston Celtics in their heyday—say, the team of 1985 to 1986? Perhaps in one game or two, but probably not in seven out of a dozen games in a row. As students of the game know, teamwork is an indispensable part of outstanding performance, and the 1985 to 1986 Celtics were famous for their self-sacrificing style of play.

The **fallacy of composition** can be convincingly illustrated, therefore, in this argument: *A team of five NBA all-stars is the best team in basketball if each of the five players is the best at his position.* The fallacy is called composition because the reasoning commits the error of arguing from the true premise that each member of a group has a certain property to the not necessarily true conclusion that the group (the composition) itself has the property. (That is, because A is the best player at forward, B is the best center, and so on, therefore, the team of A, B, . . . is the best team.)

Division

In the Bible, we are told that the apostles of Jesus were twelve and that Matthew was an apostle. Does it follow that Matthew was twelve? No. To argue in this way from a property of a group to a property of a member of that group is to commit the **fallacy of division.** The example of the apostles may not be a very tempting instance of this error; here is a classic version that is a bit more interesting. If it is true that the average American family has 1.8 children, does it follow that your brother and sister-in-law are likely to have 1.8 children? If you think it does, you have committed the fallacy of division.

Poisoning the Well

During the 1970s some critics of the Equal Rights Amendment (ERA) argued against it by pointing out that Marx and Engels, in their *Communist Manifesto*, favored equality of women and men—and therefore the ERA is immoral, undesirable, and perhaps even a communist plot. This kind of reasoning is an attempt to **poison the well;** that is, an attempt to shift attention from the merits of the argument—the validity of the reasoning, the truth of the claims—to the source or origin of the argument. Such criticism nicely deflects attention from the real issue; namely, whether the view in question is true and what the quality of evidence is in its support. The mere fact that Marx (or Hitler, for that matter) believed something does not show that the belief is false or immoral; just because some scoundrel believes the world is round, that is no reason for you to believe it is flat.

Ad Hominem

Closely allied to poisoning the well is another fallacy, **ad hominem** argument (from the Latin for "against the person"). Since arguments and theories are not natural occurrences but are the creative products of particular persons, a critic can easily yield to the temptation to attack an argument or theory by trying to impeach or undercut the credentials of its advocates.

The Genetic Fallacy

Another member of the family of related fallacies that includes poisoning the well and ad hominem is the **genetic fallacy.** Here the error takes the form of arguing against some claim by pointing out that its origin (genesis) is tainted or that it was invented by someone deserving our contempt. Thus, one might attack the ideas of the Declaration of Independence by pointing out that its principal author, Thomas Jefferson, was a slaveholder. Assuming that it is not anachronistic and inappropriate to criticize a public figure of two centuries ago for practicing slavery, and conceding that slavery is morally outrageous, it is nonetheless fallacious to attack the ideas or even the sincerity of the Declaration by attempting to impeach the credentials of its author. Jefferson's moral faults do not by themselves falsify, make improbable, or constitute counterevidence to the truth or other merits of the claims made in his writings. At most, one's faults cast doubt on one's integrity or sincerity if one makes claims at odds with one's practice.

The genetic fallacy can take other forms less closely allied to ad hominem argument. For example, an opponent of the death penalty might argue,

> Capital punishment arose in barbarous times; but we claim to be civilized; therefore, we should discard this relic of the past.

Such reasoning shouldn't be persuasive because the question of the death penalty for our society must be decided by the degree to which it serves our purposes—justice and defense against crime, presumably—to which its historic origins are irrelevant. The practices of beer- and wine-making are as old as human civilization, but their origin in antiquity is no reason to outlaw them in our time. The curious circumstances in which something originates usually play no role whatever in its validity. Anyone who would argue that nothing good could possibly come from molds and fungi is refuted by Sir Alexander Fleming's discovery of penicillin in 1928.

Appeal to Authority

The example of Jefferson can be turned around to illustrate another fallacy. One might easily imagine someone from the South in 1860 defending the slavocracy of that day by appealing to the fact that no less a person than Jefferson—a brilliant public figure, thinker, and leader by any measure—owned slaves. Or today one might defend capital punishment on the ground that Abraham Lincoln, surely one of the nation's greatest presidents, signed many death warrants during the Civil War, authorizing the execution of Union soldiers. No doubt the esteem in which such figures as Jefferson and Lincoln are deservedly held amounts to impressive endorsement for whatever acts and practices, policies and institutions, they supported. But the **authority** of these figures in itself is not *evidence* for the truth of their views, and so their authority cannot be a reason for anyone to agree with them. Obviously, Jefferson and Lincoln themselves could not support their beliefs by pointing to the fact that they held them. Because their own authority is no reason for them to believe what they believe, it is no reason for anyone else, either.

Sometimes the appeal to authority is fallacious because the authoritative person is not an expert on the issue in dispute. The fact that a high-energy physicist has won the Nobel Prize is no reason for attaching any special weight to her views on the causes of cancer, the reduction of traffic accidents, or the legalization of marijuana. On the other hand, one would be well advised to attend to her views on the advisability of ballistic missile-defense systems, for there may be a connection between the kind of research for which she received the prize and the defense research projects.

All of us depend heavily on the knowledge of various experts and authorities, and so it ill-behooves us to ignore their views. Conversely, we should resist the temptation to accord their views on diverse subjects the same respect that we grant them in the area of their expertise.

The Slippery Slope

One of the most familiar arguments against any type of government regulation is that if it is allowed, then it will be just the first step down the path that leads to ruinous interference, overregulation, and totalitarian control. Fairly often we encounter this mode of argument in the public debates over handgun control, the censorship of pornography, and physician-assisted suicide. The argument is called the **slippery slope argument** (or the **wedge argument,** from the way we use the thin end of a wedge to split solid things apart; it is also called, rather colorfully, "letting the camel's nose under the tent"). The fallacy here is in implying that the first step necessarily leads to the second, and so on down the slope to disaster, when in fact there is no necessary slide from the first step to the second at all. (Would handgun registration lead to a police state? Well, it hasn't in Switzerland.) Sometimes the argument takes the form of claiming that a seemingly innocent or even attractive principle that is being applied in a given case (censorship of pornography, to avoid promoting sexual violence) requires one for the sake of consistency to apply the same principle in other cases, only with absurd and catastrophic results (censorship of everything in print, to avoid hurting anyone's feelings).

Here's an extreme example of this fallacy in action:

> Automobiles cause more deaths than handguns do. If you oppose handguns on the ground that doing so would save lives of the innocent, you'll soon find yourself wanting to outlaw the automobile.

Does opposition to handguns have this consequence? Not necessarily. Most people accept without dispute the right of society to regulate the operation of motor vehicles by requiring drivers to have a license, a greater restriction than many states impose on gun ownership. Besides, a gun is a lethal weapon designed to kill, whereas an automobile or truck is a vehicle designed for transportation. Private ownership and use in both cases entail risks of death to the innocent. But there is no inconsistency in a society's refusal to tolerate this risk in the case of guns and its willingness to do so in the case of automobiles.

Closely related to the slippery slope is what lawyers call a **parade of horrors,** an array of examples of terrible consequences that will or might follow if we travel down a certain path. A good example appears in Justice William Brennan's opinion for the Supreme Court in *Texas v. Johnson* (p. 387), concerned with a Texas law against burning the American flag in political protest. If this law is allowed to stand, Brennan suggests, we may next find laws against burning the presidential seal, state flags, and the Constitution.

Appeal to Ignorance

In the controversy over the death penalty, the issues of deterrence and executing the innocent are bound to be raised. Because no one knows how many innocent persons have been convicted for murder and wrongfully executed, it is tempting for abolitionists to argue that the death penalty is too risky. It is equally tempting for the proponent of the death penalty to argue that since no one knows how many people have been deterred from murder by the threat of execution, we abolish it at our peril.

Each of these arguments suffers from the same flaw: the **fallacy of appeal to ignorance.** Each argument invites the audience to draw an inference from a premise that is unquestionably true—but what is that premise? It asserts that there is something "we don't know." But what we *don't* know cannot be *evidence* for (or against) anything. Our ignorance is no reason for believing anything, except perhaps that we ought to try to undertake an appropriate investigation in order to reduce our ignorance and replace it with reliable information.

Begging the Question

The argument we have just considered also illustrates another fallacy. From the fact that you live in a death-penalty state and were not murdered yesterday, we cannot infer that the death penalty was a deterrent. Yet it is tempting to make this inference, perhaps because—all unawares—we are relying on the **fallacy of begging the question.** If someone tacitly assumes from the start that the death penalty is an effective deterrent, then the fact that you weren't murdered yesterday certainly looks like evidence for the truth of that assumption. But it isn't, so long as there are competing but unexamined alternative explanations, as in this case. (The fallacy is called "begging the question," *petitio principii* in Latin, because the conclusion of the argument is hidden among its assumptions—and so the conclusion, not surprisingly, follows from the premises.)

Of course, the fact that you weren't murdered is *consistent* with the claim that the death penalty is an effective deterrent, just as someone else's being murdered is also consistent with that claim (for an effective deterrent need not be a *perfect* deterrent). In general, from the fact that two propositions are consistent with each other, we cannot infer that either is evidence for the other.

False Analogy

Argument by analogy, as we point out in Chapter 3 and as many of the selections in this book show, is a familiar and even indispensable mode of argument. But it can be treacherous because it runs the risk of the **fallacy of false analogy.** Unfortunately, we have no simple or foolproof way of distinguishing between the useful, legitimate analogies and the others. The key question to ask yourself is this: Do the two things put into analogy differ in any essential and relevant respect, or are they different only in unimportant and irrelevant aspects?

In a famous example from his discussion in support of suicide, philosopher David Hume rhetorically asked: "It would be no crime in me to divert the Nile or Danube from its course, were I able to effect such purposes. Where then is the crime of turning a few ounces of blood from their natural channel?" This is a striking analogy, except that it rests on a false assumption. No one has the right to divert the Nile or the Danube or any other major international watercourse; it would be a catastrophic crime to do so without the full consent of people living in the region, their government, and so forth. Therefore, arguing by analogy, one might well say that no one has the right to take his or her own life, either. Thus, Hume's own analogy can be used to argue against his thesis that suicide is no crime. But let us ignore the way in which his example can be turned against him. The analogy is a terrible one in any case. Isn't it obvious that the Nile, whatever its exact course, would continue to nourish Egypt and the Sudan, whereas the blood flowing out of someone's veins will soon leave that person dead? The fact that the blood is the same blood, whether in one's body or in a pool on the floor (just as the water of the Nile is the same body of water whatever path it follows to the sea) is, of course, irrelevant to the question of whether one has the right to commit suicide.

Let us look at a more complex example. During the 1960s, when the United States was convulsed over the purpose and scope of its military involvement in Southeast Asia, advocates of more vigorous U.S. military participation appealed to the so-called domino effect, supposedly inspired by a passing remark from President Eisenhower in the 1950s. The analogy refers to the way in which a row of standing dominoes will collapse, one after the other, if the first one is pushed. If Vietnam turns communist, according to this analogy, so too will its neighbors, Laos and Cambodia, followed by Thailand and then Burma, until the whole region is as communist as China to the north. The domino analogy (or metaphor) provided, no doubt, a vivid illustration and effectively portrayed the worry of many anticommunists. But did it really shed any light on the likely pattern of political and military developments in the region? The history of events there during the 1970s and 1980s did not bear out the domino analogy.

Post Hoc, Ergo Propter Hoc

One of the most tempting errors in reasoning is to ground a claim about causation on an observed temporal sequence; that is, to argue "after this, therefore because of this" (which is what the phrase **post hoc, ergo propter hoc** means in Latin). Nearly forty years ago, when the medical community first announced that smoking tobacco caused lung cancer, advocates for the tobacco industry replied that doctors were guilty of this fallacy.

These industry advocates argued that medical researchers had merely noticed that in some people, lung cancer developed *after* considerable smoking, indeed, years after; but (they insisted) this correlation was not at all the same as a causal relation between smoking and lung cancer. True enough. The claim that *A causes B* is not the same as the claim that *B* comes after *A*. After all, it was possible that smokers as a group had some other common trait and that this factor was the true cause of their cancer.

As the long controversy over the truth about the causation of lung cancer shows, to avoid the appearance of fallacious *post hoc* reasoning one needs to find some way to link the observed phenomena (the correlation of smoking and the onset of lung cancer). This step requires some further theory and preferably some experimental evidence for the exact sequence or physical mechanism, in full detail, of how ingestion of tobacco smoke is a crucial factor—and is not merely an accidental or happenstance prior event—in the subsequent development of the cancer.

Protecting the Hypothesis

In Chapter 3, we contrast *reasoning* and *rationalization* (or the finding of bad reasons for what one intends to believe anyway). Rationalization can take subtle forms, as the following example indicates. Suppose you're standing with a friend on the shore or on a pier, and you watch as a ship heads out to sea. As it reaches the horizon, it slowly disappears—first the hull, then the upper decks, and finally the tip of the mast. Because the ship (you both assume) isn't sinking, it occurs to you that you have in this sequence of observations convincing evidence that the earth's surface is curved. Nonsense, says your companion. Light waves sag, or bend down, over distances of a few miles, and so a flat surface (such as the ocean) can intercept them. Hence the ship, which appears to be going "over" the horizon, really isn't: It's just moving steadily farther and farther away in a straight line. Your friend, you discover to your amazement, is a card-carrying member of the Flat Earth Society (yes, there really is such an organization). Now most of us would regard the idea that light rays bend down in the manner required by the Flat Earther's argument as a rationalization whose sole purpose is to protect the flat-earth doctrine against counterevidence. We would be convinced it was a rationalization, and not a very good one at that, if the Flat Earther held to it despite a patient and thorough explanation from a physicist that showed modern optical theory to be quite incompatible with the view that light waves sag.

This example illustrates two important points about the *backing* of arguments. First, it is always possible to protect a hypothesis by abandoning adjacent or connected hypotheses; this is the tactic our Flat Earth friend has used. This maneuver is possible, however, only because—and this is the second point—whenever we test a hypothesis, we do so by taking for granted (usually quite unconsciously) many other hypotheses as well. So the evidence for the hypothesis we think we are confirming is impossible to separate entirely from the adequacy of the connected hypotheses. As long as we have no reason to doubt that light rays travel in straight lines (at least over distances of a few miles), our Flat Earth friend's argument is unconvincing. But once that hypothesis is itself put in doubt, the idea that looked at first to be a pathetic rationalization takes on an even more troublesome character.

There are, then, not one but two fallacies exposed by this example. The first and perhaps graver is in rigging your hypothesis so that *no matter what* observations are brought against it, you will count nothing as falsifying it. The second and subtler is in thinking that as you test one hypothesis, all of your other background beliefs are left safely to one side, immaculate and uninvolved. On the contrary, our beliefs form a corporate structure, intertwined and connected to each other with great complexity, and no one of them can ever be singled out for unique and isolated application, confirmation, or disconfirmation, to the world around us.

A CHECKLIST FOR EVALUATING AN ARGUMENT FROM A LOGICAL POINT OF VIEW

✓ Is the argument purely deductive, purely inductive, or a mixture of the two?

✓ If it is deductive, is it valid?

✓ If it is valid, are all its premises and assumptions true?

✓ If it is not valid, what fallacy does it commit?

✓ If it is not valid, are the claims at least consistent with each other?

✓ If it is not valid, can you think of additional plausible assumptions that would make it valid?

✓ If the argument is inductive, on what observations is it based?

✓ If the argument is inductive, how probable are its premises and its conclusion?

✓ In any case, can you think of evidence that would further confirm the conclusion? Disconfirm the conclusion?

Max Shulman

Having read about proper and improper arguments, you are now well equipped to read a short story on the topic.

Max Shulman (1919–1988) began his career as a writer when he was a journalism student at the University of Minnesota. Later he wrote humorous novels, stories, and plays. One of his novels, Barefoot Boy with Cheek *(1943), was made into a musical, and another,* Rally Round the Flag, Boys! *(1957), was made into a film starring Paul Newman and Joanne Woodward.* The Tender Trap *(1954), a play he wrote with Robert Paul Smith, still retains its popularity with theater groups.*

"Love Is a Fallacy" was first published in 1951, when demeaning stereotypes about women and minorities were widely accepted in the marketplace as well as the home. Thus, jokes about domineering mothers-in-law or about dumb blondes routinely met with no objection.

Love Is a Fallacy

Cool was I and logical. Keen, calculating, perspicacious, acute, and astute — I was all of these. My brain was as powerful as a dynamo, as precise as a chemist's scales, as penetrating as a scalpel. And — think of it! — I was only eighteen.

It is not often that one so young has such a giant intellect. Take, for example, Petey Bellows, my roommate at the university. Same age, same background, but dumb as an ox. A nice enough fellow, you understand, but nothing upstairs. Emotional type. Unstable. Impressionable. Worst of all, a faddist. Fads, I submit, are the very negation of reason. To be swept up in every new craze that comes along, to surrender yourself to idiocy just because everybody else is doing it — this, to me, is the acme of mindlessness. Not, however, to Petey.

One afternoon I found Petey lying on his bed with an expression of such distress on his face that I immediately diagnosed appendicitis. "Don't move," I said. "Don't take a laxative. I'll call a doctor."

"Raccoon," he mumbled thickly.

"Raccoon?" I said, pausing in my flight.   5

"I want a raccoon coat," he wailed.

I perceived that his trouble was not physical, but mental. "Why do you want a raccoon coat?"

"I should have known it," he cried, pounding his temples. "I should have known they'd come back when the Charleston came back. Like a fool I spent all my money for textbooks, and now I can't get a raccoon coat."

"Can you mean," I said incredulously, "that people are actually wearing raccoon coats again?"

"All the Big Men on Campus are wearing them. Where've you   10
been?"

"In the library," I said, naming a place not frequented by Big Men on Campus.

He leaped from the bed and paced the room. "I've got to have a raccoon coat," he said passionately. "I've got to!"

"Petey, why? Look at it rationally. Raccoon coats are unsanitary. They shed. They smell bad. They weigh too much. They're unsightly. They——"

"You don't understand," he interrupted impatiently. "It's the thing to do. Don't you want to be in the swim?"

"No," I said truthfully.   15

"Well, I do," he declared. "I'd give anything for a raccoon coat. Anything!"

My brain, that precision instrument, slipped into high gear. "Anything?" I asked, looking at him narrowly.

"Anything," he affirmed in ringing tones.

I stroked my chin thoughtfully. It so happened that I knew where to get my hands on a raccoon coat. My father had had one in his undergraduate days; it lay now in a trunk in the attic back home. It also happened that Petey had something I wanted. He didn't *have* it exactly, but at least he had first rights on it. I refer to his girl, Polly Espy.

I had long coveted Polly Espy. Let me emphasize that my desire for 20 this young woman was not emotional in nature. She was, to be sure, a girl who excited the emotions, but I was not one to let my heart rule my head. I wanted Polly for a shrewdly calculated, entirely cerebral reason.

I was a freshman in law school. In a few years I would be out in practice. I was well aware of the importance of the right kind of wife in furthering a lawyer's career. The successful lawyers I had observed were, almost without exception, married to beautiful, gracious, intelligent women. With one omission, Polly fitted these specifications perfectly.

Beautiful she was. She was not yet of pin-up proportions, but I felt sure that time would supply the lack. She already had the makings.

Gracious she was. By gracious I mean full of graces. She had an erectness of carriage, an ease of bearing, a poise that clearly indicated the best of breeding. At table her manners were exquisite. I had seen her at the Kozy Kampus Korner eating the specialty of the house—a sandwich that contained scraps of pot roast, gravy, chopped nuts, and a dipper of sauerkraut—without even getting her fingers moist.

Intelligent she was not. In fact, she veered in the opposite direction. But I believed that under my guidance she would smarten up. At any rate, it was worth a try. It is, after all, easier to make a beautiful dumb girl smart than to make an ugly smart girl beautiful.

"Petey," I said, "are you in love with Polly Espy?"   25

"I think she's a keen kid," he replied, "but I don't know if you'd call it love. Why?"

"Do you," I asked, "have any kind of formal arrangement with her? I mean are you going steady or anything like that?"

"No. We see each other quite a bit, but we both have other dates. Why?"

"Is there," I asked, "any other man for whom she has a particular fondness?"

"Not that I know of. Why?"   30

I nodded with satisfaction. "In other words, if you were out of the picture, the field would be open. Is that right?"

"I guess so. What are you getting at?"

"Nothing, nothing," I said innocently, and took my suitcase out of the closet.

"Where you going?" asked Petey.

"Home for the week end." I threw a few things into the bag.   35

"Listen," he said, clutching my arm eagerly, "while you're home, you couldn't get some money from your old man, could you, and lend it to me so I can buy a raccoon coat?"

"I may do better than that," I said with a mysterious wink and closed my bag and left.

"Look," I said to Petey when I got back Monday morning. I threw open the suitcase and revealed the huge, hairy, gamy object that my father had worn in his Stutz Bearcat in 1925.

"Holy Toledo!" said Petey reverently. He plunged his hands into the raccoon coat and then his face. "Holy Toledo!" he repeated fifteen or twenty times.

"Would you like it?" I asked.   40

"Oh yes!" he cried, clutching the greasy pelt to him. Then a canny look came into his eyes. "What do you want for it?"

"Your girl," I said, mincing no words.

"Polly?" he said in a horrified whisper. "You want Polly?"

"That's right."

He flung the coat from him. "Never," he said stoutly.   45

I shrugged. "Okay. If you don't want to be in the swim, I guess it's your business."

I sat down in a chair and pretended to read a book, but out of the corner of my eye I kept watching Petey. He was a torn man. First he looked at the coat with the expression of a waif at a bakery window. Then he turned away and set his jaw resolutely. Then he looked back at the coat, with even more longing in his face. Then he turned away, but with not so much resolution this time. Back and forth his head swiveled, desire waxing, resolution waning. Finally he didn't turn away at all; he just stood and stared with mad lust at the coat.

"It isn't as though I was in love with Polly," he said thickly. "Or going steady or anything like that."

"That's right," I murmured.

"What's Polly to me, or me to Polly?"   50

"Not a thing," said I.

"It's just been a casual kick—just a few laughs, that's all."

"Try on the coat," said I.

He complied. The coat bunched high over his ears and dropped all the way down to his shoe tops. He looked like a mound of dead raccoons. "Fits fine," he said happily.

I rose from my chair. "Is it a deal?" I asked, extending my hand.   55

He swallowed. "It's a deal," he said and shook my hand.

I had my first date with Polly the following evening. This was in the nature of a survey; I wanted to find out just how much work I had to do to get her mind up to the standard I required. I took her first to dinner. "Gee, that was a delish dinner," she said as we left the restaurant. Then I took her to a movie. "Gee, that was a marvy movie," she said as we left the theater. And then I took her home. "Gee, I had a sensaysh time," she said as she bade me good night.

I went back to my room with a heavy heart. I had gravely underestimated the size of my task. This girl's lack of information was terrifying. Nor would it be enough merely to supply her with information. First she had to be taught to *think*. This loomed as a project of no small dimensions, and at first I was tempted to give her back to Petey. But then I got to thinking about her abundant physical charms and about the way she entered a room and the way she handled a knife and fork, and I decided to make an effort.

I went about it, as in all things, systematically. I gave her a course in logic. It happened that I, as a law student, was taking a course in logic myself, so I had all the facts at my fingertips. "Polly," I said to her when I picked her up on our next date, "tonight we are going over to the Knoll and talk."

"Oo, terrif," she replied. One thing I will say for this girl: You would   60
go far to find another so agreeable.

We went to the Knoll, the campus trysting place, and we sat down under an old oak, and she looked at me expectantly: "What are we going to talk about?" she asked.

"Logic."

She thought this over for a minute and decided she liked it. "Magnif," she said.

"Logic," I said, clearing my throat, "is the science of thinking. Before we can think correctly, we must first learn to recognize the common fallacies of logic. These we will take up tonight."

"Wow-dow!" she cried, clapping her hands delightedly.   65

I winced, but went bravely on. "First let us examine the fallacy called Dicto Simpliciter."

"By all means," she urged, batting her lashes eagerly.

"Dicto Simpliciter means an argument based on an unqualified generalization. For example: Exercise is good. Therefore everybody should exercise."

"I agree," said Polly earnestly. "I mean exercise is wonderful. I mean it builds the body and everything."

"Polly," I said gently, "the argument is a fallacy. *Exercise is good* is an 70
unqualified generalization. For instance, if you have heart disease, exercise is bad, not good. Many people are ordered by their doctors *not* to exercise. You must *qualify* the generalization. You must say exercise is *usually* good, or exercise is good *for most people.* Otherwise you have committed a Dicto Simpliciter. Do you see?"

"No," she confessed. "But this is marvy. Do more! Do more!"

"It will be better if you stop tugging at my sleeve," I told her, and when she desisted, I continued. "Next we take up a fallacy called Hasty Generalization. Listen carefully: You can't speak French. I can't speak French. Petey Bellows can't speak French. I must therefore conclude that nobody at the University of Minnesota can speak French."

"Really?" said Polly, amazed. "*Nobody?*"

I hid my exasperation. "Polly, it's a fallacy. The generalization is reached too hastily. There are too few instances to support such a conclusion."

"Know any more fallacies?" she asked breathlessly. "This is more fun 75
than dancing even."

I fought off a wave of despair. I was getting nowhere with this girl, absolutely nowhere. Still, I am nothing if not persistent. I continued. "Next comes Post Hoc. Listen to this: Let's not take Bill on our picnic. Every time we take him out with us, it rains."

"I know somebody just like that," she exclaimed. "A girl back home—Eula Becker, her name is. It never fails. Every single time we take her on a picnic——"

"Polly," I said sharply, "it's a fallacy. Eula Becker doesn't *cause* the rain. She has no connection with the rain. You are guilty of Post Hoc if you blame Eula Becker."

"I'll never do it again," she promised contritely. "Are you mad at me?"

I sighed. "No, Polly, I'm not mad."   80

"Then tell me some more fallacies."

"All right. Let's try Contradictory Premises."

"Yes, let's," she chirped, blinking her eyes happily.

I frowned, but plunged ahead. "Here's an example of Contradictory Premises: If God can do anything, can He make a stone so heavy that He won't be able to lift it?"

"Of course," she replied promptly.   85

"But if He can do anything, He can lift the stone," I pointed out.

"Yeah," she said thoughtfully. "Well, then I guess He can't make the stone."

"But He can do anything," I reminded her.

She scratched her pretty, empty head. "I'm all confused," she admitted.

"Of course you are. Because when the premises of an argument con- 90
tradict each other, there can be no argument. If there is an irresistible
force, there can be no immovable object. If there is an immovable object,
there can be no irresistible force. Get it?"

"Tell me some more of this keen stuff," she said eagerly.

I consulted my watch. "I think we'd better call it a night. I'll take you
home now, and you go over all the things you've learned. We'll have
another session tomorrow night."

I deposited her at the girl's dormitory, where she assured me that
she had had a perfectly terrif evening, and I went glumly home to my
room. Petey lay snoring in his bed, the raccoon coat huddled like a great
hairy beast at his feet. For a moment I considered waking him and
telling him that he could have his girl back. It seemed clear that my
project was doomed to failure. The girl simply had a logic-proof head.

But then I reconsidered. I had wasted one evening; I might as well
waste another. Who knew? Maybe somewhere in the extinct crater of
her mind a few embers still smoldered. Maybe somehow I could fan
them into flame. Admittedly it was not a prospect fraught with hope, but
I decided to give it one more try.

Seated under the oak the next evening I said, "Our first fallacy 95
tonight is called Ad Misericordiam."

She quivered with delight.

"Listen closely," I said. "A man applies for a job. When the boss asks
him what his qualifications are, he replies that he has a wife and six children at home, the wife is a helpless cripple, the children have nothing to
eat, no clothes to wear, no shoes on their feet, there are no beds in the
house, no coal in the cellar, and winter is coming."

A tear rolled down each of Polly's pink cheeks. "Oh, this is awful,
awful," she sobbed.

"Yes, it's awful," I agreed, "but it's no argument. The man never answered the boss's question about his qualifications. Instead he appealed
to the boss's sympathy. He committed the fallacy of Ad Misericordiam.
Do you understand?"

"Have you got a handkerchief?" she blubbered.   100

I handed her a handkerchief and tried to keep from screaming while
she wiped her eyes. "Next," I said in a carefully controlled tone, "we will
discuss False Analogy. Here is an example: Students should be allowed
to look at their textbooks during examinations. After all, surgeons have
X rays to guide them during an operation, lawyers have briefs to guide
them during a trial, carpenters have blueprints to guide them when they
are building a house. Why, then, shouldn't students be allowed to look
at their textbooks during an examination?"

"There now," she said enthusiastically, "is the most marvy idea I've
heard in years."

"Polly," I said testily, "the argument is all wrong. Doctors, lawyers,
and carpenters aren't taking a test to see how much they have learned,

but students are. The situations are altogether different, and you can't make an analogy between them."

"I still think it's a good idea," said Polly.

"Nuts," I muttered. Doggedly I pressed on. "Next we'll try Hypothe- 105 sis Contrary to Fact."

"Sounds yummy," was Polly's reaction.

"Listen: If Madame Curie had not happened to leave a photographic plate in a drawer with a chunk of pitchblende, the world today would not know about radium."

"True, true," said Polly, nodding her head. "Did you see the movie? Oh, it just knocked me out. That Walter Pidgeon is so dreamy. I mean he fractures me."

"If you can forget Mr. Pidgeon for a moment," I said coldly, "I would like to point out that the statement is a fallacy. Maybe Madame Curie would have discovered radium at some later date. Maybe somebody else would have discovered it. Maybe any number of things would have happened. You can't start with a hypothesis that is not true and then draw any supportable conclusions from it."

"They ought to put Walter Pidgeon in more pictures," said Polly. "I 110 hardly ever see him any more."

One more chance, I decided. But just one more. There is a limit to what flesh and blood can bear. "The next fallacy is called Poisoning the Well."

"How cute!" she gurgled.

"Two men are having a debate. The first one gets up and says, 'My opponent is a notorious liar. You can't believe a word that he is going to say.' . . . Now, Polly, think. Think hard. What's wrong?"

I watched her closely as she knit her creamy brow in concentration. Suddenly a glimmer of intelligence — the first I had seen — came into her eyes. "It's not fair," she said with indignation. "It's not a bit fair. What chance has the second man got if the first man calls him a liar before he even begins talking?"

"Right!" I cried exultantly. "One hundred percent right. It's not fair. 115 The first man has *poisoned the well* before anybody could drink from it. He has hamstrung his opponent before he could even start. . . . Polly, I'm proud of you."

"Pshaw," she murmured, blushing with pleasure.

"You see, my dear, these things aren't so hard. All you have to do is concentrate. Think — examine — evaluate. Come now, let's review everything we have learned."

"Fire away," she said with an airy wave of her hand.

Heartened by the knowledge that Polly was not altogether a cretin, I began a long, patient review of all I had told her. Over and over and over again I cited instances, pointed out flaws, kept hammering away without letup. It was like digging a tunnel. At first everything was work, sweat, and darkness. I had no idea when I would reach the light, or even *if* I would. But I persisted. I pounded and clawed and scraped, and finally I was rewarded. I saw a chink of light. And then the chink got bigger and the sun came pouring in and all was bright.

Five grueling nights this took, but it was worth it. I had made a logi- 120 cian out of Polly; I had taught her to think. My job was done. She was worthy of me at last. She was a fit wife for me, a proper hostess for my many mansions, a suitable mother for my well-heeled children.

It must not be thought that I was without love for this girl. Quite the contrary. Just as Pygmalion loved the perfect woman he had fashioned, so I loved mine. I decided to acquaint her with my feelings at our very next meeting. The time had come to change our relationship from academic to romantic.

"Polly," I said when next we sat beneath our oak, "tonight we will not discuss fallacies."

"Aw, gee," she said, disappointed.

"My dear," I said, favoring her with a smile, "we have now spent five evenings together. We have gotten along splendidly. It is clear that we are well matched."

"Hasty Generalization," said Polly brightly.   125

"I beg your pardon," said I.

"Hasty Generalization," she repeated. "How can you say that we are well matched on the basis of only five dates?"

I chuckled with amusement. The dear child had learned her lessons well. "My dear," I said, patting her hand in a tolerant manner, "five dates is plenty. After all, you don't have to eat a whole cake to know that it's good."

"False Analogy," said Polly promptly. "I'm not a cake. I'm a girl."

I chuckled with somewhat less amusement. The dear child had 130 learned her lesson perhaps too well. I decided to change tactics. Obviously the best approach was a simple, strong, direct declaration of love. I paused for a moment while my massive brain chose the proper words. Then I began:

"Polly, I love you. You are the whole world to me, and the moon and the stars and the constellations of outer space. Please, my darling, say that you will go steady with me, for if you will not, life will be meaningless. I will languish. I will refuse my meals. I will wander the face of the earth, a shambling, hollow-eyed hulk."

There, I thought, folding my arms, that ought to do it.

"Ad Misericordiam," said Polly.

I ground my teeth. I was not Pygmalion; I was Frankenstein, and my monster had me by the throat. Frantically I fought back the tide of panic surging through me. At all costs I had to keep cool.

"Well, Polly," I said, forcing a smile, "you certainly have learned 135 your fallacies."

"You're darn right," she said with a vigorous nod.

"And who taught them to you, Polly?"

"You did."

"That's right. So you do owe me something, don't you, my dear? If I hadn't come along you never would have learned about fallacies."

"Hypothesis Contrary to Fact," she said instantly.   140

I dashed perspiration from my brow. "Polly," I croaked, "You mustn't take all these things so literally. I mean this is just classroom stuff. You know that the things you learn in school don't have anything to do with life."

"Dicto Simpliciter," she said, wagging her finger at me playfully.

That did it. I leaped to my feet, bellowing like a bull. "Will you or will you not go steady with me?"

"I will not," she replied.

"Why not?" I demanded.   145

"Because this afternoon I promised Petey Bellows that I would go steady with him."

I reeled back, overcome with the infamy of it. After he promised, after he made a deal, after he shook my hand! "That rat!" I shrieked, kicking up great chunks of turf. "You can't go with him, Polly. He's a liar. He's a cheat. He's a rat."

"Poisoning the Well," said Polly, "and stop shouting. I think shouting must be a fallacy too."

With an immense effort of will, I modulated my voice. "All right," I said. "You're a logician. Let's look at this thing logically. How could you choose Petey Bellows over me? Look at me—a brilliant student, a tremendous intellectual, a man with an assured future. Look at Petey— a knothead, a jitterbug, a guy who'll never know where his next meal is coming from. Can you give me one logical reason why you should go steady with Petey Bellows?"

"I certainly can," declared Polly. "He's got a raccoon coat."   150

Topic for Critical Thinking and Writing

After you have finished reading "Love Is a Fallacy," you may want to write an argumentative essay of 500 to 750 words on one of the following topics: (1) the story, rightly understood, is not antiwoman; (2) if the story is anti- woman, it is equally antiman; (3) the story is antiwoman but nevertheless belongs in this book; or (4) the story is antiwoman and does not belong in the book.

See the companion Web site **www.bedfordstmartins.com/ barnetbedau** for a series of brain teasers and links related to the logical point of view in argument.

9

A Moralist's View: Ways of Thinking Ethically

Elsewhere in this book we explain *deductive reasoning* (p. 298), *inductive reasoning* (p. 309), and *legal reasoning* (p. 379). More familiar and probably more important is **moral reasoning.** If truth be told, virtually every essay reprinted in this book is an example of more or less self-conscious moral reasoning. (In passing, at the outset we note that we do not draw any distinction between morals and ethics or between moral reasoning and ethical reasoning. Apart from insignificant connotations, the terms *moral* and *ethical* differ mainly in their origin, *ethical* deriving from the Greek *ethos*, meaning "custom" or "manners" and *moral* deriving from the Latin *moralis,* meaning "moral" or "ethical".)

Moral reasoning has various purposes, particularly guidance for conduct—for what someone actually does or fails to do. In this light, consider the parable Jesus tells of the Good Samaritan (Luke 10:30–37). On a journey from Jerusalem to Jericho, a man is robbed by thieves, beaten, and left nearly dead. First a priest came along, "looked on him, and passed by on the other side." Then a Levite (an assistant to a temple priest) does the same thing (implied in the story is that both the priest and the Levite are fellow countrymen of the victim and so might well be expected to come to the man's aid.) "But a certain Samaritan . . . came where he was and when he saw him, he had compassion on him." The Samaritan bound up his wounds, took him to an inn, and paid for his lodging.

Jesus tells this story to answer the question, Who is my neighbor? In context, this amounts to the question, Which of the three passersby acts toward the beaten man in a truly neighborly manner? The answer, of course, is that only the Samaritan—a person from a different culture—does.

Most of the moral reasoning in this parable is left implicit by the Gospel writer. To understand the indifference of the priest and Levite to

338

the plight of the victim, we might imagine them thinking as follows: "Nothing I have done or failed to do caused the victim to be robbed and assaulted, so I have no responsibility to interrupt my travels to care for him. Nothing binds him to me as kinship would; he and I are not neighbors in the ordinary sense of that term (persons who live nearby, in the same neighborhood), so I do not owe him assistance as I would to my kin and my immediate neighbors. His need gives him no claim on my attention. Finally, why put myself at uncertain risk in trying to help him? Perhaps the thieves are still in the vicinity, just waiting to pounce on anyone foolish enough to stop and give aid."

Clearly, Jesus implies that none of these reasons is adequate. His parable is intended in part to stretch our ordinary notion of what it means to be someone's neighbor. Jesus is in effect telling us that the beaten stranger ought to elicit the same concern and care that we would give to an assaulted family member, close friend, or immediate neighbor.

What makes Jesus' parable a story told from the moral point of view is that his implicit evaluation of the conduct of the three passersby depends on an unspoken moral principle that he believes but that he knows is not widely shared: *We ought to help the needy even at some cost or risk to ourselves.*

As a next step in the effort to deepen our grasp of moral reasoning, it is useful to be clear about what it *isn't.* To do that we need to think about two kinds of reasoning sharply contrasted to moral reasoning: *amoral* reasoning and *immoral* reasoning.

AMORAL REASONING

Amorality consists of conduct of no moral significance — that is, conduct not to be evaluated by reference to moral considerations. For example, suppose you are in the market for a used car. You want a two-door car and have narrowed your choices to three: a 1997 Honda, a 1998 Subaru, and a 1999 Toyota. No moral consideration enters your deliberation over which car to choose; morality is silent on your choice. Daily life is filled with examples of this sort, situations in which nothing of moral relevance seems to be involved, and so our decisions and choices can be made without worry over their morality or immorality. In short, for most of us, morality just does not control or pervade everything we do in life. And when we judge moral considerations to be irrelevant, we are dealing with what we regard as amoral matters.

Let us examine another example in greater detail. You are about to dine with a friend at a nice restaurant. The waiter brings you the menu, and you look it over, pondering whether to have an appetizer, order a bottle of white or red wine, choose fish or poultry for the main dish, and top it all off with dessert and coffee. Since the restaurant is noted for its cuisine, you are trying to design a meal for yourself worthy of the occasion. There is nothing particularly moral or immoral in your deliberations as you study the menu and make your choices. By eating in this restaurant, you are not depriving anyone else of their dinner, much less depriving them unfairly. You are not coercing others to turn over their food to you. You have not stolen the money to pay for your food. You are not breaking a promise to anyone to avoid this restaurant or to avoid rich and expensive restaurant food. You have no intention of leaving without paying the bill. Thus, various standard and familiar ways of acting immorally can be seen to play no role in your dinner deliberations.

On the other hand, there is no moral requirement that you dine in this restaurant or that you order this rather than that from the menu. You have no moral duty to have a feast, no obligation to anyone to have an expensive dinner. You have not promised anyone to dine in this restaurant. Your failure to dine there would flout no moral rule or principle.

Situations such as this, which call for reasoning and decision but where no moral principle or rule is involved, are without moral significance whichever way they are decided. To put this another way, in cases such as this, moral reasoning tells us we are *permitted* (neither prohibited nor required by morality) to go ahead with our restaurant meal as planned, and in this regard we may do whatever we like.

So the first of several questions that capture the idea of moral reasoning can be put this way:

- Is your (or someone else's) conduct prohibited or required by a moral rule or principle? If not, then it is probably not morally wrong: Morality permits you to act as you please.

Two kinds of considerations raised by this example deserve a closer look. First, if you are on a diet that forbids rich food, you are at risk in doing yourself some harm unless you read the menu carefully and order accordingly (no steak or other red meat, for example, and no fatty custards or sauces). The best way to treat yourself, we can probably agree, dictates caution in what you select to eat. But suppose you fail to act cautiously. Well, you are not acting immorally — although your behavior is imprudent, ill advised, and contrary to your best interests. We break no moral rule when we choose not to act in our own rational self-interest. The rule "Act always to promote your own rational self-interest" is not a moral rule.

Unless, of course, one's morality does consist of some form of self-interest, as in, for example, the views of the novelist-turned-philosopher Ayn Rand in her widely read book *The Virtue of Selfishness* (1965). Her defense of selfishness is exceptional and somewhat misleading — exceptional because very few moralists agree with her, and somewhat misleading because her main thesis — *everyone would do better if each of us pursued only our own rational self-interest* — is obviously contestable. Most moralists would insist that all of us do *not* do better if each of us acts without ever taking into account the needs of others except where they impinge on our own welfare. (For another version of a morality of self-ishness, see the essay by Garrett Hardin, p. 368.) Of course, any given moral code or moral principle is subject to criticism on moral grounds. Not all moralities—sets of moral principles that a person or a society holds—are equally reasonable, fair, or free of some other moral defect.

Second, if, for example, you are concerned about animal rights, you may see the choice between a meatless salad and a Caesar's salad as a moral issue. That is not the only way the choice of a meal may turn out to conceal a moral issue. The more expensive the dinner, the more you may feel uneasy about such self-indulgence when you could eat an adequate dinner elsewhere at one-third the cost and donate the difference to Oxfam or UNESCO. Many moralists would insist that we who are well fed in fact have a responsibility to see to it that the starving are fed. Some influential moral thinkers in recent years have gone even further, arguing that the best moral principles, preeminently the utilitarian principle that one always ought to act so as to maximize the net benefits among the available choices, require those of us in affluent nations to reduce radically our standard of living to improve the standard of living of people in the poorest nations. (See the essay by Peter Singer, p. 356.) This example nicely illustrates how something as seemingly harmless and amoral as having an expensive meal in a nice restaurant can turn out, after all, to pose a moral choice—because one's moral principles turn out to be applicable to the case in question, even if the moral principles acknowledged by others are not.

IMMORAL REASONING

The most obvious reasoning to be contrasted with moral reasoning is *immoral* reasoning. Immorality, defined abstractly, is conduct contrary to what morality requires or prohibits. Hence a person is reasoning immorally whenever he or she is contemplating judgment or conduct that violates or disregards some relevant moral rule or principle.

We are acting immorally when we use *force or fraud* in our dealings with other people and when we treat them *unfairly*. Typically we act in these ways toward others when our motives are *selfish*—that is, when we act in ways intended to gain advantage for ourselves without regard to the effects that advantage will have on others. For example,

Suppose you are short of cash and try to borrow some from a friend. You don't expect your friend simply to give you the money, so

You know you will have to promise to repay her as soon as you can, say, in a week.

But you know you really have no intention of keeping your promise to pay her back.

Nonetheless, you make the promise — well, you utter words such as "Sure, you can rely on me; I'll pay you back in a few days" — and she loans you the money. Weeks go by. Eventually your paths cross and she reminds you that you haven't yet paid her back.

What to say? Some of your options:

Laugh in her face for being so naive as to loan you the money in the first place?

Make up some phony excuse, and hope she'll accept it?

Renew your promise to pay her back but without any change in your intention not to do so?

Act tough, and threaten her if she doesn't lay off?

Each of these is an immoral tactic, and deliberating among them to choose the most effective is immoral reasoning. Why? Because each of them violates a familiar moral principle (albeit rarely formulated expressly in words). First, *promises are fraudulent if they are made with no intention to keep them.* (Underlying that principle is another one: Fraud is morally wrong.) Second, *promises ought to be kept.* Whatever else morality is, it is a constraint on acting purely out of self-interest and in a manner heedless of the consequences for others. Making fraudulent promises and unfairly breaking genuine promises are actions usually done out of selfish intentions and are likely to cause harm to others.

The discussion so far yields this important generalization:

- If the reasons for your proposed judgment and conduct are purely selfish, they are not moral reasons.

Of course, there are exceptions to the two principles mentioned in the previous paragraph. Neither principle is a rigid moral rule. Why? Because on some occasions making a fraudulent promise or breaking a sincere promise can be *excused,* and on other occasions such conduct can be *justified.* (Or so most of us in our society think when we reflect on the matter.) Both invoking a legitimate excuse or justification for breaking a moral rule and rejecting illegitimate excuses or justifications, are crucial features of everyday moral reasoning. For example, you ought to be excused for breaking a sincere promise — say, a promise to meet a friend for lunch at a certain time and place — if your car gets a flat tire on the way. On the other hand, you would be justified in breaking your promise if, for example, while driving on the way to your lunch date you are late because you stopped to help a stranded motorist change his flat tire. In general,

- We *excuse* violating a moral rule when we argue that we know breaking it was wrong but it couldn't be helped, whereas
- We *justify* violating a moral rule when we argue that doing so was the right or the best thing to do in the circumstances.

We have now identified two more questions to keep in mind as you try to assess the morality of your own or someone else's reasoning. The first is this:

- Are the reasons you offer an attempt to excuse wrongful conduct? If so, is the excuse a legitimate one?

Typical excuses include these: "It was an *accident;* he *couldn't help* it; she *didn't know it was wrong;* they did it *by mistake;* we were *forced* to do it; I was *provoked.*" The legitimacy of an excuse in any given case depends on the facts of the matter. Claiming that the harm you caused, for example, was an accident doesn't *make* it an accident. (Children are quick to learn these excuses and can be quite adept at misusing them to their own advantage.)

The second question to ask is this:

- Are the reasons you offer an attempt to justify breaking a moral rule knowingly? If so, is the proposed justification really convincing?

Typical justifications include these: "It was the *best* thing to do in the circumstances; the *sacrifice* was necessary to protect something else of greater value; *little or no harm to others will be done* if the rule is ignored; *superior orders* required me to do what I did." (Several of these justifications appear in the case of *United States v. Holmes,* p. 347.) A justification is convincing in a given case just to the extent that it invokes a moral rule or principle of greater weight or scope than the rule or principle being violated.

MORAL REASONING: A CLOSER LOOK

What does this brief excursion into amoral and immoral reasoning teach us about *moral* reasoning? Just this: Moral reasoning involves (1) reasoning from *moral* rules, principles, or standards and (2) resolving conflicts among them, thereby placing limits on what one may do with a clear conscience.

This point can be restated as follows:

- Do the reasons you propose for your conduct violate any of the relevant moral rules you accept? If not, then your morality raises no objection to your conduct.

Morality and moral reasoning can be conveniently subdivided into several narrower areas. We are sexual beings, and our pursuit of sexual experience will inevitably raise questions about the morality of our conduct. Hence we often have occasion to think about *sexual* morality—our own and that of others. *Sexual* morality can be defined as the moral rules, principles, and standards relevant to judgment and conduct in which someone's sexual behavior is at issue. Similarly, *political* morality concerns the moral rules, principles, and standards with which people ought to conduct and evaluate political activities, practices, and institutions. *Professional* ethics all involve special rules, norms, principles relevant to judgment and conduct, and these rules are often stated in the form of a *code* of ethics suitable to the judgments and conduct more or less unique to each profession (such as business, medicine, journalism, law). What is common to all such codes are prohibitions against coercion and misrepresentation, unfair advantage, and the failure to obtain informed voluntary consent from one's clients, patients, witnesses, and employees.

Second, the rules, principles, and standards that constitute a morality differ in different religions and cultures, just as they differ historically. The morality of ancient Greece was not the morality of feudal Europe or contemporary America; the morality of the Trobriand Islanders is not the same as the morality of the Kwakiutl Indians. This does not imply *moral relativism*—that is, the view that there is no rational ground on which to choose among alternative moralities. (The purely descriptive thesis that *different cultures endorse different moral codes* does not imply the evaluative thesis that *one moral code is as good as another*.) The fact that different cultures endorse different moral codes does, however, imply that there may be a need for tolerance of moral standards other than one's own.

Third, in the morality most widely shared in our society, moral rules are not rigid; they permit exceptions (as we have seen above), and they are of different importance and weight. For example, few would deny that it is more important to help a stranded motorist than to keep a lunch date. Unlike the ancient Hebrews, however, who were guided by the Ten Commandments, most of us have no book or engraved tablet where our moral principles are listed for all to study at their leisure and violate at their peril. Where, then, do a society's moral rules come from? How do we learn these rules? They come from the collective experience of peoples and cultures in their search for stability, continuity, and harmony among persons of diverse interests, talents, and preferences. And we learn them in our youth (unless we have the misfortune to be neglected by our parents and teachers) in the daily processes of socialization.

What gives these rules authority over our conduct and judgment? Indeed, what makes a rule, principle, or standard a *moral* rule, standard, or principle? These are serious philosophical questions that we cannot adequately discuss and answer here. Suffice it to say that a person's *principles* guide that person's conduct and judgment; a rule or principle counts as a *moral* rule or principle when it gives guidance regarding rational constraints on self-interested conduct. A rule or principle gives such guidance when it takes into account the legitimate and relevant interests of people generally—not just one's own interests, those of one's friends and relatives, clan, or tribe, or those of one's fellow citizens but the interests of persons generally—and does so in a manner neither deliberately nor negligently indifferent to the interests of others.

This constraining function of moral rules is most evident in the best-known Western moral code, the Ten Commandments. Apart from the first three of the Commandments, which concern people's behavior toward God, the rest—Honor thy father and thy mother, Do not kill, Do not covet thy neighbor's property, and so on—clearly amount to constraints on the pursuit of self-interest regardless of its cost to others. The immoralist flouts all such constraints; the amoralist believes that most of his and our conduct involves no moral considerations one way or the other. The rest of us, however, recognize that there are constraints on our conduct. The *moral skeptic* needs to be reminded of certain indisputable facts: Does anyone seriously believe that lying and cheating are never wrong? Or that murder, rape, assault, arson, and kidnapping are wrong only because they are against the law? Or that it is merely a matter of personal opinion or taste that we ought to help the needy and ought not to take unfair advantage of others?

To be sure, honesty requires us to admit that we do not always comply with the constraints we acknowledge—we are not saints—hence the familiar experience of feeling guilty over having knowingly done the wrong thing to somebody who deserved better of us. If morality involves constraints on the pursuit of self-interest, moral reasoning involves identifying and weighing those constraints and being prepared to explain, when appropriate, why one has not complied with them.

CRITERIA FOR MORAL RULES

Philosophers and moralists over the centuries have developed various tests or criteria against which to measure the adequacy of a moral rule. Presupposed by all these criteria is the answer to this question:

- What is the rule, principle, or standard on which you propose to act?

If you can't formulate such a rule, then the rationality of your proposed action is in doubt. (In the excerpts later in this chapter, we identify some relevant moral principles and show how they are used in practice.)

Among the questions worth asking in the evaluation of someone's conduct and the rule or rules on which it relies is this:

- Would you be willing to argue for the general adoption of whatever rules you profess?

This principle is a version of the Categorical Imperative proposed by Immanuel Kant (1724–1804): Always act so that the principle of your action could be the principle on which everyone else acts in similar situations. Could a society of utterly selfish persons accept such a principle?

Surely, a general practice of fraudulent promise-making could never pass this test.

Here's another criterion:

- Would you be willing to argue openly for the general adoption of whatever reasons you accept?

Here's yet another criterion:

- Do the reasons for your proposed conduct take into account the greatest good for the greatest number?

This is a version of the utilitarian principle (for an alternative version, see p. 341; for an application, see the essay by Peter Singer, p. 356).

A CHECKLIST FOR MORAL REASONING

What is the rule, principle, or standard on which you propose to act?

✓ Is your (or someone else's) conduct prohibited or required by a moral rule or principle? If not, then it is probably not morally right or wrong: Morality permits you to act as you please.

✓ If the reasons for your proposed judgment or conduct are purely selfish, they are not moral reasons.

✓ Are your reasons an attempt to excuse wrongful conduct? If so, is the excuse a legitimate one?

✓ Are your reasons an attempt to justify breaking a moral rule knowingly? If so, is the proposed justification convincing?

✓ Do the reasons you propose for your conduct violate any of the relevant moral rules you accept? If not, then your morality raises no objection to your conduct.

✓ What is the rule, principle, or standard on which you propose to act?

✓ Would you be willing to argue openly for the general adoption of whatever rules you accept?

✓ Would you be willing to argue openly for the general adoption of whatever reasons you accept?

✓ Do the reasons for your proposed conduct take into account the greatest good for the greatest number?

✓ Do the reasons for your proposed conduct take into account the relevant moral rights of others?

✓ Would an unbiased observer, fully informed of what you regard as all the relevant facts, approve of your reasons for your proposed conduct?

Still other criteria include the following:

- Do the reasons for your proposed conduct take into account the relevant moral rights of others?
- Would an unbiased observer, fully informed of what you regard as all the relevant facts, approve of your reasons for your proposed conduct?

Which one of these criteria is the best? Or do they all come to the same thing in practice? Answering such questions involves reasoning *about* moral principles, whereas up to now we have been discussing only reasoning *with* such principles. Reasoning about moral principles arises naturally out of reflection on reasoning with such principles. *Meta-ethics*— thinking about the nature of moral concepts, values, and norms—has been a matter of immense philosophical interest since Socrates and Plato. We must leave further development of these issues to their heirs.

In the excerpts that follow, we present two actual *moral dilemmas*— that is, two actual (not hypothetical) cases in which relevant moral principles seem to conflict and require us to choose among them, knowing that something important is being sacrificed however the issue is decided. Both of these cases raise this question: Who ought to survive when not all can do so? The first case, *United States v. Holmes*, involves a shipwreck on the high seas in 1841. The second case requires us, the well fed, to decide how to respond to famine and starvation elsewhere in the world—an issue provoked by the food shortages in Bangladesh in 1970, which led two influential thinkers—the moralist Peter Singer and the biologist Garrett Hardin—to take opposite views on the responsibility of the governments of well-fed nations and of individual persons when confronted with such disasters.

United States v. Holmes

Catastrophe at sea, especially in the North Atlantic, where giant icebergs menace the sea lanes and collision between these floating monsters and relatively frail ships of wood or steel guarantees loss of life, has haunted travelers, whalers, immigrants, explorers, and others who ventured forth by sail or steam before modern safety equipment and regulations gave some protection against the risks. Harrowing tales of drowning just short of rescue and of cannibalism among desperate survivors make these events unforgettable.

From among dozens of stories of such experiences in earlier centuries, two stand out as perhaps the most famous. The notoriety surrounding these cases is partly a result of the fact that in each, after their ordeal was over, the survivors faced charges of criminal homicide on the high seas. Perhaps the more shocking of the two cases was that of Regina v. Dudley and Stephens *in 1884. The two defendants, British sailors who survived the sinking of their ship in the South Atlantic, were charged with murdering their companion in the lifeboat, a seventeen-year-old cabin boy, so that they*

*could eat his flesh. They claimed they were justified in killing one to save the
rest because the only alternative was for all to die. Necessity, they argued,
both excused and justified their actions. Tried in London, they were convicted
and sentenced to death. The Crown commuted their sentence to six months'
imprisonment.*

The other case, the one we reprint here, is United States v. Holmes. *It
relates to events in the North Atlantic some forty years prior to those in*
Dudley and Stephens *and involved American rather than British law. No
cannibalism was involved in this case, but the victims were several. Like the
cabin boy in the other case, these victims were not chosen by lot nor did they
volunteer to die. Unlike that other case, the sole defendant in the American
case was charged not with murder but with manslaughter on the high seas;
he was duly convicted and sentenced to six months of solitary confinement in
prison and a fine of $20. In the version of this case reprinted here, we have
summarized and paraphrased some pages of the official report, the rest is
quoted verbatim from the record, which in its entirety runs to some sixteen
pages.*

SUMMARY OF THE FACTS[1]

At about 10 o'clock on the cold, wet night of April 19, 1841, in the
North Atlantic some 250 miles southeast of Cape Race in Newfoundland,
the Philadelphia-bound frigate *William Brown* struck an iceberg. Those
on board—65 Scots and Irish emigrants and a crew of 17 including 3 officers—were in immediate peril of their lives. The *William Brown* carried
only two lifeboats, a so-called jolly-boat that could safely hold 10 and a
longboat adequate for perhaps two dozen. The captain, the second mate,
six crewmen, and two passengers (a woman and a boy) quickly filled the
smaller boat. Into the larger boat clambered the first mate, 8 crewmen,
and 32 passengers—far more than the boat could safely hold. Left on
board with no hope of survival were the remaining 31 passengers;
within an hour and a half of the collision, the ship went down and they
drowned.

As dawn turned into morning the two lifeboats with their exhausted
and terrified survivors began to drift apart, but not before the captain in
the jolly-boat ordered the crew in the longboat to obey the first mate just
as they would him. The first mate, for his part, reported to the captain
that in his judgment the longboat was (in the words used later by the
court reporter) "unmanageable"—the rudder was broken, water was
leaking in through various holes, and the gunwales of the overloaded
boat were dangerously near the water. If the boat were to have any
chance of staying afloat, "it would be necessary to cast lots and throw
some overboard" (again, I quote the court reporter's words). The captain

[1]This summary is reprinted from H. A. Bedau, *Making Mortal Choices*, Oxford UP 1997, 5–8.

(as later court testimony established) replied, calling across the water, "I know what you'll have to do. . . . Don't speak of that now. Let it be the last resort." With that, the two boats parted company.

The weather turned foul during the day; rain fell steadily, and in the longboat the passengers struggled to bail the water while the crew worked the oars. But by 10 in the evening, just twenty-four hours after the collision with the iceberg (again, in the words of the court reporter), "the wind began to freshen, the sea grew heavier, and once, or oftener, the waves splashed over the boats' bow so as to wet, all over, the passengers. . . . Pieces of ice were still floating around, and . . . icebergs had been seen. . . . [T]he rain falling rather heavily . . . and the boat having considerable water in it, the [first] mate, who had been bailing for some time, gave it up, explaining 'This work won't do. Help me, God. Men, go to work.' Some of the passengers cried out, about the same time: 'The boat is sinking. . . . God have mercy on our poor souls.' But the crew did not respond to the mate's order. A few minutes later, the mate shouted to the crew, 'Men, you must go to work, or we shall all perish.' They then went to work; and . . . before they ended, 14 male passengers, and also 2 women" were thrown overboard to certain death by drowning.

It appears from the court testimony of the survivors that the selection and casting overboard of the 14 men took many hours; the last two consigned to a watery grave were not dispatched until dawn. The weather improved and early in the morning the longboat with its remaining occupants were seen and rescued by a ship. The survivors in the jolly-boat were saved by another ship, but not until after they had spent six days and nights adrift on the high seas.

A year later, in 1842, in federal court in Philadelphia, one and only one member of the crew was indicted under the provisions of a federal statute to the effect that "the punishment for certain crimes against the United States" shall be imprisonment for not more than three years and a fine of not more than a thousand dollars. The crime in question was "manslaughter on the high seas" committed by any "seaman" or other person. In the aftermath of the sinking of the *William Brown,* the sole person charged under this statute was not the ship's captain, not the first mate, but a mere crewman, Alexander William Holmes by name.

Holmes was 26, Finnish by birth, a sailor since his youth, and—once more, in the words of the court reporter—with a "frame and countenance [that] would have made an artist's model for decision and strength." He was the last crew member to leave the sinking ship, having performed heroically in rescuing passengers who otherwise would have drowned trying to escape. While in the longboat he had given to the women on board "all his clothes except his shirt and pantaloons." It was he who spotted the rescue vessel, and thanks to "his exertions the ship was made to see, and finally to save them." At the trial, the captain testified that Holmes "was always obedient to officers. I never had a better man on board ship. He was a first rate man."

What follows is an excerpt from the official court report of the case in volume 26 of *Federal Cases,* starting on p. 360.

[THE PROSECUTION]

The prosecution was conducted by Mr. Wm. M. Meredith, U.S. Dist. Atty., Mr. Dallas, and O. Hopkinson; the defense by David Paul Brown, Mr. Hazlehurst, and Mr. Armstrong.

Mr. Dallas. The prisoner is charged with "unlawful homicide," as distinguished from that sort which is malicious. His defense is that the homicide was necessary to self-preservation. First, then, we ask: Was the homicide thus necessary? That is to say, was the danger instant, overwhelming, leaving no choice of means, no moment for deliberation? For, unless the danger were of this sort, the prisoner, under any admission, had no right, without notice or consultation, or lot, to sacrifice the lives of sixteen fellow beings. Peril, even extreme peril, is not enough to justify a sacrifice such as this was. Nor would even the certainty of death be enough, if death were yet prospective. It must be instant. The law regards every man's life as of equal value. It regards it, likewise, as of sacred value. Nor may any man take away his brother's life, but where the sacrifice is indispensable to save his own. (Mr. Dallas then examined the evidence, and contended that the danger was not so extreme as is requisite to justify homicide.) But it will be answered, that death being certain, there was no obligation to wait until the moment of death had arrived. Admitting, then, the fact that death was certain, and that the safety of some persons was to be promoted by an early sacrifice of the others, what law, we ask, gives a crew, in such a case, to be the arbiters of life and death, settling, for themselves, both the time and the extent of the necessity? No. We protest against giving to seamen the power thus to make jettison of human beings, as of so much cargo; of allowing sailors, for their own safety, to throw overboard, whenever they may like, whomsoever they may choose. If the mate and seamen believed that the ultimate safety of a portion was to be advanced by the sacrifice of another portion, it was the clear duty of that officer, and of the seamen, to give full notice to all on board. Common settlement would, then, have fixed the principle of sacrifice, and, the mode of selection involving all, a sacrifice of any would have been resorted to only in dire extremity. Thus far, the argument admits that, at sea, sailor and passenger stand upon the same base, and in equal relations. But we take, third, stronger ground. The seaman, we hold, is bound, beyond the passenger, to encounter the perils of the sea. To the last extremity, to death itself, must he protect the passenger. It is his duty. It is on account of these risks that he is paid. It is because the sailor is expected to expose himself to every danger, that, beyond all mankind, by every law, his wages are secured to him. . . . No other doctrine than this one can be adopted. Promulgate as law that the prisoner is guiltless, and our marine will be disgraced in the eyes of civilized nations. The thousand ships which now traverse the ocean in safety will be consigned to the absolute power of their crews, and, worse than the dangers of the sea, will be added such as come from the violence of men more reckless than any upon earth.

[THE DEFENSE]

Mr. Armstrong opened the defense, and was followed by Mr. Brown.

We protest against the prisoner being made a victim to the reputation of the marine law of the country. It cannot be, God forbid that it should ever be, that the sacrifice of innocence shall be the price at which the name and honor of American jurisprudence is to be preserved in this country, or in foreign lands. The malediction of an unrighteous sentence will rest more heavily on the law, than on the prisoner. This court (it would be indecent to think otherwise) will administer the law, "uncaring consequences." But this case should be tried in a long-boat sunk down to its very gunwale with forty-one half naked, starved, and shivering wretches, the boat leaking from below, filling from above, a hundred leagues from land, at midnight, surrounded by ice, unmanageable from its load, and subject to certain destruction from the change of the most changeful of the elements, the winds, and the waves. To these superadd the horrors of famine and the recklessness of despair, madness, and all the prospects, past utterance, of this unutterable condition. Fairly to sit in judgment on the prisoner, we should, then, be actually translated to his situation. It was a conjuncture which no fancy can imagine. Terror had assumed the throne of reason, and passion had become judgment. Are the United States to come here, now, a year after the events, when it is impossible to estimate the elements which combined to make the risk, or to say to what extent the jeopardy was imminent? . . .

Counsel say that lots are the law of the ocean. Lots, in cases of   5
famine, where means of subsistence are wanting for all the crew, is what the history of maritime disaster records; but who has ever told of casting lots at midnight, in a sinking boat, in the midst of darkness, of rain, of terror, and of confusion? To cast lots when all are going down, but to decide who shall be spared, to cast lots when the question is, whether any can be saved, is a plan easy to suggest, rather difficult to put in practice. . . . The sailors adopted the only principle of selection which was possible in an emergency like theirs,—a principle more humane than lots. Man and wife were not torn asunder, and the women were all preserved. Lots

would have rendered impossible this clear dictate of humanity. But again: The crew either were in their ordinary and original state of subordination to their officers, or they were in a state of nature. If in the former state, they are excusable in law, for having obeyed the order of the mate,—an order twice imperatively given. Independent of the mate's general authority in the captain's absence, the captain had pointedly directed the crew to obey all the mate's orders as they would his, the captain's; and the crew had promised to do so. It imports not to declare that a crew is not bound to obey an unlawful order, for to say that this order was unlawful is to postulate what remains to be proved. Who is to judge of the unlawfulness? The circumstances were peculiar. The occasion was emergent, without precedent, or parallel. The lawfulness of the order is the very question which we are disputing; a question about which this whole community has been agitated, and is still divided; the discussion of which crowds this room with auditors past former example; a question which this court, with all its resources, is now engaged in considering, as such a question demands to be considered, most deliberately, most anxiously, most cautiously. It is no part of a sailor's duty to moralize and to speculate, in such a moment as this was, upon the orders of his superior officers. . . .

Whether the mate, if on trial here, would be found innocent, is a question which we need not decide. That question is a different one from the guilt or innocence of the prisoner, and one more difficult. But if the whole company were reduced to a state of nature, then the sailors were bound to no duty, not mutual, to the passengers. The contract of the shipping articles had become dissolved by an unforeseen and overwhelming necessity. The sailor was no longer a sailor, but a drowning man. Having fairly done his duty to the last extremity, he was not to lose the rights of a human being, because he wore a roundabout instead of a frock coat. We do not seek authorities for such doctrine. The instinct of these men's hearts is our authority,—the best authority. Whoever opposes it must be wrong, for he opposes human nature. All the contemplated conditions, all the contemplated possibilities of the voyage, were ended. The parties, sailor and passenger, were in a new state. All persons on board the vessel became equal. All became their own lawgivers; for artificial distinctions cease to prevail when men are reduced to the equality of nature. Every man on board had a right to make law with his own right hand, and the law which did prevail on that awful night having been the law of necessity, and the law of nature too, it is the law which will be upheld by this court, to the liberation of this prisoner. . . .

[THE JUDGE'S CHARGE TO THE JURY]

Baldwin, Circuit Justice, charging jury, alluded to the touching character of the case; and, after stating to the jury what was the offense laid in the indictment, his honor explained, with particularity, the distinction between murder and manslaughter. He said that malice was of the essence of murder, while want of criminal intention was consistent with the nature of manslaughter. He impressed strongly upon the jury, that the mere absence of malice did not render homicide excusable. . . .

In such cases the law neither excuses the act nor permits it to be justified as innocent; but, although inflicting some punishment, she yet looks with a benignant eye, through the thing done, to the mind and to the heart; and when, on a view of all the circumstances connected with the act, no evil spirit is discerned, her humanity forbids the exaction of life for life. . . . Where, indeed, a case does arise, embraced by this "law of necessity," the penal laws pass over such case in silence; for law is made to meet but the ordinary exigencies of life. But the case does not become "a case of necessity," unless all ordinary means of self-preservation have been exhausted. The peril must be instant, overwhelming, leaving no alternative but to lose our own life, or to take the life of another person. An illustration of this principle occurs in the ordinary case of self-defense against lawless violence. . . . And I again state that when this great "law of necessity" does apply, and is not improperly exercised, the taking of life is devested of unlawfulness.

But in applying this law, we must look not only to the jeopardy in which the parties are, but also to the relations in which they stand. . . . The passenger stands in a position different from that of the officers and seamen. It is the sailor who must encounter the hardships and perils of the voyage. Nor can this relation be changed when the ship is lost by tempest or other danger of the sea, and all on board have betaken themselves, for safety, to the small boats; for imminence of danger can not absolve from duty. The sailor is bound, as before, to undergo whatever hazard is necessary to preserve the boat and the passengers. Should the emergency become so extreme as to call for the sacrifice of life, there can be no reason why the law does not still remain the same. The passenger, not being bound either to labor or to incur the risk of life, cannot be bound to sacrifice his existence to preserve the sailor's. The captain, indeed, and a sufficient number of seamen to navigate the boat, must be preserved; for, except these abide in the ship, all will perish. But if there be more seamen than are necessary to manage the boat, the supernumerary sailors have no right, for their safety, to sacrifice the passengers. The sailors and passengers, in fact, cannot be regarded as in equal positions. The sailor (to use the language of a distinguished writer) owes more benevolence to another than to himself. He is bound to set a greater value on the life of others than on his own. And while we admit that sailor and sailor may lawfully struggle with each other for the plank which can save but one, we think that, if the passenger is on the plank, even "the law of necessity" justifies not the sailor who takes it from him. . . .

But, in addition, if the source of the danger have been obvious, and destruction ascertained to be certainly about to arrive, though at a future time, there should be consultation, and some mode of selection fixed, by which those in equal relations may have equal chance for their life. By what mode, then, should selection be made? . . . When the ship is in no danger of sinking, but all sustenance is exhausted, and a sacrifice of one person is necessary to appease the hunger of others, the selection is by lot. This mode is resorted to as the fairest mode, and, in some sort, as an appeal to God, for selection of the victim. This manner, obviously, was regarded by the mate, in parting with the captain, as the one which it was proper to adopt, in case the long-boat could not live with all who were on board on Tuesday morning. The same manner, as would appear from the response given to the mate, had already suggested itself to the captain. For ourselves, we can conceive of no mode so consonant both to humanity and to justice; and the occasion, we think, must be peculiar which will dispense with its exercise. If, indeed, the peril be instant and overwhelming, leaving no chance of means, and no moment for deliberation, then, of course, there is no power to consult, to cast lots, or in any such way to decide; but even where the final disaster is thus sudden, if it have been foreseen as certainly about to arrive, if no new cause of danger have arisen to bring on the closing catastrophe, if time have existed to cast lots, and to select the victims, then, as we have said, sortition should be adopted. In no other than this or some like way are those having equal rights put upon an equal footing, and in no other way is it possible to guard against partiality and oppression, violence, and conflict. . . .

When the selection has been made by lots, the victim yields of course to his fate, or, if he resist, force may be employed to coerce submission. Whether or not "a case of necessity" has arisen, or whether the law under which death has been inflicted have been so exercised as to hold the executioner harmless, cannot depend on his own opinion; for no man may pass upon his own conduct when it concerns the rights, and especially, when it affects the lives, of others. We have already stated to you that, by the law of the land, homicide is sometimes justifiable; and the law defines the occasions in which it is so. The transaction must, therefore, be justified to the law; and the person accused rests under obligation to satisfy those who judicially scrutinize his case that it really transcended ordinary rules. In fact, any other principle would be followed by pernicious results, and, moreover, would not be practicable in application. Opinion or belief may be assumed, whether it exist or not; and if this mere opinion of the sailors will justify them in making a sacrifice of the passengers, of course the mere opinion of the passengers would, in turn, justify these in making a sacrifice of the sailors. The passengers may have confidence in their own capacity to manage and preserve the boat, or the effort of either sailors or passengers to save the boat, may be clearly unavailing; and what, then, in a struggle against force and numbers, becomes of the safety of the seamen? Hard as is a seaman's life, would it not become yet more perilous if the passengers, who may outnumber them tenfold, should be allowed to judge when the dangers of the sea will justify a sacrifice of life? We are, therefore, satisfied, that, in requiring proof, which shall be satisfactory to you, of the existence of the necessity, we are fixing the rule which is, not merely the only one which is practicable, but, moreover, the only one which will secure the safety of the sailors themselves. . . .

[THE CASE GOES TO THE JURY]

After a few remarks upon the evidence, the case was given to the jury, who, about sixteen hours afterwards, and after having once returned to the bar, unable to agree, with some difficulty, found a verdict of guilty. The prisoner was, however, recommended to the mercy of the court. . . .

When the prisoner was brought up for sentence, the learned judge said to him, that many circumstances in the affair were of a character to commend him to regard, yet, that the case was one in which some punishment was demanded; that it was in the power of the court to inflict the penalty of an imprisonment for a term of three years, and a fine of $1,000, but, in view of all the circumstances, and especially as the prisoner had been already confined in gaol several months, that the court would make the punishment more lenient. The convict was then sentenced to undergo an imprisonment in the Eastern Penitentiary of Pennsylvania, (solitary confinement) at hard labor, for the term of six months, and to pay a fine of $20.

Topics for Critical Thinking and Writing

1. Seaman Holmes seems to have thrown passengers out of the overcrowded lifeboat as though he were acting on a principle: Save families and crew. What other possible selection principles might he have acted on, instead? Assuming that some had to be thrown overboard, what selection principle would you argue is the best one in the circumstances? Explain your views in an essay of 500 words.

2. Would you agree that in cases like this the fairest principle on which to sacrifice some for the sake of the rest is an all-inclusive lottery? Why, or why not? Could one argue that although a lottery is the fairest principle for cases of this sort, it is not the best one?

3. Holmes surely thought he was acting on the orders of the mate. If so, does that make a difference in his degree of responsibility for the deaths of those thrown overboard? Explain your answer in a 250-word essay.

4. The attorneys in this case disagreed over whether the deaths of any of the passengers in the lifeboat were "necessary." What do you think, given the facts as reported? What is the difference between deaths being necessary and deaths being highly desirable because of the greater likelihood that the others would survive?

5. Associate Justice of the U.S. Supreme Court Benjamin Cardozo (1870–1938), in commenting on the *Holmes* case, wrote in part: "When two or more are overtaken by a common disaster, there is no right on the part of one to save the lives of some by killing another. There is no rule of human jettison." He added that if none are ready to sacrifice themselves, "the human freight must be left to meet the chances of the waters." Write a 250-word essay in which you explain why you agree or disagree with Cardozo.

6. Holmes was convicted of manslaughter, sentenced to six months' solitary confinement, and fined $20. Do you think this punishment was too lenient? Too severe? Why wasn't Holmes charged with and convicted of murder?

Peter Singer

Peter Singer is the Ira W. DeCamp Professor of Bioethics at Princeton University. A native of Australia, he is a graduate of the University of Melbourne and Oxford University and the author or editor of more than two dozen books, including Animal Liberation *(1975),* Practical Ethics *(1979), and* Rethinking Life and Death *(1995). His views on several life-and-death issues have been the source of much public and scholarly controversy. This essay originally appeared in* Philosophy and Public Affairs *(Spring 1972).*

Famine, Affluence, and Morality

As I write this, in November 1971, people are dying in East Bengal from lack of food, shelter, and medical care. The suffering and death that are occurring there now are not inevitable, not unavoidable in any fatalistic sense of the term. Constant poverty, a cyclone, and a civil war have turned at least nine million people into destitute refugees; nevertheless, it is not beyond the capacity of the richer nations to give enough assistance to reduce any further suffering to very small proportions. The decisions and actions of human beings can prevent this kind of suffering. Unfortunately, human beings have not made the necessary decisions. At the individual level, people have, with very few exceptions, not responded to the situation in any significant way. Generally speaking, people have not given large sums to relief funds; they have not written to their parliamentary representatives demanding increased government assistance; they have not demonstrated in the streets, held symbolic fasts, or done anything else directed toward providing the refugees with the means to satisfy their essential needs. At the government level, no government has given the sort of massive aid that would enable the refugees to survive for more than a few days. Britain, for instance, has given rather more than most countries. It has, to date, given £14,750,000. For comparative purposes, Britain's share of the nonrecoverable development costs of the Anglo-French Concorde project is already in excess of £275,000,000, and on present estimates will reach £440,000,000. The implication is that the British government values a supersonic transport more than thirty times as highly as it values the lives of the 9 million refugees. Australia is another country which, on a per capita basis, is well up in the "aid to Bengal" table. Australia's aid, however, amounts to less than one-twelfth of the cost of Sydney's new opera house. The total amount given, from all sources, now stands at about £65,000,000. The estimated cost of keeping the refugees alive for one year is £464,000,000. Most of the refugees have now been in the camps for more than six months. The World Bank has said that India needs a minimum of £300,000,000 in assistance from other countries before the end of the year. It seems obvious that assistance on this scale will not be forthcoming. India will be forced to choose between letting the refugees starve or diverting funds from her own development program, which will mean that more of her own people will starve in the future.[1]

These are the essential facts about the present situation in Bengal. So far as it concerns us here, there is nothing unique about this situation except its magnitude. The Bengal emergency is just the latest and most acute of a series of major emergencies in various parts of the world, arising both from natural and from man-made causes. There are also many parts of the world in which people die from malnutrition and lack of food independent of any special emergency. I take Bengal as my example only because it is the present concern, and because the size of the problem has ensured that it has been given adequate publicity. Neither individuals nor governments can claim to be unaware of what is happening there.

What are the moral implications of a situation like this? In what follows, I shall argue that the way people in relatively affluent countries react to a situation like that in Bengal cannot be justified; indeed, the whole way we look at moral issues—our moral conceptual scheme—needs to be altered, and with it, the way of life that has come to be taken for granted in our society.

In arguing for this conclusion I will not, of course, claim to be morally neutral. I shall, however, try to argue for the moral position that I take, so that anyone who accepts certain assumptions, to be made explicit, will, I hope, accept my conclusion.

---

[1]There was also a third possibility: that India would go to war to enable the refugees to return to their lands. Since I wrote this paper, India has taken this way out. The situation is no longer that described above, but this does not affect my argument, as the next paragraph indicates. [All notes are Singer's.]

I begin with the assumption that suffering and death from lack of food, shelter, and medical care are bad. I think most people will agree about this, although one may reach the same view by different routes. I shall not argue for this view. People can hold all sorts of eccentric positions, and perhaps from some of them it would not follow that death by starvation is in itself bad. It is difficult, perhaps impossible, to refute such positions, and so for brevity I will henceforth take this assumption as accepted. Those who disagree need read no further.

My next point is this: If it is in our power to prevent something bad from happening, without thereby sacrificing anything of comparable moral importance, we ought, morally, to do it. By "without sacrificing anything of comparable moral importance" I mean without causing anything else comparably bad to happen, or doing something that is wrong in itself, or failing to promote some moral good, comparable in significance to the bad thing that we can prevent. This principle seems almost as uncontroversial as the last one. It requires us only to prevent what is bad, and not to promote what is good, and it requires this of us only when we can do it without sacrificing anything that is, from the moral point of view, comparably important. I could even, as far as the application of my argument to the Bengal emergency is concerned, qualify the point so as to make it: If it is in our power to prevent something very bad from happening, without thereby sacrificing anything morally significant, we ought, morally, to do it. An application of this principle would be as follows: If I am walking past a shallow pond and see a child drowning in it, I ought to wade in and pull the child out. This will mean getting my clothes muddy, but this is insignificant, while the death of the child would presumably be a very bad thing.

The uncontroversial appearance of the principle just stated is deceptive. If it were acted upon, even in its qualified form, our lives, our society, and our world would be fundamentally changed. For the principle takes, firstly, no account of proximity or distance. It makes no moral difference whether the person I can help is a neighbor's child ten yards from me or a Bengali whose name I shall never know, ten thousand miles away. Secondly, the principle makes no distinction between cases in which I am the only person who could possibly do anything and cases in which I am just one among millions in the same position.

I do not think I need to say much in defense of the refusal to take proximity and distance into account. The fact that a person is physically near to us, so that we have personal contact with him, may make it more likely that we *shall* assist him, but this does not show that we *ought* to help him rather than another who happens to be further away. If we accept any principle of impartiality, universalizability, equality, or whatever, we cannot discriminate against someone merely because he is far away from us (or we are far away from him). Admittedly, it is possible that we are in a better position to judge what needs to be done to help a person near to us than one far away, and perhaps also to provide the assistance we judge to be necessary. If this were the case, it would be a reason for helping those near to us first. This may once have been a justification for being more concerned with the poor in one's own town than with famine victims in India. Unfortunately for those who like to keep their moral responsibilities limited, instant communication and swift transportation have changed the situation. From the moral point of view, the development of the world into a "global village" has made an important, though still unrecognized, difference to our moral situation. Expert observers and supervisors, sent out by famine relief organizations or permanently stationed in famine-prone areas, can direct our aid to a refugee in Bengal almost as effectively as we could get it to someone in our own block. There would seem, therefore, to be no possible justification for discriminating on geographical grounds.

There may be a greater need to defend the second implication of my principle—that the fact that there are millions of other people in the same position, in respect to the Bengali refugees, as I am, does not make the situation significantly different from a situation in which I am the only person who can prevent something very bad from occurring. Again, of course, I admit that there is a psychological difference between the cases; one feels less guilty about doing nothing if one can point to others, similarly placed, who have also done nothing. Yet this can make no real difference to our moral obligations.[2] Should I consider that I am less obliged to pull the drowning child out of the pond if on looking around I see other people, no further away than I am, who have also noticed the child but are doing nothing? One has only to ask this question to see the absurdity of the view that numbers lessen obligation. It is a view that is an ideal excuse for inactivity; unfortunately most of the major evils—poverty, overpopulation, pollution—are problems in which everyone is almost equally involved.

The view that numbers do make a difference can be made plausible   10
if stated in this way: If everyone in circumstances like mine gave £5 to the Bengal Relief Fund, there would be enough to provide food, shelter, and medical care for the refugees; there is no reason why I should give more than anyone else in the same circumstances as I am; therefore I have no obligation to give more than £5. Each premise in this argument is true, and the argument looks sound. It may convince us, unless we notice that it is based on a hypothetical premise, although the conclusion is not stated hypothetically. The argument would be sound if the conclusion were: If everyone in circumstances like mine were to give £5, I

---

[2]In view of the special sense philosophers often give to the term, I should say that I use "obligation" simply as the abstract noun derived from "ought," so that "I have an obligation to" means no more, and no less, than "I ought to." This usage is in accordance with the definition of "ought" given by the *Shorter Oxford English Dictionary:* "the general verb to express duty or obligation." I do not think any issue of substance hangs on the way the term is used; sentences in which I use "obligation" could all be rewritten, although somewhat clumsily, as sentences in which a clause containing "ought" replaces the term "obligation."

would have no obligation to give more than £5. If the conclusion were so stated, however, it would be obvious that the argument has no bearing on a situation in which it is not the case that everyone else gives £5. This, of course, is the actual situation. It is more or less certain that not everyone in circumstances like mine will give £5. So there will not be enough to provide the needed food, shelter, and medical care. Therefore by giving more than £5 I will prevent more suffering than I would if I gave just £5.

It might be thought that this argument has an absurd consequence. Since the situation appears to be that very few people are likely to give substantial amounts, it follows that I and everyone else in similar circumstances ought to give as much as possible, that is, at least up to the point at which by giving more one would begin to cause serious suffering for oneself and one's dependents—perhaps even beyond this point to the point of marginal utility, at which by giving more one would cause oneself and one's dependents as much suffering as one would prevent in Bengal. If everyone does this, however, there will be more than can be used for the benefit of the refugees, and some of the sacrifice will have been unnecessary. Thus, if everyone does what he ought to do, the result will not be as good as it would be if everyone did a little less than he ought to do, or if only some do all that they ought to do.

The paradox here arises only if we assume that the actions in question—sending money to the relief funds—are performed more or less simultaneously, and are also unexpected. For if it is to be expected that everyone is going to contribute something, then clearly each is not obliged to give as much as he would have been obliged to had others not been giving too. And if everyone is not acting more or less simultaneously, then those giving later will know how much more is needed, and will have no obligation to give more than is necessary to reach this amount. To say this is not to deny the principle that people in the same circumstances have the same obligations, but to point out that the fact that others have given, or may be expected to give, is a relevant circumstance: Those giving after it has become known that many others are giving and those giving before are not in the same circumstances. So the seemingly absurd consequence of the principle I have put forward can occur only if people are in error about the actual circumstances—that is, if they think they are giving when others are not, but in fact they are giving when others are. The result of everyone doing what he really ought to do cannot be worse than the result of everyone doing less than he ought to do, although the result of everyone doing what he reasonably believes he ought to do could be.

If my argument so far has been sound, neither our distance from a preventable evil nor the number of other people who, in respect to that evil, are in the same situation as we are, lessens our obligation to mitigate or prevent that evil. I shall therefore take as established the principle I asserted earlier. As I have already said, I need to assert it only in its qualified form: If it is in our power to prevent something very bad from happening, without thereby sacrificing anything else morally significant, we ought, morally, to do it.

The outcome of this argument is that our traditional moral categories are upset. The traditional distinction between duty and charity cannot be drawn, or at least, not in the place we normally draw it. Giving money to the Bengal Relief Fund is regarded as an act of charity in our society. The bodies which collect money are known as "charities." These organizations see themselves in this way—if you send them a check, you will be thanked for your "generosity." Because giving money is regarded as an act of charity, it is not thought that there is anything wrong with not giving. The charitable man may be praised, but the man who is not charitable is not condemned. People do not feel in any way ashamed or guilty about spending money on new clothes or a new car instead of giving it to famine relief. (Indeed, the alternative does not occur to them.) This way of looking at the matter cannot be justified. When we buy new clothes not to keep ourselves warm but to look "well-dressed" we are not providing for any important need. We would not be sacrificing anything significant if we were to continue to wear our old clothes, and give the money to famine relief. By doing so, we would be preventing another person from starving. It follows from what I have said earlier that we ought to give money away, rather than spend it on clothes which we do not need to keep us warm. To do so is not charitable, or generous. Nor is it the kind of act which philosophers and theologians have called "supererogatory"—an act which it would be good to do, but not wrong not to do. On the contrary, we ought to give the money away, and it is wrong not to do so.

I am not maintaining that there are no acts which are charitable, or 15 that there are no acts which it would be good to do but not wrong not to do. It may be possible to redraw the distinction between duty and charity in some other place. All I am arguing here is that the present way of drawing the distinction, which makes it an act of charity for a man living at the level of affluence which most people in the "developed nations" enjoy to give money to save someone else from starvation, cannot be supported. It is beyond the scope of my argument to consider whether the distinction should be redrawn or abolished altogether. There would be many other possible ways of drawing the distinction—for instance, one might decide that it is good to make other people as happy as possible, but not wrong not to do so.

Despite the limited nature of the revision in our moral conceptual scheme which I am proposing, the revision would, given the extent of both affluence and famine in the world today, have radical implications. These implications may lead to further objections, distinct from those I have already considered. I shall discuss two of these.

One objection to the position I have taken might be simply that it is too drastic a revision of our moral scheme. People do not ordinarily judge in the way I have suggested they should. Most people reserve their moral condemnation for those who violate some moral norm, such as the norm against taking another person's property. They do not condemn those who indulge in luxury instead of giving to famine relief. But given that I did not set out to present a morally neutral description of the way people make moral judgments, the way people do in fact judge has nothing to do with the validity of my conclusion. My conclusion follows from the principle which I advanced earlier, and unless that principle is rejected, or the arguments shown to be unsound, I think the conclusion must stand, however strange it appears.

It might, nevertheless, be interesting to consider why our society, and most other societies, do judge differently from the way I have suggested they should. In a well-known article, J. O. Urmson suggests that the imperatives of duty, which tell us what we must do, as distinct from what it would be good to do but not wrong not to do, function so as to prohibit behavior that is intolerable if men are to live together in society.[3] This may explain the origin and continued existence of the present division between acts of duty and acts of charity. Moral attitudes are shaped by the needs of society, and no doubt society needs people who will observe the rules that make social existence tolerable. From the point of view of a particular society, it is essential to prevent violations of norms against killing, stealing, and so on. It is quite inessential, however, to help people outside one's own society

If this is an explanation of our common distinction between duty and supererogation, however, it is not a justification of it. The moral point of view requires us to look beyond the interests of our own society. Previously, as I have already mentioned, this may hardly have been feasible, but it is quite feasible now. From the moral point of view, the prevention of the starvation of millions of people outside our society must be considered at least as pressing as the upholding of property norms within our society.

It has been argued by some writers, among them Sidgwick and Urmson, that we need to have a basic moral code which is not too far beyond the capacities of the ordinary man, for otherwise there will be a general breakdown of compliance with the moral code. Crudely stated, this argument suggests that if we tell people that they ought to refrain from murder and give everything they do not really need to famine relief, they will do neither, whereas if we tell them that they ought to refrain from murder and that it is good to give to famine relief but not wrong not to do so, they will at least refrain from murder. The issue here is: Where should we draw the line between conduct that is required and conduct that is good although not required, so as to get the best possible 20

---

[3]J. O. Urmson, "Saints and Heroes," in *Essays in Moral Philosophy*, ed. Abraham I. Melden (Seattle and London, 1958), p. 214. For a related but significantly different view see also Henry Sidgwick, *The Methods of Ethics*, 7th ed. (London, 1907), pp. 220–21, 492–93.

result? This would seem to be an empirical question, although a very difficult one. One objection to the Sidgwick-Urmson line of argument is that it takes insufficient account of the effect that moral standards can have on the decisions we make. Given a society in which a wealthy man who gives 5 percent of his income to famine relief is regarded as most generous, it is not surprising that a proposal that we all ought to give away half our incomes will be thought to be absurdly unrealistic. In a society which held that no man should have more than enough while others have less than they need, such a proposal might seem narrowminded. What it is possible for a man to do and what he is likely to do are both, I think, very greatly influenced by what people around him are doing and expecting him to do. In any case, the possibility that by spreading the idea that we ought to be doing very much more than we are to relieve famine we shall bring about a general breakdown of moral behavior seems remote. If the stakes are an end to widespread starvation, it is worth the risk. Finally, it should be emphasized that these considerations are relevant only to the issue of what we should require from others, and not to what we ourselves ought to do.

The second objection to my attack on the present distinction between duty and charity is one which has from time to time been made against utilitarianism. It follows from some forms of utilitarian theory that we all ought, morally, to be working full time to increase the balance of happiness over misery. The position I have taken here would not lead to this conclusion in all circumstances, for if there were no bad occurrences that we could prevent without sacrificing something of comparable moral importance, my argument would have no application. Given the present conditions in many parts of the world, however, it does follow from my argument that we ought, morally, to be working full time to relieve great suffering of the sort that occurs as a result of famine or other disasters. Of course, mitigating circumstances can be adduced—for instance, that if we wear ourselves out through overwork, we shall be less effective than we would otherwise have been. Nevertheless, when all considerations of this sort have been taken into account, the conclusion remains: We ought to be preventing as much suffering as we can without sacrificing something else of comparable moral importance. This conclusion is one which we may be reluctant to face. I cannot see, though, why it should be regarded as a criticism of the position for which I have argued, rather than a criticism of our ordinary standards of behavior. Since most people are self-interested to some degree, very few of us are likely to do everything that we ought to do. It would, however, hardly be honest to take this as evidence that it is not the case that we ought to do it.

It may still be thought that my conclusions are so wildly out of line with what everyone else thinks and has always thought that there must be something wrong with the argument somewhere. In order to show that my conclusions, while certainly contrary to contemporary Western moral standards, would not have seemed so extraordinary at other times and in other places, I would like to quote a passage from a writer not normally thought of as a way-out radical, Thomas Aquinas.

> Now, according to the natural order instituted by divine providence, material goods are provided for the satisfaction of human needs. Therefore the division and appropriation of property, which proceeds from human law, must not hinder the satisfaction of man's necessity from such goods. Equally, whatever a man has in superabundance is owed, of natural right, to the poor for their sustenance. So Ambrosius says, and it is also to be found in the *Decretum Gratiani:* "The bread which you withhold belongs to the hungry; the clothing you shut away, to the naked; and the money you bury in the earth is the redemption and freedom of the penniless."[4]

I now want to consider a number of points, more practical than philosophical, which are relevant to the application of the moral conclusion we have reached. These points challenge not the idea that we ought to be doing all we can to prevent starvation, but the idea that giving away a great deal of money is the best means to this end.

It is sometimes said that overseas aid should be a government responsibility, and that therefore one ought not to give to privately run charities. Giving privately, it is said, allows the government and the non-contributing members of society to escape their responsibilities.

This argument seems to assume that the more people there are who 25 give to privately organized famine relief funds, the less likely it is that the government will take over full responsibility for such aid. This assumption is unsupported, and does not strike me as at all plausible. The opposite view — that if no one gives voluntarily, a government will assume that its citizens are uninterested in famine relief and would not wish to be forced into giving aid — seems more plausible. In any case, unless there were a definite probability that by refusing to give one would be helping to bring about massive government assistance, people who do refuse to make voluntary contributions are refusing to prevent a certain amount of suffering without being able to point to any tangible beneficial consequence of their refusal. So the onus of showing how their refusal will bring about government action is on those who refuse to give.

I do not, of course, want to dispute the contention that governments of affluent nations should be giving many times the amount of genuine, no-strings-attached aid that they are giving now. I agree, too, that giving privately is not enough, and that we ought to be campaigning actively for entirely new standards for both public and private contributions to famine relief. Indeed, I would sympathize with someone who thought that campaigning was more important than giving oneself, although I

[4]*Summa Theologica*, II–II, Question 66, Article 7, in *Aquinas, Selected Political Writings*, ed. A. P. d'Entreves, trans. J. G. Dawson (Oxford, 1948), p. 171.

doubt whether preaching what one does not practice would be very effective. Unfortunately, for many people the idea that "it's the government's responsibility" is a reason for not giving which does not appear to entail any political action either.

Another, more serious reason for not giving to famine relief funds is that until there is effective population control, relieving famine merely postpones starvation. If we save the Bengal refugees now, others, perhaps the children of these refugees, will face starvation in a few years' time. In support of this, one may cite the now well-known facts about the population explosion and the relatively limited scope for expanded production.

This point, like the previous one, is an argument against relieving suffering that is happening now, because of a belief about what might happen in the future; it is unlike the previous point in that very good evidence can be adduced in support of this belief about the future. I will not go into the evidence here. I accept that the earth cannot support indefinitely a population rising at the present rate. This certainly poses a problem for anyone who thinks it important to prevent famine. Again, however, one could accept the argument without drawing the conclusion that it absolves one from any obligation to do anything to prevent famine. The conclusion that should be drawn is that the best means of preventing famine, in the long run, is population control. It would then follow from the position reached earlier that one ought to be doing all one can to promote population control (unless one held that all forms of population control were wrong in themselves, or would have significantly bad consequences). Since there are organizations working specifically for population control, one would then support them rather than more orthodox methods of preventing famine.

A third point raised by the conclusion reached earlier relates to the question of just how much we all ought to be giving away. One possibility, which has already been mentioned, is that we ought to give until we reach the level of marginal utility — that is, the level at which, by giving more, I would cause as much suffering to myself or my dependents as I would relieve by my gift. This would mean, of course, that one would reduce oneself to very near the material circumstances of a Bengali refugee. It will be recalled that earlier I put forward both a strong and a moderate version of the principle of preventing bad occurrences. The strong version, which required us to prevent bad things from happening unless in doing so we would be sacrificing something of comparable moral significance, does seem to require reducing ourselves to the level of marginal utility. I should also say that the strong version seems to me to be the correct one. I proposed the more moderate version — that we should prevent bad occurrences unless, to do so, we had to sacrifice something morally significant — only in order to show that even on this surely undeniable principle a great change in our way of life is required. On the more moderate principle, it may not follow that we ought to reduce ourselves to the level of marginal utility, for one might hold that to reduce oneself and one's family to this level is to cause something significantly bad to happen. Whether this is so I shall not discuss, since, as I have said, I can see no good reason for holding the moderate version of the principle rather than the strong version. Even if we accepted the principle only in its moderate form, however, it should be clear that we would have to give away enough to ensure that the consumer society, dependent as it is on people spending on trivia rather than giving to famine relief, would slow down and perhaps disappear entirely. There are several reasons why this would be desirable in itself. The value and necessity of economic growth are now being questioned not only by conservationists, but by economists as well.[5] There is no doubt, too, that the consumer society has had a distorting effect on the goals and purposes of its members. Yet looking at the matter purely from the point of view of overseas aid, there must be a limit to the extent to which we should deliberately slow down our economy; for it might be the case that if we gave away, say, 40 percent of our Gross National Product, we would slow down the economy so much that in absolute terms we would be giving less than if we gave 25 percent of the much larger GNP that we would have if we limited our contribution to this smaller percentage.

I mention this only as an indication of the sort of factor that one would have to take into account in working out an ideal. Since Western societies generally consider 1 percent of the GNP an acceptable level for overseas aid, the matter is entirely academic. Nor does it affect the question of how much an individual should give in a society in which very few are giving substantial amounts.

It is sometimes said, though less often now than it used to be, that philosophers have no special role to play in public affairs, since most public issues depend primarily on an assessment of facts. On questions of fact, it is said, philosophers as such have no special expertise, and so it has been possible to engage in philosophy without committing oneself to any position on major public issues. No doubt there are some issues of social policy and foreign policy about which it can truly be said that a really expert assessment of the facts is required before taking sides or acting, but the issue of famine is surely not one of these. The facts about the existence of suffering are beyond dispute. Nor, I think, is it disputed that we can do something about it, either through orthodox methods of famine relief or through population control or both. This is therefore an issue on which philosophers are competent to take a position. The issue is one which faces everyone who has more money than he needs to support himself and his dependents, or who is in a position to take some

[5]See, for instance, John Kenneth Galbraith, *The New Industrial State* (Boston, 1967); and E. J. Mishan, *The Costs of Economic Growth* (London, 1967).

sort of political action. These categories must include practically every teacher and student of philosophy in the universities of the Western world. If philosophy is to deal with matters that are relevant to both teachers and students, this is an issue that philosophers should discuss.

Discussion, though, is not enough. What is the point of relating philosophy to public (and personal) affairs if we do not take our conclusions seriously? In this instance, taking our conclusion seriously means acting upon it. The philosopher will not find it any easier than anyone else to alter his attitudes and way of life to the extent that, if I am right, is involved in doing everything that we ought to be doing. At the very least, though, one can make a start. The philosopher who does so will have to sacrifice some of the benefits of the consumer society, but he can find compensation in the satisfaction of a way of life in which theory and practice, if not yet in harmony, are at least coming together.

Topics for Critical Thinking and Writing

1. How does Singer tell when one thing we might do is more or less "morally significant" (para. 6) than something else we might do? Do you agree with him on this point?

2. Explain whether you agree with Singer that, morally speaking, there is no difference between my coming to the aid of someone I know and love (say, my child or my parent) and coming to the aid of a stranger thousands of miles away, someone "whose name I shall never know" (para. 7) — perhaps someone whom I would thoroughly dislike if I did know him or her?

3. What is the view that "numbers lessen obligation" (para. 9), and why does Singer refer to it as an "absurdity"?

4. What does Singer mean by the affluent giving money or other resources to the needy up to "the level of marginal utility" (paras. 11 and 29)?

5. What does Singer mean by "the traditional distinction between duty and charity" (para. 14)? Why does he think this distinction collapses? Does he in fact contradict himself on this point in paragraph 15?

6. Suppose that a gift of large-scale resources by the affluent to the currently starving in some nation reduces what can be given to their successors, the next generation, when the next famine hits that nation (see paras. 27 and 28). Would Singer favor giving those resources to the currently starving or to their descendants?

7. Singer considers two objections to his position (paras. 16–21). What are they, and how does he respond to them? In an essay of 1,000 words, state concisely those objections, his replies, and your evaluation.

8. Singer refers to "the principle which I advanced earlier" (para. 17). State in a sentence what that principle is. (Hint: A version is found in para. 21.)

9. Suppose someone were to object to Singer that the plight of starving people in Africa, Asia, or elsewhere in the world is to a large extent their own fault, a result of uncontrolled overpopulation, leading to their destruction of their physical habitat and aggravated by corrupt self-government. How might Singer reply?

10. What is Singer's answer to the question, "How much, relying on his basic principle, ought the affluent give to the needy" (see para. 29)?

Garrett Hardin

Garrett Hardin is Emeritus Professor of Human Ecology at the University of California, Santa Barbara. Born in Dallas, Texas, in 1915, he received his Ph.D. in biology from Stanford in 1941 and is the author of several books, including The Limits of Altruism *(1977),* Managing the Commons *(1977),* Filters Against Folly *(1988), and most recently* The Ostrich Factor *(1998). The essay reprinted here originally appeared in* Psychology Today *(September 1974).*

Lifeboat Ethics:
The Case against Helping the Poor

Environmentalists use the metaphor of the earth as a "spaceship" in trying to persuade countries, industries, and people to stop wasting and polluting our natural resources. Since we all share life on this planet, they argue, no single person or institution has the right to destroy, waste, or use more than a fair share of its resources.

But does everyone on earth have an equal right to an equal share of its resources? The spaceship metaphor can be dangerous when used by misguided idealists to justify suicidal policies for sharing our resources through uncontrolled immigration and foreign aid. In their enthusiastic but unrealistic generosity, they confuse the ethics of a spaceship with those of a lifeboat.

A true spaceship would have to be under the control of a captain, since no ship could possibly survive if its course were determined by committee. Spaceship Earth certainly has no captain; the United Nations is merely a toothless tiger, with little power to enforce any policy upon its bickering members.

If we divide the world crudely into rich nations and poor nations, two thirds of them are desperately poor, and only one third comparatively rich, with the United States the wealthiest of all. Metaphorically each nation can be seen as a lifeboat full of comparatively rich people. In the ocean outside each lifeboat swim the poor of the world, who would like to get in, or at least to share some of the wealth. What should the lifeboat passengers do?

First, we must recognize the limited capacity of any lifeboat. For ex-   5
ample, a nation's land has a limited capacity to support a population and
as the current energy crisis has shown us, in some ways we have already
exceeded the carrying capacity of our land.

ADRIFT IN A MORAL SEA

So here we sit, say fifty people in our lifeboat. To be generous, let us
assume it has room for ten more, making a total capacity of sixty. Suppose the fifty of us in the lifeboat see 100 others swimming in the water
outside, begging for admission to our boat or for handouts. We have several options: We may be tempted to try to live by the Christian ideal of
being "our brother's keeper," or by the Marxist ideal of "to each according to his needs." Since the needs of all in the water are the same, and
since they can all be seen as "our brothers," we could take them all into
our boat, making a total of 150 in a boat designed for sixty. The boat
swamps, everyone drowns. Complete justice, complete catastrophe.

Since the boat has an unused excess capacity of ten more passengers,
we could admit just ten more to it. But which ten do we let in? How do
we choose? Do we pick the best ten, the neediest ten, "first come, first
served"? And what do we say to the ninety we exclude? If we do let an
extra ten into our lifeboat, we will have lost our "safety factor," an engineering principle of critical importance. For example, if we don't leave
room for excess capacity as a safety factor in our country's agriculture, a
new plant disease or a bad change in the weather could have disastrous
consequences.

Suppose we decide to preserve our small safety factor and admit no
more to the lifeboat. Our survival is then possible, although we shall
have to be constantly on guard against boarding parties.

While this last solution clearly offers the only means of our survival,
it is morally abhorrent to many people. Some say they feel guilty about
their good luck. My reply is simple: "Get out and yield your place to others." This may solve the problem of the guilt-ridden person's conscience,
but it does not change the ethics of the lifeboat. The needy person to
whom the guilt-ridden person yields his place will not himself feel guilty
about his good luck. If he did, he would not climb aboard. The net result
of conscience-stricken people giving up their unjustly held seats is the
elimination of that sort of conscience from the lifeboat.

This is the basic metaphor within which we must work out our solu-   10
tions. Let us now enrich the image, step by step, with substantive additions from the real world, a world that must solve real and pressing
problems of overpopulation and hunger.

The harsh ethics of the lifeboat become even harsher when we consider the reproductive differences between the rich nations and the poor
nations. The people inside the lifeboats are doubling in numbers every
eighty-seven years; those swimming around outside are doubling, on the

average, every thirty-five years, more than twice as fast as the rich. And since the world's resources are dwindling, the difference in prosperity between the rich and the poor can only increase.

As of 1973, the United States had a population of 210 million people, who were increasing by 0.8 percent per year. Outside our lifeboat, let us imagine another 210 million people (say the combined populations of Colombia, Ecuador, Venezuela, Morocco, Pakistan, Thailand, and the Philippines), who are increasing at a rate of 3.3 percent year. Put differently, the doubling time for this aggregate population is twenty-one years, compared to eighty-seven years for the Unites States.

MULTIPLYING THE RICH AND THE POOR

Now suppose the United States agreed to pool its resources with those seven countries, with everyone receiving an equal share. Initially the ratio of Americans to non-Americans in this model would be one-to-one. But consider what the ratio would be after eighty-seven years, by which time the Americans would have doubled to a population of 420 million. By then, doubling every twenty-one years, the other group would have swollen to 354 billion. Each American would have to share the available resource with more than eight people.

But, one could argue, this discussion assumes that current population trends will continue, and they may not. Quite so. Most likely the rate of population increase will decline much faster in the United States than it will in the other countries, and there does not seem to be much we can do about it. In sharing with "each according to his needs," we must recognize that needs are determined by population size, which is determined by the rate of reproduction, which at present is regarded as a sovereign right of every nation, poor or not. This being so, the philanthropic load created by the sharing ethic of the spaceship can only increase.

THE TRAGEDY OF THE COMMONS

The fundamental error of spaceship ethics, and the sharing it requires, is that it leads to what I call "the tragedy of the commons." Under a system of private property, the men who own property recognize their responsibility to care for it, for if they don't they will eventually suffer. A farmer, for instance, will allow no more cattle in a pasture than its carrying capacity justifies. If he overloads it, erosion sets in, weeds take over, and he loses the use of the pasture.

If a pasture becomes a commons open to all, the right of each to use it may not be matched by a corresponding responsibility to protect it. Asking everyone to use it with discretion will hardly do, for the considerate herdsman who refrains from overloading the commons suffers more than a selfish one who says his needs are greater. If everyone would restrain himself, all would be well; but it takes only one less than everyone to ruin a system of voluntary restraint. In a crowded world of less than perfect human beings, mutual ruin is inevitable if there are no controls. This is the tragedy of the commons.

One of the major tasks of education today should be the creation of such an acute awareness of the dangers of the commons that people will recognize its many varieties. For example, the air and water have become polluted because they are treated as commons. Further growth in the population or per-capita conversion of natural resources into pollutants will only make the problem worse. The same holds true for the fish of the oceans. Fishing fleets have nearly disappeared in many parts of the world, technological improvements in the art of fishing are hastening the day of complete ruin. Only the replacement of the system of the commons with a responsible system of control will save the land, air, water, and oceanic fisheries.

THE WORLD FOOD BANK

In recent years there has been a push to create a new commons called a World Food Bank, an international depository of food reserves to which nations would contribute according to their abilities and from which they would draw according to their needs. This humanitarian proposal has received support from many liberal international groups, and from such prominent citizens as Margaret Mead, U.N. Secretary General Kurt Waldheim, and Senators Edward Kennedy and George McGovern.

A world food bank appeals powerfully to our humanitarian impulses. But before we rush ahead with such a plan, let us recognize where the greatest political push comes from, lest we be disillusioned later. Our experience with the "Food for Peace program," or Public Law 480, gives us the answer. This program moved billions of dollars' worth of U.S. surplus grain to food-short, population-long countries during the past two decades. But when PL 480 first became law, a headline in the business magazine *Forbes* revealed the real power behind it: "Feeding the World's Hungry Millions: How It Will Mean Billions for U.S. Business."

And indeed it did. In the years 1960 to 1970, U.S. taxpayers spent a total of $7.9 billion on the Food for Peace program. Between 1948 and 1970, they also paid an additional $50 billion for other economic-aid programs, some of which went for food and food-producing machinery and technology. Though all U.S. taxpayers were forced to contribute to the cost of PL 480, certain special interest groups gained handsomely under the program. Farmers did not have to contribute the grain; the government, or rather the taxpayers, bought it from them at full market prices. The increased demand raised prices of farm products generally. The manufacturers of farm machinery, fertilizers, and pesticides benefited by the farmers' extra efforts to grow more food. Grain elevators profited from storing the surplus until it could be shipped. Railroads made money hauling it to ports, and shipping lines profited from carrying it overseas. The implementation of PL 480 required the creation of a vast government bureaucracy, which then acquired its own vested interest in continuing the program regardless of its merits.

EXTRACTING DOLLARS

Those who proposed and defended the Food for Peace program in public rarely mentioned its importance to any of these special interests. The public emphasis was always on its humanitarian effects. The combination of silent selfish interests and highly vocal humanitarian apologists made a powerful and successful lobby for extracting money from taxpayers. We can expect the same lobby to push now for the creation of a World Food Bank.

However great the potential benefit to selfish interests, it should not be a decisive argument against a truly humanitarian program. We must ask if such a program would actually do more good than harm, not only momentarily but also in the long run. Those who propose the food bank usually refer to a current "emergency" or "crisis" in terms of world food supply. But what is an emergency? Although they may be infrequent and sudden, everyone knows that emergencies will occur from time to time. A well-run family, company, organization, or country prepares for the likelihood of accidents and emergencies. It expects them, it budgets for them, it saves for them.

LEARNING THE HARD WAY

What happens if some organizations or countries budget for accidents and others do not? If each country is solely responsible for its own well-being, poorly managed ones will suffer. But they can learn from experience. They may mend their ways, and learn to budget for infrequent but certain emergencies. For example, the weather varies from year to year, and periodic crop failures are certain. A wise and competent government saves out of the production of the good years in anticipation of bad years to come. Joseph taught this policy to Pharaoh in Egypt more than 2,000 years ago. Yet the great majority of the governments in the world today do not follow such a policy. They lack either the wisdom or the competence, or both. Should those nations that do manage to put something aside be forced to come to the rescue each time an emergency occurs among the poor nations?

"But it isn't their fault!" some kindhearted liberals argue. "How can we blame the poor people who are caught in an emergency? Why must they suffer for the sins of their governments?" The concept of blame is simply not relevant here. The real question is, what are the operational consequences of establishing a world food bank? If it is open to every country every time a need develops, slovenly rulers will not be motivated to take Joseph's advice. Someone will always come to their aid. Some countries will deposit food in the world food bank, and others will withdraw it. There will be almost no overlap. As a result of such solutions to food shortage emergencies, the poor countries will not learn to mend their ways, and will suffer progressively greater emergencies as their populations grow.

POPULATION CONTROL THE CRUDE WAY

On the average, poor countries undergo a 2.5 percent increase in population each year; rich countries, about 0.8 percent. Only rich countries have anything in the way of food reserves set aside, and even they do not have as much as they should. Poor countries have none. If poor countries received no food from the outside, the rate of their population growth would be periodically checked by crop failures and famines. But if they can always draw on a world food bank in time of need, their populations can continue to grow unchecked, and so will their "need" for aid. In the short run, a world food bank may diminish that need, but in the long run it actually increases the need without limit.

Without some system of worldwide food sharing, the proportion of people in the rich and poor nations might eventually stabilize. The overpopulated poor countries would decrease in numbers, while the rich countries that had room for more people would increase. But with a well-meaning system of sharing, such as a world food bank, the growth differential between the rich and the poor countries will not only persist, it will increase. Because of the higher rate of population growth in the poor countries of the world, 88 percent of today's children are born poor, and only 12 percent rich. Year by year the ratio becomes worse, as the fast-reproducing poor outnumber the slow-reproducing rich.

A world food bank is thus a commons in disguise. People will have more motivation to draw from it than to add to any common store. The less provident and less able will multiply at the expense of the abler and more provident, bringing eventual ruin upon all who share in the commons. Besides, any system of "sharing" that amounts to foreign aid from the rich nations to the poor nations will carry the taint of charity, which will contribute little to the world peace so devoutly desired by those who support the idea of a world food bank.

As past U.S. foreign-aid programs have amply and depressingly demonstrated, international charity frequently inspires mistrust and antagonism rather than gratitude on the part of the recipient nation.

CHINESE FISH AND MIRACLE RICE

The modern approach to foreign aid stresses the export of technology and advice, rather than money and food. As an ancient Chinese proverb goes: "Give a man a fish and he will eat for a day; teach him how to fish and he will eat for the rest of his days." Acting on this advice, the Rockefeller and Ford foundations have financed a number of programs for improving agriculture in the hungry nations. Known as the "Green Revolution," these programs have led to the development of "miracle rice" and "miracle wheat," new strains that offer bigger harvests and greater resistance to crop damage. Norman Borlaug, the Nobel Prize–winning agronomist who, supported by the Rockefeller Foundation, developed "miracle wheat," is one of the most prominent advocates of a world food bank.

Whether or not the Green Revolution can increase food production 30 as much as its champions claim is a debatable but possibly irrelevant point. Those who support this well-intended humanitarian effort should first consider some of the fundamentals of human ecology. Ironically, one man who did was the late Alan Gregg, a vice president of the Rockefeller Foundation. Two decades ago he expressed strong doubts about the wisdom of such attempts to increase food production. He likened the growth and spread of humanity over the surface of the earth to the spread of cancer in the human body, remarking that "cancerous growths demand food; but, as far as I know, they have never been cured by getting it."

OVERLOADING THE ENVIRONMENT

Every human born constitutes a draft on all aspects of the environment: food, air, water, forests, beaches, wildlife, scenery, and solitude. Food can, perhaps, be significantly increased to meet a growing demand. But what about clean beaches, unspoiled forests, and solitude? If we satisfy a growing population's need for food, we necessarily decrease its per-capita supply of the other resources needed by men.

India, for example, now has a population of 600 million, which increases by 15 million each year. This population already puts a huge load on a relatively impoverished environment. The country's forests are now only a small fraction of what they were three centuries ago, and floods and erosion continually destroy the insufficient farmland that remains. Every one of the 15 million new lives added to India's population puts an additional burden on the environment, and increases the economic and social costs of crowding. However humanitarian our intent, every Indian life saved through medical or nutritional assistance from abroad diminishes the quality of life for those who remain, and for subsequent generations. If rich countries make it possible, through foreign aid, for 600 million Indians to swell to 1.2 billion in a mere twenty-eight years, as their current growth rate threatens, will future generations of Indians thank us for hastening the destruction of their environment? Will our good intentions be sufficient excuse for the consequences of our actions?

My final example of a commons in action is one for which the public has the least desire for rational discussion—immigration. Anyone who publicly questions the wisdom of current U.S. immigration policy is promptly charged with bigotry, prejudice, ethnocentrism, chauvinism, isolationism, or selfishness. Rather than encounter such accusations, one would rather talk about other matters, leaving immigration policy to wallow in the crosscurrents of special interests that take no account of the good of the whole, or the interest of posterity.

Perhaps we still feel guilty about things we said in the past. Two generations ago the popular press frequently referred to Dagos, Wops, Polacks, Chinks, and Krauts, in articles about how America was being "overrun" by foreigners of supposedly inferior genetic stock. But because the implied inferiority of foreigners was used then as justification for keeping them out, people now assume that restrictive policies could only be based on such misguided notions. There are no other grounds.

A NATION OF IMMIGRANTS

Just consider the numbers involved. Our government acknowledges 35 a net inflow of 400,000 immigrants a year. While we have no hard data on the extent of illegal entries, educated guesses put the figure at about 600,000 a year. Since the natural increase (excess of births over deaths) of the resident population now runs about 1.7 million per year, the yearly gain from immigration amounts to at least 19 percent of the total annual increase, and may be as much as 37 percent if we include the estimate for illegal immigrants. Considering the growing use of birth-control devices, the potential effect of educational campaigns by such organizations as Planned Parenthood Federation of America and Zero Population Growth, and the influence of inflation and the housing shortage, the fertility rate of American women may decline so much that immigration could account for all the yearly increase in population. Should we not at least ask if that is what we want?

For the sake of those who worry about whether the "quality" of the average immigrant compares favorably with the quality of the average resident, let us assume that immigrants and native-born citizens are of exactly equal quality, however one defines that term. We will focus here only on quantity; and since our conclusions will depend on nothing else, all charges of bigotry and chauvinism become irrelevant.

IMMIGRATION VS. FOOD SUPPLY

World food banks *move food to the people*, hastening the exhaustion of the environment of the poor countries. Unrestricted immigration, on the other hand, *moves people to the food*, thus speeding up the destruction of the environment of the rich countries. We can easily understand why poor people should want to make this latter transfer, but why should rich hosts encourage it?

As in the case of foreign-aid programs, immigration receives support from selfish interests and humanitarian impulses. The primary selfish interest in unimpeded immigration is the desire of employers for cheap labor, particularly in industries and trades that offer degrading work. In the past, one wave of foreigners after another was brought into the United States to work at wretched jobs for wretched wages. In recent years, the Cubans, Puerto Ricans, and Mexicans have had this dubious honor. The interests of the employers of cheap labor mesh well with the guilty silence of the country's liberal intelligentsia. White Anglo-Saxon Protestants are particularly reluctant to call for a closing of the doors to immigration for fear of being called bigots.

But not all countries have such reluctant leadership. Most educated Hawaiians, for example, are keenly aware of the limits of their environment, particularly in terms of population growth. There is only so much room on the islands, and the islanders know it. To Hawaiians, immigrants from the other forty-nine states present as great a threat as those from other nations. At a recent meeting of Hawaiian government officials in Honolulu, I had the ironic delight of hearing a speaker, who like most of his audience was of Japanese ancestry, ask how the country might practically and constitutionally close its doors to further immigration. One member of the audience countered: "How can we shut the doors now? We have many friends and relatives in Japan that we'd like to bring here some day so that they can enjoy Hawaii too." The Japanese-American speaker smiled sympathetically and answered: "Yes, but we have children now, and someday we'll have grandchildren too. We can bring more people here from Japan only by giving away some of the land that we hope to pass on to our grandchildren some day. What right do we have to do that?"

At this point, I can hear U.S. liberals asking: "How can you justify 40 slamming the door once you're inside? You say that immigrants should be kept out. But aren't we all immigrants, or the descendants of immigrants? If we insist on staying, must we not admit all others?" Our craving for intellectual order leads us to seek and prefer symmetrical rules and morals: a single rule for me and everybody else; the same rule yesterday, today, and tomorrow. Justice, we feel, should not change with time and place.

We Americans of non-Indian ancestry can look upon ourselves as the descendants of thieves who are guilty morally, if not legally, of stealing this land from its Indian owners. Should we then give back the land to the now living American descendants of those Indians? However morally or logically sound this proposal may be, I, for one, am unwilling to live by it and I know no one else who is. Besides, the logical consequence would be absurd. Suppose that, intoxicated with a sense of pure justice, we should decide to turn our land over to the Indians. Since all our wealth has also been derived from the land, wouldn't we be morally obliged to give that back to the Indians too?

PURE JUSTICE VS. REALITY

Clearly, the concept of pure justice produces an infinite regression to absurdity. Centuries ago, wise men invented statutes of limitations to justify the rejection of such pure justice, in the interest of preventing continual disorder. The law zealously defends property rights, but only relatively recent property rights. Drawing a line after an arbitrary time has elapsed may be unjust, but the alternatives are worse.

We are all descendants of thieves, and the world's resources are inequitably distributed. But we must begin the journey to tomorrow from the point where we are today. We cannot remake the past. We cannot safely divide the wealth equitably among all peoples so long as people reproduce at different rates. To do so would guarantee that our grandchildren, and everyone else's grandchildren, would have only a ruined world to inhabit.

To be generous with one's own possessions is quite different from being generous with those of posterity. We should call this point to the attention of those who, from a commendable love of justice and equality, would institute a system of the commons, either in the form of a world food bank, or of unrestricted immigration. We must convince them if we wish to save at least some parts of the world from environmental ruin.

Without a true world government to control reproduction and the 45 use of available resources, the sharing ethic of the spaceship is impossible. For the foreseeable future, our survival demands that we govern our actions by the ethics of a lifeboat, harsh though they may be. Posterity will be satisfied with nothing less.

Topics for Critical Thinking and Writing

1. Hardin says that "in some ways we have already exceeded the carrying capacity of our land" (para. 5). Does he tell us later what some of those ways are? Can you think of others?

2. The central analogy on which Hardin's argument rests is that human life on planet Earth is like living in an overcrowded lifeboat. Evaluate this analogy.

3. What does Hardin mean by "ethics" in the title of his essay? What, if any, ethical principle does Hardin believe should guide our conduct in lifeboat Earth?

4. What is "the tragedy" and what is "the commons" in what Hardin calls "the tragedy of the commons" (paras. 15–17)?

5. What does Hardin mean by "a truly humanitarian program" (para. 22) to alleviate future problems of hunger and starvation? Why does he think a World Food Bank would aggravate, rather than alleviate, the problem?

6. How do you react to the analogy that compares the growth of the human race over the earth to "the spread of cancer in the human body" (para. 30)?

7. Hardin's view of the relationship between population growth and available resources can be described (though he doesn't) as a zero-sum game. Do you agree with such a description? Why, or why not?

8. Hardin refers to an organization named Zero Population Growth (para. 35). In your public or college library find out about this organization, and then write a 250-word essay describing its origin and aims.

9. Hardin offers a reductio ad absurdum argument (see pp. 305–06) against large-scale restitution by the current non-native American population to the surviving native Americans (para. 41). Evaluate this argument in an essay of 250 words.

10. Hardin refers frequently (for example, para. 42) and unsympathetically to what he calls "pure justice." To what principle, exactly, is he referring by this phrase? Would you agree that this principle is, indeed, well described as "pure justice"? Why, or why not?

11. Suppose someone, after reading Hardin's essay, described it as nothing more than selfishness on a national scale. Would Hardin agree? Would he consider this a serious criticism of his analysis and proposals?

10

A Lawyer's View: Steps toward Civic Literacy

When John Adams in 1774 said that ours is "a government of law, and not of men," he meant that much of public conduct is regulated, rightly, by principles of law that by general agreement ought to be enforced and that can be altered only by our duly elected representatives, whose power is derived from our consent. In a democracy it is laws, not individuals (for instance, kings or tyrants), that govern. Adams and other early Americans rejected the view attributed to Louis XIV, "I am the state" (*L'état c'est moi*).

But what exactly the law in a given situation is often causes hot debate (as we know from watching the TV news). Whether we are ever personally called on to decide the law—as are legislators, judges, jurors, or lawyers—all of us find our daily lives constantly affected by the law. It is fitting, therefore, and even necessary that we develop **civic literacy,** the ability to understand the principles by which our government and its courts operate so that we can act appropriately. (In today's global community, our civic literacy must also include a knowledge of the ways our and others' governments function.)

From the time of Plato's *Apology*, reporting Socrates' trial before the Athenian assembly in 399 B.C. on charges of corrupting the young and preaching false gods, courtroom argument has been a staple of dramatic verbal cut-and-thrust. (Think of popular television shows such as *The Practice* and *Law and Order*.) Probably no profession prides itself more on the ability of its members to argue than does the legal profession. The uninitiated are easily intimidated by the skill with which a lawyer can marshal relevant considerations to support a client's interests. But legal argument is, after all, *argument*, and so its main features are those already discussed in Chapter 3 (such as definition, assumption, premise, deduction, conclusion, evidence, validity).

What is distinctive about legal reasoning is fairly straightforward in all but the most unusual cases.

CIVIL AND CRIMINAL CASES

Legal cases are divided into civil and criminal. In a *civil* case one party (the plaintiff) brings suit against another party (the defendant), claiming that he or she has suffered some wrong at the hands of the defendant and deserves some remedy (for instance, due to a dispute over a property boundary or over fault in a multicar accident). The judge or jury decides for or against the plaintiff based on the evidence and the relevant law. All crimes are wrongs, but not all wrongs are crimes. For instance, an automobile accident that involves negligence on the part of one of the drivers and results in harm to another is surely a wrong, but the driver responsible for the accident, even if found guilty, does not face a prison sentence (that could happen only if the accident were in fact the result of driving with gross recklessness or driving while intoxicated or were no "accident" at all). Why? Because the harm inflicted was not criminal; that is, it was not intentional, deliberate, malicious, or premeditated.

Criminal cases involve someone (the defendant) charged either with a *felony* (a serious crime like assault or battery) or with a *misdemeanor* (a less serious crime, as in *Texas v. Johnson*, p. 387). In criminal cases the state, through its prosecutor, seeks to convict the defendant as charged; the defendant, through his or her attorney, seeks an acquittal or, at worst, a conviction on a lesser charge (manslaughter instead of murder) and a milder punishment. The decision to convict or acquit on the basis of the facts submitted in evidence and the relevant law is the duty of the jury (or the judge, if there is no jury). The prosecutor and defense lawyer present what they believe are the relevant facts. Defining the relevant law is the responsibility of the trial judge. Public interest in criminal cases is often high, especially when the crime is particularly heinous. (Think of the 1995 trial of O. J. Simpson, charged with the murder of his wife and one of her friends, and the 1997 trial of Timothy McVeigh for the Oklahoma City federal building bombing.)

As you begin reading a legal case, therefore, you will want to be sure you can answer this question:

- Is the court trying to decide whether someone accused of a crime is guilty as charged, or is the court trying to resolve some noncriminal (civil) dispute?

TRIAL AND APPEAL

Most cases (civil or criminal) never go to *trial* at all. Most civil cases are settled out of court, and most criminal cases are settled with a plea bargain in which the prosecutor and the defense attorney persuade the judge to accept the defendant's guilty plea in exchange for a less severe sentence. Of the cases that are settled by trial, the losing party usually does not try to reopen, or *appeal*, the case. If, however, the losing party believes that he or she should have won, the case may be appealed for review by a higher appellate court (provided, of course, the loser can finance the appeal). The party bringing the appeal (the appellant) typically argues that because the relevant law was misstated or misapplied during the trial, the decision must be reversed and a new trial ordered. On rare occasion the issue in dispute is appealed all the way to the highest court in the nation—the U.S. Supreme Court—for a final decision. (The cases we reprint for discussion in this chapter are all cases decided by the Supreme Court.)

A pair of useful questions to answer as you work your way through a reported case are these:

- What are the events that gave rise to the legal controversy in this case?

- What are the intermediate steps the case went through before reaching the final court of appeal?

DECISION AND OPINION

With rare exceptions, only cases decided by the appellate courts are *reported*—that is, written up and published. A reported case consists of two very different elements: (1) the court's decision, or *holding,* and (2) the court's *opinion* in support of its decision. Typically, a court's decision can be stated in a sentence; it amounts to the conclusion of the court's argument. The opinion, however, is more complex and lengthy; as with most arguments, the premises of judicial reasoning and their linkages with each other involve several steps.

To illustrate, in *Texas v. Johnson* (p. 387), the U.S. Supreme Court considered a Texas statute that made it a crime to burn the American flag in political protest. The Court decided that the statute was an unconstitutional interference with freedom of speech. (The decision, as you see, can be stated concisely.)

The Court's opinion, however, runs to several pages. The gist is this: The purpose of the First Amendment (reprinted on p. 388) prohibiting abridgment of speech by the government is to protect personal expression, especially where there is a political intention or significance to the speech. Previous decisions of the Court interpreting the amendment have established that the protection of "speech" applies also to nonverbal acts; flag burning in political protest is such an act. Under certain conditions the state may regulate "speech," but in no case may the state prohibit "speech" because of its content or meaning. The Texas statute did not merely regulate the circumstances of "speech"; rather, it regulated the content or meaning of the "speech." Therefore, the statute is unconstitutional.

Thus, in reading the report of a decided case, you will want to be able to answer these two questions:

- What did the court decide?
- What reasons did the court offer to justify its decision?

MAJORITY, CONCURRING, AND DISSENTING OPINIONS

Not all appellate court decisions are unanimous ones. A court's *majority opinion* contains the ruling and reasoning of a majority of its judges. In *Texas v. Johnson*, for example, Justice William Brennan wrote the majority opinion in which four of his colleagues joined. Occasionally one or more of the judges in the majority files a *concurring opinion;* in such cases the judge agrees with the majority's decision but disagrees with its reasoning. Justice John Paul Stevens wrote a concurring opinion in *Johnson*.

In any appellate court decision, at least one judge is likely to dissent from the majority opinion and file a *dissenting opinion* explaining why. (Throughout this book we make the point that intelligent, honorable people may differ on issues of importance.) In the *Johnson* case, four judges dissented but joined in one dissenting opinion. Minority opinions have much to offer for reflection, and in many instances today's dissenting opinion becomes tomorrow's law. The most famous example is Justice John Marshall Harlan's solitary dissent in *Plessy v. Ferguson* (1896), the case that upheld "separate but equal" racial segregation; Harlan's dissent was eventually vindicated by a unanimous vote of the Supreme Court in *Brown v. Board of Education* (1954).

Thus, where there are majority, concurring, and minority opinions, you will want to think about these questions:

- On what issues do the majority and concurring opinions agree?
- On what issues do they disagree?
- Where does the minority in its dissenting opinion(s) disagree with the majority?
- Which opinion is more convincing, the majority or the minority?

FACTS AND LAW

Every court's decision is based on the relevant facts and the relevant law. What the relevant facts are is often in dispute at the trial but not on appeal; appellate court judges rarely re-examine the facts as decided by the trial court. The appellate court, however, usually restates the relevant facts in the opening paragraphs of its opinion. An old joke told among lawyers is appropriate here: "Argue the facts if the facts are on your side, argue the law if the law is on your side; if neither the law nor the facts are on your side, pound the table!"

Unfortunately, a sharp distinction between facts and law cannot always be maintained. For example, if we describe the defendant's conduct as "careless," is that a matter of fact? Or is it in part a matter of law because "careless" conduct may also be judged "negligent" conduct, and the law defines what counts as negligence?

As you read through the reported case, keep in mind these two questions:

- What are the relevant facts in the case, insofar as they can be determined by what the appellate court reported?
- Are there issues of fact omitted or ignored by the appellate court that, had they been addressed, might have shed light on the decision?

For instance, consider a case in which a cattle rancher finds one of her cows dead after it collided with a railroad train. She decides to sue for negligence and wins, and the defendant (the railroad company) appeals. Why did she sue the railroad in the first place, rather than the engineer of the train that killed her cow? Suppose the appellate court's opinion fails to mention whether there was a fence at the edge of the field to keep her cattle off the tracks; wouldn't that be relevant to deciding whether she was partly at fault for the accident? (Ought the railroad to have erected a fence on its property parallel to the track?) Information about such facts could well shed light on the strength and correctness of the court's opinion and decision.

Appellate court judges are almost entirely preoccupied with what they believe is the relevant law to deciding the case at hand. The law can come in any of several different forms: *common law principles* ("No one may enlist the courts to assist him in profiting from his own wrong"), *statutes* enacted by a legislature ("As of January 1, 1998, income taxes shall be levied according to the following formula . . ."), *ordinances* enacted by a town council ("Dogs must be leashed in public places"), a *precedent* found in a prior case decided by some appellate court ("The decision in the case before us is governed by the Supreme Court's earlier holding in . . ."), *executive orders* ("All persons of Japanese extraction currently resident in California shall be removed inland to a relocation center"), *administrative regulations* ("Milk shipped interstate must have a butterfat content not less than . . ."), as well as *constitutional interpretations* ("Statements critical of a public official but not malicious or uttered by one who knows they are false are not libelous and are permitted under the First Amendment"). Not all laws are of equal weight; as *Texas v. Johnson* shows, a state statute inconsistent with the federal Bill of Rights will be nullified, not the other way around.

Appellate court judges devote much of their attention to **interpretation,** trying to decide exactly what the relevant statute, regulation, or prior decision really means and whether it applies to the case before the court. For example, does a local ordinance prohibiting "four-wheeled vehicles" in the park apply to a nanny pushing a baby carriage? The answer often turns on what was the *purpose* of the law or the *intention* of the lawmaker.

It is not easy to decide what the lawmakers' **intention** was; lawmakers are rarely available to state for the courts what their intention was. Can we confidently infer what a legislature's intention was from the legislative history left behind in the form of debates or hearings? From what the relevant committee chairperson says it was? What if (as is typically true) the legislature never declared its intentions when it enacted a law? When a legislature creates a statute, do all those who vote for it act with the same intention? If not, which of the many intentions involved should dominate? How do we find out what those intentions were? What counts as relevant evidence for ascribing this rather than that as someone's intention?

Accordingly, as you read a reported legal case, your study of the court's opinion should lead you to ask these questions:

- Exactly what law or laws is the court trying to interpret?
- What evidence does the court cite in favor of its interpretation?

BALANCING INTERESTS

In U.S. Supreme Court cases, the decision often turns on how competing interests are to be *balanced* or weighed. This pattern of reasoning is especially relevant when one of the conflicting interests is apparently protected by the Constitution. The majority opinion in *New Jersey v. T.L.O.* (1985) (p. 397) is a good example of such balancing; there, the privacy interests of high school students are weighed (metaphorically speaking, of course — no one can literally "weigh" or "balance" anyone's interests) against the competing interest of school officials responsible for maintaining an orderly environment for teaching. The Court decided that the latter ought to prevail and concluded that "reasonable" searches are not forbidden under the Fourth Amendment's prohibition of "unreasonable searches and seizures."

This leads directly to several other questions you will want to try to answer in the legal cases you study:

- In a constitutional case, what are the conflicting interests?
- How does the Supreme Court propose to balance them?
- Why does it strike the balance one way rather than the other?

A WORD OF CAUTION

Lawyers are both officers of the court and champions for their clients' causes. In the first role they share with judges and other officials the duty to seek justice by honorable means. But in the second role lawyers often see their job as one in which they ought to bend every rule as far as they can in pursuit of their clients' interests (after all, it is the client who pays the bills). This attitude is nicely conveyed in the title of a book, *How to Argue and Win Every Time* (1995), by Gerry Spence, one of the nation's leading trial lawyers. And it is reinforced by a comment from defense attorney Alan Dershowitz: "All sides in a trial want to hide at least some of the truth."

Yet it would be wrong to see lawyers as motivated only by a ruthless desire to win at any cost. Lawyers have a civic duty to present their clients' cases in the most favorable light and to challenge whatever evidence and testimony is offered in court against them. (If you were hiring a lawyer to defend you, would you settle for anything less?) In a society such as ours—a society of law rather than of powerful individuals—it is right that accused persons be found guilty as charged only after the strongest defenses have been mounted.

To be sure, everyone concerned to argue on behalf of any claim, whether in or out of court, whether as a lawyer or in some other capacity, ought to take the challenge seriously. But it is too much to hope to "win every time"—and in fact winning is not the only, much less the highest, goal. Sometimes the other side does have the better argument, and in such cases we should be willing, indeed eager, to see the merits and to enlarge our minds.

In any case, in this book we think of argument not as a weapon for use in mortal combat but as a device for exploring the controversy or dispute under discussion, a tool for isolating the issues in contention and for helping in the evaluation of different possible outcomes. We expect you will use argument to persuade your audience to accept your views, just as a lawyer typically does; but we hope you will use argument sometimes—even often—to clarify your ideas *for yourself;* when you develop arguments for effective presentation to your colleagues and associates, you will probably improve the quality of your ideas.

A CHECKLIST FOR ANALYZING LEGAL ARGUMENTS

✓ Is the court trying to decide whether someone accused of a crime is guilty as charged, or is the court trying to resolve some noncriminal (civil) dispute?

✓ What events gave rise to the legal controversy in this case?

✓ What intermediate steps did the case go through before reaching the final court of appeal?

✓ What did the court decide?

✓ What reasons did the court offer to justify its decision?

✓ On what issues do the majority and concurring opinions agree?

✓ On what issues do they disagree?

✓ Where does the minority in its dissenting opinion(s) disagree with the majority?

✓ Which opinion is more convincing, the majority or the minority?

✓ What are the relevant facts in the case, insofar as they can be determined by what the appellate court reported?

✓ Are there issues of fact omitted or ignored by the appellate court that, had they been addressed, might have shed light on the decision?

✓ Exactly what law or laws is the court trying to interpret?

✓ What evidence does the court cite in favor of its interpretation?

✓ In constitutional cases, what are the conflicting interests?

✓ How does the Supreme Court propose to balance them?

✓ Why does it strike the balance one way rather than the other?

A CASEBOOK ON THE LAW AND SOCIETY:
What Rights Do the Constitution and the Bill of Rights Protect?

William J. Brennan Jr. and William H. Rehnquist

William J. Brennan Jr. (1906–1990), appointed to the U.S. Supreme Court in 1956 by President Dwight D. Eisenhower, established himself as a strong supporter of individual liberties. William H. Rehnquist (b. 1924), appointed in 1971 by President Richard M. Nixon because of his emphasis on law and order, came to be regarded as the most conservative member of the Court.

Texas v. Johnson (1989) concerns the right to burn the American flag in political protest. (Recall that the First Amendment to the Constitution holds that "Congress shall make no law respecting an establishment of religion, or prohibiting the free exercise thereof; or abridging the freedom of speech, or of the press; or the right of the people peaceably to assemble, and to petition the government for a redress of grievances.") The case was decided by a vote of five to four. Immediately after the Court's decision was announced, a resolution was drafted and filed in Congress to condemn the Court's decision. Also filed was the Flag Protection Act of 1989, making it a criminal offense to "knowingly mutilate, deface, burn, or trample upon" the flag. Another bill was designed to amend the Constitution so that criminal penalties for desecration of the flag would not violate the First Amendment. To date, none of these bills has left the congressional committees charged with examining them. In the excerpt that follows, legal citations have been deleted and portions of the text omitted.

Texas v. Johnson

Associate Justice Brennan delivered the opinion of the Court.

After publicly burning an American flag as a means of political protest, Gregory Lee Johnson was convicted of desecrating a flag in violation of Texas law. This case presents the question whether his conviction is consistent with the First Amendment. We hold that it is not.

I

While the Republican National Convention was taking place in Dallas in 1984, respondent Johnson participated in a political demonstration dubbed the "Republican War Chest Tour." As explained in literature distributed by the demonstrators and in speeches made by them, the purpose of this event was to protest the policies of the Reagan administration and of certain Dallas-based corporations. The demonstrators marched through the Dallas streets, chanting political slogans and stopping at several corporate locations to stage "die-ins" intended to dramatize the consequences of nuclear war. On several occasions they spray-painted the walls of buildings and overturned potted plants, but Johnson himself took no part in such activities. He did, however, accept an American flag handed to him by a fellow protestor who had taken it from a flag pole outside one of the targeted buildings.

The demonstration ended in front of Dallas City Hall, where Johnson unfurled the American flag, doused it with kerosene, and set it on fire. While the flag burned, the protestors chanted, "America, the red, white, and blue, we spit on you." After the demonstrators dispersed, a witness to the flag burning collected the flag's remains and buried them in his backyard. No one was physically injured or threatened with injury, though several witnesses testified that they had been seriously offended by the flag burning.

Of the approximately 100 demonstrators, Johnson alone was charged with a crime. The only criminal offense with which he was charged was the desecration of a venerated object in violation of Tex. Penal Code Ann.[1] After a trial, he was convicted, sentenced to one year in prison, and fined $2,000. The Court of Appeals for the Fifth District of Texas at Dallas affirmed Johnson's conviction, but the Texas Court of Criminal Appeals reversed, holding that the state could not, consistent with the First Amendment, punish Johnson for burning the flag in these circumstances. . . .

II

. . . The First Amendment literally forbids the abridgment only of 5 "speech," but we have long recognized that its protection does not end at the spoken or written word. While we have rejected "the view that an apparently limitless variety of conduct can be labeled 'speech' whenever the person engaging in the conduct intends thereby to express an idea," we have acknowledged that conduct may be "sufficiently imbued with the elements of communication to fall within the scope of the First and Fourteenth Amendments." . . .

[1]Tex. Penal Code Ann. §42.09 (1989) ["Desecration of a Venerated Object"] provides in full:

"(a) A person commits an offense if he intentionally or knowingly desecrates: (1) a public monument; (2) a place of worship or burial; or (3) a state or national flag.

"(b) For purposes of this section, 'desecrate' means deface, damage, or otherwise physically mistreat in a way that the actor knows will seriously offend one or more persons likely to observe or discover his action.

"(c) An offense under this section is a Class A misdemeanor." [Court's note.]

IV

It remains to consider whether the state's interest in preserving the flag as a symbol of nationhood and national unity justifies Johnson's conviction.

As in *Spence* [*v. Washington*], "we are confronted with a case of prosecution for the expression of an idea through activity," and "accordingly, we must examine with particular care the interests advanced by [petitioner] to support its prosecution." Johnson was not, we add, prosecuted for the expression of just any idea; he was prosecuted for his expression of dissatisfaction with the policies of this country, expression situated at the core of our First Amendment values.

Moreover, Johnson was prosecuted because he knew that his politically charged expression would cause "serious offense." If he had burned the flag as a means of disposing of it because it was dirty or torn, he would not have been convicted of flag desecration under this Texas law: Federal law designates burning as the preferred means of disposing of a flag "when it is in such condition that it is no longer a fitting emblem for display," and Texas has no quarrel with this means of disposal. The Texas law is thus not aimed at protecting the physical integrity of the flag in all circumstances, but is designed instead to protect it only against impairments that would cause serious offense to others. Texas concedes as much: "Section 42.09(b) reaches only those severe acts of physical abuse of the flag carried out in a way likely to be offensive. The statute mandates intentional or knowing abuse, that is, the kind of mistreatment that is not innocent, but rather is intentionally designed to seriously offend other individuals."

Whether Johnson's treatment of the flag violated Texas law thus depended on the likely communicative impact of his expressive conduct. Our decision in *Boos v. Barry* tells us that this restriction on Johnson's expression is content based. In *Boos*, we considered the constitutionality of a law prohibiting "the display of any sign within 500 feet of a foreign embassy if that sign tends to bring that foreign government into 'public odium' or 'public disrepute.'" Rejecting the argument that the law was content neutral because it was justified by "our international law obligation to shield diplomats from speech that offends their dignity," we held that "the emotive impact of speech on its audience is not a 'secondary effect'" unrelated to the content of the expression itself. . . .

Texas argues that its interest in preserving the flag as a symbol of nationhood and national unity survives this close analysis. Quoting extensively from the writings of this Court chronicling the flag's historic and symbolic role in our society, the state emphasizes the "'special place'" reserved for the flag in our nation. The state's argument is not that it has an interest simply in maintaining the flag as a symbol of something, no matter what it symbolizes; indeed, if that were the state's position, it 10 would be difficult to see how that interest is endangered by highly symbolic conduct such as Johnson's. Rather, the state's claim is that it has an interest in preserving the flag as a symbol of *nationhood* and *national unity*, a symbol with a determinate range of meanings. According to Texas, if one physically treats the flag in a way that would tend to cast doubt on either the idea that nationhood and national unity are the flag's referents or that national unity actually exists, the message conveyed thereby is a harmful one and therefore may be prohibited.

If there is a bedrock principle underlying the First Amendment, it is that the government may not prohibit the expression of an idea simply because society finds the idea itself offensive or disagreeable.

We have not recognized an exception to this principle even where our flag has been involved. In *Street v. New York*, we held that a state may not criminally punish a person for uttering words critical of the flag. Rejecting the argument that the conviction could be sustained on the ground that Street had "failed to show the respect for our national symbol which may properly be demanded of every citizen," we concluded that "the constitutionally guaranteed 'freedom to be intellectually . . . diverse or even contrary,' and the 'right to differ as to things that touch the heart of the existing order,' encompass the freedom to express publicly one's opinions about our flag, including those opinions which are defiant or contemptuous." Nor may the government, we have held, compel conduct that would evince respect for the flag. "To sustain the compulsory flag salute we are required to say that a Bill of Rights which guards the individual's right to speak his own mind, left it open to public authorities to compel him to utter what is not in his mind." . . .

Texas's focus on the precise nature of Johnson's expression, moreover, misses the point of our prior decisions: their enduring lesson, that the government may not prohibit expression simply because it disagrees with its message, is not dependent on the particular mode in which one chooses to express an idea. If we were to hold that a state may forbid flag burning wherever it is likely to endanger the flag's symbolic role, but allow it wherever burning a flag promotes that role—as where, for example, a person ceremoniously burns a dirty flag—we would be saying that when it comes to impairing the flag's physical integrity, the flag itself may be used as a symbol—as a substitute for the written or spoken word or a "short cut from mind to mind"—only in one direction. We would be permitting a state to "prescribe what shall be orthodox" by saying that one may burn the flag to convey one's attitude toward it and its referents only if one does not endanger the flag's representation of nationhood and national unity.

We never before have held that the government may ensure that a symbol be used to express only one view of that symbol or its referents. Indeed, in *Schacht v. United States*, we invalidated a federal statute permitting an actor portraying a member of one of our armed forces to "'wear the uniform of that armed force if the portrayal does not tend to discredit that armed force.'" This proviso, we held, "which leaves Americans free to praise the war in Vietnam but can send persons like Schacht to prison for opposing it, cannot survive in a country which has the First Amendment."

We perceive no basis on which to hold that the principle underlying 15 our decision in *Schacht* does not apply to this case. To conclude that the government may permit designated symbols to be used to communicate only a limited set of messages would be to enter territory having no discernible or defensible boundaries. Could the government, on this theory, prohibit the burning of state flags? Of copies of the presidential seal? Of the Constitution? In evaluating these choices under the First Amendment, how would we decide which symbols were sufficiently special to warrant this unique status? To do so, we would be forced to consult our own political preferences, and impose them on the citizenry, in the very way that the First Amendment forbids us to do.

There is, moreover, no indication — either in the text of the Constitution or in our cases interpreting it — that a separate juridical category exists for the American flag alone. Indeed, we would not be surprised to learn that the persons who framed our Constitution and wrote the Amendment that we now construe were not known for their reverence for the Union Jack. The First Amendment does not guarantee that other concepts virtually sacred to our nation as a whole — such as the principle that discrimination on the basis of race is odious and destructive — will go unquestioned in the marketplace of ideas. We decline, therefore, to create for the flag an exception to the joust of principles protected by the First Amendment.

It is not the state's ends, but its means, to which we object. It cannot be gainsaid that there is a special place reserved for the flag in this nation, and thus we do not doubt that the government has a legitimate interest in making efforts to "preserve the national flag as an unalloyed symbol of our country." We reject the suggestion, urged at oral argument by counsel for Johnson, that the government lacks "any state interest whatsoever" in regulating the manner in which the flag may be displayed. Congress has, for example, enacted precatory regulations describing the proper treatment of the flag, and we cast no doubt on the legitimacy of its interest in making such recommendations. To say that the government has an interest in encouraging proper treatment of the flag, however, is not to say that it may criminally punish a person for burning a flag as a means of political protest. "National unity as an end which officials may foster by persuasion and example is not in question. The problem is whether under our Constitution compulsion as here employed is a permissible means for its achievement." . . .

We are tempted to say, in fact, that the flag's deservedly cherished place in our community will be strengthened, not weakened, by our holding today. Our decision is a reaffirmation of the principles of freedom and inclusiveness that the flag best reflects, and of the conviction that our toleration of criticism such as Johnson's is a sign and source of our strength. Indeed, one of the proudest images of our flag, the one immortalized in our own national anthem, is of the bombardment it survived at Fort McHenry. It is the nation's resilience, not its rigidity, that Texas sees reflected in the flag—and it is that resilience that we reassert today.

The way to preserve the flag's special role is not to punish those who feel differently about these matters. It is to persuade them that they are wrong. "To courageous, self-reliant men, with confidence in the power of free and fearless reasoning applied through the processes of popular government, no danger flowing from speech can be deemed clear and present, unless the incidence of the evil apprehended is so imminent that it may befall before there is opportunity for full discussion. If there be time to expose through discussion the falsehood and fallacies, to avert the evil by the processes of education, the remedy to be applied is more speech, not enforced silence." And, precisely because it is our flag that is involved, one's response to the flag burner may exploit the uniquely persuasive power of the flag itself. We can imagine no more appropriate response to burning a flag than waving one's own, no better way to counter a flag burner's message than by saluting the flag that burns, no surer means of preserving the dignity even of the flag that burned than by—as one witness here did—according its remains a respectful burial. We do not consecrate the flag by punishing its desecration, for in doing so we dilute the freedom that this cherished emblem represents. . . .

Chief Justice Rehnquist dissented.

. . . Both Congress and the states have enacted numerous laws regu- 20
lating misuse of the American flag. Until 1967, Congress left the regulation of misuse of the flag up to the states. Now, however, Title 18 U.S.C. §700(a) provides that:

> Whoever knowingly casts contempt upon any flag of the United States by publicly mutilating, defacing, defiling, burning, or trampling upon it shall be fined not more than $1,000 or imprisoned for not more than one year, or both.

Congress has also prescribed, inter alia, detailed rules for the design of the flag, the time and occasion of flag's display, the position and manner of its display, respect for the flag, and conduct during hoisting, lowering, and passing of the flag. With the exception of Alaska and Wyoming, all of the states now have statutes prohibiting the burning of the flag. Most of the state statutes are patterned after the Uniform Flag Act of 1917, which in §3 provides: "No person shall publicly mutilate, deface, defile, defy, trample upon, or by word or act cast contempt upon any such flag, standard, color, ensign or shield." Most were passed by the states at about the time of World War I. . . .

The American flag, then, throughout more than two hundred years of our history, has come to be the visible symbol embodying our nation. It does not represent the views of any particular political party, and it does not represent any particular political philosophy. The flag is not simply another "idea" or "point of view" competing for recognition in the marketplace of ideas. Millions and millions of Americans regard it with an almost mystical reverence regardless of what sort of social, political, or philosophical beliefs they may have. I cannot agree that the First Amendment invalidates the act of Congress, and the laws of forty-eight of the fifty states, which make criminal the public burning of the flag.

More than eighty years ago in *Halter v. Nebraska*, this Court upheld the constitutionality of a Nebraska statute that forbade the use of representations of the American flag for advertising purposes upon articles of merchandise. The Court there said:

> For that flag every true American has not simply an appreciation but a deep affection. . . . Hence, it has often occurred that insults to a flag have been the cause of war, and indignities put upon it, in the presence of those who revere it, have often been resented and sometimes punished on the spot. . . .

But the Court insists that the Texas statute prohibiting the public burning of the American flag infringes on respondent Johnson's freedom of expression. Such freedom, of course, is not absolute. In *Chaplinsky v. New Hampshire*, a unanimous Court said:

> Allowing the broadest scope to the language and purpose of the Fourteenth Amendment, it is well understood that the right of free speech is not absolute at all times and under all circumstances. There are certain well-defined and narrowly limited classes of speech, the prevention and punishment of which have never been thought to raise any Constitutional problem. These include the lewd and obscene, the profane, the libelous, and the insulting or 'fighting' words—those which by their very utterance inflict injury or tend to incite an immediate breach of the peace. It has been well observed that such utterances are no essential part of any exposition of ideas, and are of such slight social value as a step to truth that any benefit that may be derived from them is clearly outweighed by the social interest in order and morality. . . .

The result of the Texas statute is obviously to deny one in Johnson's frame of mind one of many means of "symbolic speech." Far from being a case of "one picture being worth a thousand words," flag burning is the equivalent of an inarticulate grunt or roar that, it seems fair to say, is most likely to be indulged in not to express any particular idea, but to antagonize others. . . . The Texas statute deprived Johnson of only one rather inarticulate symbolic form of protest—a form of protest that was profoundly offensive to many—and left him with a full panoply of other symbols and every conceivable form of verbal expression to express his deep disapproval of national policy. Thus, in no way can it be said that Texas is punishing him because his hearers—or any other group of people—were profoundly opposed to the message that he sought to convey. Such opposition is no proper basis for restricting speech or expression under the First Amendment. It was Johnson's use of this particular symbol, and not the idea that he sought to convey by it or by his many other expressions, for which he was punished.

Our prior cases dealing with flag desecration statutes have left open   25 the question that the Court resolves today. In *Street v. New York*, the defendant burned a flag in the street, shouting "We don't need no damned flag" and, "if they let that happen to Meredith we don't need an American flag." The Court ruled that since the defendant might have been convicted solely on the basis of his words, the conviction could not stand, but it expressly reserved the question whether a defendant could constitutionally be convicted for burning the flag. . . .

In *Spence v. Washington*, the Court reversed the conviction of a college student who displayed the flag with a peace symbol affixed to it by means of removable black tape from the window of his apartment. Unlike the instant case, there was no risk of a breach of the peace, no one other than the arresting officers saw the flag, and the defendant owned the flag in question. The Court concluded that the student's conduct was protected under the First Amendment, because "no interest the state may have in preserving the physical integrity of a privately owned flag was significantly impaired on these facts." The Court was careful to note, however, that the defendant "was not charged under the desecration statute, nor did he permanently disfigure the flag or destroy it."

In another related case, *Smith v. Goguen*, the appellee, who wore a small flag on the seat of his trousers, was convicted under a Massachusetts flag-misuse statute that subjected to criminal liability anyone who "publicly . . . treats contemptuously the flag of the United States." The Court affirmed the lower court's reversal of appellee's conviction, because the phrase "treats contemptuously" was unconstitutionally broad and vague. The Court was again careful to point out that "certainly nothing prevents a legislature from defining with substantial specificity what constitutes forbidden treatment of United States flags." ("The flag is a national property, and the Nation may regulate those who would make, imitate, sell, possess, or use it. I would not question those statutes which proscribe mutilation, defacement, or burning of the flag or which otherwise protect its physical integrity, without regard to whether such conduct might provoke violence. . . . There would seem to be little question about the power of Congress to forbid the mutilation of the Lincoln Memorial. . . . The flag is itself a monument, subject to similar protection"); ("Goguen's punishment was constitutionally permissible for harming the physical integrity of the flag by wearing it affixed to the seat of his pants").

But the Court today will have none of this. The uniquely deep awe and respect for our flag felt by virtually all of us are bundled off under the rubric of "designated symbols" that the First Amendment prohibits the government from "establishing." But the government has not "established" this feeling; two hundred years of history have done that. The government is simply recognizing as a fact the profound regard for the American flag created by that history when it enacts statutes prohibiting the disrespectful public burning of the flag.

The Court concludes its opinion with a regrettably patronizing civics lecture, presumably addressed to the members of both houses of Congress, the members of the forty-eight state legislatures that enacted prohibitions against flag burning, and the troops fighting under that flag in Vietnam who objected to its being burned: "The way to preserve the flag's special role is not to punish those who feel differently about these matters. It is to persuade them that they are wrong." The Court's role as the final expositor of the Constitution is well established, but its role as a platonic guardian admonishing those responsible to public opinion as if they were truant school children has no similar place in our system of government. The cry of "no taxation without representation" animated those who revolted against the English Crown to found our nation—the idea that those who submitted to government should have some say as to what kind of laws would be passed. Surely one of the high purposes of a democratic society is to legislate against conduct that is regarded as evil and profoundly offensive to the majority of people—whether it be murder, embezzlement, pollution, or flag burning.

Our Constitution wisely places limits on powers of legislative majorities to act, but the declaration of such limits by this Court "is, at all times, a question of much delicacy, which ought seldom, if ever, to be decided in the affirmative, in a doubtful case." Uncritical extension of constitutional protection to the burning of the flag risks the frustration of the very purpose for which organized governments are instituted. The Court decides that the American flag is just another symbol, about which not only must opinions pro and con be tolerated, but for which the most minimal public respect may not be enjoined. The government may conscript men into the armed forces where they must fight and perhaps die for the flag, but the government may not prohibit the public burning of the banner under which they fight. I would uphold the Texas statute as applied in this case. 30

Topics for Critical Thinking and Writing

1. State the facts of this case describing Johnson's illegal conduct and the events in court, beginning with his arrest and culminating in the decision of the Supreme Court.

2. What does Justice Brennan state are the interests in conflict?

3. Why does Brennan describe Johnson's conduct as "highly symbolic" (para. 10)? What would count as less symbolic, or nonsymbolic, conduct having the same purpose as flag burning?

4. Chief Justice Rehnquist suggests (para. 24) that Johnson's flag burning is "equivalent" to "an inarticulate grunt or roar," with the intention "not to express any particular idea, but to antagonize others." Explain why you agree or disagree with these judgments.

5. Brennan cites the prior cases of *Street v. New York* and *Schacht v. United States* in his favor; Rehnquist cites several cases supporting his dissenting opinion. Which of these precedents (if any) do you find most relevant to the proper outcome of this case, and why?

6. Would it be a desecration of the flag to print the Stars and Stripes on paper towels to be sold for Fourth of July picnics? On toilet paper? Write a 250-word essay on the topic: "Desecration of the Flag: What It Is and What It Isn't."

7. In paragraph 15, Brennan uses a version of the slippery slope argument (see p. 324) in support of striking down the Texas statute. Explain whether you think this argument is effective and relevant.

8. In First Amendment cases, it is often said that the government may not restrict "speech" because of its "content" but may restrict speech in the "time, place, and manner" of expression. What might be plausible restrictions of these sorts on flag burning for political purposes?

Byron R. White
and John Paul Stevens

In January 1985, a majority of the U.S. Supreme Court, in a case called New Jersey v. T.L.O. (a student's initials), ruled six to three that a school official's search of a student who was suspected of disobeying a school regulation does not violate the Fourth Amendment's protection against unreasonable searches and seizures.

The case originated thus: An assistant principal in a New Jersey high school opened the purse of a fourteen-year-old girl who had been caught violating school rules by smoking in the lavatory. The girl denied that she ever smoked, and the assistant principal thought that the contents of her purse would show whether or not she was lying. The purse was found to contain cigarettes, marijuana, and some notes that seemed to indicate that she sold marijuana to other students. The school then called the police.

The case went through three lower courts; almost five years after the event occurred, the case reached the Supreme Court. Associate Justice Byron R. White wrote the majority opinion, joined by Chief Justice Warren E. Burger and by Associate Justices Lewis F. Powell Jr., William H. Rehnquist, and Sandra Day O'Connor. Associate Justice Harry A. Blackmun concurred in a separate opinion. Associate Justices William J. Brennan Jr., John Paul

Stevens, and Thurgood Marshall dissented in part. In the excerpt that follows, legal citations have been omitted.

New Jersey v. T.L.O.

Justice White delivered the opinion of the Court.

In determining whether the search at issue in this case violated the Fourth Amendment, we are faced initially with the question whether that amendment's prohibition on unreasonable searches and seizures applies to searches conducted by public school officials. We hold that it does.

It is now beyond dispute that "the Federal Constitution, by virtue of the Fourteenth Amendment, prohibits unreasonable searches and seizures by state officers." Equally indisputable is the proposition that the Fourteenth Amendment protects the rights of students against encroachment by public school officials.

On reargument, however, the State of New Jersey has argued that the history of the Fourth Amendment indicates that the amendment was intended to regulate only searches and seizures carried out by law enforcement officers; accordingly, although public school officials are concededly state agents for purposes of the Fourteenth Amendment, the Fourth Amendment creates no rights enforceable against them.

But this Court has never limited the amendment's prohibition on unreasonable searches and seizures to operations conducted by the police. Rather, the Court has long spoken of the Fourth Amendment's strictures as restraints imposed upon "governmental action"—that is, "upon the activities of sovereign authority." Accordingly, we have held the Fourth Amendment applicable to the activities of civil as well as criminal authorities: building inspectors, OSHA inspectors, and even firemen entering privately owned premises to battle a fire, are all subject to the restraints imposed by the Fourth Amendment.

Notwithstanding the general applicability of the Fourth Amendment   5 to the activities of civil authorities, a few courts have concluded that school officials are exempt from the dictates of the Fourth Amendment by virtue of the special nature of their authority over schoolchildren. Teachers and school administrators, it is said, act *in loco parentis* [that is, in place of a parent] in their dealings with students: Their authority is that of the parent, not the state, and is therefore not subject to the limits of the Fourth Amendment.

Such reasoning is in tension with contemporary reality and the teachings of this Court. We have held school officials subject to the commands of the First Amendment, and the Due Process Clause of the Fourteenth Amendment. If school authorities are state actors for purposes of the constitutional guarantees of freedom of expression and due process, it is difficult to understand why they should be deemed to be exercising parental rather than public authority when conducting searches of their students.

In carrying out searches and other disciplinary functions pursuant to such policies, school officials act as representatives of the state, not merely as surrogates for the parents, and they cannot claim the parents' immunity from the strictures of the Fourth Amendment.

To hold that the Fourth Amendment applies to searches conducted by school authorities is only to begin the inquiry into the standards governing such searches. Although the underlying command of the Fourth Amendment is always that searches and seizures be reasonable, what is reasonable depends on the context within which a search takes place.

[STANDARD OF REASONABLENESS]

The determination of the standard of reasonableness governing any specific class of searches requires balancing the need to search against the invasion which the search entails. On one side of the balance are arrayed the individual's legitimate expectations of privacy and personal security; on the other, the government's need for effective methods to deal with breaches of public order.

We have recognized that even a limited search of the person is a   10 substantial invasion of privacy. A search of a child's person or of a closed purse or other bag carried on her person, no less than a similar search carried out on an adult, is undoubtedly a severe violation of subjective expectations of privacy.

Of course, the Fourth Amendment does not protect subjective expectations of privacy that are unreasonable or otherwise "illegitimate." The State of New Jersey has argued that because of the pervasive supervision to which children in the schools are necessarily subject, a child has virtually no legitimate expectation of privacy in articles of personal property "unnecessarily" carried into a school. This argument has two factual premises: (1) the fundamental incompatibility of expectations of privacy with the maintenance of a sound educational environment; and (2) the minimal interest of the child in bringing any items of personal property into the school. Both premises are severely flawed.

Although this Court may take notice of the difficulty of maintaining discipline in the public schools today, the situation is not so dire that students in the schools may claim no legitimate expectations of privacy.

[PRIVACY AND DISCIPLINE]

Against the child's interest in privacy must be set the substantial interest of teachers and administrators in maintaining discipline in the classroom and on school grounds. Maintaining order in the classroom has never been easy, but in recent years, school disorder has often taken particularly ugly forms; drug use and violent crime in the schools have become major social problems. Accordingly, we have recognized that maintaining security and order in the schools requires a certain degree of flexibility in school disciplinary procedures, and we have respected the value of preserving the informality of the student-teacher relationship.

How, then, should we strike the balance between the schoolchild's legitimate expectations of privacy and the school's equally legitimate need to maintain an environment in which learning can take place? It is evident that the school setting requires some easing of the restrictions to which searches by public authorities are ordinarily subject. The warrant requirement, in particular, is unsuited to the school environment; requiring a teacher to obtain a warrant before searching a child suspected of an infraction of school rules (or of the criminal law) would unduly interfere with the maintenance of the swift and informal disciplinary procedures needed in the schools. We hold today that school officials need not obtain a warrant before searching a student who is under their authority.

The school setting also requires some modification of the level 15 of suspicion of illicit activity needed to justify a search. Ordinarily, a search—even one that may permissibly be carried out without a warrant—must be based upon "probable cause" to believe that a violation of the law has occurred. However, "probable cause" is not an irreducible requirement of a valid search.

[BALANCING OF INTERESTS]

The fundamental command of the Fourth Amendment is that searches and seizures be reasonable, and although "both the concept of probable cause and the requirement of a warrant bear on the reasonableness of a search, . . . in certain limited circumstances neither is required." Thus, we have in a number of cases recognized the legality of searches and seizures based on suspicions that, although "reasonable," do not rise to the level of probable cause. Where a careful balancing of governmental and private interests suggests that the public interest is best served by a Fourth Amendment standard of reasonableness that stops short of probable cause, we have not hesitated to adopt such a standard.

We join the majority of courts that have examined this issue in concluding that the accommodation of the privacy interests of schoolchildren with the substantial need of teachers and administrators for freedom to maintain order in the schools does not require strict adherence to the requirement that searches be based on probable cause to believe that the subject of the search has violated or is violating the law.

Rather, the legality of a search of a student should depend simply on the reasonableness, under all the circumstances, of the search. Determining the reasonableness of any search involves a twofold inquiry; first, one must consider "whether the . . . action was justified at its inception," second, one must determine whether the search as actually conducted "was reasonably related in scope to the circumstances which justified the interference in the first place."

Under ordinary circumstances, a search of a student by a teacher or other school official will be "justified at its inception" when there are reasonable grounds for suspecting that the search will turn up evidence that the student has violated or is violating either the law or the rules of the school. Such a search will be permissible in its scope when the measures adopted are reasonably related to the objectives of the search and not excessively intrusive in light of the age and sex of the student and the nature of the infraction.

This standard will, we trust, neither unduly burden the efforts of 20 school authorities to maintain order in their schools nor authorize unrestrained intrusions upon the privacy of schoolchildren. By focusing attention on the question of reasonableness, the standard will spare teachers and school administrators the necessity of schooling themselves in the niceties of probable cause and permit them to regulate their conduct according to the dictates of reason and common sense. At the same time, the reasonableness standard should insure that the interests of students will be invaded no more than is necessary to achieve the legitimate end of preserving order in the schools.

There remains the question of the legality of the search in this case. We recognize that the "reasonable grounds" standard applied by the New Jersey Supreme Court in its consideration of this question is not substantially different from the standard that we have adopted today. Nonetheless, we believe that the New Jersey court's application of that standard to strike down the search of T.L.O.'s purse reflects a somewhat crabbed notion of reasonableness. Our review of the facts surrounding the search leads us to conclude that the search was in no sense unreasonable for Fourth Amendment purposes.

Justice Stevens, dissenting.

The majority holds that "a search of a student by a teacher or other school official will be 'justified at its inception' when there are reasonable grounds for suspecting that the search will turn up evidence *that the student has violated or is violating either the law or the rules of the school.*"

This standard will permit teachers and school administrators to search students when they suspect that the search will reveal evidence of [violation of] even the most trivial school regulation or precatory guideline for students' behavior. For the Court, a search for curlers and sunglasses in order to enforce the school dress code is apparently just as important as a search for evidence of heroin addiction or violent gang activity.

A standard better attuned to this concern would permit teachers and school administrators to search a student when they have reason to believe that the search will uncover *evidence that the student is violating the*

law or engaging in conduct that is seriously disruptive of school order, or the edu-
cational process.

A standard that varies the extent of the permissible intrusion with the   25
gravity of the suspected offense is also more consistent with common-law
experience and this Court's precedent. Criminal law has traditionally recognized a distinction between essentially regulatory offenses and serious
violations of the peace, and graduated the response of the criminal justice
system depending on the character of the violation.

Topics for Critical Thinking and Writing

1. In the majority opinion Justice White says that it is "evident that the
   school setting requires some easing of the restrictions to which searches
   by public authorities are ordinarily subject" (para. 14). Does White offer
   evidence supporting what he says is "evident"? List any evidence that
   White gives or any that you can think of.

2. What argument does White give to show that the Fourth Amendment
   prohibition against "unreasonable searches and seizures" applies to the
   behavior of school officials? Do you think his argument is reasonable, or
   not? Explain.

3. On what ground does White argue that school students have "legitimate
   expectations of privacy" (para. 14) and so New Jersey is wrong in arguing the contrary?

4. What are the conflicting interests involved in the case, according to
   White? How does the Supreme Court resolve this conflict?

5. Why does White argue (para. 15) that school authorities may search
   students without first obtaining a search warrant? (By the way, who issues a search warrant? Who seeks one?) What does he mean when he
   says that the requirement of "probable cause" is "not an irreducible requirement of a valid search" (para. 15)?

6. Could a search undertaken on the principle enunciated by the Court's
   majority mean that whenever authorities perceive what they choose to
   call "disorder"—perhaps in the activity of an assembly of protesters in
   the streets of a big city—they may justify otherwise unlawful searches
   and seizures?

7. Some forty years before this case, Justice Robert H. Jackson argued
   that the schools have a special responsibility for adhering to the Constitution: "That they are educating the young for citizenship is reason
   for scrupulous protection of constitutional freedoms of the individual,
   if we are not to strangle the free mind at its source and teach youth to
   discount important principles of our government as mere platitudes."
   Similarly, in 1967 in an analogous case involving another female pupil,
   Justice Brennan argued that "schools cannot expect their students
   to learn the lessons of good citizenship when the school authorities

themselves disregard the fundamental principles underpinning our constitutional freedoms." Do you find these arguments compelling? Why, or why not?

8. Let's admit that maintaining order in schools may be extremely difficult. In your opinion, does the difficulty justify diminishing the rights of citizens? Smoking is not an illegal activity, yet in this instance a student suspected of smoking—that is, merely of violating a school rule—was searched. In an essay of 250 words, consider whether the maintenance of school discipline in such a matter justifies a search.

9. White relies on a standard of "reasonableness." Do you think this criterion is too subjective to be a proper standard to distinguish between permissible and impermissible searches? Write a 500-word essay on the standard of reasonable searches and seizures, giving a hypothetical but plausible example of a reasonable search and seizure and then of an unreasonable search and seizure.

Harry Blackmun
and
William H. Rehnquist

The first important case in which the U.S. Supreme Court decided a controversy by appeal to our "right of privacy" was in 1965 in Griswold v. Connecticut. *Plaintiffs argued that the state statute forbidding the sale of birth control devices, as well as birth control information from a licensed physician, was an unconstitutional invasion of privacy. The Court ruled in their favor, a controversial ruling because there is no explicit "right of privacy" in the Bill of Rights or elsewhere in the Constitution. The seven Justices in the majority divided over the best way to locate this right in the interstices of prior rulings, and they invoked the "penumbra" of recognized constitutional provisions as the locus of this protection.*

The storm aroused by the Court's ruling in Griswold *was as nothing compared to the raging protest eight years later caused by the Court's ruling (again, by a vote of seven to two) supporting a woman's right to choose whether to carry her pregnancy to completion or, instead, to arrange to terminate her pregnancy by abortion under the direction of a licensed physician. In 1973, when* Roe *was decided, abortion (except in special cases) was illegal in most states in the nation; the decision in* Roe *effectively nullified all such statutes. Justice Harry Blackmun, who wrote the opinion for the Court majority, proposed dividing pregnancy into three trimesters of equal length. During the first trimester, a woman's right to have an abortion was virtually absolute; not so in the second and third trimesters.*

The decision provoked a sharp and deep division between those who embraced it because it recognized a woman's autonomy and the finality of her choice and those who deplored the decision as a violation of the unborn's right to life. The struggle between "right-to-life" advocates (who would, typi-

cally, limit abortion to those rare cases where it is medically necessary to save the life of the mother) and the advocates of a "right to choose" (who favor leaving all questions of pregnancy and its termination to the decision of the pregnant woman) rages unabated. Now, three decades later, it can be said that Roe v. Wade *ranks as the most controversial decision by the Supreme Court in the past century. While it is not likely to be overturned in any future ruling by the Court, influential political forces are manifestly at work to limit its scope. Many observers have noted that, were* Roe v. Wade *up for decision today before a more conservative Supreme Court, it would be decided differently.*

Roe v. Wade

Mr. Justice Blackmun delivered the opinion of the Court. . . .

We forthwith acknowledge our awareness of the sensitive and emotional nature of the abortion controversy, of the vigorous opposing views, even among physicians, and of the deep and seemingly absolute convictions that the subject inspires. One's philosophy, one's experiences, one's exposure to the raw edges of human existence, one's religious training, one's attitudes toward life and family and their values, and the moral standards one establishes and seeks to observe, are all likely to influence and to color one's thinking and conclusions about abortion.

In addition, population growth, pollution, poverty, and racial overtones tend to complicate and not to simplify the problem.

Our task, of course, is to resolve the issue by constitutional measurement, free of emotion and of predilection. We seek earnestly to do this, and, because we do, we have inquired into, and in this opinion place some emphasis upon, medical and medical-legal history and what that history reveals about man's attitudes toward the abortion procedure over the centuries. . . .

The Texas statutes that concern us here are Articles 1191–1194 and 1196 of the State's Penal Code. These make it a crime to "procure an abortion," as therein defined, or to attempt one, except with respect to "an abortion procured or attempted by medical advice for the purpose of saving the life of the mother." Similar statutes are in existence in a majority of the states. . . .

The principal thrust of appellant's attack on the Texas statutes is that   5
they improperly invade a right, said to be possessed by the pregnant woman, to choose to terminate her pregnancy. Appellant would discover this right in the concept of personal "liberty" embodied in the Fourteenth Amendment's Due Process Clause; or in personal, marital, familial, and sexual privacy said to be protected by the Bill of Rights or its penumbras, see *Griswold v. Connecticut*, 381 U.S. 479 (1965); *Eisenstadt v. Baird*, 405 U.S. 438 (1972); id., at 460 (White, J., concurring in result);

or among those rights reserved to the people by the Ninth Amendment, *Griswold v. Connecticut,* 381 U.S., at 486 (Goldberg, J., concurring). Before addressing this claim, we feel it desirable briefly to survey, in several aspects, the history of abortion, for such insight as that history may afford us, and then to examine the state purposes and interests behind the criminal abortion laws.

It perhaps is not generally appreciated that the restrictive criminal abortion laws in effect in a majority of states today are of relatively recent vintage. Those laws, generally proscribing abortion or its attempt at any time during pregnancy except when necessary to preserve the pregnant woman's life, are not of ancient or even of common-law origin. Instead, they derive from statutory changes effected, for the most part, in the latter half of the nineteenth century. . . .

THE AMERICAN LAW

In this country, the law in effect in all but a few states until mid-nineteenth century was the pre-existing English common law. Connecticut, the first state to enact abortion legislation, adopted in 1821 that part of Lord Ellenborough's Act [in England] that related to a woman "quick with child." The death penalty was not imposed. Abortion before quickening was made a crime in that state only in 1860. In 1828, New York enacted legislation that, in two respects, was to serve as a model for early anti-abortion statutes. First, while barring destruction of an unquickened fetus as well as a quick fetus, it made the former only a misdemeanor, but the latter second-degree manslaughter. Second, it incorporated a concept of therapeutic abortion by providing that an abortion was excused if it "shall have been necessary to preserve the life of such mother, or shall have been advised by two physicians to be necessary for such purpose." By 1840, when Texas had received the common law, only eight American states had statutes dealing with abortion. It was not until after the War Between the States that legislation began generally to replace the common law. Most of these initial statutes dealt severely with abortion after quickening but were lenient with it before quickening. Most punished attempts equally with completed abortions. While many statutes included the exception for an abortion thought by one or more physicians to be necessary to save the mother's life, that provision soon disappeared and the typical law required that the procedure actually be necessary for that purpose.

Gradually, in the middle and late nineteenth century the quickening distinction disappeared from the statutory law of most states and the degree of the offense and the penalties were increased. By the end of the 1950s, a large majority of the jurisdictions banned abortion, however and whenever performed, unless done to save or preserve the life of the mother. The exceptions, Alabama and the District of Columbia, permitted abortion to preserve the mother's health. Three states permitted abortions that were not "unlawfully" performed or that were not "without lawful justification," leaving interpretation of those standards to the courts. In the past several years, however, a trend toward liberalization of abortion statutes has resulted in adoption, by about one-third of the states, of less stringent laws, most of them patterned after the ALI Model Penal Code, §230.3. . . .

It is thus apparent that at common law, at the time of the adoption of our Constitution, and throughout the major portion of the nineteenth century, abortion was viewed with less disfavor than under most American statutes currently in effect. Phrasing it another way, a woman enjoyed a substantially broader right to terminate a pregnancy than she does in most states today. At least with respect to the early stage of pregnancy, and very possibly without such a limitation, the opportunity to make this choice was present in this country well into the nineteenth century. Even later, the law continued for some time to treat less punitively an abortion procured in early pregnancy.

THE POSITION OF THE AMERICAN MEDICAL ASSOCIATION

The anti-abortion mood prevalent in this country in the late nine- 10 teenth century was shared by the medical profession. Indeed, the attitude of the profession may have played a significant role in the enactment of stringent criminal abortion legislation during that period. . . .

In 1970, after the introduction of a variety of proposed resolutions, and of a report from its Board of Trustees, a reference committee noted "polarization of the medical profession on this controversial issue"; division among those who had testified; a difference of opinion among AMA councils and committees; "the remarkable shift in testimony" in six months, felt to be influenced "by the rapid changes in state laws and by the judicial decisions which tend to make abortion more freely available;" and a feeling "that this trend will continue." On June 25, 1970, the House of Delegates adopted preambles and most of the resolutions proposed by the reference committee. The preambles emphasized "the best interests of the patient," "sound clinical judgment," and "informed patient consent," in contrast to "mere acquiescence to the patient's demand." The resolutions asserted that abortion is a medical procedure that should be performed by a licensed physician in an accredited hospital only after consultation with two other physicians and in conformity with state law, and that no party to the procedure should be required to violate personally held moral principles. Proceedings of the AMA House of Delegates 200 (June 1970). The AMA Judicial Council rendered a complementary opinion.

THE POSITION OF THE AMERICAN PUBLIC HEALTH ASSOCIATION

In October 1970, the Executive Board of the APHA adopted Standards for Abortion Services. These were five in number:

a. Rapid and simple abortion referral must be readily available through state and local public health departments, medical societies, or other nonprofit organizations.

b. An important function of counseling should be to simplify and expedite the provision of abortion services; it should not delay the obtaining of these services.

c. Psychiatric consultation should not be mandatory. As in the case of other specialized medical services, psychiatric consultation should be sought for definite indications and not on a routine basis.

d. A wide range of individuals from appropriately trained, sympathetic volunteers to highly skilled physicians may qualify as abortion counselors.

e. Contraception and/or sterilization should be discussed with each abortion patient.

Among factors pertinent to life and health risks associated with abortion were three that "are recognized as important":

a. the skill of the physician,

b. the environment in which the abortion is performed, and above all

c. the duration of pregnancy, as determined by uterine size and confirmed by menstrual history.

It was said that "a well-equipped hospital" offers more protection "to cope with unforeseen difficulties than an office or clinic without such resources. . . . The factor of gestational age is of overriding importance." Thus, it was recommended that abortions in the second trimester and early abortions in the presence of existing medical complications be performed in hospitals as inpatient procedures. For pregnancies in the first trimester, abortion in the hospital with or without overnight stay "is probably the safest practice." An abortion in an extramural facility, however, is an acceptable alternative "provided arrangements exist in advance to admit patients promptly if unforeseen complications develop." Standards for an abortion facility were listed. It was said that at present abortions should be performed by physicians or osteopaths who are licensed to practice and who have "adequate training."

THE POSITION OF THE AMERICAN BAR ASSOCIATION

At its meeting in February 1972 the ABA House of Delegates approved, with 17 opposing votes, the Uniform Abortion Act that had been drafted and approved the preceding August by the Conference of Commissioners on Uniform State Laws (1972). . . .

Three reasons have been advanced to explain historically the enact- 15
ment of criminal abortion laws in the nineteenth century and to justify
their continued existence.

It has been argued occasionally that these laws were the product of a
Victorian social concern to discourage illicit sexual conduct. Texas, however, does not advance this justification in the present case, and it appears that no court or commentator has taken the argument seriously.
The appellants and *amici* [friends of the court] contend, moreover, that
this is not a proper state purpose at all and suggest that, if it were, the
Texas statutes are overbroad in protecting it since the law fails to distinguish between married and unwed mothers.

A second reason is concerned with abortion as a medical procedure.
When most criminal abortion laws were first enacted, the procedure was
a hazardous one for the woman. This was particularly true prior to the
development of antisepsis. Antiseptic techniques, of course, were based
on discoveries by Lister, Pasteur, and others first announced in 1867, but
were not generally accepted and employed until about the turn of the
century. Abortion mortality was high. Even after 1900, and perhaps
until as late as the development of antibiotics in the 1940s, standard
modern techniques such as dilation and curettage were not nearly so
safe as they are today. Thus, it has been argued that a state's real concern
in enacting a criminal abortion law was to protect the pregnant woman,
that is, to restrain her from submitting to a procedure that placed her life
in serious jeopardy.

Modern medical techniques have altered this situation. Appellants
and various *amici* refer to medical data indicating that abortion in early
pregnancy, that is, prior to the end of the first trimester, although not
without its risk, is now relatively safe. Mortality rates for women undergoing early abortions, where the procedure is legal, appear to be as low
as or lower than the rates for normal childbirth. Consequently, any interest of the state in protecting the woman from an inherently hazardous
procedure, except when it would be equally dangerous for her to forgo
it, has largely disappeared. Of course, important state interests in the
areas of health and medical standards do remain. . . . The prevalence of
high mortality rates at illegal "abortion mills" strengthens, rather than
weakens, the state's interest in regulating the conditions under which
abortions are performed. Moreover, the risk to the woman increases as
her pregnancy continues. Thus, the state retains a definite interest in
protecting the woman's own health and safety when an abortion is proposed at a late stage of pregnancy.

The third reason is the state's interest—some phrase it in terms of
duty—in protecting prenatal life. Some of the argument for this justification rests on the theory that a new human life is present from the
moment of conception. The state's interest and general obligation to
protect life then extends, it is argued, to prenatal life. Only when the life
of the pregnant mother herself is at stake, balanced against the life she

carries within her, should the interest of the embryo or fetus not prevail. Logically, of course, a legitimate state interest in this area need not stand or fall on acceptance of the belief that life begins at conception or at some other point prior to live birth. In assessing the state's interest, recognition may be given to the less rigid claim that as long as at least *potential* life is involved, the state may assert interests beyond the protection of the pregnant woman alone. . . .

The Constitution does not explicitly mention any right of privacy. In [20] a line of decisions, however, going back perhaps as far as *Union Pacific R. Co. v. Botsford*, 141 U.S. 250, 251 (1891), the Court has recognized that a right of personal privacy, or a guarantee of certain areas or zones of privacy, does exist under the Constitution. In varying contexts, the Court or individual Justices have, indeed, found at least the roots of that right in the First Amendment, in the Fourth and Fifth Amendments, in the Ninth Amendment, or in the concept of liberty guaranteed by the first section of the Fourteenth Amendment. These decisions make it clear that only personal rights that can be deemed "fundamental" or "implicit in the concept of ordered liberty" are included in this guarantee of personal privacy. They also make it clear that the right has some extension to activities relating to marriage, procreation, contraception, family relationships, and child rearing and education.

This right of privacy, whether it be founded in the Fourteenth Amendment's concept of personal liberty and restrictions upon state action, as we feel it is, or, as the District Court determined, in the Ninth Amendment's reservation of rights to the people, is broad enough to encompass a woman's decision whether or not to terminate her pregnancy. The detriment that the state would impose upon the pregnant woman by denying this choice altogether is apparent. Specific and direct harm medically diagnosable even in early pregnancy may be involved. Maternity, or additional offspring, may force upon the woman a distressful life and future. Psychological harm may be imminent. Mental and physical health may be taxed by child care. There is also the distress, for all concerned, associated with the unwanted child, and there is the problem of bringing a child into a family already unable, psychologically and otherwise, to care for it. In other cases, as in this one, the additional difficulties and continuing stigma of unwed motherhood may be involved. All these are factors the woman and her responsible physician necessarily will consider in consultation.

On the basis of elements such as these, appellant and some *amici* argue that the woman's right is absolute and that she is entitled to terminate her pregnancy at whatever time, in whatever way, and for whatever reason she alone chooses. With this we do not agree. Appellant's arguments that Texas either has no valid interest at all in regulating the abortion decision, or no interest strong enough to support any limitation upon the woman's sole determination, are unpersuasive. The Court's decisions recognizing a right of privacy also acknowledge that some state regulation in areas protected by that right is appropriate. As noted above, a state may properly assert important interests in safeguarding health, in maintaining medical standards, and in protecting potential life. At some point in pregnancy, these respective interests become sufficiently compelling to sustain regulation of the factors that govern the abortion decision. The privacy right involved, therefore, cannot be said to be absolute. In fact, it is not clear to us that the claim asserted by some *amici* that one has an unlimited right to do with one's body as one pleases bears a close relationship to the right of privacy previously articulated in the Court's decisions. . . .

We, therefore, conclude that the right of personal privacy includes the abortion decision, but that this right is not unqualified and must be considered against important state interests in regulation.

Where certain "fundamental rights" are involved, the Court has held that regulation limiting these rights may be justified only by a "compelling state interest" . . . and that legislative enactments must be narrowly drawn to express only the legitimate state interests at stake. . . .

In the recent abortion cases, cited above, courts have recognized 25 these principles. Those striking down state laws have generally scrutinized the state's interests in protecting health and potential life, and have concluded that neither interest justified broad limitations on the reasons for which a physician and his pregnant patient might decide that she should have an abortion in the early stages of pregnancy. Courts sustaining state laws have held that the state's determinations to protect health or prenatal life are dominant and constitutionally justifiable.

A

The appellee and certain *amici* argue that the fetus is a "person" within the language and meaning of the Fourteenth Amendment. In support of this, they outline at length and in detail the well-known facts of fetal development. If this suggestion of personhood is established, the appellant's case, of course, collapses, for the fetus' right to life would then be guaranteed specifically by the Amendment. The appellant conceded as much on reargument. On the other hand, the appellee conceded on reargument that no case could be cited that holds that a fetus is a person within the meaning of the Fourteenth Amendment.

The Constitution does not define "person" in so many words. Section 1 of the Fourteenth Amendment contains three references to "person." The first, in defining "citizens," speaks of "persons born or naturalized in the United States." The word also appears both in the Due Process Clause and in the Equal Protection Clause. "Person" is used in other places in the Constitution. . . . But in nearly all these instances, the use of the word is such that it has application only postnatally. None indicates, with any assurance, that it has any possible prenatal application.

This conclusion, however, does not of itself fully answer the contentions raised by Texas, and we pass on to other considerations.

B

The pregnant woman cannot be isolated in her privacy. She carries an embryo and, later, a fetus, if one accepts the medical definitions of the developing young in the human uterus. The situation therefore is inherently different from marital intimacy, or bedroom possession of obscene material, or marriage, or procreation, or education, with which [several decided cases] were respectively concerned. As we have intimated above, it is reasonable and appropriate for a state to decide that at some point in time another interest, that of health of the mother or that of potential human life, becomes significantly involved. The woman's privacy is no longer sole and any right of privacy she possesses must be measured accordingly.

Texas urges that, apart from the Fourteenth Amendment, life begins at conception and is present throughout pregnancy, and that, therefore, the state has a compelling interest in protecting that life from and after conception. We need not resolve the difficult question of when life begins. When those trained in the respective disciplines of medicine, philosophy, and theology are unable to arrive at any consensus, the judiciary, at this point in the development of man's knowledge, is not in a position to speculate as to the answer. . . .

In areas other than criminal abortion, the law has been reluctant to endorse any theory that life, as we recognize it, begins before live birth or to accord legal rights to the unborn except in narrowly defined situations and except when the rights are contingent upon live birth. For example, the traditional rule of tort law denied recovery for prenatal injuries even though the child was born alive. That rule has been changed in almost every jurisdiction. In most states, recovery is said to be permitted only if the fetus was viable, or at least quick, when the injuries were sustained, though few courts have squarely so held. In a recent development, generally opposed by the commentators, some states permit the parents of a stillborn child to maintain an action for wrongful death because of prenatal injuries. Such an action, however, would appear to be one to vindicate the parents' interest and is thus consistent with the view that the fetus, at most, represents only the potentiality of life. Similarly, unborn children have been recognized as acquiring rights or interests by way of inheritance or other devolution of property, and have been represented by guardians *ad litem* [for the purpose of this lawsuit]. Perfection of the interests involved, again, has generally been contingent upon live birth. In short, the unborn have never been recognized in the law as persons in the whole sense.

To summarize and to repeat:

1. A state criminal abortion statute of the current Texas type, that excepts from criminality only a *lifesaving* procedure on behalf of the mother, without regard to pregnancy stage and without recognition of the other interests involved, is violative of the Due Process Clause of the Fourteenth Amendment.

(a) For the stage prior to approximately the end of the first trimester, the abortion decision and its effectuation must be left to the medical judgment of the pregnant woman's attending physician.

(b) For the stage subsequent to approximately the end of the first trimester, the state, in promoting its interest in the health of the mother, may, if it chooses, regulate the abortion procedure in ways that are reasonably related to maternal health.

(c) For the stage subsequent to viability, the state in promoting its interest in the potentiality of human life may, if it chooses, regulate, and even proscribe, abortion except where it is necessary, in appropriate medical judgment, for the preservation of the life or health of the mother.

2. The state may define the term "physician," as it has been employed in the preceding paragraphs of this . . . opinion, to mean only a physician currently licensed by the state, and may proscribe any abortion by a person who is not a physician as so defined. . . .

This holding, we feel, is consistent with the relative weights of the respective interests involved, with the lessons and examples of medical and legal history, with the lenity of the common law, and with the demands of the profound problems of the present day. The decision leaves the state free to place increasing restrictions on abortion as the period of pregnancy lengthens, so long as those restrictions are tailored to the recognized state interests. The decision vindicates the right of the physician to administer medical treatment according to his professional judgment up to the points where important state interests provide compelling justifications for intervention. Up to those points, the abortion decision in all its aspects is inherently, and primarily, a medical decision, and basic responsibility for it must rest with the physician. If an individual practitioner abuses the privilege of exercising proper medical judgment, the usual remedies, judicial and intra-professional, are available.

Our conclusion that Article 1196 is unconstitutional means, of course, that the Texas abortion statutes, as a unit, must fall. . . . [35]

Mr. Justice Rehnquist, dissenting.

The Court's opinion brings to the decision of this troubling question both extensive historical fact and a wealth of legal scholarship. While the opinion thus commands my respect, I find myself nonetheless in fundamental disagreement with those parts of it that invalidate the Texas statute in question, and therefore dissent.

I

The Court's opinion decides that a state may impose virtually no restriction on the performance of abortions during the first trimester of pregnancy. Our previous decisions indicate that a necessary predicate for such an opinion is a plaintiff who was in her first trimester of pregnancy at some time during the pendency of her lawsuit. While a party may vindicate his own constitutional rights, he may not seek vindication for the rights of others. . . . The Court's statement of facts in this case makes clear, however, that the record in no way indicates the presence of such a plaintiff. We know only that plaintiff Roe at the time of filing her complaint was a pregnant woman; for aught that appears in this record, she may have been in her *last* trimester of pregnancy as of the date the complaint was filed.

Nothing in the Court's opinion indicates that Texas might not constitutionally apply its proscription of abortion as written to a woman in that stage of pregnancy. Nonetheless, the Court uses her complaint against the Texas statute as a fulcrum for deciding that states may impose virtually no restrictions on medical abortions performed during the *first* trimester of pregnancy. In deciding such a hypothetical lawsuit, the Court departs from the longstanding admonition that it should never "formulate a rule of constitutional law broader than is required by the precise facts to which it is to be applied."

II

Even if there were a plaintiff in this case capable of litigating the issue which the Court decides, I would reach a conclusion opposite to that reached by the Court. I have difficulty in concluding, as the Court does, that the right of "privacy" is involved in this case. Texas, by the statute here challenged, bars the performance of a medical abortion by a licensed physician on a plaintiff such as Roe. A transaction resulting in an operation such as this is not "private" in the ordinary usage of that word. Nor is the "privacy" that the Court finds here even a distant relative of the freedom from searches and seizures protected by the Fourth Amendment to the Constitution, which the Court has referred to as embodying a right to privacy.

If the Court means by the term "privacy" no more than that the 40 claim of a person to be free from unwanted state regulation of consensual transactions may be a form of "liberty" protected by the Fourteenth Amendment, there is no doubt that similar claims have been upheld in our earlier decisions on the basis of that liberty. I agree with the statement of Mr. Justice Stewart in his concurring opinion[1] that the "liberty," against deprivation of which without due process the Fourteenth Amendment protects, embraces more than the rights found in the Bill of Rights. But that liberty is not guaranteed absolutely against deprivation, only against deprivation without due process of law. The test traditionally applied in the area of social and economic legislation is whether or not a law such as that challenged has a rational relation to a valid state objective. . . . The Due Process Clause of the Fourteenth Amendment undoubtedly does place a limit, albeit a broad one, on legislative power to enact laws such as this. If the Texas statute were to prohibit an abortion even where the mother's life is in jeopardy, I have little doubt that such a statute would lack a rational relation to a valid state objective under the test stated in *Williamson, supra.* But the Court's sweeping invalidation of any restrictions on abortion during the first trimester is impossible to justify under that standard, and the conscious weighing of competing factors that the Court's opinion apparently substitutes for the established test is far more appropriate to a legislative judgment than to a judicial one.

The Court eschews the history of the Fourteenth Amendment in its reliance on the "compelling state interest" test. . . . But the Court adds a new wrinkle to this test by transposing it from the legal considerations associated with the Equal Protection Clause of the Fourteenth Amendment to this case arising under the Due Process Clause of the Fourteenth Amendment. Unless I misapprehend the consequences of this transplanting of the "compelling state interest test," the Court's opinion will accomplish the seemingly impossible feat of leaving this area of the law more confused than it found it.

While the Court's opinion quotes from the dissent of Mr. Justice Holmes in *Lochner v. New York,* 198 U.S. 45, 74 (1905), the result it reaches is more closely attuned to the majority opinion of Mr. Justice Peckham in that case. As in *Lochner* and similar cases applying substantive due process standards to economic and social welfare legislation, the adoption of the compelling state interest standard will inevitably require this Court to examine the legislative policies and pass on the wisdom of these policies in the very process of deciding whether a particular state interest put forward may or may not be "compelling." The decision here to break pregnancy into three distinct terms and to outline the permissible restrictions the state may impose in each one, for example, partakes more of judicial legislation than it does of a determination of the intent of the drafters of the Fourteenth Amendment.

The fact that a majority of the states reflecting, after all, the majority sentiment in those states, have had restrictions on abortions for at least a century is a strong indication, it seems to me, that the asserted right to an abortion is not "so rooted in the traditions and conscience of our

[1]Omitted here. [Editors' note.]

people as to be ranked as fundamental." . . . Even today, when society's views on abortion are changing, the very existence of the debate is evidence that the "right" to an abortion is not so universally accepted as the appellant would have us believe.

To reach its result, the Court necessarily has had to find within the scope of the Fourteenth Amendment a right that was apparently completely unknown to the drafters of the Amendment. As early as 1821, the first state law dealing directly with abortion was enacted by the Connecticut Legislature. . . . By the time of the adoption of the Fourteenth Amendment in 1868, there were at least thirty-six laws enacted by state or territorial legislatures limiting abortion. While many states have amended or updated their laws, twenty-one of the laws on the books in 1868 remain in effect today. Indeed, the Texas statute struck down today was, as the majority notes, first enacted in 1857 and "has remained substantially unchanged to the present time."

There apparently was no question concerning the validity of this pro- 45 vision or of any of the other state statutes when the Fourteenth Amendment was adopted. The only conclusion possible from this history is that the drafters did not intend to have the Fourteenth Amendment withdraw from the states the power to legislate with respect to this matter.

III

Even if one were to agree that the case that the Court decides were here, and that the enunciation of the substantive constitutional law in the Court's opinion were proper, the actual disposition of the case by the Court is still difficult to justify. The Texas statute is struck down *in toto,* even though the Court apparently concedes that at later periods of pregnancy Texas might impose these selfsame statutory limitations on abortion. My understanding of past practice is that a statute found to be invalid as applied to a particular plaintiff, but not unconstitutional as a whole, is not simply "struck down" but is, instead, declared unconstitutional as applied to the fact situation before the Court. . . .

For all of the foregoing reasons, I respectfully dissent.

Topics for Critical Thinking and Writing

1. Abortion is nowhere mentioned in the federal Bill of Rights. Is that an insurmountable obstacle for both opponents and defenders of a woman's right to abortion who seek constitutional support for their position?

2. What does it mean for a pregnant woman to be "quick with child" (para. 7)?

3. Can a person consistently believe that (a) a woman has no right to an abortion, (b) a human embryo or fetus has an inviolable right to life, and (c) a woman may have an abortion if it is necessary to save her own

life? Explain in an essay of 500 words why you think these three propositions are or are not inconsistent.

4. Blackmun cites three reasons to explain the enactment of anti-abortion laws in nineteenth-century America (paras. 16–19). How would you rank these reasons in order of their decreasing relevance today? Write an essay of 500 words in which you state succinctly these reasons and your evaluation of them for present policy on abortion.

5. What is a "trimester" in a pregnancy (para. 13)? How, if at all, does this concept relate to the older idea of "quickening"?

6. What is a "state interest" (paras. 18–19), and why is there any such interest concerning human pregnancy and abortion?

7. Suppose someone argued that Blackmun's opinion is hopelessly confused because the issue is not the *privacy* of the pregnant woman but her *autonomy*—that is, her capacity and right to make fundamental decisions about her own life as she sees fit. Write a 250-word opinion for this case in which you defend or attack Roe's autonomy as the fundamental basis for her decision whether to abort.

8. Do you agree with the Supreme Court that a woman's right to abort a pregnancy is not an "absolute" right (paras. 22–23)? Do you agree with the Court's reasons for this conclusion? Explain.

9. Blackmun is unwilling to take any position on the question whether the human unborn is alive (para. 31). Do you share his refusal? Why, or why not?

10. Do you think the unborn human fetus is a "person" in any sense of that term (see paras. 26–27)? How about a month-old human embryo? Suppose we grant that an embryo and a fetus are *alive* (that is, neither dead nor inert) and *human* (that is, not animal or vegetable or inhuman). What do you think needs to be added to establish the personhood of the living but unborn human offspring? Or do you think it is impossible that a human embryo or fetus could be a person? Explain.

11. Rehnquist argues that an abortion is "not 'private' in the ordinary usage of that word" (para. 39). What is his reason for this view? Do you agree or not? Explain.

12. Rehnquist remarks that the complex position on abortion taken by the majority of the Court (see especially para. 33) "is far more appropriate to a legislative judgment than to a judicial one" (paras. 40 and 42). Why does he say this, do you think? Do you agree or not? Explain.

11

A Psychologist's View: Rogerian Argument

Carl R. Rogers (1902–1987), perhaps best known for his book entitled *On Becoming a Person* (1961), was a psychotherapist, not a teacher of writing. This short essay by Rogers has, however, exerted much influence on instructors who teach argument. Written in the 1950s, this essay reflects the political climate of the cold war between the United States and the Soviet Union, which dominated headlines for more than forty years (1947–1989). Several of Rogers's examples of bias and frustrated communication allude to the tensions of that era.

On the surface, many arguments seem to show *A* arguing with *B*, presumably seeking to change *B*'s mind; but *A*'s argument is really directed not to *B* but to *C*. This attempt to persuade a nonparticipant is evident in the courtroom, where neither the prosecutor (*A*) nor the defense lawyer (*B*) is really trying to convince the opponent. Rather, both are trying to convince a third party, the jury (*C*). Prosecutors do not care whether they convince defense lawyers; they don't even mind infuriating defense lawyers because their only real goal is to convince the jury. Similarly, the writer of a letter to a newspaper, taking issue with an editorial, does not expect to change the paper's policy. Rather, the writer hopes to convince a third party, the reader of the newspaper.

But suppose *A* really does want to bring *B* around to *A*'s point of view. Suppose Mary really wants to persuade the teacher to allow her little lamb to stay in the classroom. Rogers points out that when we engage in an argument, if we feel our integrity or our identity is threatened, we will stiffen our position. (The teacher may feel that his or her dignity is compromised by the presence of the lamb and will scarcely attend to Mary's argument.) The sense of threat may be so great that we are unable to consider the alternative views being offered, and we therefore remain unpersuaded. Threatened, we may defend ourselves rather than our argument, and little communication takes place. Of course, a third party might say that we or our opponent presented the more convincing case, but we, and perhaps the opponent, have scarcely listened to each other, and so the two of us remain apart.

Rogers suggests, therefore, that a writer who wishes to communicate with someone (as opposed to convincing a third party) needs to reduce the threat. In a sense, the participants in the argument need to become partners rather than adversaries. Rogers writes, "Mutual communication tends to be pointed toward solving a problem rather than toward attacking a person or group." Thus, an essay on whether schools should test students for use of drugs, need not—and probably should not—see the issue as black or white, *either/or.* Such an essay might indicate that testing is undesirable because it may have bad effects, *but in some circumstances* it may be acceptable. This qualification does not mean that one must compromise. Thus, the essayist might argue that the potential danger to liberty is so great that no circumstances justify testing students for drugs. But even such an essayist should recognize the merit (however limited) of the opposition and should grant that the position being advanced itself entails great difficulties and dangers.

A writer who wishes to reduce the psychological threat to the opposition and thus facilitate the partnership in the study of some issue can do several things:

- One can show sympathetic understanding of the opposing argument,
- One can recognize what is valid in it, and
- One can recognize and demonstrate that those who take the other side are nonetheless persons of goodwill.

Advocates of Rogerian argument are likely to contrast it with Aristotelian argument, saying that the style of argument associated with Aristotle (384–322 B.C., Greek philosopher and rhetorician)

- Is adversarial, seeking to refute other views, and
- Sees the listener as wrong, someone who now must be overwhelmed by evidence.

In contrast to the confrontational Aristotelian style, which allegedly seeks to present an airtight case that compels belief, Rogerian argument (it is said)

- Is nonconfrontational, collegial, and friendly;
- Respects other views and allows for plural truths; and
- Seeks to achieve some degree of assent rather than convince utterly.

Thus a writer who takes Rogers seriously will, usually, in the first part of an argumentative essay

1. State the problem,
2. Give the opponent's position, and
3. Grant whatever validity the writer finds in that position — for instance, will recognize the circumstances in which the position would indeed be acceptable.

Next, the writer will, if possible,

4. Attempt to show how the opposing position will be improved if the writer's own position is accepted.

Sometimes, of course, the differing positions may be so far apart that no reconciliation can be proposed, in which case the writer will probably seek to show how the problem can best be solved by adopting the writer's own position. We have discussed these matters in Chapter 5, but not from the point of view of a psychotherapist, and so we reprint Rogers's essay here.

Carl R. Rogers

Communication: Its Blocking and Its Facilitation

It may seem curious that a person whose whole professional effort is devoted to psychotherapy should be interested in problems of communication. What relationship is there between providing therapeutic help to individuals with emotional maladjustments and the concern of this conference with obstacles to communication? Actually the relationship is very close indeed. The whole task of psychotherapy is the task of dealing with a failure in communication. The emotionally maladjusted person, the "neurotic," is in difficulty first because communication within himself has broken down, and second because as a result of this his communication with others has been damaged. If this sounds somewhat strange, then let me put it in other terms. In the "neurotic" individual, parts of himself which have been termed unconscious, or repressed, or denied to awareness, become blocked off so that they no longer communicate themselves to the conscious or managing part of himself. As long as this is true, there are distortions in the way he communicates himself to others, and so he suffers both within himself, and in his interpersonal relations. The task of psychotherapy is to help the person achieve, through a special relationship with a therapist, good communication within himself. Once this is achieved he can communicate more freely and more effectively with others. We may say then that psychotherapy is good communication, within and between men. We may also turn that statement around and it will still be true. Good communication, free communication, within or between men, is always therapeutic.

It is, then, from a background of experience with communication in counseling and psychotherapy that I want to present here two ideas. I wish to state what I believe is one of the major factors in blocking or impeding communication, and then I wish to present what in our experience has proven to be a very important way to improving or facilitating communication.

I would like to propose, as an hypothesis for consideration, that the major barrier to mutual interpersonal communication is our very natural tendency to judge, to evaluate, to approve or disapprove, the statement of the person, or the other group. Let me illustrate my meaning with some very simple examples. As you leave the meeting tonight, one of the statements you are likely to hear is, "I didn't like that man's talk." Now what do you respond? Almost invariably your reply will be either approval or disapproval of the attitude expressed. Either you respond, "I didn't either. I thought it was terrible," or else you tend to reply, "Oh, I thought it was really good." In other words, your primary reaction is to evaluate what has just been said to you, to evaluate it from *your* point of view, your own frame of reference.

Or take another example. Suppose I say with some feeling, "I think the Republicans are behaving in ways that show a lot of good sound sense these days," what is the response that arises in your mind as you listen? The overwhelming likelihood is that it will be evaluative. You will find yourself agreeing, or disagreeing, or making some judgment about me such as "He must be a conservative," or "He seems solid in his thinking." Or let us take an illustration from the international scene. Russia says vehemently, "The treaty with Japan is a war plot on the part of the United States." We rise as one person to say "That's a lie!"

This last illustration brings in another element connected with my   5 hypothesis. Although the tendency to make evaluations is common in almost all interchange of language, it is very much heightened in those situations where feelings and emotions are deeply involved. So the stronger our feelings, the more likely it is that there will be no mutual element in the communication. There will be just two ideas, two feelings, two judgments, missing each other in psychological space. I'm sure you recognize this from your own experience. When you have not been emotionally involved yourself, and have listened to a heated discussion, you often go away thinking, "Well, they actually weren't talking about the same thing." And they were not. Each was making a judgment, an evaluation, from his own frame of reference. There was really nothing which could be called communication in any genuine sense. This tendency to react to any emotionally meaningful statement by forming an evaluation of it from our own point of view, is, I repeat, the major barrier to interpersonal communication.

But is there any way of solving this problem, of avoiding this barrier? I feel that we are making exciting progress toward this goal and I would like to present it as simply as I can. Real communication occurs,

and this evaluative tendency is avoided, when we listen with understanding. What does that mean? It means *to see the expressed idea and attitude from the other person's point of view, to sense how it feels to him, to achieve
his frame of reference in regard to the thing he is talking about.*

Stated so briefly, this may sound absurdly simple, but it is not. It is
an approach which we have found extremely potent in the field of psychotherapy. It is the most effective agent we know for altering the basic
personality structure of an individual, and improving his relationships
and his communications with others. If I can listen to what he can tell
me, if I can understand how it seems to him, if I can see its personal
meaning for him, if I can sense the emotional flavor which it has for
him, then I will be releasing potent forces of change in him. If I can
really understand how he hates his father, or hates the university, or
hates communists — if I can catch the flavor of his fear of insanity, or his
fear of atom bombs, or of Russia — it will be of the greatest help to him
in altering those very hatreds and fears, and in establishing realistic and
harmonious relationships with the very people and situations toward
which he has felt hatred and fear. We know from our research that
such empathic understanding — understanding *with* a person, not *about*
him — is such an effective approach that it can bring about major
changes in personality.

Some of you may be feeling that you listen well to people, and that
you have never seen such results. The chances are very great indeed
that your listening has not been of the type I have described. Fortunately I can suggest a little laboratory experiment which you can try to
test the quality of your understanding. The next time you get into an argument with your wife, or your friend, or with a small group of friends,
just stop the discussion for a moment and for an experiment, institute
this rule. "Each person can speak up for himself only *after* he has first
restated the ideas and feelings of the previous speaker accurately, and to
that speaker's satisfaction." You see what this would mean. It would
simply mean that before presenting your own point of view, it would be
necessary for you to really achieve the other speaker's frame of reference — to understand his thoughts and feelings so well that you could
summarize them for him. Sounds simple, doesn't it? But if you try it
you will discover it one of the most difficult things you have ever tried
to do. However, once you have been able to see the other's point of
view, your own comments will have to be drastically revised. You will
also find the emotion going out of the discussion, the differences being
reduced, and those differences which remain being of a rational and understandable sort.

Can you imagine what this kind of an approach would mean if
it were projected into larger areas? What would happen to a labor-
management dispute if it was conducted in such a way that labor, without necessarily agreeing, could accurately state management's point of
view in a way that management could accept; and management, without approving labor's stand, could state labor's case in a way that labor

agreed was accurate? It would mean that real communication was established, and one could practically guarantee that some reasonable solution would be reached.

If then this way of approach is an effective avenue to good communication and good relationships, as I am quite sure you will agree if you try the experiment I have mentioned, why is it not more widely tried and used? I will try to list the difficulties which keep it from being utilized.

In the first place it takes courage, a quality which is not too widespread. I am indebted to Dr. S. I. Hayakawa, the semanticist, for pointing out that to carry on psychotherapy in this fashion is to take a very real risk, and that courage is required. If you really understand another person in this way, if you are willing to enter his private world and see the way life appears to him, without any attempt to make evaluative judgments, you run the risk of being changed yourself. You might see it his way, you might find yourself influenced in your attitudes or your personality. This risk of being changed is one of the most frightening prospects most of us can face. If I enter, as fully as I am able, into the private world of a neurotic or psychotic individual, isn't there a risk that I might become lost in that world? Most of us are afraid to take that risk. Or if we had a Russian communist speaker here tonight, or Senator Joe McCarthy, how many of us would dare to try to see the world from each of these points of view? The great majority of us could not *listen;* we would find ourselves compelled to *evaluate,* because listening would seem too dangerous. So the first requirement is courage, and we do not always have it.

But there is a second obstacle. It is just when emotions are strongest that it is most difficult to achieve the frame of reference of the other person or group. Yet it is the time the attitude is most needed, if communication is to be established. We have not found this to be an insuperable obstacle in our experience in psychotherapy. A third party, who is able to lay aside his own feelings and evaluations, can assist greatly by listening with understanding to each person or group and clarifying the views and attitudes each holds. We have found this very effective in small groups in which contradictory or antagonistic attitudes exist. When the parties to a dispute realize that they are being understood, that someone sees how the situation seems to them, the statements grow less exaggerated and less defensive, and it is no longer necessary to maintain the attitude, "I am 100 percent right and you are 100 percent wrong." The influence of such an understanding catalyst in the group permits the members to come closer and closer to the objective truth involved in the relationship. In this way mutual communication is established and some type of agreement becomes much more possible. So we may say that though heightened emotions make it much more difficult to understand *with* an opponent, our experience makes it clear that a neutral, understanding, catalyst type of leader or therapist can overcome this obstacle in a small group.

This last phrase, however, suggests another obstacle to utilizing the approach I have described. Thus far all our experience has been with small face-to-face groups — groups exhibiting industrial tensions, religious tensions, racial tensions, and therapy groups in which many personal tensions are present. In these small groups our experience, confirmed by a limited amount of research, shows that this basic approach leads to improved communication, to greater acceptance of others and by others, and to attitudes which are more positive and more problem-solving in nature. There is a decrease in defensiveness, in exaggerated statements, in evaluative and critical behavior. But these findings are from small groups. What about trying to achieve understanding between larger groups that are geographically remote? Or between face-to-face groups who are not speaking for themselves, but simply as representatives of others, like the delegates at Kaesong?[1] Frankly we do not know the answers to these questions. I believe the situation might be put this way. As social scientists we have a tentative test-tube solution of the problem of breakdown in communication. But to confirm the validity of this test-tube solution, and to adapt it to the enormous problems of communication breakdown between classes, groups, and nations, would involve additional funds, much more research, and creative thinking of a high order.

Even with our present limited knowledge we can see some steps which might be taken, even in large groups, to increase the amount of listening *with,* and to decrease the amount of evaluation *about.* To be imaginative for a moment, let us suppose that a therapeutically oriented international group went to the Russian leaders and said, "We want to achieve a genuine understanding of your views and even more important, of your attitudes and feelings, toward the United States. We will summarize and resummarize the views and feelings if necessary, until you agree that our description represents the situation as it seems to you." Then suppose they did the same thing with the leaders in our own country. If they then gave the widest possible distribution to these two views, with the feelings clearly described but not expressed in name-calling, might not the effect be very great? It would not guarantee the type of understanding I have been describing, but it would make it much more possible. We can understand the feelings of a person who hates us much more readily when his attitudes are accurately described to us by a neutral third party, than we can when he is shaking his fist at us.

But even to describe such a first step is to suggest another obstacle to this approach of understanding. Our civilization does not yet have enough faith in the social sciences to utilize their findings. The opposite is true of the physical sciences. During the war[2] when a test-tube solu-

---

[1] **the delegates at Kaesong** Representatives of North and South Korea met at the border town of Kaesong to arrange terms for an armistice to hostilities during the Korean War (1950–1953). [All notes are the editors'.]
[2] **the war** World War II.

tion was found to the problem of synthetic rubber, millions of dollars and an army of talent was turned loose on the problem of using that finding. If synthetic rubber could be made in milligrams, it could and would be made in the thousands of tons. And it was. But in the social science realm, if a way is found of facilitating communication and mutual understanding in small groups, there is no guarantee that the finding will be utilized. It may be a generation or more before the money and the brains will be turned loose to exploit that finding.

In closing, I would like to summarize this small-scale solution to the problem of barriers in communication, and to point out certain of its characteristics.

I have said that our research and experience to date would make it appear that breakdowns in communication, and the evaluative tendency which is the major barrier to communication, can be avoided. The solution is provided by creating a situation in which each of the different parties come to understand the other from the *other's* point of view. This has been achieved, in practice, even when feelings run high, by the influence of a person who is willing to understand each point of view empathically, and who thus acts as a catalyst to precipitate further understanding.

This procedure has important characteristics. It can be initiated by one party, without waiting for the other to be ready. It can even be initiated by a neutral third person, providing he can gain a minimum of cooperation from one of the parties.

This procedure can deal with the insincerities, the defensive exaggerations, the lies, the "false fronts" which characterize almost every failure in communication. These defensive distortions drop away with astonishing speed as people find that the only intent is to understand, not judge.

This approach leads steadily and rapidly toward the discovery of the 20 truth, toward a realistic appraisal of the objective barriers to communication. The dropping of some defensiveness by one party leads to further dropping of defensiveness by the other party, and truth is thus approached.

This procedure gradually achieves mutual communication. Mutual communication tends to be pointed toward solving a problem rather than toward attacking a person or group. It leads to a situation in which I see how the problem appears to you, as well as to me, and you see how it appears to me, as well as to you. Thus accurately and realistically defined, the problem is almost certain to yield to intelligent attack, or if it is in part insoluble, it will be comfortably accepted as such.

This then appears to be a test-tube solution to the breakdown of communication as it occurs in small groups. Can we take this small-scale answer, investigate it further, refine it; develop it and apply it to the tragic and well-nigh fatal failures of communication which threaten the very existence of our modern world? It seems to me that this is a possibility and a challenge which we should explore.

A CHECKLIST FOR ANALYZING ROGERIAN ARGUMENT

✓ Have I stated the problem and indicated that a dialogue is possible?

✓ Have I stated at least one other point of view in a way that would satisfy its proponents?

✓ Have I been courteous to those who hold views other than mine?

✓ Have I enlarged my own understanding, to the extent that I can grant validity, at least in some circumstances, to at least some aspects of other positions?

✓ Have I stated my position and indicated the contexts in which I believe it is valid?

✓ Have I pointed out the ground that we share?

✓ Have I shown how other positions will be strengthened by accepting some aspects of my position?

See the companion Web site **www.bedfordstmartins.com/barnetbedau** for links related to Rogerian argument.

12

A Literary Critic's View: Arguing about Literature

You might think that literature—fiction, poetry (including songs), drama—is meant only to be enjoyed, not to be argued about. Yet literature is constantly the subject of argumentative writing—not all of it by teachers of English. For instance, if you glance at the current issue of *Time* or *Newsweek,* you probably will find a review of a play suggesting that the play is worth seeing or is not worth seeing. Or in the same magazine you may find an article reporting that a senator or member of Congress argued that the National Endowment for the Humanities wasted its grant money by funding research on such-and-such an author or that the National Endowment for the Arts insulted taxpayers by making an award to a writer who defamed the American family.

Probably most writing about literature, whether done by college students, their professors, journalists, members of Congress, or whomever, is devoted to interpreting, judging (evaluating), and theorizing. Let's look at each of these, drawing our examples chiefly from comments about Shakespeare's *Macbeth.*

INTERPRETING

Interpreting is a matter of setting forth the *meaning* or the meanings of a work. For some readers, a work has *a* meaning, the one intended by the writer, which we may or may not perceive. For most critics today, however, a work has *many* meanings—for instance, the meaning it had for the writer, the meanings it has accumulated over time, and the meanings it has for each of today's readers. Take *Macbeth,* a play about a Scottish king, written soon after a Scot—James VI of Scotland—had been installed as James I, King of England. The play must have meant something special to the king — we know that it was presented at court — and something a little different to the ordinary English citizen. And surely it means something different to us. For instance, few if any people today believe in the divine right of kings, although James I certainly did; and few if any people today believe in malignant witches, although witches play an important role in the tragedy. What *we* see in the play must be rather different from what Shakespeare's audience saw in it.

Many interpretations of *Macbeth* have been offered. Let's take two fairly simple and clearly opposed views:

1. Macbeth is a villain who, by murdering his lawful king, offends God's rule, so he is overthrown by God's earthly instruments, Malcolm and Macduff. Macbeth is justly punished; the reader or spectator rejoices in his defeat.

One can offer a good deal of evidence — and if one is taking this position in an essay, of course one must *argue* it — by giving supporting reasons rather than merely assert the position. Here is a second view.

2. Macbeth is a hero-villain, a man who commits terrible crimes but who never completely loses the reader's sympathy; although he is justly punished, the reader believes that with the death of Macbeth the world has become a smaller place.

Again, one *must* offer evidence in an essay that presents this thesis or indeed presents any interpretation. For instance, one might offer as evidence the fact that the survivors, especially Macduff and Malcolm, have not interested us nearly as much as Macbeth has. One might argue, too, that although Macbeth's villainy is undeniable, his conscience never deserts him — here one would point to specific passages and would offer some brief quotations. Macbeth's pained awareness of what he has done, it can be argued, enables the reader to sympathize with him continually.

Or consider an interpretation of Lady Macbeth. Is she simply evil through and through, or are there mitigating reasons for her actions? Might one argue, perhaps in a feminist interpretation, that despite her intelligence and courage she had no outlet for expression except through her husband? To make this argument, the writer might want to go beyond the text of the play, offering as evidence Elizabethan comments about the proper role of women.

JUDGING (OR EVALUATING)

Literary criticism is also concerned with such questions as these: Is *Macbeth* a great tragedy? Is *Macbeth* a greater tragedy than *Romeo and Juliet*? The writer offers an opinion about the worth of the literary work, but the opinion must be supported by an argument, expressed in sentences that offer supporting evidence.

Let's pause for a moment to think about evaluation in general. When we say "This is a great play," are we in effect saying only "I like this play"? That is, are we merely *expressing* our taste rather than *asserting* anything about something out there — something independent of our tastes and feelings? (The next few paragraphs will not answer this question, but they may start you thinking about your own answer.) Consider these three sentences:

1. It's raining outside.
2. I like vanilla.
3. This is a really good book.

If you are indoors and you say that it is raining outside, a hearer may ask for verification. Why do you say what you say? "Because," you reply, "I'm looking out the window." Or "Because Jane just came in, and she is drenched." Or "Because I just heard a weather report." If, on the other hand, you say that you like vanilla, it's almost unthinkable that anyone would ask you why. No one expects you to justify — to support, to give a reason for — an expression of taste.

Now consider the third statement, "This is a really good book." It is entirely reasonable, we think, for someone to ask you why you say that. And you reply, "Well, the characters are realistic, and the plot held my interest," or "It really gave me an insight into what life among the rich [or the poor] must be like," or some such thing. That is, statement 3 at least seems to be stating a fact, and it seems to be something we can discuss, even argue about, in a way that we cannot argue about a personal preference for vanilla. Almost everyone would agree that when we offer an aesthetic judgment we ought to be able to give reasons for it. At the very least, we might say, we hope to show *why* we evaluate the work as we do, and to suggest that if our readers try to see it from our point of view they may then accept our evaluation.

Evaluations are always based on assumptions, although these assumptions may be unstated, and in fact the writer may even be unaware of them. Some of these assumptions play the role of criteria; they control the sort of evidence the writer believes is relevant to the evaluation. What sorts of assumptions may underlie value judgments? We will mention a few, merely as examples. Other assumptions are possible, and all of these assumptions can themselves become topics of dispute:

1. A good work of art, although fictional, says something about real life.
2. A good work of art is complex yet unified.
3. A good work of art sets forth a wholesome view of life.
4. A good work of art is original.
5. A good work of art deals with an important subject.

Let's look briefly at these views, one by one.

1. *A good work of art, although fictional, says something about real life.* If you hold the view that literature is connected to life and believe that human beings behave in fairly consistent ways—that is, that each of us has an enduring "character"—you probably will judge as inferior a work in which the figures behave inconsistently or seem not to be adequately motivated. (The point must be made, however, that different literary forms or genres are governed by different rules. For instance, consistency of character is usually expected in tragedy but not in melodrama or in comedy, where last-minute reformations may be welcome and greeted with applause. The novelist Henry James said, "You will not write a good novel unless you possess the sense of reality." He is probably right—but does his view hold for the writer of farces?) In the case of *Macbeth* you might well find that the characters are consistent: Although the play begins by showing Macbeth as a loyal defender of King Duncan, Macbeth's later treachery is understandable, given the temptation and the pressure. Similarly, Lady Macbeth's descent into madness, although it may come as a surprise, may strike you as entirely plausible: At the beginning of the play she is confident that she can become an accomplice to a murder, but she has overestimated herself (or, we might say, she has underestimated her own humanity, the power of her guilty conscience, which drives her to insanity).

2. *A good work of art is complex yet unified.* If Macbeth is only a "tyrant" (Macduff's word) or a "butcher" (Malcolm's word), he is a unified character but he may be too simple and too uninteresting a character to be the subject of a great play. But, one argument holds, Macbeth in fact is a complex character, not simply a villain but a hero-villain, and the play as a whole is complex. *Macbeth* is a good work of art, one might argue, partly because it shows us so many aspects of life (courage, fear, loyalty, treachery, for a start) through a richly varied language (the diction ranges from a grand passage in which Macbeth says that his bloody hands will "incarnadine," or make red, "the multitudinous seas" to colloquial passages such as the drunken porter's "Knock, knock"). The play shows us the heroic Macbeth tragically destroying his own life, and it shows us the comic porter making coarse jokes about deceit and damnation, jokes that (although the porter doesn't know it) connect with Macbeth's crimes.

3. *A good work of art sets forth a wholesome view of life.* The idea that a work should be judged partly or largely on the moral view that it contains is widely held by the general public. (It has also been held by esteemed philosophers, notably Plato.) Thus, a story that demeans women—perhaps one that takes a casual view of rape—would be given a low rating and so would a play that treats a mass murderer as a hero.

Implicit in this approach is what is called an *instrumentalist* view—

the idea that a work of art is an instrument, a means, to some higher value. Thus, many people hold that reading great works of literature makes us better—or at least does not make us worse. In this view, a work that is pornographic or in some other way thought to be immoral will be given a low value. At the time we are writing this chapter, a law requires the National Endowment for the Arts to take into account standards of decency when making awards.

Moral judgments, it should be noted, do not come only from the conservative right; the liberal left has been quick to detect political incorrectness. In fact, except for those people who subscribe to the now unfashionable view that a work of art is an independent aesthetic object with little or no connection to the real world—something like a pretty floral arrangement or a wordless melody—most people judge works of literature largely by their content, by what the works seem to say about life. Marxist critics, for instance, have customarily held that literature should make the reader aware of the political realities of life; feminist critics are likely to hold that literature should make us aware of gender relationships—for example, aware of patriarchal power and of female accomplishments.

4. *A good work of art is original.* This assumption puts special value on new techniques and new subject matter. Thus, the *first* playwright who introduces a new subject (say, AIDS) gets extra credit, so to speak. Or to return to Shakespeare, one sign of his genius, it is held, is that he was so highly varied; none of his tragedies seems merely to duplicate another, each is a world of its own, a new kind of achievement. Compare, for instance, *Romeo and Juliet*, with its two youthful and innocent heroes, with *Macbeth*, with its deeply guilty hero. Both plays are tragedies, but we can hardly imagine two more different plays—even if a reader perversely argues that the young lovers are guilty of impetuosity and of disobeying appropriate authorities.

5. *A good work of art deals with an important subject.* Here we are concerned with theme: Great works, in this view, must deal with great themes. Love, death, patriotism, and God, say, are great themes; a work that deals with these may achieve a height, an excellence, that, say, a work describing a dog scratching for fleas may not achieve. (Of course, if the reader feels that the dog is a symbol of humanity plagued by invisible enemies, then the poem about the dog may reach the heights, but then, too, it is *not* a poem about a dog and fleas: It is really a poem about humanity and the invisible.)

The point: In writing an evaluation you must let your reader know *why* you value the work as you do. Obviously, it is not enough just to keep saying that *this* work is great whereas *that* work is not so great; the reader wants to know *why* you offer the judgments that you do, which means that you will have to set forth your criteria and then offer evidence that is in accord with them.

THEORIZING

Some literary criticism is concerned with such theoretical questions as these:

> What is tragedy? Can the hero be a villain? How does tragedy differ from melodrama?
>
> Why do tragedies—works showing good or at least interesting people destroyed—give us pleasure?
>
> Does a work of art—a play or a novel, say, a made-up world with imagined characters—offer anything that can be called "truth"? Does an experience of a work of art affect our character?
>
> Does a work of art have meaning in itself, or is the meaning simply whatever anyone wishes to say it is? Does *Macbeth* tell us anything about life, or is it just an invented story?

And, yet again, one hopes that anyone asserting a thesis concerned with any of these topics will offer evidence—will, indeed, *argue* rather than merely assert.

A CHECKLIST FOR AN ARGUMENT ABOUT LITERATURE

✓ Is your imagined reader like a typical classmate of yours, someone who is not a specialist in literature but who is open-minded and interested in hearing your point of view about a work?

✓ Is the essay supported with evidence, usually from the text itself but conceivably from other sources (such as a statement by the author, a statement by a person regarded as an authority, or perhaps the evidence of comparable works)?

✓ Is the essay inclusive? Does it take into account all relevant details (which is not to say that it includes everything the writer knows about the work—for instance, that it was made into a film or that the author died poor)?

✓ Is the essay focused? Does the thesis stay steadily before the reader?

✓ Does the essay use quotations, but as evidence, not as padding? Whenever possible, does it abridge or summarize long quotations?

✓ Are all sources fully acknowledged? (For the form of documentation, see pp. 237–54.)

EXAMPLES:
Two Students Interpret
Robert Frost's "Mending Wall"

Let's consider two competing interpretations of a poem, Robert Frost's "Mending Wall." We say "competing" because these interpretations clash head-on. Differing interpretations need not be incompatible, of course. For instance, a historical interpretation of *Macbeth*, arguing that an understanding of the context of English-Scottish politics around 1605 helps us to appreciate the play, need not be incompatible with a psychoanalytic interpretation that tells us that Macbeth's murder of King Duncan is rooted in an Oedipus complex, the king being a father figure. Different approaches thus can illuminate different aspects of the work, just as they can emphasize or subordinate different elements in the plot or characters portrayed. But, again, in the next few pages we will deal with mutually incompatible interpretations of the meaning of Frost's poem — of what Frost's poem is about.

After reading the poem and the two interpretations written by students, spend a few minutes thinking about the questions that we raise after the second interpretation.

Robert Frost

Robert Frost (1874–1963) studied for part of one term at Dartmouth College in New Hampshire, then did odd jobs (including teaching), and from 1897 to 1899 was enrolled as a special student at Harvard. He then farmed in New Hampshire, published a few poems in newspapers, did some more teaching, and in 1912 left for England, where he hoped to achieve success as a writer. By 1915 he was known in England, and he returned to the United States. By the time of his death he was the nation's unofficial poet laureate. "Mending Wall" was first published in 1914.

Mending Wall

Something there is that doesn't love a wall,
That sends the frozen-ground-swell under it,
And spills the upper boulders in the sun;
And makes gaps even two can pass abreast.
The work of hunters is another thing: 5
I have come after them and made repair
Where they have left not one stone on a stone,
But they would have the rabbit out of hiding,
To please the yelping dogs. The gaps I mean,

No one has seen them made or heard them made,   10
But at spring mending-time we find them there.
I let my neighbor know beyond the hill;
And on a day we meet to walk the line
And set the wall between us once again.
We keep the wall between us as we go.   15
To each the boulders that have fallen to each.
And some are loaves and some so nearly balls
We have to use a spell to make them balance:
"Stay where you are until our backs are turned!"
We wear our fingers rough with handling them.   20
Oh, just another kind of outdoor game,
One on a side. It comes to little more:
There where it is we do not need the wall:
He is all pine and I am apple orchard.
My apple trees will never get across   25
And eat the cones under his pines, I tell him.
He only says, "Good fences make good neighbors."
Spring is the mischief in me, and I wonder
If I could put a notion in his head:
"*Why* do they make good neighbors? Isn't it   30
Where there are cows? But here there are no cows.
Before I built a wall I'd ask to know
What I was walling in or walling out,
And to whom I was like to give offense.
Something there is that doesn't love a wall,   35
That wants it down." I could say "Elves" to him,
But it's not elves exactly, and I'd rather
He said it for himself. I see him there
Bringing a stone grasped firmly by the top
In each hand, like an old-stone savage armed.   40
He moves in darkness as it seems to me,
Not of woods only and the shade of trees.
He will not go behind his father's saying,
And he likes having thought of it so well
He says again, "Good fences make good neighbors."   45

Jonathan Deutsch
Professor Walton
English 102
March 5, 2001

          The Deluded Speaker in Frost's "Mending Wall"
          Our discussions of "Mending Wall" in high
school showed that most people think Frost is
saying that walls between people are a bad
thing and that we should not try to separate
ourselves from each other unnecessarily. Perhaps
the wall, in this view, is a symbol for race
prejudice or religious differences, and Frost is
suggesting that these differences are minor and
that they should not keep us apart. In this common view, the neighbor's words, "Good fences
make good neighbors" (lines 27 and 45) show that
the neighbor is shortsighted. I disagree with
this view, but first I want to present the evidence that might be offered for it, so that we
can then see whether it really is substantial.
          First of all, someone might claim that in
lines 23 to 26 Frost offers a good argument
against walls:

          There where it is we do not need the wall:
          He is all pine and I am apple orchard.
          My apple trees will never get across
          And eat the cones under his pines, I tell
               him.

The neighbor does not offer a valid reply to
this argument; in fact, he doesn't offer any
argument at all but simply says, "Good fences
make good neighbors."

Deutsch 2

Another piece of evidence supposedly showing that the neighbor is wrong, it is said, is
found in Frost's description of him as "an old-
stone savage" and someone who "moves in darkness" (40, 41). And a third piece of evidence
is said to be that the neighbor "will not go
behind his father's saying" (43), but he merely
repeats the saying.

There is, however, another way of looking
at the poem. As I see it, the speaker is a very
snide and condescending person. He is confident
that he knows it all and that his neighbor is
an ignorant savage; he is even willing to tease
his supposedly ignorant neighbor. For instance,
the speaker admits to "the mischief in me"
(28), and he is confident that he could tell
the truth to the neighbor but arrogantly
thinks that it would be a more effective form
of teaching if the neighbor "said it for himself" (38).

The speaker is not only unpleasantly mischievous and condescending toward his neighbor,
but he is also shallow, for he does not see the
great wisdom that there is in proverbs. The
American Heritage Dictionary of the English
Language, Third Edition, defines a proverb as
"A short, pithy saying in frequent and widespread use that expresses a basic truth."
Frost, or at least the man who speaks this
poem, does not seem to realize that proverbs
express truths. He just dismisses them, and
he thinks the neighbor is wrong not to "go behind his father's saying" (43). But there is

Deutsch 3

a great deal of wisdom in the sayings of our
fathers. For instance, in the Bible (in the Old
Testament) there is a whole book of proverbs,
filled with wise sayings such as "Reprove
not a scorner, lest he hate thee: rebuke a
wise man, and he will love thee" (9:8); "He
that trusteth in his riches shall fall"
(11:28); "The way of a fool is right in his
own eyes" (12:15; this might be said of the
speaker of "Mending Wall"); "A soft answer
turneth away wrath" (15:1); and (to cut
short what could be a list many pages long),
"Whoso diggeth a pit shall fall therein"
(26:27).

The speaker is confident that walls are unnecessary and probably bad, but he doesn't realize that even where there are no cattle, walls
serve the valuable purpose of clearly marking
out our territory. They help us to preserve our
independence and our individuality. Walls--man-
made structures--are a sign of civilization. A
wall more or less says, "This is mine, but I respect that as yours." Frost's speaker is so confident of his shallow view that he makes fun of
his neighbor for repeating that "Good fences
make good neighbors" (27, 45). But he himself
repeats his own saying, "Something there is that
doesn't love a wall" (1, 35). And at least the
neighbor has age-old tradition on his side,
since the proverb is the saying of his father.
On the other hand, the speaker has only his own
opinion, and he can't even say what the "something" is.

Deutsch 4

It may be that Frost meant for us to laugh
at the neighbor and to take the side of the
speaker, but I think it is much more likely
that he meant for us to see that the speaker is
mean-spirited (or at least given to unpleasant
teasing), too self-confident, foolishly dismissing the wisdom of the old times, and entirely unaware that he has these unpleasant
characteristics.

Felicia Alonso
Professor Walton
English 102
March 5, 2001

The Debate in Robert Frost's "Mending Wall"

I think the first thing to say about
Frost's "Mending Wall" is this: The poem is not
about a debate over whether good fences do or
do not make good neighbors. It is about two debaters: One of the debaters is on the side of
vitality, and the other is on the side of an
unchanging, fixed--dead, we might say--tra-
dition.

How can we characterize the speaker? For
one thing, he is neighborly. Interestingly, it
is <u>he</u>, and not the neighbor, who initiates the
repairing of the wall: "I let my neighbor know
beyond the hill" (line 12). This seems strange,
since the speaker doesn't see any point in this
wall, whereas the neighbor is all in favor of
walls. Can we explain this apparent contradiction? Yes; the speaker is a good neighbor,
willing to do his share of the work and willing (perhaps in order not to upset his neighbor) to maintain an old tradition even though
he doesn't see its importance. It may not be
important, he thinks, but it is really rather
pleasant, "another kind of outdoor game" (21).
In fact, sometimes he even repairs fences on
his own, after hunters have destroyed them.

Second, we can say that the speaker is on
the side of nature. "Something there is that
doesn't love a wall," he says (1, 35), and of

course, the "something" is nature itself. Nature "sends the frozen-ground-swell" under the
wall and "spills the upper boulders in the sun;
/ And makes gaps even two can pass abreast" (2--
4). Notice that nature itself makes the gaps
and that "two can pass abreast"--that is,
people can walk together in a companionable
way. It is hard to imagine the neighbor walking
side by side with anyone.

  Third, we can say that the speaker has a
sense of humor. When he thinks of trying to get
his neighbor interested in the issue, he admits
that "the mischief" is in him (28), and he
amusingly attributes his playfulness to a natural force, the spring. He playfully toys with
the obviously preposterous idea of suggesting
to his neighbor that elves caused the stones to
fall, but he stops short of making this amusing
suggestion to his very serious neighbor. Still,
the mere thought assures us that he has a playful, genial nature, and the idea also again implies that not only the speaker but also some
sort of mysterious natural force dislikes
walls.

  Finally, though, of course, he thinks he
is right and that his neighbor is mistaken, he
at least is cautious in his view. He does not
call his neighbor "an old-stone savage" (40);
rather, he uses a simile ("like") and then adds
that this is only his opinion, so the opinion
is softened quite a bit. Here is the description of the neighbor, with underlining added
to clarify my point. The neighbor is . . .

<u>like</u> an old-stone savage armed. / He moves
in darkness <u>as it seems to me</u> . . . (40-41)

Of course, the only things we know about
the neighbor are those things that the speaker
chooses to tell us, so it is not surprising
that the speaker comes out ahead. He comes out
ahead not because he is right about walls (real
or symbolic) and his neighbor is wrong--that's
an issue that is not settled in the poem. He
comes out ahead because he is a more interesting figure, someone who is neighborly, thoughtful, playful. Yes, maybe he seems to us to feel
superior to his neighbor, but we can be certain
that he doesn't cause his neighbor any embar-
rassment. Take the very end of the poem. The
speaker tells us that the neighbor

> . . . will not go behind his father's say-
> ing,
> And he likes having thought of it so well
> He says again, "Good fences make good
> neighbors."

The speaker is telling <u>us</u> that the neighbor
is utterly unoriginal and that the neighbor confuses <u>remembering</u> something with <u>thinking</u>. But
the speaker doesn't get into an argument; he
doesn't rudely challenge his neighbor and demand
reasons, which might force the neighbor to see
that he can't think for himself. And in fact we
probably like the neighbor just as he is, and we
don't want him to change his mind. The words

Alonso 4

that ring in our ears are not the speaker's but the neighbor's: "Good fences make good neighbors." The speaker of the poem is a good neighbor. After all, one can hardly be more neighborly than to let the neighbor have the last word.

Topics for Critical Thinking and Writing

1. State the thesis of each essay. Do you believe the theses are sufficiently clear and appear sufficiently early in the essays?

2. Consider the evidence that each essay offers by way of supporting its thesis. Do you find some of the evidence unconvincing? Explain.

3. Putting aside the question of which interpretation you prefer, comment on the organization of each essay. Is the organization clear? Do you want to propose some other pattern that you think might be more effective?

4. Consult the Checklist for Peer Review on page 210, and offer comments on one of the two essays. Or: If you were the instructor in the course in which these two essays were submitted, what might be your final comments on each of them? Or: Write an analysis (250–500 words) of the strengths and weaknesses of either essay.

EXERCISES: Reading a Poem and Reading Two Stories

Andrew Marvell

Andrew Marvell (1621–1678), born in Hull, England, and educated at Trinity College, Cambridge, was traveling in Europe when the civil war between the royalists and the puritans broke out in England in 1642. The pu-

*ritans were victorious and established the Commonwealth (the monarchy
was restored later, in 1660), and Marvell became a tutor to the daughter of
the victorious Lord-General. In 1657 he became an assistant to the blind
poet John Milton, who held the title of Latin Secretary (Latin was the language of international diplomacy). In 1659 Marvell was elected to represent
Hull in Parliament. As a man of letters, during his lifetime he was known
chiefly for some satiric prose and poetry; most of the writings for which he is
now esteemed were published posthumously. The following poem was first
published in 1681.*

To His Coy Mistress°

Had we but world enough, and time,
This coyness,° Lady, were no crime.
We would sit down, and think which way
To walk, and pass our long love's day.
Thou by the Indian Ganges' side   5
Shouldst rubies find; I by the tide
Of Humber° would complain. I would
Love you ten years before the Flood,
And you should, if you please, refuse
Till the Conversion of the Jews.°   10
My vegetable° love should grow
Vaster than empires and more slow;
An hundred years should go to praise
Thine eyes, and on thy forehead gaze;
Two hundred to adore each breast,   15
But thirty thousand to the rest;
An age at least to every part,
And the last age should show your heart.
For, Lady, you deserve this state,°
Nor would I love at lower rate.   20
    But at my back I always hear
Time's wingèd chariot hurrying near;
And yonder all before us lie
Deserts of vast eternity.
Thy beauty shall no more be found,   25
Nor, in thy marble vault, shall sound

Mistress Beloved woman.   **2 coyness** Reluctance.   **7 Humber** An estuary at Hull,
Marvell's birthplace.   **10 the Conversion of the Jews** Something that would take
place in the remote future, at the end of history.   **11 vegetable** Vegetative or growing.
19 state Ceremonious treatment.

My echoing song; then worms shall try°
That long-preserved virginity,
And your quaint° honour turn to dust,
And into ashes all my lust: 30
The grave's a fine and private place,
But none, I think, do there embrace.
   Now therefore, while the youthful hue
Sits on thy skin like morning dew,
And while thy willing soul transpires   35
At every pore with instant fires,
Now let us sport us while we may,
And now, like amorous birds of prey,
Rather at once our time devour
Than languish in his slow-chapt° power.   40
Let us roll all our strength and all
Our sweetness up into one ball,
And tear our pleasures with rough strife
Thorough° the iron gates of life:
Thus, though we cannot make our sun   45
Stand still,° yet we will make him run.

Topics for Critical Thinking and Writing

1. The motif that life is short and that we should seize the day (Latin: *carpe diem*) is old. Marvell's poem, in fact, probably has its ultimate source in a classical text called *The Greek Anthology*, a collection of about six thousand short Greek poems composed between the first century B.C. and the tenth century A.D. One poem goes thus, in a fairly literal translation:

   You spare your maidenhead, and to what profit? For when you come to Hades you will not find your lover, girl. Among the living are the delights of Venus, but, maiden, we shall lie in the underworld mere bones and dust.

   If you find Marvell's poem more impressive, offer reasons for your belief.

2. A student, working from the translation just given, produced this rhyming version:

   You keep your virginity, but to what end?
   Below, in Hades, you won't find your friend.

---

27 try Test.   **29 quaint** Fastidious or finicky, with a pun on a coarse word defined in an Elizabethan dictionary as "a woman's privities."   **40 slow-chapt** Slow-jawed. **44 Thorough** Through.   **45–46 we cannot . . . still** An allusion to Joshua, the ancient Hebrew who, according to the Book of Joshua (10.12–13), made the sun stand still.

> On earth we enjoy Venus' sighs and moans;
> Buried below, we are senseless bones.

What do you think of this version? Why? Prepare your own version — your instructor may divide the class into groups of four, and each group can come up with a collaborative version — and then compare it with other versions, giving reasons for your preferences.

3. Marvell's poem takes the form of a syllogism (see pp. 67–72). It can be divided into three parts:

   1. "Had we" (that is, "If we had") (line 1), a supposition, or suppositional premise;
   2. "But at my back" (line 21), a refutation;
   3. "Now therefore" (line 33), a deduction.

   Look closely at the poem and develop the argument using these three parts, devoting a few sentences to each part.

4. A student wrote of this poem:

   > As a Christian I can't accept the lover's statement that "yonder all before us lie / Deserts of vast eternity" (lines 23–24). The poem may contain beautiful lines, and it may offer clever reasoning, but the reasoning is based on what my religion tells me is wrong. I not only cannot accept the idea of the poem, but I also cannot enjoy the poem, since it presents a false view of reality.

   What assumptions is this student making about a reader's response to a work of literature? Do you agree or disagree? Why?

5. Here are three additional comments by students. For each, list the writer's assumptions, and then evaluate each comment. You may agree or disagree, in whole or in part, with any comment, but give your reasons.

   > A. The poem is definitely clever, and that is part of what is wrong with it. It is a blatant attempt at seduction. The man seems to think he is smarter than the woman he is speaking to, and he "proves" that she should go to bed with him. Since we don't hear her side of the argument, Marvell implies that she has nothing to say and that his argument is sound. What the poet doesn't seem to understand is that there is such a thing as virtue, and a woman need not sacrifice virtue just because death is inevitable.

   > B. On the surface, "To His Coy Mistress" is an attempt to persuade a woman to go to bed with the speaker, but the poem is really less about sex than it is about the terrifying shortness of life.

   > C. This is not a love poem. The speaker admits that his impulse is "lust" (line 30), and he makes fun of the girl's conception of honor and virginity. If we enjoy this poem at all, our enjoyment must be in the hope that this would-be date-rapist is unsuccessful.

6. Read the poem several times slowly, perhaps even aloud. Do certain lines seem especially moving, especially memorable? If so, which ones? Give reasons for your belief.

7. In *On Deconstruction* (1982), a study of contemporary literary theory, Jonathan Culler remarks that feminist criticism has often stressed "read-

ing as a woman." This concept, Culler says, affirms the "continuity between women's experience of social and familial structures and their experiences as readers." Do you agree with his suggestion that men and
women often interpret literary works differently? Consider Marvell's
poem in particular: Identify and discuss phrases and images in it to which
men and women readers might (or might not) respond very differently.

8. A small point, but perhaps one of some interest. In the original text, line
34 ends with *glew*, not with *dew*. Most editors assume that the printer
made an error, and—looking for a word to rhyme with *hue*—they replace *glew* with *dew*. Another possible emendation is *lew*, an archaic
word meaning "warmth." But the original reading has been defended,
as a variant of the word *glow*. Your preference? Your reasons?

Kate Chopin

*Kate Chopin (1851–1904) was born in St. Louis and named Katherine
O'Flaherty. At the age of nineteen she married a cotton broker in New Or-
leans, Oscar Chopin (the name is pronounced something like "show pan"),
who was descended from the early French settlers in Louisiana. After her
husband's death in 1883, Kate Chopin turned to writing fiction. The following story was first published in 1894.*

The Story of an Hour

Knowing that Mrs. Mallard was afflicted with a heart trouble, great
care was taken to break to her as gently as possible the news of her husband's death.

It was her sister Josephine who told her, in broken sentences,
veiled hints that revealed in half concealing. Her husband's friend
Richards was there, too, near her. It was he who had been in the newspaper office when intelligence of the railroad disaster was received,
with Brently Mallard's name leading the list of "killed." He had only
taken the time to assure himself of its truth by a second telegram, and
had hastened to forestall any less careful, less tender friend in bearing
the sad message.

She did not hear the story as many women have heard the same,
with a paralyzed inability to accept its significance. She wept at once,
with sudden, wild abandonment, in her sister's arms. When the storm of
grief had spent itself she went away to her room alone. She would have
no one follow her.

There stood, facing the open window, a comfortable, roomy armchair. Into this she sank, pressed down by a physical exhaustion that
haunted her body and seemed to reach into her soul.

She could see in the open square before her house the tops of trees   5
that were all aquiver with the new spring life. The delicious breath of
rain was in the air. In the street below a peddler was crying his wares.

The notes of a distant song which some one was singing reached her faintly, and countless sparrows were twittering in the eaves.

There were patches of blue sky showing here and there through the clouds that had met and piled one above the other in the west facing her window.

She sat with her head thrown back upon the cushion of the chair, quite motionless, except when a sob came up into her throat and shook her, as a child who has cried itself to sleep continues to sob in its dreams.

She was young, with a fair, calm face, whose lines bespoke repression and even a certain strength. But now there was a dull stare in her eyes, whose gaze was fixed away off yonder on one of those patches of blue sky. It was not a glance of reflection, but rather indicated a suspension of intelligent thought.

There was something coming to her and she was waiting for it, fearfully. What was it? She did not know; it was too subtle and elusive to name. But she felt it, creeping out of the sky, reaching toward her through the sounds, the scents, the color that filled the air.

Now her bosom rose and fell tumultuously. She was beginning to 10 recognize this thing that was approaching to possess her, and she was striving to beat it back with her will—as powerless as her two white slender hands would have been.

When she abandoned herself a little whispered word escaped her slightly parted lips. She said it over and over under her breath: "Free, free, free!" The vacant stare and the look of terror that had followed it went from her eyes. They stayed keen and bright. Her pulses beat fast, and the coursing blood warmed and relaxed every inch of her body.

She did not stop to ask if it were not a monstrous joy that held her. A clear and exalted perception enabled her to dismiss the suggestion as trivial.

She knew that she would weep again when she saw the kind, tender hands folded in death; the face that had never looked save with love upon her, fixed and gray and dead. But she saw beyond that bitter moment a long procession of years to come that would belong to her absolutely. And she opened and spread her arms out to them in welcome.

There would be no one to live for her during those coming years; she would live for herself. There would be no powerful will bending her in that blind persistence with which men and women believe they have a right to impose a private will upon a fellow creature. A kind intention or a cruel intention made the act seem no less a crime as she looked upon it in that brief moment of illumination.

And yet she had loved him—sometimes. Often she had not. What 15 did it matter! What could love, the unsolved mystery, count for in face of this possession of self-assertion which she suddenly recognized as the strongest impulse of her being.

"Free! Body and soul free!" she kept whispering.

Josephine was kneeling before the closed door with her lips to the keyhole, imploring for admission. "Louise, open the door! I beg; open the door—you will make yourself ill. What are you doing, Louise? For heaven's sake open the door."

"Go away. I am not making myself ill." No; she was drinking in a very elixir of life through that open window.

Her fancy was running riot along those days ahead of her. Spring days, and summer days, and all sorts of days that would be her own. She breathed a quick prayer that life might be long. It was only yesterday she had thought with a shudder that life might be long.

She arose at length and opened the door to her sister's importuni- 20
ties. There was a feverish triumph in her eyes, and she carried herself unwittingly like a goddess of Victory. She clasped her sister's waist, and together they descended the stairs. Richards stood waiting for them at the bottom.

Some one was opening the front door with a latchkey. It was Brently Mallard who entered, a little travel-stained, composedly carrying his gripsack and umbrella. He had been far from the scene of accident, and did not even know there had been one. He stood amazed at Josephine's piercing cry; at Richards' quick motion to screen him from the view of his wife.

But Richards was too late.

When the doctors came they said she had died of heart disease—of joy that kills.

Topics for Critical Thinking and Writing

Read the following assertions, and consider whether you agree or disagree, and why. For each assertion, draft a paragraph with your arguments.

1. The railroad accident is a symbol of the destructiveness of the industrial revolution.
2. The story claims that women rejoice in the deaths of their husbands.
3. Mrs. Mallard's death at the end is a just punishment for the joy she takes in her husband's death.
4. The story is rich in irony. Some examples: (1) The other characters think she is grieving, but she is rejoicing; (2) she prays for a long life, but she dies almost immediately; (3) the doctors say she died of "the joy that kills," but they think her joy was seeing her husband alive.
5. The story is excellent because it has a surprise ending.

Kate Chopin

For a biographical note on Chopin, see page 444. Chopin wrote the following story in 1898 but never tried to publish it, presumably because she knew it would be unacceptable to the audience of her times. "The Storm" depicts the same characters as an earlier story, "The 'Cadian Ball," in which Alcée is about to run away with Calixta when Clarisse captures him as a husband.

The Storm

I

The leaves were so still that even Bibi thought it was going to rain. Bobinôt, who was accustomed to converse on terms of perfect equality with his little son, called the child's attention to certain somber clouds that were rolling with sinister intention from the west, accompanied by a sullen, threatening roar. They were at Friedheimer's store and decided to remain there till the storm had passed. They sat within the door on two empty kegs. Bibi was four years old and looked very wise.

"Mama'll be 'fraid, yes," he suggested with blinking eyes.

"She'll shut the house. Maybe she got Sylvie helpin' her this evenin'," Bobinôt responded reassuringly.

"No; she ent got Sylvie. Sylvie was helpin' her yistiday," piped Bibi.

Bobinôt arose and going across to the counter purchased a can of   5
shrimps, of which Calixta was very fond. Then he returned to his perch on the keg and sat stolidly holding the can of shrimps while the storm burst. It shook the wooden store and seemed to be ripping great furrows in the distant field. Bibi laid his little hand on his father's knee and was not afraid.

II

Calixta, at home, felt no uneasiness for their safety. She sat at a side window sewing furiously on a sewing machine. She was greatly occupied and did not notice the approaching storm. But she felt very warm and often stopped to mop her face on which the perspiration gathered in beads. She unfastened her white sacque at the throat. It began to grow dark, and suddenly realizing the situation she got up hurriedly and went about closing windows and doors.

Out on the small front gallery[1] she had hung Bobinôt's Sunday clothes to air and she hastened out to gather them before the rain fell. As she stepped outside, Alcée Laballière rode in at the gate. She had not seen him very often since her marriage, and never alone. She stood there with Bobinôt's coat in her hands, and the big rain drops began to fall. Alcée rode his horse under the shelter of a side projection where the chickens had huddled and there were plows and a harrow piled up in the corner.

"May I come and wait on your gallery till the storm is over, Calixta?" he asked.

"Come 'long in, M'sieur Alcée."

His voice and her own startled her as if from a trance, and she seized   10
Bobinôt's vest. Alcée, mounting to the porch, grabbed the trousers and

---

[1]**gallery** Porch, or passageway along a wall, open to the air but protected by a roof supported by columns.

snatched Bibi's braided jacket that was about to be carried away by a sudden gust of wind. He expressed an intention to remain outside, but it was soon apparent that he might as well have been out in the open: the water beat in upon the boards in driving sheets, and he went inside, closing the door after him. It was even necessary to put something beneath the door to keep the water out.

"My! what a rain! It's good two years sence it rain' like that," exclaimed Calixta as she rolled up a piece of bagging and Alcée helped her to thrust it beneath the crack.

She was a little fuller of figure than five years before when she married; but she had lost nothing of her vivacity. Her blue eyes still retained their melting quality; and her yellow hair, dishevelled by the wind and rain, kinked more stubbornly than ever abut her ears and temples.

The rain beat upon the low, shingled roof with a force and clatter that threatened to break an entrance and deluge them there. They were in the dining room—the sitting room—the general utility room. Adjoining was her bed room, with Bibi's couch along side her own. The door stood open, and the room with its white, monumental bed, its closed shutters, looked dim and mysterious.

Alcée flung himself into a rocker and Calixta nervously began to gather up from the floor the lengths of a cotton sheet which she had been sewing.

"If this keeps up, *Dieu sait*[2] if the levees goin' to stan' it!" she exclaimed.   15

"What have you got to do with the levees?"

"I got enough to do! An' there's Bobinôt with Bibi out in that storm—if he only didn' left Friedheimer's!"

"Let us hope, Calixta, that Bobinôt's got sense enough to come in out of a cyclone."

She went and stood at the window with a greatly disturbed look on her face. She wiped the frame that was clouded with moisture. It was stiflingly hot. Alcée got up and joined her at the window, looking over her shoulder. The rain was coming down in sheets obscuring the view of far-off cabins and enveloping the distant wood in a gray mist. The playing of the lightning was incessant. A bolt struck a tall chinaberry tree at the edge of the field. It filled all visible space with a blinding glare and the crash seemed to invade the very boards they stood upon.

Calixta put her hands to her eyes, and with a cry, staggered backward. Alcée's arm encircled her, and for an instant he drew her close and spasmodically to him.   20

"*Bonté!*"[3] she cried, releasing herself from his encircling arm and retreating from the window, "the house'll go next! If I only knew w'ere Bibi was!" She would not compose herself; she would not be seated.

[2]**Dieu sait** God knows.
[3]**Bonté!** Goodness!

Alcée clasped her shoulders and looked into her face. The contact of her warm, palpitating body when he had unthinkingly drawn her into his arms, had aroused all the old-time infatuation and desire for her flesh.

"Calixta," he said, "don't be frightened. Nothing can happen. The house is too low to be struck, with so many tall trees standing about. There! aren't you going to be quiet? say, aren't you?" He pushed her hair back from her face that was warm and steaming. Her lips were as red and moist as pomegranate seed. Her white neck and a glimpse of her full, firm bosom disturbed him powerfully. As she glanced up at him the fear in her liquid blue eyes had given place to a drowsy gleam that unconsciously betrayed a sensuous desire. He looked down into her eyes and there was nothing for him to do but to gather her lips in a kiss. It reminded him of Assumption.[4]

"Do you remember—in Assumption, Calixta?" he asked in a low voice broken by passion. Oh! she remembered; for in Assumption he had kissed her and kissed and kissed her; until his senses would well nigh fail, and to save her he would resort to a desperate flight. If she was not an immaculate dove in those days, she was still inviolate; a passionate creature whose very defenselessness had made her defense, against which his honor forbade him to prevail. Now—well, now—her lips seemed in a manner free to be tasted, as well as her round, white throat and her whiter breasts.

They did not heed the crashing torrents, and the roar of the elements made her laugh as she lay in his arms. She was a revelation in that dim, mysterious chamber; as white as the couch she lay upon. Her firm, elastic flesh that was knowing for the first time its birthright, was like a creamy lily that the sun invites to contribute its breath and perfume to the undying life of the world.

The generous abundance of her passion, without guile or trickery, 25 was like a white flame which penetrated and found response in depths of his own sensuous nature that had never yet been reached.

When he touched her breasts they gave themselves up in quivering ecstasy, inviting his lips. Her mouth was a fountain of delight. And when he possessed her, they seemed to swoon together at the very borderland of life's mystery.

He stayed cushioned upon her, breathless, dazed, enervated, with his heart beating like a hammer upon her. With one hand she clasped his head, her lips lightly touching his forehead. The other hand stroked with a soothing rhythm his muscular shoulders.

The growl of the thunder was distant and passing away. The rain beat softly upon the shingles, inviting them to drowsiness and sleep. But they dared not yield.

The rain was over; and the sun was turning the glistening green world into a place of gems. Calixta, on the gallery, watched Alcée ride

---

[4]**Assumption** A parish (a county) in southeast Louisiana.

away. He turned and smiled at her with a beaming face; and she lifted her pretty chin in the air and laughed aloud.

III

Bobinôt and Bibi, trudging home, stopped without at the cistern to make themselves presentable. 30

"My! Bibi, w'at will yo' mama say! You ought to be ashame'. You oughtn' put on those good pants. Look at 'em! An' that mud on yo' collar! How you got that mud on yo' collar, Bibi? I never saw such a boy!" Bibi was the picture of pathetic resignation. Bobinôt was the embodiment of serious solicitude as he strove to remove from his own person and his son's the signs of their tramp over heavy roads and through wet fields. He scraped the mud off Bibi's bare legs and feet with a stick and carefully removed all traces from his heavy brogans. Then, prepared for the worst—the meeting with an over-scrupulous housewife, they entered cautiously at the back door.

Calixta was preparing supper. She had set the table and was dripping coffee at the hearth. She sprang up as they came in.

"Oh, Bobinôt! You back! My! but I was uneasy. W'ere yu been during the rain? An Bibi? he ain't wet? he ain't hurt?" She had clasped Bibi and was kissing him effusively. Bobinôt's explanations and apologies which he had been composing all along the way, died on his lips as Calixta felt him to see if he were dry, and seemed to express nothing but satisfaction at their safe return.

"I brought you some shrimps, Calixta," offered Bobinôt, hauling the can from his ample side pocket and laying it on the table.

"Shrimps! Oh, Bobinôt! you too good fo' anything!" and she gave him a smacking kiss on the cheek that resounded. "*J'vous reponds,*[5] we'll have a feas' to night! umph-umph!" 35

Bobinôt and Bibi began to relax and enjoy themselves, and when the three seated themselves at the table they laughed much and so loud that anyone might have heard them as far away as Laballière's.

IV

Alcée Laballière wrote to his wife, Clarisse, that night. It was a loving letter, full of tender solicitude. He told her not to hurry back, but if she and the babies liked it at Biloxi, to stay a month longer. He was getting on nicely; and though he missed them, he was willing to bear the separation a while longer—realizing that their health and pleasure were the first things to be considered.

---

[5]**J'vous reponds** Take my word; let me tell you.

V

As for Clarisse, she was charmed upon receiving her husband's letter. She and the babies were doing well. The society was agreeable; many of her old friends and acquaintances were at the bay. And the first free breath since her marriage seemed to restore the pleasant liberty of her maiden days. Devoted as she was to her husband, their intimate conjugal life was something which she was more than willing to forego for a while.

So the storm passed and everyone was happy.

Topics for Critical Thinking and Writing

1. Assume that you are trying to describe "The Storm" to someone who has not read it. Briefly summarize the action, and then explain why you think "The Storm" is (or is not) worth reading.

2. Chopin's title, "The Storm," in fact refers to two storms: the cyclone that sweeps through the bayou and the inner storm of passion felt by both Alcée and Calixta. Both storms erupt and subside together. Are these parallels too obvious to be effective, or does the former storm effectively lead into and provide a background for the latter?

3. Write an essay arguing that "The Storm" is (or is not) immoral or (a different thing) amoral. (By the way, because one of her slightly earlier works, a short novel called *The Awakening,* was widely condemned as sordid, Chopin was unable to find a publisher for "The Storm.")

4. You are writing to a high school teacher, urging that one of the two stories by Chopin be taught in high school. Which one do you recommend, and why?

THINKING ABOUT
THE EFFECTS OF LITERATURE

Works of art are artifacts—things constructed, made up, fashioned, just like houses and automobiles. In analyzing works of literature it is therefore customary to keep one's eye on the complex, constructed object and not simply tell the reader how one feels about it. Instead of reporting their feelings, critics usually analyze the relationships between the parts and the relationship of the parts to the whole.

For instance, in talking about literature we can examine the relationship of plot to character, of one character to another, or of one stanza in a poem to the next. Still, although we may try to engage in this sort of analysis as dispassionately as possible, we all know that inevitably we are not only examining something out there, but are also examining our own responses. Why? Because literature has an effect on us. Indeed, it probably has several kinds of effects, ranging from short-range emotional responses ("I really enjoyed this," "I burst out laughing," "It revolted me") to long-range effects ("I have always tried to live up to a line in *Hamlet*, 'This above all, to thine own self be true'"). Let's first look at, very briefly, immediate emotional responses.

Analysis usually begins with a response: "This is marvelous," or "What a bore," and we then go on to try to account for our response. A friend mentions a book or a film to us, and we say, "I couldn't stay with it for five minutes." The friend expresses surprise, and we then go on to explain, giving reasons (to the friend and also to ourselves) why we couldn't stay with it. Perhaps the book seemed too remote from life, or perhaps, on the other hand, it seemed to be nothing more than a transcript of the boring talk that we can overhear on a bus or in an elevator.

In such discussions, when we draw on our responses, as we must, the work may disappear; we find ourselves talking about ourselves. Let's take two extreme examples: "I can't abide *Huckleberry Finn*. How am I expected to enjoy a so-called masterpiece that has a character in it called 'Nigger Jim.'" Or: "T. S. Eliot's anti-Semitism is too much for me to take. Don't talk to me about Eliot's skill with meter, when he has such lines as 'Rachel, *née* Rabinovitch / Tears at the grapes with murderous paws.'"

Although everyone agrees that literature can evoke this sort of strong emotional response, not everyone agrees on how much value we should put on our personal experience. Several of the Topics for Critical Thinking and Writing on page 453 invite you to reflect on this issue.

What about the *consequences of the effects* of literature? Does literature shape our character and therefore influence our behavior? It is generally believed that it does have an effect. One hears, for example, that literature (like travel) is broadening, that it makes us aware of, and tolerant of, kinds of behavior that differ from our own and from what we see around us. One of the chief arguments against pornography, for instance, is that it desensitizes us, makes us too tolerant of abusive relationships, relationships in which people (usually men) use other people (usually women) as mere things or instruments for pleasure. (A contrary view should be mentioned: Some people argue that pornography provides a relatively harmless outlet for fantasies that otherwise might be given release in the real world. In this view, pornography acts as a sort of safety valve.)

Discussions of the effects of literature that get into the popular press almost always involve pornography, but other topics are also the subjects of controversy. For instance, in recent decades parents and educators have been much concerned with fairy tales. Does the violence in some fairy tales ("Little Red Riding Hood," "The Three Little Pigs") have a bad effect on children? Do some of the stories teach the wrong lessons, implying that women should be passive, men active ("Sleeping Beauty," for instance, in which the sleeping woman is brought to life by the action of the handsome prince)? The Greek philosopher Plato (427–347 B.C.) strongly believed that the literature we hear or read shapes our later behavior, and since most of the ancient Greek traditional stories (notably Homer's *Odyssey* and *Iliad*) celebrate acts of love and war rather than of justice, he prohibited the reading of such material in his ideal society. (We reprint a relevant passage from Plato on page 454.)

Topics for Critical Thinking and Writing

1. If you have responded strongly (favorably or unfavorably) to some aspect of the social content of a literary work—for instance, its depiction of women or of a particular minority group—in an essay of 250 to 500 words analyze the response, and try to determine whether you are talking chiefly about yourself or the work. (Two works widely regarded as literary masterpieces but nonetheless often banned from classrooms are Shakespeare's *The Merchant of Venice* and Mark Twain's *Huckleberry Finn.* If you have read either of these, you may want to write about it and your response.) Can we really see literary value—*really* see it—in a work that deeply offends us?

2. Most people believe that literature influences life—that in some perhaps mysterious way it helps to shape character. Certainly anyone who believes that some works should be censored, or at least should be made unavailable to minors, assumes that they can have a bad influence, so why not assume that other works can have a good influence?

   Read the following brief claims about literature, then choose one and write a 250-word essay offering support or taking issue with it.

   The pen is mightier than the sword. — ANONYMOUS

   The writer isn't made in a vacuum. Writers are witnesses. The reason we need writers is because we need witnesses to this terrifying century. — E. L. DOCTOROW

   When we read of human beings behaving in certain ways, with the approval of the author, who gives his benedictions to this behavior by his attitude towards the result of the behavior arranged by himself, we can be influenced towards behaving in the same way. — T. S. ELIOT

   Poetry makes nothing happen. — W. H. AUDEN

   Literature is *without proofs.* By which it must be understood that it cannot prove, not only *what* it says, but even that it is worth the trouble of saying it. — ROLAND BARTHES

   Of course the illusion of art is to make one believe that great literature is very close to life, but exactly the opposite is true. Life is amorphous, literature is formal. — FRANÇOISE SAGAN

3. At least since the time of Plato (see the piece directly following) some thoughtful people have wanted to ban certain works of literature because they allegedly stimulate the wrong sorts of pleasure or cause us to take pleasure in the wrong sorts of things. Consider, by way of

comparison, bullfighting and cockfighting. Of course, they cause pain to the animals, but branding animals also causes pain and is not banned. Bullfighting and cockfighting probably are banned in the United States largely because most of us believe that people should not take pleasure in these activities. Now to return to literature: Should some kinds of writing be prohibited because they offer the wrong sorts of pleasure?

Plato

Plato (427–347 B.C.), an Athenian aristocrat by birth, was the student of one great philosopher (Socrates) and the teacher of another (Aristotle). His legacy of more than two dozen dialogues — imaginary discussions between Socrates and one or more other speakers, usually young Athenians — has been of such influence that the whole of Western philosophy can be characterized, A. N. Whitehead wrote, as "a series of footnotes to Plato." Plato's interests encompassed the full range of topics in philosophy: ethics, politics, logic, metaphysics, epistemology, aesthetics, psychology, and education.

This selection from Plato's Republic, *one of his best-known and longest dialogues, is about the education suitable for the rulers of an ideal society. The* Republic *begins, typically, with an investigation into the nature of justice. Socrates (who speaks for Plato) convincingly explains to Glaucon that we cannot reasonably expect to achieve a just society unless we devote careful attention to the moral education of the young men who are scheduled in later life to become the rulers. (Here as elsewhere, Plato's elitism and aristocratic bias shows itself; as readers of* The Republic *soon learn, Plato is no admirer of democracy or of a classless society.) Plato cares as much about what the educational curriculum should exclude as what it should include. His special target was the common practice in his day of using for pedagogy the Homeric tales and other stories about the gods. He readily embraces the principle of censorship, as the excerpt explains, because he thinks it is a necessary means to achieve the ideal society.*

"The Greater Part of the Stories Current Today We Shall Have to Reject"

"What kind of education shall we give them then? We shall find it difficult to improve on the time-honored distinction between the physical training we give to the body and the education we give to the mind and character."

"True."

"And we shall begin by educating mind and character, shall we not?"

"Of course."

"In this education you would include stories, would you not?"   5

"Yes."

"These are of two kinds, true stories and fiction.[1] Our education must use both, and start with fiction."

"I don't know what you mean."

"But you know that we begin by telling children stories. These are, in general, fiction, though they contain some truth. And we tell children stories before we start them on physical training."

"That is so."   10

"That is what I meant by saying that we must start to educate the mind before training the body."

"You are right," he said.

"And the first step, as you know, is always what matters most, particularly when we are dealing with those who are young and tender. That is the time when they are easily molded and when any impression we choose to make leaves a permanent mark."

"That is certainly true."

"Shall we therefore readily allow our children to listen to any 15 stories made up by anyone, and to form opinions that are for the most part the opposite of those we think they should have when they grow up?"

"We certainly shall not."

"Then it seems that our first business is to supervise the production of stories, and choose only those we think suitable, and reject the rest. We shall persuade mothers and nurses to tell our chosen stories to their children, and by means of them to mold their minds and characters which are more important than their bodies. The greater part of the stories current today we shall have to reject."

"Which are you thinking of?"

"We can take some of the major legends as typical. For all, whether major or minor, should be cast in the same mold and have the same effect. Do you agree?"

"Yes: but I'm not sure which you refer to as major."   20

"The stories in Homer and Hesiod and the poets. For it is the poets who have always made up fictions and stories to tell to men."

"What sort of stories do you mean and what fault do you find in them?"

"The worst fault possible," I replied, "especially if the fiction is an ugly one."

"And what is that?"

"Misrepresenting the nature of gods and heroes, like a portrait 25 painter whose portraits bear no resemblance to their originals."

"That is a fault which certainly deserves censure. But give me more details."

[1]The Greek word *pseudos* and its corresponding verb meant not only "fiction"—stories, tales—but also "what is not true" and so, in suitable contexts, "lies": and this ambiguity should be borne in mind. [Editors' note: All footnotes are by the translator, but some have been omitted.]

"Well, on the most important of subjects, there is first and fore-most the foul story about Ouranos[2] and the things Hesiod says he did, and the revenge Cronos took on him. While the story of what Cronos did, and what he suffered at the hands of his son, is not fit as it is to be lightly repeated to the young and foolish, even if it were true; it would be best to say nothing about it, or if it must be told, tell it to a select few under oath of secrecy, at a rite which required, to restrict it still further, the sacrifice not of a mere pig but of something large and difficult to get."

"These certainly are awkward stories."

"And they shall not be repeated in our state, Adeimantus," I said. "Nor shall any young audience be told that anyone who commits hor-rible crimes, or punishes his father unmercifully, is doing nothing out of the ordinary but merely what the first and greatest of the gods have done before."

"I entirely agree," said Adeimantus, "that these stories are un-   30
suitable."

"Nor can we permit stories of wars and plots and battles among the gods; they are quite untrue, and if we want our prospective guardians to believe that quarrelsomeness is one of the worst of evils, we must cer-tainly not let them be told the story of the Battle of the Giants or embroi-der it on robes, or tell them other tales about many and various quarrels between gods and heroes and their friends and relations. On the con-trary, if we are to persuade them that no citizen has ever quarreled with any other, because it is sinful, our old men and women must tell chil-dren stories with this end in view from the first, and we must compel our poets to tell them similar stories when they grow up. But we can admit to our state no stories about Hera being tied up by her son, or Hep-haestus being flung out of Heaven by his father for trying to help his mother when she was getting a beating, nor any of Homer's Battles of the Gods, whether their intention is allegorical or not. Children cannot distinguish between what is allegory and what isn't, and opinions formed at that age are usually difficult to eradicate or change; we should therefore surely regard it as of the utmost importance that the first stories they hear shall aim at encouraging the highest excellence of character."

"Your case is a good one," he agreed, "but if someone wanted de-tails, and asked what stories we were thinking of, what should we say?"

To which I replied, "My dear Adeimantus, you and I are not engaged on writing stories but on founding a state. And the founders of a state, though they must know the type of story the poet must produce, and reject any that do not conform to that type, need not write them themselves."

---

[2]**Ouranos** (the sky), the original supreme god, was castrated by his son Cronos to separate him from Gaia (mother earth). Cronos was in turn deposed by Zeus in a struggle in which Zeus was helped by the Titans.

"True: but what are the lines on which our poets must work when they deal with the gods?"

"Roughly as follows," I said. "God must surely always be represented 35 as he really is, whether the poet is writing epic, lyric, or tragedy."

"He must."

"And in reality of course god is good, and he must be so described."

"Certainly."

"But nothing good is harmful, is it?"[3]

"I think not."   40

"Then can anything that is not harmful do harm?"

"No."

"And can what does no harm do evil?"

"No again."

"And can what does no evil be the cause of any evil?"   45

"How could it?"

"Well then; is the good beneficial?"

"Yes."

"So it must be the cause of well-being."

"Yes."   50

"So the good is not the cause of everything, but only of states of well-being and not of evil."

"Most certainly," he agreed.

"Then god, being good, cannot be responsible for everything, as is commonly said, but only for a small part of human life, for the greater part of which he has no responsibility. For we have a far smaller share of good than of evil, and while god must be held to be the sole cause of good, we must look for some factors other than god as cause of the evil."

"I think that's very true," he said.

"So we cannot allow Homer or any other poet to make such a stupid 55 mistake about the gods, as when he says that

> Zeus has two jars standing on the floor of his palace, full of fates, good
> in one and evil in the other

and that the man to whom Zeus allots a mixture of both has 'varying fortunes sometimes good and sometimes bad,' while the man to whom he allots unmixed evil is 'chased by ravening despair over the face of the earth.'[4] Nor can we allow references to Zeus as 'dispenser of good and evil.' And we cannot approve if it is said that Athene and Zeus prompted

---

[3]The reader of the following passage should bear the following ambiguities in mind: (1) the Greek word for good (*agathos*) can mean (a) morally good, (b) beneficial or advantageous; (2) the Greek word for evil (*kakos*) can also mean harm or injury; (3) the adverb of *agathos* (*eu*—the well) can imply either morally right or prosperous. The word translated "cause of" could equally well be rendered "responsible for."

[4]Quotations from Homer are generally taken from the translations by Dr. Rieu in the Penguin series. At times (as here) the version quoted by Plato differs slightly from the accepted text.

the breach of solemn treaty and oath by Pandarus, or that the strife and contentions of the gods were due to Themis and Zeus. Nor again can we let our children hear from Aeschylus that

> God implants a fault in man, when he wishes to destroy a house utterly.

No: We must forbid anyone who writes a play about the sufferings of Niobe (the subject of the play from which these last lines are quoted), or the house of Pelops, or the Trojan war, or any similar topic, to say they are acts of god; or if he does he must produce the sort of interpretation we are now demanding, and say that god's acts were good and just, and that the sufferers were benefited by being punished. What the poet must not be allowed to say is that those who were punished were made wretched through god's action. He may refer to the wicked as wretched because they needed punishment, provided he makes it clear that in punishing them god did them good. But if a state is to be run on the right lines, every possible step must be taken to prevent anyone, young or old, either saying or being told, whether in poetry or prose, that god, being good, can cause harm or evil to any man. To say so would be sinful, inexpedient, and inconsistent."

"I should approve of a law for this purpose and you have my vote for it," he said.

"Then of our laws laying down the principles which those who write or speak about the gods must follow, one would be this: *God is the cause, not of all things, but only of good.*"

"I am quite content with that," he said.

Topics for Critical Thinking and Writing

1. In the beginning of the dialogue Plato says that adults recite fictions to very young children and that these fictions help to mold character. Think of some stories that you heard or read when young, such as "Snow White and the Seven Dwarfs" or "Ali Baba and the Forty Thieves." Try to think of a story that, in the final analysis, is not in accord with what you consider to be proper morality, such as a story in which a person triumphs through trickery or a story in which evil actions—perhaps murders—are set forth without unfavorable comment. (Was it naughty of Jack to kill the giant?) On reflection, do you think children should not be told such stories? Why, or why not? Or think of the early film westerns, in which, on the whole, the Indians (except for an occasional Uncle Tonto) are depicted as bad guys and the whites (except for an occasional coward or rustler) are depicted as good guys. Many people who now have gray hair enjoyed such films in their childhood. Are you prepared to say that such films are not damaging? Or on the other hand, are you prepared to say they are damaging and should be prohibited?

2. It is often objected that censorship of reading matter and of television programs available to children underrates their ability to think for them-

selves and to discount the dangerous, obscene, and tawdry. Do you agree with this objection? Does Plato?

3. Plato says that allowing poets to say what they please about the gods in his ideal state would be "inconsistent." Explain what he means by this criticism, and then explain why you agree or disagree with it.

4. Do you believe that parents should censor the "fiction" their children encounter (literature, films, pictures, music) but that the community should not censor the "fiction" of adults? Write an essay of 500 words on one of these topics: "Censorship and Rock Lyrics"; "X-rated Films"; "Ethnic Jokes." (These topics are broadly worded; you can narrow one and offer whatever thesis you wish.)

5. Were you taught that any of the founding fathers ever acted disreputably, or that any American hero had any serious moral flaw? Or that America ever acted immorally in its dealings with other nations? Do you think it appropriate for children to hear such things?

THINKING ABOUT
GOVERNMENT FUNDING FOR THE ARTS

Our government supports the arts, including writers, by giving grants to numerous institutions. On the other hand, the amount that the government contributes is extremely small when compared to the amounts given to the arts by most European governments. Consider the following questions.

1. Should taxpayers' dollars be used to support the arts? Why, or why not?

2. What possible public benefit can come from supporting the arts? Can one argue that we should support the arts for the same reasons that we support the public schools, that is, to have a civilized society?

3. If dollars are given to the arts, should the political content of the works be taken into account, or only the aesthetic merit? Can we separate content from aesthetic merit? (The best way to approach this issue probably is to begin by thinking of a strongly political work.)

4. Is it censorship not to award public funds to writers whose work is not approved of, or is it simply a matter of refusing to reward them with taxpayers' dollars?

5. Should decisions about grants to writers be made chiefly by government officials or chiefly by experts in the field? Why?

Part Four

CURRENT ISSUES: OCCASIONS FOR DEBATE

In reading essays debating a given issue, keep in mind the questions given on page 86, "A Checklist for Analyzing an Argument." They are listed again below, with a few additional points of special relevance to debates.

A CHECKLIST FOR ANALYZING A DEBATE

✓ What is the writer's thesis?
   ✓ What claim is asserted?
   ✓ What assumptions are made?
   ✓ Are key terms defined satisfactorily?
✓ What support is offered on behalf of the claim?
   ✓ Are examples relevant and convincing?
   ✓ Are statistics relevant, accurate, and convincing?
   ✓ Are the authorities appropriate?
   ✓ Is the logic—deductive and inductive—valid?
   ✓ If there is an appeal to emotion, is this appeal acceptable?
✓ Does the writer seem fair?
   ✓ Are counterarguments considered?
   ✓ Is there any evidence of dishonesty?
Next, ask yourself the following additional questions:
✓ Do the disputants differ in
   ✓ assumptions?
   ✓ interpretations of relevant facts?
   ✓ selection of and emphasis on these facts?
   ✓ definitions of key terms?
   ✓ values and norms?
✓ What common ground do the disputants share?
✓ Which disputant seems to you to have the better overall argument? Why?

13

Abortion: Whose Right to Life Is It Anyway?

IT HAS BURNED
A HOLE IN MY SOUL
AND CHANGED ME
FOREVER.

MARGO

something inside dies after an abortion
PROJECT RACHEL • WWW.HOPEAFTERABORTION.COM
FOR HELP CALL 1-888-456-HOPE

Ellen Willis

Ellen Willis (b. 1941) was educated at Barnard College and the University of California at Berkeley. She has been a freelance writer since 1966, publishing in such journals as The New Yorker, Rolling Stone, *and the* Village Voice, *where this essay first appeared on July 16, 1985.*

Putting Women Back into the Abortion Debate

Some years ago I attended a New York Institute for the Humanities seminar on the new right. We were a fairly heterogeneous group of liberals and lefties, feminists and gay activists, but on one point nearly all of us agreed: The right-to-life movement was a dangerous antifeminist crusade. At one session I argued that the attack on abortion had significance far beyond itself, that it was the linchpin of the right's social agenda. I got a lot of supporting comments and approving nods. It was too much for Peter Steinfels, a liberal Catholic, author of *The Neoconservatives,* and executive editor of *Commonweal.* Right-to-lifers were not all right-wing fanatics, he protested. "You have to understand," he said plaintively, "that many of us see abortion as a *human life issue.*" What I remember best was his air of frustrated isolation. I don't think he came back to the seminar after that.

Things are different now. I often feel isolated when I insist that abortion is, above all, a *feminist issue.* Once people took for granted that abortion was an issue of sexual politics and morality. Now, abortion is most often discussed as a question of "life" in the abstract. Public concern over abortion centers almost exclusively on fetuses; women and their bodies are merely the stage on which the drama of fetal life and death takes place. Debate about abortion—if not its reality—has become sexlessly scholastic. And the people most responsible for this turn of events are, like Peter Steinfels, on the left.

The left wing of the right-to-life movement is a small, seemingly eccentric minority in both "progressive" and antiabortion camps. Yet it has played a critical role in the movement: By arguing that opposition to abortion can be separated from the right's antifeminist program, it has given antiabortion sentiment legitimacy in left-symp and (putatively) profeminist circles. While left antiabortionists are hardly alone in emphasizing fetal life, their innovation has been to claim that a consistent "pro-life" stand involves opposing capital punishment, supporting disarmament, demanding government programs to end poverty, and so on. This is of course a leap the right is neither able nor willing to make. It's been liberals—from Garry Wills to the Catholic bishops—who have supplied the mass media with the idea that prohibiting abortion is part of a "seamless garment" of respect for human life.

Having invented this countercontext for the abortion controversy, left antiabortionists are trying to impose it as the only legitimate context for debate. Those of us who won't accept their terms and persist in see-ing opposition to abortion, antifeminism, sexual repression, and religious sectarianism as the real seamless garment have been accused of obscur-ing the issue with demagoguery. Last year *Commonweal*—perhaps the most important current forum for left antiabortion opinion—ran an edi-torial demanding that we shape up: "Those who hold that abortion is im-moral believe that the biological dividing lines of birth or viability should no more determine whether a developing member of the species is de-nied or accorded essential rights than should the biological dividing lines of sex or race or disability or old age. This argument is open to challenge. Perhaps the dividing lines are sufficiently different. Pro-choice advocates should state their reasons for believing so. They should meet the argu-ment on its own grounds. . . ."

In other words, the only question we're allowed to debate—or the   5
only one *Commonweal* is willing to entertain—is "Are fetuses the moral equivalent of born human beings?" And I can't meet the argument on its own grounds because I don't agree that this is the key question, whose answer determines whether one supports abortion or opposes it. I don't doubt that fetuses are alive, or that they're biologically human—what else would they be? I do consider the life of a fertilized egg less precious than the well-being of a woman with feelings, self-consciousness, a his-tory, social ties; and I think fetuses get closer to being human in a moral sense as they come closer to birth. But to me these propositions are in-tuitively self-evident. I wouldn't know how to justify them to a "non-believer," nor do I see the point of trying.

I believe the debate has to start in a different place—with the rec-ognition that fertilized eggs develop into infants inside the bodies of women. Pregnancy and birth are active processes in which a woman's body shelters, nourishes, and expels a new life; for nine months she is immersed in the most intimate possible relationship with another being. The growing fetus makes considerable demands on her physical and emotional resources, culminating in the cataclysmic experience of birth. And childbearing has unpredictable consequences; it always entails some risk of injury or death.

For me all this has a new concreteness: I had a baby last year. My much-desired and relatively easy pregnancy was full of what antiabor-tionists like to call "inconveniences." I was always tired, short of breath; my digestion was never right; for three months I endured a state of hor-monal siege; later I had pains in my fingers, swelling feet, numb spots on my legs, the dread hemorrhoids. I had to think about everything I ate. I developed borderline glucose intolerance. I gained fifty pounds and am still overweight; my shape has changed in other ways that may well be permanent. Psychologically, my pregnancy consumed me—though I'd happily bought the seat on the roller coaster, I was still terrified to be so out of control of my normally tractable body. It was all bearable, even interesting—even, at times, transcendent—because I wanted a baby.

Birth was painful, exhausting, and wonderful. If I hadn't wanted a baby it would only have been painful and exhausting—or worse. I can hardly imagine what it's like to have your body and mind taken over in this way when you not only don't look forward to the result, but positively dread it. The thought appalls me. So as I see it, the key question is "Can it be moral, under any circumstances, to make a woman bear a child against her will?"

From this vantage point, *Commonweal*'s argument is irrelevant, for in a society that respects the individual, no "member of the species" in *any* stage of development has an "essential right" to make use of someone else's body, let alone in such all-encompassing fashion, without that person's consent. You can't make a case against abortion by applying a general principle about everybody's human rights; you have to show exactly the opposite—that the relationship between fetus and pregnant woman is an exception, one that justifies depriving women of their right to bodily integrity. And in fact all antiabortion ideology rests on the premise—acknowledged or simply assumed—that women's unique capacity to bring life into the world carries with it a unique obligation that women cannot be allowed to "play God" and launch only the lives they welcome.

Yet the alternative to allowing women this power is to make them impotent. Criminalizing abortion doesn't just harm individual women with unwanted pregnancies, it affects all women's sense of themselves. Without control of our fertility we can never envision ourselves as free, for our biology makes us constantly vulnerable. Simply because we are female our physical integrity can be violated, our lives disrupted and transformed, at any time. Our ability to act in the world is hopelessly compromised by our sexual being.

Ah, sex—it does have a way of coming up in these discussions, despite all. When pressed, right-to-lifers of whatever political persuasion invariably point out that pregnancy doesn't happen by itself. The leftists often give patronizing lectures on contraception (though some find only "natural birth control" acceptable), but remain unmoved when reminded that contraceptives fail. Openly or implicitly they argue that people shouldn't have sex unless they're prepared to procreate. (They are quick to profess a single standard—men as well as women should be sexually "responsible." Yes, and the rich as well as the poor should be allowed to sleep under bridges.) Which amounts to saying that if women want to lead heterosexual lives they must give up any claim to self-determination, and that they have no right to sexual pleasure without fear.

Opposing abortion, then, means accepting that women must suffer sexual disempowerment and a radical loss of autonomy relative to men: If fetal life is sacred, the self-denial basic to women's oppression is also basic to the moral order. Opposing abortion means embracing a conservative sexual morality, one that subordinates pleasure to reproduction: If fetal life is sacred, there is no room for the view that sexual passion—or even sexual love—for its own sake is a human need and a human right. Opposing abortion means tolerating the inevitable double standard, by which men may accept or reject sexual restrictions in accordance with their beliefs, while women must bow to them out of fear . . . or defy them at great risk. However much *Commonweal*'s editors and those of like mind want to believe their opposition to abortion is simply about saving lives, the truth is that in the real world they are shoring up a particular sexual culture, whose rules are stacked against women. I have yet to hear any left right-to-lifers take full responsibility for that fact or deal seriously with its political implications.

Unfortunately, their fuzziness has not lessened their appeal—if anything it's done the opposite. In increasing numbers liberals and leftists, while opposing antiabortion laws, have come to view abortion as an "agonizing moral issue" with some justice on both sides, rather than an issue—however emotionally complex—of freedom versus repression, or equality versus hierarchy, that affects their political self-definition. This above-the-battle stance is attractive to leftists who want to be feminist good guys but are uneasy or ambivalent about sexual issues, not to mention those who want to ally with "progressive" factions of the Catholic church on Central America, nuclear disarmament, or populist economics without that sticky abortion question getting in the way.

Such neutrality is a way of avoiding the painful conflict over cultural issues that continually smolders on the left. It can also be a way of coping with the contradictions of personal life at a time when liberation is a dream deferred. To me the fight for abortion has always been the cutting edge of feminism, precisely because it denies that anatomy is destiny, that female biology dictates women's subordinate status. Yet recently I've found it hard to focus on the issue, let alone summon up the militance needed to stop the antiabortion tanks. In part that has to do with second-round weariness—do we really have to go through all these things twice?—in part with my life now.

Since my daughter's birth my feelings about abortion—not as a political demand but as a personal choice—have changed. In this society, the difference between the situation of a childless woman and of a mother is immense; the fear that having a child will dislodge one's tenuous hold on a nontraditional life is excruciating. This terror of being forced into the sea-change of motherhood gave a special edge to my convictions about abortion. Since I've made that plunge voluntarily, with consequences still unfolding, the terror is gone; I might not want another child, for all sorts of reasons, but I will never again feel that my identity is at stake. Different battles with the culture absorb my energy now. Besides, since I've experienced the primal, sensual passion of caring for an infant, there will always be part of me that does want another. If I had an abortion today, it would be with conflict and sadness unknown to me when I had an abortion a decade ago. And the antiabortionists' imagery of dead babies hits me with new force. Do many women—left, feminist women—have such feelings? Is this the sort of "ambivalence about abortion" that in the present atmosphere slides so easily into self-flagellating guilt?

Some left antiabortionists, mainly pacifists—Juli Loesch, Mary Meehan, and other "feminists for life"; Jim Wallis and various writers for Wallis's radical evangelical journal *Sojourners*—have tried to square their position with concern for women. They blame the prevalence of abortion on oppressive conditions—economic injustice, lack of child care and other social supports for mothers, the devaluation of childrearing, men's exploitative sexual behavior and refusal to take equal responsibility for children. They disagree on whether to criminalize abortion now (since murder is intolerable no matter what the cause) or to build a long-term moral consensus (since stopping abortion requires a general social transformation), but they all regard abortion as a desperate solution to desperate problems, and the women who resort to it as more sinned against than sinning.

This analysis grasps an essential feminist truth: that in a male-supremacist society no choice a woman makes is genuinely free or entirely in her interest. Certainly many women have had abortions they didn't want or wouldn't have wanted if they had any plausible means of caring for a child; and countless others wouldn't have gotten pregnant in the first place were it not for inadequate contraception, sexual confusion and guilt, male pressure, and other stigmata of female powerlessness. Yet forcing a woman to bear a child she doesn't want can only add injury to insult, while refusing to go through with such a pregnancy can be a woman's first step toward taking hold of her life. And many women who have abortions are "victims" only of ordinary human miscalculation, technological failure, or the vagaries of passion, all bound to exist in any society, however utopian. There will always be women who, at any given moment, want sex but don't want a child; some of these women will get pregnant; some of them will have abortions. Behind the victim theory of abortion is the implicit belief that women are always ready to be mothers, if only conditions are right, and that sex for pleasure rather than procreation is not only "irresponsible" (i.e., bad) but something men impose on women, never something women actively seek. Ironically, left right-to-lifers see abortion as always coerced (it's "exploitation" and "violence against women"), yet regard motherhood—which for most women throughout history has been inescapable, and is still our most socially approved role—as a positive choice. The analogy to the feminist antipornography movement goes beyond borrowed rhetoric: the antiporners, too, see active female lust as surrender to male domination and traditionally feminine sexual attitudes as expressions of women's true nature.

This Orwellian version of feminism, which glorifies "female values" and dismisses women's struggles for freedom—particularly sexual freedom—as a male plot, has become all too familiar in recent years. But its use in the abortion debate has been especially muddleheaded. Somehow we're supposed to leap from an oppressive patriarchal society to the egalitarian one that will supposedly make abortion obsolete without ever allowing women to see themselves as people entitled to control their reproductive function rather than be controlled by it. How women who have no power in this most personal of areas can effectively fight for power in the larger society is left to our imagination. A "New Zealand feminist" quoted by Mary Meehan in a 1980 article in *The Progressive* says, "Accepting short-term solutions like abortion only delays the implementation of real reforms like decent maternity and paternity leaves, job protection, high-quality child care, community responsibility for dependent people of all ages, and recognition of the economic contribution of childminders"—as if these causes were progressing nicely before legal abortion came along. On the contrary, the fight for reproductive freedom is the foundation of all the others, which is why antifeminists resist it so fiercely.

As "pro-life" pacifists have been particularly concerned with refuting charges of misogyny, the liberal Catholics at *Commonweal* are most exercised by the claim that antiabortion laws violate religious freedom. The editorial quoted above hurled another challenge at the proabortion forces:

> It is time, finally, for the pro-choice advocates and editorial writers to abandon, once and for all, the argument that abortion is a religious "doctrine" of a single or several churches being imposed on those of other persuasions in violation of the First Amendment. . . . Catholics and their bishops are accused of imposing their "doctrine" on abortion, but not their "doctrine" on the needs of the poor, or their "doctrine" on the arms race, or their "doctrine" on human rights in Central America. . . .
>
> The briefest investigation into Catholic teaching would show that the church's case against abortion is utterly unlike, say, its belief in the Real Presence, known with the eyes of faith alone, or its insistence on a Sunday obligation, applicable only to the faithful. The church's moral teaching on abortion . . . is for the most part like its teaching on racism, warfare, and capital punishment, based on ordinary reasoning common to believers and nonbelievers. . . .

This is one more example of right-to-lifers' tendency to ignore the sexual ideology underlying their stand. Interesting, isn't it, how the editorial neglects to mention that the church's moral teaching on abortion jibes neatly with its teaching on birth control, sex, divorce, and the role of women. The traditional, patriarchal sexual morality common to these teachings is explicitly religious, and its chief defenders in modern times have been the more conservative churches. The Catholic and evangelical Christian churches are the backbone of the organized right-to-life movement and — a few Nathansons and Hentoffs notwithstanding — have provided most of the movement's activists and spokespeople.

Furthermore, the Catholic hierarchy has made opposition to abor- 20 tion a litmus test of loyalty to the church in a way it has done with no other political issue — witness Archbishop O'Connor's harassment of Geraldine Ferraro during her vice-presidential campaign. It's unthinkable that a Catholic bishop would publicly excoriate a Catholic office-holder or candidate for taking a hawkish position on the arms race or Central America or capital punishment. Nor do I notice anyone trying to read William F. Buckley out of the church for his views on welfare. The fact is there is no accepted Catholic "doctrine" on these matters comparable to the church's absolutist condemnation of abortion. While differing attitudes toward war, racism, and poverty cut across religious and secular lines, the sexual values that mandate opposition to abortion are the bedrock of the traditional religious world view, and the source of the most bitter conflict with secular and religious modernists. When churches devote their considerable political power, organizational resources, and money to translating those values into law, I call that imposing their religious beliefs on me — whether or not they're technically violating the First Amendment.

Statistical studies have repeatedly shown that people's views on abortion are best predicted by their opinions on sex and "family" issues, not on "life" issues like nuclear weapons or the death penalty. That's not because we're inconsistent but because we comprehend what's really at stake in the abortion fight. It's the antiabortion left that refuses to face the contradiction in its own position: you can't be wholeheartedly for "life" — or for such progressive aspirations as freedom, democracy, equality — and condone the subjugation of women. The seamless garment is full of holes.

Topics for Critical Thinking and Writing

1. What does Willis mean when she insists, in her second paragraph, that abortion is "a *feminist issue*"? Whether or not you agree, write a paragraph explaining her point. You may want to begin simply by saying, "When Ellen Willis says abortion is a '*feminist issue*,' she means . . ."

2. After describing the physical and psychological difficulties of pregnancy, Willis says (para. 8):

   in a society that respects the individual, no "member of the species" in *any* stage of development has an "essential right" to make use of someone else's body, let alone in such all-encompassing fashion, without that person's consent. You can't make a case against abortion by applying a general principle about everybody's human rights; you have to show exactly the opposite — that the relationship between fetus and pregnant woman is an exception, one that justifies depriving women of their right to bodily integrity.

Do you accept all of Willis's declarations? Any of them? Why, or why not? And (another topic) consider the expression, "without that person's consent." Suppose a woman takes no precautions against becoming pregnant—possibly she even wants to become pregnant—but at a late stage in pregnancy decides she does not wish to bear a child. Can she withdraw her "consent" at any time during her pregnancy?

3. In the previous question we asked you to consider Willis's expression "without that person's consent." Here is a related problem: The relationship between fetus and pregnant woman is different from all other relationships, but is it relevant to point out that women are not alone in having their bodies possessed, so to speak, by others? In time of war, men—but not women—are drafted; the interruption of their normal career causes considerable hardship. At the very least, a draftee is required to give up months or even several years of his life and to live in circumstances that severely interfere with his privacy and his autonomy. And of course he may in fact be required to risk—and lose—his life.

4. Do you think (in contrast to Willis) that persons who are opposed to capital punishment and to increased military spending—persons who are, so to speak, "pro-life"—must, if they are to be consistent, also oppose abortion? Why, or why not?

Randall A. Terry

Randall A. Terry is the founder of the antiabortion organization Operation Rescue. This essay originally appeared in the Boston Globe, *January 9, 1995.*

The Abortion Clinic Shootings: Why?

As the nation heard with sorrow the news of the deplorable shooting spree at abortion facilities in Brookline,[1] the question is asked: Why? Why this sudden rise of violence in this arena?

I have been intricately involved in the antiabortion movement for more than a decade. I have led thousands of people in peaceful antiabortion activism via Operation Rescue. Hence, I enjoy a perspective few have. So I submit these answers to the question "Why?"

Enemies of the babies and the antiabortion movement will argue that the conviction that abortion is murder, and the call to take nonviolent direct action to save children from death, inevitably leads to the use of lethal force. This argument is ludicrous—unless one is prepared to argue that Gandhi's nonviolent civil disobedience in India during the

---

[1] On December 30, 1994, a gunman opened fire at two abortion facilities in Brookline, Massachusetts, wounding several people, two of them fatally. [Editors' note.]

1930s led to the murder of British officials; or that Dr. Martin Luther King's nonviolent civil disobedience led to the violent actions that accompanied the civil rights movement in the United States during the 1960s.

So why, then, this recent violent outburst? Law enforcement officials need look no further than *Roe v. Wade*; abortion providers need look no further than their own instruments of death; and Congress and the president need look no further than the Freedom of Access to Clinic Entrances Act to understand the roots of the shootings.

The Supreme Court's attempt to overthrow Law (capital "L") in order to legalize and legitimize murder has led to the inevitable—a disregard of or contempt for law. I say the court's attempt, for the court can no more overturn Law and legalize murder than it can overturn the law of gravity. God's immutable commandment "Thou shalt not murder" has forever made murder illegal. The court's lawlessness is breeding lawlessness. The court cannot betray the foundation of law and civilization—the Ten Commandments—and then expect a people to act "lawful" and "civilized."

Let us look at the abortion industry itself. Abortion is murder. And just as segregation and the accompanying violence possess the seeds for further violence, likewise it appears that the Law of sowing and reaping is being visited upon the abortion industry. A society cannot expect to tear 35 million innocent babies from their mothers' wombs without reaping horrifying consequences. Was it perhaps inevitable that the violent abortion industry should itself reap a portion of what it has so flagrantly and callously sown?

Now to Congress and the judiciary. Similar to the civil rights activists, antiabortion activists have often been brutalized at the hands of police and then subjected to vulgar injustices in sundry courts of law. Add to this the Freedom of Access to Clinic Entrances Act, which turns peaceful antiabortion activists into federal felons and perhaps one can understand the frustration and anger that is growing in Americans.

The abortion industry can partly blame itself for the recent shootings. It clamored for harsh treatment of peaceful antiabortion activists, and it usually got it. Now it has to deal with an emerging violent fringe. John F. Kennedy stated, "Those who make peaceful revolution impossible will make violent revolution inevitable." One would think the pro-choice crowd would belatedly heed the late president's warning, but they haven't. They're urging an all too political Justice Department to launch a witch hunt into the lives of peaceful antiabortion activists and leaders. Make no mistake—what the pro-choice people want is to pressure law enforcement and the courts to intimidate anyone who condemns abortion as murder. Their recent public relations scam is to blame all antiabortion people for the shootings. And they will not be content until they have crushed all dissent against abortion. We must not allow them to cause us to cower in silence.

To those who support the recent shootings or herald John Salvi as a hero, I ask you: Has God authorized one person to be policeman, judge, jury, and executioner? Is it logical to leap from nonviolent life-saving activities to lethal force? Read your history! Remember the principles of Calvin, Knox, and Cromwell concerning lower magistrates. Are you likening John Salvi and Co. to Knox or Cromwell? Are you calling for revolution? Please consider these questions before calling someone who walks into a clinic and starts randomly shooting people a hero.

So what can be done to curtail this trend? First, the Freedom of Access to Clinic Entrances Act should be repealed immediately. This oppressive law is an outrage. The crushing weight of the federal government punishing peaceful protesters is the kind of thing we would expect in Communist China against political dissidents. 10

Second, the courts must stop abusing antiabortion activists. We must be accorded the same tolerance and leniency that every politically correct protester receives nationwide, i.e., small fines, two days in jail, charges dismissed, etc.

Finally, and this is most urgent, child killing must be brought to an immediate end. Whether the Supreme Court declares the personhood and inalienable right to life of preborn children or the Constitution is amended or the president signs an emancipation proclamation for children or Congress outlaws abortion outright, we must bring a swift end to the murder of innocent children.

Topics for Critical Thinking and Writing

1. In his third paragraph, Terry draws a parallel between Operation Rescue and the nonviolent civil disobedience campaigns in India led by Gandhi and in the United States led by Martin Luther King Jr. Is the analogy a good one? Why or why not?

2. Does Terry think that the Supreme Court's decision in *Roe v. Wade* (upholding a woman's right to have an abortion) *causes* violent disruption of abortion clinics? Or that it *justifies* that violence? If so, spell out the details of this causation or justification. If not, what does he mean when he says in paragraph 4 that "Law enforcement officials need look no further than *Roe v. Wade*"?

3. Why does Terry think that "abortion is murder" (see paras. 5–6)?

4. In paragraph 8 Terry cites a remark of President Kennedy: "Those who make peaceful revolution impossible will make violent revolution inevitable." Evaluate the aptness of this quotation as an explanation of violent disruption of medical services at an abortion clinic.

5. What is the purpose and the effect of Terry's choice of these words in paragraph 8: a "public relations scam," "crushed all dissent," "cower in silence"?

6. In the library, find some information about the Freedom of Access to Clinic Entrances Act (mentioned by Terry in paras. 7 and 10). Do you think its repeal, which Terry advocates, would help reduce violence at abortion clinics? Why, or why not? Why do you think this law was enacted by Congress in the first place?

7. Terry describes abortion as "child killing" (para. 12). Do you think that is a fair description? Why, or why not?

8. At the end of his essay (paras. 10–12), Terry proposes three things government ought to do to end the trend toward violence in the antiabortion movement. Do you think pro-choice advocates can accept any of these policies? Why, or why not?

9. Terry asserts that "preborn children" have an "inalienable right to life" (para. 12). What does "inalienable" mean? Suppose a pregnant woman would die because of medical complications if she carried her unborn child to birth. Do you think Terry would favor the mother dying because we must respect the "inalienable right to life" of the unborn? Does the mother, too, have such a right? How do you think he ought to resolve this conflict of rights, and why?

For topical links related to the abortion controversy, see the companion Web site:
www.bedfordstmartins.com/barnetbedau.

14

Affirmative Action: Is It Fair?

Terry Eastland

Terry Eastland, born in Dallas, Texas, and educated at Vanderbilt University, Nashville, Tennessee, and Balliol College, Oxford, is a frequent contributor to conservative journals such as the National Review, American Spectator, Commentary, *and* The Public Interest. *He is the author of several books, including* Religious Liberty in the Supreme Court: The Cases That Define the Debate over Church and State *(1995) and* Ending Affirmative Action: The Case for Colorblind Justice *(1996), from which this excerpt is taken.*

Ending Affirmative Action

One of the central and hard-won lessons of the fight for colorblindness, lasting more than a century and a quarter, was that distinctions drawn on the basis of race inevitably lead to racial discrimination. That is why the advocates of colorblindness sought the elimination of racial distinctions in the law. They sought to end the source, the raw material, of racial discrimination. The nation was the better for their efforts when, starting in the 1940s, our legal system was strengthened by the addition of a variety of antidiscrimination laws, culminating in the Civil Rights Act of 1964. Soon afterward, the founders of affirmative action, searching for ways to improve the material condition of black Americans and make amends for slavery and segregation, found the constraints of colorblind law inconvenient. They managed to loosen the colorblind strictures of the Civil Rights Act of 1964, and the federal judiciary failed to tighten them in turn. Once preferential treatment was made possible, it spread throughout the public and private sectors, and the targets of numerical affirmative action became more numerous, coming to include Hispanics, Asians, and women.

Defenders of the policy initially promised that it would be temporary—a position that implicitly recognized that it is better not to sort people on the basis of race, that colorblindness is a worthy guide. But with the first step away from colorblindness, further steps came more easily, and in time we heard less often the promise that someday we would renew our previous commitment.

Nonetheless, more than a quarter century of thinking by race and counting by race has served only to confirm and strengthen the case for colorblind law.

We now know that when government has the power to sort people on the basis of race, racial discrimination often results. Preferential treatment is never benign. Whoever would have been admitted to a school, or won the promotion or the contract, but for race, has suffered discrimination—and there is no good discrimination. The nation owes a debt of gratitude to people like Allan Bakke, Brian Weber, Randy Pech, and

Cheryl Hopwood, who have brought lawsuits challenging preferential affirmative action. They have courageously kept alive the question of the legality and morality of preferential treatment, providing often lonely witness to the principle at the heart of colorblind law—that no one in America should be discriminated against on account of race.

We know, too, that the effort to regulate on the basis of race can   5 have unanticipated consequences. Where the old advocates of colorblind law were pessimists about the very idea of racial regulation, the founders of affirmative action were optimists, confident of their ability to distinguish between benign and invidious racial classifications. They thought the world could be divided into good and bad people. The bad discriminated against blacks, either intentionally or through seemingly neutral procedures that produced adverse effects. The good—and the founders of affirmative action included themselves in this category—sought to do well by blacks. They were pure in heart, and so they could be trusted not to harm blacks.

But now we know better. It was weak-minded and dangerously naive to think that taking race into account would produce unambiguously good results for those in whose behalf it was done. Many ostensible beneficiaries of affirmative action have testified that preferential treatment often leads to self-doubt, dependency, and entitlement. To be sure, affirmative action doesn't always do that. Sometimes it "works," though the paradox of affirmative action is that its "working" is a function of how soon the recipient quits it entirely and labors under the same rules as everyone else, a sign of genuine equality that is possible only among individuals. But, as the practice of affirmative action has shown, no one knows enough confidently to predict in advance of an act of preferential treatment which effects, for better or worse, it will have upon a given recipient. This negative experience of affirmative action does not constitute an unanswerable argument against it; patients do undergo risky operations. But we do have a choice in the matter; that is, we do not have to take the risk of affirmative action. And once free of it, those now eligible for it would be able to compete and achieve on the same terms as everyone else.

There have been other unanticipated consequences as well, chief among them the stigma produced by affirmative action. Wherever affirmative action operates, the very existence of such a program will lead some people to think that every minority student or every minority employee would not have won opportunity without preferential treatment, a judgment that strips people of the respect due them as individuals. Consider, in the context of higher education, the case of the minority student admitted under affirmative action who would not have won the place without it. This student very well might have been admitted to another school, without the "help" of affirmative action. The problem, however, is that the student admitted under affirmative action is unable to erase its stigma until the individual succeeds in a nonpreferential environment. Even then, however, the number of those who know the nature of the student's achievement is likely to be very small. And the formal, pervasive nature of affirmative action, encouraged and required by so many local, state, and federal government agencies, means that the public will continue to make generalizations about minority advancement simply because it is easy to do so in the absence of particular knowledge. The generalization is that "minority" equals "affirmative action" equals "lower standards." The inference drawn is that affirmative action explains minority success. Tragically, this process of generalization and inference trails the many minorities—perhaps the majority—who make their way without the "help" of any preferential treatment.

Here the negative experience of affirmative action makes a powerful argument for colorblind law. Because affirmative action is stigmatizing, even for those who do not "benefit" from it, it is better to forego affirmative action altogether in favor of procedures for admitting students or hiring workers or awarding contracts that do not brand their targets as inferior and do not provide a basis for generalizing about minority achievement. Such procedures, of course, are those that do not distinguish on the basis of race, that do not "take race into account" in deciding who gets ahead.

Sports, fortunately, is still a world governed by such colorblind rules. No one receives preferential treatment in sports, so no one has self-doubts induced by affirmative action, no one has to "transcend" affirmative action, and no one is stigmatized by affirmative action. No one ever thinks, "Williams is in center field because of affirmative action," or "Lopez is catching because he is Hispanic." Outside of sports—which is to say, in the rest of society—the deeply human desire to be known for individual accomplishment explains why some minorities have made a point of declining participation in programs for which their race or ethnicity makes them eligible. The Hispanic law student at the University of Texas School of Law, whose academic qualifications were good enough to be admitted under the standards governing "white and others," was making an important point when he said that sometimes he wished he was wearing a shirt indicating his academic credentials. Ending affirmative action will create circumstances in which individuals will shine and, just as importantly, be seen to shine, quite on their own merits.

The longer affirmative action remains in place, the more reasons 10 there are to bring it to an end. Of course, past advocates of colorblind law could have told us how hard it would be to quit thinking and counting by race once the racial license had been granted. They knew that the human mind is creative, remarkably capable of coming up with reasons, even quite attractive ones, for why we ought to "take race into account." The founding rationale of affirmative action was to remedy the ill effects of past discrimination against blacks, but this rationale did not easily fit the other groups. So affirmative action was redefined and rejustified in terms of overcoming "underrepresentation" and achieving "diversity."

We have also heard the argument that affirmative action is necessary to prevent future discrimination. There have been other reasons offered: Affirmative action is needed to create minority role models, to stimulate the creation of minority businesses, to jump-start economic development in minority communities. With the advent at the local level of minority-dominated governments, minorities have discriminated against nonminorities by fashioning affirmative action programs that, while publicly touted in terms of one or another of the usual rationales, realistically are little more than expressions of racial politics, the ignoble triumph of minority majorities.

The use of race now threatens to produce some truly bizarre results. In large cities where new immigrants congregate, blacks who hold disproportionately more public-sector jobs stand to lose some of those jobs to "underrepresented" Hispanics. Diversity, meanwhile, is a rationale that may allow discrimination against members of traditional minority groups. Even President Clinton has said he would support laying off a black teacher instead of a white teacher if doing so would promote diversity. We cannot escape the fact that by drawing racial and ethnic lines, affirmative action—whatever its rationale—encourages Americans to think of themselves in racial and ethnic terms. That has been a recipe for resentment and chauvinism, neither of which promotes the good health of our democracy.

Fortunately, the Supreme Court has kept the light on, letting us know where home is, even in those cases where it has ruled in support of affirmative action. Those justices of the Supreme Court who consistently voted for affirmative action programs nonetheless refused to endorse group rights or to break in principle with the colorblind tradition. Equality under the Constitution, Justice Brennan wrote, is linked "with the proposition that differences in color or creed, birth or status, are neither significant nor relevant to the way in which such persons are treated." Justice Marshall declared his desire to live in a society "in which the color of a person's skin will not determine the opportunities available to him or her." And Justice Blackmun endorsed a society in which "persons will be regarded as persons," without regard to race or ethnicity.[1]

In recent years the Court has been shining the home light much more brightly. Its decisions in the *Croson* and *Adarand* cases, which speak to every government in the United States, impose strict conditions on the use of racial preferences. These decisions point us in the right direction. Citing Justice Harlan's dissent in *Plessy v. Ferguson* and the opinions in the Japanese Relocation Cases, *Croson* and *Adarand* raise the standard of colorblind law in a context that makes colorblindness even more compelling today than Harlan could have known. He made his argument for colorblind law in the context of a society made up of two races—

---

[1]See Lawrence H. Fuchs, *The American Kaleidoscope: Race, Ethnicity, and the Civic Culture* (Hanover, N.H.: Wesleyan University Press, 1995), p. 456. [All notes are the author's.]

black and white. Ours today consists of many races and ethnic groups, thanks especially to recent waves of immigration. Law that tries to distinguish among the groups and to favor one over another is bound to fail the country. Instead, we need law that can discourage the natural tendency people have to seek their own kind, law that invites people to minimize and transcend racial and ethnic differences. The best protection for every individual—of whatever race or ethnic background—is to be found in law that does not give effect to any racial views, but, as Harlan put it, provides for "equality before the law of all citizens of the United States, without regard to race."

The Supreme Court, however, has left much of the task of ending affirmative action to the American people.[2] That is just as well. Decisions by the elective branches of government to end programs containing preferences would be reached consequent to public debate, not after legal briefs have been submitted. We can take major steps toward recovering colorblind law and principle by enacting measures at the federal and state levels that would deny government the power to favor or slight anyone on account of race. If we do not take such steps, of course, the uncertain political tides may turn back to favor the supporters of affirmative action. Progress toward colorblind law will be much slower, if not impossible, if we rely exclusively on judicial decisions, for the defenders of affirmative action will respond by "mending" programs in ways that better disguise preferences but do not eliminate them. It is possible, too, that judicial progress toward colorblind law could be arrested or even reversed, if there are new Supreme Court appointees with views at odds with those of the majorities in *Croson* and *Adarand*. It falls to us to take action now.

The choice for colorblindness is the choice our own best tradition invites us to make. Our founding charter declares that "all men are created equal" and are "endowed by their Creator with certain unalienable rights," among them "life, liberty, and the pursuit of happiness." We are thereby committed to the proposition that it is individuals who have rights, not groups, and that all individuals enjoy a fundamental equality of rights. The startling character of the United States—and what it has modeled to the rest of the world—is that the individuals who have equal rights may be of any race or ethnic background.

Few Americans have stated the case for equality as cogently as Abraham Lincoln, who did so in an 1858 speech he gave in Chicago in observation of Independence Day. The challenge before Lincoln was to show

15

---

[2]As for whether the Court should declare the Constitution flatly colorblind—a position endorsed by Justices Antonin Scalia and Clarence Thomas—the issue involves complicated and controversial questions, starting with the original meaning of the Fourteenth Amendment. See Jeff Rosen, "The Colorblind Court," *The New Republic*, July 31, 1995, and Andrew Kull, *The Color-Blind Constitution* (Cambridge, Mass.: Harvard University Press, 1992), pp. 221–24.

that the truths of the Declaration of Independence were relevant to the audience before him, which included European immigrants who were not descended from those who wrote the Declaration, fought the Revolution, and framed the Constitution. Having paid honor to the "men living in that day whom we claim as our fathers and grandfathers," and having linked the principle they contended for to the nation's subsequent prosperity, Lincoln told the audience that "we hold this annual celebration to remind ourselves of all the good done . . . and how it was done and who did it, and how we are historically connected with it." He added that "we go from these meetings in better humor with ourselves—we feel more attached the one to the other, and more firmly bound to the country we inhabit." And, yes, those he was addressing were as much a part of this country as anyone else:

> We have [besides those descended from the founders] . . . among us perhaps half our people who are not descendants at all of these men, they are men who have come from Europe—German, Irish, French, and Scandinavian—men that have come from Europe themselves, or whose ancestors have come hither and settled here, finding themselves our equals in all things. If they look back through this history to trace their connection with those days by blood, they find they have none, they cannot carry themselves back into that glorious epoch and make themselves feel that they are part of us, but when they look through that old Declaration of Independence they find that those old men say that "We hold these truths to be self-evident, that all men are created equal," and then they feel that moral sentiment taught in that day evidences their relation to those men, that it is the father of all moral principle in them, and that they have a right to claim it as though they were blood of the blood, and flesh of the flesh of the men who wrote that Declaration, and so they are.[3]

As Lincoln reminds us, the Declaration included any person from anywhere—the Germans and Swedes and other Europeans whom Lincoln addressed, the slaves Lincoln freed, the Asians who began arriving on our shores just before the nation was about to rend itself in a civil war, the Hispanics from all parts of the globe, Englishmen, American Indians, Jews—in sum, everyone. The Declaration is the great leveler, teaching that the rights of one are the rights of all. It puts us all on the same footing, and it implies the necessity of colorblind law because only that kind of law fully respects the equal rights of all persons, as individuals.

Affirmative action has always been an aberration from our best principles. The time has come to end it.

---

[3]Roy P. Basler, ed., *The Collected Works of Abraham Lincoln* (New Brunswick, N.J.: Rutgers University Press, 1953), vol. 2, pp. 499–500.

Topics for Critical Thinking and Writing

1. Find out, with the help of a reference librarian, what Allan Bakke, Brian Weber, Randy Pech, or Cheryl Hopwood did to warrant commendation from Eastland (para. 4), and write a 250-word essay on what you discover.

2. What, if any, particular programs of affirmative action does Eastland mention and criticize?

3. When Eastland writes (para. 6) that "we do not have to take the risk of affirmative action," what does he mean? How do you think he would reply to someone who disagrees with him?

4. Eastland concentrates on the objections to affirmative action for African Americans; he says little about affirmative action for women. Do you think his objections apply equally well to both groups? Why, or why not?

5. Suppose one argued that affirmative action is a necessary tactic to achieve more racial and cultural diversity on campus among students, faculty, and staff and that such diversity is an end good in itself. How do you think Eastland might reply to such an argument?

6. Head Start programs, established under the Economic Opportunity Act of 1964, help prepare economically disadvantaged students to meet the rigors of academic life in school and college. Do Eastland's criticisms of affirmative action apply to Head Start?

7. Which statement do you think best characterizes Eastland's position? (a) We do not have a problem with racism, so affirmative action was never needed to solve it. (b) We do have a problem with racism, but affirmative action is not the way to solve it. (c) Affirmative action creates a problem of racism where none existed.

8. Read the essay by Burke Marshall and Nicholas deB. Katzenbach (directly following) in defense of affirmative action programs, and write a 1,000-word essay explaining why you think one essay or the other has the better argument overall.

Burke Marshall and
Nicholas deB. Katzenbach

Burke Marshall (b. 1922) received his bachelor's and law degrees from Yale University. He was an assistant attorney general from 1961 to 1965 during the Kennedy administration, working on racial issues. He is now an emeritus law professor at Yale. Nicholas deB. Katzenbach (b. 1922) graduated from Princeton University and received a law degree from Yale. He was attorney general from 1965 to 1966 during the Johnson administration and coauthor of The Political Foundations of International Law *(1961). This essay was first published in the* New York Times Magazine *(February 22, 1998).*

Not Color Blind: Just Blind

Few African American students are likely to enter the great public law schools of California and Texas in the fall. That is the direct, foreseeable consequence of a California referendum and a Texas federal court decision. So concerned were civil rights groups about the popular and legal doctrine that led to this result that they joined together to deny the U.S. Supreme Court the opportunity to decide an apparently definitive affirmative action case involving teachers in Piscataway Township, New Jersey. Do such events — especially Piscataway — foretell the end of affirmative action, or have we simply lost sight of our long-term vision of a color-blind society?

In 1989, the Piscataway school board, faced with the need to lay off a single teacher, chose to lay off a white while retaining an African American of equal seniority and qualifications. The board gave racial diversity, citing its affirmative action policy, as the sole reason for the choice. Its decision was rejected by a federal judge who found the board in violation of the 1964 Civil Rights Act. That ruling was upheld by a federal appellate court. The school board appealed to the Supreme Court. Late last year, with financial assistance from civil rights groups, the board settled the case and withdrew its appeal.

The settlement has since become a kind of raw shorthand in the national debate about affirmative action because its facts serve to make clear the core of that debate. The seeming baldness of the facts plainly told the civil rights groups' leaders that the case should not be permitted to remain in the Supreme Court, and that it would be prudent to use their funds to avoid its doing so. This may be the first time that money has been used directly to take an important public policy issue off the Court's docket.

All this arose because the case was framed to portray person-to-person competition for a job in which race alone was the decisive factor. This aspect fitted neatly with the notion, widespread among opponents of affirmative action, that it creates a zero-sum game in which there is a loser for every winner and that the game is won and lost on the basis of race. Thus it obscures the larger goal of finding and preserving room for blacks in all aspects — economic, political, educational, social — and at all levels of society.

In addition, the case involved a layoff — the loss of a specific, known   5 job — instead of a positive general decision as to what kind and mix of people are needed in a work force or in a faculty or student body. The facts fitted in not only with some legal learning — that an affirmative action program should not "unnecessarily trammel" the expectations of those not included in the program — but also more importantly with the personalization of the controversy into one in which whites are individually hurt by being deprived of their deserved opportunities, by deliberate and explicit efforts to include blacks.

These aspects of the Piscataway litigation appeared perfect for opponents of affirmative action and a legal land mine for its defenders. The former believed that the facts of the case would lead a majority of the Supreme Court to say, about affirmative action in general, that the case showed its injustices and the malevolent consequences of permitting the use of race as a factor, certainly as a decisive one, in allocating any scarce resources, like jobs or admissions to great universities. Strangely enough, the latter group—the important civil rights organizations and their lawyers as well as the Clinton administration—saw the case in the same way. Thus all concerned either hoped or feared that the Court, when faced with the rejected white teacher, would say: "Enough of this. It has gone on too long already. This is the end of affirmative action for any purpose as far as the law is concerned."

Is affirmative action really the unfair black "preference," or "reverse discrimination," policy that its critics claim and that Piscataway seems to present so starkly? Have we in fact lost sight of the larger goal of integrating blacks into our society? Or have we been so successful in achieving a "color blind" society about which Martin Luther King dreamed that the larger goal need no longer concern us?

Those who oppose affirmative action programs do not make such broad claims. They affirm the goal of an integrated society and do not contend we have yet achieved it. Critics simply argue that it is morally and constitutionally wrong to seek its achievement through race-based programs that give a "preference" to African Americans. Such programs, they maintain, are essentially wrong for the same reasons that it is wrong for whites to discriminate against blacks. It denies "equal opportunity" to whites and is antithetical to awarding jobs or promotions or college admissions on the basis of "merit."

There is no longer any dispute that overt, provable racial bias against blacks in employment or education should be unlawful. The disputed question is whether overt and provable bias is the only form of racial bias with which our society should—or can lawfully—be concerned. Certainly that bias—state supported in the Deep South and rampant throughout the country—was the immediate and most important target of the civil rights laws of the 1960s. Equally, the white majority in this country, despite deep-seated feelings of racial superiority, committed itself to achieving an integrated society. That happened, we believe, for the simple reason that it did not seem possible, then or now, for this country to maintain its democratic principles unless we could achieve Dr. King's dream. Is the elimination of overt bias all we need to do to accomplish that end?

The term "affirmative action" was first officially used in 1961 when 10 President Kennedy strengthened an existing executive order prohibiting racial discrimination by government contractors in their employment practices. It was a natural, not a provocative, term to use. In the early '60s, blacks were essentially excluded from every level and every desirable institution of society. In many places they could not enter theaters, restaurants, hotels, or even parts of public libraries, courtrooms, and legislatures. How could that condition possibly have been changed—and the nation as a whole have decided that it should be changed—without taking action affirmatively, positively, deliberately, explicitly to change it?

So it was that there was no real controversy at the national level over the basic idea of acting affirmatively about race, although debate started soon enough, as it should have, over the details of particular steps. But at that time the country saw problems of race as problems to be faced and dealt with as the racial problems they were. The label "affirmative action" became popular perhaps because it suggested that we were at long last dealing with our oldest and most difficult problem. It was applied beyond the Kennedy executive order to a variety of race-based programs, private and public, voluntary as well as legally coerced, that sought to guarantee the employment—or, in the case of educational institutions, the admission—of qualified African Americans. It preceded the Civil Rights Acts of the 1960s and was consciously aimed at racial bias at a time when individuals could not yet sue private employers. But companies' employment of qualified African Americans to insure eligibility for government contracts was measured not individual by individual but by success in achieving reasonable numbers over time.

The technique of setting goals for minority employment is important because of its capacity to deal with all forms of potential bias—overt, concealed, or even inadvertent. Most national corporations have adopted employment goals. They appreciate the economic advantages of expanding and integrating the work force and they understand the need to press hard if the overall goal of inclusion is to be obtained.

The natural inclination of predominantly white male middle managers is to hire and promote one of their own. Most of the time the decision honestly reflects their judgment as to the best candidate without conscious appreciation of how much that judgment may have been conditioned by experience in the largely segregated society we still live in. To hire or promote an African American is often viewed as risky. Will he or she be accepted by fellow workers? A white may be praised for his independence; a like-minded black is seen as not a "team player." If corporations set reasonable hiring and promotion goals and reward management for their achievement, the integration process is speeded up. Public and private policies coincide.

Critics of affirmative action in employment see it not as an effort to create a reasonably integrated work force but as a system for favoring a less-qualified African American over a better-qualified white—a system of "preference" rather than "merit." There are three difficulties with their argument.

First, critics seek to reduce what is administered as a flexible system of hiring and promoting numbers of people into a measurement of one individual against another. Affirmative action programs deal with 15 numbers of people at various times and seek to examine flexibly the results in numbers, not whether individual *A* is better than *B*. Such a program does not examine or re-examine each decision or demand precise achievement of numerical goals; it does not require a "quota," like a sales quota. It thus encourages personnel judgments, tolerating individual mistakes whether a white or a black is the victim.

Second, the critics assume that it is possible precisely to define and measure "merit." The best person for one job may not be the best for another, and vice versa; how does one square individual differences, or the "overqualified" candidate, with merit and the requirements of a particular job? Assuming that we are selecting from a pool of candidates who all meet whatever objective criteria are applicable to job performance, selection of the "best qualified" becomes a matter of subjective judgment by the employer—a judgment that involves weighing such intangibles as personality, leadership ability, motivation, dependability, enthusiasm, attitude toward authority. If critics are claiming that affirmative action has resulted in a less-competent work force because of the hiring and promotion of less-qualified blacks, neither evidence nor experience supports that conclusion.

Third, to argue that affirmative action constitutes a "preference" for African Americans is simply to argue that it distorts what would otherwise be a more efficient and fair system. Since the premise of the argument is that affirmative action constitutes a "preference" for blacks, it is fair to assume that proponents believe a "color blind" system would result in fewer blacks being employed. Why? If the pool of qualified applicants is 10 percent African American, then a color-blind system or an affirmative action program would result in about 10 percent black representation in the work force.

Thus, the word "preference" as critics use it is an effort to convert a broad employment effort into a series of individual choices or comparisons, as in Piscataway, with the additional innuendo that the fact of "preference" means a less-qualified African American will always prevail. That is a serious distortion of affirmative action.

Put differently, opponents of affirmative action in employment believe either that today the playing field is level for all races or that, absent overt racial bias, we should act as if it were. By contrast, most African Americans and many whites believe that bias still exists, though not always overtly, and that affirmative action is simply a guarantee that the playing field is not tilted.

Laws forbidding racial discrimination were relatively easy to administer when the bias was overt and widespread. The more that bias goes underground or, worse yet, is unconscious on the part of the decision maker, who believes his decision is uninfluenced by race, the more difficult and controversial that administration becomes. To label and punish unconscious bias as though it wore a hood may well be offensive. Programs of affirmative action avoid that problem while promoting the 20 integrated society we seek. They minimally interfere with discretion in making particular choices and give management a desirable latitude in exercising particular judgments.

The other use of affirmative action most commonly criticized is in college admission. Educational institutions usually create a pool of applicants who meet objective tests designed to determine if the applicant is capable of performing successfully. Tests can reasonably predict first-year performance and do not claim to do more. But selection from the pool is not confined to rank on test scores, and applicants with lower scores are admitted for many reasons. Some applicants are admitted on the basis of judgments about potential and predictions about future performance not unlike those used in employment decisions. A student from a poor school who qualifies may be seen, despite a lower score, as having great motivation and aptitude. In other cases, "merit" is measured by other abilities, like musical or athletic talent. In still others, admissions may be determined by geography, financial ability, relationship to graduates, or relationship to people important in other ways to the institution. And finally, race and national origin may be taken into account and labeled "affirmative action."

If race cannot be taken into account and admission is based on test scores alone, far fewer African Americans will qualify. That was the predictable result in California and Texas, where state institutions were forbidden to take race into account. Again, the word "preference" is unfortunate because critics use it to imply that some kind of racial bias is used to reject better-qualified whites. Most of the students admitted are in fact white, hardly a demonstration of a bias in favor of blacks, and certainly not one that can be equated with past denials of admission to blacks to our best universities.

What proponents of affirmative action in college admissions urge is simply an institutional need for qualified African Americans on the grounds that a diverse student body contributes to educational excellence and to the preparation of students to live in an integrated society. Critics do not question the educational advantage of diversity—though their prescriptions would make its achievement virtually impossible. Further, those African Americans who can qualify for the institutional admissions pool would probably not be as successful as they are without superior motivation and determination—qualities most Americans would associate with merit.

Colleges and professional schools serve as gatekeepers to professional and business careers. If African Americans can successfully do the academic work, they will importantly contribute to the public goal of an integrated society. Studies support the contention that some blacks perform better academically than some whites with better test scores and that African Americans successfully compete for employment at a comparable level with whites upon graduation.

The arguments against this "preference" are similar to those in other 25
affirmative action programs: it is anti-merit and discriminates against
whites with higher scores on admissions tests. That argument is not really worth consideration unless one is prepared to argue that all admissions should be measured exclusively by test scores. No one is prepared
to go that far. The plea for fairness based on "merit" as measured by test
scores appears to be confined to race—a plea that in our society should
be regarded with some skepticism.

Affirmative action programs, whether to avoid present bias or to
remedy the effects of three centuries of discrimination against African
Americans, are race-based. The problems they seek to cure are and always have been race-based. They stem from history—the political, economic, and social domination of blacks by a white majority that regarded
blacks as inferior. Undoubtedly there are blacks who are biased against
whites and who, given the power to do so, would discriminate against
them. Of course, given the power, it would be as morally wrong for
them to do so as it has been for whites. But discrimination by blacks
against whites is not America's problem. It is not the problem that predominantly white legislatures, businesses, and universities seek to solve
through affirmative action programs.

To speak of these white efforts as though they were racially biased
against whites and to equate them with the discriminatory practices of the
past against African Americans is to steal the rhetoric of civil rights and
turn it upside down. For racial bias to be a problem, it must be accompanied by power. Affirmative action programs are race-based not to show
preference for one race over another but to resolve that problem. Only if
one ignores that purpose and states the matter in Piscataway terms—preferring one individual over another for no reason other than race—does
there even appear to be room for argument. If problems of race are to be
solved, they must be seen as the race-based problems they are.

It is this aspect of the controversy that recent decisions of the
Supreme Court have brought into question. The Equal Protection Clause
of the Fourteenth Amendment was designed to insure that former slaves
and their descendants were entitled to the same legal protection as white
citizens. Like the Thirteenth Amendment abolishing slavery and the Fifteenth guaranteeing the right to vote regardless of race, it was clearly
and unequivocally aimed at racial problems—in today's terminology
"race based." The Equal Protection Clause has never been viewed as preventing classification of citizens for governmental reasons as long as the
legislative classification was "reasonable" in terms of its purpose.

Where that classification involved race, however, the Court determined that it must be given "strict scrutiny." In other words, given our
history both before and after the passage of the amendment, the Court
understandably thought it wise to regard any racial classifications by
overwhelmingly white legislatures with skepticism. When it was satisfied

after strict scrutiny that the classification did not have the purpose or effect of discriminating against African Americans or other ethnic minorities, the Court found legislation to be consistent with the amendment. In the context of both our history and that of the amendment, this simply forbade abuse of white political superiority that prejudiced other races or ethnic minorities.

More recently, however, a majority has edged toward pronouncing 30 the Constitution "color blind," coming close to holding legislation that uses any racial classification unconstitutional. Reading the Equal Protection Clause to protect whites as well as blacks from racial classification is to focus upon a situation that does not and never has existed in our society. Unfortunately, it casts doubt upon all forms of racial classification, however benign and however focused upon promoting integration. If such a reading is finally adopted by a majority of the Court, it would put a constitutional pall over all governmental affirmative action programs and even put similar private programs in danger of being labeled "discriminatory" against whites and therefore in violation of existing civil rights legislation—perhaps the ultimate stupidity.

The Court has, in short, never accepted as a national priority—in its terms a "compelling state interest"—the necessary race-based efforts, private and public, to include blacks in the institutional framework that constitutes America's economic, political, educational, and social life. Its recent decisions on the distribution of political power through districting outcomes have precluded race as a major factor while permitting incumbency, party affiliations, random geographic features, and boundaries drawn for obsolete historical reasons. Other lines of cases have similar outcomes for university admissions (as against unfair and educationally irrelevant factors like family ties, athletic prowess, and geography) and employment choices. It is very nearly as if this Court has simply mandated that what is the country's historic struggle against racial oppression and racial prejudice cannot be acted upon in a race-conscious way—that the law must view racial problems observable by all as if oppression and prejudice did not exist and had never existed. The Court's majority, in other words, has come very close to saying—and the hope and fear about the Piscataway case was that it would finally say at last—that courts cannot be permitted to see what is plain to everybody else.

Topics for Critical Thinking and Writing

1. What is a "zero-sum game" (para. 4), and why might it seem that affirmative action involves such a game?

2. The authors suggest that part (most?) of the original purpose behind affirmative action was "the larger goal of integrating blacks into our society" (para. 7). Do the authors explain how this was supposed to work?

3. *Affirmative action* has been defined in law and practice in several different ways. After reading this essay, how would you complete the following definition: "A given program is a program of affirmative action if and only if . . ." (Hint: Consult your reference librarian about some specific affirmative action program. For example, what made Head Start an example of affirmative action?)

4. The authors offer three replies to critics of affirmative action (paras. 14–18). Which of these replies do you think is most persuasive? Least persuasive? Explain yourself in an essay of 300 words.

5. If it had been within the power of the authors to decide the Piscataway case (paras. 1–6), how do you think they would have decided it?

6. Suppose Jones and Smith are both equally qualified for entrance to a selective college as measured in the usual ways (SAT scores, rank in high school graduating class, teacher recommendations). Only one can be admitted, however. One admission officer argues for admitting Jones because he comes from a remote part of the country and thus would help the college diversify its student body geographically. Another admission officer argues for admitting Smith because she is a member of an ethnic minority and thus would help the college diversify its student body racially. Do you think one of the two kinds of diversity is more important than the other? Why? Which candidate would you prefer to admit, and why?

7. The authors are skeptical about college admissions "based on 'merit'" (para. 25), especially when merit is measured by "test scores." Why are they skeptical? How would you define *merit* as relevant to college admission? (That is, how would you complete the following definition: "An applicant merits admission to a selective college if and only if . . .") However you define it, would you place great or little emphasis on merit in determining who is admitted to college?

For topical links related to the affirmative action debate, see the companion Web site:
www.bedfordstmartins.com/barnetbedau.

15

Gay Marriages: Should They Be Legalized?

It's not complicated:

I WANT TO MARRY THE MAN I LOVE.

Case closed!

Thomas B. Stoddard

Thomas B. Stoddard (1948–1997) was executive director of the Lambda Legal Defense and Education Fund, a gay rights organization. In 1995 New York University School of Law established a fellowship in Stoddard's name, honoring him for his work on behalf of gay and lesbian rights. This article is from the op-ed section of the New York Times, *March 4, 1988.*

Gay Marriages: Make Them Legal

"In sickness and in health, 'til death do us part." With those familiar words, millions of people each year are married, a public affirmation of a private bond that both society and the newlyweds hope will endure. Yet for nearly four years, Karen Thompson was denied the company of the one person to whom she had pledged lifelong devotion. Her partner is a woman, Sharon Kowalski, and their home state of Minnesota, like every other jurisdiction in the United States, refuses to permit two individuals of the same sex to marry.

Karen Thompson and Sharon Kowalski are spouses in every respect except the legal. They exchanged vows and rings; they lived together until November 13, 1983—when Ms. Kowalski was severely injured when her car was struck by a drunk driver. She lost the capacity to walk or to speak more than several words at a time, and needed constant care.

Ms. Thompson sought a court ruling granting her guardianship over her partner, but Ms. Kowalski's parents opposed the petition and obtained sole guardianship. They moved Ms. Kowalski to a nursing home three-hundred miles away from Ms. Thompson and forbade all visits between the two women. Last month, as part of a reevaluation of Ms. Kowalski's mental competency, Ms. Thompson was permitted to visit her partner again. But the prolonged injustice and anguish inflicted on both women hold a moral for everyone.

Marriage, the Supreme Court declared in 1967, is "one of the basic civil rights of man" (and, presumably, of woman as well). The freedom to marry, said the Court, is "essential to the orderly pursuit of happiness."

Marriage is not just a symbolic state. It can be the key to survival, emotional and financial. Marriage triggers a universe of rights, privileges, and presumptions. A married person can share in a spouse's estate even when there is no will. She is typically entitled to the group insurance and pension programs offered by the spouse's employer, and she enjoys tax advantages. She cannot be compelled to testify against her spouse in legal proceedings. 5

The decision whether or not to marry belongs properly to individuals—not the government. Yet at present, all fifty states deny that choice to millions of gay and lesbian Americans. While marriage has historically required a male partner and a female partner, history alone cannot sanctify injustice. If tradition were the only measure, most states would still limit matrimony to partners of the same race.

As recently as 1967, before the Supreme Court declared miscegenation statutes unconstitutional, sixteen states still prohibited marriages between a white person and a black person. When all the excuses were stripped away, it was clear that the only purpose of those laws was, in the words of the Supreme Court, "to maintain white supremacy."

Those who argue against reforming the marriage statutes because they believe that same-sex marriage would be "antifamily" overlook the obvious: Marriage creates families and promotes social stability. In an increasingly loveless world, those who wish to commit themselves to a relationship founded upon devotion should be encouraged, not scorned. Government has no legitimate interest in how that love is expressed.

And it can no longer be argued—if it ever could—that marriage is fundamentally a procreative unit. Otherwise, states would forbid marriage between those who, by reason of age or infertility, cannot have children, as well as those who elect not to.

As the case of Sharon Kowalski and Karen Thompson demonstrates, 10 sanctimonious illusions lead directly to the suffering of others. Denied the right to marry, these two women are left subject to the whims and prejudices of others, and of the law.

Depriving millions of gay American adults the marriages of their choice, and the rights that flow from marriage, denies equal protection of the law. They, their families and friends, together with fair-minded people everywhere, should demand an end to this monstrous injustice.

Topics for Critical Thinking and Writing

1. Study the essay as an example of ways to argue. What sorts of arguments does Stoddard offer? He does not offer statistics or cite authorities, but what *does* he do in an effort to convince the reader?

2. Stoddard draws an analogy between laws that used to prohibit marriage between persons of different races and laws that still prohibit marriage between persons of the same sex. Evaluate this analogy in an essay of 100 words.

3. Stoddard cites Karen Thompson and Sharon Kowalski (para. 2). Presumably he could have found, if he had wished, a comparable example using two men rather than two women. Do you think the effect of his essay would be better, worse, or the same if his example used men rather than women? Why?

4. Do you find adequate Stoddard's response to the charge that "same sex marriage would be 'antifamily'" (para. 8)? Why or why not?

5. One widespread assumption is that the family exists to produce children. Stoddard mentions this, but he does not mention that although gay couples cannot produce children, they can (where legally permitted to do so) adopt and rear children and thus fulfill a social need. (Also, one of the partners can even be the natural parent.) Do you think he was wise to omit this argument in behalf of same-sex marriages? Why?

6. Think about what principal claims one might make to contradict Stoddard's claims, and then write a 500-word essay defending this proposition: "Lawful marriage should be limited to heterosexual couples." Or if you believe that gay marriages should be legitimized, write an essay offering additional support to Stoddard's essay.

7. Stoddard's whole purpose is to break down the prejudice against same-sex marriages, and he seems to take for granted the appropriateness of monogamy. Yet one might argue against Stoddard that if society opened the door to same-sex marriages, it would be hard to keep the door closed to polygamy or polyandry. Write a 500-word essay exploring this question.

8. Would Stoddard's argument require him to allow marriage between a brother and a sister? A parent and a child? A human being and an animal? Why, or why not?

Lisa Schiffren

Lisa Schiffren was a speechwriter for former Vice President Dan Quayle. We reprint an essay that originally was published in the New York Times *on March 23, 1996.*

Gay Marriage, an Oxymoron

As study after study and victim after victim testify to the social devastation of the sexual revolution, easy divorce, and out-of-wedlock motherhood, marriage is fashionable again. And parenthood has transformed many baby boomers into advocates of bourgeois norms.

Indeed, we have come so far that the surprise issue of the political season is whether homosexual "marriage" should be legalized. The Hawaii courts will likely rule that gay marriage is legal, and other states will be required to accept those marriages as valid.

Considering what a momentous change this would be—a radical redefinition of society's most fundamental institution—there has been almost no real debate. This is because the premise is unimaginable to many, and the forces of political correctness have descended on the discussion, raising the cost of opposition. But one may feel the same affection for one's homosexual friends and relatives as for any other and be genuinely pleased for the happiness they derive from relationships while opposing gay marriage for principled reasons.

"Same-sex marriage" is inherently incompatible with our culture's understanding of the institution. Marriage is essentially a lifelong compact between a man and woman committed to sexual exclusivity and the creation and nurture of offspring. For most Americans, the marital union—as distinguished from other sexual relationships and legal and economic partnerships—is imbued with an aspect of holiness. Though many of us are uncomfortable using religious language to discuss social and political issues, Judeo-Christian morality informs our view of family life.

Though it is not polite to mention it, what the Judeo-Christian tradi-   5
tion has to say about homosexual unions could not be clearer. In a diverse, open society such as ours, tolerance of homosexuality is a necessity. But for many, its practice depends on a trick of cognitive dissonance that allows people to believe in the Judeo-Christian moral order while accepting, often with genuine regard, the different lives of homosexual acquaintances. That is why, though homosexuals may believe that they are merely seeking a small expansion of the definition of marriage, the majority of Americans perceive this change as a radical deconstruction of the institution.

Some make the conservative argument that making marriage a civil right will bring stability, an end to promiscuity, and a sense of fairness to gay men and women. But they miss the point. Society cares about stability in heterosexual unions because it is critical for raising healthy children and transmitting the values that are the basis of our culture.

Whether homosexual relationships endure is of little concern to society. That is also true of most childless marriages, harsh as it is to say. Society has wisely chosen not to differentiate between marriages, because it would require meddling into the motives and desires of everyone who applies for a license.

In traditional marriage, the tie that really binds for life is shared responsibility for the children. (A small fraction of gay couples may choose to raise children together, but such children are offspring of one partner and an outside contributor.) What will keep gay marriages together when individuals tire of each other?

Similarly, the argument that legal marriage will check promiscuity by gay males raises the question of how a "piece of paper" will do what the threat of AIDS has not. Lesbians seem to have little problem with monogamy or the rest of what constitutes "domestication," despite the absence of official status.

Finally, there is the so-called fairness argument. The government gives   10
tax benefits, inheritance rights, and employee benefits only to the married. Again, these financial benefits exist to help couples raise children. Tax reform is an effective way to remove distinctions among earners.

If the American people are interested in a radical experiment with same-sex marriages, then subjecting it to the political process is the right route. For a court in Hawaii to assume that it has the power to radically redefine marriage is a stunning abuse of power. To present homosexual marriage as a fait accompli, without national debate, is a serious political error. A society struggling to recover from thirty years of weakened norms and broken families is not likely to respond gently to having an institution central to most people's lives altered.

Topics for Critical Thinking and Writing

1. What is an oxymoron, and why does Schiffren think the phrases *gay marriage* and *same-sex marriage* are oxymorons?

2. In paragraph 3 Schiffren refers to "political correctness." How would you define that term? So defined, do you think political correctness is sometimes objectionable? Always objectionable? Sometimes justifiable? Always justifiable?

3. Schiffren defines marriage in paragraph 4 in such a way that a man and woman who marry with no intention of having children are deviant. She does not imply, however, that such marriages should be prohibited by law or otherwise nullified. Does consistency require her to grant that while same-sex marriages are no doubt deviant—in the sense of atypical or relatively rare—they are nonetheless legitimate?

4. Schiffren refers to "cognitive dissonance" (para. 5). What does she mean by this term, and how does she think it plays a role in our society's prevailing attitude toward homosexuality?

5. Schiffren says (para. 7), "Whether homosexual relationships endure is of little concern to society" because such relationships do not involve nurturing children. By the same token, does society have little concern for heterosexual marriages to endure where there are no children involved? Or do you think that there are other considerations that make stable intimate relations between consenting adults important to society?

6. List the reasons for same-sex marriage unions that Schiffren mentions. Which, if any, do you think are significant? Can you think of any reasons that she fails to mention?

7. In her final paragraph, Schiffren deplores the federal court in Hawaii that ratified same-sex marriage. Is it the process or the result of this decision to which she mostly objects? Do you agree with her objection? Go to your college library, find out the current status in the courts of this issue, and write a 500-word paper on the Hawaiian same-sex marriage law, how it became law, and what it provides.

8. If gay marriage is recognized as legal, are we necessarily on a slippery slope (see p. 324) that will bring us to recognition of polygamy or polyandry (perhaps heterosexual, but perhaps a marriage of a bisexual to a man and also to a woman) and incest. Why, or why not?

9. Schiffren was not replying directly to Thomas B. Stoddard (p. 492), but she probably knew his arguments. Does he make any points that you

wish she had faced? If so, what are they? If she were asked to comment on these points by Stoddard, what do you think her responses would be?

10. How would you characterize Schiffren's tone? Haughty? Earnest? Smart-alecky? (You need not come up with a one-word answer; you might say, "She is chiefly *X* but also sometimes *Y*.") Do you think her tone will help her to persuade people to accept her views?

For topical links related to the issue of gay marriage, see the companion Web site:
www.bedfordstmartins.com/barnetbedau.

16

Gun Control:
Would It Really Help?

Sarah Thompson

Sarah Thompson, a retired physician, describes herself thus on her homepage on the Internet: "Dr. Thompson is dedicated to the restoration of full civil liberties and limited constitutional government. She writes [an online] column, "The Righter," which focuses on civil liberties and individual responsibility and action." We reprint here an article that was published in American Gun Review *in October 1997.*

Concealed Carry Prevents Violent Crimes

The right of law-abiding citizens to carry concealed firearms for purposes of self-defense has become a hot and controversial topic. Claims have been made citing everything from "the presence of a firearm in the home increases the risk of homicide by 43 times" to "there are up to 2.5 million defensive uses of private firearms per year, with up to 400,000 lives saved as a result." There are people who feel endangered by the presence of a gun nearby and other people who feel vulnerable when not carrying a gun on their person. Some law enforcement agents welcome the increasing numbers of lawfully armed citizens while others view them as a deadly threat. What and where is the truth in all of this disagreement, and what are the implications for public policy?

Prior to Prohibition, there was virtually no federal gun control, and no concept of guns being "evil." Guns were seen as a threat to society only when they were possessed by blacks, and the history of gun control closely parallels the history of racism in this country. Guns were simply tools, useful for protecting one's livelihood and property, obtaining food for one's family, recreation, and when necessary, self-defense. The gun culture was an accepted and respected part of American life.

However, in a situation similar to the one we face today, Prohibition gave birth to a criminal subculture which depended on violence and guns, terrorizing law-abiding citizens. After Prohibition was repealed, these criminal organizations remained. Rather than attacking crime and criminals, the government passed the National Firearms Act in 1934, which put a $200 "transfer tax" (about $4,000 in 1996 dollars) on certain guns, particularly machine guns and short-barreled shotguns. (For comparison, a short-barreled shotgun cost only about $5!) The Federal Firearms Act followed in 1938, which required firearms dealers to obtain licenses, and started a new federal bureaucracy to "control guns."

The war on guns again escalated after the assassinations of President Kennedy, Senator Robert Kennedy, and the Reverend Martin Luther King in the 1960s. This resulted in the Federal Firearms Act of 1968 which, when compared word for word to the Nazi weapons laws of 1938, is almost identical. In the late 1980s to early 1990s, the attempted assassination of President Reagan and the wounding of his Press Secretary James Brady, and the escalation of violent, firearms-related crimes due to the failed "War on Drugs," have led to an intensification of the "War on Guns." We now have innumerable state and local laws restricting gun ownership, carrying, use, and even appearance, along with federal laws such as the Brady Act and the impending "Brady II."

To enforce these laws, the government needed to get "the people" to 5 support them, to willingly give up their Second Amendment rights and their right to self-defense. To do this, it recruited powerful spokespeople, primarily doctors and the media, to convince people that guns were bad and needed to be banned. Doctors, at least until recently, were highly re-spected professionals, scientists whose words were above questioning. The same was true of the elite medical journals. Most prestigious of all were the revered doctors and scientists who worked at the huge federal institutes of research. To their enduring shame, some of these doctors were co-opted into helping the government in its "War on Guns."

Doctors, of course, are not superhuman and they have weaknesses like everyone. Many well-meaning doctors just didn't analyze correctly what they were seeing and didn't bother to ask the right questions, since they had been trained to obey medical authorities. For example, doctors who work in emergency rooms see the horrors that misuse of guns can create. They dedicate their lives to saving lives, and watching people, es-pecially young people, die of gunshot wounds is extremely painful. This makes it easy for them to be swayed by emotion and blame the gun in-stead of the person who misused it. Of course they never see the people who use guns safely and responsibly, and they never see the people whose lives were saved by defensive gun use. It's a very one-sided view.

At the same time, there were other doctors who saw the huge amounts of money being poured into biased gun research and saw the opportunity to get grant money, have their work published, or become famous. All this required was designing research that aided the govern-ment's preconceived policy of "proving" that guns were bad in order to disarm the populace. In my opinion there is only one term that applies to people who sell their integrity and their credentials for fame and profit.

Thus since 1987 we have been bombarded with medical "experts" proclaiming that guns were the cause of nearly everything wrong in so-ciety. The media gave tremendous coverage to these studies, and rein-forced them with emotional and melodramatic stories of lives ruined by guns—by inanimate guns, not by criminals, carelessness, or their own stupidity. People, especially people raised in urban areas who had no ex-perience with guns, believed these stories. No doubt you've heard these claims, and maybe even worried that invoking your Second Amendment rights was a bad idea.

Many of these studies were funded by the National Center for Injury Prevention and Control (NCIPC), a division of the Centers for Disease Control (CDC)—funded, of course, with OUR tax dollars. That's right. Our government officials, sworn to uphold the Constitution, used our money to try to deprive us of one of our most important Constitutional rights. And the NCIPC didn't even pretend to be objective. Dr. Mark Rosenberg, former director of NCIPC, has been quoted avowing his and the CDC's desire to create a public perception of firearms as "dirty, deadly—and banned."

One common excuse for gun control, designed to sound scientific, is 10 that guns are a public health problem, that guns are "pathogens" (germs) which must be eliminated to eliminate the "disease" of gun violence.

This simply is not true. To be true, the presence of a gun would cause the disease (violence) in all those exposed to it, and in its absence, violence should not be found. (Every physician is taught the criteria for determining what is or isn't a pathogen early in medical school, so this is inexcusable.) If all those exposed to firearms attempted homicide, our streets truly would be running with blood. Approximately half of all American households own guns, yet few people are involved with homicide or other gun misuse. There are approximately 230 million guns in the United States, more than enough for each adult and teen, yet only a minuscule number of people commit homicide. And if degree of exposure to guns correlated with homicide rates, our police would be the worst offenders.

One often quoted study is the Sloan-Kellerman comparison of Seattle and Vancouver, published in the *New England Journal of Medicine.* Their methodology was simplistic and merely compared the homicide rates in the two cities, then assumed the lower rate in Vancouver was due to gun control. Obviously there are nearly infinite differences in any two cities, yet the study did not control for any differences. The difference in homicide rates could just as easily have been due to economic, cultural, or ethnic variables, differences in laws, age differences, substance abuse, or anything else. Based on their data, one could just as well conclude that the difference was due to the number of movie theaters or eating Twinkies. As a final insult to scientific research, the homicide rates before gun control were not evaluated. Homicide actually increased 25 percent after the institution of the 1977 gun law. . . .

Perhaps the most often quoted myth about the risks of gun ownership is that having a gun in one's home increases one's risk of homicide by a factor of 43. This study, by Kellerman, is full of errors and deceit, and has been widely discredited. Yet the 43 times figure continues to be repeated until it has now achieved the status of "common knowledge." Among the errors, Kellerman did not show that even ONE victim was killed with the gun kept in the home. In fact, at least 49 percent of the victims were killed by someone who did not live in the home and probably had no access to guns kept there. He assumed that the victim of the crime was the one killed, ignoring the possibility that it was the criminal, not the victim, who was killed. Finally, the study showed that substance abuse, family violence, living alone, and living in a rented home were all greater predictors of homicide than was gun ownership. Curiously, the authors have refused to make their data available to other researchers who wish to evaluate the study. Yet, as I mentioned before, this study was funded with our tax dollars.[1]

Fortunately, these fraudulent researchers at the NCIPC were finally exposed in 1996 by a coalition of physicians and criminologists who testified before the House appropriations committee. As a result, the

---

[1]These data have since been released. [*American Gun Review* editor's note.]

NCIPC's funding for so-called "gun research" was cut from the budget. Of course there were people doing well-designed, accurate research on guns and violence during this period as well. . . . But they weren't doctors, they weren't supported by the government, and the media totally ignored them. They were criminologists, sociologists, lawyers, and their studies weren't considered important, especially by the medical establishment.

Gary Kleck's book, *Point Blank: Guns and Violence in America,* was published in 1991 and received a prestigious criminology award. Although it was generally ignored by both the media and the medical researchers, it was a turning point. At last there was a comprehensive, unbiased assessment of the issues surrounding guns and violence that was available to lay people and researchers alike. In 1995 there was another breakthrough when Kleck and Gertz's study "Armed Resistance to Crime: The Prevalence and Nature of Self-Defense with a Gun" was published. This study is the first one devoted specifically to the subject of armed self-defense. Of the nearly 5,000 respondents, 222 reported a defensive gun use within the past 12 months and 313 within the past 5 years. By extrapolating to the total population, he estimated there are about 2.2 to 2.5 million defensive gun uses by civilians each year, with 1.5 to 1.9 million involving handguns! Four hundred thousand of these people felt the defensive use of a gun "almost certainly" prevented a murder. This is ten times the total number of firearms deaths from all causes in a year! Clearly the risk of allowing civilians to arm themselves for self-defense pales in comparison to the huge numbers of lives saved.

Now, in the words of David Kopel, "All of the research about concealed-carry laws has been eclipsed by a comprehensive study by University of Chicago law professor John Lott, with graduate student David Mustard." 15

This study goes far beyond any previous study both in its design and in the comprehensive data collected. Most studies of handgun effects on crime or violence use either time series or cross-sectional data. Time series data means that you look at a particular area (for example Salt Lake County) over time, either continuously or at specified times. Such studies are open to error due to the time periods chosen. If someone compared the crime rates in Salt Lake County from 1992 to 1995 (the year the "shall issue" law became effective), there would likely be little difference since few people had had the time to obtain the permits to carry concealed.

Cross-sectional data refers to comparing two or more different areas at the same time. The accuracy of these studies depends on how well the areas are matched, and how well the differences between them are controlled for in the study. As we saw with the Seattle-Vancouver study, if the cities are not well matched, it is easy to draw, or even create, the wrong conclusions. In addition, the area one chooses to study is important. Cross-sectional data from states are commonly used, since concealed carry laws are generally passed at the state level. But states are not uniform at all; they have large cities, small cities, suburban areas, rural areas, etc. Mixing data from extremely different areas, such as large population centers and rural communities together obscures important information. For example, combining statistics from Salt Lake County (urban) and Kane County (rural) and saying it represents "Utah" actually makes any statistics representing "Utah" quite misleading.

The Lott study solves these problems by using cross-sectional and time series data. They studied every county in the United States continuously from 1977 to 1992, a period of 16 years. Studying counties allowed them to separate urban from rural areas, and a sixteen-year study period is long enough to allow for any temporary, but meaningless, shift in statistics. In addition, the Lott study includes such variables as the type of crime committed, probability of arrest, of conviction, and the length of prison sentences, as well as mandatory sentencing guidelines. It also includes variables such as age, sex, race, income, population and population density. This provides a more detailed, "three-dimensional" picture of the effect of concealed carry permits on crime.

The numbers of arrests and types of crimes were provided by the FBI's Uniform Crime Report, while the information on population was collected from the Census Bureau. Additional information was obtained from state and county officials whenever possible. Other factors which could affect the results such as changes in the laws involving the use of firearms, or sentencing enhancement laws were either eliminated as possibilities or controlled for statistically.

The results of this study show that violent crimes (murder, rape, aggravated assault) decrease dramatically when "shall issue" laws are passed. At the same time, property crimes (auto theft and larceny) increase slightly. This can be explained by habitual criminals changing their preferred method of crime. It makes sense that criminals would switch from crimes where they must confront the victim and thus may get shot, to crimes of stealth where they are much less likely to confront an armed victim. Certainly a small increase in property crimes is a small price to pay for a large savings in human life and health. [20]

The statistics are dramatic. Whenever concealed carry laws went into effect in a county during this 16-year period, murders fell by 8.5 percent, rapes by 5 percent, and aggravated assaults by 7 percent. If, in 1992, all states had enacted "shall issue" laws, murders in the United States would have decreased by 1,570. There would have been 4,177 fewer rapes and over 60,000 fewer aggravated assaults. This unequivocally supports the wisdom of our Founding Fathers who guaranteed that our right to keep and bear arms "shall not be infringed."

It means that the bleeding heart gun control advocates, the Sarah Brady types weeping about dead children, and our legislators and presidents who support them, are directly responsible for the deaths of over 1,500 Americans and the rapes of over 4,000 innocent women every single year!

The anti-gunners are unable to find any scientific flaws or errors of analysis in this study. Instead they have attacked the researchers personally, just as they did to the doctors who dared speak the "politically incorrect" truth. There is no place for name-calling in either scientific research or in setting policy that affects millions of lives.

Anti-gunners might ask if allowing concealed carry would cause an increase in accidental deaths. However, the entire number of accidental deaths in the United States in 1992 was 1,409, and only 546 of these occurred in states with concealed carry laws. The total number of accidental handgun deaths per year is less than 200. At most, there would be nine more accidental deaths per year if all states passed concealed carry laws, in contrast to 1,500 lives saved.

Anti-gunners use the argument that if concealed carry were enacted, 25 every minor fender-bender or disagreement would turn into a shoot-out. Over 300,000 permits have been issued in Florida since 1986, but only five violent crimes involving permitted pistols were committed as of December 1995, and none of them resulted in a fatality. There is only one recorded instance of a permitted pistol being used in a shooting following a traffic accident, and in that case a grand jury found that the shooting was justified.

In 1993, private citizens accidentally killed 30 innocent people who they thought were committing a crime, while police killed 330 innocent people. Given the nature of police work, this is not an entirely fair comparison. However, it clearly shows the public can be trusted with concealed pistols.

Another finding is that people who carry concealed handguns protect not only themselves and their families, but the public in general, even that part of the public that protests most loudly against guns. Since by definition a concealed weapon is hidden, a criminal has no way of knowing if a prospective victim is armed, and is therefore less likely to commit a violent crime against any given person.

This is particularly important for women. Women are the victims of a disproportionate number of violent crimes. A woman who carries a gun has a much greater deterrent effect on crime than does a man. Women are usually smaller and weaker than their attackers, and the presence of a firearm equalizes this imbalance. Because the imbalance between a woman and her attacker is much greater, the benefits of carrying are also much greater. A woman carrying a gun decreases the murder rate for women by three to four times the amount a man carrying a gun decreases the murder rate for men.

While numerous studies have attempted to quantify the cost of firearms-related deaths and injuries, this is the first paper to study the economic benefits of allowing concealed carry. For the sake of consistency, the authors based their figures on estimates for the cost of various crimes used by a National Institute of Justice study published in 1996. Costs included loss of life, lost productivity, medical bills, property losses, as well as losses related to fear, pain, suffering, and decreased quality of life.

These figures are based on jury trial awards, which may not be the 30 best way to estimate economic loss. However they are the figures used in anti-gun studies and so the authors chose to use them to more clearly illustrate the economic benefits of gun ownership. The reduction in violent crime caused by concealed weapons permits provides an economic gain of $6.6 billion, compared to a much smaller economic loss of $417 million due to the increase in property crimes. The net gain is still $6.2 billion!

These results may seem like ordinary common sense. Other results seem to go against "common wisdom." For example, it has been traditional to have the most restrictive gun laws in high population, high crime, urban areas such as Los Angeles, New York City, and Washington, D.C. It is common to hear people say that "It's fine for those people who live out in the country to have guns, but people in the city shouldn't have them."

But this study shows that the effect of allowing concealed carry is much greater in high population counties and in high crime counties. For example, the murder rate in very large cities drops by 12 percent when CCW is passed, while it drops by only about 1.6 percent in an average-sized city. Data for rural areas is unreliable since the murder rates in most rural areas are so low that accurate statistical studies cannot be done. An increase from one murder per year to two would show up as a 100 percent increase in the murder rate, which is misleading when compared to cities with daily murders. However, consistent with the earlier comments on criminals switching to "safer" methods of crime, the increase in property crimes in urban areas is also greater than the increase in rural areas.

Contrary to frequently espoused theories about causes of crime, real per capita income showed only a small, though statistically significant, correlation with both violent crimes and property crimes. It would appear that living in a high population density area may contribute more to crime than does poverty, although this requires more study.

Another finding which deserves comment is that the presence of young, black males increases the rate of property crime by 22 percent and violent crime by 5 percent. However, these numbers cannot be accepted completely at face value, nor should they be used to justify racism. The history of gun control in this country reflects the history of racism. The first state and local firearms laws were designed primarily to disarm blacks, and enough damage has already been done. It is necessary to take into account studies showing that young black males are disproportionately arrested and incarcerated for crimes, and that they are disproportionately victims of crimes. In addition, they tend to live in high population areas and have low incomes, both of which are independent factors for increased crime. Finally, in view of recent allegations that the

CIA deliberately introduced drugs, guns, and thus crime, into inner city black neighborhoods, more study is necessary before any definite conclusions can be reached. Neither Professor Lott nor I believe that race is a cause of crime. . . .

While it is generally a bad idea to base policy on the results of a single study, the Lott and Mustard study is so well designed and well controlled that it is difficult, if not impossible, to argue with their findings. In addition, their results agree with those of previous researchers, most notably Kleck and Gertz. 35

Two findings stand out above all. Concealed carrying of firearms by citizens with no prior felony record or history of severe mental illness decreases violent crime, providing a large benefit both to the individuals who carry and the public as a whole. Second, arrests by law enforcement officers have a large deterrent effect on crime, while conviction has a lesser, but still important, effect.

The obvious conclusion is that concealed carry provides a very large benefit to society in terms of lives saved, violent assaults and rapes prevented, and economic savings. At the same time misuse of legally concealed weapons and accidental handgun deaths from concealed weapons are almost non-existent. Thus every effort should be made to facilitate concealed carry by law-abiding citizens. "Shall issue" permit laws should be adopted by all those states that have not yet done so. In particular, large, urban areas should actively encourage arming their good citizens and definitely should not prevent or discourage them from carrying concealed weapons.

Regulations such as gun-free zones which serve only to disarm and/or harass gun owners are counterproductive and should be eliminated at local, state and federal levels. The Supreme Court has already found gun-free school zones unconstitutional and the justices should uphold this finding in light of the current administration's repeated attempts to enact this misguided legislation. Concealed carry permits should be accepted on a reciprocal basis by all states, just as driver's licenses are, under the full faith and credit act of the Constitution.

In view of the negligible incidence of negative events resulting from concealed carry, further studies are indicated to determine whether the extensive background checks and training requirements which most states demand are even necessary. It may be that "Vermont-style"—i.e., universal concealed carry without need for a permit—is more appropriate and would remove both the financial disincentives to lawful carry as well as decrease the demand on the often overworked staff of state permitting agencies and the FBI. Further, the Constitution guarantees the right to keep and bear arms, and many people (including the author) consider the requirement for a permit, which gives them "permission" to exercise what is already an enumerated right to be both unconstitutional and offensive.

Because the beneficial effect of women carrying concealed weapons 40
far outweighs that of men carrying, women should be encouraged to
carry, and special classes designed to teach women how to safely use,
maintain and carry weapons, along with other self-defense techniques,
need to be developed and made widely available. Learning to protect
oneself from crime and violence is as important to a woman's health as
is learning to detect breast cancer or prevent heart disease. The psychological benefits to women of feeling safe are very significant, but have
yet to be studied scientifically.

In many areas, including the Salt Lake metropolitan area, there is
currently much bad feeling between some law enforcement officers who
feel citizens who carry pose a "deadly threat" to them and citizens who
feel harassed by police. Lott's study shows that this is not only unnecessary, but counterproductive. Armed citizens can protect themselves,
their families and others from violent crimes. Police cannot be everywhere simultaneously, and have no duty to protect individuals. Their
role is primarily to investigate crimes after the fact and bring perpetrators
to justice. By decreasing the number of violent crimes committed, armed
citizens actually decrease the police workload and enable them to be
more productive and apprehend a greater percentage of criminals which
in turn further decreases crime.

Armed citizens and police who are able to cooperate have a synergistic effect on decreasing crime. Both groups need to acknowledge this, accommodate to the changes in the laws, stop competing, and learn to
respect and trust each other. Law enforcement agencies, working with
citizens' groups, must develop clear written policies for police and armed
citizen interactions and disseminate these policies widely. The self-
sufficient, self-protecting gun culture must be restored to its rightful
place of respect in society, not demonized as a hotbed of terrorists. The
Second Amendment right to keep and bear arms must be unequivocally
upheld.

Those who wish to disarm the populace of this country must be exposed for the frauds they are and held responsible morally, if not legally,
for the deaths and suffering created by their misguided policies. In the
four years since 1992, those who preach gun control have contributed to
the deaths of at least six thousand innocent people whose lives they
have sworn to protect and whose freedoms they have sworn to uphold.

Topics for Critical Thinking and Writing

1. We think Thompson's opening paragraph is reasonably effective. What
   is your view of it? Why? After reading her whole article, can you think
   of ways to improve this introductory paragraph? Do so in a paragraph of
   not more than 200 words.

2. Suppose someone were to say that Thompson badly distorts the truth when she says that the government wants the public "to willingly give up . . . their right to self-defense" (para. 5). Is it fairer to say that the government wants to *regulate* the ownership, sale, and use of guns, whether for self-defense or any other purpose? How might Thompson reply to this argument?

3. Does Thompson favor unrestricted ownership, sale, and use of guns— handguns as well as long guns?

4. Thompson accuses unnamed doctors of supporting "biased gun research" "to get grant money . . . or become famous" (para. 7). Does she give any examples of such research and such doctors?

5. Ask your reference librarian to help you locate a copy of the gun research by Sloan and Kellerman published in the *New England Journal of Medicine* (para. 11). Has Thompson given a fair account of this research? Write a 300-word essay explaining why or why not.

6. In paragraph 16 and elsewhere, Thompson refers to "'shall issue' laws." What does this phrase mean? How about "CCW" (para. 32)?

7. Thompson claims that the research on comparative gun use in Seattle and Vancouver (para. 11) is of no value because "the cities are not well matched" (para. 17). After consulting with your reference librarian for useful sources of data, write a 500-word essay comparing the two cities, concluding with an account of why you agree or disagree with Thompson about how well matched these two cities are.

8. Thompson reports a decrease in murders in states permitting concealed handguns (para. 20). She does not report on accidental deaths and woundings by persons carrying a concealed weapon (see, however, para. 23). Without information of this sort, how much weight should we attach to the reported decline in murders?

9. Thompson invokes the Second Amendment to the U.S. Constitution (paras. 5, 21, 39, 42). She omits any mention of the opening clause of the amendment, which reads "A well-regulated militia, being necessary to the security of a free State . . . ." No other purpose for owning a gun is explicitly protected by the language of this amendment. How does this translate, if it does, into a right to "keep and bear arms" for other purposes?

10. Thompson claims that enthusiasts for gun control are "directly responsible for the deaths of over 1,500 Americans . . . every single year" (para. 22) and she speaks of those who are "responsible morally, if not legally" for these deaths (para. 43). Since few if any of these enthusiasts ever use, much less own, any guns themselves, how is that they are "directly responsible" for all these deaths?

11. With help from your reference librarian, find out about "road rage" in an effort to verify Thompson's claim that as of her writing (1997) or more recently, "only one" case of this sort involving a person using a concealed weapon has been recorded (para. 25).

12. Thompson is unstinting in her enthusiasm for laws permitting the carrying of concealed weapons; she favors such laws nationwide (paras. 38–40). Is there any reason, however, to believe that if *every* law-abiding citizen carried a concealed weapon, accidental killings and woundings, mistaken judgment about the need to shoot in self-defense, misguided defense of property, and impulsive use of such weapons would remain constant, so that the benefits she touts would be undiminished?

13. What does Thompson mean by the "synergistic effect on decreasing crime" (para. 42)?

Nan Desuka

Nan Desuka (1957–1985) was born in Japan but at age two was brought by her parents to Los Angeles, where she was educated. Although she most often wrote about ecology, she occasionally wrote about other controversial topics.

Why Handguns Must Be Outlawed

"Guns don't kill people—criminals do." That's a powerful slogan, much more powerful than its alternate version: "Guns don't kill people—people kill people." But this second version, though less effective, is much nearer to the whole truth. Although accurate statistics are hard to come by, and even harder to interpret, it seems indisputable that large numbers of people, not just criminals, kill, with a handgun, other people. Scarcely a day goes by without a newspaper in any large city reporting that a child has found a gun, kept by the child's parents for self-protection, and has, in playing with this new-found toy, killed himself or a playmate. Or we read of a storekeeper, trying to protect himself during a robbery, who inadvertently shoots an innocent customer. These killers are not, in any reasonable sense of the word, criminals. They are just people who happen to kill people. No wonder the gun lobby prefers the first version of the slogan, "Guns don't kill people—criminals do." This version suggests that the only problem is criminals, not you or me, or our children, and certainly not the members of the National Rifle Association.

Those of us who want strict control of handguns—for me that means the outlawing of handguns, except to the police and related service units—have not been able to come up with a slogan equal in power to "Guns don't kill people—criminals do." The best we have been able to come up with is a mildly amusing bumper sticker showing a teddy bear, with the words "Defend your right to arm bears." Humor can be a powerful weapon (even in writing *on behalf* of gun control, one slips into using the imagery of force), and our playful bumper sticker somehow deflates the self-righteousness of the gun lobby, but doesn't equal the power (again the imagery of force) of "Guns don't kill people—criminals do." For one thing, the effective alliteration of *"criminals"* and *"kill"* binds the two words, making everything so terribly simple. Criminals kill; when there are no criminals, there will be no deaths from guns.

But this notion won't do. Despite the uncertainty of some statistical evidence, everyone knows, or should know, that only about 30 percent of murders are committed by robbers or rapists (Kates, 1978). For the most part the victims of handguns know their assailants well. These victims are women killed by jealous husbands, or they are the women's lovers; or they are drinking buddies who get into a violent argument; or they are innocent people who get shot by disgruntled (and probably demented) employees or fellow workers who have (or imagine) a grudge. Or they are, as I've already said, bystanders at a robbery, killed by a storekeeper. Or they are children playing with their father's gun.

Of course this is not the whole story. Hardened criminals also have guns, and they use them. The murders committed by robbers and rapists are what give credence to Barry Goldwater's quip, "We have a crime problem in this country, not a gun problem" (1975, p. 186). But here again the half-truth of a slogan is used to mislead, used to direct attention away from a national tragedy. Different sources issue different statistics, but a conservative estimate is that handguns annually murder at least fifteen thousand Americans, accidentally kill at least another three thousand and wound at least another hundred thousand. Handguns are easily available, both to criminals and to decent people who believe they need a gun in order to protect themselves from criminals. The decent people, unfortunately, have good cause to believe they need protection. Many parts of many cities are utterly unsafe, and even the tiniest village may harbor a murderer. Senator Goldwater is right in saying there is a crime problem (that's the truth of his half-truth), but he is wrong in saying there is not also a gun problem.

Surely the homicide rate would markedly decrease if handguns were   5
outlawed. The FBI reports (Federal Bureau of Investigation, 1985) that more than 60 percent of all murders are caused by guns, and handguns are involved in more than 70 percent of these. Surely many, even most, of these handgun killings would not occur if the killer had to use a rifle, club, or knife. Of course violent lovers, angry drunks, and deranged employees would still flail out with knives or baseball bats, but some of their victims would be able to run away, with few or no injuries, and most of those who could not run away would nevertheless survive, badly injured but at least alive. But if handguns are outlawed, we are told, responsible citizens will have no way to protect themselves from criminals. First, one should remember that at least 90 percent of America's burglaries are committed when no one is at home. The householder's gun, if he or she has one, is in a drawer of the bedside table, and the gun gets lifted along with the jewelry, adding one more gun to

the estimated hundred thousand handguns annually stolen from law-abiding citizens (Shields, 1981). Second, if the householder is at home, and attempts to use the gun, he or she is more likely to get killed or wounded than to kill or deter the intruder. Another way of looking at this last point is to recall that for every burglar who is halted by the sight of a handgun, four innocent people are killed by handgun accidents.

Because handguns are not accurate beyond ten or fifteen feet, they are not the weapons of sportsmen. Their sole purpose is to kill or at least to disable a person at close range. But only a minority of persons killed with these weapons are criminals. Since handguns chiefly destroy the innocent, they must be outlawed—not simply controlled more strictly, but outlawed—to all except to law-enforcement officials. Attempts to control handguns are costly and ineffective, but even if they were cheap and effective stricter controls would not take handguns out of circulation among criminals, because licensed guns are stolen from homeowners and shopkeepers, and thus fall into criminal hands. According to Wright, Rossi, and Daly (1983, p. 181), about 40 percent of the handguns used in crimes are stolen, chiefly from homes that the guns were supposed to protect.

The National Rifle Association is fond of quoting a University of Wisconsin study that says, "gun control laws have no individual or collective effect in reducing the rate of violent crime" (cited in Smith, 1981, p. 17). Agreed—but what if handguns were not available? What if the manufacturer of handguns is severely regulated, and if the guns may be sold only to police officers? True, even if handguns are outlawed, some criminals will manage to get them, but surely fewer petty criminals will have guns. It is simply untrue for the gun lobby to assert that all criminals—since they are by definition lawbreakers—will find ways to get handguns. For the most part, if the sale of handguns is outlawed, guns won't be available, and fewer criminals will have guns. And if fewer criminals have guns, there is every reason to believe that violent crime will decline. A youth armed only with a knife is less likely to try to rob a store than if he is armed with a gun. This commonsense reasoning does not imply that if handguns are outlawed crime will suddenly disappear, or even that an especially repulsive crime such as rape will decrease markedly. A rapist armed with a knife probably has a sufficient weapon. But *some* violent crime will almost surely decrease. And the decrease will probably be significant if in addition to outlawing handguns, severe mandatory punishments are imposed on a person who is found to possess one, and even severer mandatory punishments are imposed on a person who uses one while committing a crime. Again, none of this activity will solve "the crime problem," but neither will anything else, including the "get tough with criminals" attitude of Senator Goldwater. And of course any attempt to reduce crime (one cannot realistically talk of "solving" the crime problem) will have to pay attention to our systems of bail, plea bargaining, and parole, but outlawing handguns will help.

What will the cost be? First, to take "cost" in its most literal sense, there will be the cost of reimbursing gun owners for the weapons they surrender. Every owner of a handgun ought to be paid the fair market value of the weapon. Since the number of handguns is estimated to be between 50 million and 90 million, the cost will be considerable, but it will be far less than the costs—both in money and in sorrow—that result from deaths due to handguns.

Second, one may well ask if there is another sort of cost, a cost to our liberty, to our constitutional rights. The issue is important, and persons who advocate abolition of handguns are blind or thoughtless if they simply brush it off. On the other hand, opponents of gun control do all of us a disservice by insisting over and over that the Constitution guarantees "the right to bear arms." The Second Amendment in the Bill of Rights says this: "A well-regulated militia being necessary to the security of a free State, the right of the people to keep and bear arms shall not be infringed." It is true that the founding fathers, mindful of the British attempt to disarm the colonists, viewed the presence of "a well-regulated militia" as a safeguard of democracy. Their intention is quite clear, even to one who has not read Stephen P. Halbrook's *That Every Man Be Armed*, an exhaustive argument in favor of the right to bear arms. There can be no doubt that the framers of the Constitution and the Bill of Rights believed that armed insurrection was a justifiable means of countering oppression and tyranny. The Second Amendment may be fairly paraphrased thus: "*Because* an organized militia is necessary to the security of the State, the people have the right to possess weapons." But the owners of handguns are not members of a well-regulated militia. Furthermore, nothing in the proposal to ban handguns would deprive citizens of their rifles or other long-arm guns. All handguns, however, even large ones, should be banned. "Let's face it," Guenther W. Bachmann (a vice president of Smith and Wesson) admits, "they are all concealable" (Kennedy, 1981, p. 6). In any case, it is a fact that when gun control laws have been tested in the courts, they have been found to be constitutional. The constitutional argument was worth making, but the question must now be regarded as settled, not only by the courts but by anyone who reads the Second Amendment.

Still, is it not true that "If guns are outlawed, only outlaws will have   10 guns"? This is yet another powerful slogan, but it is simply not true. First, we are talking not about "guns" but about handguns. Second, the police will have guns—handguns and others—and these trained professionals are the ones on whom we must rely for protection against criminals. Of course the police have not eradicated crime; and of course we must hope that in the future they will be more successful in protecting all citizens. But we must also recognize that the efforts of private citizens to protect themselves with handguns have chiefly taken the lives not of criminals but of innocent people.

REFERENCES

Federal Bureau of Investigation (1985). *Uniform crime reports for the United States*. Washington, DC: U.S. Department of Justice.

Goldwater, B. (1975, December). Why gun control laws don't work. *Reader's Digest, 107*, 183–188.

Halbrook, S. P. (1985). *That every man be armed: The evolution of a constitutional right*. Albuquerque: University of New Mexico Press.

Kates, D. B., Jr. (1978, September). Against civil disarming. *Harper's, 257*, 28–33.

Kennedy, E. (1981, October 5). Handguns: Preferred instruments of criminals. *Congressional Record*. Washington, DC: U.S. Government Printing Office.

Shields, P. (1981). *Guns don't die—people do*. New York: Arbor House.

Smith, A. (1981, April). Fifty million handguns. *Esquire, 96*, 16–18.

Wright, J. D., Rossi, P. H., & Daly, K. (1983). *Under the gun*. New York: Aldine.

Topics for Critical Thinking and Writing

1. Reread the first and last paragraphs, and then in a sentence or two comment on the writer's strategy for opening and closing her essay.

2. On the whole, does the writer strike you as a person who is fair or who at least is trying to be fair? Support your answer by citing specific passages that lead you to your opinion.

3. Many opponents of gun control argue that control of handguns will be only a first move down the slippery slope that leads to laws prohibiting private ownership of any sort of gun. Even if you hold this view, state as best you can the arguments that one might offer against it. (Notice that you are asked to offer arguments, not merely an assertion that it won't happen.)

4. Do you agree with Desuka that a reasonable reading of the Second Amendment reveals that individuals do not have a constitutional right to own handguns, even though the founding fathers said that "the right of the people to keep and bear arms shall not be infringed"?

5. Write a 500-word analysis of Desuka's essay (for a sample analysis see p. 142), or write a 500-word reply to her essay, responding to her main points.

6. Do you think the prohibition of handguns is feasible? Could it be enforced? Would the effort to enforce it result in worse problems than we already have? Write a 500-word essay defending or attacking the feasibility of Desuka's proposal.

For topical links related to the gun control debate, see the companion Web site:
www.bedfordstmartins.com/barnetbedau.

17

Sex Education:
Should Condoms Be
Distributed in Schools?

Rush H. Limbaugh III

Rush Limbaugh, born in Cape Girardeau, Missouri, became a Top 40 deejay in the 1960s before becoming a radio talk show host in Sacramento. In 1988 his show went national. We reprint a passage from his book The Way Things Ought to Be *(1992).*

Condoms: The New Diploma

The logic and motivation behind this country's mad dash to distribute free condoms in our public schools is ridiculous and misguided. Worse, the message conveyed by mass condom distribution is a disservice and borders on being lethal. Condom distribution sanctions, even encourages, sexual activity, which in teen years tends to be promiscuous and relegates to secondary status the most important lesson to be taught: abstinence. An analysis of the entire condom distribution logic also provides a glimpse into just what is wrong with public education today.

First things first. Advocates of condom distribution say that kids are going to have sex, that try as we might we can't stop them. Therefore they need protection. Hence, condoms. Well, hold on a minute. Just whose notion is it that "kids are going to do it anyway, you can't stop them"? Why limit the application of that brilliant logic to sexual activity? Let's just admit that kids are going to do drugs and distribute safe, untainted drugs every morning in homeroom. Kids are going to smoke, too, we can't stop them, so let's provide packs of low-tar cigarettes to the students for their after-sex smoke. Kids are going to get guns and shoot them, you can't stop them, so let's make sure that teachers have bullet-proof vests. I mean, come on! If we are really concerned about safe sex, why stop at condoms? Let's convert study halls to Safe Sex Centers where students can go to actually have sex on nice double beds with clean sheets under the watchful and approving eye of the school nurse, who will be on hand to demonstrate, along with the principal, just how to use a condom. Or even better: If kids are going to have sex, let's put disease-free hookers in these Safe Sex Centers. Hey, if safe sex is the objective, why compromise our standards?

There is something else very disturbing about all this. Let's say that Johnny and Susie are on a date in Johnny's family sedan. Johnny pulls in to his town's designated Teen Parking Location hoping to score a little affection from Susie. They move to the backseat and it isn't long before Johnny, on the verge of bliss, whips out his trusty high school-distributed condom and urges Susie not to resist him. She is hesitant, being a nice girl and all, and says she doesn't think the time is right.

"Hey, everything is okay. Nothing will go wrong. Heck, the *school gave me this condom*, they know what they're doing. You'll be fine," coos the artful and suave Johnny.

Aside from what is obviously wrong here, there is something you [5] probably haven't thought of which to me is profound. Not that long ago, school policy, including that on many college campuses, was designed to protect the girls from the natural and instinctive aggressive pursuit of young men. Chaperones, for example, were around to make sure the girls were not in any jeopardy. So much for that thinking now. The schools may just as well endorse and promote these backseat affairs. The kids are going to do it anyway.

Well, here's what's wrong. There have always been consequences to having sex. Always. Now, however, some of these consequences are severe: debilitating venereal diseases and AIDS. You can now die from having sex. It is that simple. If you look, the vast majority of adults in America have made adjustments in their sexual behavior in order to protect themselves from some of the dire consequences floating around out there. For the most part, the sexual revolution of the sixties is over, a miserable failure. Free love and rampant one-night stands are tougher to come by because people are aware of the risks. In short, we have modified our behavior. Now, would someone tell me what is so difficult about sharing this knowledge and experience with kids? The same stakes are involved. Isn't that our responsibility, for crying out loud, to teach them what's best for them? If we adults aren't responding to these new dangers by having condom-protected sex anytime, anywhere, why should such folly be taught to our kids?

Let me try the Magic Johnson example for you who remain unconvinced. Imagine that you are in the Los Angeles Lakers locker room after a game and you and Magic are getting ready to go hit the town. Outside the locker room are a bunch of young women, as there always are, and as Magic had freely admitted there always were, and that you know that the woman Magic is going to pick up and take back to the hotel has AIDS. You approach Magic and say, "Hey, Magic! Hold on! That girl you're going to take back to the hotel with you has AIDS. Here, don't worry about it. Take these condoms, you'll be fine."

Do you think Magic would have sex with that woman? Ask yourself: Would you knowingly have sex with *anyone* who has AIDS with only a condom to protect you from getting the disease? It doesn't take Einstein to answer that question. So, why do you think it's okay to send kids out into the world to do just that? Who is to know who carries the HIV virus, and on the chance your kid runs into someone who does have it, are you confident that a condom will provide all the protection he or she needs?

Doesn't it make sense to be honest with kids and tell them the best thing they can do to avoid AIDS or any of the other undesirable consequences is to abstain from sexual intercourse? It is the best way — in fact, it is the only surefire way — to guard against sexual transmission of AIDS, pregnancy, and venereal diseases. What's so terrible about saying so?

Yet, there are those who steadfastly oppose the teaching of absti-   10
nence, and I think they should be removed from any position of authority where educating children is concerned. In New York, the City Board of Education *narrowly won* (4–3) the passage of a resolution requiring the inclusion of teaching abstinence in the AIDS education program in the spring of 1992. No one was trying to eliminate anything from the program, such as condom distribution or anal sex education (which does occur in New York public school sex education classes). All they wanted

was that abstinence also be taught. Yet, the Schools Chancellor, Joseph Fernandez, vigorously fought the idea, saying it would do great damage to their existing program! Well, just how is that? The fact is that abstinence works every time it is tried. As this book went to press, the New York Civil Liberties Union was considering filing a lawsuit to stop this dangerous new addition to the curriculum. Now what in the name of God is going on here? This is tantamount to opposing a drug education program which instructs students not to use drugs because it would not be useful.

The Jacksonville, Florida, school board also decided that abstinence should be the centerpiece of their sexual education curriculum, and the liberals there were also outraged about this. What is so wrong with this? Whose agenda is being denied by teaching abstinence and just what is that agenda?

Jacksonville teachers are telling seventh-graders that "the only safe sex is no sex at all." Sex education classes provide some information about birth control and sexually transmitted diseases, but these areas are not the primary focus of the classes. Nancy Corwin, a member of the school board, admits the paradox when she says that the schools send a nonsensical message when they teach kids not to have sex but then give them condoms.

Instead of this twaddle, the Jacksonville school board has decided to teach real safe sex, which is abstinence. However, six families, along with Planned Parenthood and the ACLU, are suing the schools over this program. This bunch of curious citizens says that teaching abstinence puts the children at a greater risk of catching AIDS or other sexually transmitted diseases. Greater risk? !£#$£@! How can that be? What kind of contaminated thinking is this? The suit alleges that the schools are providing a "fear-based program that gives children incomplete, inaccurate, biased, and sectarian information." You want more? Try this: Linda Lanier of Planned Parenthood says, "It's not right to try to trick our students." Trick the students? #£&@£!? If anyone is trying to trick students, it's Planned Parenthood and this band of hedonists who try to tell kids that a condom will protect them from any consequences of sex.

Folks, here you have perhaps the best example of the culture war being waged in our country today. To say that "teaching abstinence is a trick" is absurd. Is Ms. Lanier having sex every night of the week? What adjustments has she made in her sex life because of AIDS? Does she think that a little sheath of latex will be enough to protect her?

This is terribly wrong. The Jacksonville public school system is at- 15 tempting to teach right from wrong, as opposed to teaching that sex does not have any consequences, which I believe is the selfish agenda these people hold dear. I have stated elsewhere in this book, and I state it again here, that there are many people who wish to go through life guilt-free and engage in behavior they know to be wrong and morally vacant. In order to assuage their guilt they attempt to construct and impose policies which not only allow them to engage in their chosen activities but encourage others to do so as well. There is, after all, strength in numbers.

Promiscuous and self-gratifying, of-the-moment sex is but one of these chosen lifestyles. Abortions on demand and condom distribution are but two of the policies and programs which, as far as these people are concerned, ensure there are no consequences. As one disgusted member of the Jacksonville school board said, "Every yahoo out there has a social program that they want to run through the school system. We are here for academic reasons and we cannot cure the social evils of the world."

The worst of all of this is the lie that condoms really protect against AIDS. The condom failure rate can be as high as 20 percent. Would you get on a plane—or put your children on a plane—if one in five passengers would be killed on the flight? Well, the statistic holds for condoms, folks.

Ah, but there is even more lunacy haunting the sacred halls of academe. According to the *Los Angeles Times,* administrators in the Los Angeles public schools have regretfully acknowledged that the sex education courses undertaken in the early 1970s "might" have a correlation to the rising teen pregnancy rates in their schools which can be traced to the same years. They have devised an enlightened and marvelous new approach to modernize and correct the sex education curriculum. It is called Outercourse. I am not making this up. Outercourse is, in essence, instruction in creative methods of masturbation.

"Hi, class, and welcome to Outercourse 101. I am your instructor, Mr. Reubens, from Florida, and I want to remind you that this is a hands-on course." We will know the graduates of Outercourse 101 in about forty years. They will be the people walking around with seeing-eye dogs.

Topics for Critical Thinking and Writing

1. In his second paragraph Limbaugh attempts to give a reductio ad absurdum of the proposal to distribute condoms in high school. (We discuss reductio on pp. 305–06.) Do you think this tactic of criticism as used here is successful or not? Explain.

2. Limbaugh thinks that distributing condoms in high school will encourage sex among adolescents as well as give premarital sex a stamp of approval by school authorities. Do you agree? Why, or why not?

3. In paragraph 17 Limbaugh says, "The condom failure rate can be as high as 20 percent." What do you take this statement to mean?

4. Limbaugh says that those who favor condom distribution "try to tell kids that a condom will protect them from *any* consequences of sex" (para. 13, emphasis added). Inquire at your campus health office to find out

what current medical practice advises about the likelihood of condom failure, resulting in unwanted pregnancy or in acquiring a sexually transmitted disease.

5. Make a list of the *reasons* Limbaugh gives for opposing the distribution of condoms; evaluate those reasons.

6. Limbaugh quotes (para. 16) with evident approval the public school official who complained, "Every yahoo out there has a social program that they want to run through the school system. We are here for academic reasons." Yet elsewhere Limbaugh supports prayer in the public schools. Do you think he is inconsistent or not? Explain.

Anna Quindlen

From 1986 to 1994, Anna Quindlen regularly wrote a column for the New York Times, *where this essay appeared on January 8, 1994. She is also the author of several books, including* One True Thing *(1994) and* Black and Blue *(1998).*

A Pyrrhic Victory

Pop quiz: A sixteen-year-old is appropriately treated at a school clinic after he is advised that the reason it feels as if he is going to die when he urinates is because he has a sexually transmitted disease. Told that condoms could have protected him from infection, he asks for some. A nurse tells him to wait while she looks for his name on the list of students whose parents have confidentially requested that their sons and daughters not receive them.

The student replies: (a) "No problem"; (b) "Hmmm—an interesting way to balance the reproductive health of adolescents and the rights of parents"; (c) Nothing. He sidles out of the office and not long afterward gets a whopping case of chlamydia.

Condoms, condoms, condoms. As those who oppose condom distribution in the schools gloated over an appellate court decision that said the program violated parents' rights, Alwyn Cohall, the pediatrician who oversees several school-based clinics in New York, quoted Yogi Berra. "It's déjà vu all over again," said Dr. Cohall, who has to clean up the messes made when sexually active kids don't use condoms. And he wasn't smiling.

Over the last two years the Board of Education has wasted time better spent on instructional issues giving and receiving lectures on latex. The opt-out provision its members are now likely to adopt is the "let me see if you're on the list, dear" scenario outlined above, and if you think it might have a chilling effect on a young man too self-conscious to ask for Trojans in a drugstore, then you get an A in adolescent psychology.

You get extra credit if you figure that being on the list will be scant 5
protection against disease if the young man has sex anyhow. "A victory
for parents," some have called the provision. But is it Pyrrhic?

Dr. Cohall, a champion of condom distribution, agrees that it is best
if teenagers abstain from sexual activity and talk to their parents about
issues of sex, morality, and health. But he also notes that in 1992 his
three high school clinics saw around 150 cases of sexually transmitted
diseases like condyloma, chlamydia, and the better-known gonorrhea
and syphilis.

He has a sixteen-year-old in the hospital right now who got AIDS
from her second sexual partner. And he recalls a girl who broke her leg
jumping out an apartment window because her mother found her birth
control pills, seized her by the throat, and said, according to the kid, "I
brought you into the world; I can take you out of it."

Don't you just love those little mother-daughter sex talks?

He also knows that at the heart of the balancing act between keeping
kids healthy and keeping parents involved there has always been a
covert place in which many opponents of condom distribution really
settle. It's called Fantasyland.

You could see that in the response to the rather mild commercials on 10
condom use and abstinence that the Department of Health and Human
Services unveiled this week. The general secretary of the National Conference of Catholic Bishops immediately said the ads "promote promiscuity" and the networks should reject them. At the same time ABC said
it would not run the spots during its prime-time "family-oriented"
programs.

So foolish. ABC's own *Roseanne* has been far more candid about sexuality than any of the new government public-service spots. And what
could be a better way to foment conversation with the children of the
video age than a television advertisement? Right there in your living
room you have a goad to the kind of discussion that opponents of condom distribution have always argued is the purview of parents. And you
put the ads on late at night? Do we really want to talk with our kids? Or
do we just want to talk about talking to them?

The Board of Education could do a great good if it found ways to
truly foster parent-child communication in all things, not just matters
sexual. But instead its members argue about condoms. This isn't really
about condoms, of course, but about control and the shock of adolescent
sexuality and the difficulty parents have communicating with their kids
and a deep and understandable yearning for simpler times.

While we yearn and argue, Dr. Cohall visits his sixteen-year-old
AIDS patient. Her parents' involvement may someday consist of visiting
the cemetery. Imagine how they'd feel if they put her on the no-condom
list, then put her in the hospital, then put her in the ground. Some
victory.

Topics for Critical Thinking and Writing

1. Exactly what is a Pyrrhic victory?

2. Quindlen offers three possible responses for her sixteen-year-old male student (para. 2). Write a fourth response and (if possible) a fifth response.

3. As paragraph 3 indicates, some parents argue that the distribution of condoms violates parents' rights. What parental right is at stake in the dispute over whether high schools should distribute condoms to students who seek them? Or is there no such right but instead a parental duty involved?

4. Quindlen mentions four sexually transmitted diseases. What are their names, their symptoms, and the cure in each case? (You will probably need to talk to a physician or nurse or do some library research to answer this question.)

5. Some people argue that any discussion of condoms, even in a context that advocates abstinence, in effect promotes promiscuity. Do you agree or disagree? Why?

6. Evaluate Quindlen's final paragraph as a piece of persuasive writing.

For topical links related to the sex education controversy, see the companion Web site:
www.bedfordstmartins.com/barnetbedau.

18

Women in the Military: What Is Their Role, If Any?

Mona Charen

Mona Charen, a syndicated columnist known for her conservative views, published this short essay in the Boston Globe *on August 27, 1997.*

Eight Good Reasons to Oppose Women in the Military

Most of the opinion-shaping press has presented the spectacle of the Virginia Military Institute's first female cadets as a simple story of feminism triumphant. All people of good will are presumed to be rooting for the plucky little gals as they conquer one of the last bastions of male supremacy—the military.

Here are eight reasons that the national consensus on this is wrong.

1. The male-only tradition at military academies, as in the military services themselves until recently, is not a manifestation of male dominance or an attempt to keep women in second-class status (any more than all-women's colleges are expressions of female chauvinism). It is based on fundamental differences between the sexes that no amount of political pressure can erase.

2. Men are physically stronger than women. If women object to that reality, their complaint is with God, not VMI. And while war has become more technological in recent years, physical strength is not yet irrelevant. Men are also more aggressive (though not necessarily meaner). Feminists deny this now, but remember back in the '70s, when they were arguing that the world would be so much less warlike if women ran things?

War is horrible, and it is devoutly to be hoped that mankind will someday transcend it, as we have outgrown child sacrifice and (nearly everywhere) slavery. But, until that day comes, do we not want the toughest, hardest, strongest, and most aggressive members of society to fight our wars?

3. Men do not get pregnant or nurse babies. When a woman becomes an insurance adjuster or a CEO, a pregnancy does not represent a catastrophe. But a woman warrior cannot be pregnant. (That's why the abortion rate is so high on military bases.) Will feminists next argue that keeping babies out of combat constitutes discrimination?

4. Introducing women into the military complicates morale and discipline problems. A military unit relies on camaraderie and loyalty. The rules against fraternization—widely misunderstood during the recent Kelly Flinn imbroglio—are intended to maintain morale by ensuring that no enlisted man has a close personal friendship with his commanding officer. Friendships can complicate the line of command. If your commanding officer orders you to "take that hill," you must believe he is

doing it for militarily sound reasons, not because he dislikes you or prefers to save your tent-mate.

How much more forcefully, then, can romantic love, sexual competition, and jealousy affect unit cohesion?

5. And then there is sexual harassment. In our ideological zeal to see women in the military, we have handed the sexual predators of this world a big, beautiful present. Putting young, vulnerable women into the hands of drill sergeants—who exert practically life-and-death control over their lives for a period of time—is asking for what we've got: an epidemic of abuse.

6. Feminists are now attacking military life, claiming on the one 10 hand that there are no relevant differences between the sexes that should exclude women and on the other that the trouble with the military is that it is too "phallocentric." Which is it? The feminists do not want strict equality. If they did, they would be protesting the fact that at service academies, women are not required to meet the same training standards as men.

7. The Israelis tried using women in combat but rejected the policy for several reasons. They found that men were trying to protect the women at the expense of fighting well and that the enemy was fighting harder to avoid the shame of surrendering to women. The culture of one's potential adversary is a relevant consideration. The United States is not likely to fight Canada.

8. This is not the first time feminists have claimed—in a sensitive realm—that differences between the sexes are illusory. A generation ago, they argued that differences in sexual attitudes and behavior were merely artifacts of cultural conditioning. Women were as randy as men, they argued, and deserved the chance to prove it.

Twenty-five years later, feminists are refining that view. In fact, some have become so sexually phobic that they've defined any unwelcome approach by a man to be "sexual harassment." Women are tough enough to fight wars but not able to handle a dirty joke? Hmmm.

Topics for Critical Thinking and Writing

1. Charen asserts that "Men are physically stronger than women" (her reason 2). This generalization is obviously false: Many women are stronger than some men, even if most men are stronger than most women. Is Charen ignorant of this obvious point? If not, why do you think she implicitly denies it?

2. What was the "Kelly Flinn imbroglio" (her reason 4)? Look it up in newspaper files for the spring and summer of 1997. Did that event illustrate why women ought not to be in the military? Or did it show something else?

3. In her reason 5, regarding sexual harassment, is Charen assuming that it is impossible—or just very difficult, time-consuming, and perhaps expensive—to prevent "young, vulnerable women" from being abused by "drill sergeants"?

4. Is it reasonable to reply to Charen that many of her complaints vanish if women are not put into combat situations alone or only with other women? Has she given any reasons to bar women, say, from being army helicopter pilots? Or communication specialists? Or artillery spotters?

5. Women have been military nurses near the front lines in many wars during the past century. Why doesn't Charen object to women in such a role?

Vivian Norwood

The preceding essay by Mona Charen was syndicated in the Boston Globe. *Vivian Norwood, of Somerville, Massachusetts, read the essay and responded with this comment, which the* Globe *published on August 30, 1997.*

Eight Reasons Women Should Be in the Military

In response to Mona Charen's "Eight Good Reasons to Oppose Women in the Military," (op-ed, August 27):

1. Women deserve and have earned the right to protect their homes, families, and country by serving in the military.

2. A recent study by the National Aeronautics and Space Administration found that women resist extreme heat, cold, and pressure better than men. It also showed that women are more resistant to disease than men and that women, under high stress and isolation, deal better with the situation than men.

3. A woman warrior cannot be pregnant. I don't think many people would dispute that fact. However, a woman is not an animal. Women can control their sexual needs, often better than most men.

4. Women are just as capable of developing camaraderie and loyalty   5 as men. Men and women are equally capable of understanding the prohibition against fraternization between the ranks.

5. The military has always had a problem with hazing among men. Hazing is simply another form of inappropriate harassment. The military cannot blame women for this problem. Sexual predators of either sex do not belong in the military. There is a difference between wanting aggressive soldiers and filling the military with criminals.

6. By saying that the military is "phallocentric," feminists mean that the military has a bias against allowing women to join. This does not change the fact that women should be allowed to join. The military has to change.

Women should meet all the required training standards for a soldier. However, the military should not set those standards higher or more rigidly than necessary to keep women out.

7. The people the United States fights in wars and other conflicts are usually fighting on their native ground. They are fighting for their homes and families as well as for their lives and their countries. Often they are driven by religious zeal. Being beaten by a woman is of little consideration.

8. Women and men are the same. Women and men are different. 10 The paradox of these two facts has been the subject of debate for hundreds of years. I do not expect that we will solve it anytime soon. In the meantime, we must work toward a fair and practical solution for all people.

Topics for Critical Thinking and Writing

1. On what basis does Norwood assert that women "deserve and have earned the right" to serve in the armed forces (her reason 1)? What's the difference between saying (a) women ought to be allowed to serve in the armed forces and (b) women deserve and have the right to such service?

2. Charen (her reason 3) and Norwood (her reason 3) agree that pregnant women have no place in combat situations. How significant an obstacle is pregnancy, do you think, to having women serve in the military?

3. Does Norwood's position come down to the proposition that, as she says, "Women and men are the same. Women and men are different" (her reason 8) and that the similarities outweigh the differences so far as military service is concerned?

4. In warfare, male soldiers frequently treat women in occupied territories with contempt, sexual abuse, and violence. Do you think the presence of women in military service side by side with men would be likely to reduce such violence, increase it, or have no significant effect?

For topical links related to the women in the military controversy, see the companion Web site: **www.bedfordstmartins.com/barnetbedau.**

Part Five

CURRENT ISSUES:
CASEBOOKS

19

Business Ethics: Do Corporations Have a Social Responsibility?

WHY ARE YOU BUYING YOUR FOOD FROM A TOBACCO COMPANY?

Did you know that every product pictured here is owned by Philip Morris, the world's largest cigarette company? Chances are you've been helping to promote Marlboro cigarettes without even knowing it. Now you can withdraw that support by personally boycotting these products. It's like giving money to a health organization that is working to find a cure for cancer — but in this case, you're taking money from a corporation that causes it. So next time you go to buy food — try it. You'll like it.

<www.adbusters.org>

Product list valid as of Feb 1999

Milton Friedman

Milton Friedman, winner of a Nobel Prize in economics in 1976, was born in 1912 in Brooklyn and educated at Rutgers University, the University of Chicago, and Columbia University. A leading conservative economist, Friedman was a Distinguished Professor at the University of Chicago and has had an influence far beyond the academic world through his writings for the general public. The essay that we reprint here first appeared in the New York Times Magazine *on September 13, 1970.*

The Social Responsibility of Business Is to Increase Its Profits

When I hear businessmen speak eloquently about the "social responsibilities of business in a free-enterprise system," I am reminded of the wonderful line about the Frenchman who discovered at the age of 70 that he had been speaking prose all his life. The businessmen believe that they are defending free enterprise when they declaim that business is not concerned "merely" with profit but also with promoting desirable "social" ends; that business has a "social conscience" and takes seriously its responsibilities for providing employment, eliminating discrimination, avoiding pollution, and whatever else may be the catchwords of the contemporary crop of reformers. In fact they are — or would be if they or anyone else took them seriously — preaching pure and unadulterated socialism. Businessmen who talk this way are unwitting puppets of the intellectual forces that have been undermining the basis of a free society these past decades.

The discussions of the "social responsibilities of business" are notable for their analytical looseness and lack of rigor. What does it mean to say that "business" has responsibilities? Only people can have responsibilities. A corporation is an artificial person and in this sense may have artificial responsibilities, but "business" as a whole cannot be said to have responsibilities, even in this vague sense. The first step toward clarity in examining the doctrine of the social responsibility of business is to ask precisely what it implies for whom.

Presumably, the individuals who are to be responsible are businessmen, which means individual proprietors or corporate executives. Most of the discussion of social responsibility is directed at corporations, so in what follows I shall mostly neglect the individual proprietors and speak of corporate executives.

In a free-enterprise, private-property system, a corporate executive is an employee of the owners of the business. He has direct responsibility to his employers. That responsibility is to conduct the business in accordance with their desires, which generally will be to make as much money as possible while conforming to the basic rules of the society, both those embodied in law and those embodied in ethical custom. Of course, in some cases his employers may have a different objective. A group of persons might establish a corporation for an eleemosynary purpose—for example, a hospital or a school. The manager of such a corporation will not have money profit as his objectives but the rendering of certain services.

In either case, the key point is that, in his capacity as a corporate executive, the manager is the agent of the individuals who own the corporation or establish the eleemosynary institution, and his primary responsibility is to them.

Needless to say, this does not mean that it is easy to judge how well he is performing his task. But at least the criterion of performance is straightforward, and the persons among whom a voluntary contractual arrangement exists are clearly defined.

Of course, the corporate executive is also a person in his own right. As a person, he may have many other responsibilities that he recognizes or assumes voluntarily—to his family, his conscience, his feelings of charity, his church, his clubs, his city, his country. He may feel impelled by these responsibilities to devote part of his income to causes he regards as worthy, to refuse to work for particular corporations, even to leave his job, for example, to join his country's armed forces. If we wish, we may refer to some of these responsibilities as "social responsibilities." But in these respects he is acting as a principal, not an agent; he is spending his own money or time or energy, not the money of his employers or the time or energy he has contracted to devote to their purposes. If these are "social responsibilities," they are the social responsibilities of individuals, not of business.

What does it mean to say that the corporate executive has a "social responsibility" in his capacity as businessman? If this statement is not pure rhetoric, it must mean that he is to act in some way that is not in the interest of his employers. For example, that he is to refrain from increasing the price of the product in order to contribute to the social objective of preventing inflation, even though a price increase would be in the best interests of the corporation. Or that he is to make expenditures on reducing pollution beyond the amount that is in the best interests of the corporation or that is required by law in order to contribute to the social objective of improving the environment. Or that, at the expense of corporate profits, he is to hire "hardcore" unemployed instead of better qualified available workmen to contribute to the social objective of reducing poverty.

In each of these cases, the corporate executive would be spending someone else's money for a general social interest. Insofar as his actions in accord with his "social responsibility" reduce returns to stockholders, he is spending their money. Insofar as his actions raise the price to customers, he is spending the customers' money. Insofar as his actions lower the wages of some employees, he is spending their money.

The stockholders or the customers of the employees could separately 10 spend their own money on the particular action if they wished to do so. The executive is exercising a distinct "social responsibility," rather than serving as an agent of the stockholders or the customers or the employees, only if he spends the money in a different way than they would have spent it.

But if he does this, he is in effect imposing taxes, on the one hand, and deciding how the tax proceeds shall be spent, on the other.

This process raises political questions on two levels: principle and consequences. On the level of political principle, the imposition of taxes and the expenditure of tax proceeds are governmental functions. We have established elaborate constitutional, parliamentary, and judicial provisions to control these functions, to assure that taxes are imposed so far as possible in accordance with the preferences and desires of the public—after all, "taxation without representation" was one of the battle cries of the American Revolution. We have a system of checks and balances to separate the legislative function of imposing taxes and enacting expenditures from the executive function of collecting taxes and administering expenditure programs and from the judicial function of mediating disputes and interpreting the law.

Here the businessman—self-selected or appointed directly or indirectly by stockholders—is to be simultaneously legislator, executive, and jurist. He is to decide whom to tax by how much and for what purpose, and he is to spend the proceeds—all this guided only by general exhortations from on high to restrain inflation, improve the environment, fight poverty, and so on and on.

The whole justification for permitting the corporate executive to be selected by the stockholders is that the executive is an agent serving the interests of his principal. This justification disappears when the corporate executive imposes taxes and spends the proceeds for "social" purposes. He becomes in effect a public employee, a civil servant, even though he remains in name an employee of a private enterprise. On grounds of political principle, it is intolerable that such civil servants—insofar as their actions in the name of social responsibility are real and not just window-dressing,—should be selected as they are now. If they are to be civil servants, then they must be elected through a political process. If they are to impose taxes and make expenditures to foster "social" objectives, then political machinery must be set up to make the assessment of taxes and to determine through a political process the objectives to be served.

This is the basic reason why the doctrine of "social responsibility" in- 15 volves the acceptance of the socialist view that political mechanisms, not market mechanisms, are the appropriate way to determine the allocation of scarce resources to alternative uses.

On the grounds of consequences, can the corporate executive in fact discharge his alleged "social responsibilities"? On the other hand, suppose he could get away with spending the stockholders' or customers' or employees' money. How is he to know how to spend it? He is told that he must contribute to fighting inflation. How is he to know what action of his will contribute to that end? He is presumably an expert in running his company—in producing a product or selling it or financing it. But nothing about his selection makes him an expert on inflation. Will his holding down the price of his product reduce inflationary pressure? Or, by leaving more spending power in the hands of his customers, simply divert it elsewhere? Or, by forcing him to produce less because of the lower price, will it simply contribute to shortages? Even if he could answer these questions, how much cost is he justified in imposing on his stockholders, customers, and employees for this social purpose? What is his appropriate share and what is the appropriate share of others?

And, whether he wants to or not, can he get away with spending his stockholders', customers', or employees' money? Will not the stockholders fire him? (Either the present ones or those who take over when his actions in the name of social responsibility have reduced the corporation's profits and the price of its stock.) His customers and his employees can desert him for other producers and employers less scrupulous in exercising their social responsibilities.

This facet of "social responsibility" doctrine is brought into sharp relief when the doctrine is used to justify wage restraint by trade unions. The conflict of interest is naked and clear when union officials are asked to subordinate the interest of their members to some more general purpose. If the union officials try to enforce wage restraint, the consequence is likely to be wildcat strikes, rank-and-file revolts, and the emergence of strong competitors for their jobs. We thus have the ironic phenomenon that union leaders—at least in the United States—have objected to government interference with the market far more consistently and courageously than have business leaders.

The difficulty of exercising "social responsibility" illustrates, of course, the great virtue of private competitive enterprise—it forces people to be responsible for their own actions and makes it difficult for them to "exploit" other people for either selfish or unselfish purposes. They can do good—but only at their own expense.

Many a reader who has followed the argument this far may be 20 tempted to remonstrate that it is all well and good to speak of government's having the responsibility to impose taxes and determine expenditures for such "social" purposes as controlling pollution or training the hard-core unemployed, but that the problems are too urgent to wait on the slow course of political processes, that the exercise of social responsibility by businessmen is a quicker and surer way to solve pressing current problems.

Aside from the question of fact—I share Adam Smith's skepticism about the benefits that can be expected from "those who affected to trade for the public good"—this argument must be rejected on grounds of principle. What it amounts to is an assertion that those who favor the taxes and expenditures in question have failed to persuade a majority of their fellow citizens to be of like mind and that they are seeking to attain by undemocratic procedures what they cannot attain by democratic procedures. In a free society, it is hard for "evil" people to do "evil," especially since one man's good is another's evil.

I have, for simplicity, concentrated on the special case of the corporate executive, except only for the brief digression on trade unions. But precisely the same argument applies to the newer phenomenon of calling upon stockholders to require corporations to exercise social responsibility (the recent G.M. crusade for example). In most of these cases, what is in effect involved is some stockholders trying to get other stockholders (or customers or employees) to contribute against their will to "social" causes favored by the activists. Insofar as they succeed, they are again imposing taxes and spending the proceeds.

The situation of the individual proprietor is somewhat different. If he acts to reduce the returns of his enterprise in order to exercise his "social responsibility," he is spending his own money, not someone else's. If he wishes to spend his money on such purposes, that is his right, and I cannot see that there is any objection to his doing so. In the process, he, too, may impose costs on employees and customers. However, because he is far less likely than a large corporation or union to have monopolistic power, any such side effects will tend to be minor.

Of course, in practice the doctrine of social responsibility is frequently a cloak for actions that are justified on other grounds rather than a reason for those actions.

To illustrate, it may well be in the long-run interest of a corporation 25 that is a major employer in a small community to devote resources to providing amenities to that community or to improving its government. That may make it easier to attract desirable employees, it may reduce the wage bill or lessen losses from pilferage and sabotage or have other worthwhile effects. Or it may be that, given the laws about the deductibility of corporate charitable contributions, the stockholders can contribute more to charities they favor by having the corporation make the gift than by doing it themselves, since they can in that way contribute an amount that would otherwise have been paid as corporate taxes.

In each of these—and many similar—cases, there is a strong temptation to rationalize these actions as an exercise of "social responsibility." In the present climate of opinion, with its widespread aversion to "capitalism," "profits," the "soulless corporation," and so on, this is one way for a corporation to generate goodwill as a byproduct of expenditures that are entirely justified in its own self-interest.

It would be inconsistent of me to call on corporate executives to refrain from this hypocritical window-dressing because it harms the foundations of a free society. That would be to call on them to exercise a "social responsibility"! If our institutions and the attitudes of the public make it in their self-interest to cloak their actions in this way, I cannot summon much indignation to denounce them. At the same time, I can express admiration for those individual proprietors or owners of closely held corporations or stockholders of more broadly held corporations who disdain such tactics as approaching fraud.

Whether blameworthy or not, the use of the cloak of social responsibility, and the nonsense spoken in its name by influential and prestigious businessmen, does clearly harm the foundations of a free society. I have been impressed time and again by the schizophrenic character of many businessmen. They are capable of being extremely far-sighted and clear-headed in matters that are internal to their businesses. They are incredibly short-sighted and muddle-headed in matters that are outside their businesses but affect the possible survival of business in general. This short-sightedness is strikingly exemplified in the calls from many businessmen for wage and price guidelines or controls or income policies. There is nothing that could do more in a brief period to destroy a market system and replace it by a centrally controlled system than effective governmental control of prices and wages.

The short-sightedness is also exemplified in speeches by businessmen on social responsibility. This may gain them kudos in the short run. But it helps to strengthen the already too prevalent view that the pursuit of profits is wicked and immoral and must be curbed and controlled by external forces. Once this view is adopted, the external forces that curb the market will not be the social consciences, however highly developed, of the pontificating executives; it will be the iron fist of government bureaucrats. Here, as with price and wage controls, businessmen seem to me to reveal a suicidal impulse.

The political principle that underlies the market mechanism is unanimity. In an ideal free market resting on private property, no individual can coerce any other, all cooperation is voluntary, all parties to such cooperation benefit or they need not participate. There are no values, no "social" responsibilities in any sense other than the shared values and responsibilities of individuals. Society is a collection of individuals and of the various groups they voluntarily form.

The political principle that underlies the political mechanism is conformity. The individual must serve a more general social interest — whether that be determined by a church or a dictator or a majority. The individual may have a vote and say in what is to be done, but if he is overruled, he must conform. It is appropriate for some to require others to contribute to a general social purpose whether they wish to or not.

Unfortunately, unanimity is not always feasible. There are some respects in which conformity appears unavoidable, so I do not see how one can avoid the use of the political mechanism altogether.

But the doctrine of "social responsibility" taken seriously would extend the scope of the political mechanism to every human activity. It does not differ in philosophy from the most explicitly collectivist doctrine. It differs only by professing to believe that collectivist ends can be attained without collectivist means. That is why, in my book *Capitalism and Freedom*, I have called it a "fundamentally subversive doctrine" in a free society, and have said that in such a society, "there is one and only one social responsibility of business—to use its resources and engage in activities designed to increase its profits so long as it stays within the rules of the game, which is to say, engages in open and free competition without deception or fraud."

Topics for Critical Thinking and Writing

1. Friedman characterizes the ideology he opposes as "socialism" (paras. 1 and 15). On the basis of Friedman's remarks, complete the following sentence: "A person is an advocate of socialism if and only if . . ."

2. Friedman suggests that "one man's good is another's evil" (para. 21)—an ethical thesis of radical subjectivism and relativism. Has Friedman given adequate (even any) reasons for the reader to agree? Must a free-market economist, such as Friedman, hold such a view? What evidence can you think of that supports or undermines his thesis?

3. Friedman attacks the idea that "'business' has responsibilities" (see paras. 2–3). Yet his final paragraph clearly tells us what he thinks the "social responsibility of business" is. Has Friedman contradicted himself?

4. Friedman strongly opposes "effective governmental control of prices and wages" (para. 28). Some economists, however, believe that during national emergencies scarcity of goods and services (whatever the cause) leads to inflation unless constrained by wage and price controls. Ask your reference librarian to help you research our most recent experience with national wage and price controls. What on balance seem to have been the benefits (if any) and the harms (if any)?

5. Friedman says that corporate executives who spend the corporation's money "for a general social interest" (para. 9) are "in effect imposing taxes . . . and deciding how the tax proceeds shall be spent" (para. 11). Is the use of the word *tax* effective? Is it fair? Notice that paragraphs 12, 13, and 14, as well as some later paragraphs, also speak of taxes.

6. "The socialist view," Friedman says in paragraph 15, is "that political mechanisms, not market mechanisms, are the appropriate way to determine the allocation of scarce resources to alternative uses." Suppose a fellow student told you that he or she found this passage puzzling. How would you clarify it?

7. Some persons in business have replied to Friedman by arguing that because the owners of today's corporations are rarely involved in running them, the corporations can properly be viewed not as private property but as social institutions able to formulate goals of their own. These people argue that the managers of a corporation are public trustees of a multipurpose organization and are empowered to promote the interests

not only of stockholders but also of employees and the general public. What do you think are the strengths and the weaknesses of this reply?

Letters of Response to Milton Friedman from Timothy Mellon, Richard A. Liroff, and Yale Roe

The following letters in response to Milton Friedman's article were published in the New York Times Magazine *on October 4, 1970.*

To the Editor:

I would like to take exception to the underlying assumption of the "Friedman doctrine" ("The Social Responsibility of Business Is to Increase Its Profits," by Milton Friedman, Sept. 13) that the only demand upon the businessman by the stockholder "generally will be to make as much money as possible. . . ."

I speak not only as an investor in American corporations but also as a "stockholder" in other institutions: my government, my community, my family, my society. As multiple stockholders, we all make complex and sometimes conflicting demands upon these institutions. When we demand that automobiles be designed so as not to foul the air, we are weighing a 1 percent reduction in corporate profits against a 10 percent increase in the cost of remaining healthy. When we applaud efforts to hire the "hard-core unemployed," we are mindful as much of the staggering economic and social costs of welfare and urban renewal as we are of the horrifying plight of many of these individuals. Stockholders seek not to incapacitate the corporate mechanism but to maximize our overall economic and social portfolio. This I do not believe to be "pure unadulterated socialism."

Timothy Mellon
Guilford, Conn.

To the Editor:

Milton Friedman clearly indicates why there is a need for vigorous government taxation and regulation of industry's environmental pollution, for if it is the objective of each business organization to maximize profits, each can readily do so by forcing society at large to absorb the costs of environmental pollution rather than internalizing such costs and thereby reducing net profits.

It is incumbent upon the government to use its taxation authority (an authority which, according to Friedman, must be respected and obeyed by the corporate executive) to levy effluent taxes that will make it financially irresponsible and disadvantageous to pollute our skies and water and which will force individual companies to internalize the costs of combating their pollution rather than passing such costs on to those individuals residing downwind and downstream from them.

Richard A. Liroff
Graduate Student, Department of Political Science,
Northwestern University, Evanston, Ill.

To the Editor:

Here is the key fallacy in Milton Friedman's "What's good for General Motors is good for America" argument. It is becoming quite apparent that all will not necessarily be well with the world just because each man honestly pursues his own private gain. It is becoming apparent that with the best of intentions, and scrupulously observing all laws, a corporate executive may do harm to people.

The corporate executives whose industries have poured harmful ingredients into our lakes have usually done so without violating laws and in conscientious efforts to maximize profits. Likewise, those men have poisoned our air.

Mr. Friedman certainly makes a strong case that the executive who spends money for social responsibility takes from the stockholders without their consent. But by the same token, the executive who pollutes the streams takes from the public without *their* consent. Between the alternative of imposing on his own stockholders and imposing on the public, the executive should lean toward the former because he is still in a position to generate for them a net gain. After all, if Mr. Friedman is to argue that an executive has no right to involve the corporation in activities that are *for* the public, it would follow that he has no right to act *against* that same public.

Yale Roe
Winnetka, Ill.

Topics for Critical Thinking and Writing

1. How might Friedman reply to Timothy Mellon's claim that "to maximize our overall economic and social portfolio" is not "pure unadulterated socialism"?

2. Richard Liroff and Yale Roe insist that corporations, not the public, ought to pay the costs of conducting business in a pollution-free environment, even though this will reduce corporate profits. Do you agree or not? In any case, are Liroff and Roe advocating what Friedman would call "socialism"?

Robert D. Haas

Robert D. Haas was chairman of the board and chief executive officer of Levi Strauss & Company. We reprint part of a speech that he delivered at a two-day conference of a business research organization, the Conference Board, on May 4, 1994.

Ethics: A Global Business Challenge

Because Levi Strauss & Company operates in many countries and diverse cultures, we take special care in selecting contractors and those countries where our goods are produced. We do this to ensure that our products are being made in a manner consistent with our values and that protects our brand image and corporate reputation. So, in 1991, we developed a set of Global Sourcing Guidelines.

Our guidelines describe the business conduct we require of our contractors. For instance, the guidelines ban the use of child or prison labor. They stipulate certain environmental requirements. They limit working hours and mandate regularly scheduled days off. Workers must have the right of free association and not be exploited. At a minimum, wages must comply with the law and match prevailing local practice, and working conditions must be safe and healthy. We also expect our business partners to be law abiding and to conduct all of their business affairs in an ethical way.

In developing our guidelines, we also recognized that there are certain issues beyond the control of our contractors, so we produced a list of "country selection" criteria. For example, we will not source in countries where conditions, such as the human rights climate, would run counter to our values and have an adverse effect on our global brand image or damage our corporate reputation.

Similarly, we will not source in countries where circumstances threaten our employees while traveling, where the legal climate makes it difficult or jeopardizes our trademarks, and where political or social turmoil threatens our commercial interest.

Since adopting our guidelines, we've terminated our business rela-   5
tionships with about 5 percent of our contractors and required workplace improvements of another 25 percent. Likewise, we announced a phased withdrawal from contracting in China and exited Burma due to human rights concerns, although we remain hopeful that the human rights climate in these countries will improve so we can alter these decisions.

In the process of creating our guidelines, we formed a working group of 15 employees from a broad cross section of the company. The working group spent nine months formulating our guidelines. In crafting these guidelines, they used our principle-based decision-making model to guide their deliberations.

Drafting these guidelines was difficult. Applying them has proven even more challenging.

When we were rolling out our guidelines—which included extensive on-site audits of each of our 700 contractors worldwide—we discovered that two of our manufacturing contractors in Bangladesh and one in Turkey employed underage workers. This was a clear violation of our guidelines, which prohibit the use of child labor. At the outset, it appeared that we had two options:

- Instruct our contractors to fire these children, knowing that many are the sole wage earners for their families and that if they lost their jobs, their families would face extreme hardships; or we could
- Continue to employ underage children, ignoring our stance against the use of child labor.

By referencing our ethical guidelines to decision making we came up with a different approach and one that we believe helped to minimize adverse ethical consequences.

The contractors agreed to pay the underage children their salaries 10 and benefits while they go to school full-time. We agreed to pay for books, tuition, and uniforms. When the children reach legal working age, they will be offered jobs in the plant. Due to these efforts, 35 children have attended school in Bangladesh, while another six are currently in school in Turkey.

And how did we benefit from this situation?

We were able to retain quality contractors that play an important role in our worldwide sourcing strategy. At the same time, we were able to honor our values and protect our brands.

Applying our sourcing guidelines has forced us to find creative solutions to vexing ethical dilemmas. Clearly, at times, adhering to these standards has added costs. To continue working for us, some contractors have added emergency exits and staircases, increased ventilation, reduced crowding, improved bathroom facilities, and invested in water-treatment systems. The costs of these requirements have been passed on to us—at least in part—in the form of higher product prices. In other cases, we have foregone less expensive sources of production due to unsatisfactory working conditions or concerns about the country of origin.

Conventional wisdom holds that these added costs put us at a competitive disadvantage. Yes, they limit our options somewhat and squeeze profit margins in the near-term. But over the years, we've found that decisions which emphasize cost to the exclusion of all other factors don't serve a company's and its shareholders' long-term interests.

Moreover, as a company that invests hundreds of millions of adver- 15
tising dollars each year to create consumer preference for our products,
we have a huge stake in protecting that investment. In today's world, a
television exposé on working conditions can undo years of effort to build
brand loyalty. Why squander your investment when, with foresight and
commitment, reputational problems can be prevented?

But you don't have to take my word for it.

There is a growing body of evidence that shows a positive correlation
between good corporate citizenship and financial performance. Studies
by leading research groups such as Opinion Research Corporation and
Yankelovich Partners, respected scholars and socially responsible investment firms underscore the point that companies which look beyond
solely maximizing wealth and profits and are driven by values and a
sense of purpose outperform those companies that focus only on short-
term gain.

Companies with strong corporate reputations have been shown to
outperform the S&P 500, have higher sales, sustain greater profits, and
have stocks that outperform the market. These are results that no
bottom-line fixated manager can ignore.

Similarly, a recent study suggests that how a company conducts itself
affects consumer purchasing decisions and customer loyalty. A vast majority—84 percent—of the American public agrees that a company's
reputation can well be the deciding factor in terms of what product or
service they buy.

These findings mirror our own experience. Our values-driven ap- 20
proach has helped us

- Identify contractors who want to work for Levi Strauss & Co. to
  achieve our "blue ribbon" certification, enhancing their own business stature;
- We have gained retailer and consumer loyalty. Retailers feel good
  about having us as business partners because of our commitment
  to ethical practices. Today's consumer has more products to choose
  from and more information about those products. A company's
  reputation forms a part of the consumer's perceptions of the product and influences purchasing decisions.

At the same time,

- We're better able to attract, retain, and motivate the most talented
  employees, because the company's values more closely mirror
  their own personal values.
- Because government and community leaders view us as a responsible corporate citizen we have been welcomed to do business in
  established and emerging markets.

Let me conclude with a few last thoughts.

We are living in an environment in which ethical standards and behaviors are being increasingly challenged. Addressing these dilemmas becomes even more difficult when you overlay the complexities of different cultures and values systems that exist throughout the world. For example, in some cultures honesty will take precedence over caring — "tell the truth even if it hurts"; whereas other cultures find caring, or "saving face," as the predominant value.

As you grapple with some fictitious ethical quandaries over the next two days, I encourage you to ask yourselves these questions:

- "How much am I willing to compromise my principles?"
- "Are there times when I'm willing to risk something I value for doing the right thing?"

For me and my associates at Levi Strauss & Co. I think the answers 25 have become clear: Ethics must trump all other considerations. Ultimately, there are important commercial benefits to be gained from managing your business in a responsible and ethical way that best serves your enterprise's long-term interests. The opposite seems equally clear: the dangers of not doing so are profound.

Michael Josephson, a noted ethics expert, defined ethics this way: "Ethics is about character and courage and how we meet the challenge when doing the right thing will cost more than we want to pay."

The good news is that courage carries with it a great reward — the prospect of sustained responsible commercial success. I think that's what each of us wants our legacy to be. And I believe ultimately our key stakeholders — all of them — will accept nothing less.

Topics for Critical Thinking and Writing

1. How did Levi Strauss respond to the use of child labor in Bangladesh (para. 10)? Can you think of other possible responses besides the three that Haas mentions? Are any of them superior, in your judgment, to what Levi Strauss actually did?

2. Did the use of child labor in Bangladesh pose an "ethical dilemma" for Levi Strauss? Haas seems to think so (para. 13). Do you agree? Why, or why not?

3. Why does Haas believe that companies are wrong to ignore or violate ethical standards because their "added costs put [them] at a competitive disadvantage" (para. 14)?

4. Haas lists six guidelines (para. 2) that he says govern the business conduct of Levi Strauss's contractors. Do you think his list of principles is complete? What other important principles or values should it also include?

5. Haas mentions several corporate "values" (paras. 3, 12, 20) that his company integrates with its ethical principles. How would you define the difference between an ethical principle and a corporate value?

6. Let's assume that everything Haas says about the way Levi Strauss conducts its business is true. And let's assume that at least some of the competing companies do *not* adhere to the principles he sets forth—for instance, by using child labor. Has Haas said anything that you will take into account when you buy your next pair of jeans? Why, or why not?

Donella Meadows

Donella Meadows (1942–2001) cowrote the environmental study The Limits of Growth, *and at the time of her death was an adjunct professor of environmental studies at Dartmouth College in New Hampshire. This essay originally appeared in* Valley News, *a regional newspaper, on June 30, 1990.*

Not Seeing the Forest for the Dollar Bills

The U.S. Fish and Wildlife Service has finally declared the spotted owl an endangered species. The decision will, if the administration enforces the law of the land, drastically cut back logging in the owl's habitat—old-growth forest in the Pacific Northwest.

The logging companies are fighting back. They will go to court to "dispute the science" behind the finding. Knowing that the science is not on their side, they have also leaned on the administration not to enforce the law. And they are trying to get the law changed.

The law in question is the Endangered Species Act. The companies want it to take into account economic considerations. If it did, they say over and over to the press, the politicians, and the public, we would never choose to sacrifice 28,000 jobs for an owl.

That is not the choice at all, of course. The choice is not between an owl and jobs, but between a forest and greed.

The spotted owl is, like every other species, the holder of a unique   5 genetic code that is millions of years old and irreplaceable. Even more important, the owl is a canary, in the old miners' sense—a sign that all is well. It is an indicator species, a creature high up the food chain that depends upon a large area of healthy land for its livelihood.

Every thriving family of spotted owls means that 4,000 acres of forests are well. The trees are living their full lives and returning stored nutrients to the soil when they die. Two hundred other vertebrates that live in the forest are well, as are 1,500 insects and spiders and untold numbers of smaller creatures. The spongy soil under the trees is storing and filtering rain, controlling floods and droughts, keeping the streams clear and pure.

When old-growth is clear-cut, the trees and the owls disappear and so does everything else. Burned slash releases to the sky nutrients that have been sequestered and recycled by living things for 500 years. What's left of the soil bleeds downhill as from an open wound. Waters cloud and silt, flood and dry up. The temperature goes up, the humidity goes down. It will take hundreds of years to regather the nutrients, re-build the soil, and restore the complex system of the intact forest, *if* there is still old-growth forest around to recolonize, and *if* the forest compa-nies stay away.

They are unlikely to stay away. On their own land, they replant with a single, commercially valuable, fast-growing species and call it a forest. It bears as much resemblance to a 500-year-old natural forest as a sub-urb of identical ticky-tacky houses bears to a Renaissance cathedral. Ecologists call such plantations "cornfields." It's not at all certain how many cycles of these cornfields will be possible, given the loss of soil and nutrients when they are cut every fifty years or so.

In the past ten years, 13,000 forest-related jobs were lost in Oregon alone, though the annual cut increased. The jobs were lost to automa-tion and to moving mills offshore, not to the Endangered Species Act.

The forest companies are interested not in jobs or forests, but in mul- 10 tiplying money. Old-growth forests yield higher profit than second-growth plantations. Therefore 85 percent of the old growth is already gone. The companies have stripped it from their own lands. Nearly all that remains is on federal land, owned by you and me. In Washington and Oregon, 2.4 million acres of old growth are left, of which 800,000 are protected in national parks. The rest, in national forests, is marked for cutting.

Our elected representatives are selling off old-growth logging rights in national forests at a rate of about 100,000 acres per year, and at a loss. Taxpayers are subsidizing this process. At the present cutting rate, all but the last protected bits will be gone in about twenty years. The owls will be on their way out—the 800,000 acres remaining will be too frag-mented to sustain them. The jobs will be gone, not because of owls, but because of rapacious forestry.

If loggers and their communities cannot be sustained by second-growth cutting on private lands, then they were in trouble anyway. A compassionate nation would look for a dignified way to help them build a viable economy. It wouldn't sacrifice the biological treasure of an intact forest to keep them going twenty more years. That's the kind of behavior we are righteously telling the Brazilians to stop.

The Endangered Species Act should not take into account economic considerations. Economics doesn't know how to value a species or a for-est. Its logic drives people to exploit resources to the point of extinction. The Endangered Species Act tells us that extinction is morally unaccept-able. It was enacted by a Congress and president in a wise mood, to express a higher value than a bottom line. It should not be weakened. It should be enforced.

Topics for Critical Thinking and Writing

1. In a few sentences summarize Meadows's essay.

2. In a sentence or two state her thesis.

3. In paragraphs 3 and 13 Meadows refers to the Endangered Species Act. What, exactly, does the act provide? Write a 250-word summary of the act. (You probably will want to consult with your college reference librarian to find the text of this law and some details concerning its enactment by Congress.)

4. In paragraphs 3 and 4 Meadows says that the choice is not between 28,000 jobs and an owl but "between a forest and greed." Do you think she has properly formulated the choice? Do you think the choice *is* between the owl and jobs? Or would you put the choice differently? Explain.

5. What do you think are Meadows's strongest points? Her weakest points?

6. In paragraph 5 Meadows says that the spotted owl is "the holder of a unique genetic code that is millions of years old and irreplaceable." In her final paragraph she says that "extinction is morally unacceptable." Suppose someone were to reply, "Extinction is nature's way. Countless species—all of the dinosaurs, for instance—have become extinct." What reply might Meadows offer?

Philip H. Knight

In April 2000, a majority of voting students at the University of Oregon agreed to support the Worker Rights Consortium, an organization already endorsed by several dozen other institutions of higher learning. According to the WRC's homepage, "The Worker Rights Consortium (WRC) is a nonprofit organization that supports and verifies licensee compliance with production codes of conduct. These codes of conduct have been developed by colleges and universities across the country to ensure that goods are produced under conditions that respect the basic rights of workers." Manufacturers of sports apparel, which frequently draw on cheap labor in countries such as Guatemala and Pakistan, have come under attack for their sweatshop conditions and their exploitation of women and children. When the University of Oregon announced that because a majority of its voting students supported the WRC, it too would support the WRC, Nike's chief executive officer, Philip Knight, an alumnus of Oregon, said that he would no longer donate money to the university. Because Knight had already donated $50 million to the school, his words, published in the Oregon Daily Emerald, *received much attention on the campus and off. Predictably, controversy arose.*

Statement from Nike Founder and CEO Philip H. Knight Regarding the University of Oregon

In recent days there have been numerous media reports and speculation regarding my personal philanthropy and relationship with the University of Oregon. As a lifelong Duck and in fairness to the many alumnus at Nike and around Oregon, I feel obligated to address this personally.

I was shocked on Friday morning, April 14, at 9 A.M. to find out that the University of Oregon had joined the Worker Rights Consortium (WRC). With this move the university inserted itself into the new global economy where I make my living. And inserted itself on the wrong side, fumbling a teachable moment.

Nike did not invent the global economy but has been determined to be a leader and to show its good citizenship. We are very, very serious about providing good factory working conditions and continuously improving the work experience for all 500,000 people who make Nike products. We also have been consistent in calling for one strong external code and one monitoring system for the entire industry that puts us all on a level playing field.

We believe the president's and the Department of Labor's Fair Labor Association (FLA), representing a coalition of human, consumer, and labor rights groups, industry, and universities, is such a system although it is taking too long to get active.

Regardless of whether either the FLA or WRC get up and running, we are committed to having the best monitoring and remediation 5 process possible and to be open. Should anyone doubt that, today I have directed our labor practices department to begin a program to publish the results of all PricewaterhouseCoopers factory monitoring visits on our Web site beginning in May—warts and all. We have nothing to hide.

Because this issue has been so important to students on college campuses such as the University of Oregon, last fall we invited students to become monitors. Tomorrow we will be releasing the student monitors' reports on 32 of our college-licensed apparel manufacturers.

Frankly, we are frustrated that factory monitoring is badly misconstrued. For us one of the great hurdles and real handicaps in the dialogue has been the complexity of the issue. For real progress to be made, all key participants have to be at the table. That's why the FLA has taken so long to get going. The WRC is supported by the AFL-CIO and its affiliated apparel workers' union, UNITE. Their main aim, logically and understandably, however misguided, is to bring apparel jobs back to the United States. Among WRC rules, no company can participate in setting standards or monitoring. It has an unrealistic living wage provision. And its "gotcha" approach to monitoring doesn't do what good monitoring should—measure conditions and make improvements.

As even our most severe critics acknowledge, Nike, because of the strength of its trademark on campuses, not because of its actions in overseas factories, has been the specific target of criticism. We have been called "evil" by some.

Let's recap some of the things this "evil" company has done over the past several years:

- Increased minimum age requirements for footwear workers to an industry-high 18 years of age
- Increased wages for Indonesian footwear workers by more than 70 percent
- Established community-based micro-loan programs and on-site, after hours continuing education for our footwear factory workers
- Significantly improved indoor air quality in our footwear factories consistent with OSHA guidelines
- Disclosed the U.S. and global locations of the 45 factories that produce collegiate licensed apparel

If you want to begin to understand this issue, ask University of Ore- 10
gon President Dave Frohnmayer one question: Ask him if he will sign a pledge that all contractors and subcontractors of the University of Oregon as well as the university itself meet the WRC's "living wage" provision. Not just Nike. All of us. No university, including the University of Oregon, can meet the WRC living wage and other code standards for food service employees, grounds keepers, clerical personnel, or teaching assistants.

My history with the University of Oregon goes back a long way. My father graduated from the university in 1934. From the time I was 14 years old it was the only college for me. The late Bill Bowerman, my mentor and cofounder of Nike, was a graduate as well as track coach there for 24 years. There is a strong emotional attachment for me with the university. I personally have given $50 million to the University of Oregon — $30 million for academics, and $20 million for athletics.

Nike has a lot of pride and has been my life. It is the source of any dollars I am able to give. To accept the University of Oregon's endorsement of the WRC would be to place my company, our employees, our university-related manufacturers, and their employees in unknown hands under undefined monitoring that has no protocols, no credibility, no role for the companies whose businesses are being monitored, and no independence. It would be a sell-out of my company, my fellow employees, and the progress we have worked so hard to make in our factories both here and abroad. I am simply not able to do that.

Nike will honor its contractual commitment. But for me personally, there will be no further donations of any kind to the University of Oregon. At this time, this is not a situation that can be resolved. The bonds of trust, which allowed me to give at a high level, have been shredded.

Topics for Critical Thinking and Writing

1. Check the Internet to find out what the WRC (para. 2) and the FLA (para. 4) advocate. Do you agree with Knight's criticisms of the WRC (paras. 7 and 12)? Based on your research, which organization do you think is better? Explain why.

2. Knight asserts that "No university . . . can meet the WRC living wage and other code standards" (para. 10). What are those standards, and why can't they be met, do you think? (See "Labor 101" on p. 551, para. 4.)

3. What is the point Knight is making (para. 11) by informing the reader of his and his family's long-standing connections with the University of Oregon?

4. If you were Knight, would you have abruptly terminated all personal donations to the University of Oregon (para. 13)? Can you think of another response that he might have made but didn't?

Letters of Response to Philip H. Knight

We reprint three letters of response from the online edition of the Oregon Daily Emerald (www.dailyemerald.com), *the University newspaper.*

April 28

I am a little concerned about the discourse that has risen out of the Worker Rights Consortium protests. Although I understand the rationale for promoting the WRC from the perspective of the protesters, I don't see anyone making the connection in global, economic terms, which I feel is more important than sweatshop labor, Nike funding, or governance: namely, our relationship with capitalism.

The main tenet of capitalism is inequality or the ability of one to subjugate another for profit. To protest against the effects of capitalism without addressing their cause is like putting a Band-Aid on a bullet wound. The content of the protest shows that there is a large unawareness of capitalism, due mainly to its persuasiveness and the promotion of capitalism as the only avenue to democracy and (oddly enough) equality.

If capitalism is to remain, expect inequality, domination, and expansion. If, however, we are able to view individual issues in relation to capitalism on a level that is above individuals or nations or even international relations, we can find the nature or essence of the problem: not apathy or stupidity or powerlessness, but our own constructed system of economic exchange.

C. H.
Student

Topics for Critical Thinking and Writing

1. Read the essay by Milton Friedman (p. 530), and ask yourself if Friedman would agree with C. H.'s characterization (para. 2) of capitalism as "inequality or the ability of one to subjugate another for profit."

2. What, in your own words, is C. H. advocating in the closing paragraph of his letter?

April 28

Something really needs to be done.

It is not about Nike CEO Phil Knight or Nike or even money. It is about a respectable university such as ours joining an extremist highly politicized Worker Rights Consortium that is backed and funded by American labor groups who don't even care about workers in other countries.

Shame on the 17,000-strong student body if they let a handful of [protesters] affect the future and the integrity of my alma mater. What do these students know about working conditions in other countries? Do they realize that Nike and other companies often pay salaries that are much higher than what local governments can afford and that the foreign workers do not appreciate one bit what WRC is trying to do to "protect" their rights?

Knight is not the only one who will pull donations. A lot of alumni are absolutely disgusted, and I am one of them. Do something before it is too late! Get out there; organize a rally! Show the administration that you are not going to allow the university back into mediocrity!

M. Z.
Alumnus

Topic for Critical Thinking and Writing

Evaluate the arguments raised in M. Z.'s letter.

May 4

There is more than enough blame to go around for the Worker Rights Consortium fiasco, and yes, not all of the blame should be directed at the students. However, by your own reporting, only about 2,000 students took enough interest in the subject to press the issue. Where were the remaining 15,000 students who could have stopped the movement in its tracks by voicing their opposition? Now that the university is going to pay a heavy price for this inappropriate and highly questionable course of action, everyone is pointing fingers at someone else to take the blame. Yes, 2,000 students were too emotional and the administration was derelict in its duty to look out for what was best for the university.

Ultimately, the final responsibility rests with the university president [Dave Frohnmayer], and this sad and pathetic lack of common sense is going to cost the university and thousands of future students and faculty the benefit of increased funding for educational facilities and programs, all in the name of some social-political agenda that has no place in the official policy of the university.

Perhaps the best advice would be to adhere to my mother's old adage, "Engage brain before opening mouth!"

D. F.
Alumnus

Topics for Critical Thinking and Writing

1. D. F. says, "Ultimately, the final responsibility rests with the university president" (para. 2). If you had been the president of the University of Oregon, and a majority of the voting students voted to endorse the WRC, what would you have done? Rejected the vote on the grounds that only a small minority of enrolled students voted? Rejected the vote on the grounds that it would be irresponsible of you as president to allow the university to suffer a financial loss that would be damaging to future students? Accepted the vote and perhaps even applauded the students' highly developed sense of morality? You may want to put your

response in the form of an open letter of 250 to 500 words written by President Frohnmayer, addressed to the university community, and published in the *Oregon Daily Emerald.*

2. Imagine that you are the president of the University of Oregon. Write a letter to Knight, seeking to persuade him to continue to be a generous benefactor of the university.

Anonymous

In the wake of the Nike controversy, the following editorial was originally published in the Wall Street Journal *on May 12, 2000.*

Labor 101

Remember when Corporate Enemy No. 1 on campus was Dow Chemical, manufacturer of napalm? In the demonology of today, Dow Chemical has been replaced by Nike, maker of tennis shoes.

The Worker Rights Consortium, which now boasts 48 member colleges and universities, is demanding that companies such as Nike ensure that overseas factory hands are paid according to a "living wage" formula. Their case would be far more persuasive, however, if their members agreed first to apply that same formula to their own workers on campus.

That was Nike founder Phil Knight's point when he announced he was cutting off donations to his alma mater, the University of Oregon, after waking up to read in the local paper that the university had joined the WRC: This is no small thing, for not only is Nike one of the Oregon Ducks' leading suppliers but Mr. Knight has over the years personally donated $50 million to the school. His move comes, moreover, as the campus antisweatshop movement is reaching a fever pitch and Nike itself has pulled out of deals with two other universities—Michigan and Brown—over what it says are high-handed university efforts to insert unworkable labor guarantees into contracts.

At the heart of these disputes is the notion of a "living wage." The WRC defines it as a wage that "provides for the basic needs (housing, energy, nutrition, clothing, health care, education, potable water, childcare, transportation, and savings) of an average family unit of employees in the garment manufacturing employment sector of the country divided by the average number of adult wage earners in the family unit." Note the complete lack of reference to anything linking wages to, say, productivity.

Yet at the same time that university officials are moving to decree   5
what others should pay a Guatemalan shirt-maker, on their own turf they take a more Adam Smith-like line. Activists themselves are begin-

ning to note the discrepancy. Just this week actors Matt Damon and Ben Affleck—whose father worked as a janitor at Harvard—appeared on the front lines of the Harvard Living Wage Campaign, whose bid for a $10.25-per-hour living wage for all service workers was just rejected by a faculty panel.

Closer to Nike's home, the pay scales for the University of Oregon show that when it comes to the cafeteria workers or custodians who toil on campus—the "marginalized" workers, in labor parlance—the university is as living-wage challenged as any multinational. Food service workers, for example, can start at $14,500 a year. That's barely a third of the $34,019 living wage for a single adult with two children in Oregon as calculated by a joint study by the University of Washington's Northwest Policy Center and the Northwest Federation of Community Organizations.

Up to now, one of the most difficult things for global companies to get across to those in the ivory towers is just how complicated issues such as the "living wage" really are. Perhaps the growing agitation for our universities to abide by this same formula on their own campuses will do the trick.

Topics for Critical Thinking and Writing

1. Why was Dow Chemical once "Corporate Enemy No. 1" (para. 1)?

2. Do you think that "wages" ought to be linked with "productivity" (para. 4), as the editorial implies? Why, or why not?

3. Is it inconsistent and hypocritical, as the editorial implies, for a university to pay its "marginalized" (para. 6) employees noticeably less than what the WRC defines as a "living wage" (para. 4) and at the same time to insist that corporations like Nike pay their overseas workers a "living wage" (para. 2)?

Thomas L. Friedman

The following comments on Nike CEO Philip H. Knight and the University of Oregon appeared as an editorial in the New York Times *on June 20, 2000.*

Knight Is Right

Some things are true even though Phil Knight, the chairman of Nike, believes them.

Mr. Knight recently made news by suddenly withdrawing a contemplated $30 million gift to the University of Oregon after the university balked at joining a coalition—the Fair Labor Association (FLA)—that was formed by human rights groups, colleges, the U.S. government, and companies such as Nike to alleviate global sweatshop conditions. Oregon opted to join an alternative group being pushed on college campuses, the Worker Rights Consortium (WRC), which also plans to combat sweatshops but refuses to cooperate with any companies, such as Nike.

The natural assumption is that Mr. Knight is wrong. The truth is, Nike has a shameful past when it comes to tolerating sweatshops. But on the question of how best to remedy those conditions in the future—which Nike has now agreed to do—Mr. Knight is dead *right* and Oregon wrong: The best way to create global governance—over issues from sweatshops to the environment—when there is no global government is to build coalitions, in which enlightened companies, consumers, and social activists work together to forge their own rules and enforcement mechanisms. That's what the FLA represents and it's what the WRC doesn't.

We've heard plenty this year about the downsides of globalization. The question is what to do about it. The more radical protesters, such as the WRC, want to trash multinationals and get the World Trade Organization to set rules for workers and the environment, not just for trade. And what practical effect have the protesters had so far? Zero.

So what to do? Well, it comes down to this: Do you want a make a point or do you want to make a difference? The FLA was formed to make a difference. The WRC was formed to make a point.   5

The FLA was founded four years ago, and it now includes the Lawyers Committee for Human Rights, the National Council of Churches, the International Labor Rights Fund, 135 universities, and major apparel companies such as Liz Claiborne, Levi Strauss, Nike, Reebok, and Adidas. After long talks, this diverse group agreed on a nine-point code for any apparel factory anywhere in the world—including rules against forced labor and child labor, as well as freedom of association, minimum wages, maximum working hours, lighting, bathrooms, and safety. They also agreed on a system of independent monitoring, surprise inspections, and follow-ups, which is now being tested in five developing countries.

Companies whose factories comply will be able to sew an "FLA" label into their clothing, and the 135 universities have agreed that their logos will go only on FLA-made products. Global brands can't afford any longer to be associated with sweatshops, and the FLA creates a credible system for empowering consumers to punish dirty companies and reward improving ones.

The WRC, by contrast, is backed by protectionist U.S. unions, such as Unite, that don't want any system that would give a stamp of approval to any production outside the U.S. That's one reason the WRC won't work with companies. But that means the WRC has no way of consistently monitoring factories or following up remedies, and it is only focused on clothing sold on college campuses.

It's good that there's a WRC out there noisily protesting sweatshops and embarrassing companies. But the WRC is not a substitute for the FLA, which has a comprehensive strategy for upgrading the whole apparel industry. It's a pity that some cowardly college presidents—intimidated by a few vocal and often uninformed students—have quit the FLA in favor of the WRC.

"If you want to improve people's lives in the absence of a global gov- 10 ernment, you need to align the economic interests of the better global companies with the social interests of the least advantaged people," said Sam Brown, the 1960s antiwar activist, former U.S. ambassador and now director of the FLA. "We need to make these companies our allies, not our opponents. We won't change the world overnight. But it is foolish to dismiss the FLA because it does not go far enough or fast enough. The issue is how to get from here to there, and the FLA has a real strategy for harnessing U.S. consumer power to change the lives and working conditions of real people."

Topics for Critical Thinking and Writing

1. Friedman refers to "globalization" (para. 4) but doesn't explain what it means. What is globalization?

2. If a group on your campus advocated that your college join the WRC, would you support that position? Would you support your college's endorsement of the FLA? Would you endorse neither group? Explain your view.

Louise Lee and Aaron Bernstein

The following essay, by staff writers, appeared in BusinessWeek *on June 12, 2000. Louise Lee covers Nike from San Mateo, and Aaron Bernstein covers workplace issues from Washington, D.C.*

Who Says Student Protests Don't Matter?

For several years, Nike, Gap, and most other leading U.S. garment makers have tried to placate antisweatshop activists by hiring auditors to inspect their overseas factories. But the industry has refused to make the audits public. Executives have insisted that they shouldn't have to air their dirty laundry until the factories—which are often owned by contractors—have a chance to fix any problems.

So it was a coup for activists when Nike Inc. declared on April 24 that it would release the complete audits of the 600 plants that manufacture its shoes and apparel—gory details and all. Nike's reluctant move testifies to the surprising effectiveness of the three-year-old United Students against Sweatshops. USAS, which has chapters on 50-odd campuses and supporters at dozens more, has mounted a growing campaign of pickets, rallies, and sit-ins to pressure garment makers. So far, it has prompted 48 colleges to join the Worker Rights Consortium (WRC), including all nine campuses of the University of California and athletic powerhouses such as the University of Michigan. USAS formed the WRC as an independent body to inspect factories that produce for the collegiate-licensing market. "They are gaining in strength," says James A. Koehne, general manager of the college division of VF Corporation's Jansport unit, which makes clothes for 2,000 colleges.

Still, USAS may set back its own cause if it pushes the WRC idea too hard. Students have been pressuring universities to join the WRC and quit the Fair Labor Association, the leading auditing system, which grew out of a presidential task force of human-rights groups and companies such as Nike and Liz Claiborne Inc. Students see the FLA as an industry tool that provides cover for abuses rather than exposing them. Already, USAS has persuaded a half-dozen colleges to quit the FLA. If USAS discredits the FLA, it could collapse.

That would be bad news for the antisweatshop effort. The FLA may not be as strict as USAS, but it has been working for two years to develop an effective system and hire competent auditors. The WRC has only just formed a board of directors, composed of students, university officials, and human-rights experts, and it could take years for the new group to get up and running.

What's more, the WRC's planned source of revenue is the fee that 5 companies pay colleges to license their names. This would underwrite a system to monitor the college market. But that's less than 2 percent of the $200 billion U.S. garment industry. A much bigger scheme is needed to impact even a sample of the thousands of other factories that produce goods for the general public. The FLA, funded by major companies, is better positioned for that gargantuan task.

Rather than pit the WRC against the more established group, USAS should try to complement the FLA. The WRC wants to set higher standards by insisting on the publication of factory locations and audits. That's an important role for the consortium, but tackling sweatshops worldwide requires a more comprehensive system. "There's no inconsistency between the FLA being an industrywide code and other initiatives such as the WRC that try to keep the system honest," says Mike Posner, head of the Lawyers Committee for Human Rights, which helped form the FLA.

Still, students have gained more clout than they thought possible just last fall, when USAS began pressuring the industry to clean up its act. In October, Nike agreed to disclose the locations of 42 plants in 11 countries that make college apparel. Nike and others had for years insisted that such a move would let rivals steal its sourcing secrets. But knowing plant locations is a big deal to activists because it helps them know where to look for abuses. Nike's move to disclose has prompted dozens of companies, such as Jansport and Reebok International Ltd., to release the locations of their factories.

Plenty of resistance remains. Nike CEO Phil Knight has withdrawn $30 million he was giving to his alma mater, the University of Oregon, after it joined the WRC. And Nike still won't reveal the sites of its other 560-odd factories. Levi Strauss & Company won't release such information outside the FLA, to which it belongs. Still, arguments against disclosure are more difficult to make now. "Nike was the first; now others will have to follow," says Jeremy Blasi, a senior at the University of California at Berkeley.

USAS scored another win when Nike agreed to publicize its factory audits. For years, human-rights groups have denounced corporate inspections as shams because they're funded by the manufacturer being inspected. Companies have defended the process. Now, critics will be able to see how audits are performed and compare them with their own research.

The real test for USAS will come as it sorts out the WRC's role. If the WRC ever succeeds in launching inspections, Nike and others that sell at WRC colleges will have to submit to its conditions or give up the sales. In any case, students have shown that the industry can go a lot further than execs had insisted was possible. 10

Topics for Critical Thinking and Writing

1. The authors concede that "The FLA may not be as strict as USAS" (para. 4). How "strict" is the FLA? What does "strict" mean in this context?

2. Are any student activists on your campus or a neighboring college trying to persuade college administrators to join the WRC? If so, write an account of their activities and successes (if any) so far.

For topical links related to the discussion of business ethics, see the companion Web site: **www.bedfordstmartins.com/barnetbedau.**

20

The Death Penalty:
Can It Ever Be Justified?

Edward I. Koch

Edward I. Koch (b. 1924), long active in Democratic politics, was mayor of New York from 1978 to 1989. This essay first appeared in The New Republic *on April 15, 1985.*

Death and Justice:
How Capital Punishment Affirms Life

Last December a man named Robert Lee Willie, who had been convicted of raping and murdering an eighteen-year-old woman, was executed in the Louisiana state prison. In a statement issued several minutes before his death, Mr. Willie said: "Killing people is wrong. . . . It makes no difference whether it's citizens, countries, or governments. Killing is wrong." Two weeks later in South Carolina, an admitted killer named

Joseph Carl Shaw was put to death for murdering two teenagers. In an appeal to the governor for clemency, Mr. Shaw wrote: "Killing was wrong when I did it. Killing is wrong when you do it. I hope you have the courage and moral strength to stop the killing."

It is a curiosity of modern life that we find ourselves being lectured on morality by cold-blooded killers. Mr. Willie previously had been convicted of aggravated rape, aggravated kidnapping, and the murders of a Louisiana deputy and a man from Missouri. Mr. Shaw committed another murder a week before the two for which he was executed, and admitted mutilating the body of the fourteen-year-old girl he killed. I can't help wondering what prompted these murderers to speak out against killing as they entered the deathhouse door. Did their newfound reverence for life stem from the realization that they were about to lose their own?

Life is indeed precious, and I believe the death penalty helps to affirm this fact. Had the death penalty been a real possibility in the minds of these murderers, they might well have stayed their hand. They might have shown moral awareness before their victims died, and not after. Consider the tragic death of Rosa Velez, who happened to be home when a man named Luis Vera burglarized her apartment in Brooklyn. "Yeah, I shot her," Vera admitted. "She knew me, and I knew I wouldn't go to the chair."

During my twenty-two years in public service, I have heard the pros and cons of capital punishment expressed with special intensity. As a district leader, councilman, congressman, and mayor, I have represented constituencies generally thought of as liberal. Because I support the death penalty for heinous crimes of murder, I have sometimes been the subject of emotional and outraged attacks by voters who find my position reprehensible or worse. I have listened to their ideas. I have weighed their objections carefully. I still support the death penalty. The reasons I maintain my position can be best understood by examining the arguments most frequently heard in opposition.

1. The death penalty is "barbaric." Sometimes opponents of capital punishment horrify with tales of lingering death on the gallows, of faulty electric chairs, or of agony in the gas chamber. Partly in response to such protests, several states such as North Carolina and Texas switched to execution by lethal injection. The condemned person is put to death painlessly, without ropes, voltage, bullets, or gas. Did this answer the objections of death penalty opponents? Of course not. On June 22, 1984, the *New York Times* published an editorial that sarcastically attacked the new "hygienic" method of death by injection, and stated that "execution can never be made humane through science." So it's not the method that really troubles opponents. It's the death itself they consider barbaric.

Admittedly, capital punishment is not a pleasant topic. However, one does not have to like the death penalty in order to support it any more than one must like radical surgery, radiation, or chemotherapy in order to find necessary these attempts at curing cancer. Ultimately we may learn how to cure cancer with a simple pill. Unfortunately, that day has not yet arrived. Today we are faced with the choice of letting the cancer spread or trying to cure it with the methods available, methods that one day will almost certainly be considered barbaric. But to give up and do nothing would be far more barbaric and would certainly delay the discovery of an eventual cure. The analogy between cancer and murder is imperfect, because murder is not the "disease" we are trying to cure. The disease is injustice. We may not like the death penalty, but it must be available to punish crimes of cold-blooded murder, cases in which any other form of punishment would be inadequate and, therefore, unjust. If we create a society in which injustice is not tolerated, incidents of murder—the most flagrant form of injustice—will diminish.

2. No other major democracy uses the death penalty. No other major democracy—in fact, few other countries of any description—are plagued by a murder rate such as that in the United States. Fewer and fewer Americans can remember the days when unlocked doors were the norm and murder was a rare and terrible offense. In America the murder rate climbed 122 percent between 1963 and 1980. During that same period, the murder rate in New York City increased by almost 400 percent, and the statistics are even worse in many other cities. A study at M.I.T. showed that based on 1970 homicide rates a person who lived in a large American city ran a greater risk of being murdered than an American soldier in World War II ran of being killed in combat. It is not surprising that the laws of each country differ according to differing conditions and traditions. If other countries had our murder problem, the cry for capital punishment would be just as loud as it is here. And I dare say that any other major democracy where 75 percent of the people supported the death penalty would soon enact it into law.

3. An innocent person might be executed by mistake. Consider the work of Hugo Adam Bedau, one of the most implacable foes of capital punishment in this country. According to Mr. Bedau, it is "false sentimentality to argue that the death penalty should be abolished because of the abstract possibility that an innocent person might be executed." He cites a study of the seven thousand executions in this country from 1892 to 1971, and concludes that the record fails to show that such cases occur. The main point, however, is this. If government functioned only when the possibility of error didn't exist, government wouldn't function at all. Human life deserves special protection, and one of the best ways to guarantee that protection is to assure that convicted murderers do not kill again. Only the death penalty can accomplish this end.

In a recent case in New Jersey, a man named Richard Biegenwald was freed from prison after serving eighteen years for murder; since his release he has been convicted of committing four murders. A prisoner named Lemuel Smith, who, while serving four life sentences for murder (plus two life sentences for kidnapping and robbery) in New York's Green Haven Prison, lured a woman corrections officer into the chaplain's office and strangled her. He then mutilated and dismembered her body. An additional life sentence for Smith is meaningless. Because New York has no death penalty statute, Smith has effectively been given a license to kill.

But the problem of multiple murder is not confined to the nation's penitentiaries. In 1981, ninety-one police officers were killed in the line of duty in this country. Seven percent of those arrested in the cases that have been solved had a previous arrest for murder. In New York City in 1976 and 1977, eighty-five persons arrested for homicide had a previous arrest for murder. Six of these individuals had two previous arrests for murder, and one had four previous murder arrests. During those two years the New York police were arresting for murder persons with a previous arrest for murder on the average of one every eight and a half days. This is not surprising when we learn that in 1975, for example, the median time served in Massachusetts for homicide was less than two and a half years. In 1976 a study sponsored by the Twentieth Century Fund found that the average time served in the United States for first-degree murder is ten years. The median time served may be considerably lower.

4. Capital punishment cheapens the value of human life. 10
On the contrary, it can be easily demonstrated that the death penalty strengthens the value of human life. If the penalty for rape were lowered, clearly it would signal a lessened regard for the victim's suffering, humiliation, and personal integrity. It would cheapen their horrible experience, and expose them to an increased danger of recurrence. When we lower the penalty for murder, it signals a lessened regard for the value of the victim's life. Some critics of capital punishment, such as columnist Jimmy Breslin, have suggested that a life sentence is actually a harsher penalty for murder than death. This is sophistic nonsense. A few killers may decide not to appeal a death sentence, but the overwhelming majority make every effort to stay alive. It is by exacting the highest penalty for the taking of human life that we affirm the highest value of human life.

5. The death penalty is applied in a discriminatory manner. This factor no longer seems to be the problem it once was. The appeals process for a condemned prisoner is lengthy and painstaking. Every effort is made to see that the verdict and sentence were fairly arrived at. However, assertions of discrimination are not an argument for ending the death penalty but for extending it. It is not justice to exclude everyone from the penalty of the law if a few are found to be so favored. Justice requires that the law be applied equally to all.

6. Thou Shalt Not Kill. The Bible is our greatest source of moral inspiration. Opponents of the death penalty frequently cite the sixth of the Ten Commandments in an attempt to prove that capital punishment is divinely proscribed. In the original Hebrew, however, the Sixth Commandment reads "Thou Shalt Not Commit Murder," and the Torah specifies capital punishment for a variety of offenses. The biblical viewpoint has been upheld by philosophers throughout history. The greatest thinkers of the nineteenth century—Kant, Locke, Hobbes, Rousseau, Montesquieu, and Mill—agreed that natural law properly authorizes the sovereign to take life in order to vindicate justice. Only Jeremy Bentham was ambivalent. Washington, Jefferson, and Franklin endorsed it. Abraham Lincoln authorized executions for deserters in wartime. Alexis de Tocqueville, who expressed profound respect for American institutions, believed that the death penalty was indispensable to the support of social order. The United States Constitution, widely admired as one of the seminal achievements in the history of humanity, condemns cruel and inhuman punishment, but does not condemn capital punishment.

7. The death penalty is state-sanctioned murder. This is the defense with which Messrs. Willie and Shaw hoped to soften the resolve of those who sentenced them to death. By saying in effect, "You're no better than I am," the murderer seeks to bring his accusers down to his own level. It is also a popular argument among opponents of capital punishment, but a transparently false one. Simply put, the state has rights that the private individual does not. In a democracy, those rights are given to the state by the electorate. The execution of a lawfully condemned killer is no more an act of murder than is legal imprisonment an act of kidnapping. If an individual forces a neighbor to pay him money under threat of punishment, it's called extortion. If the state does it, it's called taxation. Rights and responsibilities surrendered by the individual are what give the state its power to govern. This contract is the foundation of civilization itself.

Everyone wants his or her rights, and will defend them jealously. Not everyone, however, wants responsibilities, especially the painful responsibilities that come with law enforcement. Twenty-one years ago a woman named Kitty Genovese was assaulted and murdered on a street in New York. Dozens of neighbors heard her cries for help but did nothing to assist her. They didn't even call the police. In such a climate the criminal understandably grows bolder. In the presence of moral cowardice, he lectures us on our supposed failings and tries to equate his crimes with our quest for justice.

The death of anyone—even a convicted killer—diminishes us all. 15
But we are diminished even more by a justice system that fails to function. It is an illusion to let ourselves believe that doing away with capital
punishment removes the murderer's deed from our conscience. The
rights of society are paramount. When we protect guilty lives, we give
up innocent lives in exchange. When opponents of capital punishment
say to the state, "I will not let you kill in my name," they are also saying
to murderers: "You can kill in your *own* name as long as I have an excuse for not getting involved."

It is hard to imagine anything worse than being murdered while
neighbors do nothing. But something worse exists. When those same
neighbors shrink back from justly punishing the murderer, the victim
dies twice.

Topics for Critical Thinking and Writing

1. In paragraph 6 Koch draws an analogy between cancer and murder and
   observes that imperfect as today's cures for cancer are, "to give up and
   do nothing would be far more barbaric." What is the relevance of this
   comment in the context of the analogy and the dispute over the death
   penalty?

2. In paragraph 8 Koch describes a convicted but unexecuted recidivist
   murderer as someone who "has effectively been given a license to kill."
   But a license to kill, as in a deer-hunter's license, entitles the holder to
   engage in lawful killing. (Think of the fictional hero James Bond—
   Agent 007—who, we are told, had a "license to kill.") What is the difference between having a license and "effectively" having one? How
   might the opponent of the death penalty reply to Koch's position here?

3. Koch distinguishes between the "median time" served by persons convicted of murder but not sentenced to death and the "average time"
   they serve, and he adds that the former "may be considerably lower"
   than the latter (para. 9). Explain the difference between a "median" and
   an "average" (review the section on statistics, p. 80). Is knowing one of
   these more important for certain purposes than the other? Why?

4. Koch identifies seven arguments against the death penalty, and he rejects them all. Which of the seven arguments seems to you to be the
   strongest objection to the death penalty? Which the weakest? Why?
   Does Koch effectively refute the strongest argument? Can you think of
   any argument(s) against the death penalty that he neglects?

5. Koch says he supports the death penalty "for heinous crimes of murder"
   (para. 4). Does he imply that all murders are heinous crimes or only
   some? If the latter, what criteria seem to you to be the appropriate ones
   to distinguish the heinous murders from the rest? Why these criteria?

6. Koch asserts that the death penalty "strengthens the value of human
   life" (para. 10). Yet opponents of the death penalty often claim the

reverse, arguing that capital punishment undermines the idea that human life is precious. Write an essay of 500 words in which you explain what it means to assert that life is precious and why one of the two positions — support for or opposition to the death penalty — best supports (or is consistent with) this principle.

David Bruck

David Bruck (b. 1949) graduated from Harvard College and received his law degree from the University of South Carolina. His practice is devoted almost entirely to the defense of persons under death sentence, through the South Carolina Office of Appellate Defense. The essay reprinted here originally appeared on May 20, 1985, in The New Republic *as a response to the essay by Edward I. Koch (p. 557).*

The Death Penalty

Mayor Ed Koch contends that the death penalty "affirms life." By failing to execute murderers, he says, we "signal a lessened regard for the value of the victim's life." Koch suggests that people who oppose the death penalty are like Kitty Genovese's neighbors, who heard her cries for help but did nothing while an attacker stabbed her to death.

This is the standard "moral" defense of death as punishment: Even if executions don't deter violent crime any more effectively than imprisonment, they are still required as the only means we have of doing justice in response to the worst of crimes.

Until recently, this "moral" argument had to be considered in the abstract, since no one was being executed in the United States. But the death penalty is back now, at least in the southern states, where every one of the more than thirty executions carried out over the last two years has taken place. Those of us who live in those states are getting to see the difference between the death penalty in theory, and what happens when you actually try to use it.

South Carolina resumed executing prisoners in January with the electrocution of Joseph Carl Shaw. Shaw was condemned to death for helping to murder two teenagers while he was serving as a military policeman at Fort Jackson, South Carolina. His crime, propelled by mental illness and PCP, was one of terrible brutality. It is Shaw's last words ("Killing was wrong when I did it. It is wrong when you do it. . . .") that so outraged Mayor Koch: He finds it "a curiosity of modern life that we are being lectured on morality by cold-blooded killers." And so it is.

But it was not "modern life" that brought this curiosity into being. It 5
was capital punishment. The electric chair was J. C. Shaw's platform. (The mayor mistakenly writes that Shaw's statement came in the form of a plea to the governor for clemency: Actually Shaw made it only seconds

before his death, as he waited, shaved and strapped into the chair, for the switch to be thrown.) It was the chair that provided Shaw with celebrity and an opportunity to lecture us on right and wrong. What made this weird moral reversal even worse is that J. C. Shaw faced his own death with undeniable dignity and courage. And while Shaw died, the TV crews recorded another "curiosity" of the death penalty—the crowd gathered outside the death-house to cheer on the executioner. Whoops of elation greeted the announcement of Shaw's death. Waiting at the penitentiary gates for the appearance of the hearse bearing Shaw's remains, one demonstrator started yelling, "Where's the beef?"

For those who had to see the execution of J. C. Shaw, it wasn't easy to keep in mind that the purpose of the whole spectacle was to affirm life. It will be harder still when Florida executes a cop-killer named Alvin Ford. Ford has lost his mind during his years of death-row confinement, and now spends his days trembling, rocking back and forth, and muttering unintelligible prayers. This has led to litigation over whether Ford meets a centuries-old legal standard for mental competency. Since the Middle Ages, the Anglo-American legal system has generally prohibited the execution of anyone who is too mentally ill to understand what is about to be done to him and why. If Florida wins its case, it will have earned the right to electrocute Ford in his present condition. If it loses, he will not be executed until the state has first nursed him back to some semblance of mental health.[1]

We can at least be thankful that this demoralizing spectacle involves a prisoner who is actually guilty of murder. But this may not always be so. The ordeal of Lenell Jeter—the young black engineer who recently served more than a year of a life sentence for a Texas armed robbery that he didn't commit—should remind us that the system is quite capable of making the very worst sort of mistake. That Jeter was eventually cleared is a fluke. If the robbery had occurred at 7 P.M. rather than 3 P.M., he'd have had no alibi, and would still be in prison today. And if someone had been killed in that robbery, Jeter probably would have been sentenced to death. We'd have seen the usual execution-day interviews with state officials and the victim's relatives, all complaining that Jeter's appeals took too long. And Jeter's last words from the gurney would have taken their place among the growing literature of death-house oration that so irritates the mayor.

Koch quotes Hugo Adam Bedau, a prominent abolitionist, to the effect that the record fails to establish that innocent defendants have been executed in the past. But this doesn't mean, as Koch implies, that it hasn't happened. All Bedau was saying was that doubts concerning exe-

---

[1] Florida lost its case to execute Ford. On June 26, 1986, the Supreme Court barred execution of convicted murderers who have become so insane that they do not know that they are about to be executed and do not understand the reason for their sentence. If Ford regains his sanity, however, he can be executed. [Editors' note.]

cuted prisoners' guilt are almost never resolved. Bedau is at work now on an effort to determine how many wrongful death sentences may have been imposed: His list of murder convictions since 1900 in which the state eventually *admitted* error is some four hundred cases long. Of course, very few of these cases involved actual executions: The mistakes that Bedau documents were uncovered precisely because the prisoner was alive and able to fight for his vindication. The cases where someone is executed arc the very cases in which we're least likely to learn that we got the wrong man.

I don't claim that executions of entirely innocent people will occur very often. But they will occur. And other sorts of mistakes already have. Roosevelt Green was executed in Georgia two days before J. C. Shaw. Green and an accomplice kidnapped a young woman. Green swore that his companion shot her to death after Green had left, and that he knew nothing about the murder. Green's claim was supported by a statement that his accomplice made to a witness after the crime. The jury never resolved whether Green was telling the truth, and when he tried to take a polygraph examination a few days before his scheduled execution, the state of Georgia refused to allow the examiner into the prison. As the pressure for symbolic retribution mounts, the courts, like the public, are losing patience with such details. Green was electrocuted on January 9, while members of the Ku Klux Klan rallied outside the prison.

Then there is another sort of arbitrariness that happens all the 10 time. Last October, Louisiana executed a man named Ernest Knighton. Knighton had killed a gas station owner during a robbery. Like any murder, this was a terrible crime. But it was not premeditated, and is the sort of crime that very rarely results in a death sentence. Why was Knighton electrocuted when almost everyone else who committed the same offense was not? Was it because he was black? Was it because his victim and all twelve members of the jury that sentenced him were white? Was it because Knighton's court-appointed lawyer presented no evidence on his behalf at his sentencing hearing? Or maybe there's no reason except bad luck. One thing is clear: Ernest Knighton was picked out to die the way a fisherman takes a cricket out of a bait jar. No one cares which cricket gets impaled on the hook.

Not every prisoner executed recently was chosen that randomly. But many were. And having selected these men so casually, so blindly, the death penalty system asks us to accept that the purpose of killing each of them is to affirm the sanctity of human life.

The death penalty states are also learning that the death penalty is easier to advocate than it is to administer. In Florida, where executions have become almost routine, the governor reports that nearly a third of his time is spent reviewing the clemency requests of condemned prisoners. The Florida Supreme Court is hopelessly backlogged with death cases. Some have taken five years to decide, and the rest of the Court's work waits in line behind the death appeals. Florida's death row currently holds more than 230 prisoners. State officials are reportedly considering building a special "death prison" devoted entirely to the isolation and electrocution of the condemned. The state is also considering the creation of a special public defender unit that will do nothing else but handle death penalty appeals. The death penalty, in short, is spawning death agencies.

And what is Florida getting for all of this? The state went through almost all of 1983 without executing anyone: Its rate of intentional homicide declined by 17 percent. Last year Florida executed eight people — the most of any state, and the sixth highest total for any year since Florida started electrocuting people back in 1924. Elsewhere in the United States last year, the homicide rate continued to decline. But in Florida, it actually rose by 5.1 percent.

But these are just the tiresome facts. The electric chair has been a centerpiece of each of Koch's recent political campaigns, and he knows better than anyone how little the facts have to do with the public's support for capital punishment. What really fuels the death penalty is the justifiable frustration and rage of people who see that the government is not coping with violent crime. So what if the death penalty doesn't work? At least it gives us the satisfaction of knowing that we got one or two of the sons of bitches.

Perhaps we want retribution on the flesh and bone of a handful of 15 convicted murderers so badly that we're willing to close our eyes to all of the demoralization and danger that come with it. A lot of politicians think so, and they may be right. But if they are, then let's at least look honestly at what we're doing. This lottery of death both comes from and encourages an attitude toward human life that is not reverent, but reckless.

And that is why the mayor is dead wrong when he confuses such fury with justice. He suggests that we trivialize murder unless we kill murderers. By that logic, we also trivialize rape unless we sodomize rapists. The sin of Kitty Genovese's neighbors wasn't that they failed to stab her attacker to death. Justice does demand that murderers be punished. And common sense demands that society be protected from them. But neither justice nor self-preservation demands that we kill men whom we have already imprisoned.

The electric chair in which J. C. Shaw died earlier this year was built in 1912 at the suggestion of South Carolina's governor at the time, Cole Blease. Governor Blease's other criminal justice initiative was an impassioned crusade in favor of lynch law. Any lesser response, the governor insisted, trivialized the loathsome crimes of interracial rape and murder. In 1912, a lot of people agreed with Governor Blease that a proper regard for justice required both lynching and the electric chair. Eventually we are going to learn that justice requires neither.

Topics for Critical Thinking and Writing

1. After three introductory paragraphs, Bruck devotes two paragraphs to Shaw's execution. In a sentence or two, state the point he is making in his discussion of this execution. Then in another sentence or two (or three), indicate the degree to which this point refutes Edward I. Koch's argument.

2. In paragraph 7, Bruck refers to the case of Lenell Jeter, an innocent man who was condemned to a life sentence. Evaluate this point as a piece of evidence used to support an argument against the death penalty.

3. In paragraph 8, Bruck says that "the state eventually *admitted* error" in some four hundred cases. He goes on: "Of course, very few of these cases involved actual executions." How few is "very few"? Why do you suppose Bruck doesn't specify the number? If it is only, say, two, in your opinion does that affect Bruck's point?

4. Discussing the case of Roosevelt Green (para. 9), Bruck points out that Green offered to take a polygraph test but "the state of Georgia refused to allow the examiner into the prison." In a paragraph evaluate the state's position on this matter.

5. In paragraph 13 Bruck points out that although "last year" (1984) the state executed eight people, the homicide rate in Florida rose 5.1 percent, whereas elsewhere in the United States the homicide rate declined. What do you make of these figures? What do you think Edward I. Koch (p. 557) would make of them?

6. In his next-to-last paragraph Bruck says that Koch "suggests that we trivialize murder unless we kill murderers. By that logic, we also trivialize rape unless we sodomize rapists." Do you agree that this statement brings out the absurdity of Koch's thinking?

7. Evaluate Bruck's final paragraph (a) as a concluding paragraph and (b) as a piece of argumentation.

8. Bruck, writing early in 1985, stresses that all the "more than thirty" executions in the nation "in the last two years" have taken place in the South (para. 3). Why does he think this figure points to a vulnerability in Koch's argument? Would Bruck's argument here be spoiled if some executions were to occur outside of the South? (By the way, where exactly have most of the recent executions in the nation occurred?)

9. Bruck argues that the present death-penalty system—in practice even if not in theory—utterly fails to "affirm the sanctity of human life" (para. 11). Do you think Bruck would, or should, concede that at least in theory it is possible for a death-penalty system to be no more offensive to the value of human life than, say, a system of imprisonment is offensive to the value of human liberty or a system of fines is offensive to the value of human property?

10. Can Bruck be criticized for implying that cases like those he cites — Shaw, Ford, Green, and Knightson in particular—are the rule rather

than the exception? Does either Bruck or Koch cite any evidence to help settle this question?

11. Write a paragraph explaining which of these events seems to you to be the more unseemly: a condemned prisoner, on the threshold of execution, lecturing the rest of us on the immorality of killing; or the crowd that bursts into cheers outside a prison when it learns that a scheduled execution has been carried out.

Potter Stewart

After the U.S. Supreme Court decided Furman v. Georgia *in 1972, requiring states either to abolish the death penalty or revise their statutes to avoid the "arbitrariness" to which the Court objected in* Furman, *state legislatures reacted in one of two ways. A few states enacted mandatory death penalties, giving the trial court no alternative to a death sentence once the defendant was convicted. Most states, including Georgia, tightened up their procedures by imposing new requirements on the trial and appellate courts in death penalty cases. In 1976 these new statutes were challenged, and in a series of decisions the Court (by a seven to two majority) settled two crucial questions: (1) The death penalty was not "a per se [as such] violation" of the Eighth Amendment (prohibiting "cruel and unusual punishments") and the Fourteenth Amendment (guaranteeing "equal protection of the laws"), and (2) several kinds of new death penalty statutes were constitutionally unobjectionable. The most important of these cases was* Gregg v. Georgia; *we reprint excerpts from the majority opinion by Associate Justice Potter Stewart (1915–1985). (Justice Stewart had voted against the death penalty in* Furman, *but four years later he switched sides, evidently believing that his objections of 1972 were no longer relevant.) In the following opinion, the citations referring to legal documents have been omitted.*

Gregg v. Georgia

The Georgia statute, as amended after our decision in *Furman v. Georgia*, retains the death penalty for six categories of crime: murder, kidnapping for ransom or where the victim is harmed, armed robbery, rape, treason, and aircraft hijacking. The capital defendant's guilt or innocence is determined in the traditional manner, either by a trial judge or a jury, in the first stage of a bifurcated trial. . . .

After a verdict, finding, or plea of guilty to a capital crime, a presentence hearing is conducted before whoever made the determination of guilt. The sentencing procedures are essentially the same in both bench and jury trials. At the hearing:

> [T]he judge [or jury] shall hear additional evidence in extenuation, mitigation, and aggravation of punishment, including the record of any prior criminal convictions and pleas of guilty or pleas of nolo contendere of the defendant, or the absence of any prior conviction and

pleas: Provided, however, that only such evidence in aggravations as the State has made known to the defendant prior to his trial shall be admissible. The judge [or jury] shall also hear argument by the defendant or his counsel and the prosecuting attorney . . . regarding the punishment to be imposed.

The defendant is accorded substantial latitude as to the types of evidence that he may introduce. Evidence considered during the guilt stage may be considered during the sentencing stage without being resubmitted.

In the assessment of the appropriate sentence to be imposed the judge is also required to consider or to include in his instructions to the jury "any mitigating circumstances or aggravating circumstances otherwise authorized by law and any of [ten] statutory aggravating circumstances which may be supported by the evidence. . . ." The scope of the nonstatutory aggravating or mitigating circumstances is not delineated in the statute. Before a convicted defendant may be sentenced to death, however, except in cases of treason or aircraft hijacking, the jury, or the trial judge in cases tried without a jury, must find beyond a reasonable doubt one of the ten aggravating circumstances specified in the statute.[1] The sentence of death may be imposed only if the jury (or judge) finds one of the statutory aggravating circumstances and then elects to impose that sentence. If the verdict is death the jury or judge must specify the aggravating circumstance(s) found. In jury cases, the trial judge is bound by the jury's recommended sentence.

In addition to the conventional appellate process available in all criminal cases, provision is made for special expedited direct review by the Supreme Court of Georgia of the appropriateness of imposing the sentence of death in the particular case. The court is directed to consider "the punishment as well as any errors enumerated by way of appeal," and to determine

1. whether the sentence of death was imposed under the influence of passion, prejudice, or any other arbitrary factor, and
2. whether, in cases other than treason or aircraft hijacking, the evidence supports the jury's or judge's finding of a statutory aggravating circumstance as enumerated in §27.2534.1 (b), and
3. whether the sentence of death is excessive or disproportionate to the penalty imposed in similar cases, considering both the crime and the defendant.

If the court affirms a death sentence, it is required to include in its decision reference to similar cases that it has taken into consideration.

. . . We now consider specifically whether the sentence of death for the crime of murder is a per se violation of the Eighth and Fourteenth Amendments to the Constitution. We note first that history and precedent strongly support a negative answer to this question.

The imposition of the death penalty for the crime of murder has a long history of acceptance both in the United States and in England. The common-law rule imposed a mandatory death sentence on all convicted murderers. And the penalty continued to be used into the twentieth century by most American states, although the breadth of the common-law rule was diminished, initially by narrowing the class of murders to be punished by death and subsequently by widespread adoption of laws expressly granting juries the discretion to recommend mercy.

It is apparent from the text of the Constitution itself that the existence of capital punishment was accepted by the Framers. At the time the Eighth Amendment was ratified, capital punishment was a common sanction in every state. Indeed, the First Congress of the United States enacted legislation providing death as the penalty for specified crimes. The Fifth Amendment, adopted at the same time as the Eighth, contemplated the continued existence of the capital sanction by imposing certain limits on the prosecution of capital cases:

> No person shall be held to answer for a capital, or otherwise infamous crime, unless on a presentment or indictment of a Grand Jury . . . ; nor shall any person be subject for the same offense to be twice put in jeopardy of life or limb; . . . nor be deprived of life, liberty, or property, without due process of law. . . .

And the Fourteenth Amendment, adopted over three-quarters of a century later, similarly contemplates the existence of the capital sanction in providing that no state shall deprive any person of "life, liberty, or property" without due process of law.

Four years ago, the petitioners in *Furman* and its companion cases predicated their argument primarily upon the asserted proposition that standards of decency had evolved to the point where capital punishment no longer could be tolerated. The petitioners in those cases said, in effect, that the evolutionary process had come to an end, and that standards of decency required that the Eighth Amendment be construed finally as prohibiting capital punishment for any crime regardless of its depravity and impact on society. This view was accepted by two Justices. Three other Justices were unwilling to go so far; focusing on the procedures by which convicted defendants were selected for the death penalty rather than on the actual punishment inflicted, they joined in the conclusion that the statutes before the Court were constitutionally invalid.

The petitioners in the capital cases before the Court today renew the "standards of decency" argument, but developments during the four years since *Furman* have undercut substantially the assumptions upon which their argument rested. Despite the continuing debate, dating back to the nineteenth century, over the morality and utility of capital punishment, it is now evident that a large proportion of American society continues to regard it as an appropriate and necessary criminal sanction.

The most marked indication of society's endorsement of the death 10
penalty for murder is the legislative response to *Furman*. The legislatures
of at least thirty-five states have enacted new statutes that provide for
the death penalty for at least some crimes that result in the death of another person. And the Congress of the United States, in 1974, enacted a
statute providing the death penalty for aircraft piracy that results in
death. . . .

In the only statewide referendum occurring since *Furman* and
brought to our attention, the people of California adopted a constitutional amendment that authorized capital punishment, in effect negating
a prior ruling by the Supreme Court of California in *People v. Anderson*,
that the death penalty violated the California Constitution.

The jury also is a significant and reliable objective index of contemporary values because it is so directly involved. . . .

It may be true that evolving standards have influenced juries in recent decades to be more discriminating in imposing the sentence of
death. But the relative infrequency of jury verdicts imposing the death
sentence does not indicate rejection of capital punishment per se.
Rather, the reluctance of juries in many cases to impose the sentence
may well reflect the humane feeling that this most irrevocable of sanctions should be reserved for a small number of extreme cases. Indeed,
the actions of juries in many states since *Furman* are fully compatible
with the legislative judgments, reflected in the new statutes, as to the
continued utility and necessity of capital punishment in appropriate
cases. At the close of 1974 at least 254 persons had been sentenced to
death since *Furman*, and by the end of March 1976, more than 460 persons were subject to death sentences. . . .

The death penalty is said to serve two principal social purposes: retribution and deterrence of capital crimes by prospective offenders.

In part, capital punishment is an expression of society's moral out- 15
rage at particularly offensive conduct. This function may be unappealing
to many, but it is essential in an ordered society that asks its citizens to
rely on legal processes rather than self-help to vindicate their wrongs.

> The instinct for retribution is part of the nature of man, and channeling
> that instinct in the administration of criminal justice serves an impor-
> tant purpose in promoting the stability of a society governed by law.
> When people begin to believe that organized society is unwilling or un-
> able to impose upon criminal offenders the punishment they "deserve,"
> then there are sown the seeds of anarchy — of self-help, vigilante jus-
> tice, and lynch law. *Furman v. Georgia* (Stewart, J., concurring).

"Retribution is no longer the dominant objective of the criminal law,"
Williams v. New York, but neither is it a forbidden objective nor one inconsistent with our respect for the dignity of men. . . . Indeed, the decision that capital punishment may be the appropriate sanction in extreme

cases is an expression of the community's belief that certain crimes are themselves so grievous an affront to humanity that the only adequate response may be the penalty of death.[2]

Statistical attempts to evaluate the worth of the death penalty as a deterrent to crimes by potential offenders have occasioned a great deal of debate. The results simply have been inconclusive. As one opponent of capital punishment has said:

> [A]fter all possible inquiry, including the probing of all possible methods of inquiry, we do not know, and for systematic and easily visible reasons cannot know, what the truth about this "deterrent" effect may be. . . .
>
> The inescapable flaw is . . . that social conditions in any state are not constant through time, and that social conditions are not the same in any two states. If an effect were observed (and the observed effects, one way or another, are not large) then one could not at all tell whether any of this effect is attributable to the presence or absence of capital punishment. A "scientific" — that is to say, a soundly based — conclusion is simply impossible, and no methodological path out of this tangle suggests itself. C. Black, *Capital Punishment: The Inevitability of Caprice and Mistake* 25–26 (1974).

Although some of the studies suggest that the death penalty may not function as a significantly greater deterrent than lesser penalties, there is no convincing empirical evidence either supporting or refuting this view. We may nevertheless assume safely that there are murderers, such as those who act in passion, for whom the threat of death has little or no deterrent effect. But for many others, the death penalty undoubtedly is a significant deterrent. There are carefully contemplated murders, such as murder for hire, where the possible penalty of death may well enter into the cold calculus that precedes the decision to act.[3] And there are some categories of murder, such as murder by a life prisoner, where other sanctions may not be adequate. . . .

In sum, we cannot say that the judgment of the Georgia legislature that capital punishment may be necessary in some cases is clearly wrong. Considerations of federalism, as well as respect for the ability of a legislature to evaluate, in terms of its particular state, the moral consensus concerning the death penalty and its social utility as a sanction, require us to conclude, in the absence of more convincing evidence, that the infliction of death as a punishment for murder is not without justification and thus is not unconstitutionally severe.

Finally, we must consider whether the punishment of death is disproportionate in relation to the crime for which it is imposed. There is no question that death as a punishment is unique in its severity and irrevocability. But we are concerned here only with the imposition of capital punishment for the crime of murder, and when a life has been taken deliberately by the offender,[4] we cannot say that the punishment is invariably disproportionate to the crime. It is an extreme sanction, suitable to the most extreme of crimes.

We hold that the death penalty is not a form of punishment that 20 may never be imposed, regardless of the circumstances of the offense, regardless of the character of the offender, and regardless of the procedure followed in reaching the decision to impose it. . . .

While some have suggested that standards to guide a capital jury's sentencing deliberations arc impossible to formulate, the fact is that such standards have been developed. When the drafters of the Model Penal Code faced this problem, they concluded "that it is within the realm of possibility to point to the main circumstances of aggravation and of mitigation that should be weighed *and weighed against each other* when they are presented in a concrete case" (emphasis in original). While such standards are by necessity somewhat general, they do provide guidance to the sentencing authority and thereby reduce the likelihood that it will impose a sentence that fairly can be called capricious or arbitrary. Where the sentencing authority is required to specify the factors it relied upon in reaching its decision, the further safeguard of meaningful appellate review is available to ensure that death sentences are not imposed capriciously or in a freakish manner.

In summary, the concerns expressed in *Furman* that the penalty of death not be imposed in an arbitrary or capricious manner can be met by a carefully drafted statute that ensures that the sentencing authority is given adequate information and guidance. As a general proposition these concerns are best met by a system that provides for a bifurcated proceeding at which the sentencing authority is apprised of the information relevant to the imposition of sentence and provided with standards to guide its use of the information.

For the reasons expressed in this opinion, we hold that the statutory system under which Gregg was sentenced to death does not violate the Constitution. Accordingly, the judgment of the Georgia Supreme Court is affirmed.

NOTES

1. The statute provides in part:
   (a) The death penalty may be imposed for the offenses of aircraft hijacking or treason, in any case.
   (b) In all cases of other offenses for which the death penalty may be authorized, the judge shall consider, or he shall include in his instructions to the jury for it to consider, any mitigating circumstances or aggravating circumstances otherwise authorized by law and any of the following statutory aggravating circumstances which may be supported by the evidence:
      (1) The offense of murder, rape, armed robbery, or kidnapping was committed by a person with a prior record of conviction for a capital felony, or the offense of murder was committed

by a person who has a substantial history of serious assaultive criminal convictions.

(2) The offense of murder, rape, armed robbery, or kidnapping was committed while the offender was engaged in the commission of another capital felony, or aggravated battery, or the offense of murder was committed while the offender was engaged in the commission of burglary or arson in the first degree.

(3) The offender by his act of murder, armed robbery, or kidnapping knowingly created a great risk of death to more than one person in a public place by means of a weapon or device which would normally be hazardous to the lives of more than one person.

(4) The offender committed the offense of murder for himself or another, for the purpose of receiving money or any other thing of monetary value.

(5) The murder of a judicial officer, former judicial officer, district attorney or solicitor or former district attorney or solicitor during or because of the exercise of his official duty.

(6) The offender caused or directed another to commit murder or committed murder as an agent or employee of another person.

(7) The offense of murder, rape, armed robbery, or kidnapping was outrageously or wantonly vile, horrible or inhuman in that it involved torture, depravity of mind, or an aggravated battery to the victim.

(8) The offense of murder was committed against any peace officer, corrections employee or fireman while engaged in the performance of his official duties.

(9) The offense of murder was committed by a person in, or who has escaped from, the lawful custody of a peace officer or place of lawful confinement.

(10) The murder was committed for the purpose of avoiding, interfering with, or preventing a lawful arrest or custody in a place of lawful confinement, of himself or another.

(c) The statutory instructions as determined by the trial judge to be warranted by the evidence shall be given in charge and in writing to the jury for its deliberation. The jury, if its verdict be a recommendation of death, shall designate in writing, signed by the foreman of the jury, the aggravating circumstance or circumstances which it found beyond a reasonable doubt. In non-jury cases the judge shall make such designation. Except in cases of treason or aircraft hijacking, unless at least one of the statutory aggravating circumstances enumerated is so found, the death penalty shall not be imposed.

The Supreme Court of Georgia recently held unconstitutional the portion of the first circumstance encompassing persons who have a "substantial history of serious assaultive criminal convictions" because it did not set "sufficiently 'clear and objective standards.'"

2. Lord Justice Denning, Master of the Rolls of the Court of Appeal in England, spoke to this effect before the British Royal Commission on Capital Punishment:

Punishment is the way in which society expresses its denunciation of wrong-doing: and, in order to maintain respect for law, it is essential that the punishment inflicted for grave crimes should adequately reflect the revulsion felt by the great majority of citizens for them. It is a mistake to consider the objects of punishment as being deterrent or reformative or preventive and nothing else. . . . The truth is that some crimes are so outrageous that society insists on adequate punishment, because the wrong-doer deserves it, irrespective of whether it is a deterrent or not.

A contemporary writer has noted more recently that opposition to capital punishment "has much more appeal when the discussion is merely academic than when the community is confronted with a crime, or a series of crimes, so gross, so heinous, so cold-blooded that anything short of death seems an inadequate response." Raspberry, Death Sentence, *Washington Post*, Mar. 12, 1976, p. A27, cols. 5–6.

3. Other types of calculated murders, apparently occurring with increasing frequency, include the use of bombs or other means of indiscriminate killings, the extortion murder of hostages or kidnap victims, and the execution-style killing of witnesses to a crime.

4. We do not address here the question whether the taking of the criminal's life is a proportionate sanction where no victim has been deprived of life — for example, when capital punishment is imposed for rape, kidnapping, or armed robbery that does not result in the death of any human being.

Topics for Critical Thinking and Writing

1. What features of Georgia's new death penalty statute does Justice Stewart point to in arguing that the new statute will prevent the problems found in the old statute?

2. Since the new Georgia statute upheld by the Supreme Court in its *Gregg* decision does nothing to affect the discretion the prosecutor has in deciding whether to seek the death penalty in a murder case, and nothing to affect the complete discretion the governor has in deciding whether to extend clemency, can it be argued that despite the new death-penalty statutes like Georgia's, the problems that gave rise to the decision in *Furman* will probably reappear?

3. How important do you think public opinion is in determining what the Bill of Rights means? Does it matter to the meaning of "cruel and unusual punishment" that most Americans profess to favor the death penalty? (Think of parallel cases: Does it matter to the meaning of "due process of law," "the right to bear arms," "an impartial jury" — all protected in the Bill of Rights — what a majority of the public thinks?)

4. In 1976, when the Supreme Court decided *Gregg*, it also decided *Woodson v. North Carolina*; in that case the Court held unconstitutional under the Eighth and Fourteenth Amendments a *mandatory* death penalty for anyone convicted of first-degree murder. Do you think North Carolina's statute was a reasonable response to objections to the death penalty at the time of *Furman* based on the alleged arbitrary and discriminatory administration of that penalty? Why, or why not?

5. Stewart mentions the kinds of murder where he thinks the death penalty might be a better deterrent than life imprisonment. What are they? What reasons might be given for or against agreeing with him?

6. A year after *Gregg* was decided, the Supreme Court ruled in *Coker v. Georgia* that the death penalty for rape was unconstitutional under the Eighth and Fourteenth Amendments. Do you think that Stewart's opinion in *Gregg* silently implies that *only* murder is punishable by death? (What about a death penalty for treason? Espionage? Kidnapping for ransom? Large-scale illegal drug trafficking?) In an essay of 500 words, argue either for or against that conclusion.

Harry Blackmun

Harry Blackmun (1908–1999) was born in Nashville, Illinois, and educated at Harvard, where he received his undergraduate and law degrees. He was appointed to the United States Supreme Court in 1970 as a conservative, but when he retired in 1994, he was regarded as a liberal. Blackmun became a national figure in 1973 when he wrote the majority opinion in Roe v. Wade, *a case that (although it placed limits on abortion) asserted that the right to privacy includes "a woman's decision whether or not to terminate her pregnancy." We reprint his dissent from the Supreme Court's order denying review in a Texas death-penalty case,* Callins v. Collins, *510 U.S. 1141 (1994). In his first sentence, Blackmun says that Callins "will be executed by the State of Texas," and though in 1994 Callins received a stay of execution, he, in fact, was executed in 1997.*

Dissenting Opinion in Callins v. Collins

Bruce Edwin Callins will be executed by the State of Texas. . . . Intravenous tubes attached to his arms will carry the instrument of death, a toxic fluid designed specifically for the purpose of killing human beings. The witnesses, standing a few feet away, will behold Callins, no longer a defendant, an appellant, or a petitioner, but a man, strapped to a gurney, and seconds away from extinction.

Within days, or perhaps hours, the memory of Callins will begin to fade. The wheels of justice will churn again, and somewhere, another jury or another judge will have the unenviable task of determining whether some human being is to live or die.

We hope, of course, that the defendant whose life is at risk will be represented by competent counsel, someone who is inspired by the awareness that a less-than-vigorous defense truly could have fatal consequences for the defendant. We hope that the attorney will investigate all aspects of the case, follow all evidentiary and procedural rules, and appear before a judge who is still committed to the protection of defendants' rights even now, as the prospect of meaningful judicial oversight has diminished. In the same vein, we hope that the prosecution, in urging the penalty of death, will have exercised its discretion wisely, free from bias, prejudice, or political motive and will be humbled, rather than emboldened, by the awesome authority conferred by the State.

But even if we can feel confident that these actors will fulfill their roles to the best of their human ability, our collective conscience will remain uneasy. Twenty years have passed since this Court declared that the death penalty must be imposed fairly, and with reasonable consistency or not at all (see *Furman v. Georgia,* 1972), and, despite the effort of the states and courts to devise legal formulas and procedural rules to meet this daunting challenge, the death penalty remains fraught with arbitrariness, discrimination, caprice, and mistake.

This is not to say that the problems with the death penalty today are   5 identical to those that were present twenty years ago. Rather, the problems that were pursued down one hole with procedural rules and verbal formulas have come to the surface somewhere else, just as virulent and pernicious as they were in their original form. Experience has taught us that the constitutional goal of eliminating arbitrariness and discrimination from the administration of death . . . can never be achieved without compromising an equally essential component of fundamental fairness: individualized sentencing. (See *Lockett v. Ohio,* 1978.)

It is tempting, when faced with conflicting constitutional commands, to sacrifice one for the other or to assume that an acceptable balance between them already has been struck. In the context of the death penalty, however, such jurisprudential maneuvers are wholly inappropriate. The death penalty must be imposed "fairly, and with reasonable consistency, or not at all." (*Eddings v. Oklahoma,* 1982).

To be fair, a capital sentencing scheme must treat each person convicted of a capital offense with that "degree of respect due the uniqueness of the individual. . . ." That means affording the sentencer the power and discretion to grant mercy in a particular case, and providing avenues for the consideration of any and all relevant mitigating evidence that would justify a sentence less than death.

Reasonable consistency, on the other hand, requires that the death penalty be inflicted evenhandedly, in accordance with reason and objective standards, rather than by whim, caprice, or prejudice.

Finally, because human error is inevitable and because our criminal justice system is less than perfect, searching appellate review of death sentences and their underlying convictions is a prerequisite to a constitutional death penalty scheme.

On their face, these goals of individual fairness, reasonable consis- 10 tency, and absence of error appear to be attainable: Courts are in the very business of erecting procedural devices from which fair, equitable, and reliable outcomes are presumed to flow. Yet, in the death penalty area, this Court, in my view, has engaged in a futile effort to balance these constitutional demands and now is retreating not only from the *Furman* promise of consistency and rationality but from the requirement of individualized sentencing as well.

Having virtually conceded that both fairness and rationality cannot be achieved in the administration of the death penalty (*McClesky v. Kemp*, 1987), the Court has chosen to deregulate the entire enterprise, replacing, it would seem, substantive constitutional requirements with mere aesthetics and abdicating its statutorily and constitutionally imposed duty to provide meaningful judicial oversight to the administration of death by the states.

From this day forward, I no longer shall tinker with the machinery of death. For more than twenty years I have endeavored—indeed, I have struggled, along with a majority of this Court—to develop procedural and substantive rules that would lend more than the mere appearance of fairness to the death penalty endeavor. . . . Rather than continue to coddle the Court's delusion that the desired level of fairness has been achieved and the need for regulation eviscerated, I feel morally and intellectually obligated simply to concede that the death penalty experiment has failed. It is virtually self-evident to me now that no combination of procedural rules or substantive regulations ever can save the death penalty from its inherent constitutional deficiencies. The basic question—does the system accurately and consistently determine which defendants "deserve" to die?—cannot be answered in the affirmative. . . . The problem is that the inevitability of factual, legal, and moral error gives us a system that we know must wrongly kill some defendants, a system that fails to deliver the fair, consistent and reliable sentences of death required by the Constitution. . . .

There is little doubt now that *Furman*'s essential holding was correct. Although most of the public seems to desire, and the Constitution appears to permit, the penalty of death, it surely is beyond dispute that if the death penalty cannot be administered consistently and rationally, it may not be administered at all. . . .

Delivering on the *Furman* promise, however, has proved to be another matter. *Furman* aspired to eliminate the vestiges of racism and the effects of poverty in capital sentencing; it deplored the "wanton" and "random" infliction of death by a government with constitutionally limited power. *Furman* demanded that the sentencer's discretion be directed and limited by procedural rules and objective standards in order to minimize the risk of arbitrary and capricious sentences of death.

In the years following *Furman*, serious efforts were made to comply 15 with its mandate. State legislatures and appellate courts struggled to provide judges and juries with sensible and objective guidelines for determining who should live and who should die. Some states attempted to define who is "deserving" of the death penalty through the use of carefully chosen adjectives, reserving the death penalty for those who commit crimes that are "especially heinous, atrocious, or cruel," or "wantonly vile, horrible, or inhuman." Other states enacted mandatory death penalty statutes, reading *Furman* as an invitation to eliminate sentencer discretion altogether. . . .

Unfortunately, all this experimentation and ingenuity yielded little of what *Furman* demanded. It soon became apparent that discretion could not be eliminated from capital sentencing without threatening the fundamental fairness due a defendant when life is at stake. Just as contemporary society was no longer tolerant of the random or discriminatory infliction of the penalty of death . . . evolving standards of decency required due consideration of the uniqueness of each individual defendant when imposing society's ultimate penalty.

This development in the American conscience would have presented no constitutional dilemma if fairness to the individual could be achieved without sacrificing the consistency and rationality promised in *Furman*. But over the past two decades, efforts to balance these competing constitutional commands have been to no avail. Experience has shown that the consistency and rationality promised in *Furman* are inversely related to the fairness owed the individual when considering a sentence of death. A step toward consistency is a step away from fairness. . . .

While one might hope that providing the sentencer with as much relevant mitigating evidence as possible will lead to more rational and consistent sentences, experience has taught otherwise. It seems that the decision whether a human being should live or die is so inherently subjective, rife with all of life's understandings, experiences, prejudices, and passions, that it inevitably defies the rationality and consistency required by the Constitution. . . .

The consistency promised in *Furman* and the fairness to the individual demanded in *Lockett* are not only inversely related but irreconcilable in the context of capital punishment. Any statute or procedure that could effectively eliminate arbitrariness from the administration of death would also restrict the sentencer's discretion to such an extent that the sentencer would be unable to give full consideration to the unique characteristics of each defendant and the circumstances of the offense.

By the same token, any statute of procedure that would provide the sentencer with sufficient discretion to consider fully and act upon the unique circumstances of each defendant would "thro(w) open the back door to arbitrary and irrational sentencing." . . .   20

In my view, the proper course when faced with irreconcilable constitutional commands is not to ignore one or the other, nor to pretend that the dilemma does not exist, but to admit the futility of the effort to harmonize them. This means accepting the fact that the death penalty cannot be administered in accord with our Constitution. . . .

Perhaps one day this Court will develop procedural rules or verbal formulas that actually will provide consistency, fairness, and reliability in a capital-sentencing scheme. I am not optimistic that such a day will come. I am more optimistic, though, that this Court eventually will conclude that the effort to eliminate arbitrariness while preserving fairness "in the infliction of (death) is so plainly doomed to failure that it and the death penalty must be abandoned altogether." (*Godfrey v. Georgia*, 1980. . . .) I may not live to see that day, but I have faith that eventually it will arrive. The path the Court has chosen lessens us all.

Topics for Critical Thinking and Writing

1. Who is the "we" to whom Blackmun refers when he says "We hope . . ." (para. 3)? We on the U.S. Supreme Court? We who are inclined to support the death penalty? We the people of Texas? We Americans? Or is this merely the so-called editorial "we" and of no substantive significance at all?

2. What does Blackmun mean by contrasting "procedural and substantive rules" of law (para. 12)?

3. Assuming for the sake of the argument that Blackmun's criticisms of what he elsewhere called "the machinery of death" are correct, what do you think accounts for the failure of the criminal justice system in death-penalty states over the past generation (since *Furman v. Georgia* was decided in 1972) to operate "fairly, and with reasonable consistency" (para. 6) in accordance with "reason and objective standards" (para. 8)?

4. What does Blackmun mean when he says that "consistency and rationality" in death-penalty cases are "inversely related to the fairness owed the individual" offender (paras. 17 and 19)?

5. Blackmun claims that the appellate courts (of Texas? of all death-penalty states? of the federal government?) have failed to give "meaningful judicial oversight to the administration of death by the states" (para. 11). After reading Blackmun's opinion, explain in an essay of 500 words what you think such "meaningful oversight" ought to involve.

Helen Prejean

Sister Helen Prejean, born in Baton Rouge, has been a member of the Order of the Sisters of St. Joseph of Medaille since 1957. In 1993, she achieved international fame with her book Dead Man Walking: An Eyewitness Account of the Death Penalty in the United States, *based on her experiences counseling prisoners on death row in Louisiana prisons. An excerpt is printed here. A film with the same title, starring Susan Sarandon (as Sister Helen) and Sean Penn, was released in 1995. When confronted with the argument that the death penalty is appropriate revenge for society to take on a murderer, Sister Helen said, "I would not want my death avenged — especially by government,* which can't be trusted to control its own bureaucrats or collect taxes equitably or fill a pothole, much less decide which of its citizens to kill." *The title is the editors'.*

Executions Are Too Costly — Morally

I think of the running debate I engage in with "church" people about the death penalty. "Proof texts" from the Bible usually punctuate these discussions without regard for the cultural context or literary genre of the passages invoked. (Will D. Campbell, a Southern Baptist minister and writer, calls this use of scriptural quotations "biblical quarterbacking.")

It is abundantly clear that the Bible depicts murder as a crime for which death is considered the appropriate punishment, and one is hard-pressed to find a biblical "proof text" in either the Hebrew Testament or the New Testament which unequivocally refutes this. Even Jesus' admonition "Let him without sin cast the first stone," when he was asked the appropriate punishment for an adulteress (John 8:7) — the Mosaic law prescribed death — should be read in its proper context. This passage is an "entrapment" story, which sought to show Jesus' wisdom in besting his adversaries. It is not an ethical pronouncement about capital punishment.

Similarly, the "eye for eye" passage from Exodus, which pro-death penalty advocates are fond of quoting, is rarely cited in its original context, in which it is clearly meant to limit revenge.

The passage, including verse 22, which sets the context reads:

> If, when men come to blows, they hurt a woman who is pregnant and she suffers a miscarriage, though she does not die of it, the man responsible must pay the compensation demanded of him by the woman's master; he shall hand it over after arbitration. But should she die, you shall give life for life, eye for eye, tooth for tooth, hand for hand, foot for foot, burn for burn, wound for wound, stroke for stroke. (Exodus 21:22–25)

In the example given (patently patriarchal: the woman is considered   5
the negotiable property of her male master), it is clear that punishment is to be measured out according to the seriousness of the offense. If the child is lost but not the mother, the punishment is less grave than if both mother and child are lost. *Only* an eye for an eye, *only* a life for a life is the intent of the passage. Restraint was badly needed. It was not uncommon for an offended family or clan to slaughter entire communities in retaliation for an offense against one of their members.

Even granting the call for restraint in this passage, it is nonetheless clear — here and in numerous other instances throughout the Hebrew Bible — that the punishment for murder was death.

But we must remember that such prescriptions of the Mosaic Law were promulgated in a seminomadic culture in which the preservation of a fragile society — without benefit of prisons and other institutions — demanded quick, effective, harsh punishment of offenders. And we should note the numerous other crimes for which the Bible prescribes death as punishment:

contempt of parents (Exodus 21:15, 17; Leviticus 24:17);

trespass upon sacred ground (Exodus 19:12–13; Numbers 1:51; 18:7);

sorcery (Exodus 22:18; Leviticus 20:27);

bestiality (Exodus 22:19; Leviticus 20:15–16);

sacrifice to foreign gods (Exodus 22:20; Deuteronomy 13:1–9);

profaning the sabbath (Exodus 31:14);

adultery (Leviticus 20:10; Deuteronomy 22:22–24);

incest (Leviticus 20:11–13);

homosexuality (Leviticus 20:13);

and prostitution (Leviticus 21:19; Deuteronomy 22:13–21).

And this is by no means a complete list.

But no person with common sense would dream of appropriating such a moral code today, and it is curious that those who so readily invoke the "eye for an eye, life for life" passage are quick to shun other biblical prescriptions which also call for death, arguing that modern societies have evolved over the three thousand or so years since biblical times and no longer consider such exaggerated and archaic punishments appropriate.

Such nuances are lost, of course, in "biblical quarterbacking," and   10
more and more I find myself steering away from such futile discussions. Instead, I try to articulate what I personally believe about Jesus and the ethical thrust he gave to humankind: an impetus toward compassion, a preference for disarming enemies without humiliating and destroying them, and a solidarity with poor and suffering people.

So, what happened to the impetus of love and compassion Jesus set blazing into history?

The first Christians adhered closely to the way of life Jesus had taught. They died in amphitheaters rather than offer homage to worldly emperors. They refused to fight in emperors' wars. But then a tragic diversion happened, which Elaine Pagels has deftly explored in her book *Adam, Eve, and the Serpent:* in 313 C.E. (Common Era) the Emperor Constantine entered the Christian church.

Pagels says, "Christian bishops, once targets for arrest, torture, and execution, now received tax exemptions, gifts from the imperial treasury, prestige, and even influence at court; the churches gained new wealth, power and prominence."

Unfortunately, the exercise of power practiced by Christians in alliance with the Roman Empire—with its unabashed allegiance to the sword—soon bore no resemblance to the purely moral persuasion that Jesus had taught.

In the fifth century, Pagels points out, Augustine provided the theo-   15
logical rationale the church needed to justify the use of violence by

church and state governments. Augustine persuaded church authorities that "original sin" so damaged every person's ability to make moral choices that external control by church and state authorities over people's lives was necessary and justified. The "wicked" might be "coerced by the sword" to "protect the innocent," Augustine taught. And thus was legitimated for Christians the authority of secular government to "control" its subjects by coercive and violent means—even punishment by death.

In the latter part of the twentieth century, however, two flares of hope—Mohandas K. Gandhi and Martin Luther King—have demonstrated that Jesus' counsel to practice compassion and tolerance even toward one's enemies can effect social change. Susan Jacoby, analyzing the moral power that Gandhi and King unleashed in their campaigns for social justice, finds a unique form of aggression:

"'If everyone took an eye for an eye,' Gandhi said, 'the whole world would be blind.' But Gandhi did not want to take anyone's eye; he wanted to force the British out of India. . . .'"

> Nonviolence and nonaggression are generally regarded as interchangeable concepts—King and Gandhi frequently used them that way—but nonviolence, as employed by Gandhi in India and by King in the American South, might reasonably be viewed as a highly disciplined form of aggression. If one defines aggression in the primary dictionary sense of "attack," nonviolent resistance proved to be the most powerful attack imaginable on the powers King and Gandhi were trying to overturn. The writings of both men are filled with references to love as a powerful force against oppression, and while the two leaders were not using the term "force" in the military sense, they certainly regarded nonviolence as a tactical weapon as well as an expression of high moral principle. The root meaning of Gandhi's concept of *satyagraha* . . . is "holding on to truth" . . . Gandhi also called *satyagraha* the "love force" or "soul force" and explained that he had discovered "in the earliest stages that pursuit of truth did not permit violence being inflicted on one's opponent, but that he must be weaned from error by patience and sympathy. . . . And patience means self-suffering." So the doctrine came to mean vindication of truth, not by the infliction of suffering on the opponent, but on one's self.
>
> King was even more explicit on this point: the purpose of civil disobedience, he explained many times, was to force the defenders of segregation to commit brutal acts in public and thus arouse the conscience of the world on behalf of those wronged by racism. King and Gandhi did not succeed because they changed the hearts and minds of southern sheriffs and British colonial administrators (although they did, in fact, change some minds) but because they *made the price of maintaining control too high for their opponents* [emphasis mine].

That, I believe, is what it's going to take to abolish the death penalty in this country: we must persuade the American people that government killings are too costly for us, not only financially, but—more important—morally.

The death penalty *costs* too much. Allowing our government to kill citizens compromises the deepest moral values upon which this country was conceived: the inviolable dignity of human persons.

I have no doubt that we will one day abolish the death penalty in   20
America. It will come sooner if people like me who know the truth about executions do our work well and educate the public. It will come slowly if we do not. Because, finally, I know that it is not a question of malice or ill will or meanness of spirit that prompts our citizens to support executions. It is, quite simply, that people don't know the truth of what is going on. That is not by accident. The secrecy surrounding executions makes it possible for executions to continue. I am convinced that if executions were made public, the torture and violence would be unmasked, and we would be shamed into abolishing executions. We would be embarrassed at the brutalization of the crowds that would gather to watch a man or woman be killed. And we would be humiliated to know that visitors from other countries—Japan, Russia, Latin America, Europe—were watching us kill our own citizens—we, who take pride in being the flagship of democracy in the world.

Topics for Critical Thinking and Writing

1. Suppose you interpret the "eye for eye" passage from Exodus (paras. 3–6) not as a "call for restraint" but as support for the death penalty. Does that mean no exceptions whatsoever—that everyone who kills another must be sentenced to death and executed? Would that require abandoning the distinction between murder and manslaughter or between first- and second-degree murder?

2. Prejean lists ten different crimes for which the Bible prescribes death as the punishment (para. 7) and says "no person with common sense would dream of appropriating [them] today" (para. 9). Do you agree? In an essay of 500 words, defend or criticize the proposition that the death penalty ought to be confined to the crime of first-degree murder.

3. Do you think that someone who endorses the biblical doctrine of "life for life, eye for eye" (para. 4) is also required by consistency to endorse the death penalty for some or all of the ten nonhomicidal crimes Prejean mentions (para. 7)? Explain.

4. In deciding whether to impose the death penalty for serious crimes, what guidance do you think a secular society, such as ours, ought to accept from the Bible? In an essay of 500 words, defend or criticize this thesis: "Biblical teachings ought to play a central role in deciding how we use the death penalty."

5. Prejean does not propose any alternative to the death penalty. Presumably she would favor some form of imprisonment for crimes involving

death. She claims that the death penalty is inconsistent with "the invio-lable dignity of human persons" (para. 19). Does consistency require her also to reject flogging? Solitary confinement in prison? Life imprison-ment without the possibility of parole? Write a 500-word essay on this theme: "Severe Punishment and the Inviolable Dignity of Human Persons."

6. Prejean thinks that if executions were made public, Americans would soon decide to oppose the death penalty (para. 20). Do you agree? Write a 500-word essay for or against the following proposition: "Executions held in public would soon lead to public rejection of the death penalty."

Alex Kozinski and Sean Gallagher

Alex Kozinski is a judge on the Ninth U.S. Circuit Court of Appeals. Sean Gallagher was his law clerk when the two of them wrote this essay, pub-lished in the New York Times *on March 8, 1995.*

For an Honest Death Penalty

It is a staple of American politics that there is very strong support for the death penalty; in opinion polls, roughly 70 percent consistently favor it. Yet the popular will on this issue has been thwarted.

To be sure, we have many capital trials, convictions, and death sen-tences; we have endless and massively costly appeals; and a few people do get put to death every year. But compared to the number of death sentences, the number of executions is minuscule, and the gap is widen-ing fast.

In 1972, the Supreme Court struck down all existing death penalty statutes and emptied the nation's death rows. Almost immediately states began passing death penalty laws to comply with the Court's reinterpreta-tion of the Eighth Amendment. Since then more than 5,000 men and a handful of women have been given the death sentence; about 2,000 of those sentences have been set aside; fewer than 300 have been carried out.

THE WILL OF THE MAJORITY THWARTED

The reasons are complex, but they boil down to this: The Supreme Court's death penalty case law reflects an uneasy accommodation be-tween the will of the popular majority, who favor capital punishment, and the objections of a much smaller—but ferociously committed—mi-nority, who view it as a barbaric anachronism.

Assuaging death penalty opponents, the Court has devised a number   5 of extraordinary safeguards applicable to capital cases; but responding to complaints that these procedures were used for obstruction and delay, it has also imposed various limitations and exceptions to these safeguards. This pull and tug has resulted in a procedural structure—what Justice Harry A. Blackmun called a "machinery of death"—that is remarkably time-consuming, painfully cumbersome, and extremely expensive.

No one knows precisely how large a slice of our productive resources we force-feed to this behemoth, but we can make some educated guesses. To begin with, while 80 to 90 percent of all criminal cases end in plea bargains, capital cases almost always go to trial, and the trials are vastly more complex than their noncapital counterparts. If the defendant is sentenced to death, the case shuttles between the state and Federal courts for years, sometimes decades.

The Robert Alton Harris case, for example, found its way to the California Supreme Court six times; it was reviewed in Federal district court on five occasions, and each time it was appealed to the Ninth Circuit. The U.S. Supreme Court reviewed the case once on the merits, though on five other occasions it considered and declined Mr. Harris's request for review. Before Mr. Harris was executed in 1992, his case was reviewed by at least thirty judges and justices on more than twenty occasions over thirteen years.

State and local governments pay for the prosecution as well as for the defense team—which consists of at least two lawyers and a battery of investigators and experts; much of this money is spent even if the defendant eventually gets a lesser sentence. California reportedly spends $90 million a year on the death penalty. Once the case gets into Federal court, the United States starts picking up the defense tab and the sums can be daunting. In one recent case, a Federal district court paid defense lawyers more than $400,000, which didn't include the appeal or petition to the Supreme Court. Our own estimate is that death cases, on the average, cost taxpayers about a million dollars more than their noncapital counterparts. With 3,000 or so inmates on death row, to paraphrase Senator Everett Dirksen, pretty soon you get into real money.

Another significant cost is the burden on the courts. More than a quarter of the opinions published by the California Supreme Court from 1987 to 1993 involved death penalty cases. Since capital appeals are mandatory while appeals in other cases are discretionary, much of this burden is borne by other litigants who must vie for a diminished share of that court's attention. Estimating the judicial resources devoted to a capital case in the Federal courts is difficult, but a fair guess would be ten times those in other cases.

Perhaps the most significant cost of the death penalty is the lack of 10 finality. Death cases raise many more issues, and far more complex issues, than other criminal cases; convictions are attacked with more gusto and reviewed with more vigor in the courts. As a result, fully 40 percent of the death sentences imposed since 1972 have been vacated, sometimes five, ten or fifteen years after trial. One worries about the effect on the families of the victims, who have to endure the possibility—often the reality—of retrials, evidentiary hearings and last-minute stays of execution for years after the crime.

What are we getting in return? Even though we devote vast resources to the task, we come nowhere near executing the number of people we put on death row, and probably never will. We sentence about 250 inmates to death every year but have never executed more than forty. Just to keep up with the number of new death row inmates, states would have to sextuple the pace of executions; to eliminate the backlog, there would have to be one execution a day for the next twenty-six years.

This reality moots much of the traditional debate about the death penalty. Death penalty opponents have certainly not won the popular battle: despite relentless assaults, the public remains firmly committed to capital punishment. Nor have opponents won the moral battle: most of us continue to believe that those who show utter contempt for human life by committing remorseless, premeditated murder justly forfeit the right to their own life.

Other arguments against the death penalty also fall flat. For example, the fear that an innocent person may be convicted also applies to noncapital cases; no one, after all, can give back the twenty years someone wrongfully spends behind bars. Our system is therefore heavily geared to give the criminal defendant the benefit of the doubt. Wrongfully convicted defendants are rare; wrongfully convicted capital defendants are even rarer. The case where the innocent defendant is saved from the electric chair because the one-armed man shows up and confesses happens only in the movies.

Death penalty opponents are winning the war nevertheless. Unable to stop the majority altogether, they have managed to vastly increase the cost of imposing the death penalty while reducing the rate of executions to a trickle. This trend is not likely to be reversed. Even if we were willing to double or triple the resources we devote to the death penalty, even if we could put all other civil and criminal cases handled by the state and Federal courts on the back burner, it would be to no avail.

The great stumbling block is the lawyers: the jurisprudence of death   15
is so complex, so esoteric, so harrowing, this is the one area where there aren't nearly enough lawyers willing and able to handle all the current cases. In California, for example, almost half the pending death penalty appeals—more than 100—are on hold because the state can't find lawyers to handle them.

We are thus left in a peculiar limbo: we have constructed a machine that is extremely expensive, chokes our legal institutions, visits repeated trauma on victims' families, and ultimately produces nothing like the benefits we would expect from an effective system of capital punishment. This is surely the worst of all worlds.

Only two solutions suggest themselves, one judicial and the other political. The judicial solution would require a wholesale repudiation of the Supreme Court's death penalty jurisprudence. This is unlikely to happen. Over the last quarter-century, the Court has developed a substantial body of case law, consisting of some four score opinions, premised on the proposition that death *is* different and we must exercise extraordinary caution before taking human life. As we learned a few years back in the area of abortion, conservative justices are reluctant to reverse such major constitutional judgments.

A political solution may be no easier to achieve, but it's all we have left. The key to any such solution lies with the majority, precisely those among us who consistently strive for imposition of the death penalty for an ever-widening circle of crimes.

The majority must come to understand that this is a self-defeating tactic. Increasing the number of crimes punishable by death, widening the circumstances under which death may be imposed, obtaining more guilty verdicts and expanding death row populations will do nothing to insure that the very worst members of our society are put to death. The majority must accept that we may be willing and able to carry out thirty, forty, maybe fifty executions a year but that we cannot—will not—carry out one a day, every day, for the foreseeable future.

Once that reality is accepted, a difficult but essential next step is to 20 identify where we want to spend our death penalty resources. Instead of adopting a very expansive list of crimes for which the death penalty is an option, state legislatures should draft narrow statutes that reserve the death penalty for only the most heinous criminals. Everyone on death row is very bad, but even within that depraved group, it's possible to make moral judgments about how deeply someone has stepped down the rungs of Hell. Hitler was worse than Eichmann, though both were unspeakably evil by any standard; John Wayne Gacy, with two dozen or so brutal deaths on his conscience, must be considered worse than John Spenkelink, who killed only once.

Differentiating among depraved killers would force us to do some painful soul-searching about the nature of human evil, but it would have three significant advantages. First, it would mean that in a world of limited resources and in the face of a determined opposition, we will sentence to death only those we intend to execute. Second, it would insure that those who suffer the death penalty are the worst of the very bad—mass murderers, hired killers, airplane bombers, for example. This must be better than loading our death rows with many more than we can possibly execute, and then picking those who will die essentially at random.

Third, a political solution would put the process of accommodating divergent viewpoints back into the political arena, where it belongs. This would mean that the people, through their elected representatives, would reassert meaningful control over the process, rather than letting the courts and chance perform the accommodation on an ad hoc, irrational basis.

It will take a heroic act of will for the majority to initiate a political compromise on this emotionally charged issue. But as with democracy itself, the alternatives are much worse.

Topics for Critical Thinking and Writing

1. The authors, writing in 1995, reported that "roughly 70 percent" of the American public "consistently favor" the death penalty (para. 1). Consult the reference librarian in your college library, and verify whether this is true according to the most recent public-opinion polls (Gallup, Harris, or other polling agencies).

2. The authors say that "compared to the number of death sentences, the number of executions is minuscule" (para. 2). Verify this claim by consulting the most recent issue of *Capital Punishment* (issued by the U.S. Department of Justice, Bureau of Justice Statistics). Exactly how many death sentences and executions occurred last year?

3. The authors cite the case of Robert Alton Harris and the multiple reviews his conviction and sentence received in the state and federal courts (para. 7). Is the reader supposed to infer from this case that (a) the courts are being manipulated by a convicted murderer who doesn't want to die, (b) the courts give extraordinary attention to capital cases to avoid making an irreversible mistake, or (c) neither of the above?

4. The authors say, "One worries about the effect [of these delays] on the families of the victims" (para. 10). This concern for the victims' families assumes that the defendants are guilty and were proved guilty by fair trials. Is it equally appropriate to worry about the effect on the families of defendants who were not guilty or were not proved guilty by a fair trial?

5. The authors identify three costs associated with the death penalty in this country (paras. 8–10). How would you rank their relative importance? Explain your view in an essay of 250 words.

6. The authors refer to "the benefits we would expect from an effective system of capital punishment" (para. 16), but they never tell us what those benefits are. Write a 500-word essay on this topic: "The (Alleged) Benefits of an Ideal Death-Penalty System."

7. Why do the authors insist that increasing the number of crimes punishable by death or increasing the number of persons sentenced to death "will do nothing to insure that the very worst members of our society are put to death" (para. 19)?

8. What is the "political solution" (para. 22) to the death penalty in our society that the authors favor? Do you agree or disagree with them? Why? Explain your position in an essay of 350 words.

> For topical links related to the death penalty debate, see the companion Web site:
> **www.bedfordstmartins.com/barnetbedau.**

21

Drugs: Should Their Sale and Use Be Legalized?

"Your condition is serious, Mr. Reynolds, but fortunately I recently scored some excellent weed that should alleviate your symptoms."

William J. Bennett

William J. Bennett, born in Brooklyn in 1943, was educated at Williams College, the University of Texas, and Harvard Law School. Today he is most widely known as the author of The Book of Virtues: A Treasury of Great Moral Stories *(1993), but he has also been a public servant, Secretary of Education, and a director of the National Drug Control Policy. In 1989, during his tenure as "drug czar," he delivered at Harvard the address that we reprint.*

Drug Policy and the Intellectuals

. . . The issue I want to address is our national drug policy and the intellectuals. Unfortunately, the issue is a little one-sided. There is a very great deal to say about our national drug policy, but much less to say about the intellectuals—except that by and large, they're against it. Why they should be against it is an interesting question, perhaps more a social-psychological question than a properly intellectual one. But whatever the reasons, I'm sorry to say that on properly intellectual grounds the arguments mustered against our current drug policy by America's intellectuals make for very thin gruel indeed.

I should point out, however, that in the fields of medical and scientific research, there is indeed serious and valuable drug-related work going on. But in the great public policy debate over drugs, the academic and intellectual communities have by and large had little to contribute, and little of that has been genuinely useful or for that matter mentally distinguished.

The field of national drug policy is wide open for serious research and serious thinking on both the theoretical and the practical levels; treatment and prevention; education; law enforcement and the criminal-justice system; the proper role of the federal government versus state and local jurisdictions; international diplomacy and foreign intelligence—these are only a few of the areas in which complex questions of policy and politics need to be addressed and resolved if our national drug strategy is to be successful. But apart from a handful of exceptions—including Mark Moore and Mark Kleiman here at the Kennedy School, and Harvard's own, or ex-own, James Q. Wilson—on most of these issues the country's major ideas factories have not just shut down, they've hardly even tooled up.

It's not that most intellectuals are indifferent to the drug issue, though there may be some of that, too. Rather, they seem complacent and incurious. They've made up their minds, and they don't want to be bothered with further information or analysis, further discussion or debate, especially when it comes from Washington. What I read in the opinion columns of my newspaper or in my monthly magazine or what I hear from the resident intellectual on my favorite television talk show is something like a developing intellectual consensus on the drug question. That consensus holds one or both of these propositions to be self-evident: (a) *that the drug problem in America is absurdly simple, and easily solved;* and (b) *that the drug problem in America is a lost cause.*

As it happens, each of these apparently contradictory propositions is   5 false. As it also happens, both are disputed by the *real* experts on drugs in the United States—and there are many such experts, though not the kind the media like to focus on. And both are disbelieved by the American people, whose experience tells them, emphatically, otherwise.

The consensus has a political dimension, which helps account for its seemingly divergent aspect. In some quarters of the far Right there is a tendency to assert that the drug problem is essentially a problem of the inner city, and therefore that what it calls for, essentially, is quarantine. "If those people want to kill themselves off with drugs, let them kill themselves off with drugs," would be a crude but not too inaccurate way of summarizing this position. But this position has relatively few adherents. On the Left, it is something else, something much more prevalent. There we see whole cadres of social scientists, abetted by whole armies of social workers, who seem to take it as catechism that the problem facing us isn't drugs at all, it's poverty, or racism, or some other equally large and intractable social phenomenon. If we want to eliminate the drug problem, these people say, we must first eliminate the "root causes" of drugs, a hopelessly daunting task at which, however, they also happen to make their living. Twenty-five years ago, no one would have suggested that we must first address the root causes of racism before fighting segregation. We fought it, quite correctly, by passing laws against unacceptable conduct. The causes of racism was an interesting question, but the moral imperative was to end it as soon as possible and by all reasonable means: education, prevention, the media and not least of all, the law. So too with drugs.

What unites these two views of the drug problem from opposite sides of the political spectrum is that they issue, inevitably, in a policy of neglect. To me that is a scandalous position, intellectually as well as morally scandalous. For I believe, along with those I have named as the real experts on drugs, and along with most Americans, that the drug problem is not easy but difficult — very difficult in some respects. But at the same time, and again along with those same experts and with the American people, I believe it is not a lost cause but a solvable one. I will return to this theme, but let me pause here to note one specific issue on which the Left/Right consensus has lately come to rest; a position around which it has been attempting to build national sentiment. That position is legalization.

It is indeed bizarre to see the likes of Anthony Lewis and William F. Buckley lining up on the same side of an issue; but such is the perversity that the so-called legalization debate engenders. To call it a "debate," though, suggests that the arguments in *favor* of drug legalization are rigorous, substantial, and serious. They are not. They are, at bottom, a series of superficial and even disingenuous ideas that more sober minds recognize as a recipe for a public policy disaster. Let me explain.

Most conversations about legalization begin with the notion of "taking the profit out of the drug business." But has anyone bothered to examine carefully how the drug business works? As a recent *New York Times* article vividly described, instances of drug dealers actually earning huge sums of money are relatively rare. There are some who do, of course, but most people in the crack business are the low-level "runners" who do not make much money at all. Many of them work as prostitutes or small-time criminals to supplement their drug earnings. True, a lot of naive kids are lured into the drug world by visions of a life filled with big money and fast cars. That's what they think the good life holds for them. But the reality is far different. Many dealers, in the long run, wind up smoking more crack than they sell. Their business becomes a form of slavery: long hours, dangerous work, small pay, and, as the *Times* pointed out, no health benefits either. In many cases, steady work at McDonald's over time would in fact be a step *up* the income scale for these kids. What does straighten them out, it seems, is not a higher minimum wage, or less stringent laws, but the dawning realization that dealing drugs invariably leads to murder or to prison. And that's exactly why we have drug laws—to make drug use a wholly unattractive choice.

Legalization, on the other hand, removes that incentive to stay away 10 from a life of drugs. Let's be honest—there are some people who are going to smoke crack whether it is legal or illegal. But by keeping it illegal, we maintain the criminal sanctions that persuade most people that the good life cannot be reached by dealing drugs.

The big lie behind every call for legalization is that making drugs legally available would "solve" the drug problem. But has anyone actually thought about what that kind of legalized regime would look like? Would crack be legal? How about PCP? Or smokable heroin? Or ice? Would they all be stocked at the local convenience store, perhaps just a few blocks from an elementary school? And how much would they cost? If we taxed drugs and made them expensive, we would still have the black market and crime problems that we have today; if we sold them cheap to eliminate the black market cocaine at, say, $10 a gram—then we would succeed in making a daily dose of cocaine well within the allowance budget of most sixth-graders. When pressed, the advocates of legalization like to sound courageous by proposing that we begin by legalizing marijuana. But they have absolutely nothing to say on the tough questions of controlling other, more powerful drugs, and how they would be regulated.

As far as marijuana is concerned, let me say this: I didn't have to become drug czar to be opposed to legalized marijuana. As Secretary of Education I realized that, given the state of American education, the last thing we needed was a policy that made widely available a substance that impairs memory, concentration, and attention span; why in God's name foster the use of a drug that makes you stupid?

Now what would happen if drugs were suddenly made legal? Legalization advocates deny that the amount of drug use would be affected. I would argue that if drugs are easier to obtain, drug use will soar. In fact, we have just undergone a kind of cruel national experiment in which drugs became cheap and widely available: That experiment is called the crack epidemic. When powder cocaine was expensive and hard to get, it was found almost exclusively in the circles of the rich, the famous, or the privileged. Only when cocaine was dumped into the country, and a $3 vial of crack could be bought on street corners did we see cocaine use skyrocket, this time largely among the poor and disadvantaged. The lesson is clear: If you're in favor of drugs being sold in stores like aspirin, you're in favor of boom times for drug users and drug addicts. With legalization, drug use will go up, way up.

When drug use rises, who benefits and who pays? Legalization advocates think that the cost of enforcing drug laws is too great. But the real question—the question they never ask—is what does it cost not to enforce those laws. The price that American society would have to pay for legalized drugs, I submit, would be intolerably high. We would have more drug-related accidents at work, on the highways, and in the airways. We would have even bigger losses in worker productivity. Our hospitals would be filled with drug emergencies. We would have more school kids on dope, and that means more dropouts. More pregnant women would buy legal cocaine, and then deliver tiny, premature infants. I've seen them in hospitals across the country. It's a horrid form of child abuse, and under a legalization scheme, we will have a lot more of it. For those women and those babies, crack has the same effect whether it's legal or not. Now, if you add to that the costs of treatment, social welfare, and insurance, you've got the price of legalization. So I ask you again, who benefits, who pays?

What about crime? To listen to legalization advocates, one might   15 think that street crime would disappear with the repeal of our drug laws. They haven't done their homework. Our best research indicates that most drug criminals were into crime well before they got into drugs. Making drugs legal would just be a way of subsidizing their habit. They would continue to rob and steal to pay for food, for clothes, for entertainment. And they would carry on with their drug trafficking by undercutting the legalized price of drugs and catering to teenagers, who, I assume, would be nominally restricted from buying drugs at the corner store.

All this should be old news to people who understand one clear lesson of prohibition. When we had laws against alcohol, there was less consumption of alcohol, less alcohol-related disease, fewer drunken brawls, and a lot less public drunkenness. And contrary to myth, there is no evidence that Prohibition caused big increases in crime. No one is suggesting that we go back to Prohibition. But at least we should admit that legalized alcohol, which is responsible for some 100,000 deaths a year, is hardly a model for drug policy. As Charles Krauthammer has pointed out, the question is not which is worse, alcohol or drugs. The question is can we accept both legalized alcohol *and* legalized drugs? The answer is no.

So it seems to me that on the merits of their arguments, the legalizers have no case at all. But there is another, crucial point I want to make on this subject, unrelated to costs or benefits. Drug use—especially heavy drug use—destroys human character. It destroys dignity and autonomy, it burns away the sense of responsibility, it subverts productivity, it makes a mockery of virtue. As our Founders would surely recognize, a citizenry that is perpetually in a drug-induced haze doesn't bode well for the future of self-government. Libertarians don't like to hear this, but it is a truth that everyone knows who has seen drug addiction up close. And don't listen to people who say drug users are only hurting themselves: They hurt parents, they destroy families, they ruin friendships. And let me remind this audience, here at a great university, that drugs are a threat to the life of the mind; anyone who values that life should have nothing but contempt for drugs. Learned institutions should regard drugs as the plague.

That's why I find the surrender of many of America's intellectuals to arguments for drug legalization so odd and so scandalous. For the past three months, I have been traveling the country, visiting drug-ridden neighborhoods, seeing treatment and prevention programs in action, talking to teachers, cops, parents, kids. These, it seems, are the real drug experts—they've witnessed the problem firsthand. But unlike some prominent residents of Princeton, Madison, Cambridge, or Palo Alto, they refuse to surrender. They are in the community, reclaiming their neighborhoods, working with police, setting up community activities, getting addicts into treatment, saving their children.

Too many American intellectuals don't know about this and seem not to want to know. Their hostility to the national war on drugs is, I think, partly rooted in a general hostility to law enforcement and criminal justice. That's why they take refuge in pseudosolutions like legalization, which stress only the treatment side of the problem. Whenever discussion turns to the need for more police and stronger penalties, they cry that our constitutional liberties are in jeopardy. Well, yes, they are in jeopardy, but not from drug *policy:* On this score, the guardians of our Constitution can sleep easy. Constitutional liberties are in jeopardy, instead, from drugs themselves, which every day scorch the earth of our common freedom. Yes, sometimes cops go too far, and when they do they should be held accountable. But these excursions from the law are the exception. Meanwhile drug dealers violate our rights everyday as a rule, as a norm, as their modus operandi. Why can't our civil libertarians see that?

When we are not being told by critics that law enforcement threat- 20 ens our liberties, we are being told that it won't work. Let me tell you that law enforcement does work and why it must work. Several weeks ago I was in Wichita, Kansas, talking to a teenage boy who was now in his fourth treatment program. Every time he had finished a previous round of treatment, he found himself back on the streets, surrounded by the same cheap dope and tough hustlers who had gotten him started in the first place. He was tempted, he was pressured, and he gave in. Virtually any expert on drug treatment will tell you that, for most people, no therapy in the world can fight temptation on that scale. As long as drugs are found on any street corner, no amount of treatment, no amount of education can finally stand against them. Yes, we need drug treatment and drug education. But drug treatment and drug education need law enforcement. And that's why our strategy calls for a bigger criminal justice system: as a form of drug *prevention*.

To the Americans who are waging the drug war in their own front yards every day, this is nothing new, nothing startling. In the San Jose section of Albuquerque, New Mexico, just two weeks ago, I spoke to Rudy Chavez and Jack Candelarla, and police chief Sam Baca. They had wanted to start a youth center that would keep their kids safe from the depredations of the street. Somehow it never worked—until together they set up a police station right in the heart of drug-dealing territory. Then it worked. Together with the cops, the law-abiding residents cleared the area, and made it safe for them and their children to walk outside their homes. The youth center began to thrive.

Scenes like this are being played out all across the country. I've seen them in Tulsa, Dallas, Tampa, Omaha, Des Moines, Seattle, New York. Americans—many of them poor, black, or Hispanic—have figured out what the armchair critics haven't. Drugs may threaten to destroy their neighborhoods, but *they* refuse to stand by and let it happen. *They* have discovered that it is possible not only to fight back, but to win. In some elite circles, the talk may be only of the sad state of the helpless and the hopeless, but while these circles talk on, the helpless and the hopeless themselves are carrying out a national drug policy. They are fighting back.

When I think of these scenes I'm reminded of what John Jacob, president of the Urban League, said recently: Drugs are destroying more black families than poverty ever did. And I'm thankful that many of these poor families have the courage to fight drugs now, rather than declaring themselves passive victims of root causes.

America's intellectuals—and here I think particularly of liberal intellectuals—have spent much of the last nine years decrying the social programs of two Republican administrations in the name of the defenseless poor. But today, on the one outstanding issue that disproportionately hurts the poor—that is wiping out many of the poor—where are the liberal intellectuals to be found? They are on the editorial and op-ed pages, and in magazines like this month's *Harper's*, telling us with an ignorant sneer that our drug policy won't work. Many universities, too, which have been quick to take on the challenges of sexism, racism, and ethnocentrism, seem content on the drug issue to wag a finger at us, or to point it mindlessly at American society in general. In public policy schools, there is no shortage of arms control scholars. Isn't it time we had more drug control scholars?

The current situation won't do. The failure to get serious about the drug issue is, I think, a failure of civic courage—the kind of courage shown by many who have been among the main victims of the drug scourge. But it betokens as well a betrayal of the self-declared mission of intellectuals as the bearers of society's conscience. There may be reasons for this reluctance, this hostility, this failure. But I would remind you 25 that not all crusades led by the U.S. government, enjoying broad popular support, are brutish, corrupt, and sinister. What is brutish, corrupt, and sinister is the murder and mayhem being committed in our cities' streets. One would think that a little more concern and serious thought would come from those who claim to care so deeply about America's problems.

So I stand here this afternoon with a simple message for America's pundits and academic cynics: Get serious about drug policy. We are grappling with complicated, stubborn policy issues, and I encourage you to join us. Tough work lies ahead, and we need serious minds to focus on how we should use the tools that we have in the most effective way.

I came to this job with realistic expectations. I am not promising a drug-free America by next week, or even by next year. But that doesn't mean that success is out of reach. Success will come — I've seen a lot of it already — in slow, careful steps. Its enemies are timidity, petulance, false expectations. But its three greatest foes remain surrender, despair, and neglect. So, for the sake of their fellow citizens, I invite America's deep thinkers to get with the program, or at the very least, to get in the game.

Topics for Critical Thinking and Writing

1. In paragraph 6, Bennett draws a parallel between racism and drug abuse and suggests that society ought to fight the one (drug abuse) as it successfully fought the other (racism). What do you think of this parallel? Explain.

2. Bennett identifies two propositions on the issue of drug abuse that he believes are accepted by "consensus" thinking in America (para. 4). What are these propositions, and what is Bennett's view of them? How does he try to convince the reader to agree with him?

3. What are Bennett's main objections to solving the problem of drug abuse by legalizing drugs?

4. At the time he gave this lecture, Bennett was a cigarette smoker trying to break the habit. Do you see any inconsistency in his opposing legalized marijuana and tolerating (and even using) legalized tobacco?

5. What measures besides stricter law enforcement does Bennett propose for wide-scale adoption to reduce drug abuse? Why does he object to relying only on such measures?

James Q. Wilson

James Q. Wilson is Collins Professor of Management and Public Policy at the University of California at Los Angeles. He is the author of Thinking about Crime *(1975) and* Bureaucracy *(1989), the coauthor of* Crime and Human Nature *(1985), and the coeditor of* Drugs and Crime *(1990). The essay that we reprint appeared originally in February 1990 in* Commentary, *a conservative magazine.*

Against the Legalization of Drugs

In 1972, the president appointed me chairman of the National Advisory Council for Drug Abuse Prevention. Created by Congress, the Council was charged with providing guidance on how best to coordinate the national war on drugs. (Yes, we called it a war then, too.) In those days, the drug we were chiefly concerned with was heroin. When I took office, heroin use had been increasing dramatically. Everybody was worried that this increase would continue. Such phrases as "heroin epidemic" were commonplace.

That same year, the eminent economist Milton Friedman published an essay in *Newsweek* in which he called for legalizing heroin. His argument was on two grounds: As a matter of ethics, the government has no right to tell people not to use heroin (or to drink or to commit suicide); as a matter of economics, the prohibition of drug use imposes costs on society that far exceed the benefits. Others, such as the psychoanalyst Thomas Szasz, made the same argument.

We did not take Friedman's advice. (Government commissions rarely do.) I do not recall that we even discussed legalizing heroin, though we did discuss (but did not take action on) legalizing a drug, cocaine, that many people then argued was benign. Our marching orders were to figure out how to win the war on heroin, not to run up the white flag of surrender.

That was 1972. Today, we have the same number of heroin addicts that we had then — half a million, give or take a few thousand. Having that many heroin addicts is no trivial matter; these people deserve our attention. But not having had an increase in that number for over fifteen years is also something that deserves our attention. What happened to the "heroin epidemic" that many people once thought would overwhelm us?

The facts are clear: A more or less stable pool of heroin addicts has been getting older, with relatively few new recruits. In 1976 the average age of heroin users who appeared in hospital emergency rooms was about twenty-seven; ten years later it was thirty-two. More than two-thirds of all heroin users appearing in emergency rooms are now over the age of thirty. Back in the early 1970s, when heroin got onto the national political agenda, the typical heroin addict was much younger, often a teenager. Household surveys show the same thing—the rate of opiate use (which includes heroin) has been flat for the better part of two decades. More fine-grained studies of inner-city neighborhoods confirm this. John Boyle and Ann Brunswick found that the percentage of young blacks in Harlem who use heroin fell from 8 percent in 1970–71 to about 3 percent in 1975–76.

Why did heroin lose its appeal for young people? When the young blacks in Harlem were asked why they stopped, more than half mentioned "trouble with the law" or "high cost" (and high cost is, of course, directly the result of law enforcement). Two-thirds said that heroin hurt their health; nearly all said they had had a bad experience with it. We need not rely, however, simply on what they said. In New York City in 1973–75, the street price of heroin rose dramatically and its purity sharply declined, probably as a result of the heroin shortage caused by the success of the Turkish government in reducing the supply of opium base and of the French government in closing down heroin-processing laboratories located in and around Marseilles. These were short-lived gains for, just as Friedman predicted, alternative sources of supply— mostly in Mexico—quickly emerged. But the three-year heroin shortage interrupted the easy recruitment of new users.

Health and related problems were no doubt part of the reason for the reduced flow of recruits. Over the preceding years, Harlem youth had watched as more and more heroin users died of overdoses, were poisoned by adulterated doses, or acquired hepatitis from dirty needles. The word got around: Heroin can kill you. By 1974 new hepatitis cases and drug-overdose deaths had dropped to a fraction of what they had been in 1970.

Alas, treatment did not seem to explain much of the cessation in drug use. Treatment programs can and do help heroin addicts, but treatment did not explain the drop in the number of *new* users (who by definition had never been in treatment) nor even much of the reduction in the number of experienced users.

No one knows how much of the decline to attribute to personal observation as opposed to high prices or reduced supply. But other evidence suggests strongly that price and supply played a large role. In 1972 the National Advisory Council was especially worried by the prospect that U.S. servicemen returning to this country from Vietnam would bring their heroin habits with them. Fortunately, a brilliant study by Lee Robins of Washington University in St. Louis put that fear to rest. She measured drug use of Vietnam veterans shortly after they had returned home. Though many had used heroin regularly while in Southeast Asia, most gave up the habit when back in the United States. The reason: Here, heroin was less available and sanctions on its use were more pronounced. Of course, if a veteran had been willing to pay enough— which might have meant traveling to another city and would certainly have meant making an illegal contact with a disreputable dealer in a threatening neighborhood in order to acquire a (possibly) dangerous dose—he could have sustained his drug habit. Most veterans were unwilling to pay this price, and so their drug use declined or disappeared.

RELIVING THE PAST

Suppose we had taken Friedman's advice in 1972. What would have happened? We cannot be entirely certain, but at a minimum we would have placed the young heroin addicts (and, above all, the prospective addicts) in a very different position from the one in which they actually 10 found themselves. Heroin would have been legal. Its price would have been reduced by 95 percent (minus whatever we chose to recover in taxes). Now that it could be sold by the same people who make aspirin, its quality would have been assured—no poisons, no adulterants. Sterile hypodermic needles would have been readily available at the neighborhood drugstore, probably at the same counter where the heroin was sold. No need to travel to big cities or unfamiliar neighborhoods—heroin could have been purchased anywhere, perhaps by mail order.

There would no longer have been any financial or medical reason to avoid heroin use. Anybody could have afforded it. We might have tried to prevent children from buying it, but as we have learned from our efforts to prevent minors from buying alcohol and tobacco, young people have a way of penetrating markets theoretically reserved for adults. Returning Vietnam veterans would have discovered that Omaha and Raleigh had been converted into the pharmaceutical equivalent of Saigon.

Under these circumstances, can we doubt for a moment that heroin use would have grown exponentially? Or that a vastly larger supply of new users would have been recruited? Professor Friedman is a Nobel Prize–winning economist whose understanding of market forces is profound. What did he think would happen to consumption under his legalized regime? Here are his words: "Legalizing drugs might increase the number of addicts, but it is not clear that it would. Forbidden fruit is attractive, particularly to the young."

Really? I suppose that we should expect no increase in Porsche sales if we cut the price by 95 percent, no increase in whiskey sales if we cut the price by a comparable amount—because young people only want fast cars and strong liquor when they are "forbidden." Perhaps Friedman's uncharacteristic lapse from the obvious implications of price theory can be explained by a misunderstanding of how drug users are recruited. In his 1972 essay he said that "drug addicts are deliberately made by pushers, who give likely prospects their first few doses free." If drugs were legal it would not pay anybody to produce addicts, because everybody would buy from the cheapest source. But as every drug expert knows, pushers do not produce addicts. Friends or acquaintances do. In fact, pushers are usually reluctant to deal with nonusers because a nonuser could be an undercover cop. Drug use spreads in the same way any fad or fashion spreads: Somebody who is already a user urges his friends to try, or simply shows already-eager friends how to do it.

But we need not rely on speculation, however plausible, that lowered prices and more abundant supplies would have increased heroin usage. Great Britain once followed such a policy and with almost exactly those results. Until the mid-1960s, British physicians were allowed to prescribe heroin to certain classes of addicts. (Possessing these drugs without a doctor's prescription remained a criminal offense.) For many years this policy worked well enough because the addict patients were typically middle-class people who had become dependent on opiate painkillers while undergoing hospital treatment. There was no drug culture. The British system worked for many years, not because it prevented drug abuse but because there was no problem of drug abuse that would test the system.

All that changed in the 1960s. A few unscrupulous doctors began passing out heroin in wholesale amounts. One doctor prescribed almost six hundred thousand heroin tablets—that is, over thirteen pounds—in just one year. A youthful drug culture emerged with a demand for drugs far different from that of the older addicts. As a result, the British government required doctors to refer users to government-run clinics to receive their heroin.

But the shift to clinics did not curtail the growth in heroin use. Throughout the 1960s the number of addicts increased—the late John Kaplan of Stanford estimated by fivefold—in part as a result of the diversion of heroin from clinic patients to new users on the streets. An addict would bargain with the clinic doctor over how big a dose he would receive. The patient wanted as much as he could get, the doctor wanted to give as little as was needed. The patient had an advantage in this conflict because the doctor could not be certain how much was really needed. Many patients would use some of their "maintenance" dose and sell the remaining part to friends, thereby recruiting new addicts. As the clinics learned of this, they began to shift their treatment away from heroin and toward methadone, an addictive drug that, when taken orally, does not produce a "high" but will block the withdrawal pains associated with heroin abstinence.

Whether what happened in England in the 1960s was a miniepidemic or an epidemic depends on whether one looks at numbers or at rates of change. Compared to the United States, the numbers were small. In 1960 there were sixty-eight heroin addicts known to the British government; by 1968 there were two thousand in treatment and many more who refused treatment. (They would refuse in part because they did not want to get methadone at a clinic if they could get heroin on the street.) Richard Hartnoll estimates that the actual number of addicts in England is five times the number officially registered. At a minimum, the number of British addicts increased by thirtyfold in ten years; the actual increase may have been much larger.

In the early 1980s the numbers began to rise again, and this time nobody doubted that a real epidemic was at hand. The increase was estimated to be 40 percent a year. By 1982 there were thought to be twenty thousand heroin users in London alone. Geoffrey Pearson reports that many cities—Glasgow, Liverpool, Manchester, and Sheffield among them—were now experiencing a drug problem that once had been largely confined to London. The problem, again, was supply. The country was being flooded with cheap, high-quality heroin, first from Iran and then from Southeast Asia.

The United States began the 1960s with a much larger number of heroin addicts and probably a bigger at-risk population than was the case in Great Britain. Even though it would be foolhardy to suppose that the British system, if installed here, would have worked the same way or with the same results, it would be equally foolhardy to suppose that a combination of heroin available from leaky clinics and from street dealers who faced only minimal law-enforcement risks would not have produced a much greater increase in heroin use than we actually experienced. My guess is that if we had allowed either doctors or clinics to prescribe heroin, we would have had far worse results than were produced in Britain, if for no other reason than the vastly larger number of addicts with which we began. We would have had to find some way to police thousands (not scores) of physicians and hundreds (not dozens) of clinics. If the British civil service found it difficult to keep heroin in the hands of addicts and out of the hands of recruits when it was dealing with a few hundred people, how well would the American civil service have accomplished the same tasks when dealing with tens of thousands of people?

BACK TO THE FUTURE

Now cocaine, especially in its potent form, crack, is the focus of attention. Now as in 1972 the government is trying to reduce its use. Now as then some people are advocating legalization. Is there any more reason to yield to those arguments today than there was almost two decades ago?[1] 20

I think not. If we had yielded in 1972 we almost certainly would have had today a permanent population of several million, not several hundred thousand, heroin addicts. If we yield now we will have a far more serious problem with cocaine.

Crack is worse than heroin by almost any measure. Heroin produces a pleasant drowsiness and, if hygienically administered, has only the physical side effects of constipation and sexual impotence. Regular heroin use incapacitates many users, especially poor ones, for any productive work or social responsibility. They will sit nodding on a street corner, helpless but at least harmless. By contrast, regular cocaine use leaves the user neither helpless nor harmless. When smoked (as with crack) or injected, cocaine produces instant, intense, and short-lived euphoria. The experience generates a powerful desire to repeat it. If the drug is readily available, repeat use will occur. Those people who

---

[1]I do not here take up the question of marijuana. For a variety of reasons—its widespread use and its lesser tendency to addict—it presents a different problem from cocaine or heroin. For a penetrating analysis, see Mark Kleiman, *Marijuana: Costs of Abuse, Costs of Control* (Greenwood Press, 217 pp.). [Wilson's note.]

progress to "bingeing" on cocaine become devoted to the drug and its effects to the exclusion of almost all other considerations—job, family, children, sleep, food, even sex. Dr. Frank Gawin at Yale and Dr. Everett Ellinwood at Duke report that a substantial percentage of all high-dose, binge users become uninhibited, impulsive, hypersexual, compulsive, irritable, and hyperactive. Their moods vacillate dramatically, leading at times to violence and homicide.

Women are much more likely to use crack than heroin, and if they are pregnant, the effects on their babies are tragic. Douglas Besharov, who has been following the effects of drugs on infants for twenty years, writes that nothing he learned about heroin prepared him for the devastation of cocaine. Cocaine harms the fetus and can lead to physical deformities or neurological damage. Some crack babies have for all practical purposes suffered a disabling stroke while still in the womb. The long-term consequences of this brain damage are lowered cognitive ability and the onset of mood disorders. Besharov estimates that about thirty thousand to fifty thousand such babies are born every year, about seven thousand in New York City alone. There may be ways to treat such infants, but from everything we now know the treatment will be long, difficult, and expensive. Worse, the mothers who are most likely to produce crack babies are precisely the ones who, because of poverty or temperament, are least able and willing to obtain such treatment. In fact, anecdotal evidence suggests the crack mothers are likely to abuse their infants.

The notion that abusing drugs such as cocaine is a "victimless crime" is not only absurd but dangerous. Even ignoring the fetal drug syndrome, crack-dependent people are, like heroin addicts, individuals who regularly victimize their children by neglect, their spouses by improvidence, their employers by lethargy, and their co-workers by carelessness. Society is not and could never be a collection of autonomous individuals. We all have a stake in ensuring that each of us displays a minimal level of dignity, responsibility, and empathy. We cannot, of course, coerce people into goodness, but we can and should insist that some standards must be met if society itself—on which the very existence of the human personality depends—is to persist. Drawing the line that defines those standards is difficult and contentious, but if crack and heroin use do not fall below it, what does?

The advocates of legalization will respond by suggesting that my picture is overdrawn. Ethan Nadelmann of Princeton argues that the risk of legalization is less than most people suppose. Over twenty million Americans between the ages of eighteen and twenty-five have tried cocaine (according to a government survey), but only a quarter million use it daily. From this Nadelmann concludes that at most 3 percent of all young people who try cocaine develop a problem with it. The implication is clear: Make the drug legal and we only have to worry about 3 percent of our youth.

25

The implication rests on a logical fallacy and a factual error. The fallacy is this: The percentage of occasional cocaine users who become binge users *when the drug is illegal* (and thus expensive and hard to find) tells us nothing about the percentage who will become dependent when the drug is legal (and thus cheap and abundant). Drs. Gawin and Ellinwood report, in common with several other researchers, that controlled or occasional use of cocaine changes to compulsive and frequent use "when access to the drug increases" or when the user switches from snorting to smoking. More cocaine more potently administered alters, perhaps sharply, the proportion of "controlled" users who become heavy users.

The factual error is this: The federal survey Nadelmann quotes was done in 1985, *before* crack had become common. Thus the probability of becoming dependent on cocaine was derived from the responses of users who snorted the drug. The speed and potency of cocaine's action increases dramatically when it is smoked. We do not yet know how greatly the advent of crack increases the risk of dependency, but all the clinical evidence suggests that the increase is likely to be large.

It is possible that some people will not become heavy users even when the drug is readily available in its most potent form. So far there are no scientific grounds for predicting who will and who will not become dependent. Neither socioeconomic background nor personality traits differentiate between casual and intensive users. Thus, the only way to settle the question of who is correct about the effect of easy availability on drug use, Nadelmann or Gawin and Ellinwood, is to try it and see. But the social experiment is so risky as to be no experiment at all, for if cocaine is legalized and if the rate of its abusive use increases dramatically, there is no way to put the genie back in the bottle, and it is not a kindly genie.

HAVE WE LOST?

Many people who agree that there are risks in legalizing cocaine or heroin still favor it because, they think, we have lost the war on drugs. "Nothing we have done has worked" and the current federal policy is just "more of the same." Whatever the costs of greater drug use, surely they would be less than the costs of our present, failed efforts.

That is exactly what I was told in 1972—and heroin is not quite as 30 bad a drug as cocaine. We did not surrender and we did not lose. We did not win, either. What the nation accomplished then was what most efforts to save people from themselves accomplish: The problem was contained and the number of victims minimized, all at a considerable cost in law enforcement and increased crime. Was the cost worth it? I think so, but others may disagree. What are the lives of would-be addicts worth? I recall some people saying to me then, "Let them kill themselves." I was appalled. Happily, such views did not prevail.

Have we lost today? Not at all. High-rate cocaine use is not commonplace. The National Institute of Drug Abuse (NIDA) reports that less than 5 percent of high-school seniors used cocaine within the last thirty days. Of course this survey misses young people who have dropped out of school and miscounts those who lie on the questionnaire, but even if we inflate the NIDA estimate by some plausible percentage, it is still not much above 5 percent. Medical examiners reported in 1987 that about 1,500 died from cocaine use; hospital emergency rooms reported about 30,000 admissions related to cocaine abuse.

These are not small numbers, but neither are they evidence of a nationwide plague that threatens to engulf us all. Moreover, cities vary greatly in the proportion of people who are involved with cocaine. To get city-level data we need to turn to drug tests carried out on arrested persons, who obviously are more likely to be drug users than the average citizen. The National Institute of Justice, through its Drug Use Forecasting (DUF) project, collects urinalysis data on arrestees in twenty-two cities. As we have already seen, opiate (chiefly heroin) use has been flat or declining in most of these cities over the last decade. Cocaine use has gone up sharply, but with great variation among cities. New York, Philadelphia, and Washington, D.C., all report that two-thirds or more of their arrestees tested positive for cocaine, but in Portland, San Antonio, and Indianapolis the percentage was one-third or less.

In some neighborhoods, of course, matters have reached crisis proportions. Gangs control the streets, shootings terrorize residents, and drug dealing occurs in plain view. The police seem barely able to contain matters. But in these neighborhoods—unlike at Palo Alto cocktail parties—the people are not calling for legalization, they are calling for help. And often not much help has come. Many cities are willing to do almost anything about the drug problem except spend more money on it. The federal government cannot change that; only local voters and politicians can. It is not clear that they will.

It took about ten years to contain heroin. We have had experience with crack for only about three or four years. Each year we spend perhaps $11 billion on law enforcement (and some of that goes to deal with marijuana) and perhaps $2 billion on treatment. Large sums, but not sums that should lead anyone to say, "We just can't afford this any more."

The illegality of drugs increases crime, partly because some users turn to crime to pay for their habits, partly because some users are stimulated by certain drugs (such as crack or PCP) to act more violently or ruthlessly than they otherwise would, and partly because criminal organizations seeking to control drug supplies use force to manage their markets. These also are serious costs, but no one knows how much they would be reduced if drugs were legalized. Addicts would no longer steal to pay black-market prices for drugs, a real gain. But some, perhaps a great deal, of that gain would be offset by the great increase in the number of addicts. These people, nodding on heroin or living in the delusion-ridden high of cocaine, would hardly be ideal employees. Many would steal simply to support themselves, since snatch-and-grab, opportunistic crime can be managed even by people unable to hold a regular job or plan an elaborate crime. Those British addicts who get their supplies from government clinics are not models of law-abiding decency. Most are in crime, and though their per-capita rate of criminality may be lower thanks to the cheapness of their drugs, the total volume of crime they produce may be quite large. Of course, society could decide to support all unemployable addicts on welfare, but that would mean that gains from lowered rates of crime would have to be offset by large increases in welfare budgets.

Proponents of legalization claim that the costs of having more' addicts around would be largely if not entirely offset by having more money available with which to treat and care for them. The money would come from taxes levied on the sale of heroin and cocaine.

To obtain this fiscal dividend, however, legalization's supporters must first solve an economic dilemma. If they want to raise a lot of money to pay for welfare and treatment, the tax rate on the drugs will have to be quite high. Even if they themselves do not want a high rate, the politicians' love of "sin taxes" would probably guarantee that it would be high anyway. But the higher the tax, the higher the price of the drug, and the higher the price the greater the likelihood that addicts will turn to crime to find the money for it and that criminal organizations will be formed to sell tax-free drugs at below-market rates. If we managed to keep taxes (and thus prices) low, we would get that much less money to pay for welfare and treatment and more people could afford to become addicts. There may be an optimal tax rate for drugs that maximizes revenue while minimizing crime, bootlegging, and the recruitment of new addicts, but our experience with alcohol does not suggest that we know how to find it.

THE BENEFITS OF ILLEGALITY

The advocates of legalization find nothing to be said in favor of the current system except, possibly, that it keeps the number of addicts smaller than it would otherwise be. In fact, the benefits are more substantial than that.

First, treatment. All the talk about providing "treatment on demand" implies that there is a demand for treatment. That is not quite right. There are some drug-dependent people who genuinely want treatment and will remain in it if offered; they should receive it. But there are far more who want only short-term help after a bad crash; once stabilized and bathed, they are back on the street again, hustling. And even many of the addicts who enroll in a program honestly wanting help drop out after a short while when they discover that help takes time and commitment. Drug-dependent people have very short time horizons and a weak capacity for commitment. These two groups—those looking for a quick fix and those unable to stick with a long-term fix—are not easily helped. Even if we increase the number of treatment slots—as we should—we would have to do something to make treatment more effective.

One thing that can often make it more effective is compulsion. 40 Douglas Anglin of UCLA, in common with many other researchers, has found that the longer one stays in a treatment program, the better the chances of a reduction in drug dependency. But he, again like most other researchers, has found that dropout rates are high. He has also found, however, that patients who enter treatment under legal compulsion stay in the program longer than those not subject to such pressure. His research on the California civil commitment program, for example, found that heroin users involved with its required drug-testing program had over the long term a lower rate of heroin use than similar addicts who were free of such constraints. If for many addicts compulsion is a useful component of treatment, it is not clear how compulsion could be achieved in a society in which purchasing, possessing, and using the drug were legal. It could be managed, I suppose, but I would not want to have to answer the challenge from the American Civil Liberties Union that it is wrong to compel a person to undergo treatment for consuming a legal commodity.

Next, education. We are now investing substantially in drug-education programs in the schools. Though we do not yet know for certain what will work, there are some promising leads. But I wonder how credible such programs would be if they were aimed at dissuading children from doing something perfectly legal. We could, of course, treat drug education like smoking education: Inhaling crack and inhaling tobacco are both legal, but you should not do it because it is bad for you. That tobacco is bad for you is easily shown; the Surgeon General has seen to that. But what do we say about crack? It is pleasurable, but devoting yourself to so much pleasure is not a good idea (though perfectly legal)? Unlike tobacco, cocaine will not give you cancer or emphysema, but it will lead you to neglect your duties to family, job, and neighborhood? Everybody is doing cocaine, but you should not?

Again, it might be possible under a legalized regime to have effective drug-prevention programs, but their effectiveness would depend heavily, I think, on first having decided that cocaine use, like tobacco use, is purely a matter of practical consequences; no fundamental moral significance attaches to either. But if we believe—as I do—that dependency on certain mind-altering drugs *is* a moral issue and that their illegality rests in part on their immorality, then legalizing them undercuts, if it does not eliminate altogether, the moral message.

That message is at the root of the distinction we now make between nicotine and cocaine. Both are highly addictive; both have harmful physical effects. But we treat the two drugs differently, not simply because nicotine is so widely used as to be beyond the reach of effective prohibition, but because its use does not destroy the user's essential humanity. Tobacco shortens one's life, cocaine debases it. Nicotine alters one's habits, cocaine alters one's soul. The heavy use of crack, unlike the heavy use of tobacco, corrodes those natural sentiments of sympathy and duty that constitute our human nature and make possible our social life. To say, as does Nadelmann, that distinguishing morally between tobacco and cocaine is "little more than a transient prejudice" is close to saying that morality itself is but a prejudice.

THE ALCOHOL PROBLEM

Now we have arrived where many arguments about legalizing drugs begin: Is there any reason to treat heroin and cocaine differently from the way we treat alcohol?

There is no easy answer to that question because, as with so many 45 human problems, one cannot decide simply on the basis either of moral principles or of individual consequences; one has to temper any policy by a commonsense judgment of what is possible. Alcohol, like heroin, cocaine, PCP, and marijuana, is a drug—that is, a mood-altering substance—and consumed to excess it certainly has harmful consequences: auto accidents, barroom fights, bedroom shootings. It is also, for some people, addictive. We cannot confidently compare the addictive powers of these drugs, but the best evidence suggests that crack and heroin are much more addictive than alcohol.

Many people, Nadelmann included, argue that since the health and financial costs of alcohol abuse are so much higher than those of cocaine or heroin abuse, it is hypocritical folly to devote our efforts to preventing cocaine or drug use. But as Mark Kleiman of Harvard has pointed out, this comparison is quite misleading. What Nadelmann is doing is showing that a *legalized* drug (alcohol) produces greater social harm than *illegal* ones (cocaine and heroin). But of course. Suppose that in the 1920s we had made heroin and cocaine legal and alcohol illegal. Can anyone doubt that Nadelmann would now be writing that it is folly to continue our ban on alcohol because cocaine and heroin are so much more harmful?

And let there be no doubt about it—widespread heroin and cocaine use are associated with all manner of ills. Thomas Bewley found that the mortality rate of British heroin addicts in 1968 was twenty-eight times as high as the death rate of the same age group of nonaddicts, even though in England at the time an addict could obtain free or low-cost heroin and clean needles from British clinics. Perform the following mental experiment: Suppose we legalized heroin and cocaine in this country. In what proportion of auto fatalities would the state police report that the driver was nodding off on heroin or recklessly driving on a coke high? In what proportion of spouse-assault and child-abuse cases would the local police report that crack was involved? In what proportion of industrial accidents would safety investigators report that the forklift or drill-press operator was in a drug-induced stupor or frenzy? We do not know exactly what the proportion would be, but anyone who asserts that it would not be much higher than it is now would have to believe that these drugs have little appeal except when they are illegal. And that is nonsense.

An advocate of legalization might concede that social harm—perhaps harm equivalent to that already produced by alcohol—would follow from making cocaine and heroin generally available. But at least, he might add, we would have the problem "out in the open" where it could be treated as a matter of "public health." That is well and good, *if* we knew how to treat—that is, cure—heroin and cocaine abuse. But we do not know how to do it for all the people who would need such help. We are having only limited success in coping with chronic alcoholics. Addictive behavior is immensely difficult to change, and the best methods for changing it—living in drug-free therapeutic communities, becoming faithful members of Alcoholics Anonymous or Narcotics Anonymous—require great personal commitment, a quality that is, alas, in short supply among the very persons—young people, disadvantaged people—who are often most at risk for addiction.

Suppose that today we had, not fifteen million alcohol abusers, but half a million. Suppose that we already knew what we have learned from our long experience with the widespread use of alcohol. Would we make whiskey legal? I do not know, but I suspect there would be a lively debate. The surgeon general would remind us of the risks alcohol poses to pregnant women. The National Highway Traffic Safety Administration would point to the likelihood of more highway fatalities caused by drunk drivers. The Food and Drug Administration might find that there is a nontrivial increase in cancer associated with alcohol consumption. At the same time the police would report great difficulty in keeping illegal whiskey out of our cities, officers being corrupted by bootleggers, and alcohol addicts often resorting to crime to feed their habit. Libertarians, for their part, would argue that every citizen has a right to drink anything he wishes and that drinking is, in any event, a "victimless crime."

However the debate might turn out, the central fact would be that 50 the problem was still, at that point, a small one. The government cannot legislate away the addictive tendencies in all of us, nor can it remove completely even the most dangerous addictive substances. But it can cope with harms when the harms are still manageable.

SCIENCE AND ADDICTION

One advantage of containing a problem while it is still containable is that it buys time for science to learn more about it and perhaps to discover a cure. Almost unnoticed in the current debate over legalizing drugs is that basic science has made rapid strides in identifying the underlying neurological processes involved in some forms of addiction. Stimulants such as cocaine and amphetamines alter the way certain brain cells communicate with one another. That alteration is complex and not entirely understood, but in simplified form it involves modifying the way in which a neurotransmitter called dopamine sends signals from one cell to another.

When dopamine crosses the synapse between two cells, it is in effect carrying a message from the first cell to activate the second one. In certain parts of the brain that message is experienced as pleasure. After the message is delivered, the dopamine returns to the first cell. Cocaine apparently blocks this return, or "reuptake," so that the excited cell and others nearby continue to send pleasure messages. When the exaggerated high produced by cocaine-influenced dopamine finally ends, the brain cells may (in ways that are still a matter of dispute) suffer from an extreme lack of dopamine, thereby making the individual unable to experience any pleasure at all. This would explain why cocaine users often feel so depressed after enjoying the drug. Stimulants may also affect the way in which other neurotransmitters, such as serotonin and noradrenaline, operate.

Whatever the exact mechanism may be, once it is identified it becomes possible to use drugs to block either the effect of cocaine or its tendency to produce dependency. There have already been experiments using desipramine, imipramine, bromocriptine, carbamazepine, and other chemicals. There are some promising results.

Tragically, we spend very little on such research, and the agencies funding it have not in the past occupied very influential or visible posts in the federal bureaucracy. If there is one aspect of the "war on drugs" metaphor that I dislike, it is its tendency to focus attention almost exclusively on the troops in the trenches, whether engaged in enforcement or treatment, and away from the research-and-development efforts back on the home front where the war may ultimately be decided.

I believe that the prospects of scientists in controlling addiction will 55 be strongly influenced by the size and character of the problem they face. If the problem is a few hundred thousand chronic, high-dose users of an illegal product, the chances of making a difference at a reasonable cost will be much greater than if the problem is a few million chronic users of legal substances. Once a drug is legal, not only will its use increase but many of those who then use it will prefer the drug to the treatment: They will want the pleasure, whatever the cost to themselves or their families, and they will resist—probably successfully—any effort to wean them away from experiencing the high that comes from inhaling a legal substance.

IF I AM WRONG . . .

No one can know what our society would be like if we changed the law to make access to cocaine, heroin, and PCP easier. I believe, for reasons given, that the result would be a sharp increase in use, a more widespread degradation of the human personality, and a greater rate of accidents and violence.

I may be wrong. If I am, then we will needlessly have incurred heavy costs in law enforcement and some forms of criminality. But if I am right, and the legalizers prevail anyway, then we will have consigned millions of people, hundreds of thousands of infants, and hundreds of neighborhoods to a life of oblivion and disease. To the lives and families destroyed by alcohol we will have added countless more destroyed by cocaine, heroin, PCP, and whatever else a basement scientist can invent.

Human character is formed by society; indeed, human character is inconceivable without society, and good character is less likely in a bad society. Will we, in the name of an abstract doctrine of radical individualism, and with the false comfort of suspect predictions, decide to take the chance that somehow individual decency can survive amid a more general level of degradation?

I think not. The American people are too wise for that, whatever the academic essayists and cocktail-party pundits may say. But if Americans today are less wise than I suppose, then Americans at some future time will look back on us now and wonder, what kind of people were they that they could have done such a thing?

Topics for Critical Thinking and Writing

1. Wilson objects to the idea that using cocaine is a "victimless crime" (para. 24; see also para. 49). A crime is said to be "victimless" when the offender consents to the act and those who do not consent are not harmed. Why does it matter to Wilson, do you think, whether using illegal drugs is a victimless crime?

2. Wilson accuses Ethan Nadelmann, an advocate of legalization, of committing "a logical fallacy and a factual error" (para. 26). What is the fallacy, and what is the error?

3. Wilson raises the question of whether we "won" or "lost" the war on heroin in the 1970s and whether we will do any better with the current war on cocaine (paras. 30–31). What would you regard as convincing evidence that we are winning the war on drugs? Losing it?

4. In his criticism of those who would legalize drugs, Wilson points to what he regards as an inescapable "economic dilemma" (para. 37). What is this dilemma? Do you see any way around it?

5. Economists tell us that we can control the use of a good or service by controlling the cost (thus probably reducing the demand), by ignoring the cost and controlling the supply, or by doing both. In the war on drugs, which of these three strategies does Wilson apparently favor, and why?

Milton Friedman

Milton Friedman, winner of a Nobel Prize in economics, was born in Brooklyn in 1912. Educated at Rutgers University, the University of Chicago, and Columbia University, Friedman, a leading conservative economist, has had considerable influence on economic thought in America through his academic and popular writings. We reprint a piece that appeared in the New York Times *in 1998.*

There's No Justice in the War on Drugs

Twenty-five years ago, President Richard M. Nixon announced a "War on Drugs." I criticized the action on both moral and expediential grounds in my *Newsweek* column of May 1, 1972, "Prohibition and Drugs":

> On ethical grounds, do we have the right to use the machinery of government to prevent an individual from becoming an alcoholic or a drug addict? For children, almost everyone would answer at least a qualified yes. But for responsible adults, I, for one, would answer no. Reason with the potential addict, yes. Tell him the consequences, yes. Pray for and with him, yes. But I believe that we have no right to use force, directly or indirectly, to prevent a fellow man from committing suicide, let alone from drinking alcohol or taking drugs.

That basic ethical flaw has inevitably generated specific evils during the past quarter century, just as it did during our earlier attempt at alcohol prohibition.

1. The use of informers. Informers are not needed in crimes like robbery and murder because the victims of those crimes have a strong incentive to report the crime. In the drug trade, the crime consists of a transaction between a willing buyer and willing seller. Neither has any incentive to report a violation of law. On the contrary, it is in the self-interest of both that the crime not be reported. That is why informers are needed. The use of informers and the immense sums of money at stake inevitably generate corruption—as they did during Prohibition. They also lead to violations of the civil rights of innocent people, to the shameful practices of forcible entry and forfeiture of property without due process.

As I wrote in 1972: "Addicts and pushers are not the only ones corrupted. Immense sums are at stake. It is inevitable that some relatively low-paid police and other government officials—and some high-paid ones as well—will succumb to the temptation to pick up easy money."

2. Filling the prisons. In 1970, 200,000 people were in prison. Today, 1.6 million people are. Eight times as many in absolute number,   5 six times as many relative to the increased population. In addition, 2.3 million are on probation and parole. The attempt to prohibit drugs is by far the major source of the horrendous growth in the prison population.

There is no light at the end of that tunnel. How many of our citizens do we want to turn into criminals before we yell "enough"?

3. Disproportionate imprisonment of blacks. Sher Hosonko, at the time Connecticut's director of addiction services, stressed this effect of drug prohibition in a talk given in June 1995:

> Today in this country, we incarcerate 3,109 black men for every 100,000 of them in the population. Just to give you an idea of the drama in this number, our closest competitor for incarcerating black men is South Africa. South Africa — and this is pre–Nelson Mandela and under an overt public policy of apartheid — incarcerated 729 black men for every 100,000. Figure this out: In the land of the Bill of Rights, we jail over four times as many black men as the only country in the world that advertised a political policy of apartheid.

4. Destruction of inner cities. Drug prohibition is one of the most important factors that have combined to reduce our inner cities to their present state. The crowded inner cities have a comparative advantage for selling drugs. Though most customers do not live in the inner cities, most sellers do. Young boys and girls view the swaggering, affluent drug dealers as role models. Compared with the returns from a traditional career of study and hard work, returns from dealing drugs are tempting to young and old alike. And many, especially the young, are not dissuaded by the bullets that fly so freely in disputes between competing drug dealers — bullets that fly only because dealing drugs is illegal. Al Capone epitomizes our earlier attempt at Prohibition; the Crips and Bloods epitomize this one.

5. Compounding the harm to users. Prohibition makes drugs exorbitantly expensive and highly uncertain in quality. A user must associate with criminals to get the drugs, and many are driven to become criminals themselves to finance the habit. Needles, which are hard to get, are often shared, with the predictable effect of spreading disease. Finally, an addict who seeks treatment must confess to being a criminal in order to qualify for a treatment program. Alternatively, professionals who treat addicts must become informers or criminals themselves.

6. Undertreatment of chronic pain. The Federal Department of 10 Health and Human Services has issued reports showing that two-thirds of all terminal cancer patients do not receive adequate pain medication, and the numbers are surely higher in nonterminally ill patients. Such serious undertreatment of chronic pain is a direct result of the Drug Enforcement Agency's pressures on physicians who prescribe narcotics.

7. Harming foreign countries. Our drug policy has led to thousands of deaths and enormous loss of wealth in countries like Colombia, Peru, and Mexico, and has undermined the stability of their governments. All because we cannot enforce our laws at home. If we did, there would be no market for imported drugs. There would be no Cali cartel. The foreign countries would not have to suffer the loss of sovereignty involved in letting our "advisers" and troops operate on their soil, search their vessels, and encourage local militaries to shoot down their planes. They could run their own affairs, and we, in turn, could avoid the diversion of military forces from their proper function.

Can any policy, however high-minded, be moral if it leads to widespread corruption, imprisons so many, has so racist an effect, destroys our inner cities, wreaks havoc on misguided and vulnerable individuals, and brings death and destruction to foreign countries?

Topics for Critical Thinking and Writing

1. State in one sentence the thesis of Friedman's essay.

2. Which of the seven reasons Friedman cites in favor of revising our "war on drugs" do you find most convincing? Explain why, in a short essay of 100 words.

3. Friedman distinguishes between "moral and expediential" objections to current drug policy (para. 1). What does he mean by this distinction? Which kind of objection do you think is the most persuasive? Why?

4. If a policy, a practice, or an individual act is unethical or immoral, then it violates some ethical standard or moral norm. What norms or standards does Friedman think our current drug policy violates?

5. Does Friedman favor a policy toward addictive (and currently illegal) drugs like our policy toward alcohol? Explain in an essay of 250 words how the two policies might differ.

Elliott Currie

Elliott Currie, a graduate of Roosevelt University in Chicago, was a lecturer in the Legal Studies Program at the University of California, Berkeley, and vice chair of the Eisenhower Foundation in Washington, D.C., an organization that supports drug-abuse-prevention programs. We reprint an essay that appeared in the journal Dissent *in 1993; the essay is a slightly revised version of a chapter that first appeared in one of Currie's books,* Reckoning: Drugs, the Cities, and the American Future *(1993).*

Toward a Policy on Drugs

One of the strongest implications of what we now know about the causes of endemic drug abuse is that the criminal-justice system's effect on the drug crisis will inevitably be limited. That shouldn't surprise us in the 1990s; it has, after all, been a central argument of drug research since the 1950s. Today, as the drug problem has worsened, the limits of the law are if anything even clearer. But that does not mean that the justice system has no role to play in a more effective strategy against drugs. Drugs will always be a "law-enforcement problem" in part, and the real job is to define what we want the police and the courts to accomplish.

We will never, for reasons that will shortly become clear, punish our way out of the drug crisis. We can, however, use the criminal-justice system, in small but significant ways, to improve the prospects of drug users who are now caught in an endless loop of court, jail, and street. And we can use law enforcement, in small but significant ways, to help strengthen the ability of drug-ridden communities to defend themselves against violence, fear, and demoralization. Today the criminal-justice system does very little of the first and not enough of the second. But doing these things well will require far-reaching changes in our priorities. Above all, we will have to shift from an approach in which discouraging drug use through punishment and fear takes central place to one that emphasizes three very different principles: the reintegration of drug abusers into productive life, the reduction of harm, and the promotion of community safety.

This is a tall order, but, as we shall see, something similar is being practiced in many countries that suffer far less convulsing drug problems than we do. Their experience suggests that a different and more humane criminal-justice response to drugs is both possible and practical. Today, there is much debate about the role of the justice system in a rational drug policy—but for the most part, the debate is between those who would intensify the effort to control drugs through the courts and prisons and those who want to take drugs out of the orbit of the justice system altogether. I do not think that either approach takes sufficient account of the social realities of drug abuse; and both, consequently, exaggerate the role of regulatory policies in determining the shape and seriousness of the problem. But those are not the only alternatives. In between, there is a range of more promising strategies—what some Europeans call a "third way"—that is more attuned to those realities and more compatible with our democratic values.

One response to the failure of the drug war has been to call for more of what we've already done—even harsher sentences, still more money for jails and prisons—on the grounds that we have simply not provided enough resources to fight the war effectively. That position is shared by the Bush administration and many Democrats in Congress as well. But the strategy of upping the ante cannot work; and even to attempt it on a large scale would dramatically increase the social costs that an overreliance on punishment has already brought. We've seen that the effort to contain the drug problem through force and fear has already distorted our justice system in fundamental ways and caused a rippling of secondary costs throughout the society as a whole. Much more of this would alter the character of American society beyond recognition. And it would not solve the drug problem.

Why wouldn't more of the same do the job?   5

To understand why escalating the war on drugs would be unlikely to make much difference—short of efforts on a scale that would cause unprecedented social damage—we need to consider how the criminal-justice system is, in theory, *supposed* to work to reduce drug abuse and drug-related crime. Criminologists distinguish between two mechanisms by which punishment may decrease illegal behavior. One is "incapacitation," an unlovely term that simply means that locking people up will keep them—as long as they are behind bars—from engaging in the behavior we wish to suppress. The other is "deterrence," by which we mean either that people tempted to engage in the behavior will be persuaded otherwise by the threat of punishment ("general deterrence"), or that individuals, once punished, will be less likely to engage in the behavior again ("specific deterrence"). What makes the drug problem so resistant to even very heavy doses of criminalization is that neither mechanism works effectively for most drug offenders—particularly those most heavily involved in the drug subcultures of the street.

The main reason why incapacitation is unworkable as a strategy against drug offenders is that there are so many of them that a serious attempt to put them all—or even just the "hard core"—behind bars is unrealistic, even in the barest fiscal terms. This is obvious if we pause to recall the sheer number of people who use hard drugs in the United States. Consider the estimates of the number of people who have used drugs during the previous year provided annually by the NIDA (National Institute on Drug Abuse) Household Survey—which substantially *understates* the extent of hard-drug use. Even if we exclude the more than 20 million people who used marijuana in the past year, the number of hard-drug users is enormous: the survey estimates over six million cocaine users in 1991 (including over a million who used crack), about 700,000 heroin users, and 5.7 million users of hallucinogens and inhalants. Even if we abandon the aim of imprisoning less serious hard-drug users, thus allowing the most conservative accounting of the costs of incapacitation, the problem remains staggering: by the lowest estimates, there are no fewer than two million hard-core abusers of cocaine and heroin alone.

If we take as a rough approximation that about 25 percent of America's prisoners are behind bars for drug offenses, that gives us roughly 300,000 drug offenders in prison at any given point—and this after several years of a hugely implemented war mainly directed at lower-level dealers and street drug users. We have seen what this flood of offenders has done to the nation's courts and prisons, but what is utterly sobering is that even this massive effort at repression has barely scratched the surface: according to the most optimistic estimate, we may at any point be incarcerating on drug-related charges about one-eighth of the country's hard-core cocaine and heroin abusers. And where drug addiction is truly endemic, the disparity is greater. By 1989 there were roughly 20,000 drug offenders on any given day in New York State's prisons, but there were an estimated 200,000 to 250,000 *heroin* addicts in New York City alone. To be sure, these figures obscure the fact that many prisoners behind bars for *non*drug offenses are also hard-core drug users; but the figures are skewed in the other direction by the large (if unknown) number of active drug dealers who are not themselves addicted.

Thus, though we cannot quantify these proportions with any precision, the basic point should be clear: the pool of *serious* addicts and active dealers is far, far larger than the numbers we now hold in prison—even in the midst of an unprecedented incarceration binge that has made us far and away the world's leader in imprisonment rates.

What would it mean to expand our prison capacity enough to put the *majority* of hard-core users and dealers behind bars for long terms? To triple the number of users and low-level dealers behind bars, even putting two drug offenders to a cell, would require about 300,000 new cells. At a conservative estimate of about $100,000 per cell, that means a $30 billion investment in construction alone. If we then assume an equally conservative estimate of about $25,000 in yearly operating costs per inmate, we add roughly $15 billion a year to our current costs. Yet this would leave the majority of drug dealers and hard-core addicts still on the streets and, of course, would do nothing to prevent new ones from emerging in otherwise unchanged communities to take the place of those behind bars.

It is not entirely clear, moreover, what that huge expenditure would, in fact, accomplish. For if the goal is to prevent the drug dealing and other crimes that addicts commit, the remedy may literally cost more than the disease. Although drug addicts do commit a great deal of crime, most of them are very minor ones, mainly petty theft and small-time drug dealing. This pattern has been best illuminated in the study of Harlem heroin addicts by Bruce Johnson and his co-workers. Most of the street addicts in this study were "primarily thieves and small-scale drug distributors who avoided serious crimes, like robbery, burglary, assault." The average income per nondrug crime among these addicts was $35. Even among the most criminally active group—what these researchers called "robber-dealers"—the annual income from crime amounted on average to only about $21,000, and for the great majority—about 70 percent—of less active addict-criminals, it ranged from $5,000 to $13,000. At the same time, the researchers estimated that the average cost per day of confining one addict in a New York City jail cell was roughly $100, or $37,000 a year. Putting these numbers together, Johnson and his co-workers came to the startling conclusion that it would cost considerably more to lock up all of Harlem's street addicts than to simply let them continue to "take care of business" on the street.

If we cannot expect much from intensified criminalization, would the legalization of hard drugs solve the drug crisis?

No: it would not. To understand why, we need to consider the claims for legalization's effects in the light of what we know about the roots and meanings of endemic drug abuse. First, however, we need to step back in order to sort out exactly what we *mean* by "legalization"—a frustratingly vague and often confused term that means very different things to different interpreters. Many, indeed, who argue most vehemently one way or the other about the merits of legalization are not really clear just what it is they are arguing *about*.

At one end of the spectrum are those who mean by legalization the total deregulation of the production, sale, and use of all drugs—hard and soft. Advocates of this position run the gamut from right-wing economists to some staunch liberals, united behind the principle that government has no business interfering in individuals' choice to ingest whatever substances they desire. Most who subscribe to that general view would add several qualifiers: for example, that drugs (like alcohol) should not be sold to minors, or that drug advertising should be regulated or prohibited, or (less often) that drugs should be sold only in government-run stores, as alcohol is in some states. But these are seen as necessary, if sometimes grudging, exceptions to the general rule that private drug transactions should not be the province of government intervention. For present purposes, I will call this the "free-market" approach to drug control, and describe its central aim as the "deregulation" of the drug market.

Another approach would not go so far as to deregulate the drug   15 trade, but would opt for the controlled dispensation of drugs to addicts who have been certified by a physician, under strict guidelines as to amounts and conditions of use. Something like this "medical model," in varying forms, guided British policy toward heroin after the 1920s. Under the so-called British system, addicts could receive heroin from physicians or clinics—but the private production and distribution of heroin was always subject to strong penalties, as was the use of the drug except in its medical or "pharmaceutical" form. (A small-scale experiment in cocaine prescription is presently being tried in the city of Liverpool.) Since the seventies, the British have largely abandoned prescribing heroin in favor of methadone—a synthetic opiate that blocks the body's craving for heroin but, among other things, produces less of a pleasurable "high" and lasts considerably longer. The practice of dispensing methadone to heroin addicts came into wide use in the United States in the 1960s and remains a major form of treatment. Methadone prescription, of course, does not "legalize" heroin, and the possession or sale of methadone itself is highly illegal outside of the strictly controlled medical relationship.

Still another meaning sometimes given to legalization is what is more accurately called the "decriminalization" of drug *use*. We may continue to define the production and sale of certain drugs as crimes and subject them to heavy penalties, but not punish those who only *use* the drugs (or have small amounts in their possession), or punish them very lightly — with small fines, for example, rather than jail. Something close to this is the practice in Holland, which is often wrongly perceived as a country that has legalized drugs. Though drug use remains technically illegal, Dutch policy is to focus most law-enforcement resources on sales, especially on larger traffickers, while dealing with users mainly through treatment programs and other social services, rather than the police and courts.

Another aspect of Dutch policy illustrates a further possible meaning of legalization: we may selectively decriminalize *some* drugs, in some amounts, and not others. The Dutch, in practice — though not in law — have tolerated both sale and use of small amounts of marijuana and hashish, but not heroin or cocaine. A German court has recently ruled that possession of small amounts of hashish and marijuana is not a crime, and, indeed, marijuana possession has largely been decriminalized in some American states, though usually as a matter of practical policy rather than legislation.

Let me make my own view clear. I think much would be gained if we followed the example of some European countries and moved toward decriminalization of the drug user. I also think there is a strong argument for treating marijuana differently from the harder drugs, and that there is room for careful experiment with strictly controlled medical prescription for some addicts. For reasons that will become clear, decriminalization is not a panacea; it will not end the drug crisis, but it could substantially decrease the irrationality and inhumanity of our present punitive war on drugs.

The free-market approach, on the other hand, is another matter entirely. Some variant of that approach is more prominent in drug-policy debates in the United States than in other developed societies, probably because it meshes with a strongly individualistic and antigovernment political culture. Indeed, the degree to which the debate over drug policy has been dominated by the clash between fervent drug "warriors" and equally ardent free-market advocates is a peculiarly American phenomenon. Much of that clash is about philosophical principles, and addressing those issues in detail would take more space than we have. My aim here is simply to examine the empirical claims of the free-market perspective in the light of what we know about the social context of drug abuse. Here the free-market view fails to convince. It greatly exaggerates the benefits of deregulation while simultaneously underestimating the potential costs.

There is no question that the criminalization of drugs produces nega- 20 tive secondary consequences—especially in the unusually punitive form that criminalization has taken in the United States. Nor is there much question that this argues for a root-and-branch rethinking of our current punitive strategy—to which we'll return later in this essay—especially our approach to drug *users*.

But proponents of full-scale deregulation of hard drugs also tend to gloss over the very real primary costs of drug abuse—particularly on the American level—and to exaggerate the degree to which the multiple pathologies surrounding drug use in America are simply an unintended result of a "prohibitionist" regulatory policy. No country now legalizes the sale of hard drugs. Yet no other country has anything resembling the American drug problem. That alone should tell us that more than prohibition is involved in shaping the magnitude and severity of our drug crisis. But there is more technical evidence as well. It confirms that much (though, of course, not all) of the harm caused by endemic drug abuse is intrinsic to the impact of hard drugs themselves (and the street cultures in which drug abuse is embedded) within the context of a glaringly unequal, depriving, and deteriorating society. And it affirms that we will not substantially reduce that harm without attacking the social roots of the extraordinary demand for hard drugs in the United States. Just as we cannot punish our way out of the drug crisis, neither will we escape its grim toll by deregulating the drug market.

The most important argument for a free-market approach has traditionally been that it would reduce or eliminate the crime and violence now inextricably entwined with addiction to drugs and with the drug trade. In this view it is precisely the illegality of drug use that is responsible for drug-related crime—which, in turn, is seen as by far the largest part of the overall problem of urban violence. Criminal sanctions against drugs, as one observer insists, "cause the bulk of murders and property crime in major urban areas." Because criminalization makes drugs far more costly than they would otherwise be, addicts are forced to commit crimes in order to gain enough income to afford their habits. Moreover, they are forced to seek out actively criminal people in order to obtain their drugs, which exposes them to even more destructive criminal influences. At the same time, the fact that the drug trade is illegal means both that it is hugely profitable and that the inevitable conflicts and disputes over "turf" or between dealers and users cannot be resolved or moderated by legal mechanisms, and hence are usually resolved by violence.

For all of these reasons, it is argued, outlawing drugs has the unintended, but inevitable, effect of causing a flood of crime and urban violence that would not exist otherwise and sucking young people, especially, into a bloody drug trade. If we legalize the sale and use of hard drugs, the roots of drug-related violence would be severed, and much of the larger crisis of criminal violence in the cities would disappear.

But the evidence suggests that although this view contains an element of truth, it is far too simplistic—and that it relies on stereotypical assumptions about the relationship between drugs and crime that have been called into serious question since the classic drug research of the 1950s. In particular, the widely held notion that most of the crime committed by addicts can be explained by their need for money to buy illegal drugs does not fit well with the evidence.

In its popular form, the drugs-cause-crime argument is implicitly 25 based on the assumption that addict crime is caused by pharmacological compulsion—as a recent British study puts it, on a kind of "enslavement" model in which the uncontrollable craving for drugs forces an otherwise law-abiding citizen to engage in crime for gain. As we've seen, however, a key finding of most of the research into the meaning of drug use and the growth of drug subcultures since the 1950s has been that the purely pharmacological craving for drugs is by no means the most important motive for drug use. Nor is it clear that those cravings are typically so uncontrollable that addicts are in any meaningful sense "driven" to crime to satisfy them.

On the surface, there is much to suggest a strong link between crime and the imperatives of addiction. The studies of addict crime by John Ball and Douglas Anglin and their colleagues show not only that the most heavily addicted commit huge numbers of crimes, but also that their crime rates seem to increase when their heroin use increases and to fall when it declines. Thus, for example, heroin addicts in Ball's study in Baltimore had an average of 255 "crime days" per year when they were actively addicted, versus about 65 when they were not. In general, the level of property crime appears in these studies to go up simultaneously with increasing intensity of drug use. One explanation, and perhaps the most common one, is that the increased need for money to buy drugs drives addicts into more crime.

But a closer look shows that things are considerably more complicated. To begin with, it is a recurrent finding that most people who both abuse drugs and commit crimes began committing the crimes *before* they began using drugs—meaning that their need for drugs cannot have caused their initial criminal involvement (though it may have accelerated it later). George Vaillant's follow-up study of addicts and alcoholics found, for example, that, unlike alcoholics, heroin addicts had typically been involved in delinquency and crime well before they began their career of substance abuse. While alcoholics seemed to become involved in crime as a *result* of their abuse of alcohol, more than half of the heroin addicts (versus just 5 percent of the alcoholics) "were known to have been delinquent *before* drug abuse." A federal survey of drug use among prison inmates in 1986, similarly, found that three-fifths of those who had ever used a "major drug" regularly—that is, heroin, cocaine, methadone, PCP, or LSD—had not done so until after their first arrest.

Other studies have found that for many addicts, drug use and crime seem to have begun more or less *independently* without one clearly causing the other. This was the finding, for example, in Charles Faupel and Carl Klockars's study of hard-core heroin addicts in Wilmington, Delaware. "All of our respondents," they note, "reported some criminal activity prior to their first use of heroin." Moreover, "perhaps most importantly, virtually all of our respondents reported that they believed that their criminal and drug careers began independently of one another, although both careers became intimately interconnected as each evolved."

More recent research shows that the drugs-crime relationship may be even more complex than this suggests. It is not only that crime may precede drug use, especially heavy or addictive use, or that both may emerge more or less independently; it is also likely that there are several *different* kinds of drugs-crime connections among different types of drug users. David Nurco of the University of Maryland and his colleagues, for example, studying heroin addicts in Baltimore and New York City, found that nine different kinds of addicts could be distinguished by the type and severity of their crimes. Like earlier researchers, they found that most addicts committed large numbers of crimes—mainly drug dealing and small-scale property crime, notably shoplifting, burglary, and fencing. Others were involved in illegal gambling and what the researchers called "deception crimes"—including forgery and con games—and a relatively small percentage had engaged in violent crime. On the whole, addicts heavily involved in one type of crime were not likely to be involved in others; as the researchers put it, they tended to be either "dealers or stealers," but rarely both. About 6 percent of the addicts, moreover, were "uninvolved"—they did not commit crimes either while addicted or before, or during periods of nonaddiction interspersed in the course of their longer addiction careers.

The most troubling group of addicts—what the researchers called 30 "violent generalists"—were only about 7 percent of the total sample, but they were extremely active—and very dangerous; they accounted for over half of all the violent crimes committed by the entire sample. Moreover, revealingly, the violent generalists were very active in serious crime *before* they became addicted to narcotics as well as during periods of nonaddiction thereafter—again demonstrating that the violence was not dependent on their addiction itself. Nurco and his colleagues measured the addicts' criminal activity by what they called "crime days" per year. Addicts were asked how many days they had committed each of several types of crime; since on any given day they might have committed more than one type of crime, the resulting figure could add up to more than the number of days in the year. The violent generalists averaged an astonishing 900 crime days a year over the course of their careers. The rates were highest during periods when they were heavily addicted to drugs. But even *before* they were addicted, they averaged 573 crime days, and 491 after their addiction had ended. Indeed, the most active group of violent generalists engaged in more crime *prior* to addiction than any other group did *while* addicted. And they continued to commit crimes—often violent ones—long after they had ceased to be addicted to narcotics.

None of this is to deny that serious addiction to heroin or other illegal drugs can accelerate the level of crime among participants in the drug culture, or stimulate crime even in some users who are otherwise not criminal. Higher levels of drug use *do* go hand in hand with increased crime, especially property crime. Certainly, many addicts mug, steal, or sell their bodies for drugs. The point is that—as the early drug researchers discovered in the 1950s—both crime and drug abuse tend to be spawned by the same set of unfavorable social circumstances, and they interact with one another in much more complex ways than the simple addiction-leads-to-crime view proposes. Simply providing drugs more easily to people enmeshed in the drug cultures of the cities is not likely to cut the deep social roots of addict crime.

If we take the harms of drug abuse seriously, and I think we must, we cannot avoid being deeply concerned about anything that would significantly increase the availability of hard drugs within the American social context; and no one seriously doubts that legalization would indeed increase availability, and probably lower prices for many drugs. In turn, increased availability—as we know from the experience with alcohol—typically leads to increased consumption, and with it increased social and public-health costs. A growing body of research, for example, shows that most alcohol-related health problems, including deaths from cirrhosis and other diseases, were far lower during Prohibition than afterward, when per capita alcohol consumption rose dramatically (by about 75 percent, for example, between 1950 and 1980). It is difficult to imagine why a similar rise in consumption—and in the associated public-health problems—would not follow the full-scale legalization of cocaine, heroin, methamphetamine, and PCP (not to mention the array of as yet undiscovered "designer" drugs that a legalized corporate drug industry would be certain to develop).

If consumption increased, it would almost certainly increase most among the strata already most vulnerable to hard-drug use—thus exacerbating the social stratification of the drug crisis. It is among the poor and near-poor that offsetting measures like education and drug treatment are least effective and where the countervailing social supports and opportunities are least strong. We would expect, therefore, that a free-market policy applied to hard drugs would produce the same results it has created with the *legal* killer drugs, tobacco and alcohol—namely, a widening disparity in use between the better-off and the disadvantaged. And that disparity is already stunning. According to a recent study by Colin McCord and Howard Freeman of Harlem Hospital, between 1979 and 1981—that is, *before* the crack epidemic of the eighties—Harlem blacks were 283 times as likely to die of drug dependency as whites in the general population. Drug deaths, combined with deaths from cirrhosis, alcoholism, cardiovascular disease, and homicide, helped to give black men in Harlem a shorter life expectancy than men in Bangladesh. This is the social reality that the rather abstract calls for the legalization of hard-drug sales tend to ignore.

Topics for Critical Thinking and Writing

1. Currie claims that "Drugs will always be a 'law-enforcement problem'" (para. 1). Why do you think he believes this? Is the evidence he offers adequate to support this troubling judgment?

2. Currie mentions what he regards as "small but significant ways" (para. 2) to reduce the place of drugs in our lives. What are they? Why do you think he doesn't mention (a) curbing the manufacture of illegal addictive drugs, (b) vigorously reducing imports into the U.S. of illegal addictive drugs, and (c) aggressively educating the public on the harm illegal addictive drugs cause their users?

3. Why does Currie think that "escalating the war on drugs," with its reliance on "incapacitation" and "deterrence," is doomed to ineffectiveness (para. 6)? Are you persuaded? Explain.

4. Currie eventually states his own views (para. 18). Do you think the essay would have been more effective if he had stated his views in his opening paragraph? Why, or why not?

5. Currie stresses the uniqueness of the drug problem in the United States. What do you think explains "the magnitude and severity of our drug crisis" (para. 21)? Farmers in other countries produce more illegal addictive drugs than ours do. Other countries have graver problems of poverty than we do. Gross manifest disparities between rich and poor are not unique to the United States. So what's the explanation? Does Currie tell us?

6. Why does Currie reject the drugs-cause-crime argument (para. 24)?

For topical links related to the discussion of the legalization of drugs, see the companion Web site:
www.bedfordstmartins.com/barnetbedau.

22

Euthanasia: Should Doctors Intervene at the End of Life?

DOONESBURY ©1998 G. B. Trudeau. Reprinted with permission of UNIVERSAL PRESS SYNDICATE. All rights reserved.

Ellen Goodman

Ellen Goodman, educated at Radcliffe College, worked as a reporter for Newsweek *and the* Detroit Free Press. *Since 1967 she has written for the* Boston Globe, *and since 1972 her column has been nationally syndicated. This column appeared in the* Boston Globe *in February 1980, the year she won a Pulitzer Prize for journalism.*

Who Lives? Who Dies? Who Decides?

Some have called it a Right to Die case. Others have labeled it a Right to Live case. One group of advocates has called for "death with dignity." Others have responded accusingly, "euthanasia."

At the center of the latest controversy about life and death, medicine and law, is a seventy-eight-year-old Massachusetts man whose existence hangs on a court order.

On one point, everyone agrees: Earle Spring is not the man he used to be. Once a strapping outdoorsman, he is now strapped to a wheelchair. Once a man with a keen mind, he is now called senile by many, and mentally incompetent by the courts. He is, at worst, a member of the living dead; at best, a shriveled version of his former self.

For more than two years, since his physical and then mental health began to deteriorate, Earle Spring has been kept alive by spending five hours on a kidney dialysis machine three times a week. Since January 1979, his family has pleaded to have him removed from the life-support system.

They believe deeply that the Earle Spring who was would not want   5
to live as the Earle Spring who is. They believe they are advocates for the right to die in peace.

In the beginning, the courts agreed. Possibly for the first time, they ruled last month in favor of withdrawing medical care from an elderly patient whose mind had deteriorated. The dialysis was stopped.

But then, in a sudden intervention, an outside nurse and doctor visited Earle Spring and testified that he was alert enough to "make a weak expression of his desire to live." And so the treatments were resumed.

Now, while the courts are waiting for new and more thorough evidence about Spring's mental state, the controversy rages about legal procedures; no judge ever visited Spring, no psychiatrist ever testified. And even more important, we are again forced to determine one person's right to die or to live.

This case makes the Karen Ann Quinlan story seem simple in comparison. Quinlan today hangs onto her "life" long after her "plug was pulled." But when the New Jersey court heard that case, Quinlan had no will. She had suffered brain death by any definition.

The Spring story is different. He is neither competent nor comatose.   10
He lives in a gray area of consciousness. So the questions also range over the gray area of our consciences.

What should the relationship be between mental health and physical treatment? Should we treat the incompetent as aggressively as the competent? Should we order heart surgery for one senile citizen? Should we take another off a kidney machine? What is the mental line between a life worth saving and the living dead? Who is to decide?

Until recently, we didn't have the technology to keep an Earle Spring alive. Until recently, the life-and-death decisions about the senile elderly or the retarded or the institutionalized were made privately between families and medical people. Now, increasingly, in states like Massachusetts, they are made publicly and legally.

Clearly there are no absolutes in this case. No right to die. No right to live. We have to take into account many social as well as medical factors. How much of the resources of a society or a family should be allotted to a member who no longer recognizes it? How many sacrifices should the healthy and vital make for the terminally or permanently ill and disabled?

In England, where kidney dialysis machines are scarce, Earle Spring would never have remained on one. In America, one Earle Spring can decimate the energy and income of an entire family.

But the Spring case is a crucial, scary one that could affect all those 15 living under that dubious sentence "incompetent" or that shaky diagnosis "senile." So it seems to me that if there is one moment a week when the fog lifts and when this man wants to live, if there is any mental activity at all, then disconnecting him from life would be a dangerous precedent, far more dangerous than letting him continue.

The court ruled originally in favor of taking Spring off the machine. It ruled that this is what Earle Spring would have wanted. I have no doubt that his family believes it. I have no doubt of their affection or their pain.

But I remember, too, what my grandfather used to say: No one wants to live to be one hundred until you ask the man who is ninety-nine. Well, no one, including Earle Spring, wants to live to be senile. But once senile, he may well want to live. We simply have to give him the benefit of the doubt. Any doubt.

Topics for Critical Thinking and Writing

1. Suppose you were in the condition of Earle Spring, as described by Goodman (paras. 3, 4, and 10). Would you want to be kept alive? In an essay of 250 words, explain why, or why not.

2. Goodman invites us to think about the relationship between "mental health and physical treatment" (para. 11). She concludes that we have to give everyone, no matter what mental condition he or she is in, "the benefit of the doubt" (para. 17). Does she give any argument for this conclusion? If so, what is it, and what do you think of it? If not, invent an argument that you think she might accept.

3. Goodman declares, "Clearly there are no absolutes in this case. No right to die. No right to live" (para. 13). Why does she hold this view, do you think? Could there be a right to die (or to live) that is not "absolute"?

What sort of right to die, or to live, do you think *you* have — if any? Explain your view in an essay of 500 words.

Terry Golway

Terry Golway regularly publishes a column in America, *a Roman Catholic magazine. In the essay that we reprint, he responds in part to Ellen Goodman, though he is writing not about the Goodman essay that we reprint in this chapter (p. 627) but about another of her essays. This essay was first published on May 10, 1997, so when Golway speaks of "the next century's way of life" (para. 9), he is speaking of the twenty-first century. The title of the essay is the editors'.*

The Culture of Death

There are times, friends, when those who hold human life to be sacred seem as exotic and old-fashioned as the Amish farmers of Lancaster County, Pennsylvania. There are days when it is possible to envision a time in the not very distant future when people in short pants and sneakers, with cameras hanging from their necks, will gawk at sturdy, God-fearing, life-affirming folk and wonder in amazement that such people could exist in the modern world.

The morning newspaper has brought a dispatch from the Netherlands about the joys of euthanasia. It was ever so earnest — why, there wasn't even an attempt at cheap irony: A country called the Netherlands has become the international capital of euthanasia, the place to be if you're in pain (or perhaps even if you're not) and you wish (or maybe you don't) to be dispatched to the netherworld.

The writer, the syndicated columnist Ellen Goodman, made predictably reasonable arguments on behalf of needle-wielding Dutch doctors. No doubt you will take comfort in knowing that there are layers upon layers of bureaucracy one must hurdle before winning the "right" to die! And the doctors — they are ever so careful about deciding who shall die and who shall not! It is positively uplifting! The Dutch, you see, have been thinking a lot about this business of euthanasia.

Apparently yet another wide-eyed American has been dazzled by the sophistication and the cool rationality of the Old World. "Holland has grappled longer and more publicly with the end-of-life issues that we are only now beginning to confront seriously," the columnist wrote. And, she added, the Dutch bristle when they hear that coarse, unthinking and church-going Americans believe that they are "ridding themselves of the old and the handicapped."

Of course they are doing no such thing. They are merely getting rid   5
of people who want to be gotten rid of. For the most part. Nearly always.

As in any activity—baseball, omelette-making, euthanasia—there's the occasional error. But why focus on the botched ground ball when you can feast your eyes on a glorious home run!

In the course of this starry-eyed glimpse of the doctors who slip their patients the ultimate mickey, the columnist conceded that, sure, mistakes have been made. "The most troubling discovery is that 900 to 1,000 patients a year die from what they call 'involuntary euthanasia,'" Goodman wrote. In the rational, reasonable world in which a fair number of our cultural and media elites reside, the doctor-assisted killing of 900 to 1,000 people a year is merely "troubling." If you want to get the elite really outraged, really motivated, you'll have to do something a bit more hideous. Try proposing vouchers for parents of parochial-school children.

In what, in another age, would have been the central point of this discussion, the columnist noted in passing that "it's a weak point...that the Dutch laws don't make a distinction between mental and physical suffering." Now, are you ready for this year's award for best use of a euphemism by a columnist? Here goes: "Not long ago, a psychiatrist performed euthanasia on a physically healthy woman who had lost her children and was in deep despair."

Performed euthanasia? Back in the old days, we simple folk would have used a less grandiose verb—*murdered*. Ah, but in preparing Americans for that fine day when trained physicians dispose of the unwanted, we mustn't use judgmental language. So, you see, psychiatrists who believe their patients are in deep despair don't *kill* them. Why, only a coarse American would use such a word. Kindly souls that these Dutch doctors are, they, in their humane way, *perform euthanasia.*

Those who are selling the culture of death as the next century's way of life have chosen as their role model a country in which a psychiatrist can kill you if he or she thinks you're too depressed, a country where physicians dispense with 900 to 1,000 people a year without the patient's consent. Rather than recoil with horror, the merchants of death would like to see America adopt similarly enlightened policies.

It's fair to say that many of the people preparing the way for euthanasia in America, who regard a few "involuntary" cases as sufficient price to pay for a greater "good," are vociferous opponents of capital punishment. But what is capital punishment but the state performing a form of involuntary euthanasia on an unwanted population? Those who treasure the gift of life and who oppose its taking, whether by government or by physician, have a relentless consistency to their arguments. The cultural leftists who support abortion and suicide on demand, but who turn squeamish on the matter of capital punishment, ought to spend some time thinking through their arguments. They might discover, as pro-lifers have said for years, that on matters of life and death, it is a slippery slope indeed.

The matter-of-fact arguments on behalf of the Dutch way of death, the use of the absurd phrase "performed euthanasia" in the work of a well-known syndicated columnist—these are signs that the forces of darkness are gathering.

Those who have a different view of life can take some comfort and draw some succor from the knowledge that the late Cardinal Joseph Bernardin's autobiography remains on the best-seller list. Clearly his example continues to inspire, and his arguments against the culture of death remain cogent, vital and—we can only hope and pray—decisive.

Topics for Critical Thinking and Writing

1. Who are the "Amish farmers of Lancaster County," and what is "exotic and old fashioned" about their way of life (para. 1)?

2. Read paragraph 2 carefully: Does Golway imply that in the Netherlands people who are not in severe pain and who do not want to die can be euthanized? Justify your interpretation.

3. Consider the metaphor of baseball for euthanasia (para. 5). What is implied by "a glorious home run"?

4. In paragraph 6, Golway speaks of "the elite." Who do you suppose are the people he has in mind? Is the term "the elite" a good term to describe these people? Explain.

5. What does Golway mean (quoting Ellen Goodman) by "involuntary euthanasia" (paras. 6 and 10)? Euthanasia against the wishes of the patient? Or euthanasia of a person incompetent to give or withhold consent? Does it matter which interpretation is implied?

6. Golway suggests (para. 10) that it is inconsistent to oppose the death penalty and yet to favor euthanasia. Do you agree? Explain.

7. Golway's essay uses a considerable amount of verbal irony. Point out two or three examples. (On irony, see page 83.) Would you say that he himself is guilty of the "cheap irony" that he deplores in his second paragraph? Why, or why not?

Cecil McIver

Cecil McIver has practiced medicine for more than fifty years. The essay we reprint is a publication of the Hemlock Society, an organization that (in the words of its homepage on the Internet) "believes that people who want to retain their dignity and choices at the end of life should have the option of a peaceful and gentle death."

Assisted Dying as a Moral and Ethical Choice: A Physician's View

WHAT IS MEANT BY PHYSICIAN ASSISTANCE IN DYING?

During the past century there has been a growing feeling in America, and in other countries too, that hopelessly ill people who are suffering greatly despite the best available medical care, and who have no expectation of ever obtaining relief of their suffering, and who are mentally competent and not acting under any undue influence, and who request assistance in bringing their lives to an end, should be able to receive the assistance of a physician to do that.

The Hemlock Society's proposal, which was the subject of a court case in Florida in 1997, was slightly more focused than that — it sought assistance in dying only for adults with a life expectation of six months or less.

IS THERE EVER A NEED FOR ASSISTANCE IN DYING?

Whilst more people die in an acceptable degree of comfort, for some, dying is a most distressing experience. The things that can make dying so distressing include physical pain, mental distress, and the knowledge that the suffering is pointless in the sense that it has to be borne without hope of subsequent improvement in health or relief in suffering. People can tolerate a lot of mental and physical suffering if they know that it has a purpose, but when there is no purpose suffering can become unbearable. At the tail end of their lives some people simply don't want to be forced to endure such stress.

There have not been many scientific studies on the problems associated with dying but there was an informative article in the *Journal of the American Medical Association* in November of 1995. It reported findings of a study conducted at five large hospitals on 5,000 patients, over a period of five years, and some of the results were:

- 50 percent of patients who were able to communicate said that they experienced moderate or severe pain half the time in their final days.

- 38 percent of terminal patients spent ten or more days in a coma, attached to a ventilator, or in intensive care, where they were isolated from their families.

- 31 percent of terminally ill patients spent all or most of their family's savings in their dying days.

- The average cost of terminal care in this study was estimated to have been about $100,000.

The conclusion of the director of this study was that "this is not the   5
picture of the end of life that I would like to face or that most Americans
would like to face."

The natural hope was that problems of dying patients could be
solved by better pain control, and more tender, loving care. There was a
second part to the study in which, over a two-year period, the investigators tried to determine whether "aggressive intervention by nurse advocates and efforts to improve communication would affect these
conditions." The conclusion was these efforts did not change the situation for the better. Terminal patients in the second study group spent the
same amount of time in intensive care units, in comas, or hooked up to
ventilators before dying. The costs of care remained the same, and complaints of pain actually increased in the groups of patients receiving better communication. The director of the study commented: "our society
needs to create a better vision of living well while dying," and "we live in
a health care system focused on treating disease, and we do that very
well, but we don't know when to stop."

There is no doubt in my mind that physician assistance in dying is
appropriate under certain circumstances.

HOW SHOULD WE DEAL
WITH DIFFERENCES OF OPINION
ON MORAL AND LEGAL ISSUES?

Morality and legality are, or should be, closely coupled. Morality
should provide the theoretical basis for our concepts of right and wrong,
and the legal system should codify, police, and enforce our moral conclusions. When laws are based on fundamental and universal moral
principles, they must be inflexible. However, when a law is based on sec-
tarian opinions, it should accommodate differences of opinion.

Providing assistance in dying in the proper circumstances might be
an act of murder in the eyes of some people, but it is an act of love in the
eyes of others. It is not taking a life with malice aforethought—quite the
opposite in fact—and it is perfectly consistent with the Golden Rule.

HOW DO WE ARRIVE AT THE MORAL
POSITIONS WHICH ARE THE UNDERPINNING
OF OUR LEGAL SYSTEM?

In a recent encyclical entitled *Fides et Ratio* (Faith and Reason), the   10
Pope considered the question of how we arrive at our moral concepts.
The Pope acknowledged that in the past the church had placed too much
emphasis on Faith, and too little on Reason, and he encouraged a greater
emphasis on Reason. However, whilst encouraging his flock to be more
adventurous in exploring the rational basis for their beliefs, he also

warned that the conclusions reached from the exercise of reason must not contradict postulates of faith!

Should Reason be reduced to be no more than the servant of Faith? Can we rely on Faith to provide us with answers to the ultimate existential questions? We cannot! One man's faith is another man's heresy, and there is no way of reconciling the divergent faiths of the many different religions. Faith has not led people in only one direction as one would expect of a reliable guide. Catholics, Protestants, Jews, Hindus, Muslims, Mormons, Seventh Day Adventists, and adherents of all the approximately two thousand different religions, all have beliefs which are, to a greater or lesser degree, irreconcilable. Faith is like a signpost with a thousand different arms all labeled "This way to the truth" but all pointing in different, and often opposite, directions. Faith cannot be relied upon as a certain guide to truth. Reason is the only tool at our disposal with which we can examine and analyze the evidence on which our beliefs must be based.

WHAT DOES REASON TELL US ABOUT MORALITY?

Reason tells us that the Golden Rule is the basis of morality and, on this point, Reason and Faith are in agreement. The Golden Rule has been incorporated into the doctrines of many religions, and there are many versions of it. For example:

- The Mahabharata, a Hindu text dating back some hundreds of years of B.C.E., states it this way: "This is the sum of all true righteousness: deal with others as thou wouldst thyself be dealt with. Do nothing to thy neighbor that thou wouldst not have him do to thee thereafter."

- A Jewish version of the Golden Rule, found in the Talmud, is: "What is hateful to you, do not to your fellow: that is the whole law: all the rest is interpretation."

- An Old Testament version found in Leviticus may be the most familiar version in our society: "Thou shalt love they neighbor as thyself."

- In the New Testament it is found in this form: "As ye would that men should do to you, do ye also to them."

A second basic principle, again based on logic, concerns accountability: "Competent persons are responsible for their decisions and actions and accountable for all the reasonably foreseeable consequences of those decisions and actions."

Assistance in dying is justified by three considerations:

- Firstly, a doctor must always act in his patient's best interests.
- Secondly, dying is sometimes in a patient's best interests.

- Thirdly, if the doctor agrees with his patient that dying is in the latter's best interests, it becomes his obligation to provide such assistance.

That dying can sometimes be in a patient's best interest is a realization that first came to me in the 1940s, during the war. After bombing raids in London, victims of the air raids were sometimes brought to the hospital in such a serious condition that there was no possibility of healing them. Pain relief and tender loving care was all we could offer whilst they died. Death was a blessing to them.

Some terminally ill persons find themselves in the same situation   15 today and would be better off dead. Had my patients in this predicament asked me to ease them into the next world, and had it been legal to do so, I have no doubt that I would have been justified in cutting short their misery and giving them a comfortable passage out of this life. Nothing positive was achieved by not doing so, and much needless suffering was inflicted on both patients and family by not doing so.

WHAT IS THE PRESENT ATTITUDE IN THE UNITED STATES TO ASSISTANCE IN DYING?

Hard data on this question are difficult to come by, but polls in the past five decades report the percentage of people supporting physician assistance in dying has risen steadily from 37 percent in 1947 to 75 percent in 1996. A poll taken on the attitudes of physicians in Oregon and Michigan in November 1995 showed that, among the 70 percent of physicians who responded to the questions, a majority were in favor of physician assistance in dying by a ratio of about two to one. Patients were included in that poll, and a majority of them, too, were in favor of physician assistance in dying. People with strong religious convictions were more likely to be opposed but there were religious people, nonreligious people, agnostics and atheists on both sides of the fence.

The reaction of my patients and friends to my involvement in the debate are in broad agreement with the results of the polls: it would certainly appear that the support for the concept of physician assistance in dying is widespread and growing.

LET US NOW CONSIDER SOME OF THE ARGUMENTS WHICH HAVE BEEN ADVANCED AGAINST PHYSICIAN AID IN DYING.

I have selected nine arguments to address . . . that good palliative care would eliminate the need for assistance in dying, that it would start us on the slippery slope leading who knows where, that the vast majority of people requesting it are incompetent to make such a request, that it is contrary to traditional values, that it contravenes the Hippocratic oath, that it is fundamentally incompatible with the physicians' role as healer, that it would be impossible to regulate, that it has not worked well in practice, and that it is against God's law.

1. Good palliative care would eliminate the need for physician assistance in dying, it has been claimed. In his testimony to the Supreme Court a couple of years ago, Cardinal Law, Archbishop of Boston, said this: "By and large, seriously ill patients do not want assisted suicide: they want decent health care, control of their pain, and the same kind of love and support that everyone needs when vulernable and dependent on others."

The Cardinal is absolutely right. Seriously ill people want and deserve decent health care, and the problems of the terminally ill can usually be made tolerable by such care. But even the best care cannot make the lives of all terminally ill patients tolerable, and that is the crux of the problem. What do we do for those patients who want assistance in dying, despite receiving the best possible care, because living has become so intolerable that dying has become a better option than living? 20

Good palliative care can manage pain and other physical problems, although sometimes at a high cost from the patient's point of view, and loving care can usually keep existential problems within a tolerable range. But even the best palliative and supportive care cannot always make life tolerable, and at the tail end of their lives some people simply want to bring their useless suffering to a close. And, like the majority of people, I think they have a right to make that choice, and to receive help from those of us who are prepared to offer it.

2. Physician assistance in dying would lead to discrimination against the less privileged and most defenseless members of society. I have greater faith in the American people and the American medical profession than to believe that. It is inconceivable to me that the poor here would be systematically discriminated against in that manner, and pressured into dying before their time. *A greater danger is that people will continue to be pressured into living when the time for dying has come.*

Polls indicate that most requests for assistance in dying come not from the least privileged members of society but from the most privileged, and this is in accordance with my experience. In fact, I cannot recall having ever had such a request from a patient who could be considered underprivileged. I don't know the reason for this, but I surmise that the privileged are more accustomed to exercising control over their lives, and that they therefore find the helplessness and hopelessness of terminal illness particularly difficult to tolerate. Sadly, the poor may be better at tolerating dreadful conditions because they have more experience of having had to do that.

3. It has been said people requesting physician assistance in dying are unlikely to be competent to make that request. Suicidologists tell us that at least 95 percent of suicidal patients are depressed, and therefore incompetent to make a request for assistance in dying. However, those figures have no relevance whatsoever to the subject of physician assistance in dying; 95 percent of physically healthy people who are suicidal may be depressed, as claimed, and therefore mentally or emotionally incompetent to make life and death decisions, but that is no reason to infer that 95 percent of terminally ill people who wish to terminate their suffering are in the same category. The two groups are not comparable.

The Hemlock Society, and many other organizations with a similar agenda all around the world, have thousands of members, and we are neither suicidal nor incompetent. We don't want to die; however, we know we are going to die, and when the time for dying comes we want the right to manage the process of our dying, should it become intolerable. Is that a sign of mental or emotional incompetence? We don't think so.

Also, there is no reason to suppose that the incidence of mental incompetence rises dramatically on the deathbed. Like all physicians in primary care I have seen a lot of people die, and whilst the mental and emotional stress of dying can be severe, it does not make the majority of competent people incompetent on their deathbeds. And the suggestion that all terminally ill people requesting assistance in dying should be subjected to full-scale psychological testing prior to receiving such assistance, were this to be legalized, is not only absurd but cruel.

4. Physician assistance in dying cannot be reconciled with our traditional values. Traditional values, which are usually regional values rather than universal values, must not be considered sacrosanct, simply because they have been accepted long enough, to have become traditional. All values must be kept under constant scrutiny to ensure that they are worthy, in fact, to be regarded as standards against which our conduct should be judged. History is replete with examples of "traditional values" which have been employed to defend activities which are absolutely indefensible. The countries of our western hemisphere, for example, have fought religious wars, tortured and killed "heretics," hanged "witches," engaged in slavery, dispossessed native peoples of their land, practiced racial segregation, etc. The medieval church in the Inquisition turned its victims over to the civil authorities to be burned to death since its "traditional values" did not permit the shedding of blood! We have advanced since then, but we have a long way to go before we can claim to be a truly civilized society.

5. Physician assistance in dying cannot be reconciled with the Hippocratic oath. I was never asked to take the Hippocratic oath and I would not have taken an oath to Apollo, Aesculapius, and other putative gods, had I been asked to do so. Of course, the principle of the Hippocratic oath—namely, that a physician should never do anything that is not in the best interests of his patient—is the fundamental basis of the unwritten contract between patients and physicians. Keeping a patient alive, when dying has become a better option for the patient than living, is not in the patient's best interests.

6. Physician assistance in dying is "fundamentally incompatible with the physician's role as a healer." The American Medical Association has made this pronouncement. With respect, I disagree. Physicians cannot heal all the time, and our responsibilities are not confined to healing. A physician's responsibility is to use his/her skills in the best interests of the patient, whatever those happen to be—to heal when possible, to comfort always, and when neither healing nor comforting is possible, to do then whatever is in the patient's best interests.

Sometimes, dying is in a patient's best interests, and if it is, and if the patient requests assistance in dying, it becomes the physician's responsibility to help that person, provided that is in accord with the physician's own ethical values. 30

The American Medical Association went on to state: "Physician-assisted suicide could, it is argued, undermine the trust that is essential to the doctor-patient relationship by blurring the time-honored line between healing and harming." Helping patients terminate their lives when it is in their best interest to do so can hardly be construed as harming them. *Forcing patients to live when it is no longer in their best interest to do so is certainly causing harm!*

7. Physician assistance in dying would be impossible to regulate. There is no reason to believe this. The regulations governing assistance in dying should be made very simple for two reasons: Firstly, the dying patient has enough problems to deal with without adding to them unnecessarily. Secondly, complicated and burdensome controls are all too often self-defeating.

It would be reasonable to require all physicians who are considering the possibility of assisting a patient to die to obtain a consultation from a fellow physician. The consulting physician should be drawn from a panel of consultants who have had several years experience in medicine, who are highly regarded in the community, and who are in agreement with the concept of physician assistance in dying. The duty of the consultant would be to confirm that the patient was terminally ill, mentally competent, receiving optimum care, acting under no undue pressure, and resolutely requesting assistance in dying. If assistance was later provided, that fact should be recorded in a confidential manner on the death certificate, or on an accompanying document, and all cases in which assistance in dying had been provided should be reviewed confidentially by a committee of peers at regular meetings convened for this purpose.

8. The practice of physician assistance in dying has not worked well in practice. The only country in which physician assistance in dying has been tried over any length of time is Holland. It has not been legalized there, but it has been practiced there for two decades, with the unwritten understanding that a blind eye will be turned provided guidelines are followed. The Dutch people have seen fit to continue the practice of providing assistance in dying, from which it must be concluded that they are satisfied with the scheme of things despite its shortcomings. Less than 5 percent of deaths in Holland have been attributed to "active intervention by physicians."

Opponents of physician assistance in dying have quoted the Dutch 35 figures as evidence that no scheme for assistance in dying can work because it is inherently incapable of regulation and bound to slide down a *slippery slope*. There is no reason to believe that this has been the case in Holland, or that it would be the case in America. In Oregon, only 15 patients died under the Death with Dignity Act in the first year and 26 in the second—out of a total of almost 60,000 deaths during that period.

9. Physician assistance in dying is against God's law. There is no consensus to this point. The Reverend Dr. Donald Miller, rector of the Episcopal church in San Mateo, California, said this: "When a terminally ill patient's suffering becomes intolerable despite every effort, this is a medical emergency that requires a compassionate response. Physician assistance in dying should be the response of last resort . . . subject to religious safeguards." Reverend Miller was speaking from personal experience. In his words: "Towards the end, my father entreated me to end his misery, a task for which I possessed neither sufficient skills nor courage. I am still ashamed of that, and would not willingly let others down as I did my father."

THE NINTH CIRCUIT COURT OF APPEALS HAD THIS TO SAY ABOUT PHYSICIAN ASSISTANCE IN DYING

"A competent terminally ill adult, having lived nearly the full measure of his life, has a strong liberty interest in choosing a dignified and humane death rather than being reduced at the end of his existence to a childlike state of helplessness, diapered, sedated, incontinent. Those who believe strongly that death must come without assistance are free to follow that creed, be they doctors or patients. They are not free, however, to force their religious convictions or their philosophies on members of a democratic society, and to compel those whose values differ from theirs to die painful, protracted, and agonizing deaths."

ONE OF THE MAJOR DIFFICULTIES WE FACE IN OUR GENERATION IS THE ADJUSTMENT WE HAVE TO MAKE TO OUR RAPIDLY CHANGING CONCEPTS ABOUT THE UNIVERSE WE LIVE IN, AND THE ROLE WE PLAY IN IT

Inevitably, dogma and superstition are gradually being replaced by reason and knowledge as the basis for our beliefs. The universe is not 15 thousand years old, more or less, but 15 *million* thousand years old, more or less. The earth is not the center of the universe but merely a relatively tiny speck of matter in a system of unimaginable dimensions. Man was not created; he evolved from lower animals, as even the Pope conceded some time ago.

It is not credible that we men and women are the sole reason and purpose for which everything else in the universe exists, or that the universe and all that's in it is simply here for man's benefit. Genesis is a wonderfully poetic account of creation, but it cannot any longer be regarded as an accurate account of how our universe came into being. Would the universe grind to a halt if mankind was to disappear in a mass extinction such as that which wiped out the dinosaurs some millions of years ago? I doubt it. A little humility is in order when considering our place in the overall scheme of things.

FINALLY, I WOULD LIKE TO TOUCH ON THE PRINCIPLE OF THE "DOUBLE EFFECT"

Preservation of life is almost always a physician's dominant objective, but in terminal illness preservation of life may no longer be a goal of treatment at all. When the termination of suffering has become more important than the preservation of life, and the patient wishes to terminate his suffering as quickly as possible, it can be appropriate to end life as a means of terminating suffering. 40

At the present time such action is considered to be criminal, but it is considered perfectly proper to render the patient stuporous and to withhold sustenance, in the certain knowledge that this course of action will result in the patient's death within a matter of days. Death is then attributed to "natural causes," and accountability for the death is denied on the basis that death was not the intent of the treatment but merely an unintended outcome.

This argument does not hold water. We are accountable for all the reasonably foreseeable outcomes of our actions and decisions. How can the predictable outcomes of voluntary actions deliberately taken be considered "unintended"? When actions have multiple predictable outcomes, we must weigh these against each other and decide whether, on balance, the action is justifiable.

In terminal illness, actions which hasten death, whether over a period of minutes or days, can be justified by circumstances. The quick and deliberate ending of life, when dying has become a better option than living and when it is in the patient's best interests, can be an act of virtue, love, and compassion.

In the same circumstances, measures which predictably terminate life slowly, whatever the "intent" of the physician, are *not* morally superior. The relationship between the treatment and the ensuing death is no less real, just less obvious. In both instances, the patient's death is accelerated as a direct result of the physician's intervention.

When death is imminent, dying deliberately in the bosom of the 45 family, at a time and in a manner of one's choosing, having done all one can do to tie up loose ends, is what many people desire. Having seen all kinds of dying, it is certainly what I want for myself, and what I want for myself, I must try and obtain for others, too.

Topics for Critical Thinking and Writing

1. Where does the Hemlock Society get its name? (Hint: Think Socrates in Athens in the fifth century B.C.; see page 818.)

2. McIver opens his essay (para. 1) by laying down four necessary and sufficient conditions that justify physician intervention to end a life. Do you agree that each of these conditions is necessary? Are the four together sufficient? Or do you think it is impossible to specify such conditions? Is the list he gives here of necessary and sufficient conditions the same as the list he gives later in paragraph 32?

3. The Hemlock Society added a fifth condition (para. 2). Would you add it, too?

4. McIver mentions the Golden Rule (paras. 9 and 12) and implies that he accepts it as relevant to the issue of providing physician assistance in dying. Are you willing to decide this issue by relying on the Golden Rule? Why, or why not?

5. McIver thinks that "Faith" (para. 11) (in what?) cannot provide an adequate moral guide. Review his reasons carefully. How might someone who disagrees with him reply?

6. How can dying "sometimes be in a patient's best interest" (paras. 14–15)? Isn't being alive a necessary condition of *any* interests a person might have?

7. Suppose someone were to argue that physician assistance in dying, like suicide or murder, fails to show adequate respect for the value of human life. How might McIver reply?

8. McIver identifies nine arguments (paras. 19–36) that, if sound, would undermine his position. Which of these arguments do you think is the strongest? Which the weakest? Explain why in an essay of 300 words.

9. What does McIver mean when he refers to "existential problems within a tolerable range" (para. 21)?

10. The most widespread objection to physician assistance in dying is that it puts us on the first step of a "slippery slope" (para. 35) leading to grave abuses. Does McIver address this challenge among his nine questions? If not, why not? If so, what is his answer, and how adequate do you think it is? (For slippery slope, see p. 324.)

11. McIver mentions the Hippocratic oath (para. 28) but does not tell us what it says of relevance to physician assistance in dying. Ask your reference librarian to help you find a copy of the oath. What (if anything) is its relevance to the issue? Would you agree with McIver in refusing to acknowledge its authority and finality? Why, or why not?

12. What is the principle of "double effect" (para. 40), and what is its relevance to the issue of physician assistance in dying? Do you think there is an important moral distinction between (a) using drugs with the intention that the patient die in as little pain and suffering as is possible and (b) using drugs with the intention that the patient be relieved of pain and suffering and also knowing that the patient will die in the process? What is McIver's position on these questions?

James Rachels

James Rachels, professor of philosophy at the University of Alabama at Birmingham, is the author of several books, including The End of Life: Euthanasia and Morality *(1986) and* Can Ethics Provide Answers? And Other Essays in Moral Philosophy *(1997). The article reprinted here appeared in the* New England Journal of Medicine *in 1975.*

Active and Passive Euthanasia

The distinction between active and passive euthanasia is thought to be crucial for medical ethics. The idea is that it is permissible, at least in some cases, to withhold treatment and allow a patient to die, but it is never permissible to take any direct action designed to kill the patient. This doctrine seems to be accepted by most doctors, and it is endorsed in a statement adopted by the House of Delegates of the American Medical Association on December 4, 1973:

> The intentional termination of the life of one human being by another—mercy killing—is contrary to that for which the medical profession stands and is contrary to the policy of the American Medical Association. The cessation of the employment of extraordinary means to prolong the life of the body when there is irrefutable evidence that biological death is imminent is the decision of the patient and/or his immediate family. The advice and judgment of the physician should be freely available to the patient and/or his immediate family.

However, a strong case can be made against this doctrine. In what follows I will set out some of the relevant arguments, and urge doctors to reconsider their views on this matter.

To begin with a familiar type of situation, a patient who is dying of incurable cancer of the throat is in terrible pain, which can no longer be satisfactorily alleviated. He is certain to die within a few days, even if present treatment is continued, but he does not want to go on living for those days since the pain is unbearable. So he asks the doctor for an end to it, and his family joins in the request.

Suppose the doctor agrees to withhold treatment, as the conventional doctrine says he may. The justification for his doing so is that the patient is in terrible agony, and since he is going to die anyway, it would be wrong to prolong his suffering needlessly. But now notice this. If one simply withholds treatment, it may take the patient longer to die, and so he may suffer more than he would if more direct action were taken and a lethal injection given. This fact provides strong reason for thinking that, once the initial decision not to prolong his agony has been made, active euthanasia is actually preferable to passive euthanasia, rather than the reverse. To say otherwise is to endorse the option that leads to more suffering rather than less, and is contrary to the humanitarian impulse that prompts the decision not to prolong his life in the first place.

Part of my point is that the process of being "allowed to die" can be relatively slow and painful, whereas being given a lethal injection is relatively quick and painless. Let me give a different sort of example. In the United States about one in six hundred babies is born with Down's syndrome. Most of these babies are otherwise healthy—that is, with only the usual pediatric care, they will proceed to an otherwise normal infancy. Some, however, are born with congenital defects such as intestinal obstructions that require operations if they are to live. Sometimes, the parents and the doctor will decide not to operate, and let the infant die. Anthony Shaw describes what happens then:

> When surgery is denied [the doctor] must try to keep the infant from
> suffering while natural forces sap the baby's life away. As a surgeon
> whose natural inclination is to use the scalpel to fight off death, stand-
> ing by and watching a salvageable baby die is the most emotionally ex-
> hausting experience I know. It is easy at a conference, in a theoretical
> discussion to decide that such infants should be allowed to die. It is alto-
> gether different to stand by in the nursery and watch as dehydration
> and infection wither a tiny being over hours and days. This is a terrible
> ordeal for me and the hospital staff — much more so than for the par-
> ents who never set foot in the nursery.[1]

I can understand why some people are opposed to all euthanasia, and
insist that such infants must be allowed to live. I think I can also understand why other people favor destroying these babies quickly and painlessly. But why should anyone favor letting "dehydration and infection
wither a tiny being over hours and days"? The doctrine that says that a
baby may be allowed to dehydrate and wither, but may not be given an
injection that would end its life without suffering, seems so patently
cruel as to require no further refutation. The strong language is not intended to offend, but only to put the point in the clearest possible way.

My second argument is that the conventional doctrine leads to deci-   5
sions concerning life and death made on irrelevant grounds.

Consider again the case of the infants with Down's syndrome who
need operations for congenital defects unrelated to the syndrome to live.
Sometimes, there is no operation, and the baby dies, but when there is
no such defect, the baby lives on. Now, an operation such as that to remove an intestinal obstruction is not prohibitively difficult. The reason
why such operations are not performed in these cases is, clearly, that the
child has Down's syndrome and the parents and the doctor judge that
because of that fact it is better for the child to die.

But notice that this situation is absurd, no matter what view one
takes of the lives and potentials of such babies. If the life of such an infant is worth preserving, what does it matter if it needs a simple operation? Or, if one thinks it better that such a baby should not live on, what
difference does it make that it happens to have an unobstructed intestinal tract? In either case, the matter of life and death is being decided on
irrelevant grounds. It is the Down's syndrome, and not the intestines,
that is the issue. The matter should be decided, if at all, on that basis, and
not be allowed to depend on the essentially irrelevant question of
whether the intestinal tract is blocked.

What makes this situation possible, of course, is the idea that when
there is an intestinal blockage, one can "let the baby die," but when
there is no such defect there is nothing that can be done, for one must
not "kill" it. The fact that this idea leads to such results as deciding life or

---

[1]Anthony Shaw, "Doctor, Do We Have a Choice?" *New York Times Magazine*, January 30,
1972, p. 54. [Rachels's note.]

death on irrelevant grounds is another good reason why the doctrine would be rejected.

One reason why so many people think that there is an important moral difference between active and passive euthanasia is that they think killing someone is morally worse than letting someone die. But is it? Is killing, in itself, worse than letting die? To investigate this issue, two cases may be considered that are exactly alike except that one involves killing whereas the other involves letting someone die. Then, it can be asked whether this difference makes any difference to the moral assessments. It is important that the cases be exactly alike, except for this one difference, since otherwise one cannot be confident that it is this difference and not some other that accounts for any variation in the assessments of the two cases. So, let us consider this pair of cases:

In the first, Smith stands to gain a large inheritance if anything should happen to his six-year-old cousin. One evening while the child is taking his bath, Smith sneaks into the bathroom and drowns the child, and then arranges things so that it will look like an accident.

In the second, Jones also stands to gain if anything should happen to his six-year-old cousin. Like Smith, Jones sneaks in planning to drown the child in his bath. However, just as he enters the bathroom Jones sees the child slip and hit his head, and fall face down in the water. Jones is delighted; he stands by, ready to push the child's head back under if it is necessary, but it is not necessary. With only a little thrashing about, the child drowns all by himself, "accidentally," as Jones watches and does nothing.

Now Smith killed the child, whereas Jones "merely" let the child die. That is the only difference between them. Did either man behave better, from a moral point of view? If the difference between killing and letting die were in itself a morally important matter, one should say that Jones's behavior was less reprehensible than Smith's. But does one really want to say that? I think not. In the first place, both men acted from the same motive, personal gain, and both had exactly the same end in view when they acted. It may be inferred from Smith's conduct that he is a bad man, although the judgment may be withdrawn or modified if certain further facts are learned about him — for example, that he is mentally deranged. But would not the very same thing be inferred about Jones from his conduct? And would not the same further considerations also be relevant to any modification of this judgment? Moreover, suppose Jones pleaded, in his own defense, "After all, I didn't do anything except just stand there and watch the child drown. I didn't kill him; I only let him die." Again, if letting die were in itself less bad than killing, this defense should have at least some weight. But it does not. Such a "defense" can only be regarded as a grotesque perversion of moral reasoning. Morally speaking, it is no defense at all.

Now, it may be pointed out, quite properly, that the cases of euthanasia with which doctors are concerned are not like this at all. They do not involve personal gain or the destruction of normal healthy children. Doctors are concerned only with cases in which the patient's life is of no further use to him, or in which the patient's life has become or will soon become a terrible burden. However, the point is the same in these cases: The bare difference between killing and letting die does not, in itself, make a moral difference. If a doctor lets a patient die, for humane reasons, he is in the same moral position as if he had given the patient a lethal injection for humane reasons. If his decision was wrong — if, for example, the patient's illness was in fact curable — the decision would be equally regrettable no matter which method was used to carry it out. And if the doctor's decision was the right one, the method used is not in itself important.

The AMA policy statement isolates the crucial issue very well; the crucial issue is "the intentional termination of the life of one human being by another." But after identifying this issue, and forbidding "mercy killing," the statement goes on to deny that the cessation of treatment is the intentional termination of life. This is where the mistake comes in, for what is the cessation of treatment, in these circumstances, if it is not "the intentional termination of the life of one human being by another?" Of course it is exactly that, and if it were not, there would be no point to it.

Many people will find this judgment hard to accept. One reason, I 15 think, is that it is very easy to conflate the question of whether killing is, in itself, worse than letting die, with the very different question of whether most actual cases of killing are more reprehensible than most actual cases of letting die. Most actual cases of killing are clearly terrible (think, for example, of all the murders reported in the newspapers), and one hears of such cases every day. On the other hand, one hardly ever hears of a case of letting die, except for the actions of doctors who are motivated by humanitarian reasons. So one learns to think of killing in a much worse light than of letting die. But this does not mean that there is something about killing that makes it in itself worse than letting die, for it is not the bare difference between killing and letting die that makes the difference in these cases. Rather, the other factors — the murderer's motive of personal gain, for example, contrasted with the doctor's humanitarian motivation — account for different reactions to the different cases.

I have argued that killing is not in itself any worse than letting die; if my contention is right, it follows that active euthanasia is not any worse than passive euthanasia. What arguments can be given on the other side? The most common, I believe, is the following:

> The important difference between active and passive euthanasia is that, in passive euthanasia, the doctor does not do anything to bring about the patient's death. The doctor does nothing, and the patient dies of whatever ills already afflict him. In active euthanasia, however, the doctor does something to bring about the patient's death: He kills him. The doctor who gives the patient with cancer a lethal injection has him-

self caused his patient's death; whereas if he merely ceases treatment, the cancer is the cause of the death.

A number of points need to be made here. This first is that it is not exactly correct to say that in passive euthanasia the doctor does nothing, for he does do one thing that is very important: He lets the patient die. "Letting someone die" is certainly different, in some respects, from other types of action—mainly in that it is a kind of action that one may perform by way of not performing certain other actions. For example, one may let a patient die by way of not giving medication, just as one may insult someone by way of not shaking his hand. But for any purpose of moral assessment, it is a type of action nonetheless. The decision to let a patient die is subject to moral appraisal in the same way that a decision to kill him would be subject to moral appraisal: It may be assessed as wise or unwise, compassionate or sadistic, right or wrong. If a doctor deliberately let a patient die who was suffering from a routinely curable illness, the doctor would certainly be to blame for what he had done, just as he would be to blame if he had needlessly killed the patient. Charges against him would then be appropriate. If so, it would be no defense at all for him to insist that he didn't "do anything." He would have done something very serious indeed, for he let his patient die.

Fixing the cause of death may be very important from a legal point of view, for it may determine whether criminal charges are brought against the doctor. But I do not think that this notion can be used to show a moral difference between active and passive euthanasia. The reason why it is considered bad to be the cause of someone's death is that death is regarded as a great evil—and so it is. However, if it has been decided that euthanasia—even passive euthanasia—is desirable in a given case, it has also been decided that in this instance death is not greater an evil than the patient's continued existence. And if this is true, the usual reason for not wanting to be the cause of someone's death simply does not apply.

Finally, doctors may think that all of this is only of academic interest—the sort of thing that philosophers may worry about but that has no practical bearing on their own work. After all, doctors must be concerned about the legal consequences of what they do, and active euthanasia is clearly forbidden by the law. But even so, doctors should also be concerned with the fact that the law is forcing upon them a moral doctrine that may be indefensible, and has a considerable effect on their practices. Of course, most doctors are not now in the position of being coerced in this matter, for they do not regard themselves as merely going along with what the law requires. Rather, in statements such as the AMA policy statement that I have quoted, they are endorsing this doctrine as a central point of medical ethics. In that statement, active euthanasia is condemned not merely as illegal but as "contrary to that for which the medical profession stands," whereas passive euthanasia is approved. However, the preceding considerations suggest that there is really no moral difference between the two, considered in themselves (there may be important moral differences in some cases in their *consequences*, but, as I pointed out, these differences may make active euthanasia, and not passive euthanasia, the morally preferable option). So, whereas doctors may have to discriminate between active and passive euthanasia to satisfy the law, they should not do any more than that. In particular, they should not give the distinction any added authority and weight by writing it into official statements of medical ethics.

Topics for Critical Thinking and Writing

1. Explain the distinction between "active and passive euthanasia" (para. 1). Why do you think the American Medical Association attaches importance to the distinction?

2. Rachels argues that in certain cases, "active euthanasia is actually preferable to passive euthanasia" (para. 3). What is his argument? Do you think it ought to persuade a person who already favors "passive" euthanasia to perform "active" euthanasia in cases of the sort Rachels describes? Why, or why not?

3. What is Rachels's "second argument" (para. 5), and what is it supposed to prove? Do you think it succeeds? Explain.

4. Rachels asks whether "killing someone is morally worse than letting someone die" (para. 9). He argues that it is not. What is his argument? Does it persuade you? Why, or why not?

5. Rachels opens his essay by discussing a genuine case of a newborn with Down's syndrome (para. 4), but eventually he is forced to construct purely hypothetical cases (paras. 10–11). Do you think that the persuasive power of his argument suffers when he shifts to hypothetical cases? Or does it improve? Or doesn't it matter whether he is discussing actual or only hypothetical cases? Explain.

6. The principal thesis of Rachels's essay is that "the bare difference between killing and letting die does not, in itself, make a moral difference" (para. 13). Summarize his argument for this thesis.

Timothy M. Quill

Timothy M. Quill, born in 1949, was educated at Amherst College and at the University of Rochester School of Medicine. He now teaches at the University of Rochester and is division head of internal medicine at the Genesee Hospital in Rochester, New York. The essay here first appeared on March 7, 1991, in the New England Journal of Medicine, *a publication read chiefly by physicians. Quill later expanded on the ideas in this essay in a book entitled*

Death and Dignity: Making Choices and Taking Charge *(1993). In 1996 he published* A Midwife through the Dying Process: Stories of Healing and Hard Choices at the End of Life.

Death and Dignity: A Case of Individualized Decision Making

Diane was feeling tired and had a rash. A common scenario, though there was something subliminally worrisome that prompted me to check her blood count. Her hematocrit was 22, and the white-cell count was 4.3 with some metamyelocytes and unusual white cells. I wanted it to be viral, trying to deny what was staring me in the face. Perhaps in a repeated count it would disappear. I called Diane and told her it might be more serious than I had initially thought—that the test needed to be repeated and that if she felt worse, we might have to move quickly. When she pressed for the possibilities, I reluctantly opened the door to leukemia. Hearing the word seemed to make it exist. "Oh, shit!" she said. "Don't tell me that." Oh, shit! I thought, I wish I didn't have to.

Diane was no ordinary person (although no one I have ever come to know has been really ordinary). She was raised in an alcoholic family and had felt alone for much of her life. She had vaginal cancer as a young woman. Through much of her adult life, she had struggled with depression and her own alcoholism. I had come to know, respect, and admire her over the previous eight years as she confronted these problems and gradually overcame them. She was an incredibly clear, at times brutally honest, thinker and communicator. As she took control of her life, she developed a strong sense of independence and confidence. In the previous three and a half years, her hard work had paid off. She was completely abstinent from alcohol, she had established much deeper connections with her husband, college-age son, and several friends, and her business and her artistic work were blossoming. She felt she was really living fully for the first time.

Not surprisingly, the repeated blood count was abnormal, and detailed examination of the peripheral-blood smear showed myelocytes. I advised her to come into the hospital, explaining that we needed to do a bone marrow biopsy and make some decisions relatively rapidly. She came to the hospital knowing what we would find. She was terrified, angry, and sad. Although we knew the odds, we both clung to the thread of possibility that it might be something else.

The bone marrow confirmed the worst: acute myelomonocytic leukemia. In the face of this tragedy, we looked for signs of hope. This is an area of medicine in which technological intervention has been successful, with cures 25 percent of the time—long-term cures. As I probed the costs of these cures, I heard about induction chemotherapy (three weeks in the hospital, prolonged neutropenia, probable infectious complications, and

hair loss; 75 percent of patients respond, 25 percent do not). For the survivors, this is followed by consolidation chemotherapy (with similar side
effects; another 25 percent die, for a net survival of 50 percent). Those still
alive, to have a reasonable chance of long-term survival, then need bone
marrow transplantation (hospitalization for two months and whole-body
irradiation, with complete killing of the bone marrow, infectious complications, and the possibility for graft-versus-host disease—with a survival
of approximately 50 percent, to 25 percent of the original group). Though
hematologists may argue over the exact percentages, they don't argue
about the outcome of no treatment—certain death in days, weeks, or at
most a few months.

Believing that delay was dangerous, our oncologist broke the news   5
to Diane and began making plans to insert a Hickman catheter and begin
induction chemotherapy that afternoon. When I saw her shortly thereafter, she was enraged at his presumption that she would want treatment, and devastated by the finality of the diagnosis. All she wanted to
do was go home and be with her family. She had no further questions
about treatment and in fact had decided that she wanted none. Together
we lamented her tragedy and the unfairness of life. Before she left, I felt
the need to be sure that she and her husband understood that there was
some risk in delay, that the problem was not going to go away, and that
we needed to keep considering the options over the next several days.
We agreed to meet in two days.

She returned in two days with her husband and son. They had
talked extensively about the problem and the options. She remained
very clear about her wish not to undergo chemotherapy and to live
whatever time she had left outside the hospital. As we explored her
thinking further, it became clear that she was convinced she would die
during the period of treatment and would suffer unspeakably in the
process (from hospitalization, from lack of control over her body, from
the side effects of chemotherapy, and from pain and anguish). Although
I could offer support and my best effort to minimize her suffering if she
chose treatment, there was no way I could say any of this would not
occur. In fact, the last four patients with acute leukemia at our hospital
had died very painful deaths in the hospital during various stages of
treatment (a fact I did not share with her). Her family wished she would
choose treatment but sadly accepted her decision. She articulated very
clearly that it was she who would be experiencing all the side effects of
treatment and that odds of 25 percent were not good enough for her
to undergo so toxic a course of therapy, given her expectations of
chemotherapy and hospitalization and the absence of a closely matched
bone marrow donor. I had her repeat her understanding of the treatment, the odds, and what to expect if there were no treatment. I clarified
a few misunderstandings, but she had a remarkable grasp of the options
and implications.

I have been a long-time advocate of active, informed patient choice of treatment or nontreatment, and of a patient's right to die with as much control and dignity as possible. Yet there was something about her giving up a 25 percent chance of long-term survival in favor of almost certain death that disturbed me. I had seen Diane fight and use her considerable inner resources to overcome alcoholism and depression, and I half expected her to change her mind over the next week. Since the window of time in which effective treatment can be initiated is rather narrow, we met several times that week. We obtained a second hematology consultation and talked at length about the meaning and implications of treatment and nontreatment. She talked to a psychologist she had seen in the past. I gradually understood the decision from her perspective and became convinced that it was the right decision for her. We arranged for home hospice care (although at that time Diane felt reasonably well, was active, and looked healthy), left the door open for her to change her mind, and tried to anticipate how to keep her comfortable in the time she had left.

Just as I was adjusting to her decision, she opened up another area that would stretch me profoundly. It was extraordinarily important to Diane to maintain control of herself and her own dignity during the time remaining to her. When this was no longer possible, she clearly wanted to die. As a former director of a hospice program, I know how to use pain medicines to keep patients comfortable and lessen suffering. I explained the philosophy of comfort care, which I strongly believe in. Although Diane understood and appreciated this, she had known of people lingering in what was called relative comfort, and she wanted no part of it. When the time came, she wanted to take her life in the least painful way possible. Knowing of her desire for independence and her decision to stay in control, I thought this request made perfect sense. I acknowledged and explored this wish but also thought that it was out of the realm of currently accepted medical practice and that it was more than I could offer or promise. In our discussion, it became clear that preoccupation with her fear of a lingering death would interfere with Diane's getting the most out of the time she had left until she found a safe way to ensure her death. I feared the effects of a violent death on the family, the consequences of an ineffective suicide that would leave her lingering in precisely the state she dreaded so much, and the possibility that a family member would be forced to assist her, with all the legal and personal repercussions that would follow. She discussed this at length with her family. They believed that they should respect her choice. With this in mind, I told Diane that information was available from the Hemlock Society that might be helpful to her.

A week later she phoned me with a request for barbiturates for sleep. Since I knew that this was an essential ingredient in a Hemlock Society suicide, I asked her to come to the office to talk things over. She was more than willing to protect me by participating in a superficial conversation about her insomnia, but it was important to me to know how she planned to use the drugs and to be sure that she was not in despair or overwhelmed in a way that might color her judgment. In our discussion, it was apparent that she was having trouble sleeping, but it was also evident that the security of having enough barbiturates available to commit suicide when and if the time came would leave her secure enough to live fully and concentrate on the present. It was clear that she was not despondent and that in fact she was making deep, personal connections with her family and close friends. I made sure that she knew how to use the barbiturates for sleep, and also that she knew the amount needed to commit suicide. We agreed to meet regularly, and she promised to meet with me before taking her life, to ensure that all other avenues had been exhausted. I wrote the prescription with an uneasy feeling about the boundaries I was exploring—spiritual, legal, professional, and personal. Yet I also felt strongly that I was setting her free to get the most out of the time she had left and to maintain dignity and control on her own terms until her death.

The next several months were very intense and important for Diane. 10 Her son stayed home from college, and they were able to be with one another and say much that had not been said earlier. Her husband did his work at home so that he and Diane could spend more time together. She spent time with her closest friends. I had her come into the hospital for a conference with our residents, at which she illustrated in a most profound and personal way the importance of informed decision making, the right to refuse treatment, and the extraordinarily personal effects of illness and interaction with the medical system. There were emotional and physical hardships as well. She had periods of intense sadness and anger. Several times she became very weak, but she received transfusions as an outpatient and responded with marked improvement of symptoms. She had two serious infections that responded surprisingly well to empirical courses of oral antibiotics. After three tumultuous months, there were two weeks of relative calm and well-being, and fantasies of a miracle began to surface.

Unfortunately, we had no miracle. Bone pain, weakness, fatigue, and fevers began to dominate her life. Although the hospice workers, family members, and I tried our best to minimize the suffering and promote comfort, it was clear that the end was approaching. Diane's immediate future held what she feared the most—increasing discomfort, dependence, and hard choices between pain and sedation. She called up her closest friends and asked them to come over to say goodbye, telling them that she would be leaving soon. As we had agreed, she let me know as well. When we met, it was clear that she knew what she was doing, that she was sad and frightened to be leaving, but that she would be even more terrified to stay and suffer. In our tearful goodbye, she promised a reunion in the future at her favorite spot on the edge of Lake Geneva, with dragons swimming in the sunset.

Two days later her husband called to say that Diane had died. She had said her final goodbyes to her husband and son that morning and asked them to leave her alone for an hour. After an hour, which must have seemed an eternity, they found her on the couch, lying very still and covered by her favorite shawl. There was no sign of struggle. She seemed to be at peace. They called me for advice about how to proceed. When I arrived at their house, Diane indeed seemed peaceful. Her husband and son were quiet. We talked about what a remarkable person she had been. They seemed to have no doubts about the course she had chosen or about their cooperation, although the unfairness of her illness and the finality of her death were overwhelming to us all.

I called the medical examiner to inform him that a hospice patient had died. When asked about the cause of death, I said, "acute leukemia." He said that was fine and that we should call a funeral director. Although acute leukemia was the truth, it was not the whole story. Yet any mention of suicide would have given rise to a police investigation and probably brought the arrival of an ambulance crew for resuscitation. Diane would have become a "coroner's case," and the decision to perform an autopsy would have been made at the discretion of the medical examiner. The family or I could have been subject to criminal prosecution, and I to professional review, for our roles in support of Diane's choices. Although I truly believe that the family and I gave her the best care possible, allowing her to define her limits and directions as much as possible, I am not sure the law, society, or the medical profession would agree. So I said "acute leukemia" to protect all of us, to protect Diane from an invasion into her past and her body, and to continue to shield society from the knowledge of the degree of suffering that people often undergo in the process of dying. Suffering can be lessened to some extent, but in no way eliminated or made benign, by the careful intervention of a competent, caring physician, given current social constraints.

Diane taught me about the range of help I can provide if I know people well and if I allow them to say what they really want. She taught me about life, death, and honesty and about taking charge and facing tragedy squarely when it strikes. She taught me that I can take small risks for people that I really know and care about. Although I did not assist in her suicide directly, I helped indirectly to make it possible, successful, and relatively painless. Although I know we have measures to help control pain and lessen suffering, to think that people do not suffer in the process of dying is an illusion. Prolonged dying can occasionally be peaceful, but more often the role of the physician and family is limited to lessening but not eliminating severe suffering.

I wonder how many families and physicians secretly help patients over the edge into death in the face of such severe suffering. I wonder 15 how many severely ill or dying patients secretly take their lives, dying alone in despair. I wonder whether the image of Diane's final aloneness will persist in the minds of her family, or if they will remember more the intense, meaningful months they had together before she died. I wonder whether Diane struggled in that last hour, and whether the Hemlock Society's way of death by suicide is the most benign. I wonder why Diane, who gave so much to so many of us, had to be alone for the last hour of her life. I wonder whether I will see Diane again, on the shore of Lake Geneva at sunset, with dragons swimming on the horizon.

Topics for Critical Thinking and Writing

1. Do you think Diane's refusal to fight her leukemia (para. 5) shows— dare we say it?—that she was a coward in the face of death? When Dr. Quill says (para. 7) that her refusal "disturbed me," is he tacitly and evasively making just such a judgment? Or do his reservations have another source and meaning?

2. Dr. Quill refers to his belief that a patient has the "right to die with as much control and dignity as possible" (para. 7). How would you define human dignity? What do you think are appropriate criteria for dying with dignity? What is an undignified death—and how can it be avoided? Write an essay of 500 words explaining these ideas.

3. The reader is told that Diane wanted to "maintain control of herself and her own dignity during the time remaining to her" (para. 8; cf. para. 11). What is the evidence that she succeeded or failed? Explain in an essay of 250 words whether you think she succeeded, or not.

4. Did Quill lie to the county medical examiner when he reported Diane's death as caused by "acute leukemia" (para. 13)? If not, why not? If he did, do you think the lie was justified? Why, or why not? Write an essay of 500 words in which you argue for your position on these questions.

> For topical links related to the issue of euthanasia, see the companion Web site:
> **www.bedfordstmartins.com/barnetbedau.**

23

Juvenile Crime: How Should Society Respond?

Rita Kramer

Rita Kramer, the author of At a Tender Age: Violent Youth and Juvenile Justice *(1988) and other books, published this article in the* Wall Street Journal *(May 27, 1992).*

Juvenile Justice Is Delinquent

Anyone who reads newspapers or watches TV is familiar with scenes of urban violence in which the faces of those who rob and rape, maim and kill get younger and younger. On the streets, in the subways, and even in the schools, juvenile crime has taken on a character unthinkable when the present justice system was set up to deal with it. That system, like so many of the ambitious social programs designed in the '60s, has had unintended results. Instead of solving society's ills, it has added to them.

The juvenile justice system now in place in most parts of the country is not very different from New York's Family Court. Originally conceived to protect children (defined by different states as those under age sixteen, seventeen, or eighteen) who ran afoul of the law, it was designed to function as a kind of wise parent providing rehabilitation.

The 1950s delinquent, who might have been a shoplifter, a truant, or a car thief, would not be treated like an adult criminal. He was held to be, in the wording of the New York statute, "not criminally responsible . . . by reason of infancy." He would be given a hearing (not a trial) closed to the press and public and the disposition (not a sentence) would remain sealed, so the juvenile would not be stigmatized by youthful indiscretion. The optimistic belief was that under the guidance of social workers he would undergo a change of character.

It was a dream destined to become a nightmare. In the early 1960s, the character of juvenile court proceedings underwent a radical transformation. Due process was interpreted to grant youthful "respondents" (not defendants) not only the services of a lawyer, but also the protections the criminal justice system affords adults, who are liable to serious penalties if found guilty.

In the hands of Legal Aid Society lawyers (and sometimes sympathetic judges), the juvenile system focuses on the minutiae of procedural technicalities at the expense of fact-finding, in order to achieve the goal of "getting the kid off." The question is not whether a teenage boy has beaten up a homeless old man, shot a storekeeper, or sodomized a little girl. He may even admit the act. The question is whether his admission can be invalidated because a police officer forgot to have him initial his responses to the Miranda warnings in the proper place or whether the arresting officer had probable cause to search him for the loaded gun that was found on him.

It has become the lawyer's job not only to protect his young client from punishment, but from any possibility of rehabilitation in the system's various facilities. The best interests of the child or adolescent have been reinterpreted to mean his legal rights, even when the two are in opposition. He now has the right to continue the behavior that brought him into the juvenile court, which he leaves with the knowledge that his behavior had no real negative consequences to him.

Even when there are consequences, they are mild indeed, a fact not lost on his peers. Eighteen months in a facility that usually has TV, a basketball court, and better food and medical care than at home is the worst that all but the most violent repeat offenders have to fear in New York. The system, based on a person's age and not his crimes, fails either to restrain or retrain him.

As juvenile courts were changing, so were juvenile criminals. As recently as the early '70s, the majority of cases before children's and family courts were misdemeanors. In New York City, the most common charge was "jostling," pickpocketing without physical contact. By 1991, robbery—a charge that involves violence against people—had outpaced drug-related offenses as the largest category of crimes by juveniles. Between 1987 and 1991, the fastest-growing crime by juveniles was loaded gun possession, and metal detectors and spot police checks had become routine in some inner-city high schools.

Cases of violent group assault—"kids" causing serious physical injury "for fun"—had increased dramatically. Predatory behavior was becoming a form of entertainment for some of the urban young, white as well as black and Hispanic. Last year, according to Peter Reinharz, chief of New York City's Family Court Division, 85 percent of the young offenders brought into Family Court were charged with felonies. "These are dangerous people," Mr. Reinharz says. "We hardly ever see the nonviolent any more."

Nationwide figures compiled by the FBI's Uniform Crime Reporting   10
Program in 1990 showed the highest number of arrests of youth for violent offenses—homicide, armed robbery, rape, aggravated assault—in the more than twenty-five years that the statistics have been compiled. Juvenile arrest rates, after rising steadily from the mid-1960s through the 1970s, remained relatively constant until the 1989–90 statistics revealed a 26 percent increase in the number of youths arrested for murder and non-negligent manslaughter, while arrests for robbery had increased by 16 percent, and those for aggravated assault by 17 percent.

But the system still defines juveniles as children rather than as criminals, a distinction that makes little sense to their victims or to the rest of the public. Family Court turns the worst juvenile offenders over to the adult system for trial, but they are still sentenced as juveniles.

When anything does happen it's usually so long after the event, so short in duration, and so ineffective that it's no wonder the young men who rob, maim, rape, and terrorize don't perceive those actions as having any serious consequences. Eighty percent of chronic juvenile offenders (five or more arrests) go on to adult criminal careers.

Is it possible to change these young criminals? And what should be done to protect the community from them?

The first necessity is legislation to open juvenile court proceedings to the public and the press. It makes no sense to protect the privacy of those who are a palpable menace to their neighbors or scruple about "stigmatizing" them. A repeat offender should know the authorities will make use of his past record in deciding what to do with him next time. At present, a young habitual criminal is born again with a virgin record when he reaches the age to be dealt with by the adult system.

Opening court records would also make it possible to undertake follow-up studies to find out what works and what doesn't in the various detention facilities and alternative programs designed to rehabilitate. Taxpayers have a right to know what outcomes they are getting for the $85,000 a year it costs to keep a juvenile offender in a secure facility in New York state. 15

Intervention should occur early, while there is still time to try measures that might make a difference. First offenders should be required to make restitution to their victims or perform community service. A second arrest should be followed by stronger measures. For those who have families who undertake to be responsible for them, there should be intensive supervision by well-trained probation officers with manageable caseloads. For those who require placement out of the home, it should include intensive remedial schoolwork and practical training in some job-related skill. The youth should remain long enough for such efforts to have some hope of proving effective.

Sanctions should be swift and sure. Once arrested, a court appearance should follow without delay, preferably on the same day, so that there is a clear connection made between behavior and its consequences. Placement in appropriately secure institutions, locked away from the community for definite periods of time, should be the immediate and inevitable response to repeated acts of violence. And incarceration should involve some form of work that helps defray its cost to the community, not just a period of rest and recreation. Young criminals should know that is what they can expect.

A growing cadre of violent teenage boys are growing up with mothers who are children and no resident fathers. What they need most of all is structure and supervision. We may not be able to change attitudes, but we can change behavior. While there is no evidence that any form of therapy can really change a violent repeat offender into someone with empathy for others, it has been demonstrated that the one thing that can result in impulse control is the certainty of punishment.

The present system actually encourages the young to continue their criminal behavior by showing them that they can get away with it. No punishment means a second chance at the same crimes. A significant number of boys arrested for violent crimes were out on parole at the time of the arrest.

They think of the system as a game they can win. "They can't do 20 nothing to me, I ain't sixteen yet" is a repeated refrain in a system that breeds contempt for the law and for the other institutions of society. It is time to acknowledge its failure and restructure the system so that "juvenile justice" ceases to be an oxymoron. We owe it to the law-abiding citizens who share the streets and schools with the violent few to protect the rights of the community and not just those of its victimizers.

Topics for Critical Thinking and Writing

1. In her fifth paragraph Kramer indicates her distress with a system that allows a guilty juvenile to be released because the police failed to comply with some procedural details. But the requirement that police comply with details was generated by police misconduct. If adults can be released because the police fail to act according to all of the standard procedures, why shouldn't juveniles also be released for the same reasons?

2. Kramer says (para. 6) that the current juvenile justice system has made it the defendant's lawyer's job "to protect his young client . . . from any possibility of rehabilitation." Explain her reasoning.

3. Kramer says (para. 7) that if a youthful offender is put away, it is "in a facility that usually has TV, a basketball court, and better food and medical care than at home." Let's assume she is right. Why do you suppose the government provides TV, a basketball court, and better food and medical care than the youth probably has at home? If you were running things, what would you change? Would you, for instance, do away with television sets or provide medical care that is below the national standard? Explain.

4. "But the system," Kramer says in paragraph 11, "still defines juveniles as children rather than as criminals, a distinction that makes little sense to their victims." Does she have a point here? Or might it also be said that of course the victims are distressed, but the feelings of the victims are irrelevant to a society that is trying to deal intelligently and humanely with youthful offenders? Explain.

5. In paragraph 18 Kramer says that "it has been demonstrated that the one thing that can result in impulse control is the certainty of punishment." She offers no evidence. Do you accept her statement? Why, or why not (because it seems self-evident? because it is a principle that guides your own life?)? Explain.

6. Kramer says (para. 19): "The present system actually encourages the young to continue their criminal behavior by showing them that they can get away with it." What evidence, if any, does she offer to support this sentence? If she does not support it, should she have, or is it self-evident?

7. In her final paragraph Kramer indicates that the reason we must reform the system is "to protect the rights of the community." Earlier in the essay, however, she also indicated the desirability of helping youthful offenders to reform their conduct. What do you make of the fact that she does not continue this point into her final paragraph?

8. Kramer reports a sudden increase (26 percent) in violent crimes by juveniles in the years 1989 and 1990 (para. 10). If your library receives the FBI's annual *Uniform Crime Reports* or the *Sourcebook of Criminal Justice Statistics,* consult one of these sources and determine whether in the years since 1990 juvenile crime has continued to increase, has leveled off, or has decreased.

9. In paragraph 18 Kramer mentions the "growing cadre of violent teenage boys . . . growing up with . . . no resident fathers." She ends this paragraph insisting on the "certainty of punishment" for such boys. Why do you suppose she doesn't instead recommend measures to punish the fathers of these boys for neglecting them?

10. List the measures Kramer recommends to decrease juvenile crime. Does she cite any evidence to show that these reforms really would reduce such crime? Can you think of reasons to believe in or to doubt their efficacy?

George Horan

In this letter to the Los Angeles Times *(July 13, 1992), Father George Horan, Catholic chaplain for the Los Angeles County's Men's Central Jail, responds to a news item reporting that persons convicted of three felonies — even if a felony was committed while a minor — will be sentenced to life in prison.*

Juvenile Felonies

Re "Juvenile Felonies Can Now Count toward Three Strikes," July 4:

Perhaps before we certify juveniles to adult court, or before we sentence someone to spend the rest of his or her life in prison under three-strikes for juvenile crimes, we should undergo a "fitness" hearing to determine whether we have met our responsibilities: Did this juvenile have two nurturing, loving, and caring parents? Was he or she abused, sexually, physically, or emotionally? Did teachers and school administrators take time to make sure this juvenile mastered basic skills? Was the religious community a welcoming and accepting part of this child's life? Did this juvenile receive appropriate medical care?

I believe that everyone, no matter what age, should be held accountable to victims and to the community for violent criminal activity and that incarceration is sometimes appropriate as punishment or to protect others. But before we are permitted to throw away the life of a juvenile into an adult prison cell, we must be held to certain standards in our community treatment of this child, otherwise we must consider ourselves unfit to throw away the life of this child like so much useless trash.

Those of us who are Christian might spend some time reflecting on the words of our Gospel, "What you do to the least of these, you do to me" (Matthew 25:40).

Father George Horan
Catholic Chaplain
L.A. County's Men's Central Jail

Topics for Critical Thinking and Writing

1. Suppose a skeptic were to reply to Horan that it's all very well to suggest that the community be subjected to a "'fitness' hearing" (para. 1) before sentencing juveniles to prison for long terms, but that society cannot really deal with the complex, lengthy, and controversial investigations such hearings would require. How might Horan reply?

2. The three paragraphs of Horan's letter (we are disregarding the opening citation) might be published in any sequence — the first paragraph might be last, for instance — and the letter would still be coherent. Explain and evaluate the structure of the letter as it stands.

Robert L. Sexton

Robert L. Sexton teaches economics at Pepperdine University, in Malibu, California. We reprint an article that originally appeared in the Journal of Social, Political, and Economic Studies *in January 1996.*

Tackling Juvenile Crime

Last year a 14-year-old drug runner in the District of Columbia shot and killed three people on the same day. The drug dealer for whom the juvenile worked was convicted of felony murder, but the juvenile served a total of only 26 months in juvenile detention for the three killings. He was back on the street taunting local police before his 17th birthday.

Washington Post, July 31, 1991

A vast majority of states in the United States do not gain jurisdiction over young offenders in criminal courts until they reach the age of eighteen (Hamparian, 1987). As a result, the law has little control over juvenile crime and there is much recidivism. This situation could be ameliorated without the use of additional scarce resources by redefining the age at which offenders are treated as adults to, say 16, or lower yet if it is politically feasible. According to Siegel and Senna (1991, p. 418), numerous authorities in the field believe that most youths over the age of 14 can be held accountable for their own actions.

All regulations require enforcement if they are to be effective. While this is a rather obvious point, much research proceeds as if somehow regulations are self-enforcing. The present paper illustrates the advantage of recognizing the role of enforcement costs in the selection of statute stringency. In most contexts, those setting standards (the legislature) rarely consider enforcement efforts, perhaps tacitly assuming full compliance. The failure to consider enforcement costs in statute writing may be regarded as an institutional inefficiency that may be a result of the formal separation from the legislative policing units.

This paper is an extension of analysis by Becker (1968) of optimal trade-offs between fines and real resource-using enforcement efforts. This analysis has particular relevance to statutes as well, since one may well be able to reduce the number of crimes, especially those of a recidivist nature, committed by juveniles by lowering the age at which one defines adults in criminal courts.[1]

According to Becker (1968), heavy enforcement costs are expensive and may not be essential. That is, a policy of high fines and constant or lower enforcement costs could reduce average crime rates. Increased fines are relatively costless as a social solution to the enforcement of criminal behavior. The solution presented in this paper is quite similar, but instead of increased fines as a deterrent, the age at which juveniles would be tried as adults would be lowered.

THE GROWING JUVENILE CRIME PROBLEM

A recent report from the U.S. Department of Justice highlights the alarming increase in juvenile crime from 1988–1992—aggravated assault cases were up 80 percent; homicides increased 55 percent; robberies went up 52 percent; and forcible rape cases rose by 27 percent. In 1990, more than a third of all murders in the United States were committed by individuals under the age of 21. Among 18-year-olds the homicide rate doubled between 1985 and 1992. During that same period the rate for 16-year-olds increased 138 percent while homicidal rates for adults declined by 20 percent. Thus, most of the increase in homicides from 1985 to 1992 was due to a surge in killings by the young. The rates of juvenile crime differ markedly between different ethnic groups, but the principles here discussed would apply equally to juvenile offenders irrespective of ethnic background.

[1]For a mathematical treatment of this issue, see Sexton, Graves, and Lee, "Lowering the Age Requirement for Adult Courts: An Analytical Framework," *Atlantic Economic Journal*, Volume 21, Number 4, December 1990.

Overall, the American juvenile crime rate is rising. According to Uniform Crime Reports, juvenile arrests were up 11 percent from 1993–1994. Even more disturbing is the fact that while 15- and 16-year-olds make up only a small proportion of our population, they commit a large percentage of all violent crime. There are presently 40 million children now under the age of ten, and projections show the number of teenagers increasing by almost 25 percent by the year 2005. If the current trend continues, violent crimes will reach horrific levels.

The fact that teenagers are committing more violent acts at an earlier age is undoubtedly responsible for the rising growth in the nation's violent-crime rate. And the age cohort responsible for much of the recent youth violence is the smallest it has been in recent years. But what can effectively be done about juvenile crime when federal and state governments are under severe budgetary constraints?

LOWERING THE AGE REQUIREMENT ON ADULT COURTS

The influence of drugs, drug money, gang-related incidents, and the ease of acquiring a lethal weapon are all contributing factors to the juvenile crime problem. In the past, we have tried two approaches to reducing the inordinate amount of crime: increasing the budget for law enforcement and imposing more stringent statutes and stiffer penalties on those apprehended. However, one particularly effective way to increase the sentence or fine for juvenile offenses that has not been considered seriously is to reduce the age requirement for adult courts.

According to a 1989 U.S. Department of Justice Report, "The Juvenile Courts' Response to Violent Crimes," only 5 percent of juveniles are tried in the federal system as adults. Lowering the age requirement to say 15 or 16 years of age for "adult" courts might be an effective strategy for all cases. The cost to society of a trial is the same regardless of the age of the criminal, and it is no secret that juvenile courts are considerably more lenient than adult courts. In light of the persistent recidivism among juvenile criminals, it makes sense that if tried as adults they could be given longer sentences and required to spend time in state prisons rather than in juvenile detention centers.

One serious problem in dealing with young offenders is the lack of data regarding serious crimes committed before the age of 18. Under current laws in most states, felonies and misdemeanors committed by minors are not made public. Hence, many apparent first-time offenders appearing in adult courts have in fact committed many serious crimes as juveniles, but the evidence is not available. If offending youths of 16 years and above were tried as adults, their criminal records would be disclosed at an earlier age. This is important because past criminal records have a lot to do with current sentencing. Another advantage of having greater access to juvenile criminal records is that prosecutors can increase the probability of convicting the right person.

The Bureau of Justice Statistics has estimated that 38 percent of inmates incarcerated for murder in a state prison in 1986 had a prior juvenile conviction. The same study found that 54 percent of state prisoners convicted of robbery as adults had a juvenile record.

There is also a need to maintain an up-to-date computerized record of criminal history data that is reliable and accurate so that judges can detain dangerous suspects before trial. Lacking this information, serious criminals are too often released pending trial and put back on the streets where they commit fresh crimes while awaiting trial for their previous offense.

Access to the crime records of youthful repeat offenders at an earlier age, and the threat of spending more time in prison, rather than less time in a juvenile detention center, would have a significant deterrent effect and would protect innocent citizens from much violent juvenile crime. Since the vast majority of states do not grant adult jurisdiction over young offenders in criminal courts until the age of 18, it is not surprising that criminal activity is so prevalent among the young, since they pay such a low "price" for it.

Some might be concerned that first-time juvenile offenders might be prosecuted to the full extent of the law in adult courts, spend time in state prisons, and consequently turn into hardened criminals. However, this is not a compelling argument, since most juvenile crime is committed by repeat juvenile offenders and sentencing for first-time juvenile offenders, even if tried in adult courts, would not be the same as that for repeat offenders. It is true that it would be possible to lower the juvenile crime rate by enforcing existing laws more rigorously, but this is unlikely to happen because of the high cost of additional police equipment and a larger police force, and a simple adjustment of the age at which youths may be tried as adults would achieve massive benefits at virtually no additional cost.

JUVENILE COURTS

The critics of harsher punishments for juveniles may ask, "Why are   15 we attacking the Juvenile Court? Do we really believe that the adult courts will produce better results. Or that youths coming out of the state penitentiary are more likely to become model citizens than kids coming out of a juvenile institution?" We need to look at the facts:

Firstly, the number of juveniles waived to adult courts is relatively small, and until the adult court age is lowered (at the very least for repeat juvenile offenders) we will not accurately know the impact that adult courts would have on crime rates. However, the fact is that research appears to confirm that waivers of youths into adult courts for serious offenses increase the certainty of punishment. A study by Donna Martin

Hamparian (1987) found that 91 percent of the waived youths were convicted.

Secondly, the most serious or intractable juveniles are not currently always those who are waived to adult courts. A recent analysis of Florida juveniles that were waived to adult courts revealed that "very few of the juveniles were dangerous or repeat offenders." Rather most were charged with property offenses. These findings are consistent with those of M. A. Bortner (1986), who found that remanded juveniles were not typically dangerous or retractable. Consequently, it sometimes appears, as in the Florida case, that adult courts are lenient on juveniles when these have been arrested for non-violent crimes. It may be assumed that they would be more severe with those arrested for violent crimes, especially if they have already had a serious crime record.

Thirdly, is the fact that most juvenile crime is committed by "chronic offenders." According to Marvin Wolfgang's well-known study of Philadelphia youths, chronic juvenile offenders committed 65–75 percent of serious crimes (Wolfgang, 1987). Furthermore, the hardcore juvenile offenders committed most of the crimes and were rarely punished. He found that only 14 percent of the first five arrests resulted in punishment. And those few who were imprisoned committed fewer and less serious crimes after their release. This study casts serious doubt on the juvenile justice system's ability to rehabilitate chronic offenders.

And chronic offenders appears to be the serious problem. In 1988, Beck et al. (1988) in a Bureau of Justice Statistics study that focused on state-operated juvenile facilities, found that almost 43 percent of the juveniles detained had been arrested more than 5 times and more than 20 percent had been arrested more than 10 times. Again the conclusion from this study confirms that the arrest and juvenile court experience did little to deter repeat offenders. A 1990 study found that youths who spent 14 months in a California Youth Authority institution had a re-arrest rate of 70 percent. All of these studies cast serious doubt on the juvenile justice system's ability to rehabilitate chronic offenders.

The juvenile justice system has their counterpart to adult court plea 20 bargaining. Department of Justice statistics reveal that only 60 percent of all children arrested by the police are actually referred to juvenile courts. The others are either warned, parents are notified, or they are referred to social service programs.

If we are to make any progress towards controlling violent juvenile crime, court records on juveniles must be opened. Repeat juvenile offenders should know that the authorities have access to past records and will use that information when handing down their sentences. After all, don't taxpayers have a right to know what they're getting for $85,000 a year—the cost of keeping a juvenile offender in a secure facility in the state of New York?

The average cost per year for adult prisoners is $28,000. Most would probably agree that in order to keep repeat juvenile offenders off the streets we need to open juvenile court records, enforce strict laws, and apply firm uniform sentencing provisions. This will have two effects: One, keep chronic juvenile offenders in prison for longer periods of time, and two, deter others from pursuing careers as criminals.

GUNS

According to a National Institute of Justice study guns are increasingly involved in juvenile homicides. From 1976 to 1985 a gun was used in roughly 60 percent of juvenile homicides. In 1992 the number of juvenile murders using guns doubled while those homicides without guns remained stable. Statutes that mandate even tighter handgun control and/or automatic waiver to adult courts for juveniles in possession of handguns could help mitigate the rise in handgun use.

CONCLUSIONS

For the most part, politicians have ignored strategies that would minimize enforcement costs in the "war against juvenile crime." Since these costs are substantial, there is a clear economic advantage in favor of introducing a lower adult court age limit rather than far more costly and less well targeted increases in police budgets. And the recent explosion in teenage violence by many of those less than 18 years of age might lead to a political acceptance of an adult court age limit of 16 years or younger for juvenile offenders.

Of course, it would be naive to exclusively blame the juvenile justice 25 system for the increases in violent juvenile crime. And any solution to the problem will have to also address issues such as education and family values. Educational vouchers, especially in the inner cities where they are needed the most might be an effective first step. A voucher program could give rise to alternative high school programs that include vocational training. It is time that we look for some fresh, cost-controlled solutions, to handling the growth in juvenile crime.

REFERENCES

Beck, A. J., S. A. Kline, and L. Greenfield. (1988). *Survey of Youth in Custody, 1987.* Washington, DC: U.S. Department of Justice, Bureau of Justice Statistics.

Becker, G. S. (1968). "Crime and Punishment: An Economic Approach." *Journal of Political Economy*, 2:76, 169–217.

Bortner, M. A. (1986). "Traditional Rhetoric, Organizational Realities: Remand of Juveniles to Adult Courts." *Crime and Delinquency*, 32, 53–73.

Hamparian, Donna, et al. (1982, rev. 1987). *Youth in Adult Courts.* Washington, DC: U.S. Government Printing Office.

Sexton, Robert, Philip Graves, and Dwight Lee. (1990). "Lowering the Age Requirement for Adult Courts: An Analytical Framework." *Atlantic Economic Journal*, 21:4, 67–70.

Siegel, Larry J., and Joseph Senna. (1991). *Juvenile Delinquency: Theory, Practice and Law* (3rd ed.). St. Paul: West.

Wolfgang, Marvin E., Terence P. Thornberry, and Robert B. Figlio. (1987). *From Boy to Man: From Delinquency to Crime.* Chicago: University of Chicago Press.

Topics for Critical Thinking and Writing

1. What does Sexton mean by "statute stringency" (para. 2; cf. para. 8)? Is he for or against it?

2. Sexton assumes throughout his article that greater severity in punishment will reduce juvenile crime and that too little severity has increased juvenile crime in recent years. Does he give any evidence that supports these assumptions? What are the objectionable costs (not necessarily economic costs) of basing punitive policies and programs for youths under eighteen on these assumptions?

3. From time to time the newspapers report that a judge has refused to sentence a young offender to adult prison because of the virtual certainty that the offender will be victimized—assaulted or raped—by older prisoners. Is the likelihood of such abuse a good argument against Sexton's proposal to lower the age at which a person can be tried as an adult?

4. How might Sexton reply to the following objection: "You favor reducing the age at which *all* juveniles (defined as anyone under eighteen) can be treated as adults for the purpose of trial and punishment, yet you admit that the evidence shows that *most* of the violent crime committed by juveniles is done by 'chronic offenders' (paras. 18–19), who constitute only a *small* fraction of all juvenile offenders. Why jeopardize the future of all juvenile offenders to punish more severely the few?"

For topical links related to the issue of juvenile crime, see the companion Web site:
www.bedfordstmartins.com/barnetbedau.

24

Privacy:
What Are Its Limits?

Amitai Etzioni

Amitai Etzioni, university professor at George Washington University, previously taught sociology at Columbia University for twenty years. He is the editor of The Responsive Community *and the author of more than a dozen books, the most recent of which is* The Limits of Privacy *(1999). Etzioni served as senior advisor to the White House from 1979 to 1980 and as the president of the American Sociological Association from 1994 to 1995.*

Less Privacy Is Good for Us (and You)

Despite the fact that privacy is not so much as mentioned in the Constitution and that it was only shoehorned in some thirty-four years ago, it is viewed by most Americans as a profound, inalienable right.

The media is loaded with horror stories about the ways privacy is not so much nibbled away as it is stripped away by bosses who read your e-mail, neighbors who listen in on your cell phones, and E-Z passes that allow tollbooth operators to keep track of your movements. A typical headline decries the "End of Privacy" (Richard A. Spinello, in an issue of *America,* a Catholic weekly) or "The Death of Privacy" (Joshua Quittner, in *Time*).

It is time to pay attention to the other half of the equation that defines a good society: concerns for public health and safety that entail some rather justifiable diminution of privacy.

Take the HIV testing of infants. New medical data—for instance, evidence recently published by the prestigious *New England Journal of Medicine*—show that a significant proportion of children born to mothers who have HIV can ward off this horrible disease but only on two conditions: that their mothers not breast-feed them and that they immediately be given AZT. For this to happen, mothers must be informed that they have HIV. An estimated two-thirds of infected mothers are unaware. However, various civil libertarians and some gay activists vehemently oppose such disclosure on the grounds that when infants are tested for HIV, in effect one finds out if the mother is a carrier, and thus her privacy is violated. While New York State in 1996, after a very acrimonious debate, enacted a law that requires infant testing and disclosure of the findings to the mother, most other states have so far avoided dealing with this issue.

Congress passed the buck by asking the Institute of Medicine (IOM) to   5 conduct a study of the matter. The IOM committee, dominated by politically correct people, just reported its recommendations. It suggested that all pregnant women be asked to consent to HIV testing as part of routine prenatal care. There is little wrong with such a recommendation other than it does not deal with many of the mothers who are drug addicts or otherwise live at society's margins. Many of these women do not show up for prenatal care, and they are particularly prone to HIV, according to a study published in the American Health Association's *Journal of School Health*. To save the lives of their children, they must be tested at delivery and treated even if this entails a violation of mothers' privacy.

Recently a suggestion to use driver's licenses to curb illegal immigration has sent the Coalition for Constitutional Liberties, a large group of libertarians, civil libertarians, and privacy advocates, into higher orbit than John Glenn ever traversed. The coalition wrote:

> This plan pushes us to the brink of tyranny, where citizens will not be allowed to travel, open bank accounts, obtain health care, get a job, or purchase firearms without first presenting the proper government papers.
> The authorizing section of the law . . . is reminiscent of the totalitarian dictates by Politburo members in the former Soviet Union, not the Congress of the United States of America.

Meanwhile, Wells Fargo is introducing a new device that allows a person to cash checks at its ATM machines because the machines recognize faces. Rapidly coming is a whole new industry of so-called biometrics that uses natural features such as voice, hand design, and eye pattern to recognize a person with the same extremely high reliability provided by the new DNA tests.

It's true that as biometrics catches on, it will practically strip Americans of anonymity, an important part of privacy. In the near future, a person who acquired a poor reputation in one part of the country will find it much more difficult to move to another part, change his name, and gain a whole fresh start. Biometrics see right through such assumed identities. One may hope that future communities will become more tolerant of such people, especially if they openly acknowledge the mistakes of their past and truly seek to lead a more prosocial life. But they will no longer be able to hide their pasts.

Above all, while biometrics clearly undermines privacy, the social benefits it promises are very substantial. Specifically, each year at least half a million criminals become fugitives, avoiding trial, incarceration, or serving their full sentences, often committing additional crimes while on the lam. People who fraudulently file for multiple income tax refunds using fake identities and multiple Social Security numbers cost the nation between $1 billion and $5 billion per year. Numerous divorced parents escape their financial obligations to their children by avoiding detection when they move or change jobs. (The sums owed to children are variously estimated as running between $18 billion to $23 billion a year.) Professional and amateur criminals, employing fraudulent identification documentation to make phony credit card purchases, cost credit card companies and retail businesses an indeterminate number of billions of dollars each year. The United States loses an estimated $18 billion a year to benefit fraud committed by illegal aliens using false IDs. A 1998 General Accounting Office report estimates identity fraud to cost $10 billion annually in entitlement programs alone.

People hired to work in child care centers, kindergartens, and 10 schools cannot be effectively screened to keep out child abusers and sex offenders, largely because when background checks are conducted, convicted criminals escape detection by using false identification and aliases. Biometrics would sharply curtail all these crimes, although far from wipe them out singlehandedly.

The courts have recognized that privacy must be weighed against considerations of public interest but have tended to privilege privacy and make claims for public health or safety clear several high hurdles. In recent years these barriers have been somewhat lowered as courts have become more concerned with public safety and health. Given that these often are matters of state law and that neither legislatures nor courts act in unison, the details are complex and far from all pointing in one direction. But, by and large, courts have allowed mandatory drug testing of those who directly have the lives of others in their hands, including pilots, train engineers, drivers of school buses, and air traffic controllers, even though such testing violates their privacy. In case after case, the courts have disregarded objections to such tests by civil libertarians who argue that such tests constitute "suspicionless" searches, grossly violate privacy, and—as the ACLU puts it—"condition Americans to a police state."

All this points to a need to recast privacy in our civic culture, public policies, and legal doctrines. We should cease to treat it as unmitigated good, a sacred right (the way Warren and Brandeis referred to in their famous article and many since) or one that courts automatically privilege.

Instead, privacy should rely squarely on the Fourth Amendment, the only one that has a balance built right into its text. It recognizes both searches that wantonly violate privacy ("unreasonable" ones) and those that enhance the common good to such an extent that they are justified, even if they intrude into one's privacy. Moreover, it provides a mechanism to sort out which searches are in the public interest and which violate privacy without sufficient cause, by introducing the concept of warrants issued by a "neutral magistrate" presented with "probable cause." Warrants also limit the invasion of privacy "by specification of the person to be seized, the place to be searched, and the evidence to be sought." The Fourth may have become the Constitutional Foundation of privacy a long time ago if it was not for the fact that *Roe v. Wade* is construed as a privacy right, and touching it provokes fierce opposition. The good news, though, is that even the advocates of choice in this area are now looking to base their position on some other legal grounds, especially the Fourteenth Amendment.

We might be ready to treat privacy for what it is: one very important right but not one that trumps most other considerations, especially of public safety and health.

Topics for Critical Thinking and Writing

1. Etzioni says that the right of privacy "was only shoehorned" into the Constitution "some thirty-four years ago" (para. 1)—that is, in 1965. Look up the U.S. Supreme Court case of *Griswold v. Connecticut,* and write a 250-word essay explaining how this right figured in that decision.

2. Who are the "politically correct people" to whom the author refers (para. 5)? What determines whether a policy or a practice is politically correct?

3. Etzioni obviously favors some invasions of privacy—but on what grounds? Where and why does he draw the line between justifiable and unjustifiable invasions of privacy? Write a 250-word essay answering that question.

4. The author takes for granted the value of privacy—that is, the value each of us attaches to keeping truths about ourselves from becoming public knowledge. Is the value of privacy only or mainly in its role as a means to other ends? Or is there something about privacy of intrinsic value in itself? Explain your own views in an essay of 500 words.

5. Who should bear the burden of persuasion: those who want to violate someone's privacy or those who do not want their privacy invaded, even for a good cause?

6. Ask your reference librarian to help you locate the "famous article" by Samuel Warren and Louis Brandeis (para. 12) that initially and influentially defended the right to privacy. What were the circumstances in which they defended this right, and what arguments did they offer to that purpose?

Simson Garfinkel

Simson Garfinkel was born in Cambridge, Massachusetts, in 1965, where he still resides. Educated at the Massachusetts Institute of Technology and Columbia University, he is a high-tech entrepreneur and journalist. Among his eight books are PGP: Pretty Good Privacy *(1995) and* Database Nation: The Death of Privacy in the Twenty-First Century *(2000), whose first chapter we partly reprint here.*

Privacy under Attack

WHAT DO WE MEAN BY PRIVACY?

. . . I wish I had a better word [than *privacy*] to express the aspect of individual liberty that is under attack by advanced technology as we enter the new millennium.

For decades, people have warned that pervasive databanks and surveillance technology are leading inevitably to the death of privacy and democracy. But these days, many people who hear the word *privacy* think about those kooks living off in the woods with their shotguns: these folks get their mail at post office boxes registered under assumed names, grow their own food, use cash to buy what they can't grow for themselves, and constantly worry about being attacked by the federal government—or by space aliens. If you are not one of these people, you may well ask, "Why should I worry about my privacy? I have nothing to hide."

The problem with this word *privacy* is that it falls short of conveying the really big picture. Privacy isn't just about hiding things. It's about self-possession, autonomy, and integrity. As we move into the computerized world of the twenty-first century, privacy will be one of our most important civil rights. But this right of privacy isn't the right of people to close their doors and pull down their window shades—perhaps because they want to engage in some sort of illicit or illegal activity. It's the right of people to control what details about their lives stay inside their own houses and what leaks to the outside.

To understand privacy in the next century, we need to rethink what privacy really means today:

- It's not about the man who wants to watch pornography in complete anonymity over the Internet. It's about the woman who's afraid to use the Internet to organize her community against a proposed toxic dump—afraid because the dump's investors are sure to dig through her past if she becomes too much of a nuisance.

- It's not about people speeding on the nation's highways who get automatically generated tickets mailed to them thanks to a computerized speed trap. It's about lovers who will take less joy in walking around city streets or visiting stores because they know they're being photographed by surveillance cameras everywhere they step.

- It's not about the special prosecutors who leave no stone unturned in their search for corruption or political misdeeds. It's about good, upstanding citizens who are now refusing to enter public service because they don't want a bloodthirsty press rummaging through their old school reports, computerized medical records, and e-mail.

- It's not about the searches, metal detectors, and inquisitions that have become a routine part of our daily lives at airports, schools, and federal buildings. It's about a society that views law-abiding citizens as potential terrorists, yet does little to effectively protect its citizens from the real threats to their safety.

Today, more than ever before, we are witnessing the daily erosion of personal privacy and freedom. We're victims of a war on privacy that's being waged by government eavesdroppers, business marketers, and nosy neighbors.   5

Most of us recognize that our privacy is at risk. According to a 1996 nationwide poll conducted by Louis Harris & Associates, one in four Americans (24 percent) has "personally experienced a privacy invasion"[1]—up from 19 percent in 1978. In 1995, the same survey found that 80 percent of Americans felt that "consumers have lost all control over how personal information about them is circulated and used by companies."[2] Ironically, both the 1995 and 1996 surveys were paid for by Equifax, a company that earns nearly two billion dollars each year from collecting and distributing personal information.

We know our privacy is under attack. The problem is that we don't know how to fight back.

THE ROLE OF TECHNOLOGY

Today's war on privacy is intimately related to the dramatic advances in technology we've seen in recent years. . . . [U]nrestrained technology ends privacy. Video cameras observe personal moments; computers store personal facts; and communications networks make personal information widely available throughout the world. Although some specialty technology may be used to protect personal information and autonomy, the overwhelming tendency of advanced technology is to do the reverse.

Privacy is fundamentally about the power of the individual. In many ways, the story of technology's attack on privacy is really the story of how institutions and the people who run them use technology to gain control over the human spirit, for good and ill. That's because technology by itself doesn't violate our privacy or anything else: it's the people using this technology and the policies they carry out that create violations.

Many people today say that in order to enjoy the benefits of modern 10 society, we must necessarily relinquish some degree of privacy. If we want the convenience of paying for a meal by credit card or paying for a toll with an electronic tag mounted on our rear view mirror, then we must accept the routine collection of our purchases and driving habits in a large database over which we have no control. It's a simple bargain, albeit a Faustian one.

I think this tradeoff is both unnecessary and wrong. It reminds me of another crisis our society faced back in the 1950s and 1960s — the environmental crisis. Then, advocates of big business said that poisoned rivers and lakes were the necessary costs of economic development, jobs, and an improved standard of living. Poison was progress: anybody who argued otherwise simply didn't understand the facts.

Today we know better. Today we know that sustainable economic development *depends* on preserving the environment. Indeed, preserving the environment is a prerequisite to the survivability of the human race. Without clean air to breathe and clean water to drink, we will all surely die. Similarly, in order to reap the benefits of technology, it is more important than ever for us to use technology to protect personal freedom.

Blaming technology for the death of privacy isn't new. In 1890, two Boston lawyers, Samuel Warren and Louis Brandeis, argued in the *Harvard Law Review* that privacy was under attack by "recent inventions and business methods." They contended that the pressures of modern society required the creation of a "right of privacy," which would help protect what they called "the right to be let alone."[3] Warren and Brandeis refused to believe that privacy had to die for technology to flourish. Today, the Warren-Brandeis article is regarded as one of the most influential law review articles ever published.[4] And the article's significance has increased with each passing year, as the technological invasions that worried Warren and Brandeis have become more commonplace.

Privacy-invasive technology does not exist in a vacuum, of course. That's because technology itself exists at a junction between science, the market, and society. People create technology to fill specific needs, real or otherwise. And technology is regulated, or not, as people and society see fit.

Few engineers set out to build systems designed to crush privacy and 15 autonomy, and few businesses or consumers would willingly use or purchase these systems if they understood the consequences. What happens more often is that the privacy implications of a new technology go unnoticed. Or if the privacy implications are considered, they are misunderstood. Or if they are understood correctly, errors are made in implementation. In practice, just a few mistakes can turn a system designed to protect personal information into one that destroys our secrets.

How can we keep technology and the free market from killing our privacy? One way is by being careful and informed consumers. But I believe that government has an equally important role to play.

THE ROLE OF GOVERNMENT

With everything we've heard about Big Brother, how can we think of government as anything but the enemy of privacy? While it's true that federal laws and actions have often damaged the cause of privacy, I believe that the federal government may be our best hope for privacy protection as we move into the new millennium.

The biggest privacy failure of American government has been its failure to carry through with the impressive privacy groundwork that was laid in the Nixon, Ford, and Carter administrations. It's worth taking a look back at that groundwork and how it may serve us today.

The 1970s were a good decade for privacy protection and consumer rights. In 1970, Congress passed the Fair Credit Reporting Act. Elliot Richardson, who at the time was President Nixon's secretary of health, education, and welfare (HEW), created a commission in 1973 to study the impact of computers on privacy. After years of testimony in Congress, the commission found all the more reason for alarm and issued a landmark report in 1973.

The most important contribution of the Richardson report was a bill of 20 rights for the computer age, which it called the Code of Fair Information Practices (see [the box on p. 676]). That Code remains the most significant American thinking on the topic of computers and privacy to this day.

The biggest impact of the HEW report wasn't in the United States, but in Europe. In the years after the report was published, practically every European country passed laws based on these principles. Many created data protection commissions and commissioners to enforce the laws.[5] Some believe that one reason for this interest in electronic privacy was Europe's experience with Nazi Germany in the 1940s. Hitler's secret police used the records of governments and private organizations in the

CODE OF FAIR INFORMATION PRACTICES

The Code of Fair Information Practices is based on five principles:

- There must be no personal data record-keeping systems whose very existence is secret.
- There must be a way for a person to find out what information about the person is in a record and how it is used.
- There must be a way for a person to prevent information about the person that was obtained for one purpose from being used or made available for other purposes without the person's consent.
- There must be a way for a person to correct or amend a record of identifiable information about the person.
- Any organization creating, maintaining, using, or disseminating records of identifiable personal data must assure the reliability of the data for their intended use and must take precautions to prevent misuses of the data.

Source: Department of Health, Education, and Welfare, 1973.

countries he invaded to round up people who posed the greatest threat to the German occupation; postwar Europe realized the danger of allowing potentially threatening private information to be collected, even by democratic governments that might be responsive to public opinion.

But here in the United States, the idea of institutionalized data protection faltered. President Jimmy Carter showed interest in improving medical privacy, but he was quickly overtaken by economic and political events. Carter lost the election of 1980 to Ronald Reagan, whose aides saw privacy protection as yet another failed Carter initiative. Although several privacy protection laws were signed during the Reagan/Bush era, the leadership for these bills came from Congress, not the White House. The lack of leadership stifled any chance of passing a nationwide data protection act.

In fact, while most people in the federal government were ignoring the cause of privacy, some were actually pursuing an antiprivacy agenda. In the early 1980s, the federal government initiated numerous "computer matching" programs designed to catch fraud and abuse. (Unfortunately, because of erroneous data, these programs often penalized innocent individuals.[6]) In 1994, Congress passed the Communications Assistance to Law Enforcement Act, which gave the government dramatic new powers for wiretapping digital communications. In 1996, Congress passed a law requiring states to display Social Security numbers on driver's licenses, and another law requiring that all medical patients in the United States be issued unique numerical identifiers, even if they paid their own bills. Fortunately, the implementation of those 1996 laws has been delayed, largely thanks to a citizen backlash.

Continuing the assault, both the Bush and Clinton administrations waged an all-out war against the rights of computer users to engage in private and secure communications. Starting in 1991, both administrations floated proposals for use of "Clipper" encryption systems that would have given the government access to encrypted personal communications. President Clinton also backed the Communications Decency Act (CDA), which made it a crime to transmit sexually explicit information to minors—and, as a result, might have required Internet providers to deploy far-reaching monitoring and censorship systems. When a court in Philadelphia found the CDA unconstitutional, the Clinton administration appealed the decision all the way to the Supreme Court—and lost.

Finally, the U.S. government's restrictions on the export of encryp- 25 tion technology have effectively restrained the widespread use of this technology for personal privacy protection within the United States.

As we move forward into the twenty-first century, the United States needs to take personal privacy seriously again. The final chapter of this book explores ways our government might get back on track, and suggests a federal privacy agenda for the twenty-first century.

FIGHTING BACK

Privacy is certainly on the ropes in America today, but so was the environment in 1969. Thirty years ago, the Cuyahoga River in Ohio caught on fire and Lake Erie was proclaimed dead. Times have certainly changed. Today it's safe to eat fish that are caught in the Cuyahoga, Lake Erie is alive again, and the overall environment in America is the cleanest it's been in decades.

There are signs around us indicating that privacy is getting ready to make a comeback as well. The war against privacy is commanding more and more attention in print, on television, and on the Internet. People are increasingly aware of how their privacy is compromised on a daily basis. Some people have begun taking simple measures to protect their privacy, measures like making purchases with cash and refusing to provide their Social Security numbers—or providing fake ones. And a small but growing number of people are speaking out for technology *with* privacy, and putting their convictions into practice by developing systems or services that protect, rather than attack, our privacy.

Over the past few decades, we've learned that technology is flexible, and that when it invades our privacy, the invasion is usually the result of a conscious choice. We now know, for instance, that when a representative from our bank says:

> I'm sorry that you don't like having your Social Security number
> printed on your bank statement, but there is no way to change it.

that representative is actually saying:

> Our programmers made a mistake by telling the computer to put your Social Security number on your bank statement, but we don't think it's a priority to change the program. Take your business elsewhere.

Today we are relearning this lesson and discovering how vulnerable 30 business and government can be to public pressure. Consider these three examples from the past decade:

- *Lotus Development Corporation.* In 1990, Lotus and Equifax teamed up to create a CD-ROM product called "Lotus Marketplace: Households" that would have included names, addresses, and demographic information on every household in the United States, so small businesses could do the same kind of target marketing that big businesses have been doing since the 1960s. The project was canceled when more than 30,000 people wrote to Lotus demanding that their names be taken out of the database.

- *Lexis-Nexis.* In 1996, Lexis-Nexis suffered an embarrassing public relations debacle when it was revealed that their P-TRAK database service was publishing the Social Security numbers of most U.S. residents. Thousands of angry consumers called the company's switchboard, effectively shutting it down for a week. Lexis-Nexis discontinued the display of Social Security numbers 11 days after the product was introduced.

- *Social Security Administration (SSA).* In 1997, it was the U.S. Social Security Administration's turn to suffer the public's wrath. The press informed U.S. taxpayers that the SSA was making detailed tax history information about them available over the Internet. The SSA argued that its security provisions—requiring that taxpayers enter their name, date of birth, state of birth, and mother's maiden name—were sufficient to prevent fraud. But tens of thousands of Americans disagreed, several U.S. senators investigated the agency, and the service was promptly shut down. When the service was reactivated some months later, the detailed financial information could not be downloaded over the Internet.

Technology is not autonomous; it simply empowers choices made by government, business, and individuals. One of the big lessons of the environmental movement is that it's possible to shape these choices through the political process. This, I believe, justifies the involvement of government on the privacy question.

NOTES

1. Harris-Equifax, *Consumer Privacy Survey.* Conducted for Equifax by Louis Harris and Associates in association with Dr. Alan Westin of Columbia University, Equifax, Atlanta, GA, 1996.

2. Harris-Equifax, *Consumer Privacy Survey.* Conducted for Equifax by Louis Harris and Associates in association with Dr. Alan Westin of Columbia University, Equifax, Atlanta, GA, 1995.
3. Samuel Warren and Louis Brandeis, "The Right of Privacy," *Harvard Law Review* 4 (1890), 193. Although the phrase "the right to be let alone" is commonly attributed to Warren and Brandeis, the article attributes the phrase to the nineteenth-century judge Thomas M. Cooley.
4. Turkington et al., *Privacy: Cases and Materials.*
5. David H. Flaherty, *Protecting Privacy in Surveillance Societies* (University of North Carolina Press, 1989). In 1989, David H. Flaherty, the privacy commissioner of British Columbia, published a revised set of Twelve Data Protection Principles and Practices for Government Personal Information Systems. These 12 principles are (emphasis supplied by David Flaherty in May 1997):

> The principles of *publicity and transparency* (openness) concerning government personal information systems (no secret databanks).
> The principles of *necessity* and relevance governing the collection and storage of personal information.
> The principle of reducing the collection, use, and storage of personal information to the maximum extent possible.
> The principle of *finality* (the purpose and ultimate administrative uses for personal information need to be established in advance).
> The principle of establishing and requiring *responsible keepers* for personal information systems.
> The principle of controlling *linkages,* transfers, and interconnections involving personal information.
> The principle of requiring informed *consent* for the collection of personal information.
> The principle of requiring accuracy and completeness in personal information systems.
> The principle of *data trespass,* including civil and criminal penalties for unlawful abuses of personal information.
> The requirement of special rules for protecting sensitive personal information.
> The right of access to, and correction of, personal information systems.
> The *right to be forgotten,* including the ultimate anonymization or destruction of almost all personal information.

6. One federal match program compared a database that had the names of people who had defaulted on their student college loans with another database that had the names of federal employees. The match then automatically garnished the wages of the federal employees to pay for the defaulted loans. The problem with this match, and others, was that there were many false matches that were the result of incorrect data or similar-sounding names. And because the wages were automatically garnished, victims of this match were required to prove their innocence—that is, to prove that the match was erroneous.

Topics for Critical Thinking and Writing

1. What's wrong with the word *privacy* that leads the author to "wish [he] had a better word" for his purposes (para. 1)?

2. Does the author think that everyone has something to hide and that the best way to keep it hidden is to protect our privacy? Or does he believe there are other reasons for protecting our privacy? Explain what you think about his position on privacy in an essay of 500 words.

3. Given what the author says about control (para. 3) and power (para. 9), complete the following definition: "A person's privacy is violated by another person's intrusion if and only if . . . "

4. What is "a Faustian bargain" (para. 10), and how does it come by that name?

5. The author mentions "autonomy" (para. 15) as related to but distinct from privacy. Explain autonomy so that its relation to privacy is clear. (Hint: Is a person's privacy a necessary condition of that person's autonomy? Could a person be fully autonomous and yet have little or no privacy?)

6. Summarize in a sentence the story the author tells about how privacy has fared in national politics over the past several decades (paras. 22–30).

7. Drawing only on the first five paragraphs, set forth your impression of the writer. Does he seem intelligent? Knowledgeable? Engaging? Is he the sort of person you might want to meet? Why, or why not? (In your answer, be sure to make specific references to the text.)

8. Has Garfinkel pretty much convinced you that (a) there is a serious problem and (b) you can take actions that will solve or at least reduce the problem? Explain.

Nadine Strossen

Nadine Strossen, president of the American Civil Liberties Union, published the following essay on IntellectualCapital.com in 1998. It evoked an abundant response, from which we reprint (following her essay) a selection of e-mails, including a response by Strossen.

Everyone Is Watching You

In 1949, a young English author named Eric Blair opened his latest novel with a scene in an apartment building where on each landing, a poster with an "enormous face gazed from the wall. It was so contrived that the eyes follow you about when you move."

You probably know Blair better by his pen name — George Orwell. The book, of course, was *1984,* and the poster bore the now-clichéd caption, "Big Brother is watching you." But even Blair's vivid imagination did not accurately predict the future. Today, the more appropriate caption would be, "Everyone Is Watching You."

"Everyone" includes banks, automated teller machines, parking lots, shopping centers, stadiums, and convenience stores. Also government offices, schools, businesses, and workplaces. Whether cruising through a toll booth, or buying a gallon of milk, or strolling in the park, private citizens increasingly are forfeiting their privacy whenever they venture out of their homes — or even, for that matter, while we are at home.

Consider the chilling story of Barbara Katende, who recently told the *New York Times* that she had spotted a camera on a rooftop about 200 yards from her apartment. A rooftop she had seen, but not thought about, every time she stood before her sixth-floor window with the blinds open, lounging around in her underwear or in nothing at all. The camera monitors traffic. But it has a powerful zoom lens and can turn in any direction. A technician who controls traffic cameras from a Manhattan studio told the *Times*, "If you can see the Empire State Building, we can see you."

Cities all over the country, including our nation's capital, are installing cameras to record citizens' every coming-and-going on the streets, sidewalks, and parks. In Tempe, Arizona, officials struck a rotating camera — nicknamed "Sneaky Peak" — atop the municipal building. 5

Why? Why not? "It's the biggest hit on our Web page," a Tempe official told the *Washington Post*.

Even more chillingly, new "face recognition" technology makes it possible to instantly identify individuals who are captured on video through complicated searches of facial images stored in government databases. As CNN commented, this is "a wonderful way for government to spy on its citizens who went to the antigovernment rally."

Why the mania for surveillance? Many claim that we need to trade privacy for safety. But even many law-enforcement officials believe, based on their actual experience, that video surveillance does not effectively detect or deter crime.

A number of cities that previously used video cameras — for example, Miami Beach, Florida, Newark, New Jersey, White Plains, New York, and Fredricksburg, Virginia — have abandoned them, concluding that they were not worth the expense. Surveillance cameras that had been mounted for 22 months in New York City's Times Square led to only 10 arrests before they were dismantled, prompting the *New York Times* to dub them, "one of the greatest flops along the Great White Way."

Even in Blair's United Kingdom, where video-surveillance cameras 10 are the most pervasive and powerful, the government itself has concluded that they have not demonstrably improved public safety. As noted by a report in the *Telegraph*, "A series of studies, including one by

the Home Office itself, suggest that" video surveillance "has merely
pushed crime into others areas or that its initial impact fades rapidly."

Just last September, the police department in Oakland, California,
urged the city council to reject a video-surveillance project that the police department itself initially had recommended, but about which it had
second thoughts—in terms of both privacy and efficiency. As Oakland's
police chief told the city council, "There is no conclusive way to establish
that the presence of video surveillance cameras resulted in the prevention or reduction of crime."

Moreover, responding to a detailed letter of concern from the American Civil Liberties Union, the Oakland city attorney concluded that a
"method of surveillance may be no greater than that which can be
achieved by the naked eye. [T]he California Supreme Court has held
that 'precious liberties' . . . do not simply shrink as the government acquires new means of infringing upon them.'"

I applaud the California supreme court's ruling, which echoes the
pro-privacy principles first declared by U.S. Supreme Court Justice Louis
Brandeis in a famous 1928 dissent. Unfortunately, the Brandeisian view
of privacy—which he defined as "the right to be let alone, the most
comprehensive of rights"—remains a minority position among current
judges. The Supreme Court, for example, has held that the Constitution
only protects expectations of privacy that society considers "reasonable."
This creates a downward spiral: The more government and others invade
our privacy, the fewer "reasonable expectations" of privacy we have,
which means that government and others may intrude even further into
our privacy, etc., etc.

Given the foreshortened view of constitutional privacy that is currently enforced by our courts, we have to develop other avenues of legal
protection—most importantly, federal and state statutes. Here, too, we
now have only a patchwork of protection.

We must, therefore, take political and other direct action to remedy 15
the current lack of legal protection against the ubiquitous electronic
"peeping Toms." Urge your community to oppose cameras in public
places. If you notice a camera in an odd place, find out why it is there
and what it is supposed to be recording. Tell businesses that record every
transaction on camera that you will not be shopping there anymore. Before taking a job, let the employer know that you object to secret taping.
And, most importantly, urge your elected officials to introduce laws limiting surveillance.

E-mail Responses to
Nadine Strossen

Here we give a selection of e-mail responses that Strossen's article evoked. Typographical errors have not been corrected.

5/28/98

Dave

We have had the cop on the corner for over a hundred years, watching. He had a circle of vision of about 200 yards diameter. If the young lady in the story had lived in that 200 yard circle, she would have been observed by the government. What has changed is that the circle of vision is now about 2000 yards diameter. That and the cop on the corner of 50–100 years ago would have walked over to the womans house and ask her to act responsibly. All a camera can do is replace 100 cops on the corner with one. The garantee of the government is to be secure in our person and our homes, and it was done to provide for the pursuit of happiness. A camera can help to provide that security and that avenue of pursuit. The real question I have is this: is the decision of police departments to abandon video surveilance an outcome of Rodney King?

5/29/98

Merwyn R. Markel

There still are some situations where individuals may have no reasonable expectation of privacy. These include public areas and unshaded 6th floor windows in urban areas, where they may easily be seen, and may want to be seen, by others. Government has as much right to post cameras as to patrol police officers in the former former areas, and for some strange reason I can't get too concerned about people parading semi-nude and nude and then complaining when they are observed in the latter areas.

5/29/98

Merwyn R. Markel

By insisting government curtail its observation in public areas does ACLU really want to protect the right of persons to conduct criminal activities out of sight of law enforcement personnel?

5/29/98

Wilson Lee, San Diego, CA

Merwyn, I don't think the ACLU is arguing that criminals should be allowed to commit crimes, but rather that there are better ways—which don't infringe upon our privacy rights—to enforce laws against criminal behavior than using blanket video surveillance. Those cameras are pretty much equivalent to warrantless searches of innocent people.

5/30/98
Merwyn R. Markel
   Wilson Lee: I don't think you adequately dealt with my first post. Cameras in public places don't "search" innocent people; they mearly record what is there for anyone present to see. I can't escape the conclusion that the ACLU just wants goverment to give criminals what the ACLU considers a sporting chance. Of course without using video cameras, government has and continues to unjustifiably if not illegally intrude on the privacy of its citizens. Some of the ways it does so include: (a) gathering information about them that they do not vluntarily disclose, whether or not it then discloses that information to unauthorized parties for political or other unauthorized purposes, and (b) obtaining information from citizens under the promise that it will not be used to their detrament, and then breaking that promise. Category (a) includes EEOC's requirement that all employers of 15 or more persons gather and report the percentages of "minorities" and females they employ, and the 500 FBI files on political opponents that just happened to be turned over to White House personnel. Example (b) includes a government agency asking an employment applicant to disclose his race and sex on a document it promises to use only for "statistical puropses" and then managing to associate it with the applicant anyway to deny him a job he was better qualified for than the successful applicant. Now why, do you suppose, Nadine and the ACLU don't mention such intrusions of our privacy?

5/30/98
Wilson Lee, San Diego, CA
   Merwyn: Perhaps calling surveillance cameras warrantless searches may have been hyperbolic on my part. But I still think we have some reasonable expectations of privacy, even in public places. And I'm not sure a surveillance camera is equivalent in power to posting police officers. For one, a police officer wouldn't be able to search databases to instantly identify the faces of those being surveilled. The point is not that criminals will get away with more without surveillance. That may be true, to a certain extent. But having some crimes go unpunished costs our society less than giving the government more power. Even if you ignore the issue of constitutional rights, on purely pragmatic terms, surveillance fails the test because its efficacy in preventing crime is unproven, simlar to how capital punishment fails as a deterrent (but that's a debate for another article). I agree that we should be able to keep

control over our private information. I can't speak for the ACLU, but I imagine that the lack of mention of such other privacy violations in the article does not imply that they don't take issue with them.

5/31/98
Merwyn R. Markel

Wilson Lee: You say "surveilence fails the test [of fairness or constitutionality, I assume] because its efficacy in preventing crime is unproven." I humbly suggest that we don't need "proof" to justify doing what seems reasonable, even when its constutionality is challenged. I'd like to see a judicial decision that says otherwise. It is reasonable to believe that many if not all criminals would not commit their crimes if they thought they were being observed doing so by law enforcement officers or recorded doing so by law enforcement cameras. It is also resonable to believe that such surveilence will assist government law enforcement personnel to detect and apprehend criminals, which is still a prime responsibility of government. The "proof" Nadine mentions is, assumining her claims about it are correct, merely "proof" that in specific past situations electronic surveilence was found—correctly or incorrectly—to deter crime less than certain government officials thought justified by the cost. That says nothing about the efficacy of other past or future surveilence programs or situations. The efficacy of science to prove something today and the opposite tomorrow hardly needs proof. For similar reasons, I welcome future discussions about capital punishment.

6/1/98
Nadine Strossen

A couple of you . . . make a point that is often raised in opposition to pro-privacy arguments, namely: If you've got nothing to hide, why should you care about privacy? This is a variation on the theme that only criminals would benefit from increasing privacy protection. Nothing could be further from the truth. I pride myself on being a law-abiding person, and on holding myself to high moral standards even in arenas where no one can observe my behavior. In other words, it is extremely important to me that I conduct myself consistent with my own moral standards especially when I am being judged only by my own conscience, rather than for the benefit of some outside observer/evaluator. . . . So, when I want to stop someone from observing my behavior, it's not because I believe my behavior is illegal or immoral. Rather, it's because my behavior is my private business—and that of the others with whom I affirmatively choose to share it. Think of this analogy: I'm not ashamed of my nude body, but that doesn't mean I want government or private Peeping Toms to look at it! In short, I—and every other law-abiding citizen—has something very important to hide: our privacy.

Topics for Critical Thinking and Writing

1. Do you consider surveillance cameras in "banks, automated teller machines, parking lots, shopping centers, stadiums, and convenience stores" (para. 3) an unreasonable invasion of your privacy? Explain.

2. Strossen refers to a "famous 1928 dissent" by Justice Brandeis (para. 13); the case is *Olmstead v. United States*. With the help of your reference librarian, locate a copy of this case, and read Brandeis's dissent. Then summarize it in an essay of 250 words.

3. The U.S. Supreme Court has held, Strossen tells us, "that the Constitution only protects expectations of privacy that society considers 'reasonable'" (para. 13). Look back at paragraph 4, in which Strossen tells us that Barbara Katende sometimes stood nude before her sixth-floor window. Would you say that Katende had a "reasonable" expectation of privacy? Why, or why not?

4. In "Dave," a comparison with "50–100 years ago" is offered. How convincing do you find this argument? Why?

5. "Dave" also mentions Rodney King. Who is he, and why is it apt to mention him in the context?

6. Two of the letter writers, "Dave" and "Merwyn R. Markel" draw an analogy between police observation and camera observation. Do you think the analogy is a good one, or not? Explain your view in an essay of 250 words.

7. Do you agree with "Wilson Lee" (5/29/98) that surveillance "cameras are pretty much equivalent to warrantless searches of innocent people"? In your response, consider also the later postings that we print.

8. "Merwyn R. Markel" ends his posting of 5/30/98 with a question. What do you think his own answer to the question would be?

9. "Wilson Lee" (5/30/98) says that "having some crimes go unpunished costs our society less than giving the government more power." How would you support or refute this assertion?

10. Write a response to Nadine Strossen's posting of 6/1/98 (but don't send it). Consider especially the analogy that she offers.

11. Strossen recommends that you "tell businesses that record every transaction on camera that you will not be shopping there anymore" (para. 15). Is this reasonable advice? Are you prepared to follow it? Why, or why not?

Judith Wagner DeCew

Judith Wagner DeCew is a professor of philosophy and associate dean at Clark University, Worcester, Massachusetts. She has served on the faculty at the Massachusetts Institute of Technology and has been a research fellow at the Bunting Institute and also at Harvard Law School. Her book In Pursuit of Privacy: Law, Ethics, and the Rise of Technology *(1995), from which this selection is drawn, was nominated for the Herbert Jacob Book Prize of the Law and Society Association.*

The Feminist Critique of Privacy

. . . There has been extensive debate among philosophers and legal theorists about what privacy means, whether and how it can be defined, and the scope of protection it can and should afford. Reactions to recent Supreme Court confirmation hearings have made it clear that many in the public and in Congress are unwilling to give up the privacy protection they currently enjoy. They view privacy, as I do, as a valuable shield for protecting a sphere within which we can act free of scrutiny and intrusion by others.

In contrast, many feminists have called attention to the "darker side of privacy," citing its potential to shield domination, repression, degradation, and physical harm to women and others without power. It might be thought that this feminist critique of privacy is powerful enough to defeat my thesis that we can and must view privacy as a meaningful concept with significant value for a wide range of claims associated with tort, Fourth Amendment, and other constitutional law. I argue . . . , to the contrary, that we may support many concerns raised by the feminist critique of privacy without abandoning the concept of privacy and the significant benefits a strong right of privacy affords.

Perhaps the most prominent version of this critique of privacy is articulated by Catharine MacKinnon. She begins by observing that

> the idea of privacy embodies a tension between precluding public exposure or governmental intrusion on the one hand, and autonomy in the sense of protecting personal self-action on the other. This is a tension, not just two facets of one right. The liberal state resolves this tension by identifying the threshold of the state at its permissible extent of penetration into a domain that is considered free by definition: the private sphere. By this move the state secures "an inviolable personality" by

The full text has been edited, and the endnotes have accordingly been renumbered. [Editors' note.]

ensuring "autonomy of control over the intimacies of personal
identity."[1] The state does this by centering its self-restraint on body and
home, especially bedroom. By staying out of marriage and the family —
essentially meaning sexuality, that is, heterosexuality — from contraception through pornography to the abortion decision, the law of privacy
proposes to guarantee individual bodily integrity, personal exercise of
moral intelligence, and freedom of intimacy. But have women's rights
to access to those values been guaranteed? The law of privacy instead
translates traditional liberal values into the rhetoric of individual rights
as a means of subordinating those rights to specific social imperatives.[2]

MacKinnon is of course correct that privacy has developed in law to protect both (i) an "individual interest in avoiding disclosure of personal
matters," as well as limiting governmental intrusion on and regulation of
these matters, and (ii) an "interest in independence in making certain
kinds of important decisions" regarding body, home, and lifestyle.[3] Many
legal theorists have taken these to be clearly separable interests, whereas
I have argued [elsewhere] that there are deeper similarities and connections between the two than is usually acknowledged.[4] Following most
legal theorists, MacKinnon treats protection from public exposure and
governmental intrusion as separate from and in tension with protection
of autonomous decision making. Perhaps her reason is that she finds
these goals incompatible: safeguarding (i) precludes guaranteeing (ii).

A serious difficulty, MacKinnon believes, is that the state merges
these two interests by drawing the line where state intrusion is no longer
justified at those matters concerning body, home, and the heterosexual
family, asserting that in this way it is protecting personal autonomy. But,
MacKinnon continues, the move to ensure autonomy in intimate relations with respect to the body, home, and family relations does nothing
to help women, since the values of individual bodily integrity, exercise
of moral intelligence, and freedom of intimacy are not guaranteed to
women. The fundamental flaw, according to MacKinnon, is that underlying privacy protection in the law is a liberal ideal of the private: as long
as the public does not interfere, autonomous individuals interact freely
and equally. But this presumes that women are, like men, free and
equal, an assumption MacKinnon finds patently false. When the private
is defined as personal, intimate, autonomous, and individual, it is on her
view defined by reference to characteristics most feminists believe
women do not possess. The law of privacy thus presumes a liberal conception of rights with false assumptions about women. Moreover, privacy is just one instance where our legal system fails to recognize and
take into account the preexisting oppression and inequality of women.
For MacKinnon, privacy represents yet another domain where women
are deprived of power and are deprived of recourse under the law, all on
the suspect theory that "the government best promotes freedom when it
stays out of existing social relationships."[5]

MacKinnon continues her argument in even stronger language: 5

> For women the measure of the intimacy has been the measure of the op-
> pression. This is why feminism has had to explode the private. This is
> why feminism has seen the personal as the political. The private is public
> for those for whom the personal is political. In this sense, for women
> there is no private, either normatively or empirically. Feminism con-
> fronts the fact that women have no privacy to lose or to guarantee.
> Women are not inviolable. Women's sexuality is not only violable, it is —
> hence, women are — seen in and as their violation. To confront the fact
> that women have no privacy is to confront the intimate degradation of
> women as the public order. The doctrinal choice of privacy in the abor-
> tion context thus reaffirms and reinforces what the feminist critique of
> sexuality criticizes: the public/private split.[6]

MacKinnon appears to be making two distinct but related claims here.
The first is that women have no privacy, and hence protecting privacy
provides no benefit at all for women. Privacy protection may even be a
positive detriment to women, giving men the legal right to treat their
wives and partners (and children) unequally or even brutally.[7] The second claim is that feminism has demonstrated the importance of criticizing the split between public and private domains, and thus "has had to
explode the private." Let us consider each in turn.

Why is it that women have no privacy to lose or guarantee? Mac-
Kinnon's answer appears to be that because women are violable and violated, they have no zone of autonomy within which to control their
destinies. In particular, in the realm of sexuality, often viewed as a para-
digmatic example of the private, women do not have control. Men can
and often do maintain their power over women in such intimate circumstances. Although sexual intimacy, and activities within the home and
family, may be private in the sense of being withheld from public view
and shielded from governmental intrusion, they are not private in the
sense of being areas where women have control over their decision
making.

This argument is easily refuted. Note first that I have already shown,
contrary to MacKinnon, that although privacy law does in part protect
one's ability to make intimate and personal choices, it does not follow
that privacy is merely equivalent to autonomy or control over decision
making. Privacy and autonomy are distinct concepts and can and should
be differentiated.[8] Second, even if women do in fact often lose control in
the domain of intimate sexual relations, it does not follow that they have
no interest in the value of protecting a zone for autonomous decision
making. MacKinnon often repeats her claim that women have no
privacy that can be taken away. That women are in fact violated in private contexts, however, implies nothing about the worth of protecting a

zone within which they can have the power to limit intrusions and violations. In short, descriptive facts about actual limitations on privacy fail to imply anything about the normative value of seeking privacy protection for women.

MacKinnon's second point in this passage underscores the importance of rejecting the public/private split. The public/private distinction has captured the imagination of many feminist scholars. In fact a substantial portion of feminist theory and political struggle over the past two hundred years has been concerned with deconstructing the traditional notion, going back as far as Aristotle, of a public (male) political realm and a private (female) domestic realm.[9] Some of the most influential work in feminist political theory, philosophy, and legal theory takes this paradigm as its starting point in analyzing women's oppression. Carole Pateman goes so far as to claim that the public/private dichotomy "is, ultimately, what the feminist movement is about."[10] Yet despite this emphasis on the public/private distinction, it is difficult to clarify what the feminist critique of it entails. Feminist scholars such as Ruth Gavison and Pateman have made clear that there is no single or privileged version.[11] There are, to the contrary, a multiplicity of interwoven ways of understanding attacks on the public/private dichotomy. As regards MacKinnon in particular, it is not clear what she means by the need to "explode" the private. She appears to believe there is no distinction between public and private because there is no private realm for women at all. Does she also mean to say that there *should* be no public/private distinction? . . .

I believe we can agree with MacKinnon that whenever distinguishing public and private realms renders the domestic arena unsuitable for scrutiny, then the distinction works to the detriment of women. But what is the alternative? If the line between public and private is sometimes indeterminate, does it follow that nothing is or should be private? If there is no distinction between public and private, is everything public? Should every part of our lives be open to public appraisal? Indeed, on one interpretation of MacKinnon's view that we must "explode" the public/private distinction and that "the private is public," we must totally reject any realm of the private and apparently must conclude that everything is public. Thus rejection of the dichotomy is accomplished by collapsing the private into the public. Others have viewed this as a plausible reading of the feminist critique of privacy. For example, in a recent discussion of the public and private, Jean Bethke Elshtain describes one form of the feminist critique:

> In its give-no-quarter form in radical feminist argument, any distinction
> between the personal and the political was disdained. Note that the
> claim was not that the personal and political are interrelated in ways
> previously hidden by male-dominated political ideology and practice, or
> that the personal and political might be analogous to each other along
> certain axes of power and privilege. Rather, there was a collapse of one

into the other: The personal *is* political. Nothing personal was exempt from political definition, direction, and manipulation—not sexual intimacy, not love, not parenting. The total collapse of public and private as central distinctions in an enduring democratic drama followed, at least in theory. The private sphere fell under a thoroughgoing politicized definition. Everything was grist for a voracious publicity mill; nothing was exempt, there was nowhere to hide.[12]

A similar understanding of the feminist critique of privacy is echoed 10 by Ruth Gavison, who observes, "Usually, when the dichotomy between public and private is challenged, the argument is that all is (or should be) public." Yet Gavison quickly notes that feminists often equivocate when confronted with the implications of this rejection of the public/private split:

> But once we look at particular questions, it is rare to find feminists who argue consistently either that everything should be regulated by the state, or that the family and all other forms of intimate relationships should disappear in favor of public communities that . . . police the different ways in which members interact. When pushed, feminists explicitly deny this is their ideal. . . . [I]t is hard to specify even one context or dimension of the distinction in which the claim is that the whole category of the private is useless.[13]

Thus, even if women are often vulnerable and exploited in the private, domestic sphere, we may ask whether it follows that women have *no* interest in values of accessibility privacy as freedom from intrusion and expressive privacy as control over certain intimate and personal decisions and relationships. Are there *no* contexts in which women wish to keep the state out of their lives? MacKinnon often writes as if she would respond affirmatively, especially in her argument against privacy protection and in favor of equality analysis in feminist jurisprudence.[14] Nevertheless, I suspect the answer must be no, even for MacKinnon. Anita Allen has suggested that an analogy between privacy and liberty is helpful here. Just as the harm that results from the exercise of individual liberty does not lead to the rejection of liberty, similarly there is inadequate reason to reject privacy completely based on harm done in private.[15]

MacKinnon believes that the public/private distinction perpetuates the subjection of women in the domestic sphere, encouraging a policy of nonintervention by the state. She seems then to be making a further point as well: that male power over women is affirmatively embodied in privacy law. In the words of Susan Moller Okin, "The protection of the privacy of a domestic sphere in which inequality exists is the protection of the right of the strong to exploit and abuse the weak."[16] Batterers and child molesters rely on the shroud of secrecy that surrounds abuse to maintain their power. Thus many have worked to make the state more responsive to the abuse of women by rejecting legal privacy protection for the family. MacKinnon concludes,

> The right of privacy is a right of men "to be let alone" to oppress women one at a time. It embodies and reflects the private sphere's existing definition of womanhood. This instance of liberalism—applied to women as if they were persons, gender neutral—reinforces the division between public and private which is not gender neutral. It is an ideological division that lies about women's shared experience. . . . It polices the division between public and private, a very material division that keeps the private beyond public redress and depoliticizes women's subjection within it.[17]

The insights of this critique of privacy underscore how important it is to take care when viewing public and private categories differently. Feminists have correctly identified the ways in which the distinction can be dangerous if it is used to devalue the work of women in domestic roles, to silence them politically by categorizing them as having no public voice or value, and to allow the continuation of abuse and degradation under the cover of a private sphere unavailable for public censure. Thus MacKinnon and other feminists are right to urge that the distinction not be used to justify differential social and legal treatment of women. The "privacy" of the family, for example, should not be invoked to mask exploitation and battering of family members.

On one hand, it seems clear that defenders of privacy have too often ignored the role of *individual* male power, and sexual and physical abuse, in domestic contexts. On the other hand, focus on domestic violence ignores *state-sponsored* expressions of control over women. Consider, for example, intrusions such as government sterilization programs and the interventions involved in state control over welfare programs, including the withdrawal of benefits from women upon the birth of additional children.[18]

Consequently, this first interpretation of MacKinnon's sweeping critique may ultimately lead to a view stronger than she means to endorse. Rejecting the public/private distinction in this way obscures the difference between individual and institutional expressions of (male) power. On this reading, MacKinnon highlights the very real existence of domination by individual men over women, then argues for the rejection of privacy, and thereby implies everything should remain public. In doing so, she fails to address the need to differentiate between justified and unjustified uses of state power over individuals.[19] Governmental regulation might refer to reasonable laws regarding family matters, such as giving women the right to charge husbands with rape. Or it might mean that the state will reveal and regulate all the embarrassing details. There is, moreover, an important difference between a government that protects a woman's decision to charge her husband with rape and one that forces her to do so. Evaluating the justifiability of state intervention requires specifying what kind of regulation is at issue.[20] We may decry violations of women by individual men, and may well defend the role of the state to intervene—reasonably, firmly, and effectively—given evidence of domestic violence. Exploitation and abuse *should* be matters of public concern. But that need not imply that there is never value in making a distinction between public and private. We need not be committed to the view that there should be *no* limitations on state interference in individual, personal, and intimate affairs. We need not be pushed to agree that there should be *no* private realm within which women can live their lives free from state policing and intrusion.

In short, on this first interpretation of her critique of privacy, MacKinnon correctly emphasizes the need to limit individual violations and intrusions on women by men, but at the same time she underemphasizes the need to limit intrusions by the state.

Some may believe, however, that this first interpretation of MacKinnon's argument is unsympathetic and actually misses a central point of the feminist critique of privacy. Other readers of MacKinnon's critique dispute the view that rejecting the public/private split merely collapses one side of the dichotomy onto the other.[21] On this alternative interpretation, that is neither the feminist point nor an implication of the feminist position. To the contrary, feminists want to do away with the whole public/private dichotomy *as it has been understood in the past.* Thus feminists stress that they do not intend to have the state insinuating itself into the most intimate parts of people's lives. They are instead emphasizing that the state must stop ignoring the unbelievable abuses that have been protected in the name of privacy; this is, they believe, a position that is not captured by the public/private distinction as it has been known and used. According to this account, whether or not it is successfully captured by MacKinnon, feminists are talking about a position that bypasses the public/private distinction in a different way. . . .

Carole Pateman reiterates the feminist challenge to the separation and opposition between public and private spheres as central categories of political liberalism, where domestic family life is paradigmatically private. Pateman believes that "the dichotomy between the private and the public obscures the subjection of women to men within an apparently universal, egalitarian and individualist order. . . . The essential feminist argument is that the doctrine of 'separate but equal,' and the ostensible individualism and egalitarianism of liberal theory, obscure the patriarchal reality of a social structure of inequality and the domination of women by men."[22] But she emphasizes that feminists reject the claim that a public/private dichotomy is inevitable:

> They [feminists] argue that a proper understanding of liberal social life is possible only when it is accepted that the two spheres, the domestic (private) and civil society (public) held to be separate and opposed, are inextricably interrelated; they are the two sides of the single coin of

liberal-patriarchalism. . . . [Furthermore,] feminist critiques insist that
an alternative to the liberal conception must also encompass the relationship between public and domestic life.[23]

What is needed, on Pateman's view, is a feminist theoretical perspective that takes account of social relationships between men and women
within the context of interpretations of both the public and the private.
Work by political theorists such as John Stuart Mill,[24] as well as practical
experience from the feminist movement, has shown that women's place
in the private sphere cannot simply be augmented by extending to
women a role in the public sphere. The spheres are not additive but inte-
grally related. As Pateman notes, "These feminist critiques of the dichotomy between private and public stress that the categories refer to
two *interrelated* dimensions of the structure of liberal-patriarchalism;
they do not necessarily suggest that no distinction can or should be
drawn between the personal and political aspects of social life" (emphasis mine).[25] In sum, Pateman views the feminist critique of privacy as
stressing rejection of the dichotomy *as it has been understood,* but she concludes that the "separate" worlds of private and public life are closely interrelated and that both are necessary dimensions of a future, democratic
feminist social order. An adequate account, after acknowledging that
public and private are not necessarily in harmony, will develop a social
theory in which these categories are distinct but interrelated, rather than
totally separate or opposed.

Pateman's approach also highlights another dimension of feminist
perspectives on the public/private split. The well-known slogan "the personal is political" is often taken to be one of feminism's most significant
lessons. Whom one sleeps with, whether one has an abortion, whether
one seeks reproduction-assisting technologies, whether one is a religious
fundamentalist, and so on—all these choices have political implications.
Moreover, personal circumstances and family life are regulated and
structured by public factors, including legislation concerning rape and
sexuality, marriage and divorce, and policies on child care and welfare.
What feminists are trying to articulate in this strand of argument is that
the public/private dichotomy is misleading in critical ways because it fails
to reflect the interconnections between public and private. . . .

Clearly the feminist critique of privacy is multifaceted, and there is
no question that . . . Pateman acknowledge[s] the difficulties of the pub-
lic/private dichotomy and the damaging effects of accepting it as it has
been defended in the past. Both, however, appear to agree that absent
domination and abuse, there may be great value for women as well as
men in preserving a sanctuary where we can live free from scrutiny and
the pressure to conform, free to express our identities through relationships and choices about our bodies and lifestyles, without government
intrusion. Nevertheless, this clearly leads to a challenge for . . . Pateman,

as well as other feminists like Gavison, Allen, Elshtain, and myself, who are unwilling to jettison privacy completely. Given the lingering influence, in our culture and law, of the separate spheres analysis—that women belong in the home and men in public positions—it may take much time and effort to address the difficulties of preserving the two spheres in some form while extricating them from their gendered past and gendered connotations.[26] Perhaps MacKinnon believes that these difficulties are insurmountable.

It is now clear, however, that the feminist critique of privacy, on either of the interpretations I have examined, does not undermine my defense of a broad conception of privacy. Exploding the public/private distinction by collapsing it to leave all public is an unacceptable and even dangerous alternative, granting excessive power to the state. While we may often find it difficult to determine when official intervention is warranted, defending privacy as a shield to ward off unjustified individual and institutional intrusions in our personal lives remains an essential component of both our moral and legal systems if we are to preserve both peace of mind and bodily integrity. Alternatively, recognizing the insidious effects of the dichotomy, including the continued subordination of women, and rejecting the distinction as it has been understood in the past are compatible with retaining a meaningful concept of privacy in a theory of a new social order as envisioned by such feminists as . . . Pateman.

20

NOTES

1. Tom Gerety, "Redefining Privacy," 12 *Harvard Civil Rights–Civil Liberties Law Review* 233, 236 (1977).
2. Catharine MacKinnon, *Toward a Feminist Theory of the State* (Cambridge: Harvard University Press, 1989), 187. In this passage, she cites Kenneth I. Karst, "The Freedom of Intimate Association," 89 *Yale Law Journal* 624 (1980); Tom Grey, "Eros, Civilization, and the Burger Court," 43 *Law and Contemporary Problems* 83 (1980); and others.
3. Whalen v. Roe, 429 U.S. 589, 599, 600 (1977).
4. For example, see Louis Henkin, "Privacy and Autonomy," 74 *Columbia Law Review* 1410 (1974), and Hyman Gross, "The Concept of Privacy," 42 *New York Law Review* 34 (1967), on the separation of the interests. See also Judith Wagner DeCew, "The Scope of Privacy in Law and Ethics," *Law and Philosophy* 5 (1986), 145–173, on connections between them. Others who take this latter view include Ferdinand Schoeman, *Privacy and Social Freedom* (Cambridge: Cambridge University Press, 1992), and Julie Inness, *Privacy, Intimacy, and Isolation* (Oxford: Oxford University Press, 1992).
5. MacKinnon, *Toward a Feminist Theory of the State*, 164–165.
6. Ibid., 191.
7. The old rape shield laws, for example, made it impossible for women to claim their husbands had raped them.
8. See . . . William Parent, "Privacy, Morality, and the Law," *Philosophy and Public Affairs* 12 (1983), 269–288, for examples and discussion of this point.

9. See Carole Pateman, "Feminist Critiques of the Public/Private Dichotomy," in *The Disorder of Women: Democracy, Feminism, and Political Theory* (Stanford: Stanford University Press, 1989), 127, for example, on enfranchising women.

10. Ibid., 118. Also quoted in Susan Moller Okin, *Justice, Gender, and the Family* (New York: Basic Books, 1989), 111.

11. See Ruth Gavison, "Feminism and the Public/Private Distinction," 45 *Stanford Law Review* 1 (1992). She reviews and carefully assesses many different interpretations of the feminist critique of the public/private distinction.

12. Jean Bethke Elshtain, *Democracy on Trial* (New York: Basic Books, 1995), 43.

13. Gavison, "Feminism and the Public/Private Distinction," 28, 28–29.

14. Another who seems to endorse this view is Supreme Court Justice Ruth Bader Ginsberg, "Some Thoughts on Autonomy and Equality in Relation to *Roe v. Wade*," 63 *North Carolina Law Review* 375 (1985). See also Kenneth L. Karst, "Foreword: Equal Citizenship under the Fourteenth Amendment," 91 *Harvard Law Review* 1 (1977). For replies to this approach, see Gavison, "Feminism and the Public/Private Distinction," 31–35.

15. Anita Allen, *Uneasy Access: Privacy for Women in a Free Society* (Totowa, N.J.: Rowman and Littlefield, 1988), 40. But see my review of her book in *Philosophical Review* 101 (1992), 709–711, describing why this reply is incomplete.

16. Okin, *Justice, Gender, and the Family,* 174. See also MacKinnon, *Toward a Feminist Theory of the State,* 244.

17. MacKinnon, *Toward a Feminist Theory of the State,* 194.

18. See, for example, Frances Olsen, "The Myth of State Intervention in the Family," 18 *University of Michigan Journal of Law Reform* 835 (1985), for an explanation of the government's pervasive involvement in black women's lives. I am grateful to Barbara Schulman for stressing this distinction.

19. Jean Bethke Elshtain's critique of this feminist view is related to my own yet differs in that it is based on political considerations. Calling attention to a serious problem that puts democracy on trial, she writes, "if there are no distinctions between public and private, personal and political, it follows that there can be no differentiated activity or set of institutions that are genuinely political, the purview of citizens and the bases of order, legitimacy, and purpose in a democratic community" (*Democracy on Trial,* 44).

20. See the proceedings of Changing Perspectives of the Family, a symposium held April 16, 1994, at the Constitutional Law Resource Center at Drake University, Des Moines, Iowa, for a contemporary discussion of the implications of changing perspectives of the family in both constitutional law and family law and for a discussion of the degree to which the state may organize and control intimate relationships.

21. I am indebted to Joan Callahan for emphasizing the importance of this interpretation.

22. Pateman, "Feminist Critiques," 120.

23. Ibid., 121–122, 123.

24. John Stuart Mill, *The Subjection of Women* (1869; reprint, Indianapolis: Hackett, 1988).

25. Pateman, "Feminist Critiques," 133.

26. I owe this point to Diana Meyers. She has suggested that the debate over privacy may have an important pragmatic dimension as well. Those who believe the battery of women is so pervasive, and the need to expose it to stop the abuse so urgent, that it almost always compromises women's autonomy (whether women acknowledge that or not) will be drawn to MacKinnon's full-blown critique of privacy. Those who believe domestic violence, despite its severity, can be addressed without giving up the value of privacy will be attracted to a more moderate approach.

Topics for Critical Thinking and Writing

1. In the second paragraph, DeCew refers to "claims [of privacy] associated with tort [and] Fourth Amendment" issues. What do you think these claims might be?

2. The author tells us that "Privacy and autonomy are distinct concepts" (para. 7). How does she distinguish them? Write a 500-word essay on the theme "Privacy versus Autonomy."

3. What do you think MacKinnon means when she says that "feminism has had to explode the private" (para. 5)? On what basis does she claim that "women have no privacy to lose or to guarantee" (para. 5)? Do you agree? Explain.

4. Explain what DeCew means by the "public/private split" (para. 8). Does she accept or reject this "split"?

5. The author mentions the slogan "the personal is political" (para. 18). Explain in a sentence or two what you think this slogan means.

For topical links related to the issue of privacy, see the companion Web site:
www.bedfordstmartins.com/barnetbedau.

25

Sexual Harassment:
Is There Any Doubt about
What It Is?

**"I'd like you to keep your ears open,
make sure our office is safe from any
charges of sexual harassment.
Thanks, babe."**

Tufts University

Many colleges and universities have drawn up statements of policy concerning sexual harassment. The following statement is fairly typical in that it seeks to define sexual harassment, to suggest ways of stopping it (these range from informal discussion to a formal grievance procedure), and to indicate resources that can provide help.

What Is Sexual Harassment?

Sexual harassment is a form of sex discrimination and violates federal and state law and university policy. Tufts University, its agents, supervisory employees, employees, and students shall be held liable for their acts of sexual harassment and are subject to appropriate university disciplinary action and personal liability. Sexual harassment is prohibited at Tufts University.

Sexual harassment, whether between people of different sexes or the same sex, is defined to include but is not limited to, unwanted sexual advances, unwelcome requests for sexual favors, and other behavior of a sexual nature when:

1. submission to such conduct is made either explicitly or implicitly a term and condition of an individual's employment or academic status; or
2. submission to, or rejection of, such conduct by an individual is used as a basis for employment or academic decisions affecting him or her; or
3. such conduct, whether verbal or physical, has the purpose or effect of unreasonably interfering with the individual's work or academic performance or of creating an intimidating, hostile, or offensive environment in which to work or to learn.

Any member of the Tufts community who feels that he or she has been sexually harassed should feel free to use the procedure described in this pamphlet without threat of intimidation, retaliation, or harassment.

WHO ARE THE PARTICIPANTS?

Sexual harassment can involve

- instructor and instructor
- professor and student
- teaching assistant and student
- supervisor and employee
- student and student
- staff member and student
- other relationships among colleagues, peers, and co-workers

The following behavior may constitute sexual harassment: 5

- lewd remarks, whistles, or personal reference to one's anatomy
- unwanted physical contact such as patting, pinching, or constant brushing against a person's body
- subtle or overt pressure for sexual favors

- persistent and offensive sexual jokes and comments
- display of pictures of a sexual nature
- persistent and unwanted requests for dates
- e-mail messages of an offensive sexual nature

The consequences to a person responsible for sexual harassment can include

- termination
- demotion
- denial of a promotion
- suspension
- letter of reprimand

It is unlawful to retaliate against an employee or student for filing a complaint of sexual harassment or for cooperating in an investigation of a complaint of sexual harassment.

HOW TO STOP SEXUAL HARASSMENT

If you are experiencing some form of sexual harassment, you need to know that Tufts provides several options to assist you. Since each situation is as distinct as the persons involved, the preferences of the complainant—including the need for confidentiality—will determine which option is most appropriate. Both informal and formal resolution options are available at Tufts. The only alternative we do not recommend is that you do nothing.

If you believe you are being or have been sexually harassed, you should consider taking the following steps immediately:

1. You may want to keep track of dates, places, times, witnesses, and the nature of the harassment. Save any letters, cards, or notes in a safe place.
2. Seek the advice of or report the incident to any of the individuals listed as sexual harassment resource persons. You may also seek the assistance of the Counseling Center, campus chaplains, Health Services psychiatrist, or Health Services counselor.

You may also consider using the following strategies: 10

1. Say "no" to your harasser. Say it firmly without smiling and apologizing.
2. Tell your harasser, in writing, that you object to this behavior. Describe the specific behaviors which are offensive or threatening, and keep a copy.
3. Utilize the Tufts University sexual harassment grievance procedure.

WHERE TO FIND HELP?

On each campus there are university sexual harassment resource persons who are available to provide informal and formal resolution options. Efforts will be made to protect your confidentiality. Each, however, has a duty to assure resolution and report the incident to the Office of Equal Opportunity, which may limit the ability to maintain confidentiality. The Tufts University sexual harassment resource persons are: [At this point the brochure gives a list of names of Tufts deans and organizations (for instance, Asian American Center; Health Education Program; Lesbian, Gay, Bisexual Resource Center) as well as outside organizations (for instance, Equal Employment Opportunity Commission), with telephone numbers.]

RESOLUTION BY INFORMAL DISCUSSION

Any student or employee who believes that he/she has been sexually harassed should first attempt to resolve the problem through discussion with the other party. In cases in which discussing the problem with that person presents particular stress or difficulties, the complainant has the right to consult on an informal basis with a supervisor, an administrator, the Office of Equal Opportunity, Human Resources, or a sexual harassment resource person. Efforts will be made to protect your confidentiality. The complainant may bring an associate to that meeting if desired. If there has been no resolution within a reasonable period of time, the sexual harassment grievance procedure shall then be instituted if desired.

SEXUAL HARASSMENT
GRIEVANCE PROCEDURE

If the problem has not been resolved to the satisfaction of the complainant through informal discussion, she/he has the right to file a grievance in accordance with the following procedure.

A. Where to File the Grievance?
If the person alleged to be responsible for the harassment is:
1. a staff member or an administrator—file with the vice president for Human Resources or campus Human Resources manager;
2. a faculty member—file with the appropriate dean of college/ school or provost;
3. a student—file with the appropriate dean of students or dean of the college/school.

B. What Should Be Filed?
The grievance should be in writing and should summarize the 15 harassment complained of, the person alleged to be responsible, and the resolution sought.

C. When Should the Grievance Be Filed?

The grievance should normally be filed within ninety (90) days of the incident(s) giving rise to the complaint. The university may extend this period if it finds that there are extenuating circumstances.

D. How Will the Grievance Be Processed?

1. If the person alleged to be responsible for the harassment is a student, the grievance will be processed through the discipline procedure applicable to that student.
2. If the person alleged to be responsible for the harassment is a staff member, administrator, or faculty member, the person with whom the grievance is filed will notify the special assistant to the president for affirmative action, who will attempt to resolve it by discussion, investigation, or other steps that he/she deems appropriate. The special assistant to the president for affirmative action may appoint a hearing panel to review the matter. The complainant will be informed by the special assistant to the president for affirmative action or his/her designee of the action taken.
3. If a hearing panel is appointed, it will conduct an investigation which may, if the panel deems appropriate, include a hearing. The findings and recommendations of the panel will be sent to the president.
4. The president or his/her designee will review the findings and recommendations of the panel and may review other facts relating to the grievance. The decision of the president or his/her designee is binding and shall not be subject to review under any other grievance procedure in effect at Tufts University.

Topics for Critical Thinking and Writing

1. Where, if at all, would you draw the line between harmless, inoffensive flirtation and sexual harassment?

2. Is it, or should it be, a necessary condition for an act to qualify as sexual harassment that the aggressor persist in behavior the victim doesn't want after the victim has said "Stop!"? What position does the Tufts policy take on this issue?

3. Evaluate the four-part grievance procedure described in the Tufts statement. Can you think of ways it might be improved to be fairer? More efficient? Should the accused have the right to face his or her accusers? Should the victim's testimony require corroboration? Explain your answers to these questions in an essay of 500 words.

4. The list headed "Who Are the Participants?" does not include "student and instructor" or "student and staff member," though it includes the

reverse relationships. Can you conceive of situations in which a student harasses an instructor or a staff member?

5. If your school has a comparable statement of policy, study it closely, partly by comparing it with the Tufts policy. Then (assuming that your school's statement does not in every respect satisfy you), set forth (with supporting reasons) the revisions you would make in it.

Ellen Goodman

Ellen Goodman, educated at Radcliffe College, worked as a reporter for Newsweek *and the* Detroit Free Press. *Since 1967 she has written for the* Boston Globe, *and since 1972 her column has been nationally syndicated. The essay that we reprint appeared in the* Boston Globe *in October 1991.*

The Reasonable Woman Standard

Since the volatile mix of sex and harassment exploded under the Capitol dome, it hasn't just been senators scurrying for cover. The case of the professor and judge has left a gender gap that looks more like a crater.[1]

We have discovered that men and women see this issue differently. Stop the presses. Sweetheart, get me rewrite.

On the *Today* show, Bryant Gumbel asks something about a man's right to have a pinup on the wall and Katie Couric says what she thinks of that. On the normally sober *MacNeil/Lehrer* hour the usual panel of legal experts doesn't break down between left and right but between male and female.

On a hundred radio talk shows, women are sharing experiences and men are asking for proof. In ten thousand offices, the order of the day is the nervous joke. One boss asks his secretary if he can still say "good morning," or is that sexual harassment. Heh, heh. The women aren't laughing.

Okay boys and girls, back to your corners. Can we talk? Can we   5
hear?

The good news is that women have stopped rolling their eyes at each other and started speaking out. The bad news is that we may each assume the other gender not only doesn't understand but can't understand. "They don't get it" becomes "they can't get it."

[1]Professor Anita Hill, of the University of Oklahoma Law School, accused Clarence Thomas of sexually harassing her while he was her supervisor. The accusations were made before the Senate Judiciary Committee in hearings to confirm Thomas's appointment to a seat on the U.S. Supreme Court. During the televised hearings, several senators were widely regarded as having treated Hill badly. [Editors' note.]

Let's start with the fact that sexual harassment is a concept as new as date rape. Date rape, that should-be oxymoron, assumes a different perspective on the part of the man and the woman. His date, her rape. Sexual harassment comes with some of the same assumptions. What he labels sexual, she labels harassment.

This produces what many men tend to darkly call a "murky" area of the law. Murky however is a step in the right direction. When everything was clear, it was clearly biased. The old single standard was [a] male standard. The only options a working woman had were to grin, bear it, or quit.

Sexual harassment rules are based on the point of view of the victim, nearly always a woman. The rules ask, not just whether she has been physically assaulted, but whether the environment in which she works is intimidating or coercive. Whether she feels harassed. It says that her feelings matter.

This, of course, raises all sorts of hackles about women's *feelings*, 10
women's *sensitivity*. How can you judge the sensitivity level of every single woman you work with? What's a poor man to do?

But the law isn't psychiatry. It doesn't adapt to individual sensitivity levels. There is a standard emerging by which the courts can judge these cases and by which people can judge them as well. It's called "the reasonable woman standard." How would a reasonable woman interpret this? How would a reasonable woman behave?

This is not an entirely new idea, although perhaps the law's belief in the reasonableness of women is. There has long been a "reasonable man" in the law not to mention a "reasonable pilot," a "reasonable innkeeper," a "reasonable train operator."

Now the law is admitting that a reasonable woman may see these situations differently than a man. That truth—available in your senator's mailbag—is also apparent in research. We tend to see sexualized situations from our own gender's perspective. Kim Lane Scheppele, a political science and law professor at the University of Michigan, summarizes the miscues this way: "Men see the sex first and miss the coercion. Women see the coercion and miss the sex."

Does that mean that we are genetically doomed to our double vision? Scheppele is quick to say no. Our justice system rests on the belief that one person can get in another's head, walk in her shoes, see things from another perspective. And so does our hope for change.

If a jury of car drivers can understand how a "reasonable pilot" 15
would see one situation, a jury of men can see how a reasonable woman would see another event. The crucial ingredient is empathy.

Check it out in the office tomorrow. He's coming on, she's backing off, he keeps coming. Read the body language. There's a *Playboy* calendar on the wall and a PMS joke in the boardroom and the boss is just being friendly. How would a reasonable woman feel?

At this moment, when the air is crackling with hostility and consciousness-raising has the hair sticking up on the back of many necks, guess what? Men can "get it." Reasonable men.

Topics for Critical Thinking and Writing

1. Goodman is a journalist, which means in part that her writing is lively. Point to two or three sentences that you would not normally find in a textbook, and evaluate them. (Example: "Okay boys and girls, back to your corners," para. 5.) Are the sentences you have selected effective? Why, or why not?

2. Why does Goodman describe date rape as a "should-be oxymoron" (para. 7)?

3. In paragraphs 11 and 12 Goodman speaks of "the reasonable woman standard." In recent years several cases have come to the courts in which women have said that they are harassed by posters of nude women in the workplace. Such posters have been said to create an "intimidating, hostile, or offensive environment." (a) What do you think Goodman's opinion would be? (b) Imagine that you are a member of the jury deciding such a case. What is your verdict? Why?

4. According to Goodman's account of the law (paras. 8–13), the criterion for sexual harassment is whether the "reasonable woman" would regard the "environment" in which she works (or studies) as "intimidating" or "coercive," thus causing her to "feel harassed." In a 500-word essay describe three hypothetical cases, one of which you believe clearly involves sexual harassment, a second that clearly does not, and a third that is a borderline case.

5. Given what Goodman says about sexual harassment, can men be victims of sexual harassment? Why, or why not?

Ellen Frankel Paul

Ellen Frankel Paul teaches political science at Bowling Green State University. Among the many books that she has written, edited, or coedited are Equity and Gender *(1989),* Self-Interest *(1997),* Democracy *(1999), and* The Right to Privacy *(2000). The essay that we reprint here was originally published in* Society *in 1991.*

Bared Buttocks and Federal Cases

Women in American society are victims of sexual harassment in alarming proportions. Sexual harassment is an inevitable corollary to class exploitation; as capitalists exploit workers, so do males in positions of authority exploit their female subordinates. Male professors, supervisors, and apartment managers in ever increasing numbers take advantage of the financial dependence and vulnerability of women to extract sexual concessions.

These are the assertions that commonly begin discussions of sexual harassment. For reasons that will be adumbrated below, dissent from the prevailing view is long overdue. Three recent episodes will serve to frame this disagreement.

Valerie Craig, an employee of Y & Y Snacks, Inc., joined several coworkers and her supervisor for drinks after work one day in July of 1978. Her supervisor drove her home and proposed that they become more intimately acquainted. She refused his invitation for sexual relations, whereupon he said that he would "get even" with her. Ten days after the incident she was fired from her job. She soon filed a complaint of sexual harassment with the Equal Employment Opportunity Commission (EEOC), and the case wound its way through the courts. Craig prevailed, the company was held liable for damages, and she received back pay, reinstatement, and an order prohibiting Y & Y from taking reprisals against her in the future.

Carol Zabowicz, one of only two female forklift operators in a West Bend Company warehouse, charged that her coworkers over a four-year period 1978–1982 sexually harassed her by such acts as: asking her whether she was wearing a bra; two of the men exposing their buttocks between ten and twenty times; a male coworker grabbing his crotch and making obscene suggestions or growling; subjecting her to offensive and abusive language; and exhibiting obscene drawings with her initials on them. Zabowicz began to show symptoms of physical and psychological stress, necessitating several medical leaves, and she filed a sexual harassment complaint with the EEOC. The district court judge remarked that "the sustained, malicious, and brutal harassment meted out . . . was more than merely unreasonable; it was malevolent and outrageous." The company knew of the harassment and took corrective action only after the employee filed a complaint with the EEOC. The company, was, therefore, held liable, and Zabowicz was awarded back pay for the period of her medical absence, and a judgment that her rights were violated under the Civil Rights Act of 1964.

On September 17, 1990, Lisa Olson, a sports reporter for the *Boston Herald,* charged five football players of the just-defeated New England Patriots with sexual harassment for making sexually suggestive and offensive remarks to her when she entered their locker room to conduct a post-game interview. The incident amounted to nothing short of "mind rape," according to Olson. After vociferous lamentations in the media, the National Football League fined the team and its players $25,000 each. The National Organization for Women called for a boycott of Remington electric shavers because the owner of the company, Victor Kiam, also own[ed] the Patriots and allegedly displayed insufficient sensitivity at the time when the episode occurred.

All these incidents are indisputably disturbing. In an ideal world—
one needless to say far different from the one that we inhabit or are ever
likely to inhabit—women would not be subjected to such treatment in
the course of their work. Women, and men as well, would be accorded
respect by coworkers and supervisors, their feelings would be taken into
account, and their dignity would be left intact. For women to expect reverential treatment in the workplace is utopian, yet they should not have
to tolerate outrageous, offensive sexual overtures and threats as they go
about earning a living.

One question that needs to be pondered is: What kinds of undesired
sexual behavior women should be protected against by law? That is,
what kind of actions are deemed so outrageous and violate a woman's
rights to such extent that the law should intervene, and what actions
should be considered inconveniences of life, to be morally condemned
but not adjudicated? A subsidiary question concerns the type of legal
remedy appropriate for the wrongs that do require redress. Before directly addressing these questions, it might be useful to diffuse some of
the hyperbole adhering to the sexual harassment issue.

Surveys are one source of this hyperbole. If their results are accepted
at face value, they lead to the conclusion that women are disproportionately victims of legions of sexual harassers. A poll by the Albuquerque
Tribune found that nearly 80 percent of the respondents reported that
they or someone they knew had been victims of sexual harassment. The
Merit Systems Protection Board determined that 42 percent of the
women (and 14 percent of men) working for the federal government
had experienced some form of unwanted sexual attention between 1985
and 1987, with unwanted "sexual teasing" identified as the most prevalent form. A Defense Department survey found that 64 percent of
women in the military (and 17 percent of the men) suffered "uninvited
and unwanted sexual attention" within the previous year. The United
Methodist Church established that 77 percent of its clergywomen experienced incidents of sexual harassment, with 41 percent of these naming a
pastor or colleague as the perpetrator, and 31 percent mentioning
church social functions as the setting.

A few caveats concerning polls in general, and these sorts of polls in
particular, are worth considering. Pollsters looking for a particular social
ill tend to find it, usually in gargantuan proportions. (What fate would
lie in store for a pollster who concluded that child abuse, or wife beating,
or mistreatment of the elderly had dwindled to the point of negligibility!)
Sexual harassment is a notoriously ill-defined and almost infinitely ex-
pandable concept, including everything from rape to unwelcome neck
massaging, discomfiture upon witnessing sexual overtures directed at
others, yelling at and blowing smoke in the ears of female subordinates,
and displays of pornographic pictures in the workplace. Defining sexual
harassment, as the United Methodists did, as "any sexually related behavior that is unwelcome, offensive or which fails to respect the rights of

others," the concept is broad enough to include everything from "unsolicited suggestive looks or leers [or] pressures for dates" to "actual sexual assaults or rapes." Categorizing everything from rape to "looks" as sexual harassment makes us all victims, a state of affairs satisfying to radical feminists, but not very useful for distinguishing serious injuries from the merely trivial.

Yet, even if the surveys exaggerate the extent of sexual harassment, however defined, what they do reflect is a great deal of tension between the sexes. As women in ever increasing numbers entered the workplace in the last two decades, as the women's movement challenged alleged male hegemony and exploitation with ever greater intemperance, and as women entered previously all-male preserves from the board rooms to the coal pits, it is lamentable, but should not be surprising, that this tension sometimes takes sexual form. Not that sexual harassment on the job, in the university, and in other settings is a trivial or insignificant matter, but a sense of proportion needs to be restored and, even more importantly, distinctions need to be made. In other words, sexual harassment must be deideologized. Statements that paint nearly all women as victims and all men and their patriarchal, capitalist system as perpetrators, are ideological fantasy. Ideology blurs the distinction between being injured—being a genuine victim—and merely being offended. An example is this statement by Catharine A. MacKinnon, a law professor and feminist activist:

> Sexual harassment perpetuates the interlocked structure by which women have been kept sexually in thrall to men and at the bottom of the labor market. Two forces of American society converge: men's control over women's sexuality and capital's control over employees' work lives. Women historically have been required to exchange sexual services for material survival, in one form or another. Prostitution and marriage as well as sexual harassment in different ways institutionalize this arrangement.

Such hyperbole needs to be diffused and distinctions need to be drawn. Rape, a nonconsensual invasion of a person's body, is a crime clear and simple. It is a violation of the right to the physical integrity of the body (the right to life, as John Locke or Thomas Jefferson would have put it). Criminal law should and does prohibit rape. Whether it is useful to call rape "sexual harassment" is doubtful, for it makes the latter concept overly broad while trivializing the former.

Intimidation in the workplace of the kind that befell Valerie Craig— that is, extortion of sexual favors by a supervisor from a subordinate by threatening to penalize, fire, or fail to reward—is what the courts term *quid pro quo*[1] sexual harassment. Since the mid-1970s, the federal courts have treated this type of sexual harassment as a form of sex

---

[1] ***quid pro quo*** This for that, or one thing in return for another (Latin). [Editors' note.]

discrimination in employment proscribed under Title VII of the Civil Rights Act of 1964. A plaintiff who prevails against an employer may receive such equitable remedies as reinstatement and back pay, and the court can order the company to prepare and disseminate a policy against sexual harassment. Current law places principal liability on the company, not the harassing supervisor, even when higher management is unaware of the harassment and, thus, cannot take any steps to prevent it.

Quid pro quo sexual harassment is morally objectionable and analogous to extortion: The harasser extorts property (i.e., use of the woman's body) through the leverage of fear for her job. The victim of such behavior should have legal recourse, but serious reservations can be held about rectifying these injustices through the blunt instrument of Title VII: In egregious cases the victim is left less than whole (for back pay will not compensate her for ancillary losses), and no prospects for punitive damages are offered to deter would-be harassers. Even more distressing about Title VII is the fact that the primary target of litigation is not the actual harasser, but rather the employer. This places a double burden on a company. The employer is swindled by the supervisor because he spent his time pursuing sexual gratification and thereby impairing the efficiency of the workplace by mismanaging his subordinates, and the employer must endure lengthy and expensive litigation, pay damages, and suffer loss to its reputation. It would be fairer to both the company and the victim to treat sexual harassment as a tort—that is, as a private wrong or injury for which the court can assess damages. Employers should be held vicariously liable only when they know of an employee's behavior and do not try to redress it.

As for the workplace harassment endured by Carol Zabowicz—the bared buttocks, obscene portraits, etc.—that too should be legally redressable. Presently, such incidents also fall under the umbrella of Title VII, and are termed hostile environment sexual harassment, a category accepted later than *quid pro quo* and with some judicial reluctance. The main problem with this category is that it has proven too elastic: cases have reached the courts based on everything from off-color jokes to unwanted, persistent sexual advances by coworkers. A new tort of sexual harassment would handle these cases better. Only instances above a certain threshold of egregiousness or outrageousness would be actionable. In other words, the behavior that the plaintiff found offensive would also have to be offensive to the proverbial "reasonable man" of the tort law. That is, the behavior would have to be objectively injurious rather than merely subjectively offensive. The defendant would be the actual harasser not the company, unless it knew about the problem and failed to act. Victims of scatological jokes, leers, unwanted offers of dates, and other sexual annoyances would no longer have their day in court.

A distinction must be restored between morally offensive behavior [15] and behavior that causes serious harm. Only the latter should fall under the jurisdiction of criminal or tort law. Do we really want legislators and judges delving into our most intimate private lives, deciding when a look is a leer, and when a leer is a Civil Rights Act offense? Do we really want courts deciding, as one recently did, whether a school principal's disparaging remarks about a female school district administrator was sexual harassment and, hence, a breach of Title VII, or merely the act of a spurned and vengeful lover? Do we want judges settling disputes such as the one that arose at a car dealership after a female employee turned down a male coworker's offer of a date and his colleagues retaliated by calling her offensive names and embarrassing her in front of customers? Or another case in which a female shipyard worker complained of an "offensive working environment" because of the prevalence of pornographic material on the docks? Do we want the state to prevent or compensate us for any behavior that someone might find offensive? Should people have a legally enforceable right not to be offended by others? At some point, the price for such protection is the loss of both liberty and privacy rights.

Workplaces are breeding grounds of envy, personal grudges, infatuation, and jilted loves, and beneath a fairly high threshold of outrageousness, these travails should be either suffered in silence, complained of to higher management, or left behind as one seeks other employment. No one, female or male, can expect to enjoy a working environment that is perfectly stress-free, or to be treated always and by everyone with kindness and respect. To the extent that sympathetic judges have encouraged women to seek monetary compensation for slights and annoyances, they have not done them a great service. Women need to develop a thick skin in order to survive and prosper in the workforce. It is patronizing to think that they need to be recompensed by male judges for seeing a few pornographic pictures on a wall. By their efforts to extend sexual harassment charges to even the most trivial behavior, the radical feminists send a message that women are not resilient enough to ignore the run-of-the-mill, churlish provocation from male coworkers. It is difficult to imagine a suit by a longshoreman complaining of mental stress due to the display of nude male centerfolds by female coworkers. Women cannot expect to have it both ways: equality where convenient, but special dispensations when the going gets rough. Equality has its price and that price may include unwelcome sexual advances, irritating and even intimidating sexual jests, and lewd and obnoxious colleagues.

Egregious acts—sexual harassment per se—must be legally redressable. Lesser but not trivial offenses, whether at the workplace or in other more social settings, should be considered moral lapses for which the offending party receives opprobrium, disciplinary warnings, or penalties, depending on the setting and the severity. Trivial offenses, dirty jokes, sexual overtures, and sexual innuendoes do make many women feel intensely discomfited, but, unless they become outrageous through persistence or content, these too should be taken as part of life's annoyances. The perpetrators should be either endured, ignored, rebuked, or avoided, as circumstances and personal inclination dictate. Whether Lisa Olson's experience in the locker room of the New England Patriots falls into the second or third category is debatable. The media circus triggered by the incident was certainly out of proportion to the event.

As the presence of women on road gangs, construction crews, and oil rigs becomes a fact of life, the animosities and tensions of this transition period are likely to abate gradually. Meanwhile, women should "lighten up," and even dispense a few risqué barbs of their own, a sure way of taking the fun out of it for offensive male bores.

Topics for Critical Thinking and Writing

1. Reread the first paragraph, trying *not* to bring to it your knowledge of what Paul says in the rest of the essay. What was your response? Then, in light of what you know about the entire essay, explain Paul's strategy in beginning this way.

2. Paul occasionally uses a word that probably is not part of everyone's vocabulary, such as "adumbrated" (paragraph 2), "adjudicated" (7), "hegemony" (10), "deideologized" (10), and "ancillary" (13). What is your response? Is the essay needlessly obscure? Are some words not part of everyday speech but appropriate here? Explain.

3. How, if at all, does Paul define "sexual harassment" (see especially paras. 9–10)? How would you define it? Consider what is common to the three cases of sexual harassment with which Paul opens her essay (paras. 3–5).

4. Paul asserts that women ought to be prepared to encounter a certain amount of inappropriate behavior in the workplace. Are you satisfied with the reasons she gives? Explain.

5. Paul thinks Title VII places an unfair burden on employers whose employees are guilty of sexual harassment because the employer may not know about the employee's misbehavior (paras. 12–13). Suppose one argues that employers ought to know about such harassment and ought to take steps to prevent it. How might Paul reply?

6. Paul distinguishes between "offensive behavior" and harm (para. 15) and the behavior that causes each. Can you think of cases of sexual harassment (actual or hypothetical) in which the distinction is blurred? If so, explain.

7. If you have read Ellen Goodman's "The Reasonable Woman Standard" (p. 711), compare Goodman's views with Paul's. On what significant points do they disagree?

Sarah J. McCarthy

As Sarah J. McCarthy indicates in this essay, she is the owner of a small restaurant. The essay originally appeared in the December 9, 1991, issue of Forbes, a business-oriented magazine.

Cultural Fascism

On the same day that Ted Kennedy asked forgiveness for his personal "shortcomings," he advocated slapping lottery-size punitive damages on small-business owners who may be guilty of excessive flirting or whose employees may be guilty of talking dirty. Senator Kennedy expressed regrets that the new civil rights bill caps punitive damages for sexual harassment as high as $300,000 (depending on company size), and he promises to push for increases next year. Note that the senators have voted to exempt themselves from punitive damages.

I am the owner of a small restaurant/bar that employs approximately twenty young males whose role models range from Axl Rose to John Belushi. They work hard in a high-stress, fast-paced job in a hot kitchen and at times they are guilty of colorful language. They have also been overheard telling Pee-Wee Herman jokes and listening to obnoxious rock lyrics. They have discussed pornography and they have flirted with waitresses. One chef/manager has asked out a pretty blonde waitress probably a hundred times in three years. She seems to enjoy the game, but always says no. Everyone calls everyone else "Honey"—it's a ritual, a way of softening what sound like barked orders: "I need the medium-rare shish kebab *now!*"

"Honey" doesn't mean the same thing here as it does in women's studies departments or at the EEOC.[1] The auto body shop down the street has pinups. Perhaps under the vigilant eyes of the feminist political correctness gestapo we can reshape our employees' behavior so they act more like nerds from the Yale women's studies department. The gestapo will not lack for potential informers seeking punitive damages and instant riches.

With the Civil Rights Bill of 1991 we are witnessing the most organized and systematic assault on free speech and privacy since the McCarthy era. The vagueness of the sexual harassment law, combined with our current litigation explosion, is a frightening prospect for small businesses. We are now financially responsible for sexually offensive verbal behavior, even if we don't know it is occurring, under a law that provides no guidelines to define "offensive" and "harassment." This is a cultural fascism unmatched since the Chinese communists outlawed hand-holding, decorative clothing, and premarital sex.

[1]**EEOC** Equal Employment Opportunity Commission. [Editors' note.]

This law is detrimental even to the women it professes to help. I am   5
a feminist, but the law has made me fearful of hiring women. If one of
our cooks or managers—or my husband or sons—offends someone, it
could cost us $100,000 in punitive damages and legal expenses. There
will be no insurance fund or stockholders or taxpayers to pick up the tab.

When I was a feminist activist in the 1970s, we knew the dangers of
a pedestal—it was said to be as confining as any other small place. As we
were revolted and outraged by the woman-hatred in violent pornography, we reminded each other that education, not laws, was the solution
to our problems. In Women against Sexist Violence in Pornography and
Media, in Pittsburgh, we were well aware of the dangers of encroaching
on the First Amendment. Free speech was, perhaps more than anything
else, what made our country grow into a land of enlightenment and diversity. The lesbians among us were aware that the same laws used to
censor pornography could be used against them if their sexual expressions were deemed offensive.

We admired powerful women writers such as Marge Piercy and
poets like Robin Morgan who swooped in from nowhere, writing break-
your-chains poems about women swinging from crystal chandeliers like
monkeys on vines and defecating in punch bowls. Are we allowed to
talk about these poems in the current American workplace?

The lawyers—the prim women and men who went to the politically
correct law schools—believe with sophomoric arrogance that the solution to all the world's problems is tort litigation. We now have eternally
complicated questions of sexual politics judged by the shifting standards
of the reasonable prude.

To the leadership of the women's movement: You do women a disservice. You ladies—and I use that term intentionally—have trivialized
the women's movement. You have made us ladies again. You have not
considered the unintended effects of your sexual harassment law. You
are saying that too many things men say and do with each other are too
rough-and-tumble for us. Wielding the power of your $300,000 law-
suits, you are frightening managers into hiring men over women. I
know that I am so frightened. You have installed a double pane of glass
on the glass ceiling with the help of your white knight and protector,
Senator Kennedy.

You and your allies tried to lynch Clarence Thomas. You alienate   10
your natural allies. Men and women who wanted to work shoulder to
shoulder with you are now looking over their shoulders. You have made
women into china dolls that if broken come with a $300,000 price tag.
The games, intrigue, nuances, and fun of flirting have been made into
criminal activity.

We women are not as delicate and powerless as you think. We do
not want victim status in the workplace. Don't try to foist it on us.

Topics for Critical Thinking and Writing

1. Reread McCarthy's opening paragraph. What is her point? How effective do you think this paragraph is as the opening of an argumentative essay?

2. In her third paragraph McCarthy speaks of "the feminist political correctness gestapo." What does she mean by this phrase, and why does she use it?

3. In paragraph 8 McCarthy refers to "tort litigation." Explain the phrase.

4. In her second paragraph McCarthy suggests that in "a high-stress, fast-paced" environment with young (and presumably not highly educated) males, "colorful language," "dirty jokes," and "obnoxious rock lyrics" are to be expected. Would you agree that a woman who takes a job in such an environment cannot reasonably complain that this sort of behavior constitutes sexual harassment? Explain.

5. How do you think McCarthy would define sexual harassment? That is, how according to her views should we complete the following sentence: "Person A sexually harasses person B if and only if . . ."?

6. Read the essay by Ellen Goodman (p. 703), and explain in a brief essay of 100 words where she and Sarah J. McCarthy differ. With whom do you agree? Why?

For topical links related to the sexual harassment debate, see the companion Web site:
www.bedfordstmartins.com/barnetbedau.

26

Video Violence: Do Children Need to Be Protected?

Leonard D. Eron

Leonard D. Eron, professor of psychology at the University of Michigan and a student of TV violence since 1957, is chair of the American Psychological Association's Commission on Violence and Youth. This essay originated in a panel discussion sponsored by the Harvard School of Public Health in 1992.

The Television Industry Must Police Itself

A recent summary of over two hundred studies, published in 1990, offers convincing evidence that the observation of violence, as seen in standard everyday television entertainment, does affect the aggressive behavior of the viewer. . . .

What can be done? As soon as the suggestion for action comes up, the TV industry raises the issue of censorship, violation of First Amendment rights, and abrogation of the Constitution. For many years now Western European countries have monitored TV and films and have not permitted the showing of excess violence, especially during child viewing hours. I have never heard of any complaints by citizens in those democratic countries that their rights have been violated. But in the United States, youth violence is a public health problem, so designated by the Centers for Disease Control [and Prevention]. . . . No one is claiming that TV violence is the sole cause of the epidemic. However, it is certainly *one* of the causes, and one which we at least can do something about. Is it too much to ask the industry to police itself? It has done so before with some success.

I don't favor censorship and I am jealous of my First Amendment rights. But I don't think some serious self-regulation and monitoring by the TV and film industry is a threat to our constitutional rights.

It would be appropriate for the FCC to require stations to document what they have done to lower the violence in their programming before their licenses are renewed. . . .

In the spring [of 1992] we had to face the implications of the uncontrolled violence in Los Angeles. TV cannot escape its share of the responsibility for this outburst. We know that children living in the inner city watch more TV than other children. Children living in the inner city are increasingly surrounded by violence — at home, in the neighborhood, on the way to and from school. They are constantly dodging bullets, cowering in hallways, hiding under tables, because the streets are so dangerous from drive-by shootings and other violence. They spend more and more time indoors watching TV.

And what do they see on TV? More violence. This validates what the children have seen in the neighborhood. It makes violence normative — everyone's doing it, not just in their neighborhood but all over. TV represents violence as an appropriate way to solve interpersonal problems, to get what you want out of life, avenge slights and insults, and make up for perceived injustices.

Topics for Critical Thinking and Writing

1. In his first paragraph Eron asserts that a summary of studies shows "convincing evidence that the observation of violence . . . does affect the aggressive behavior of the viewer." Design a study that you think might show the effects of observing violence.

2. Eron says (para. 2) that censorship of violence on TV in Western European countries has led to no complaints "in those democratic countries that their rights have been violated." How might Eron respond if you pointed out to him that those countries do not have a First Amendment that guarantees their citizens "freedom of speech" and "freedom of the press"?

3. Eron thinks (para. 4) that TV stations ought to be required to show "what they have done to lower the violence" in their programs. How do you think the quantity or quality of violence ought to be measured?

4. If, as Eron admits (para. 5), inner-city children live in a world "surrounded by violence," why does he think that reducing fictional portrayals of violence on television will have a beneficial effect?

5. Violence on television is of many kinds — for instance, fictional stories of police, news images of war or murder, nature films of animals preying on other animals, and cartoons of animals knocking other animals around. Do you think episodes in cartoons such as *Bugs Bunny* and *Tom and Jerry* may stimulate children to act violently? Explain.

6. Get a copy of the week's *TV Guide,* turn on your television set, and devote twelve hours (from 10 A.M. to 10 P.M.) gathering your own data firsthand on TV violence. Then write an essay of 750 words explaining your methodology and your conclusions for or against this thesis: "There Is Too Much Violence Shown on Television during Prime-Time Viewing Hours."

Ernest F. Hollings

Ernest F. Hollings was the ranking Democrat of the Senate Committee on Commerce, Science, and Transportation at the time he wrote this essay. It was originally published in the New York Times *(November 23, 1993) as part of a dialogue called "TV Violence: Survival vs. Censorship," along with an essay by Floyd Abrams (p. 719).*

Save the Children

Imagine an intruder entering your home, seizing your children, and forcing them to watch 8,000 murders and 100,000 acts of violence. A monstrous crime? Yes. A crime that would do untold psychological harm to your children? No question about it.

Wake up, parents. Chances are that your child is the victim I just described. The statistics come from the American Psychological Association, which reported in 1992 that by the end of elementary school, the average American child has watched that many acts of violence on television. Saturday morning children's programming leads the way in mayhem and gore, showing an average of thirty-two violent acts per hour.

Enough! It is time for decent Americans to rescue our children from this threat. To that end, I have co-sponsored with Senator Daniel K. Inouye the Children's Protection from Violent Programming Act of 1993, which would ban the broadcast or cable transmission of violent programming during hours when children make up a substantial share of the audience.

At a hearing before the committee in October, TV executives claimed that they have cleaned up their prime-time programming, created monitoring committees, and shown good faith. But we've heard these same hollow pledges for four decades.

Testifying, Attorney General Janet Reno remarked, "Don't things   5
seem upside-down when violent programming is turning television into one more obstacle that parents and teachers have to overcome in order to raise their children?"

First and foremost, the bill to fight TV violence is intended to benefit children—many of them unsupervised, all of them impressionable and vulnerable.

More than one thousand studies—including reports by the Surgeon General, the National Institute of Mental Health, and others—have demonstrated a direct link between exposure to violence in the media and aggressive, violent behavior.

Shamefully, Hollywood and the TV networks have thumbed their nose at this crisis. And they have mobilized to defeat the bill. Many media executives acknowledge the harmful effects of violent programming on children, but insist it isn't their responsibility. Their solution: Parents should supervise children's viewing.

But what about the millions of kids whose viewing is unsupervised? A civic leader from South Central Los Angeles told the Commerce Committee that 80 percent of children in inner-city neighborhoods are latchkey kids—kids who return from school to parentless homes, where they spend four to five hours an afternoon, unsupervised, in front of the electronic baby sitter.

Some TV executives claim the bill infringes on their First Amend-   10
ment right to free speech. Not so, responded Attorney General Reno, testifying that the Supreme Court has upheld a "compelling state interest" in protecting the physical and psychological well-being of children. Under this principle, we have restricted sexual indecency on TV for decades. The same principle applies to violence.

Bear in mind that the legislation in no way seeks to control what adults watch. Premium cable channels such as HBO and Showtime are not covered. Networks and cable channels would remain free to broad-cast violent programming during hours when children are not a substan-tial part of the audience.

For Hollywood, violence and sex translate into profits and market share. This is its corporate bottom line. But our society has a different bottom line. The proposed legislation gives concerned Americans a chance to fight back. If the TV and cable industries have no sense of shame, we must take it upon ourselves to stop licensing their violence-saturated programming.

Topics for Critical Thinking and Writing

1. In his first paragraph Hollings speaks of the "8,000 murders and 100,000 acts of violence" that children are likely to see by the time they com-plete elementary school. Drawing on your own experience, what sorts of people are treated violently on television?

2. Do you think that the murders and acts of violence you saw on televi-sion when you were young influenced your behavior? Often? Some-times? Rarely? Never? Explain.

3. If you do not think you were influenced by seeing violence on televi-sion, do you think that other young people were? If so, why were they influenced but not you?

4. Some researchers argue that although televised violence may increase aggressiveness, it may also have other effects. For instance, it may in-crease fearfulness of becoming a victim, or it may increase callousness toward violence directed at others. Drawing on your own experience, can you support these views? Explain.

5. Hollings reports (para. 2) that a typical Saturday morning's worth of tele-vision for children shows "an average of thirty-two violent acts per hour." On a convenient Saturday morning, turn on your television, and do some channel surfing between 8 A.M. and noon. How many "violent acts" did you see? What was your criterion of a "violent act"? Does your research incline you to agree or disagree with the data that Hollings reported?

6. If, as Hollings says in paragraph 9, "80 percent of children in inner-city neighborhoods are latchkey kids," and if we assume that many of their households have not only a TV set but also a VCR and that children know how to operate a VCR, what's to keep these children from watch-ing all the violence they want by the simple expedient of plugging in a suitable videocassette?

Floyd Abrams

Floyd Abrams, a lawyer, has represented the New York Times, *other newspa-pers, and broadcasters. This essay was first published, along with the preceding essay by Senator Ernest F. Hollings (p. 717), in the* New York Times *(November 23, 1993), as part of a dialogue called "TV Violence: Survival vs. Censorship."*

Save Free Speech

As the Senate Commerce Committee's hearings on television violence drew to a close, two Senators argued about a movie.

Senator Conrad Burns had just seen *Rudy* in a theater. Although the movie was violent, he thought it was a "wonderful" and "delightful" story about a Notre Dame football player that the entire family should see on TV.

Senator Byron L. Dorgan disagreed. Seeing the movie in a theater was one thing, he said. Allowing it to come out of "a television box in the living room" was something else.

The exchange was illuminating. We cannot even agree on which violence children should not see. Should it include *Roots* and *Lonesome Dove*? *The War of the Roses* and *True Grit*? Or is the problem only "bad" violence, the sordid and frightening depiction, cited by Senator Paul Simon, of some fiend on the attack with a chainsaw?

Laws don't have vocabularies that distinguish between good and bad   5 violence. Adjectives help when we speak to each other—words like "sordid" and "frightening." Even a word like "bad." But these are not and cannot be the words of legislation.

If they were, we would need a constantly monitoring Federal Communications Commission deciding on matters of subjective taste and psychological reality: which violence is constructive, which gratuitous. We would, in short, need a national censorship board. But that is the world of the Ayatollah, not ours.

Even objective criteria would not help. How many bullets are too many? How much violence is too much? Does it matter if the movie is *Glory* or *Gettysburg*? Or the latest remake of *Nightmare on Elm Street*? Or if the characters are Tom or Jerry?

One proposal is that Congress should bar the showing of *any* act of violence on TV in the evening before, say, 11 P.M. That is the heart of the legislation proposed by Senators Ernest F. Hollings and Daniel K. Inouye.

No program or film with any violence, whatever its artistic value or potential social benefit, could thus be shown at a time when most adults and most children watch TV. Not *Rudy*. Not *A Streetcar Named Desire*. We could watch *Married with Children* but not *War and Remembrance*, *Star Search* but not *Star Wars*.

This is censorship, plain and simple. It is no less so because the legis-   10 lation is designed to protect children. As the Supreme Court Justice Felix Frankfurter put it in a 1957 opinion, we may not "reduce the adult population" to material "fit for children."

Justice Lewis Powell added a related conclusion in an opinion seventeen years later: "Speech that is neither obscene as to youths nor subject to some other legitimate prescription cannot be suppressed solely to protect the young from ideas or images that a legislative body thinks unsuitable for them."

That is precisely what all of the antiviolence legislation before Congress seeks to do. Much of it is justified on the ground that since Congress can regulate "indecency" on TV, it should be permitted to regulate violence as well.

But the depiction of violence, some of which is contained in the greatest works of literature and film, is hardly equivalent to that of "indecent material"—material that a much disputed 5–4 Supreme Court opinion in 1978 concluded "surely lies at the periphery of First Amendment concern."

Whatever the correctness of that ruling, there is nothing peripheral to the First Amendment of much of the TV programming that so many in Congress seek to regulate. Senator Burns was right: It is not for Congress to choose whether or when we see *Rudy* on TV. And he was right about something else. Legislation in this area cannot be passed "that would stay within the Constitution."

Topics for Critical Thinking and Writing

1. Abrams argues that reasonable people cannot agree on how to distinguish between "good and bad violence" (para. 5). Try to formulate a distinction—perhaps working with three or four of your classmates. Begin with examples that seem obvious, and then work toward a grayer area but where you still think a line can be drawn. If you can think of an example that in your opinion could go on either side, briefly summarize the example, and explain why you think it cannot be firmly classified.

2. Abrams argues that just because "Congress can regulate 'indecency,'" it doesn't follow that Congress can or ought to regulate violence (para. 12). How would Abrams reply to these objections: (1) Surely, depictions of violence can be far more harmful to the young than any depictions of indecency. (2) If publishers can comply with regulations against indecency, there is no good reason that movie and television producers cannot also comply with regulations against violence. (3) Censorship of violence is no more unreasonable than censorship of indecency—and since we have the latter, why not have the former, too?

3. How might Hollings reply to Abrams's point that under the Hollings-Inouye plan, families could not watch, say, *A Streetcar Named Desire* before 11 P.M.?

Richard Rhodes

Richard Rhodes was born in Kansas City in 1937 and educated at Yale University. As a journalist he has written for numerous magazines and papers, including Newsweek, Harper's, Playboy, *and* Rolling Stone, *but he is also known as a novelist and as a writer of books about science and technology.* The Making of the Atomic Bomb *(1987) won the National Book Award, the National Book Circle Award, and the Pulitzer Prize for nonfiction. This essay first appeared in the* New York Times *on September 17, 2000.*

Hollow Claims about Fantasy Violence

The moral entrepreneurs are at it again, pounding the entertainment industry for advertising its Grand Guignolesque confections to children. If exposure to this mock violence contributes to the development of violent behavior, then our political leadership is justified in its indignation at what the Federal Trade Commission has reported about the marketing of violent fare to children. Senators John McCain and Joseph Lieberman have been especially quick to fasten on the FTC report as they make an issue of violent offerings to children.

But is there really a link between entertainment and violent behavior?

The American Medical Association, the American Psychological Association, the American Academy of Pediatrics, and the National Institute of Mental Health all say yes. They base their claims on social science research that has been sharply criticized and disputed within the social science profession, especially outside the United States. In fact, no direct, causal link between exposure to mock violence in the media and subsequent violent behavior has ever been demonstrated, and the few claims of modest correlation have been contradicted by other findings, sometimes in the same studies.

History alone should call such a link into question. Private violence has been declining in the West since the media-barren late Middle Ages, when homicide rates are estimated to have been 10 times what they are in Western nations today. Historians attribute the decline to improving social controls over violence—police forces and common access to courts of law—and to a shift away from brutal physical punishment in child-rearing (a practice that still appears as a common factor in the background of violent criminals today).

The American Medical Association has based its endorsement of the media violence theory in major part on the studies of Brandon Centerwall, a psychiatrist in Seattle. Dr. Centerwall compared the murder rates for whites in three countries from 1945 to 1974 with numbers for television set ownership. Until 1975, television broadcasting was banned in South Africa, and "white homicide rates remained stable" there, Dr. Centerwall found, while corresponding rates in Canada and the United States doubled after television was introduced.

A spectacular finding, but it is meaningless. As Franklin E. Zimring and Gordon Hawkins of the University of California at Berkeley subsequently pointed out, homicide rates in France, Germany, Italy, and Japan either failed to change with increasing television ownership in the same period or actually declined, and American homicide rates have

5

more recently been sharply declining despite a proliferation of popular media outlets—not only movies and television but also video games and the Internet.

Other social science that supposedly undergirds the theory, too, is marginal and problematic. Laboratory studies that expose children to selected incidents of televised mock violence and then assess changes in the children's behavior have sometimes found more "aggressive" behavior after the exposure—usually verbal, occasionally physical.

But sometimes the control group, shown incidents judged not to be violent, behaves more aggressively afterward than the test group; sometimes comedy produces the more aggressive behavior; and sometimes there's no change. The only obvious conclusion is that sitting and watching television stimulates subsequent physical activity. Any kid could tell you that.

As for those who claim that entertainment promotes violent behavior by desensitizing people to violence, the British scholar Martin Barker offers this critique: "Their claim is that the materials they judge to be harmful can only influence us by trying to make us be the same as them. So horrible things will make us horrible—not horrified. Terrifying things will make us terrifying—not terrified. To see something aggressive makes us feel aggressive—not aggressed against. This idea is so odd, it is hard to know where to begin in challenging it."

Even more influential on national policy has been a 22-year study 10 by two University of Michigan psychologists, Leonard D. Eron and L. Rowell Huesmann, of boys exposed to so-called violent media. The Telecommunications Act of 1996, which mandated the television V-chip, allowing parents to screen out unwanted programming, invoked these findings, asserting, "Studies have shown that children exposed to violent video programming at a young age have a higher tendency for violent and aggressive behavior later in life than children not so exposed."

Well, not exactly. Following 875 children in upstate New York from third grade through high school, the psychologists found a correlation between a preference for violent television at age 8 and aggressiveness at age 18. The correlation—0.31—would mean television accounted for about 10 percent of the influences that led to this behavior. But the correlation only turned up in one of three measures of aggression: the assessment of students by their peers. It didn't show up in students' reports about themselves or in psychological testing. And for girls, there was no correlation at all.

Despite the lack of evidence, politicians can't resist blaming the media for violence. They can stake out the moral high ground confident that the First Amendment will protect them from having to actually write legislation that would be likely to alienate the entertainment industry. Some use the issue as a smokescreen to avoid having to confront gun control.

But violence isn't learned from mock violence. There is good evidence—causal evidence, not correlational—that it's learned in personal violent encounters, beginning with the brutalization of children by their parents or their peers.

The money spent on all the social science research I've described was diverted from the National Institute of Mental Health budget by reducing support for the construction of community mental health centers. To this day there is no standardized reporting system for emergency-room findings of physical child abuse. Violence is on the decline in America, but if we want to reduce it even further, protecting children from real violence in their real lives—not the pale shadow of mock violence—is the place to begin.

Topics for Critical Thinking and Writing

1. What do you make of the first words of the essay: "The moral entrepreneurs are at it again"? That is, what tone do the words "moral entrepreneurs" and "at it again" convey? The second sentence begins "If exposure to this mock violence contributes to the development of violent behavior . . ." Do you think a reader is supposed to believe that "mock violence" *does* contribute to the development of violent behavior or that it does *not* contribute? And what do you make of the term "mock violence"? How does this expression differ from, say, "violence on television"?

2. To what is Rhodes referring when he mentions "Grand Guignolesque confections" (para. 1)?

3. What is the best answer in Rhodes's essay to his own question, "Is there really a link between entertainment and violent behavior?" (para. 2): (a) There is no such link; (b) there may be such a link, but all we have is inadequate evidence to support such a claim; (c) there is no causal connection, but there is a correlation; (d) none of the above.

4. Rhodes refers in paragraph 8 to the "control group" and to the "test group." What do these technical terms mean?

5. In paragraphs 7 through 11, Rhodes dismisses studies that claim to show that children who witness violence on television become more "aggressive" after the exposure. Are you satisfied with his dismissal of the alleged evidence? Why, or why not?

6. What would you say is Rhodes's thesis? Where does he come closest to stating it? How effective do you think his organization is? Why?

7. What, if anything, does Rhodes think causes juvenile violence, and what, if anything, does he think we can and should do about it?

Letters of Response to Richard Rhodes from Jill Andrews, Robert B. Harris, Gregory J. Hanson, and Frank Sciulli

The following letters of response to Richard Rhodes were published in the New York Times *on September 19, 2000.*

To the Editor:

Re "Hollow Claims about Fantasy Violence," by Richard Rhodes (op-ed, Sept. 17):

Just 30 years ago, there were no police officers in our high schools, nor was there any need for them. While violent movies and violent music do not always lead, in any direct way, to real violence, they do set a tone and a mood. And they do send the message that in America, violence is an answer to almost any problem.

Censorship is not the answer, but movie makers and music makers need to be far more responsible.

Jill Andrews
Arlington, Va., Sept. 17, 2000

To the Editor:

Richard Rhodes has it right in his critique of violence on television and its effect on young viewers (op-ed, Sept. 17). Most children know the difference between fantasy and reality. It's the real violence that should concern us. The real role models for young men and boys are real men in sports and in their homes.

We continue to train boys to be violent men by offering them highly paid athletes who fight, trash-talk, and assault officials.

Domestic violence is all too common. Our sons witness the violence and want to model the behavior of real men.

So rather than look outside our homes for the cause of the violence in our young men and boys, try looking at how we encourage our sons to be violent, angry, competitive achievers who use violence as a means to an end.

Robert B. Harris
Lancaster, Calif., Sept. 17, 2000

To the Editor:

Richard Rhodes tears apart studies that purport to show a correlation between media violence and violence in the public arena ("Hollow Claims about Fantasy Violence," op-ed, Sept. 17).

Then he speculates that many politicians "use the issue as a smoke-screen to avoid having to confront gun control." So Hollywood is as pure as the driven snow, while guns are the problem.

It seems to me that too many politicians advocate gun control in order to avoid having to confront the human decay of our society and the Hollywood elite that has perpetrated it.

Gregory J. Hanson
Poughkeepsie, N.Y., Sept. 17, 2000

To the Editor:

Richard Rhodes (op-ed, Sept. 17) argues persuasively that no evidence links the mock violence portrayed in the media to violence by real people. In fact, both are reflections of a culture that encourages such behavior.

Society at large endorses violence and killing to resolve issues, and people elect political leaders who have this attitude.

The death penalty is society's ultimate violence. There is no evidence that it accomplishes more than a "good" feeling of retribution, which some call justice. If political leaders wish to lead on the issue of violence in society, they should focus less on fantasy violence and pay more attention to socially approved real violence.

Frank Sciulli
Irvington, N.Y., Sept. 17, 2000

Topics for Critical Thinking and Writing

1. In her letter, Jill Andrews claims that media violence "do[es] not always lead . . . to real violence" but that it sets "a tone and a mood" in which real violence does occur. Describe this distinction more precisely.

2. Robert B. Harris in his letter declares that "Domestic violence is all too common" and "Our sons witness [such] violence" (para. 3). Presumably girls witness the same violence and yet do not act as violently as boys. Why? Or is Harris wrong about what causes the violence he deplores?

Dave Grossman and Gloria DeGaetano

Lt. Col. Dave Grossman (U.S.A. ret.), a West Point professor of psychology and of medical science, trains medical and health professionals to deal with and prevent killing. He is the author of On Killing: The Psychological Cost of Learning to Kill in War and Society *(1995). Gloria DeGaetano, a specialist in the field of media evidence, is the author of* Screen Smarts: A Family Guide to Media Literacy *(1996). We reprint a chapter from their recent book,* Stop Teaching Our Kids to Kill: A Call to Action against TV, Movie, and Video Game Violence *(1999).*

"It's Important to Feel Something When You Kill"

Like most technologies, video game technology has changed drastically in the last few years. Arcades may look much the same on the surface as they did a decade or two ago, but the games have become far more violent, sophisticated, and addictive. Pac-Man they are not. In case you haven't made a trip to a video arcade lately or peered over your child's shoulder while he's standing in front of the television pointing and shooting something that looks suspiciously like a real weapon, then you should. If Pong—or, for that matter, Pac-Man and Super Mario Brothers—is your point of reference, think again. We must assume that what we know of the more benign, outdated games of the 1970s and 1980s, even of the early 1990s, and the research regarding them, cannot be considered valid for the games that have been put on the market in the last five years.[1] It's a whole new world, and it's evolving at a rate that is hard for parents to keep pace with.

How fast a rate? Consider this: During the last two decades interactive video games have emerged as one of the most popular forms of entertainment, particularly among teens. According to the nonprofit organization Mediascope, "Globally, annual video game revenues now exceed $18 billion. In the United States alone, video game revenues exceed $10 billion annually, nearly double the amount Americans spend going to the movies. On average, American children who have home video game systems play with them about ninety minutes a day."[2]

The kids are changing with the technology—how could they not be? They are riding the technology curve in a way we are not and never can. On many levels it's wonderful to have them exposed to this brave new cyberworld; the opportunities for them to learn, the resources at their fingertips, are tremendous and hard to fathom. The World Wide Web is like a vast, almost limitless encyclopedia, and unlike *Encyclopedia Britannica,* kids can talk to it and it talks back. So it's especially disconcerting to see armies of these very kids wandering through cyberspace mutilating and killing everything in their path—and having a great time doing it. It's the dark side of heightened technology, but one to which we ought to be paying much closer attention.

More than any other aspect of these new video games, it's the accuracy of the simulations—the carnage, the blood, the guts—that is so advanced. Realism is the Holy Grail of the video game industry. And the latest technology leaves little to the imagination—the simulations seem less fake, and therefore more effective. Compare it, if you will, to a well-made horror movie with a very believable plot, set in a town not unlike your own, with characters that could be right out of your neighborhood. The reality of it will undoubtedly affect you, more so certainly than watching a low-budget picture like *Godzilla.*

So, immersed as we are in technology in all facets of our lives, it's   5
not hard to understand why children's games are more advanced and sophisticated—they're like everything else these days. But the fact that, in the last few years, video game manufacturers have chosen to amplify gruesome violence (note that 49 percent of young teens indicate a preference for violent games, while only 2 percent prefer educational ones),[3] to make it a mainstay in their products, seems a direct result of where the television and movie industry have taken *their* content.

The relationship between viewing violent television and films and being attracted to these elevated forms of interactive violent video games is well documented. We've talked a lot about the desensitizing effect on-screen violence has on kids, and how it fosters a need for more graphic, real-life displays of carnage and mayhem to keep kids interested. The entertainment industry knows this better than anyone, and the makers of these games are way past the curve. Graphically violent video games like Doom, Postal, Duke Nukem, and Mortal Kombat serve up just what the doctor did not order.

And you can see why. The real selling point with these games is that you get to pull the trigger, you inflict the damage, rather than just watching someone else do it. As graphic as the violence is on TV and in movies, it can't quite compete with a medium where you, not an actor, can control the action. It's a whole new level of involvement—and it's terrifying.

Any teacher or coach of young people will tell you that hands-on experience is what teaches best. Repetition of movements and the hand-eye connection are invaluable for learning most skills. And, especially with children, hands-on learning is usually a lot more fun and interesting than the alternatives. It's precisely this that makes interactive video games so potent a learning tool. As researcher Patricia Greenfield points out, "Video games are the first medium to combine visual dynamism with an active participatory role for the child."[4] Television, film, and video game violence may all be imaginary, but the latter lets you put your hands on it, aim, and fire. We don't think we have to tell you how deadly the combination can be of viewing ultraviolent images with the amusement park fun of shooting at things until they drop.

So it's no surprise that violent games are very habit-forming. Parents we have spoken to are alarmed at not just the violent images in the games but the amount of time their children spend playing them. If nothing else, it proves how effective these things are. More than 60 percent of children report that they play video games longer than they intend to play.[5] The interactive quality, the intensity of the violence, the physiological reactions, all serve to connect the player's feelings of exhilaration and accomplishment directly to the violent images. And "good" feelings keep the player wanting to play. Countless parents try desperately to keep video game play within certain time limits, but it's a huge challenge . . . a parental battle we often lose. Once kids get hooked, it's difficult to unhook them. Both home and arcade games make extensive use of reinforcement schedules for both the acquisition and maintenance of the habit. According to Jane Healey, in her classic book *Endangered Minds*,[6] here are the basic elements that make video games addictive:

1. The player experiences feelings of mastery and control. The less sense of power the child or teen feels in his or her life, the more this element may become important as an addictive factor. (In

fact, studies show that generally boys' preferences for violent video games are associated with low self-competence — in school, in personal relationships, and in general behavior.[7] For girls, more time playing video or computer games is associated with lower self-esteem.)[8]

2. The level of play is exactly calibrated to the player's ability level. Rather than coping with the challenging problems in the real world, young people are easily drawn into following the more made-to-order sequence in video games.

3. The player receives immediate and continual reinforcement, which make the games particularly addictive.

4. The player can escape life and be immersed in a constructed reality that seems to be totally in his/her control. (We all know that one of the anxieties of being young is a lack of control. Parents, teachers, clergy, and caregivers tell you what to do, and it's not always very much fun. It's one reason why children have active imaginations and like to construct their own worlds. And it's usually healthy for them to do so — if they are exercising their own imagination. Video game manufacturers understand this desire — and they give kids all the things they want, and for as long as they're willing to stick with it.)

As children and youth are playing these games for ten or more hours   10 a week, they are not solving and negotiating conflicts with their peers, and they are missing priceless opportunities to gain needed cooperative learning and social skills. Instead, the world constructed for them by video game manufacturers comes to determine their ability levels for successful negotiation with people in the real world. The more they become inept at dealing effectively with real-world people and situations, the more likely it is that they will lose themselves in the video games, particularly violent ones that ensure feelings of control, mastery, and exhilaration. And as the real world of slowness and struggle, decisions and demands becomes less appealing, children's psychological and physiological systems become more affected by violent video games.

In a study on arcade use among adolescents, "regular" arcade visitors varied from the more "casual" visitors (those who visited less often) in their orientation to, and experience in, arcades.[9] Regular visitors were more likely to score positively on indices screening for addiction. This study raised important questions about children's vulnerabilities to potentially addictive technologies and their access to violent video games at arcades.

But children do not have to go to arcades to become addicted to video games. Home video games can have the same effect. "A definite drug response" is how Dr. Donald Shifrin, a pediatrician and the American Academy of Pediatrics representative on the National Television Violence Study, describes what he sees when children and teens play video games at home: "When youngsters get into video games, the object is excitement. The child then builds a tolerance for that level of excitement. Now the child mimics drug-seeking behavior . . . initially there's experimentation, behavior to seek the drug for increasing levels of excitement, and then there is habituation, when more and more of the drug is actually necessary for these feelings of excitement. There is no need to have a video game system in the house, especially for young children. There is no middle ground for me on this. I view it as a black-and-white issue like helmets for bike safety. If parents want, rent a video game for a day and then return it. Everyone goes to Disneyland for a day. No one goes there daily."[10]

Are children and teens who regularly play violent video games in a permanent state of arousal? We know that merely watching violent imagery physiologically arouses both children and adults. Early experiments using physiological measures of arousal such as galvanic skin response, heart rate, and respiratory changes found that children are emotionally responsive to even animated television violence. If being a spectator to the sensational arouses our children, what happens when they get to engage in the simulated slaughter?

The effects of violent video games on young adults' arousal levels, hostile feelings, and aggressive thoughts have been measured. Results indicated that college students who had played a violent virtual reality game had a higher heart rate, reported more dizziness and nausea, and exhibited more aggressive thoughts in a posttest than those who had played a nonviolent game.[11]

Another study examined differences in cardiovascular reactions and hostility following nonviolent play and violent video game play.[12] The subjects were thirty male college undergraduate students. Only male subjects were used because most video games are male oriented, males frequent video game arcades more often than do females, and the gender gap in video game play widens with age until the undergraduate years. Hostility and cardiovascular reactivity were examined after subjects played either a nonviolent game of billiards or a violent video game. The video game, Mortal Kombat, was presented in either a less violent (MK1) or a more violent (MK2) version. Results indicated that subjects who played the video game had higher heart rate reactivity than those who played billiards. Subjects who played the MK2 version showed greater systolic blood pressure reactivity than those who played the MK1 version or billiards. Subjects who played MK2 scored higher on the hostility measures than those who played MK1, who in turn scored higher than those who played billiards.

These two studies indicate that adults, with fully developed brains and central nervous systems, can be impacted negatively by violent video games. What about children and teens whose brains and response mechanisms are in the process of development? They are much more vulnerable to physiological arousal and conditioning effects.

A real—and the newest—concern we have with our children's exposure to violent video games is what the devices teach them physically. The mechanical, interactive quality of a "First Person Shooter" game like Doom or 007 Golden Eye makes it so much more dangerous to society than images on a television screen, however violent. "Why?" we are constantly asked. "It's a game. It may be violent and it's probably better our children weren't exposed to it, but . . ." Well, it's a lot more than that. Certain types of these "games" are actually killing simulators, and they teach our kids to kill, much the same way the astronauts on Apollo 11 learned how to fly to the moon without ever leaving the ground. Believe it or not, simulators can be that good. Sounds far-fetched, we know. But consider the following.

The military learned in World War II that there is a vast gulf, a leap, between being an ordinary citizen and being someone who can aim and fire a gun at another human being with intent to kill, even in war. They discovered that firing at bull's-eye targets in training did not properly prepare soldiers for combat. Bull's-eye targets are not humans; they are not even simulated humans. And shooting at a bull's-eye target may teach someone the mechanics of aiming a gun, pulling the trigger, and dealing with the recoil, but it doesn't teach what it takes to look at another human being in the eyes, lift up a weapon, and knowingly try to take their life. Soldiers in that war spent a lot of time firing their guns into the air or not at all. In fact, the firing rate was a mere 15 percent among riflemen, which, from a military perspective, is like a 15 percent literacy rate among librarians.[13]

The army's first simulators used "simulated people" or silhouettes as targets, and that appears to have been sufficient to increase the firing manyfold. But pop-up targets, firing ranges, and bullets are expensive (bullets for a 9 mm pistol cost over twenty cents each). Improved technology now allows these communities to train on computer simulators—to learn how to shoot, where to shoot, how to maneuver through possibly deadly combat situations, how to tell enemy from friend, and, most important, how to kill. The entire event of killing in combat can be simulated by a computer.

There are three things you need in order to shoot and kill effectively 20 and efficiently. From a soldier in Vietnam to an eleven-year-old in Jonesboro, anyone who does not have all three will essentially fail in any endeavor to kill. First, you need a gun. Next you need the skill to hit a target with that gun. And finally you need the will to use that gun. The gun, the skill, and the will. Of these three factors, the military knows that the killing simulators take care of two out of three by nurturing both the skill and the will to kill a fellow human being.

Operant conditioning is a very powerful procedure of stimulus-response training, which gives a person the skill to act under stressful conditions. A benign example is the use of flight simulators to train pilots. An airline pilot in training sits in front of a flight simulator for endless, mind-numbing hours; he is taught to react in a certain way when a particular stimulus warning light goes on. When another warning light goes on, a different reaction is necessary. Stimulus-response, stimulus-response, stimulus-response. One day the pilot is actually flying a jumbo jet, the plane is going down, and three hundred people are screaming behind him. He's scared out of his wits, but he does the right thing. Why? Because he's been conditioned to respond in a particular way to this crisis situation. He reacts from a conditioned response rather than making a cerebral decision. Thinking too much in these types of situations may mean that you will be dead before you do something effective.

Today soldiers learn to fire at realistic, man-shaped silhouettes that pop up in their field of vision. This "simulated" human being is the conditioning stimulus. The trainee has only a split second to engage the target. The conditioned response is to shoot the target, and then it drops. Stimulus-response, stimulus-response, stimulus-response—soldiers and police officers experience hundreds of repetitions of this. Later, when they're out on the battlefield or walking a beat and somebody pops up with a gun, reflexively they will shoot, and shoot to kill.

These devices are used extensively, and the scientific data on their effectiveness is exhaustive. It began with flight simulators and tank crew simulators half a century ago. Their introduction is undeniably responsible for increasing the firing rate from 15 to 20 percent in World War II to 95 percent in Vietnam. In the Falklands war, the Argentine soldiers, trained to fire at bull's-eye targets, had a firing rate of approximately 10 to 15 percent. The British, trained to kill using modern methods, had well over a 90 percent firing rate. Thus we know that, all other factors being equal, 75 percent to 80 percent of the killing on the modern battlefield is a direct result of the simulators.[14]

Now these simulators are in our homes and arcades—in the form of violent video games! If you don't believe us, you should know that one of the most effective and widely used simulators developed by the United States Army in recent years, MACS (Multipurpose Arcade Combat Simulator), is nothing more than a modified Super Nintendo game (in fact, it closely resembles the popular game Duck Hunt, except with a plastic M16 firing at typical military targets on a TV screen). It is an excellent, ubiquitous military marksmanship-training device. The FATS trainer (Fire Arms Training Simulator), used by most law enforcement agencies in this country, is more or less identical to the ultraviolent video arcade game Time Crisis. Both teach the user (or player) to hit a target, both help rehearse the act of killing, and both come complete with guns that have recoil—the slide slams back when the trigger is pulled.

In a bold advertising campaign, the brochure for the home version of 25 this game, in particular, asserts: "Time Crisis uses the revolutionary Guncon, the most advanced light gun ever made for any home system. The Guncon connects to the video output of the PlayStation and it actually stores the screen image in the gun button so players can duck and reload. . . . It's time we got the handguns off the streets and back where they belong—in the hands of America's youth."[15]

We're not the only ones suggesting that violent video games and military simulators share the same technology. The wording in this ad for the game device WingMan Force puts it as bluntly as is possible: "[WingMan Force is] based on the same exacting technology used for aerospace, medical and military simulators. It uses high-precision steel cable drives so you can actually feel the detailed environment of your favorite games . . ."[16] The ad goes on to remind us, "Psychiatrists say it is important to feel something when you kill."

The military and law enforcement agencies across the country are none too pleased that these devices are in the hands of civilians, especially kids. In a lawsuit against the video game manufacturers that has come out of the killings in Paducah, Kentucky, the heads of several major national and international law enforcement training organizations have offered to testify that these video games are identical to law enforcement firearms training devices, except with the safety catch turned off. That should say a lot. The video game industry boasts about the real quality of their products; the military and police are wondering why on earth such technology is on the street. What more proof do we need that these games are anything *but* games?

Across America we are reaping the bitter harvest of this "training" as ever more kids shoot their girlfriends or their teachers or other individuals that they have grudges against. A horrific development in this is that rather than just stopping with their intended target, these kids keep firing—and a simple grudge turns into a mass murder. The point is, these games are indeed affecting our children and we can't hide behind the myriad other excuses when kids "go off." Because when they do, they do so in all the ways these games train them—to kill every living person in front of them until they run out of bullets or run out of targets. That results in a lot of dead bodies.

Michael Carneal, the fourteen-year-old boy who walked into a Paducah school and opened fire on a prayer group meeting that was breaking up, never moved his feet during his rampage. He never fired far to the right or left, never far up or down. He simply fired once at everything that popped up on his "screen." It is not natural to fire once at each target. The normal, almost universal, response is to fire at a target until it drops and then move on to the next target. This is the defensive reaction that will save our lives, the human instinctual reaction—eliminate the threat quickly. Not to shoot once and then go on to another target before the first threat has been eliminated. But most video games teach you to fire at each target only once, hitting as many targets as you can as fast as you can in order to rack up a high score. And many video games give bonus effects . . . for head shots. It's awful to note that of Michael Carneal's eight shots he had eight hits, all head and upper torso, three dead and one paralyzed. And this from a kid who, prior to stealing that gun, had never shot a real handgun in his life!

In South Carolina a boy named Wesley Schafer had put hundreds of 30 dollars into point-and-shoot video games. One day he and a buddy of his decided it would be fun to rob the local convenience store. They walked in and Schafer pointed a .38 caliber pistol at the clerk's head. The clerk turned to look at him, and the defendant shot reflexively from a range of about six feet. The bullet hit the clerk right between the eyes and killed him. Afterward, police asked the boy what had happened and why he'd done it. Killing the clerk clearly was not part of their plan—it was being videotaped from six different directions. Schafer responded, with great anguish and confusion, "I don't know; it was a mistake; it wasn't supposed to happen."[17] Stimulus-response.

In the Jonesboro, Arkansas, shootings, one of the two children (eleven and thirteen) involved had a fair bit of experience shooting real guns, but the other boy, to the best of our knowledge, had none. These two avid video game players fired a combined total of twenty-seven shots from a range of over one hundred yards, and hit fifteen people.[18] They strategically trapped their victims, lined them up, and shot with deadly accuracy. Battle-scarred veterans and military analysts reacted with amazement at the accuracy of their shooting, on one hand, and the military strategy involved in setting up their "kill zone," on the other. Both skills are taught by an array of home and arcade video games.

The incident that really brought the issue to the public's attention, though, was the Columbine High School massacre, in Littleton, Colorado. It was well documented that Dylan Klebold and Eric Harris were literally obsessed with playing the video game Doom and other such games. And they were very good at it. These boys, like the other boys mentioned, practiced for hundreds and hundreds of hours, perfecting their craft. Therefore, it should not be altogether surprising that their killing spree resembled something out of the cyberworld of a typical Doom scenario. (In fact, Eric Harris reprogrammed his edition of Doom so that it looked like his neighborhood, complete with the houses of the people he hated.) They moved from room to room, stalking their prey and killing almost everyone in their path. And, not unlike most kids' response to video game mayhem, Dylan Klebold and Eric Harris laughed the killings off.

The realism of a game like Doom, played on the home computer, can be extreme, especially with the multitude of "add-on" packages available to upgrade systems. For example, in the wake of the Columbine massacre, many in the game industry claimed that Doom, played only with a mouse or keyboard, can't possibly teach a player real combat skills. First, we have to understand that even when Doom is played with a mouse, it is still a good enough combat simulator that the Marine Corps uses a modified version of it (called Marine Doom) to teach recruits how to kill. They use it as a tactical training device, as opposed to teaching motor skills—although when used with a pistol grip joystick it has some value there, too. Its primary value is in developing the will to kill by repeatedly rehearsing the act until it feels natural.

It's safe to say that such technology is much more dangerous in the hands of kids than among soldiers and cops—these above examples prove that, as does common sense. There often are no safeguards at home and in arcades, no supervision, nor anyone around to put this technology into perspective for a child. In the military and law enforcement worlds, the right option is often not to shoot, and recruits receive extensive training about this. Often, recruits are reprimanded, punished, or even "failed" and kicked out for making too many mistakes—that is, for shooting the wrong targets. But when a kid puts his quarter in a video machine, there is *always* the intention to shoot. There is never an incentive not to shoot. And there's always some stimulus to keep excitement high, heart rate up, thinking functions closed down. This process is extraordinarily powerful and frightening. The result is ever more home-made pseudosociopaths who kill reflexively, even when they don't intend to.

The Duke Nukem series provides a good current example of just how 35 gruesome and explicit the violence of the home video games has recently become.[19] In this popular "shooter" game, the player is behind a weapon of choice, shooting everything in sight to get to the next level in order to shoot everything in sight. The "shooter," Duke, who is controlled by the player and looks somewhat like the Terminator, moves through pornography shops, where he finds posters of scantily clad women he can use for target practice. In advanced levels, bonus points are awarded for the murder of female prostitutes, women who are usually naked. Duke often encounters defenseless, bound women, some of whom are even conveniently tied to columns and plead, "Kill me, kill me."

A game called Postal takes the horror one step further. The user gets to "go postal" and receives points for killing as many innocent victims as possible while they beg for mercy. Likewise Redneck Rampage, where you can do the same with farm animals and farmers. The latest technology permits you to scan pictures of your fellow students and teachers from your high school yearbook and "morph" them onto the faces of the people you kill. Like many "First Person Shooter" games, Quake is often played with a joystick, which is really more like a pistol grip complete with trigger, that lets the child point (and thereby move the gun on the screen) and shoot (by pulling the trigger, which causes the gun on the screen to fire and recoil). Then there is House of the Dead, in which you blow away chunks of the bodies you fire at and get clean kills only for head shots; and CarnEvil, where you fire a pump-action shotgun and learn how to handle that skill. A new game on the market, Kingpin: Life of Crime, is raising a lot of eyebrows due to its heightened realism and level of violence. Experts are saying it makes other current games look like B movies. For example, a player can shoot a character in fifteen different places "and see the damage done—including exit wounds"; the game comes with a soundtrack from the popular rap group Cypress Hill; and your "enemies" like to remind you that they'll "kick your ass." One ad for the game's release is drawing a lot of fire from parental watchdog groups. It says: "You're Gonna Die."

It's interesting to note that the makers of games like Kingpin assiduously deny that their game is meant for kids or marketed to that group. Indeed, many such games carry warnings and are labeled for a "mature" audience, and they do have increasingly large adult followings. But deny it or not, these games (the word itself suggests that the core audience is young) easily get into the hands of kids. The makers of the games, distributors, store owners, and parents are not exactly as vigilant about stopping children from buying them as they would be if we were talking about, say, cigarettes or pornography. "Unfortunately, video games are stuck with the kiddie label," said Gary Eng Walk in an article in *Entertainment Weekly*, "and everyone . . . tends to drop their guard when letting the rough stuff find its way to the under-seventeen crowd."[20] He's right, up to a point. It's hard to deny that many video game producers have actively sought out the "kiddie" label for their products. Obviously, we can't lump all games together, but it's impossible not to see the blatant marketing to children that is going on at all levels. The language of the ads, the highly effective packaging, the million-dollar promotion campaigns are all aimed at fairly young audiences. Either that or extremely immature adults. It's worth noting that the aforementioned Duke Nukem 3-D is available at toy stores. In many toy stores the ultra-violent video games are not in a different area, hidden from innocent eyes. In fact, the larger stores arrange their video games alphabetically. Duke Nukem, rated M for mature audiences, seventeen and older, is shelved next to Eggs of Steel, a kiddie game about an animated egg.[21] Duke action figures, which are becoming popular with boys eight years old and younger, can be ordered on-line.

The gaming industry can talk all they want about the age groups they're aiming their products at, but the truth is that if ratings were strictly enforced, they would lose countless young consumers. It's no mystery that most people don't even know a rating system exists—it's hard to tell. Even Doug Lowenstein, of the Interactive Digital Association, admits there is a problem. "[The ratings system] simply doesn't have the visibility and the awareness it should have," he says.[22] "When you talk to everyone from reporters to politicians, and these people think there isn't a system, then it tells you that you have work to do." Indeed.

Leafing through any game magazine can be an eye-opener. "Fatalities can be the best part of Mortal Kombat." (Mortal Kombat action toys are labeled "For children four and up.") A new game for your child's enjoyment is "as easy as killing babies with axes." Another one is "more fun than shooting your neighbor's cat."[23] Capcom's latest Street Fighter proclaims, "The killer in me is just beginning."[24] Robert Lindsey, head of sales and marketing for the U.S. unit of Japan's Capcom, acknowledges that teenagers are an important audience: "I refer [to] them as my early adapters — if I get them on board, I know I'll get everyone else."

The on-line availability of violent video games is a big part of the [40] problem. Label first-person shooter sites with any warning you want, there's still really nothing to stop a kid with access to a computer from seeing what's there, communicating with other players, and ordering an array of products. In fact, warnings can serve the opposite purpose; most kids we know see them not as a caution but as an advertisement. They want the game to be more violent, more adult. It gives the product validity. Kids have to get past the manned ticket counter to see restricted films; they have to provide proper identification that they are old enough to buy cigarettes and alcohol; but there are no such obstacles in their way if they want to learn all there is to know about Kingpin and other "mature" video games.

So with all the evidence to suggest that these games are dangerous — that they're modeled after military killing simulators, that they are super-violent and graphic, that the user is rewarded for killing, and that kids are playing with these games way too often and for too long — it is particularly egregious that they are being marketed to kids, and marketed in ways that highlight all that is bad for them. What kind of message does this send? Well, yet another on-line ad for Kingpin gives us a pretty good indication: "The Creators of Redneck Rampage are about to bring you a new, urban drama that finally proves that crime pays."[25] As we ourselves tolerate these games and even label them fun, we are also telling our children that slower-paced, less emotionally arousing screen fare is boring. Arouse instead of awaken; excite instead of examine; splatter instead of study — this is what we're telling them. And they're listening.

NOTES

1. Eugene Provenzo, in *The Social Effects of Electronic Games: An Annotated Bibliography*, ed. Joel Federman, S. Carbone, Helen Chen, and William Munn. Studio City: Mediascope, 1996, ii.
2. Federman, Carbone, Chen, and Munn, *The Social Effects of Electronic Games*, i.
3. Jeanne B. Funk, "Reevaluating the Impact of Video Games," *Clinical Pediatrics*, vol. 32, no. 2, 1993, 86–90.
4. Eugene Provenzo, *Video Kids* (Cambridge: Harvard University Press, 1991), 47–48.
5. Mark D. Griffiths and N. Hunt, "Computer Game Playing in Adolescence: Prevalence and Demographic Indicators," *Journal of Community and Applied Social Psychology*, vol. 5, 1995, 189–193.
6. Jane M. Healy, *Endangered Minds: Why Kids Don't Think and What to Do about It* (New York: Simon and Schuster, 1990), 207.
7. Funk, "Reevaluating the Impact of Video Games."
8. Jeanne B. Funk and Debra D. Buchman, "Playing Violent Video and Computer Games and Adolescent Self-Concept," *Journal of Communication*, vol. 46, Spring 1996, 19–32.

9. Sue Fisher, "Identifying Video Game Addiction in Children and Adolescents," *Addictive Behaviors*, vol. 19, 545–553.
10. Donald Shifrin, interview with Gloria DeGaetano, June 22, 1999.
11. Sandra L. Calvert and Siu-Lan Tan, "Impact of Virtual Reality on Young Adults' Physiological Arousal and Aggressive Thoughts: Interaction versus Observation," *Journal of Applied Developmental Psychology*, vol. 5, no. 1, 125–139.
12. Mary E. Ballard and J. Rose Wiest, "Mortal Kombat: The Effects of Violent Video Technology on Males' Hostility and Cardiovascular Responding," March 8, 1995, paper presented at the sixty-first Biennial Meeting of the Society for Research in Child Development, Indianapolis, March 30–April 2, 1995.
13. S. L. A. Marshall, *Men against Fire*. Gloucester: Peter Smith, 1978, 51.
14. Ken Murray, Lt. Col. Dave Grossman, and R. W. Kentridge, "Behavioral Psychology," in *Encyclopedia of Violence, Peace and Conflict*. San Diego: Academic Press, 1999.
15. Jack Thompson, correspondence with Dave Grossman, June 1999.
16. Advertising copy in *PC Gamer*, cited by President Clinton in his national speech on media violence after the Littleton, Colorado, massacre, June 1, 1999.
17. Wesley Schafer, interviews with Dave Grossman, Union, S.C., January 1998.
18. Law enforcement officers, interviews with Dave Grossman after the Jonesboro massacre, March 1998.
19. Media Watch Online: "Duke's the King Baby," *http://www.mediawatch.com*.
20. Gary Eng Walk, "All Gore," *Entertainment Weekly*, Summer Double Issue 1999, 143.
21. Susan Nielsen, "A Beginner's Guide to Becoming a Video Game Prude," *Seattle Times*, February 21, 1999, B7–8.
22. Mark Boal, "One Step ahead of the Law," *http://www.salon.com*, July 19, 1999.
23. Nielsen, "A Beginner's Guide."
24. "Game Makers Downplay Violent Role," *USA Today*, Internet site, ctc8229 .htm at *http://www.usatoday.com*, 2.
25. "Kingpin: Life of Crime," *http://www.interplay.com/kingpin*.

Topics for Critical Thinking and Writing

1. The authors declare (para. 7) that the "new level of involvement" in interactive video games is "terrifying." What's so terrifying about these games? Is there any evidence that playing such games leads to real-world violence? Do only adults who are unfamiliar with these games cry out with alarm?

2. A source cited by the authors claims that these games produce "a definite drug response" (para. 12). They state that these games are "potentially addictive technologies" (para. 11). Is this hyperbole? Complete the following sentence: "Interactive video games are potentially addictive because . . ." (Queries: Are the authors using the term *addictive* literally or metaphorically? How are you using it?)

3. Consider the research findings on college students cited in paragraph 14. Suppose someone argued that they are worthless since the "more ag-

gressive thoughts" exhibited by the students who participated in the study are not specified. For example, did the students fantasize using a chain saw to cut down a neighbor's tree? Or using a chain saw to cut down the neighbor? How might the authors reply be consistent with their overall thesis?

4. When the editors of this book were young, they used toy guns in mock street battles with their friends. Playing cowboys and Indians, they littered the sidewalks with the "dead." As adults, neither of the editors went on to become a serial killer. Do the authors of this article and the sources they cite show conclusively that playing violent interactive video games will lead today's children to commit violent acts as adults?

5. What is "operant conditioning" (para. 21), and how is it used to turn an ordinary twenty-something male into a physically aggressive combat soldier?

6. Suppose someone were to object that using military simulators to teach soldiers how to fire their weapons (paras. 24–25) sheds no light whatsoever on the results of playing violent video games, and that the use of rapid-fire 9 mm handguns by criminals sheds no light on their use by the police. How might the authors reply?

7. Why is the story about Michael Carneal (para. 29) relevant, since the authors never claim that he spent weeks (or even days) before the slaughter absorbed in playing the violent video games in a local arcade (or at home)?

8. The several cases cited by the authors (paras. 30–33) provide a positive correlation between frequent playing of violent video games and actual murder. But thousands of boys play these games without becoming murderers. (a) Is the correlation so weak as to be insignificant? (b) Does the weak correlation suggest that other factors beyond playing these games must be present in a youth's life to turn him into a killer? (c) If so, what might such factors be?

For topical links related to the issue of television and video game violence, see the companion Web site: **www.bedfordstmartins.com/barnetbedau.**

Part Six

ENDURING QUESTIONS: ESSAYS, STORIES, POEMS, AND A PLAY

27

What Is the Ideal Society?

Thomas More

The son of a prominent London lawyer, More (1478–1535) served as a page in the household of the Archbishop of Canterbury, went to Oxford University, and then studied law in London. More's charm, brilliance, and gentle manner caused Erasmus, the great Dutch humanist who became his friend during a visit to London, to write to a friend: "Did nature ever create anything kinder, sweeter, or more harmonious than the character of Thomas More?"

More served in Parliament, became a diplomat, and after holding several important positions in the government of Henry VIII, rose to become Lord Chancellor. But when Henry married Anne Boleyn, broke from the Church of Rome, and established himself as head of the Church of England, More refused to subscribe to the Act of Succession and Supremacy. Condemned to death as a traitor, he was executed in 1535, nominally for treason but really because he would not recognize the king rather than the pope as the head of his church. A moment before the ax fell, More displayed a bit of the whimsy for which he was known: When he put his head on the block, he brushed his beard aside, commenting that his beard had done no offense to the king. In 1886 the Roman Catholic Church beatified More, and in 1935, the four-hundredth anniversary of his death, it canonized him as St. Thomas More.

More wrote Utopia *(1514–15) in Latin, the international language of the day. The book's name, however, is Greek for "no place" (ou topos), with a pun on "good place" (eu topos). Utopia owes something to Plato's* Republic *and something to then-popular accounts of voyagers such as Amerigo Vespucci.* Utopia *purports to record an account given by a traveler named Hytholodaeus (Greek for "learned in nonsense"), who allegedly visited Utopia. The work is playful, but it is also serious. In truth, it is hard to know exactly where it is serious and how serious it is. One inevitably wonders, for example, if More the devoted Roman Catholic could really have*

*advocated euthanasia. And could More the persecutor of heretics really have
approved of the religious tolerance practiced in Utopia? Is he perhaps in effect saying, "Let's see what reason, unaided by Christian revelation, can tell
us about an ideal society"? But if so, is he nevertheless also saying, very
strongly, that Christian countries, though blessed with the revelation of
Christ's teachings, are far behind these unenlightened pagans? Utopia has
been widely praised by all sorts of readers—from Roman Catholics to communists—but for all sorts of reasons. The selection presented here is about
one-twelfth of the book (in a translation by Paul Turner).*

From *Utopia*

[A DAY IN UTOPIA]

And now for their working conditions. Well, there's one job they all
do, irrespective of sex, and that's farming. It's part of every child's education. They learn the principles of agriculture at school, and they're taken
for regular outings into the fields near the town, where they not only
watch farm work being done, but also do some themselves, as a form of
exercise.

Besides farming which, as I say, is everybody's job, each person is
taught a special trade of his own. He may be trained to process wool or
flax, or he may become a stonemason, a blacksmith, or a carpenter.
Those are the only trades that employ any considerable quantity of
labor. They have no tailors or dressmakers, since everyone on the island
wears the same sort of clothes—except that they vary slightly according
to sex and marital status—and the fashion never changes. These clothes
are quite pleasant to look at, they allow free movement of the limbs,
they're equally suitable for hot and cold weather—and the great thing
is, they're all home-made. So everybody learns one of the other trades I
mentioned, and by everybody I mean the women as well as the men—
though the weaker sex are given the lighter jobs, like spinning and
weaving, while the men do the heavier ones.

Most children are brought up to do the same work as their parents,
since they tend to have a natural feeling for it. But if a child fancies some
other trade, he's adopted into a family that practices it. Of course, great
care is taken, not only by the father, but also by the local authorities, to
see that the foster father is a decent, respectable type. When you've
learned one trade properly, you can, if you like, get permission to
learn another—and when you're an expert in both, you can practice
whichever you prefer, unless the other one is more essential to the
public.

The chief business of the Stywards[1]—in fact, practically their only
business—is to see that nobody sits around doing nothing, but that

---

[1]**Stywards** In Utopia, each group of thirty households elects a styward; each town has
two hundred stywards, who elect the mayor. [All notes are the editors'.]

everyone gets on with his job. They don't wear people out, though, by keeping them hard at work from early morning till late at night, like cart horses. That's just slavery—and yet that's what life is like for the working classes nearly everywhere else in the world. In Utopia they have a six-hour working day—three hours in the morning, then lunch—then a two-hour break—then three more hours in the afternoon, followed by supper. They go to bed at 8 P.M., and sleep for eight hours. All the rest of the twenty-four they're free to do what they like—not to waste their time in idleness or self-indulgence, but to make good use of it in some congenial activity. Most people spend these free periods on further education, for there are public lectures first thing every morning. Attendance is quite voluntary, except for those picked out for academic training, but men and women of all classes go crowding in to hear them—I mean, different people go to different lectures, just as the spirit moves them. However, there's nothing to stop you from spending this extra time on your trade, if you want to. Lots of people do, if they haven't the capacity for intellectual work, and are much admired for such public-spirited behavior.

After supper they have an hour's recreation, either in the gardens   5
or in the communal dining-halls, according to the time of year. Some people practice music, others just talk. They've never heard of anything so silly and demoralizing as dice, but they have two games rather like chess. The first is a sort of arithmetical contest, in which certain numbers "take" others. The second is a pitched battle between virtues and vices, which illustrates most ingeniously how vices tend to conflict with one another, but to combine against virtues. It also shows which vices are opposed to which virtues, how much strength vices can muster for a direct assault, what indirect tactics they employ, what help virtues need to overcome vices, what are the best methods of evading their attacks, and what ultimately determines the victory of one side or the other.

But here's a point that requires special attention, or you're liable to get the wrong idea. Since they only work a six-hour day, you may think there must be a shortage of essential goods. On the contrary, those six hours are enough, and more than enough to produce plenty of everything that's needed for a comfortable life. And you'll understand why it is, if you reckon up how large a proportion of the population in other countries is totally unemployed. First you have practically all the women—that gives you nearly 50 percent for a start. And in countries where the women *do* work, the men tend to lounge about instead. Then there are all the priests, and members of so-called religious orders—how much work do they do? Add all the rich, especially the landowners, popularly known as nobles and gentlemen. Include their domestic staffs—I mean those gangs of armed ruffians that I mentioned before. Finally, throw in all the beggars who are perfectly hale and hearty, but pretend to be ill as an excuse for being lazy. When you've counted them up, you'll be surprised to find how few people actually produce what the human race consumes.

And now just think how few of these few people are doing essential work—for where money is the only standard of value, there are bound to be dozens of unnecessary trades carried on, which merely supply luxury goods or entertainment. Why, even if the existing labor force were distributed among the few trades really needed to make life reasonably comfortable, there'd be so much overproduction that prices would fall too low for the workers to earn a living. Whereas, if you took all those engaged in nonessential trades, and all who are too lazy to work—each of whom consumes twice as much of the products of other people's labor as any of the producers themselves—if you put the whole lot of them on to something useful, you'd soon see how few hours' work a day would be amply sufficient to supply all the necessities and comforts of life—to which you might add all real and natural forms of pleasure.

[THE HOUSEHOLD]

But let's get back to their social organization. Each household, as I said, comes under the authority of the oldest male. Wives are subordinate to their husbands, children to their parents, and younger people generally to their elders. Every town is divided into four districts of equal size, each with its own shopping center in the middle of it. There the products of every household are collected in warehouses, and then distributed according to type among various shops. When the head of a household needs anything for himself or his family, he just goes to one of these shops and asks for it. And whatever he asks for, he's allowed to take away without any sort of payment, either in money or in kind. After all, why shouldn't he? There's more than enough of everything to go round, so there's no risk of his asking for more than he needs—for why should anyone want to start hoarding, when he knows he'll never have to go short of anything? No living creature is naturally greedy, except from fear of want—or in the case of human beings, from vanity, the notion that you're better than people if you can display more superfluous property than they can. But there's no scope for that sort of thing in Utopia.

[UTOPIAN BELIEFS]

The Utopians fail to understand why anyone should be so fascinated by the dull gleam of a tiny bit of stone, when he has all the stars in the sky to look at—or how anyone can be silly enough to think himself better than other people, because his clothes are made of finer woollen thread than theirs. After all, those fine clothes were once worn by a sheep, and they never turned it into anything better than a sheep.

Nor can they understand why a totally useless substance like gold 10 should now, all over the world, be considered far more important than human beings, who gave it such value as it has, purely for their own convenience. The result is that a man with about as much mental agility as a lump of lead or a block of wood, a man whose utter stupidity is paralleled only by his immorality, can have lots of good, intelligent people at his beck and call, just because he happens to possess a large pile of gold coins. And if by some freak of fortune or trick of the law—two equally effective methods of turning things upside down—the said coins were suddenly transferred to the most worthless member of his domestic staff, you'd soon see the present owner trotting after his money, like an extra piece of currency, and becoming his own servant's servant. But what puzzles and disgusts the Utopians even more is the idiotic way some people have of practically worshipping a rich man, not because they owe him money or are otherwise in his power, but simply because he's rich—although they know perfectly well that he's far too mean to let a single penny come their way, so long as he's alive to stop it.

They get these ideas partly from being brought up under a social system which is directly opposed to that type of nonsense, and partly from their reading and education. Admittedly, no one's allowed to become a full-time student, except for the very few in each town who appear as children to possess unusual gifts, outstanding intelligence, and a special aptitude for academic research. But every child receives a primary education, and most men and women go on educating themselves all their lives during those free periods that I told you about. . . .

In ethics they discuss the same problems as we do. Having distinguished between three types of "good," psychological, physiological, and environmental, they proceed to ask whether the term is strictly applicable to all of them, or only to the first. They also argue about such things as virtue and pleasure. But their chief subject of dispute is the nature of human happiness—on what factor or factors does it depend? Here they seem rather too much inclined to take a hedonistic view, for according to them human happiness consists largely or wholly in pleasure. Surprisingly enough, they defend this self-indulgent doctrine by arguments drawn from religion—a thing normally associated with a more serious view of life, if not with gloomy asceticism. You see, in all their discussions of happiness they invoke certain religious principles to supplement the operations of reason, which they think otherwise ill-equipped to identify true happiness.

The first principle is that every soul is immortal, and was created by a kind God, Who meant it to be happy. The second is that we shall be rewarded or punished in the next world for our good or bad behavior in this one. Although these are religious principles, the Utopians find rational grounds for accepting them. For suppose you didn't accept them? In that case, they say, any fool could tell you what you ought to do. You should go all out for your own pleasure, irrespective of right and wrong. You'd merely have to make sure that minor pleasures didn't interfere with major ones, and avoid the type of pleasure that has painful aftereffects. For what's the sense of struggling to be virtuous, denying yourself the pleasant things of life, and deliberately making yourself uncomfortable, if there's nothing you hope to gain by it? And what *can* you hope to gain by it, if you receive no compensation after death for a thoroughly unpleasant, that is, a thoroughly miserable life?

Not that they identify happiness with every type of pleasure—only with the higher ones. Nor do they identify it with virtue—unless they belong to a quite different school of thought. According to the normal view, happiness is the *summum bonum*[2] toward which we're naturally impelled by virtue—which in their definition means following one's natural impulses, as God meant us to do. But this includes obeying the instinct to be reasonable in our likes and dislikes. And reason also teaches us, first to love and reverence Almighty God, to Whom we owe our existence and our potentiality for happiness, and secondly to get through life as comfortably and cheerfully as we can, and help all other members of our species to do so too.

The fact is, even the sternest ascetic tends to be slightly inconsistent 15
in his condemnation of pleasure. He may sentence *you* to a life of hard labor, inadequate sleep, and general discomfort, but he'll also tell you to do your best to ease the pains and privations of others. He'll regard all such attempts to improve the human situation as laudable acts of humanity—for obviously nothing could be more humane, or more natural for a human being, than to relieve other people's sufferings, put an end to their miseries, and restore their *joie de vivre*, that is, their capacity for pleasure. So why shouldn't it be equally natural to do the same thing for oneself?

Either it's a bad thing to enjoy life, in other words, to experience pleasure—in which case you shouldn't help anyone to do it, but should try to save the whole human race from such a frightful fate—or else, if it's good for other people, and you're not only allowed, but positively obliged to make it possible for them, why shouldn't charity begin at home? After all, you've a duty to yourself as well as to your neighbor, and, if Nature says you must be kind to others, she can't turn round the next moment and say you must be cruel to yourself. The Utopians therefore regard the enjoyment of life—that is, pleasure—as the natural object of all human efforts, and natural, as they define it, is synonymous with virtuous. However, Nature also wants us to help one another to enjoy life, for the very good reason that no human being has a monopoly of her affections. She's equally anxious for the welfare of every member of the species. So of course she tells us to make quite sure that we don't pursue our own interests at the expense of other people's.

On this principle they think it right to keep one's promises in private life, and also to obey public laws for regulating the distribution of

---

[2]***summum bonum*** Latin for "the highest good."

"goods"—by which I mean the raw materials of pleasure—provided such laws have been properly made by a wise ruler, or passed by common consent of a whole population, which has not been subjected to any form of violence or deception. Within these limits they say it's sensible to consult one's own interests, and a moral duty to consult those of the community as well. It's wrong to deprive someone else of a pleasure so that you can enjoy one yourself, but to deprive yourself of a pleasure so that you can add to someone else's enjoyment is an act of humanity by which you always gain more than you lose. For one thing, such benefits are usually repaid in kind. For another, the mere sense of having done somebody a kindness, and so earned his affection and goodwill, produces a spiritual satisfaction which far outweighs the loss of a physical one. And lastly—a belief that comes easily to a religious mind—God will reward us for such small sacrifices of momentary pleasure, by giving us an eternity of perfect joy. Thus they argue that, in the final analysis, pleasure is the ultimate happiness which all human beings have in view, even when they're acting most virtuously.

Pleasure they define as any state or activity, physical or mental, which is naturally enjoyable. The operative word is *naturally*. According to them, we're impelled by reason as well as an instinct to enjoy ourselves in any natural way which doesn't hurt other people, interfere with greater pleasures, or cause unpleasant aftereffects. But human beings have entered into an idiotic conspiracy to call some things enjoyable which are naturally nothing of the kind—as though facts were as easily changed as definitions. Now the Utopians believe that, so far from contributing to happiness, this type of thing makes happiness impossible— because, once you get used to it, you lose all capacity for real pleasure, and are merely obsessed by illusory forms of it. Very often these have nothing pleasant about them at all—in fact, most of them are thoroughly disagreeable. But they appeal so strongly to perverted tastes that they come to be reckoned not only among the major pleasures of life, but even among the chief reasons for living.

In the category of illusory pleasure addicts they include the kind of person I mentioned before, who thinks himself better than other people because he's better dressed than they are. Actually he's just as wrong about his clothes as he is about himself. From a practical point of view, why is it better to be dressed in fine woollen thread than in coarse? But he's got it into his head that fine thread is naturally superior, and that wearing it somehow increases his own value. So he feels entitled to far more respect than he'd ever dare to hope for, if he were less expensively dressed, and is most indignant if he fails to get it.

Talking of respect, isn't it equally idiotic to attach such importance to 20 a lot of empty gestures which do nobody any good? For what real pleasure can you get out of the sight of a bared head or a bent knee? Will it cure the rheumatism in your own knee, or make you any less weak in the head? Of course, the great believers in this type of artificial pleasure are those who pride themselves on their "nobility." Nowadays that merely means that they happen to belong to a family which has been rich for several generations, preferably in landed property. And yet they feel every bit as "noble" even if they've failed to inherit any of the said property, or if they have inherited it and then frittered it all away.

Then there's another type of person I mentioned before, who has a passion for jewels, and feels practically superhuman if he manages to get hold of a rare one, especially if it's a kind that's considered particularly precious in his country and period—for the value of such things varies according to where and when you live. But he's so terrified of being taken in by appearances that he refuses to buy any jewel until he's stripped off all the gold and inspected it in the nude. And even then he won't buy it without a solemn assurance and a written guarantee from the jeweler that the stone is genuine. But my dear sir, why shouldn't a fake give you just as much pleasure, if you can't, with your own eyes, distinguish it from a real one? It makes no difference to you whether it's genuine or not—any more than it would to a blind man!

And now, what about those people who accumulate superfluous wealth, for no better purpose than to enjoy looking at it? Is their pleasure a real one, or merely a form of delusion? The opposite type of psychopath buries his gold, so that he'll never be able to use it, and may never even see it again. In fact, he deliberately loses it in his anxiety not to lose it—for what can you call it but lost, when it's put back into the earth, where it's no good to him, or probably to anyone else? And yet he's tremendously happy when he's got it stowed away. Now, apparently, he can stop worrying. But suppose the money is stolen, and ten years later he dies without ever knowing it has gone. Then for a whole ten years he has managed to survive his loss, and during that period what difference has it made to him whether the money was there or not? It was just as little use to him either way.

Among stupid pleasures they include not only gambling—a form of idiocy that they've heard about but never practiced—but also hunting and hawking. What on earth is the fun, they ask, of throwing dice onto a table? Besides, you've done it so often that, even if there was some fun in it at first, you must surely be sick of it by now. How can you possibly enjoy listening to anything so disagreeable as the barking and howling of dogs? And why is it more amusing to watch a dog chasing a hare than to watch one dog chasing another? In each case the essential activity is running—if running is what amuses you. But if it's really the thought of being in at the death, and seeing an animal torn to pieces before your eyes, wouldn't pity be a more appropriate reaction to the sight of a weak, timid, harmless little creature like a hare being devoured by something so much stronger and fiercer?

So the Utopians consider hunting below the dignity of free men, and leave it entirely to butchers, who are, as I told you, slaves. In their view hunting is the vilest department of butchery, compared with which all the others are relatively useful and honorable. An ordinary butcher slaughters livestock far more sparingly, and only because he has to, whereas a hunter kills and mutilates poor little creatures purely for his own amusement. They say you won't find that type of blood lust even among animals, unless they're particularly savage by nature, or have become so by constantly being used for this cruel sport.

There are hundreds of things like that, which are generally regarded   25
as pleasures, but everyone in Utopia is quite convinced that they've got nothing to do with real pleasure, because there's nothing naturally enjoyable about them. Nor is this conviction at all shaken by the argument that most people do actually enjoy them, which would seem to indicate an appreciable pleasure content. They say this is a purely subjective reaction caused by bad habits, which can make a person prefer unpleasant things to pleasant ones, just as pregnant women sometimes lose their sense of taste, and find suet or turpentine more delicious than honey. But however much one's judgment may be impaired by habit or ill health, the nature of pleasure, as of everything else, remains unchanged.

Real pleasures they divide into two categories, mental and physical. Mental pleasures include the satisfaction that one gets from understanding something, or from contemplating truth. They also include the memory of a well-spent life, and the confident expectation of good things to come. Physical pleasures are subdivided into two types. First there are those which fill the whole organism with a conscious sense of enjoyment. This may be the result of replacing physical substances which have been burnt up by the natural heat of the body, as when we eat or drink. Or else it may be caused by the discharge of some excess, as in excretion, sexual intercourse, or any relief of irritation by rubbing or scratching. However, there are also pleasures which satisfy no organic need, and relieve no previous discomfort. They merely act, in a mysterious but quite unmistakable way, directly on our senses, and monopolize their reactions. Such is the pleasure of music.

Their second type of physical pleasure arises from the calm and regular functioning of the body—that is, from a state of health undisturbed by any minor ailments. In the absence of mental discomfort, this gives one a good feeling, even without the help of external pleasures. Of course, it's less ostentatious, and forces itself less violently on one's attention than the cruder delights of eating and drinking, but even so it's often considered the greatest pleasure in life. Practically everyone in Utopia would agree that it's a very important one, because it's the basis of all the others. It's enough by itself to make you enjoy life, and unless you have it, no other pleasure is possible. However, mere freedom from pain, without positive health, they would call not pleasure but anesthesia.

Some thinkers used to maintain that a uniformly tranquil state of health couldn't properly be termed a pleasure since its presence could only be detected by contrast with its opposite—oh yes, they went very thoroughly into the whole question. But that theory was exploded long ago, and nowadays nearly everybody subscribes to the view that health is most definitely a pleasure. The argument goes like this—illness involves pain, which is the direct opposite of pleasure, and illness is the direct opposite of health, therefore health involves pleasure. They don't think it matters whether you say that illness *is* or merely *involves* pain. Either way it comes to the same thing. Similarly, whether health *is* a pleasure, or merely *produces* pleasure as inevitably as fire produces heat, it's equally logical to assume that where you have an uninterrupted state of health you cannot fail to have pleasure.

Besides, they say, when we eat something, what really happens is this. Our failing health starts fighting off the attacks of hunger, using the food as an ally. Gradually it begins to prevail, and, in this very process of winning back its normal strength, experiences the sense of enjoyment which we find so refreshing. Now, if health enjoys the actual battle, why shouldn't it also enjoy the victory? Or are we to suppose that when it has finally managed to regain its former vigor—the one thing that it has been fighting for all this time—it promptly falls into a coma, and fails to notice or take advantage of its success? As for the idea that one isn't conscious of health except through its opposite, they say that's quite untrue. Everyone's perfectly aware of feeling well, unless he's asleep or actually feeling ill. Even the most insensitive and apathetic sort of person will admit that it's delightful to be healthy—and what is delight, but a synonym for pleasure?

They're particularly fond of mental pleasures, which they consider of 30 primary importance, and attribute mostly to good behavior and a clear conscience. Their favorite physical pleasure is health. Of course, they believe in enjoying food, drink, and so forth, but purely in the interests of health, for they don't regard such things as very pleasant in themselves—only as methods of resisting the stealthy onset of disease. A sensible person, they say, prefers keeping well to taking medicine, and would rather feel cheerful than have people trying to comfort him. On the same principle it's better not to need this type of pleasure than to become addicted to it. For, if you think that sort of thing will make you happy, you'll have to admit that your idea of perfect felicity would be a life consisting entirely of hunger, thirst, itching, eating, drinking, rubbing, and scratching—which would obviously be most unpleasant as well as quite disgusting. Undoubtedly these pleasures should come right at the bottom of the list, because they're so impure. For instance, the pleasure of eating is invariably diluted with the pain of hunger, and not in equal proportions either—for the pain is both more intense and more prolonged. It starts before the pleasure, and doesn't stop until the pleasure has stopped too.

So they don't think much of pleasures like that, except insofar as they're necessary. But they enjoy them all the same, and feel most grateful to Mother Nature for encouraging her children to do things that have to be done so often, by making them so attractive. For just think how dreary life would be, if those chronic ailments, hunger and thirst, could only be cured by foul-tasting medicines, like the rarer types of disease!

They attach great value to special natural gifts such as beauty, strength, and agility. They're also keen on the pleasures of sight, hearing, and smell, which are peculiar to human beings—for no other species admires the beauty of the world, enjoys any sort of scent, except as a method of locating food, or can tell the difference between a harmony and a discord. They say these things give a sort of relish to life.

However, in all such matters they observe the rule that minor pleasures mustn't interfere with major ones, and that pleasure mustn't cause pain—which they think is bound to happen, if the pleasure is immoral. But they'd never dream of despising their own beauty, overtaxing their strength, converting their agility into inertia, ruining their physique by going without food, damaging their health, or spurning any other of Nature's gifts, unless they were doing it for the benefit of other people or of society, in the hope of receiving some greater pleasure from God in return. For they think it's quite absurd to torment oneself in the name of an unreal virtue, which does nobody any good, or in order to steel oneself against disasters which may never occur. They say such behavior is merely self-destructive, and shows a most ungrateful attitude toward Nature—as if one refused all her favors, because one couldn't bear the thought of being indebted to her for anything.

Well, that's their ethical theory, and short of some divine revelation, they doubt if the human mind is capable of devising a better one. We've no time to discuss whether it's right or wrong—nor is it really necessary, for all I undertook was to describe their way of life, not to defend it.

[TREATMENT OF THE DYING]

As I told you, when people are ill, they're looked after most sympathetically, and given everything in the way of medicine or special food that could possibly assist their recovery. In the case of permanent invalids, the nurses try to make them feel better by sitting and talking to them, and do all they can to relieve their symptoms. But if, besides being incurable, the disease also causes constant excruciating pain, some priests and government officials visit the person concerned, and say something like this: 35

"Let's face it, you'll never be able to live a normal life. You're just a nuisance to other people and a burden to yourself—in fact you're really leading a sort of posthumous existence. So why go on feeding germs? Since your life's a misery to you, why hesitate to die? You're imprisoned in a torture chamber—why don't you break out and escape to a better world? Or say the word, and we'll arrange for your release. It's only common sense to cut your losses. It's also an act of piety to take the advice of a priest, because he speaks for God."

If the patient finds these arguments convincing, he either starves himself to death, or is given a soporific and put painlessly out of his misery. But this is strictly voluntary, and, if he prefers to stay alive, everyone will go on treating him as kindly as ever.

[THE SUMMING UP]

Well, that's the most accurate account I can give you of the Utopian Republic. To my mind, it's not only the best country in the world, but the only one that has any right to call itself a republic. Elsewhere, people are always talking about the public interest, but all they really care about is private property. In Utopia, where's there's no private property, people take their duty to the public seriously. And both attitudes are perfectly reasonable. In other "republics" practically everyone knows that, if he doesn't look out for himself, he'll starve to death, however prosperous his country may be. He's therefore compelled to give his own interests priority over those of the public; that is, of other people. But in Utopia, where everything's under public ownership, no one has any fear of going short, as long as the public storehouses are full. Everyone gets a fair share, so there are never any poor men or beggars. Nobody owns anything, but everyone is rich—for what greater wealth can there be than cheerfulness, peace of mind, and freedom from anxiety? Instead of being worried about his food supply, upset by the plaintive demands of his wife, afraid of poverty for his son, and baffled by the problem of finding a dowry for his daughter, the Utopian can feel absolutely sure that he, his wife, his children, his grandchildren, his great-grandchildren, his great-great-grandchildren, and as long a line of descendants as the proudest peer could wish to look forward to, will always have enough to eat and enough to make them happy. There's also the further point that those who are too old to work are just as well provided for as those who are still working.

Now, will anyone venture to compare these fair arrangements in Utopia with the so-called justice of other countries?—in which I'm damned if I can see the slightest trace of justice or fairness. For what sort of justice do you call this? People like aristocrats, goldsmiths, or moneylenders, who either do no work at all, or do work that's really not essential, are rewarded for their laziness or their unnecessary activities by a splendid life of luxury. But laborers, coachmen, carpenters, and farmhands, who never stop working like cart horses, at jobs so essential that, if they *did* stop working, they'd bring any country to a standstill within twelve months—what happens to them? They get so little to eat, and have such a wretched time, that they'd be almost better off if they *were* cart horses. Then at least, they wouldn't work quite such long hours, their food wouldn't be very much worse, they'd enjoy it more, and they'd have no fears for the future. As it is, they're not only ground down by unrewarding toil in the present, but also worried to death by the prospect of a poverty-stricken old age—since their daily wages aren't enough to support them for one day, let alone leave anything over to be saved up when they're old.

Can you see any fairness or gratitude in a social system which lav- 40 ishes such great rewards on so-called noblemen, goldsmiths, and people like that, who are either totally unproductive or merely employed in producing luxury goods or entertainment, but makes no such kind provision for farmhands, coal heavers, laborers, carters, or carpenters, without whom society couldn't exist at all? And the climax of ingratitude comes when they're old and ill and completely destitute. Having taken advantage of them throughout the best years of their lives, society now forgets all the sleepless hours they've spent in its service, and repays them for all the vital work they've done, by letting them die in misery. What's more, the wretched earnings of the poor are daily whittled away by the rich, not only through private dishonesty, but through public legislation. As if it weren't unjust enough already that the man who contributes most to society should get the least in return, they make it even worse, and then arrange for injustice to be legally described as justice.

In fact, when I consider any social system that prevails in the modern world, I can't, so help me God, see it as anything but a conspiracy of the rich to advance their own interests under the pretext of organizing society. They think up all sorts of tricks and dodges, first for keeping safe their ill-gotten gains, and then for exploiting the poor by buying their labor as cheaply as possible. Once the rich have decided that these tricks and dodges shall be officially recognized by society—which includes the poor as well as the rich—they acquire the force of law. Thus an unscrupulous minority is led by its insatiable greed to monopolize what would have been enough to supply the needs of the whole population. And yet how much happier even these people would be in Utopia! There, with the simultaneous abolition of money and the passion for money, how many other social problems have been solved, how many crimes eradicated! For obviously the end of money means the end of all those types of criminal behavior which daily punishments are powerless to check: fraud, theft, burglary, brawls, riots, disputes, rebellion, murder, treason, and black magic. And the moment money goes, you can also say goodbye to fear, tension, anxiety, overwork, and sleepless nights. Why, even poverty itself, the one problem that has always seemed to need money for its solution, would promptly disappear if money ceased to exist.

Let me try to make this point clearer. Just think back to one of the years when the harvest was bad, and thousands of people died of starvation. Well, I bet if you'd inspected every rich man's barn at the end of that lean period you'd have found enough corn to have saved all the lives that were lost through malnutrition and disease, and prevented anyone from suffering any ill effects whatever from the meanness of the weather and the soil. Everyone could so easily get enough to eat, if it weren't for that blessed nuisance, money. There you have a brilliant invention which was designed to make food more readily available. Actually it's the only thing that makes it unobtainable.

I'm sure that even the rich are well aware of all this, and realize how much better it would be to have everything one needed, than lots of things one didn't need — to be evacuated altogether from the danger area, than to dig oneself in behind a barricade of enormous wealth. And I've no doubt that either self-interest, or the authority of our Savior Christ — Who was far too wise not to know what was best for us, and far too kind to recommend anything else — would have led the whole world to adopt the Utopian system long ago, if it weren't for that beastly root of all evils, pride. For pride's criterion of prosperity is not what you've got yourself, but what other people haven't got. Pride would refuse to set foot in paradise, if she thought there'd be no underprivileged classes there to gloat over and order about — nobody whose misery could serve as a foil to her own happiness, or whose poverty she could make harder to bear, by flaunting her own riches. Pride, like a hellish serpent gliding through human hearts — or shall we say, like a sucking-fish that clings to the ship of state? — is always dragging us back, and obstructing our progress toward a better way of life.

But as this fault is too deeply ingrained in human nature to be easily eradicated, I'm glad that at least one country has managed to develop a system which I'd like to see universally adopted. The Utopian way of life provides not only the happiest basis for a civilized community, but also one which, in all human probability, will last forever. They've eliminated the root causes of ambition, political conflict, and everything like that. There's therefore no danger of internal dissension, the one thing that has destroyed so many impregnable towns. And as long as there's unity and sound administration at home, no matter how envious neighboring kings may feel, they'll never be able to shake, let alone to shatter, the power of Utopia. They've tried to do so often enough in the past, but have always been beaten back.

Topics for Critical Thinking and Writing

1. More, writing early in the sixteenth century, was living in a primarily agricultural society. Laborers were needed on farms, but might More have had any other reason for insisting (para. 1) that all people should do some farming and that farming should be part of "every child's education"? Do you think everyone should put in some time as a farmer? Why, or why not?

2. More indicates that in the England of his day many people loafed or engaged in unnecessary work (producing luxury goods, for one thing), putting an enormous burden on those who engaged in useful work. Is this condition, or any part of it, true of our society? Explain.

3. The Utopians cannot understand why the people of other nations value gems, gold, and fine clothes. If you value any of these, can you offer an explanation?

4. What arguments can you offer against the Utopians' treatment of persons who are incurably ill and in pain? (You may get some ideas from the essays by Ellen Goodman, p. 627, and Terry Golway, p. 629.)

5. Summarize More's report of the Utopians' idea of pleasure. (This summary will probably take three or four paragraphs.)

6. More's Utopians cannot understand why anyone takes pleasure in gambling or in hunting. If either activity gives you pleasure, in an essay of 500 words explain why, and offer an argument on behalf of your view.

7. As More makes clear in the part we entitle "The Summing Up," in Utopia there is no private property. In a sentence or two summarize the reasons he gives for this principle, and then in a paragraph evaluate them.

Niccolò Machiavelli

Niccolò Machiavelli (1469–1527) was born in Florence at a time when Italy was divided into five major states: Venice, Milan, Florence, the Papal States, and Naples. Although these states often had belligerent relations with one another as well as with lesser Italian states, under the Medici family in Florence they achieved a precarious balance of power. In 1494, however, Lorenzo de' Medici, who had ruled from 1469 to 1492, died, and two years later Lorenzo's successor was exiled when the French army arrived in Florence. Italy became a field where Spain, France, and Germany competed for power. From 1498 to 1512 Machiavelli held a high post in the diplomatic service of the Florentine Republic, but when the French army reappeared and the Florentines in desperation recalled the Medici, Machiavelli lost his post, was imprisoned, tortured, and then exiled. Banished from Florence, he nevertheless lived in fair comfort on a small estate nearby, writing his major works and hoping to obtain an office from the Medici. In later years he was employed in a few minor diplomatic missions, but even after the collapse and expulsion of the Medici in 1527 and the restoration of the republic, he did not regain his old position of importance. He died shortly after the restoration.

Our selection comes from The Prince, *which Machiavelli wrote in 1513 during his banishment hoping that it would interest the Medici and thus restore him to favor; but the book was not published until 1532, five years after his death. In this book of twenty-six short chapters, Machiavelli begins by examining different kinds of states, but the work's enduring power resides in the discussions (in Chapters 15–18, reprinted here) of qualities necessary to a prince—that is, a head of state. Any such examination obviously is based in part on assumptions about the nature of the citizens of the realm.*

This selection was taken from a translation edited by Peter Bondanella and Mark Musa.

From *The Prince*

ON THOSE THINGS FOR WHICH MEN, AND PARTICULARLY PRINCES, ARE PRAISED OR BLAMED

Now there remains to be examined what should be the methods and procedures of a prince in dealing with his subjects and friends. And because I know that many have written about this, I am afraid that by writing about it again I shall be thought of as presumptuous, since in discussing this material I depart radically from the procedures of others. But since my intention is to write something useful for anyone who understands it, it seemed more suitable to me to search after the effectual truth of the matter rather than its imagined one. And many writers have imagined for themselves republics and principalities that have never been seen nor known to exist in reality; for there is such a gap between how one lives and how one ought to live that anyone who abandons what is done for what ought to be done learns his ruin rather than his preservation: for a man who wishes to make a vocation of being good at all times will come to ruin among so many who are not good. Hence it is necessary for a prince who wishes to maintain his position to learn how not to be good, and to use this knowledge or not to use it according to necessity.

Leaving aside, therefore, the imagined things concerning a prince, and taking into account those that are true, I say that all men, when they are spoken of, and particularly princes, since they are placed on a higher level, are judged by some of these qualities which bring them either blame or praise. And this is why one is considered generous, another miserly (to use a Tuscan word, since "avaricious" in our language is still used to mean one who wishes to acquire by means of theft; we call "miserly" one who excessively avoids using what he has); one is considered a giver, the other rapacious; one cruel, another merciful; one treacherous, another faithful; one effeminate and cowardly, another bold and courageous; one humane, another haughty; one lascivious, another chaste; one trustworthy, another cunning; one harsh, another lenient; one serious, another frivolous; one religious, another unbelieving; and the like. And I know that everyone will admit that it would be a very praiseworthy thing to find in a prince, of the qualities mentioned above, those that are held to be good; but since it is neither possible to have them nor to observe them all completely, because human nature does not permit it, a prince must be prudent enough to know how to escape the bad reputation of those vices that would lose the state for him, and must protect himself from those that will not lose it for him, if this is possible; but if he cannot, he need not concern himself unduly if he ignores these less serious vices. And, moreover, he need not worry about incurring the bad reputation of those vices without which it would be difficult to hold his state; since, carefully taking everything into account, one will discover that something which appears to be a virtue, if pursued, will end in his destruction; while some other thing which seems to be a vice, if pursued, will result in his safety and his well-being.

ON GENEROSITY AND MISERLINESS

Beginning, therefore, with the first of the above-mentioned qualities, I say that it would be good to be considered generous; nevertheless, generosity used in such a manner as to give you a reputation for it will harm you; because if it is employed virtuously and as one should employ it, it will not be recognized and you will not avoid the reproach of its opposite. And so, if a prince wants to maintain his reputation for generosity among men, it is necessary for him not to neglect any possible means of lavish display; in so doing such a prince will always use up all his resources and he will be obliged, eventually, if he wishes to maintain his reputation for generosity, to burden the people with excessive taxes and to do everything possible to raise funds. This will begin to make him hateful to his subjects, and, becoming impoverished, he will not be much esteemed by anyone; so that, as a consequence of his generosity, having offended many and rewarded few, he will feel the effects of any slight unrest and will be ruined at the first sign of danger; recognizing this and wishing to alter his policies, he immediately runs the risk of being reproached as a miser.

A prince, therefore, unable to use this virtue of generosity in a manner which will not harm himself if he is known for it, should, if he is wise, not worry about being called a miser; for with time he will come to be considered more generous once it is evident that, as a result of his parsimony, his income is sufficient, he can defend himself from anyone who makes war against him, and he can undertake enterprises without overburdening his people, so that he comes to be generous with all those from whom he takes nothing, who are countless, and miserly with all those to whom he gives nothing, who are few. In our times we have not seen great deeds accomplished except by those who were considered miserly; all others were done away with. Pope Julius II, although he made use of his reputation for generosity in order to gain the papacy, then decided not to maintain it in order to be able to wage war; the present King of France has waged many wars without imposing extra taxes on his subjects, only because his habitual parsimony has provided for the additional expenditures; the present King of Spain, if he had been considered generous, would not have engaged in nor won so many campaigns.

Therefore, in order not to have to rob his subjects, to be able to defend himself, not to become poor and contemptible, and not to be forced to become rapacious, a prince must consider it of little importance if he incurs the name of miser, for this is one of those vices that permits him to rule. And if someone were to say: Caesar with his generosity came to rule the empire, and many others, because they were generous and known to be so, achieved very high positions; I reply: You are either already a prince or you are on the way to becoming one; in the first instance such generosity is damaging; in the second it is very necessary to be thought generous. And Caesar was one of those who wanted to gain the principality of Rome; but if, after obtaining this, he had lived and had not moderated his expenditures, he would have destroyed that empire. And if someone were to reply: There have existed many princes who have accomplished great deeds with their armies who have been reputed to be generous; I answer you: A prince either spends his own money and that of his subjects or that of others; in the first case he must be economical; in the second he must not restrain any part of his generosity. And for that prince who goes out with his soldiers and lives by looting, sacking, and ransoms, who controls the property of others, such generosity is necessary; otherwise he would not be followed by his troops. And with what does not belong to you or to your subjects you can be a more liberal giver, as were Cyrus, Caesar, and Alexander; for spending the wealth of others does not lessen your reputation but adds to it; only the spending of your own is what harms you. And there is nothing that uses itself up faster than generosity, for as you employ it you lose the means of employing it, and you become either poor or despised or, in order to escape poverty, rapacious and hated. And above all other things a prince must guard himself against being despised and hated; and generosity leads you to both one and the other. So it is wiser to live with the reputation of a miser, which produces reproach without hatred, than to be forced to incur the reputation of rapacity, which produces reproach along with hatred, because you want to be considered as generous.

ON CRUELTY AND MERCY AND WHETHER IT IS BETTER TO BE LOVED THAN TO BE FEARED OR THE CONTRARY

Proceeding to the other qualities mentioned above, I say that every prince must desire to be considered merciful and not cruel; nevertheless, he must take care not to misuse this mercy. Cesare Borgia[1] was considered cruel; nonetheless, his cruelty had brought order to Romagna, united it, restored it to peace and obedience. If we examine this carefully, we shall see that he was more merciful than the Florentine people,

---

[1]**Cesare Borgia** The son of Pope Alexander VI, Cesare Borgia (1476–1507) was ruthlessly opportunistic. Encouraged by his father, in 1499 and 1500 he subdued the cities of **Romagna**, the region including Ferrara and Ravenna. [All notes are the editors' unless otherwise specified.]

who, in order to avoid being considered cruel, allowed the destruction of Pistoia.[2] Therefore, a prince must not worry about the reproach of cruelty when it is a matter of keeping his subjects united and loyal; for with a very few examples of cruelty he will be more compassionate than those who, out of excessive mercy, permit disorders to continue, from which arise murders and plundering; for these usually harm the community at large, while the executions that come from the prince harm one individual in particular. And the new prince, above all other princes, cannot escape the reputation of being called cruel, since new states are full of dangers. And Virgil, through Dido, states: "My difficult condition and the newness of my rule make me act in such a manner, and to set guards over my land on all sides."[3]

Nevertheless, a prince must be cautious in believing and in acting, nor should he be afraid of his own shadow; and he should proceed in such a manner, tempered by prudence and humanity, so that too much trust may not render him imprudent nor too much distrust render him intolerable.

From this arises an argument: whether it is better to be loved than to be feared, or the contrary. I reply that one should like to be both one and the other; but since it is difficult to join them together, it is much safer to be feared than to be loved when one of the two must be lacking. For one can generally say this about men: that they are ungrateful, fickle, simulators and deceivers, avoiders of danger, greedy for gain; and while you work for their good they are completely yours, offering you their blood, their property, their lives, and their sons, as I said earlier, when danger is far away; but when it comes nearer to you they turn away. And that prince who bases his power entirely in their words, finding himself stripped of other preparations, comes to ruin; for friendships that are acquired by a price and not by greatness and nobility of character are purchased but are not owned, and at the proper moment they cannot be spent. And men are less hesitant about harming someone who makes himself loved than one who makes himself feared because love is held together by a chain of obligation which, since men are a sorry lot, is broken on every occasion in which their own self-interest is concerned; but fear is held together by a dread of punishment which will never abandon you.

A prince must nevertheless make himself feared in such a manner that he will avoid hatred, even if he does not acquire love; since to be feared and not to be hated can very well be combined; and this will always be so when he keeps his hands off the property and the women of his citizens and his subjects. And if he must take someone's life, he

---

[2]**Pistoia** A town near Florence; Machiavelli suggests that the Florentines failed to treat dissenting leaders with sufficient severity.
[3]In *Aeneid* I, 563–64, **Virgil** (70–19 B.C.) puts this line into the mouth of **Dido,** the queen of Carthage.

should do so when there is proper justification and manifest cause; but, above all, he should avoid the property of others; for men forget more quickly the death of their father than the loss of their patrimony. Moreover, the reasons for seizing their property are never lacking; and he who begins to live by stealing always finds a reason for taking what belongs to others; on the contrary, reasons for taking a life are rarer and disappear sooner.

But when the prince is with his armies and has under his command 10 a multitude of troops, then it is absolutely necessary that he not worry about being considered cruel; for without that reputation he will never keep an army united or prepared for any combat. Among the praiseworthy deeds of Hannibal[4] is counted this: that, having a very large army, made up of all kinds of men, which he commanded in foreign lands, there never arose the slightest dissension, neither among themselves nor against their prince, both during his good and his bad fortune. This could not have arisen from anything other than his inhuman cruelty, which, along with his many other abilities, made him always respected and terrifying in the eyes of his soldiers; and without that, to attain the same effect, his other abilities would not have sufficed. And the writers of history, having considered this matter very little, on the one hand admire these deeds of his and on the other condemn the main cause of them.

And that it be true that his other abilities would not have been sufficient can be seen from the example of Scipio,[5] a most extraordinary man not only in his time but in all recorded history, whose armies in Spain rebelled against him; this came about from nothing other than his excessive compassion, which gave to his soldiers more liberty than military discipline allowed. For this he was censured in the senate by Fabius Maximus, who called him the corruptor of the Roman militia. The Locrians, having been ruined by one of Scipio's officers, were not avenged by him, nor was the arrogance of that officer corrected, all because of his tolerant nature; so that someone in the senate who tried to apologize for him said that there were many men who knew how not to err better than they knew how to correct errors. Such a nature would have, in time, damaged Scipio's fame and glory if he had maintained it during the empire; but, living under the control of the senate, this harmful characteristic of his not only concealed itself but brought him fame.

I conclude, therefore, returning to the problem of being feared and loved, that since men love at their own pleasure and fear at the pleasure of the prince, a wise prince should build his foundation upon that which belongs to him, not upon that which belongs to others: He must strive only to avoid hatred, as has been said.

---

[4]**Hannibal** The Carthaginian general (247–183 B.C.) whose crossing of the Alps with elephants and full baggage train is one of the great feats of military history.
[5]**Scipio** Publius Cornelius Scipio Africanus the Elder (235–183 B.C.), the conqueror of Hannibal in the Punic Wars. The mutiny of which Machiavelli speaks took place in 206 B.C.

HOW A PRINCE SHOULD KEEP HIS WORD

How praiseworthy it is for a prince to keep his word and to live by integrity and not by deceit everyone knows; nevertheless, one sees from the experience of our times that the princes who have accomplished great deeds are those who have cared little for keeping their promises and who have known how to manipulate the minds of men by shrewdness; and in the end they have surpassed those who laid their foundations upon honesty.

You must, therefore, know that there are two means of fighting: one according to the laws, the other with force; the first way is proper to man, the second to beasts; but because the first, in many cases, is not sufficient, it becomes necessary to have recourse to the second. Therefore, a prince must know how to use wisely the natures of the beast and the man. This policy was taught to princes allegorically by the ancient writers, who described how Achilles and many other ancient princes were given to Chiron[6] the Centaur to be raised and taught under his discipline. This can only mean that, having a half-beast and half-man as a teacher, a prince must know how to employ the nature of the one and the other; and the one without the other cannot endure.

Since, then, a prince must know how to make good use of the nature 15 of the beast, he should choose from among the beasts the fox and the lion; for the lion cannot defend itself from traps and the fox cannot protect itself from wolves. It is therefore necessary to be a fox in order to recognize the traps and a lion in order to frighten the wolves. Those who play only the part of the lion do not understand matters. A wise ruler, therefore, cannot and should not keep his word when such an observance of faith would be to his disadvantage and when the reasons which made him promise are removed. And if men were all good, this rule would not be good; but since men are a sorry lot and will not keep their promises to you, you likewise need not keep yours to them. A prince never lacks legitimate reasons to break his promises. Of this one could cite an endless number of modern examples to show how many pacts, how many promises have been made null and void because of the infidelity of princes; and he who has known best how to use the fox has come to a better end. But it is necessary to know how to disguise this nature well and to be a great hypocrite and a liar: and men are so simpleminded and so controlled by their present necessities that one who deceives will always find another who will allow himself to be deceived.

I do not wish to remain silent about one of these recent instances. Alexander VI[7] did nothing else, he thought about nothing else, except to

---

[6]**Chiron** (Kī'ron) A centaur (half man, half horse), who was said in classical mythology to have been the teacher not only of Achilles but also of Theseus, Jason, Hercules, and other heroes.

[7]**Alexander VI** Pope from 1492 to 1503; father of Cesare Borgia.

deceive men, and he always found the occasion to do this. And there never was a man who had more forcefulness in his oaths, who affirmed a thing with more promises, and who honored his word less; nevertheless, his tricks always succeeded perfectly since he was well acquainted with this aspect of the world.

Therefore, it is not necessary for a prince to have all of the above-mentioned qualities, but it is very necessary for him to appear to have them. Furthermore, I shall be so bold as to assert this; that having them and practicing them at all times is harmful; and appearing to have them useful; for instance, to seem merciful, faithful, humane, forthright, religious, and to be so; but his mind should be disposed in such a way that should it become necessary not to be so, he will be able and know how to change to the contrary. And it is essential to understand this: that a prince, and especially a new prince, cannot observe all those things by which men are considered good, for in order to maintain the state he is often obliged to act against his promise, against charity, against humanity, and against religion. And therefore, it is necessary that he have a mind ready to turn itself according to the way the winds of Fortune and the changeability of affairs require him; and, as I said above, as long as it is possible, he should not stray from the good, but he should know how to enter into evil when necessity commands.

A prince, therefore, must be very careful never to let anything slip from his lips which is not full of the five qualities mentioned above: He should appear, upon seeing and hearing him, to be all mercy, all faithfulness, all integrity, all kindness, all religion. And there is nothing more necessary than to seem to possess this last quality. And men in general judge more by their eyes than their hands; for everyone can see but few can feel. Everyone sees what you seem to be, few perceive what you are, and those few do not dare to contradict the opinion of the many who have the majesty of the state to defend them; and in the actions of all men, and especially of princes, where there is no impartial arbiter, one must consider the final result.[8] Let a prince therefore act to seize and to maintain the state; his methods will always be judged honorable and will be praised by all; for ordinary people are always deceived by appearances and by the outcome of a thing; and in the world there is nothing but ordinary people; and there is no room for the few, while the many have a place to lean on. A certain prince of the present day, whom I shall refrain from naming, preaches nothing but peace and faith, and to both one and the other he is entirely opposed; and both, if he had put them into practice, would have cost him many times over either his reputation or his state.

---

[8]The Italian original, *si guarda al fine*, has often been mistranslated as "the ends justify the means," something Machiavelli never wrote. [Translators' note.]

Topics for Critical Thinking and Writing

1. In the opening paragraph, Machiavelli claims that a ruler who wishes to keep in power must "learn how not to be good" — that is, must know where and when to ignore the demands of conventional morality. In the rest of the excerpt, does he give any convincing evidence to support this claim? Can you think of any recent political event in which a political leader violated the requirements of morality, as Machiavelli advises?

2. Machiavelli says in paragraph 1 that "a man who wishes to make a vocation of being good at all times will come to ruin among so many who are not good." (By the way, the passage is ambiguous. "At all times" is, in the original, a squinting modifier. It may look backward to "being good" or forward to "will come to ruin," but Machiavelli probably means, "A man who at all times wishes to make a vocation of being good will come to ruin among so many who are not good.") Is this view realistic or cynical? (What is the difference between these two?) Assume for the moment that the view is realistic. Does it follow that society requires a ruler who must act according to the principles Machiavelli sets forth?

3. In his second paragraph Machiavelli claims that it is impossible for a ruler to exhibit *all* the conventional virtues (trustworthiness, liberality, and so on). Why does he make this claim? Do you agree with it?

4. In paragraph 4 Machiavelli cites as examples Pope Julius II, the King of France, the King of Spain, and other rulers. Is he using these examples to illustrate his generalizations or to provide evidence for them? If you think he is using them to provide evidence, how convincing do you find the evidence? (Consider: Could Machiavelli be arguing from a biased sample?)

5. In paragraphs 6 to 10 Machiavelli argues that it is sometimes necessary for a ruler to be cruel, and so he praises Cesare Borgia and Hannibal. What in human nature, according to Machiavelli, explains this need to have recourse to cruelty? (By the way, how do you think *cruelty* should be defined here?)

6. Machiavelli says that Cesare Borgia's cruelty brought peace to Romagna and that, on the other hand, the Florentines who sought to avoid being cruel in fact brought pain to Pistoia. Can you think of recent episodes supporting the view that cruelty can be beneficial to society? If so, restate Machiavelli's position, using these examples from recent history. Then go on to write two paragraphs, arguing on behalf of your two examples. Or if you believe that Machiavelli's point here is fundamentally wrong, explain why, again using current examples.

7. In *The Prince*, Machiavelli is writing about how to be a successful ruler. He explicitly says he is dealing with things as they are, not things as they should be. Do you think that in fact one can write usefully about statecraft without considering ethics? Explain. Or you may want to think about it in this way: The study of politics is often called *political science*. Machiavelli can be seen as a sort of scientist, objectively analyzing the

nature of governing—without offering any moral judgments. In an essay of 500 words argue for or against the view that the study of politics is rightly called *political science*.

8. In paragraph 18 Machiavelli declares that "one must consider the final result." Taking account of the context, do you think the meaning is that (a) any end, goal, or purpose of anyone justifies using any means to reach it or (b) the end of governing the state, nation, or country justifies using any means to achieve it? Or do you think Machiavelli means both? Something else entirely?

9. In 500 words argue that an important contemporary political figure does or does not act according to Machiavelli's principles.

10. If you have read the selection from Thomas More's *Utopia* (p. 744), write an essay of 500 words on one of these two topics: (1) why More's book is or is not wiser than Machiavelli's or (2) why one of the books is more interesting than the other.

11. More and Machiavelli wrote their books at almost exactly the same time. Write a dialogue of two or three double-spaced typed pages in which the two men argue about the nature of the state. (During the argument, they will have to reveal their assumptions about the nature of human beings and the role of government.)

Thomas Jefferson

Thomas Jefferson (1743–1826) was a congressman, the governor of Virginia, the first secretary of state, and the president of the United States, but he said he wished to be remembered for only three things: drafting the Declaration of Independence, writing the Virginia Statute for Religious Freedom, and founding the University of Virginia. All three were efforts to promote freedom.

Jefferson was born in Virginia and educated at William and Mary College in Williamsburg, Virginia. After graduating he studied law, was admitted to the bar, and in 1769 was elected to the Virginia House of Burgesses, his first political office. In 1776 he went to Philadelphia as a delegate to the second Continental Congress, where he was elected to a committee of five to write the Declaration of Independence. Jefferson drafted the document, which was then subjected to some changes by the other members of the committee and by the Congress. Although he was unhappy with the changes (especially with the deletion of a passage against slavery), his claim to have written the Declaration is just.

The Declaration of Independence

When in the course of human events, it becomes necessary for one people to dissolve the political bands which have connected them with another, and to assume among the Powers of the earth, the separate and equal station to which the Laws of Nature and of Nature's God entitle them, a decent respect to the opinions of mankind requires that they should declare the causes which impel them to the separation.

We hold these truths to be self-evident, that all men are created equal, that they are endowed by their Creator with certain unalienable Rights, that among these are Life, Liberty and the pursuit of Happiness.

That to secure these rights, Governments are instituted among Men, deriving their just powers from the consent of the governed.

That whenever any Form of Government becomes destructive of these ends, it is the Right of the People to alter or to abolish it, and to institute a new Government, laying its foundation on such principles and organizing its powers in such form, as to them shall seem most likely to effect their Safety and Happiness. Prudence, indeed, will dictate that Governments long established should not be changed for light and transient causes; and accordingly all experience hath shown that mankind are more disposed to suffer, while evils are sufferable, than to right themselves by abolishing the forms to which they are accustomed. But when a long train of abuses and usurpations pursuing invariably the same Object evinces a design to reduce them under absolute Despotism, it is their right, it is their duty, to throw off such government, and to provide new Guards for their future security.

Such has been the patient sufferance of these Colonies; and such is   5
now the necessity which constrains them to alter their former Systems of Government. The history of the present King of Great Britain is a history of repeated injuries and usurpations, all having in direct object the establishment of an absolute Tyranny over these States. To prove this, let Facts be submitted to a candid world.

He has refused his Assent to Laws, the most wholesome and necessary for the public good.

He has forbidden his Governors to pass Laws of immediate and pressing importance, unless suspended in their operation till his Assent should be obtained; and when so suspended, he has utterly neglected to attend to them.

He has refused to pass over Laws for the accommodation of large districts of people, unless those people would relinquish the right of Representation in the Legislature, a right inestimable to them and formidable to tyrants only.

He has called together legislative bodies at places unusual, uncomfortable, and distant from the depository of their Public Records, for the sole purpose of fatiguing them into compliance with his measures.

He has dissolved Representative Houses repeatedly, for opposing   10
with manly firmness his invasions on the rights of the people.

He has refused for a long time, after such dissolutions, to cause others to be elected; whereby the Legislative Powers, incapable of Annihilation, have returned to the People at large for their exercise; the State remaining in the mean time exposed to all the dangers of invasion from without, and convulsions within.

He has endeavored to prevent the population of these States, for that purpose obstructing the Laws of Naturalization of Foreigners; refusing to pass others to encourage their migration hither, and raising the conditions of new Appropriations of Lands.

He has obstructed the Administration of Justice, by refusing his Assent to Laws for establishing Judiciary Powers.

He has made Judges dependent on his Will alone, for the tenure of their offices, and the amount and payment of their salaries.

He has erected a multitude of New Offices, and sent hither swarms 15 of Officers to harass our People, and eat out their substance.

He has kept among us, in time of peace, Standing Armies without the consent of our Legislature.

He has affected to render the Military independent of and superior to the Civil Power.

He has combined with others to subject us to jurisdictions foreign to our constitution, and unacknowledged by our laws; giving his Assent to their acts of pretended Legislation:

For quartering large bodies of armed troops among us:

For protecting them, by a mock Trial, from Punishment for any Mur- 20 ders which they should commit on the Inhabitants of these States:

For cutting off our Trade with all parts of the world:

For imposing Taxes on us without our Consent:

For depriving us in many cases, of the benefits of Trial by Jury:

For transporting us beyond Seas to be tried for pretended offenses:

For abolishing the free System of English Laws in a Neighbouring 25 Province, establishing therein an Arbitrary government, and enlarging its boundaries so as to render it at once an example and fit instrument for introducing the same absolute rule into these Colonies:

For taking away our Charters, abolishing our most valuable Laws, and altering fundamentally the Forms of our Governments.

For suspending our own Legislatures, and declaring themselves invested with Power to legislate for us in all cases whatsoever.

He has abdicated Government here, by declaring us out of his Protection and waging War against us.

He has plundered our seas, ravaged our Coasts, burnt our towns and destroyed the Lives of our people.

He is at this time transporting large Armies of foreign Mercenaries to 30 compleat the works of death, desolation and tyranny, already begun with circumstances of Cruelty & perfidy scarcely paralleled in the most barbarous ages, and totally unworthy the Head of a civilized nation.

He has constrained our fellow Citizens taken Captive on the high Seas to bear Arms against their Country, to become the executioners of their friends and Brethren, or to fall themselves by their Hands.

He has excited domestic insurrections amongst us, and has endeavored to bring on the inhabitants of our frontiers, the merciless Indian Savages, whose known rule of warfare is an undistinguished destruction of all ages, sexes and conditions.

In every stage of these Oppressions We Have Petitioned for Redress in the most humble terms: Our repeated petitions have been answered only by repeated injury. A Prince, whose character is thus marked by every act which may define a Tyrant, is unfit to be the ruler of a free People.

Nor have We been wanting in attention to our British brethren. We have warned them from time to time of attempts by their legislature to extend an unwarrantable jurisdiction over us. We have reminded them of the circumstances of our emigration and settlement here. We have appealed to their native justice and magnanimity and we have conjured them by the ties of our common kindred to disavow these usurpations, which would inevitably interrupt our connections and correspondence. They too have been deaf to the voice of justice and of consanguinity. We must, therefore, acquiesce in the necessity, which denounces our Separation, and hold them, as we hold the rest of mankind, Enemies in War, in Peace Friends.

We, therefore, the Representatives of the United States of America, 35 in General Congress, Assembled, appealing to the Supreme Judge of the world of the rectitude of our intentions, do, in the Name, and by Authority of the good People of these Colonies, solemnly publish and declare, That these United Colonies are, and of Right ought to be, Free and Independent States; that they are Absolved from all Allegiance to the British Crown, and that all political connection between them and the State of Great Britain, is and ought to be totally dissolved; and that as Free and Independent States, they have full power to levy War, conclude Peace, contract Alliances, establish Commerce, and so all the other Acts and Things which Independent States may of right do. And for the support of this Declaration, with a firm reliance on the protection of Divine Providence, we mutually pledge to each other our lives, our Fortunes and our sacred Honor.

Topics for Critical Thinking and Writing

1. According to the first paragraph, for what audience was the Declaration written? What other audiences do you think the document was (in one way or another) addressed to?

2. The Declaration states that it is intended to "prove" that the acts of the government of George III had as their "direct object the establishment of an absolute Tyranny" in the American colonies (para. 5). Write an essay of 500 to 750 words showing whether the evidence offered in the

Declaration "proves" this claim to your satisfaction. (You will, of course, want to define *absolute tyranny*.) If you think further evidence is needed to "prove" the colonists' point, indicate what this evidence might be.

3. Paying special attention to the paragraphs beginning "That whenever any Form of Government" (para. 4), "In every stage" (para. 33), and "Nor have We been wanting" (para. 34), in a sentence or two set forth the image of themselves that the colonists seek to convey.

4. In the Declaration of Independence it is argued that the colonists are entitled to certain things and that under certain conditions they may behave in a certain way. Make explicit the syllogism that Jefferson is arguing.

5. What evidence does Jefferson offer to support his major premise? His minor premise?

6. In paragraph 2 the Declaration cites "certain unalienable Rights" and mentions three: "Life, Liberty and the pursuit of Happiness." What is an unalienable right? If someone has an unalienable (or inalienable) right, does that imply that he or she also has certain duties? If so, what are these duties? John Locke, a century earlier (1690), asserted that all men have a natural right to "life, liberty, and property." Do you think the decision to drop "property" and substitute "pursuit of Happiness" improved Locke's claim? Explain.

7. The Declaration ends thus: "We mutually pledge to each other our lives, our Fortunes and our sacred Honor." Is it surprising that honor is put in the final, climactic position? Is this a better ending than "our Fortunes, our sacred Honor, and our lives," or than "our sacred Honor, our lives, and our Fortunes?" Why?

8. King George III has asked you to reply, on his behalf, to the colonists, in 500 to 750 words. Write his reply. (Caution: A good reply will probably require you to do some reading about the period.)

9. Write a declaration of your own, setting forth in 500 to 750 words why some group is entitled to independence. You may want to argue that adolescents should not be compelled to attend school, that animals should not be confined in zoos, or that persons who use drugs should be able to buy them legally. Begin with a premise, then set forth facts illustrating the unfairness of the present condition, and conclude by stating what the new condition will mean to society.

Elizabeth Cady Stanton

Elizabeth Cady Stanton (1815–1902), a lawyer's daughter and journalist's wife, proposed in 1848 a convention to address the "social, civil, and religious condition and rights of women." Responding to Stanton's call, women and men from all over the Northeast convened in the village of Seneca Falls, New York. Her Declaration, adopted by the Seneca Falls Convention—but only after vigorous debate and some amendments by others—became the platform for the women's movement in this country.

Declaration of Sentiments and Resolutions

When, in the course of human events, it becomes necessary for one portion of the family of man to assume among the people of the earth a position different from that which they have hitherto occupied, but one to which the laws of nature and of nature's God entitle them, a decent respect to the opinions of mankind requires that they should declare the causes that impel them to such a course.

We hold these truths to be self-evident: that all men and women are created equal; that they are endowed by their Creator with certain inalienable rights; that among these are life, liberty and the pursuit of happiness; that to secure these rights governments are instituted, deriving their just powers from the consent of the governed. Whenever any form of government becomes destructive of these ends, it is the right of those who suffer from it to refuse allegiance to it, and to insist upon the institution of a new government, laying its foundation on such principles, and organizing its powers in such form, as to them shall seem most likely to effect their safety and happiness. Prudence, indeed, will dictate that governments long established should not be changed for light and transient causes; and accordingly all experience hath shown that mankind are more disposed to suffer, while evils are sufferable, than to right themselves by abolishing the forms to which they were accustomed. But when a long train of abuses and usurpations, pursuing invariably the same object, evinces a design to reduce them under absolute despotism, it is their duty to throw off such government, and to provide new guards for their future security. Such has been the patient sufferance of the women under this government, and such is now the necessity which constrains them to demand the equal station to which they are entitled.

The history of mankind is a history of repeated injuries and usurpations on the part of man toward woman, having in direct object the establishment of an absolute tyranny over her. To prove this, let facts be submitted to a candid world.

He has never permitted her to exercise her inalienable right to the elective franchise.

He has compelled her to submit to laws, in the formation of which   5
she had no voice.

He has withheld from her rights which are given to the most ignorant and degraded men — both natives and foreigners.

Having deprived her of this first right of a citizen, the elective franchise, thereby leaving her without representation in the halls of legislation, he has oppressed her on all sides.

He has made her, if married, in the eye of the law, civilly dead.

He has taken from her all right in property, even to the wages she earns.

He has made her, morally, an irresponsible being, as she can commit   10
many crimes with impunity, provided they be done in the presence of

her husband. In the covenant of marriage, she is compelled to promise obedience to her husband, he becoming to all intents and purposes, her master—the law giving him power to deprive her of her liberty, and to administer chastisement.

He has so framed the laws of divorce, as to what shall be the proper causes, and in case of separation, to whom the guardianship of the children shall be given, as to be wholly regardless of the happiness of women—the law, in all cases, going upon a false supposition of the supremacy of man, and giving all power into his hands.

After depriving her of all rights as a married woman, if single, and the owner of property, he has taxed her to support a government which recognizes her only when her property can be made profitable to it.

He has monopolized nearly all the profitable employments, and from those she is permitted to follow, she receives but a scanty remuneration. He closes against her all the avenues to wealth and distinction which he considers most honorable to himself. As a teacher of theology, medicine, or law, she is not known.

He has denied her the facilities for obtaining a thorough education, all colleges being closed against her.

He allows her in Church, as well as State, but a subordinate position,   15
claiming Apostolic authority for her exclusion from the ministry, and, with some exceptions, from any public participation in the affairs of the Church.

He has created a false public sentiment by giving to the world a different code of morals for men and women, by which moral delinquencies which exclude women from society, are not only tolerated, but deemed of little account in man.

He has usurped the prerogative of Jehovah himself, claiming it as his right to assign for her a sphere of action, when that belongs to her conscience and to her God.

He has endeavored, in every way that he could, to destroy her confidence in her own powers, to lessen her self-respect, and to make her willing to lead a dependent and abject life.

Now, in view of this entire disfranchisement of one-half the people of this country, their social and religious degradation—in view of the unjust laws above mentioned, and because women do feel themselves aggrieved, oppressed, and fraudulently deprived of their most sacred rights, we insist that they have immediate admission to all the rights and privileges which belong to them as citizens of the United States.

In entering upon the great work before us, we anticipate no small   20
amount of misconception, misrepresentation, and ridicule; but we shall use every instrumentality within our power to effect our object. We shall employ agents, circulate tracts, petition the State and National legislatures, and endeavor to enlist the pulpit and the press in our behalf. We hope this Convention will be followed by a series of Conventions embracing every part of the country.

[The following resolutions were discussed by Lucretia Mott, Thomas and Mary Ann McClintock, Amy Post, Catharine A. F. Stebbins, and others, and were adopted:]

Whereas, The great precept of nature is conceded to be, that "man shall pursue his own true and substantial happiness." Blackstone in his Commentaries remarks, that this law of Nature being coeval with mankind, and dictated by God himself, is of course superior in obligation to any other. It is binding over all the globe, in all countries, and at all times; no human laws are of any validity if contrary to this, and such of them as are valid, derive all their force, and all their validity, and all their authority, mediately and immediately, from this original; therefore,

Resolved, That such laws as conflict, in any way, with the true and substantial happiness of woman, are contrary to the great precept of nature and of no validity, for this is "superior in obligation to any other."

Resolved, That all laws which prevent woman from occupying such a station in society as her conscience shall dictate, or which place her in a position inferior to that of man, are contrary to the great precept of nature, and therefore of no force or authority.

Resolved, That woman is man's equal — was intended to be so by the Creator, and the highest good of the race demands that she should be recognized as such.

Resolved, That the women of this country ought to be enlightened in   25
regard to the laws under which they live, that they may no longer publish their degradation by declaring themselves satisfied with their present position, nor their ignorance, by asserting that they have all the rights they want.

Resolved, That inasmuch as man, while claiming for himself intellectual superiority, does accord to woman moral superiority, it is preeminently his duty to encourage her to speak and teach, as she has an opportunity, in all religious assemblies.

Resolved, That the same amount of virtue, delicacy, and refinement of behavior that is required of woman in the social state, should also be required of man, and the same transgressions should be visited with equal severity on both man and woman.

Resolved, That the objection of indelicacy and impropriety, which is so often brought against woman when she addresses a public audience, comes with a very ill-grace from those who encourage, by their attendance, her appearance on the stage, in the concert, or in feats of the circus.

Resolved, That woman has too long rested satisfied in the circumscribed limits which corrupt customs and a perverted application of the Scriptures have marked out for her, and that it is time she should move in the enlarged sphere which her great Creator has assigned her.

Resolved, That it is the duty of the women of this country to secure to   30
themselves their sacred right to the elective franchise.

Resolved, That the equality of human rights results necessarily from the fact of the identity of the race in capabilities and responsibilities.

Resolved, therefore, That, being invested by the Creator with the same capabilities, and the same consciousness of responsibility for their exercise, it is demonstrably the right and duty of woman, equally with man, to promote every righteous cause by every righteous means; and especially in regard to the great subjects of morals and religion, it is self-evidently her right to participate with her brother in teaching them, both in private and in public, by writing and by speaking, by any instrumentalities proper to be used, and in any assemblies proper to be held; and this being a self-evident truth growing out of the divinely implanted principles of human nature, any custom or authority adverse to it, whether modern or wearing the hoary sanction of antiquity, is to be regarded as a self-evident falsehood, and at war with mankind.

[At the last session Lucretia Mott offered and spoke to the following resolution:]

Resolved, That the speedy success of our cause depends upon the zealous and untiring efforts of both men and women, for the overthrow of the monopoly of the pulpit, and for the securing to woman an equal participation with men in the various trades, professions, and commerce.

Topics for Critical Thinking and Writing

1. Stanton echoes the Declaration of Independence because she wishes to associate her ideas and the movement she supports with a document and a movement that her readers esteem. And she must have believed that if readers esteem the Declaration of Independence, they must grant the justice of her goals. Does her strategy work, or does it backfire by making her essay seem strained?

2. When Stanton insists that women have an "inalienable right to the elective franchise" (para. 4), what does she mean by "inalienable"?

3. Stanton complains that men have made women, "in the eye of the law, civilly dead" (para. 8). What does she mean by "civilly dead"? How is it possible for a person to be biologically alive and yet civilly dead?

4. Stanton objects that women are "not known" as teachers of "theology, medicine, or law" (para. 13). Is this still true today? Do some research in your library, and then write three 100-word biographical sketches, one each on a well-known woman professor of theology, medicine, and law.

5. How might you go about proving (rather than merely asserting) that, as paragraph 24 says, "woman is man's equal—was intended to be so by the Creator"?

6. The Declaration claims that women have "the same capabilities" as men (para. 32). Yet in 1848 Stanton and the others at Seneca Falls knew, or should have known, that history recorded no example of a woman philosopher comparable to Plato or Kant, a composer comparable to Beethoven or Chopin, a scientist comparable to Galileo or Newton, or a mathematician comparable to Euclid or Descartes. Do these facts contradict the Declaration's claim? If not, why not? How else but by different intellectual capabilities do you think such facts can be explained?

7. Stanton's Declaration is over 150 years old. Have all of the issues she raised been satisfactorily resolved? If not, which ones remain?

8. In our society, children have very few rights. For instance, a child cannot decide to drop out of elementary school or high school, and a child cannot decide to leave his or her parents to reside with some other family that he or she finds more compatible. Whatever your view of children's rights, compose the best Declaration of the Rights of Children that you can.

Martin Luther King Jr.

Martin Luther King Jr. (1929–1968) was born in Atlanta and educated at Morehouse College, Crozer Theological Seminary, and Boston University. In 1954 he was called to serve as a Baptist minister in Montgomery, Alabama. During the next two years he achieved national fame when, using a policy of nonviolent resistance, he successfully led the boycott against segregated bus lines in Montgomery. He then organized the Southern Christian Leadership Conference, which furthered civil rights, first in the South and then nationwide. In 1964 he was awarded the Nobel Peace Prize. Four years later he was assassinated in Memphis, Tennessee, while supporting striking garbage workers.

The speech presented here was delivered from the steps of the Lincoln Memorial, in Washington, D.C., in 1963, the hundredth anniversary of the Emancipation Proclamation. King's immediate audience consisted of more than two hundred thousand people who had come to demonstrate for civil rights.

I Have a Dream

I am happy to join with you today in what will go down in history as the greatest demonstration for freedom in the history of our nation.

Five score years ago, a great American, in whose symbolic shadow we stand today, signed the Emancipation Proclamation. This momentous decree came as a great beacon light of hope to millions of Negro slaves who had been seared in the flames of withering injustice. It came as a joyous daybreak to end the long night of their captivity. But one hundred years later, the Negro still is not free. One hundred years later, the life of the Negro is still sadly crippled by the manacles of segregation and the chains of discrimination. One hundred years later, the Negro lives on a lonely island of poverty in the midst of a vast ocean of material prosperity. One hundred years later, the Negro is still anguished in the corners of American society and finds himself in exile in his own land. And so we have come here today to dramatize a shameful condition.

In a sense we have come to our nation's capital to cash a check. When the architects of our republic wrote the magnificent words of the Constitution and the Declaration of Independence, they were signing a promissory note to which every American was to fall heir. This note was the promise that all men—yes, black men as well as white men—would be guaranteed the inalienable rights of life, liberty, and the pursuit of happiness.

It is obvious today that America has defaulted on this promissory note insofar as her citizens of color are concerned. Instead of honoring this sacred obligation, America has given the Negro people a bad check, a check which has come back marked "insufficient funds." But we refuse to believe that the bank of justice is bankrupt. We refuse to believe that there are insufficient funds in the great vaults of opportunity of this nation; and so we have come to cash this check, a check that will give us upon demand the riches of freedom and the security of justice.

We have also come to this hallowed spot to remind America of the fierce urgency of *now*. This is no time to engage in the luxury of cooling off or to take the tranquilizing drug of gradualism. *Now* is the time to make real promises of democracy. *Now* is the time to rise from the dark and desolate valley of segregation to the sunlit path of racial justice. *Now* is the time to lift our nation from the quicksands of racial injustice to the solid rock of brotherhood. *Now* is the time to make justice a reality for all of God's children. 5

It would be fatal for the nation to overlook the urgency of the moment. This sweltering summer of the Negro's legitimate discontent will not pass until there is an invigorating autumn of freedom and equality. Nineteen sixty-three is not an end, but a beginning. And those who hope that the Negro needed to blow off steam and will now be content will have a rude awakening if the nation returns to business as usual. There will be neither rest nor tranquility in America until the Negro is granted his citizenship rights. The whirlwinds of revolt will continue to shake the foundations of our nation until the bright day of justice emerges.

But there is something that I must say to my people who stand on the warm threshold which leads into the palace of justice. In the process of gaining our rightful place, we must not be guilty of wrongful deeds. Let us not seek to satisfy our thirst for freedom by drinking from the cup of bitterness and hatred. We must forever conduct our struggle on the high plane of dignity and discipline. We must not allow our creative protest to degenerate into physical violence. Again and again we must rise to the majestic heights of meeting physical force with soul force. And the marvelous new militancy which has engulfed the Negro community must not lead us to a distrust of all white people; for many of our white brothers, as evidenced by their presence here today, have come to realize that their destiny is tied up with our destiny, and they have come to realize that their freedom is inextricably bound to our freedom.

We cannot walk alone. And as we walk we must make the pledge that we shall always march ahead. We cannot turn back. There are those who are asking the devotees of civil rights, "When will you be satisfied?" We can never be satisfied as long as the Negro is the victim of the unspeakable horrors of police brutality. We can never be satisfied as long as our bodies, heavy with the fatigue of travel, cannot gain lodging in the motels of the highways and the hotels of the cities. We cannot be satisfied as long as the Negro's basic mobility is from a smaller ghetto to a larger one. We can never be satisfied as long as our children are stripped of their selfhood and robbed of their dignity by signs stating "For Whites Only." We cannot be satisfied as long as the Negro in Mississippi cannot vote and a Negro in New York believes he has nothing for which to vote. No, no, we are not satisfied, and we will not be satisfied until justice rolls down like waters and righteousness like a mighty stream.[1]

I am not unmindful that some of you have come here out of great trials and tribulations. Some of you have come fresh from narrow jail cells. Some of you have come from areas where your quest for freedom left you battered by the storms of persecution and staggered by the winds of police brutality. You have been the veterans of creative suffering. Continue to work with the faith that unearned suffering is redemptive.

Go back to Mississippi, and go back to Alabama. Go back to South   10
Carolina. Go back to Georgia. Go back to Louisiana. Go back to the slums and ghettos of our Northern cities, knowing that somehow this situation can and will be changed. Let us not wallow in the valley of despair.

I say to you today, my friends, even though we face the difficulties of today and tomorrow, I still have a dream. It is a dream deeply rooted in the American dream. I have a dream that one day this nation will rise up and live out the true meaning of its creed: "We hold these truths to be self-evident, that all men are created equal." I have a dream that one day, on the red hills of Georgia, sons of former slaves and the sons of former slave owners will be able to sit down together at the table of brotherhood. I have a dream that one day even the state of Mississippi, a state sweltering with the heat of injustice, sweltering with the heat of oppression, will be transformed into an oasis of freedom and justice. I have a dream that my four little children will one day live in a nation where they will not be judged by the color of their skin, but by the content of their character.

---

[1]**justice . . . stream** A quotation from the Hebrew Bible: Amos 5:24. [All notes are the editors'.]

I have a dream today. I have a dream that one day down in Alabama—with its vicious racists, with its governor's lips dripping with the words of interposition and nullification—one day right there in Alabama, little black boys and black girls will be able to join hands with little white boys and white girls as sisters and brothers.

I have a dream today. I have a dream that one day every valley shall be exalted and every hill and mountain shall be made low, the rough places will be made plain and the crooked places will be made straight, and the glory of the Lord shall be revealed, and all flesh shall see it together.[2]

This is our hope. This is the faith that I go back to the South with. And with this faith we will be able to hew out of the mountain of despair a stone of hope. With this faith we will be able to transform the jangling discords of our nation into a beautiful symphony of brotherhood. With this faith we will be able to work together, to play together, to struggle together, to go to jail together, to stand up for freedom together, knowing that we will be free one day.

And this will be the day—this will be the day when all of God's children will be able to sing with new meaning: 15

> My country, 'tis of thee,
> Sweet land of liberty,
>   Of thee I sing;
> Land where my fathers died,
> Land of the Pilgrim's pride,
> From every mountainside
> Let freedom ring.

And if America is to be a great nation, this must become true.

And so let freedom ring from the prodigious hilltops of New Hampshire. Let freedom ring from the mighty mountains of New York. Let freedom ring from the heightening Alleghenies of Pennsylvania. Let freedom ring from the snow-capped Rockies of Colorado. Let freedom ring from the curvaceous slopes of California.

But not only that. Let freedom ring from Stone Mountain of Georgia. Let freedom ring from Lookout Mountain of Tennessee. Let freedom ring from every hill and molehill of Mississippi. "From every mountainside let freedom ring."

And when this happens—when we allow freedom to ring, when we let it ring from every village and every hamlet, from every state and every city—we will be able to speed up that day when all of God's children, Black men and white men, Jews and Gentiles, Protestants and Catholics, will be able to join hands and sing in the words of the old Negro spiritual: "Free at last! Free at last! Thank God Almighty. We are free at last!"

---

[2]**every valley . . . see it together** Another quotation from the Hebrew Bible: Isaiah 40:4–5.

Topics for Critical Thinking and Writing

1. Analyze the rhetoric—the oratorical art—of the second paragraph. What, for instance, is gained by saying "five score years ago" instead of "a hundred years ago"? By metaphorically calling the Emancipation Proclamation "a great beacon light"? By saying that "Negro slaves . . . had been seared in the flames of withering injustice"? And what of the metaphors "daybreak" and "the long night of . . . captivity"?

2. Do the first two paragraphs make an effective opening? Why?

3. In the third and fourth paragraphs King uses the metaphor of a bad check. Rewrite the third paragraph *without* using any of King's metaphors, and then in a paragraph evaluate the difference between King's version and yours.

4. King's highly metaphoric speech appeals to emotions. But it also offers *reasons*. What reasons, for instance, does King give to support his belief that African Americans should not resort to physical violence?

5. When King delivered the speech, his audience at the Lincoln Memorial was primarily African American. Do you think that the speech is also addressed to other Americans? Explain.

6. The speech can be divided into three parts: paragraphs 1 through 6; paragraphs 7 ("But there is") through 10; and paragraph 11 ("I say to you today, my friends") to the end. Summarize each of these three parts in a sentence or two so that the basic organization is evident.

7. King says (para. 11) that his dream is "deeply rooted in the American dream." First, what is the American dream, as King seems to understand it? Second, how does King establish his point—that is, what evidence does he use to convince us—that his dream is the American dream? (On this second issue, one might start by pointing out that in the second paragraph King refers to the Emancipation Proclamation. What other relevant documents does he refer to?)

8. King delivered his speech in 1963, nearly forty years ago. In an essay of 500 words argue that the speech still is—or is not—relevant. Or write an essay of 500 words in which you state what you take to be the "American dream," and argue that it now is or is not readily available to African Americans.

Edward Bellamy

Edward Bellamy (1850–1898), born in Chicopee Falls, Massachusetts, studied law, was admitted to the bar, but then turned to journalism and to writing fiction. Short stories and three novels brought him a modest success, but with Looking Backward *(1888) his name became a household word. The book is in the tradition of Thomas More's* Utopia *(1514–1515), but where More presents a vision of an ideal society by setting his story in a remote place, Bellamy presents a vision of an ideal society (state socialism) by setting his story in a remote time.*

In the book, young Julian West is hypnotized in Boston in 1887 and wakes up 113 years later in the year 2000. When West, a rather naive fellow, tells the people of this new society about life in the late nineteenth century, Bellamy is able to present an unflattering view of his age; and when the people of 2000 tell West what their lives are like, Bellamy suggests to his readers the sort of society that provides amply for all its members. We give about one-tenth of the book.

Looking Backward

CHAPTER 1

I first saw the light in the city of Boston in the year 1857. "What!" you say, "eighteen fifty-seven? That is an odd slip. He means nineteen fifty-seven, of course." I beg pardon, but there is no mistake. It was about four in the afternoon of December the 26th, one day after Christmas, in the year 1857, not 1957, that I first breathed the east wind of Boston, which, I assure the reader, was at that remote period marked by the same penetrating quality characterizing it in the present year of grace, 2000.

These statements seem so absurd on their face, especially when I add that I am a young man apparently of about thirty years of age, that no person can be blamed for refusing to read another word of what promises to be a mere imposition upon his credulity. Nevertheless I earnestly assure the reader that no imposition is intended, and will undertake, if he shall follow me a few pages, to entirely convince him of this. If I may, then, provisionally assume, with the pledge of justifying the assumption, that I know better than the reader when I was born, I will go on with my narrative. As every schoolboy knows, in the latter part of the nineteenth century the civilization of to-day, or anything like it, did not exist, although the elements which were to develop it were already in ferment. Nothing had, however, occurred to modify the immemorial division of society into the four classes, or nations, as they may be more fitly called, since the differences between them were far greater than those between any nations nowadays, of the rich and the poor, the educated and the ignorant. I myself was rich and also educated, and possessed, therefore, all the elements of happiness enjoyed by the most fortunate in that age. Living in luxury, and occupied only with the pursuit of the pleasures and refinements of life, I derived the means of my support from the labor of others, rendering no sort of service in return. My parents and grand-parents had lived in the same way, and I expected that my descendants, if I had any, would enjoy a like easy existence.

But how could I live without service to the world? you ask. Why should the world have supported in utter idleness one who was able to render service? The answer is that my great-grandfather had accumulated a sum of money on which his descendants had ever since lived. The sum, you will naturally infer, must have been very large not to have been exhausted in supporting three generations in idleness. This, however, was not the fact. The sum had been originally by no means large. It was, in fact, much larger now that three generations had been supported upon it in idleness, than it was at first. This mystery of use without consumption, of warmth without combustion, seems like magic, but was merely an ingenious application of the art now happily lost but carried to great perfection by your ancestors, of shifting the burden of one's support on the shoulders of others. The man who had accomplished this, and it was the end all sought, was said to live on the income of his investments. To explain at this point how the ancient methods of industry made this possible would delay us too much. I shall only stop now to say that interest on investments was a species of tax in perpetuity upon the product of those engaged in industry which a person possessing or inheriting money was able to levy. It must not be supposed that an arrangement which seems so unnatural and preposterous according to modern notions was never criticised by your ancestors. It had been the effort of lawgivers and prophets from the earliest ages to abolish interest, or at least to limit it to the smallest possible rate. All these efforts had, however, failed, as they necessarily must so long as the ancient social organizations prevailed. At the time of which I write, the latter part of the nineteenth century, governments had generally given up trying to regulate the subject at all.

By way of attempting to give the reader some general impression of the way people lived together in those days, and especially of the relations of the rich and poor to one another, perhaps I cannot do better than to compare society as it then was to a prodigious coach which the masses of humanity were harnessed to and dragged toilsomely along a very hilly and sandy road. The driver was hunger, and permitted no lagging, though the pace was necessarily very slow. Despite the difficulty of drawing the coach at all along so hard a road, the top was covered with passengers who never got down, even at the steepest ascents. These seats on top were very breezy and comfortable. Well up out of the dust, their occupants could enjoy the scenery at their leisure, or critically discuss the merits of the straining team. Naturally such places were in great demand and the competition for them was keen, every one seeking as the first end in life to secure a seat on the coach for himself and to leave it to his child after him. By the rule of the coach a man could leave his seat to whom he wished, but on the other hand there were many accidents by which it might at any time be wholly lost. For all that they were so easy, the seats were very insecure, and at every sudden jolt of the coach persons were slipping out of them and falling to the ground, where they were instantly compelled to take hold of the rope and help to drag the coach on which they had before ridden so pleasantly. It was naturally regarded as a terrible misfortune to lose one's seat, and the apprehension that this might happen to them or their friends was a constant cloud upon the happiness of those who rode.

But did they think only of themselves? you ask. Was not their very luxury rendered intolerable to them by comparison with the lot of their brothers and sisters in the harness, and the knowledge that their own weight added to their toil? Had they no compassion for fellow beings from whom fortune only distinguished them? Oh, yes; commiseration was frequently expressed by those who rode for those who had to pull the coach, especially when the vehicle came to a bad place in the road, as it was constantly doing, or to a particularly steep hill. At such times, the desperate straining of the team, their agonized leaping and plunging under the pitiless lashing of hunger, the many who fainted at the rope and were trampled in the mire, made a very distressing spectacle, which often called forth highly creditable displays of feeling on the top of the coach. At such times the passengers would call down encouragingly to the toilers of the rope, exhorting them to patience, and holding out hopes of possible compensation in another world for the hardness of their lot, while others contributed to buy salves and liniments for the crippled and injured. It was agreed that it was a great pity that the coach should be so hard to pull, and there was a sense of general relief when the specially bad piece of road was gotten over. This relief was not, indeed, wholly on account of the team, for there was always some danger at these bad places of a general overturn in which all would lose their seats.

It must in truth be admitted that the main effect of the spectacle of the misery of the toilers at the rope was to enhance the passengers' sense of the value of their seats upon the coach, and to cause them to hold on to them more desperately than before. If the passengers could only have felt assured that neither they nor their friends would ever fall from the top, it is probably that, beyond contributing to the funds for liniments and bandages, they would have troubled themselves extremely little about those who dragged the coach.

I am well aware that this will appear to the men and women of the twentieth century an incredible inhumanity, but there are two facts, both very curious, which partly explain it. In the first place, it was firmly and sincerely believed that there was no other way in which Society could get along, except the many pulled at the rope and the few rode, and not only this, but that no very radical improvement even was possible, either in the harness, the coach, the roadway, or the distribution of the toil. It had always been as it was, and it always would be so. It was a pity, but it could not be helped, and philosophy forbade wasting compassion on what was beyond remedy.

The other fact is yet more curious, consisting in a singular hallucination which those on the top of the coach generally shared, that they were not exactly like their brothers and sisters who pulled at the rope, but of finer clay, in some way belonging to a higher order of beings who might justly expect to be drawn. This seems unaccountable, but, as I once rode on this very coach and shared that very hallucination, I ought to be believed. The strangest thing about the hallucination was that those who had but just climbed up from the ground, before they had outgrown the marks of the rope upon their hands, began to fall under its influence. As for those whose parents and grand-parents before them had been so fortunate as to keep their seats on the top, the conviction they cherished of the essential difference between their sort of humanity and the common article was absolute. The effect of such a delusion in moderating fellow feeling for the sufferings of the mass of men into a distant and philosophical compassion is obvious. To it I refer as the only extenuation I can offer for the indifference which, at the period I write of, marked my own attitude toward the misery of my brothers.

In 1887 I came to my thirtieth year. Although still unmarried, I was engaged to wed Edith Bartlett. She, like myself, rode on the top of the coach. That is to say, not to encumber ourselves further with an illustration which has, I hope, served its purpose of giving the reader some general impression of how we lived then, her family was wealthy. In that age, when money alone commanded all that was agreeable and refined in life, it was enough for a woman to be rich to have suitors; but Edith Bartlett was beautiful and graceful also.

My lady readers, I am aware, will protest at this. "Handsome she might have been," I hear them saying, "but graceful never, in the costumes which were the fashion at that period, when the head covering was a dizzy structure a foot tall, and the almost incredible extension of the skirt behind by means of artificial contrivances more thoroughly dehumanized the form than any former device of dressmakers. Fancy any one graceful in such a costume!" The point is certainly well taken, and I can only reply that while the ladies of the twentieth century are lovely demonstrations of the effect of appropriate drapery in accenting feminine graces, my recollection of their great-grandmothers enables me to maintain that no deformity of costume can wholly disguise them.

Our marriage only waited on the completion of the house which I was building for our occupancy in one of the most desirable parts of the city, that is to say, a part chiefly inhabited by the rich. For it must be understood that the comparative desirability of different parts of Boston for residence depended then, not on natural features, but on the character of the neighboring population. Each class or nation lived by itself, in quarters of its own. A rich man living among the poor, an educated man among the uneducated, was like one living in isolation among a jealous and alien race. When the house had been begun, its completion by the winter of 1886 had been expected. The spring of the following year found it, however, yet incomplete, and my marriage still a thing of the future. The cause of a delay calculated to be particularly exasperating to an ardent lover was a series of strikes, that is to say, concerted refusals to work on the part of the brick-layers, masons, carpenters, painters, plumbers, and other trades concerned in house building. What the specific causes of these strikes were I do not remember. Strikes had become so common at that period that people had ceased to inquire into their particular grounds. In one department of industry or another, they had been nearly incessant ever since the great business crisis of 1873. In fact it had come to be the exceptional thing to see any class of laborers pursue their avocation steadily for more than a few months at a time. . . .

CHAPTER V

When, in the course of the evening the ladies retired, leaving Dr. Leete and myself alone, he sounded me as to my disposition for sleep, saying that if I felt like it my bed was ready for me; but if I was inclined to wakefulness nothing would please him better than to bear me company. "I am a late bird, myself," he said, "and, without suspicion of flattery, I may say that a companion more interesting than yourself could scarcely be imagined. It is decidedly not often that one has a chance to converse with a man of the nineteenth century."

Now I had been looking forward all the evening with some dread to the time when I should be alone, on retiring for the night. Surrounded by these most friendly strangers, stimulated and supported by their sympathetic interest, I had been able to keep my mental balance. Even then, however, in pauses of the conversation I had had glimpses, vivid as lightning flashes, of the horror of strangeness that was waiting to be faced when I could no longer command diversion. I knew I could not sleep that night, and as for lying awake and thinking, it argues no cowardice, I am sure, to confess that I was afraid of it. When, in reply to my host's question, I frankly told him this, he replied that it would be strange if I did not feel just so, but that I need have no anxiety about sleeping; whenever I wanted to go to bed, he would give me a dose which would insure me a sound night's sleep without fail. Next morning, no doubt, I would awake with the feeling of an old citizen.

"Before I acquire that," I replied, "I must know a little more about the sort of Boston I have come back to. You told me when we were upon the house-top that though a century only had elapsed since I fell asleep, it had been marked by greater changes in the conditions of humanity than many a previous millennium. With the city before me I could well believe that, but I am very curious to know what some of the changes have been. To make a beginning somewhere, for the subject is doubtless a large one, what solution, if any, have you found for the labor question? It was the Sphinx's riddle[1] of the nineteenth century, and when I

---

[1]In Greek mythology, the sphinx, a winged monster with the head of a woman and the body of a lion, asked this riddle: "What goes on four legs in the morning, two at noon, and three in the evening?" Those who did not know the answer—man—were killed. [Editors' note.]

dropped out the Sphinx was threatening to devour society, because the answer was not forthcoming. It is well worth sleeping a hundred years to learn what the right answer was, if, indeed, you have found it yet."

"As no such thing as the labor question is known nowadays," replied 15 Dr. Leete, "and there is no way in which it could arise, I suppose we may claim to have solved it. Society would indeed have fully deserved being devoured if it had failed to answer a riddle so entirely simple. In fact, to speak by the book, it was not necessary for society to solve the riddle at all. It may be said to have solved itself. The solution came as the result of a process of industrial evolution which could not have terminated otherwise. All that society had to do was to recognize and coöperate with that evolution, when its tendency had become unmistakable."

"I can only say," I answered, "that at the time I fell asleep no such evolution had been recognized."

"It was in 1887 that you fell into this sleep, I think you said."

"Yes, May 30th, 1887."

My companion regarded me musingly for some moments. Then he observed, "And you tell me that even then there was no general recognition of the nature of the crisis which society was nearing? Of course, I fully credit your statement. The singular blindness of your contemporaries to the signs of the times is a phenomenon commented on by many of our historians, but few facts of history are more difficult for us to realize, so obvious and unmistakable as we look back seem the indications, which must also have come under your eyes, of the transformation about to come to pass. I should be interested, Mr. West, if you would give me a little more definite idea of the view which you and men of your grade of intellect took of the state and prospects of society in 1887. You must, at least, have realized that the widespread industrial and social troubles, and the underlying dissatisfaction of all classes with the inequalities of society, and the general misery of mankind, were portents of great changes of some sort."

"We did, indeed, fully realize that," I replied. "We felt that society 20 was dragging anchor and in danger of going adrift. Whither it would drift nobody could say, but all feared the rocks."

"Nevertheless," said Dr. Leete, "the set of the current was perfectly perceptible if you had but taken pains to observe it, and it was not toward the rocks, but toward a deeper channel."

"We had a popular proverb," I replied, "that 'hindsight is better than foresight,' the force of which I shall now, no doubt, appreciate more fully than ever. All I can say is, that the prospect was such when I went into that long sleep that I should not have been surprised had I looked down from your house-top to-day on a heap of charred and moss-grown ruins instead of this glorious city."

Dr. Leete had listened to me with close attention and nodded thoughtfully as I finished speaking. "What you have said," he observed, "will be regarded as a most valuable vindication of Storiot, whose account of your era has been generally thought exaggerated in its picture of the gloom and confusion of men's minds. That a period of transition like that should be full of excitement and agitation was indeed to be looked for; but seeing how plain was the tendency of the forces in operation, it was natural to believe that hope rather than fear would have been the prevailing temper of the popular mind."

"You have not yet told me what was the answer to the riddle which you found," I said. "I am impatient to know by what contradiction of natural sequence the peace and prosperity which you now seem to enjoy could have been the outcome of an era like my own."

"Excuse me," replied my host, "but do you smoke?" It was not till 25 our cigars were lighted and drawing well that he resumed. "Since you are in the humor to talk rather than to sleep, as I certainly am, perhaps I cannot do better than to try to give you enough idea of our modern industrial system to dissipate at least the impression that there is any mystery about the process of its evolution. The Bostonians of your day had the reputation of being great askers of questions, and I am going to show my descent by asking you one to begin with. What should you name as the most prominent feature of the labor troubles of your day?"

"Why, the strikes, of course," I replied.

"Exactly; but what made the strikes so formidable?"

"The great labor organizations."

"And what was the motive of these great organizations?"

"The workmen claimed they had to organize to get their rights from 30 the big corporations," I replied.

"That is just it," said Dr. Leete; "the organization of labor and the strikes were an effect, merely, of the concentration of capital in greater masses than had ever been known before. Before this concentration began, while as yet commerce and industry were conducted by innumerable petty concerns with small capital, instead of a small number of great concerns with vast capital, the individual workman was relatively important and independent in his relations to the employer. Moreover, when a little capital or a new idea was enough to start a man in business for himself, workingmen were constantly becoming employers and there was no hard and fast line between the two classes. Labor unions were needless then, and general strikes out of the question. But when the era of small concerns with small capital was succeeded by that of the great aggregations of capital, all this was changed. The individual laborer, who had been relatively important to the small employer, was reduced to insignificance and powerlessness over against the great corporation, while at the same time the way upward to the grade of employer was closed to him. Self-defense drove him to union with his fellows.

"The records of the period show that the outcry against the concentration of capital was furious. Men believed that it threatened society with a form of tyranny more abhorrent than it had ever endured. They believed that the great corporations were preparing for them the yoke of a baser servitude than had ever been imposed on the race, servitude not to men but to soulless machines incapable of any motive but insatiable greed. Looking back, we cannot wonder at their desperation, for certainly humanity was never confronted with a fate more sordid and hideous than would have been the era of corporate tyranny which they anticipated.

"Meanwhile, without being in the smallest degree checked by the clamor against it, the absorption of business by ever larger monopolies continued. In the United States there was not, after the beginning of the last quarter of the century, any opportunity whatever for individual enterprise in any important field of industry, unless backed by a great capital. During the last decade of the century, such small businesses as still remained were fast-failing survivals of a past epoch, or mere parasites on the great corporations, or else existed in fields too small to attract the great capitalists. Small businesses, as far as they still remained, were reduced to the condition of rats and mice, living in holes and corners, and counting on evading notice for the enjoyment of existence. The railroads had gone on combining till a few great syndicates controlled every rail in the land. In manufactories, every important staple was controlled by a syndicate. These syndicates, pools, trusts, or whatever their name, fixed prices and crushed all competition except when combinations as vast as themselves arose. Then a struggle, resulting in a still greater consolidation, ensued. The great city bazaar crushed its country rivals with branch stores, and in the city itself absorbed its smaller rivals till the business of a whole quarter was concentrated under one roof, with a hundred former proprietors of shops serving as clerks. Having no business of his own to put his money in, the small capitalist, at the same time that he took service under the corporation, found no other investment for his money but its stocks and bonds, thus becoming doubly dependent upon it.

"The fact that the desperate popular opposition to the consolidation of business in a few powerful hands had no effect to check it proves that there must have been a strong economical reason for it. The small capitalists, with their innumerable petty concerns, had in fact yielded the field to the great aggregations of capital, because they belonged to a day of small things and were totally incompetent to the demands of an age of steam and telegraphs and the gigantic scale of its enterprises. To restore the former order of things, even if possible, would have involved returning to the day of stage-coaches. Oppressive and intolerable as was the régime of the great consolidations of capital, even its victims, while they cursed it, were forced to admit the prodigious increase of efficiency which had been imparted to the national industries, the vast economies effected by concentration of management and unity of organization, and to confess that since the new system had taken the place of the old the wealth of the world had increased at a rate before undreamed of. To be sure this vast increase had gone chiefly to make the rich richer, increasing the gap between them and the poor; but the fact remained that, as a means merely of producing wealth, capital had been proved efficient in proportion to its consolidation. The restoration of the old system with the subdivision of capital, if it were possible, might indeed bring back a greater equality of conditions, with more individual dignity and freedom, but it would be at the price of general poverty and the arrest of material progress.

"Was there, then, no way of commanding the services of the mighty 35 wealth-producing principle of consolidated capital without bowing down to a plutocracy like that of Carthage? As soon as men began to ask themselves these questions, they found the answer ready for them. The movement toward the conduct of business by larger and larger aggregations of capital, the tendency toward monopolies, which had been so desperately and vainly resisted, was recognized at last, in its true significance, as a process which only needed to complete its logical evolution to open a golden future to humanity.

"Early in the last century the evolution was completed by the final consolidation of the entire capital of the nation. The industry and commerce of the country, ceasing to be conducted by a set of irresponsible corporations and syndicates of private persons at their caprice and for their profit, were intrusted to a single syndicate representing the people, to be conducted in the common interest for the common profit. The nation, that is to say, organized as the one great business corporation in which all other corporations were absorbed; it became the one capitalist in the place of all other capitalists, the sole employer, the final monopoly in which all previous and lesser monopolies were swallowed up, a monopoly in the profits and economies of which all citizens shared. The epoch of trusts had ended in The Great Trust. In a word, the people of the United States concluded to assume the conduct of their own business, just as one hundred odd years before they had assumed the conduct of their own government, organizing now for industrial purposes on precisely the same grounds that they had then organized for political purposes. At last, strangely late in the world's history, the obvious fact was perceived that no business is so essentially the public business as the industry and commerce on which the people's livelihood depends, and that to entrust it to private persons to be managed for private profit is a folly similar in kind, though vastly greater in magnitude, to that of surrendering the functions of political government to kings and nobles to be conducted for their personal glorification."

"Such a stupendous change as you describe," said I, "did not, of course, take place without great bloodshed and terrible convulsions."

"On the contrary," replied Dr. Leete, "there was absolutely no violence. The change had been long foreseen. Public opinion had become fully ripe for it, and the whole mass of the people was behind it. There was no more possibility of opposing it by force than by argument. On the other hand the popular sentiment toward the great corporations and those identified with them had ceased to be one of bitterness, as they came to realize their necessity as a link, a transition phase, in the evolution of the true industrial system. The most violent foes of the great private monopolies were now forced to recognize how invaluable and indispensable had been their office in educating the people up to the point of assuming control of their own business. Fifty years before, the consolidation of the industries of the country under national control would have seemed a very daring experiment to the most sanguine. But by a series of object lessons, seen and studied by all men, the great corporations had taught the people an entirely new set of ideas on this subject. They had seen for many years syndicates handling revenues greater than those of states, and directing the labors of hundreds of thousands of men with an efficiency and economy unattainable in smaller operations. It had come to be recognized as an axiom that the larger the business the simpler the principles that can be applied to it; that, as the machine is truer than the hand, so the system, which in a great concern does the work of the master's eye in a small business, turns out more accurate results. Thus it came about that, thanks to the corporations themselves, when it was proposed that the nation should assume their functions, the suggestion implied nothing which seemed impracticable even to the timid. To be sure it was a step beyond any yet taken, a broader generalization, but the very fact that the nation would be the sole corporation in the field would, it was seen, relieve the undertaking of many difficulties with which the partial monopolies had contended."

CHAPTER VI

Dr. Leete ceased speaking, and I remained silent, endeavoring to form some general conception of the changes in the arrangements of society implied in the tremendous revolution which he had described.

Finally I said, "The idea of such an extension of the functions of government is, to say the least, rather overwhelming." 40

"Extension!" he repeated, "where is the extension?"

"In my day," I replied, "it was considered that the proper functions of government, strictly speaking, were limited to keeping the peace and defending the people against the public enemy, that is, to the military and police powers."

"And, in heaven's name, who are the public enemies?" exclaimed Dr. Leete. "Are they France, England, Germany, or hunger, cold, and nakedness? In your day governments were accustomed, on the slightest international misunderstanding, to seize upon the bodies of citizens and deliver them over by hundreds of thousands to death and mutilation, wasting their treasures the while like water; and all this oftenest for no imaginable profit to the victims. We have no wars now, and our governments no war powers, but in order to protect every citizen against hunger, cold, and nakedness, and provide for all his physical and mental needs, the function is assumed of directing his industry for a term of years. No, Mr. West, I am sure on reflection you will perceive that it was in your age, not in ours, that the extension of the functions of governments was extraordinary. Not even for the best ends would men now allow their governments such powers as were then used for the most maleficent."

"Leaving comparisons aside," I said, "the demagoguery and corruption of our public men would have been considered, in my day, insuperable objections to any assumption by government of the charge of the national industries. We should have thought that no arrangement could be worse than to entrust the politicians with control of the wealth-producing machinery of the country. Its material interests were quite too much the football of parties as it was."

"No doubt you were right," rejoined Dr. Leete, "but all that is 45 changed now. We have no parties or politicians, and as for demagoguery and corruption, they are words having only an historical significance."

"Human nature itself must have changed very much," I said.

"Not at all," was Dr. Leete's reply, "but the conditions of human life have changed, and with them the motives of human action. The organization of society with you was such that officials were under a constant temptation to misuse their power for the private profit of themselves or others. Under such circumstances it seems almost strange that you dared entrust them with any of your affairs. Nowadays, on the contrary, society is so constituted that there is absolutely no way in which an official, however ill-disposed, could possibly make any profit for himself or any one else by a misuse of his power. Let him be as bad an official as you please, he cannot be a corrupt one. There is no motive to be. The social system no longer offers a premium on dishonesty. But these are matters which you can only understand as you come, with time, to know us better."

"But you have not yet told me how you have settled the labor problem. It is the problem of capital which we have been discussing," I said. "After the nation had assumed conduct of the mills, machinery, railroads, farms, mines, and capital in general of the country, the labor question still remained. In assuming the responsibilities of capital the nation had assumed the difficulties of the capitalist's position."

"The moment the nation assumed the responsibilities of capital those difficulties vanished," replied Dr. Leete. "The national organization of labor under one direction was the complete solution of what was, in your day and under your system, justly regarded as the insoluble labor problem. When the nation became the sole employer, all the citizens, by virtue of their citizenship, became employees, to be distributed according to the needs of industry."

"That is," I suggested, "you have simply applied the principle of uni- 50 versal military service, as it was understood in our day, to the labor question."

"Yes," said Dr. Leete, "that was something which followed as a matter of course as soon as the nation had become the sole capitalist. The people were already accustomed to the idea that the obligation of every citizen, not physically disabled, to contribute his military services to the defense of the nation was equal and absolute. That it was equally the duty of every citizen to contribute his quota of industrial or intellectual services to the maintenance of the nation was equally evident, though it was not until the nation became the employer of labor that citizens were able to render this sort of service with any pretense either of universality or equity. No organization of labor was possible when the employing power was divided among hundreds or thousands of individuals and corporations, between which concert of any kind was neither desired, nor indeed feasible. It constantly happened then that vast numbers who desired to labor could find no opportunity, and on the other hand, those who desired to evade a part or all of their debt could easily do so."

"Service, now, I suppose, is compulsory upon all," I suggested.

"It is rather a matter of course than of compulsion," replied Dr. Leete. "It is regarded as so absolutely natural and reasonable that the idea of its being compulsory has ceased to be thought of. He would be thought to be an incredibly contemptible person who should need compulsion in such a case. Nevertheless, to speak of service being compulsory would be a weak way to state its absolute inevitableness. Our entire social order is so wholly based upon and deduced from it that if it were conceivable that a man could escape it, he would be left with no possible way to provide for his existence. He would have excluded himself from the world, cut himself off from his kind, in a word, committed suicide."

"Is the term of service in this industrial army for life?"

"Oh, no; it both begins later and ends earlier than the average working period in your day. Your workshops were filled with children and old men, but we hold the period of youth sacred to education and the period of maturity, when the physical forces begin to flag, equally sacred to ease and agreeable relaxation. The period of industrial service is twenty-four years, beginning at the close of the course of education at twenty-one and terminating at forty-five. After forty-five, while discharged from labor, the citizen still remains liable to special calls, in case of emergencies causing a sudden great increase in the demand for labor, till he reaches the age of fifty-five, but such calls are rarely, in fact almost never, made. The fifteenth day of October of every year is what we call Muster Day, because those who have reached the age of twenty-one are then mustered into the industrial service, and at the same time those who, after twenty-four years' service, have reached the age of forty-five, are honorably mustered out. It is the great day of the year with us, whence we reckon all other events, our Olympiad, save that it is annual." 55

CHAPTER IX

Dr. and Mrs. Leete were evidently not a little startled to learn, when they presently appeared, that I had been all over the city alone that morning, and it was apparent that they were agreeably surprised to see that I seemed so little agitated after the experience.

"Your stroll could scarcely have failed to be a very interesting one," said Mrs. Leete, as we sat down to table soon after. "You must have seen a good many new things."

"I saw very little that was not new," I replied. "But I think what surprised me as much as anything was not to find any stores on Washington Street, or any banks on State. What have you done with the merchants and bankers? Hung them all, perhaps, as the anarchists wanted to do in my day?"

"Not so bad as that," replied Dr. Leete. "We have simply dispensed with them. Their functions are obsolete in the modern world."

"Who sells you things when you want to buy them?" I inquired.   60

"There is neither selling nor buying nowadays; the distribution of goods is effected in another way. As to the bankers, having no money we have no use for those gentry."

"Miss Leete," said I, turning to Edith, "I am afraid that your father is making sport of me. I don't blame him, for the temptation my innocence offers must be extraordinary. But, really, there are limits to my credulity as to possible alterations in the social system."

"Father had no idea of jesting, I am sure," she replied, with a reassuring smile.

The conversation took another turn then, the point of ladies' fashions in the nineteenth century being raised, if I remember rightly, by Mrs. Leete, and it was not till after breakfast, when the doctor had invited me up to the house-top, which appeared to be a favorite resort of his, that he recurred to the subject.

"You were surprised," he said, "at my saying that we got along with-   65 out money or trade, but a moment's reflection will show that trade existed and money was needed in your day simply because the business of production was left in private hands, and that, consequently, they are superfluous now."

"I do not at once see how that follows," I replied.

"It is very simple," said Dr. Leete. "When innumerable different and independent persons produced the various things needful to life and comfort, endless exchanges between individuals were requisite in order that they might supply themselves with what they desired. These exchanges constituted trade, and money was essential as their medium. But as soon as the nation became the sole producer of all sorts of commodities, there was no need of exchanges between individuals that they might get what they required. Everything was procurable from one source, and nothing could be procured anywhere else. A system of direct distribution from the national storehouses took the place of trade, and for this money was unnecessary."

"How is this distribution managed?" I asked.

"On the simplest possible plan," replied Dr. Leete. "A credit corresponding to his share of the annual product of the nation is given to every citizen on the public books at the beginning of each year, and a credit card issued him with which he procures at the public storehouses, found in every community, whatever he desires whenever he desires it. This arrangement, you will see, totally obviates the necessity for business transactions of any sort between individuals and consumers. Perhaps you would like to see what our credit cards are like.

"You observe," he pursued as I was curiously examining the piece of 70 pasteboard he gave me, "that this card is issued for a certain number of dollars. We have kept the old word, but not the substance. The term, as we use it, answers to no real thing, but merely serves as an algebraical symbol for comparing the values of products with one another. For this purpose they are all priced in dollars and cents, just as in your day. The value of what I procure on this card is checked off by the clerk, who pricks out of these tiers of squares the price of what I order."

"If you wanted to buy something of your neighbor, could you transfer part of your credit to him as consideration?" I inquired.

"In the first place," replied Dr. Leete, "our neighbors have nothing to sell us, but in any event our credit would not be transferable, being strictly personal. Before the nation could even think of honoring any such transfer as you speak of, it would be bound to inquire into all the circumstances of the transaction, so as to be able to guarantee its absolute equity. It would have been reason enough, had there been no other, for abolishing money, that its possession was no indication of rightful title to it. In the hands of the man who had stolen it or murdered for it, it was as good as in those which had earned it by industry. People nowadays interchange gifts and favors out of friendship, but buying and selling is considered absolutely inconsistent with the mutual benevolence and disinterestedness which should prevail between citizens and the sense of community of interest which supports our social system. According to our ideas, buying and selling is essentially anti-social in all its tendencies. It is an education in self-seeking at the expense of others, and no society whose citizens are trained in such a school can possibly rise above a very low grade of civilization."

"What if you have to spend more than your card in any one year?" I asked.

"The provision is so ample that we are more likely not to spend it all," replied Dr. Leete. "But if extraordinary expenses should exhaust it, we can obtain a limited advance on the next year's credit, though this practice is not encouraged, and a heavy discount is charged to check it. Of course if a man showed himself a reckless spendthrift he would receive his allowance monthly or weekly instead of yearly, or if necessary not be permitted to handle it all."

"If you don't spend your allowance, I suppose it accumulates?" 75

"That is also permitted to a certain extent when a special outlay is anticipated. But unless notice to the contrary is given, it is presumed that the citizen who does not fully expend his credit did not have occasion to do so, and the balance is turned into the general surplus."

"Such a system does not encourage saving habits on the part of citizens," I said.

"It is not intended to," was the reply. "The nation is rich, and does not wish the people to deprive themselves of any good thing. In your day, men were bound to lay up goods and money against coming failure of the means of support and for their children. This necessity made parsimony a virtue. But now it would have no such laudable object, and, having lost its utility, it has ceased to be regarded as a virtue. No man any more has any care for the morrow, either for himself or his children, for the nation guarantees the nurture, education, and comfortable maintenance of every citizen from the cradle to the grave."

"That is a sweeping guarantee!" I said. "What certainty can there be that the value of a man's labor will recompense the nation for its outlay on him? On the whole, society may be able to support all its members, but some must earn less than enough for their support, and others more; and that brings us back once more to the wages question, on which you have hitherto said nothing. It was at just this point, if you remember, that our talk ended last evening; and I say again, as I did then, that here I should suppose a national industrial system like yours would find its main difficulty. How, I ask once more, can you adjust satisfactorily the comparative wages or remuneration of the multitude of avocations, so unlike and so incommensurable, which are necessary for the service of society? In our day the market rate determined the price of labor of all sorts, as well as of goods. The employer paid as little as he could, and the worker got as much. It was not a pretty system ethically, I admit; but it did, at least, furnish us a rough and ready formula for settling a question which must be settled ten thousand times a day if the world was ever going to get forward. There seemed to us no other practicable way of doing it."

"Yes," replied Dr. Leete, "it was the only practicable way under a 80 system which made the interests of every individual antagonistic to those of every other; but it would have been a pity if humanity could never have devised a better plan, for yours was simply the application to the mutual relations of men of the devil's maxim, "Your necessity is my opportunity." The reward of any service depended not upon its difficulty, danger, or hardship, for throughout the world it seems that the most perilous, severe, and repulsive labor was done by the worst paid classes; but solely upon the strait of those who needed the service."

"All that is conceded," I said. "But, with all its defects, the plan of settling prices by the market rate was a practical plan; and I cannot conceive what satisfactory substitute you can have devised for it. The government being the only possible employer, there is of course no labor market or market rate. Wages of all sorts must be arbitrarily fixed by the government. I cannot imagine a more complex and delicate function than that must be, or one, however performed, more certain to breed universal dissatisfaction."

"I beg your pardon," replied Dr. Leete, "but I think you exaggerate the difficulty. Suppose a board of fairly sensible men were charged with settling the wages for all sorts of trades under a system which, like ours, guaranteed employment to all, while permitting the choice of avocations. Don't you see that, however unsatisfactory the first adjustment might be, the mistakes would soon correct themselves? The favored trades would have too many volunteers, and those discriminated against would lack them till the errors were set right. But this is aside from the purpose, for, though this plan would, I fancy, be practicable enough, it is no part of our system."

"How, then, do you regulate wages?" I once more asked.

Dr. Leete did not reply till after several moments of meditative silence. "I know, of course," he finally said, "enough of the old order of things to understand just what you mean by that question; and yet the present order is so utterly different at this point that I am a little at loss how to answer you best. You ask me how we regulate wages; I can only reply that there is no idea in the modern social economy which at all corresponds with what was meant by wages in your day."

"I suppose you mean that you have no money to pay wages in," said 85 I. "But the credit given the worker at the government storehouse answers to his wages with us. How is the amount of the credit given respectively to the workers in different lines determined? By what title does the individual claim his particular share? What is the basis of allotment?"

"His title," replied Dr. Leete, "is his humanity. The basis of his claim is the fact that he is a man."

"The fact that he is a man!" I repeated, incredulously. "Do you possibly mean that all have the same share?"

"Most assuredly."

The readers of this book never having practically known any other arrangement, or perhaps very carefully considered the historical accounts of former epochs in which a very different system prevailed, cannot be expected to appreciate the stupor of amazement into which Dr. Leete's simple statement plunged me.

"You see," he said, smiling, "that it is not merely that we have no 90 money to pay wages in, but, as I said, we have nothing at all answering to your idea of wages."

By this time I had pulled myself together sufficiently to voice some of the criticisms which, man of the nineteenth century as I was, came uppermost in my mind, upon this to me astounding arrangement. "Some men do twice the work of others!" I exclaimed. "Are the clever workmen content with a plan that ranks them with the indifferent?"

"We leave no possible ground for any complaint of injustice," replied Dr. Leete, "by requiring precisely the same measure of service from all."

"How can you do that, I should like to know, when no two men's powers are the same?"

"Nothing could be simpler," was Dr. Leete's reply. "We require of each that he shall make the same effort; that is, we demand of him the best service it is in his power to give."

"And supposing all do the best they can," I answered, "the amount 95 of the product resulting is twice greater from one man than from another."

"Very true," replied Dr. Leete; "but the amount of the resulting product has nothing whatever to do with the question, which is one of desert. Desert is a moral question, and the amount of the product a material quantity. It would be an extraordinary sort of logic which should try to determine a moral question by a material standard. The amount of the effort alone is pertinent to the question of desert. All men who do their best, do the same. A man's endowments, however godlike, merely fix the measure of his duty. The man of great endowments who does not do all he might, though he may do more than a man of small endowments who does his best, is deemed a less deserving worker than the latter, and dies a debtor to his fellows. The Creator sets men's tasks for them by the faculties he gives them; we simply exact their fulfillment."

"No doubt that is very fine philosophy," I said; "nevertheless it seems hard that the man who produces twice as much as another, even if both do their best, should have only the same share."

"Does it, indeed, seem so to you?" responded Dr. Leete. "Now, do you know, that seems very curious to me? The way it strikes people nowadays is, that a man who can produce twice as much as another with the same effort, instead of being rewarded for doing so, ought to be punished if he does not do so. In the nineteenth century, when a horse pulled a heavier load than a goat, I suppose you rewarded him. Now, we should have whipped him soundly if he had not, on the ground that, being much stronger, he ought to. It is singular how ethical standards change." The doctor said this with such a twinkle in his eye that I was obliged to laugh.

"I suppose," I said, "that the real reason that we rewarded men for their endowments, while we considered those of horses and goats merely as fixing the service to be severally required of them, was that the animals, not being reasoning beings, naturally did the best they could, whereas men could only be induced to do so by rewarding them according to the amount of their product. That brings me to ask why, unless human nature has mightily changed in a hundred years, you are not under the same necessity."

"We are," replied Dr. Leete. "I don't think there has been any 100 change in human nature in that respect since your day. It is still so constituted that special incentives in the form of prizes, and advantages to be gained, are requisite to call out the best endeavors of the average man in any direction."

"But what inducement," I asked, "can a man have to put forth his best endeavors when, however much or little he accomplishes, his income remains the same? High characters may be moved by devotion to the common welfare under such a system, but does not the average man tend to rest back on his oar, reasoning that it is of no use to make a special effort, since the effort will not increase his income, nor its withholding diminish it?"

"Does it then really seem to you," answered my companion, "that human nature is insensible to any motives save fear of want and love of luxury, that you should expect security and equality of livelihood to leave them without possible incentives to effort? Your contemporaries did not really think so, though they might fancy they did. When it was a question of the grandest class of efforts, the most absolute self-devotion, they depended on quite other incentives. Not higher wages, but honor and the hope of men's gratitude, patriotism and the inspiration of duty, were the motives which they set before their soldiers when it was a question of dying for the nation, and never was there an age of the world when those motives did not call out what is best and noblest in men. And not only this, but when you come to analyze the love of money which was the general impulse to effort in your day, you find that the dread of want and desire of luxury was but one of several motives which the pursuit of money represented; the others, and with many the more influential, being desire of power, of social position, and reputation for ability and success. So you see that though we have abolished poverty and the fear of it, and inordinate luxury with the hope of it, we have not touched the greater part of the motives which underlay the love of money in former times, or any of those which prompted the supremer sorts of effort. The coarser motives, which no longer move us, have been replaced by higher motives wholly unknown to the mere wage earners of your age. Now that industry of whatever sort is no longer self-service, but service of the nation, patriotism, passion for humanity, impel the worker as in your day they did the soldier. The army of industry is an army, not alone by virtue of its perfect organization, but by reason also of the ardor of self-devotion which animates its members.

"But as you used to supplement the motives of patriotism with the love of glory, in order to stimulate the valor of your soldiers, so do we. Based as our industrial system is on the principle of requiring the same unit of effort from every man, that is, the best he can do, you will see that the means by which we spur the workers to do their best must be a very essential part of our scheme. With us, diligence in the national service is the sole and certain way to public repute, social distinction, and official power. The value of a man's services to society fixes his rank in it. Compared with the effect of our social arrangements in impelling men to be zealous in business, we deem the object-lessons of biting poverty and wanton luxury on which you depended a device as weak and uncertain as it was barbaric. The lust of honor even in your sordid day notoriously impelled men to more desperate effort than the love of money could." . . .

Topics for Critical Thinking and Writing

1. Bellamy's character Julian West expresses some reservations about being a man who could "live on the income of his investments" (para. 3). What are those reservations, and do you share them? Why, or why not?

2. How, if at all, do you think the elaborate metaphor of society as a coach driven by hunger and hauled by the poor for the benefit of the rich (paras. 4–8) differs from a contemporary free-market capitalist society?

3. In an essay of 500 words, discuss the similarities and differences between our economic system in the year 2000 and the portrait of 2000 that Dr. Leete gives in Chapter V of the selection.

4. Obtain from your college library, or some other source, a copy of Karl Marx's *Communist Manifesto,* written just forty years before Bellamy's *Looking Backward.* On what features does the communist society depicted by Marx and the society depicted by Dr. Leete in paragraphs 46 through 55 differ?

5. Why does the fictional Julian West declare that the economic system with which he was familiar, one in which "The employer paid as little as he could, and the worker got as much [as he could] . . . was not a pretty system ethically" (para. 79)? Do you agree with his judgment?

6. Suppose someone were to reply to Dr. Leete that in every society different material incentives were necessary to elicit productive efforts from the talented and energetic and that society depends on those efforts because merely trying as hard as one can at whatever job one holds (cf. para. 96) does not guarantee any useful results. How might Dr. Leete reply? Do you find his reply persuasive? Explain.

7. The questions that are always asked about books such as *Looking Backward* are (a) is the writer's vision practical — that is, might this imagined world really come into existence or has the writer misunderstood human nature?, and (b) is the writer's vision desirable — that is, would we want to live in the world described in the book? In an essay of 500 to 750 words, give your response to both of these questions, as applied to *Looking Backward.*

W. H. Auden

Wystan Hugh Auden (1907–1973) was born in York, England, and educated at Oxford University. In the 1930s his witty left-wing poetry earned him wide acclaim as the leading poet of his generation. In 1939 he came to the United States, becoming a citizen in 1946, though he returned to England for his last years. Much of Auden's poetry is characterized by a combination of colloquial diction and technical dexterity. The poem reprinted here was originally published in 1940.

The Unknown Citizen

(To JS/07/M/378
This Marble Monument
Is Erected by the State)

He was found by the Bureau of Statistics to be
One against whom there was no official complaint,
And all the reports on his conduct agree
That, in the modern sense of an old-fashioned word, he was a saint,
For in everything he did he served the Greater Community.   5
Except for the War till the day he retired
He worked in a factory and never got fired,
But satisfied his employers, Fudge Motors Inc.
Yet he wasn't a scab or odd in his views,
For his Union reports that he paid his dues,   10
(Our report on his Union shows it was sound)
And our Social Psychology workers found
That he was popular with his mates and liked a drink.
The Press are convinced that he bought a paper every day
And that his reactions to advertisements were normal in every way.   15
Policies taken out in his name prove that he was fully insured,
And his Health-card shows he was once in hospital but left it cured.
Both Producers Research and High-Grade Living declare
He was fully sensible to the advantages of the Installment Plan
And had everything necessary to the Modern Man,   20
A phonograph, radio, a car and a frigidaire.
Our researches into Public Opinion are content
That he held the proper opinions for the time of year;
When there was peace, he was for peace; when there was war, he went.
He was married and added five children to the population,   25
Which our Eugenist says was the right number for a parent of his
     generation,
And our teachers report that he never interfered with their education.
Was he free? Was he happy? The question is absurd:
Had anything been wrong, we should certainly have heard.

Topics for Critical Thinking and Writing

1. Who is the narrator in Auden's poem, and on what sort of occasion is he speaking? How do you know?

2. France, Great Britain, and the United States all have monuments to "The Unknown" (formerly "The Unknown Soldier"). How is Auden's proposed monument like and unlike these war memorials?

3. The poem ends by asking "Was he free? Was he happy?" and the questions are dismissed summarily. Is that because the answers are so obvious? What answers (obvious or subtle) do you think the poem offers to these questions?

4. Evaluate the poem, making clear the reasons behind your evaluation. (On literary evaluations, see pp. 426–29.)

5. If you have read the selection from Thomas More's *Utopia* (p. 744), write an essay of 500 to 750 words—in More's voice—setting forth More's response to Auden's poem.

Langston Hughes

Langston Hughes (1902–1967), an African American writer, was born in Joplin, Missouri, but after his parents divorced, he lived with his grandmother in Lawrence, Kansas, then in Cleveland, and then for fifteen months in Mexico with his father. He returned to the United States in 1921 and spent a year at Columbia University, served as a merchant seaman, and worked in a Paris nightclub, where he showed some of his poems to Dr. Alain Locke, a strong advocate of African American literature. Encouraged by Locke, when Hughes returned to the United States, he studied at the University of Pennsylvania and Lincoln University, where he earned a bachelor's degree. He continued to write, publishing fiction, plays, essays, and biographies; he also founded theaters, gave public readings, and was, in short, a highly visible presence. Esquire magazine first published an abridged version of "Let America Be America Again" in 1936.

Let America Be America Again

Let America be America again.
Let it be the dream it used to be.
Let it be the pioneer on the plain
Seeking a home where he himself is free.

(America never was America to me.)   5

Let America be the dream the dreamers dreamed—
Let it be that great strong land of love
Where never kings connive nor tyrants scheme
That any man be crushed by one above.

(It never was America to me.)   10

O, let my land be a land where Liberty
Is crowned with no false patriotic wreath,
But opportunity is real, and life is free,
Equality is in the air we breathe.

(There's never been equality for me,   15
Nor freedom in this "homeland of the free.")

Say, who are you that mumbles in the dark?
And who are you that draws your veil across the stars?

I am the poor white, fooled and pushed apart,
I am the Negro bearing slavery's scars.   20
I am the red man driven from the land,
I am the immigrant clutching the hope I seek—
And finding only the same old stupid plan
Of dog eat dog, of mighty crush the weak.

I am the young man, full of strength and hope,   25
Tangled in that ancient endless chain
Of profit, power, gain, of grab the land!
Of grab the gold! Of grab the ways of satisfying need!
Of work the men! Of take the pay!
Of owning everything for one's own greed!   30

I am the farmer, bondsman to the soil.
I am the worker sold to the machine.
I am the Negro, servant to you all.
I am the people, humble, hungry, mean—
Hungry yet today despite the dream.   35
Beaten yet today—O, Pioneers!
I am the man who never got ahead,
The poorest worker bartered through the years.

Yet I'm the one who dreamt our basic dream
In that Old World while still a serf of kings,   40
Who dreamt a dream so strong, so brave, so true,
That even yet its mighty daring sings
In every brick and stone, in every furrow turned
That's made America the land it has become.
O, I'm the man who sailed those early seas   45
In search of what I meant to be my home—
For I'm the one who left dark Ireland's shore,
And Poland's plain, and England's grassy lea,
And torn from Black Africa's strand I came
To build a "homeland of the free."   50

The free?

Who said the free? Not me?
Surely not me? The millions on relief today?
The millions shot down when we strike?
The millions who have nothing for our pay?   55
For all the dreams we've dreamed
And all the songs we've sung

And all the hopes we've held
And all the flags we've hung,
The millions who have nothing for our pay—   60
Except the dream that's almost dead today.

O, let America be America again—
The land that never has been yet—
And yet must be—the land where *every* man is free.
The land that's mine—the poor man's, Indian's, Negro's, ME—   65
Who made America,
Whose sweat and blood, whose faith and pain,
Whose hand at the foundry, whose plow in the rain,
Must bring back our mighty dream again.

Sure, call me any ugly name you choose—   70
The steel of freedom does not stain.
From those who live like leeches on the people's lives,
We must take back our land again,
America!

O, yes,   75
I say it plain,
America never was America to me,
And yet I swear this oath—
America will be!

Out of the rack and ruin of our gangster death,   80
The rape and rot of graft, and stealth, and lies,
We, the people, must redeem
The land, the mines, the plants, the rivers.
The mountains and the endless plain—
All, all the stretch of these great green states—   85
And make America again!

Topics for Critical Thinking and Writing

1. Hughes says in line 1, "Let America be America again," but do you suppose America ever was what he seems to assume that it once was? For instance, might not his "pioneer" (line 3) have been sexist and racist? Or is it evident that contemporary society is morally inferior to early American society?

2. In line 24 Hughes speaks of a system "of dog eat dog," where the "mighty crush the weak," and in line 27 he speaks of a system of "profit, power, gain, of grab the land." Do you believe that this charge can be lodged today against our system of capitalism? Explain.

3. When *Esquire* magazine bought the poem, it bought only the first fifty lines. Why do you suppose the magazine declined to publish the re-

mainder? Because the latter part is less good as poetry? Because it is too radical? In an essay of 500 words compare the two versions (lines 1–50 and 1–86), and indicate which version you would publish if you were an editor today and why.

Ursula K. Le Guin

Ursula K. Le Guin was born in 1929 in Berkeley, California, the daughter of a distinguished mother (Theodora Kroeber, a folklorist) and father (Alfred L. Kroeber, an anthropologist). After graduating from Radcliffe College, she earned a master's degree at Columbia University; in 1952 she held a Fulbright Fellowship for study in Paris, where she met and married Charles Le Guin, a historian. She began writing in earnest while bringing up three children. Although her work is most widely known to buffs of science fiction, because it usually has larger moral or political dimensions it interests many other readers who normally do not care for sci-fi.

Le Guin has said that she was prompted to write the following story by a remark she encountered in William James's "The Moral Philosopher and the Moral Life." James suggests there that if millions of people could be "kept permanently happy on the one simple condition that a certain lost soul on the far-off edge of things should lead a life of lonely torment," our moral sense "would make us immediately feel" it would be "hideous" to accept such a bargain. This story first appeared in New Dimensions 3 *(1973).*

The Ones Who Walk Away from Omelas

With a clamor of bells that set the swallows soaring, the Festival of Summer came to the city Omelas, bright-towered by the sea. The rigging of the boats in harbor sparkled with flags. In the streets between houses with red roofs and painted walls, between old moss-grown gardens and under avenues of trees, past great parks and public buildings, processions moved. Some were decorous: old people in long stiff robes of mauve and gray, grave master workmen, quiet, merry women carrying their babies and chatting as they walked. In other streets the music beat faster, a shimmering of gong and tambourine, and the people went dancing, the procession was a dance. Children dodged in and out, their high calls rising like the swallows' crossing flights over the music and the singing. All the processions wound towards the north side of the city, where on the great water-meadow called the Green Fields boys and girls, naked in the bright air, with mudstained feet and ankles and long, lithe arms, exercised their restive horses before the race. The horses wore no gear at all but a halter without bit. Their manes were braided with streamers of silver, gold, and green. They flared their nostrils and pranced and boasted to one another; they were vastly excited, the horse being the only animal who has adopted our ceremonies as his own. Far off to the north and west the mountains stood up half encircling Omelas on her bay. The air of morning was so clear that the snow still crowning the Eighteen Peaks burned with white-gold fire across the miles of sunlit air, under the dark blue of the sky. There was just enough wind to make the banners that marked the racecourse snap and flutter now and then. In the silence of the broad green meadows one could hear the music winding through the city streets, farther and nearer and ever approaching, a cheerful faint sweetness of the air that from time to time trembled and gathered together and broke out into the great joyous clanging of the bells.

Joyous! How is one to tell about joy? How describe the citizens of Omelas?

They were not simple folk, you see, though they were happy. But we do not say the words of cheer much any more. All smiles have become archaic. Given a description such as this one tends to make certain assumptions. Given a description such as this one tends to look next for the King, mounted on a splendid stallion and surrounded by his noble knights, or perhaps in a golden litter borne by great-muscled slaves. But there was no king. They did not use swords, or keep slaves. They were not barbarians. I do not know the rules and laws of their society, but I suspect that they were singularly few. As they did without monarchy and slavery, so they also got on without the stock exchange, the advertisement, the secret police, and the bomb. Yet I repeat that these were not simple folk, not dulcet shepherds, noble savages, bland utopians. They were not less complex than us. The trouble is that we have a bad habit, encouraged by pedants and sophisticates, of considering happiness as something rather stupid. Only pain is intellectual, only evil interesting. This is the treason of the artist: a refusal to admit the banality of evil and the terrible boredom of pain. If you can't lick 'em, join 'em. If it hurts, repeat it. But to praise despair is to condemn delight, to embrace violence is to lose hold of everything else. We have almost lost hold, we can no longer describe a happy man, nor make any celebration of joy. How can I tell you about the people of Omelas? They were not naïve and happy children—though their children were, in fact, happy. They were mature, intelligent, passionate adults whose lives were not wretched. O miracle! But I wish I could describe it better. I wish I could convince you. Omelas sounds in my words like a city in a fairy tale, long ago and far away, once upon a time. Perhaps it would be best if you imagined it as your own fancy bids, assuming it will rise to the occasion, for certainly I cannot suit you all. For instance, how about technology? I think that there would be no cars or helicopters in and above the streets; this follows from the fact that the people of Omelas are happy people. Happiness is based on a just discrimination of what is necessary, what is neither necessary nor destructive, and what is destructive. In the middle category, however—that of the unnecessary but undestructive, that of comfort, luxury, exuberance, etc.—they could perfectly well have central heating, subway trains, washing machines, and all kinds of marvelous devices not yet invented here, floating light-sources, fuelless power, a cure for the common cold. Or they could have none of that: it doesn't matter. As you like it. I incline to think that people from towns up and down the coast have been coming in to Omelas during the last days before the Festival on very fast little trains and double-decked trams, and that the train station of Omelas is actually the handsomest building in town, though plainer than the magnificent Farmers' Market. But even granted trains, I fear that Omelas so far strikes some of you as goody-goody. Smiles, bells, parades, horses, bleh. If so, please add an orgy. If an orgy would help, don't hesitate. Let us not, however, have temples from which issue beautiful nude priests and priestesses already half in ecstasy and ready to copulate with any man or woman, lover or stranger, who desires union with the deep godhead of the blood, although that was my first idea. But really it would be better not to have any temples in Omelas—at least, not manned temples. Religion yes, clergy no. Surely the beautiful nudes can just wander about, offering themselves like divine soufflés to the hunger of the needy and the rapture of the flesh. Let them join the processions. Let tambourines be struck above the copulations, and the glory of desire be proclaimed upon the gongs, and (a not unimportant point) let the offspring of these delightful rituals be beloved and looked after by all. One thing I know there is none of in Omelas is guilt. But what else should there be? I thought that first there were no drugs, but that is puritanical. For those who like it, the faint insistent sweetness of *drooz* may perfume the ways of the city, *drooz* which first brings a great lightness and brilliance to the mind and limbs, and then after some hours a dreamy languor, and wonderful visions at last of the very arcana and inmost secrets of the Universe, as well as exciting the pleasure of sex beyond all belief; and it is not habit-forming. For more modest tastes I think there ought to be beer. What else, what else belongs in the joyous city? The sense of victory, surely, the celebration of courage. But as we did without clergy, let us do without soldiers. The joy built upon successful slaughter is not the right kind of joy; it will not do; it is fearful and it is trivial. A boundless and generous contentment, a magnanimous triumph felt not against some outer enemy but in communion with the finest and fairest in the souls of all men everywhere and the splendor of the world's summer: this is what swells the hearts of the people of Omelas, and the victory they celebrate is that of life. I really don't think many of them need to take *drooz*.

Most of the processions have reached the Green Fields by now. A marvelous smell of cooking goes forth from the red and blue tents of the provisioners. The faces of small children are amiably sticky; in the benign grey beard of a man a couple of crumbs of rich pastry are entangled. The youths and girls have mounted their horses and are beginning to group around the starting line of the course. An old woman, small, fat, and laughing, is passing out flowers from a basket, and tall young men wear her flowers in their shining hair. A child of nine or ten sits at the edge of the crowd, alone, playing on a wooden flute. People pause to listen, and they smile, but they do not speak to him, for he never ceases playing and never sees them, his dark eyes wholly rapt in the sweet, thin magic of the tune.

He finishes, and slowly lowers his hands holding the wooden flute.   5

As if that little private silence were the signal, all at once a trumpet sounds from the pavilion near the starting line: imperious, melancholy, piercing. The horses rear on their slender legs, and some of them neigh in answer. Sober-faced, the young riders stroke the horses' necks and soothe them, whispering, "Quiet, quiet, there my beauty, my hope. . . ." They begin to form in rank along the starting line. The crowds along the racecourse are like a field of grass and flowers in the wind. The Festival of Summer has begun.

Do you believe? Do you accept the festival, the city, the joy? No? Then let me describe one more thing.

In a basement under one of the beautiful public buildings of Omelas, or perhaps in the cellar of one of its spacious private homes, there is a room. It has one locked door, and no window. A little light seeps in dustily between cracks in the boards, secondhand from a cobwebbed window somewhere across the cellar. In one corner of the little room a couple of mops, with stiff, clotted, foul-smelling heads, stand near a rusty bucket. The floor is dirt, a little damp to the touch, as cellar dirt usually is. The room is about three paces long and two wide: a mere broom closet or disused tool room. In the room a child is sitting. It could be a boy or a girl. It looks about six, but actually is nearly ten. It is feeble-minded. Perhaps it was born defective, or perhaps it has become imbecile through fear, malnutrition, and neglect. It picks its nose and occasionally fumbles vaguely with its toes or genitals, as it sits hunched in the corner farthest from the bucket and the two mops. It is afraid of the mops. It finds them horrible. It shuts its eyes, but it knows the mops are still standing there; and the door is locked; and nobody will come. The door is always locked; and nobody ever comes, except that sometimes—the child has no understanding of time or interval—sometimes the door rattles terribly and opens, and a person, or several people, are there. One of them may come in and kick the child to make it stand up. The others never come close, but peer in at it with frightened, disgusted eyes. The food bowl and the water jug are hastily filled, the door is locked, the eyes disappear. The people at the door never say anything, but the child, who has not always lived in the tool room, and can remember sunlight and its mother's voice, sometimes speaks. "I will be good," it says. "Please let me out. I will be good!" They never answer. The child used to scream for help at night, and cry a good deal, but now it only makes a kind of whining, "eh-haa, eh-haa," and it speaks less and less often. It is so thin there are no calves to its legs; its belly protrudes; it lives on a half-bowl of corn meal and grease a day. It is naked. Its buttocks and thighs are a mass of festered sores, as it sits in its own excrement continually.

They all know it is there, all the people of Omelas. Some of them have come to see it, others are content merely to know it is there. They all know that it has to be there. Some of them understand why, and some do not, but they all understand that their happiness, the beauty of their city, the tenderness of their friendships, the health of their children, the wisdom of their scholars, the skill of their makers, even the abundance of their harvest and the kindly weathers of their skies, depend wholly on this child's abominable misery.

This is usually explained to children when they are between eight 10 and twelve, whenever they seem capable of understanding; and most of those who come to see the child are young people, though often enough an adult comes, or comes back, to see the child. No matter how well the matter has been explained to them, these young spectators are always shocked and sickened at the sight. They feel disgust, which they had thought themselves superior to. They feel anger, outrage, impotence, despite all the explanations. They would like to do something for the child. But there is nothing they can do. If the child were brought up into the sunlight out of that vile place, if it were cleaned and fed and comforted, that would be a good thing, indeed; but if it were done, in that day and hour all the prosperity and beauty and delight of Omelas would wither and be destroyed. Those are the terms. To exchange all the goodness and grace of every life in Omelas for that single, small improvement: to throw away the happiness of thousands for the chance of the happiness of one: that would be to let guilt within the walls indeed.

The terms are strict and absolute; there may not even be a kind word spoken to the child.

Often the young people go home in tears, or in a tearless rage, when they have seen the child and faced this terrible paradox. They may brood over it for weeks or years. But as time goes on they begin to realize that even if the child could be released, it would not get much good of its freedom: a little vague pleasure of warmth and food, no doubt, but little more. It is too degraded and imbecile to know any real joy. It has been afraid too long ever to be free of fear. Its habits are too uncouth for it to respond to humane treatment. Indeed, after so long it would probably be wretched without walls about it to protect it, and darkness for its eyes, and its own excrement to sit in. Their tears at the bitter injustice dry when they begin to perceive the terrible justice of reality, and to accept it. Yet it is their tears and anger, the trying of their generosity and the acceptance of their helplessness, which are perhaps the true source of the splendor of their lives. Theirs is no vapid, irresponsible happiness. They know that they, like the child, are not free. They know compassion. It is the existence of the child, and their knowledge of its existence, that makes possible the nobility of their architecture, the poignancy of their music, the profundity of their science. It is because of the child that they are so gentle with children. They know that if the wretched one were not there snivelling in the dark, the other one, the flute-player, could make no joyful music as the young riders line up in their beauty for the race in the sunlight of the first morning of summer.

Now do you believe in them? Are they not more credible? But there is one more thing to tell, and this is quite incredible.

At times one of the adolescent girls or boys who go to see the child does not go home to weep or rage, does not, in fact, go home at all. Sometimes also a man or woman much older falls silent for a day or two, and then leaves home. These people go out into the street, and walk down the street alone. They keep walking, and walk straight out of the city of Omelas, through the beautiful gates. They keep walking across the farmlands of Omelas. Each one goes alone, youth or girl, man or woman. Night falls; the traveler must pass down village streets, between the houses with yellow-lit windows, and on out into the darkness of the fields. Each alone, they go west or north, towards the mountains. They go on. They leave Omelas, they walk ahead into the darkness, and they do not come back. The place they go towards is a place even less imaginable to most of us than the city of happiness. I cannot describe it at all. It is possible that it does not exist. But they seem to know where they are going, the ones who walk away from Omelas.

Topics for Critical Thinking and Writing

1. Summarize the point of the story—not the plot, but what the story adds up to, what the author is getting at. Next, set forth what you would probably do (and why) if you were born in Omelas.

2. Consider the narrator's assertion that happiness "is based on a just discrimination of what is necessary" (para. 3).

3. Do you think the story implies a criticism of contemporary American society? Explain.

28

How Free Is the Will
of the Individual
within Society?

Plato

Plato (427–347 B.C.), an Athenian aristocrat by birth, was the student of one great philosopher (Socrates) and the teacher of another (Aristotle). His legacy of more than two dozen dialogues—imaginary discussions between Socrates and one or more other speakers, usually young Athenians—has been of such influence that the whole of Western philosophy can be characterized, A. N. Whitehead wrote, as "a series of footnotes to Plato." Plato's interests encompassed the full range of topics in philosophy: ethics, politics, logic, metaphysics, epistemology, aesthetics, psychology, and education.

The selection reprinted here, Crito, *is the third of four dialogues telling the story of the final days of Socrates (469–399 B.C.). The first in the sequence,* Euthyphro, *portrays Socrates in his typical role, questioning someone about his beliefs (in this case, the young aristocrat, Euthyphro). The discussion is focused on the nature of piety, but the conversation breaks off before a final answer is reached—perhaps none is possible—because Socrates is on his way to stand trial before the Athenian assembly. He has been charged with "preaching false gods" (heresy) and "corrupting the youth" by causing them to doubt or disregard the wisdom of their elders. (How faithful to any actual event or discussion* Euthyphro *and Plato's other Socratic dialogues really are, scholars cannot say with assurance.)*

In Apology, *the second dialogue in the sequence, Plato (who remains entirely in the background, as he does in all the dialogues) recounts Socrates' public reply to the charges against him. During the speech, Socrates explains his life, reminding his fellow citizens that if he is (as the oracle had pronounced) "the wisest of men," then it is only because he knows that he doesn't know what others believe or pretend they do know. The dialogue ends with Socrates being found guilty and duly sentenced to death.*

The third in the series is Crito, *but we will postpone comment on it for a moment and glance at the fourth dialogue,* Phaedo, *in which Plato portrays Socrates' final philosophical discussion. The topic, appropriately, is whether the soul is immortal. It ends with Socrates, in the company of his closest friends, bidding them a last farewell and drinking the fatal cup of hemlock.*

Crito, the whole text of which is reprinted here, is the debate provoked by Crito, an old friend and admirer of Socrates. He visits Socrates in prison and urges him to escape while he still has the chance. After all, Crito argues, the guilty verdict was wrong and unfair, few Athenians really want to have Socrates put to death, his family and friends will be distraught, and so forth. Socrates will not have it. He patiently but firmly examines each of Crito's arguments and explains why it would be wrong to follow his advice.

Plato's Crito *thus ranks with Sophocles' tragedy* Antigone *as one of the first explorations in Western literature of the perennial theme of our responsibility for obeying laws that challenge our conscientious moral convictions. Antigone concludes that she must disobey the law of Creon, tyrant of Thebes; Socrates concludes that he must obey the law of democratic Athens. In* Crito, *we have not only a superb illustration of Socratic dialogue and argument but also a portrait of a virtuous thinker at the end of a long life, reflecting on its course and on the moral principles that have guided him. We see Socrates living an "examined life," the only life he thought was worth living.*

This translation is by Hugh Tredennick.

Crito

(**SCENE:** *A room in the State prison at Athens in the year 399 B.C. The time is half an hour before dawn, and the room would be almost dark but for the light of a little oil lamp. There is a pallet bed against the back wall. At the head of it a small table supports the lamp; near the foot of it Crito is sitting patiently on a stool. He is an old man, kindly, practical, simple-minded; at present he is suffering from acute emotional strain. On the bed lies Socrates asleep. He stirs, yawns, opens his eyes, and sees Crito.*)

SOCRATES: Here already, Crito? Surely it is still early?

CRITO: Indeed it is.

SOCRATES: About what time?

CRITO: Just before dawn.

SOCRATES: I wonder that the warder paid any attention to you.   5

CRITO: He is used to me now, Socrates, because I come here so often; besides, he is under some small obligation to me.

SOCRATES: Have you only just come, or have you been here for long?

CRITO: Fairly long.

SOCRATES: Then why didn't you wake me at once, instead of sitting by my bed so quietly?

CRITO: I wouldn't dream of such a thing, Socrates. I only wish I were   10 not so sleepless and depressed myself. I have been wondering at you, because I saw how comfortably you were sleeping; and I deliberately didn't wake you because I wanted you to go on being as comfortable as you could. I have often felt before in the course of my life how fortunate you are in your disposition, but I feel it more than ever now in your present misfortune when I see how easily and placidly you put up with it.

SOCRATES: Well, really, Crito, it would be hardly suitable for a man of my age to resent having to die.

CRITO: Other people just as old as you are get involved in these misfortunes, Socrates, but their age doesn't keep them from resenting it when they find themselves in your position.

SOCRATES: Quite true. But tell me, why have you come so early?

CRITO: Because I bring bad news, Socrates; not so bad from your point of view, I suppose, but it will be very hard to bear for me and your other friends, and I think that I shall find it hardest of all.

SOCRATES: Why, what is this news? Has the boat come in from Delos— 15 the boat which ends my reprieve when it arrives?[1]

CRITO: It hasn't actually come in yet, but I expect that it will be here today, judging from the report of some people who have just arrived from Sunium and left it there. It's quite clear from their account that it will be here today; and so by tomorrow, Socrates, you will have to—to end your life.

SOCRATES: Well, Crito, I hope that it may be for the best; if the gods will it so, so be it. All the same, I don't think it will arrive today.

CRITO: What makes you think that?

SOCRATES: I will try to explain. I think I am right in saying that I have to die on the day after the boat arrives?

CRITO: That's what the authorities say, at any rate.   20

SOCRATES: Then I don't think it will arrive on this day that is just beginning, but on the day after. I am going by a dream that I had in the night, only a little while ago. It looks as though you were right not to wake me up.

CRITO: Why, what was the dream about?

SOCRATES: I thought I saw a gloriously beautiful woman dressed in white robes, who came up to me and addressed me in these words: "Socrates, to the pleasant land of Phthia on the third day thou shalt come."

CRITO: Your dream makes no sense, Socrates.

SOCRATES: To my mind, Crito, it is perfectly clear.   25

CRITO: Too clear, apparently. But look here, Socrates, it is still not too late to take my advice and escape. Your death means a double calamity for me. I shall not only lose a friend whom I can never possibly replace, but besides a great many people who don't know you and me very well will be sure to think that I let you down, because I could have saved you if I had been willing to spend the money; and what could be more contemptible than to get a name for thinking more of money than of your

---

[1]**Delos . . . arrives** Ordinarily execution was carried out immediately after sentencing, but the day before Socrates' trial was the first day of an annual ceremony that involved sending a ship to Delos. When the ship was absent—in this case for about a month—executions could not be performed. As Crito goes on to say, Socrates could easily escape, and indeed he could have left the country before being tried. [All notes are the editors'.]

friends? Most people will never believe that it was you who refused to leave this place although we tried our hardest to persuade you.

SOCRATES: But my dear Crito, why should we pay so much attention to what "most people" think? The really reasonable people, who have more claim to be considered, will believe that the facts are exactly as they are.

CRITO: You can see for yourself, Socrates, that one has to think of popular opinion as well. Your present position is quite enough to show that the capacity of ordinary people for causing trouble is not confined to petty annoyances, but has hardly any limits if you once get a bad name with them.

SOCRATES: I only wish that ordinary people *had* unlimited capacity for doing harm; then they might have an unlimited power for doing good; which would be a splendid thing, if it were so. Actually they have neither. They cannot make a man wise or stupid; they simply act at random.

CRITO: Have it that way if you like; but tell me this, Socrates. I hope that you aren't worrying about the possible effects on me and the rest of your friends, and thinking that if you escape we shall have trouble with informers for having helped you to get away, and have to forfeit all our property or pay an enormous fine, or even incur some further punishment? If any idea like that is troubling you, you can dismiss it altogether. We are quite entitled to run that risk in saving you, and even worse, if necessary. Take my advice, and be reasonable. 30

SOCRATES: All that you say is very much in my mind, Crito, and a great deal more besides.

CRITO: Very well, then, don't let it distress you. I know some people who are willing to rescue you from here and get you out of the country for quite a moderate sum. And then surely you realize how cheap these informers are to buy off; we shan't need much money to settle them; and I think you've got enough of my money for yourself already. And then even supposing that in your anxiety for my safety you feel that you oughtn't to spend my money, there are these foreign gentlemen staying in Athens who are quite willing to spend theirs. One of them, Simmias of Thebes, has actually brought the money with him for this very purpose; and Cebes and a number of others are quite ready to do the same. So as I say, you mustn't let any fears on these grounds make you slacken your efforts to escape; and you mustn't feel any misgivings about what you said at your trial, that you wouldn't know what to do with yourself if you left this country. Wherever you go, there are plenty of places where you will find a welcome; and if you choose to go to Thessaly, I have friends there who will make much of you and give you complete protection, so that no one in Thessaly can interfere with you.

Besides, Socrates, I don't even feel that it is right for you to try to do what you are doing, throwing away your life when you might save it.

You are doing your best to treat yourself in exactly the same way as your enemies would, or rather did, when they wanted to ruin you. What is more, it seems to me that you are letting your sons down too. You have it in your power to finish their bringing up and education, and instead of that you are proposing to go off and desert them, and so far as you are concerned they will have to take their chance. And what sort of chance are they likely to get? The sort of thing that usually happens to orphans when they lose their parents. Either one ought not to have children at all, or one ought to see their upbringing and education through to the end. It strikes me that you are taking the line of least resistance, whereas you ought to make the choice of a good man and a brave one, considering that you profess to have made goodness your object all through life. Really, I am ashamed, both on your account and on ours your friends'; it will look as though we had played something like a coward's part all through this affair of yours. First, there was the way you came into court when it was quite unnecessary—that was the first act; than there was the conduct of the defense—that was the second; and finally, to complete the farce, we get this situation, which makes it appear that we have let you slip out of our hands through some lack of courage and enterprise on our part, because we didn't save you, and you didn't save yourself, when it would have been quite possible and practicable, if we had been any use at all.

There, Socrates; if you aren't careful, besides the suffering there will be all this disgrace for you and us to bear. Come, make up your mind. Really it's too late for that now; you ought to have it made up already. There is no alternative; the whole thing must be carried through during this coming night. If we lose any more time, it can't be done, it will be too late. I appeal to you, Socrates, on every ground; take my advice and please don't be unreasonable!

SOCRATES: My dear Crito, I appreciate your warm feelings very 35 much—that is, assuming that they have some justification; if not, the stronger they are, the harder they will be to deal with. Very well, then; we must consider whether we ought to follow your advice or not. You know that this is not a new idea of mine; it has always been my nature never to accept advice from any of my friends unless reflection shows that it is the best course that reason offers. I cannot abandon the principles which I used to hold in the past simply because this accident has happened to me; they seem to me to be much as they were, and I respect and regard the same principles now as before. So unless we can find better principles on this occasion, you can be quite sure that I shall not agree with you; not even if the power of the people conjures up fresh hordes of bogies to terrify our childish minds, by subjecting us to chains and executions and confiscations of our property.

Well, then, how can we consider the question most reasonably? Suppose that we begin by reverting to this view which you hold about people's opinions. Was it always right to argue that some opinions should be taken seriously but not others? Or was it always wrong? Perhaps it was right before the question of my death arose, but now we can see clearly that it was a mistaken persistence in a point of view which was really irresponsible nonsense. I should like very much to inquire into this problem, Crito, with your help, and to see whether the argument will appear in any different light to me now that I am in this position, or whether it will remain the same; and whether we shall dismiss it or accept it.

Serious thinkers, I believe, have always held some such view as the one which I mentioned just now: that some of the opinions which people entertain should be respected, and others should not. Now I ask you, Crito, don't you think that this is a sound principle?—You are safe from the prospect of dying tomorrow, in all human probability; and you are not likely to have your judgment upset by this impending calamity. Consider, then; don't you think that this is a sound enough principle, that one should not regard all the opinions that people hold, but only some and not others? What do you say? Isn't that a fair statement?

CRITO: Yes, it is.

SOCRATES: In other words, one should regard the good ones and not the bad?

CRITO: Yes.   40

SOCRATES: The opinions of the wise being good, and the opinions of the foolish bad?

CRITO: Naturally.

SOCRATES: To pass on, then: What do you think of the sort of illustration that I used to employ? When a man is in training, and taking it seriously, does he pay attention to all praise and criticism and opinion indiscriminately, or only when it comes from the one qualified person, the actual doctor or trainer?

CRITO: Only when it comes from the one qualified person.

SOCRATES: Then he should be afraid of the criticism and welcome the   45
praise of the one qualified person, but not those of the general public.

CRITO: Obviously.

SOCRATES: So he ought to regulate his actions and exercises and eating and drinking by the judgment of his instructor, who has expert knowledge, rather than by the opinions of the rest of the public.

CRITO: Yes, that is so.

SOCRATES: Very well. Now if he disobeys the one man and disregards his opinion and commendations, and pays attention to the advice of the many who have no expert knowledge, surely he will suffer some bad effect?

CRITO: Certainly.   50

SOCRATES: And what is this bad effect? Where is it produced?—I mean, in what part of the disobedient person?

CRITO: His body, obviously; that is what suffers.

SOCRATES: Very good. Well now, tell me, Crito—we don't want to go through all the examples one by one—does this apply as a general rule, and above all to the sort of actions which we are trying to decide about: just and unjust, honorable and dishonorable, good and bad? Ought we to be guided and intimidated by the opinion of the many or by that of the one—assuming that there is someone with expert knowledge? Is it true that we ought to respect and fear this person more than all the rest put together; and that if we do not follow his guidance we shall spoil and mutilate that part of us which, as we used to say, is improved by right conduct and destroyed by wrong? Or is this all nonsense?

CRITO: No, I think it is true, Socrates.

SOCRATES: Then consider the next step. There is a part of us which is   55 improved by healthy actions and ruined by unhealthy ones. If we spoil it by taking the advice of nonexperts, will life be worth living when this part is once ruined? The part I mean is the body; do you accept this?

CRITO: Yes.

SOCRATES: Well, is life worth living with a body which is worn out and ruined by health?

CRITO: Certainly not.

SOCRATES: What about the part of us which is mutilated by wrong actions and benefited by right ones? Is life worth living with this part ruined? Or do we believe that this part of us, whatever it may be, in which right and wrong operate, is of less importance than the body?

CRITO: Certainly not.   60

SOCRATES: It is really more precious?

CRITO: Much more.

SOCRATES: In that case, my dear fellow, what we ought to consider is not so much what people in general will say about us but how we stand with the expert in right and wrong, the one authority, who represents the actual truth. So in the first place your proposition is not correct when you say that we should consider popular opinion in questions of what is right and honorable and good, or the opposite. Of course one might object "All the same, the people have the power to put us to death."

CRITO: No doubt about that! Quite true, Socrates; it is a possible objection.

SOCRATES: But so far as I can see, my dear fellow, the argument   65 which we have just been through is quite unaffected by it. At the same time I should like you to consider whether we are still satisfied on this point: that the really important thing is not to live, but to live well.

CRITO: Why, yes.

SOCRATES: And that to live well means the same thing as to live honorably or rightly?

CRITO: Yes.

SOCRATES: Then in the light of this agreement we must consider whether or not it is right for me to try to get away without an official discharge. If it turns out to be right, we must make the attempt; if not, we must let it drop. As for the considerations you raise about expense and reputation and bringing up children, I am afraid, Crito, that they represent the reflections of the ordinary public, who put people to death, and would bring them back to life if they could, with equal indifference to reason. Our real duty, I fancy, since the argument leads that way, is to consider one question only, the one which we raised just now: Shall we be acting rightly in paying money and showing gratitude to these people who are going to rescue me, and in escaping or arranging the escape ourselves, or shall we really be acting wrongly in doing all this? If it becomes clear that such conduct is wrong, I cannot help thinking that the question whether we are sure to die, or to suffer any other ill effect for that matter, if we stand our ground and take no action, ought not to weigh with us at all in comparison with the risk of doing what is wrong.

CRITO: I agree with what you say, Socrates; but I wish you would 70
consider what we ought to *do*.

SOCRATES: Let us look at it together, my dear fellow; and if you can challenge any of my arguments, do so and I will listen to you; but if you can't, be a good fellow and stop telling me over and over again that I ought to leave this place without official permission. I am very anxious to obtain your approval before I adopt the course which I have in mind; I don't want to act against your convictions. Now give your attention to the starting point of this inquiry—I hope that you will be satisfied with my way of stating it—and try to answer my questions to the best of your judgment.

CRITO: Well, I will try.

SOCRATES: Do we say that one must never willingly do wrong, or does it depend upon circumstance? Is it true, as we have often agreed before, that there is no sense in which wrongdoing is good or honorable? Or have we jettisoned all our former convictions in these last few days? Can you and I at our age, Crito, have spent all these years in serious discussions without realizing that we were no better than a pair of children? Surely the truth is just what we have always said. Whatever the popular view is, and whether the alternative is pleasanter than the present one or even harder to bear, the fact remains that to do wrong is in every sense bad and dishonorable for the person who does it. Is that our view, or not?

CRITO: Yes, it is.

SOCRATES: Then in no circumstances must one do wrong.   75

CRITO: No.

SOCRATES: In that case one must not even do wrong when one is wronged, which most people regard as the natural course.

CRITO: Apparently not.

SOCRATES: Tell me another thing, Crito: Ought one to do injuries or not?

CRITO: Surely not, Socrates. 80

SOCRATES: And tell me: Is it right to do an injury in retaliation, as most people believe, or not?

CRITO: No, never.

SOCRATES: Because, I suppose, there is no difference between injuring people and wronging them.

CRITO: Exactly.

SOCRATES: So one ought not to return a wrong or an injury to any 85 person, whatever the provocation is. Now be careful, Crito, that in making these single admissions you do not end by admitting something contrary to your real beliefs. I know that there are and always will be few people who think like this; and consequently between those who do think so and those who do not there can be no agreement on principle; they must always feel contempt when they observe one another's decisions. I want even you to consider very carefully whether you share my views and agree with me, and whether we can proceed with our discussion from the established hypothesis that it is never right to do a wrong or return a wrong or defend one's self against injury by retaliation; or whether you dissociate yourself from any share in this view as a basis for discussion. I have held it for a long time, and still hold it; but if you have formed any other opinion, say so and tell me what it is. If, on the other hand, you stand by what we have said, listen to my next point.

CRITO: Yes, I stand by it and agree with you. Go on.

SOCRATES: Well, here is my next point, or rather question. Ought one to fulfill all one's agreements, provided that they are right, or break them?

CRITO: One ought to fulfill them.

SOCRATES: Then consider the logical consequence. If we leave this place without first persuading the State to let us go, are we or are we not doing an injury, and doing it in a quarter where it is least justifiable? Are we or are we not abiding by our just agreements?

CRITO: I can't answer your question, Socrates; I am not clear in my 90 mind.

SOCRATES: Look at it in this way. Suppose that while we were preparing to run away from here (or however one should describe it) the Laws and Constitution of Athens were to come and confront us and ask this question: "Now, Socrates, what are you proposing to do? Can you deny that by this act which you are contemplating you intend, so far as you have the power, to destroy us, the Laws, and the whole State as well? Do you imagine that a city can continue to exist and not be turned upside down, if the legal judgments which are pronounced in it have no force but are nullified and destroyed by private persons?"—how shall we answer this question, Crito, and others of the same kind? There is much that could be said, especially by a professional advocate, to protest against the invalidation of this law which enacts that judgments once pronounced shall be binding. Shall we say "Yes, I do intend to destroy the laws, because the State wronged me by passing a faulty judgment at my trial"? Is this to be our answer, or what?

CRITO: What you have just said, by all means, Socrates.

SOCRATES: Then what supposing the Laws say, "Was there provision for this in the agreement between you and us, Socrates? Or did you undertake to abide by whatever judgments the State pronounced?" If we expressed surprise at such language, they would probably say: "Never mind our language, Socrates, but answer our questions; after all, you are accustomed to the method of question and answer. Come now, what charge do you bring against us and the State, that you are trying to destroy us? Did we not give you life in the first place? Was it not through us that your father married your mother and begot you? Tell us, have you any complaint against those of us Laws that deal with marriage?" "No, none," I should say. "Well, have you any against the laws which deal with children's upbringing and education, such as you had yourself? Are you not grateful to those of us Laws which were instituted for this end, for requiring your father to give you a cultural and physical education?" "Yes," I should say. "Very good. Then since you have been born and brought up and educated, can you deny, in the first place, that you were our child and servant, both you and your ancestors? And if this is so, do you imagine that what is right for us is equally right for you, and that whatever we try to do to you, you are justified in retaliating? You did not have equality of rights with your father, or your employer (supposing that you had had one), to enable you to retaliate; you were not allowed to answer back when you were scolded or to hit back when you were beaten, or to do a great many other things of the same kind. Do you expect to have such license against your country and its laws that if we try to put you to death in the belief that it is right to do so, you on your part will try your hardest to destroy your country and us its Laws in return? And will you, the true devotee of goodness, claim that you are justified in doing so? Are you so wise as to have forgotten that compared with your mother and father and all the rest of your ancestors your country is something far more precious, more venerable, more sacred, and held in greater honor both among gods and among all reasonable men? Do you not realize that you are even more bound to respect and placate the anger of your country than your father's anger? That if you cannot persuade your country you must do whatever it orders, and patiently submit to any punishment that it imposes, whether it be flogging or imprisonment? And if it leads you out to war, to be wounded or killed, you must comply, and it is right that you should do so; you must not give way or retreat or abandon your position. Both in war and in the law courts and everywhere else you must do whatever your city and your country commands, or else persuade it in accordance with universal justice; but violence is a sin even against your parents, and it is a far greater sin against your country"—What shall we say to this, Crito?—that what the Laws say is true, or not?

CRITO: Yes, I think so.

SOCRATES: "Consider, then, Socrates," the Laws would probably con- 95
tinue, "whether it is also true for us to say that what you are now trying to do to us is not right. Although we have brought you into the
world and reared you and educated you, and given you and all your fellow citizens a share in all the good things at our disposal, nevertheless
by the very fact of granting our permission we openly proclaim this
principle: that any Athenian, on attaining to manhood and seeing for
himself the political organization of the State and us its Laws, is permitted, if he is not satisfied with us, to take his property and go away wherever he likes. If any of you chooses to go to one of our colonies,
supposing that he should not be satisfied with us and the State, or to
emigrate to any other country, not one of us Laws hinders or prevents
him from going away wherever he likes, without any loss of property.
On the other hand, if any one of you stands his ground when he can
see how we administer justice and the rest of our public organization,
we hold that by so doing he has in fact undertaken to do anything that
we tell him; and we maintain that anyone who disobeys is guilty of
doing wrong on three separate counts: first because we are his parents,
and secondly because we are his guardians; and thirdly because, after
promising obedience, he is neither obeying us nor persuading us to
change our decision if we are at fault in any way; and although all our
orders are in the form of proposals, not of savage commands, and we
give him the choice of either persuading us or doing what we say, he is
actually doing neither. These are the charges, Socrates, to which we say
that you will be liable if you do what you are contemplating; and you
will not be the least culpable of your fellow countrymen, but one of the
most guilty." If I said "Why do you say that?" they would no doubt
pounce upon me with perfect justice and point out that there are very
few people in Athens who have entered into this agreement with them
as explicitly as I have. They would say "Socrates, we have substantial evidence that you are satisfied with us and with the State. You would not
have been so exceptionally reluctant to cross the borders of your country if you had not been exceptionally attached to it. You have never left
the city to attend a festival or for any other purpose, except on some
military expedition; you have never traveled abroad as other people do,
and you have never felt the impulse to acquaint yourself with another
country or constitution; you have been content with us and with our
city. You have definitely chosen us, and undertaken to observe us in all
your activities as a citizen; and as the crowning proof that you are satisfied with our city, you have begotten children in it. Furthermore, even
at the time of your trial you could have proposed the penalty of banishment, if you had chosen to do so; that is, you could have done then
with the sanction of the State what you are now trying to do without it.
But whereas at that time you made a noble show of indifference if you
had to die, and in fact preferred death, as you said, to banishment, now
you show no respect for your earlier professions, and no regard for us,

the Laws, whom you are trying to destroy; you are behaving like the lowest type of menial, trying to run away in spite of the contracts and undertakings by which you agreed to live as a member of our State. Now first answer this question: Are we or are we not speaking the truth when we say that you have undertaken, in deed if not in word, to live your life as a citizen in obedience to us?" What are we to say to that, Crito? Are we not bound to admit it?

CRITO: We cannot help it, Socrates.

SOCRATES: "It is a fact, then," they would say, "that you are breaking covenants and undertakings made with us, although you made them under no compulsion or misunderstanding, and were not compelled to decide in a limited time; you had seventy years in which you could have left the country, if you were not satisfied with us or felt that the agreements were unfair. You did not choose Sparta or Crete—your favorite models of good government—or any other Greek or foreign state; you could not have absented yourself from the city less if you had been lame or blind or decrepit in some other way. It is quite obvious that you stand by yourself above all other Athenians in your affection for this city and for us its Laws;—who would care for a city without laws? And now, after all this, are you not going to stand by your agreement? Yes, you are, Socrates, if you will take our advice; and then you will at least escape being laughed at for leaving the city.

"We invite you to consider what good you will do to yourself or your friends if you commit this breach of faith and stain your conscience. It is fairly obvious that the risk of being banished and either losing their citizenship or having their property confiscated will extend to your friends as well. As for yourself, if you go to one of the neighboring states, such as Thebes or Megara, which are both well governed, you will enter them as an enemy to their constitution[2] and all good patriots will eye you with suspicion as a destroyer of law and order. Incidentally you will confirm the opinion of the jurors who tried you that they gave a correct verdict; a destroyer of laws might very well be supposed to have a destructive influence upon young and foolish human beings. Do you intend, then, to avoid well governed states and the higher forms of human society? And if you do, will life be worth living? Or will you approach these people and have the impudence to converse with them? What arguments will you use, Socrates? The same which you used here, that goodness and integrity, institutions and laws, are the most precious possessions of mankind? Do you not think that Socrates and everything about him will appear in a disreputable light? You certainly ought to think so. But perhaps you will retire from this part of the world and go to Crito's friends in Thessaly? That is the home of indiscipline and laxity, and no doubt they would enjoy hearing the amusing story of how you

---

[2]**as an enemy to their constitution** As a lawbreaker.

managed to run away from prison by arraying yourself in some costume or putting on a shepherd's smock or some other conventional runaway's disguise, and altering your personal appearance. And will no one comment on the fact that an old man of your age, probably with only a short time left to live, should dare to cling so greedily to life, at the price of violating the most stringent laws? Perhaps not, if you avoid irritating anyone. Otherwise, Socrates, you will hear a good many humiliating comments. So you will live as the toady and slave of all the populace, literally 'roistering in Thessaly,' as though you had left this country for Thessaly to attend a banquet there; and where will your discussions about goodness and uprightness be then, we should like to know? But of course you want to live for your children's sake, so that you may be able to bring them up and educate them. Indeed! by first taking them off to Thessaly and making foreigners of them, so that they may have that additional enjoyment? Or if that is not your intention, supposing that they are brought up here with you still alive, will they be better cared for and educated without you, because of course your friends will look after them? Will they look after your children if you go away to Thessaly, and not if you go away to the next world? Surely if those who profess to be your friends are worth anything, you must believe that they would care for them.

"No, Socrates; be advised by us your guardians, and do not think more of your children or of your life or of anything else than you think of what is right; so that when you enter the next world you may have all this to plead in your defense before the authorities there. It seems clear that if you do this thing, neither you nor any of your friends will be the better for it or be more upright or have a cleaner conscience here in this world, nor will it be better for you when you reach the next. As it is, you will leave this place, when you do, as the victim of a wrong done not by us, the Laws, but by your fellow men. But if you leave in that dishonorable way, returning wrong for wrong and evil for evil, breaking your agreements and covenants with us, and injuring those whom you least ought to injure—yourself, your friends, your country, and us—then you will have to face our anger in your lifetime, and in that place beyond when the laws of the other world know that you have tried, so far as you could, to destroy even us their brothers, they will not receive you with a kindly welcome. Do not take Crito's advice, but follow ours."

That, my dear friend Crito, I do assure you, is what I seem to hear 100 them saying, just as a mystic seems to hear the strains of music; and the sound of their arguments rings so loudly in my head that I cannot hear the other side. I warn you that, as my opinion stands at present, it will be useless to urge a different view. However, if you think that you will do any good by it, say what you like.

CRITO: No, Socrates, I have nothing to say.

SOCRATES: Then give it up, Crito, and let us follow this course, since God points out the way.

Topics for Critical Thinking and Writing

1. State as precisely as you can all the arguments Crito uses to try to convince Socrates that he ought to escape. Which of these arguments seems to you to be the best? The worst? Why?

2. Socrates says to Crito, "I cannot abandon the principles which I used to hold in the past simply because this accident [the misfortune of being convicted by the Athenian assembly and then sentenced to death] has happened to me" (para. 35). Does this remark strike you as self-righteous? Stubborn? Smug? Stupid? Explain.

3. Socrates declares that "serious thinkers" have always held the view that "some of the opinions which people entertain should be respected, and others should not" (para. 37). There are two main alternatives to this principle: (a) One should respect *all* the opinions that others hold, and (b) one should respect *none* of the opinions of others. Socrates attacks (a) but he ignores (b). What are his objections to (a)? Do you find them convincing? Can you think of any convincing arguments against (b)?

4. As Socrates shows in his reply to Crito, he seems ready to believe (para. 63) that there are "expert[s] in right and wrong"—that is, persons with expert opinion or even authoritative knowledge on matters of right and wrong conduct—and that their advice should be sought and followed. Do you agree? Consider the thesis that there are no such experts, and write a 500-word essay defending or attacking it.

5. Socrates, as he comments to Crito, believes that "it is never right to do a wrong or return a wrong or defend one's self against injury by retaliation" (para. 85). He does not offer any argument for this thesis in the dialogue (although he does elsewhere). It was a very strange doctrine in his day, and even now it is not generally accepted. Write a 1,000-word essay defending or attacking this thesis.

6. Socrates seems to argue that (a) no one ought to do wrong, (b) it would injure the state for someone in Socrates' position to escape, and (c) this act would break a "just agreement" between the citizen and his state; therefore, (d) no one in Socrates' position should escape. Do you think this argument is valid? If not, what further assumptions would be needed to make it valid? Do you think the argument is sound (that is, both valid and true in all its premises)? If not, explain. If you had to attack premise (b) or (c), which do you think is the more vulnerable, and why?

7. In the imaginary speech by the Laws of Athens to Socrates, especially in paragraph 93, the Laws convey a picture of the supremacy of the state over the individual—and Socrates seems to assent to this picture. Do you? Why, or why not?

8. The Laws (para. 95) claim that if Socrates were to escape, he would be "guilty of doing wrong on three separate counts." What are they? Do you agree with all or any? Why, or why not? Read the essay by Martin Luther King Jr., "Letter from Birmingham Jail" (p. 839), and decide how King would have responded to the judgment of the Laws of Athens.

9. At the end of their peroration (para. 99), the Laws of Athens say to Socrates: Take your punishment as prescribed, and at your death "you will leave this place . . . as the victim of a wrong done not by us, the Laws, but by your fellow men." To what wrong do the Laws allude? Do you agree that it is men and not laws who perpetrated this wrong? If you were in Socrates' position, would it matter to you if you were being wronged not by laws but only by men? Explain.

10. Compose a letter from Socrates to Martin Luther King Jr. in which Socrates responds to King's "Letter from Birmingham Jail" (p. 839).

Samuel Johnson and James Boswell

James Boswell (1740–1795), Scottish lawyer and writer, is known chiefly as the author of one of the world's great biographies, The Life of Samuel Johnson, LL.D. *(1791), in which he reports the conversations of England's leading man of letters at the time. Samuel Johnson (1709–1784) was a poet, essayist, and critic of distinction, but he lives chiefly in Boswell's biography; the anecdotes and conversations that Boswell reports are better known than Johnson's own writings.*

We reprint a page from Boswell's Life, *in which Johnson and Boswell, along with a clergyman named Dr. Mayo, discuss prescience (knowledge of actions before they occur). The discussion, which took place on April 15, 1778, begins with Mayo asking Johnson if he has read the writings of Jonathan Edwards (1703–1758), the American theologian who had written on freedom of the will and on grace (usually defined as God's all-powerful gift enabling human beings—all of whom are sinful at birth—to enjoy eternal life).*

Do We Have Free Will?

DR. MAYO (TO DR. JOHNSON): Pray, Sir, have you read Edwards, of New England, on grace?

JOHNSON: No, sir.

BOSWELL: It puzzled me so much as to the freedom of the will, by stating, with wonderful acute ingenuity, our being actuated by a series of motives which we cannot resist, that the only relief I had was to forget it.

MAYO: But he makes the proper distinction between moral and physical necessity.

BOSWELL: Alas, sir, they come both to the same thing. You may be   5 bound as hard by chains when covered by leather, as when the iron appears. The argument for the moral necessity of human actions is always, I observe, fortified by supposing universal prescience to be one of the attributes of the Deity.

JOHNSON: You are surer that you are free, than you are of prescience; you are surer that you can lift up your finger or not as you please, than you are of any conclusion from a deduction of reasoning. But let us consider a little the objection from prescience. It is certain I am either to go home tonight or not; that does not prevent my freedom.

BOSWELL: That it is certain you are *either* to go home or not, does not prevent your freedom; because the liberty of choice between the two is compatible with that certainty. But if *one* of these events be certain *now*, you have no *future* power of volition. If it be certain you are to go home tonight, you *must* go home.

JOHNSON: If I am well acquainted with a man, I can judge with great probability how he will act in any case, without his being restrained by my judging. God may have this probability increased to certainty.

BOSWELL: When it is increased to certainty, freedom ceases, because that cannot be certainly foreknown, which is not certain at the time; but if it be certain at the time, it is a contradiction in terms to maintain that there can be afterwards any *contingency* dependent upon the exercise of will or anything else.

JOHNSON: All theory is against the freedom of the will; all experience 10
for it.

Topics for Critical Thinking and Writing

1. What does Dr. Mayo mean in paragraph 4 by "the proper distinction between moral and physical necessity"? What does Boswell mean in the following paragraph when he says "they come both to the same thing"?

2. Do you think that if "universal prescience" (that is, the ability to predict with certainty everything that we will do) is "one of the attributes of the Deity" (para. 5), then we must lack free will?

3. Johnson observes in the final paragraph that "all theory is against the freedom of the will; all experience for it." Theory of what? Experience of what? Explain in no more than 100 words what Johnson means.

4. Boswell says, "If it be certain you are to go home tonight, you *must* go home" (para. 7). Do you agree? Would Walter T. Stace (see p. 831)? When Boswell says this, is he implying that in such cases one has no free will? If not, what do you think he means?

George Orwell

George Orwell was the pen name adopted by Eric Blair (1903–1950), an Englishman born in India. Orwell was educated at Eton, in England, but in 1921 he went back to the East and served for five years as a police officer in Burma (now Myanmar). Disillusioned with colonial imperialism, he returned to Europe, doing odd jobs while writing novels and stories. In 1936 he fought in the Spanish Civil War on the side of the Republicans, an experience he reported in Homage to Catalonia *(1938). His last years were spent writing in England. His best-known work probably is the satiric allegory*

1984 *(1949), showing a totalitarian state in which the citizens are perpetually under the eye of Big Brother. The following essay is from* Shooting an Elephant and Other Essays *(1950).*

Shooting an Elephant

In Moulmein, in Lower Burma, I was hated by large numbers of people — the only time in my life that I have been important enough for this to happen to me. I was sub-divisional police officer of the town, and in an aimless, petty kind of way anti-European feeling was very bitter. No one had the guts to raise a riot, but if a European woman went through the bazaars alone somebody would probably spit betel juice over her dress. As a police officer I was an obvious target and was baited whenever it seemed safe to do so. When a nimble Burman tripped me up on the football field and the referee (another Burman) looked the other way, the crowd yelled with hideous laughter. This happened more than once. In the end the sneering yellow faces of young men that met me everywhere, the insults hooted after me when I was at a safe distance, got badly on my nerves. The young Buddhist priests were the worst of all. There were several thousands of them in the town and none of them seemed to have anything to do except stand on street corners and jeer at Europeans.

All this was perplexing and upsetting. For at that time I had already made up my mind that imperialism was an evil thing and the sooner I chucked up my job and got out of it the better. Theoretically — and secretly, of course — I was all for the Burmese and all against their oppressors, the British. As for the job I was doing, I hated it more bitterly than I can perhaps make clear. In a job like that you see the dirty work of Empire at close quarters. The wretched prisoners huddling in the stinking cages of the lock-ups, the grey, cowed faces of the long-term convicts, the scarred buttocks of the men who had been flogged with bamboos — all these oppressed me with an intolerable sense of guilt. But I could get nothing into perspective. I was young and ill-educated and I had had to think out my problems in the utter silence that is imposed on every Englishman in the East. I did not even know that the British Empire is dying, still less did I know that it is a great deal better than the younger empires that are going to supplant it. All I knew was that I was stuck between my hatred of the empire I served and my rage against the evil-spirited little beasts who tried to make my job impossible. With one part of my mind I thought of the British Raj[1] as an unbreakable tyranny, as something clamped down, in *saecula saeculorum*,[2] upon the will of prostrate peoples; with another part I thought that the greatest joy in the world would be to drive a bayonet into a Buddhist priest's guts. Feelings

---

[1]**British Raj** British imperial government in India and Burma. [All notes are the editors'.]
[2]**in *saecula saeculorum*** Forever (Latin). A term used in Christian liturgy.

like these are the normal by-products of imperialism; ask any Anglo-Indian official, if you can catch him off duty.

One day something happened which in a roundabout way was enlightening. It was a tiny incident in itself, but it gave me a better glimpse than I had had before of the real nature of imperialism—the real motives for which despotic governments act. Early one morning the sub-inspector at a police station the other end of the town rang me up on the 'phone and said that an elephant was ravaging the bazaar. Would I please come and do something about it? I did not know what I could do, but I wanted to see what was happening and I got on to a pony and started out. I took my rifle, an old .44 Winchester and much too small to kill an elephant, but I thought the noise might be useful *in terrorem*.[3] Various Burmans stopped me on the way and told me about the elephant's doings. It was not, of course, a wild elephant, but a tame one which had gone "must."[4] It had been chained up, as tame elephants always are when their attack of "must" is due, but on the previous night it had broken its chain and escaped. Its mahout, the only person who could manage it when it was in that state, had set out in pursuit, but had taken the wrong direction and was now twelve hours' journey away, and in the morning the elephant had suddenly reappeared in the town. The Burmese population had no weapons and were quite helpless against it. It had already destroyed somebody's bamboo hut, killed a cow and raided some fruit-stalls and devoured the stock; also it had met the municipal rubbish van and, when the driver jumped out and took to his heels, had turned the van over and inflicted violences upon it.

The Burmese sub-inspector and some Indian constables were waiting for me in the quarter where the elephant had been seen. It was a very poor quarter, a labyrinth of squalid bamboo huts, thatched with palm-leaf, winding all over a steep hillside. I remember that it was a cloudy, stuffy morning at the beginning of the rains. We began questioning the people as to where the elephant had gone and, as usual, failed to get any definite information. That is invariably the case in the East; a story always sounds clear enough at a distance, but the nearer you get to the scene of events the vaguer it becomes. Some of the people said that the elephant had gone in one direction, some said that he had gone in another, some professed not even to have heard of any elephant. I had almost made up my mind that the whole story was a pack of lies, when we heard yells a little distance away. There was a loud, scandalized cry of "Go away, child! Go away this instant!" and an old woman with a switch in her hand came round the corner of a hut, violently shooing away a crowd of naked children. Some more women followed, clicking their tongues and exclaiming; evidently there was something that the children ought not to have seen. I rounded the hut and saw a man's

[3] *in terrorem* As a warning.
[4] "**must**" Into sexual heat.

dead body sprawling in the mud. He was an Indian, a black Dravidian coolie, almost naked, and he could not have been dead many minutes. The people said that the elephant had come suddenly upon him round the corner of the hut, caught him with its trunk, put its foot on his back and ground him into the earth. This was the rainy season and the ground was soft, and his face had scored a trench a foot deep and a couple of yards long. He was lying on his belly with arms crucified and head sharply twisted to one side. His face was coated with mud, the eyes wide open, the teeth bared and grinning with an expression of unendurable agony. (Never tell me, by the way, that the dead look peaceful. Most of the corpses I have seen looked devilish.) The friction of the great beast's foot had stripped the skin from his back as neatly as one skins a rabbit. As soon as I saw the dead man I sent an orderly to a friend's house nearby to borrow an elephant rifle. I had already sent back the pony, not wanting it to go mad with fright and throw me if it smelt the elephant.

The orderly came back in a few minutes with a rifle and five cartridges, and meanwhile some Burmans had arrived and told us that the elephant was in the paddy fields below, only a few hundred yards away. As I started forward practically the whole population of the quarter flocked out of the houses and followed me. They had seen the rifle and were all shouting excitedly that I was going to shoot the elephant. They had not shown much interest in the elephant when he was merely ravaging their homes, but it was different now that he was going to be shot. It was a bit of fun to them, as it would be to an English crowd; besides they wanted the meat. It made me vaguely uneasy. I had no intention of shooting the elephant—I had merely sent for the rifle to defend myself if necessary—and it is always unnerving to have a crowd following you. I marched down the hill, looking and feeling a fool, with the rifle over my shoulder and an ever-growing army of people jostling at my heels. At the bottom, when you got away from the huts, there was a metalled road and beyond that a miry waste of paddy fields a thousand yards across, not yet ploughed but soggy from the first rains and dotted with coarse grass. The elephant was standing eight yards from the road, his left side towards us. He took not the slightest notice of the crowd's approach. He was tearing up bunches of grass, beating them against his knees to clean them and stuffing them into his mouth.

I had halted on the road. As soon as I saw the elephant I knew with perfect certainty that I ought not to shoot him. It is a serious matter to shoot a working elephant—it is comparable to destroying a huge and costly piece of machinery—and obviously one ought not to do it if it can possibly be avoided. And at that distance, peacefully eating, the elephant looked no more dangerous than a cow. I thought then and I think now that his attack of "must" was already passing off; in which case he would merely wander harmlessly about until the mahout came back and caught him. Moreover, I did not in the least want to shoot him. I decided that I would watch him for a little while to make sure that he did not turn savage again, and then go home.

But at that moment I glanced round at the crowd that had followed me. It was an immense crowd, two thousand at the least and growing every minute. It blocked the road for a long distance on either side. I looked at the sea of yellow faces above the garish clothes—faces all happy and excited over this bit of fun, all certain that the elephant was going to be shot. They were watching me as they would watch a conjurer about to perform a trick. They did not like me, but with the magical rifle in my hands I was momentarily worth watching. And suddenly I realized that I should have to shoot the elephant after all. The people expected it of me and I had got to do it; I could feel their two thousand wills pressing me forward, irresistibly. And it was at this moment, as I stood there with the rifle in my hands, that I first grasped the hollowness, the futility of the white man's dominion in the East. Here was I, the white man with his gun, standing in front of the unarmed native crowd—seemingly the leading actor of the piece; but in reality I was only an absurd puppet pushed to and fro by the will of those yellow faces behind. I perceived in this moment that when the white man turns tyrant it is his own freedom that he destroys. He becomes a sort of hollow, posing dummy, the conventionalized figure of a sahib. For it is the condition of his rule that he shall spend his life in trying to impress the "natives," and so in every crisis he has got to do what the "natives" expect of him. He wears a mask, and his face grows to fit it. I had got to shoot the elephant. I had committed myself to doing it when I sent for the rifle. A sahib has got to act like a sahib; he has got to appear resolute, to know his own mind and do definite things. To come all that way, rifle in hand, with two thousand people marching at my heels, and then to trail feebly away, having done nothing—no, that was impossible. The crowd would laugh at me. And my whole life, every white man's life in the East, was one long struggle not to be laughed at.

But I did not want to shoot the elephant. I watched him beating his bunch of grass against his knees, with that preoccupied grandmotherly air that elephants have. It seemed to me that it would be murder to shoot him. At that age I was not squeamish about killing animals, but I had never shot an elephant and never wanted to. (Somehow it always seems worse to kill a *large* animal.) Besides, there was the beast's owner to be considered. Alive, the elephant was worth at least a hundred pounds; dead, he would only be worth the value of his tusks, five pounds, possibly. But I had got to act quickly. I turned to some experienced-looking Burmans who had been there when we arrived, and asked them how the elephant had been behaving. They all said the same thing; he took no notice of you if you left him alone, but he might charge if you went too close to him.

It was perfectly clear to me what I ought to do. I ought to walk up to within, say, twenty-five yards of the elephant and test his behavior.

If he charged, I could shoot; if he took no notice of me, it would be safe to leave him until the mahout came back. But also I knew that I was going to do no such thing. I was a poor shot with a rifle and the ground was soft mud into which one would sink at every step. If the elephant charged and I missed him, I should have about as much chance as a toad under a steam-roller. But even then I was not thinking particularly of my own skin, only of the watchful yellow faces behind. For at that moment, with the crowd watching me, I was not afraid in the ordinary sense, as I would have been if I had been alone. A white man mustn't be frightened in front of "natives"; and so, in general, he isn't frightened. The sole thought in my mind was that if anything went wrong those two thousand Burmans would see me pursued, caught, trampled on and reduced to a grinning corpse like that Indian up the hill. And if that happened it was quite probable that some of them would laugh. That would never do. There was only one alternative. I shoved the cartridges into the magazine and lay down on the road to get a better aim.

The crowd grew very still, and a deep, low, happy sigh, as of people 10 who see the theatre curtain go up at last, breathed from innumerable throats. They were going to have their bit of fun after all. The rifle was a beautiful German thing with cross-hair sights. I did not then know that in shooting an elephant one would shoot to cut an imaginary bar running from ear-hole to ear-hole. I ought, therefore, as the elephant was sideways on, to have aimed straight at his ear-hole; actually I aimed several inches in front of this, thinking the brain would be further forward.

When I pulled the trigger I did not hear the bang or feel the kick—one never does when a shot goes home—but I heard the devilish roar of glee that went up from the crowd. In that instant, in too short a time, one would have thought, even for the bullet to get there, a mysterious, terrible change had come over the elephant. He neither stirred nor fell, but every line of his body had altered. He looked suddenly stricken, shrunken, immensely old, as though the frightful impact of the bullet had paralyzed him without knocking him down. At last, after what seemed a long time—it might have been five seconds, I dare say—he sagged flabbily to his knees. His mouth slobbered. An enormous senility seemed to have settled upon him. One could have imagined him thousands of years old. I fired again into the same spot. At the second shot he did not collapse but climbed with desperate slowness to his feet and stood weakly upright, with legs sagging and head dropping. I fired a third time. That was the shot that did for him. You could see the agony of it jolt his whole body and knock the last remnant of strength from his legs. But in falling he seemed for a moment to rise, for as his hind legs collapsed beneath him he seemed to tower upward like a huge rock toppling, his trunk reaching skywards like a tree. He trumpeted, for the first and only time. And then down he came, his belly towards me, with a crash that seemed to shake the ground even where I lay.

I got up. The Burmans were already racing past me across the mud. It was obvious that the elephant would never rise again, but he was not dead. He was breathing very rhythmically with long rattling gasps, his great mound of a side painfully rising and falling. His mouth was wide open—I could see far down into caverns of pale pink throat. I waited a long time for him to die, but his breathing did not weaken. Finally I fired my two remaining shots into the spot where I thought his heart must be. The thick blood welled out of him like red velvet, but still he did not die. His body did not even jerk when the shots hit him, the tortured breathing continued without a pause. He was dying, very slowly and in great agony, but in some world remote from me where not even a bullet could damage him further. I felt that I had got to put an end to that dreadful noise. It seemed dreadful to see the great beast lying there, powerless to move and yet powerless to die, and not even to be able to finish him. I sent back for my small rifle and poured shot after shot into his heart and down his throat. They seemed to make no impression. The tortured gasps continued as steadily as the ticking of a clock.

In the end I could not stand it any longer and went away. I heard later that it took him half an hour to die. Burmans were bringing dahs[5] and baskets even before I left, and I was told they had stripped his body almost to the bones by the afternoon.

Afterwards, of course, there were endless discussions about the shooting of the elephant. The owner was furious, but he was only an Indian and could do nothing. Besides, legally I had done the right thing, for a mad elephant has to be killed, like a mad dog, if its owner fails to control it. Among the Europeans opinion was divided. The older men said I was right, the younger men said it was a damn shame to shoot an elephant for killing a coolie, because an elephant was worth more than any damn Coringhee coolie. And afterwards I was very glad that the coolie had been killed; it put me legally in the right and it gave me a sufficient pretext for shooting the elephant. I often wondered whether any of the others grasped that I had done it solely to avoid looking a fool.

Topics for Critical Thinking and Writing

1. Did Orwell shoot the elephant of his own free will? Or did he shoot the elephant because he *had* to shoot it? What does he say about this? Do you find his judgment convincing, or not? Write a 500-word essay explaining your answer.

2. Was Orwell justified in shooting the elephant? Did he do the right thing in killing it? In the aftermath, did he think he did the right thing? Do you? Write a 500-word essay explaining your answers.

[5]**dahs** Large knives.

3. Orwell says that "as soon as I saw the elephant I knew with perfect certainty that I ought not to shoot him" (para. 6). How could he claim to "know" this, when moments later he did shoot the elephant?

4. Orwell says in passing, "Somehow it always seems worse to kill a *large* animal" (para. 8). Explain why you think Orwell says this and whether you agree.

5. A biographer who did research on Orwell in Burma reported that he could find no supporting documentation, either in the local newspapers or in the files of the police, that this episode ever occurred. Suppose that Orwell made it up. If so, is your response different? Explain.

6. If, pressured by circumstances, you have ever acted against what you might think is your reason or your nature, report the experience, and give your present evaluation of your behavior.

Walter T. Stace

Walter T. Stace (1886–1967), a professor of philosophy at Princeton University for many years, was the author of several books, including Religion and the Modern Mind *(1952), from which this selection is taken. The title is the editors'.*

Is Determinism Inconsistent with Free Will?

The second great problem which the rise of scientific naturalism has created for the modern mind concerns the foundations of morality. The old religious foundations have largely crumbled away, and it may well be thought that the edifice built upon them by generations of men is in danger of collapse. A total collapse of moral behavior is, as I pointed out before, very unlikely. For a society in which this occurred could not survive. Nevertheless the danger to moral standards inherent in the virtual disappearance of their old religious foundations is not illusory.

I shall first discuss the problem of free will, for it is certain that if there is no free will there can be no morality. Morality is concerned with what men ought and ought not to do. But if a man has no freedom to choose what he will do, if whatever he does is done under compulsion, then it does not make sense to tell him that he ought not to have done what he did and that he ought to do something different. All moral precepts would in such case be meaningless. Also if he acts always under compulsion, how can he be held morally responsible for his actions? How can he, for example, be punished for what he could not help doing?

It is to be observed that those learned professors of philosophy or psychology who deny the existence of free will do so only in their professional moments and in their studies and lecture rooms. For when it comes to doing anything practical, even of the most trivial kind, they invariably behave as if they and others were free. They inquire from you at dinner whether you will choose this dish or that dish. They will ask a child why he told a lie, and will punish him for not having chosen the way of truthfulness. All of which is inconsistent with a disbelief in free will. This should cause us to suspect that the problem is not a real one; and this, I believe, is the case. The dispute is merely verbal, and is due to nothing but a confusion about the meanings of words. It is what is now fashionably called a semantic problem.

How does a verbal dispute arise? Let us consider a case which, although it is absurd in the sense that no one would ever make the mistake which is involved in it, yet illustrates the principle which we shall have to use in the solution of the problem. Suppose that someone believed that the word "man" means a certain sort of five-legged animal; in short that "five-legged animal" is the correct *definition* of man. He might then look around the world, and rightly observing that there are no five-legged animals in it, he might proceed to deny the existence of men. This preposterous conclusion would have been reached because he was using an incorrect definition of "man." All you would have to do to show him his mistake would be to give him the correct definition; or at least to show him that his definition was wrong. Both the problem and its solution would, of course, be entirely verbal. The problem of free will, and its solution, I shall maintain, is verbal in exactly the same way. The problem has been created by the fact that learned men, especially philosophers, have assumed an incorrect definition of free *will*, and then finding that there is nothing in the world which answers to their definition, have denied its existence. As far as logic is concerned, their conclusion is just as absurd as that of the man who denies the existence of men. The only difference is that the mistake in the latter case is obvious and crude, while the mistake which the deniers of free will have made is rather subtle and difficult to detect.

Throughout the modern period, until quite recently, it was assumed, both by the philosophers who denied free will and by those who defended it, that *determinism is inconsistent with free will*. If a man's actions were wholly determined by chains of causes stretching back into the remote past, so that they could be predicted beforehand by a mind which knew all the causes, it was assumed that they could not in that case be free. This implies that a certain definition of actions done from free will was assumed, namely that they are actions *not* wholly determined by causes or predictable beforehand. Let us shorten this by saying that free will was defined as meaning indeterminism. This is the incorrect definition which has led to the denial of free will. As soon as we see what the true definition is we shall find that the question whether the world is deterministic, as Newtonian science implied, or in a measure indeterministic, as current physics teaches, is wholly irrelevant to the problem.

Of course there is a sense in which one can define a word arbitrarily in any way one pleases. But a definition may nevertheless be called correct or incorrect. It is correct if it accords with a *common usage* of the word defined. It is incorrect if it does not. And if you give an incorrect definition, absurd and untrue results are likely to follow. For instance, there is nothing to prevent you from arbitrarily defining a man as a five-legged animal, but this is incorrect in the sense that it does not accord with the ordinary meaning of the word. Also it has the absurd result of leading to a denial of the existence of men. This shows that *common usage is the criterion for deciding whether a definition is correct or not.* And this is the principle which I shall apply to free will. I shall show that indeterminism is not what is meant by the phrase "free will" *as it is commonly used.* And I shall attempt to discover the correct definition by inquiring how the phrase is used in ordinary conversation.

Here are a few samples of how the phrase might be used in ordinary conversation. It will be noticed that they include cases in which the question whether a man acted with free will is asked in order to determine whether he was morally and legally responsible for his acts.

JONES: I once went without food for a week.
SMITH: Did you do that of your own free will?
JONES: No. I did it because I was lost in a desert and could find no food.

But suppose that the man who had fasted was Mahatma Gandhi. The conversation might then have gone:

GANDHI: I once fasted for a week.
SMITH: Did you do that of your own free will?
GANDHI: Yes. I did it because I wanted to compel the British Government to
    give India its independence.

Take another case. Suppose that I had stolen some bread, but that I was as truthful as George Washington. Then, if I were charged with the crime in court, some exchange of the following sort might take place:

JUDGE: Did you steal the bread of your own free will?
STACE: Yes. I stole it because I was hungry.

Or in different circumstances the conversation might run: 10

JUDGE: Did you steal of your own free will?
STACE: No. I stole because my employer threatened to beat me if I did not.

At a recent murder trial in Trenton some of the accused had signed confessions, but afterwards asserted that they had done so under police duress. The following exchange might have occurred:

JUDGE: Did you sign this confession of your own free will?
PRISONER: No. I signed it because the police beat me up.

Now suppose that a philosopher had been a member of the jury. We could imagine this conversation taking place in the jury room.

FOREMAN OF THE JURY: The prisoner says he signed the confession because he was beaten, and not of his own free will.
PHILOSOPHER: This is quite irrelevant to the case. There is no such thing as free will.
FOREMAN: Do you mean to say that it makes no difference whether he signed because his conscience made him want to tell the truth or because he was beaten?
PHILOSOPHER: None at all. Whether he was caused to sign by a beating or by some desire of his own — the desire to tell the truth, for example — in either case his signing was causally determined, and therefore in neither case did he act of his own free will. Since there is no such thing as free will, the question whether he signed of his own free will ought not to be discussed by us.

The foreman and the rest of the jury would rightly conclude that the philosopher must be making some mistake. What sort of a mistake could it be? There is only one possible answer. The philosopher must be using the phrase "free will" in some peculiar way of his own which is not the way in which men usually use it when they wish to determine a question of moral responsibility. That is, he must be using an incorrect definition of it as implying action not determined by causes.
Suppose a man left his office at noon, and were questioned about it. Then we might hear this:

JONES: Did you go out of your own free will?
SMITH: Yes. I went out to get my lunch.

But we might hear: 15

JONES: Did you leave your office of your own free will?
SMITH: No. I was forcibly removed by the police.

We have now collected a number of cases of actions which, in the ordinary usage of the English language, would be called cases in which people have acted of their own free will. We should also say in all these cases that they *chose* to act as they did. We should also say that they could have acted otherwise, if they had chosen. For instance, Mahatma Gandhi was not compelled to fast; he chose to do so. He could have eaten if he had wanted to. When Smith went out to get his lunch, he chose to do so. He could have stayed and done some more work, if he had wanted to. We have also collected a number of cases of the opposite kind. They are cases in which men were not able to exercise their free will. They had no choice. They were compelled to do as they did. The man in the desert did not fast of his own free will. He had no choice in the matter. He was compelled to fast because there was nothing for him to eat. And so with the other cases. It ought to be quite easy, by an inspection of these cases, to tell what we ordinarily mean when we say that a man did or did not exercise free will. We ought therefore to be able to extract from them the proper definition of the term. Let us put the cases in a table:

Free Acts	Unfree Acts
Gandhi fasting because he wanted to free India.	The man fasting in the desert because there was no food.
Stealing bread because one is hungry.	Stealing because one's employer threatened to beat one.
Signing a confession because one wanted to tell the truth.	Signing because the police beat one.
Leaving the office because one wanted one's lunch.	Leaving because forcibly removed.

It is obvious that to find the correct definition of free acts we must discover what characteristic is common to all the acts in the left-hand column, and is, at the same time, absent from all the acts in the right-hand column. This characteristic which all free acts have, and which no unfree acts have, will be the defining characteristic of free will.

Is being uncaused, or not being determined by causes, the characteristic of which we are in search? It cannot be, because although it is true that all the acts in the right-hand column have causes, such as the beating by the police or the absence of food in the desert, so also do the acts in the left-hand column. Mr. Gandhi's fasting was caused by his desire to free India, the man leaving his office by his hunger, and so on. Moreover there is no reason to doubt that these causes of the free acts were in turn caused by prior conditions, and that these were again the results of causes, and so on back indefinitely into the past. Any physiologist can tell us the causes of hunger. What caused Mr. Gandhi's tremendously powerful desire to free India is no doubt more difficult to discover. But it must have had causes. Some of them may have lain in peculiarities of his glands or brain, others in his past experiences, others in his heredity, others in his education. Defenders of free will have usually tended to deny such facts. But to do so is plainly a case of special pleading, which is unsupported by any scrap of evidence. The only reasonable view is that all human actions, both those which are freely done and those which are not, are either wholly determined by causes, or at least as much determined as other events in nature. It may be true, as the physicists tell us, that nature is not as deterministic as was once thought. But whatever degree of determinism prevails in the world, human actions appear to be as much determined as anything else. And if this is so, it cannot be the case that what distinguishes actions freely chosen from those which are not free is that the latter are determined by causes while the former are not. Therefore, being uncaused or being undetermined by causes, must be an incorrect definition of free will.

What, then, is the difference between acts which are freely done and those which are not? What is the characteristic which is present to all the acts in the left-hand column and absent from all those in the right-hand column? It is not obvious that, although both sets of actions have causes, the causes of those in the left-hand column are *of a different kind* from the causes of those in the right-hand column? The free acts are all caused by desires, or motives, or by some sort of internal psychological states of the agent's mind. The unfree acts, on the other hand, are all caused by physical forces or physical conditions, outside the agent. Police arrest means physical force exerted from the outside; the absence of food in the desert is a physical condition of the outside world. We may therefore frame the following rough definitions. *Acts freely done are those whose immediate causes are psychological states in the agent. Acts not freely done are those whose immediate causes are states of affairs external to the agent.*

It is plain that if we define free will in this way, then free will certainly exists, and the philosopher's denial of its existence is seen to be what it is—nonsense. For it is obvious that all those actions of men which we should ordinarily attribute to the exercise of their free will, or of which we should say that they freely chose to do them, are in fact actions which have been caused by their own desires, wishes, thoughts, emotions, impulses, or other psychological states. 20

In applying our definition we shall find that it usually works well, but that there are some puzzling cases which it does not seem exactly to fit. These puzzles can always be solved by paying careful attention to the ways in which words are used, and remembering that they are not always used consistently. I have space for only one example. Suppose that a thug threatens to shoot you unless you give him your wallet, and suppose that you do so. Do you, in giving him your wallet, do so of your own free will or not? If we apply our definition, we find that you acted freely, since the immediate cause of the action was not an actual outside force but the fear of death, which is a psychological cause. Most people, however, would say that you did not act of your own free will but under compulsion. Does this show that our definition is wrong? I do not think so. Aristotle, who gave a solution of the problem of free will substantially the same as ours (though he did not use the term "free will") admitted that there are what he called "mixed" or borderline cases in which it is difficult to know whether we ought to call the acts free or compelled. In the case under discussion, though no actual force was used, the gun at your forehead so nearly approximated to actual force that we tend to say the case was one of compulsion. It is a borderline case.

Here is what may seem like another kind of puzzle. According to our view an action may be free though it could have been predicted beforehand with certainty. But suppose you told a lie, and it was certain beforehand that you would tell it. How could one then say, "You could have told the truth"? The answer is that it is perfectly true that you could have told the truth *if* you had wanted to. In fact you would have done so, for in that case the causes producing your action, namely your desires, would have been different, and would therefore have produced different effects. It is a delusion that predictability and free will are incompatible. This agrees with common sense. For if, knowing your character, I predict that you will act honorably, no one would say when you do act honorably, that this shows you did not do so of your own free will.

Since free will is a condition of moral responsibility, we must be sure that our theory of free will gives a sufficient basis for it. To be held morally responsible for one's actions means that one may be justly punished or rewarded, blamed or praised, for them. But it is not just to punish a man for what he cannot help doing. How can it be just to punish him for an action which it was certain beforehand that he would do? We have not attempted to decide whether, as a matter of fact, all events, including human actions, are completely determined. For that question is irrelevant to the problem of free will. But if we assume for the purposes of argument that complete determinism is true, but that we are nevertheless free, it may then be asked whether such a deterministic free will is compatible with moral responsibility. For it may seem unjust to punish a man for an action which it could have been predicted with certainty beforehand that he would do.

But that determinism is incompatible with moral responsibility is as much a delusion as that it is incompatible with free will. You do not excuse a man for doing a wrong act because, knowing his character, you felt certain beforehand that he would do it. Nor do you deprive a man of a reward or prize because, knowing his goodness or his capabilities, you felt certain beforehand that he would win it.

Volumes have been written on the justification of punishment. But so far as it affects the question of free will, the essential principles involved are quite simple. The punishment of a man for doing a wrong act is justified, either on the ground that it will correct his own character, or that it will deter other people from doing similar acts. The instrument of punishment has been in the past, and no doubt still is, often unwisely used; so that it may often have done more harm than good. But that is not relevant to our present problem. Punishment, if and when it is justified, is justified only on one or both of the grounds just mentioned. The question then is how, if we assume determinism, punishment can correct character or deter people from evil actions.

Suppose that your child develops a habit of telling lies. You give him a mild beating. Why? Because you believe that his personality is such that the usual motives for telling the truth do not cause him to do so. You therefore supply the missing cause, or motive, in the shape of pain and the fear of future pain if he repeats his untruthful behavior. And you hope that a few treatments of this kind will condition him to the habit of truth-telling, so that he will come to tell the truth without the infliction of pain. You assume that his actions are determined by causes, but that the usual causes of truth-telling do not in him produce their usual effects. You therefore supply him with an artificially injected motive, pain and fear, which you think will in the future cause him to speak truthfully.

The principle is exactly the same where you hope, by punishing one man, to deter others from wrong actions. You believe that the fear of punishment will cause those who might otherwise do evil to do well.

We act on the same principle with nonhuman, and even with inanimate, things, if they do not behave in the way we think they ought to behave. The rose bushes in the garden produce only small and poor blooms, whereas we want large and rich ones. We supply a cause which will produce large blooms, namely fertilizer. Our automobile does not go properly. We supply a cause which will make it go better, namely oil in the works. The punishment for the man, the fertilizer for the plant, and the oil for the car are all justified by the same principle and in the same way. The only difference is that different kinds of things require different kinds of causes to make them do what they should. Pain may be the appropriate remedy to apply, in certain cases, to human beings, and oil to the machine. It is, of course, of no use to inject motor oil into the boy or to beat the machine.

Thus we see that moral responsibility is not only consistent with determinism, but requires it. The assumption on which punishment is based is that human behavior is causally determined. If pain could not be a cause of truth-telling there would be no justification at all for punishing lies. If human actions and volitions were uncaused, it would be useless either to punish or reward, or indeed to do anything else to correct people's bad behavior. For nothing that you could do would in any way influence them. Thus moral responsibility would entirely disappear. If there were no determinism of human beings at all, their actions would be completely unpredictable and capricious, and therefore irresponsible. And this is in itself a strong argument against the common view of philosophers that free will means being undetermined by causes.

Topics for Critical Thinking and Writing

1. Stace asserts that "if there is no free will there can be no morality" (para. 2). What is his reasoning (see para. 23)? Do you agree?

2. "The dispute is merely verbal," Stace proclaims in paragraph 3. What "dispute"? Why "merely verbal"? What would Stace say to someone who insists that the existence or nonexistence of free will is a question of *fact*?

3. What is *determinism* (para. 5)? Why does Stace seem to think that philosophers are strongly inclined to believe in it?

4. Stace claims that he will show that "indeterminism is not what is meant by . . . 'free will' *as it is commonly used*" (para. 6). What is his argument? What does he think *free will* means as the term is "commonly used"? Are you convinced? Why, or why not? Write a 500-word paper answering these questions.

5. Stace insists that "all human actions . . . are . . . at least as much determined as other events in nature" (para. 18). How might one argue against this?

6. Complete the following definition so that it captures Stace's view: "When Smith did *X*, he acted freely if and only if . . ."

7. Stace mentions some "puzzling cases" (para. 21) that do not quite fit, he admits, his analysis of free will. Give an example of such a case, and explain why it is puzzling.

8. Why does Stace conclude in paragraph 22 that "it is a delusion that predictability and free will are incompatible"? Do you agree? Why, or why not?

9. It seems paradoxical to assert, as Stace does in his last paragraph, that "moral responsibility is not only consistent with determinism, but requires it." Explain Stace's view here in no more than 250 words.

Martin Luther King Jr.

Martin Luther King Jr. (1929–1968) was born in Atlanta and educated at Morehouse College, Crozer Theological Seminary, and Boston University. In 1954 he was called to serve as a Baptist minister in Montgomery, Alabama. During the next two years he achieved national fame when, using a policy of nonviolent resistance, he successfully led the boycott against segregated bus lines in Montgomery. He then organized the Southern Christian Leadership Conference, which furthered civil rights, first in the South and then nationwide. In 1964 he was awarded the Nobel Peace Prize. Four years later he was assassinated in Memphis, Tennessee, while supporting striking garbage workers.

In 1963 Dr. King was arrested in Birmingham, Alabama, for participating in a march for which no parade permit had been issued by city officials. In jail he wrote a response to a letter that eight local clergymen had published in a newspaper. Their letter, titled "A Call for Unity," is printed here, followed by King's response.

Letter from Birmingham Jail

A CALL FOR UNITY

April 12, 1963

We the undersigned clergymen are among those who, in January, issued "An Appeal for Law and Order and Common Sense," in dealing with racial problems in Alabama. We expressed understanding that honest convictions in racial matters could properly be pursued in the courts, but urged that decisions of those courts should in the meantime be peacefully obeyed.

Since that time there had been some evidence of increased forebearance and a willingness to face facts. Responsible citizens have undertaken to work on various problems which cause racial friction and unrest. In Birmingham, recent public events have given indication that we all have opportunity for a new constructive and realistic approach to racial problems.

However, we are now confronted by a series of demonstrations by some of our Negro citizens, directed and led in part by outsiders. We recognize the natural impatience of people who feel that their hopes are slow in being realized. But we are convinced that these demonstrations are unwise and untimely.

We agree rather with certain local Negro leadership which has called for honest and open negotiation of racial issues in our area. And we believe this kind of facing of issues can best be accomplished by citizens of our own metropolitan area, white and Negro, meeting with their knowledge and experience of the local situation. All of us need to face that responsibility and find proper channels for its accomplishment.

Just as we formerly pointed out that "hatred and violence have no sanction in our religious and political traditions," we also point out that such actions as incite to hatred and violence, however technically peaceful those actions may be, have not contributed to the resolution of our local problems. We do not believe that these days of new hope are days when extreme measures are justified in Birmingham.

We commend the community as a whole, and the local news media and law enforcement officials in particular, on the calm manner in which these demonstrations have been handled. We urge the public to continue to show restraint should the demonstrations continue, and the law enforcement officials to remain calm and continue to protect our city from violence.

We further strongly urge our own Negro community to withdraw support from these demonstrations, and to unite locally in working peacefully for a better Birmingham. When rights are consistently denied, a cause should be pressed in the courts and in negotiations among local leaders, and not in the streets. We appeal to both our white and Negro citizenry to observe the principles of law and order and common sense.

C.C.J. Carpenter, D.D., L.L.D., Bishop of Alabama; Joseph A. Durick, D.D., Auxiliary Bishop, Diocese of Mobile-Birmingham; Rabbi Milton L. Grafman, Temple Emanu-El, Birmingham, Alabama; Bishop Paul Hardin, Bishop of the Alabama–West Florida Conference of the Methodist Church; Bishop Nolan B. Harmon, Bishop of the North Alabama Conference of the Methodist Church; George M. Murray, D.D., L.L.D., Bishop Coadjutor, Episcopal Diocese of Alabama; Edward V. Ramage, Moderator, Synod of the Alabama Presbyterian Church in the United

States; Earl Stallings, Pastor, First Baptist Church, Birmingham, Alabama.

LETTER FROM BIRMINGHAM JAIL

April 16, 1963

My Dear Fellow Clergymen:

While confined here in the Birmingham city jail, I came across your recent statement calling my present activities "unwise and untimely."[1] Seldom do I pause to answer criticism of my work and ideas. If I sought to answer all the criticisms that cross my desk, my secretaries would have little time for anything other than such correspondence in the course of the day, and I would have no time for constructive work. But since I feel that you are men of genuine good will and that your criticisms are sincerely set forth, I want to try to answer your statement in what I hope will be patient and reasonable terms.

I think I should indicate why I am here in Birmingham, since you have been influenced by the view which argues against "outsiders coming in." I have the honor of serving as president of the Southern Christian Leadership Conference, an organization operating in every southern state, with headquarters in Atlanta, Georgia. We have some eighty-five affiliated organizations across the South, and one of them is the Alabama Christian Movement for Human Rights. Frequently we share staff, educational, and financial resources with our affiliates. Several months ago the affiliate here in Birmingham asked us to be on call to engage in a nonviolent direct-action program if such were deemed necessary. We readily consented, and when the hour came we lived up to our promise. So I, along with several members of my staff, am here because I was invited here. I am here because I have organizational ties here.

But more basically, I am in Birmingham because injustice is here. Just as the prophets of the eighth century B.C. left their villages and carried their "thus saith the Lord" far beyond the boundaries of their home towns, and just as the Apostle Paul left his village of Tarsus and carried the gospel of Jesus Christ to the far corners of the Greco-Roman world, so am I compelled to carry the gospel of freedom beyond my own home town. Like Paul, I must constantly respond to the Macedonian call for aid.

---

[1]This response to a published statement by eight fellow clergymen from Alabama (Bishop C.C.J. Carpenter, Bishop Joseph A. Durick, Rabbi Milton L. Grafman, Bishop Paul Hardin, Bishop Nolan B. Harmon, the Reverend George M. Murray, the Reverend Edward V. Ramage, and the Reverend Earl Stallings) was composed under somewhat constricting circumstances. Begun on the margins of the newspaper in which the statement appeared while I was in jail, the letter was continued on scraps of writing paper supplied by a friendly Negro trusty, and concluded on a pad my attorneys were eventually permitted to leave me. Although the text remains in substance unaltered, I have indulged in the author's prerogative of polishing it for publication. [King's note.]

Moreover, I am cognizant of the interrelatedness of all communities and states. I cannot sit idly by in Atlanta and not be concerned about what happens in Birmingham. Injustice anywhere is a threat to justice everywhere. We are caught in an inescapable network of mutuality; tied in a single garment of destiny. Whatever affects one directly, affects all indirectly. Never again can we afford to live with the narrow, provincial "outside agitator" idea. Anyone who lives inside the United States can never be considered an outsider anywhere within its bounds.

You deplore the demonstrations taking place in Birmingham. But your statement, I am sorry to say, fails to express a similar concern for the conditions that brought about the demonstrations. I am sure that none of you would want to rest content with the superficial kind of social analysis that deals merely with effects and does not grapple with underlying causes. It is unfortunate that demonstrations are taking place in Birmingham, but it is even more unfortunate that the city's white power structure left the Negro community with no alternative.

In any nonviolent campaign there are four basic steps: collection of the facts to determine whether injustices exist; negotiation; self-purification; and direct action. We have gone through all these steps in Birmingham. There can be no gainsaying the fact that racial injustice engulfs this community. Birmingham is probably the most thoroughly segregated city in the United States. Its ugly record of brutality is widely known. Negroes have experienced grossly unjust treatment in the courts. There have been more unsolved bombings of Negro homes and churches in Birmingham than in any other city in the nation. These are the hard, brutal facts of the case. On the basis of these conditions, Negro leaders sought to negotiate with the city fathers. But the latter consistently refused to engage in good-faith negotiation.

Then, last September, came the opportunity to talk with leaders of Birmingham's economic community. In the course of the negotiations, certain promises were made by the merchants—for example, to remove the stores' humiliating racial signs. On the basis of these promises, the Reverend Fred Shuttleworth and the leaders of the Alabama Christian Movement for Human Rights agreed to a moratorium on all demonstrations. As the weeks and months went by, we realized that we were the victims of a broken promise. A few signs, briefly removed, returned; the others remained.

As in so many past experiences, our hopes had been blasted, and the shadow of deep disappointment settled upon us. We had no alternative except to prepare for direct action, whereby we would present our very bodies as a means of laying our case before the conscience of the local and the national community. Mindful of the difficulties involved, we decided to undertake a process of self-purification. We began a series of workshops on nonviolence, and we repeatedly asked ourselves: "Are you able to accept blows without retaliating?" "Are you able to endure the ordeal of jail?" We decided to schedule our direct-action program for the Easter season, realizing that except for Christmas, this is the main shopping period of the year. Knowing that a strong economic-withdrawal program would be the by-product of direct action, we felt that this would be the best time to bring pressure to bear on the merchants for the needed change.

Then it occurred to us that Birmingham's mayoralty election was coming up in March, and we speedily decided to postpone action until after election day. When we discovered that the Commissioner of Public Safety, Eugene "Bull" Connor, had piled up enough votes to be in the run-off, we decided again to postpone action until the day after the run-off so that the demonstrations could not be used to cloud the issues. Like many others, we waited to see Mr. Connor defeated, and to this end we endured postponement after postponement. Having aided in this community need, we felt that our direct-action program could be delayed no longer.

You may well ask: "Why direct action? Why sit-ins, marches, and so forth? Isn't negotiation a better path?" You are quite right in calling for negotiation. Indeed, this is the very purpose of direct action. Nonviolent direct action seeks to create such a crisis and foster such a tension that a community which has constantly refused to negotiate is forced to confront the issue. It seeks so to dramatize the issue that it can no longer be ignored. My citing the creation of tension as part of the work of the nonviolent-resister may sound rather shocking. But I must confess that I am not afraid of the word "tension." I have earnestly opposed violent tension, but there is a type of constructive, nonviolent tension which is necessary for growth. Just as Socrates felt that it was necessary to create a tension in the mind so that individuals could rise from the bondage of myths and half-truths to the unfettered realm of creative analysis and objective appraisal, so must we see the need for nonviolent gadflies to create the kind of tension in society that will help men rise from the dark depths of prejudice and racism to the majestic heights of understanding and brotherhood.

The purpose of our direct-action program is to create a situation so crisis-packed that it will inevitably open the door to negotiation. I therefore concur with you in your call for negotiation. Too long has our beloved Southland been bogged down in a tragic effort to live in monologue rather than dialogue.

One of the basic points in your statement is that the action that I and my associates have taken in Birmingham is untimely. Some have asked: "Why didn't you give the new city administration time to act?" The only answer that I can give to this query is that the new Birmingham administration must be prodded about as much as the outgoing one, before it will act. We are sadly mistaken if we feel that the election of Albert Boutwell as mayor will bring the millennium to Birmingham. While Mr. Boutwell is a much more gentle person than Mr. Connor, they are both segregationists, dedicated to maintenance of the status quo. I have hope that Mr. Boutwell will be reasonable enough to see the futility of massive resistance to desegregation. But he will not see this without pressure from devotees of civil rights. My friends, I must say to you that we have not made a single gain in civil rights without determined legal and nonviolent pressure. Lamentably, it is an historical fact that privileged groups seldom give up their privileges voluntarily. Individuals may see the moral light and voluntarily give up their unjust posture; but as Reinhold Niebuhr[2] has reminded us, groups tend to be more immoral than individuals.

We know through painful experience that freedom is never voluntarily given by the oppressor; it must be demanded by the oppressed. Frankly, I have yet to engage in a direct-action campaign that was "well timed" in the view of those who have not suffered unduly from the disease of segregation. For years now I have heard the word "Wait!" It rings in the ear of every Negro with piercing familiarity. This "Wait" has almost always meant "Never." We must come to see, with one of our distinguished jurists, that "justice too long delayed is justice denied."[3]

We have waited for more than 340 years for our constitutional and God-given rights. The nations of Asia and Africa are moving with jetlike speed toward gaining political independence, but we still creep at horse-and-buggy pace toward gaining a cup of coffee at a lunch counter. Perhaps it is easy for those who have never felt the stinging darts of segregation to say, "Wait." But when you have seen vicious mobs lynch your mothers and fathers at will and drown your sisters and brothers at whim; when you have seen hate-filled policemen curse, kick, and even kill your black brothers and sisters; when you see the vast majority of your twenty million Negro brothers smothering in an airtight cage of poverty in the midst of an affluent society; when you suddenly find your tongue twisted and your speech stammering as you seek to explain to your six-year-old daughter why she can't go to the public amusement park that has just been advertised on television, and see tears welling up in her eyes when she is told that Funtown is closed to colored children, and see ominous clouds of inferiority beginning to form in her little mental sky, and see her beginning to distort her personality by developing an unconscious bitterness toward white people; when you have to concoct an answer for a five-year-old son who is asking: "Daddy, why do white people treat colored people so mean?"; when you take a cross-country drive and find it necessary to sleep night after night in the uncomfortable corners of your automobile because no motel will accept you; when you are humiliated day in and day out by nagging signs reading "white" and "colored"; when your first name be-

---

[2]**Reinhold Niebuhr** Niebuhr (1892–1971) was a minister, political activist, author, and professor of applied Christianity at Union Theological Seminary. [All notes are the editors' unless otherwise specified.]

[3]**justice . . . denied** A quotation attributed to William E. Gladstone (1809–1898), British statesman and prime minister.

comes "nigger," your middle name becomes "boy" (however old you are) and your last name becomes "John," and your wife and mother are never given the respected title "Mrs."; when you are harried by day and haunted by night by the fact that you are a Negro, living constantly at tiptoe stance, never quite knowing what to expect next, and are plagued with inner fears and outer resentments; when you are forever fighting a degenerating sense of "nobodiness" — then you will understand why we find it difficult to wait. There comes a time when the cup of endurance runs over, and men are no longer willing to be plunged into the abyss of despair. I hope, sirs, you can understand our legitimate and unavoidable impatience.

You express a great deal of anxiety over our willingness to break   15
laws. This is certainly a legitimate concern. Since we so diligently urge people to obey the Supreme Court's decision of 1954 outlawing segregation in the public schools, at first glance it may seem rather paradoxical for us consciously to break laws. One may well ask: "How can you advocate breaking some laws and obeying others?" The answer lies in the fact that there are two types of laws: just and unjust. I would be the first to advocate obeying just laws. One has not only a legal but a moral responsibility to obey just laws. Conversely, one has a moral responsibility to disobey unjust laws. I would agree with St. Augustine that "an unjust law is no law at all."

Now, what is the difference between the two? How does one determine whether a law is just or unjust? A just law is a man-made code that squares with the moral law or the law of God. An unjust law is a code that is out of harmony with the moral law. To put it in the terms of St. Thomas Aquinas: An unjust law is a human law that is not rooted in eternal law and natural law. Any law that uplifts human personality is just. Any law that degrades human personality is unjust. All segregation statutes are unjust because segregation distorts the soul and damages the personality. It gives the segregator a false sense of superiority and the segregated a false sense of inferiority. Segregation, to use the terminology of the Jewish philosopher Martin Buber, substitutes an "I-it" relationship for an "I-thou" relationship and ends up relegating persons to the status of things. Hence segregation is not only politically, economically, and sociologically unsound, it is morally wrong and sinful. Paul Tillich[4] has said that sin is separation. Is not segregation an existential expression of man's tragic separation, his awful estrangement, his terrible sinfulness? Thus it is that I can urge men to obey the 1954 decision of the Supreme Court, for it is morally right; and I can urge them to disobey segregation ordinances, for they are morally wrong.

---

[4]**Paul Tillich** Tillich (1886–1965), born in Germany, taught theology at several German universities, but in 1933 he was dismissed from his post at the University of Frankfurt because of his opposition to the Nazi regime. At the invitation of Reinhold Niebuhr, he came to the United States and taught at Union Theological Seminary.

Let us consider a more concrete example of just and unjust laws. An unjust law is a code that a numerical or power majority group compels a minority group to obey but does not make binding on itself. This is *difference* made legal. By the same token, a just law is a code that a majority compels a minority to follow and that it is willing to follow itself. This is *sameness* made legal.

Let me give another explanation. A law is unjust if it is inflicted on a minority that, as a result of being denied the right to vote, had no part in enacting or devising the law. Who can say that the legislature of Alabama which set up that state's segregation laws was democratically elected? Throughout Alabama all sorts of devious methods are used to prevent Negroes from becoming registered voters, and there are some counties in which, even though Negroes constitute a majority of the population, not a single Negro is registered. Can any law enacted under such circumstances be considered democratically structured?

Sometimes a law is just on its face and unjust in its application. For instance, I have been arrested on a charge of parading without a permit. Now, there is nothing wrong in having an ordinance which requires a permit for a parade. But such an ordinance becomes unjust when it is used to maintain segregation and to deny citizens the First Amendment privilege of peaceful assembly and protest.

I hope you are able to see the distinction I am trying to point out. In no sense do I advocate evading or defying the law, as would the rabid segregationist. That would lead to anarchy. One who breaks an unjust law must do so openly, lovingly, and with a willingness to accept the penalty. I submit that an individual who breaks a law that conscience tells him is unjust, and who willingly accepts the penalty of imprisonment in order to arouse the conscience of the community over its injustice, is in reality expressing the highest respect for law. 20

Of course, there is nothing new about this kind of civil disobedience. It was evidenced sublimely in the refusal of Shadrach, Meshach, and Abednego to obey the laws of Nebuchadnezzar, on the ground that a higher moral law was at stake. It was practiced superbly by the early Christians, who were willing to face hungry lions and the excruciating pain of chopping blocks rather than submit to certain unjust laws of the Roman Empire. To a degree, academic freedom is a reality today because Socrates practiced civil disobedience. In our own nation, the Boston Tea Party represented a massive act of civil disobedience.

We should never forget that everything Adolf Hitler did in Germany was "legal" and everything the Hungarian freedom fighters did in Hungary was "illegal." It was "illegal" to aid and comfort a Jew in Hitler's Germany. Even so, I am sure that, had I lived in Germany at the time, I would have aided and comforted my Jewish brothers. If today I lived in a Communist country where certain principles dear to the Christian faith are suppressed, I would openly advocate disobeying that country's antireligious laws.

I must make two honest confessions to you, my Christian and Jewish brothers. First, I must confess that over the past few years I have been gravely disappointed with the white moderate. I have almost reached the regrettable conclusion that the Negro's great stumbling block in his stride toward freedom is not the White Citizen's Counciler or the Ku Klux Klanner, but the white moderate, who is more devoted to "order" than to justice; who prefers a negative peace which is the absence of tension to a positive peace which is the presence of justice; who constantly says: "I agree with you in the goal you seek, but I cannot agree with your methods or direct action"; who paternalistically believes he can set the timetable for another man's freedom; who lives by a mythical concept of time and who constantly advises the Negro to wait for a "more convenient season." Shallow understanding from people of good will is more frustrating than absolute misunderstanding from people of ill will. Lukewarm acceptance is much more bewildering than outright rejection.

I had hoped that the white moderate would understand that law and order exist for the purpose of establishing justice and that when they fail in this purpose they become the dangerously structured dams that block the flow of social progress. I had hoped that the white moderate would understand that the present tension in the South is a necessary phase of the transition from an obnoxious negative peace, in which the Negro passively accepted his unjust plight, to a substantive and positive peace, in which all men will respect the dignity and worth of human personality. Actually, we who engage in nonviolent direct action are not the creators of tension. We merely bring to the surface the hidden tension that is already alive. We bring it out in the open, where it can be seen and dealt with. Like a boil that can never be cured so long as it is covered up but must be opened with all its ugliness to the natural medicines of air and light, injustice must be exposed, with all the tension its exposure creates, to the light of human conscience and the air of national opinion before it can be cured.

In your statement you assert that our actions, even though peaceful, 25 must be condemned because they precipitate violence. But is this a logical assertion? Isn't this like condemning a robbed man because his possession of money precipitated the evil act of robbery? Isn't this like condemning Socrates because his unswerving commitment to truth and his philosophical inquiries precipitated the act by the misguided populace in which they made him drink hemlock? Isn't this like condemning Jesus because his unique God-consciousness and never-ceasing devotion to God's will precipitated the evil act of crucifixion? We must come to see that, as the federal courts have consistently affirmed, it is wrong to urge an individual to cease his efforts to gain his basic constitutional rights because the quest may precipitate violence. Society must protect the robbed and punish the robber.

I had also hoped that the white moderate would reject the myth concerning time in relation to the struggle for freedom. I have just received a letter from a white brother in Texas. He writes: "All Christians know that the colored people will receive equal rights eventually, but it is possible that you are in too great a religious hurry. It has taken Christianity almost two thousand years to accomplish what it has. The teachings of Christ take time to come to earth." Such an attitude stems from a tragic misconception of time, from the strangely irrational notion that there is something in the very flow of time that will inevitably cure all ills. Actually, time itself is neutral; it can be used either destructively or constructively. More and more I feel that the people of ill will have used time much more effectively than have the people of good will. We will have to repent in this generation not merely for the hateful words and actions of the bad people but for the appalling silence of the good people. Human progress never rolls in on wheels of inevitability; it comes through the tireless efforts of men willing to be co-workers with God, and without this hard work, time itself becomes an ally of the forces of social stagnation. We must use time creatively, in the knowledge that the time is always ripe to do right. Now is the time to make real the promise of democracy and transform our pending national elegy into a creative psalm of brotherhood. Now is the time to lift our national policy from the quicksand of racial injustice to the solid rock of human dignity.

You speak of our activity in Birmingham as extreme. At first I was rather disappointed that fellow clergymen would see my nonviolent efforts as those of an extremist. I began thinking about the fact that I stand in the middle of two opposing forces in the Negro community. One is a force of complacency, made up in part of Negroes who, as a result of long years of oppression, are so drained of self-respect and a sense of "somebodiness" that they have adjusted to segregation; and in part of a few middle-class Negroes who, because of a degree of academic and economic security and because in some ways they profit by segregation, have become insensitive to the problems of the masses. The other force is one of bitterness and hatred, and it comes perilously close to advocating violence. It is expressed in the various black nationalist groups that are springing up across the nation, the largest and best-known being Elijah Muhammad's Muslim movement. Nourished by the Negro's frustration over the continued existence of racial discrimination, this movement is made up of people who have lost faith in America, who have absolutely repudiated Christianity, and who have concluded that the white man is an incorrigible "devil."

I have tried to stand between these two forces, saying that we need emulate neither the "do-nothingism" of the complacent nor the hatred and despair of the black nationalist. For there is the more excellent way of love and nonviolent protest. I am grateful to God that, through the influence of the Negro church, the way of nonviolence became an integral part of our struggle.

If this philosophy had not emerged, by now many streets of the South should, I am convinced, be flowing with blood. And I am further convinced that if our white brothers dismiss as "rabble-rousers" and "outside agitators" those of us who employ nonviolent direct action, and if they refuse to support our nonviolent efforts, millions of Negroes will, out of frustration and despair, seek solace and security in black-nationalist ideologies—a development that would inevitably lead to a frightening racial nightmare.

Oppressed people cannot remain oppressed forever. The yearning 30 for freedom eventually manifests itself, and that is what has happened to the American Negro. Something within has reminded him of his birthright of freedom, and something without has reminded him that it can be gained. Consciously or unconsciously, he has been caught up by the *Zeitgeist*,[5] and with his black brothers of Africa and his brown and yellow brothers of Asia, South America, and the Caribbean, the United States Negro is moving with a sense of great urgency toward the promised land of racial justice. If one recognizes this vital urge that has engulfed the Negro community, one should readily understand why public demonstrations are taking place. The Negro has many pent-up resentments and latent frustrations, and he must release them. So let him march; let him make prayer pilgrimages to the city hall; let him go on freedom rides—and try to understand why he must do so. If his repressed emotions are not released in nonviolent ways, they will seek expression through violence; this is not a threat but a fact of history. So I have not said to my people: "Get rid of your discontent." Rather, I have tried to say that this normal and healthy discontent can be channeled into the creative outlet of nonviolent direct action. And now this approach is being termed extremist.

But though I was initially disappointed at being categorized as an extremist, as I continued to think about the matter I gradually gained a measure of satisfaction from the label. Was not Jesus an extremist for love: "Love your enemies, bless them that curse you, do good to them that hate you, and pray for them which despitefully use you, and persecute you." Was not Amos an extremist for justice: "Let justice roll down like waters and righteousness like an ever-flowing stream." Was not Paul an extremist for the Christian gospel: "I bear in my body the marks of the Lord Jesus." Was not Martin Luther an extremist: "Here I stand; I cannot do otherwise, so help me God." And John Bunyan: "I will stay in jail to the end of my days before I make a butchery of my conscience." And Abraham Lincoln: "This nation cannot survive half slave and half free." And Thomas Jefferson: "We hold these truths to be self-evident, that all men are created equal. . . ." So the question is not whether we will be extremists, but what kind of extremists we will be. Will we be extremists for hate or for love? Will we be extremists for the preservation of injustice or for the extension of justice? In that dramatic scene on Calvary's hill three men were crucified. We must never forget that all three

[5]*Zeitgeist* German for "spirit of the age."

were crucified for the same crime—the crime of extremism. Two were extremists for immorality, and thus fell below their environment. The other, Jesus Christ, was an extremist for love, truth, and goodness, and thereby rose above his environment. Perhaps the South, the nation, and the world are in dire need of creative extremists.

I had hoped that the white moderate would see this need. Perhaps I was too optimistic; perhaps I expected too much. I suppose I should have realized that few members of the oppressor race can understand the deep groans and passionate yearnings of the oppressed race, and still fewer have the vision to see that injustice must be rooted out by strong, persistent, and determined action. I am thankful, however, that some of our white brothers in the South have grasped the meaning of this social revolution and committed themselves to it. They are still all too few in quantity, but they are big in quality. Some—such as Ralph McGill, Lillian Smith, Harry Golden, James McBride Dabbs, Ann Braden, and Sarah Patton Boyle—have written about our struggle in eloquent and prophetic terms. Others have marched with us down nameless streets of the South. They have languished in filthy, roach-infested jails, suffering the abuse and brutality of policemen who view them as "dirty nigger-lovers." Unlike so many of their moderate brothers and sisters, they have recognized the urgency of the moment and sensed the need for powerful "action" antidotes to combat the disease of segregation.

Let me take note of my other major disappointment. I have been so greatly disappointed with the white church and its leadership. Of course, there are some notable exceptions. I am not unmindful of the fact that each of you has taken some significant stands on this issue. I commend you, Reverend Stallings, for your Christian stand on this past Sunday, in welcoming Negroes to your worship service on a nonsegregated basis. I commend the Catholic leaders of this state for integrating Spring Hill College several years ago.

But despite these notable exceptions, I must honestly reiterate that I have been disappointed with the church. I do not say this as one of those negative critics who can always find something wrong with the church. I say this as a minister of the gospel, who loves the church; who was nurtured in its bosom; who has been sustained by its spiritual blessings and who will remain true to it as long as the cord of life shall lengthen.

When I was suddenly catapulted into the leadership of the bus 35 protest in Montgomery, Alabama, a few years ago, I felt we would be supported by the white church. I felt that the white ministers, priests, and rabbis of the South would be among our strongest allies. Instead, some have been outright opponents, refusing to understand the freedom movement and misrepresenting its leaders; all too many others have been more cautious than courageous and have remained silent behind the anesthetizing security of stained-glass windows.

In spite of my shattered dreams, I came to Birmingham with the hope that the white religious leadership of this community would see the justice of our cause and, with deep moral concern, would serve as the channel through which our just grievances could reach the power structure. I had hoped that each of you would understand. But again I have been disappointed.

I have heard numerous southern religious leaders admonish their worshipers to comply with a desegregation decision because it is the law, but I have longed to hear white ministers declare: "Follow this decree because integration is morally right and because the Negro is your brother." In the midst of blatant injustices inflicted upon the Negro, I have watched white churchmen stand on the sideline and mouth pious irrelevancies and sanctimonious trivialities. In the midst of a mighty struggle to rid our nation of racial and economic injustice, I have heard many ministers say: "Those are social issues, with which the gospel has no real concern." And I have watched many churches commit themselves to a completely otherworldly religion which makes a strange, unbiblical distinction between body and soul, between the sacred and the secular.

I have traveled the length and breadth of Alabama, Mississippi, and all the other southern states. On sweltering summer days and crisp autumn mornings I have looked at the South's beautiful churches with their lofty spires pointing heavenward. I have beheld the impressive outlines of her massive religious-education buildings. Over and over I have found myself saying: "What kind of people worship here? Who is their God? Where were their voices when the lips of Governor Barnett dripped with words of interposition and nullification? Where were they when Governor Wallace gave a clarion call for defiance and hatred? Where were their voices of support when bruised and weary Negro men and women decided to rise from the dark dungeons of complacency to the bright hills of creative protest?"

Yes, these questions are still in my mind. In deep disappointment I have wept over the laxity of the church. But be assured that my tears have been tears of love. There can be no deep disappointment where there is not deep love. Yes, I love the church. How could I do otherwise? I am in the rather unique position of being the son, the grandson, and the great-grandson of preachers. Yes, I see the church as the body of Christ. But, Oh! How we have blemished and scarred that body through social neglect and through fear of being nonconformists.

There was a time when the church was very powerful—in the time 40 when the early Christians rejoiced at being deemed worthy to suffer for what they believed. In those days the church was not merely a thermometer that recorded the ideas and principles of popular opinion; it was a thermostat that transformed the mores of society. Whenever the early Christians entered a town, the people in power became disturbed and immediately sought to convict the Christians for being "disturbers of the peace" and "outside agitators." But the Christians pressed on, in the conviction that they were "a colony of heaven," called to obey God rather than man. Small in number, they were big in commitment. They were too God-intoxicated to be "astronomically intimidated." By their effort and example they brought an end to such ancient evils as infanticide and gladiatorial contests.

Things are different now. So often the contemporary church is a weak, ineffectual voice with an uncertain sound. So often it is an archdefender of the status quo. Far from being disturbed by the presence of the church, the power structure of the average community is consoled by the church's silent—and often even vocal—sanction of things as they are.

But the judgment of God is upon the church as never before. If today's church does not recapture the sacrificial spirit of the early church, it will lose its authenticity, forfeit the loyalty of millions, and be dismissed as an irrelevant social club with no meaning for the twentieth century. Every day I meet young people whose disappointment with the church has turned into outright disgust.

Perhaps I have once again been too optimistic. Is organized religion too inextricably bound to the status quo to save our nation and the world? Perhaps I must turn my faith to the inner spiritual church, the church within the church, as the true *ekklesia*[6] and the hope of the world. But again I am thankful to God that some noble souls from the ranks of organized religion have broken loose from the paralyzing chains of conformity and joined us as active partners in the struggle for freedom. They have left their secure congregations and walked the streets of Albany, Georgia, with us. They have gone down the highways of the South on tortuous rides for freedom. Yes, they have gone to jail with us. Some have been dismissed from their churches, have lost the support of their bishops and fellow ministers. But they have acted in the faith that right defeated is stronger than evil triumphant. Their witness has been the spiritual salt that has preserved the true meaning of the gospel in these troubled times. They have carved a tunnel of hope through the dark mountain of disappointment.

I hope the church as a whole will meet the challenge of this decisive hour. But even if the church does not come to the aid of justice, I have no despair about the future. I have no fear about the outcome of our struggle in Birmingham, even if our motives are at present misunderstood. We will reach the goal of freedom in Birmingham and all over the nation, because the goal of America is freedom. Abused and scorned though we may be, our destiny is tied up with America's destiny. Before the pilgrims landed at Plymouth, we were here. Before the pen of Jefferson etched the majestic words of the Declaration of Independence across the pages of history, we were here. For more than two centuries our forebears labored in this country without wages; they made cotton king; they built the homes of their masters while suffering gross injustice and shameful humiliation—and yet out of a bottomless vitality they con-

---

[6]*ekklesia*: Greek for "a gathering or assembly of citizens."

tinue to thrive and develop. If the inexpressible cruelties of slavery could not stop us, the opposition we now face will surely fail. We will win our freedom because the sacred heritage of our nation and the eternal will of God are embodied in our echoing demands.

Before closing I feel impelled to mention one other point in your ⁴⁵ statement that has troubled me profoundly. You warmly commended the Birmingham police force for keeping "order" and "preventing violence." I doubt that you would have so warmly commended the police force if you had seen its dogs sinking their teeth into unarmed, nonviolent Negroes. I doubt that you would so quickly commend the policemen if you were to observe their ugly and inhumane treatment of Negroes here in the city jail; if you were to watch them push and curse old Negro women and young Negro girls; if you were to see them slap and kick old Negro men and young boys; if you were to observe them, as they did on two occasions, refuse to give us food because we wanted to sing our grace together. I cannot join you in your praise of the Birmingham police department.

It is true that the police have exercised a degree of discipline in handling the demonstrators. In this sense they have conducted themselves rather "nonviolently" in public. But for what purpose? To preserve the evil system of segregation. Over the past few years I have consistently preached that nonviolence demands that the means we use must be as pure as the ends we seek. I have tried to make clear that it is wrong to use immoral means to attain moral ends. But now I must affirm that it is just as wrong, or perhaps even more so, to use moral means to preserve immoral ends. Perhaps Mr. Connor and his policemen have been rather nonviolent in public, as was Chief Pritchett in Albany, Georgia, but they used the moral means of nonviolence to maintain the immoral end of racial injustice. As T. S. Eliot has said: "The last temptation is the greatest treason: To do the right deed for the wrong reason."

I wish you had commended the Negro sit-inners and demonstrators of Birmingham for their sublime courage, their willingness to suffer, and their amazing discipline in the midst of great provocation. One day the South will recognize its real heroes. They will be the James Merediths, with the noble sense of purpose that enables them to face jeering and hostile mobs, and with the agonizing loneliness that characterizes the life of the pioneer. They will be old, oppressed, battered Negro women, symbolized in a seventy-two-year-old woman in Montgomery, Alabama, who rose up with a sense of dignity and with her people decided not to ride segregated buses, and who responded with ungrammatical profundity to one who inquired about her weariness: "My feets is tired, but my soul is at rest." They will be the young high school and college students, the young ministers of the gospel and a host of their elders, courageously and nonviolently sitting in at lunch counters and willingly going to jail for conscience's sake. One day the South will know that when these disinherited children of God sat down at lunch counters, they were in reality standing up for what is best in the American dream and for the most sacred values in our Judaeo-Christian heritage, thereby bringing our nation back to those great wells of democracy which were dug deep by the founding fathers in their formulation of the Constitution and the Declaration of Independence.

Never before have I written so long a letter. I'm afraid it is much too long to take your precious time. I can assure you that it would have been much shorter if I had been writing from a comfortable desk, but what else can one do when he is alone in a narrow jail cell, other than write long letters, think long thoughts, and pray long prayers?

If I have said anything in this letter that overstates the truth and indicates an unreasonable impatience, I beg you to forgive me. If I have said anything that understates the truth and indicates my having a patience that allows me to settle for anything less than brotherhood, I beg God to forgive me.

I hope this letter finds you strong in the faith. I also hope that circ- 50 cumstances will soon make it possible for me to meet each of you, not as an integrationist or a civil-rights leader but as a fellow clergyman and a Christian brother. Let us all hope that the dark clouds of racial prejudice will soon pass away and the deep fog of misunderstanding will be lifted from our fear-drenched communities, and in some not too distant tomorrow the radiant stars of love and brotherhood will shine over our great nation with all their scintillating beauty.

> Yours for the cause of Peace and Brotherhood,
> Martin Luther King Jr.

Topics for Critical Thinking and Writing

1. In his first five paragraphs of the "Letter," how does King assure his audience that he is not a meddlesome intruder but a man of good will?

2. In paragraph 3 King refers to Hebrew prophets and to the Apostle Paul and later (para. 10) to Socrates. What is the point of these references?

3. In paragraph 11 what does King mean when he says that "our beloved Southland" has long tried to "live in monologue rather than dialogue"?

4. King begins paragraph 23 with "I must make two honest confessions to you, my Christian and Jewish brothers." What would have been gained or lost if he had used this paragraph as his opening?

5. King's last three paragraphs do not advance his argument. What do they do?

6. Why does King advocate breaking unjust laws "openly, lovingly" (para. 20)? What does he mean by these words? What other motives or attitudes do these words rule out?

7. Construct two definitions of *civil disobedience,* and explain whether and to what extent it is easier (or harder) to justify civil disobedience, depending on how you have defined the expression.

8. If you feel that you wish to respond to King's letter on some point, write a letter nominally addressed to King. You may, if you wish, adopt the persona of one of the eight clergymen whom King initially addressed.

9. King writes (para. 46) that "nonviolence demands that the means we use must be as pure as the ends we seek." How do you think King would evaluate the following acts: (a) occupying a college administration building to protest the administration's unsatisfactory response to a racial incident on campus or its failure to hire minority persons as staff and faculty; (b) occupying an abortion clinic to protest abortion? Set down your answer in an essay of 500 words.

10. Compose a letter from Martin Luther King Jr. in which King responds to Plato's "Crito."

Stanley Milgram

Stanley Milgram (1933–1984) taught at Yale and Harvard Universities and at the Graduate Center, City University of New York. In 1963, while at Yale, he devised an experiment that tested the willingness of people to submit to the authority of an experimenter even if it meant they would violate their conscience by inflicting pain on another person during the course of the experiment. He published his research on conformity in a book, Obedience to Authority *(1974), which was nominated for the National Book Award.*

The Perils of Obedience

Obedience is as basic an element in the structure of social life as one can point to. Some system of authority is a requirement of all communal living, and it is only the person dwelling in isolation who is not forced to respond, with defiance or submission, to the commands of others. For many people, obedience is a deeply ingrained behavior tendency, indeed a potent impulse overriding training in ethics, sympathy, and moral conduct.

The dilemma inherent in submission to authority is ancient, as old as the story of Abraham, and the question of whether one should obey when commands conflict with conscience has been argued by Plato, dramatized in *Antigone*, and treated to philosophic analysis in almost every historical epoch. Conservative philosophers argue that the very fabric of society is threatened by disobedience, while humanists stress the primacy of the individual conscience.

The legal and philosophic aspects of obedience are of enormous import, but they say very little about how most people behave in concrete situations. I set up a simple experiment at Yale University to test how much pain an ordinary citizen would inflict on another person simply because he was ordered to by an experimental scientist. Stark authority was pitted against the subjects' strongest moral imperatives against hurting others, and, with the subjects' ears ringing with the screams of the victims, authority won more often than not. The extreme willingness of adults to go to almost any lengths on the command of an authority constitutes the chief finding of the study and the fact most urgently demanding explanation.

In the basic experimental design, two people come to a psychology laboratory to take part in a study of memory and learning. One of them is designated as a "teacher" and the other a "learner." The experimenter explains that the study is concerned with the effects of punishment on learning. The learner is conducted into a room, seated in a kind of miniature electric chair; his arms are strapped to prevent excessive movement, and an electrode is attached to his wrist. He is told that he will be read lists of simple word pairs, and that he will then be tested on his ability to remember the second word of a pair when he hears the first one again. Whenever he makes an error, he will receive electric shocks of increasing intensity.

The real focus of the experiment is the teacher. After watching the   5
learner being strapped into place, he is seated before an impressive shock generator. The instrument panel consists of thirty lever switches set in a horizontal line. Each switch is clearly labeled with a voltage designation ranging from 15 to 450 volts. The following designations are clearly indicated for groups of four switches, going from left to right: Slight Shock, Moderate Shock, Strong Shock, Very Strong Shock, Intense Shock, Extreme Intensity Shock, Danger: Severe Shock. (Two switches after this last designation are simply marked XXX.)

When a switch is depressed, a pilot light corresponding to each switch is illuminated in bright red; an electric buzzing is heard; a blue light, labeled "voltage energizer," flashes; the dial on the voltage meter swings to the right; and various relay clicks sound off.

The upper left-hand corner of the generator is labeled SHOCK GENERATOR, TYPE ZLB, DYSON INSTRUMENT COMPANY, WALTHAM, MASS. OUTPUT 15 VOLTS–450 VOLTS.

Each subject is given a sample 45-volt shock from the generator before his run as teacher, and the jolt strengthens his belief in the authenticity of the machine.

The teacher is a genuinely naïve subject who has come to the laboratory for the experiment. The learner, or victim, is actually an actor who receives no shock at all. The point of the experiment is to see how far a person will proceed in a concrete and measurable situation in which he is ordered to inflict increasing pain on a protesting victim.

Conflict arises when the man receiving the shock begins to show   10
that he is experiencing discomfort. At 75 volts, he grunts; at 120 volts, he complains loudly; at 150, he demands to be released from the experiment. As the voltage increases, his protests become more vehement and emotional. At 285 volts, his response can be described only as an agonized scream. Soon thereafter, he makes no sound at all.

For the teacher, the situation quickly becomes one of gripping tension. It is not a game for him; conflict is intense and obvious. The manifest suffering of the learner presses him to quit; but each time he hesitates to administer a shock, the experimenter orders him to continue. To extricate himself from this plight, the subject must make a clear break with authority.

The subject, Gretchen Brandt, is an attractive thirty-one-year-old medical technician who works at the Yale Medical School. She had emigrated from Germany five years before.[1]

On several occasions when the learner complains, she [Brandt] turns to the experimenter coolly and inquires, "Shall I continue?" She promptly returns to her task when the experimenter asks her to do so. At the administration of 210 volts, she turns to the experimenter, remarking firmly, "Well, I'm sorry, I don't think we should continue."

EXPERIMENTER: The experiment requires that you go on until he has learned all the word pairs correctly.

BRANDT: He has a heart condition, I'm sorry. He told you that before.   15

EXPERIMENTER: The shocks may be painful but they are not dangerous.

BRANDT: Well, I'm sorry, I think when shocks continue like this, they *are* dangerous. You ask him if he wants to get out. It's his free will.

EXPERIMENTER: It is absolutely essential that we continue. . . .

BRANDT: I'd like you to ask him. We came here of our free will. If he wants to continue I'll go ahead. He told you he had a heart condition. I'm sorry. I don't want to be responsible for anything happening to him. I wouldn't like it for me either.

EXPERIMENTER: You have no other choice.   20

BRANDT: I think we are here on our own free will. I don't want to be responsible if anything happens to him. Please understand that.

She refuses to go further and the experiment is terminated.

The woman is firm and resolute throughout. She indicates in the interview that she was in no way tense or nervous, and this corresponds to her controlled appearance during the experiment. She feels that the last shock she administered to the learner was extremely painful and reiterates that she "did not want to be responsible for any harm to him."

The woman's straightforward, courteous behavior in the experiment, lack of tension, and total control of her own action seem to make disobedience a simple and rational deed. Her behavior is the very embodiment of what I envisioned would be true for almost all subjects.

---

[1]Names of subjects described in this piece have been changed. [Milgram's note.]

AN UNEXPECTED OUTCOME

Before the experiments, I sought predictions about the outcome from
various kinds of people—psychiatrists, college sophomores, middle-class
adults, graduate students, and faculty in the behavioral sciences. With remarkable similarity, they predicted that virtually all subjects would refuse
to obey the experimenter. The psychiatrists, specifically, predicted that
most subjects would not go beyond 150 volts, when the victim makes his
first explicit demand to be freed. They expected that only 4 percent would
reach 300 volts, and that only a pathological fringe of about one in a thousand would administer the highest shock on the board.

These predictions were unequivocally wrong. Of the forty subjects in
the first experiment, twenty-five obeyed the orders of the experimenter
to the end, punishing the victim until they reached the most potent
shock available on the generator. After 450 volts were administered
three times, the experimenter called a halt to the session. Many obedient
subjects then heaved sighs of relief, mopped their brows, rubbed their
fingers over their eyes, or nervously fumbled cigarettes. Others displayed
only minimal signs of tension from beginning to end.

When the very first experiments were carried out, Yale undergraduates
were used as subjects, and about 60 percent of them were fully obedient. A
colleague of mine immediately dismissed these findings as having no relevance to "ordinary" people, asserting that Yale undergraduates are a highly
aggressive, competitive bunch who step on each other's necks on the slightest provocation. He assured me that when "ordinary" people were tested,
the results would be quite different. As we moved from the pilot studies to
the regular experimental series, people drawn from every stratum of New
Haven life came to be employed in the experiment: professionals, white-
collar workers, unemployed persons, and industrial workers. *The experiment's total outcome was the same as we had observed among the students.*

Moreover, when the experiments were repeated in Princeton, Munich, Rome, South Africa, and Australia, the level of obedience was invariably somewhat *higher* than found in the investigation reported in
this article. Thus one scientist in Munich found 85 percent of his subjects
obedient.

Fred Prozi's reactions, if more dramatic than most, illuminate the
conflicts experienced by others in less visible form. About fifty years old
and unemployed at the time of the experiment, he has a good-natured,
if slightly dissolute, appearance, and he strikes people as a rather ordinary fellow. He begins the session calmly but becomes tense as it proceeds. After delivering the 180-volt shock, he pivots around in his chair
and, shaking his head, addresses the experimenter in agitated tones:

PROZI: I can't stand it. I'm not going to kill that man in there. You
hear him hollering?

EXPERIMENTER: As I told you before, the shocks may be painful, but . . .

PROZI: But he's hollering. He can't stand it. What's going to happen to him?

EXPERIMENTER (his voice is patient, matter-of-fact): The experiment requires that you continue, Teacher.

PROZI: Aaah, but, unh, I'm not going to get that man sick in there — know what I mean?

EXPERIMENTER: Whether the learner likes it or not, we must go on, 35 through all the word pairs.

PROZI: I refuse to take the responsibility. He's in there hollering!

EXPERIMENTER: It's absolutely essential that you continue, Prozi.

PROZI (indicating the unused questions): There's too many left here, I mean, Jeez, if he gets them wrong, there's too many of them left. I mean, who's going to take the responsibility if anything happens to that gentleman?

EXPERIMENTER: I'm responsible for anything that happens to him. Continue, please.

PROZI: All right. (Consults list of words.) The next one's "Slow — 40 walk, truck, dance, music." Answer, please. (A buzzing sound indicates the learner has signaled his answer.) Wrong. A hundred and ninety-five volts. "Dance." (Zzumph!)

LEARNER (yelling): Let me out of here! My heart's bothering me! (Teacher looks at experimenter.)

EXPERIMENTER: Continue, please.

LEARNER (screaming): Let me out of here! You have no right to keep me here! Let me out of here, my heart's bothering me, let me out!

PROZI (shakes head, pats the table nervously): You see, he's hollering. Hear that? Gee, I don't know.

EXPERIMENTER: The experiment requires . . .   45

PROZI (interrupting): I know it does, sir, but I mean—hunh! He don't know what he's getting in for. He's up to 195 volts! (Experiment continues, through 210 volts, 225 volts, 240 volts, 255 volts, 270 volts, at which point Prozi, with evident relief, runs out of word-pair questions.)

EXPERIMENTER: You'll have to go back to the beginning of that page and go through them again until he's learned them all correctly.

PROZI: Aw, no. I'm not going to kill that man. You mean I've got to keep going up with the scale? No sir. He's hollering in there. I'm not going to give him 450 volts.

EXPERIMENTER: The experiment requires that you go on.

LEARNER: Ohhh. I absolutely refuse to answer anymore. (Shouting 50 urgently now.) Let me out of here! You can't hold me here! Get me out. Get-me-out-of-here!

EXPERIMENTER: Continue. The next word is "Green," please.

PROZI: "Green—grass, hat, ink, apple." (Nothing happens. No answering buzz. Just gloomy silence.)

PROZI: I don't think he is going to answer.

EXPERIMENTER: If the learner doesn't answer in a reasonable time, about four or five seconds, consider the answer wrong. And follow the same procedures you have been doing for wrong answers. Say, "Wrong," tell him the number of volts, give him the punishment, read him the correct answer. Continue, please.

PROZI: "Green—grass, hat, ink, apple." Answer, please. (More si- 55 lence. Subject just sits there.)

EXPERIMENTER: Go on with the procedure, please.

PROZI: Three hundred and fifteen volts. The answer is "ink." (Zzumph!)

LEARNER: Ohh. Ooohh.

PROZI (relieved to hear response): Next one . . .

LEARNER: I absolutely refuse to answer. 60

PROZI: You got to. You get a shock if you don't answer. (Experiment continues with learner refusing to answer, and, finally, failing even to grunt or groan. At 375 volts, the subject stands up.)

PROZI: I think something's happened to that fellow in there. I don't get no answer. He was hollering at less voltage. Can't you check in and see if he's all right, please?

EXPERIMENTER (with same detached calm): Not once we've started. Please continue, Teacher.

PROZI (sits down, sighs deeply): "Cool—day, shade, water, paint." Answer, please. Are you all right in there? Are you all right?

EXPERIMENTER: Please continue, Teacher. Continue, please. (Subject 65 pushes lever. Zzumph!)

PROZI (swiveling around in his chair): Something's happened to that man in there. (Swiveling back.) Next one. "Low—dollar, necklace, moon, paint." (Turning around again.) Something's happened to that man in there. You better check in on him, sir. He won't answer or nothing.

EXPERIMENTER: Continue. Go on, please.

PROZI: You accept all responsibility?

EXPERIMENTER: The responsibility is mine. Correct. Please go on. (Subject returns to his list, starts running through words as rapidly as he can read them, works through to 450 volts.)

PROZI: That's that. 70

EXPERIMENTER: Continue using the 450 switch for each wrong answer. Continue, please.

PROZI: But I don't get anything!

EXPERIMENTER: Please continue. The next word is "white."

PROZI: Don't you think you should look in on him, please?

EXPERIMENTER: Not once we've started the experiment. 75

PROZI: What if he's dead in there? (Gestures toward the room with the electric chair.) I mean, he told me he can't stand the shock, sir. I don't mean to be rude, but I think you should look in on him. All you

have to do is look in on him. All you have to do is look in the door. I
don't get no answer, no noise. Something might have happened to the
gentleman in there, sir.

EXPERIMENTER: We must continue. Go on, please.

PROZI: You mean keep giving him what? Four-hundred-fifty volts,
what he's got now?

EXPERIMENTER: That's correct. Continue. The next word is "white."

PROZI (now at a furious pace): "White — cloud, horse, rock, house." 80
Answer, please. The answer is "horse." Four hundred and fifty volts.
(Zzumph!) Next word, "Bag — paint, music, clown, girl." The answer is
"paint." Four hundred and fifty volts. (Zzumph!) Next word is "Short —
sentence, movie . . ."

EXPERIMENTER: Excuse me, Teacher. We'll have to discontinue the
experiment.

PECULIAR REACTIONS

Morris Braverman, another subject, is a thirty-nine-year-old social
worker. He looks older than his years because of his bald head and serious demeanor. His brow is furrowed, as if all the world's burdens were
carried on his face. He appears intelligent and concerned.

When the learner refuses to answer and the experimenter instructs
Braverman to treat the absence of an answer as equivalent to a wrong
answer, he takes his instruction to heart. Before administering 300 volts
he asserts officiously to the victim, "Mr. Wallace, your silence has to be
considered as a wrong answer." Then he administers the shock. He offers
half-heartedly to change places with the learner, then asks the experimenter, "Do I have to follow these instructions literally?" He is satisfied
with the experimenter's answer that he does. His very refined and authoritative manner of speaking is increasingly broken up by wheezing
laughter.

The experimenter's notes on Mr. Braverman at the last few
shocks are:

- Almost breaking up now each time gives shock. Rubbing face to
  hide laughter.
- Squinting, trying to hide face with hand, still laughing.
- Cannot control his laughter at this point no matter what he does.
- Clenching fist, pushing it onto table.

In an interview after the session, Mr. Braverman summarizes the ex- 85
periment with impressive fluency and intelligence. He feels the experiment may have been designed also to "test the effects on the teacher of
being in an essentially sadistic role, as well as the reactions of a student
to a learning situation that was authoritative and punitive." When asked
how painful the last few shocks administered to the learner were, he

indicates that the most extreme category on the scale is not adequate (it read EXTREMELY PAINFUL) and places his mark at the edge of the scale with an arrow carrying it beyond the scale.

It is almost impossible to convey the greatly relaxed, sedate quality of his conversation in the interview. In the most relaxed terms, he speaks about his severe inner tension.

EXPERIMENTER: At what point were you most tense or nervous?

MR. BRAVERMAN: Well, when he first began to cry out in pain, and I realized this was hurting him. This got worse when he just blocked and refused to answer. There was I. I'm a nice person, I think, hurting somebody, and caught up in what seemed a mad situation . . . and in the interest of science, one goes through with it.

When the interviewer pursues the general question of tension, Mr. Braverman spontaneously mentions his laughter.

"My reactions were awfully peculiar. I don't know if you were 90 watching me, but my reactions were giggly, and trying to stifle laughter. This isn't the way I usually am. This was a sheer reaction to a totally impossible situation. And my reaction was to the situation of having to hurt somebody. And being totally helpless and caught up in a set of circumstances where I just couldn't deviate and I couldn't try to help. This is what got me."

Mr. Braverman, like all subjects, was told the actual nature and purpose of the experiment, and a year later he affirmed in a questionnaire that he had learned something of personal importance: "What appalled me was that I could possess this capacity for obedience and compliance to a central idea, i.e., the value of a memory experiment, even after it became clear that continued adherence to this value was at the expense of violation of another value, i.e., don't hurt someone who is helpless and not hurting you. As my wife said, 'You can call yourself Eichmann.' I hope I deal more effectively with any future conflicts of values I encounter."

THE ETIQUETTE OF SUBMISSION

One theoretical interpretation of this behavior holds that all people harbor deeply aggressive instincts continually pressing for expression, and that the experiment provides institutional justification for the release of these impulses. According to this view, if a person is placed in a situation in which he has complete power over another individual, whom he may punish as much as he likes, all that is sadistic and bestial in man comes to the fore. The impulse to shock the victim is seen to flow from the potent aggressive tendencies, which are part of the motivational life of the individual, and the experiment, because it provides social legitimacy, simply opens the door to their expression.

It becomes vital, therefore, to compare the subject's performance when he is under orders and when he is allowed to choose the shock level.

The procedure was identical to our standard experiment, except that the teacher was told that he was free to select any shock level on any of the trials. (The experimenter took pains to point out that the teacher could use the highest levels on the generator, the lowest, any in between, or any combination of levels.) Each subject proceeded for thirty critical trials. The learner's protests were coordinated to standard shock levels, his first grunt coming at 75 volts, his first vehement protest at 150 volts.

The average shock used during the thirty critical trials was less than 60 volts—lower than the point at which the victim showed the first signs of discomfort. Three of the forty subjects did not go beyond the very lowest level on the board, twenty-eight went no higher than 75 volts, and thirty-eight did not go beyond the first loud protest at 150 volts. Two subjects provided the exception, administering up to 325 and 450 volts, but the overall result was that the great majority of people delivered very low, usually painless, shocks when the choice was explicitly up to them.

This condition of the experiment undermines another commonly offered explanation of the subjects' behavior—that those who shocked the victim at the most severe levels came only from the sadistic fringe of society. If one considers that almost two-thirds of the participants fall into the category of "obedient" subjects, and that they represented ordinary people drawn from working, managerial, and professional classes, the argument becomes very shaky. Indeed, it is highly reminiscent of the issue that arose in connection with Hannah Arendt's 1963 book, *Eichmann in Jerusalem.* Arendt contended that the prosecution's effort to depict Eichmann as a sadistic monster was fundamentally wrong, that he came closer to being an uninspired bureaucrat who simply sat at his desk and did his job. For asserting her views, Arendt became the object of considerable scorn, even calumny. Somehow, it was felt that the monstrous deeds carried out by Eichmann required a brutal, twisted personality, evil incarnate. After witnessing hundreds of ordinary persons submit to the authority in our own experiments, I must conclude that Arendt's conception of the banality of evil comes closer to the truth than one might dare imagine. The ordinary person who shocked the victim did so out of a sense of obligation—an impression of his duties as a subject—and not from any peculiarly aggressive tendencies.

This is, perhaps, the most fundamental lesson of our study: Ordinary people, simply doing their jobs, and without any particular hostility on their part, can become agents in a terrible destructive process. Moreover, even when the destructive effects of their work become patently clear, and they are asked to carry out actions incompatible with fundamental standards of morality, relatively few people have the resources needed to resist authority.

Many of the people were in some sense against what they did to the learner, and many protested even while they obeyed. Some were totally convinced of the wrongness of their actions but could not bring themselves to make an open break with authority. They often derived satisfaction from their thoughts and felt that—within themselves, at least—they had been on the side of the angels. They tried to reduce strain by obeying the experimenter but "only slightly," encouraging the learner, touching the generator switches gingerly. When interviewed, such a subject would stress that he had "asserted my humanity" by administering the briefest shock possible. Handling the conflict in this manner was easier than defiance.

The situation is constructed so that there is no way the subject can stop shocking the learner without violating the experimenter's definitions of his own competence. The subject fears that he will appear arrogant, untoward, and rude if he breaks off. Although these inhibiting emotions appear small in scope alongside the violence being done to the learner, they suffuse the mind and feelings of the subject who is miserable at the prospect of having to repudiate the authority to his face. (When the experiment was altered so that the experimenter gave his instructions by telephone instead of in person, only a third as many people were fully obedient through 450 volts.) It is a curious thing that a measure of compassion on the part of the subject—an unwillingness to "hurt" the experimenter's feelings—is part of those binding forces inhibiting his disobedience. The withdrawal of such deference may be as painful to the subject as to the authority he defies.

DUTY WITHOUT CONFLICT

The subjects do not derive satisfaction from inflicting pain, but they often like the feeling they get from pleasing the experimenter. They are proud of doing a good job, obeying the experimenter under difficult circumstances. While the subjects administered only mild shocks on their own initiative, one experimental variation showed that, under orders, 30 percent of them were willing to deliver 450 volts even when they had to forcibly push the learner's hand down on the electrode.

Bruno Batta is a thirty-seven-year-old welder who took part in the variation requiring the use of force. He was born in New Haven, his parents in Italy. He has a rough-hewn face that conveys a conspicuous lack of alertness. He has some difficulty in mastering the experimental procedure and needs to be corrected by the experimenter several times. He shows appreciation for the help and willingness to do what is required. After the 150-volt level, Batta has to force the learner's hand down on the shock plate, since the learner himself refuses to touch it.

When the learner first complains, Mr. Batta pays no attention to him. His face remains impassive, as if to dissociate himself from the learner's disruptive behavior. When the experimenter instructs him to force the learner's hand down, he adopts a rigid, mechanical procedure. He tests the generator switch. When it fails to function, he immediately forces the learner's hand onto the shock plate. All the while he maintains the same rigid mask. The learner, seated alongside him, begs him to stop, but with robotic impassivity he continues the procedure.

What is extraordinary is his apparent total indifference to the learner; he hardly takes cognizance of him as a human being. Meanwhile, he relates to the experimenter in a submissive and courteous fashion.

At the 330-volt level, the learner refuses not only to touch the shock plate but also to provide any answers. Annoyed, Batta turns to him, and chastises him: "You better answer and get it over with. We can't stay here all night." These are the only words he directs to the learner in the course of an hour. Never again does he speak to him. The scene is brutal and depressing, his hard, impassive face showing total indifference as he subdues the screaming learner and gives him shocks. He seems to derive no pleasure from the act itself, only quiet satisfaction at doing his job properly.

When he administers 450 volts, he turns to the experimenter and asks, "Where do we go from here, Professor?" His tone is deferential and expresses his willingness to be a cooperative subject, in contrast to the learner's obstinacy. 105

At the end of the session he tells the experimenter how honored he has been to help him, and in a moment of contrition, remarks, "Sir, sorry it couldn't have been a full experiment."

He has done his honest best. It is only the deficient behavior of the learner that has denied the experimenter full satisfaction.

The essence of obedience is that a person comes to view himself as the instrument for carrying out another person's wishes, and he therefore no longer regards himself as responsible for his actions. Once this critical shift of viewpoint has occurred, all of the essential features of obedience follow. The most far-reaching consequence is that the person feels responsible *to* the authority directing him but feels no responsibility *for* the content of the actions that the authority prescribes. Morality does not disappear—it acquires a radically different focus: The subordinate person feels shame or pride depending on how adequately he has performed the actions called for by authority.

Language provides numerous terms to pinpoint this type of morality: *Loyalty, duty, discipline* all are terms heavily saturated with moral meaning and refer to the degree to which a person fulfills his obligations to authority. They refer not to the "goodness" of the person per se but to the adequacy with which a subordinate fulfills his socially defined role. The most frequent defense of the individual who has performed a heinous act under command of authority is that he has simply done his duty. In asserting this defense, the individual is not introducing an alibi concocted for the moment but is reporting honestly on the psychological attitude induced by submission to authority.

For a person to feel responsible for his actions, he must sense that the behavior has flowed from "the self." In the situation we have studied, subjects have precisely the opposite view of their actions—namely, they see them as originating in the motives of some other person. Subjects in the experiment frequently said, "If it were up to me, I would not have administered shocks to the learner."

Once authority has been isolated as the cause of the subject's behavior, it is legitimate to inquire into the necessary elements of authority and how it must be perceived in order to gain his compliance. We conducted some investigations into the kinds of changes that would cause the experimenter to lose his power and to be disobeyed by the subject. Some of the variations revealed that

- *The experimenter's physical presence has a marked impact on his authority.* As cited earlier, obedience dropped off sharply when orders were given by telephone. The experimenter could often induce a disobedient subject to go on by returning to the laboratory.

- *Conflicting authority severely paralyzes action.* When two experimenters of equal status, both seated at the command desk, gave incompatible orders, no shocks were delivered past the point of their disagreement.

- *The rebellious action of others severely undermines authority.* In one variation, three teachers (two actors and a real subject) administered a test and shocks. When the two actors disobeyed the experimenter and refused to go beyond a certain shock level, thirty-six of forty subjects joined their disobedient peers and refused as well.

Although the experimenter's authority was fragile in some respects, it is also true that he had almost none of the tools used in ordinary command structures. For example, the experimenter did not threaten the subjects with punishment—such as loss of income, community ostracism, or jail—for failure to obey. Neither could he offer incentives. Indeed, we should expect the experimenter's authority to be much less than that of someone like a general, since the experimenter has no power to enforce his imperatives, and since participation in a psychological experiment scarcely evokes the sense of urgency and dedication found in warfare. Despite these limitations, he still managed to command a dismaying degree of obedience.

I will cite one final variation of the experiment that depicts a dilemma that is more common in everyday life. The subject was not ordered to pull the lever that shocked the victim, but merely to perform a subsidiary task (administering the word-pair test) while another person administered the shock. In this situation, thirty-seven of forty adults continued to the highest level on the shock generator. Predictably, they excused their behavior by saying that the responsibility belonged to the man who actually pulled the switch. This may illustrate a dangerously typical arrangement in a complex society: It is easy to ignore responsibility when one is only an intermediate link in a chain of action.

The problem of obedience is not wholly psychological. The form and shape of society and the way it is developing have much to do with it. There was a time, perhaps, when people were able to give a fully human response to any situation because they were fully absorbed in it as human beings. But as soon as there was a division of labor things changed. Beyond a certain point, the breaking up of society into people carrying out narrow and very special jobs takes away from the human quality of work and life. A person does not get to see the whole situation but only a small part of it, and is thus unable to act without some kind of overall direction. He yields to authority but in doing so is alienated from his own actions.

Even Eichmann was sickened when he toured the concentration 115 camps, but he had only to sit at a desk and shuffle papers. At the same time the man in the camp who actually dropped Cyclon-b into the gas chambers was able to justify *his* behavior on the ground that he was only following orders from above. Thus there is a fragmentation of the total human act; no one is confronted with the consequences of his decision to carry out the evil act. The person who assumes responsibility has evaporated. Perhaps this is the most common characteristic of socially organized evil in modern society.

Topics for Critical Thinking and Writing

1. Milgram says that "the dilemma inherent in submission to authority is ancient, as old as the story of Abraham" (para. 2). What is the story of Abraham to which he refers? And what is the "dilemma inherent in submission"? (Review the section on dilemmas, p. 304.)

2. Describe the Milgram experiments in an essay of 150 words. In a sentence, what conclusion does Milgram himself draw from the experiments?

3. Read the essay by Walter T. Stace (p. 831), and decide whether he would regard the dialogue between the experimenter and Brandt (paras. 14–21) as a good example of people acting of their own "free will." Is the experimenter correct when he tells her "You have no other choice"?

4. Milgram explains that prior to the experiment he asked various people to predict the results; these predictions were "unequivocally wrong" (para. 26). Explain, if you can, why these groups predicted a very different outcome from what actually happened.

5. Did the experimenter ever threaten the subjects in the experiments? Use coercion? What is your evidence, one way or the other?

6. Milgram eventually offers "one theoretical interpretation" of the behavior of the experimenters (para. 92). What is that interpretation? Do you think it is plausible?

7. What, according to Milgram (para. 108), is "the essence of obedience"? Does an obedient person, in this sense of the term, cease to act of his own free will? Explain why or why not in an essay of 250 words.

8. Suppose someone were to criticize Milgram for his experiments, arguing that they were unethical because they were based fundamentally on deceiving the subjects about what they were really doing. How might Milgram reply?

Thomas Hardy

Thomas Hardy (1840–1928) was born in Dorset, England, the son of a stonemason. Despite great obstacles, he studied the classics and architecture, and in 1862 he moved to London to study and practice as an architect. Ill health forced him to return to Dorset, where he continued to work as an architect and to write. Best known for his novels, Hardy ceased writing fiction after the hostile reception of Jude the Obscure *in 1896 and turned to writing lyric poetry. We print a poem of 1902.*

The Man He Killed

"Had he and I but met
By some old ancient inn,
We should have sat us down to wet
Right many a nipperkin°!

"But ranged an infantry,   5
And staring face to face,
I shot at him as he at me,
And killed him in his place.

"I shot him dead because—
Because he was my foe,   10
Just so: my foe of course he was;
That's clear enough; although

"He thought he'd 'list, perhaps,
Off-hand like—just as I—
Was out of work—had sold his traps°—   15
No other reason why.

"Yes; quaint and curious war is!
You shoot a fellow down
You'd treat if met where any bar is,
Or help to half-a-crown."   20

---

4 nipperkin Cup.   **15 traps** Personal belongings. [Both notes are the editors'.]

Topics for Critical Thinking and Writing

1. Hardy published this poem in 1902, at the conclusion of the Boer War (1899–1902, also called the South African War), a war between the Boers (Dutch) and the British for possession of part of Africa. The speaker of the poem is an English veteran of the war. Do you think such a poem might just as well have been written by an English (or American) soldier in World War II? Explain.

2. Characterize the speaker. What sort of man does he seem to be? Pay special attention to the punctuation in the third and fourth stanzas — what do the pauses indicated by the dashes, the colons, and the semicolon tell us about him? — and pay special attention to the final stanza, in which he speaks of war as "quaint and curious" (line 17). Do you think that Hardy too would speak of war this way? Why, or why not? Can you imagine an American soldier in the Vietnam War speaking of the war as "quaint and curious"? Explain.

T. S. Eliot

Thomas Stearns Eliot (1888–1965) was born into a New England family that had moved to St. Louis. He attended a preparatory school in Massachusetts, graduated from Harvard University, and then continued his studies in literature in France, Germany, and England. In 1914 he began working for Lloyds Bank in London, and three years later he published his first book of poems, which included "Prufrock." In 1925 he joined a publishing firm, and in 1927 he became a British citizen and a member of the Church of England. In 1948 he received the Nobel Prize for Literature.

The Love Song of J. Alfred Prufrock

> *S'io credesse che mia risposta fosse*
> *A persona che mai tornasse al mondo,*
> *Questa fiamma staria senza più scosse.*
> *Ma perciocchè giammai di questo fondo*
> *Non torno vivo alcun, s' i' odo il vero,*
> *Senza tema d'infamia ti rispondo.*°

Let us go then, you and I,
When the evening is spread out against the sky

S'io . . . rispondo The Italian epigraph that begins the poem is a quotation from Dante's *Divine Comedy* (1321). In this passage, a damned soul in Hell who had sought absolution before committing a crime addresses Dante, thinking that his words will never reach the earth. He says: "If I thought that my answer were to someone who could ever return to the world, this flame would be still, without further motion. But because no one has ever returned alive from this depth, if what I hear is true, without fear of shame I answer you." [All notes are the editors'.]

Like a patient etherised upon a table;
Let us go, through certain half-deserted streets,
The muttering retreats   5
Of restless nights in one-night cheap hotels
And sawdust restaurants with oyster-shells:
Streets that follow like a tedious argument
Of insidious intent
To lead you to an overwhelming question . . .   10
Oh, do not ask, "What is it?"
Let us go and make our visit.

In the room the women come and go
Talking of Michelangelo.

The yellow fog that rubs its back upon the window-panes,   15
The yellow smoke that rubs its muzzle on the window-panes
Licked its tongue into the corners of the evening,
Lingered upon the pools that stand in drains,
Let fall upon its back the soot that falls from chimneys,
Slipped by the terrace, made a sudden leap,   20
And seeing that it was a soft October night,
Curled once about the house, and fell asleep.

And indeed there will be time
For the yellow smoke that slides along the street,
Rubbing its back upon the window-panes;   25
There will be time, there will be time
To prepare a face to meet the faces that you meet;
There will be time to murder and create,
And time for all the works and days° of hands
That lift and drop a question on your plate;   30
Time for you and time for me,
And time yet for a hundred indecisions,
And for a hundred visions and revisions,
Before the taking of a toast and tea.

In the room the women come and go   35
Talking of Michelangelo
And indeed there will be time
To wonder, "Do I dare?" and, "Do I dare?"
Time to turn back and descend the stair,
With a bald spot in the middle of my hair—   40
[They will say: "How his hair is growing thin!"]
My morning coat, my collar mounting firmly to the chin,
My necktie rich and modest, but asserted by a simple pin—

---

29 works and days The title of a poem on farm life by Hesiod (Greek, eighth century B.C.).

[They will say: "But how his arms and legs are thin!"]
Do I dare   45
Disturb the universe?
In a minute there is time
For decisions and revisions which a minute will reverse.

For I have known them all already, known them all:—
Have known the evenings, mornings, afternoons,   50
I have measured out my life with coffee spoons;
I know the voices dying with a dying fall°
Beneath the music from a farther room.
          So how should I presume?

And I have known the eyes already, known them all—   55
The eyes that fix you in a formulated phrase,
And when I am formulated, sprawling on a pin,
When I am pinned and wriggling on the wall,
Then how should I begin
To spit out all the butt-ends of my days and ways?   60
          And how should I presume?

And I have known the arms already, known them all—
Arms that are braceleted and white and bare
[But in the lamplight, downed with light brown hair!]
Is it perfume from a dress   65
That makes me so digress?
Arms that lie along a table, or wrap about a shawl.
          And should I then presume?
          And how should I begin?

                    . . . . .

Shall I say, I have gone at dusk through narrow streets   70
And watched the smoke that rises from the pipes
Of lonely men in shirt-sleeves, leaning out of windows? . . .

I should have been a pair of ragged claws
Scuttling across the floors of silent seas.

                    . . . . .

And the afternoon, the evening, sleeps so peacefully!   75
Smoothed by long fingers,
Asleep . . . tired . . . or it malingers,
Stretched on the floor, here beside you and me.
Should I, after tea and cakes and ices,
Have the strength to force the moment to its crisis?   80
But though I have wept and fasted, wept and prayed,

---

52 dying fall Echoes Shakespeare's *Twelfth Night* 1.1.4.

Though I have seen my head [grown slightly bald]
    brought in upon a platter,°
I am no prophet — and here's no great matter;
I have seen the moment of my greatness flicker,
And I have seen the eternal Footman hold my coat, and
    snicker,   85
And in short, I was afraid.

And would it have been worth it, after all,
After the cups, the marmalade, the tea,
Among the porcelain, among some talk of you and me,
Would it have been worth while,   90
To have bitten off the matter with a smile,
To have squeezed the universe into a ball
To roll° it toward some overwhelming question,
To say: "I am Lazarus,° come from the dead,
Come back to tell you all, I shall tell you all" —   95
If one, settling a pillow by her head,
    Should say: "That is not what I meant at all.
    That is not it, at all."

And would it have been worth it, after all,
Would it have been worth while,   100
After the sunsets and the dooryards and the sprinkled streets,
After the novels, after the teacups, after the skirts
    that trail along the floor —
And this, and so much more? —
It is impossible to say just what I mean!
But as if a magic lantern threw the nerves in patterns
    on a screen: 105
Would it have been worth while
If one, settling a pillow or throwing off a shawl,
And turning toward the window, should say:
    "That is not it at all,
    That is not what I meant, at all."   110

     · · · · ·

No! I am not Prince Hamlet,° nor was meant to be;

---

82 head ... platter Alludes to John the Baptist, whose head was delivered on a platter to Salome.   **92–93 ball to roll** Echoes Andrew Marvell's "To His Coy Mistress," lines 41–42 (see p. 441).   **94 Lazarus** Mentioned twice in the New Testament: Luke 16.19–31 tells of a poor man named Lazarus, who is carried by angels to Abraham's bosom, whereas a rich man is tormented in the underworld; the rich man, concerned about his brothers who are still on earth, asks Abraham to send Lazarus back to earth to warn them, but Abraham refuses. The other reference to Lazarus — possibly but not certainly the same man — is in John 11; this Lazarus rises from the dead at the command of Jesus. **111 Prince Hamlet** The next few lines allude to lesser figures in Shakespeare's tragedy, specifically to Polonius, a self-satisfied fatuous courtier.

Am an attendant lord, one that will do
To swell a progress, start a scene or two,
Advise the prince; no doubt, an easy tool.
Deferential, glad to be of use,   115
Politic, cautious, and meticulous;
Full of high sentence,° but a bit obtuse;
At times, indeed, almost ridiculous—
Almost, at times, the Fool.

I grow old . . . I grow old . . .   120
I shall wear the bottoms of my trousers rolled.

Shall I part my hair behind? Do I dare to eat a peach?
I shall wear white flannel trousers, and walk upon the beach.
I have heard the mermaids singing, each to each.
I do not think that they will sing to me.   125

I have seen them riding seaward on the waves
Combing the white hair of the waves blown back
When the wind blows the water white and black.

We have lingered in the chambers of the sea
By sea-girls wreathed with seaweed red and brown   130
Till human voices wake us, and we drown.

Topics for Critical Thinking and Writing

1. One of the most famous images of the poem compares the evening to "a patient etherised upon a table" (lines 2–3). Does the image also suggest that individuals—for instance, Prufrock—may not be fully conscious and therefore are not responsible for their actions or their inactions?

2. Are lines 57 to 60 meant to evoke the reader's pity for the speaker? If not, what (if any) response are these lines intended to evoke?

3. The speaker admits he is "At times, indeed, . . . / Almost . . . the Fool" (lines 118–19). Where, if at all, in the poem do we see him not at all as a fool?

4. Do you take the poem to be a criticism of an individual, a society, neither, or both? Why?

5. Evaluate this critical judgment, offering evidence to support your view: "The poem is obscure: It begins in Italian, and it includes references that most readers can't know. It is not at all uplifting. In fact, in so far as it is comprehensible, it is depressing. These are not the characteristics of a great poem."

---

117 full of high sentence Full of thoughtful sayings; comes from Chaucer's description of the Oxford student in *The Canterbury Tales.*

6. The poem is chiefly concerned with the thoughts of a man, J. Alfred Prufrock. Do you think it therefore is of more interest to men than to women? Explain.

7. The speaker describes the streets he walks as "follow[ing] like a tedious argument" (line 8). Is the simile apt? When do you think an argument becomes tedious?

Susan Glaspell

Susan Glaspell (1882–1948) was born in Davenport, Iowa, and educated at Drake University in Des Moines. In 1903 she married George Cram Cook and, with Cook and other writers, actors, and artists, in 1915 founded the Provincetown Players, a group that remained vital until 1929. Glaspell wrote Trifles *(1916) for the Provincetown Players, but she also wrote stories, novels, and a biography of her husband. In 1931 she won the Pulitzer Prize for* Alison's House, *a play about the family of a deceased poet who in some ways resembles Emily Dickinson.*

Trifles

(**SCENE:** *The kitchen in the now abandoned farmhouse of John Wright, a gloomy kitchen, and left without having been put in order—unwashed pans under the sink, a loaf of bread outside the breadbox, a dish towel on the table—other signs of incompleted work. At the rear the outer door opens, and the Sheriff comes in, followed by the County Attorney and Hale. The Sheriff and Hale are men in middle life, the County Attorney is a young man; all are much bundled up and go at once to the stove. They are followed by the two women—the Sheriff's Wife first; she is a slight wiry woman, a thin nervous face. Mrs. Hale is larger and would ordinarily be called more comfortable looking, but she is disturbed now and looks fearfully about as she enters. The women have come in slowly and stand close together near the door.*)

COUNTY ATTORNEY *(rubbing his hands)*. This feels good. Come up to the fire, ladies.

MRS. PETERS *(after taking a step forward)*. I'm not—cold.

SHERIFF *(unbuttoning his overcoat and stepping away from the stove as if to the beginning of official business)*. Now, Mr. Hale, before we move things about, you explain to Mr. Henderson just what you saw when you came here yesterday morning.

COUNTY ATTORNEY. By the way, has anything been moved? Are things just as you left them yesterday?

SHERIFF *(looking about)*. It's just the same. When it dropped below zero   5 last night, I thought I'd better send Frank out this morning to make a fire for us—no use getting pneumonia with a big case on; but I told him not to touch anything except the stove—and you know Frank.

COUNTY ATTORNEY. Somebody should have been left here yesterday.

SHERIFF. Oh—yesterday. When I had to send Frank to Morris Center for that man who went crazy—I want you to know I had my hands full yesterday. I knew you could get back from Omaha by today, and as long as I went over everything here myself—

COUNTY ATTORNEY. Well, Mr. Hale, tell just what happened when you came here yesterday morning.

HALE. Harry and I had started to town with a load of potatoes. We came along the road from my place; and as I got here, I said, "I'm going to see if I can't get John Wright to go in with me on a party telephone." I spoke to Wright about it once before, and he put me off, saying folks talked too much anyway, and all he asked was peace and quiet—I guess you know about how much he talked himself; but I thought maybe if I went to the house and talked about it before his wife, though I said to Harry that I didn't know as what his wife wanted made much difference to John—

COUNTY ATTORNEY. Let's talk about that later, Mr. Hale. I do want to talk 10 about that, but tell now just what happened when you got to the house.

HALE. I didn't hear or see anything; I knocked at the door, and still it was all quiet inside. I knew they must be up, it was past eight o'clock. So I knocked again, and I thought I heard somebody say, "Come in." I wasn't sure, I'm not sure yet, but I opened the door—this door *(indicating the door by which the two women are still standing)*, and there in that rocker—*(pointing to it)* sat Mrs. Wright. *(They all look at the rocker.)*

COUNTY ATTORNEY. What—was she doing?

HALE. She was rockin' back and forth. She had her apron in her hand and was kind of—pleating it.

COUNTY ATTORNEY. And how did she—look?

HALE. Well, she looked queer. 15

COUNTY ATTORNEY. How do you mean—queer?

HALE. Well, as if she didn't know what she was going to do next. And kind of done up.

COUNTY ATTORNEY. How did she seem to feel about your coming?

HALE. Why, I don't think she minded—one way or other. She didn't pay much attention. I said, "How do, Mrs. Wright, it's cold, ain't it?" And she said, "Is it?"—and went on kind of pleating at her apron. Well, I was surprised; she didn't ask me to come up to the stove, or to set down, but just sat there, not even looking at me, so I said, "I want to see John." And then she—laughed. I guess you would call it a laugh. I thought of Harry and the team outside, so I said a little sharp: "Can't I see John?" "No," she says, kind o' dull like. "Ain't he home?" says I. "Yes," says she, "he's home." "Then why can't I see him?" I asked her, out of patience. "'Cause he's dead," says she. "*Dead?*" says I. She just nodded her head, not getting a bit excited, but rockin' back and forth. "Why—where is he?" says I, not knowing what to say. She just pointed upstairs—like that *(himself pointing to the room above)*. I got up, with the idea of going up there. I walked from there to here—then I says, "Why, what did he die of?" "He died of a rope around his neck," says she, and just went on pleatin' at her apron. Well, I went out and called Harry. I thought I might—need help. We went upstairs, and there he was lyin'—

COUNTY ATTORNEY. I think I'd rather have you go into that upstairs, where   20
you can point it all out. Just go on now with the rest of the story.

HALE. Well, my first thought was to get that rope off. I looked . . . *(Stops, his face twitches.)* . . . but Harry, he went up to him, and he said, "No, he's dead all right, and we'd better not touch anything." So we went back downstairs. She was still sitting that same way. "Has anybody been notified?" I asked. "No," says she, unconcerned. "Who did this, Mrs. Wright?" said Harry. He said it businesslike—and she stopped pleatin' of her apron. "I don't know," she says. "You don't *know*?" says Harry. "No," says she. "Weren't you sleepin' in the bed with him?" says Harry. "Yes," says she, "but I was on the inside." "Somebody slipped a rope round his neck and strangled him, and you didn't wake up?" says Harry. "I didn't wake up," she said after him. We must 'a looked as if we didn't see how that could be, for after a minute she said, "I sleep sound." Harry was going to ask her more questions, but I said maybe we ought to let her tell her story first to the coroner, or the sheriff, so Harry went fast as he could to Rivers' place, where there's a telephone.

COUNTY ATTORNEY. And what did Mrs. Wright do when she knew that you had gone for the coroner?

HALE. She moved from that chair to this over here . . . *(Pointing to a small chair in the corner.)* . . . and just sat there with her hands held together and looking down. I got a feeling that I ought to make some conversation, so I said I had come in to see if John wanted to put in a telephone, and at that she started to laugh, and then she stopped and looked at me—scared. *(The County Attorney, who has had his notebook out, makes a note.)* I dunno, maybe it wasn't scared. I wouldn't like to say it was. Soon Harry got back, and then Dr. Lloyd came, and you, Mr. Peters, and so I guess that's all I know that you don't.

COUNTY ATTORNEY *(looking around)*. I guess we'll go upstairs first—and then out to the barn and around there. *(To the Sheriff.)* You're convinced that there was nothing important here—nothing that would point to any motive?

SHERIFF. Nothing here but kitchen things. *(The County Attorney, after again*   25
looking around the kitchen, opens the door of a cupboard closet. He gets up on a chair and looks on a shelf. Pulls his hand away, sticky.)

COUNTY ATTORNEY. Here's a nice mess. *(The women draw nearer.)*

MRS. PETERS *(to the other woman)*. Oh, her fruit; it did freeze. *(To the Lawyer.)* She worried about that when it turned so cold. She said the fire'd go out and her jars would break.

SHERIFF. Well, can you beat the women! Held for murder and worryin' about her preserves.

COUNTY ATTORNEY. I guess before we're through she may have something more serious than preserves to worry about.

HALE. Well, women are used to worrying over trifles. *(The two women* 30 *move a little closer together.)*

COUNTY ATTORNEY *(with the gallantry of a young politician).* And yet, for all their worries, what would we do without the ladies? *(The women do not unbend. He goes to the sink, takes a dipperful of water from the pail and, pouring it into a basin, washes his hands. Starts to wipe them on the roller towel, turns it for a cleaner place.)* Dirty towels! *(Kicks his foot against the pans under the sink.)* Not much of a housekeeper, would you say, ladies?

MRS. HALE *(stiffly).* There's a great deal of work to be done on a farm.

COUNTY ATTORNEY. To be sure. And yet . . . *(With a little bow to her.)* . . . I know there are some Dickson county farmhouses which do not have such roller towels. *(He gives it a pull to expose its full length again.)*

MRS. HALE. Those towels get dirty awful quick. Men's hands aren't always as clean as they might be.

COUNTY ATTORNEY. Ah, loyal to your sex, I see. But you and Mrs. Wright 35 were neighbors. I suppose you were friends, too.

MRS. HALE *(shaking her head).* I've not seen much of her of late years. I've not been in this house — it's more than a year.

COUNTY ATTORNEY. And why was that? You didn't like her?

MRS. HALE. I liked her all well enough. Farmers' wives have their hands full, Mr. Henderson. And then —

COUNTY ATTORNEY. Yes — ?

MRS. HALE *(looking about).* It never seemed a very cheerful place.   40

COUNTY ATTORNEY. No — it's not cheerful. I shouldn't say she had the homemaking instinct.

MRS. HALE. Well, I don't know as Wright had, either.

COUNTY ATTORNEY. You mean they didn't get on very well?

MRS. HALE. No, I don't mean anything. But I don't think a place'd be any cheerfuller for John Wright's being in it.

COUNTY ATTORNEY. I'd like to talk more of that a little later. I want to get 45 the lay of things upstairs now. *(He goes to the left, where three steps lead to a stair door.)*

SHERIFF. I suppose anything Mrs. Peters does'll be all right. She was to take in some clothes for her, you know, and a few little things. We left in such a hurry yesterday.

COUNTY ATTORNEY. Yes, but I would like to see what you take, Mrs. Peters, and keep an eye out for anything that might be of use to us.

MRS. PETERS. Yes, Mr. Henderson. *(The women listen to the men's steps on the stairs, then look about the kitchen.)*

MRS. HALE. I'd hate to have men coming into my kitchen, snooping around and criticizing. *(She arranges the pans under the sink which the Lawyer had shoved out of place.)*

MRS. PETERS. Of course it's no more than their duty.   50

MRS. HALE. Duty's all right, but I guess that deputy sheriff that came out to make the fire might have got a little of this on. *(Gives the roller towel a pull.)* Wish I'd thought of that sooner. Seems mean to talk about her for not having things slicked up when she had to come away in such a hurry.

MRS. PETERS *(who has gone to a small table in the left rear corner of the room, and lifted one end of a towel that covers a pan).* She had bread set. *(Stands still.)*

MRS. HALE *(eyes fixed on a loaf of bread beside the breadbox, which is on a low shelf at the other side of the room. Moves slowly toward it).* She was going to put this in there. *(Picks up loaf, then abruptly drops it. In a manner of returning to familiar things.)* It's a shame about her fruit. I wonder if it's all gone. *(Gets up on the chair and looks.)* I think there's some here that's all right, Mrs. Peters. Yes—here; *(Holding it toward the window.)* this is cherries, too. *(Looking again.)* I declare I believe that's the only one. *(Gets down, bottle in her hand. Goes to the sink and wipes it off on the outside.)* She'll feel awful bad after all her hard work in the hot weather. I remember the afternoon I put up my cherries last sum- mer. *(She puts the bottle on the big kitchen table, center of the room. With a sigh, is about to sit down in the rocking chair. Before she is seated realizes what chair it is; with a slow look at it, steps back. The chair, which she has touched, rocks back and forth.)*

MRS. PETERS. Well, I must get those things from the front room closet. *(She goes to the door at the right, but after looking into the other room steps back.)* You coming with me, Mrs. Hale? You could help me carry them. *(They go into the other room; reappear, Mrs. Peters carrying a dress and skirt, Mrs. Hale following with a pair of shoes.)*

MRS. PETERS. My, it's cold in there. *(She puts the cloth on the big table, and* 55
hurries to the stove.)

MRS. HALE *(examining the skirt).* Wright was close. I think maybe that's why she kept so much to herself. She didn't even belong to the Ladies' Aid. I suppose she felt she couldn't do her part, and then you don't enjoy things when you feel shabby. She used to wear pretty clothes and be lively, when she was Minnie Foster, one of the town girls singing in the choir. But that—oh, that was thirty years ago. This all you was to take in?

MRS. PETERS. She said she wanted an apron. Funny thing to want, for there isn't much to get you dirty in jail, goodness knows. But I sup- pose just to make her feel more natural. She said they was in the top drawer in this cupboard. Yes, here. And then her little shawl that al- ways hung behind the door. *(Opens stair door and looks.)* Yes, here it is. *(Quickly shuts door leading upstairs.)*

MRS. HALE *(abruptly moving toward her).* Mrs. Peters?

MRS. PETERS. Yes, Mrs. Hale?

MRS. HALE. Do you think she did it?   60

MRS. PETERS *(in a frightened voice)*. Oh, I don't know.

MRS. HALE. Well, I don't think she did. Asking for an apron and her little shawl. Worrying about her fruit.

MRS. PETERS *(starts to speak, glances up, where footsteps are heard in the room above. In a low voice)*. Mr. Peters says it looks bad for her. Mr. Henderson is awful sarcastic in speech, and he'll make fun of her sayin' she didn't wake up.

MRS. HALE. Well, I guess John Wright didn't wake when they was slipping that rope under his neck.

MRS. PETERS. No, it's strange. It must have been done awful crafty and 65
still. They say it was such a—funny way to kill a man, rigging it all up like that.

MRS. HALE. That's just what Mr. Hale said. There was a gun in the house. He says that's what he can't understand.

MRS. PETERS. Mr. Henderson said coming out that what was needed for the case was a motive; something to show anger or—sudden feeling.

MRS. HALE *(who is standing by the table)*. Well, I don't see any signs of anger around here. *(She puts her hand on the dish towel which lies on the table, stands looking down at the table, one half of which is clean, the other half messy.)* It's wiped here. *(Makes a move as if to finish work, then turns and looks at loaf of bread outside the breadbox. Drops towel. In that voice of coming back to familiar things.)* Wonder how they are finding things upstairs? I hope she had it a little more red-up there. You know, it seems kind of *sneaking*. Locking her up in town and then coming out here and trying to get her own house to turn against her!

MRS. PETERS. But, Mrs. Hale, the law is the law.

MRS. HALE. I s'pose 'tis. *(Unbuttoning her coat.)* Better loosen up your 70
things, Mrs. Peters. You won't feel them when you go out. *(Mrs. Peters takes off her fur tippet, goes to hang it on hook at the back of room, stands looking at the under part of the small corner table.)*

MRS. PETERS. She was piecing a quilt. *(She brings the large sewing basket, and they look at the bright pieces.)*

MRS. HALE. It's log cabin pattern. Pretty, isn't it? I wonder if she was goin' to quilt or just knot it? *(Footsteps have been heard coming down the stairs. The Sheriff enters, followed by Hale and the County Attorney.)*

SHERIFF. They wonder if she was going to quilt it or just knot it. *(The men laugh, the women look abashed.)*

COUNTY ATTORNEY *(rubbing his hands over the stove)*. Frank's fire didn't do much up there, did it? Well, let's go out to the barn and get that cleared up. *(The men go outside.)*

MRS. HALE *(resentfully)*. I don't know as there's anything so strange, our 75
takin' up our time with little things while we're waiting for them to get the evidence. *(She sits down at the big table, smoothing out a block with decision.)* I don't see as it's anything to laugh about.

MRS. PETERS *(apologetically)*. Of course they've got awful important things on their minds. *(Pulls up a chair and joins Mrs. Hale at the table.)*

MRS. HALE (*examining another block*). Mrs. Peters, look at this one. Here, this is the one she was working on, and look at the sewing! All the rest of it has been so nice and even. And look at this! It's all over the place! Why, it looks as if she didn't know what she was about! (*After she has said this, they look at each other, then start to glance back at the door. After an instant Mrs. Hale has pulled at a knot and ripped the sewing.*)

MRS. PETERS. Oh, what are you doing, Mrs. Hale?

MRS. HALE (*mildly*). Just pulling out a stitch or two that's not sewed very good. (*Threading a needle.*) Bad sewing always made me fidgety.

MRS. PETERS (*nervously*). I don't think we ought to touch things.   80

MRS. HALE. I'll just finish up this end. (*Suddenly stopping and leaning forward.*) Mrs. Peters?

MRS. PETERS. Yes, Mrs. Hale?

MRS. HALE. What do you suppose she was so nervous about?

MRS. PETERS. Oh—I don't know. I don't know as she was nervous. I sometimes sew awful queer when I'm just tired. (*Mrs. Hale starts to say something, looks at Mrs. Peters, then goes on sewing.*) Well, I must get these things wrapped up. They may be through sooner than we think. (*Putting apron and other things together.*) I wonder where I can find a piece of paper, and string.

MRS. HALE. In that cupboard, maybe.   85

MRS. PETERS (*looking in cupboard*). Why, here's a birdcage. (*Holds it up.*) Did she have a bird, Mrs. Hale?

MRS. HALE. Why, I don't know whether she did or not—I've not been here for so long. There was a man around last year selling canaries cheap, but I don't know as she took one; maybe she did. She used to sing real pretty herself.

MRS. PETERS (*glancing around*). Seems funny to think of a bird here. But she must have had one, or why should she have a cage? I wonder what happened to it?

MRS. HALE. I s'pose maybe the cat got it.

MRS. PETERS. No, she didn't have a cat. She's got that feeling some people   90
have about cats—being afraid of them. My cat got in her room, and she was real upset and asked me to take it out.

MRS. HALE. My sister Bessie was like that. Queer, ain't it?

MRS. PETERS (*examining the cage*). Why, look at this door. It's broke. One hinge is pulled apart.

MRS. HALE (*looking, too*). Looks as if someone must have been rough with it.

MRS. PETERS. Why, yes. (*She brings the cage forward and puts it on the table.*)

MRS. HALE. I wish if they're going to find any evidence they'd be about it.   95
I don't like this place.

MRS. PETERS. But I'm awful glad you came with me, Mrs. Hale. It would be lonesome for me sitting here alone.

MRS. HALE. It would, wouldn't it? (*Dropping her sewing.*) But I tell you what I do wish, Mrs. Peters. I wish I had come over sometimes when *she* was here. I—(*Looking around the room.*)—wish I had.

MRS. PETERS. But of course you were awful busy, Mrs. Hale—your house and your children.

MRS. HALE. I could've come. I stayed away because it weren't cheerful—and that's why I ought to have come. I—I've never liked this place. Maybe because it's down in a hollow, and you don't see the road. I dunno what it is, but it's a lonesome place and always was. I wish I had come over to see Minnie Foster sometimes. I can see now— *(Shakes her head.)*

MRS. PETERS. Well, you mustn't reproach yourself, Mrs. Hale. Somehow we   100
just don't see how it is with other folks until—something comes up.

MRS. HALE. Not having children makes less work—but it makes a quiet house, and Wright out to work all day, and no company when he did come in. Did you know John Wright, Mrs. Peters?

MRS. PETERS. Not to know him; I've seen him in town. They say he was a good man.

MRS. HALE. Yes—good; he didn't drink, and kept his word as well as most, I guess, and paid his debts. But he was a hard man, Mrs. Peters. Just to pass the time of day with him. *(Shivers.)* Like a raw wind that gets to the bone. *(Pauses, her eye falling on the cage.)* I should think she would 'a' wanted a bird. But what do you suppose went with it?

MRS. PETERS. I don't know, unless it got sick and died. *(She reaches over and swings the broken door, swings it again; both women watch it.)*

MRS. HALE. You weren't raised around here, were you? *(Mrs. Peters shakes*   105
her head.) You didn't know—her?

MRS. PETERS. Not till they brought her yesterday.

MRS. HALE. She—come to think of it, she was kind of like a bird herself—real sweet and pretty, but kind of timid and—fluttery. How—she—did—change. *(Silence; then as if struck by a happy thought and relieved to get back to everyday things.)* Tell you what, Mrs. Peters, why don't you take the quilt in with you? It might take up her mind.

MRS. PETERS. Why, I think that's a real nice idea, Mrs. Hale. There couldn't possible be any objection to it, could there? Now, just what would I take? I wonder if her patches are in here—and her things. *(They look in the sewing basket.)*

MRS. HALE. Here's some red. I expect this has got sewing things in it. *(Brings out a fancy box.)* What a pretty box. Looks like something somebody would give you. Maybe her scissors are in here. *(Opens box. Suddenly puts her hand to her nose.)* Why— *(Mrs. Peters bends nearer, then turns her face away.)* There's something wrapped up in this piece of silk.

MRS. PETERS. Why, this isn't her scissors.   110

MRS. HALE *(lifting the silk)*. Oh, Mrs. Peters—it's— *(Mrs. Peters bends closer.)*

MRS. PETERS. It's the bird.

MRS. HALE *(jumping up)*. But, Mrs. Peters—look at it. Its neck! Look at its neck! It's all—other side *to*.

MRS. PETERS. Somebody—wrung—its neck. *(Their eyes meet. A look of growing comprehension of horror. Steps are heard outside. Mrs. Hale slips box under quilt pieces, and sinks into her chair. Enter Sheriff and County Attorney, Mrs. Peters rises.)*

COUNTY ATTORNEY *(as one turning from serious things to little pleasantries).* 115
Well, ladies, have you decided whether she was going to quilt it or knot it?

MRS. PETERS. We think she was going to—knot it.

COUNTY ATTORNEY. Well, that's interesting, I'm sure. *(Seeing the birdcage.)*
Has the bird flown?

MRS. HALE *(putting more quilt pieces over the box).* We think the—cat got it.

COUNTY ATTORNEY *(preoccupied).* Is there a cat? *(Mrs. Hale glances in a quick covert way at Mrs. Peters.)*

MRS. PETERS. Well, not now. They're superstitious, you know. They leave. 120

COUNTY ATTORNEY *(to Sheriff Peters, continuing an interrupted conversation).* No
sign at all of anyone having come from the outside. Their own rope.
Now let's go up again and go over it piece by piece. *(They start upstairs.)* It would have to have been someone who knew just the—
*(Mrs. Peters sits down. The two women sit there not looking at one another,
but as if peering into something and at the same time holding back. When
they talk now, it is the manner of feeling their way over strange ground, as if
afraid of what they are saying, but as if they cannot help saying it.)*

MRS. HALE. She liked the bird. She was going to bury it in that pretty box.

MRS. PETERS *(in a whisper).* When I was a girl—my kitten—there was a
boy took a hatchet, and before my eyes—and before I could get
there—*(Covers her face an instant.)* If they hadn't held me back, I
would have—*(Catches herself, looks upstairs where steps are heard, falters
weakly.)*—hurt him.

MRS. HALE *(with a slow look around her).* I wonder how it would seem
never to have had any children around. *(Pause.)* No, Wright
wouldn't like the bird—a thing that sang. She used to sing. He killed
that, too.

MRS. PETERS *(moving uneasily).* We don't know who killed the bird.   125

MRS. HALE. I knew John Wright.

MRS. PETERS. It was an awful thing was done in this house that night,
Mrs. Hale. Killing a man while he slept, slipping a rope around his
neck that choked the life out of him.

MRS. HALE. His neck. Choked the life out of him. *(Her hand goes out and
rests on the birdcage.)*

MRS. PETERS *(with a rising voice).* We don't know who killed him. We don't
know.

MRS. HALE *(her own feeling not interrupted).* If there'd been years and years 130
of nothing, then a bird to sing to you, it would be awful—still, after
the bird was still.

MRS. PETERS *(something within her speaking).* I know what stillness is. When
we homesteaded in Dakota, and my first baby died—after he was
two years old, and me with no other then—

MRS. HALE *(moving).* How soon do you suppose they'll be through, looking for evidence?

MRS. PETERS. I know what stillness is. *(Pulling herself back.)* The law has got to punish crime, Mrs. Hale.

MRS. HALE *(not as if answering that)*. I wish you'd seen Minnie Foster when she wore a white dress with blue ribbons and stood up there in the choir and sang. *(A look around the room.)* Oh, I *wish* I'd come over here once in a while! That was a crime! That was a crime! Who's going to punish that?

MRS. PETERS *(looking upstairs)*. We mustn't—take on.   135

MRS. HALE. I might have known she needed help! I know how things can be—for women. I tell you, it's queer, Mrs. Peters. We live close together and we live far apart. We all go through the same things—it's all just a different kind of the same thing. *(Brushes her eyes, noticing the bottle of fruit, reaches out for it.)* If I was you, I wouldn't tell her her fruit was gone. Tell her it *ain't*. Tell her it's all right. Take this in to prove it to her. She—she may never know whether it was broke or not.

MRS. PETERS *(takes the bottle, looks about for something to wrap it in; takes petticoat from the clothes brought from the other room, very nervously begins winding this around the bottle. In a false voice)*. My, it's a good thing the men couldn't hear us. Wouldn't they just laugh! Getting all stirred up over a little thing like a—dead canary. As if that could have anything to do with—with—wouldn't they *laugh!* (The men are heard coming downstairs.)

MRS. HALE *(under her breath)*. Maybe they would—maybe they wouldn't.

COUNTY ATTORNEY. No, Peters, it's all perfectly clear except a reason for doing it. But you know juries when it comes to women. If there was some definite thing. Something to show—something to make a story about—a thing that would connect up with this strange way of doing it. *(The women's eyes meet for an instant. Enter Hale from outer door.)*

HALE. Well, I've got the team around. Pretty cold out there.   140

COUNTY ATTORNEY. I'm going to stay here a while by myself. *(To the Sheriff.)* You can send Frank out for me, can't you? I want to go over everything. I'm not satisfied that we can't do better.

SHERIFF. Do you want to see what Mrs. Peters is going to take in? *(The Lawyer goes to the table, picks up the apron, laughs.)*

COUNTY ATTORNEY. Oh, I guess they're not very dangerous things the ladies have picked up. *(Moves a few things about, disturbing the quilt pieces which cover the box. Steps back.)* No, Mrs. Peters doesn't need supervising. For that matter, a sheriff's wife is married to the law. Ever think of it that way, Mrs. Peters?

MRS. PETERS. Not—just that way.

SHERIFF *(chuckling)*. Married to the law. *(Moves toward the other room.)* I just   145
want you to come in here a minute, George. We ought to take a look at these windows.

COUNTY ATTORNEY *(scoffingly)*. Oh, windows!

SHERIFF. We'll be right out, Mr. Hale. *(Hale goes outside. The Sheriff follows the County Attorney into the other room. Then Mrs. Hale rises, hands tight together, looking intensely at Mrs. Peters, whose eyes take a slow turn, finally meeting Mrs. Hale's. A moment Mrs. Hale holds her, then her own eyes point the way to where the box is concealed. Suddenly Mrs. Peters throws back quilt pieces and tries to put the box in the bag she is carrying. It is too big. She opens box, starts to take the bird out, cannot touch it, goes to pieces, stands there helpless. Sound of a knob turning in the other room. Mrs. Hale snatches the box and puts it in the pocket of her big coat. Enter County Attorney and Sheriff.)*

COUNTY ATTORNEY *(facetiously)*. Well, Henry, at least we found out that she was not going to quilt it. She was going to—what is it you call it, ladies?

MRS. HALE *(her hand against her pocket)*. We call it—knot it, Mr. Henderson.

Topics for Critical Thinking and Writing

1. Obviously the dead canary in the box isn't evidence that Mrs. Wright has killed her husband. So what is the point of the dead canary in the play?

2. Do you think the play is immoral? Explain.

3. Assume that Minnie is indicted for murder and that you are asked to serve as Minnie's defense lawyer. If you somehow know that the evidence of the canary has been suppressed, would you accept the case? Why, or why not? (It is unlawful for *prosecutors* to suppress evidence, but it is not unlawful for defense lawyers to withhold incriminating evidence that they are aware of.)

4. Assume that you have accepted Minnie's case. In 500 words set forth the defense you will offer for her. (Take any position that you wish. You may, for example, argue that she committed justifiable homicide or that—on the basis of her behavior as reported by Mr. Hale—she is innocent by reason of insanity.)

5. Assume that Minnie has been found guilty. Compose the speech she might give before being sentenced.

6. "*Trifles* is badly dated. It cannot speak to today's audience." In an essay of 500 words evaluate this view: Offer an argument supporting or rejecting it, or take a middle position.

Mitsuye Yamada

Mitsuye Yamada, the daughter of Japanese immigrants to the United States, was born in Japan in 1923, during her mother's return visit to her native land. Yamada was raised in Seattle, but in 1942 she and her family were incarcerated and then relocated to a camp in Idaho, when Executive Order 9066 (signed by President Franklin D. Roosevelt in 1941) gave military authorities the right to remove any and all persons from "military areas." In 1954 she became an American citizen. A professor of English at Cypress Junior College in San Luis Obispo, California, Yamada is the author of poems and stories.

Yamada's poem concerns the compliant response to Executive Order 9066, which brought about the incarceration and relocation of the entire Japanese and Japanese American population on the Pacific coast — about 112,000 people. More than two-thirds of the people moved were native-born citizens of the United States. (The 158,000 Japanese residents of the Territory of Hawaii were not affected.) There was virtually no protest at the time, but in recent years the order has been widely regarded as an outrageous infringement on liberty, and some younger Japanese Americans cannot fathom why their parents and grandparents complied with it. This poem first appeared in Camp Notes and Other Poems *in 1976.*

To the Lady

The one in San Francisco who asked:
Why did the Japanese Americans let
the government put them in
those camps without protest?

Come to think of it I   5
    should've run off to Canada
    should've hijacked a plane to Algeria
    should've pulled myself up from my
    bra straps
    and kicked'm in the groin   10
    should've bombed a bank
    should've tried self-immolation
    should've holed myself up in a
    woodframe house
    and let you watch me   15
    burn up on the six o'clock news
    should've run howling down the street
    naked and assaulted you at breakfast
    by AP wirephoto
    should've screamed bloody murder   20
    like Kitty Genovese°

    Then
YOU would've
    come to my aid in shining armor
    laid yourself across the railroad track   25

---

21 Kitty Genovese In 1964 Kitty Genovese of Kew Gardens, New York, was stabbed to death when she left her car and walked toward her home. Thirty-eight persons heard her screams, but no one came to her assistance. [Editors' note.]

marched on Washington
tattooed a Star of David on your arm
written six million enraged
letters to Congress

But we didn't draw the line   30
anywhere
law and order Executive Order 9066
social order moral order internal order

YOU let'm
I let'm   35
All are punished.

Topics for Critical Thinking and Writing

1. Has the lady's question (lines 2–4) ever crossed your mind? If so, what answers did you think of?

2. What, in effect, is the speaker really saying in lines 5 to 21? And in lines 22 to 29?

3. What possible arguments can you offer for and against the removal of Japanese Americans in 1942?

4. Do you think the survivors of the relocation are entitled to some sort of redress? Why, or why not? If you think they merit compensation, what should the compensation be?

29

What Are the Grounds of Religious Faith?

The Hebrew Bible

Among the books in the Hebrew Bible (usually called the Old Testament by Christians) is the Book of Psalms (psalm is from the Greek psalmoi, songs of praise), or the Psalter (Greek, psalterion, a stringed instrument). The Book of Psalms contains about 150 songs, prayers, and meditations. The number is a bit imprecise for several reasons: For instance, in the Hebrew Bible the numbering from Psalm 10 to Psalm 148 is one digit ahead of the numbering in Bibles used in the Christian church, which joins 9 and 10, and 114 and 115, but which divides both 116 and 147 into two.

The Hebrew text attributes seventy-three of the psalms to David, who reigned circa 1010–970 B.C. David is said to have been a musician (1 Samuel 16:23; Amos 6:5), but these attributions are no longer accepted by scholars, who point out that although some of the psalms may indeed go back to the tenth century B.C., some others may be as late as 200 B.C. The book in fact is a compilation of earlier collections from hundreds of years of Hebrew history.

The psalms are of various types—for instance, lamentations, songs of thanksgiving, songs of sacred history, and songs of praise. Psalm 19 is a song of praise. We give it in the King James Version (1611); later translations are recognized as more accurate, but none is regarded as the literary equal of the King James Version.

Psalm 19

The heavens declare the glory of God; and the firmament[1] sheweth his handywork.

---

[1]**firmament** Dome of the sky. [All notes are the editors'.]

2 Day unto day uttereth speech, and night unto night sheweth knowledge.

3 There is no speech nor language, where their voice is not heard.

4 Their line is gone out through all the earth, and their words to the end of the world. In them hath he set a tabernacle for the sun,

5 Which is as a bridegroom coming out of his chamber, and rejoiceth as a strong man to run a race.

6 His going forth is from the end of the heaven, and his circuit unto the ends of it: and there is nothing hid from the heat thereof.

7 The law of the Lord is perfect, converting the soul: the testimony of the Lord is sure, making wise the simple.

8 The statutes of the Lord are right, rejoicing the heart: the commandment of the Lord is pure, enlightening the eyes.

9 The fear[2] of the Lord is clean, enduring for ever: the judgments of the Lord are true and righteous altogether.

10 More to be desired are they than gold, yea, than much fine gold: sweeter also than honey and the honeycomb.

11 Moreover by them is thy servant warned: and in keeping of them there is great reward.

12 Who can understand his errors? cleanse thou me from secret faults.[3]

13 Keep back thy servant also from presumptuous sins; let them not have dominion over me: then shall I be upright, and I shall be innocent from the great transgression.

14 Let the words of my mouth, and the meditation of my heart, be acceptable in thy sight, O Lord, my strength, and my redeemer.

Topics for Critical Thinking and Writing

1. In Psalm 19, probably most readers will agree about the structure of the poem: verses 1 to 6 are on nature, 7 to 11 are on the law, and 12 to 14 are a prayer. How might you state the *argument* of verses 1 to 6? Of verses 7 to 11?

2. Do you think these three units cohere into a whole? For instance, does it make sense to say that the second unit is connected to the first by the idea that just as nothing is hidden from the heat of the sun (6), in like manner "the law of the Lord" is everywhere? Is such a reading appropriate, or is it strained? Explain.

[2]**fear** Often emended in later translations to *word*.
[3]**secret faults** Unconscious violations of God's will.

Paul

Paul (A.D. 5?–67?), known as Saul before his conversion from Judaism to Christianity, was a native of Tarsus, a commercial town in the land that is now Turkey. Tarsus was part of the Roman empire, and Saul, though a Jew, was a Roman citizen. After attending a rabbinical school in Jerusalem, Saul set out for Damascus in A.D. 33 or 34 to suppress Christianity there, but on the way he saw a blinding light, heard the voice of Jesus, and experienced a conversion, described in Acts of the Apostles 9:1–22. In later years he traveled widely, preaching Christianity to Jews and gentiles. Between 59 and 61 he was imprisoned in Rome, and he may have been convicted and executed, but nothing certain is known about his death.

Paul seems to have been the first Christian missionary to Corinth, a Roman colony in Greece, a little to the west of Athens. After his initial visit, probably from 50 to 52, he is reported to have gone to Judea, Syria, Ephesus, and elsewhere. While at Ephesus, however, he heard reports of disorders in Corinth. His letter of response, probably written in about 54, was incorporated into the New Testament as 1 Corinthians, one of his two extant epistles addressed to the Christian community at Corinth. From this letter we reprint Chapter 15.

It is not entirely clear what doctrine(s) of resurrection Paul is opposing in this passage. Perhaps some members of the church did not believe in any form of life after death; perhaps others believed that the resurrection took place at baptism; and perhaps others debated the nature of the resurrection body.

The Interpreter's Bible, 10:12, outlines the fifty-eight verses of Chapter 15 thus:

A. *The resurrection of Jesus (1–19)*
  1. *The tradition concerning the fact (1–11)*
  2. *The significancy of the resurrection (12–19)*
B. *The eschatological drama [i.e., concern with ultimate things, such as death and heaven] (20–34)*
  1. *The order of events (20–28)*
  2. *Ad hominem rebuttal (29–34)*
C. *The resurrection body (35–50)*
  1. *Various types of body (35–41)*
  2. *A spiritual body (42–50)*
D. *The Christian confidence (51–58)*

The translation used here is the Authorized Version (1611), also known as the King James Version.

1 Corinthians 15

Moreover, brethren, I declare unto you the gospel which I preached unto you, which also ye have received, and wherein ye stand;

2 By which also ye are saved, if we keep in memory what I preached unto you, unless ye have believed in vain.

3 For I delivered unto you first of all that which I also received, how that Christ died for our sins according to the scriptures;

4 And that he was buried, and that he rose again the third day according to the scriptures:

5 And that he was seen of Cephas, then of the twelve:

6 After that, he was seen of above five hundred brethren at once; of whom the greater part remain unto this present, but some are fallen asleep.

7 After that, he was seen of James; then of all the apostles.

8 And last of all he was seen of me also, as of one born out of due time.

9 For I am the least of the apostles, that am not meet to be called an apostle, because I persecuted the church of God.

10 But by the grace of God I am what I am: and his grace which was bestowed upon me was not in vain; but I laboured more abundantly than they all: yet not I, but the grace of God which was with me.

11 Therefore whether it were I or they, so we preach, and so ye believed.

12 Now if Christ be preached that he rose from the dead, how say some among you that there is no resurrection of the dead?

13 But if there be no resurrection of the dead, then is Christ not risen:

14 And if Christ be not risen, then is our preaching vain, and your faith is also vain.

15 Yea, and we are found false witnesses of God; because we have testified of God that he raised up Christ: whom he raised not up, if so be that the dead rise not.

16 For if the dead rise not, then is not Christ raised:

17 And if Christ be not raised, your faith is vain; ye are yet in your sins.

18 Then they also which are fallen asleep in Christ are perished.

19 If in this life only we have hope in Christ, we are of all men most miserable.

20 But now is Christ risen from the dead, and become the first fruits of them that slept.

21 For since by man came death, by man came also the resurrection of the dead.

22 For as in Adam all die, even so in Christ shall all be made alive.

23 But every man in his own order: Christ the first fruits; afterward they that are Christ's at his coming.

24 Then cometh the end, when he shall have delivered up the kingdom to God, even the Father; when he shall have put down all rule and all authority and power.

25 For he must reign, till he hath put all enemies under his feet.

26 The last enemy that shall be destroyed is death.

27 For he hath put all things under his feet. But when he saith all things are put under him, it is manifest that he is excepted, which did put all things under him.

28 And when all things shall be subdued unto him, then shall the Son also himself be subject unto him that put all things under him, that God may be all in all.

29 Else what shall they do which are baptized for the dead, if the dead rise not at all? why are they then baptized for the dead?

30 And why stand we in jeopardy every hour?

31 I protest by your rejoicing which I have in Christ Jesus our Lord, I die daily.

32 If after the manner of men I have fought with beasts at Ephesus, what advantageth it me, if the dead rise not? let us eat and drink; for to-morrow we die.

33 Be not deceived: evil communications corrupt good manners.

34 Awake to righteousness, and sin not; for some have not the knowledge of God: I speak this to your shame.

35 But some man will say, How are the dead raised up? and with what body do they come?

36 Thou fool, that which thou sowest is not quickened, except it die:

37 And that which thou sowest, thou sowest not that body that shall be, but bare grain, it may chance of wheat, or of some other grain:

38 But God giveth it a body as it hath pleased him, and to every seed his own body.

39 All flesh is not the same flesh: but there is one kind of flesh of men, another flesh of beasts, another of fishes, and another of birds.

40 There are also celestial bodies, and bodies terrestrial: but the glory of the celestial is one, and the glory of the terrestrial is another.

41 There is one glory of the sun, and another glory of the moon, and another glory of the stars: for one star differeth from another star in glory.

42 So also is the resurrection of the dead. It is sown in corruption; it is raised in incorruption:

43 It is sown in dishonour; it is raised in glory: it is sown in weakness; it is raised in power:

44 It is sown a natural body; it is raised a spiritual body. There is a natural body, and there is a spiritual body.

45 And so it is written, The first man Adam was made a living soul; the last Adam was made a quickening spirit.

46 Howbeit that was not first which is spiritual, but that which is natural; and afterward that which is spiritual.

47 The first man is of the earth, earthy: the second man is the Lord from heaven.

48 As is the earthy, such are they also that are earthy: and as is the heavenly, such are they also that are heavenly.

49 And as we have borne the image of the earthy, we shall also bear the image of the heavenly.

50 Now this I say, brethren, that flesh and blood cannot inherit the kingdom of God; neither doth corruption inherit incorruption.

51 Behold, I shew you a mystery; We shall not all sleep, but we shall all be changed,

52 In a moment, in the twinkling of an eye, at the last trump: for the trumpet shall sound, and the dead shall be raised incorruptible, and we shall be changed.

53 For this corruptible must put on incorruption, and this mortal must put on immortality.

54 So when this corruptible shall have put on incorruption, and this mortal shall have put on immortality, then shall be brought to pass the saying that is written, Death is swallowed up in victory.

55 O death, where is thy sting? O grave, where is thy victory?

56 The sting of death is sin; and the strength of sin is the law.

57 But thanks be to God, which giveth us the victory through our Lord Jesus Christ.

58 Therefore, my beloved brethren, be ye stedfast, unmoveable, always abounding in the work of the Lord, forasmuch as ye know that your labour is not in vain in the Lord.

Topics for Critical Thinking and Writing

1. Why is belief in the resurrection of Christ important to Paul? What evidence does he offer to support his belief in it?

2. What leads Paul to the conclusion that the dead are resurrected? What evidence does he offer to support this belief? What conclusion, according to Paul, follows if the dead are not resurrected?

3. In verse 22 Paul speaks of people who are "in Adam" and of others who are "in Christ." Explain the distinction to someone who finds it puzzling. (If you find it puzzling, check a guide to the Bible, such as *The Interpreter's Bible*, or *A New Catholic Commentary on Holy Scripture*, ed. Reginald C. Fuller et al.)

4. What mistaken belief, according to Paul, leads people to conclude that we should (as he says in verse 32) "eat and drink; for tomorrow we die"?

5. In verses 35 to 50 Paul insists again on bodily resurrection of human beings. In 35 to 44 he uses an analogy to explain that the body that dies and the body that is resurrected are continuous and yet also are different. Put his analogy into your own words. Do you think analogy is an effective way of making this point? Why? In verse 45 Paul uses a different argument, contrasting Adam ("the first man Adam") with Christ ("the last Adam"). Why do you think he drops the analogy and now offers this evidence? How in verses 46 to 47 does Paul bring the two points together?

6. In verse 55 Paul says, "O death, where is thy sting? O grave, where is thy victory?" In a paragraph summarize the beliefs (expressed in this selection) that lead Paul to the conclusion that death and the grave are conquered.

Bertrand Russell

Bertrand Russell (1872–1970), born in England, made his academic reputation as a mathematician and logician, but he won a popular reputation as a philosopher and social critic. Among his highly readable books are History of Western Philosophy *(1945) and* Why I Am Not a Christian *(1957).*

A pacifist during World War I, Russell was imprisoned in 1916 and deprived of his teaching position at Cambridge University. His unorthodox opinions continued to cause him personal difficulties. In 1938 he was offered a post at the City College of New York, but a judge refused to grant him a visa because of Russell's allegedly dangerous views on sex. During the last two decades of his life, Russell's criticism of American foreign policy made him an especially provocative figure in this country.

Reprinted here is one of his most famous essays on religion, delivered as a lecture on March 6, 1927, to the National Secular Society, South London Branch, at Battersea Town Hall. An amusing note: On one occasion when he was imprisoned, the jailer asked him his religion. Russell replied that he was an atheist, a remark that puzzled the jailer, but the man, wishing to be friendly, replied, "Ah well, we all believe in the same God, don't we?"

Why I Am Not a Christian

As your Chairman has told you, the subject about which I am going to speak to you tonight is "Why I Am Not a Christian." Perhaps it would be as well, first of all, to try to make out what one means by the word *Christian*. It is used these days in a very loose sense by a great many people. Some people mean no more by it than a person who attempts to live a good life. In that sense I suppose there would be Christians in all sects and creeds; but I do not think that that is the proper sense of the word, if only because it would imply that all the people who are not Christians — all the Buddhists, Confucians, Mohammedans, and so on — are not trying to live a good life. I do not mean by a Christian any person who tries to live decently according to his lights. I think that you must have a certain amount of definite belief before you have a right to call yourself a Christian. The word does not have quite such a full-blooded meaning now as it had in the times of St. Augustine and St. Thomas Aquinas. In those days, if a man said that he was a Christian it was known what he meant. You accepted a whole collection of creeds which were set out with great precision, and every single syllable of those creeds you believed with the whole strength of your convictions.

WHAT IS A CHRISTIAN?

Nowadays it is not quite that. We have to be a little more vague in our meaning of Christianity. I think, however, that there are two different items which are quite essential to anybody calling himself a

Christian. The first is one of a dogmatic nature—namely, that you must believe in God and immortality. If you do not believe in those two things, I do not think that you can properly call yourself a Christian. Then, further than that, as the name implies, you must have some kind of belief about Christ. The Mohammedans, for instance, also believe in God and in immortality, and yet they would not call themselves Christians. I think you must have at the very lowest the belief that Christ was, if not divine, at least the best and wisest of men. If you are not going to believe that much about Christ, I do not think you have any right to call yourself a Christian. Of course, there is another sense, which you find in *Whitaker's Almanack* and in geography books, where the population of the world is said to be divided into Christians, Mohammedans, Buddhists, fetish worshipers, and so on; and in that sense we are all Christians. The geography books count us all in, but that is a purely geographical sense, which I suppose we can ignore. Therefore I take it that when I tell you why I am not a Christian I have to tell you two different things: first, why I do not believe in God and in immortality; and, secondly, why I do not think that Christ was the best and wisest of men, although I grant him a very high degree of moral goodness.

But for the successful efforts of unbelievers in the past, I could not take so elastic a definition of Christianity as that. As I said before, in olden days it had a much more full-blooded sense. For instance, it included the belief in hell. Belief in eternal hell-fire was an essential item of Christian belief until pretty recent times. In this country, as you know, it ceased to be an essential item because of a decision of the Privy Council, and from that decision the Archbishop of Canterbury and the Archbishop of York dissented; but in this country our religion is settled by Act of Parliament, and therefore the Privy Council was able to override their Graces and hell was no longer necessary to a Christian. Consequently I shall not insist that a Christian must believe in hell.

THE EXISTENCE OF GOD

To come to this question of the existence of God: It is a large and serious question, and if I were to attempt to deal with it in any adequate manner I should have to keep you here until Kingdom Come, so that you will have to excuse me if I deal with it in a somewhat summary fashion. You know, of course, that the Catholic Church has laid it down as a dogma that the existence of God can be proved by the unaided reason. That is a somewhat curious dogma, but it is one of their dogmas. They had to introduce it because at one time the freethinkers adopted the habit of saying that there were such and such arguments which mere reason might urge against the existence of God, but of course they knew as a matter of faith that God did exist. The arguments and the reasons were set out at great length, and the Catholic Church felt that they must stop it. Therefore they laid it down that the existence of God can be proved by the unaided reason and they had to set up what they considered were arguments to prove it. There are, of course, a number of them, but I shall take only a few.

The First Cause Argument. Perhaps the simplest and easiest to 5 understand is the argument of the First Cause. (It is maintained that everything we see in this world has a cause, and as you go back in the chain of causes further and further you must come to a First Cause, and to that First Cause you give the name of God.) That argument, I suppose, does not carry very much weight nowadays, because, in the first place, cause is not quite what it used to be. The philosophers and the men of science have got going on cause, and it has not anything like the vitality it used to have; but, apart from that, you can see that the argument that there must be a First Cause is one that cannot have any validity. I may say that when I was a young man and was debating these questions very seriously in my mind, I for a long time accepted the argument of the First Cause, until one day, at the age of eighteen, I read John Stuart Mill's *Autobiography,* and I there found this sentence: "My father taught me that the question 'Who made me?' cannot be answered, since it immediately suggests the further question 'Who made God?'" That very simple sentence showed me, as I still think, the fallacy in the argument of the First Cause. If everything must have a cause, then God must have a cause. If there can be everything without a cause, it may just as well be the world as God, so that there cannot be any validity in that argument. It is exactly of the same nature as the Hindu's view that the world rested upon an elephant and the elephant rested upon a tortoise; and when they said, "How about the tortoise?" the Indian said, "Suppose we change the subject." The argument is really no better than that. There is no reason why the world could not have come into being without a cause; nor, on the other hand, is there any reason why it should not have always existed. There is no reason to suppose that the world had a beginning at all. The idea that things must have a beginning is really due to the poverty of our imagination. Therefore, perhaps, I need not waste any more time upon the argument about the First Cause.

The Natural Law Argument. Then there is a very common argument from natural law. That was a favorite argument all through the eighteenth century, especially under the influence of Sir Isaac Newton and his cosmogony. People observed the planets going around the sun according to the law of gravitation, and they thought that God had given a behest to these planets to move in that particular fashion, and that was why they did so. That was, of course, a convenient and simple explanation that saved them the trouble of looking any further for explanations of the law of gravitation. Nowadays we explain the law of gravitation in a somewhat complicated fashion that Einstein has introduced. I do not propose to give you a lecture on the law of gravitation, as interpreted by Einstein, because that again would take some time; at any rate, you no longer have the sort of natural law that you had in the Newtonian system, where, for some reason that nobody could understand, nature behaved in a uniform fashion. We now find that a great many things we thought were natural laws are really human conventions. You know that even in the remotest depths of stellar space there are still three feet to a yard. That is, no doubt, a very remarkable fact, but you would hardly call it a law of nature. And a great many things that have been regarded as laws of nature are of that kind. On the other hand, where you can get down to any knowledge of what atoms actually do, you will find they are much less subject to law than people thought, and that the laws at which you arrive are statistical averages of just the sort that would emerge from chance. There is, as we all know, a law that if you throw dice you will get double sixes only about once in thirty-six times, and we do not regard that as evidence that the fall of the dice is regulated by design; on the contrary, if the double sixes came every time we should think that there was design. The laws of nature are of that sort as regards a great many of them. They are statistical averages such as would emerge from the laws of chance; and that makes this whole business of natural law much less impressive than it formerly was. Quite apart from that, which represents the momentary state of science that may change tomorrow, the whole idea that natural laws imply a lawgiver is due to a confusion between natural and human laws. Human laws are behests commanding you to behave a certain way, in which way you may choose to behave, or you may choose not to behave; but natural laws are a description of how things do in fact behave, and being a mere description of what they in fact do, you cannot argue that there must be somebody who told them to do that, because even supposing that there were, you are then faced with the question "Why did God issue just those natural laws and no others?" If you say that he did it simply from his own good pleasure, and without any reason, you then find that there is something which is not subject to law, and so your train of natural law is interrupted. If you say, as more orthodox theologians do, that in all the laws which God issues he had a reason for giving those laws rather than others—the reason, of course, being to create the best universe, although you would never think it to look at it—if there were a reason for the laws which God gave, then God himself was subject to law, and therefore you do not get any advantage by introducing God as an intermediary. You have really a law outside and anterior to the divine edicts, and God does not serve your purpose, because he is not the ultimate lawgiver. In short, this whole argument about natural law no longer has anything like the strength that it used to have. I am traveling on in time in my review of the arguments. The arguments that are used for the existence of God change their character as time goes on. They were at first hard intellectual arguments embodying certain quite definite fallacies. As we come to modern times they become less respectable intellectually and more and more affected by a kind of moralizing vagueness.

The Argument from Design. The next step in this process brings us to the argument from design. You all know the argument from design: Everything in the world is made just so that we can manage to live in the world, and if the world was ever so little different, we could not manage to live in it. That is the argument from design. It sometimes takes a rather curious form; for instance, it is argued that rabbits have white tails in order to be easy to shoot. I do not know how rabbits would view that application. It is an easy argument to parody. You all know Voltaire's remark, that obviously the nose was designed to be such as to fit spectacles. That sort of parody has turned out to be not nearly so wide of the mark as it might have seemed in the eighteenth century, because since the time of Darwin we understand much better why living creatures are adapted to their environment. It is not that their environment was made to be suitable to them but that they grew to be suitable to it, and that is the basis of adaptation. There is no evidence of design about it.

When you come to look into this argument from design, it is a most astonishing thing that people can believe that this world, with all the things that are in it, with all its defects, should be the best that omnipotence and omniscience have been able to produce in millions of years. I really cannot believe it. Do you think that, if you were granted omnipotence and omniscience and millions of years in which to perfect your world, you could produce nothing better than the Ku Klux Klan or the Fascists? Moreover, if you accept the ordinary laws of science, you have to suppose that human life and life in general on this planet will die out in due course: It is a stage in the decay of the solar system; at a certain stage of decay you get the sort of conditions of temperature and so forth which are suitable to protoplasm, and there is life for a short time in the life of the whole solar system. You see in the moon the sort of thing to which the earth is tending—something dead, cold, and lifeless.

I am told that that sort of view is depressing, and people will sometimes tell you that if they believed that, they would not be able to go on living. Do not believe it; it is all nonsense. Nobody really worries much about what is going to happen millions of years hence. Even if they think they are worrying much about that, they are really deceiving themselves. They are worried about something much more mundane, or it may merely be a bad digestion; but nobody is really seriously rendered unhappy by the thought of something that is going to happen to this world millions and millions of years hence. Therefore, although it is of course a gloomy view to suppose that life will die out—at least I suppose we may say so, although sometimes when I contemplate the things that people do with their lives I think it is almost a consolation—it is not such as to render life miserable. It merely makes you turn your attention to other things.

The Moral Arguments for Deity. Now we reach one stage fur- 10
ther in what I shall call the intellectual descent that the Theists have made in their argumentations, and we come to what are called the moral arguments for the existence of God. You all know, of course, that there used to be in the old days three intellectual arguments for the existence of God, all of which were disposed of by Immanuel Kant in the *Critique of Pure Reason;* but no sooner had he disposed of those arguments than he invented a new one, a moral argument, and that quite convinced him. He was like many people: In intellectual matters he was skeptical, but in moral matters he believed implicitly in the maxims that he had imbibed at his mother's knee. That illustrates what the psychoanalysts so much emphasize—the immensely stronger hold upon us that our very early associations have than those of later times.

Kant, as I say, invented a new moral argument for the existence of God, and that in varying forms was extremely popular during the nineteenth century. It has all sorts of forms. One form is to say that there would be no right or wrong unless God existed. I am not for the moment concerned with whether there is a difference between right and wrong, or whether there is not: That is another question. The point I am concerned with is that, if you are quite sure there is a difference between right and wrong, you are then in this situation: Is that difference due to God's fiat or is it not? If it is due to God's fiat, then for God himself there is no difference between right and wrong, and it is no longer a significant statement to say that God is good. If you are going to say, as theologians do, that God is good, you must then say that right and wrong have some meaning which is independent of God's fiat, because God's fiats are good and not bad independently of the mere fact that he made them. If you are going to say that, you will then have to say that it is not only through God that right and wrong came into being, but that they are in their essence logically anterior to God. You could, of course, if you liked, say that there was a superior deity who gave orders to the God who made this world, or could take up the line that some of the gnostics took up—a line which I often thought was a very plausible one—that as a matter of fact this world that we know was made by the devil at a moment when God was not looking. There is a good deal to be said for that, and I am not concerned to refute it.

The Argument for the Remedying of Injustice. Then there is another very curious form of moral argument, which is this: They say that the existence of God is required in order to bring justice into the world. In the part of this universe that we know there is great injustice, and often the good suffer, and often the wicked prosper, and one hardly knows which of those is the more annoying; but if you are going to have justice in the universe as a whole you have to suppose a future life to redress the balance of life here on earth. So they say that there must be a God, and there must be heaven and hell in order that in the long run there may be justice. That is a very curious argument. If you looked at the matter from a scientific point of view, you would say, "After all, I know only this world. I do not know about the rest of the universe, but so far as one can argue at all on probabilities one would say that probably this world is a fair sample, and if there is injustice here the odds are that there is injustice elsewhere also." Supposing you got a crate of oranges that you opened, and you found all the top layer of oranges bad, you would not argue, "The underneath ones must be good, so as to redress the balance." You would say, "Probably the whole lot is a bad consignment"; and that is really what a scientific person would argue about the universe. He would say, "Here we find in this world a great deal of injustice, and so far as that goes that is a reason for supposing that justice does not rule in the world; and therefore so far as it goes it affords a moral argument against deity and not in favor of one." Of course I know that the sort of intellectual arguments that I have been talking to you about are not what really moves people. What really moves people to believe in God is not any intellectual argument at all. Most people believe in God because they have been taught from early infancy to do it, and that is the main reason.

Then I think that the next most powerful reason is the wish for safety, a sort of feeling that there is a big brother who will look after you. That plays a very profound part in influencing people's desire for a belief in God.

THE CHARACTER OF CHRIST

I now want to say a few words upon a topic which I often think is not quite sufficiently dealt with by Rationalists, and that is the question whether Christ was the best and the wisest of men. It is generally taken for granted that we should all agree that that was so. I do not myself. I think that there are a good many points upon which I agree with Christ a great deal more than the professing Christians do. I do not know that I could go with Him all the way, but I could go with Him much further than most professing Christians can. You will remember that He said, "Resist not evil: But whosoever shall smite thee on thy right cheek, turn to him the other also." That is not a new precept or a new principle. It was used by Lao-tse and Buddha some 500 or 600 years before Christ, but it is not a principle which as a matter of fact Christians accept. I have no doubt that the present Prime Minister,[1] for instance, is a most sincere Christian, but I should not advise any of you to go and smite him on one cheek. I think you might find that he thought this text was intended in a figurative sense.

Then there is another point which I consider excellent. You will re- 15 member that Christ said, "Judge not lest ye be judged." That principle I do not think you would find was popular in the law courts of Christian countries. I have known in my time quite a number of judges who were very earnest Christians, and none of them felt that they were acting contrary to Christian principles in what they did. Then Christ says, "Give to him that asketh of thee, and from him that would borrow of thee turn not thou away." That is a very good principle. Your Chairman has reminded you that we are not here to talk politics, but I cannot help observing that the last general election was fought on the question of how desirable it was to turn away from him that would borrow of thee, so that one must assume that the Liberals and Conservatives of this country are composed of people who do not agree with the teaching of Christ, because they certainly did very emphatically turn away on that occasion.

Then there is one other maxim of Christ which I think has a great deal in it, but I do not find that it is very popular among some of our Christian friends. He says, "If thou wilt be perfect, go and sell that which thou hast, and give to the poor." That is a very excellent maxim, but, as I say, it is not much practiced. All these, I think, are good maxims, although they are a little difficult to live up to. I do not profess to live up to them myself; but then, after all, it is not quite the same thing as for a Christian.

DEFECTS IN CHRIST'S TEACHING

Having granted the excellence of these maxims, I come to certain points in which I do not believe that one can grant either the superlative wisdom or the superlative goodness of Christ as depicted in the Gospels; and here I may say that one is not concerned with the historical question. Historically it is quite doubtful whether Christ ever existed at all, and if He did we do not know anything about Him, so that I am not concerned with the historical question, which is a very difficult one. I am concerned with Christ as He appears in the Gospels, taking the Gospel narrative as it stands, and there one does find some things that do not seem to be very wise. For one thing, He certainly thought that His second coming would occur in clouds of glory before the death of all the people who were living at that time. There are a great many texts that prove that. He says, for instance, "Ye shall not have gone over the cities of Israel till the Son of Man be come." Then He says, "There are some

---

[1]Stanley Baldwin (1867–1947). [Editors' note.]

standing here which shall not taste death till the Son of Man comes into His kingdom"; and there are a lot of places where it is quite clear that He believed that His second coming would happen during the lifetime of many then living. That was the belief of His earlier followers, and it was the basis of a good deal of His moral teaching. When He said, "Take no thought for the morrow," and things of that sort, it was very largely because He thought that the second coming was going to be very soon, and that all ordinary mundane affairs did not count. I have, as a matter of fact, known some Christians who did believe that the second coming was imminent. I knew a parson who frightened his congregation terribly by telling them that the second coming was very imminent indeed, but they were much consoled when they found that he was planting trees in his garden. The early Christians did really believe it, and they did abstain from such things as planting trees in their gardens, because they did accept from Christ the belief that the second coming was imminent. In that respect, clearly He was not so wise as some other people have been, and He was certainly not superlatively wise.

THE MORAL PROBLEM

Then you come to moral questions. There is one very serious defect to my mind in Christ's moral character, and that is that He believed in hell. I do not myself feel that any person who is really profoundly humane can believe in everlasting punishment. Christ certainly as depicted in the Gospels did believe in everlasting punishment, and one does find repeatedly a vindictive fury against those people who would not listen to His preaching—an attitude which is not uncommon with preachers, but which does somewhat detract from superlative excellence. You do not, for instance, find that attitude in Socrates. You find him quite bland and urbane toward the people who would not listen to him; and it is, to my mind, far more worthy of a sage to take that line than to take the line of indignation. You probably all remember the sort of things that Socrates was saying when he was dying, and the sort of things that he generally did say to people who did not agree with him.

You will find that in the Gospels Christ said, "Ye serpents, ye generation of vipers, how can ye escape the damnation of hell." That was said to people who did not like His preaching. It is not really to my mind quite the best tone, and there are a great many of these things about hell. There is, of course, the familiar text about the sin against the Holy Ghost: "Whosoever speaketh against the Holy Ghost it shall not be forgiven him neither in this World nor in the world to come." That text has caused an unspeakable amount of misery in the world, for all sorts of people have imagined that they have committed the sin against the Holy Ghost, and thought that it would not be forgiven them either in this world or in the world to come. I really do not think that a person with a

proper degree of kindliness in his nature would have put fears and terrors of that sort into the world.

Then Christ says, "The Son of Man shall send forth His angels, and 20
they shall gather out of His kingdom all things that offend, and them
which do iniquity, and shall cast them into a furnace of fire; there shall
be wailing and gnashing of teeth"; and He goes on about the wailing and
gnashing of teeth. It comes in one verse after another, and it is quite
manifest to the reader that there is a certain pleasure in contemplating
wailing and gnashing of teeth, or else it would not occur so often. Then
you all, of course, remember about the sheep and the goats; how at the
second coming He is going to divide the sheep from the goats, and He is
going to say to the goats, "Depart from me, ye cursed, into everlasting
fire." He continues, "And these shall go away into everlasting fire." Then
He says again, "If thy hand offend thee, cut it off; it is better for thee to
enter into life maimed, than having two hands to go into hell, into the
fire that never shall be quenched; where the worm dieth not and the fire
is not quenched." He repeats that again and again also. I must say that I
think all this doctrine, that hell-fire is a punishment for sin, is a doctrine
of cruelty. It is a doctrine that put cruelty into the world and gave the
world generations of cruel torture; and the Christ of the Gospels, if you
could take Him as His chroniclers represent Him, would certainly have to
be considered partly responsible for that.

There are other things of less importance. There is the instance of
the Gadarene swine, where it certainly was not very kind to the pigs to
put the devils into them and make them rush down the hill to the sea.
You must remember that He was omnipotent, and He could have made
the devils simply go away; but He chose to send them into the pigs. Then
there is the curious story of the fig tree, which always rather puzzled me.
You remember what happened about the fig tree. "He was hungry; and
seeing a fig tree afar off having leaves, He came if haply He might find
anything thereon; and when He came to it He found nothing but leaves,
for the time of figs was not yet. And Jesus answered and said unto it:
'No man eat fruit of thee hereafter for ever' . . . and Peter . . . saith unto
Him: 'Master, behold the fig tree which thou cursedst is withered
away.'" This is a very curious story, because it was not the right time of
year for figs, and you really could not blame the tree. I cannot myself
feel that either in the matter of wisdom or in the matter of virtue Christ
stands quite as high as some other people known to history. I think I
should put Buddha and Socrates above Him in those respects.

THE EMOTIONAL FACTOR

As I said before, I do not think that the real reason why people accept religion has anything to do with argumentation. They accept religion on emotional grounds. One is often told that it is a very wrong

thing to attack religion, because religion makes men virtuous. So I am told; I have not noticed it. You know, of course, the parody of that argument in Samuel Butler's book, *Erewhon Revisited*. You will remember that in *Erewhon* there is a certain Higgs who arrives in a remote country, and after spending some time there he escapes from that country in a balloon. Twenty years later he comes back to that country and finds a new religion in which he is worshipped under the name of the "Sun Child," and it is said that he ascended into heaven. He finds that the Feast of the Ascension is about to be celebrated, and he hears Professors Hanky and Panky say to each other that they never set eyes on the man Higgs, and they hope they never will; but they are the high priests of the religion of the Sun Child. He is very indignant, and he comes up to them, and he says, "I am going to expose all this humbug and tell the people of Erewhon that it was only I, the man Higgs, and I went up in a balloon." He was told, "You must not do that, because all the morals of this country are bound round this myth, and if they once know that you did not ascend into heaven they will all become wicked"; and so he is persuaded of that and he goes quietly away.

That is the idea — that we should all be wicked if we did not hold to the Christian religion. It seems to me that the people who have held to it have been for the most part extremely wicked. You find this curious fact, that the more intense has been the religion of any period and the more profound has been the dogmatic belief, the greater has been the cruelty and the worse has been the state of affairs. In the so-called ages of faith, when men really did believe the Christian religion in all its completeness, there was the Inquisition, with its tortures; there were millions of unfortunate women burned as witches; and there was every kind of cruelty practiced upon all sorts of people in the name of religion.

You find as you look around the world that every single bit of progress in humane feeling, every improvement in the criminal law, every step toward the diminution of war, every step toward better treatment of the colored races, or every mitigation of slavery, every moral progress that there has been in the world, has been consistently opposed by the organized churches of the world. I say quite deliberately that the Christian religion, as organized in its churches, has been and still is the principal enemy of moral progress in the world.

HOW THE CHURCHES HAVE RETARDED PROGRESS

You may think that I am going too far when I say that that is still so. 25 I do not think that I am. Take one fact. You will bear with me if I mention it. It is not a pleasant fact, but the churches compel one to mention facts that are not pleasant. Supposing that in this world that we live in today an inexperienced girl is married to a syphilitic man; in that case the Catholic Church says, "This is an indissoluble sacrament. You must endure celibacy or stay together. And if you stay together, you must not use birth control to prevent the birth of syphilitic children." Nobody whose natural sympathies have not been warped by dogma, or whose moral nature was not absolutely dead to all sense of suffering, could maintain that it is right and proper that that state of things should continue.

That is only an example. There are a great many ways in which, at the present moment, the church, by its insistence upon what it chooses to call morality, inflicts upon all sorts of people undeserved and unnecessary suffering. And of course, as we know, it is in its major part an opponent still of progress and of improvement in all the ways that diminish suffering in the world, because it has chosen to label as morality a certain narrow set of rules of conduct which have nothing to do with human happiness; and when you say that this or that ought to be done because it would make for human happiness, they think that has nothing to do with the matter at all. "What has human happiness to do with morals? The object of morals is not to make people happy."

FEAR, THE FOUNDATION OF RELIGION

Religion is based, I think, primarily and mainly upon fear. It is partly the terror of the unknown and partly, as I have said, the wish to feel that you have a kind of elder brother who will stand by you in all your troubles and disputes. Fear is the basis of the whole thing—fear of the mysterious, fear of defeat, fear of death. Fear is the parent of cruelty, and therefore it is no wonder if cruelty and religion have gone hand in hand. It is because fear is at the basis of those two things. In this world we can now begin a little to understand things, and a little to master them by help of science, which has forced its way step by step against the Christian religion, against the churches, and against the opposition of all the old precepts. Science can help us to get over this craven fear in which mankind has lived for so many generations. Science can teach us, and I think our own hearts can teach us, no longer to look around for imaginary supports, no longer to invent allies in the sky, but rather to look to our own efforts here below to make this world a fit place to live in, instead of the sort of place that the churches in all these centuries have made it.

WHAT WE MUST DO

We want to stand upon our own feet and look fair and square at the world—its good facts, its bad facts, its beauties, and its ugliness; see the world as it is and be not afraid of it. Conquer the world by intelligence and not merely by being slavishly subdued by the terror that comes from it. The whole conception of God is a conception derived from the ancient Oriental despotisms. It is a conception quite unworthy of free men.

When you hear people in church debasing themselves and saying that they are miserable sinners, and all the rest of it, it seems contemptible and not worthy of self-respecting human beings. We ought to stand up and look the world frankly in the face. We ought to make the best we can of the world, and if it is not so good as we wish, after all it will still be better than what these others have made of it in all these ages. A good world needs knowledge, kindliness, and courage; it does not need a regretful hankering after the past or a fettering of the free intelligence by the words uttered long ago by ignorant men. It needs a fearless outlook and a free intelligence. It needs hope for the future, not looking back all the time toward a past that is dead, which we trust will be far surpassed by the future that our intelligence can create.

Topics for Critical Thinking and Writing

1. Russell's talk was originally delivered to the National Secular Society. What sort of a group do you think this Society was? Do you imagine that the audience approved or disapproved of the talk? Do you think that to some extent the talk was geared to the taste of this audience? What evidence can you offer for your view?

2. In a sentence summarize Russell's first paragraph, and in another sentence summarize his second paragraph. Finally, write a third sentence, this one describing and evaluating Russell's strategy in beginning his essay with these two paragraphs.

3. Read and reread Russell's third paragraph, about hell. In the last sentence of this paragraph, he says, "Consequently I shall not insist that a Christian must believe in hell." "Consequently," of course, suggests that what follows is logically derived from what precedes. State in your own words the reason that Russell offers for the conclusion here. What do you think Russell thought of that reason?

4. In paragraph 8 Russell wonders why an omnipotent and omniscient creator would "produce nothing better than the Ku Klux Klan or the Fascists." Even if you do not believe in an omnipotent and omniscient creator, try to write a one-paragraph response to this point.

5. Many Christians would say that they believe in God because Jesus believed in God. They would add that because historical evidence supports their belief that Jesus did indeed live and die and was resurrected, there can be no reason to doubt Jesus' teachings. Why, in your opinion, does Russell not comment on this argument?

6. Russell discusses the meaning of the term "Christian" and offers his own definition. Look up in two unabridged dictionaries the definitions of this term, and explain whether Russell's definition agrees with all or any of those in the dictionaries. (By the way, do the dictionaries fully agree with each other?)

7. In paragraph 15 Russell says that many Christians do not practice certain teachings of Jesus. Suppose he is right. Does this failing show that Jesus' teachings are wrong? Or that it is unreasonable to believe in Jesus? What, exactly, does Russell's argument prove?

8. In paragraph 21, setting forth what he takes to be some of Jesus' unpleasant teachings and doings, Russell refers to one episode in which exorcised devils entered into swine (Matthew 8:28–34; Mark 5:1–20) and another in which Jesus cursed a fig tree (Matthew 21:19; Mark 11:13–14). In the library examine several Christian commentaries on the Bible (for instance, D. E. Nineham's *The Gospel of St. Mark* or *The Interpreter's One-Volume Commentary on the Bible*) to see what explanations believers have offered. Do you find any of these explanations adequate? Why, or why not?

9. In paragraph 24 Russell asserts that "every single bit of progress in humane feeling . . . has been consistently opposed by the organized churches of the world." What evidence does he offer? What evidence can you offer to support or to refute this view?

10. Russell states and criticizes five arguments for God's existence. Whether or not you find any of these arguments wholly convincing, which of them seems to you to be the strongest and which the weakest? In an essay of 500 words explain your evaluation. Optional: If you believe in God's existence, does it matter to you whether any of these arguments survived Russell's criticisms? Explain.

11. In paragraph 27 Russell says that "fear" is the basis of religion. Many Christians would disagree and would insist that love is the basis of Christianity. On this issue, where do you stand? Why?

12. In his final paragraph Russell says that people who debase themselves and call themselves "miserable sinners" in fact are "contemptible." If you have done things of which you have been deeply ashamed, do you think your confession (even if only to yourself) is "contemptible"?

13. Putting aside your own views of Christianity, in an essay of 500 to 750 words assess the strengths and the weaknesses of Russell's essay as an argument.

Joseph Addison

Joseph Addison (1672–1719), an English essayist and poet, was perhaps the most influential literary critic of his day. His essays, written chiefly for two newspapers (The Tatler *and* The Spectator*), were immensely popular and they remain highly esteemed today, at least by teachers of English. In one issue of* The Spectator *(#465, August 23, 1712) Addison published the poem that we reprint here, a version of Psalm 19. He called it simply "Ode." (An ode is a song of praise, specifically of an exalted subject such as heroism, or one's nation, or God.) In the essay he introduced the poem thus:*

The Supreme Being has made the best Arguments for his own Existence, in the Formation of the Heavens and the Earth, and these are Arguments which a Man of Sense cannot forbear attending to, who is out of the Noise and Hurry of Human Affairs. Aristotle says, that should a Man live under Ground, and there converse with Works of Art and Mechanism, and should afterwards be brought up into the open Day, and see the several Glories of the Heav'n and Earth, he would immediately pronounce them the Works of such a Being as we define God to be.

What Addison is here offering is his version of the Argument from Design — that the world obviously is a designed thing, like, say, a watch and therefore must have a designer, God.

Ode

The Spacious Firmament on high,
With all the blue Etherial Sky,
And spangled Heav'ns, a Shining Frame,
Their great Original proclaim:
Th'unwearied Sun, from Day to Day,   5
Does his Creator's Power display,
And publishes to every land
The Work of an Almighty Hand.

Soon as the Evening Shades prevail,
The Moon takes up the wondrous Tale,   10
And nightly to the listning Earth
Repeats the Story of her Birth:
Whilst all the Stars that round her burn,
And all the Planets, in their turn,
Confirm the Tidings as they rowl,   15
And spread the truth from Pole to Pole.

What though, in solemn Silence, all
Move round the dark terrestrial Ball?
What tho' nor real Voice nor Sound
Amid their radiant Orbs be found?   20
In Reason's Ear they all rejoice,
And utter forth a glorious Voice,
For ever singing, as they shine,
"The Hand that made us is Divine."

Topics for Critical Thinking and Writing

1. In a sentence or two summarize Addison's argument for the existence of God.

2. In the biographical note we mention the Argument from Design—the idea that the universe is a complex, functioning thing and therefore must have been made by a creator. Some Christian theologians argued that because the universe functions perfectly, we can infer the perfection of the creator. What objections, if any, can be offered against the basic argument, and against the amplified argument that we can infer the qualities of the creator from the creation?

Emily Dickinson

Emily Dickinson (1830–1886) was born into a prosperous New England family in Amherst, Massachusetts. Although she spent her seventeenth year a few miles away, at Mount Holyoke Seminary (now Mount Holyoke College), in the next twenty years she left Amherst only five or six times, and in her final twenty years she may never have left her house.

Dickinson's attitude toward religion seems to have been decidedly untraditional. She apparently disliked the patriarchal deity of the Hebrew Bible, whom she calls "Burglar! Banker—Father!"; she mentioned to a correspondent that the members of her family were all religious, except for her and that they "address an Eclipse every morning—whom they call their 'Father.'"

Papa above!

Papa above!
Regard a Mouse
O'erpowered by the Cat!
Reserve within thy kingdom
A "Mansion" for the Rat!   5

Snug in seraphic Cupboards
To nibble all the day,
While unsuspecting Cycles°
Wheel solemnly away!

Topics for Critical Thinking and Writing

1. In the Gospel according to St. John, 14:2, Jesus says, "In my Father's house are many mansions." What does this mean, and is it relevant to this poem?

2. Some readers take the poem to be a satire on religious faith. Do you agree? Explain.

---

8 Cycles Long periods, eons. [Editors' note.]

Emily Dickinson
Those — dying, then

Those — dying, then
Knew where they went
They went to God's Right Hand —
The Hand is amputated now
And God cannot be found —   5

The abdication of Belief
Makes the Behavior small —
Better an ignis fatuus
Than no illume at all —

Topics for Critical Thinking and Writing

1. In a sentence or two, state the point of the poem.

2. Is the image in line 4 in poor taste? Explain.

3. What is an *ignis fatuus*? In what ways does it connect visually with traditional images of hell and heaven?

Gerard Manley Hopkins

Gerard Manley Hopkins (1844–1889) was born near London and was educated at Oxford University, where he studied the classics. A convert from Anglicanism to Roman Catholicism, he was ordained a Jesuit priest in 1877. Hopkins published only a few poems during his lifetime, partly because he believed that the pursuit of literary fame was incompatible with his vocation as a priest and partly because he was aware that his highly individual style might puzzle readers. Especially in the last few years of his short life Hopkins experienced what religious mystics call "the dark night of the soul," agonizing sensations of weakness or unworthiness. "I cannot produce anything at all," he wrote, in a note typical of this period, "not only the luxuries like poetry, but the duties almost of my position." We cannot, of course, speak confidently about Hopkins's state of mind, but his doubt seems to have centered not in belief in God but in Hopkins's own ability to live up to the faith that he held.

Hopkins wrote "Thou Art Indeed Just, Lord" shortly before he died. He prefaces the poem with a quotation from a Latin translation of the Hebrew Bible, Jeremiah 12, which he translates in the first two and a·half lines of his poem. But the "&c" at the end of the Latin quotation indicates that Hopkins had additional biblical verses in mind. In this chapter, Jeremiah accuses God of injustice. We quote part of the chapter, from the New Jerusalem Bible, a Roman Catholic translation. (Yahweh, regarded by

many modern scholars as the best approximation of the Hebrew YHWH, *is
more usually given as Jehovah.)*

> *Your uprightness is too great, Yahweh,*
> *for me to dispute with you.*
> *But I should like to discuss some points of justice with you:*
> *Why is it that the way of the wicked prospers?*
> *Why do all treacherous people thrive?*
> *You plant them, they take root,*
> *they flourish, yes, and bear fruit.*
> *You are on their lips,*
> *yet far from their heart.*
> *You know me, Yahweh, you see me,*
> *you probe my heart, which is close to yours. . . .*

Thou Art Indeed Just, Lord

> *Justus quidem tu es, Domine, si disputem tecum; verumtamen
> justa loquar ad te: Quare via impiorum prosperatur? &c.*

Thou art indeed just, Lord, if I contend
With thee; but, sir, so what I plead is just.
Why do sinners' ways prosper? and why must
Disappointment all I endeavor end?

Wert thou my enemy, O thou my friend,   5
How wouldst thou worse, I wonder, than thou dost
Defeat, thwart me? Oh, the sots and thralls of lust
Do in spare hours more thrive than I that spend,

Sir, life upon thy cause. See, banks and brakes°
Now, leavèd how thick! lacèd they are again   10
With fretty chervil, look, and fresh wind shakes

Them; birds build—but not I build; no, but strain,
Time's eunuch, and not breed one work that wakes.
Mine, O thou lord of life, send my roots rain.

Topics for Critical Thinking and Writing

1. Do you find it inappropriate for a priest to "contend" with God (line 1)?
   To suggest (line 3) that "sinners' ways prosper"? Explain.

2. The title and first line assure us the poet thinks the Lord is "just," yet the
   poet offers no evidence to support that judgment. Is this a flaw in the
   poem? Why, or why not?

9 brakes Thickets.

3. In lines 9 to 12 Hopkins comments excitedly about natural phenomena that are flourishing all around him—the leafy thickets, the abundant chervil (an aromatic plant used in soups and stews), the birds building nests—and suggests that he is less productive than they. Does it make sense for human beings to compare their productivity with that of other living things?

Robert Frost

Robert Frost (1874–1963) studied for part of one term at Dartmouth College in New Hampshire, did odd jobs (including teaching), and from 1897 to 1899 was enrolled as a special student at Harvard. He then farmed in New Hampshire, published a few poems in newspapers, did some more teaching, and in 1912 left for England, where he hoped to achieve success as a writer. By 1915 he was known in England, and he returned to the United States. By the time of his death he was the nation's unofficial poet laureate. This poem was first published in 1936.

Design

I found a dimpled spider, fat and white,
On a white heal-all,° holding up a moth
Like a white piece of rigid satin cloth—
Assorted characters of death and blight
Mixed ready to begin the morning right,   5
Like the ingredients of a witches' broth—
A snow-drop spider, a flower like froth,
And dead wings carried like a paper kite.

What had that flower to do with being white,
The wayside blue and innocent heal-all?   10
What brought the kindred spider to that height,
Then steered the white moth thither in the night?
What but design of darkness to appall?—
If design govern in a thing so small.

Topics for Critical Thinking and Writing

1. The poem is a sonnet, divided into an octave (the first eight lines) and a sestet (the next six). How does the structure shape the thought?

2. What meanings of the word *design* come to your mind? Which of these meanings are relevant to the poem?

---

2 heal-all A flower, which is normally blue. [Editors' note.]

Leslie Marmon Silko

Leslie Marmon Silko characterizes herself as "Laguna, Mexican, white." She was born in 1948 in Albuquerque, New Mexico, and grew up on the La-guna Pueblo Reservation some fifty miles to the west. After graduating from the University of New Mexico in 1969, Silko entered law school but soon left to become a writer. She taught for two years at Navajo Community College at Many Farms, Arizona, and then went to Alaska for two years where she studied Eskimo-Aleut culture and worked on a novel, Ceremony. *After returning to the Southwest, she taught at the University of Arizona and then at the University of New Mexico.*

In addition to writing stories, novels, and poems, Silko wrote the screen-play for Marlon Brando's film Black Elk. *In 1981 she was awarded one of the so-called genius grants from the MacArthur Foundation, which supports "exceptionally talented individuals." This story was first published by the* New Mexico Quarterly *in 1969.*

The Man to Send Rain Clouds

ONE

They found him under a big cottonwood tree. His Levi jacket and pants were faded light-blue so that he had been easy to find. The big cottonwood tree stood apart from a small grove of winterbare cottonwoods which grew in the wide, sandy arroyo. He had been dead for a day or more, and the sheep had wandered and scattered up and down the arroyo. Leon and his brother-in-law, Ken, gathered the sheep and left them in the pen at the sheep camp before they returned to the cottonwood tree. Leon waited under the tree while Ken drove the truck through the deep sand to the edge of the arroyo. He squinted up at the sun and unzipped his jacket—it sure was hot for this time of year. But high and northwest the blue mountains were still deep in snow. Ken came sliding down the low, crumbling bank about fifty yards down, and he was bringing the red blanket.

Before they wrapped the old man, Leon took a piece of string out of his pocket and tied a small gray feather in the old man's long white hair. Ken gave him the paint. Across the brown wrinkled forehead he drew a streak of white and along the high cheekbones he drew a strip of blue paint. He paused and watched Ken throw pinches of corn meal and pollen into the wind that fluttered the small gray feather. Then Leon painted with yellow under the old man's broad nose, and finally, when he had painted green across the chin, he smiled.

"Send us rain clouds, Grandfather." They laid the bundle in the back of the pickup and covered it with a heavy tarp before they started back to the pueblo.

They turned off the highway onto the sandy pueblo road. Not long after they passed the store and post office they saw Father Paul's car coming toward them. When he recognized their faces he slowed his car and waved for them to stop. The young priest rolled down the car window.

"Did you find old Teofilo?" he asked loudly.   5

Leon stopped the truck. "Good morning, Father. We were just out to the sheep camp. Everything is O.K. now."

"Thank God for that. Teofilo is a very old man. You really shouldn't allow him to stay at the sheep camp alone."

"No, he won't do that any more now."

"Well, I'm glad you understand. I hope I'll be seeing you at Mass this week—we missed you last Sunday. See if you can get old Teofilo to come with you." The priest smiled and waved at them as they drove away.

TWO

Louise and Teresa were waiting. The table was set for lunch, and the   10
coffee was boiling on the black iron stove. Leon looked at Louise and then at Teresa.

"We found him under a cottonwood tree in the big arroyo near the sheep camp. I guess he sat down to rest in the shade and never got up again." Leon walked toward the old man's bed. The red plaid shawl had been shaken and spread carefully over the bed, and a new brown flannel shirt and pair of stiff new Levis were arranged neatly beside the pillow. Louise held the screen door open while Leon and Ken carried in the red blanket. He looked small and shriveled, and after they dressed him in the new shirt and pants he seemed more shrunken.

It was noontime now because the church bells rang the Angelus.[1] They ate the beans with hot bread, and nobody said anything until after Teresa poured the coffee.

Ken stood up and put on his jacket. "I'll see about the gravediggers. Only the top layer of soil is frozen. I think it can be ready before dark."

Leon nodded his head and finished his coffee. After Ken had been gone for a while, the neighbors and clanspeople came quietly to embrace Teofilo's family and to leave food on the table because the gravediggers would come to eat when they were finished.

THREE

The sky in the west was full of pale-yellow light. Louise stood out-   15
side with her hands in the pockets of Leon's green army jacket that was too big for her. The funeral was over, and the old men had taken their

[1] **Angelus** A devotional prayer commemorating the Annunciation (the angel Gabriel's an- nouncement of the incarnation of God in the human form of Jesus). [Editors' note.]

candles and medicine bags and were gone. She waited until the body was laid into the pickup before she said anything to Leon. She touched his arm, and he noticed that her hands were still dusty from the corn meal that she had sprinkled around the old man. When she spoke, Leon could not hear her.

"What did you say? I didn't hear you."

"I said that I had been thinking about something."

"About what?"

"About the priest sprinkling holy water for Grandpa. So he won't be thirsty."

Leon stared at the new moccasins that Teofilo had made for the 20 ceremonial dances in the summer. They were nearly hidden by the red blanket. It was getting colder, and the wind pushed gray dust down the narrow pueblo road. The sun was approaching the long mesa where it disappeared during the winter. Louise stood there shivering and watching his face. Then he zipped up his jacket and opened the truck door. "I'll see if he's there."

FOUR

Ken stopped the pickup at the church, and Leon got out; and then Ken drove down the hill to the graveyard where people were waiting. Leon knocked at the old carved door with its symbols of the Lamb. While he waited he looked up at the twin bells from the king of Spain with the last sunlight pouring around them in their tower.

The priest opened the door and smiled when he saw who it was. "Come in! What brings you here this evening?"

The priest walked toward the kitchen, and Leon stood with his cap in his hand, playing with the earflaps and examining the living room — the brown sofa, the green armchair, and the brass lamp that hung down from the ceiling by links of chain. The priest dragged a chair out of the kitchen and offered it to Leon.

"No thank you, Father. I only came to ask you if you would bring your holy water to the graveyard."

The priest turned away from Leon and looked out the window at the 25 patio full of shadows and the dining-room windows of the nuns' cloister across the patio. The curtains were heavy, and the light from within faintly penetrated; it was impossible to see the nuns inside eating supper. "Why didn't you tell me he was dead? I could have brought the Last Rites anyway."

Leon smiled. "It wasn't necessary, Father."

The priest stared down at his scuffed brown loafers and the worn hem of his cassock. "For a Christian burial it was necessary."

His voice was distant, and Leon thought that his blue eyes looked tired.

"It's O.K., Father, we just want him to have plenty of water."

The priest sank down in the green chair and picked up a glossy mis- 30 sionary magazine. He turned the colored pages full of lepers and pagans without looking at them.

"You know I can't do that, Leon. There should have been the Last Rites and a funeral Mass at the very least."

Leon put on his green cap and pulled the flaps down over his ears. "It's getting late, Father. I've got to go."

When Leon opened the door Father Paul stood up and said, "Wait." He left the room and came back wearing a long brown overcoat. He followed Leon out the door and across the dim churchyard to the adobe steps in front of the church. They both stooped to fit through the low adobe entrance. And when they started down the hill to the graveyard only half of the sun was visible above the mesa.

The priest approached the grave slowly, wondering how they had managed to dig into the frozen ground; and then he remembered that this was New Mexico, and saw the pile of cold loose sand beside the hole. The people stood close to each other with little clouds of steam puffing from their faces. The priest looked at them and saw a pile of jackets, gloves, and scarves in the yellow, dry tumbleweeds that grew in the graveyard. He looked at the red blanket, not sure that Teofilo was so small, wondering if it wasn't some perverse Indian trick—something they did in March to ensure a good harvest—wondering if maybe old Teofilo was actually at sheep camp corraling the sheep for the night. But there he was, facing into a cold dry wind and squinting at the last sunlight, ready to bury a red wool blanket while the faces of the parishioners were in shadow with the last warmth of the sun on their backs.

His fingers were stiff, and it took them a long time to twist the lid off 35 the holy water. Drops of water fell on the red blanket and soaked into dark icy spots. He sprinkled the grave and the water disappeared almost before it touched the dim, cold sand; it reminded him of something—he tried to remember what it was, because he thought if he could remember he might understand this. He sprinkled more water; he shook the container until it was empty, and the water fell through the light from sundown like August rain that fell while the sun was still shining, almost evaporating before it touched the wilted squash flowers.

The wind pulled at the priest's brown Franciscan robe and swirled away the corn meal and pollen that had been sprinkled on the blanket. They lowered the bundle into the ground, and they didn't bother to untie the stiff pieces of new rope that were tied around the ends of the blanket. The sun was gone, and over on the highway the eastbound lane was full of headlights. The priest walked away slowly. Leon watched him climb the hill, and when he had disappeared within the tall, thick walls, Leon turned to look up at the high blue mountains in the deep snow that reflected a faint red light from the west. He felt good because it was finished, and he was happy about the sprinkling of the holy water; now the old man could send them big thunderclouds for sure.

Topics for Critical Thinking and Writing

1. Why do Leon and Ken decorate the body of the old man (para. 2)? Why do they conceal this from Father Paul?

2. Why do Catholic priests sprinkle holy water on the body of a person about to be buried? Why does Louise think it is to keep her grandfather from being thirsty (para. 19)? Why does Leon think sprinkling the grave will bring "big thunderclouds for sure" (para. 36)? Are we to suppose that she and Leon don't understand the Christian ritual? Or that they reject it? (See especially paras. 24–29.)

3. How well does Leon understand the priest? How well does the priest understand Leon? Have the Indians made an unwitting fool of Father Paul? What do you think he would think if he knew what the Indians had said to one another behind his back?

4. Do you think the story is in any way offensive to Christians, specifically to Catholics? Explain.

5. Did you enjoy the story? If so, presumably you think it is a good story, *good* here being an aesthetic judgment and probably having nothing to do with moral judgment. In any case, evaluate the story, supporting your evaluation with reasons.

Judith Ortiz Cofer

Born in Puerto Rico in 1952 of a Puerto Rican mother and a United States mainland father who served in the Navy, Judith Ortiz Cofer was educated both in Puerto Rico and on the mainland. After earning a bachelor's and a master's degree in English, she did further graduate work at Oxford University and then taught English in Florida. She has published seven volumes of poetry. This poem first appeared in Triple Crown: Chicano, Puerto Rican, and Cuban American Poetry *(1987).*

Latin Women Pray

Latin women pray
In incense sweet churches
They pray in Spanish to an Anglo God
With a Jewish heritage.
And this Great White Father   5
Imperturbable in his marble pedestal
Looks down upon his brown daughters
Votive candles shining like lust
In his all seeing eyes
Unmoved by their persistent prayers.   10

Yet year after year
Before his image they kneel

Margarita Josefina Maria and Isabel
All fervently hoping
That if not omnipotent   15
At least he be bilingual

Topics for Critical Thinking and Writing

1. The Hebrew Bible tells us (Genesis 1:26) that "God said, Let us make man in our image." Some cynic, reversing the idea, has observed that men make God in their own image. (Montesquieu, the eighteenth-century French philosopher, put it a bit differently: "If triangles made a god, they would give him three sides.") Is this poem with its reference to "an Anglo God" and a "Great White Father" spoken in the same spirit? Is the poem at all serious, or is it just a mildly amusing joke? Support your answer with reasons.

2. C. S. Lewis in *A Grief Observed* (1961) wrote, "Can a mortal ask questions which God finds unanswerable? Quite easily, I think. All nonsense questions are unanswerable." Do you imagine that a devout person who believes that God has not answered his or her prayers might find this comment acceptable? Explain.

Leonard D. Eron, "The Television Industry Must Police Itself" from Harvard School of Public Health panel discussion, 1992. Copyright © 1992 by Leonard D. Eron. Reprinted with the permission of the author.

Amitai Etzioni, "Less Privacy Is Good for Us" from *The Limits of Privacy* by Amitai Etzioni. Reprinted by permission of the author.

Milton Friedman, "The Social Responsibility of Business Is to Increase Its Profits" from the *New York Times,* March 19, 1970 (Magazine). Copyright © 1970 by the New York Times Company. "There's No Justice in the War on Drugs" from the *New York Times,* January 17, 1998. Copyright © 1998 by the New York Times Company. All of the above by permission of the *New York Times.*

Thomas Friedman, "Knight Is Right" from the *New York Times,* June 20, 2000. Copyright © 2000 by the New York Times Company. Reprinted by permission of the *New York Times.*

Robert Frost, "Design" by Robert Frost from *The Poetry of Robert Frost,* edited by Edward Connery Lathem, Copyright 1936 by Robert Frost. Copyright 1964 by Lesley Frost Ballantine, © 1969 by Henry Holt & Co., LLC. Reprinted by permission of Henry Holt and Company, LLC.

Simson Garfinkel, "Privacy under Attack" from *Database Nation* by Simson Garfinkel. © 2000 by O'Reilly & Associates, Inc. 101 Morris St., Sebastopol, CA 95472.

"God—Guns—Guts." © Mark Antam/THE IMAGE WORKS, PO Box 443, Woodstock, NY 12498. All Rights Reserved.

Terry Golway, "The Culture of Death" from *America,* May 10, 1997. Copyright © 1997. Reprinted by permission of America Press, Inc. All rights reserved.

Paul Goodman, "A Proposal to Abolish Grading" from *Compulsory Miseducation and the Community of Scholars* by Paul Goodman (Horizon, 1966). Reprinted by permission of Sally Goodman.

Ellen Goodman, "The Reasonable Woman Standard" and "Who Lives? Who Dies? Who Decides?" © 1980, 1991, the Boston Globe Newspaper Co./ Washington Post Writers Group. Reprinted with permission.

Dave Grossman and Gloria DeGaetano, "It's Important to Feel Something When You Kill" from *Stop Teaching Our Kids to Kill* by Dave Grossman and Gloria DeGaetano. Copyright © 1999 by Dave Grossman and Gloria DeGaetano. Used by permission of Crown Publishers, a division of Random House, Inc.

Robert D. Haas, "Ethics: A Global Business Challenge" (excerpt), May 4, 1994. Reprinted by permission of the author and *Vital Speeches of the Day.*

Garrett Hardin, "Lifeboat Ethics" from *Psychology Today* magazine, September 1974. Copyright © 1974 Sussex Publishers, Inc.

Ernest F. Hollings, "Save the Children" from the *New York Times,* November 23, 1993. Copyright © 1993 by the New York Times Company. Reprinted with the permission of the *New York Times.*

George Horan, "Juvenile Felonies" from the *Los Angeles Times,* June 13, 1992. Reprinted by permission of the author.

Langston Hughes, "Let America Be America Again" from *The Collected Poems of Langston Hughes* by Langston Hughes. Copyright © 1994 by The Estate of Langston Hughes. Used by permission of Alfred A. Knopf, a division of Random House, Inc.

"I'd Like You To Keep Your Ears Open . . . Thanks, Babe." © 1997 by Randy Glasbergen.

"It Has Burned a Hole in My Soul . . . " *Client:* Project Rachel; *Agency:* Hannon McKendry, Grand Rapids, MI.

"It's Not Complicated: I Want to Marry the Man I Love." © Joel Gordon 1996.

Jeff Jacoby, "Bring Back Flogging" from the *Boston Globe,* February 26, 1997. Copyright © 1997. Reprinted with the permission of the *Boston Globe.*

Susan Jacoby, "A First Amendment Junkie" from the *New York Times,* January 26, 1978. Copyright © 1978 by Susan Jacoby. Reprinted with the permission of Georges Borchardt, Inc. for the author.

Elizabeth Joseph, "My Husband's Nine Wives" from the *New York Times,* May 23, 1991. Copyright © 1991 by the New York Times Company. Reprinted by permission of the *New York Times.*

Nicholas deB Katzenbach, "Not Color Blind: Just Blind" from the *New York Times,* February 22, 1998 (Magazine). Copyright © 1998. Reprinted by permission of the author.

"Keep Planned Parenthood out of Our Schools." © Rob Nelson/Black Star Publishing/PictureQuest.

Jean Kilbourne, "Own This Child" from *Deadly Persuasion: Why Women and Girls Must Fight the Addictive Power of Advertising.* Reprinted by permission of The Free Press, a division of Simon & Schuster, Inc. Copyright © 1999, by Jean Kilbourne.

Martin Luther King Jr., "I Have a Dream" and "Letter from Birmingham Jail" reprinted by arrangement with The Heirs to the Estate of Martin Luther King Jr., c/o Writers House Inc. as agent for the proprietor. Copyright 1963 by Martin Luther King Jr., copyright renewed 1991 by Coretta Scott King.

Philip Knight, "Statement from Nike Founder and CEO Philip H. Knight Regarding the University of Oregon" from the Oregon *Daily Emerald* online; www.dailyemerald.com. Reprinted by permission of the Oregon Daily Emerald.

Edward I. Koch, "Death and Justice: How Capital Punishment Affirms Life" from *The New Republic,* April 15, 1985. Copyright © 1985 by The New Republic, Inc. Reprinted with the permission of *The New Republic.*

Alex Kozinski and Sean Gallagher, "For an Honest Death Penalty" from the *New York Times,* March 8, 1995. Copyright © 1995 by the New York Times Company. Reprinted by permission of the *New York Times.*

Rita Kramer, "Juvenile Justice Is Delinquent" from the *Wall Street Journal,* May 27, 1992. Copyright © 1992 by Dow Jones & Company, Inc. Reprinted with the permission of the author and the *Wall Street Journal.* All rights reserved.

Charles R. Lawrence III, "On Racist Speech" from the *Chronicle of Higher Education,* October 25, 1989. Copyright © 1989 by Charles R. Lawrence III. Reprinted by permission of the author.

Louise Lee and Aaron Bernstein, "Who Says Student Protests Don't Matter?" from *BusinessWeek,* June 12, 2000.

Ursula K. Le Guin, "The Ones Who Walk Away from Omelas" from *New Dimensions 3.* Copyright © 1973 by Ursula K. Le Guin. Reprinted with the permission of the author and the author's agent, Virginia Kidd.

Michael Levin, "The Case for Torture" from *Newsweek,* June 7, 1982. Reprinted by permission of Michael Levin.

Rush Limbaugh III, "Condoms: The New Diploma" reprinted with permission of Pocket Books, a Division of Simon & Schuster, from *The Way Things Ought to Be* by Rush H. Limbaugh III. Copyright © 1992 by Rush Limbaugh.

Niccolò di Bernardo Machiavelli, "The Prince" translated by Mark Musa and Peter Bondanella, from *The Portable Machiavelli,* edited by Peter Bondanella & Mark Musa. Copyright © 1979 by Viking Penguin, Inc. Used by permission of Viking Penguin, a division of Penguin Putnam, Inc.

Sarah J. McCarthy, "Cultural Fascism" from *Forbes,* December 9, 1991. Copyright © 1991 by Forbes, Inc. Reprinted with the permission of *Forbes* Magazine.

Cecil McIver, "Assisted Dying as a Moral and Ethical Choice: A Physician's View." Reprinted by permission of The Hemlock Society USA & Hemlock Foundation.

Donella Meadows, "Not Seeing the Forest for the Dollar Bills" from *Valley News*, White River Junction (Vermont), June 30, 1990. Copyright © 1990 by Donella Meadows. Reprinted with the permission of the author.

"Migrant Mother." (two photos by Dorothea Lange) Reproduced from the Collections of the Library of Congress.

Stanley Milgram, "The Perils of Obedience" from *Harper's* 24, December 1973. Copyright © 1973 by Stanley Milgram. Reprinted with the permission of Alexandra Milgram.

Thomas More, excerpt from *Utopia*, translated by Paul Turner. Copyright © 1961 by Paul Turner. Reprinted with the permission of Penguin Books Ltd.

"National Iwo Jima Memorial Monument." Parks & History Assoc. Photo by Bill Clark, courtesy of National Park Service.

Nicholas Negroponte, "Being Asynchronous" from *Being Digital* by Nicholas Negroponte. Copyright © 1995 by Nicholas Negroponte. Used by permission of Alfred A. Knopf, a division of Random House, Inc.

Vivian Norwood, "Eight Reasons Women Should Be in the Military" from the *Boston Globe*, August 30, 1997. Republished with the permission of the *Boston Globe*. Permission conveyed through Copyright Clearance Center, Inc.

"Of Course I'm Against the Death Penalty." Pat Oliphant. © Washington Star. Reprinted with permission Los Angeles Times Syndicate. From the *Times Record*, January 19, 1971.

George Orwell, "Shooting an Elephant" from *Shooting an Elephant and Other Essays* by George Orwell. Copyright 1950 by Sonia Brownell Orwell and renewed 1978 by Sonia Pitt-Rivers. Reprinted by permission of Harcourt, Inc. "Shooting an Elephant" (Copyright © George Orwell 1936) reproduced by permission of A M Heath & Co. Ltd. on behalf of Bill Hamilton as the Literary Executor of the Estate of the Late Sonia Brownell Orwell and Martin Secker & Warburg Ltd.

Ellen Frankel Paul, "Bared Buttocks and Federal Cases" from *Society*, May/June 1991. Reprinted by permission of Transaction Publishers.

Plato, "Crito" from *The Last Days of Socrates*, translated by Hugh Tredennick. Copyright © 1954, © 1959, 1969 by Hugh Tredennick. "The Greater Part of the Stories Current Today We Shall Have to Reject" from *The Republic*, translated by Desmond Lee. Copyright © 1955, 1974 by H. D. P. Lee. Reprinted with the permission of Penguin Books Ltd.

Katha Pollitt, "It Takes Two: A Modest Proposal for Holding Fathers Equally Accountable" from *The Nation*, January 30, 1995. Originally appeared in the *Boston Globe*, January 17, 1995. Copyright © 1995 The Nation Company L. P. Reprinted with permission of *The Nation*.

"Portrait of Guiliano de' Medici." © The Metropolitan Museum of Art, The Jules Bache Collection, 1949. (49.7.12).

Sister Helen Prejean, "Executions Are Too Costly — Morally" (editors' title) Pages 193–197 from *Dead Man Walking* by Helen Prejean. Copyright © 1993 by Helen Prejean. Used by permission of Random House, Inc.

Timothy M. Quill, "Death and Dignity: A Case of Individualized Decision Making" from *The New England Journal of Medicine* 324 (1991). Copyright © 1991 by the Massachusetts Medical Society. Reprinted with the permission of *The New England Journal of Medicine*.

Anna Quindlen, "A Pyrrhic Victory" from the *New York Times*, January 8, 1994. Copyright © 1994 by the New York Times Company. Reprinted with the permission of the *New York Times*.

James Rachels, "Active and Passive Euthanasia" from *The New England Journal of Medicine* 292 (1975). Copyright © 1975 by the Massachusetts Medical Society. Reprinted with the permission of *The New England Journal of Medicine*.

Diane Ravitch, "In Defense of Testing" from *Time*, September 11, 2000. Copyright © 2000 Time Inc. Reprinted by permission.

Anna Lisa Raya, "It's Hard Enough Being Me" from *Columbia College Today*, Winter/Spring 1994. Reprinted by permission of the author.

Richard Rhodes, "Hollow Claims about Fantasy Violence" from the *New York Times*, September 17, 2000. Copyright © 2000 by the New York Times Company. Reprinted by permission of the *New York Times*.

Carl R. Rogers, "Communication: Its Blocking and Its Facilitation" Reprinted with the permission of the author.

Bertrand Russell, "Why I Am Not a Christian" reprinted with the permission of Simon & Schuster from *Why I Am Not a Christian* by Bertrand Russell. Copyright © 1957 by George Allen & Unwin Ltd.

Lisa Schiffren, "Gay Marriage, an Oxymoron" from the *New York Times*, March 23, 1996. Copyright © 1996 by the New York Times Company. Reprinted with the permission of the *New York Times*.

Stanley S. Scott, "Smokers Get a Raw Deal" from the *New York Times*, December 29, 1984. Copyright © 1984 by the New York Times Company. Reprinted with the permission of the *New York Times*.

"Seattle: WTO Riot." © Reuters New Media Inc./CORBIS #UT0011724.

Robert L. Sexton, "Tackling Juvenile Crime" from *Journal of Social, Political and Economic Studies* 21:2, Summer, 1996, pages 191–197. Reprinted by permission of the Council for Social and Economic Studies, Washington, D.C.

"Should I Answer This Questionnaire about Internet Privacy?" By permission of Bruce Beattie, Florida and Copley News Service.

Max Shulman, "Love Is a Fallacy" from *Love Is a Fallacy*. Copyright © 1951, 1979 by Max Shulman. Permissions to reprint granted by Harold Matson Co., Inc.

John Silber, "Students Should Not Be above the Law" from the *New York Times*, May 9, 1996. Copyright © 1996 by the New York Times Company. Reprinted with permission of the *New York Times*.

Leslie Marmon Silko, "The Man to Send Rain Clouds" from *Storyteller* by Leslie Marmon Silko. Copyright © 1981 by Leslie Marmon Silko. Reprinted with the permission of The Wylie Agency.

Peter Singer, "Animal Liberation" from the *New York Review of Books*, April 15, 1973. Copyright © 1973 by Peter Singer. Reprinted with the permission of the author. "Famine, Affluence and Morality" from *Philosophy and Public Affairs*, Spring 1972. Reprinted by permission of Princeton University Press.

W. T. Stace, "Is Determinism Inconsistent with Free Will?" from *Religion and the Modern Mind* by W. T. Stace. Copyright 1952 by W. T. Stace, renewed © 1980 by Blanche Stace. Reprinted by permission of HarperCollins Publishers, Inc.

Thomas Stoddard, "Gay Marriages: Make Them Legal" from the *New York Times*, March 4, 1989. Copyright © 1989 by the New York Times Company. Reprinted with the permission of the *New York Times*.

Nadine Strossen, "Everyone Is Watching You" from the ACLU Web site <www.intellectualcapital.com> May 28, 1998. Reprinted by permission of the author.

Nate Stulman, "Goofing-Off with Computers" from the *New York Times*, March 15, 1999. Copyright © 1999 by the New York Times Company. Reprinted by permission of the *New York Times*.

Ronald Takaki, "The Harmful Myth of Asian Superiority" from the *New York Times*, June 16, 1990. Copyright © 1990 by the New York Times Company. Reprinted with the permission of the *New York Times*.

Stuart Taylor Jr., "School Prayer: When Constitutional Principles Clash" from *National Journal*, July 15, 2000 in "Opening Argument." Copyright 2001 by National Journal Group, Inc. All rights reserved. Reprinted by permission.

"The Terror of War: Children on Route 1 near Trang Bang." (Huynh Cong (Nick) Ut) © AP/Worldwide Photos.

Randall Terry, "The Abortion Clinic Shootings: Why?" from the *Boston Globe,* January 9, 1995. Copyright © 1995 by Randall Terry. Reprinted with the permission of the author.

"They Finally Found an Answer to Overcrowded Prisons." ACLU *Client:* ACLU; *Agency:* DeVito/Verdi, New York, NY.

Sarah Thompson, "Concealed Carry Prevents Violent Crimes," *American Gun Review,* October 1, 1997. Reprinted by permission of the author.

"Tomb of the Unknown Soldier." © Bettmann/CORBIS.

"Tomb of the Unknown Soldier." © Rob Crandall/Stock, Boston Inc./Picture Quest.

Tufts University, "What Is Sexual Harassment?" Reprinted with the permission of Tufts University.

"Utne Reader: A New Renaissance?" Illustration by Daniel Craig, Art Director: Lynn Phelps.

"Vietnam Veterans Memorial." Parks & History Assoc. Photo by Terry Adams, courtesy of National Park Service.

"Warning! Our Homes Are in Danger *Now!"* National Archives © National Archives.

"Why Are You Buying Your Food from a Tobacco Company?" Ad Busters Image courtesy of <www.adbusters.org>.

Ellen Willis, "Putting Women Back into the Abortion Debate" from *No More Nice Girls* by Ellen Willis. Copyright © 1993 by Ellen Willis. Reprinted by permission of Wesleyan University Press.

James Q. Wilson, "Against the Legalization of Drugs" from *Commentary,* February 1990. Copyright © 1990 by James Q. Wilson. Reprinted with the permission of the author and *Commentary.* "Just Take Away Their Guns" from the *New York Times,* March 20, 1994. Copyright © 1994 by the New York Times Company. Reprinted with the permission of the *New York Times.*

"Women in the Military." © Christophe Loviny/CORBIS.

Mitsuye Yamada, "To the Lady" from *Camp Notes and Other Writings,* copyright © 1992 by Mitsuye Yamada. Reprinted by permission of Rutgers University Press.

"Your condition is serious . . . alleviate your symptoms." © The New Yorker Collection 1997: Mick Stevens from cartoonbank.com. All rights reserved.

Index of Authors
and Titles

Index of Terms

Directory to Documentation Models in MLA Format

abortion ■ affirmative action ■ animal rights ■ business
ethics ■ campus discipline ■ computers in college ■
corporal punishment ■ death penalty ■ drug legalization
■ euthanasia ■ fourth amendment ■ freedom of
speech ■ gay marriages ■ gun control ■ immigration
■ juvenile crime ■ model minorities ■ polygamy ■
pornography ■ prayer in school ■ privacy ■ sex education
■ sexual harassment ■ standardized tests ■ televised trials
■ video violence ■ women in the military

CURRENT ISSUES
AND
ENDURING QUESTIONS

A GUIDE TO CRITICAL THINKING
AND ARGUMENT, WITH READINGS

What Is the Ideal Society? How Free Is the Will of
the Individual within Society? What Are the Grounds
of Religious Faith?

Sylvan Barnet ■ Hugo Bedau

Resources for Teaching

CURRENT ISSUES
AND
ENDURING QUESTIONS
A Guide to
Critical Thinking and Argument,
with Readings

SIXTH EDITION

SYLVAN BARNET

Professor of English, Tufts University

HUGO BEDAU

Professor of Philosophy, Tufts University

Bedford/St. Martin's   BOSTON ◆ NEW YORK

For information, write: Bedford/St. Martin's, 75 Arlington Street, Boston, MA 02116
(617-399-4000)

ISBN: 0–312–39455–1

Instructors who have adopted *Current Issues and Enduring Questions: A Guide to Critical Thinking and Argument, with Readings,* Sixth Edition, as a textbook for a course are authorized to duplicate portions of this manual for their students.

Preface

Like the book they accompany, these notes are the work of two people — one a teacher of literature and composition, the other a teacher of philosophy. No single set of notes can fully satisfy all instructors or even be of much use to all instructors, but we hope that our alliance has enabled us to produce some notes that will have something of interest for almost everyone.

THE SCOPE OF THESE NOTES

If the two of us have succeeded in being of some use, it is partly because we have different approaches and partly because we do not methodically treat every anthologized essay in the same way. We treat *all* of the essays and literary works — some briefly, some extensively, some chiefly from a rhetorician's point of view, some chiefly from a philosopher's point of view. We have, however, always kept in mind that because teachers of composition courses devote many hours to reading students' papers, they have correspondingly fewer hours to devote to working up the background for unfamiliar essays. We have therefore provided background on such matters as affirmative action, animal rights, gay marriage, and immigration, so that an instructor who happens to be relatively unfamiliar with one or another of these topics nevertheless can teach with ease the essays we reprint.

Beyond providing background on specialized topics, in these notes we simply touch on some of the matters we discuss in our classes. We realize that something is artificial here; what one does in class depends heavily on the students and on the stage in the term at which one is studying an essay. And of course what one does in class depends even more heavily on one's ideas of what teaching is. Still, we hope instructors will scan these comments and will find at least some of them useful; if the comments seem utterly wrongheaded, they may nevertheless be useful in providing material to react against.

THE SYLLABUS

All instructors will have their own ideas about how to use the text in a composition course. Which essays are assigned, and in what sequence and at what pace, will depend partly on whether you require a short research paper, several short research papers, or a long research paper. Still, our suggestion (for what it is worth) is to teach the first six chapters (Parts One and Two) in sequence.

Part One: In Chapter 1 we would glance fairly briefly at the essay by John Silber and the reply by Judith H. Christie and would spend more time on the casebook on testing — paying attention not only to the reasoning but also to the tone of the writers. Similarly, in Chapter 2 we would deal briefly with Susan Jacoby's essay (it is discussed in the text), and would spend considerably more time on the four essays that constitute the casebook on free speech. We should mention that Chapter 10, A Lawyer's View: Steps Toward Civic Literacy (in Part Three), is highly relevant to the material on free speech. If your course introduces the notion of civic literacy, you probably will want to teach at least part of Chapter 10, which contains very readable Supreme Court opinions on three fascinating cases — the first on burning the flag as an act of political protest, the second on searching a student suspected of disobeying school regulations, and the third (*Roe v. Wade*) on whether the right to privacy includes a women's decision to terminate pregnancy. The question, in our minds, is whether to discuss one or more of these issues in conjunction with Chapter 2 or to postpone such discussion until the class has read all of Parts One and Two. In any case, whether we turn directly from Chapter 2 to Chapter 3 or whether we pause to use some of the material from Chapter 10, when we do turn to Chapter 3, we probably will teach two or three of the six essays (Takaki, Wilson, Ephron, Levin, Raya, Brady) and then spend at least a half of one period on the casebook concerning computers in college.

To cover Part One (Chapters 1–3) will take about four meetings if at the beginning of the course you give only brief writing assignments, or five or six meetings if you require substantial writing to accompany the reading assignments. In our discussions of these chapters in this manual we offer a few suggestions about essays printed later in the book that go well with the early chapters, but we don't think it is necessary to supplement these first three chapters. (In teaching Chapter 3 — on syllogisms, evidence, and so on — instructors who wish to inform students about the Toulmin model will want to supplement the chapter with Chapter 7, which is devoted to that topic. Also relevant to Chapter 3 is Chapter 8, A Logician's View: Deduction, Induction, Fallacies, a fuller and somewhat more difficult discussion of topics set forth in Chapter 3. Our suggestion is this: If you have strong students and you wish to emphasize the role of logic in persuasive writing, assign Chapter 8. We also spend part of a class hour discussing the images in Chapter 3, in particular Lange's *Migrant Mother* and the anonymous poster entitled *Our Homes Are in Danger Now!*, partly because students enjoy discussing them and partly because later in the term we may ask our students to analyze images in the casebooks.

Although Part One includes some discussion of writing (especially concerning annotating and summarizing), our chief discussion of writing is in Part Two (Chapters 4–6): writing an analysis of an argument, writing an argument, and using sources to write a research paper. Each chapter in Part Two can be covered in a meeting, but most instructors probably will want to give two meetings to Chapter 4, Writing an Analysis of an Argument — one to discuss Scott's editorial and the student's analysis of it and another to discuss the arguments in at least two of the eight other essays included in the chapter. In connection with these chapters on writing an argument — especially in connection with Chapter 5, where we talk about the audience as a collaborator — you may also want to assign Chapter 11 in Part Three, A Psychologist's View: Rogerian Argument.

Part Three, Further Views on Argument, contains four chapters already mentioned, A Philosopher's View: The Toulmin Model, A Logician's View: Deduction, Induction, Fallacies, A Lawyer's View: Steps toward Civic Literacy, and A Psychologist's View: Rogerian Argument. It also contains two chapters that we have not yet mentioned, A Moralist's View: Ways of Thinking Ethically and A Literary Critic's View: Arguing about Literature. This last chapter can stand alone, but it is especially useful as preparation for some of the readings in Part Six, Enduring Questions: Essays, Stories, Poems, and a Play.

Part Four, each chapter of which contains a pair of sharply opposed arguments, lets students examine strong, for the most part unnuanced, statements. If Rogerian argument interests you (it is the subject of Chapter 11), you may want to examine one or more of these debates in Rogerian terms, inviting students to search for common ground, in effect asking them to act as mediators or facilitators.

Part Five offers eight Current Issues (for example, Business Ethics, Euthanasia, Sexual Harassment), and Part Six offers three Enduring Questions (What Is the Ideal Society?, How Free Is the Will of the Individual within Society?, and What Are the Grounds of Religious Faith?). Each topic is represented by several voices — in no case fewer than four and in one case as many as eleven. The chapters concerned with Enduring Questions (Chapters 27–29) include some literary selections — poems by Joseph Addison, W. H. Auden, Judith Ortiz Cofer, Emily Dickinson, T. S. Eliot, Robert Frost, Thomas Hardy, Gerard Manley Hopkins, Langston Hughes, Mitsuye Yamada; stories by Ursula K. Le Guin, and Leslie Marmon Silko; a play by Susan Glaspell. If you teach some of this literary material, you may also want to assign by way of preparation Chapter 12, A Literary Critic's View, which includes two stories by Kate Chopin and two poems.

Although any essay in the book can be taken by itself, we hope that you will assign most or even all of the essays within at least one thematic chapter (Chapters 19–29). But of course good arguments can be made for being more selective, and again, much will depend on the abilities of the students and on your overall aims. Chapters 20 (on the death penalty), 21 (drugs), 22 (euthanasia), and 24 (privacy) are probably the thematic chapters that lend themselves most easily to abridgment. On the other hand, some chapters lend themselves easily to expansion. For instance, in Chapter 28 one might take Glaspell's *Trifles* and add Elizabeth Cady Stanton's "Declaration" (from Chapter 27), Judy Brady's "I Want a Wife" (from Chapter 3), and Ellen Willis's "Putting Women Back into the Abortion Debate" (from Chapter 13).

EXERCISES

All of the essays and literary selections in the text are followed by exercises, but in these notes we include some additional topics for discussion and writing.

CONTENTS

Part Six
ENDURING QUESTIONS:
ESSAYS, STORIES, POEMS, AND A PLAY   122

Part One

CRITICAL THINKING AND READING

1
Critical Thinking (p. 3)

Although the ideas in this introductory chapter are pretty straightforward, many of them will be new to some students, and we have therefore tried to illustrate them with a fairly extended discussion of just one example — the West Virginia law in 1989 that restricts a driver's license to those over eighteen, unless they are still in school, in which case they are eligible for a license at sixteen.

It's extremely instructive to see that sometimes a great deal can be extracted from very little, in this instance from one statute on a perfectly ordinary matter. We've tried to present in the manageable scope of this humdrum example many of the considerations discussed in greater detail elsewhere in the book. This example gives the student a real taste of what critical thinking, reading, and writing involve as well as of what lies ahead in the rest of the book.

John Silber

Students Should Not Be above the Law (p. 10)

John Silber, trained at Yale as a philosopher and president of Boston University from 1971 to 1997, is the paradigm of a tough-talking Texas academic. (Those attracted by his ideas in the essay we reprint might want to look also at his book, *Straight Shooting* (1989), in which a selection of his occasional writings is reprinted.) During his long tenure at the helm of Boston University he earned the respect (except when he earned the fury) of students, faculty, and alumni for the firm way he fought with all constituencies to improve the caliber of the university, using methods that were less than democratic. Some of the flavor of his style is unmistakably conveyed in the essay we reprint.

Silber's essay has been subjected to considerable discussion in the text, focusing on his assumptions. By the time that discussion is finished, however, we have looked at more than his assumptions, and so there is little need here to dwell further on his argumentative niceties.

A useful research project for students would be to interview the dean of students (or another responsible campus official) to find out what policy, with what disciplinary actions, their college has regarding on-campus conduct by students that would make them subject to arrest if done off campus. Are the policies and practices on your campus subject to Silber's criticisms? If so, how do your college officials reply to his arguments?

Judith H. Christie

What about the Faculty? (p. 14)

Judith Christie's objection to John Silber's essay is simply that his complaint is not as inclusive as it ought to be. By confining his attention to the way university officials indulgently treat student criminal conduct, Silber fails to object to the way those same officials look the other way when male faculty take advantage of their female students.

Her letter raises at least two questions: First, is she right that there is no good reason for protecting faculty from being "held accountable [off campus] for their behavior"? Second, is she right that the problem of sexual harassment by male faculty is "routinely" ignored by university officials? As to the former question, we agree with her; there is even less reason to protect adult faculty from the legal consequences of their misbehavior than there is to protect postadolescent undergraduates.

As to the latter question, we have no data on the point; our impression is that she may be right about prevailing practices, until fairly recently. Now, however, on the campuses we know best our impression is that women students are much more empowered and are far more capable of bringing (or threatening) charges against predatory male faculty than their mothers were.

Christie fails to notice two other points of interest. First, many (most?) colleges and universities have made great strides in developing their own disciplinary procedures where sexual harassment by faculty is concerned. Second, it is by no means obvious that a woman student (or young female faculty member, for that matter) is always better off pursuing off-campus legal remedies than she is by being content with on-campus remedies.

For a fuller discussion of sexual harassment, see Chapter 25 and our discussion in the manual at p. 112.

A Casebook on Examining Assumptions: What Values Do Tests Have?

First, a few words about testing. The negative view seems to be that

1. Tests damage students in two ways: (a) tests often discourage "true" learning; and (b) tests result in classifying students, with the result that those students who for one reason or another do not do well on tests are classified to their disadvantage;

2. Tests damage teachers, who (so to speak) teach the test (or "teach for the test") rather than teach the subject they are genuinely interested in.

Critics of testing often note that those who advocate tests are fond of using such words as "standards," "success," "accountability," and "evaluation" and, on the other hand, are not likely to use such words as "excitement," "involvement," and "inquiring minds." Further, critics of testing point out that (1) a student may have a bad day, just as a baseball player may have a season average of .330 but in any given ballgame may not get a hit and (2) a student may not be skilled at taking tests — perhaps because he or she can't work under pressure — but may nevertheless be talented even within the field of the test.

On the other hand, those who defend tests (see, for instance, the essay by Diane Ravitch in Chapter 1 of the text) are likely to say that we *need* to "assess" and "evaluate" so that we can help students advance in their education. But they also point out that tests help to protect society: Who wants drivers on the road who have not passed a driving test?

Paul Goodman

A Proposal to Abolish Grading (p. 16)

Our first question asks about Goodman's assumption when he suggests in his opening paragraph that a few "prestigious" universities should abolish grading and use tests only for pedagogic purposes that the instructors find appropriate. As we see it, Goodman assumes that (1) students will then study because of "the beauty of the subject" (para. 2) and (2) most other schools, when they see that the prestigious universities no longer use grades, will similarly adopt the practice of using tests only for pedagogic purposes. Not surprisingly, he doesn't offer any evidence to support these assumptions.

Although presumably all or almost all instructors do regard their subjects as beautiful or at least as inherently interesting, it may well be that some students who *need* the subject for professional reasons (let's say, statistics, for an economist) are unable to perceive the beauty of the subject. Second, we can ask if the less prestigious schools will or should follow the doings of Ivy League schools. Quite possibly a procedure that works well for very bright students who are financially well-off (not all students in Ivy League schools come from rich families, of course, but most of the lower-income students who are in the elite schools are there on substantial scholarships) will not work well for students who are average and who are financially pressed. Further, many students at top institutions probably (speaking a bit broadly) come to college with expectations and study habits that are different from those of students who attend less distinguished institutions. Our point: Although we find Goodman's essay attractive, he does not come anywhere near to building a compelling case.

He could easily have strengthened his case, and we suggest that in teaching the essay you ask students *how* he might have strengthened it. For instance, he says that a test can be used for "pedagogic purposes," but he does not explain how an instructor might indicate a student's weaknesses without grading the test. There are ways, and students can probably set them forth.

But in discussing this essay in class the danger is that students will confirm Goodman's worst fears. Students will argue *for* grading because they want to be admitted to veterinary school, because they need grades on a transcript to apply to a four-year college, or because (they say) they wouldn't work hard in courses without grades. A difficulty in teaching this essay, then, is focusing discussion on the function of grading in *education*, not in *certification*, and of course education is Goodman's real topic.

Leon Botstein

A Tyranny of Standardized Tests (p. 19)

Surely Botstein is correct when he says, "Quickness of recall does not indicate depth of understanding" (para. 6). In college, instructors sometimes use tests that do not require quickness of recall (tests that are not timed or open-book tests), but it is probably true that in elementary school and high school almost all tests are ruled by the clock. And surely it is true that (1) some students do not work well when they are under pressure and (2) even a student who normally is skilled in taking tests may have a bad day, perhaps because she couldn't get a good night's sleep since her sibling was coughing all night.

Botstein is chiefly concerned with *learning*, and he does grant that "Testing can and must be linked to learning" (para. 12). But do tests have other legitimate purposes too, such as *certification*? A topic worth thinking about.

A word about question 4, in which we call attention to Botstein's use of analogy in paragraphs 8 and 10. In paragraph 8 he writes, "When we go for a medical checkup, we are evaluated not only in terms of an objective standard of health but on the progress or deterioration in our own particular bodies since the last examination." In paragraph 10 he asks, "Would we tolerate a system in sports where the calls of umpires and linesmen remained a secret until the next season and the hits and errors of particular players were never revealed or justified?" Well, as we try to explain in the text when we talk about analogy, an analogy involves a comparison between *un*like things that are alleged to be *like* in some particular respect. If we say, "Don't change horses in midstream," and we are talking about an election in difficult times, we are saying that choosing a new leader in uncertain times is like mounting a horse in difficult circumstances. The figure is effective, but surely an election is very different from mounting a horse, and what is true about changing horses may not be true about changing a leader.

Speaking a bit broadly, we can say that reasoning by analogy can be effective if the similarities are highly relevant to the conclusion. Thus, people who said that the climate of northern California is similar to the climate of southern France and therefore that northern California ought to be suitable for viticulture found by experiment that indeed the analogy worked. The conclusion turned out to be right: California is like France in X; therefore, it probably is like France in Y. But if someone had said (to take a ridiculous instance) that because the population of eastern Canada equaled the population of southern France, eastern Canada ought to be suitable for viticulture, the speaker would be wrong. Why? Because climate is closely related to viticulture, whereas size of population is not. In our view, Botstein's analogy between a medical examination — really a physical checkup — and a school test is bizarre. A medical examination is not the same thing (despite the word *examination*) as an examination in a Spanish class; we see almost no relevance between the similarities and the conclusion. Similarly, the analogy in paragraph 10 between testing in school and the calls of umpires and linesmen in a game seems to us to be based on virtually no relevant similarities; the calls of umpires in a baseball game are nothing like the evaluations of teachers who are teaching English grammar or who are teaching how the Electoral College works. A game cannot proceed without the umpire's immediate call, but learning can certainly proceed without an immediate call from the teacher.

If you talk about analogy in class, we urge you to assign Max Shulman's "Love Is a Fallacy" (Chapter 8, p. 329), where analogy — Shulman's example concerns examinations — is hilariously treated (paras. 101–03).

A very few words about the four letters that Botstein's essay stimulated.

Janet Rudolph makes several sound points: A test measures "only a small portion of a child's intellectual reservoir," it "is often used . . . to pigeonhole students, guiding important choices like college placement and future employment," and it does not usually "measure creativity, music, and artistic ability, ethics, human relationships or independent thinking." Probably most educators (as well as parents and children) would agree. The question remains, however, whether her conclusion is sound: "Tests are a very poor, even destructive measure of a person." Or perhaps we should say that her conclusion may well be true if indeed tests are the sole measure of judging a person. If, on the other hand, they are combined with personal statements, interviews, auditions, and letters of recommendation, perhaps one can argue that they have their function and their place.

Jerome Henkin provides an interesting example of what is commonly called "anecdotal evidence." Drawing on his experience, he cites an instance that is quite moving. But what does it prove about the value or lack of value of tests?

Batya Lewton, writing about timed tests, also draws on her experience, though she goes beyond a single example. Presumably advocates of timed tests might well say that there is a place and a need for both kinds.

Sidney Wilson broadens the issue. He agrees (in a subordinate clause) that better kinds of tests might well be helpful but argues (in the independent clause — the more important part of the sentence) that Botstein's essay has the unfortunate effect of reinforcing the idea that education will improve markedly if we can only develop better tests. For Wilson, what is needed is not better tests but better teachers, and he suggests we will get better teachers if we pay for them. (Our guess is that Botstein would agree — and also that he would explain that he was not addressing the largest problem in education but only one specific topic.)

Diane Ravitch

In Defense of Testing (p. 24)

We like Ravitch's opening paragraph — a punchy short sentence followed by two longer sentences that offer concrete details to support the initial broad generalization. Here is the paragraph:

> No one wants to be tested. We would all like to get a driver's license without answering questions about right of way or showing that we can parallel park a car. Many future lawyers and doctors probably wish they could join their profession without taking an exam.

Given the title of the essay, "In Defense of Testing," however, we know what is coming: "But tests and standards are a necessary fact of life." So far she hasn't proved anything or, rather, hasn't proved anything other than that she can hold a reader's attention by writing clearly. And that's quite a lot.

In her third and fourth paragraphs she looks at the harm that tests have done. It's always a good strategy to grant that your side of the argument has its weaknesses and the other side has its strengths. But, she argues, we now see clearly that the proper role of tests is not to "ration" education but to "improve" it. Hard to quarrel with her here. The fifth paragraph continues the rosy view ("enormous benefits"), and the sixth tells us what "good tests" should be like. Her final paragraph opens with a sentence that probably engenders assent from almost all readers ("Performance in education means the mastery of both knowledge and skills") though perhaps a hypersensitive reader sniffs danger: "Performance" — a word used by persons who value credentials too highly; "mastery" — a word that is not only sexist but that has a faint aroma of cruelty. And then the bombshell: "This is why it is reasonable to test teachers to make sure they know their subject matter as well as how to teach it to young children." Well, we should have seen it coming. Ravitch's title is "In Defense of Testing," so why shouldn't testing refer to teachers as well as to students? Still, her essay is almost entirely directed toward the testing of students, not teachers.

2
Critical Reading: Getting Started (p. 27)

The major points made in this chapter — that one should read carefully and that making a summary helps one to grasp an argument — are obvious, and perhaps that's why students often ignore them. Our experience suggests that students often fail to grasp the main points of an argument not because it is especially difficult but merely because they do not read it carefully. But if they do read it carefully (aided by writing a summary), they are likely to find ideas arising — differences with the author — and therefore the process of writing a summary of someone else's ideas can be a way of generating ideas of one's own. Drawing on the assumptions in Chapter 1, it may be useful to ask students to underline any explicit assumptions that the writer makes (these will probably appear in the summary) and then to think about, and to jot down, any assumptions present but *not* stated.

Nicholas Negroponte

Being Asynchronous (p. 33)

We include this short essay chiefly to distinguish between *paraphrase* and *summary*, a distinction many students are unaware of. We think it is essential that they grasp the distinction and that they put this knowledge to use when they are writing arguments in which they draw on sources. In such writing, summary is almost inevitable, but paraphrase ought to be rare, reserved chiefly for notably difficult passages in a source.

Negroponte is the apostle of high-tech communication, so we were surprised at the technological hurdles we had to overcome when we telephoned Massachusetts Institute of technology, asked to be connected with Negroponte, heard the connection being made, and received a message, "The voice mailbox is full." A second telephone call to MIT's switchboard gave us an operator who said she would connect us with the Media Lab, of which Negroponte is the director. This call did indeed go through, but the person on the other end of the line was not in the Media Lab but in the Humanities Department. A day or two later we did get into touch with Negroponte, and he generously provided whatever information we asked for — but we have forgotten what we asked for.

Suggested Topic for Writing

Do you agree with Negroponte that answering machines "should *always* answer the telephone"? Explain. (Our own view: If the answering machine always answers the phone, we need not explain, while eating, that we do not want another credit card. On the other hand, we are uneasy about keeping friends at bay and seeming a bit rude. A few of our friends always let the machine answer, which means that we have to endure their message ("This is such-and-such a number; no one is here to answer your call, but if you wish to leave a message or to send a fax, please wait for the beep and . . ."), and they then pick the phone up after we say, "Hi, this is X, and I was calling about . . . ." We are not happy with this arrangement, but, in our experience, most students support Negroponte's position.

Susan Jacoby

A First Amendment Junkie (p. 36)

With Susan Jacoby's essay we hope to show that even where the language is informal, the topic familiar, and the argument fairly easy, a second or third reading may reveal things not perceived in a quick scanning.

At this stage in the course we are less intent on exploring the pros and cons of the issue than on teaching how to read, how to summarize, and how to become aware of explicit and implicit assumptions. "How to read" includes developing awareness of persona and tone, and it is worth discussing the title (even though it is the editors', because the original title was simply "Hers," the unvarying title of a weekly column in the *New York Times*), and worth discussing the ways in which Jacoby establishes a persona.

Although in the text we do not discuss the role of a persona until Chapter 4, preliminary discussion in class can help to pave the way for the student's later encounter with the topic. Because a writer's choice of a persona depends partly on the audience, it is appropriate to discuss this essay *as an argument for readers of a specific newspaper*. It's not a bad idea to ask students to read a couple of issues of the *Times*. Students who have been taught to write in a somewhat stiff, impersonal manner may be surprised to learn from Jacoby (and other columnists in the paper) that they can use "I," and they can even use colloquial diction ("junkie") in some contexts.

Our second question in the text, on Jacoby's next-to-last paragraph, is prompted by our thought that although the essay is always clear, she makes some leaps. The women who favor censorship in paragraph 1 are, on the whole, women who see pornography as one kind of violence against women. Paragraph 5 gets into kiddie porn — a related issue, but not the same issue. Probably Jacoby introduces it to dissociate herself from the extreme position of some opponents of censorship. (It is usually a good idea to distance oneself from extremists who share one's views.) But the issue of young people surfaces again in paragraphs 13 and 14. There is, of course, a connection between Jacoby's arguments that parents should protect the young and her argument that adult-oriented pornography, however objectionable, should not be censored. The connection is that it is the job of adults to fulfill their responsibilities, and not to "shift responsibility from individuals to institutions" (para. 13).

Question 3, on the final paragraph, aims at getting students to see that a final paragraph need not begin "Thus we see" and need not summarize all the points argued earlier.

Question 5, about what is or is not permitted under the "absolute interpretation of the First Amendment," is meant to provoke some thought about whether anyone does or should want the free-speech clause to include protection of offensive and possibly harmful acts — when the acts are wholly verbal (as seems tolerated by Justice Black's remark quoted in Jacoby's para. 2). Falsely shouting "Fire!" in a crowded theater may be no more than a speech act, but it was Justice Holmes's famous example of speech *not* protected by the First Amendment because in a context of utterance such as his example provides, these words would cause "a clear and present danger" of *harm* (and not merely annoyance, offense, or other hostile feelings) to the innocent.

For a discussion of constitutional law on the First Amendment, see Archibald Cox, *Freedom of Expression* (1981). An older book, still of great value, is Thomas I. Emerson's *The System of Freedom of Expression* (1970). A more recent book on the subject is by Anthony Lewis, *Make No Law* (1991).

Note: We discuss in the text, on page 294, Jacoby's essay from the point of view of the Toulmin method.

(text pp. 36–41)

A NOTE ON HATE SPEECH

The argument about whether hate speech (for example, racial epithets) should be permitted on the campus is not likely to go away, nor is it likely to be answered definitively. Here are the chief arguments that we have encountered.

Arguments in favor of restricting speech on the campus:

1. Speech demeaning a person's color, creed, sex, sexual orientation, or other personal attributes creates a hostile learning environment — a workplace in which work cannot be done — and thus such speech infringes on the rights of others. Sometimes this argument is supported by a comparison with sexual harassment: The courts have upheld regulations against sexual harassment in the workplace. Thus, if women have a right to work in a nonthreatening environment, then students have a right to study in an atmosphere free of racial (or other) harassment. But how exact is the comparison?

2. Limitation of such speech is allowable under the "fighting-words" doctrine. A face-to-face insult using four-letter words or other epithets and addressed to an individual or small group is not intended to discover truth or initiate dialogue but rather is an attempt to injure and inflame. Such language is not protected by the First Amendment, according to the Supreme Court in *Chaplinsky v. New Hampshire* (1942). (In this case, a man shouted into the face of a police officer that he was a "Goddamned racketeer and a damned fascist.")

3. A college or university fosters unlimited inquiry, *not* unlimited speech. Hate speech does not lead to advances in knowledge.

4. Outlawing hate speech would not mean that there would be limitations on discussions even of heinous ideas, in situations that allow for rebuttal or for persons to choose not to attend.

Arguments against restricting speech on campus:

1. Restrictions against remarks about race, creed, and so forth violate the rights of free speech under the First Amendment. Such remarks do not come under the fighting-words doctrine, since it is not clear that they will produce violence, especially if they are comments about groups rather than specific individuals.

2. By tolerating (rather than suppressing) such speech, we are in a better position to diagnose the real problems that give rise to racist speech and can try to face them directly, not indirectly through regulation and prohibition.

3. We all need to develop a thicker skin to merely verbal utterances that offend. If we don't, then either we will foolishly attempt to protect *everyone* from whatever speech offends them, or we will yield the platform and rostrum to whoever is nastiest among us. Either way threatens disaster; the best remedy for bad speech is still better speech, not silence.

4. Exactly which words are to be prohibited? When three students at the University of Wisconsin complained that they had been called "rednecks," the administration told them that "redneck" is "not a demeaning term." Or consider the word "Negro," once considered a polite term, used by African Americans both privately and publicly, but now regarded by many as demeaning. Another example: "Queer" used to be, and for many people still is, a demeaning term for a homosexual, but in the last few years many homosexuals have themselves used the term, as in the group called Queer Nation.

The Supreme Court decided (June 1992) that an ordinance against hate speech enacted by the city of St. Paul was unconstitutional. The ordinance banned any action "which one knows . . . arouses anger, alarm, or resentment in others on the basis of race, color, creed, religion or gender." The case did not concern speech on the campus, but it did concern expression of racial hate — the burning of a cross on the lawn of a black family that had recently moved into a white neighborhood. In *R.A.V. v. St. Paul*, Justice Scalia, writing for the majority of five (Kennedy, Rehnquist, Scalia, Souter, Thomas) held that government may not opt for "silencing speech on the basis of its content."

The majority opinion, holding that the St. Paul law was impermissibly narrow, acknowledged that hate speech directed at race or religion was hurtful, but did not concede that there was any difference in kind between a racial epithet and, for instance, an insult directed at union membership or political affiliation. The court made the point that burning a cross on someone's lawn is "reprehensible," but it insisted that "St. Paul has sufficient means [such as trespassing laws] to prevent such behavior without adding the First Amendment to the fire."

The other four justices agreed that the St. Paul ordinance was unconstitutional, but they would have struck it down on the less sweeping ground that it was written in too broad a manner. The justices who did not sign the majority opinion (Blackmun, O'Connor, Stevens, White) were troubled by the refusal of the majority to see that certain kinds of hate speech are especially evil. Justice White, for instance, said that the city's

> selective regulation reflects the city's judgment that harms based on race, color, creed, religion, or gender are more pressing public concerns than the harms caused by other fighting words. . . . In light of our nation's long and painful experience with discrimination, this determination is plainly reasonable.

Justice Stevens, in a footnote, glancing at the Los Angeles riots earlier in the year, wrote:

> One need look no further than the recent social unrest in the nation's cities to see that race-based threats may cause more harm to society and to individuals than other threats. . . . Until the nation matures beyond that condition, laws such as St. Paul's ordinance will remain reasonable and justifiable.

In short, the justices who refrained from joining the majority valued free speech not as something good in itself but as something instrumental. That is, they valued speech on the ground that it serves a constructive purpose by helping to create a better informed electorate and therefore a better country. In this view, speech that is harmful need not be protected.

According to a report in the *New York Times*, June 24, 1992, a spokesman for the American Council on Education said that the consequences of the decision for colleges and universities are unclear. Private institutions face fewer constitutional restraints, the report said, than do public institutions, but it is thought that those educational institutions with codes will probably modify them. For instance, after a federal court in 1989 declared unconstitutional the code of University of Michigan in Ann Arbor, the university adopted a provisional code prohibiting

> physical acts or threats or verbal slurs, invectives or epithets referring to an individual's race, ethnicity, religion, sex, sexual orientation, creed, national origin, ancestry, age, or handicap made with the purpose of injuring the person to whom the words or actions are directed and that are not made as part of a discussion or exchange of an idea, ideology, or philosophy.

You might want to ask your students to evaluate the Michigan provisional code.

A Casebook for Critical Reading:
Should Some Kinds of Speech Be Censored? (p. 42)

Susan Brownmiller

Let's Put Pornography Back in the Closet (p. 43)

First, a point made by Wendy Kaminer in an essay in *Take Back the Night*, edited by Laura Lederer (the book in which Susan Brownmiller's essay also appears): Feminists such as Brownmiller in recent years have been arguing that pornography is not merely dirty (obscene) but is, by virtue of images of violence against women, a threat to society. The distinction, Kaminer explains, is important. "Obscenity" is not constitutionally protected, but it is very narrowly defined. According to the Supreme Court ruling in *Miller v. California* (1973), obscene material is material "that the average person, applying community standards . . . would find . . . as a whole, appeals to the prurient interest" and "taken as a whole, lacks serious artistic, political, or scientific value." It is extremely difficult to prove in court that a work is obscene. Moreover, although almost any piece of hard-core pornography probably fits this description, enforcement of obscenity laws is difficult because the government may not prohibit publication of any material before the courts decide it is obscene. Each book or magazine must individually be judged obscene before it may be enjoined. Kaminer points out that a store with one thousand books cannot be closed because of fifty or even five hundred obscenity convictions. The stock that has not been judged obscene can be sold.

The newer view of pornography, developed especially by Catharine MacKinnon and Andrea Dworkin, sees it not merely as obscenity but as material that depicts the subjugation of women. Pornography is said to represent violence against women, thereby impeding their chances of achieving equal opportunity. It should be mentioned, by the way, that although some feminists oppose pornography on the grounds that it is humiliating to women, other feminists argue that (l) modern feminism is itself linked to sexual liberation, and (2) feminists who fear pornography unwittingly reinforce the notion that women are sexually passive.

Brownmiller, claiming that the battle for free speech has on the whole been won, asserts that pornography is not chiefly a matter of free speech, but she, like MacKinnon and Dworkin, politicizes the issue and thereby tends to legitimize pornography. That is, by seeing it as political speech, these writers bring it into a constitutionally protected area. Of course if they can demonstrate that pornography is a threat to society — a "clear and present danger" — then they will have put it in an area *not* constitutionally protected, but it is very difficult to prove that something is a "clear and present danger." (Cf. question 3.)

A February 1986 ruling of the Supreme Court is relevant. The Court ruled *un*constitutional an Indianapolis ordinance that forbade pornography on the ground that it is a form of discrimination against women. The ordinance, drafted with the help of MacKinnon and Dworkin, defined pornography as "the graphic sexually explicit subordination of women, whether in pictures or in words," if it showed them enjoying "pain or humiliation" or if they were in "positions of servility or submission or display." Brownmiller is especially concerned about images of these sorts. Although the Supreme Court did not explain why it declared the ordinance unconstitutional, perhaps we can guess the rationale by considering the explanation of Judge Frank Easterbrook, for the court of appeals, when he ruled against the city ordinance. Easterbrook said that the Indianapolis law "discriminates on the grounds of the content of speech" by establishing "an 'approved' view of women." "This is thought control," he said, for this law attempted to silence explicit speech that did not conform to a particular view of women. He also pointed out that the law could be applied to Homer's epics and to Joyce's *Ulysses*.

Now to look, briefly, a little more closely at Brownmiller's essay. She begins by calling free speech "one of the great foundations on which our democracy rests," thus putting herself on the side of virtue, a good strategy when arguing. Brownmiller then goes on to indicate that she would not burn *Ulysses*, *Lady Chatterley's Lover*, and the *Tropic* books. Again she is on the side of virtue, or at least of classic liberal thought. In short, Brownmiller devotes her first seven paragraphs to showing that she is for democracy and the arts. In paragraph 8 she says she is "not opposed to sex and desire," again establishing her credentials as a liberal. In paragraph 9 she briefly explains why feminists *do* object to pornography (it degrades women), and the remainder of the essay (less than half of the total) amplifies the point. In paragraph 14 she raises an important point that we glanced at earlier in this commentary — not all speech is protected — but, again as we suggested, although the Constitution does not protect a person who falsely shouts "Fire!" in a crowded theater (a "clear and present danger"), there is some question about whether pornography represents such a danger. Still, by mentioning false advertising and the cry of "Fire," paragraph 14 effectively suggests that pornography is not necessarily protected.

Charles R. Lawrence III

On Racist Speech (p. 46)

So-called hate speech on campus in recent years has provoked anger and dismay among students, faculty, staff, and the public at large. Any attempt to control such speech by official regulation seems likely to be on a collision course with the First Amendment. Or so most academic administrators concluded, after *Doe v. University of Michigan* (1989). In that case, regulations restricting free speech on the Michigan campus out of a desire to resist "a rising tide of racial intolerance and harassment on campus," were permanently enjoined by Judge Avern Cohn. Judge Cohn of course had no difficulty permitting regulations as to time, place, and manner of speech. His concern was about the way the university's regulations governed *content*. He held that any regulations against the content of "speech" on no stronger ground than that it was "offensive" — even "gravely so [to] large numbers of people" — was unconstitutionally vague and overbroad.

Charles Lawrence is himself African American (see his para. 15) (by the way, he's the brother of Sara Lawrence Lightfoot, author of the widely acclaimed *Balm in Gilead: Journey of a Healer* [1988]), and he presents a measured defense of narrowly drawn regulations against hate speech. No enemy of the First Amendment (see paras. 1 and 14–19), he nonetheless doubts whether its defenders really will act on the proposition, touted by the American Civil Liberties Union in its perennial defense of the First Amendment, that the best remedy for bad speech is more and better speech (para. 17).

Lawrence's position (question 2) is clear from the opening sentence of paragraph 8: If regulations of conduct on campus are needed to protect minority students from harassment and personal vilification, then "equal educational opportunity" is the "compelling justification" for them. We would agree; a few students have no right to make campus life intolerable for others by language, gesture, or symbol that interferes with their rightful access to all the campus has to offer.

But we would also urge that before any such regulations are adopted, one needs to reflect carefully on several basic facts. Everyone finds some words or pictures offensive, but what offends one does not always offend others. Not everything that is offensive is seriously harmful (or counts as harassment). Finally, not everything offensive can be prevented. We all need to develop a thick skin to the merely offensive, lest we find ourselves provoked into violent response or timidly cowering before verbal bullies. We all also need to cultivate a civil environment, free of insulting, degrading, and offensive behavior, verbal or otherwise, especially on a college campus.

Part of what makes the whole hate speech issue so controversial and difficult are the uncertainties that surround the key words "assaultive speech," "verbal vilification," and the like (question 5). Lawrence does not attempt to define these terms explicitly, nor does he provide illustrative and convincing examples of verbal conduct that is "assaultive" or "vilifying." (Students could be usefully asked to give some such examples — genuine or hypothetical — themselves and then see whether they can give sensible definitions of these terms.) Nor does Lawrence draft a model set of regulations for hate speech that would prevent (or make liable to punishment for) the harm such speech causes and still pass constitutional muster.

We suspect that Lawrence would deny that straight white males (question 4) are as vulnerable to insulting posters and the like as are certain other classes of students (blacks, women, gays). The reason is that political power and social status have traditionally been the preserve of white males, so that as a class they are relatively immune to the power of offensive language to degrade and intimidate. Of course, Lawrence might still argue (as we would) that straight white males ought not to have to endure insults because of their race or sexual orientation and that regulations protecting women or blacks or homosexuals from vilification ought to be extended equally to all classes of students.

Derek Bok

Protecting Freedom of Expression on the Campus (p. 51)

Like Charles R. Lawrence III (see the previous essay in the chapter), Derek Bok is trained as a lawyer, avows his personal allegiance to the First Amendment, and speaks from a position of concern about racially provocative speech and symbols on a private university campus. (This last point is important because the courts seem to agree that *private* colleges and universities are not bound by the First Amendment as are public institutions. Notice that in paragraph 9, Bok rightly refuses to use this reason for favoring regulations of free speech on the Harvard campus.) But where Lawrence speaks in measured tones on behalf of the victims of "hate speech," Bok seems to speak for the vast majority of bystanders, those who are neither victims nor offenders where hate speech is concerned.

Bok offers three very different reasons for opposing attempts to curtail hate speech. First, unlike Lawrence he is doubtful whether the class of harmful verbal and graphic symbols can be suitably defined so that they can be regulated without infringing on full freedom of expression (para. 10). Second, even if such regulations could be drafted and enforced, they would not change racist attitudes or bring greater mutual respect and decency to campus life (para. 11). Finally, irrepressible adolescents will gleefully "test the limits" of these regulations, thereby aggravating the nuisance and trying the patience of deans and disciplinary committees (para. 12). From our own experience we are strongly inclined to agree with Bok on all these points, even if they do not constitute the last word on the subject.

What constructive measures against hate speech does Bok recommend? First, prospective victims ought to learn to "ignore" nasty and hateful speech; second, the rest of the campus community ought to counsel and persuade would-be vilifiers to mend their ways lest they do grave harm to some of their fellow students (para. 13). Sensible advice, indeed — but perhaps too easily issued by one who himself is neither black, female, gay, or (it would appear) in any other way a member of a group specially vulnerable to verbal assault. Indeed, we can understand how some will judge Bok's counsels to be unimaginative and deeply disappointing.

Notice, too, that although Bok cites several grounds for restricting speech (para. 7), they do not include the ground Lawrence mentioned in the previous essay — namely, ensuring equal educational opportunity to minority students.

Jean Kilbourne

"Own This Child" (p. 53)

Hardly a week goes by when one does not encounter in a national magazine an article complaining that advertisements are deceptive, with their "Buy me and you will have friends," or "Use-this-perfume-and-you-will-be irresistible," and their meaningless assertions such as "New, improved," and "Doctors say." And hardly a day goes by when a college instructor does not find in the mail a brochure that claims the newest textbook has been "classroom tested" and will hold the interest of students. In the extract that we print, Kilbourne is less concerned with such deceptive claims than she is with the fact that advertisers aim material at children. Still, just as we scrutinize the language of advertisers, we ought to scrutinize the language of those who attack advertisers. What are we to make, for instance, of Kilbourne's assertion that because we do not prohibit advertisements aimed at children one might "conclude that we are a nation that hates its children" (para. 2)?

For us, one of the most interesting points that she raises (aside from the question of whether advertisements aimed at children should be prohibited) appears in paragraphs 7 to 10, where she talks about businesses that give schools funds or supplies in exchange for the opportunity to get their names in front of kids' eyes. "Cash-strapped and underfunded schools accept this dance with the devil" (para. 9). We imagine that our third question, in which we ask if a school should reject funds for a "Nike concert," will provide good class discussion. Incidentally, can one go further? All colleges accept money from donors and name buildings for them. Indeed, some colleges are named for generous donors, and plenty of schools — perhaps especially business and engineering schools — have buildings and professorships that are obviously connected with a particular business (the Ford Laboratory, the Toyota Professor). Should elementary schools and secondary schools adopt the practice, so we might have the Toys R Us Playroom, Nike Gymnasium, perhaps even Coca-Cola High School (known familiarly as Coke High)?

A word about question 6, in which we call attention to Kilbourne's distress that today's kids drink more soda than milk (see her final paragraph), and we ask where the reader may have encountered the idea that milk is more healthful than soda. We ourselves are inclined to believe that milk is good for people, but, on reflection we realize that we learned this idea from our parents, who learned it from ads sponsored by the dairy industry. It happens that on the day we were drafting this page, we came across an item in the *New York Times*, September 26, 2000, called "Debate over Milk," which reports that a nonprofit group called Physician's Committee for Responsible Medicine has taken on the Nutrition Dairy Council (very much a for-profit group, we guess, since it essentially is in the business of advertising milk). The Physicians Committee claims that cow's milk has various harmful effects on children, and apparently at least some of their claims may be true. In any case, our point is that although Kilbourne deplores advertising, her belief that milk is healthful probably is the result of exposure to ads.

3
Critical Reading: Getting Deeper into Arguments (p. 59)

This chapter may seem to hold our major discussion of arguing, for in it we talk about definitions, assumptions, induction, deduction, and evidence (and we do think it is essential reading for students) but we think that the next three chapters — Writing an Analysis of an Argument, Developing an Argument of Your Own, and Using Sources are equally important. Moreover, for especially strong students, Part Three will be valuable. It includes a summary of the Toulmin method for analyzing arguments and then offers further discussion of deduction and induction from a philosophic point of view. It also includes a survey of fallacies (Chapter 8), Carl R Rogers's "Communication: Its Blocking and Its Facilitation" (Chapter 11), and Max Shulman's entertaining and informative "Love Is a Fallacy" (Chapter 8).

Nothing is particularly difficult in the chapter; most students should have no trouble with it, including its section on analyzing images, its short essays and its brief casebook on computers.

Note: In our discussion of *analogy* we give Judith Thomson's example in which (during the course of an argument on abortion) she invites the reader to imagine that he or she wakes up and finds that a violinist whose body has not been functioning adequately has been hooked up to the reader's body. Thomson's essay originally appeared in *Philosophy and Public Affairs* 1.1 (Fall 1971): 47–66, and is reprinted in her book *Rights, Restitution, and Risk* (1986).

IMAGES FOR ANALYSIS

Dorothea Lange

Migrant Mother (p. 98)

We think most students will agree that the more tightly framed image is more moving. The other is interesting, but the lamp in the lower left, the lean-to, the landscape at the right, and the faces of the two children — especially the appealing face of the child resting her chin on the mother's shoulder — provide distractions. In the famous image, which is more symmetrical than the other and which almost surely puts us in mind of traditional paintings of the Madonna and child, the two faceless children have turned to the mother for comfort. Further, the mother's hand touches her chin, somewhat suggesting the pose of Rodin's *The Thinker*, but whereas Rodin's muscular man is an image of strength — mental as well as physical — Lange's migrant mother is an image of powerlessness. We can admire her courage, and we know that her children love her because they turn to her for comfort, but we also know that however hard she thinks, she is not going to solve her problem.

Anonymous

Our Homes Are In Danger Now! *(p. 99)*

We think it is interesting that although Hitler is shown, a specific Japanese person (Emperor Hirohito or General and later Prime Minister Tojo) is not shown. Apparently during World War II, no single Japanese face was sufficiently familiar to American viewers so that it could stand for Japanese aggression. Perhaps behind this failure to identify an individual Japanese is the common Western idea that "They all look alike."

Why does Hitler have a gun and the Japanese a knife? There is no need to comment on the gun, but probably the knife suggests the racist idea that Asians are more primitive than Caucasians.

The globe that Hitler and the Japanese are grabbing shows the United States, and the text ("OUR HOMES ARE IN DANGER *NOW!*") is given visual form by little houses on the map. Speaking of little houses, why is the image of the American response — a bomber and a tank, encircled by the words "*OUR JOB* KEEP 'EM FIRING" — so small? Presumably to emphasize our vulnerability. We Americans are the little kids on the block, menaced by hulking bullies.

Daniel Craig

A New Renaissance? (p. 100)

First, a few words about portraiture. It is almost universally agreed that a portrait ought to provide a likeness — it should show the viewer what the subject's face looks like — and it should also reveal personality, the mind of the sitter. The idea here is that our faces reveal our intellectual abilities ("The stupidity is written all over his face") and our moral nature ("What a good mother she must be"). Presumably this belief that faces tell the viewer something is tied to the belief that, as Orwell said, "At 50, everyone has the face he deserves"; if we are mean-spirited we will have a mean-spirited face, and if we are intelligent we will have an intelligent face. Camus says pretty much the same thing: "After a certain age every man is responsible for his face." Probably the idea that there is an art or science of face-reading is of a piece with palm-reading and phrenology, but it is widespread, and indeed we find ourselves subscribing to it.

It is tempting to believe that faces are, so to speak, autobiographical, but we should keep in mind Duncan's words in *Macbeth*: "There's no art / To find the mind's construction in the face." We should remember too, or students should be told, that until the Renaissance, painted portraits were not much concerned with an image of what the subject looked like. Rather, they were chiefly concerned with presenting the subject as the *sort* of person he or she was — a queen, a saint, or a warrior — and stereotypical attributes (a throne, a halo, or a sword), as well as an appropriate costume would do the trick. Mere faces were interchangeable. In Europe, with the Renaissance came an interest in individualism and in portraiture that closely reproduced what the eye saw. Of course, the social status of the sitter was still identified by the setting, garments, and attributes — books for the scholar — but the emphasis was on what might be thought of as a scientific accuracy in depicting physical appearance. The painter was a sort of cartographer, mapping the human face, and if he had ideas about his sitter's personality, he was supposed to keep them to himself. To some extent, then, the Renaissance portrait painter was himself a sort of Mr. Spock, guided not by emotions but by pure rationality, looking clearly and telling the truth rather than flattering or expressing preconceived ideas.

Daniel Craig's Renaissance-style image of Mr. Spock perhaps was prompted by the title of the essay, "A New Renaissance?," an essay summed up on the *Utne Reader* cover with these words: "High tech may rule today, but tomorrow belongs to the human spirit." Given this title and given Western technology's close association with the Renaissance (think of Leonardo's drawings of machines), it is not surprising that the artist who was assigned to produce an illustration for the cover decided to use a Renaissance style for the portrait of one of popular culture's best-known (if fictional) high-tech leaders. There probably is no need to spend much time in class on the style of Renaissance portraiture, and if you ask your students to talk about the style of Renaissance portraiture, they may confess they have few ideas about the subject, but if you remind them of Leonardo's *Mona Lisa* and then ask them whether the picture of Spock is closer to Leonardo, van Gogh, Picasso, or Walt Disney, they will find that indeed they *do* have some idea about the conventions of Renaissance portraiture.

Ordinarily an image of this sort might be used to diminish and thus to spoof its subject — that is, to cause the viewer to think about the disparity between the subject and the image. Thus, *The New Yorker* showed Monica Lewinsky as *Mona Lisa*, but in the case of this *Utne Reader* cover the aim surely is not to deride. True, inevitably the picture provokes a bit of a smile — a familiar modern face in Renaissance clothing and moreover the face of a guy with pointy ears — but presumably it stimulates reflection rather than mockery. According to the cover article, "The original Renaissance in fifteenth-century Italy confronted a medieval mindset that diminished human achievement and exalted God's omnipotence. In the same spirit, these new Renaissance women and men [such as Riane Eisler, Duane Elgin, and Barbara Marx Hubbard] challenge the prevailing dogma of our era: the idea that the Market and high technology are omnipotent forces whose decrees we must blindly obey" (44). "The renaissance they're working for is a rebirth of high-level human ingenuity in the service of human ends, not market commands or technological wonders — a total rethinking of the terms of political and social change" (47).

Ronald Takaki

The Harmful Myth of Asian Superiority (p. 102)

In his first paragraph Ronald Takaki introduces the term *model minority*, a term our fifth question asks students to consider. Takaki couples this term with being financially "successful," and it's our impression that when Asian Americans are said to be a "model minority" the term does usually imply financial success, conjuring up images of prosperous merchants, engineers, lawyers, and so on. But it's our impression, too, that the term also implies three other things: academic success (strong undergraduate work and graduate or professional work), family stability, and a low crime rate. Takaki is scarcely concerned with these matters, though in paragraph 7 he mentions "gangs" of Asian Americans (an indirect glance at crime), and in paragraphs 8 to 10 he touches on Asian American laborers — though it turns out, in paragraph 12, that some Korean greengrocers are highly educated.

Chiefly Takaki is concerned with disproving the myth of financial success, and he wants to do this for two reasons: The myth is harmful to Asian Americans (because the rest of America mistakenly thinks this minority is doing very well), and it is harmful to African Americans (because the rest of America uses the Asian Americans as a stick to beat the African Americans). To demonstrate that the financial success of the Asian Americans is a myth, Takaki introduces statistics — and indeed it is partly because of his statistics and because of his comments on the possible deceptiveness of some figures that we include Takaki's essay in this chapter. As early as his fourth paragraph he points out that statistics may be misleading. He doesn't cite specific figures, but he says, (convincingly, we think) that it's not enough to point to "figures on the high earnings of Asian Americans relative to Caucasians." Why not? Because, he says, Asian Americans tend to be concentrated in places with a high cost of living (Hawaii, California, New York). This is a telling point. Again, even without giving specific figures, he sets the reader thinking, giving the reader cause to be skeptical about the figures.

The bulk of the essay (paras. 4–14) is devoted to the finances of Asian Americans, but surely Takaki's purpose in demythologizing Asian Americans is twofold: to say something that will help Asian Americans and to say something that will help African Americans. Although African Americans are mentioned in only paragraphs 3 and 15, their appearance is significant, especially because one of the two appearances is in the final paragraph.

This essay makes use of statistics and also calls attention to the misuse of statistics. You may want to invite students to examine Takaki's statistics. We wonder, for instance, exactly how significant it is that "Twenty-five percent of the people in New York City's Chinatown lived below the poverty level in 1980" (para. 8). For the figure to be meaningful one would probably have to know what percentage of the rest of America lived below the poverty level in 1980. And in any case, why cite a figure from 1980 in an essay written in 1990? That's a long time ago; surely there must be a more recent figure.

You may want to invite the class to bring in some statistics on this or another issue, perhaps gathered from an article in *Time* or *Newsweek* or a textbook, and to discuss their possible limitations.

James Q. Wilson

Just Take Away Their Guns (p. 105)

Our question 1 goes to the heart of this essay: What sentence in James Wilson's essay best expresses his thesis? We suggest the answer is in this sentence in paragraph 4, when Wilson writes: "The most effective way to reduce illegal gun-carrying is to encourage the police to take guns away from people who carry them without a permit." Why do we focus on this sentence? First, it echoes the title of the essay ("Just Take Away Their Guns"). As we suggest elsewhere in the text, a good title will often signal the writer's main thesis. Second, the quoted sentence implies that the *goal* of gun control is to get guns out of the hands of those most likely to use them illegally, and that the *best means to this end* is authorizing the police to stop and frisk. Any careful reader of Wilson's essay will see that it is this second point and its ramifications that get most of Wilson's attention in the rest of the article.

Our second question is intended to get the student to look carefully at the research Wilson cites and to evaluate just what that research implies. One cannot infer that displaying or firing guns in self-defense actually prevented victimization in all, most, or even many of the million cases where guns were used for this purpose. Nor are we told in how many of these million cases the gun user was under a misapprehension (no robbery or other crime was in the offing) or in how many other cases children or others in the household caused accidental deaths or injuries by firearms. So on balance we do not know anything from this research about the extent to which safety in the home was increased (or decreased) by the availability and use of firearms by ordinary citizens to prevent crimes. The only legitimate use of the statistics Wilson reports here is the very limited use he himself makes of them in the final sentence of his paragraph.

How might a defender of gun control respond to Wilson's barb quoted in our question 3? In his twelfth paragraph, Wilson thinks it is "politically absurd" for a citizen in crime-infested America to seek laws that "forbid or severely restrict the sale of guns." This is the preface to his remark we quote in the question.

Before proceeding with a reply, as the question asks, we draw the reader's attention to the extreme and perhaps misleading generalization in his remark quoted above. Are the restrictions and prohibitions to which he refers here confined only to handguns? Or does he think all restrictions on firearms of whatever sort are "politically absurd?" We do not think it is "politically absurd" for the government to forbid outright all sales of automatic weapons, dumdum bullets, antitank weapons, and the like except to authorized purchasers. Perhaps Wilson would agree. If so, he might have easily made that clear.

More to the point, we think the gun-control advocate might reply to Wilson's challenge along these lines:

First, no government can hope to shield its citizens against all criminal harms, even if by deterrence and incapacitation, not to mention moral education, government does keep crime from overwhelming us. (Ask the class: How many of you were the victims of crime earlier today? Earlier this week? This month? How many of you were *not* victims only because you used a weapon to frighten off a would-be assailant?) So it is unfair to describe our "government" as "having failed to protect" our persons and property. Its successes vastly outnumber its failures.

Second, society has to weigh *all* the consequences of our current virtually uncontrolled gun ownership practices against the alternative of varying degrees of restriction and prohibition. It is not enough just to look at the ways in which guns in the hands of the citizenry have deterred crime. Those successes have to be measured against the many costs that Wilson nowhere mentions (notably, suicides and other killings and accidents that would not have occurred except for the availability at all hours of loaded handguns).

In our question 5, we ask the reader to confront the racial impact of Wilson's proposal, which he candidly mentions. We agree with his prediction: Widespread use of stop-and-frisk practices aimed at removing guns from those without permits to possess them will in practice do exactly what he says. Is this a fatal objection to his proposal? Yes, if you think that young black males have enough problems already without the added burden of heightened attention from the police, or that stop-and-frisk practices will lead mainly to more shoot-outs with police on the mean streets of urban America. No, if you think that black neighborhoods are far more likely to be victimized by black offenders than are white neighborhoods, that the best way to protect the bulk of the black population is to get illegal guns out of the hands of would-be black offenders, and that the best way to do this is to encourage adoption of Wilson's stop-and-frisk proposal.

Nora Ephron

The Boston Photographs (p. 109)

Many people get agitated when images that they take to be pornographic are published in magazines or are hung on museum walls. Your students know this, but they may not know that until quite recently many people thought that images of violence should not be shown. Respectable newspapers did not show the blood-spattered corpses of gangland killings. That sort of image was left to the tabloids. The chief exceptions were photographs of persons killed in a war, and these were usually acceptable only if the dead seemed intact and asleep. Severed limbs, decapitated bodies, and agonized faces were not tolerated. But exactly why were they not tolerated?

"All the news that's fit to print" was and still is the slogan of the *New York Times*. And just as some news stories were judged unprintable — let's say stories about prostitution and abortion — so were some images. Probably the idea behind this informal code was that such stories and images pander to a taste that ought not to be nourished. We are reminded of Thomas Babington Macaulay's comment on bearbaiting: "The Puritan hated bear-baiting not because it gave pain to the bear, but because it gave pleasure to the spectators." An astute remark, not merely a wisecrack at the expense of Puritans. Why, indeed, do we in the United States prohibit cockfighting in all but three states? Surely not merely because a few birds suffer for relatively brief periods — a tiny number, when compared with the enormous numbers of birds that suffer for months until they have grown large enough to be slaughtered for food. Presumably forty-seven states prohibit cockfighting because their citizens think — rightly — that spectators ought not to take pleasure in the sight of birds maiming each other. The idea is as old as Plato: Our base appetites ought not to be nourished.

To get back to certain kinds of pictures of violence. The idea behind censoring them was that these images appeal to impulses that ought to be suppressed, not nourished. It is pretty hard for anyone today to favor censorship, but when you look at the pictures in James Allen et al., *Without Sanctuary: Lynching Photography in America* (2000), and you learn that some of these horrifying images of burned and castrated bodies were printed as picture postcards and inscribed with playful comments (e.g., "This is the barbecue we had last night"), well, one understands what Plato and the Puritans were getting at.

In our text, the most horrifying image is not reproduced in Ephron's essay but is Huynh Cong (Nick) Ut's photograph on page 96, "The Terror of War" (1972). This picture, which was widely printed in newspapers, is said to have played an enormous role in turning American public opinion against the war in Vietnam. (For details, see Denise Chong, *The Girl in the Picture: The Story of Kim Phuc, the Photograph, and the Vietnam War* [2000].) Conceivably, some people take pleasure in the horror in depicts, but surely its publication was justified by its message: "What is going on over there is unbelievably horrifying." On June 8, 1972, American-backed South Vietnamese pilots trying to kill Vietcong troops dropped napalm canisters near a pagoda where villagers had taken refuge. The girl in the center of the picture had torn off her clothing in an effort to free herself from the searing napalm jelly. A viewer looks with horror at the picture, but — and we say this with much unease — part of our interest in the photograph probably is aesthetic. In its terrifying way, it is a beautiful photograph, admirably composed, the sort of composition that Cartier-Bresson called "the decisive moment," the moment when the flux of the world suddenly takes shape and seems to say something. The four figures nearest to the camera run forward, but they take us back relentlessly. The boy at the extreme left shows his agony in his wide-open mouth and his slightly contorted posture; the naked girl in the center, vulnerable in her nudity, is by virtue of her outstretched arms in a posture that reminds a viewer of the crucified Jesus; the small boy toward the right (like the smaller boy who is the second figure from the left) is apparently too young to understand the horror, but the girl who holds his hand reveals her terror in her face. And behind them, apparently walking rather than running, apparently a relentless and unemotional force (we can see no expression on their faces) pushing these victims forward, are four soldiers (one is almost totally hidden by the girl at the right). And still further back, behind the soldiers, a flat backdrop of the smoking village.

Is this photo merely an image of a most regrettable incident — like, say, a fire in Boston that kills a woman who falls from an unstable fire escape? Or does it have meaning? And, if so, what is its meaning? Ephron doesn't talk about this image, but she does make a relevant point in her next-to-last paragraph, when she talks about car wrecks and says that newspapers will print images of wrecked cars but not of dead bodies: "But the significance of fatal automobile accidents is not that a great deal of steel is twisted but that people die. Why not show it?" And in her final paragraph she introduces an aesthetic element when she says, of the Boston photographs, "They deserve to be printed because they are great pictures, breathtaking pictures of something that happened. That they disturb readers is exactly as it should be: that's why photojournalism is often more powerful than written journalism."

In short, although doubtless there are some people who enjoy the violence depicted in some images, images of the sort that Ephron is talking about (photos by Stanley Forman) and images like Ut's rivet our attention because — one can hardly dare to say it — the horror is transformed by the artistry. This is *not* to say that the horror is diminished. Far from it; the horror is made memorable, enduring, and perhaps even eternal.

Michael Levin

The Case for Torture (p. 115)

As Professor Levin knows, torture has not received positive press in recent decades, even though it continues to be widely practiced as an interrogation technique in many parts of the world. As the social philosopher Henry Shue has noted, "No other practice except slavery is so universally and unanimously condemned in law and human convention." To which the authors of Amnesty International's *Report on Torture* (1975) added: "At the same time the practice of torture has reached epidemic proportions."

Identifying torture as a human-rights violation did not rise to the level of international human-rights law until after World War II. The basis for all later international prohibitions is Article 5 of the Universal Declaration of Human Rights (1948), which declares that "No one shall be subjected to torture or to cruel, inhumane or degrading treatment of punishment." The same language appears in Article 7 of the International Covenant on Civil and Political Rights (1976). Under the authority of the United Nations Convention against Torture and Other Cruel, Inhuman or Degrading Treatment or Punishment (1984) a special U.N. Committee against Torture has been established. How effective these provisions have been in suppressing torture and punishing torturers is another matter.

No doubt the principal current source of popular awareness of and opposition to torture is Amnesty International, whose Campaign for the Abolition of Torture began in 1972 and continues to the present.

Hypothetical cases to the side (questions 1 and 2), we have difficulty accepting the criterion Levin offers (which we quote) to demark the justified from the unjustified use of torture. (In this vein consider our suggested reply to Levin in question 4.) How many innocent lives need to be saved before torture is justified? Levin does not tell us (how could he?). Above all, how do we avoid the all-too-obvious slippery slope: Once we openly allow torture in the kind of cases Levin accepts, how are we to keep others from loosening the criteria to include persons "very probably" guilty? Or applying the criteria on the basis of an imperfect grasp of the relevant facts? Or turning prematurely to torture when other possibly effective interrogation methods might work? To us, Levin seems remarkably complacent about this nest of problems.

On the other hand, we are reluctant to embrace an absolute human right forbidding torture. Candor requires us to admit that we have no better alternative to offer for the kind of hypothetical cases Levin conjures up. The cases have been designed in such a way that it is all but impossible to reject his conclusion. What one can say is that his hypothetical cases bear little relation to the kinds of cases in which we know torturers today and in the past have done their work.

In addition to Amnesty's *Report on Torture* (1975), two other books might be mentioned because of the light they shed on the actual use of torture — a story quite remote from the considerations that inspire Levin's defense. One is Edward Peters, *Torture* (1985), a historical survey of torture from Greek and Roman times to the recent past. The other is *The Breaking of Bodies and Minds* (1985), edited by Eric Stover and Elena O. Nightingale, full of stories of recent vintage that record the terrors of those at the mercy of torturers.

Anna Lisa Raya (student essay)

It's Hard Enough Being Me (p. 118)

As we say in our headnote in the text, Raya published this essay while she was an undergraduate. Your students may very well find that they can do just as well.

If you have looked at the questions that we pose in the text, you have probably guessed that we think Raya is a bit unclear about *why* she "had to define [herself] according to the broad term 'Latina'" (para. 1). The closest she comes, we think, to offering an explanation is when she says that in "El Sereno, I felt like I was part of a majority, whereas at the College I am a minority" (para. 2).

But even this sentence, we think, doesn't say *why* she "had" to define herself. Pressure from the majority? From the minority? Again, she says (para. 8), "To be fully Latina in college . . . I *must* know Spanish." But (again) *who* demands that she be "fully Latina"? As we read the essay, we are inclined to guess that the demand comes from Latinos and Latinas who emphasize their heritage and want Raya to celebrate it, but we don't think she is explicit on the point. She ends by asserting — briefly, in Spanish and in English — that she will be herself. We think this ending is rhetorically effective since it uses both languages.

There is, however, a further difficulty, something we raise in our fourth question in the text. Exactly what does it mean to be true to oneself? Of course, we can say that we don't steal (we are not that sort of person) or that we don't cheat (again, we are not that sort of person). But isn't "the self" really constructed out of relationships to others? We are loving (or neglectful) parents or children; we are serious (or frivolous) students; we are serious (or casual) about advancing in a career, and so on. We have many selves (parent, child, student, worker), and it is not always easy to know *which* self we must be true to.

Judy Brady

I Want a Wife (p. 120)

Incidental passages of satire, employing an ironic voice, appear throughout the book, but Judy Brady's essay, like Jonathan Swift's "A Modest Proposal" in the next chapter, is satiric from beginning to end. Since our book is chiefly about argument (reasoning) rather than about the broader topic of persuasion, we discuss irony very briefly. And because of our emphasis on engaging the audience's goodwill by presenting oneself as benign, and because of Carl Rogers's point about reducing the sense of threat to the reader (see Chapter 11), we advise students to think twice before they use irony in their arguments. Still, Brady's essay offers an opportunity to talk about the power of verbal irony or satire — in Frank O'Connor's definition, "The intellectual dagger opposing the real dagger."

In talking about this satire, one can point out that in "I Want a Wife," as in much other satire, the persona more or less appears as an innocent eye, a speaker who merely describes, in a simple, objective way, what is going on. (The reader, not the speaker, says, "This is outrageous." The speaker never explicitly states her thesis.) Thus, in the essay Brady is not a creature with a name but merely a member of a class. She is simply "a Wife." We then get the terrifying list of things that a Wife finds thrust on her. These are scarcely described in detail, but the mere enumeration of the chores becomes, by the volume of its unadorned accumulation, comic — and stinging. One is reminded of John Dryden's comment, in *Origin and Progress of Satire* (1692), distinguishing between invective (direct abuse) and verbal irony:

> How easy is it to call "rogue" and "villain," and that wittily. But how hard to make a man appear a fool, a blockhead, or a knave, without using any of those opprobrious terms.

Whether things have changed since 1971, when Brady's essay first appeared in *Ms.*, is a question that might be argued. One might also ask (though of course one doesn't expect a balanced view in satire) if things in 1971 really were the way Brady saw them. Did marriage really offer nothing to a wife? No love, no companionship, no security? Were all husbands childish and selfish, and all wives selfless?

A Casebook: How Valuable Are Computers in College?

Nate Stulman (student essay)

The Great Campus Goof-Off Machine (p. 123)

There probably are two separate issues here: (1) Do many or even most students waste time playing computer games and writing needless e-mail messages? and (2) are computers and the Internet of great use to most college students? Stulman's answer is yes to the first question and no to the second, and he concludes that schools have erred in making Internet connections available. But even if one agrees that students waste time with computers, one need not agree that the schools have erred. Perhaps those students who waste great amounts of time playing games need better counseling, and perhaps their instructors need to show them how computers are relevant to courses other than courses in computer science and mathematics. Some of the letters of response take this line. In the first letter Mark Casell (a professor of political science) says that he suggests "Web-based resources to help with researching and writing papers." David Schwartz asserts that students in fields other than computer science and math need computers, but his case would be stronger if he gave an example or if he spoke with the authority either of a professor or of a student who in fact had found the computer invaluable in such-and-such a field. Jo Manning, a reference librarian, does speak from a position of authority and is admirably specific in mentioning the MLA database and Lexis-Nexis — though as a professor of English who in fact makes very little use of the MLA database, the writer of this comment remains unconvinced.

Since I have just introduced myself, I'll go a bit further in this autobiographical comment: It may be that I don't find the MLA database of much help because I don't know how to use it properly, but for the most part I don't think that I or my students need to turn up lots of sources. What they need to do is to think hard and write thoughtfully about a few sources, and such material is usually easily located.

Having said this, I want to repeat that I believe Stulman errs in thinking that *because* many students goof off, the Internet is not highly useful. The logic here is odd. Further, his assertion that it is useful chiefly for students in computer science and math is contradicted by the experience of some of the letter-writers — students as well as professors. One of the students, Paul Hogarth, offers an analogy: High school and college students get in car accidents all the time; does that mean they shouldn't drive? If they "get in accidents all the time," indeed maybe they shouldn't drive!

It's our guess that many students will admit that they waste an enormous amount of time and will nevertheless insist that the Internet connections are important. Such a twofold statement makes sense to us.

Part Two

CRITICAL WRITING

4
Writing an Analysis of an Argument (p. 133)

Although we offer incidental comments about *writing* in Chapters 2 and 3 — with comments on audience, tone, organization, and so on — this chapter and Chapter 5 contain our primary discussions of writing.

In Chapter 11 we reprint Carl R. Rogers's "Communication: Its Blocking and Its Facilitation," an essay that has interested many teachers of rhetoric because of its emphasis on psychological aspects of persuasion. The essay is fairly short and easy, and because it is mainly about a writer's interaction with an audience, it may well be assigned in conjunction with this chapter.

If you want to give a writing assignment *not* based on a reading assignment, this suggestion may be useful:

Write a letter (150 to 300 words) to the editor of a newspaper, responding to an editorial or to a published letter. Hand in the material you are responding to, along with your essay.

Stanley S. Scott

Smokers Get a Raw Deal (p. 138)

Because the student's essay on Stanley S. Scott's "Smokers Get a Raw Deal" is (we believe) an excellent analysis, we don't want to offer a comment on Scott here, but you may want your class to think about some of these questions on his essay:

1. Why does Scott think that today "smokers must put up with virtually unenforceable laws"? Is he right?

2. Scott cites four examples of the use of force by antismokers provoked by smokers. Why does Scott think this use of force is unjustified? What do you think?

3. Scott uses the device of "the slippery slope" or "the thin edge of the wedge" (on this device, see the discussion in Chapter 8 in the text) to attack militant antismokers. He suggests that if antismokers get their way today, then the next thing someone will attack is personal choice over "ice cream, cake, and cookies." Do you think that this argumentative strategy is effective, or is it a ridiculous exaggeration? (*Note:* Another way to read Scott's maneuver is to see it as a reductio ad absurdum; that is, he argues that the obvious absurdity of policing personal choice over desserts reveals the error of trying to stop smoking. Scott implies that the principle invoked by those who favor policing desserts is identical with the principle that would suffice to prohibit smoking. Reductio is discussed in the text, in Chapter 8.)

Elizabeth Joseph

My Husband's Nine Wives (p. 147)

Joseph speaks of "polygamy, or plural marriage" (para. 3), thereby defining *polygamy*. Many students think *polygamy* refers only to a system in which a man has several wives or mates at one time, but of course it can also refer to a system in which a woman has several mates or husbands at one time. Perhaps it is a bit pedantic to tell students that the former system is polygyny and the latter polyandry — but we do tell them, or, rather, we get students in the class to come up with these words.

Exactly why is plural marriage outlawed in the United States and in many other countries? We think it is worth asking this question of students because most of them unthinkingly assume it is immoral. If you ask students why slavery or torture or cannibalism (or for that matter, deceptive advertising or plagiarism) should be outlawed, they can probably come up with answers that satisfy pretty much everyone in the class, but if you ask them why plural marriage should be outlawed, they may find, to their surprise, that they can't give compelling reasons. It has been our experience that most students simply believe polygamy is wrong, and that is that. They may have very strong convictions about the issue, but probably few have bothered to think about it.

In her third paragraph, Joseph mentions that "Polygamists believe that the Old Testament mandates the practice of plural marriage." She doesn't give any citations, but Genesis 29.15–30 unambiguously indicates that polygyny was accepted. Further, the patriarchs took concubines, especially if the wife did not conceive children (Genesis 16.1–2). (Doubtless there are replies — for instance, God created one wife for Adam — but our point is not to assemble all possible biblical citations on the issue. Rather, our point is to indicate that polygamy has been widely practiced and certainly was practiced by the patriarchs. For a quick review of the topic, see *The Anchor Bible Dictionary* 4:563.) If someone argues that gay marriage should be outlawed because, it is alleged, the Bible condemns it, is that person committed to permitting polygyny because the Bible accepts it? And, again putting aside the testimony of the Bible, exactly why should plural marriages be outlawed? We think it is useful to press students to come up with reasons. In our experience, many students take refuge in statements such as "It's unnatural," "It's obvious why men shouldn't be allowed to have more than one wife," "It's clearly immoral," and "It exploits women." Joseph herself says in her final paragraph that "plural marriage isn't for everyone." Agreed, but you might ask your students (and we ask them in the fourth question in the text) whether it should be a legal option.

For most of the world's history, marriage has been used for social, economic, and political purposes to establish or confirm relationships. Arranged marriages still are fairly common in some societies. In recent centuries, the idea of love has been added to the picture, but Joseph shrewdly puts her case not in terms of the Bible and not in terms of love but (para. 3) in terms of the needs of "the modern career woman." She offers some concrete evidence: Polygyny offers baby-sitters, cooks, and, on occasion, freedom from unwanted sexual demands of her husband (para. 13).

Who could ask for anything more?

Jeff Jacoby

Bring Back Flogging (p. 149)

Our society takes pretty much for granted that punishment for crimes will take the form of imprisonment, except for juveniles and first-offenders, who may be offered probation instead. But the prison (as distinct from the jail, traditionally used only to detain accused persons prior to trial) is a relatively new invention in England and the United States, dating only from the end of the eighteenth century (see Michel Foucault, *Discipline and Punish: The Birth of the Prison* [1977] and Michael Ignatieff, *A Just Measure of Pain: The Penitentiary in the Industrial Revolution, 1750–1850* [1978]). Corporal punishments — the stocks, flogging, branding, mutilation, and hanging — are as old as recorded history, and some of these modes of punishment remain in use today — for example, in Saudi Arabia. Except for the death penalty, all such practices have been abandoned in the United States, and probably few would survive constitutional challenge were a legislature foolish enough to reintroduce them.

The case of flogging (or whipping) is different. Whipping survived in Delaware until 1952; in 1989 a bill was filed in the Delaware legislature to bring back the whipping post (see *New York Times*, Jan. 29, 1989), but it failed to pass. It may come as a surprise to learn that the U.S. Supreme Court has yet to rule on the constitutionality of this classic mode of punishment. And for reasons Jeff Jacoby offers in his essay — inexpensiveness, brevity of duration, humiliation of offenders, and above all, physical pain — it retains a certain attractiveness in some quarters. Not until 1983, however, in the book *Just and Painful: A Case for the Corporal Punishment of Criminals* by criminologist Graeme Newman, did anyone in recent years seriously defend flogging. (Newman proposed electric shocks, carefully calibrated to suit the desert of the offender, followed by whipping if the offender recidivates, and incarceration only after repeated convictions of violent crimes.)

Our question 3 goes to the heart of the issue, as Jacoby realizes: Is it true that flogging (in whatever form and degree) is more degrading or brutal than imprisonment, and on that ground — entirely apart from any other consideration — ought to be abolished? Jacoby raises the issue and disposes of it with a rhetorical question ("Where is it written," etc.?; para. 12). Flogging always brings to mind scenes of merciless beating; but such brutality is not necessary. It also often has overtones of sadistic pleasure aroused by the sight of naked flesh being turned to a bloody pulp; but, again, that is not necessary. Some opponents of flogging as punishment (including the authors of this manual) are repelled by the whole idea and cannot imagine ourselves inflicting such punishment on anyone, no matter what the crime, or of encouraging others to do it for us. But is this mere sentimentality, or is detesting such a practice a good enough reason for opposing it? Perhaps one can argue that when the abuses of imprisonment that Jacoby rightly reminds us of are compared with the abuses of flogging that Jacoby ignores, it is far from clear that a reasonable and humane person ought to join him in preferring flogging.

Katha Pollitt

It Takes Two: A Modest Proposal for Holding Fathers Equally Accountable (p. 152)

Katha Pollitt's title appropriately echoes Jonathan Swift's title (the subject of our seventh question) because her subject is, like Swift's, the impoverished (especially women and their children) and also because her weapon, like Swift's, is irony. Pollitt cannot expect or even hope that any of her devastating proposals will be put into practice, but she does succeed (we think) in making readers see the absurdity of the sort of talk that is exemplified in Mayor Barry's view, a view that Pollitt says is widely held.

She begins her sixth paragraph by saying — very earnestly and sounding a bit naive, somewhat like Swift's earnest but uncomprehending projector — that her point is not to demonize men, "but fair's fair." Well, who can disagree with a call for fair play, even if the expression "fair's fair" sounds a bit childish? She then goes on, with a straight face, to set forth five proposals that hit home — that is, proposals that make demands of men that are roughly equivalent to the demands many people wish to make of women on welfare. Her point, of course, is to call attention to what men can get away with. She ends by returning to the idea of justice: "As I was saying, fair's fair." And by now it is hard to disagree with a point she made earlier, in her fifth paragraph: "It is not the mother's care that welfare replaces, but the father's cash."

David Cole

Five Myths about Immigration (p. 155)

Before looking at David Cole's article, we will (1) give some history and (2) survey the chief arguments for and against keeping the gate open.

In 1924 the law provided a national-origins quota system that favored northern and western Europe and severely restricted immigration from everywhere else. This system was replaced in 1965 by a law (with amendments) that said there were three reasons to award visas to immigrants:

1. An immigrant might possess certain job skills, especially skills that this country needs. (Relatively few visas were awarded on this basis.)

2. An immigrant might be a refugee from war or from political persecution and so eligible for "political asylum."

3. An immigrant might be related to an American citizen or to a legal alien (the "family reunification policy").

In 1965, when this policy was formulated, there was little immigration from Latin America, the Caribbean, and Asia. Today, 90 percent of all immigration to the United States comes from those areas. Upward of 80 percent are people of color. Whatever our policy is, it is *not* racist. What about numbers, rather than percentages? The peak decade for immigration was 1901 to 1910, when about 8.7 million immigrants arrived, chiefly from southern and eastern Europe. Some authorities say that 1981 to 1990 matched this, if illegal immigrants are included, but in any case in 1901 to 1910 the total U.S. population was less than one-third of what it is today. After 1910, immigration declined sharply; in all of the 1930s only about 500,000 immigrants came to the United States, and in all of the 1940s there were only about 1 million including refugees from Hitler. The figure now is about 1.5 million annually, plus an unknown number (the usual guess is half a million annually). In 1970 Latino immigration was 4.5 percent; in 1990 it was 9 percent.

What about ethnic identity? In the middle of the century, when Nathan Glazer and Daniel Patrick Moynihan wrote *The Melting Pot* (1963), they found that the ethnic groups that had arrived between 1880 and 1920 retained their identity. Will Herberg, in *Protestant, Catholic, Jew* (rev. ed. 1960), found that at best there was a "triple melting pot" — that is, people married outside of their ethnic group but still within their religious group. Thus, Italian Americans for the most part married Catholics, but these Catholics might be Irish; similarly, German Jews married Jews, but they might be Russian Jews. From 1980 onward, however, religious identity too was shaken. For instance, half of all Italian Americans born after World War II married non-Catholics; 40 percent of Jews marrying in the 1980s married Gentiles (according to Robert C. Christopher, *Crashing the Gates* [1989]).

In selecting material for our text, we read fairly widely, and we noticed that certain arguments kept recurring. Because instructors may find it useful to have the chief arguments on both sides, we list them. Please understand that we are not endorsing any of these arguments; we are just reporting them.

(text pp. 155–159)

Chief Arguments in Favor
of a Relatively Open Door

1. *Immigrants provide cheap labor and do not displace native-born workers.* Immigrants work as gardeners, farm laborers, domestic helpers, restaurant employees, and so on. They do not displace American workers, since Americans (white and African American) will not take these jobs at the current wages. If the wages had to be increased, the jobs would vanish. In 1980 the Mariel boatlift brought 125,000 Cubans, increasing Miami's workforce by 7 percent virtually overnight, but it had no effect on the wages of skilled or unskilled labor, black or white. Further, job losses are more than offset by new jobs generated by immigrants; after all, immigrants need housing, food, and so on, and therefore they are a new market.

2. *Immigrants provide high-tech knowledge.* Silicon Valley depends largely on immigrant engineers, microchip designers, and so on.

3. *Immigrants stimulate the economy.* Many immigrants have founded companies, thereby generating thousands of jobs.

4. *Immigrants are assimilating at the usual rate.* Despite assertions that immigrants today are not assimilating, they are in fact assimilating in pretty much the same ways that their predecessors did. Their children marry outside of the group (in California, nearly half of the native-born Asians and Latinos marry into other ethnic groups), their grandchildren often do not know the language of the immigrants, and so on. The charge that immigrants do not assimilate is an old one; for instance, it was regularly said of the Irish in the nineteenth century.

5. *Immigrants are not a threat to the peace of the cities.* San Jose, California, is the eleventh-largest city in the United States, with a white population less than 50 percent, but it has the lowest murder and robbery rates of any major city in the United States, and it has virtually no ethnic conflict. El Paso is 70 percent Latino, but it has one of the lowest rates of serious crime or murder; the robbery rate is one-half of that of Seattle, an overwhelmingly white city of similar size. Hawaii, too — the state with the lowest percentage of whites in the United States — has a low rate for serious crime and little ethnic conflict.

6. *Immigrants may cost us something in the short run, but in the long run they add to the country.* They are energetic workers, increasing the supply of goods and services with their labor, and increasing the demand for goods and services by spending their wages. Refugees — the immigrant group that gains the most public sympathy — are the immigrants who cost the government the most in welfare and in Medicaid.

7. *Immigrants from developing societies are likely to have strong family structures.* We fret that immigrants from developing nations are likely to be poorer and less well educated than those from Europe, but they come from traditional societies with strong moral codes. The collapse of family values originated not with the arrival of Haitians but in the white Anglo communities, where, for instance, today 22 percent of the children are born out of wedlock.

8. *We are a nation of immigrants; our strength is derived from our openness to all cultures.* The fear of immigrants is now in large measure a fear of cultures new to the United States, and a fear of persons of color. In some instances, it is rooted in hostility to what one writer calls "anti-progressive Iberian values" — that is, the values of Roman Catholic Latinos.

Chief Arguments in Favor of Shutting the Door, or Keeping It Only Narrowly Ajar

1. *Immigrants cost the United States money.* (1) Since most immigrants are at the low end of the wage scale, and (2) since they have children of school age, they cost local governments more in services (especially education, health services, and welfare) than they pay in sales and income taxes. Moreover, (3) they constitute a disproportionate percentage of prisoners (in California, 20 percent of the prison population).

2. *Today's immigrants are not assimilating at the rate that earlier immigrants assimilated.* In the past, most immigrants came from England, Ireland, or Europe, and they were glad to put the old country behind them. Many never returned to the countries of their birth, partly because they had no affection for those countries and partly because the trip was long and costly. Today, many Latinos fly back and forth between the United States and Central or South America, thereby keeping up their cultural ties with the country of origin. And in fact the new emphasis on multiculturalism encourages them to retain their identity rather than to enter into the melting pot. The result is the nation's loss of a common culture, a common language.

    The culture of our country is essentially northern European and Christian. The vast increase in Latinos and Asians brings into question whether we will continue to have a national identity.

3. *Immigrants deprive Americans of jobs.* By working in substandard conditions and for substandard wages, immigrants keep wages low and they deprive citizens of jobs. In California and in Texas it is especially evident that immigrants have displaced unskilled native-born workers.

4. *Immigrants today are less skilled than those of the past.* Because they are less skilled, they are more likely to become a burden to the state.

5. *Immigration is unfair to countries from where the immigrants come.* Among the immigrants from developing nations are some who are politically dissatisfied or who are economically unfulfilled. These are precisely the people who can improve their own countries; this brain drain is unfair to those countries. (The usual reply to this is to say that such people emigrate precisely because they cannot exercise their talent in their native countries because of various obstacles.)

6. *It is nonsense to justify immigration today by saying, "We are a nation of immigrants."* First of all, most nations are nations of immigrants. For instance, England was invaded by the Vikings, by people from Germanic areas, and later by the Norman French. Even the supposedly homogeneous Japanese are believed to have experienced several waves of prehistoric immigration from Korea. Second, that immigration was good for us in the past does not mean it still is good for us. The times have changed. For instance, today the country is heavily populated, and, second, the immigrants come from different cultures.

The Two Basic Questions

Finally, it is probably appropriate to say that both sides agree there are two basic questions:

1. Which and how many immigrants ought we take? (The usual answer to the first part of this question is, "People like me.")

2. How ought we enforce the law — that is, what measures can reduce illegal immigration? (About 95 percent of the illegal border crossings come from Mexico — but many of these illegal entrants do not stay in this country. Further, many illegal immigrants do *not* enter surreptitiously; they enter legally, but stay beyond the time specified on their visas.)

Now, at last, for a few comments about Cole's essay. His use of the word "Myths" in his title suggests that he subscribes to the old adage, "The best defense is a strong offense." His basic strategy, clearly, is to say that *X, Y,* and *Z* are untrue — with the implication that his own views must therefore be true.

In the course of his opening attack he introduces the Know-Nothings (properly called the Native American party), the anti-immigrant and anti-Catholic (specifically, anti-Irish) movement in the 1850s. Subgroups of secret societies formed (for example, the Order of the Star-Spangled Banner), but when members were asked awkward questions about their beliefs they replied with a stock statement, to the effect that they knew nothing, hence the nickname.

In short, Cole begins by introducing the Know-Nothings, a most unpleasant bunch who were associated with hatred of immigrants, and he then announces that the persons he opposes subscribe not to "mistakes" or "errors" but to myths — enduring, attractive-looking falsehoods. All in all, a rhetorically effective beginning. We are surprised, however, that he does not repeat the powerful word "myths." For instance, he could have said, "Myth No. 1," "Myth No. 2," and so on, and he could have explained why he calls them myths rather than mistakes, errors, falsehoods, or whatever.

In the third paragraph he introduces the point that he is descended from the poor Irish whom the Know-Nothings wanted to keep out, the idea being that he is a decent guy so we can see how wrong these foes of immigrants were. In the next paragraph he clarifies the point; yesterday it was the Irish, but since the Irish — "they" — have now become "us," of course today's unwanted immigrants go by a different name. The "they" of our times, he says, "are Latin Americans (most recently, Cubans), Haitians and Arab Americans, among others."

We don't need to comment on Cole's "myths," except to say, first, that some of the things in our list of pros and cons at the beginning of this discussion may be useful in evaluating his views, and, second, in his discussion of the myth concerning the costs of immigrants (paras. 10–14), he does in fact grudgingly admit that on the local level immigrants may cost the community money: "At most, such figures suggest that some redistribution of federal and state monies may be appropriate" (para. 11).

Let's end by returning to Cole's rhetoric. We think his final paragraph is effective. In it he returns to the "they" versus "us" of his opening (paras. 3–4), and he more or less appeals to the decency of his readers: "I was always taught that we will be judged by how we treat others." The implication is that we should be decent, just, and so on, and that we do not at present treat immigrants fairly or humanely. He hasn't quite proved this — one might, for a start, insist that he could show a little more sympathy for the taxpayers in some communities (Texas and California) — but probably most readers will agree that he comes across as a decent fellow and that he has given us some things to think about.

Stuart Taylor Jr.

School Prayer: When Constitutional Principles Clash (p. 159)

Taylor opens his article about as provocatively as one could, raising the possibility that it might be unconstitutional for nonsectarian texts — such as the three he mentions — to be recited, read, or sung. How could it possibly be the case that reciting the Declaration of Independence (one of his examples) might be unconstitutional? (How about reciting the Bill of Rights? Could that be unconstitutional?) Taylor says that these possibilities arise from "a plausible reading" (para. 2) of a recent Supreme Court decision holding that a high school's "policy of allowing an elected student leader to *pray* [our emphasis] over the public address system at football games" was unconstitutional.

We disagree, and we would think all but a maverick few students of constitutional law would see a world of difference between authorized prayer at a public school function and authorized recitation of the Declaration of Independence. Taylor's remarkable "plausible reading" of the Court's decision depends on the mention of God in the Declaration, the Pledge, and the national anthem (not to speak of our coinage). No problem arises over the possible unconstitutionality of reciting the Bill of Rights because God goes unmentioned in that text. But if Taylor is right, we are in trouble elsewhere. In the Gettysburg Address, Lincoln invokes the deity without doubt — can't recite that on school property. "The Battle Hymn of the Republic" refers to "the coming of the Lord" — can't sing that in class. What about sessions of the state and national legislature (but not the Supreme Court or other courts), which open with a prayer? We can hardly deny that the word *God* is occasionally used in our public life. Is this usage now at risk? And is that a bad thing?

Taylor seems to us to be slightly amused by these possible implications, and in the course of laying out his argument he suppresses an important distinction. In his seventh paragraph he formulates what he calls "two untenable propositions" (we think he means that each is untenable, not that together they are untenable): Requiring or even permitting prayers in school or on school grounds amounts to (1) "'coercion' of nonbelievers and religious minorities" because they are required to (2) "participate in an act of religious worship."

But there is no "prayer" in the Declaration of Independence, nor is there any prayer in the Pledge of Allegiance or in the national anthem. In other words, if the issue is *prayer* — and praying, not saying the word *God*, was the issue in the case before the Supreme Court (reread Taylor's second paragraph) — we see no likelihood that a majority of the Supreme Court, staunch religious antiestablishmentarians though they may be, will see as their next step the disallowance of any mention of the deity in a school setting. So we think Taylor's (mock?) worries about the Court sliding down another slippery slope (para. 14, our question 5) are unfounded.

At the end of his article, Taylor mentions as a related issue another recent decision by the Supreme Court, in this case overturning a Louisiana school board's three-part constraint on the teaching of evolution (para. 15). This issue we think is important. Taylor is unhappy with the Court's ruling that the board's constraints constituted an "establishment of religion" (para. 16). He is especially unhappy that the Court failed to present any opinion of its own and instead merely endorsed the ruling of the lower appellate court.

Leaving that issue to the side, could it be argued that the teaching of evolution involved "coercion" of any children in the classroom — say, those who were being reared in a fundamentalist Christian household? If not, then the case is unlike the one Taylor discusses first, and we are left with nothing but the possible offensiveness of the principles of natural selection (call it "godless evolution" if you wish) to those of a different persuasion. But why should the teaching of evolution be thought to be any more coercive than the teaching of correct spelling? Or correct arithmetic? And why should biology teachers in Louisiana classrooms be told that they must present their views on evolution without any "intention to influence" their student's opinions (as the school board's constraint requires)? And, above all, why is it *not* an "establishment of religion" for "the Biblical version of Creation" to be protected by school policy from being criticized from the perspective of belief in the theory

32

of evolution? We think interesting and provocative classroom discussion can be aroused by reflecting on these questions.

M. Scott Peck

Living Is the Mystery (p. 163)

Dr. Peck opens his essay by complaining that "We don't even have a generally agreed-upon definition of the word [*euthanasia*]." This comes as a surprise to us. We think that a word's etymology often is a good guide to its meaning and hence to its definition, and in this case the word is derived from the Greek meaning "a good death." The various options Peck mentions do not go to the issue of what the word *means*; they go to the very different issue of whether such acts are *justified*. Thus, he asks whether "euthanasia requires the patient's consent." No, it doesn't: A good death for a person in a permanent vegetative state might be done without the patient's consent. In most cases, however, consent is a necessary condition of justified euthanasia. Certainly, all agree that even a good death contrary to the patient's express wishes is ill-disguised murder and thus obviously unjustified.

We are also a bit concerned over what verges on an imputation of cowardice in those who would avoid what Peck calls "existential suffering" in the course of their dying. When he says "they [meaning those tempted to seek euthanasia for themselves] have a lot to learn from being assisted to face this problem rather than being assisted to kill themselves in order to avoid it" (para. 2), this strikes us as rather condescending counsel from someone in good health addressed to those in acute distress. Here, for example, is an account of the wretched misery that afflicted Jonathan Swift (as reported by the ethicist Joseph Fletcher): "His mind crumbled to pieces. . . . at times the pain in his blinded eyes was so intense he had to be restrained from tearing them out with his own hands. . . . For the last three years of his life, he could do nothing but sit and drool; and when he finally died it was only after convulsions that lasted thirty-six hours." Are we to take seriously a proposal for a dose of "existential suffering" for anyone in Swift's situation? Who is in a position to preach courage to those like Swift? (In his third paragraph, Peck comes close to admitting that he knows he isn't.) To be sure, not everyone tempted to seek physician assistance in dying is a companion in misery with Swift. But that only points up the fact behind dispute that not every case of would-be euthanasia is justified or the best thing to do in the circumstances.

If we turn to consider Peck's three reasons for opposing legalized euthanasia (our question 5), we will pass over the first (in his fourth paragraph) since it is persuasive only with those who share his religious outlook on life. We think his second reason — permitting some but not all requests for euthanasia would lead us "into a legal quagmire" — is pretty unconvincing. Society constantly uses laws and regulations to draw lines dividing the permissible from the impermissible. What reason is there to think that in this context it cannot be done because it would land us in a "legal quagmire"? His third reason is more interesting. He thinks legalizing euthanasia in any form and to any degree *now* would be putting last things first. To argue the point he reels off a string of claimed "rights" that "need to be decided first" but does not make clear why they do and why the issue is best formulated in terms of a basketful of "rights."

Two final points. First, we strongly favor, as does Peck, increased availability of hospice care for the terminally ill (see his penultimate paragraph). Who could reasonably oppose this? But when he says "The first order of business should be to establish that dying patients have a constitutional right to competent hospice care," we part company. All that is required to guarantee improved hospice care is suitable state and federal legislation. Amending the Constitution (or trying to find wiggle room for the Supreme Court in the interstices of prior cases interpreting the Bill of Rights) seems to us needless. Besides, we already know that hospice care is not enough in all cases; intractable pain is beyond the powers of hospice care. The hospice movement typically refuses physician intervention to end life in the toughest cases even when there is no other remedy for those like Swift.

Second, Peck's desire to "enlarge" and "heat up" the public debate over euthanasia (the final paragraph) has already taken place, thanks to Jack Kevorkian. As much as we do not approve of his methods and his purposes, to the extent they are self-centered, we give him credit for forcing the nation to confront this problem. If anyone deserves our grudging thanks for moving this issue onto the public agenda, it is Kevorkian.

Peter Singer

Animal Liberation (p. 166)

This essay is an earlier version of text that became the opening chapter of Peter Singer's remarkably influential *Animal Liberation: A New Ethics for Our Treatment of Animals* (1975). In his book, Singer elaborates all his basic ideas, and especially "speciesism" (para. 13), to which he devotes a whole chapter.

Speciesism is the arbitrary favorable preference for members of our own species, and its logical consequence is an equally arbitrary but indifferent or hostile attitude toward lower species. Whether the analogy to racism, sexism, and other *-isms* is as instructive as Singer implies is another matter. In any case, he argues (para. 19) that the "case for animal liberation" does not depend on the analogy.

What, then, is animal liberation? Singer never says in so many words (cf. para. 3), but it amounts to, or at least can be stated as, a series of Dos and Don'ts: Don't kill animals to eat their flesh or to clothe your body, don't experiment on animals to save human lives or to reduce human misery, don't remove animals from their natural habitat. In short, don't treat animals as you would not like to be treated yourself.

Singer's opening paragraph is a model for the use of analogy to gain the high ground right from the start. Each of his readers will be able to identify with one or another of the groups he mentions that has been discriminated against in the past and so is immediately but unwittingly vulnerable to the "expansion of our moral horizons" about to unfold.

Singer worries (para. 12; our question 3) whether having intentions is necessarily, albeit mysteriously, connected with having the capacity to use language. We doubt that it is, and he does, too. Surely anyone who spends time with dogs and cats readily ascribes intentions to them ("He's trying to catch the stick when you throw it," "She's waiting to pounce on the mouse as soon as it moves"), and this use of intentional thinking is no more anthropomorphic than is ascribing intentions to other people. To insist that the latter is intelligible but the former isn't, because other people can speak a language whereas animals can't, pretty obviously begs the question. To insist that no creature can have an intention unless it can state what its intentions are is far too broad a thesis to defend; it would entail that many human creatures do not have intentions, or act intentionally, when we believe they do. And so even if animals can't use language, because they lack the capacity, they may yet have minds enough to warrant a concern about how we intentionally treat them.

On what grounds does Singer base drawing the line where he does to demark the creatures that deserve our concern from those that don't? Why not draw the

(text pp. 166–178)

line elsewhere, particularly at the point that divides the living from the nonliving (not dead but inorganic or inert)? It wouldn't be at all satisfactory for Singer to answer: "Because I talk about creatures that can feel, and I don't about those that can't," although this reading seems to be true. But this can't be his answer because he does not want his argument to turn on who cares about what; he knows that most of us simply do not and will not easily come to care about animal welfare. A better line for him to take would be to refer to the *interests* of creatures and to the *equality* of their interests (para. 6), on the ground that only creatures with a capacity to suffer have interests, the first and foremost of which is to diminish their own suffering, pain, and discomfort. But on closer inspection, is it not still true that *all living* things have interests? Surely, a dogwood tree in the front yard has an interest in air, water, sunlight, and space to grow, even if it feels no pain when it is denied these things or when its leaves are plucked or — heaven forfend! — its branches slashed. To reason in this manner is to tie the concept of having an interest in something to the concept of something being good for a thing (water is surely good for a plant). But this is not what Singer does; rather, he ties a creature's interests to what it can feel (see how he handles the case of the year-old infant in para. 15).

When one goes in the other direction, as some have (for example, Christopher Stone, in his *Should Trees Have Standing?* [1988]), a whole environmental ethic begins to unfold, but with alarming consequences, for even all but the most scrupulous vegetarianism will neglect and even ruthlessly violate the interests of other living entities.

If we enlarge our moral community to include plants as well as animals — because all living entities have interests and because one interest is as good as another "from the point of view of the universe" (the criterion proposed by the utilitarian Henry Sidgwick, which Singer invokes in his *Animal Liberation*, 5) — what will our moral principles permit us to eat? Not much, perhaps only unfruitful food, such as some of the surfeit of seeds and nuts produced by plants, and dead flesh, perhaps including even human flesh (our question 10). Killing to eat may be entirely ruled out, but eating what is dead isn't unless one appeals to some other moral principles besides the utilitarian notions Singer relies on.

This discussion can be put into an argument of this form: Because we have to eat to live, either we eat things that have interests or we don't. If we do, then we violate the equal interests of other creatures and thus act immorally. If we don't, then we can't kill living plants to eat them, any more than we can kill living animals to eat them. Instead, our survival depends on eating dropped fruit and seeds and carrion. Some readers will regard this argument as a reductio ad absurdum of Singer's position. Others will argue that it shows how difficult it is to formulate moral principles that we can really live by consistently and self-consciously.

Although persons who in journals debate with Singer often say that he subscribes to "animal rights," Singer has repeatedly denied that he believes that animals have "rights." Setting forth his disagreement with Tom Regan's *The Case for Animal Rights* (1983), Singer discusses the point at some length in the *New York Review of Books*, January 17, 1985, pp. 46–52. In a letter in the issue of April 25, 1985, p. 57, he reaffirms his point. Singer explains that his view is utilitarian; he grants that conceivably there would be circumstances in which an experiment on an animal stands to reduce human suffering so much that it would be permissible to carry it out even if it involved some harm to the animal. (This would be true, he says in his letter of April 25, 1985, even if the animal were a human being.) In this letter he explains that, as a utilitarian, he advocates stopping animal experiments because

1. The suffering of an immense number of animals would be spared,

2. "The benefits lost would be uncertain," and

3. "The incentive thus provided for the speedy development of alternative methods of conducting research [would be] the most powerful imaginable."

Jonathan Swift

A Modest Proposal (p. 179)

Our discussion in these notes of Judy Brady's "I Want a Wife" (p. 120) offers a few general comments on satire, some of which are relevant to Jonathan Swift.

Unlike Brady's essay, where the title in conjunction with the author's name immediately alerts the reader that the essay cannot be taken straight, Swift's essay does not provide an obvious clue right away. In fact, some students don't perceive the irony until it is pointed out to them. Such imperceptiveness is entirely understandable. Swift's language is somewhat remote from twentieth-century language, and in any case students don't expect satire in a collection of arguments. Moreover, it's hard today to know when a projector (the eighteenth-century name for someone with a bright idea) is kidding. A student who has not understood that "A Modest Proposal" is a satire may be extremely embarrassed on learning the truth in public. To avoid this possibility we usually begin the discussion by talking about Swift as a satirist who is known chiefly through *Gulliver's Travels,* and so on.

Most commentators on "A Modest Proposal" have concentrated on the persona of the speaker — his cool use of statistics, his way of regarding human beings as beasts ("a child just dropped from its dam," in para. 4, for example, or his reference to wives as "breeders," in para. 6), and, in short, his unawareness of the monstrosity of his plan to turn the children into "sound, useful members of the commonwealth" (para. 2), a plan that, by destroying children, will supposedly make the proposer "a preserver of the nation" (para. 2). Much of this complacent insensitivity and even craziness is apparent — on rereading — fairly early, as in the odd reference (para. 1) to "three, four, or six children" (what happened to five?), or, for that matter, in the phrases already quoted from paragraph 2. And of course it is true that one object of Swift's attack is the persona, a figure who, despite his profession that he is rational, practical, and compassionate, perhaps can be taken as an emblem of English indifference to Irish humanity. (But the speaker is an Irishman, not an Englishman.) More specifically, the leading object of attack can be said to be political reformers, especially those who heartlessly bring statistics ("I calculate," "I have reckoned," "I have already computed") where humane feelings should rule.

It is less often perceived, however, that the satire is also directed against the Irish themselves, with whom Swift was, by this time, fed up. "Satire" is almost too mild a word for the vehemence of "savage indignation" (Swift's own epitaph refers to his *saeva indignatio*) with which Swift denounces the Irish. Yes, he in effect says, the English treat the Irish abominably, but the Irish take no reasonable steps to help themselves. Even in so small a detail as the proposer's observation that his plan would cause husbands to stop beating pregnant wives (para. 26), we hear criticism not of the English but of the Irish. The chief denunciation of the Irish is evident, however, in the passage beginning with paragraph 29, in which Swift lists the "other expedients" that indeed the Irish themselves could (but do not) undertake to alleviate their plight.

In short, commentators who see Swift's essay simply as a scathing indictment of English hardheartedness are missing much of the point. One can almost go so far as to say that Swift's satire against the projector is directed not only against his impracticality and his unconscious cruelty but also against his folly in trying to help a nation that, out of stupidity and vanity, obstinately refuses to help itself. The projector sees the Irish as mere flesh; Swift at this time apparently saw them as something more exasperating, flesh that is stupid and vain. Swift was, we think, more than half in earnest when he had his crazy projector say, "I desire the reader will observe, that I calculate my remedy for this one individual kingdom of Ireland and for no other that was, is, or, I think ever can be upon earth."

If you wish students to do some research, you can ask them to look at Swift's "Irish Tracts" (*Prose Works*, ed. Herbert Davis, 12: 1–90, especially *Intelligencer* 19: 54–61), where they will find Swift arguing for the "other expedients" that his projector dismisses.

Related points:

1. This essay has ample material to demonstrate the use of the method that Aristotle calls "the ethical proof"; that is, the pleader's use of his or her ethical character to persuade an audience. (Of course, here it backfires: We soon see a monster, not a benevolist.) Thus, in paragraph 1 the author shows his moral sensibility in using such expressions as "melancholy object" and "helpless infants." Also relevant is the projector's willingness to listen to other views — which he then of course always complacently rejects. (One might ask students to examine this issue through the eyes of Carl Rogers, who in his essay in Chapter 11 of the text urges writers to regard the views of the opposition sympathetically, not merely as points to be dismissed.)

2. A scattering of anti–Roman Catholic material (for example, references to "papists") indicates that the speaker, for all his insistence on his objectivity, is making a prejudiced appeal to emotions.

3. Instructors interested in satiric techniques will probably want to call attention to Swift's abundant use of diminution, such as people reduced to animals and to statistics.

Additional Topics for Critical Thinking and Writing

1. Drawing only on the first three paragraphs, write a brief characterization (probably three or four sentences) of the speaker — that is, of the persona whom Swift invents. Do not talk about Swift the author; talk only about the anonymous speaker of these three paragraphs. Support your assertions by quoting words or phrases from the paragraphs.

2. In an essay of 150 to 250 words, characterize the speaker of "A Modest Proposal," and explain how Swift creates this character. You may want to make use of your answer to the previous question, pointing out that at first we think such-and-such, but later, picking up clues that Swift provides, we begin to think thus-and-so. You may wish, also, to devote a few sentences to the last paragraph of Swift's essay.

3. What is the speaker arguing for? What is Swift arguing for?

4. Write a modest proposal of your own, suggesting a solution to some great social problem. Obvious topics include war, crime, and racism, but choose any topic that almost all people agree is a great evil. Do not choose a relatively controversial topic, such as gay rights, vivisection, gun control, or right-to-work laws. Your proposed solution should be, like Swift's, outrageous, but your essay should not be silly. In the essay you should satirize some identifiable way of thinking.

5. The same basic assignment as the previous one, but this time write an essay on a topic that *is* controversial and on which you have strong feelings.

5

Developing an Argument of Your Own (p. 187)

In this chapter we try to help students get and develop ideas, chiefly by urging them (1) to ask themselves questions, (2) to write and rewrite, (3) to think of their audience as their collaborator, and (4) to submit drafts to peers for review. We think instructors will agree with us on the value of these practices. The trick is to convince students that even students who are pretty good writers will profit by working along these lines and, similarly, that even students who have difficulty writing *can* write interesting and effective papers if they make use of these suggestions.

All writers have their own methods of writing. Some can write only with a pen, whereas others can write only with a word processor; Balzac believed he needed the smell of rotten apples to stimulate his pen. Still, allowing for individual needs, we think it is honest to tell students that, in general, the sooner they begin an assignment, and the more they think about it and put their thoughts into notes and drafts, the better their essay will be. In an effort to make this point, we give in the text Emily Andrews's preliminary notes and second thoughts, as well as the final version of her essay.

Emily Andrews (student essay)

Why I Don't Spare "Spare Change" (p. 214)

As our comments in the text indicate, we think the essay is an effective piece of writing, but you may disagree, and you may want students to discuss its strengths and weaknesses and perhaps even to write a critical analysis or a response.

6
Using Sources (p. 218)

In our teaching, we try to inculcate the idea that the "research paper" is not a genre found only in the land of Freshman English or even in the larger realm of College Writing but is something that flourishes (under different descriptions, of course) wherever writing is required. That is, we try to help students to see that when, say, one writes a letter to a school newspaper, complaining that a coach has been fired, one first does (or ought to do) a little homework, finding out the won-lost record to strengthen the letter. And of course almost all reports written for businesses require research.

Students are more likely to work enthusiastically on their papers if they understand that using sources is an activity in which all literate people sometimes engage. In fact, students engage in research all the time — for instance, when they consult a book of baseball statistics or a catalog of recordings or when they talk with friends to find out what courses they should take next semester.

To give students some practice in finding materials (and in learning something), you might ask them to produce a bibliography of recent writings on, say, pornography, racist speech, or euthanasia, with summaries of two or three articles.

Part Three

FURTHER VIEWS ON ARGUMENT

7
A Philosopher's View:
The Toulmin Model (p. 289)

Of the many attempts by philosophers in recent decades to explain the logic of ordinary argumentation — and to do so in a manner that the general reader (especially undergraduates and faculty not trained in formal logic) can grasp — none has been as well received as the work of Stephen Toulmin. Toulmin began his career at Cambridge at the end of Wittgenstein's tenure there as a professor and in recent years has been on the philosophy faculty of the University of Southern California.

Why Toulmin's model of argumentation should have proved so popular where others have failed is not entirely clear to us. No doubt his reputation as a philosopher among philosophers has helped; but that is hardly the whole story because few philosophers teach informal logic and fewer still use his book *The Uses of Argument* (1958, 1969) to do it. Surely his desire to avoid forcing every kind of argument into some version of an Aristotelian syllogism is attractive. Perhaps it is mostly that the six-step model he offers with its untechnical nomenclature ("claim," "ground," and so on) is relatively more user-friendly than what the competition has to offer. Whatever the explanation, we think instructors using this book, especially those making their first acquaintance with Toulmin's method here, will find it rewarding to study (if not also to teach).

8
A Logician's View:
Deduction, Induction, Fallacies (p. 298)

The purpose of this chapter is to develop at somewhat greater length the tools of reasoning introduced in Chapter 3. Here, in two dozen pages, we divide the subject into three natural and familiar parts: deductive reasoning, inductive reasoning, and fallacious reasoning.

To take them in reverse order, we identify and illustrate eighteen fallacies. The list can be extended; for example, in the latest edition of his standard textbook, *With Good Reason*, 5th ed. (1994), S. Morris Engel identifies and discusses a dozen more. Few instructors will want to introduce their students even to all the fallacies that we discuss; but we would hope that instructors would find it useful to dwell on a few from time to time. Here, we want to mention a popular fallacy (of the sort that logicians call "formal") that does not appear in our text or in Engel's textbook: the fallacy of *denying the antecedent*.

Consider this argument:

(1) If it's raining, then the streets will be wet.

(2) It isn't raining.

(3) Therefore, the streets aren't wet.

This argument has the obvious form: if *p* then *q*; not *p*; therefore not *q*. The trouble is that this argument form is invalid; to see why, just consider the example above. Surely, it is possible the streets *are* wet — for example, a catch basin overflowed, the street cleaners flushed down the street — despite no rain at all. This argument is invalid because of its form, and we cannot trust any argument of this form. It has a related invalid argument form that is almost equally popular; its name is *affirming the consequent*, and this is its form: if *p* then *q*; *q*; therefore *p*. We leave it to your imagination to see why this form of argument is also invalid.

A large fraction (we cannot be more precise) of our daily reasoning is inductive, and to the few pages in Chapter 3 devoted to this topic we have added seven or eight more pages in this chapter. In the pages below our aim has been to take a couple of examples (involving fatality, or the risk thereof, caused by smoking) as the skeleton on which to hang our discussion of evidence, observation, inference, probability, confirmation, and related concepts essential to inductive reasoning. Brief though our discussion is, we think that at a minimum it should help instructors make these important concepts more accessible and useable by students and thus add to their available tools for diagnosing and constructing arguments.

Finally, we begin the chapter with a discussion of deduction, amplifying what we offered as a bare-bones introduction in Chapter 3. Here we offer another dozen terms (*dilemma, hypothetical syllogism*, and so on) that are standard vocabulary for the discussion of formal deductive reasoning. Some instructors may find it useful to work their way through our discussion with their students in class (perhaps in conjunction with the parallel material found in Chapter 3). Most instructors, we suspect, will find this material of use mainly for occasional reference. All (at least all instructors) can profit to greater or lesser degree merely by (carefully) reading these pages once over.

Max Shulman

Love Is a Fallacy (p. 329)

There are lots of laughs here, but the piece *does* teach effectively; students are more likely to remember Max Shulman's discussion of fallacies than ours. One can also use the story — especially the first paragraph — to talk about style. Read the first sentence aloud in class ("Cool was I and logical") and ask students what sorts of expectations are set up. Most will see that he *must* be kidding. And so on through the paragraph, to "And think of I — I was only eighteen."

9
A Moralist's View:
Ways of Thinking Ethically (p. 338)

United States v. Holmes (p. 348)

Holmes might have relied on other selection principles (question 1): save the most lives possible; first person grabbed, first overboard; save the best; last in, first out (the principle of seniority); decimation; shared disaster (see below); sailor's duty of self-sacrifice. Class discussion of one or more of these principles will prove stimulating, and no doubt other principles will emerge from the discussion as well.

The issue of a lottery (question 2) is bound to arise and has certain attractions, notably its treatment of all the surviving sailors and passengers on a par with each other. But is it not plausible to argue that, under the circumstances, it was virtually impossible to conduct a lottery — and so some other principle must be relied on? And could the passengers realistically hope to manage the lifeboat without at least some sailors to help?

The defense of superior orders (question 3) has a troubled history. Nazi soldiers and guards appealed to this defense after World War II. After the massacre of civilians at My Lai, American soldiers claimed they acted under superior orders. Is it reasonable to say in either case that ordinary soldiers *ought* to have known that their acts were wrong, even if in fact they didn't, and so had no legitimate excuse of superior orders — that those orders ought not to have been obeyed?

Justice Cardozo (question 5) in effect tells us that in situations like that faced by Holmes and the others in the lifeboat, the principle they must act on is shared disaster. That is, they must take their chances with the boat and the weather, since no one volunteered to sacrifice himself for the rest.

Several sources worth mentioning will deepen one's appreciation of the issues raised in this case. First, there is the brief discussion by Edmund Cahn in his much-admired book *The Moral Decision* (1956), pp. 61–71. More recently, there is the fascinating book by A.W.B. Simpson, *Cannibalism and the Common Law* (1984), in which most of chapter 9 is given over to the *Holmes* case. The most recent and the longest discussion is by H. A. Bedau in his book *Making Mortal Choices* (1997), pp. 3–37 and notes on pp. 107–11. Finally, in the 1970s, a film for television starring Martin Sheen was made of Holmes's trial.

Peter Singer

Famine, Affluence, and Morality (p. 356)

Singer opens his essay with a bang; before we know it, we are confronted with the plight of the famine-ridden east Bengali (now Bangladeshi) and the sorry response of affluent nations that had the wherewithal but not the will to provide massive relief. Having plunged us into the thick of things, he then backs off and begins to lay out his argument. He starts (paras. 5–6) with what he thinks are two pretty uncontroversial principles: "suffering and death from lack of food [etc.] are bad," and "if it is within our power to prevent something bad from happening, without thereby sacrificing anything of comparable moral importance, we ought, morally, to do it." He rightly points out (para. 7) that true devotion to his second principle would require major changes in our (personal and national) behavior. By the time he is finished, he has laid out an argument of far-reaching consequences, much more radical than is hinted at by his innocuous initial principles.

Regarding question 2, there is of course a "difference" between aiding one's child and aiding a perfect stranger one has never met and never will meet. Singer's position is that there is no *moral* difference. That is, morality is indifferent to propinquity: Affluent persons have no less a responsibility to aid a distant stranger than they have to aid someone nearby. Other factors of no moral significance — say, the greater effectiveness of aiding those who are nearer but whose plight is no greater than others at a great remove — may have a role to play in one's final decision of whom to aid. As for the failure of others (nations or persons) to do their fair share toward famine prevention and relief, that does not lessen (it also does not increase) our obligation to do so.

Much in this argument turns on what "morally significant" means and when two acts have or lack the same moral significance. In paragraph 14, Singer gives an example. Contrast (1) buying new clothes solely or mainly to keep up with the latest fashion trends with (2) buying new clothes to replace those that are worn out. Singer believes that failing to do 1 does not involve a sacrifice of anything morally significant, whereas failing to do 2 does. To put it another way, Singer argues that satisfying needs has a moral priority over gratifying the taste for luxury (example 1). This is not a new idea, nor is it controversial. Most of us are pretty alert to satisfying our own needs before we give ourselves luxuries. We are not equally good, however, at denying ourselves luxuries to satisfy the needs of others.

Singer strikes out in a novel direction when he undertakes to break down the familiar distinction between charity and obligation (paras. 14–19), at least to the extent of being able to say of the affluent (persons and nations) that they ought to use their surplus wealth to aid the hungry and that "to do so is not charitable, or generous." Most readers will find this puzzling and unconvincing. Singer wants to argue that if we ought to perform a certain act, then doing so cannot be either charitable or generous of us. Who, then, is in a position to act charitably or generously? It would seem to be only the poor and the hungry; their gifts and grants (if any) can be described as charitable and generous because they have no duty to act in this manner. We think (and perhaps Singer would agree) that distinguishing charity from obligation is of no great practical importance. What is important is whether the affluent ought to act as Singer counsels, not whether those acts are charitable or generous.

Notice that although Singer is a utilitarian, he is a utilitarian with a difference. Utilitarianism comes in many forms; the central feature of Singer's version (not original with him) is what is called *negative utilitarianism*. That is, as his second principle indicates, he thinks we ought to act so as to avoid causing harm or bad things to people. He does not endorse the idea (prominent in the writings of the great nineteenth-century utilitarians, Jeremy Bentham and John Stuart Mill) that we ought to act so as to bring about the greatest happiness or good things for people — or, as he puts it, "working full time to increase the balance of happiness over misery" (para. 21).

Singer's final position focuses on the question, How much ought we to be giving away for famine relief? His answer is: "we ought to give until we reach the level of marginal utility" (para. 29). He explains "marginal utility" (our question 4) in this context as "the level at which by giving more, I would cause as much suffering to myself or my dependents as I would relieve by my gift." He does not shrink from the fact that to act in this way would be to reduce oneself to "very near the material circumstances of a Bengali refugee." He shows some sympathy at the predictable reluctance of most readers to agree and comments that this is the "strong" version of his conclusion; "the more moderate version" we have met earlier in his second principle (see above). In either its strong or its moderate version, Singer's overall argument is a serious challenge to conventional thinking.

For those who wish to deepen their understanding of the causes of famine and what morality has to say about its prevention and relief, perhaps the best book is still *Faces of Hunger: An Essay on Poverty, Justice and Development* (1986) by the English philosopher Onora O'Neill. She largely agrees with Singer's position in the article we reprint, but she has a distinctive approach to the topic all her own.

Garrett Hardin

Lifeboat Ethics: The Case against Helping the Poor (p. 368)

Hardin's essay is probably the most widely read and controversial of any that have attempted to alert the reading public to environmental dangers — indeed, catastrophes — that lie ahead if we (the affluent nations) continue on our current path of sticking on a Band-Aid here and there in response to famine, AIDS, and the other major killers in the third world. Hardin's great predecessor — the Reverend Thomas Malthus (1766–1834) — goes unmentioned in his essay. Two centuries ago, Malthus warned that population was increasing at an exponential rate, that food supply could increase only at a linear rate, that millions would eventually starve as the number of hungry mouths outstripped the capacity to feed them, and that the cycle would repeat itself endlessly.

Published two years after the essay by Peter Singer (p. 356), Hardin's recommendations are diametrically opposed to Singer's. Where Singer relies on utilitarian principles and tries to show why we ought to aid the starving, Hardin relies on national self-interest (or is it just plain selfishness?) (see questions 3 and 11), for he urges us to abandon the starving, the hungry, the homeless in other nations, and to sharply curtail immigration — exactly as he thinks any sensible survivors in a lifeboat would do toward the others less fortunate who are slowly drowning in the merciless seas. And notice, too, how he tacitly disagrees with Singer in implying the not implausible view that we have a greater responsibility toward our kith and kin that we do for utter strangers near or far (paras. 42–45).

At the heart of his argument is what he calls "the tragedy of the commons" (para. 15), a phrase he coined and a concept now invariably employed in the ongoing discussion of these issues. The idea is worth a closer look. A common is essentially anything owned and used by the community at large. Some commons are modest in scale, such as the grassy meadow in the center of a typical New England village used in earlier days for sheep and cattle grazing by any or all of the local herders. Others, like the air, seem virtually infinite in scope and therefore inexhaustible. What is tragic about a common is that without a social mechanism for protecting it from ruinous exploitation by whoever gets there first, its exhaustion and destruction are inevitable. Uncontrolled population growth and unrestricted immigration merely speed up the process. In Hardin's own words, "If everyone would restrain himself, all would be well; but it takes only one less than everyone to ruin a system of voluntary restraint. . . . [M]utual ruin is inevitable if there are no controls" (para. 16). Perhaps Hardin would prefer (see paras. 1–3) that, like a spaceship, earth should be ruled by those with the authority to do so, including making the hard decisions on which collective survival depends.

To return to his analogy, if a lifeboat is treated as a common, it is bound to swamp, and all will perish. If it is treated as the private property of those who got into it first, then at least some will survive. To be sure, the survivors may not get in first but rather may get and keep a seat despite the pressure of others of take those seats for themselves. And while "First come, first served" may be a good principle for running an Oklahoma land rush a century ago or for queuing at a ticket booth for tonight's movie, few will abide by it where their own lives are at stake: Voluntary adherence to the principle "First come" will be defeated in practice by those who choose to act on the principle "To the victor belongs the spoils."

Central to the debate over Hardin's tough-minded advice is the adequacy of his lifeboat analogy — that human life on planet earth is essentially like living on a lifeboat but that the constraints evident in the lifeboat are hidden and obscured in various ways in life on earth. We are disturbed by Hardin's ugly metaphor of the human race as a "cancerous growth" (para. 30, our question 6), but we cannot see how he is wrong in believing that unchecked growth in human population will eventually make human life and society as we know them today all but impossible. What is insidious, of course, is that the "cancer" is slow growing and piecemeal adjustments year after year mask its relentless progress. Is it unreasonable to hope that social factors Hardin neglects will cause human population growth to decline and that international legal controls will slowly but steadily make their presence felt, thereby keeping Lifeboat Earth afloat? We do not expect to be around to see for ourselves.

10
A Lawyer's View:
Steps toward Civic Literacy (p. 379)

From the very first edition of our book in 1987, we have reprinted material from notable legal cases for three reasons: Judges are unusually articulate and rational in their reasoning, and so they provide valuable models for study; decided cases are rarely unanimous, especially where the stakes are high and the issues complex, so the reader has a perfect opportunity to watch trained minds at work, arguing for their preferred interpretation of the facts and the relevant law; finally, the issues raised and resolved in the courtrooms of the land are among the most dramatic to be found anywhere, so for sheer interest we want to expose our students to judicial opinions in at least a few such cases.

In this edition of our text we have expanded considerably the number and variety of materials gleaned from legal cases. In addition to the three cases and six judicial opinions presented here in Chapter 10, we also reprint two Supreme Court opinions on the death penalty (Chapter 20). Taken together, these materials provide a rich variety of legal reasoning for study, discussion, and writing.

We have subtitled this chapter Steps toward Civic Literacy because the law — its sources, interpretation, administration, and evaluation — is essential to the life of a constitutional democracy. We laugh readily at jokes about the unscrupulous and unprincipled behavior of lawyers (Shakespeare's suggestion, it will be recalled, was "The first thing we do, let's kill all the lawyers"). But the fact remains that legal reasoning, argument, and decision making are indispensable for our society. They provide the vehicles for discourse and debate about the most fundamental issues we face, and they are not the property of lawyers alone. If civic illiteracy is the inability to carry on intelligent and intelligible discussion on matters of public concern and our shared political life within the framework of a settled (but not rigid) Constitution, then the remedy is developing interest in and skill at discourse that addresses such issues and disposes of them in a reasoned, publicly accessible manner.

A Casebook on the Law and Society:
What Rights Do the Constitution and the Bill of Rights Protect?

William J. Brennan Jr. and William H. Rehnquist

Texas v. Johnson (p. 387)

Texas v. Johnson held that burning the American flag in political protest is protected by the First Amendment. The case involved Gregory ("Joey") Johnson, a member of the Revolutionary Communist Youth Brigade, who burned an American flag near the site of the 1984 Republican Convention in Dallas.

In the 5 to 4 decision, Justice William Brennan wrote the opinion in favor of Johnson, and Justice William Rehnquist wrote the main dissent. That Thurgood Marshall and Harry Blackmun joined Brennan in what is thought of as a "liberal" opinion was no surprise, but that Antonin Scalia and Anthony Kennedy (two conservative appointees) also joined Brennan was a surprise to many. On the other side, along with Rehnquist, were John Paul Stevens, Sandra Day O'Connor, and Byron White.

Justice Rehnquist (subsequently appointed Chief Justice) rejected the idea that burning the flag was a form of symbolic speech:

> Flag burning is the equivalent of an inarticulate grunt or roar that, it seems fair to say, is most likely to be indulged in not to express any particular idea, but to antagonize others.

Stevens, arguing that the flag is a symbol "worthy of protection from unnecessary desecration," cited instances where the government might legitimately restrict free expression. Among his examples: writing graffiti on the Washington Monument, projecting movie messages on the Lincoln Memorial, and extinguishing the eternal flame at John Kennedy's grave. Students might be invited to compare these actions. (Such acts of vandalism clearly would not be protected by the Court's ruling. Similarly, a person who damaged a flag flying in a public building could still be charged with vandalism or trespassing.)

Although Rehnquist did not think Joey Johnson's action was "speech," Johnson had something to say about the decision: "I think it was great to see a symbol of international plunder and murder go up in flames."

The decision in this case was a blow to many self-described patriots, especially in Congress, which moved swiftly in the aftermath to file a bill amending the Constitution so that flag-burning in political protest would not be protected by the First Amendment. The proposed bill would further permit enactment of statutes making such acts criminal offenses. So far, these efforts have not succeeded, and so the decision in this case still stands: Desecration of the nation's flag for political purposes cannot be prohibited by law.

Justice Brennan describes Johnson's conduct as "highly symbolic" (para. 10). Why (our question 3)? The flag is obviously a symbol; it is not a straightforward assertion or a nonverbal gesture. And it is highly symbolic because of the way it uniquely stands for the nation or the government, or both. Nonsymbolic conduct having the same purpose as flag-burning in this case would consist of *words* of protest explicitly criticizing the Reagan administration (para. 2). Less symbolic conduct might include a poster parade, songs specially written for the occasion, and other quasi-verbal modes of expression conveying a message of discontent with the Reagan administration.

As we note in question 8, the First Amendment as interpreted by the Supreme Court permits "time, place, and manner" (but *not* content) restrictions; regulations to such effect are a perfectly reasonable constraint on bad judgment or awkward and unnecessary interferences with the conduct of others. In this case, any of the following would probably be permissible restrictions based on time, place, or manner: burning the flag inside the Republican convention headquarters; burning it while surrounded with inflammable materials; burning the flag by drenching it first in gasoline, followed by throwing more gasoline on it as it burned.

Chief Justice Rehnquist's judgment that Johnson's behavior was the "equivalent" of an "inarticulate grunt or roar" (para. 27 and our question 4) seems to us to reveal a lack of imagination on his part. It is difficult to tell just what, if any, political message could be communicated by "a grunt or roar" — except possibly to show approval or disapproval of some immediately prior and clearly political statement. Grunts and roars are more like expletives; they command attention, express (ambiguously) the utterer's attitude of the moment, but signify little. Burning the flag, by contrast, clearly expresses disapproval with some national law or policy, the prevailing political mood, or the incumbent government; thus it clearly has *political* significance. Burning some other piece of cloth, a rag or towel, has no political significance whatever. Choice of the object (the flag) and the circumstances (a political party convention) makes the act (burning the flag) one of unquestionable political significance.

Byron R. White and John Paul Stevens

New Jersey v. T.L.O. (p. 397)

The footnote in our text gives the background to the case.

Notice first (para. 1) that the Supreme Court could have held that the search of students by school officials does not violate the Constitution because the bar to "unreasonable searches and seizures" does not apply to school officials, and so they are free to do whatever they want in this vein. Not so, argues Justice Byron White — and a good thing, too, because even though a public school principal or teacher is not a law enforcement officer, he or she still acts with public authority in conducting searches of schoolchildren on school premises during school hours. As White says (para. 7), "school officials act as representatives of the State, not merely as surrogates for the parents, and they cannot claim the parents' immunity from the strictures of the Fourth Amendment."

(By the way, Justice White mentions the Fourteenth Amendment in paragraph 2, but that amendment makes no mention of "unreasonable searches and seizures." This language appears only in the Fourth Amendment, and there it is directed solely to *federal* officers. In this case, that language is applied to *state* law and practice, under the authority of the Fourteenth Amendment as interpreted by the Court.)

The Court grants recognition to the privacy interests of the schoolchildren (paras. 10–11) but promptly weighs them against the security and disciplinary interests of the teachers (para. 13). Does it come as a surprise that the latter is said to outweigh the former? An obvious problem here is what is left of student privacy if it is subject to such weighing.

Essential to the Court's reasoning is whether the searches were "unreasonable" (para. 18). The Court offers two rather abstract criteria to define a reasonable search (end of para. 18) and then promptly reformulates them in paragraph 19 so as to be more obviously applicable to searches on school grounds. With that formulation serving in effect as the major premise of the Court's argument, the Court then adds as the minor premise the factual claim (para. 21) that the criteria are satisfied by the way the New Jersey officials conducted the search. The Court concludes its argument by judging the search to have been a constitutionally permissible one.

The four-paragraph dissent of Justice Stevens divides into two parts. First, he criticizes the standard for justifiable searches and seizures proposed by the Court majority (para. 2). Second, he proposes a tighter standard (para. 3). What is tighter about the standard he proposes? He would require a reasonable belief that the student in question is about to "seriously disrupt" the class or other school activity. Whether his proposal is better than the one adopted by the Court we leave for the class to discuss.

Harry Blackmun and William H. Rehnquist

Roe v. Wade (p. 403)

With his opinion for the Supreme Court in this case, Justice Blackmun joined his predecessor on the Court, Chief Justice Earl Warren, as one of the two most reviled Supreme Court judges of the twentieth century. The enmity and fury that

Warren aroused in the 1950s for his role in ending racial segregation — in a line of decisions beginning with *Brown v. Board of Education* (1954) — was matched by the anger and vilification heaped on Blackmun in the 1970s and 1980s for his role in legalizing abortion in the United States.

At the heart of Blackmun's opinion is the proposition that laws prohibiting abortion are an unwarranted invasion of the pregnant woman's *privacy*. Justice Rehnquist, in his dissent (paras. 39–40), makes it clear that he finds this proposition unpersuasive. Our question 7 addresses this issue but not as a question of constitutional law. If you think of your right of privacy as a right to keep information about yourself from becoming public property regardless of your consent, then it is hard to see how privacy plays a prominent, much less a dominant, role in a pregnant woman's decision to abort. Autonomy, however, is quite clearly implicated: If your autonomy consists in your capacity for self-determination and in actions exercising that capacity, then nothing could be more relevant to a pregnant woman's autonomy than her decision whether to carry her pregnancy to term. Why, then, do we hear not a word in Blackmun's opinion about women's autonomy?

The short answer is that the Supreme court had by 1972 already recognized a role for protecting privacy but had recognized no such role for protecting autonomy. The most important privacy case prior to *Roe v. Wade* is *Griswold v. Connecticut* (1965), cited by Blackmun in paragraph 5. In that case the Court held unconstitutional a Connecticut statute forbidding doctors to inform their patients about birth control and forbidding pharmacists to sell birth control materials. The Court grounded this decision in a constitutionally protected right of privacy — not, perhaps, the most plausible basis, at least not when compared with grounding it on the autonomy of persons to use their own judgment whether to disconnect their sexual conduct from any procreative intention.

To put all this another way (see question 1), by the late 1960s the Supreme Court had teased out of the broad and vague concept of protected *liberty* (an explicitly protected constitutional value) a role for protected *privacy* that was implicit in the Bill of Rights and that had been slowly emerging explicitly in the Court's opinions and decisions. (We have deleted dozens of references in Justice Blackmun's opinion in which he cites decided cases of support of privacy as a hitherto latent constitutional value.) Critics (such as the defeated Supreme Court nominee Robert Bork) ranged from those who insisted there was no constitutional protection available for privacy at all, apart from liberty, to those who allowed that there was such protection but that it did not extend to a right of a woman to have an abortion.

One of the weakest aspects of Justice Blackmun's opinion, in our judgment, is his position on "when life begins" (paras. 30–31, our question 9). So far as the human fetus is concerned, there are only three possibilities: The fetus (indeed, the embryo) is alive, dead, or inert. The second and third of these three options are absurd. Similarly, there is no denying that the embryo and fetus are human; of course they are. What really matters is not whether the fetus is *alive* or *human* — surely it is — but whether in its embryonic or fetal state it is anything more than a potential person, whether potential persons have any rights, and whether those rights (if any) always or ever prevail over the woman's rights of liberty, privacy, and autonomy. We are not so foolish as to try to resolve these questions here.

11
A Psychologist's View:
Rogerian Argument (p. 416)

Carl R. Rogers

Communication: Its Blocking and Its Facilitation (p. 418)

An occasional student has told us that Carl Rogers is "merely trying to apply psychology" to outwit his opponent, but we believe this interpretation is mistaken. Rogers was much concerned with reducing tension so that issues could be more easily discussed, not with deceiving the parties involved. Still, it is easy to see how students might think that "psychology" is a weapon to be wielded — something akin to bluffing at poker — in order to win. We are reminded of the advice that an old actor gave to a young one: "The most important thing is sincerity. When you can fake *that*, you can do anything."

It's not hard to find comments about argument that come close to the actor's view. Consider, for instance, Samuel Butler's "It is not he who gains the exact point in dispute who scores most in controversy, but he who has shown the most forbearance and the better temper." Or Lord Chesterfield's advice to his son: "If you would convince others, seem open to conviction yourself." But Butler's concern with scoring most and Chesterfield's use of *seem* (as opposed to *be*) set their comments sharply apart from Rogers's. Similarly, consider Ben Franklin: "Those disputing, contradicting, and confuting people are general unfortunate in their affairs. They get victory, sometimes, but they never get good will, which be of more use to them." Rogers would probably agree, but he would rightly claim that he is not concerned with gaining goodwill so that it will be of "use" to him; he is concerned with helping the world to achieve peace.

Much closer to Rogers than Butler, Chesterfield, or Franklin is Pascal: "When we wish to correct with advantage, and to show another that he errs, we must notice from what side he views the matter, for on that side it is usually true." Close — but still short of Rogers's view, since Rogers recognizes not only that the other side may be right from its own point of view but may indeed be right enough so that we can come to accept at least part of that point of view. Consider these key statements:

> The whole task of psychotherapy is the task of dealing with a failure in communication.
> (para. 1)

> If you really understand another person in this way, if you are willing to enter his private world and see the way life appears to him, without any attempt to make evaluative judgments, you run the risk of being changed yourself. You might see it his way, you might find yourself influenced in your attitudes or your personality.
> (para. 11)

We imagine that most people would agree with Rogers in theory, but some opposing voices have been heard. For us, the most telling objection is that Rogers speaks as a white male — that is, as a member of the group that for centuries has done most of the speaking and has done very little listening. His advice — in effect, "Calm down, listen to me, and see things from my point of view" — is good advice for people like Rogers but is less useful (we have heard it said) for women, gays and lesbians, blacks, Hispanics, and other marginalized people. Some members of these groups say that they have listened long enough, and that it is now their turn to speak out and to speak out forcefully. Let straight white males, they argue, do the listening for a change.

One other point must be made about Rogerian argument. Rogers was talking about *talking*, about people who are actually facing their hearers. But instructors who use our book are for the most part concerned with *writing*, and they may wonder if Rogers's essay is relevant to writers. We offer two short answers: (1) assign and discuss the essay, and (2) urge students to make use of the checklist in the text (p. 424) when they write their next essays. We think that if students read the essay and pay attention to the checklist, they not only will write better essays but may become better people.

12
A Literary Critic's View:
Arguing about Literature (p. 425)

Classroom discussion usually centers on the meaning of a work, and almost always someone raises the question, "Do you really think that's what the author intended?" But ever since the publication of W. K. Wimsatt Jr. and Monroe C. Beardsley's "The Intentional Fallacy," *Sewanee Review* 54 (Summer 1946), conveniently reprinted in W. K. Wimsatt Jr., *The Verbal Icon* (1954), it has been impossible (we think) to talk easily about the author's intention.

To begin with, most authors have not in any explicit way set forth their intentions: We have, for example, *Hamlet*, but not Shakespeare's comment on his intention in the drama, and we have Robert Frost's "Design" (Chapter 29) but not Frost's comment on his intention in the poem. Nevertheless, students may say that if an author has stated what he or she intended, we should interpret the work accordingly. But we might respectfully point out that the stated intention is not always fulfilled in the work. The author doubtless intended to write a great work — but does this intention mean that the work is great? The author intended to write a serious work — but we may find it absurd. Does the author's intention make the work less absurd? Or, conversely, the writer may have intended only to earn money —a famous instance is Dr. Johnson, hurriedly writing *Rasselas* to pay the costs of his mother's funeral but nevertheless producing a masterpiece. Wimsatt and Beardsley have taught us that the work "means" what the work itself says, not what the author says he or she meant it to mean. In the words of Lillian Hellman, "The writer's intention hasn't anything to do with what he achieves." Or, in the words of D. H. Lawrence (quoted from memory), "Trust the tale, not the teller."

Although "The Intentional Fallacy" remains the classic text, you may want to suggest that students interested in this topic should read Beardsley's later comments on intention in his *Aesthetics: Problems in the Philosophy of Criticism* (1958) and in his *The Possibility of Criticism* (1970).

The proper question to ask, we believe, is not "What did the author mean?" but, rather, "What does the text say?" We can, of course, try to see what the work meant in its own day — that is, in its historical context. For instance, if we are thinking about *The Merchant of Venice* or about *Othello* we can try to collect information about Elizabethan attitudes toward Jews or toward Moors, but even with such material we will not be able to say much about Shakespeare's intention. *The Merchant of Venice* contains at least one extended passage (3.1.55–65) in which Shylock is presented far more sympathetically than any Jew in any other Elizabethan text (did Shakespeare perhaps find Shylock coming to life, and did he give him better lines than he intended?) and as for *Othello*, well, no other Elizabethan drama has a tragic hero who is Moor. The mere fact that Shakespeare alone made a Moor the central figure in a tragedy — a genre that displayed human greatness — suggests that we will not get much insight into Othello by seeing how other dramatists represented Moors or, for that matter, even by seeing how Shakespeare represented Moors in other plays (*Titus Andronicus* and *The Merchant of Venice*). To read *Othello* is to see a Moor who is incontestably different from the Moors in all other Elizabethan plays (including Shakespeare's other plays), and we do great injustice to the heroic Othello if we push him into the mold of "the Elizabethan Moor," which in effect means the Moor as depicted by people who were not Shakespeare.

Let's take a particular passage in T. S. Eliot's "The Love Song of J. Alfred Prufrock" (Chapter 28). After the epigraph from Dante the poem begins thus: "Let us go then, you and I." Who is the "you"? In this manual we suggest that "Prufrock" is an internal monologue in which the timid self ("I") addresses his own amorous self as "you." (We don't say that *every* "you" in the poem is the amorous self.) It happens that a reader asked Eliot (apparently in the mid-1940s, some thirty years after Eliot wrote the poem) who the "you" is, and Eliot replied:

> As for THE LOVE SONG OF J. ALFRED PRUFROCK anything I say now must be somewhat conjectural, as it was written so long ago that my memory may deceive me; but I am prepared to assert that the "you" in THE LOVE SONG is merely some friend or companion, presumably of the male sex, whom the speaker is at that moment addressing. . . .
> — Kristian Smidt, *Poetry and Belief in the Work of T. S. Eliot* (1961), 85.

Several points are worth noting: (1) The statement was made long after the poem was written, and Eliot grants that any such late statement "must be somewhat conjectural"; (2) he nevertheless is "prepared to assert" that the "you" is "some friend or companion"; (3) although he is prepared to make this assertion, the assertion itself is rather imprecise (there is a difference between a "friend" and a "companion") and he immediately goes on to reveal (by saying "presumably of the male sex") that he himself no longer has (if he ever did have) a clear idea of who the "you" is. How helpful, then, is his comment? True, if one wants to say that the author is the decisive authority, presumably one can rule out the view that the "you" in the poem is (for the most part) the amorous self, the self urging the timid self to go forward. But, we suggest, the test is to read the poem to see if the suggestion makes sense.

Eliot himself occasionally commented at some length on the topic of intention. For instance, in "The Social Function of Poetry" (1945) after saying that "a great deal more goes to the making of poetry than the conscious purpose of the poet," he went on to add, "And in recent times, a reason why we have become more cautious in accepting a poet's expressed intention as evidence of what he was really doing, is that we have all become more conscious of the role of the unconscious." And in "The Frontiers of Criticism" (1956) he mentions, of a published interpretation of "Prufrock" that he had recently read, "[The author set forth] an attempt to find out what the poem really meant — whether that was what I had meant it to mean or not. And for that I was grateful." Possibly Eliot's expression of gratitude is spoken with tongue in cheek (though we do not think so), but even if one does think Eliot is being ironic, the case for the authority of the author's interpretation is undermined; the author may (or may not) be speaking ironically, so how much weight can we give to his comments? In any case, in the context of the entire essay, it is clear that Eliot really does believe that a work cannot be reduced to what the author "intended."

One last quotation from Eliot, this one from *The Use of Poetry and the Use of Criticism* (1933), 130:

> A poet can try, of course, to give an honest report of the way in which he himself writes: the result may, if he is a good observer, be illuminating. And in one sense, but a very limited one, he knows better what his poems "mean" than can anyone else; he may know the history of their composition, the material which has gone in and come out in an unrecognisable form, and he knows what he was trying to do and what he was meaning to mean. But what a poem means is as much what it means to others as what it means to the author; and indeed, in the course of time a poet may become merely a reader in respect to his own works, forgetting his original meaning.

These sentences make sense, but we also see the force of the commonsense view that a competent author shapes the material so that it embodies his meaning. This meaning may change during the process of composition — the writer finds his or her intention shifting and therefore revises the work — but, in this view, the creator of a work does know, at the end, what the meaning of the work is. Notice that we say "a competent author." Obviously an incompetent author may compose a work that is inadvertently incoherent or ludicrous and be unaware of the result. But a competent author, in this view, shapes the work — admittedly modifying the original intention as the work proceeds — and at the end has produced a work in which all of the elements cohere, and on whose meaning he or she can comment. This, we say, is a commonsense view; the only trouble, again, is that most writers have *not* commented on their works (for example, Chaucer, Shakespeare), and those writers who have commented (for example, Eliot) have often made inconclusive remarks. Aside from Eliot, none of the poets, story writers, or dramatists represented in this book have commented on the works we reprint.

Robert Frost

Mending Wall (p. 431)

Some critics applaud the neighbor in Robert Frost's "Mending Wall," valuing his respect for barriers. For an extreme version, see Robert Hunting, "Who Needs Mending?" *Western Humanities Review* 17 (Winter 1963): 88–89. The gist of this faction is that the neighbor wisely realizes — as the speaker does not — that individual identity depends on respect for boundaries. Such a view sees the poem as a Browningesque dramatic monologue like "My Last Duchess," in which the self-satisfied speaker unknowingly gives himself away.

Richard Poirier, in *Robert Frost* (1977), makes the interesting point that it is not the neighbor (who believes that "good fences make good neighbors") who initiates the ritual of mending the wall; rather, it is the speaker: "I let my neighbor know beyond the hill." Poirier suggests that "if fences do not 'make good neighbors,' the *making* of fences can," for it makes for talk — even though the neighbor is hopelessly taciturn. For a long, judicious discussion of the poem, see John C. Kemp, *Robert Frost: The Poet as Regionalist* (1979), 13–25.

Andrew Marvell

To His Coy Mistress (p. 441)

First, we touch on our final question, the emendation of "glew" to "dew" in line 35. This emendation has found wide acceptance, but the original reading may be right, not in the ordinary sense of glue, of course, but in a sense that H. Grierson suggested, "a shining gum found on some trees."

Probably most of the discussion in class will concentrate on the structure of the poem and the question of whether the poem is offensively sexist. As for the tripartite structure, which we call attention to in a question in the text, we want to make two points here. First, we do not see it as a Hegelian matter of thesis/antithesis/synthesis, although many readers do see it this way. We see it, as we indicate in the text, as a matter of a supposition, a refutation, and a deduction.

The supposition is somewhat comic, with the lover offering to devote two hundred years to the praise of each breast, and it is even somewhat bawdy in his offer to devote "thirty thousand to the rest": After all, what can "the rest" be, after he has praised her forehead, eyes, and breasts? This apparently leisurely state might at first thought seem to be ideal for a lover, but, when one thinks about it, one perceives its barrenness: "We would sit down, and think which way / To walk, and pass our long love's day" (lines 2–3). Nothing is fulfilled: "An age at least to every part, / and the last age should show your heart" (lines 17–18), which is to say that after centuries of praising this or that part, the last age — an unimaginably long period — would be devoted to praising the countless good qualities of her heart, for instance her generosity, kindness, piety, and whatever else. It all sounds rather barren.

The second unit begins with lines that are among the most famous in English literature, "But at my back I always hear / Time's wingéd chariot hurrying near" (lines 21–22). These lines seem to introduce swiftness and vitality into the poem; but when one comes to think further about this unit, one notices that at least so far as the man and the woman are concerned, they don't do much here either. In the "deserts of vast eternity," her beauty will *not* be found; his song will *not* be heard; they will *not* embrace. The chief actors will be the worms, who will "try" her virginity. If in the first unit the speaker spoofs the woman, showing her as a caricature of the disdainful mistress, in the second unit he savagely attacks her verbally, with talk of graves and worms. And here, too, as we have just said, nothing much happens.

In the third unit, there is plenty of (imagined) action, action that they share, unlike the earlier action of the speaker praising the beloved or of her refusing his offers. This joint action, sexual union, is indicated by "we," "us," and "our." But the imagery and the emotion are not what we might have expected. The savagery persists, notably in the images of "fire" and "birds of prey" (rather than the doves of Venus, which we might expect in a love poem) and in the verbs "devour" and "tear." Instead of time devouring the lovers, they devour time, but now we feel that the speaker's assertions lacerate himself as well as the beloved.

This gets us to our main point: We see the poem not so much as primarily a love poem or even as a poem of seduction (which is what disturbs many students), but as primarily a poem about the desperate condition of human beings, as the speaker sees it. To this extent, what interests a reader (we think) is the emotional states through which the speaker moves, from teasing the beloved (the first unit), to twisting the knife (the second unit), to forcing himself to face the facts that he has been thrusting under her eyes (the third unit).

Kate Chopin

The Story of an Hour (p. 444)

The first sentence of Kate Chopin's story, of course, proves to be essential to the end, though during the middle of the story the initial care to protect Mrs. Mallard from the "sad message" seems almost comic. Students may assume, too easily, that Mrs. Mallard's "storm of grief" is hypocritical. They may not notice that the renewal after the first shock is stimulated by the renewal of life around her ("the tops of trees . . . were all aquiver with the new spring of life") and that before she achieves a new life, Mrs. Mallard first goes through a sort of death and then tries to resist renewal: Her expression "indicated a suspension of intelligent thought," she felt something "creeping out of the sky," and she tried to "beat it back with her will," but she soon finds herself "drinking the elixir of life through that open window," and her thoughts turn to "spring days, and summer days."

Implicit in the story is the idea that her life as a wife — which she had thought was happy — was in fact a life of repression or subjugation, and the awareness comes to her only at this late stage. The story has two surprises: The change from grief to joy proves not to be the whole story, for we get the second surprise, the husband's return and Mrs. Mallard's death. The last line ("the doctors . . . said she had died . . . of joy that kills") is doubly ironic: The doctors wrongly assume that she was overjoyed to find that her husband was alive, but they were not wholly wrong in guessing that her last day of life brought her great joy.

In a sense, moreover, the doctors are right (though not in the sense they mean) in saying that she "died of heart disease." That is, if we take the "heart" in a metaphorical sense to refer to love and marriage, we can say that the loss of her new freedom from her marriage is unbearable. This is not to say (though many students do say it) that her marriage was miserable. The text explicitly says "she had loved him — sometimes." The previous paragraph in the story nicely calls attention to certain aspects of love — a satisfying giving of the self — and yet also to a most unpleasant yielding to force: "There would be no one to live for her during those coming years; she would live for herself. There would be no powerful will bending her in that blind persistence with which men and women believe they have a right to impose a private will upon a fellow-creature."

A biographical observation: Chopin's husband died in 1882, and her mother died in 1885. In 1894 in an entry in her diary she connected the two losses with her growth. "If it were possible for my husband and my mother to come back to earth, I feel that I would unhesitatingly give up every thing that has come into my life since they left it and join my existence again with theirs. To do that, I would have to forget the past ten years of my growth — my real growth."

Having said what we have to say about the story, we now offer our own responses to the critical assertions in the text to which we ask students to respond.

1. We don't think the railroad accident is a symbol of the destructiveness of the industrial revolution. In our view, something in a text becomes symbolic by virtue of being emphasized, perhaps by being presented at considerable length, or perhaps by being repeated at intervals. Nothing in the story connects the train with the industrial revolution; it is not, for instance, said to have altered the landscape, changing what was once an agrarian community into an industrial community. On the other hand, we think that in this story the coming of spring *is* symbolic of new life. Why? For one thing, Chopin explicitly says in the fifth paragraph that the "tops of trees . . . were all aquiver with the new spring life." She goes on to talk of "the delicious breath of rain" and of sparrows twittering. The rain of course is refreshing, and it is a fact that water brings about renewed life. Further, literary tradition (cf. Chaucer's reference to April showers at the start of *The Canterbury Tales*) has given spring showers a symbolic meaning. Sparrows are associated with sexuality (the sparrow is an attribute of Aphrodite), but we don't usually bring this up in class because Chopin mentions the sparrows only briefly and because students are not likely to know of the tradition. (This point seems to us not worth arguing.) A few paragraphs later Chopin tells us that something was coming toward Mrs. Mallard "out of the sky, reaching toward her through the sounds, the scents, the color that filled the air." Surely, therefore, it is reasonable to say that Chopin is emphasizing the season — its sounds, scents, and colors. A few paragraphs later, Chopin tells us that Mrs. Mallard was thinking of "spring days, summer days." In short, *in the story* spring is given an emphasis that the train is not, and so we tend to think that the spring is not just the spring but is something more, something whose implications we should attend to.

2. To say that the story claims that women rejoice in the deaths of their husbands seem to us to be a gross overgeneralization. The story is about one particular woman. True, in reading any work we may find ourselves saying, "Yes, life is sometimes like that," or some such thing, but nothing in the story suggests that it is about "women," and certainly nothing suggests that Mrs. Mallard's response toward the death of her husband is *typical* of "women."

3. The view that her death at the end of the story is a just punishment strikes us as going far beyond the text; we find no evidence that Chopin judges Mrs. Mallard harshly, and we think we can point to contrary evidence — for instance, to the sympathetic way in which her response is set forth.

4. We do not agree that the story is good *because* it has a surprise ending — but we also do not condemn it because of the ending. True, some critics would argue that surprise endings are tricks, that such endings are far less important than plausible characters, and so on. Our own view is that if a story offers virtually nothing but a surprise ending, it is probably a weak story — one can hardly read it a second time with any interest — but a certain amount of surprise surely is desirable. Most, maybe all, realistic prose fictions make use of foreshadowing; expectations are set up, but they are fulfilled in slightly unexpected ways. We are reminded of a passage in E. M. Forster's *Aspects of the Novel* (1927):

> Shock, followed by the feeling, "Oh, that's all right," is a sign that all is well with plot: characters, to be real, ought to run smoothly, but a plot ought to cause surprise.

Of course, one might argue that this view is arbitrary; here is a chance to ask students what values they might establish — what makes them say that a story is good or bad or so-so.

Kate Chopin

The Storm (p. 447)

Chopin wrote this story in 1898 but never tried to publish it, presumably because she knew it would be unacceptable to the taste of the age. "The Storm" depicts the same characters as an earlier story, "The 'Cadian Ball," in which Alcée is about to run away with Calixta when Clarisse captures him as a husband.

Our first question in the text is intended to give students a chance to practice writing a *short* summary and then an argument setting forth an evaluation. In our experience, most students who write on this topic will argue that the story is "broadening," a few will argue that it is immoral, and a few (we regard these with special approval) will argue that it should be read because it is highly entertaining.

Our second question also calls for an evaluation, this one of the parallel between the inner and the outer storms. Obviously there is no right answer to the question, but this is not to say that some answers cannot be more convincing than others. A good answer will offer evidence.

Our third question, asking if the story is immoral, is more or less discussed below, when we talk about the matter of cynicism. As for the fourth question (the letter to a high school teacher, indicating which story might be more effective in high school), we have found that a majority of our students recommend "The Story of an Hour," largely on the grounds that high school students may not be ready for "The Storm" but also because a fair number of our students read "The Story of an Hour" in high school, know it better, and therefore feel more comfortable with it.

Here now are some thoughts on topics that regularly come up when we teach "The Storm."

The characters of Calixta and Bobinôt. In Part I, Bobinôt buys a can of shrimp because Calixta is fond of shrimp. Our own impression is that this detail is provided chiefly to show Bobinôt's interest in pleasing his wife, but Per Seyersted, in *Kate Chopin* (1969), finds a darker meaning. Seyersted suggests (223) that shrimp "may represent a conscious allusion to the potency often denoted by sea foods." (To the best of our knowledge, this potency is attributed only to oysters, but perhaps we lead sheltered lives.) At the beginning of Part II Calixta is "sewing furiously on a sewing machine," and so readers gather that she is a highly industrious woman, presumably a more than usually diligent housekeeper. The excuses Bobinôt frames on the way home (Part III) suggest that he is somewhat intimidated by his "overscrupulous housewife." Calixta is genuinely concerned about the welfare of her somewhat simple husband and of her child. The affair with Alcée by no means indicates that she is promiscuous or, for that matter, unhappy with her family. We don't think her expressions of solicitude for the somewhat childlike Bobinôt are insincere. We are even inclined to think that perhaps her encounter with Alcée has heightened her concern for her husband. (At least, to use the language of reader-response criticism, this is the way we "naturalize" — make sense out of — the gap or blank in the narrative.)

Alcée's letter to his wife. The letter suggests that he thinks his affair with Calixta may go on for a while, but we take it that the affair is, like the storm (which gives its title to the story), a passing affair. It comes about unexpectedly and "naturally": Alcée at first takes refuge on the gallery, with no thought of entering the house but because the gallery does not afford shelter, Calixta invites him in, and then a lightning bolt drives her (backward) into his arms. The experience is thoroughly satisfying, and it engenders no regrets, but presumably it will be treasured rather than repeated, despite Alcée's thought when he writes his letter.

Clarisse's response. By telling us, in Part V, that Clarisse is delighted at the thought of staying a month longer in Biloxi, Chopin diminishes any blame that a reader might attach to Alcée. That is, although Alcée is unfaithful to his wife, we see that his wife doesn't regret his absence: "Their intimate conjugal life was something which she was more than willing to forego for a while."

Is the story cynical? We don't think so, since cynicism involves a mocking or sneering attitude, whereas in this story Chopin regards her characters affectionately. Blame is diminished not only by Clarisse's letter but by other means. We learn that at an earlier time, when Calixta was a virgin, Alcée's "honor forbade him to prevail." And, again, by associating the affair with the storm, Chopin implies that this moment of passion is in accord with nature. Notice also that the language becomes metaphoric during the scene of passion. For instance, Calixta's "lips were as red and as moist as pomegranate seed," and her "passion . . . was like a white flame," suggesting that the characters are transported to a strange (though natural) world. There is, of course, the implication that people are less virtuous than they seem to be, but again, Chopin scarcely seems to gloat over this fact. Rather, she suggests that the world is a fairly pleasant place in which there is enough happiness to go all around. "So the storm passed and everyone was happy." There is no need to imagine further episodes in which, for instance, Calixta and Alcée deceive Bobinôt; nor is there any need to imagine further episodes in which Calixta and Alcée regret their moment of passion.

Two additional points. First, there seems to be a suggestion of class distinction between Calixta and Alcée though both are Creoles. Calixta uses some French terms, and her speech includes such expressions as "An' Bibi? he ain't wet? Ain't hurt"? Similarly Bobinôt's language, though it does not include any French terms, departs from Standard English. On the other hand, Alcée speaks only Standard English. Possibly, however, the distinctions in language are also based, at least partly based, on gender as well as class; Calixta speaks the language of an uneducated woman largely confined to her home, whereas Alcée — a man who presumably deals with men in a larger society — speaks the language of the Anglo world. But if gender is relevant, how can one account for the fact that Bobinôt's language resembles Calixta's, and Clarisse's resembles Alcée's? A tentative answer: Bobinôt, like Calixta, lives in a very limited world, whereas Clarisse is a woman of the world. We see Clarisse only at the end of the story, and there we hear her only through the voice of the narrator, but an expression such as "The society was agreeable" suggests that her language (as might be expected from a woman rich enough to take a long vacation) resembles her husband's, not Calixta's.

Plato

"The Greater Part of the Stories Current Today We Shall Have to Reject" (p. 454)

This excerpt from Plato's *Republic* is a passage near the end of Book II, in which Socrates undertakes to describe the proper education for that handful of the young intended to become the guardians or rulers of the ideal state. (Throughout the dialogue, we hear nothing about how the rest of the population is to be educated, that presumably being a matter of no interest.) After explaining the importance of "gymnastics," or bodily training, Socrates turns to "music," or training for the soul. To be fair, one must not carry Platonic-Socratic admonitions out of context; nevertheless, there is some reason to believe that — unlike Socrates, who relied on the free air of Athens to carry out his ideas about education of the citizenry — Plato, the son of an Athenian nobleman, really did believe that a stricter regimen involving some censorship of the prevailing methods was appropriate.

Plato's argument for discarding the Homeric tales about the gods depends on accepting the principle that whatever is good can be the cause only of good things — hence the gods, being wholly good, cannot cause any of the bad things that the prevailing mythology attributes to them. Plato knows that the gods are wholly good only because that is part of his implicit definition of deity — as though he had said, "I [we?] wouldn't call it divine unless it was (morally) good."

Plato even goes so far as to allege that in his ideal state, it would be "sinful, inexpedient, and inconsistent" to permit the poets to say that "those who were punished were made wretched through god's action." Presumably, he thinks it would be inconsistent to allow this statement (question 3) because it would contradict something that the elder guardian-teachers themselves avow; namely, that (as Plato says at the end of the excerpt) "God is the cause, not of all things, but only of good." Thus, when a poet presents a story in which a god is depicted as making a person "wretched" (and we assume that being made wretched is not a "good" thing, but that getting your deserved punishment is), this interpretation contradicts the doctrine above because it makes the god out to be the cause of something not "good."

Some will complain that Plato assumes, on no explicit evidence, that "children cannot distinguish between what is allegory and what isn't," and he shows throughout that he underestimates the capacity of children to distinguish the silly from the serious, the cheap from the dear, and the obscene from the respectful (our question 2). It is, of course, an empirical question — and not an easy one to answer — whether children can make these distinctions. But it is needless to speculate whether they can make them in the abstract or in a wholly nonsocial environment. As we remember our childhood and that of our friends, we testify that we had no great difficulty in making these distinctions and that an unremitting diet of Saturday afternoon B-grade films at the local movie palace or the standard TV fare of the 1950s did not hopelessly muddle our values and our sense of reality. Obviously, we did not feed only on such stuff, any more than children today see nothing except what is on the most violent television shows. Even if we overestimate our own ability as youngsters to sort the wheat from the chaff, we doubt that the best way to develop judgment about what is harmful, tasteless, offensive, and worse is to deny all access to the meretricious, salacious, and blasphemous. Even if this is too serene (or radical) a view to gain favor, one must eventually face the question *quis custodiet custodies*, or who shall guard the guardians? Plato does not need to worry about this problem because he, unlike the rest of us, deals by definition with an ideal state and its appropriately ideal government, one that is incapable of the provinciality of every known board of public censorship.

Part Four

CURRENT ISSUES: OCCASIONS FOR DEBATE

Most of the essays in Part Four (six debates) are fairly short. Those on gay marriage and on gun control are close to the usual 500-word freshman essay.

As we suggested earlier, you may want to use one or more of these pairs when assigning the first five chapters, in discussions of such matters as assumptions, evidence, and tone.

Because these topics have inspired much writing in the last few years, they can be used to introduce students to ways of finding recent sources, as through the *Readers' Guide to Periodical Literature*, the *New York Times Index*, and the *Social Sciences Index*. Each pair of debates can, however, be taken by itself. By the time a student has read both sides of one debate, he or she is in a pretty good position to write an essay on the issue or to analyze one of the arguments.

13

Abortion:
Whose Right to Life Is It Anyway? (p. 463)

The problem of abortion, at least from the moral point of view, can be posed as a choice among three options: (1) Abortion is morally wrong under all circumstances; or (2) it is morally permissible under all circumstances (and maybe even required in some imaginable situations); or (3) it is permissible under some but not under other circumstances — the challenge then being to spell out the relevant circumstances. The two essays we reprint here position themselves quite differently with regard to these three basic options. Ellen Willis clearly tolerates abortion under various unspecified circumstances and argues for such toleration. Randall Terry, however, presupposes but does not directly argue his opposition to abortion under all circumstances and addresses instead the secondary issue of whether violent protests of abortion are justified.

Ellen Willis

Putting Women Back into the Abortion Debate (p. 464)

Ellen Willis's personal narrative approach to this heated issue in her opening paragraph is soon replaced by a more vigorously argumentative style. She makes it clear that she supports abortion where appropriate, as an expression of woman's autonomy. Her view is not pro-abortion (true enthusiasts for abortion are hard to find, we hope); rather, it is pro-choice. Here is her central comment: "I do consider the life of a fertilized egg less precious than the well-being of a woman with feelings, self-consciousness, a history, social ties" (para. 5). No wonder she says that abortion is "a *feminist issue*" (para. 2).

The reader of Willis's essay may well wonder just how much her views have changed (see para. 14) since the birth of her child. Part of what has changed, she makes clear, is that she thinks the abortion decision — at least for her, in any future pregnancy — is much more complex and fraught with emotion than it was before she became a mother. Her worries about "self-flagellating guilt" raise an important and troubling aspect of the moral psychology that pro-choice women may discover in the aftermath of an abortion.

Willis does not attempt to draw any lines defining permissible in contrast to impermissible abortions. Where does she stand, for instance, on abortion of a viable human fetus? She does not even hint an answer. What about an abortion based on early diagnosis during pregnancy that the fetus has some crippling and irremedial abnormality? Silence. So some of the central issues debated in the abortion controversy cannot readily be illuminated by careful discussion of Willis's essay.

Additional Topics for Critical Thinking and Writing

1. Willis mentions several propositions that she regards as "intuitively self-evident." Identify these propositions; do you agree that they are self-evident? Has she left off her list some other equally self-evident truths that bear on the abortion controversy? Why should it matter to her argument whether these propositions are "intuitively self-evident," rather than merely true?

2. What is Willis's point in juxtaposing Anatole France's old quip about the rich as well as the poor being allowed to sleep under bridges with the claim that "men as well as women should be sexually 'responsible' "?

3. Willis insists that the abortion controversy should be viewed as an issue of "freedom versus repression, or equality versus hierarchy." What does she mean by these oppositions? Do you agree that these are the best way to frame the issue? Explain.

4. What evidence does Willis cite to support her claim that "the Catholic hierarchy has made opposition to abortion a litmus test of loyalty to the church"?

5. Do you agree that there is such a thing as "the right's antifeminist program" (para. 3)? Whether or not you agree, what do you think Willis would point to if asked for evidence that the right is antifeminist?

6. In her next-to-last sentence Willis says that antiabortionists "condone the subjugation of women." Reread the essay, and then write a paragraph that begins thus:

   > In "Putting Women Back into the Abortion Debate," Ellen Willis argues that antiabortionists "condone the subjugation of women."

   Then complete the paragraph, summarizing as accurately as possible her arguments on behalf of this thesis. Do not simply restate the thesis; rather, concisely describe the evidence she offers.

Randall A. Terry

The Abortion Clinic Shootings: Why? (p. 471)

Whereas Ellen Willis presents the issue of abortion as a "feminist issue" and implies that there is no fundamental objection to a woman's exercise of choice to end her pregnancy for any of a wide variety of reasons flowing out of her own personal situation as a woman, Randall Terry presupposes that abortion is forbidden on essentially religious grounds. He never mentions, but surely accepts, the pro-life position classically expressed for Roman Catholics in the papal encyclical *Humanae Vitae* (On Human Life) issued under the name of Pope Paul VI in 1968 and reaffirmed in a much expanded discussion in 1995 by Pope John Paul II in *Evangelium Vitae* (The Gospel of Life).

"Although there is no direct and explicit call to protect human life at its very beginning, specifically life not yet born," the new encyclical concedes, "denying life" to the unborn "is completely foreign to the religious and cultural way of thinking of the People of God." Later, we are told: "The human being is to be respected and treated as a person from the moment of conception." If so, then deliberately causing the death of a human fetus is murder. This is precisely the view of Terry: Abortion under any circumstances and for any reason is morally wrong. Thus Terry sees himself and other antiabortion activists as warriors in God's cause, saving innocent human lives from undeserved destruction. So much by way of sketching the moral background for his views on violence.

Terry implies that it is "ludicrous" — well, anyway, inconsistent and perhaps hypocritical — to condemn opponents of abortion for violence at abortion clinics and not to condemn Gandhi and King for the violence that accompanied their nonviolent direct action movements. We think the analogy is a poor one (our first question). What Terry calls "the violent actions that accompanied the civil rights movement in the United States during the 1960s" were *not* caused by King or his followers; these violent outcomes were caused by the White Citizens Councils, the Ku Klux Klan, and other white supporters in defense of segregation, Jim Crow, and a whole host of unconstitutional laws, ordinances, and social practices. Occasional violence by King's supporters was regularly criticized by King. Much the same story is to be told about Gandhi's efforts in South Africa and India.

A better parallel for Terry's purposes would be the violence against slavery by John Brown and other radical abolitionists prior to the Civil War: Would those who oppose slavery condemn the use of violence to attack the spread of "the peculiar institution" after the Dred Scott decision (1857), when (like abortion today) slavery was deemed not unconstitutional and when nonviolent measures could not reasonably be expected to end slavery in any foreseeable future? That's a tough question worth exploring.

When Terry describes abortion as "child killing," he is tacitly assimilating the status of unborn humans to the status of born but not yet adolescent or adult humans — an effective rhetorical device, since few if any Americans who favor a woman's right to choose abortion also favor infanticide, much less other kinds of "child killing." Thus "child killing" is the inverse of phrases like "ethnic cleansing" — the euphemism the Serbs have used to redescribe their atrocities in Bosnia in recent years.

It does strike us as extreme and misleading, however, to describe a pre-embryonic fertilized human ovum as a "child" — or, indeed, to describe any nonviable humane fetus in this way. "Child," "infant," "neonate," "youngster" — these and other familiar terms are not synonyms, and none has a meaning that permits application to the unborn without distortion and misrepresentation. But of course both the friends and the enemies of abortion will choose their language for maximum rhetorical effect, hoping in this way to arouse sympathy for their position that more disciplined argument probably cannot secure. Whether it is more illuminating to think of a human embryo as the earliest stage of a "child" and thus as a potential "person" or whether it is better to think of it only as a clump of living tissue is not something to be settled in haste or by fiat.

When Terry ascribes an "inalienable right to life" to the unborn (see our question 9), it is not altogether clear to us what he means. An inalienable right is usually explained as a right that cannot be alienated — that is, given away, sold, or traded in exchange for something else. Thus, our right to vote is legally inalienable.

Inalienable rights can, however, be waived, and they can be forfeited. Physician-assisted suicide does the former, and supporters of the death penalty believe that murder does the latter.

However, like other rights, inalienable rights are not absolute; that is, other morally relevant considerations can prevail over such a right. If Terry thinks unborn humans have an *absolute* right to life, then he has a tough proposition to defend, as our hypothetical example in question 9 indicates. But if he means what he says, then the fetus's inalienable right to life settles little or nothing about the morality of abortion, since inalienability by itself does not tell us anything about when such a right does or ought to prevail over other competing moral considerations.

14
Affirmative Action: Is It Fair? (p. 475)

From its inception over thirty years ago in President Johnson's Executive Order 11246 (1965) to the present moment, affirmative action has been one of the most controversial set of social programs created by federal law and practiced, voluntarily or not, in countless industries, businesses, and offices. These programs were a natural outcome of the civil rights movement of the 1960s, once it was realized that purely formal equality of opportunity (that is, nullification of legal segregation and Jim Crow laws) was not by itself enough to ensure progress of minorities in all avenues of employment and careers. Something else was needed, and needed promptly, if the promise of "equal opportunity" was not to be a mockery for those so long denied *any* opportunity because of their race and color. Affirmative action programs — with their "minority set-asides," "goals," and "quotas" — were the result.

Affirmative action as it affects (white) women was a parallel development and to date has been far more successful by every measure in advancing the interests of women than have been those programs designed solely to increase equality of opportunity for nonwhites.

Affirmative action continues to be in the forefront of domestic political controversy. One of the most prominent arenas of controversy is college admissions. In California, Proposition 209 (prohibiting race as a factor in determining public college admissions) has resulted in a severe drop in the enrollment of minority applicants (excluding Asian Americans, who do extremely well in competition with every other group of applicants, including whites). *Time* reports (April 20, 1998) that African Americans, Native Americans, and Latinos, who together constitute 34 percent of the state's population, amount to only 10 percent of that year's admissions. According to a report in the *New York Times* (April 12, 1998), however, this has stiffened the spine of advocates of affirmative action. The *Times* also reports (April 5, 1998) that anti-affirmative action legislation like Proposition 209 was defeated in thirteen state legislatures during 1997. And (according to the same source) it has caused prominent neoconservatives, such as James Q. Wilson and Nathan Glazer, to rethink their hostility to affirmative action. Only yesterday they shared the outlook of Terry Eastland (see the text at p. 476); now they are reported as having suddenly realized that affirmative action in college admissions is the only way to prevent thousands of African American youngsters from losing their best opportunity to enter the middle class.

Those users of our text who would like to see a fuller account of the actual effects of affirmative action as measured by the available statistics should consult the recent tome by Stephan Thernstrom and Abigail Thernstrom, *America in Black and White* (1997). Their reading of the data convinces them that considerable progress in raising the accomplishments of African Americans over the past generation owes little or nothing to affirmative action. Not surprisingly, several reviewers of their book have severely criticized that interpretation.

Terry Eastland

Ending Affirmative Action (p. 476)

When Terry Eastland says (para. 6) that "we do not have to take the risk of affirmative action," we wonder what alternative he proposes that is less risky (see our question 3). (Could it be that he just wants minorities to work harder and score higher — and if they fail, then what?) Just what measures within reason could we adopt, after abandoning all forms of affirmative action, to improve prospects for equality of opportunity for African American youths?

Here's a thought, not original with us but worthy of class discussion: Why not adopt new policies of college admission, for example, where the basis for special admission advantages is not race but socioeconomic class? What would the details of such a program look like? (For example, we could give an edge on admissions to applicants whose parents earn less than $30,000 and who are not themselves college graduates.) Would Eastland attack that kind of alternative, too? (After all, poor people are disproportionately black, and conversely.)

Eastland, like other critics of affirmative action, is quick to blame such programs for "encourag[ing] Americans to think of themselves in racial and ethnic terms" (para. 11; cf. our question 7). Does he mean to imply, or suggest, that until such programs were invented in the late 1960s, Americans never (well, hardly ever) thought of themselves in such terms? Perhaps today's college students, who have never known our society without affirmative action programs, might be inclined to agree. But others like us, who grew up in racially segregated America, knew from earliest youth what it was like to "think in racial and ethnic terms." It would be an outrageous distortion of the facts to put the blame for that error (if error it is) on three decades of affirmative action.

Burke Marshall and Nicholas deB. Katzenbach

Not Color Blind: Just Blind (p. 483)

During the 1990s, affirmative action was subject to widespread criticism and some disillusionment among its supporters. What began in the 1960s as an effort to create employment and educational opportunities for nonwhites traditionally denied them because of their race or color became increasingly attacked as "reverse discrimination," by means of which more qualified whites were denied jobs, promotions, and other benefits in favor of less qualified nonwhites. At present the future of affirmative action programs is far from certain.

The most thorough recent essay in its defense we have seen is the one we reprint by Marshall and Katzenbach. As the headnote to their article suggests (p. 482), they write against a background of firsthand acquaintance with the theory and practice of affirmative action programs from their inception. Among its other values, this essay provides a capsule history of affirmative action (paras. 7–12) and explains why such programs were needed — and are still needed. They also explain some of the key terms in which the controversy over affirmative action is formulated — especially "merit," "preference," "goals," and "color blind."

Conspicuous by its absence in their essay is any mention of *quotas*, the worst aspect of affirmative action according to its critics. Had Katzenbach and Marshall chosen to expand on this concept, they might have said something like the following. First, racial *quotas* — a fixed number or percentage of minority persons to be added to a workforce or other group — are rare. Quotas were introduced into affirmative action programs by the courts in response to the failure of employers and unions to make a good-faith effort to achieve *goals* for minority hires and trainees. Thus quotas have a punitive dimension wholly lacking in goals and were a last resort for failure to make progress toward the goal of a racially integrated workforce.

The case of *Local 28 v. Equal Employment Opportunity Commission* (19860) is one of the most dramatic in which the futile attempt to get a group (in this case a New York City sheet metal union) to remedy its racist practices led to a court-ordered quota of trainees. Local 28's refusal to admit any nonwhites into its membership was so blatant and extensive that it is difficult to imagine anyone familiar with the details of the case concluding that the courts overreached themselves in forcing Local 28 to comply with a quota of minority trainees, a quota that began as a goal.

Critics of affirmative action have often argued that for most practical purposes, racial goals often become de facto quotas. This allegedly happens because employers or unions, afraid that some court will judge them to be not in compliance with their goal, decide on their own to treat that goal as if it were a strict quota. How extensive this tactic has been over the past four decades and how much harm it has caused is undetermined.

Unmentioned by Katzenbach and Marshall in their essay is the important social science research that tends to show that career-enhancing benefits flow from affirmative action college admission programs. This evidence may be found in *The Shape of the River: Long-Term Consequences of Considering Race in College and University Admissions* (1998), by Derek Bok (former president of Harvard) and William G. Bowen (former president of Princeton). The inferences from the data central to the Bok-Bowen research have been challenged in another major treatise on the subject, *American in Black and White*, coauthored by Stephen Thernstrom (a professor at Harvard) and his wife, Abigail Thernstrom.

The future of affirmative action in college admissions received a severe setback in 1996, when the U.S. Court of Appeals for the Fifth Circuit ruled against race-based admission by universities under its jurisdiction (Texas, Louisiana, Mississippi). On the heels of that ruling, public initiatives in California and Washington prohibited preferential treatment in their public universities for minority applicants. Legal rulings in the opposite direction emerged four years later. In early December 2000, U.S. District Court judge Patrick J. Duggan ruled in favor of the University of Michigan's use of race in admission decisions. (The background to this case is told in Nicholas Lemann, "The Empathy Defense," *The New Yorker*, Dec. 18, 2000.) Especially prominent in the Michigan ruling was the court's judgment that affirmative action programs "expand the reasoning skills of white students and increase their likelihood of community involvement" (*New York Times*, Dec. 17, 2000). This ruling came on the heels of a similar judicial ruling in Washington. With the federal courts sharply divided, only the Supreme Court can resolve the disagreement.

15
Gay Marriages: Should They Be Legalized? (p. 491)

First, some background: In 1989, when we first chose an essay on gay marriage — perhaps the first such essay to be used in a college textbook — very little had been published on the topic. It now seems that we were about one minute ahead of the time; the issue is now a regular feature not only in college textbooks but in the daily newspapers. The chief arguments, pro and con, seem to be these:

Pro

1. Various human rights acts are violated if gay marriage is denied. For example, in Washington, D.C., the Human Rights Act of 1977 says, "Every individual shall have an equal opportunity . . . to participate in all aspects of life." The choice of one's marital partner is protected by the Constitution, which guarantees each person's right to "life, liberty, and the pursuit of happiness." In pursuing happiness, one ought to be allowed to marry a person whom one loves. It was on this ground that laws forbidding miscegenation were struck down.

2. Marriage gives societal recognition to a relationship.

3. Marriage confers numerous material benefits, such as pensions, health coverage, property rights, even citizenship.

4. Until 1967 interracial marriage was prohibited in about one-third of the states in this country. Opponents of interracial marriage argued, like today's opponents of gay marriage, that it threatened traditional values. We now see that this position was wrong.

5. Marriage — not "civil union" or "domestic partnership" — is what some gays want. They do not wish the sort of "separate but equal" status that "civil union" and "domestic partnership" imply, for such terms in effect stigmatize the relationship as something less than a loving relationship between two human beings. True, they cannot without a third party produce a child — but neither can an infertile or sterile heterosexual couple.

6. The fact that the Bible does not sanction homosexual relationships is irrelevant. In our society, church and state are separate. And if the bible's view of marraig were relevant, today we would tolerate polygamy and would regard wives as the property of their husbands.

Con

1. It is unnatural, illegal, unsanctioned by the Bible, and a threat to traditional values.

2. Such a marriage cannot produce children, and a marriage that lacks children is especially vulnerable. "Children are the strongest cement of marriage" (Richard A. Posner, *Sex and Reason* [1992], 305). This argument assumes, among other things, that gay persons cannot adopt children or do not have children from a former marriage or noncommital children.

3. If there are children (adopted or from a previous marriage) in a gay marriage, they are at a disadvantage because children need a father and a mother.

4. Males seek variety, and so a union of two men is doubly unstable (Posner says, p. 306, "The male taste for variety in sexual partners makes the prospect for sexual fidelity worse in a homosexual than in a heterosexual marriage").

Although the right to marry is recognized as a fundamental right protected by the due process clause of the Fourteenth Amendment, no state (as of January 2001) recognizes gay marriages — but see the last paragraph of this introductory note. State courts have routinely defined the right as conditional, the right being interpreted as freedom only to enter a heterosexual marriage. This interpretation is based on the traditional view of marriage. It should be mentioned, however, that some states now recognize "domestic partnerships" for same-sex couples, which means that financial benefits (pensions, inheritance, etc.) are available. In 1993, when Hawaii seemed about the recognize marriage (rather than mere "partnership"), other states grew nervous, fearing that they would have to recognize as legitimate a same-sex marriage recognized by Hawaii. In fact, Hawaii did not recognize gay marriage, but in February 1995 Utah legislators voted to deny recognition to marriages performed elsewhere that do not conform to Utah law. As of April 1998, twenty-eight states have officially barred gay marriages. Further, in 1996 President Clinton signed the Defense of Marriage Act, which denies partners in gay marriages federal tax, pension, and other benefits.

Several cities in California, however, have given legal recognition to the "domestic partnership" of homosexual couples and of unmarried heterosexual couples. (We will also see, in a moment, that the New York Court of Appeals — the highest court in the state — ruled in 1988 that a longtime gay union can be regarded as a "family.") For instance, Berkeley has extended health benefits to the unmarried partners of city workers. In 1989 a law in San Francisco authorized a plan whereby domestic partners are accorded the same hospital visitation rights as are accorded to married couples, and extended to city employees the bereavement leave policy that previously had been limited to married couples. (Cities may extend family benefits to their unmarried employees, but federal law prohibits cities from requiring private companies to do the same.) The San Francisco ordinance defines a domestic partnership as consisting of "two people who have chosen to share one another's lives in an intimate and committed relationship." The two must live together and be jointly responsible for basic living expenses. Neither may be married to anyone else. The couple publicly registers (the fee is $35), in the same way that other couples file for marriage licenses, and the partners must file a notice of termination if their relationship ends. (Roughly speaking, the idea that a gay couple can constitute a family is based on the idea that a family is defined by functions. In 1987 the California State Task Force on the Changing Family, established by the state legislature, said that the functions of the family include maintaining the physical health and the safety of members, providing conditions for emotional growth, helping to shape a "belief system," and encouraging shared responsibility.)

On April 25, 2000, Vermont passed a bill allowing same-sex couples to enter into a "civil union." Civil-union partners are guaranteed various rights in areas of child custody, family leave, inheritance, and insurance.

Thomas B. Stoddard

Gay Marriages: Make Them Legal (p. 492)

Thomas Stoddard's short essay is interesting in itself, but it may also be used in connection with several of the essays in Chapter 27, What Is the Ideal Society? Paragraph 4, for instance, quotes the Supreme Court's declaration that marriage is "one of the basic civil rights of man." One might also cite *Loving v. Virginia* (1966). ("Loving" is a man, not an action, and "Virginia" is the state, not a woman.) In this case the Supreme Court of the United States held that "the freedom to marry has long been recognized as one of the vital personal rights essential to the orderly pursuit of happiness by free men." (The Court's language is unfortunately sexist, but, as someone has pointed out, in legal language "the male embraces the female.") In the eyes of many, however, homosexuality is a moral disorder, and gay people have no legitimate claim to protection of civil rights. One argument against official attempts to legalize homosexual relations is that the government should seek to treat and rehabilitate homosexuals rather than legitimize homosexuality.

Stoddard begins effectively, we think, first by starting with a cherished quotation and then by showing us that a loving couple was prevented (at least for a while) from living together, "in sickness and in health." His choice of an example — a real example and so not one that can easily be dismissed as far-fetched — is worth discussing in class. He might have chosen two men, one of whom was incapacitated by AIDS, but he chose two women, one of whom was injured by a drunk driver. First, why women rather than men? It's probably true to say that the general public — and that is the public that Stoddard is addressing in this op-ed piece from the *New York Times* — is less disturbed by two women living together than by two men living together. (The reasons for this difference in attitude are worth thinking about.) Second, by choosing a person who was injured by a drunk driver, he gains the reader's sympathy for the couple and for his own position. The woman is clearly an innocent victim. Not everyone sees a homosexual male with AIDS as an innocent victim.

A second point about the way the essay develops: Stoddard holds off discussing the financial advantages of legalizing gay marriages until his fifth paragraph. That is, he begins by engaging our sympathies, or at least our sentiments, and only after quietly appealing to our emotions does he turn to financial matters. (Marriage of course confers legal, financial, social, and, presumably, psychological benefits.) The financial matters are legitimate concerns, but if he began with them he might seem to be trivializing love and marriage. Stoddard mentions inheritance without a will (this, by the way, is allowed in Sweden), insurance, pension programs, and tax advantages. He omits at least one other important benefit that marriage can confer: A citizen who marries an alien can enable the spouse to become a citizen. (At the end of our discussion of Stoddard's argument we will return to the issue of benefits conferred by marriage.)

Paragraph 6 introduces the point that traditional marriage was often limited to partners of the same race. (Doubtless in this country the aim was to prevent whites and blacks from marrying. Thus, in Virginia the law prohibited Caucasians from marrying non-Caucasians, but it did not care in the least if an African American married a Native American or an Asian. Although the law doubtless was aimed at black-white marriages, it also prohibited Caucasian-Asian marriages. In the 1950s a Caucasian friend of ours who taught in Virginia married a Japanese American woman and therefore had to leave the state or face prison.)

The eighth paragraph addresses what probably is the most common objection to gay marriages: They are antifamily. Stoddard responds by arguing that since marriage "promotes social stability," in our "increasingly loveless world" gay marriages "should be encouraged, not scorned." Moreover, if marriage were only a device to develop families, sterile couples should be refused permission to marry. Since sterile couples are permitted to marry, gays should also be permitted (para. 9). The gist of the idea, thus, is: Marriage is a union of a loving couple; gays can be loving couples; therefore gays should be allowed (legally) to marry. (Here we might add that the view that marriage exists as a protected legal institution primarily to ensure the propagation of the human race, though often stated by the Supreme Court in the past, is no longer strongly held, and many legal scholars doubt that the Supreme Court will in the future take this position. The prevailing view now is that if children are born, they are born as a result of a loving union, but even if no children are born, there remains the loving union.)

The next-to-last paragraph returns to the lesbian couple of the opening. Because students often have trouble ending their essays, we call their attention to the often-used device of tying up the package, at the end, by glancing at the beginning. Of course one can't always finish this way, but it is usually worth thinking about relating the end to the beginning. In any case such thought may stimulate the writer to alter the beginning or to think further about organization. Strictly speaking, Stoddard does not end with Thompson and Kowalski, since he uses them in his penultimate rather than in his final paragraph, but his reference to the couple helps to unite the essay and to bring it to its close.

The final paragraph consists of two sentences, the first essentially a summary (but, mercifully, without such unnecessary words as "Thus we have seen"), the second essentially a vigorous call to justice. Having set forth his argument (with supporting evidence) in previous paragraphs, Stoddard now feels he can call a spade a spade, and he uses stock terms of moral judgment: "fair-minded people" and "monstrous injustice." This last sentence is especially worth discussing in class: Is such language acceptable? That is, has Stoddard earned (so to speak) the right to talk this way, or is the language not much more than hot air? (Our own feeling is this: The essay has made some interesting points, and we understand that the writer now feels entitled to speak rather broadly, but we wish his last sentence were not so familiar.)

Our fifth question asks students to consider whether Stoddard was wise not to introduce the issue of gay couples adopting children. We think he was wise not to get into this issue. Given the fairly widespread belief that gays seduce children and encourage children to become gay, some readers who might be willing to entertain the idea that gays should be able to benefit financially from marriage would draw back from allowing marriage if it meant also allowing gays to adopt children.

Probably similar considerations made it advisable for Stoddard not to enlarge his topic to include polygamy or polyandry. He is not seeking to call into question the whole idea of monogamy, what is sometimes called "natural marriage" (one male and one female); rather, he just wants to enlarge the idea a bit, so that it will accommodate two persons of the same sex. There is no reason, then, for him to ally himself with people whom his readers may consider to be cranks, sex fiends, cultists, and other assorted nuts.

Midway in our discussion of this essay we said that we would comment further on the benefits conferred by marriage. In 1988 a relevant case was decided in New York by the State Court of Appeals. Two gay men in New York City had lived together for more than ten years, sharing a one-bedroom rent-controlled apartment. They had also shared their friends, their business, their checking account, and their vacations. When one of the men died, the landlord sought to evict the survivor. Under rent-control guidelines, a landlord may not evict either "the surviving spouse of the deceased tenant or some other member of the deceased tenant's family who has been living with the tenant." When the issue was first litigated, a lower court decided in favor of the tenant, but the owners of the building appealed, and the Appellate Division in 1988 overthrew the decision. The Appellate Division's ruling held that the tenant's lawyers had not persuasively proved that the legislature intended to give protection under rent-control laws to "nontraditional family relationships." It noted, too, that homosexual couples "cannot yet legally marry," and it said that it was up to the legislature "as a matter of public policy" to grant some form of legal status to a homosexual relationship.

In the appeal the Legal Aid Society spoke of the two men as living in a "loving and committed relationship, functioning in every way as a family." Advocates of the case argued that because the legislature won't act, the courts — though reluctant to make a policy decision by giving gay partners certain legal rights — ought to act. In fact, the court did rule (4 to 2) that a gay couple could be considered to be a family under New York City's rent-control laws. This decision was the first by a state's highest court to find that a long-term gay relationship qualified as a family. In the majority opinion Judge Vito J. Titone wrote that protection against eviction

> should not rest on fictitious legal distinctions or genetic history, but instead should find its foundation in the reality of family life. . . . In the context of eviction, a more realistic, and certainly equally valid, view of a family includes two adult lifetime partners whose relationship is long-term and characterized by an emotional and financial commitment and interdependence.

The factors that judges and other officials should consider, Judge Titone wrote, include the "exclusivity and longevity" of the relationship, the "level of emotional and financial commitment," the way in which a couple has "conducted their everyday lives and held themselves out to society," and "the reliance placed upon one another for daily family services." Judge Titone's characterization of heterosexual marriage as a "fictitious legal distinction" amazed many observers, who said they might expect such a description from a gay activist but not from a judge.

It is important to realize, however, that the New York decision, which applies also to heterosexuals living together, was narrowly written to deal only with New York City's rent-control regulations. The court avoided ruling on constitutional grounds, which could have opened the possibility of homosexuals qualifying for health insurance benefits normally limited to a spouse or family member.

Stoddard was concerned with this case. When the case was being argued, the *New York Times* quoted him as saying,

> There may be no real alternative to a declaration of new policy from the court. [The court is] dealing with a class of people who are underrepresented in the Legislature, who do not have a strong voice in the democratically elected branches of government and who need the assistance and recognition of the judicial branch to have basic necessities of life preserved for them.

This quotation makes evident a connection between Stoddard's essay and the issue of abortion: Who should decide — the legislatures or the courts? Speaking broadly, the pro-choice people want the courts to decide; they want a ruling that will make unconstitutional the efforts of certain state legislatures to limit abortion. On the other hand, the right-to-life people want the legislatures to be able to establish certain conditions, or limitations. Or put it this way: The right-to-lifers argue that the people (through their elected representatives) ought to make the law; the pro-choicers argue that the courts must act to protect the minority from the tyranny of the majority. Similarly, Stoddard is saying, in the newspaper account, that the judicial branch must come to the aid of underrepresented people. On the other hand, at least in the present climate of opinion, the court might decide that a new definition of marriage is beyond its competence, especially in the absence of any action by the state legislatures showing a willingness to broaden the definition.

A final point: Stoddard does not offer any details about the laws or rituals that might establish gay marriages, but some other advocates have proposed the following:

1. The couple would go to a justice of the peace, who would be authorized by statute to perform the ceremony, or would go to a clergy person.

2. Divorce proceedings would be the same as for heterosexual divorces.

3. A married couple would have all of the financial benefits that are now available to heterosexual married couples.

It may be worth mentioning that it would not follow that homosexual couples would be allowed to adopt children, since in the adoption "the best interest" of the child is the overriding concern. Thus, a legislature might sanction same-sex marriages but might also assert that the psychological climate in such marriages is ill suited to the raising of children. The burden then would be on the couple to prove the contrary. Such legislation would of course not satisfy the gay community.

(text pp. 494–497)

Lisa Schiffren

Gay Marriage, an Oxymoron (p. 494)

Based on what we have read, it seems to us that most people who favor gay marriage believe that marriage is for love, so gays ought to be allowed to marry, whereas most people who oppose gay marriage say that marriage is for having children (and therefore deserves to be favored by the government), so gays should not be allowed to marry. The view that marriage is for children, not for love, perhaps sounds odd, but probably in the past it was commonplace. Even today it is dominant in some societies (for instance, Japan) where arranged marriages are still not unusual and where many men have mistresses.

If marriage is for children, it makes sense for the government to do what it can to help couples to stay together. But, advocates for gay marriage argue, gays can have children (1) through adoption, (2) through prior marriages, and (3) for lesbian couples, through artificial insemination. Shouldn't the government help such unions to be stable? Conservatives are likely to respond: Most gays do not have children, but even if they do, they ought not to have them because a healthy family normally requires a father and a mother as models of adult male and female behavior.

To the argument that the government helps marriages because it is in society's interest for children to be born into stable relationships, one can respond that some heterosexual couples either cannot have children or do not want to have them, and yet these couples receive the benefits of marriage. If the point of marriage is to establish a stable relationship in which stable children will be reared, why should the government favor the marriage of a sterile couple or of a man to a woman who has passed menopause? Lisa Schiffren faces this issue in paragraph 7, when she says, "Whether homosexual relationships endure is of little concern to society. This is also true of most childless marriages, harsh as it is to say." What answer can be made?

It will be interesting to see what sorts of responses are offered in class. Perhaps some students will argue that an important purpose of marriage — straight or gay — is to *provide sustenance*, to nourish a partner who is ill or depressed, to provide love, if that is not an outdated concept. Of course nothing prevents one person from loving another and providing sustenance in a time of need, married or not, but perhaps marriage — a socially recognized institution — helps a partner to remain a loving partner. The act of taking vows publicly may provide cement in the relationship, and perhaps even persons who are not especially well disposed toward homosexuality may think it is better for there to be homosexual partners than homosexual individuals drifting around.

In paragraph 10 Schiffren turns briefly to the "fairness argument," the argument that the government offers tax advantages and other benefits only to married couples, and homosexuals can't marry. She restates the view that "these financial benefits exist to help couples raise children," but she does not face the question: Why should childless couples also benefit? A possible answer would be that only in the instance of postmenopausal women could one safely predict that the marriage will be childless, and who is going to initiate legislation that will take away benefits from older couples?

16
Gun Control: Would It Really Help? (p. 498)

Sarah Thompson

Concealed Carry Prevents Violent Crimes (p. 499)

Our uneasiness with statistical evidence is apparent in our discussion of statistics in Chapter 3. We are aware that we are not sophisticated in this area; when we read an argument that uses statistics, we are inclined to say, "Hm, well, that's impressive," but then we read a counterargument, perhaps one that asserts the statistics are flawed because . . . , and we find ourselves agreeing with the counterargument. Further, like most people, we are familiar with a comment that Mark Twain attributed to Disraeli, "There are three kinds of lies: lies, damned lies, and statistics," Jean Baudrillard made a less familiar but equally forceful comment: "Like dreams, statistics are a form of wish fulfillment."

Whatever the merits of her case, we do think Dr. Thompson is unduly confident about the statistics that she uses. Notice, for instance, that in her final paragraph she says, "In the four years since 1992, those who preach gun control have contributed to the deaths of at least six thousand innocent people." This assertion is probably of a piece with an assertion she rejects in her first paragraph when she says that advocates of gun control claim to have saved 400,000 lives. Probably all such figures are based on dubious extrapolations and can be countered by other figures, equally dubious.

The difficulty of getting useful statistics seems evident to us in Thompson's comment (para. 10) on the Sloan-Kellerman study, which compares Seattle and Vancouver and suggests that gun control laws account for the lower rate of homicide in Vancouver. Thompson says, plausibly, that "There are nearly infinite differences in any two cities," and she goes on to say that "the difference in homicide rates could just as easily have been due to economic, cultural, or ethnic variables, differences in laws, age difference, substance abuse, or anything else." But of course the researchers chose cities that they believed were comparable in significant aspects. In any case, Thompson does *not* specify even one difference that might convince her readers that the cities are not comparable; she merely asserts (as we just heard) that they aren't comparable and that is that. Nevertheless, she says, "As we saw with the Seattle-Vancouver study, if the cities are not well matched, it is easy to draw, or even create, the wrong conclusions" (para. 17). By saying "As we saw," she incorrectly suggests that she actually demonstrated (rather than merely asserted) that Seattle and Vancouver are not well matched. Also worth noting here is her implication that studies comparing cities *can* be valid, if (to use her own words) the cities are "well matched"; she earlier (para. 10) strongly implies that comparisons between cities are pointless because of the innumerable variables.

In our view, Thompson comes across as terrifically eager, deeply sincere, but not a careful thinker and not a particularly effective writer. Her opening paragraph indeed is clear and sets the stage, but as the essay goes on, we think she gets careless. She speaks about "powerful spokespeople" and "doctors and the media" who are recruited to convince the public that guns are bad, but for the most part Thompson does not name names or even give citations of the studies that she angrily dismisses. (You may want some of your students to look at the Sloan-Kellerman study in the *New England Journal of Medicine*, Nov. 10, 1988.)

Notice, too, that although she insists more than once that individuals have a "constitutional right to keep and bear arms" (paras. 37 and 40), she shows no awareness that this right is much disputed. True, the Second Amendment does say "A well regulated militia, being necessary to the security of a free state, the right of the people to keep and bear arms, shall not be infringed." But the meaning of these words is not so clear as Thompson suggests. In 1939 the U.S. Supreme Court held that this amendment guarantees only a collective right for states to arm their militias, and this opinion endured until 1999, when Judge Sam R. Cummings, in a federal Circuit Court of Appeals in Texas, ruled that a citizen has a constitutional right to possess a gun. Several recent books are devoted to interpreting the amendment. Joyce Lee Malcolm, in *To Keep and Bear Arms: The Origins of an Anglo-American Right* (1991), argues that an individual right to weapons goes back to the English Declaration of Rights (1689), which was imported to America and became the Second Amendment. But other scholars say the English Declaration was limited by class and religion and way always subject to regulation. Michael A. Bellesiles, in *Arming American: The Origins of an Anglo-American Right* (1991), argues that contrary to popular belief, in early America few people owned guns, and the drafters of the Second Amendment were *not* thinking about guaranteeing an individual right to guns. Both sides of the controversy invoke Patrick Henry. The pro-gun people call attention to his statement that "The great object is that every man be armed . . . everyone who is able may have a gun." The other side, however, gives the rest of the quotation: "But we have learned, by experience, that, necessary as it is to have arms, and though our Assembly has, by a succession of laws for many years, endeavored to have the militia completely armed, it is still far from being the case. When this power is given up to Congress without limitation or bounds, how will your militia be armed?" That is, the gun-control people say, Patrick Henry was talking about an armed militia, not about the right of an individual to possess a gun.

Back to Sarah Thompson's essay, briefly. For obvious reasons she has little to say in response to those persons who call attention to fatal accidents involving guns, especially accidents involving children. As we see it, her first allusion (quite veiled) to the issue is in paragraph 8, where she speaks of people who lose their lives because of "carelessness, or their own stupidity." In paragraph 14 she speaks of "the number of firearm deaths from all causes in a year," a figure that of course includes accidental deaths, but she does not single these deaths out. And in paragraph 23 she says, "In 1993, private citizens accidentally killed 30 innocent people who they thought were committing a crime," but that's about it, so far as the argument goes concerning accidental deaths.

In short, we think Thompson's strength is in her passion; her weakness is in her lack of attention to detail and lack of attention to certain powerful arguments commonly offered by the opposition. And can we say that her final paragraph goes over the top?

> Those who wish to disarm the popular of this country must be exposed for the frauds they are and held responsible morally, if not legally, for the deaths and suffering created by their misguided policies. In the four years since 1992, those who preach gun control have contributed to the deaths of at least six thousand innocent people whose lives they have sworn to protect and whose freedoms they have sworn to uphold.

There is a lot here that one might quarrel with, but we will simply ask, who are these people who have "sworn" to protect others? And is it appropriate to characterize as a "fraud" someone whose policy is "misguided"?

Nan Desuka

Why Handguns Must Be Outlawed (p. 509)

First, a mechanical point that you may wish to mention to students: This essay uses the American Psychological Association (APA) system of documentation.

Nan Desuka denigrates statistics (para. 1) but uses them when they suit her purpose. Probably Desuka's expression of caution about statistics is a way of disarming the opposition because the latter can provide troublesome figures. Moreover, by hinting that the statistics are uncertain and hard to interpret, Desuka presumably implies that the ones *she* offers are reliable and unambiguous. Notice, too, that in her first paragraph she relies on concrete examples — a child or a customer killed accidentally. These examples are the stuff of newspaper accounts, and whatever their statistical probability, we know that such things happen, and so to some extent we are drawn to the author's side.

In the first two paragraphs, largely a warm-up, Desuka seeks to move the reader away from the neat but (she claims) misleading slogans of the gun lobby. Paragraphs 4 and 5, using statistics, are more clearly argumentative. Paragraph 7 advances in some detail a position (handguns should be sold only to police officers) that was briefly introduced in the first sentence of the second paragraph. Notice, too, that this paragraph, like some other passages, conveys a sense of moderation, in order to gain agreement. The author concedes that her proposed solution will not solve the crime problem — but she argues that it will "reduce" crime and that it's a step in the right direction. (Notice, for comparison, that in the next essay the author also makes a concession. This point can be connected to Carl Rogers's essay in Chapter 11.)

In paragraphs 8 and 9 she examines two objections to her proposal, one in each paragraph (cost in dollars and cost in liberty). In the final paragraph she returns to the opening motif of slogans (the tried-and-true formula of ending by echoing the beginning, which is what we are getting at in question 1), and she also repeats the assertion (not really documented in the essay) that handguns usually take the lives of innocent people.

A NOTE ON STATISTICS AND GUN CONTROL

It is hard to know the worth of the statistics that each side regularly produces in this long-running controversy. Take the study with which we are familiar, an article by Arthur Kellermann and Donald Reay in the *New England Journal of Medicine* 314.24 (1986): 1557–60. The authors examined police records of gun-related deaths in King County, Washington (Seattle and surrounding communities), from 1978 to 1983 and found that of 743 deaths, 398 occurred in the home where the weapon was kept. Of these 398, 9 were classified as self-protection, 333 were suicides, 41 were criminal homicides, 12 were accidents, and 3 (all self-inflicted) were of uncertain classification. On the basis of these figures, the researchers argued that a handgun or rifle kept in the home is more likely to kill residents than to protect them. But Paul Blackman, of the National Rifle Association, pointed out that Kellermann and Reay counted only deaths and thus in no way measured, for example, the benefits that accrued when intruders were wounded or frightened away by the use of firearms. Kellermann agreed but countered that the study also omitted nonfatal gunshot injuries of residents in unsuccessful suicide attempts, family arguments, and accidents. The gist of his response is that although the study was limited, a gun in the home probably does more harm than good. Still, one feels the strength of Blackman's point — and one can hardly envision a statistical study that can include a count of crimes *not* committed because the would-be criminal avoids a household that possesses a gun.

17

Sex Education: Should Condoms Be Distributed in Schools? (p. 514)

First, some background: According to studies, in 1994, 53 percent of teenagers were sexually active. Of these, 52.8 percent used condoms. Actually, the data represent only teenagers in school, and other surveys indicate that dropouts are more likely to engage in high-risk sexual behavior.

The writers of this manual live in the Boston area and are more aware of local sex education programs than of programs elsewhere, but probably things are pretty much the same — that is, equally controversial — in most parts of the country. In any case, some details (taken from newspapers in March 1995) of activities in Boston may be useful in teaching the essays by Rush Limbaugh and Anna Quindlen.

The Massachusetts State Departments of Education and of Public Health have urged local districts to create AIDS-prevention programs. Twenty-three school districts, including Boston, offer junior high and high school students some form of condom availability. Programs vary — for example, from providing vending machines in lavatories to providing school nurses who dispense condoms and who also dispense information about the spread of AIDS through sexual intercourse. Everyone agrees that AIDS is a problem and that young people are at risk, but there is bitter disagreement about how to halt the spread.

Forty-three other Massachusetts communities have rejected the idea of making condoms available as part of a comprehensive AIDS-prevention program. In Falmouth, where there is a program of condom distribution, four families have fought the plan in the courts, arguing that it violates the First Amendment right to religious expression and also that it interferes with constitutionally protected "family privacy rights." (Falmouth has no provision for parents to opt out of the program — that is, for parents to inform the school that condoms are not to be available to their children — in the manner mentioned by Quindlen in the first paragraph of her article.) Essentially the argument is (as Limbaugh says) that the program endangers rather than safeguards students. Some studies have shown an increase in sexual activity among teenagers when condoms are available. And condoms can fail, resulting in exposure to sexually transmitted diseases or pregnancy, or both.

Attorneys for the Falmouth School Committee say the plan is legal and that it does not violate constitutional rights because student participation is voluntary. They also say that no parent can expect to agree completely with school officials on every issue: "The right of privacy does not guarantee that raising children will not in some instances be made more difficult by school programs, including those related to sexuality."

A coalition of civil libertarians and health care providers sides with the Falmouth School Committee, arguing that a parental-consent or opt-out provision (1) would prevent some sexually active students from using the program and (2) would deprive all students of anonymity in obtaining condoms because their identities would be checked against a master list of those whose parents objected to the program. If the policy is changed, allegedly there will be an increase in unwanted pregnancy, disease, and early death.

A few other details: A report issued by the Henry J. Kaiser Family Foundation in October 2000 indicated that an overwhelming majority of parents — in all regions of the country and in all socioeconomic groups — want schools to provide *more* sex education once students become teenagers. They want discussions of abstinence, how to avoid pregnancy (including information about how to obtain and use birth-control devices), abortion, sexually transmitted diseases (including of course AIDS), and sexual orientation. According to a summaru in the *New York Times,* Oct. 4, 2000, nearly two-thirds of the parents say the sex-education course should be at least half of a semester; three out of four parents want teachers to discuss homosexuality and sexual orientation. According to the *Times,* this report will not change the views of the Family Research Council, a conservative group that favors abstinence until marriage and that does not approve of schools giving any instruction about using condoms or giving information about how to obtain birth control devices.

Rush H. Limbaugh III

Condoms: The New Diploma (p. 515)

Rush Limbaugh is noted for his confidence and for his freewheeling style, both of which are evident here. The opening paragraph speaks of "this country's mad dash" to distribute condoms in a "ridiculous and misguided" program. The second paragraph offers an engaging reductio ad absurdum in the loose sense of the term. (In the strict sense, reductio is proof of the falsity of a principle by demonstrating that its logical consequence involves an absurdity. We don't think that Limbaugh in fact shows that the logical consequence of the program is the provision of "disease-free hookers in . . . Safe Sex Centers." In the loose sense, reductio is the practice of taking an argument to impractical lengths. And this is something that Limbaugh does, in a very entertaining way.)

When we first read "Condoms: The New Diploma" we found ourselves laughing out loud at the final paragraph. One can indeed sympathize with Limbaugh's impatience with some of what passes for sex education. It certainly sounds as if the program in Outercourse, which he claims is offered in the Los Angeles public schools and which he describes (caricatures?) as "creative methods of masturbation," is not a satisfactory solution. Still, what *are* the best solutions? One might at first think that this is a matter for parents to discuss with their children, but, as Anna Quindlen argues in her essay and as no one (we think) will deny, some children do not have parents who are competent to offer advice, and other children have parents who will not offer advice.

Anna Quindlen

A Pyrrhic Victory (p. 519)

Essentially Anna Quindlen argues that the schools must offer condoms because otherwise there will be an increase in the spread of AIDS among young people. Her assumption is that many parents can't or won't (or are not around to) discuss sexual matters with their children.

Quindlen doesn't have Rush Limbaugh's skills as a writer of comedy, but she knows how to shape her sentences. Students might be invited to study the rhetoric of the final paragraph, where she employs a contrast ("While we yearn and argue, Dr. Cohall visits his 16-year-old AIDS patient"), and where she uses repetition effectively: "Imagine how [the parents will] feel if they *put her* on a no-condom list, then *put her* in the hospital, then *put her* in the ground." And in the final words, "Some victory," she comes back to her title, "A Pyrrhic Victory," thus providing a sense of closure.

18
Women in the Military:
What Is Their Role, If Any? (p. 522)

First, although each of our two authors gives a list of arguments, we want to set forth, very briefly, the chief arguments that we have collected from a number of discussions on this topic.

IN FAVOR OF WOMEN SERVING

1. Women have served effectively in wars throughout history (think of Joan of Arc). True, until World War II, women usually served in auxiliary positions (such as nurses), and they were not combatants on the battlefield, but modern warfare is such that the distinction between combat zones and noncombat zones is increasingly blurred. Indeed, in modern warfare, supply lines, and support forces are sometimes attacked before the combat forces are attacked.

2. Women have the right to serve their country; to deny them this right is to discriminate against them.

3. Although women are in general smaller than men and have less upper-body strength, with proper physical training women can perform all the assignments necessary.

4. Our society is founded on the idea that competition is good. The addition of competent women to the pool increases the element of competition and results in better fighting forces.

5. It is alleged that women will interfere with the spirit of male camaraderie, but in fact groups containing men and women can have strong bonds of friendship.

6. Although it is alleged that men are more aggressive than women and that fighting forces need highly aggressive personnel, the women who volunteer for the military and who successfully complete the required training programs presumably have the appropriate spirit.

7. Women in the armed forces must be allowed to serve in combat, partly because if they don't serve in combat (1) they are accused of getting favored treatment and (2) their chances for promotion are diminished (the higher ranks are largely populated by combat veterans).

AGAINST WOMEN SERVING

1. Although the distinction between combat zones and noncombat zones is sometimes blurred, certain areas clearly are combat areas, and in such areas women are subject to capture and therefore are subject to rape. Men, too, are occasionally subject to rape but not to the degree that women are.

2. It is not a matter of whether women have a right to serve. The armed forces exist to protect the nation, and we therefore need an effective fighting force. The needs of the nation outweigh any claim of civil rights.

3. Women in general do not have the bodily strength needed in certain situations. For instance, a woman might be unable to carry a wounded comrade to safety. And four-man teams that carried heavy ammunition have been replaced by six-person teams (men and women) because women do not always have the requisite strength. Thus, more bodies are needed to do a job, which means costs and risks are increased.

4. The presence of women does not bring out a healthy spirit of competition; rather it brings out sexual feelings, which may interfere with getting jobs done efficiently (because sexual relationships will blur relationships in the chain of command).

5. An armed force needs a strong sense of camaraderie, and the friendships of men and women are not at all the same as the male-bonding that exists in all-male groups.

6. Women — including those who volunteer for the armed forces — as a group are more nurturing and less aggressive than men, but a fighting force needs disciplined aggressive people, not nurturing people. Further, aggressive men *are* likely to engage in sexual harassment. This sort of behavior is deplorable, and indeed it is intolerable in certain kinds of life, but it is inevitable and must to a degree be accepted in a military force. The only way to avoid it is to keep women out of the military.

7. The presence of women requires special facilities (separate sleeping quarters, separate latrines). These can be costly and in some combat circumstances impossible to provide. For instance, space is so tight in attack submarines that it is impossible to provide separate facilities.

8. Women get pregnant and nurse babies. During the Gulf War one ship, the *Arcadia* (dubbed *The Love Boat*) lost 36 women of its 360 women sailors to pregnancy. (These women were removed from active duty because it was felt that they could not engage in heavy labor without endangering the fetus.) A fighting force cannot afford to lose 10 percent of its members.

Mona Charen

Eight Good Reasons to Oppose Women in the Military (p. 523)

We find Charen's essay a bit less clear than it should be, given her eight numbered points. The first point is that the male-oriented tradition at the military academies "is based on fundamental differences between the sexes," but she doesn't specify these differences. Her second point is that men are physically stronger than women — but shouldn't this assertion be part of her first point? And her third point is that men don't get pregnant and nurse babies — again something that we take to be part of her first point (that men and women are different).

All of her points are worth discussing, but we wish that each of her numbered items was indeed a new point. And is her eighth point a point? The gist: Feminists claim that women are tough enough to serve in the armed forces, but they complain of sexual harassment. How does this assertion qualify as a "good reason" for keeping women out of the military? At most it says that feminists are inconsistent — a sweeping and in our view irrelevant charge.

One further thought: It seems evident to us that Mona Charen's agenda includes commenting not only on the particular issue of women in the military but also on the views of feminists. This motif is introduced in her first paragraph, when she says that the presence of a female cadet at VMI is heralded "as a simple story of feminism triumphant." In making her second point she says, "feminists deny" that women are insufficiently aggressive to serve, but (she says) they used to say that if women ran things, the world would be less warlike. In making her third point she says, "Will feminists next argue that keeping babies out of combat constitutes discrimination?" Feminists come in for another rap on the knuckles in Charen's sixth point, in her eighth point, and in her final paragraph. Our own view is that this subtext — this running battle with feminists — gets in the way of her argument about whether women should serve in the military.

Vivian Norwood

Eight Reasons Women Should Be in the Military (p. 525)

Norwood's response is brisk, though of course in so short a piece she cannot face all of the arguments and all of the ramifications that have become part of the controversy. For instance, she does not really confront the issue of pregnancy — Charen's and Norwood's third point. Norwood merely says that "Women can control their sexual needs, often better than most men." Probably true, but as we indicated in our introductory remarks, the fact is that some women in the military have become pregnant when on active duty. Norwood's final paragraph, her eighth point, probably is as good a response as any, given the severe limitations of space: "We must work toward a fair and practical solution for all people." Surely no one can argue with that.

Part Five

CURRENT ISSUES: CASEBOOKS

19

Business Ethics: Do Corporations Have a Social Responsibility? (p. 529)

Milton Friedman

The Social Responsibility of Business Is to Increase Its Profits (p. 530)

Some background may be useful, especially with reference to the last question that we give in the text. Roughly speaking, the old ideology (to which, again roughly speaking, we can say Adam Smith and Milton Friedman subscribe) held that a business produces goods and services, with the intention of selling them at a profit. Anything goes, so long as the business obeys the law. The new ideology holds that a business must not only obey the law but also go beyond its legal obligations and exercise moral judgment.

The tremendous impact on and power over our society exerted by corporations also casts doubt on their private character. Some thinkers argue that social power inevitably implies social responsibility and suggest that those who fail to exercise a responsibility commensurate with their power will lose that power. As the power of business has grown, we have become increasingly aware of the external costs corporations have passed on to society at large — for example pollution, hazardous products, and job dissatisfaction. These costs in turn call into question a basic assumption of the old ideology that what is good for the individual is good for society. (On this point — essentially "What's good for General Motors is good for the country" — see our comment, below, on the letter by Yale Roe.)

We think the letters responding to Friedman are thoughtful and well written, and we discuss them in terms of tone as well as in terms of their arguments. Mellon, beginning directly but courteously ("I would like to take exception to the underlying assumption of the 'Friedman doctrine'"), picks up the word "stockholder." In his second paragraph he says, "I speak not only as an investor in American corporations, but also as a 'stockholder' in other institutions: my Government, my community, my family, my society. As multiple stockholders." Friedman probably would reply that Mellon is merely playing with words, and of course Mellon is not literally a "stockholder" in the government, but we think his metaphoric use of the word is effective — that is, it helps Mellon to make his point forcefully.

Notice, too, Mellon's use of parallels — not only in "my Government, my community, my family, my society" but also in later passages, such as "When we demand" and "When we applaud."

Richard A. Liroff, in his letter, briskly begins by asserting that Friedman's article indicates the need for something that Friedman deplores — increased taxation. His letter is perhaps a trifle inflated ("incumbent," "effluent," "disadvantageous," "internalize"), but it is clear, and he rightly assumed that readers of the *New York Times* could handle these words.

Yale Roe's letter is clear and in passages effectively written, but we wish his first three sentences were a bit tighter. He writes:

> Here is the key fallacy in Miilton Friedman's "What's good for General Motors is good for America" argument. It is becoming quite apparent that all will not necessarily be well with the world just because each man honestly pursues his own private gain. It is becoming apparent that with the best of intentions and scrupulously observing all laws, a corporate executive may do harm to people.

His opening words, "Here is a key fallacy," pretty much sets the reader to expect a colon at the end of the sentence and then a concise, forceful statement of the fallacy. Instead, however, we merely get in the next sentence an assertion that "it is becoming apparent" — pretty dead words, those — that such-and-such is the case. Then a third sentence, which has the virtue of picking up words from the preceding sentence, though, unfortunately, the words ("It is becoming apparent") are, as we have just said, lifeless. He fails to offer a telling detail in the sentences that supposedly reveal the fallacy. We are not saying that the writing is very bad, just that it isn't notably good. Still, it does have a lively quotation in it, Charles Wilson's infamous remark, made while testifying before the Senate Armed Services Committee in 1952, "What's good for General Motors is good for the country." Wilson was president of General Motors, and his remark caused much indignation and much mirth.

Robert D. Haas

Ethics: A Global Business Challenge (p. 539)

As we indicate in our headnote in the text, this material was originally a talk. You may want to call attention to some of its informal passages, such as the sentence beginning "So" in the first paragraph. You may also want to call attention to some usages (such as "principle-based-decision-making model" and "By referencing our ethical guidelines to decision making") that grate on our ears and perhaps yours but that probably did not grate on the ears of Haas's listeners because the terms are common in the trade. We are not keen on a compound noun made up of five words, and we are not keen on "reference" as a verb, but apparently this sort of language is common in business, and we can hardly object to a speaker who uses language that his audience is comfortable with. Haas's tone throughout is informal, and we imagine that his auditors enjoyed the talk, even if they disagreed with aspects of it.

It's probably fair to say that his basic point is this: It pays to run a business according to decent ethical principles. We hope this formula is true, and we hope Levi Strauss adheres to it and is successful. But we have heard that Levi Strauss is not in good financial shape and has been steadily losing its share of the market. Whether (if our understanding is true) this is because Levi Strauss's business methods reduce its profit or because of other factors — such as poor management, bad decisions about style, or whatever — we do not know. And we do not know if their competitors are less ethical. But it may be interesting to hear a class discuss our last question: Would they buy jeans from Levi Strauss if they heard that the company was ethically superior to some other company whose jeans they normally bought? By the way, the issue implicitly comes up again later in this chapter in Thomas Friedman's editorial about Phil Knight and Nike. Friedman explains that the label of the Fair Labor Association (FLA) can be sewn into garments made by approved companies, thereby (Friedman says) "empowering consumers to punish dirty companies and reward improving ones." But *do* students look for the FLA label?

Donella Meadows

Not Seeing the Forest for the Dollar Bills (p. 543)

In our discussion of the preceding essay, and in our introductory paragraphs to this part of the manual, we give some background that we think may be useful in teaching Donella Meadows's essay.

We think that Meadows does a good job, given the severe limits of space, in explaining the conservationists' point that the issue is not simply one of preserving or not preserving owls — though Meadows is by no means willing to give up the owls (in para. 5 she characterizes the spotted owl as "the holder of a unique genetic code that is millions of years old and irreplaceable").

Does she do an equally good job, in paragraph 8, in explaining the difference between a natural forest and a tree farm? The tree farm, she says, "bears as much resemblance to a 500-year-old natural forest as a suburb of identical ticky-tacky houses bears to a Renaissance cathedral. Ecologists call such plantations 'cornfields.'" We find the comparison to a Renaissance cathedral suggestive but perhaps a bit confusing. In fact, we wonder if she really meant a Renaissance cathedral (Renaissance cathedrals are usually massive, stolid things, such as St. Peter's in Rome); it's our hunch that she meant a Gothic cathedral (lofty, with light filtering through stained glass windows). In any case, we do find the basic contrast (a forest is to a tree farm as a cathedral is to a tacky suburban house) suggestive, even though we ourselves live in tacky suburban houses. (It occurs to us, however, that some suburbanites will not be delighted with her figure.) Her other assertion in this passage, that ecologists call tree farms "cornfields," we find less interesting. The term is meant to belittle, but the fact that ecologists have a contemptuous name for something they don't like is not much of an argument.

Metaphor is fairly rare in Meadows's essay. On the whole she does not use figures, though in paragraph 5 she does effectively say that the spotted owl "is a canary, in the old miners' sense." (Caged canaries were introduced into mines to detect the presence of gas; if the birds died, gas was present and the miners beat a hasty retreat.) In general, instead of using figurative language she relies on what might be called an unadorned style ("this is not the choice at all, of course") or a plain style adorned with a few statistics ("in the past ten years, 13,000 forest-related jobs were lost"). Further, she relies on an appeal to self-interest (coupled with the assumption that the reader is the ordinary person, not a business magnate). Thus, in paragraph 11 she tells us that "our elected representatives are selling off old growth logging rights. . . . Taxpayers are subsidizing this process." But the self-interest is not a narrow self-interest; she assumes we are a "compassionate nation" (para. 12) and that there are some things on which we put "a higher value than a bottom line" (paras. 13). She is always tough-minded, however, at least in her style. Notice, for instance, the two final sentences, short, punchy assertions about the Endangered Species Act: "It should not be weakened. It should be enforced."

Philip H. Knight

Statement from Nike Founder and CEO Philip H. Knight Regarding the University of Oregon (p. 546)

Note: Last minute update on the controversy. On 3 March 2001, the very day that proofs arrived for these pages, we read in a newspaper that the Oregon Board of Higher Education adopted a policy that in effect prohibits the University of Oregon from belonging either to the student-backed WRC or the Nike-backed Fair Labor Association. The gist: The policy prohibits the university from limiting competition except for a few reasons, such as evidence of illegal activity on the part of a manufacturer. The WRC and the FLA both required adherence to codes that set rules on wages, workplace conditions, etc. for companies that produce goods carrying the university name or logo. The Board of Higher Education's policy also blocks enforcement of the university's own code of conduct for such companies. Plenty here to argue about.

Knight's statement is the first of a cluster of materials we give concerning Knight's announcement that because the University of Oregon endorsed the Workers Rights Consortium he would no longer be a major benefactor of the University (he had given $50 million).

In this age when public figures regularly employ speech writers and publicists to speak for them, it is amazing to see that Knight speaks for himself. How do we know? No professional could have written such a plodding piece as this. Look again at the first paragraph, with its "In recent days there have been numerous media reports and speculation regarding my personal philanthropy and relationship with the University of Oregon." Why "In recent days" when "Recently" will do? Why "there have been numerous media reports" when he could have said "the media have widely reported"? And so on. (OK, maybe even a professional writer would have treated "media" as singular, but that's a mere detail.) This guy needs to take a course in composition. Caution: An instructor who calls attention to Knight's weak writing runs the risk of being asked by a student, "If you're so smart, why aren't you rich?" Still, we do think it is worth glancing at Knight's prose, not to make fun of it but to show that it can be strengthened.

Most discussion in class will probably center on the issue of whether Knight acted reasonably in stopping his donations, and this discussion may in part depend on whether one subscribes to the WRC's insistence that companies pay "a living wage," a point that Knight raises in paragraph 10. This matter of a living wage is picked up in the anonymous editorial entitled "Labor 101," where the term is defined and where the point is made that many universities do *not* pay "a living wage" to some of their employees (such as groundskeepers and food handlers), if "a living wage" is defined as enough to support a single adult with two children. Why, one might ask, should Nike have to pay all its workers in Pakistan "a living wage" when the American university does not pay all of its own workers a living wage?

The letters responding to Knight are, of course, varied. C.H.'s letter goes beyond Nike in its indictment; it indicts capitalism. M.Z., supporting Knight, angrily says that the students know nothing about working conditions abroad, and he adds that Nike and other companies often pay workers at a higher rate than prevails. His final paragraph exhorts students to "do something before it is too late," and he urges them "not . . . to allow the University back into mediocrity," the implication being that without large donations the university cannot be very good.

D.F. says, "There is more than enough blame to go around." He blames the students as a whole for letting a small number of them set the policy, and he blames the president for accepting this policy. He never discusses the merits of the case — the morality of the action — but merely asserts that funds that would have greatly helped future students have been forsaken "all in the name of some social-political agenda that has no place in the official policy of the University." One wonders if D.F. disapproves of the doings at Oregon because he disapproves of a particular political agenda or if he disapproves because he thinks that under no circumstances should universities be concerned about working conditions abroad. That is, would he also reject the "social-political agenda" of a group that argued, for instance, we should not buy products that are made by slave laborers in a country that persecutes Christians? Of course we don't know D.F.'s position, but the issue may well arise in class.

Anonymous

Labor 101 (p. 551)

In our comment on Knight's letter we have already glanced at this essay, with its discussion of the "living wage." If you assign Knight's essay, we suggest that you also assign this editorial. The writer makes a good point — universities do not pay all of their employees a "living wage" — but our sense is that the writer's real purpose was to trash the universities, which he or she regards as leftist and hypocritical. Classroom discussion concerning wages on campus may or may not make for lively discussion. We have lived through times of radical activism when students were much concerned with the circumstance of campus workers and through times when students couldn't care less.

Thomas L. Freidman

Knight Is Right (p. 552)

This piece seems judicious to us. Of course it is *meant* to sound judicious, so perhaps we have been taken in. But in any case we think it is worth discussing. The title probably is not the author's — material published in newspapers seldom has a title that the author provided — and the rhyme ("Knight is right") is perhaps a bit too cute, but we think the first paragraph is effective, partly because of its wryness. The second paragraph makes the point that Nike has had a "shameful past when it comes to tolerating sweatshops," so in effect the writer assures us that he is not simply a rugged individualist who supports unrestricted capitalism. That is, he shows his awareness of the other side, in this case arguments of the people who oppose Knight. The third paragraph introduces his main point, that what is needed is the building of coalitions, and this is (he says) what the FLA stands for and what the WRC does not stand for.

In his seventh paragraph he introduces the point about the FLA's label, sewn into clothing, a topic that connects with a question we ask concerning Haas's essay: When students buy clothing, do they care about the morals of the manufacturer? In the final paragraph he uses a quotation, usually a way of ending effectively. (Many students have trouble writing a final paragraph. Among the scraps of advice that we give them is this: Consider using a quotation in your final paragraph.)

Louise Lee and Aaron Bernstein

Who Says Student Protests Don't Matter? (p. 554)

This piece is largely devoted to reporting rather than to arguing, but we include it because it encourages students to take an active role in significant issues, because it gives useful background information, and because it does get into the realm of opinion and argument when it suggests (para. 3) that the "USAS may set back its own cause if it pushes the WRC idea too hard." A reader feels — or at least *we* feel — that the writers here are quietly arguing that the USAS should not press too hard. As the essay goes on, the writers speak more directly: first they say that USAS "may set back its cause" (para. 3), and then they become prescriptive: "USAS should try to complement the FLA" (para. 6).

If you assign this piece, you may want to suggest that when the students read it, they should distinguish between reporting and arguing and between objective and subjective passages. They will quickly see that it is hard to give "Just the facts, ma'am, just the facts." Almost as soon as one asserts a fact, one starts to comment on it, to interpret it, and to use it as part of an argument. Or as Mark Twain wryly put it, "Get your facts first, and then you can distort them as much as you please."

20
The Death Penalty:
Can It Ever Be Justified? (p. 557)

The continuing salience of the death penalty in our society (as well as the apparent popularity of the topic with users of the book) encourages us again in this edition to devote several essays to the topic. Indeed, we reprint enough material to permit a modest research paper to be written on the strength of this chapter alone. We have kept the debate between former mayor of New York Ed Koch and death penalty attorney David Bruck and two other essays (by Sister Helen Prejean and by Alex Kozinski and Sean Gallagher), and we have added excerpts from the opinions in *Gregg v. Georgia* (1976) and *Callins v. Collins* (1994), two Supreme Court death penalty decisions.

As a preface to these essays, here are some basic facts about the death penalty as of spring 2001.

About 3,700 people are currently under sentence of death in thirty-eight states (twelve states have no death penalty), all convicted of some form of criminal homicide. About 20,000 persons are homicide victims each year, about 14,000 persons are convicted of these crimes, and about 250 are sentenced to death. The overwhelming majority of persons on death row are male (nearly 99 percent); about half are white and the rest nonwhite (including about 1,500, or 40 percent, who are African American). In 80 percent of the executions, the murder victim was white.

In the years since 1976, when the Supreme Court validated the constitutionality of the death penalty, 675 persons have been executed. Executions ranged from zero per year in 1978 and 1980 to 25 in 1987 and 98 in 1999. The vast majority have occurred in the South; Texas has executed the most (235) and five states (Colorado, Idaho, Kentucky, Ohio, Wyoming) have executed but one; nine of the death penalty jurisdictions have executed none. Eleven states still use the electric chair, five use the gas chamber, three use hanging, three use the firing squad, and thirty-two use lethal injection; sixteen allow the prisoner to choose between alternatives (for example, hanging or lethal injection).

Eight states permit a prisoner of any age to be sentenced to death and executed; Florida in 1991 sentenced a fifteen-year-old boy to death. In recent years, two-thirds of those on death row had a prior felony conviction; 9 percent had a prior conviction of criminal homicide.

The elapsed time between conviction and execution is considerable — ten to fifteen years is not uncommon — owing principally to the appeals taken in state and federal courts. In recent years, roughly 40 percent of all death sentences have been reversed on appeal in federal courts. (It is not known how many are reinstituted by state courts after either retrial or resentencing.)

Our six excerpts in this chapter do not attempt to present the "human" side of the death penalty — the experiences of the condemned waiting for execution on death row, the frustration inflicted on surviving relatives and friends of the deceased victim by the delays in carrying out the death sentence, the impossible demands made on attorneys on both sides to meet court-imposed deadlines. From among the many books devoted to these aspects of the whole controversy two deserve mention. One is *Dead Man Walking* (1993), by a Roman Catholic nun, Sister Helen Prejean, focusing on her experiences in Louisiana. (We reprint an excerpt from this book, but it is focused on a different aspect of the whole subject.) The film of that title made from her book, available on videocassette, has proved to be a remarkable stimulus to classroom discussion. The other book is *Among the Lowest of the Dead* (1995), by a journalist, David von Drehle, based on his extensive study of Florida's death row prisoners. Neither book is devoted primarily to the argument pro or con, but each adds immeasurably to a better understanding of the impact of the current death penalty system on individual lives.

Elsewhere in the world, according to Amnesty International, seventy-three countries have abolished the death penalty either by law or custom, including all of Western Europe and all the eastern nations that were satellites of the former USSR (except Poland, which has had since 1988 an unofficial moratorium on executions).

Edward I. Koch

Death and Justice: How Capital Punishment Affirms Life (p. 557)

The controversy over the death penalty is a perennial focus of high school debate, and some students will have encountered the issue there. Extensive discussion of almost every claim advanced or contested by Mayor Koch and by David Bruck (author of the essay following) can be found in the scholarly literature on the subject; for starters, look at *The Death Penalty in America: Current Controversies* (1997), edited by Hugo Bedau. An unusually extensive exchange in a modified debate format, between John Conrad and Ernest van den Haag, can be found in their book, *The Death Penalty: A Debate* (1983).

Koch opens with several examples that hold our attention. They allow him to get the ironist's advantage by the end of his second paragraph ("their newfound reverence for life"), and they hint at his combative style, which helped make his autobiographical book, *Mayor* (1984), into a best seller.

Koch's essay is a bit unusual among those in the text because he adopts the strategy of advancing his side of the argument by succinctly stating and then criticizing the arguments of the other side. Because he is in control, of course, the other side has to be content with his selection and emphasis; by allowing the other side no more than a one-sentence statement per argument, he makes it look pretty unconvincing.

Koch's concluding paragraphs (15 and 16) are particularly strong, because he manages to show his sensitivity to a major claim by the opposition ("the death of . . . even a convicted killer . . . diminishes us all"), even as he implies that the alternative he favors is nevertheless better than the one he opposes. The important details of his own position (question 5) he leaves unspecified.

David Bruck

The Death Penalty (p. 563)

David Bruck's style of argument can be usefully contrasted to Edward Koch's. Bruck begins, not as Koch did with an example or two (Bruck offers his first example only at para. 4), but with a brief recap of Koch's central position — that morality requires society to execute the convicted murderer. Then, instead of a patient (tedious?) argument-by-argument examination of Koch's position, Bruck tries to make headway by rubbing our noses in some of the disturbing details about the plight of persons on death row that, he implies, cast a different light on the morality of executions.

He then directly challenges (paras. 7–8) one of Koch's principal factual contentions about the possibility of erroneous executions. While we're at it, we can correct Bruck when he writes that Hugo Bedau's research involved about 400 cases "in which the state eventually *admitted* error." The research showed that the state admitted error in 309 out of 350 cases — and also that no state has ever admitted executing an innocent person, although Bedau reports that his research shows twenty-three such erroneous executions since 1900. Subsequent to the Koch-Bruck debate, this research has been published in a book, *In Spite of Innocence* (1992), by Michael Radelet, Hugo Bedau, and Constance Putnam.

Worry over convicting the innocent in capital cases reached a new degree of intensity during 2000. In Illinois, prompted by the fact that in recent years as many death row prisoners had been released because of their innocence as had been executed, Governor George Ryan declared a statewide moratorium on executions, to last until he could be assured that effective remedial procedures were in place. Thus Illinois became the first capital punishment jurisdiction to comply with the 1996 recommendation from the House of Delegates of the American Bar Association, urging a nationwide moratorium on the death penalty until procedures were introduced to ensure fairness, due process, and competent counsel for capital defendants. Much of the background to Governor Ryan's decision is discussed in the recent book *Actual Innocence* (2000) by Barry Scheck, Peter Neufeld, and Jim Dwyer. They relate the stories of recent cases (many, but not all, of them involving the use of DNA evidence to exonerate the innocent) that show just how easy it is for the innocent to be convicted and sentenced to death.

In the Koch-Bruck debate, the mayor had the last word, although we didn't reprint it in the text. His objections to Bruck's rebuttal may be found in *The New Republic* (May 20, 1985, p. 21). The main assertion in Koch's response is that "a truly civilized society need not shrink from imposing capital punishment as long as its procedures for determining guilt and passing sentence are constitutional and just." The reader of Koch's original article may well wonder where in it he succeeded in showing that these "procedures" in our society, as actually administered, are "just."

A word about question 4, on the polygraph or "lie detector." The so-called lie detector does not, of course, detect lies. It records physiological phenomena such as abnormal perspiration that are commonly associated with lying. Opponents say it is based on the premise that there is a "Pinocchio effect," a bodily response unique to lying. Opponents of the polygraph argue that the effects recorded, such as an increased heart rate or blood presence, can have other causes. That is, these changes may reflect personal anxieties apart from lying, and, on the other hand, the symptoms may be suppressed by persons who in fact are lying. Wu-Tai Chin, the CIA employee who spied for China for thirty years, "passed" polygraph tests many times. The American Psychological Association, after a two-year study, concluded flatly that polygraph tests are "unsatisfactory." It is also noteworthy that findings from polygraphs are not admitted as evidence in federal courts.

Potter Stewart

Gregg v. Georgia (p. 568)

In this case, Justice Brennan and Justice Marshall were the sole dissenters (as they were to be, until their retirements, in every death penalty case where the majority upheld the conviction and the sentence).

Question 2 requires the reader to make a sharp distinction between the normative principles asserted by Brennan in *Furman* and the factual claims about the death penalty (its affront to human dignity, its needless severity, and so on) on which

Brennan relied. Theoretically, Justice Stewart or anyone else who disagrees with Brennan could do so in any of the following ways: One could (1) reject both Brennan's four principles and his factual claims about the death penalty, (2) reject the principles but agree on the facts, or (3) accept the principles but reject the factual claims. As we examine Justice Stewart's opinion, although he never mentions Justice Brennan by name, we think alternative (1) most nearly describes his position: Stewart does not reject all of Brennan's principles, nor does he reject all of Brennan's factual claims, but he does reject some of both.

As to question 3, it is perhaps worth noting that the House of Delegates of the American Bar Association, meeting in Houston in early 1997, urged a national moratorium on the death penalty until such time as trial and appellate procedures in death penalty cases could be brought into conformity with the requirements of due process of law. For the considerations that lie behind the ABA's position, see *The Death Penalty in America: Current Controversies*, ed. Hugo A. Bedau (1997). It might also be noted that for the first time in over three decades, not a single member of the current Supreme Court is on record as being opposed to the death penalty on constitutional grounds.

Regarding the mandatory death penalty ruled unconstitutional in *Woodson v. North Carolina* (1976) (see question 5), the Court argued that such penalties had been all but completely rejected as "unduly harsh and unworkably rigid" and that they fail "to allow the particularized consideration of relevant aspects of the character and record of each convicted defendant." A decade later, in *Sumner v. Shuman* (1987), the Court went so far as to rule that a mandatory death penalty even for a convicted murderer who murdered again while in prison under a life sentence was unconstitutional.

In discussing question 7, it should be noted that when Congress enacted the Violent Crime Control and Law Enforcement Act of 1994 and the Anti-Terrorism and Effective Death Penalty Act of 1996, the death penalty was authorized for several nonhomicidal crimes. As of 2000, however, the Supreme Court has not ruled on the constitutionality of such punishments.

Harry Blackmun

Dissenting Opinion in Callins v. Collins (p. 576)

Justice Blackmun (who died in 1998) had an unusual judicial career where the death penalty is concerned. In the mid-1960s, in the Arkansas case of *Maxwell v. Bishop* (Maxwell was an African American sentenced to death for the rape of a white woman), Blackmun upheld the conviction and sentence in his role as a U.S. Court of Appeals judge. Appointed to the U.S. Supreme Court in 1970, he rendered a tortured dissenting opinion in the *Furman* case two years later, as he struggled unsuccessfully to resolve the tension between his personal opposition to the death penalty and his inability to find a convincing constitutional argument to support that opinion.

After more than two decades on the Court, during which time he confronted scores of capital cases, he emerged toward the end of his life as a staunch opponent of the death penalty, for reasons he explains in his dissent in the *Callins* case of 1994, which we reprint. Paramount in his thinking was the failure of what he called "the machinery of death" — a failure of the criminal justice system compounded out of the racial discrimination and arbitrariness of the decision making in capital cases, faults supposedly cured years earlier by the "new" capital statutes enacted in many states after *Furman*.

Blackmun's dissent is characteristic of most contemporary opposition to the death penalty in America. The focus is on the death penalty *as administered*, not on the death penalty as an abstract matter of right or wrong or even as an unconstitutional "cruel and unusual punishment." It is this emphasis on "the machinery of death" that prompted the American Bar Association's House of Delegates in 1997 to call for a nationwide moratorium on executions until the malfunctioning "machinery" could be repaired. The first such moratorium took effect in Illinois in 2000, with what results it is too early to say.

Friends of the death penalty have replied to the kind of argument that Justice Blackmun relies on by insisting that in theory the death penalty can be freed of its current faults, such as they are, and it is the faults, not the death penalty as such, that ought to be abolished. Until they are, the death penalty as such cannot be repudiated as a violation of "equal protection of the laws," of "due process of law," or of any other constitutional principle. Students ought to try to discuss what to make of this reply to Blackmun.

Helen Prejean

Executions Are Too Costly — Morally (p. 581)

Sister Helen Prejean has proved to be the most influential figure — speaker, lobbyist, film consultant, writer, and spiritual adviser to men on death row — currently opposing the death penalty in the United States. Her humor, warmth, and compassion have been much admired, and she has earned the respect of many whose lives have been ravaged by the murder of a loved one — whether in a crime of homicide or in a legally authorized execution. She has brought to the public debate a down-home human approach noticeably absent from much of the discourse on this subject.

The excerpt we reprint from her popular book, *Dead Man Walking*, is devoted largely to examining the biblical support for (or opposition to) capital punishment. She neglects to mention what many think is the best single passage in the Bible on this subject, Genesis 4:9–16 — God's response to Cain for murdering his brother, Abel. God punishes Cain in three ways: He is exiled, he is cursed, and he is stigmatized (so that others will recognize him for the murderer he is). Perhaps no other passage in the Bible so personalizes God's punishment meted out to a murderer — not perhaps a perfect paradigm for how today's opponents of the death penalty would have murderers punished but worthy of their thoughtful reflection.

The Judeo-Christian posture on the death penalty is a long story. A small fraction of it is related in paragraphs 11 through 15. Those who seek more must consult the hefty recent monograph by James J. Megivern, *The Death Penalty: An Historical and Theological Survey* (1997). Professor Megivern explains how the Christian church at the time of the First Crusade (1095) abandoned its early commitment to pacifism in favor of Christian triumphalism with sword in hand, led by Pope Gregory VII (1073–1085), his successor Pope Urban II (1042–1099), and St. Bernard of Clairvaux (1090–1153). Their enemies were infidels (read Jews and Moslems) and soon thereafter Christian heretics. According to Megivern, the epitome of this transformation in the Christian ethic of war and peace, of violence and pacifism, appears in the *Chanson d'Antioche*, "the greatest of the vernacular epics of the First Crusade." Christ is portrayed as hanging on the cross and assuring the good thief to his side that "from over the seas will come a new race which will take *revenge* on the death of the father." Thus, as Megivern notes, was brought to pass a "total reversal of the actual teachings of Jesus."

92

585

Alex Kozinski and Sean Gallagher

For an Honest Death Penalty (p. 585)

Judge Kozinski (often mentioned as a possible future Justice of the U.S. Supreme Court) and his junior colleague advance a line of argument that tries to carve a middle way between outright across-the-board abolition of the death penalty, at the one extreme, and, at the other extreme, the haphazard system that Justice Blackmun has so vigorously criticized elsewhere (see his dissenting opinion in *Callins v. Collins*, reprinted at p. 576 and written about the same time as the Kozinski and Gallagher essay). This is their "political solution" (see question 8) to the death penalty controversy.

Note the world-weary tone in which they write. Kozinski and Gallagher find no merit in any of the standard arguments against the death penalty (see especially paras. 11–12), although they ignore the question of deterrence (and thus we don't know quite what they think of that argument). They seem to rest their case for the Death Penalty Lite on the proposition that the great majority of the public wants it (para. 1) and the public is right: "premeditated murder[ers] justly forfeit the right to their own life" (para. 12). What seems to exercise them is mainly the cost and inefficiency of the present death penalty system; they profess no deep concerns over the morality of that system.

We have to confess some doubt whether their goal of reserving the death penalty "for only the most heinous criminals" (para. 20) is really within reach. When the post-*Furman* death penalty statutes were enacted in the mid-1970s, their proponents strongly believed that this is exactly what these statutes would do: They had narrowed the death penalty so that it reached only the worst among the bad. But Kozinski and Gallagher fully concede that this effort has proved to be a failure. One really must wonder, therefore, whether it is within the wisdom of any legislature to craft narrow death penalty statutes that will reach only "the most heinous criminals" so long as lay juries have the final decision in applying these statutes. Those who agree with Kozinski and Gallagher might well ponder the words of a much-respected Supreme Court Justice, John Marshall Harlan (not an avowed opponent of the death penalty by any means). In 1971 he wrote: "To identify before the fact those characteristics of criminal homicide and their perpetrators which call for the death penalty, and to express these characteristics in language which can be fairly understood and applied by the sentencing authority, appear to be tasks which are beyond present human ability."

20
Drugs: Should Their Sale and Use
Be Legalized? (p. 591)

Next to AIDS, drugs — their use and abuse and the costs of the efforts to control them — may well be the nation's most publicized if not its most pressing social problem. Unlike AIDS, however, drug use leaves few of the users dead; and many of those who do die from drugs do not do so from overdosing or suicide but from shoot-outs in turf wars and busted deals. The four essays we present take several divergent views of the problem and its solution.

In his inaugural address early in 1989, President Bush reassured the nation by declaring "This scourge will end." A few months later, in a special broadcast on the drug problem, he reported that although "23 million Americans were using drugs" regularly in 1985, that number had dropped in 1988 by "almost 9 million." The president credited this gain to his administration's four-point campaign: tougher penalties, more effective enforcement, expanded treatment programs, and education to reach the young who have not yet started to use drugs. An enthusiastic elaboration of the government's efforts is presented in the articles we reprint by William Bennett, the nation's first drug czar (a good guy, not to be confused with a "drug kingpin," who is a bad guy) and by James Q. Wilson.

Others are more skeptical. Here are some of the disturbing facts reported in a review article, "What Ever Happened to the 'War on Drugs'?" by Michael Massing in the June 11, 1992, issue of *New York Review of Books*.

How many people are using illegal drugs and how frequently? According to a 1990 household survey reported by the National Institute of Drug Abuse, some 12.9 million of us used such drugs within a month prior to the survey, 11 percent fewer than in 1988 (these figures do not quite jibe with those reported by President Bush). More frequent (weekly) users dropped by 23 percent, from 862,000 in 1988 to 662,000 in 1990. Among adolescents, cocaine use had dropped almost by half. But in 1991, the same agency reported that monthly users of cocaine had jumped 18 percent over 1990, to 1.9 million people. Weekly users had also increased, back to 1988 levels. Emergency hospital visits from cocaine abuse had risen 30 percent over 1990. And heroin was making a return engagement. But casual use of drugs among the middle class continued its steady decline from the mid-1980s. Does all this sound like we are winning or losing the war on drugs?

What about treatment for those who want to shake the drug habit? During President Reagan's first term (again relying on data provided by Michael Massing in his survey), funds for treatment centers (adjusted for inflation) dropped by nearly 40 percent. During Reagan's second term, when crack cocaine reached epidemic proportions in the nation's inner cities, treatment centers were overwhelmed. Both the numbers of those seeking help and the extent of the treatment they needed had grown enormously. With the cocaine-related death of college basketball star Len Bias fresh on everyone's mind, the Bush administration approved a budget of $1.6 billion for treatment centers run by the states, an increase of 50 percent over the funds provided by his predecessor. But even this increase failed to meet the demand for treatment.

Turning from the issues of salience and success in the war on drugs, what is it costing us? In a 1990 article by Ethan Nadelmann, "Should Some Illegal Drugs Be Legalized?" in *Issues in Science and Technology*, we are told that the nation spent

93

(text pp. 591–598)

$10 billion to enforce our drug laws in 1987, perhaps twice that amount in 1990. Between 40 percent and 50 percent of all felony convictions are for drug offenses. In 1989 alone, "between three-quarters of a million and a million people were arrested . . . on drug charges." To this we must add the indirect costs. International enforcement, interdiction, and domestic enforcement — all essential elements in the government's strategy — have yet to succeed. To put it simply, we need to keep two things in mind. First, we have so far failed to keep drugs from being brought into the country. All the drugs illegal in this country and in wide use nevertheless (opium and heroin, cannabis, coca and cocaine) are native to many foreign countries and are a major cash crop in much of the world. Second, we have not succeeded in drying up demand despite granting substantial resources to law enforcement to do so.

Literature on the drug problem continues to roll off the presses; of the five books in Massing's review survey, we recommend especially *The Search for Rational Drug Control,* by Franklin E. Zimring and Gordon Hawkins, an author team highly regarded for their shelf of books on virtually every problem in criminal justice.

William J. Bennett

Drug Policy and the Intellectuals (p. 592)

William Bennett gives a vigorous defense of the national drug policy he was assigned to carry out by the Bush administration. He attacks intellectuals (the only two he names are the liberal columnist Anthony Lewis and the conservative spokesman William F. Buckley Jr. in para. 8; but he alludes to a host of unnamed "prominent residents" on the campuses of Princeton, Wisconsin, Harvard, and Stanford in para. 18) for their faults in blinding themselves and the nation to the evils of legalizing drug use, a policy supported (he says) by "a series of superficial and even disingenuous ideas" (para. 8).

Here's a quick summary of Bennett's seven-point argument against the legalization of drugs (question 3): (1) criminalizing drugs provides an incentive to stay out of the business (para. 10); (2) no one has figured out how to carry out a policy of legalization of drugs across the board, from marijuana to PCP (para. 11); (3) if drugs are legalized, their use will "soar" (para. 13), thereby increasing the harm and suffering to the users; (4) the cost to the nation of more drug use would be "intolerably high" (para. 14); (5) drug-related crimes would not decrease at all (para. 15); (6) the terrible problems we have with legalized alcohol are a foretaste of the even graver problems we would have were all drugs legalized (para. 16); (7) apart from all the foregoing, "heavy drug use destroys character," "dignity and autonomy" (para. 17). We have to admit Bennett makes a pretty convincing argument, spiced with barbs at "America's pundits and academic cynics" along the way.

Were someone to accuse Bennett of hypocrisy or inconsistency (question 4), he might well reply in the same manner that he does regarding legalization of alcohol (para. 16): No doubt it would be a futile effort for society now to make tobacco use illegal; yet he would be better off (as he might well admit) if he had never acquired the nicotine habit and if he could get rid of it. But whether he can is his personal medical problem; there is no inconsistency in his urging a policy to the effect that everyone (himself included) avoid harmful illegal drugs, even if he is unable to cease using a harmful legal drug himself. Of course, he might also take another line, that nicotine addiction is not as harmful as addiction to any illegal drug. But that is an empirical claim, and it is far from clear whether it is true.

James Q. Wilson

Against the Legalization of Drugs (p. 599)

This essay alongside William Bennett's reminds us of the "good cop/bad cop" routine in police interrogation. We debated whether to include both these essays, since the argument in each is pretty much the same. But the tone is so different — James Wilson thoughtful and patient, Bennett using words as though they were clubs — that we thought this difference itself is worth some reflection. (Students might well be set the task of reading these two essays as a pair and explaining what, if anything, is different in the two arguments and, that apart, which essay has the more persuasive, effective tone.)

The idea of "victimless crimes" (our question 1) gained prominence in the 1960s, as part of an argument for decriminalizing various drug and sex offenses, as well as gambling. When consenting adults engage in illegal practices that harm no one (or harm only themselves), so the argument went, they have committed a victimless crime. But such acts ought to be decriminalized because the criminal law in such cases is improperly invading privacy, liberty, and autonomy. (John Stuart Mill made this argument famous, although he did not use the term *victimless crimes*.) Wilson seems to object to this argument on two grounds (para. 24). First, he rejects the criterion of state intervention as too narrow: "Society is not and could never be," he says, "a collection of autonomous individuals." So we need the criminal law here and there for admittedly paternalistic purposes. Consequently, even if drug abuse were a victimless crime, Wilson might not approve of its legalization. Second, he rejects the factual minor premise of the victimless crime argument; drug use is harmful not only to the user but to others who have not or cannot consent (there is "fetal drug syndrome," for example).

Wilson is a skillful, polished arguer, and we draw attention to some of these features of his essay in two of our questions (the second and the fourth). The "economic dilemma" that the drug legalizers face, to which Wilson refers in his paragraph 37 (our fourth question), can be formulated somewhat more briefly than he does, as follows: Tax money from legalized drugs will pay for the cost of regulation and treatment of users, abusers, and addicts, or it will not. If it does, then the tax rate on drugs must be set quite high; but this will lead to tax evasion and crime and a black market in drugs. If tax money from drugs does not fully finance the costs of regulation and treatment, then we will have more addicts and either inadequately financed treatment centers or less tax money for other public needs. But none of these alternatives is acceptable. Therefore, we cannot reasonably legalize drugs in the expectation that taxing them (as alcohol and tobacco are now taxed) will enable society to pay for the costs.

Like any dilemma worthy of the name (see our discussion of the dilemma in the text), this one has a disjunctive tautology as its major premise (that is, the premise states two exhaustive and exclusive alternatives). Such a premise is invulnerable to criticism. Criticism can be directed, however, at each of the two other conditional premises ("if . . . then . . ."), as they are empirical generalizations and vulnerable on factual grounds. Or criticism can be focused on the premise that expresses how unacceptable the dilemma is. Perhaps one of these alternatives is not so bad after all, especially when compared with the costs of losing the war on drugs. One way to develop that thought would be by constructing a counterdilemma, showing the awkward consequences of *not* legalizing drugs. (Here, we leave that task for another day.)

In his criticism of Nadelmann (paras. 25–26), Wilson accuses him of "a logical fallacy and a factual error." The fallacy is to infer (1) the percentage of occasional cocaine users who become "binge users" when the drug is *legal* from (2) the percentage who become "binge users" when (as at present) the drug is *illegal*. Why does Wilson think this is a fallacy? To be sure, (1) and (2) are quite independent propositions, and it is possible that the percentage of users would grow (rather than stay roughly constant, as Nadelmann infers) as soon as the drug is legalized. But by how much? At what rate? In the face of antidrug education? These unanswered questions apart, what Wilson needs to show us is that in general, or perhaps in some closely parallel case, the number of those who do X when doing X is illegal has no relationship to the number of those who do X when doing X is legal. But Wilson hasn't shown this at all.

As for the "factual error," it looks to us as though Wilson has caught Nadelmann in an error (see para. 27).

Milton Friedman

There's No Justice in the War on Drugs (p. 613)

Milton Friedman is the nation's best-known free-market economist and the author of many books, including *Capitalism and Freedom* (1962). He and his fellow conservatives seem to be divided over the nation's "War on drugs." Some, like William Bennett, strongly favor fighting the use of illegal drugs with unrelenting fervor. Others, believing that drug use harms only or principally the user, oppose government interference (either in the form of regulation or outright prohibition) and favor using free-market methods to control its use. Friedman is of the latter persuasion. He hints at reasons of this sort in his paragraph 2, where he quotes himself from 1972. There, in a phrase, his position was this: Persuasion, yes; coercion, no.

What is surprising about Friedman's essay is that he does not rely on free-market reasoning. It's not that he rejects such reasoning; it's rather that he invokes what he describes as "ethical" considerations of several different sorts. They constitute a variety of objections, each of which represents one kind of empirical consequence of the policy of the past quarter century but inadequately foreseen when the war on drugs was launched with much fanfare by President Nixon in 1972.

Regarding question 1, here is one way the thesis of his essay might be stated in a sentence: "The unethical consequences of the nation's war on drugs far outweigh whatever advantages have been or might be gained." (This version is inspired by the rhetorical question Friedman asks at the end of his essay, in para. 13.)

As to question 2 (and also question 4), an "expediential" objection to the war on drugs would be any claim that its harmful consequences (for example, in tempting the police into corruption) outweigh its good consequences. A moral (or ethical) objection would be that our drug policies violate some moral norm, standard, or principle (for example, the principle that adults ought to be left free of governmental interference to act as they wish — including using drugs — so long as they do not harm others).

Elliott Currie

Toward a Policy on Drugs (p. 616)

Currie's position on the drug controversy (our question 4) includes three steps: (1) move toward decriminalizing the drug user (but not necessarily the trafficker), (2) treat marijuana (use as well as dealing?) "differently" from (he means more leniently than) "the harder drugs" (mainly heroin and cocaine, we surmise), and (3) permit medical experimentation with certain drugs (which ones he does not say, but marijuana is the obvious example) (para. 18). These recommendations (all adopted in one way or another, he says, by "some European countries") fall well short of radical decriminalization of drugs, but if Currie is right, to go any further is to cause predictable costs and harms that make radical decriminalization the wrong social policy.

Is Currie convincing that these steps, and these only, are a reasonable compromise between those who want to carry on the "war on drugs" no matter what the costs and those who want all aspects of drug use, sale, and manufacture to be permitted by law? (He presented these views nearly a decade ago, and we suspect he would say today that precious little progress has been made over this period to bring any of these three recommendations to come to pass.) We do not have a better proposal to offer, and we think at the very least that his middle way between the two extremes deserves careful thought. The prospect of ideas such as his receiving careful thought at the highest levels in our governments, state and federal, are not encouraging.

In our question 2 we mention three possible steps to reduce the role of drugs in our lives, steps Currie does not mention. Why doesn't he? As a guess, we suggest this. He would reject our first suggestion (curbing manufacture of illegal drugs) because either most of the drugs in question are not manufactured in the United States or the one that mainly is (marijuana) he wants largely to decriminalize. Perhaps he would reject our second suggestion (reducing imports of illegal drugs) on the grounds that federal agencies have tried for years to do precisely this but to little effect and that tax dollars to curb heavy drug importing can be more effectively spent elsewhere. As for our third suggestion (aggressive public education), perhaps he could argue it is implicit and is presupposed in much of what he says.

The evident uniqueness of the magnitude of the drug problem in this country troubles us. Currie mentions the issue (para. 21), but he offers no explanation for our unfortunate plight. We mention (question 5) three possible explanations that seem to us unconvincing. We don't have a fourth to offer for contemplation. So long as there is no convincing and generally accepted explanation, it seems likely to us that the drug problem will not abate. Meanwhile, the human cost in our drug policies ought to terrify and infuriate. In New York, for example, drug laws enacted during the Rockefeller administration (as reported by the Fortune Society) mandate a fifteen-years-to-life sentence for the sale of two ounces or the possession of four ounces of an illegal drug. Is there any convincing reason why our society ought to persist in enacting and enforcing such laws? We earnestly doubt it.

22
Euthanasia: Should Doctors Intervene at the End of Life? (p. 626)

The five essays in this chapter (along with the passage on euthanasia from More's *Utopia*, reprinted in the text in our Chapter 27, What Is the Ideal Society?) and the essay by Peck in Chapter 4 present a diversity of views on the issue of euthanasia. None of the essays (with the possible exception of the one by James Rachels) is so difficult as to pose serious challenge to students.

Here, we will depart from our frequent practice of prefatory general comment when introducing a chapter with multiple essays on a given topic, in favor of piecemeal commentary — except for one preliminary observation. The topic of euthanasia is of personal importance to most students only to the extent they know of the plight of their aging grandparents. Of far more interest to them, given their age, is the topic of suicide. Teenage suicide, by every report, is a serious national problem (even if less frequent, say, than teen-age pregnancy or teenage drug addiction). Not infrequently, a student of ours has in fact a record of attempted suicide or had a suicidal classmate in high school or college. For this reason, if no other, we think it is likely students can discuss euthanasia more effectively than suicide, as an issue of life and death; student emotional involvement in it is far less intense.

Ellen Goodman

Who Lives? Who Dies? Who Decides? (p. 627)

We like the alliterative title and the way it ends by stressing the need for *decision*, perhaps even despite our inability to give really confident answers to the two questions ("Who lives? Who dies?") that precede it.

Today's students will not immediately recognize the name of Karen Ann Quinlan, mentioned in Ellen Goodman's ninth paragraph. Quinlan became the focus of national attention in the late 1970s because she posed the terrible problem (increasingly common) of the impact of medical technology on the helpless and comatose. A woman in her twenties, Quinlan suffered an accident of undetermined nature (possibly a drug overdose) that left her in an irreversibly chronic vegetative state, alive thanks only to life support systems (intubation, artificial respiration). Her parents wanted her taken off the respirator, in the belief that she would promptly die of suffocation and that, given her state, this is what she would have wanted for herself. Over the protests of the hospital, the New Jersey courts eventually (in 1976) granted them their wish — only to discover that she lived on without the help of the respirator. Eventually, in 1985, she did die.

Goodman focuses on the little-known case of Earle Spring. She does not shrink from portraying his plight (her paras. 3–4) nor the cost of his treatment ("one Earle Spring can decimate the energy and income of an entire family"). Yet she sides unequivocally with those who want to "give him the benefit of the doubt. Any doubt" (the final paragraph). What is her argument? She concedes "there are no absolutes" that apply to this case (para. 13). Rather, she relies on two things. First, there is a fact of the matter: Spring recently had a lucid moment in which (according to "an outside nurse and doctor") he made " 'a weak expression of his desire to live'" (para. 7). Second, there is a principle involved: "if there is any mental activity at all, then disconnecting him [or anyone, we assume] from life would be a dangerous precedent, far more dangerous than letting him continue" to live (para. 15). Notice that his consent to be kept alive, or not to be allowed to die, is not crucial to her argument (is that a weakness in her principle above?). What is crucial is the presence in Spring of "mental activity" of whatever sort. This is what requires us to give him "the benefit of the doubt." Question 2 focuses on this argument of hers.

Question 3 is not one students can be expected to answer with any finality. If you are tempted to use it as a writing assignment, we urge you first to spend some time in class discussing the subject. Keep in mind that a right counts as *absolute* just in case no other moral consideration overrides or undermines it; if one acts in a given way, claiming it is based on an absolute right, the implication is that any moral objection to the act is outweighed. In the game of moral conduct, absolute rights are nothing less than trumps (an epigram popularized by the legal philosopher Ronald Dworkin; see his book *Taking Rights Seriously* [1977]).

Terry Golway

The Culture of Death (p. 629)

In discussions of euthanasia and physician-assisted dying, it is important to keep distinct various kinds of such cases (question 5). *Voluntary* euthanasia means that the dying person gave his or her informed and uncoerced consent to die. Cases of *nonvoluntary* euthanasia (a term Golway doesn't use) are cases where the dying person does not — probably because he or she cannot — give such consent. *Involuntary* euthanasia is death contrary to the desires of the patient. Few would debate the point that involuntary euthanasia is murder. Only die-hard opponents would claim that voluntary euthanasia is murder, though it certainly is homicide. Most of the controversy concerns the middle group, those who are helped to die but who gave no consent or dissent. It does not help Golway's case that he fails to make these distinctions, and writes (para. 9) that "900 to 1000 people a year" in Holland are being put to death "without [their] consent." Does he mean contrary to their wishes? There is no evidence to support such a claim. Or does he mean without any consent, which they could not in the nature of the case give or withhold? He does get it half right a little later when he refers to capital punishment (para. 10) as "involuntary" — but surely he is wrong to describe death in the electric chair as a kind of euthanasia. Even to call it eugenic killing is too much of a stretch.

Which brings us to his paragraph 7 (and our question 7). We certainly agree with him that psychiatrists authorizing the death of their patients in "deep despair" — presumably for no better reason than their despair — are a dangerous menace let loose on society. But Golway doesn't tell us enough about the case to know what to think. The case seems clearly to fall in the class above called nonvoluntary. Nothing suggests that the dead woman's attending psychiatrist put her to death against her will; her "deep despair" suggests — but does not really establish — that she could not give rational, informed, voluntary consent to her own death. And she is not a terminally ill patient, it seems. Until we have further evidence, it seems incautious to agree with Golway that this woman was "murdered" by her doctor.

We cannot forebear sharing with the reader our acute discomfort at the tone of Golway's essay, especially at the leaden irony and ill-disguised sneers aimed at the Dutch doctors and their medical practice, which includes physician-assisted dying in certain cases. His essay was written the year before the definitive treatise on the subject was published. We refer to *Euthanasia and Law in the Netherlands* (1998), which we discuss in our comments on the essay we reprint from Dr. McIver (p. 632). If Golway had had the benefit of reading this book, he might have tempered his tone and provided a more persuasive argument for his own case.

(text pp. 629–642)

In our commentary on the views of Dr. McIver (below), we have quoted the text of the new Dutch law on physician-assisted euthanasia. Students might be asked to write a 500-word paper on the extent to which Golway's criticisms are or are not appropriate under this new law, assuming it is enforced strictly.

Cecil McIver

Assisted Dying as a Moral and Ethical Choice: A Physician's View (p. 632)

The Hemlock Society (question 1) takes its name from the poison hemlock, which Socrates is reported to have swallowed in 399 B.C., thereby carrying out the death sentence of the Athenian court. As the name for a voluntary euthanasia society, however, "Hemlock" is a bit misleading, since Socrates was (so far as we know) in good health at the time of his death, had no desire to die by his own hand (much less by the hand of another), and was not in the care of a physician. In fact, none of the conditions laid down by Dr. McIver (in para. 1) for justifiable physician assistance in dying apply to the case of Socrates.

Whether one should add as a fifth condition (question 3) that the patient and the doctor both know "the suffering is pointless," in the sense that "it has to be borne without hope of subsequent improvement," we agree that insofar as physician assistance in dying can be justifiable at all, satisfying this condition certainly increases the likelihood of justification. The interesting question is whether it is a necessary condition of any possible justification. We (speaking for ourselves) would hesitate to go that far. Think of the case where the suffering is not "pointless" in the sense defined above but where the prospect of future well-being is remote or slight. We can imagine a patient who is extremely ill deciding that the struggle to endure the pain (perhaps accompanied with some disablement in normal functioning) demands too much courage to bear. Pain and its attendant burdens need not be "pointless" to be judged by the patient to be a bad bargain.

As we review the nine arguments McIver discusses (question 8), we do not find any of them utterly convincing. Surely the weakest is the ninth (para. 37), invoking God's law. To some readers this will seem to be the strongest, we grant. But exactly what is the divine ordinance violated by this practice? If one is attracted to the Golden Rule argument (para. 12) and believes it to be divinely ordained (consult Matthew 7:12), at least for professing Christians, then it is hard to see how this objection has much weight.

But what is the best objection of the nine? Perhaps a version of the seventh (para. 33), formulated this way: Physician assistance in dying would be difficult to regulate in any case, and it is not obvious that were it to be authorized under strict regulations, dying and terminally ill patients would be much better off than they are now, with many primary care physicians willing to use their own private judgment to hasten death in cases they deem appropriate. We are not ready to endorse this objection because it depends on empirical factors we are not competent to judge. Still, it is worth pondering — and is less of a straw man than the seventh objection as McIver formulates it.

The slippery slope objection to physician assistance in dying (our question 10) is explicit in McIver's eighth objection (paras. 35–36) and is implicit in the seventh objection (paras. 33–34). To claim that physician assistance in dying cannot be adequately regulated (which is the gravamen of both the seventh and eighth objections) is to imply that there will be cases — possibly a slow but steady increase in the number of cases — in which doctors will cause the death of their patients but ought not to have done so. McIver is evidently not as worried about this possibility as many of his critics would be. He meets it head on by pointing to actual experiences in Holland and in Oregon. We are not familiar with any recent studies on the experience in Oregon. Holland is another story — a story that has been told in great detail and scope by John Griffiths, Alex Bood, and Heleen Weyers in their treatise *Euthanasia and Law in the Netherlands* (1998), published by the Amsterdam University Press. Without attempting here to convey the full range of their research findings, we can say that any reader of their work is bound to come away with the conclusion that the slippery slope objection is considerably overrated. They end their study by saying "[A] reasonable observer would have to conclude, we think, that there is no significant evidence that the frequency of termination of life without an explicit request is higher in the Netherlands than it used to be; and if there had been any increase, it is almost certainly the result of things (medical technology; demographic changes) that have nothing to do with legalization of euthanasia" (p. 301).

In Holland, the most recent development (reported in the *New York Times* of Nov. 27, 2000, p. A3) is the enactment by the lower house of Parliament of the following guidelines for physician-assisted euthanasia.

> The physician must be convinced that the patient's request is voluntary and well considered. The physician must be convinced that the patient is facing unremitting and unbearable suffering. The patient does not have to be terminally ill. The patient must have a correct and clear understanding of his or her situation and prognosis. The physician, together with the patient, must reach the conclusion that there is no reasonable alternative that is acceptable to the patient. The decision to die must be the patient's own. The physician must consult at least one other independent doctor who has examined the patient. The physician must end the patient's life in a medically appropriate manner.

The bill was passed 104 to 40 and (after endorsement by the Senate) will become law in 2001. Students might well be asked to write a 500-word essay evaluating the similarities and differences between this new Dutch law and McIver's proposals.

The most hotly contested issue raised by the demand for physician assistance in dying is whether improved palliative care (paras. 20–21) could obviate the need for such assistance. What we have here is the dispute between the hospice movement (which places great reliance on medication to alleviate pain) and Hemlock (which argues, as McIver does in para. 21, that some pain cannot be alleviated except at the cost of making the remaining days or weeks of terminally ill intolerable). Most Hemlock supporters are prepared to grant that palliative care can and ought to be improved and made widely available. Few hospice supporters are willing to grant that in some cases there is no feasible and humane alternative to physician assistance in dying.

Our question 12 asks for an evaluation of the principle of double effect. Unfortunately, McIver doesn't formulate the principle, so we will do it for him: The double effect mentioned in the principle is actually two different effects that one's act may cause: the intentional effect and the unintentional effect. It is not intended because it is morally wrong. Thus, in the context of euthanasia or physician-assisted dying, although it is morally wrong to act with the intention of killing another person, it is permissible to act in a manner that one knows in advance will bring about the death of another person, provided one's intention in so acting is to do good. Thus, increasing the dose of morphine with the intention of alleviating acute pain is permissible because acting with the intention of alleviating pain is a good thing to do — even if one knows that the dose will kill the patient.

McIver implicitly rejects the distinction because he sees nothing morally wrong in administering a drug with the intention of ending the patient's life — provided, of course, that the necessary conditions that he has laid down to justify such an act have been satisfied.

James Rachels

Active and Passive Euthanasia (p. 642)

Patients have the right to refuse treatment or any form of medical intervention; but they do not have the right to receive whatever treatment or intervention they demand. Consequently, as things currently stand, they do not have the right to ask (much less demand) that a doctor put them out of their misery. The right to refuse undoubtedly underlies the AMA's position that tolerates "cessation of . . . extraordinary means to prolong the life of the body," or "passive" euthanasia, but rejects "mercy killing" (and hence "active" euthanasia) because that involves acting with the "intention" to "terminate" the patient's life. This bears on our first question.

The essence of James Rachels's argument that active euthanasia is sometimes preferable to passive euthanasia (question 2) is essentially utilitarian. That is, he assumes the criterion of right conduct is reduction of human suffering; accordingly, letting someone die by slow starvation and dehydration (the result of withholding nourishment) may take longer, or otherwise be more painful, than directly injecting some lethal but painless drug.

Now one can argue against such a view in any of three ways. First, one can reject the utilitarian criterion or at least limit its application in this context. Second, one can challenge the factual premise, according to which it is more painful to be allowed to die than to be put to death. Third, one can concede both premises but insist that a utilitarian must take other things into account besides the pain and suffering of the dying person — such as whether the practice of directly killing the dying would result in "slippery slope" objections that might outweigh the good done through pain reduction in direct killing of the dying.

As we note in question 6, Rachels's main purpose is to destroy our commonsense confidence that "the bare difference between killing and letting die" makes "a moral difference." Rachels argues that "killing is not in itself any worse than letting die" (para. 16). His principal argument is based on a pair of hypothetical cases he carefully constructs in paragraphs 10 and 11, and his own discussion of these cases in paragraph 12. If your students are like ours, they will quickly get to the heart of the matter by discussing this pair of cases.

One might wonder, however, whether Rachels has proved his point. Has he shown that there is no *moral difference whatever* between killing and letting die — or only that *in certain cases,* like the hypothetical cases he invents, there is no moral difference? And isn't there an enormous range of cases of letting die, where the moral judgment to be placed on the person who lets another die varies with a range of obvious factors (risk to the bystander, cost and likely effectiveness of the intervention, fault of the dying person for his or her current plight)? But if this is true, then there are moral differences among cases of letting die; so perhaps one ought to be cautious in concluding that there are no moral differences whatever between a case of killing and a case of letting die.

As for the "mistake" (para. 14) that Rachels thinks the AMA makes in its position statement, which he quoted in his first paragraph, we are again not sure there is any such mistake. If a doctor at a patient's request withdraws further life support, Rachels says that such action is "the intentional termination of the life of one human being by another." Is it? Can't the doctor who accedes to the patient's request argue as follows: "To act as my patient requests, I withhold all further medical intervention with this patient. I believe the patient has made this request in the expectation that his death will result. I believe he is right." But does the action in question, based on the hypothesized beliefs, amount to *acting with the intention to terminate the patient's life*? It is not obvious that it does. For suppose that after the doctor ended medical intervention, the patient miraculously lived on painlessly. Would the doctor necessarily construe that happy event as an outcome contrary to his intentions? Not unless his intentions had been to murder the patient. But in the normal case of letting a patient die, the doctor had no such intentions, and so the happy miracle does not thwart his intentions at all.

Timothy M. Quill

Death and Dignity: A Case of Individualized Decision Making (p. 649)

We think there is something inevitably *un*dignified about human death, at least what we have seen of it, with the result that the concept of "death with dignity" is not easy to explain and even harder to implement. Dr. Timothy Quill's essay helps us to come to grips with the problems surrounding this idea and how to put it into practice. (So does an essay by W. A. Parent, "Constitutional Values and Human Dignity," in the book he edited with Michael E. Meyer, *The Constitution of Rights* [1992], on which we rely in what follows.) What can we say, briefly, about the idea of human dignity? Roughly, this: You treat me with dignity, we suggest, because you *respect* me as a fellow human being, which disallows you from treating me *arbitrarily,* or *debasing* me simply because I am different from you (say, dying rather than healthily alive). My dignity is caught up with my *moral rights,* and so your failure to treat me with dignity flouts those rights.

Quill wants his patient, Diane, to "die with as much control and dignity as possible." This requires him to accede to her wishes insofar as he cannot dismiss them as impulsive, absurd, irrational, insincere, delusionary, or in some other way not a true expression of her desires as an adult, rational, normal albeit sick and dying person. Clearly, as Quill reports Diane's views (see especially the opening lines of para. 8), she connected her "dignity" with her ability to "maintain control of herself" — that is, with her ability to implement her desires in actions that she could accept as plausibly rational. This amounts to saying that for Diane, her dignity was essentially connected to her sense of herself as an *autonomous* person: self-conscious, self-determining, self-critical, self-activating. These features of autonomy are absent in infancy, and they vanish under the assault of fatal diseases. Diane fully expected to watch the loss of these abilities in herself, and she eventually does (see para. 11). At a critical moment she gave herself the fatal dose of barbiturates she had carefully accumulated for the purpose (para. 9). Without Quill's help, however, this might have been impossible; and he cooperated with her, if we can trust his account, only because "she was not in despair or overwhelmed in a way that might color her judgment." To put this in terms of human dignity, Quill assured himself that Diane's request deserved his respect because she was acting autonomously and within her rights, and so he acted accordingly. (We have here sketched some of the ideas that deserve exploration by students answering questions 2 and 3.)

Of course, Quill lied to the medical examiner; Diane did not die of "acute leukemia" — although she probably would have before long, if she had not fatally dosed herself first with barbiturates. And Quill knew this was how she died; he had helped her make this final exit, as he well knew. So the only question to be discussed is whether his lie was justified. We think it was, but we leave to students answering question 4 the task of spelling out a plausible argument to defend that judgment.

23
Juvenile Crime: How Should
Society Respond? (p. 655)

First, a bit of background. The *New York Times* (Dec. 15, 2000, p. A22) cited Justice Department figures to claim that "A six-year decline in the rate of homicide arrests has brought the 1999 rate down 68 percent from its 1993 peak to the lowest level since 1966." The article defined juveniles as youths ten to seventeen years old and stated that their arrest rate for four major violent crimes — murder, rape, robbery, and aggravated assault — had plunged 36 percent from the 1994 peak and reached the lowest point since 1988. Why? Three reasons are given: (1) the decline of crack cocaine and the gangs that sold it, (2) expanded after-school crime prevention programs, and (3) big-city policy crackdowns on illegal guns.

The article also said that juvenile-arrest rates for drug abuse violations and for curfew and loitering violations also fell.

Rita Kramer

Juvenile Justice Is Delinquent (p. 656)

Rita Kramer's opening paragraph strikes us as effective; she begins by appealing to our own experience ("Anyone who reads newspapers or watches TV"), and we think, "Yes, yes, I know what you mean. I agree." Further, her prose is lucid and forceful ("On the streets, in the subways, and even in the schools"), and for those of us who care about writing, clear, vigorous prose always makes an argument seem at least moderately respectable.

You may want to invite students to talk about Kramer's persona. What sort of person does she seem to be? What words or phrases or sentences — to say nothing of ideas — make students imagine her the way they do? The discussion might begin by concentrating on the first paragraph. Notice that in the next-to-last sentence of this paragraph, she strongly censures the social programs of the 1960s without seeming mean-spirited; the programs were "ambitious," but they have "had unintended results." The last sentence of the paragraph is a bit strong. These social programs are part of a system that, "instead of solving society's ills. . . . has added to them."

By the end of the third paragraph Kramer has explained the juvenile justice system — that is, has provided what she takes to be the background necessary for a reader to know — before she goes on to offer her argument more directly. We say "more directly" because, naturally, she has been arguing her case from the very beginning — from the title, which announced the point of view.

A word about the sixth question in the text. In the early part of the essay, Kramer expresses concern for juveniles (the hope that their character can be changed) and for the victims of juveniles. By the end of the essay, the concern for the well-being of the young offenders has disappeared, and it is evident that Kramer has little faith in reforming them; rather, her concern is now solely for "the rights of the community."

A small query: In paragraph 19 Kramer says that "a significant number of boys arrested for violent crimes were out on parole at the time of the arrest." How big is "a significant number"? Ten percent? Twenty? Fifty? We think that Kramer would have done much better if she had given a specific number.

Addendum: In 1998 two Jonesboro, Arkansas boys, ages eleven and thirteen, shot and killed four girls and a teacher and wounded nine other students. Under Arkansas law children under fourteen cannot be tried as adults, and if they are convicted as juveniles, they cannot be incarcerated beyond their twenty-first birthday. In practice, most juvenile offenders are released when they become eighteen. On the other hand, twenty-seven states do not have age restrictions that prevent prosecuting juveniles as adults. The youngest age at which someone can be sentenced to death in the United States is sixteen; of the thirty-eight states that allow the death penalty, twenty have expressly set the minimum age at sixteen. Since the reinstatement of the death penalty in 1976, nine Americans, all males, have been executed for crimes committed as juveniles — that is, crimes committed between their sixteenth and eighteenth birthdays. But because of the appeals process, all were in their twenties or thirties before they were executed.

What about punishing the parents of juveniles offenders? Child access prevention laws (CAP laws), on the books in forty-two states, hold parents, as legal guardians, accountable if their guns are used by children. For instance, in Florida adults may be given five years and a $5,000 fine if a minor obtains a firearm and causes injury or death. The chief point of such laws is prevention, not punishment, and we are told that statistical evidence indicates that the laws have reduced unintentional deaths caused by children. You may want to ask your class to discuss the pros and cons of holding adults responsible.

George Horan

Juvenile Felonies (p. 660)

The burden of Father Horan's opening paragraph is that where a crucial condition — loving parents, concerned teachers, responsible adults, caring priests — is absent in the life of a youngster, childhood or adolescent delinquency is likely to erupt and that its cause is *our* failure as parents, teachers, and other concerned adults to rear that person properly in the first place.

Horan's questions ("Did teachers . . . ?" "Was he or she . . . ?") are all rhetorical; the reader immediately can tell what answers are expected. It seems impossible for these questions to be answered in the affirmative ("Yes, the child always received adequate health care. Yes, teachers gave personal attention to the child") and yet the child or adolescent still becomes a delinquent. The possibility that much or even any delinquency has a different etiology than that implied by those rhetorical questions is simply not considered.

Well, what is the story of causation where juvenile delinquency is concerned? It is a commonplace of conservative opinion to point out that *not every* child neglected or abused becomes a youthful criminal. Yet all students of the subject insist that children who have been neglected or abused are *more likely* to end up as delinquents than are children who have been spared such harms. A good recent account of what clinical study can reveal on this topic is found in *Ghosts from the Nursery: Tracing the Roots of Violence* (1998) by Robin Karr-Morse and Meredith S. Wiley. The authors urge that the earlier in the child's life constructive interventions can be arranged (and destructive interventions avoided), the greater the likelihood children will grow up as we would want them to.

Plausible though Horan's viewpoint is, we must not underestimate the difficulty in putting his views into practice. He says we adults, parents, teachers, and the like "must be held to certain standards in our community treatment" of children at risk before we have any right to abandon them to the mercies of prison. But just what are these standards? Who is to hold us to them? What measures are to be used to do this? We are not told. Of course, one cannot expect adequate answers to such questions in such a brief essay. But they must be asked and answered if Horan's humane and earnest recommendations are to be taken seriously.

Robert L. Sexton

Tackling Juvenile Crime (p. 661)

The essay by Sexton is representative of a widespread attitude in this country that juvenile crime is out of control and the remedy is treating older juveniles as if they were adults — thus making them liable to more severe sanctions. This attitude is based on the assumption that the cause of this crime wave is excessive and sentimental leniency among legislators, police, prosecutors, judges, parents — indeed, the majority of the adult public that has any contact with juvenile crime.

Sexton adopts and explains his views against the background of three decades of work by social scientists exploiting the "economic" approach to crime and punishment. (He is himself an economist, not a criminologist or penologist — and one might well wonder whether his academic training qualifies him to pronounce on the causes and remedies of juvenile crime.) We learn this in his third paragraph when he informs the reader that "This paper is an extension of analysis by Becker [1968] of optimal trade-offs between fines and real resource-using enforcement efforts." And he next cites a paper he coauthored that was published in an economics journal (see his note 1 to para. 3).

If we may say so, there seems to us a kind of mindlessness (or is it heartlessness?) running through the whole essay. It boils down to something like this:

Problem: The juvenile crime rate is rising (see para. 6).

Question: What is the cheapest way to reduce that rate?

Answer: Lower the age to fourteen at which juveniles may be treated like adults in criminal courts. "A simple adjustment of the age at which youths may be tried as adults would achieve massive benefits at virtually no additional cost" (para. 14).

Question: Are there any adverse consequences of this tactic in the war on juvenile crime?

Answer: None we are aware of. Next question.

The obvious possible downside to Sexton's proposal — turning young boys into "hardened criminals" (para. 14) — evokes this response: "This is not a compelling argument." Why? Because "most juvenile crime is committed by repeat juvenile offenders, and sentencing for first time juvenile offenders, even if tried in adult courts, would not be the same [that is, as severe] as that for repeat offenders." Sexton is saying in effect that repeat juvenile offenders are already "hardened criminals," so punishing them as adults is entirely appropriate and will not make them any worse than they already are. We are not convinced.

Even if Sexton is right about "hardened" juvenile recidivists, time in an adult prison is almost certainly going to make a fourteen-year-old boy worse, not better, and he will eventually be released. We doubt that it is really reasonable to put a fourteen-year-old recidivist juvenile in prison with "hardened" adult criminals. (Think about it: A fourteen-year-old becomes a recidivist because he was committing crimes at twelve or thirteen.) How can such a policy really be cost-effective over the long run? As a separate point, it is reasonable to assume that boys who are fourteen, fifteen, or sixteen are more impulsive, less capable of self-control, and more likely to have illusionary views about their immunity from arrest than are boys eighteen and older. So there is no guarantee that the desired increased deterrence will result from a liability to increased punitive severity.

Students might be asked to write a 500-word paper on how Sexton would reply to the views of Horan (p. 660).

24
Privacy: What Are Its Limits? (p. 668)

Amitai Etzioni

Less Privacy Is Good for Us (and You) (p. 668)

Although this essay is graceless, we think it makes a good introduction to the topic, partly because it is short, partly because it does not go into subtleties, and partly because it lucidly sets forth a basic issue: How do we balance a right to privacy against considerations of the public interest? We say the essay in graceless. We have in mind such things as the use of *media* as a singular noun (para. 2) (common of course, but still not widely accepted) and the use of *rather* to modify "justifiable diminution of privacy" (para. 3) (the diminution may be justifiable in some instances and not others, but that is different from saying something is "rather justifiable"). He tells us that biometrics will lead to "substantial" benefits (para. 9), a word that seems grotesquely cautious when in the next paragraph he speaks of recovering billions of dollars from criminals, persons who falsify their income taxes, and divorced parents who change their identity to escape their financial obligations to their children.

But, again, in our view these infelicities do not prevent the essay from being a useful way of getting into an important aspect of the topic. Readers will differ in their evaluation of Etzioni's position, but it is our guess that most students will accept his concluding formulation: Privacy is "one very important right, but not one that trumps most other considerations, especially of public safety and health."

Etzioni says in his next-to-last paragraph that "Privacy should rely squarely on the Fourth Amendment." This amendment distinguishes between searches that are "unreasonable" (and therefore violate privacy) and searches that are acceptable because they are supported by evidence of "probably cause." In Etzioni's view, the latter searches are "those that enhance the common good to such an extent that they are justified, even if they intrude into one's privacy." We quote the amendment:

> The right of the people to be secure in their persons, houses, papers, and effects, against unreasonable searches and seizures, shall not be violated, and no warrants shall issue but upon probable cause, supported by oath or affirmation, and particularly describing the place to be searched, and the persons or thing to be seized.

Simson Garfinkel

Privacy under Attack (p. 672)

Garfinkel tells us (para. 3) that our "right of privacy" is "the right of people to control what details about their lives stay inside their own houses and what leaks to the outside." If that is the *right* of privacy, then privacy itself is exercising that control, and an invasion of privacy (question 3) occurs when we lose that control to another who has acquired information about our lives without our permission. Garfinkel is thus correct when he says that "Privacy is fundamentally about the power of the individual" (para. 9).

Let us consider the concept of privacy in relation to its two most important elements — *autonomy* and *liberty* (our fifth question). Privacy is essential for autonomy to be exercised because if our privacy is invaded, then we no longer fully control our choices: That loss of privacy requires us to take into account the knowledge that others have about our private lives. Privacy is also necessary for *liberty* or freedom to be experienced because if information about my life ends up without my consent in the hands of others, then my conduct is impeded: My loss of privacy entails a loss of liberty.

Garfinkel is less interested in these conceptual relationships among privacy, liberty, and autonomy than he is in the magnitude and scope of the threats to privacy that increasingly lie ahead (paras. 4–5), thanks to technological developments (para. 8).

He thinks we are all tempted, and often yield to the temptation, to "enjoy the benefits of modern society" at the price of losing "some degree of privacy" (para. 10) — a "Faustian bargain," he declares. Faust, it will be recalled (question 4), gave his eternal soul to the devil in exchange for a few decades of earthly delights. If that is what one risks when using a credit card to pay for a nice dinner out (his example), then we are all headed for eternal torments.

As a side issue, Garfinkel mentions (para. 13) the famous *Harvard Law Review* article by Samuel Warren and Louis Brandeis, "The Right to Privacy." Warren was the scion of a Boston Brahmin family. He and Brandeis had been classmates at Harvard Law School and prior to 1890, when the article was published, had been law partners in Boston. The article was prompted by rather commonplace events, explained as follows by A. T. Mason in his biography of Brandeis: "On January 25, 1883, Warren had married Miss Mabel Bayard, daughter of Senator Thomas Francis Bayard, Sr. They set up housekeeping in Boston's exclusive Back Bay section and began to entertain elaborately. The *Saturday Evening Gazette*, which specialized in 'blue blood items,' naturally reported their activities in lurid detail. This annoyed Warren, who took the matter up with Brandeis. The article was the result." Warren and his wife had nothing to hide, but they regarded the regular reporting of their hospitality as an invasion of their privacy, and they were right: They had lost control over who could witness (at second hand) the dinners and entertainments in their house.

Garfinkel frequently mentions a parallel between the movement of the 1950s and 1960s to protect the environment and the incipient movement of today to protect privacy (para. 11). His point seems to be that we are winning the war to preserve the environment and that we can do the same thing to preserve our privacy in the face of government and corporate efforts to invade and control it. Of course he is right when he says (para. 12) that "Without clean air to breathe and water to drink, we will all surely die." But do we, does government, do corporations in fact act on this knowledge? The newspapers every day report yet another place where the physical environment has been degraded, poisoned, or otherwise made uninhabitable. Couldn't one argue that both our privacy and our physical environment are equally at risk as we enter the new century? Students might be set to write a 500-word essay developing an argument on Garfinkel's parallel, either supporting or rejecting it.

Nadine Strossen

Everyone Is Watching You (p. 680)

The title is catchy, but of course it is *obviously* not true. Strossen defends the aptness of her title (para. 3), but her list of privacy invaders ("banks, . . . workplaces") falls well short of "everyone." Her entire worry seems to focus on surveillance cameras. But not every street has such cameras recording whoever strolls down the sidewalk. We do not wish to quibble over her use of the inclusive pronoun; we grant that her list of invaders is broad enough to alert us to their lurking in many corners of everyday life, enough to properly alarm us.

We also hesitate to agree with her that our current lifestyles find us "increasingly . . . forfeiting [our] privacy" (para. 3). Normally, one "forfeits" something as a penalty or punishment for wrongdoing. But no such wrongdoing is involved in this context; what is involved is a *loss* of privacy.

Strossen considers and rejects the argument that "we need to trade privacy for safety" (para. 8). We find the anecdotal evidence she cites (paras. 9–11) convincing, as far as it goes. What, however, about the principle itself? Strossen neither endorses nor rejects it. We think it is certainly reasonable to trade a certain amount of privacy for safety. Think, for example, of the x-ray screening of our baggage we all experience as we queue up to board the plane. We have no idea how many mad bombers, angry jilted lovers, drunks, or others who arrive at the gate with a loaded gun are prevented from boarding, thanks to the x-ray surveillance. But we are reassured by the practice every time we have to ride a plane. Reasonable people, of course, can disagree over *how much* privacy to sacrifice to secure a given increment in safety. But the principle itself seems to us unassailable. We wish Strossen had explicitly conceded that point. (Could she claim she had done so, implicitly?)

Strossen is a law professor and president of the American Civil Liberties Union and thus sees herself (rightly) to be a staunch defender of personal privacy; she is skeptical, if not downright hostile, regarding laws that infringe on that privacy. Naturally, she endorses the rulings of the California Supreme Court striking down "methods of surveillance" that invade our privacy with little or no gain in public safety (paras. 12–13). She is less enthusiastic about the current majority on the U.S. Supreme Court and encourages us to "take political or other direct action" to remedy the Court's inaction (para. 15).

What measures does she recommend? (1) Join with others to protest cameras in public places (does that mean cameras are acceptable in bank lobbies or airport terminals?). (2) If you see one in a public place, "find out why it is there" (arrive at the airport or bank an hour or so early, so you can ask some questions?). (3) Refuse to shop at businesses that photorecord all transactions (a tall order today). (4) Tell a prospective employer that "you object to secret taping" (how about taping that is obvious because the camera is visible?). (5) Urge elected officials to enact laws "limiting surveillance" ("limiting" it in what ways and by what methods?). We grant that an alarmed and concerned citizenry is our safest protection against excessive public and private invasions of our privacy. But we suspect that most of us will quietly acquiesce in these current invasions without much if any protest.

Judith Wagner DeCew

The Feminist Critique of Privacy (p. 687)

By the way, the author's name is pronounced as though it were spelled "Dekew."

This is one of the more challenging essays in our book; most readers are unlikely to fully grasp it on a first reading. The reason is twofold. First, the targets of DeCew's analysis are views on privacy from law professor Catharine MacKinnon, whose prose demands patience and care. Second, the reader has to watch DeCew struggle again and again to make MacKinnon's views sufficiently clear so that they can be fairly and effectively criticized. That, too, requires the reader's patience and care. So let us start out modestly.

In answer to question 1 (and see also DeCew's para. 2), the Fourth Amendment in the federal Bill of Rights protects us "against unreasonable searches and seizures" — that is, against unwarranted invasions of our private property (things that can be "searched" or "seized"). A tort is any harmful wrong to a person (other than a breach of contract or a crime) for which a court will provide a remedy — that is, an invasion of personal safety or privacy where harm is inflicted, typically unintentionally but negligently.

How might a feminist critique of privacy undermine or trivialize the protections that a right of privacy provides or ought to provide? That is the great topic of this essay. The answer comes initially in the paragraph in which DeCew first quotes MacKinnon — a paragraph that she paraphrases and interprets and makes much more accessible. Perhaps the best epigrammatic expression of MacKinnon's position comes at the beginning of DeCew's fifth paragraph, when MacKinnon is quoted as stating that "The private is public for those for whom the personal is political." Some class discussion could usefully be devoted to unpacking this sentence. Readers should find DeCew's interpretation of this phrase and the two claims it contains helpful (para. 5 following the MacKinnon quotation).

Perhaps the best restatement of MacKinnon's position by DeCew (para. 6) leads DeCew to open the next paragraph by stating flatly that MacKinnon's argument — now that we can at last see what it comes to — "is easily refuted." Perhaps. But it takes DeCew the next couple of paragraphs to explain that refutation.

DeCew insists that although MacKinnon blurs the point, "privacy and autonomy are distinct concepts" (para. 7) (question 2), and we fully agree. But we won't pursue the matter here because we have discussed these two distinct concepts elsewhere, in our discussion of the essay by Simson Garfinkel (this manual, p. 108) and in our comments on *Roe v. Wade* (this manual, p. 48).

We encounter the so-called public/private split first at the end of MacKinnon's remarks in the middle of paragraph 5 and again when DeCew undertakes to "reconstruct" it (para. 8) (question 4). We sympathize with her when she says that, important though his "split" is, "it is difficult to clarify what the feminist critique of it entails." DeCew thinks MacKinnon thinks "there is no distinction between public and private because there is no private realm for women at all" (para. 8). DeCew is reluctant to follow MacKinnon here (and so are we) because a mare's nest of questions arises once you take seriously the idea that there is not and cannot be any private realm for women at all (para. 9). Further light is shed on this point by DeCew's review of the relevant ideas of Jean Bethke Elshtain (para. 9) and Ruth Gavison (para. 10).

Is it really true, as MacKinnon claims (in DeCew's interpretation), that "women have no privacy" (para. 5)? Or is this just exaggeration to catch our attention in a way that a more accurate statement ("many women have little privacy in matters of great importance to them, and some women have none") fails to do? What, after all, is the legitimate role for rhetorical exaggeration in a serious argument? Consider another of her remarks in this vein: "The right of privacy is a right of men 'to be let alone'" (para. 11). The phrase "to be let alone" comes from the famous law review article by Brandeis and Warren, which we discuss in connection with Garfinkel's essay (this manual, p.108). It is difficult, indeed impossible, for us to see the Brandeis-Warren defense of privacy in that article as a protective device for "men 'to be let alone.'" Another epigrammatic exaggeration from MacKinnon? Or a deep penetration below the surface of the concept of privacy? We leave it for the reader to judge.

25

Sexual Harassment:
Is There Any Doubt about What It Is? (p. 698)

Of the four pieces that we reprint, none will cause students any difficulty. We begin the unit with the Tufts University statement, and then continue with Ellen Goodman, who in a very readable middle-of-the-road piece argues that *of course* there is such a thing as sexual harassment and it is fairly widespread and fairly easily identifiable.

At some point in the discussion you may want to tell students what the Equal Employment Opportunity Commission (EEOC) says about the issue. Here are its "Guidelines on Sexual Harassment," from Title VII, Part 1604.11:

> Harassment on the basis of sex is a violation of Sec. 703 of Title VII. Unwelcome sexual advances, requests for sexual favors, and other verbal or physical conduct of a sexual nature constitute sexual harassment when (1) submission to such conduct is made either explicitly or implicitly a term or condition of an individual's employment, (2) submission to or rejection of such conduct by an individual is used as the basis for employment decisions affecting such individual, or (3) such conduct has the purpose or effect of unreasonably interfering with an individual's work performance or creating an intimidating, hostile, or offensive working environment.

This passage has been fairly widely copied and adapted in codes issued by universities. Here, for instance, is a passage from the University of Minnesota's "Policy Statement on Sexual Harassment." We have italicized the additions.

> For the purposes of this policy, sexual harassment is defined as follows: Unwelcome sexual advances, requests for sexual favors, and other verbal or physical conduct of a sexual nature constitute sexual harassment when (1) submission to such conduct is made either explicitly or implicitly a term or condition of an individual's employment *or academic advancement*, (2) submission to or rejection of such conduct by an individual is used as the basis for employment decisions *or academic decisions* affecting such individual, or (3) such conduct has the purpose or effect of unreasonably interfering with an individual's work performance *or academic performance* or creating an intimidating, hostile, or offensive working *or academic* environment.

Tufts University

What Is Sexual Harassment? (p. 699)

The policy statement, as it stands, is not an argument and does not include any argument. The statement also does not define *sexual harassment*. However, both an implicit definition and an implicit argument can be detected; here's one way of formulating each, beginning in premise (1) with the definition:

(1) Sexual harassment consists of unwanted, unwelcome sexual attention by one person from another.

(2) Such attention can create an intimidating, hostile social environment for the victim.

(3) Whoever creates such an environment ought to be disciplined and, if appropriate, punished.

(4) Therefore, whoever sexually harasses another ought to be disciplined and, if appropriate, punished.

The argument as it stands is valid; whether it is sound (that is, proves its conclusion) depends mostly on whether premise (3) is acceptable. We think it is, and so do most opponents of sexual harassment.

In principle, of course, sexual harassment can occur between men and between women, but the predominant mode is heterosexual harassment, with the male party the harasser and the female the one who is harassed.

There is, to be sure, some vagueness in the definition of sexual harassment. Perhaps the most important question is this: Does an unsolicited sexual advance (for example, a hug or a kiss) by a man constitute sexual harassment of a woman if she doesn't want it? Or does it count as harassment only if she also *says* she doesn't want it, and he refuses to take no for an answer and *persists* anyway? The Tufts policy (perhaps all too typically) does not make it clear whether the former as well as the latter qualifies as sexual harassment. Some feminists are in controversy with the law on this point. Gloria Steinem, founder the National Women's Political Caucus and of *Ms.* magazine, for example, recently made it clear that for her, there is no sexual harassment until the woman has said no to the advancing male (*New York Times*, Mar. 22, 1998). That provoked a critic to point out that the EEOC has ruled that a no first was not necessary provided the unwanted conduct was "unusually severe" (*New York Times*, Mar. 28, 1998). Taking sexual harassment' seriously was not encouraged when a first-grader in North Carolina was suspended from school for kissing a classmate on the cheek (*New York Times*, Mar. 22, 1998).

Sexual harassment of women by men in the workplace, as a special category of sex discrimination, was outlawed under Title VII of the Civil Rights Act of 1964; the Supreme Court upheld that interpretation in 1968 in *Meritor Savings Bank v. Vinson*. (To this day no federal statute defines *sexual harassment* and makes it unlawful.) With the confirmation hearings in the Senate for Supreme Court nominee Clarence Thomas in 1991, sexual harassment (charged against him by his former assistant, Anita Hill) suddenly went to the head of the national agenda, where it remains today, having been enormously stimulated during the second Clinton administration when charges of sexual harassment were filed against the president by Paula Jones. Under the law, an unwanted sexual overture will not normally count as sexual harassment unless some adverse effect on the unwilling recipient can be shown, for example, denial of a promotion by the employer because the employee refused to submit to the overture. In April 1998 Paula Jones's suit against the president was dismissed by the trial judge in part because she could show no adverse effects on her career from her refusal to submit to the alleged harassment. During 1997, more than 17,000 lawsuits charging sexual harassment were filed with the EEOC (*New York Times*, Mar. 19, 1998).

Colleges and universities are, of course, free to develop their own codes of sexual harassment. The Tufts policy deviates from the prevailing law by not requiring the complainant to show she suffered adverse effects from rejecting unwanted attentions (see the "or" at the end of item (1) in para. (2)).

A good exercise, either in class or as a take-home assignment, would be to try to revise the Tufts policy so that its conception of sexual harassment and the ensuing disciplinary procedures more nearly conform to what the student thinks appropriate — assuming, of course, that there are ways to improve the Tufts policy.

(text pp. 703–711)

Ellen Goodman

The Reasonable Woman Standard (p. 703)

Our first question following the essay invites students to talk about Ellen Goodman's style. We think part of a classroom session might well be devoted to stylistic matters, though of course stylistic matters (at least in our view) are in the final analysis matters of content. Consider, for example, the end of paragraph 4:

> One boss asks his secretary if he can still say "good morning," or is that sexual harassment. Heh, heh. The women aren't laughing.

What, one might ask the class, is that "heh, heh" doing here? Whether Goodman is imitating the boss, who laughs at his own little joke, or whether she is mockingly speaking in her own person, pretending to laugh at the idiotic joke and thus making clear that the joke *is* idiotic, the point is evident: It is not amusing when men make jokes about the sexual harassment of women. Men may pretend to be kidding, or they may even believe that they are kidding, but the jokes reveal either an unwillingness to recognize a serious problem, or, more often, they reveal a continued attempt to put women down. That is, the jokes are a way of ridiculing women, who are rightly concerned about a serious problem. Our laborious comment on Goodman's sentences shows, by way of contrast, how effective her colloquial language is. A less colloquial style probably could not have made this point so pointedly.

Although the essay is loosely organized, the thesis is clear enough: Men should try to imagine (and they *can* do this) how a reasonable woman would feel. This may sound a bit murky, but, as Goodman says, "When everything was clear, it was clearly biased. The old single standard was a male standard" (para. 8). She goes on (after a passage in which she ironically asks, "What's a poor man to do?"), to indicate that in fact males *can* empathize sufficiently, just as jurors do when they must put themselves into the role of a reasonable innkeeper or a reasonable train operator — or, for that matter, a reasonable man.

Ellen Frankel Paul

Bared Buttocks and Federal Cases (p. 705)

Professor Paul opens her essay with a strongly worded indictment against American men for their sexual harassment of women "in alarming proportions." She then turns (paras. 1–5) to some examples of such harassment. So far, however, we have no definition of this key concept in the discussion; we are left to define the term on the wing, as it were, from the examples she gives (question 3). Eventually she rightly notes (para. 9) that the term "is notoriously ill-defined" — all the more reason for her to help out the reader sooner rather than later. The first indications of how she might define it do not come until her comments on the United Methodist position on the issue (para. 9).

The effect of her silence, intentional or not, is to make it virtually impossible to know what to make of one statistic she cites (para. 8). When she reports that "nearly 80 percent of the respondents reported that they or someone they knew had been victims of sexual harassment," what did these respondents (or those who polled their views) think was the sexual harassment these women had experienced? Would we agree? Without any definition we are at a loss to respond reasonably to this information.

Here's a test: Would Paul accept the definition of the term used in the Tufts statement on the subject (p. 699)? Or perhaps the version in the law specified by EEOC (this manual, p. 112)? Your students might well be asked to write a 250-word paper in which they compare one of those policy statements with their own proposed definition of sexual harassment as it figures in Paul's essay.

In passing we note a rather odd remark from Paul. She observes, "For women to expect reverential treatment in the workplace is utopian" (para. 6). Normally things described as "utopian" are things we'd love to have, but realistically won't be lucky enough to obtain. Does Paul really want us to think that it would be a marvelous idea, just too good to be true, if women were given "reverential treatment in the workplace"? We think the idea is, well, silly and not utopian at all, and an example of the very hyperbole she condemns two paragraphs later. With apologies to Coventry Patmore (author of "The Angel in the House"), Paul seems to be recommending the angel in the workplace, and we find that as objectionable as the angel in the house.

We heartily endorse the cautions Paul urges on readers in paragraph 10, especially when she says "a sense of proportion needs to be restored" to the discussion (and accusations) of sexual harassment. She singles out the exaggerations of Catharine MacKinnon as representative of the failure to make appropriate distinctions. Paul herself relies on the distinction between the "objectively injurious" and the "subjectively offensive" (para. 14) and between "serious harm" and the "morally offensive" (para. 15). Harmful sexual harassment, she argues, deserves to be treated as a crime or a tort. Offensive harassment she dismisses as unworthy of attention by the courts. She urges women to raise their threshold of the "outrageous" (para. 16) by enduring discomfort "in silence," complaining "to higher management," or getting a different job. "Women," she says, "need to develop a thick skin in order to survive and prosper in the workforce."

We expect many feminists will bridle at these suggestions. But before they do, shouldn't they consider whether the alternatives aren't really worse? What is to be done with "offensive male bores" (her closing phrase) whose bad judgment, lack of self-discipline, and failures of sympathy and imagination make women uncomfortable? Their "trivial offenses, dirty jokes, sexual overtures, and sexual innuendoes" (para. 17) can cause intense discomfort. Is the solution to go to court seeking an injunction, demanding compensation, or threatening prosecution? If legal resources such as these are inappropriate overkill, what is left but confrontation, persuasion, mockery, and anger at those who mistreat women in these offensive but not harmful ways?

Sarah J. McCarthy

Cultural Fascism (p. 712)

Sarah McCarthy's argument appeared in *Forbes*, a business-oriented magazine, so it is not surprising that it takes the line it does. It is pretty hard-hitting, beginning with the title, "Cultural Fascism," a theme that is picked up in paragraph 3, where McCarthy speaks of her opponents as "the feminist political correctness gestapo" — that is, as comparable to the hated Nazi secret service police.

To return to the beginning of the essay: The first paragraph uses an ad hominem argument, calling attention to the fact that the call for "lottery-size punitive damages" for sexual harassment (McCarthy *does* have a gift for metaphor!) comes from Senator Ted Kennedy, widely regarded as a womanizer and as the man responsible for the death of a women who worked for him. The point here is, in effect, "Look who is setting himself up as the defender of women." Still, we find the paragraph powerful, especially since it ends by calling attention to the fact that the senators have voted to exempt themselves from punitive damages. There may be good reasons for their vote, but (at least as McCarthy presents the matter) they do seem like a bunch of rogues.

In the second half of the essay McCarthy several times asserts that she was a feminist activist. She does not, in our view, convincingly support this assertion: She just talks about the good old days when there were "powerful woman writers" (para. 7) and contrasts them with today, an age of "lawyers — prim women and men who went to the politically correct law schools" (para. 8). These New Age feminists, in her view, regard women as "china dolls" and therefore do a disservice to women who, she knows from her experience in the restaurant business, can take the rough stuff that men dish out.

Additional Topics for Critical Thinking and Writing

1. In the text, in question 5, we ask students to provide what McCarthy might offer as a definition of sexual harassment. You may want to vary the assignment by calling attention to the fact that the American Civil Liberties Union has argued that sexual harassment should be defined as expression that (1) is directed at a specific employee — rather than, for instance, a pin-up calendar visible to all passersby — and that (2) "demonstrably hinders or completely prevents his or her continuing to function as an employee." Do you agree with this position, or do you think it is too restricted? Explain.

2. Do you think that only someone who has suffered economic harm — for instance, someone who has been denied raises or who has been fired — should be able to allege that a supervisor has created a "hostile environment"? (This position would mean that a supervisor who repeatedly asked for a date or who made suggestive comments but who did not damage the employee financially would not be said to have created a hostile environment.)

26
Video Violence:
Do Children Need to Be Protected? (p. 715)

Much as Mark Twain once observed about the weather, so with video violence: Everyone talks about it, but no one does much about it. The main problems are (1) What, if any, forms of violence does television viewing tend to cause, and why? and (2) What, if any, forms of censorship — from government regulation to station and network self-censorship — are consistent with the constitutional protections of free "speech" (including vivid portrayals of violence and death)? The five essays we have reprinted take divergent views of these two problems.

In her 1991 book, *Deadly Consequences*, Deborah Prothrow-Stith reported much the same data that are summarized in Leonard Eron's essay below. She adds that "while the case is not air-tight, two Surgeon Generals have publicly supported the thesis that an overdose of media can trigger aggressive behavior" and that this conclusion has been supported as well by the American Medical Association, the American Pediatric Association, the American Academy of Child Psychiatry, and the American Psychological Association.

Prothrow-Stith also reports some details about Eron's research not mentioned in his own essay. Observations by his team of researchers of hundreds of young boys revealed that those who showed a "preference for T.V. violence" turned out to be more likely to commit aggression. "In fact," she reports, the research showed that "the leading predictor of how aggressive a young male would be at nineteen turned out to be the violence of the television he preferred at age eight." She adds that probation officers familiar with juvenile violence agree that "young males growing up in poverty, in homes that lack non-violent male role models, are the most vulnerable to television's violence-promoting message."

So, although watching violence on television by itself may not cause much copycat violence among youthful viewers, it may well do so if the viewers also are growing up without adequate adult supervision, are victims of child abuse, are exposed to drugs, are members of a youth gang, or are (also) marginalized because of their race or color.

Leonard D. Eron

The Television Industry Must Police Itself (p. 716)

Designing an interesting and significant method for measuring the quality and quantity of violence on television (our question 3) could be a good way to focus class discussion. Suppose you wanted to describe the quality and quantity of violence depicted during a one-hour show. You might tape it (so that you could study various scenes more carefully) and then answer the following questions: (1) How many different persons were victims of the acts of violence (knifing, shooting, fighting without weapons, and so on) shown on the show? (2) What exactly was shown in each such act? Just the corpse? A bloodied face? A bomb explosion with bodies flying in all directions? (3) How many total seconds were such acts on the screen? (4) What proportion of the whole show consisted in these violent scenes? (5) Who were the victims: children, women, storekeepers, police, bystanders, Mafia hit men? (6) Was the violence depicted as excused (caused by accident, say) or justified (necessary to save lives of the innocent, for example)? Or was it criminal violence against the innocent? (7) What attitude toward the violence was indicated by the characters involved? Did they deplore it? Ignore it? Approve of it? Finally, (8) you might want to consider how much violence is shown on a typical day during the television news programs (actual violence in our society, not the fictional kind), in comparison with that shown as entertainment. Even if the class does not, or is not in a position to, actually answer these questions about a given show, a discussion built around identifying the relevant questions would be instructive.

Ernest F. Hollings

Save the Children (p. 717)

Our question 3 touches on points raised in our introductory remarks to this chapter (this guide, p. 117), and before discussing the question in class you might reread what we said there about various factors present or absent in childhood and youth that bear on whether television violence tends to arouse and justify aggressive acts.

The Hollings-Inouye Children's Protection from Violent Programming Act (para. 3) did not become law. It nevertheless served as a threat and thus inspired some self-censorship among TV executives. Liberal though we are, we do not have any hesitation in favoring forms of self-discipline — including some self-restraint by those whose business is business — that result in severely limiting the quality and quantity of violent entertainment on television (and, while we're at it, in the movies as well).

Floyd Abrams

Save Free Speech (p. 720)

Abrams's essay is bound to stimulate discussion because of the many examples of films and television shows he cites to make his chief point: "We cannot even agree on which violence children should not see" (para. 4). Of course, his position results in a misleading exaggeration: we cannot agree about *all* the shows that children should not see, but it does not follow that we cannot agree about *any* such shows or about enough cases to make it worthwhile to develop criteria for the cases that we do agree about.

To put the point another way — and it is a general and an extremely important point in argumentative analysis — controversial *borderline cases* do not negate the uncontroversial *paradigm cases* at opposite ends of the full spectrum of cases, and we can agree to censor and not to censor those paradigms.

While we would not underestimate the difficulty in developing such criteria (our question 1), we also think that the quotation from Justice Powell that Abrams cites (para. 11) is not very much to the point. Those who favor some form of censorship to reduce violence on television do so in the belief that watching violence in the forms and at the rates at which many young children now do is a causal factor in their aggressive behavior toward others. Powell's remarks, like those Abrams quotes from Justice Frankfurter (para. 10), have nothing to do with disputing or undermining the desirability of reducing such causes of violence. Instead, Powell acknowledges that some "speech" (that is, violent television entertainment) *is* "subject to . . . legitimate prescription." One can hardly use the words of Frankfurter and Powell, in which they rightly object to paternalistic interventions, the efforts to insulate violence on television from any form of content regulation.

Of course, if you see no causal relationship between watching violence on television and engaging in aggressive violence, then censorship is surely unreasonable as well as unnecessary. But Abrams does not challenge the research that Leonard Eron and Senator Hollings cite to this point, and so his argument fails to come to grips with the problem.

Richard Rhodes

Hollow Claims about Fantasy Violence (p. 722)

The title introduces Rhodes's chief point: The claims that people make about "fantasy violence" (in the essay itself he uses the term "mock violence") are "hollow." (His puzzling shift from "fantasy violence" to "mock violence" — two terms for the same thing — was probably introduced by a well-meaning editor who thought the term "mock violence" in a title would not be clear. We very much believe that one should not shift terms and engage in what Fowler calls "elegant variation.") The violence offered by the entertainment industry is not in fact violence, he argues, but is merely "mock violence," an imitation of violence. One thinks of the clever painting by Magritte, showing a pipe, under which is written, "This is not a pipe." And of course Magritte is right: It is not a pipe but only a picture of a pipe. Violence on the screen is not real violence but "mock violence" or "fantasy violence." Having said this, admittedly the question still remains: Can mock violence have a harmful effect?

Our first question directs students to examine Rhodes's tone in his expressions such as "moral entrepreneurs" and "are at it again." Most students will easily hear the contempt in Rhodes's voice. We think this opening paragraph is satisfactory, but we also think that a reader does not want to hear this sort of sarcasm for more than a paragraph. Fortunately, Rhodes pretty much drops this tone after the first paragraph. Rhodes wisely, however, does continue to use the term "mock violence" (paras. 7 and 13) and suggests it when he speaks of "real violence" (para. 14).

His second paragraph consists of only one sentence: "But is there really a link between entertainment and violent behavior?" This paragraph, by virtue of its brevity, is powerful, and readers who have read the first paragraph attentively will know that this second paragraph clearly signals Rhodes's position: No, there isn't a connection.

His third paragraph cites the opposing view — always a good thing to do in an argument — and goes on to dismiss it. Remaining paragraphs, too, are largely devoted to dismissing the charge that the media induce violent behavior. He asserts that "There is good evidence . . . that [violence is] learned in personal violent encounters, beginning with the brutalization of children by their parents" (para. 13) and that the money spent on the studies that he rejects ought to have been spent on "the construction of community mental health centers" so that we could go about "protecting children from real violence in their real lives" (para. 14). In short, "fantasy" or "mock" violence is, for Rhodes, not the problem; the problem is "real violence in real lives."

The letters of response cannot develop extended arguments, but surely Jill Andrews could have done a little more than merely assert that "violent movies and violent music . . . send the message that in America, violence is an answer to almost any problem." She might at least have specified a piece of "violent music" or a film or two. Robert B. Harris supports Rhodes, picks up his use of "fantasy," and suggests that "It's the real violence that should concern us." He then goes on to suggest that this real violence is seen in "highly paid athletes who fight, trash-talk and assault officials." Nothing in his letter establishes that fantasy violence is harmless, but he does turn our thought toward something in real life that may induce violence in youngsters. Gregory J. Hanson's hostility to Rhodes is evident, we think, in his first sentence ("Richard Rhodes tears apart studies"), but if a reader somehow missed Hanson's attitude toward Rhodes here, it is unmistakable in the next paragraph: "So Hollywood is as pure as the driven snow, while guns are the problem." Rhodes never said Hollywood was pure; he said that films don't induce violence in youngsters. The last letter, by Frank Sciulli, supports Rhodes, picks us his terms "mock violence" and "fantasy violence," continues Rhodes's point about society being violent, but then introduces a specific point that Rhodes had not made (and indeed may not subscribe to): "The death penalty is society's ultimate violence." (By the way, we are surprised that neither of the letter writers who support Rhodes quotes Rap Brown, "Violence . . . is as American as cherry pie." Has this 1960s phrase dropped from public memory?)

Dave Grossman and Gloria DeGaetano

"It's Important to Feel Something When You Kill" (p. 726)

First, a few words about violent video games. We claim no expertise here, but we have read that such games are far less popular than some people claim. A newspaper article (*Boston Globe Magazine*, Dec. 10, 2000) said that the top three computer games are *Roller Coaster Tycoon* (the player runs an amusement park), *Sim-City 3000* (a city-building simulation), and *Who Wants to Be a Millionaire?*, all of which are said to be nonviolent. A violent game does not appear until the fifth slot. (We do not vouch for the rankings.)

We also have read that despite charges to the contrary, the youngsters who most frequently play are *not* playing in isolation or withdrawing from companionship. Defenders of the games say that because a player soon learns the programmed moves, he or she needs a real-life competitor and plays with friends or with strangers found via the Internet.

The essay by Grossman and DeGaetano will not cause students any difficulty. The language is close to ordinary speech ("In case you haven't made a trip to a video arcade," para. 1, and "How fast a rate? Consider this," para. 2). In fact, we think the authors may have delivered much of this material as lectures to concerned parents. But to say that the essay is an easy read is not to say that there is nothing to discuss in class. On the contrary, the evidence that the authors present should be evaluated. What do students make, for instance, of the authors' claim that "More than 60 percent of children report that they play video games longer than they intend to play"? (para. 9). We can easily accept the statistic, but what does it prove? Probably more than 60 percent of children who skate will report that they skated longer than they intended to or stayed visiting a friend longer than they intended to. Every parent knows that kids often forget the clock: "Where is Annie? She said she would be home by now!"

Grossman and DeGaetano are also concerned with children who have low self-esteem. But if the games help to build self-esteem, isn't that a good thing? Don't sports sometimes help to build self-esteem? The child who builds a model ship or wins the prize as the best speaker of Spanish gains in self-esteem, and such a gain is usually said to be valuable. The question, then, as we see it is this: Do the authors establish that the self-esteem gained from doing well in playing a violent game ("mock violent," Richard Rhodes would insist) is in fact a bad thing?

One other thing: The authors do not face the question of whether these games may not have a cathartic effect. That is, it can be argued that the games serve a social purpose, allowing youngsters to release — to harmlessly discharge —

aggressive feelings. This is the view that Aristotle took when he replied to Plato's charge that Greek tragedies had a bad effect on the spectators because the plays stimulated passions and passions ought to be kept in check. True, exactly what Aristotle meant by *catharsis* is disputed — did he say that the passions are purged, or rather that they are purified? — but the gist of his point is clear: Tragedy serves a useful purpose by stimulating emotions and then purging or purifying them.

ENDURING QUESTIONS: ESSAYS, STORIES, POEMS, AND A PLAY

27
What Is the Ideal Society? (p. 743)

We at first thought of having a section titled "Utopia," but as we worked on it the idea seemed needlessly limited, and "Utopia" gave way to the present chapter. Still, several of the readings we give here are utopian. The utopian element in this section allows us here to introduce a comment by Gertrude Himmelfarb, in *Marriage and Morals among the Victorians* (1986):

> "Utopian" is one of the more ambiguous words in our vocabulary. To some it signifies an ideal that is commendable if not entirely realistic, a goal to aspire to, a vision of excellence that leads us, if not to the best, then at least to the better — a benign and altogether innocent image. To others it suggests exactly the opposite, a dangerous illusion which tempts us, in the name of the best, to reject the better and end up with the worse. The yearning for perfection that makes reality seem irredeemably flawed creates so large a discrepancy between the ideal and the reality that nothing less will suffice than a total transformation of reality — of society, the polity, the economy, above all, of human nature.

Thomas More

From *Utopia (p. 743)*

For a sampling of the amazing variety of interpretations of Thomas More's *Utopia*, one has only to look at the essays reprinted in the Norton Critical Edition of *Utopia* (1975), edited by Robert M. Adams. *Utopia* has been seen, for example, as a book advocating Christianity (in particular, Roman Catholicism), communism, or colonialism. It seems fairly clear to us, however, that More is not advocating any of these things, at least not as an end in itself. Rather, in this humanistic work he is giving his version of an ideal state based on *reason* alone. But he is a Christian speaking to Christians; presumably his sixteenth-century readers were supposed to say to themselves, "If people without revelation can achieve this degree of decency, surely we, with Christ's help, can achieve more. Our society is far inferior to Utopia; let us strive to equal and then to surpass it."

Perhaps the best short essay on *Utopia* is Edward Surtz's introduction to the Yale paper edition, though Father Surtz sees the book as more Christian than do many other commentators. Among Surtz's points are these:

1. The Utopians are typically Renaissance people, balancing Epicureanism with Christianity, having the best of both worlds. They pursue personal pleasure "until it conflicts with social or religious duties, that is, with the just claims of God or fellow citizens" (p. xiv). The term "pleasure" covers many kinds of actions, from scratching an itch to doing virtuous deeds.

2. Utopian communism "is not an end in itself but the best means to the end: pleasure for all the citizens collectively as well as individually" (p. xiv). "The

ultimate Utopian ideal of communism is . . . to be of one mind. . . . Sharing material possessions can succeed only if there is first one heart and soul in all" (p. xv).

3. Modern critics too often emphasize More's political, social, and economic innovations and neglect his opinions on education, ethics, philosophy, and religion.

4. More's Utopians are not saints; some are even criminals. More does *not* believe, as some moderns do, that people can be conditioned (brainwashed) to think they are freely cooperating in a society that in fact enslaves them. More's Utopians have some leeway, as in the choice of an occupation and in the use of leisure. Believing in the immutability of the soul, they believe that one's final end is not worship of the state but union with the Absolute.

Most students, when asked for the meaning of *Utopian,* will come up with such pejorative words as *unrealistic, impractical, escapist.* They will be surprised, then, to see how realistic More's view of human nature is. He is fully aware, for instance, of such vices as laziness and, especially, pride — not only in non-Utopian countries but even in Utopia. Indeed, he seems to feel that most of our ills are due to pride. To restrain pride, almost all Utopians must engage in manual labor and must wear a simple garment, and, again to restrain pride, there is no private property. Notice that More does not put the blame for our wicked actions entirely on private property or on any other economic factors. True, he does say that Europeans greedily seek to attain superfluities because they fear they may some day be in want, but it is evident that even Utopia has wrongdoers. That is, even the Utopian system cannot prevent some people from engaging in wicked behavior. More does think, however, that some systems allow our wicked natures to thrive, and so he devises a political, economic, and social system that keeps down pride (the root of the other deadly sins).

But it is not only pride that is kept in check. Utopia is severely regulated in many ways. For instance, Utopians are free to do what they wish during their leisure time — provided that they don't loaf, gamble, or hunt. Similarly, they are free to talk — provided that they don't talk politics, except at special times. Discussion of state affairs, except at the appointed times and places, is punishable by death. Orwell's Big Brother is present in More's Utopia, but R. W. Chambers is probably right when he argues (in his *Thomas More* [1935]) that Utopia is founded not on terrorism but on "religious enthusiasm," in particular on faith in God and in the immortality of the soul. Still, even "religious enthusiasm" has, for many readers, something unpleasant about it — something too monastic, too rigid, too disciplined, too cold.

Although one understands and sympathizes with More's condemnation of the pride that engenders social injustice, one can't help but feel that Utopia, with its rational distribution of labor and its evening lectures on edifying topics, is the poorer for lacking the messy vitality of life. (In Utopia, everything seems terribly static: The constitution doesn't change, population is fixed, clothing is uniform, freedom of thought is limited.) On the other hand, we must remember that in the Europe of More's day (and still in much of the world) the masses had to toil from sunrise to sunset to live at a subsistence level. Today's college students (and their professors) find More's Utopia overly restrictive, but they should remember that (1) it is a society of material prosperity for all citizens and a society with a good deal of leisure and (2) it was freer and more tolerant than any of the European societies of its day.

Additional Topics for Critical Thinking and Writing

1. Can it be said that whatever the merits or weaknesses of More's proposal, he has astutely diagnosed the problems of society?

2. More's spokesman says that European society "is a conspiracy of the rich to advance their own interests under the pretext of organizing society" (para. 4). Can the same be said of our society? Explain.

3. Is More's view of human nature "utopian" in the modern sense of the word — that is, is it uncharacteristically benign? Explain.

Niccolò Machiavelli

From *The Prince* (p. 758)

Harvey Mansfield Jr., in the introduction to his translation of *The Prince* (1985), argues that for Machiavelli the only moral laws are those made by human beings: "The rules or laws that exist are those made by governments or other powers acting under necessity, and they must be obeyed out of the same necessity. Whatever is necessary may be called just or reasonable, but justice is no more reasonable than what a person's prudence tells him he must acquire for himself, or submit to, because men cannot afford justice in any sense that transcends their own preservation" (p. xi).

This reading seems, in a way, much like Marx, who argues that ideology (including ideas of justice) is created by the ruling class, though Marx also seems to believe that because this class achieved power through historical necessity, its ideals — during the period in which it holds power — indeed are true. Witness Marx's praise of the bourgeoisie for redeeming the masses from the "idiocies" of rural life.

Perhaps the heart of the issue is this: Although we may believe that we should be governed by people of honor, Machiavelli (and most utilitarians) would argue that personal goodness and political usefulness are distinct things. A person may be an adulterer, a liar, a sadist, or whatever but may still be an effective guardian of the state. Or, expressed more mildly, a governor may sometimes have to sacrifice personal morality for the safety of the state. Bernard Williams argues, in *Public and Private Morality* (Stuart Hampshire, ed. [1978]) that to preserve civilized life, we need politicians who can bring themselves to behave more badly than we ourselves could do. We want them to be as good as possible — and certainly not to be people who act wickedly on a whim or take pleasure in acting wickedly — but to be able to sacrifice personal moral values for political ones. (This idea makes for lively class discussion.)

A related point: If a leader is widely regarded as immoral, he or she loses an important strength, the goodwill of the public. A small example: A senator who is known to have extramarital affairs can probably survive and can be an effective and even an important senator, but a senator who is regarded as a lecher probably cannot.

On the question of whether cruelty may be beneficial to the state: Machiavelli apparently believed that before a state can be justly ruled, there must be a ruler, and to survive the ruler must be cunning and ruthless. One wonders, of course, if a person with these qualities will also act reasonably, using power for the well-being of the state rather than for purely personal goals. Machiavelli, living in the turmoil of early sixteenth-century Italy, concentrates on the qualities necessary for a leader to survive. Thomas More (see the previous selection in the text), on the other hand, shows us a Utopia with almost no political problems, and thus he can concentrate on the morality of the state rather than on the personal characteristics of the governors. Or put it this way: In Machiavelli, it is the ruler against his rivals and his subjects, whereas in More it is society against the individual's unruly passions.

Additional Topics for Critical Thinking and Writing

1. Imitating Machiavelli's style, notably his use of contrasting historical examples, write an essay of 500 words, presenting an argument on behalf of your own view of some quality necessary in a leader today. You may, for example, want to argue that a leader must be a master of television appearances or must be truthful, compassionate, or versed in history. Your essay will, in a sense, be one chapter in a book called *The Prince Today*.

2. James M. Burns's biography of President Franklin Delano Roosevelt (1882–1945) is titled *Roosevelt: The Lion and the Fox* (1956). Judging from your rereading of Chapter XVIII of *The Prince*, indicate in a paragraph the characteristics of Roosevelt that the biographer is suggesting by this title. Read Burns's biography, and write a 1,000-word essay in which you evaluate the aptness of the title, given the facts about Roosevelt's career and Machiavelli's views.

Thomas Jefferson

The Declaration of Independence (p. 766)

In discussing almost any argument (for that matter, in discussing any writing) it is usually helpful to consider the intended or imagined *audience(s)*. With minimal assistance students can see that the Declaration of Independence has several audiences (question 1). These audiences can perhaps be described thus:

1. The "candid world" (para. 5), addressed out of "a decent respect to the opinions of mankind" (para. 1);

2. The King and his ministers (the grievances are blamed on them);

3. The British people (students who do a research paper on the Declaration will learn that some passages censuring the British people were deleted to maintain good relations);

4. France (the Declaration announces that the "United Colonies" have "full power to levy War, conclude Peace, contract Alliances, establish Commerce, and to do all other Acts and Things which Independent States may of right do") (most historians see in these words a bid for foreign aid — military supplies from France); and

5. Those colonists who were not eager for independence.

Attention may be given to the *speaker* of the Declaration — that is, to the self-image (question 3) that the colonists present. Jefferson refers to "a decent respect to the opinions of mankind" (para. 1), and he admits that "Governments long established should not be changed for light and transient causes" (para. 4). Notice too his assertion that "We have petitioned for redress in the most humble terms" (para. 33). In short, the colonists present themselves not as radicals or firebrands but as patient, long-suffering people who are willing to put their case before the tribunal of the world. Notice such words as *duty, necessary,* and *necessity.* They are not rebels; rather, they have been "plundered" and "ravaged" and are exerting a right — the right of the people to alter or to abolish a government that fails to fulfill the legitimate purpose of government (para. 4).

Some attention in class can also be profitably given to discussing the *structure* of the work:

1. The first sentence announces the colonists' purpose, explaining "the causes which impel them to the separation."

2. The core of the document is an exposition of the causes, in two sections:

   a. Theoretical and general justification (for example, "self-evident" truths) and

   b. The list of despotic British actions.

3. The Declaration concludes with the response of the colonies (the signers pledge their lives).

Students can also be shown how the explicit assumptions of the Declaration —

1. All men are created equal and are endowed with "unalienable rights."

2. Governments are instituted to preserve these rights.

3. People have a duty and a right to throw off a despotic government.

— can be cast into this *syllogism:*

1. If a government is despotic, the people have a right to overthrow it and to form a new government.

2. The British government of the American colonies is despotic.

3. Therefore, the people have a right to overthrow it and to form a new government.

The major premise is not argued but is asserted as an "unalienable right." The minor premise is arrived at inductively (instances are cited, and a generalization is drawn from them).

Additional Topics for Critical Thinking and Writing

1. The Declaration is an argument for revolution in a particular society. Investigate conditions in some society (for examaple, Cuba, China, Iran, El Salvador, Nicaragua), and argue that, on the grounds of the Declaration, people in that society do — or do not — have the right to revolt.

2. Read Chapter 19 of John Locke's *Essay Concerning Civil Government* (first published in 1690), and write a 500-word essay in which you identify all those passages or ideas found in Locke that appear also in the Declaration. Are there any ideas in Locke's chapter that have *no* parallel in the Declaration, but that nevertheless seem to you to be relevant to its purpose and content?

Elizabeth Cady Stanton

Declaration of Sentiments and Resolutions (p. 771)

Stanton's Declaration of 1848 is the historic precursor of the decade-long effort that finally failed in 1982 to enact an Equal Rights Amendment (ERA) to the Constitution. The Fourteenth Amendment, enacted twenty years after the Seneca Falls Convention, did provide that no state "shall . . . deprive any person of life, liberty, or property without due process of law, nor deny any person within its jurisdiction the equal protection of the laws." At face value, that might look like the rejection of gender as a basis for lawful discrimination. Opponents of ERA in the 1970s who professed sympathy with feminist claims for constitutional equality often pointed to the language quoted as if that settled the matter. Not so, however.

The term *male* entered the Constitution in the Fourteenth Amendment itself (see section 2), thereby helping to etch more clearly the implicit and historic male bias of the Constitution and the laws from the beginning and indicating that "due process" and "equal protection" were not to be given a gender-free reading. An Illinois case of 1873 settled this issue for decades. Arguing that she was entitled under the Fourteenth Amendment to be admitted to the bar, Myra Bradwell unsuccessfully fought her case through the state courts to the U.S. Supreme Court. The language of the majority's decision enshrined in constitutional interpretation the worst excesses of male chauvinism (see *Bradwell v. Illinois*, 83 U.S. 130 [1873]). Even the right to vote ("elective franchise") (para. 4) was not incorporated into the Constitution until 1920 (the Nineteenth Amendment). Full equality of the sexes under the laws and the Constitution, whether or not it is a good thing, still does not exist in our society.

Civil death (question 3) is the ultimate extreme to which a person can be reduced: denial by law of all civil rights, privileges, immunities, and liberties. (Not even prisoners on death row, today, suffer civil death.) Stanton elaborates the point (paras. 9–11). It was commonplace among feminists of the previous century to point out that marriage under law was functionally equivalent to civil death.

It was not, however, functionally equivalent to chattel slavery (which was to last another fifteen years after the Seneca Falls Convention; not surprisingly, the women who organized the convention were staunch abolitionists). It might be a useful classroom exercise for students to explore the differences under law in the 1840s between the status of American white women, as the Declaration reports it, and the status of American black slaves. An excellent source for slave law is A. Leon Higginbotham Jr., *In the Matter of Color* (1978).

Martin Luther King Jr.

I Have a Dream (p. 775)

The setting (the steps of the Lincoln Memorial, in Washington, D.C., on the centennial of the Emancipation Proclamation) plays an important part in this speech. By the way, few students know that the Emancipation Proclamation did not in fact free any slaves. In 1862 President Lincoln announced that he would declare free the slaves of any state that did not return to the Union. None of the states that had seceded accepted the invitation to return, and so on January 1, 1863, he announced the Emancipation Proclamation. It did not apply to slaves in states such as Maryland and Kentucky that had chosen to stay in the Union, and of course it had no force in the Confederacy. Still, the symbolic importance of the Proclamation was and is immense, and it is part of King's speech.

King's association with Lincoln is evident not only in the setting but also in the language. The opening words, "Five Score," evoke the "Four score and seven years ago" of the Gettysburg Address; and Lincoln himself was evoking the language of the Bible. King's speech, too, richly evokes the Bible ("dark and desolate valley," "God's children," "cup of bitterness," "trials and tribulations," "storms of persecution," "every hill and mountain shall be made low, the rough places will be made straight, and the glory of the Lord shall be revealed, and all flesh shall see it together" — this last from Isaiah 40:4–5).

Another symbol, in addition to Lincoln and to the Bible, is the "American dream" (para. 11, but foreshadowed in the title of the speech), which King, like most other Americans, identifies with the remark in the Declaration of Independence that "All men are created equal." King also identifies his dream (and himself) with "My country, 'tis of thee," and (in the final paragraph) with black spirituals.

The exalted language of the Bible and the Declaration is joined with the humble language of commerce, the "promissory note," the "bad check" of paragraphs 3 and 4, and the whole (because it is a speech) is rich in evocative repetition, especially parallelisms (again a biblical device).

All these devices and allusions are fairly obvious, and that is part of their point. King is emphasizing that speaker and audience share a culture; and though the immediate audience, in Washington, was predominantly black, King knew that his words would also reach a larger audience of whites — whites who share this culture.

The structure (question 6) is this: The first part gives a historical perspective; the second, an exhortation not to fall into evil; the third, an exposition of the dream, a picture of the better world that they can help to bring about.

Additional Topic for Critical Thinking and Writing

King's speech stresses the twin themes of equality and freedom and does not suggest that the two might be in tension or conflict with each other. Do you agree that there is no tension? Try to state precisely the freedom(s) and equalities for which King pleads. Is our society any closer to achieving these goals today, do you think, than in 1963?

Edward Bellamy

Looking Backward (p. 780)

Although the selection from Bellamy is one of the longest in our book, the following comment is short. This is not because there is nothing to say about *Looking Backward* but because the text is lucid and because we are convinced that the best way to treat it in class is to assign one or both of the writing topics that we suggest in the book — either a Bellamy-like vision of life a hundred years from now or an evaluation of the practicability of Bellamy's vision.

Inevitably discussion in class focuses on Bellamy's socialistic vision — a society with nationalized industry and economic stability — made possible (in his view) by technology (and presumably by the fundamental goodness of human nature). But we do want to call attention to the extended metaphor that looks at the wretched society of his day (para. 4). He compares

> society as it then was to a prodigious coach which the masses of humanity were harnessed to and dragged toilsomely along a very hilly and sandy road. The driver was hunger, and permitted no lagging though the pace was necessarily very slow. Despite the difficulty of drawing the coach at all along so hard a road, the top was covered with passengers who never got down, even at the steepest ascents. These seats on top were very breezy and comfortable. Well up out of the dust, their occupants could enjoy the scenery at their leisure, or critically discuss the merits of the straining team. Naturally such places were in great demand and the competition for them was keen, every one seeking as the first end in life to secure a seat on the coach for himself and to leave it to his child after him.

Here is Bellamy's view of a capitalistic world of struggle.

Let's assume for the moment that Bellamy's metaphor is apt or at least that it was apt for his day: Life for most people was very hard, but for a few people it was easy. How are we to feel about this fact? Here is Andrew Carnegie's view, published in 1889, only a year after the publication of *Looking Backward:*

> While the law [of competition] may be sometimes hard for the individual, it is best for the race, because it insures the survival of the fittest in every department. We accept and welcome, therefore, as conditions to which we must accommodate ourselves, great inequality of environment, the concentration of business, industrial and commercial, in the hands of a few, and the law of competition between these, as being not only beneficial, but essential for the future progress of the race.

Andrew Carnegie is not kidding; he expresses mild concern for the losers ("While the law may be sometimes hard for the individual"), but picking up Herbert Spencer's words, "the survival of the fittest" (a moralized interpretation of what Darwin called "the struggle for existence"), he sees the fierce struggle as unquestionably "best for the race."

Bellamy, as readers of *Looking Backward* know, did indeed think that the capitalistic struggle that led toward larger and larger monopolies indeed would prove best for the race, but not because the system would produce the increasingly hardy specimens that social Darwinists valued and called "better." In Bellamy's view, the future socialistic state would come into being because "large responsible corporations" would be replaced by "a single syndicate representing the people . . . conducted in the common interest for the common people." This "syndicate" would, in the absence of competition, be able to produce goods efficiently and therefore cheaply. Since there would be enough goods for all, greed would disappear, and people would be motivated not by a desire for money or for what money can buy but by patriotism and "passion for humanity." Bellamy's symbol for his collectivist idea is the canopy that is lowered over streets on rainy days, replacing individual umbrellas.

Bellamy, in the extended metaphor of the coach, in a marvelous ironic passage (para. 5) glances at the alleged benevolence of the fortunate people who ride on top of the coach:

> But did they think only of themselves? you ask. Was not their very luxury rendered intolerable to them by comparison with the lot of their brothers and sisters in the harness, and the knowledge that their own weight added to their toil? Had they no compassion for fellow beings from whom fortune only distinguished them? Oh, yes: commiseration was frequently expressed by those who rode for those who had to pull the coach, especially when the vehicle came to a bad place in the road, as it was constantly doing, or to a particularly steep hill. At such times, the desperate straining of the team, their agonized leaping and plunging under the pitiless lashing of hunger, the many who fainted at the rope and were trampled in the mire, make a very distressing spectacle, which often called forth highly creditable displays of feeling on the top of the coach. At such times the passengers would call down encouragingly to the toilers of the rope, exhorting them to patience, and holding out hopes of possible compensation in another world for the hardness of their lot, while others contributed to buy salves and liniments for the crippled and the injured. It was agreed that it was a great pity that the coach should be so hard to pull, and there was a sense of great relief when the specially bad piece of road was gotten over. The relief was not, indeed, wholly on account of the team, for there was always some danger at these bad places of a general overturn in which all would lose their seats.

The metaphor is not really necessary to his view of his Utopian world. In fact, in its representation of the seated passengers it introduces questions about the inherent stupidity or hypocrisy of human nature that perhaps the rest of the book forgets about. But it seems to us much too good to be omitted, and we suggest that it is worth discussing in class, both as a piece of writing and as an analysis of human nature. (Bellamy, it should be added, believed that people in his ideal world had indeed become "purified" — were made better — by the change in the social system.)

One other point: *Looking Backward* is unusual among utopian writings because it not only depicts a utopia but also explains how this ideal world came into being. Bellamy had seen a variety of small utopian communities come and go, and he had concluded that what was needed was not a group of few like-minded people but a new kind of state. Some fifty years before the publication of *Looking Backward*, Alexis de Tocqueville had said that America was characterized by "equality of condition" but that the Industrial Revolution had changed all that. As we mentioned a moment ago, Bellamy envisioned the transformation of private monopolies into a single state monopoly. Today, few people are so sanguine, and whatever utopias we have are of the small, old sort.

W. H. Auden

The Unknown Citizen (p. 799)

In "The Unknown Citizen" the speaker's voice is obviously not the poet's. The speaker — appropriately unidentified in a poem about a society without individuals — is apparently a bureaucrat. For such a person, a "saint" is not one who is committed to spiritual values but one who causes no trouble.

Additional Topics for Critical Thinking and Writing

1. What is W. H. Auden satirizing in "The Unknown Citizen"? (Students might be cautioned to spend some time thinking about whether Auden is satirizing the speaker, the citizen, conformism, totalitarianism, technology, or what.)

2. Write a prose eulogy of 250 words satirizing contemporary conformity or, if you prefer, contemporary individualism.

3. Was he free? Was he happy? Argue your view.

4. In a paragraph or two, sketch the values of the speaker of the poem, and then sum them up in a sentence or two. Finally, in as much space as you feel you need, judge these values.

Langston Hughes

Let America Be America Again (p. 800)

It is sometimes difficult to remember that poets (or at least some of them) once were regarded as national bards, celebrating the ideals of society. On the whole, today we distrust public oratory, and we are much more comfortable with the idea of the poet as the reporter of private feelings. In short, we prefer the private lyric to such public lyric forms as the ode and the hymn. People who believe that poetry ought to address public themes are likely to complain that poetry has turned inward on itself and has retreated from life. They may point out that although there are all sorts of poetry festivals and public readings, the poetry is likely to be confessional — for instance, the expression of the emotions of an abandoned woman, a gay man, or the child of immigrant Jews or Hispanics. In fact, such poems are deeply rooted in the politics and social practices of our age. (For an example, see Mitsuye Yamada, "To the Lady," p. 885.)

Still, it must be said that poems explicitly about the nation — patriotic poems — are now rare. We can hardly imagine a poet today writing something like "Barbara Frietchie" (the stuff of our school days), "Paul Revere's Ride," or "O Captain, My Captain." Today we seem chiefly to value what Harold Bloom has crankily called "The Poetry of Resentment." Hughes did not by any means write the sort of poetry that Bloom castigates, but the Hughes poems that we value most highly do seem to come directly from the life that he observed closely — for instance, his poems about prostitution and poverty in Harlem. But there is another Hughes, the Hughes who for a while saw himself as an heir to Walt Whitman and especially to Carl Sandburg, and it was in this role that he wrote "Let America Be America Again." Although the influence of Whitman and Sandburg was great, Hughes of course drew also on black sources. In particular, the motif that America has been America (the land of the free) only for some whites was common in black prose — for instance, in the writings of Frederick Douglass. Hughes also drew, very evidently, on radical socialist thought, and doubtless that is why (as we indicate in question 3) *Esquire* published only the first fifty lines. Lines 1–50 offer a strong indictment, but they stop short of preaching revolution. The gist of the idea in these lines is that America today should be true to its original ideals, the ideals of the founding fathers. No one can disapprove of this ideal. But Hughes goes a bit further: Blacks, he says, have not shared in this society ("America never was America to me"), and early in the poem he links the marginalization of blacks with that of poor whites (line 19) and immigrants (line 45). True enough; almost everyone would grant, "Yes, it's not just that today we have lost some of our ideals; we failed from the start to extend them to all of our people." But beyond line 50 the poem gets more radical, as Hughes specifies additional victims — unemployed people on relief (line 53) and Native Americans (line 65). The suggestion that injustice extended to groups beyond blacks must have sounded menacing enough even to the liberal editors of *Esquire*, but in line 73 we hear (and the editors of *Esquire* must have heard) a still more radical note, a call to revolution: "We must take back our land again" and "We, the people, must redeem / The land, the mines, the plants, the rivers" (lines 82–84). The editors doubtless knew that this talk of the redemptive power of "the people," especially as opposed to the "leeches" of line 72, was the voice of the extreme left wing. Our own view, for what it is worth, is that the shorter poem (lines 1–50, as opposed to 1–86) is the better poem, partly — we confess, because the call to "take back" the land is left unexplained.

Ursula K. Le Guin

The Ones Who Walk away from Omelas (p. 803)

When Thomas More called his book *Utopia*, he punned on the Greek "good place" (*eu topos*) and on "no place" (*ou topos*). Like all of the rest of us, he knew that the fully happy society is "no place," if only because accidents, disease, and death are part of life. Le Guin's narrator gives us a fairly detailed description of an imagined happy society — Omelas is "bright-towered by the sea," the old celebrants in the festival wear "long stiff robes of mauve and grey," and the boys and girls are "naked in the bright air, with mud-stained feet and ankles and long, lithe arms" —but the narrator also is vague about many things that we would dearly like to know. For instance, although the narrator tells us that there is no king and there are no slaves in Omelas, the narrator also makes a confession, "I do not know the rules and laws of their society." The story includes other confessions of ignorance, and at one point the narrator, aware that the narrative thus far has been unconvincing and fairy-tale like (for example, those bright towers by the sea), almost gives up and urges the reader to imagine Omelas "as your own fancy bids."

Doubtless Le Guin is vague about important matters because she — like everyone else — cannot depict a convincing Utopia that can withstand scrutiny. But she is also vague for a more important reason: She is not earnestly writing a Utopian tale like, say, Edward Bellamy's *Looking Backward*. Rather, she is raising a moral problem, or, more exactly, she is amplifying a problem that William James had raised. Omelas need not be a convincing presentation of the perfectly happy life, and indeed the narrator makes Omelas most convincing when he (or she?) prefaces the information about the suffering child with these words: "Do you believe? Do you accept the festival, the city, the joy? No? Then let me describe one more thing." When we learn about the wretched child, Omelas becomes much more believable, for we are all aware that much of our happiness in fact depends on the suffering of others. These others may be the exploited workers whose painful labor allows us to eat and dress well; they may be the sick, whose ills make some physicians prosperous; they may be the aggrieved, whose lawsuits pay the college tuition for the children of lawyers; they may even be the suffering animals whose pain in medical laboratories may help to alleviate our own pain. In short, whoever we are, some of our happiness depends on the misfortunes of other creatures — and at times we are aware of this fact. Le Guin's happy city now becomes easily understandable: It is an image not of an ideal world but of our world.

Where a parable usually evokes a fairly clear moral and leaves us in little doubt about how we ought to act, this story leaves us puzzled. It heightens our awareness of a cruel fact of society, but it does not tell us how we can reform our society. Put another way, where does one go when one walks away from Omelas? Can we really envisage the possibility of a happy life that is not in any way based on suffering and injustice somewhere? Is the story therefore pointless, mere fantasy, mere escapism? Presumably Le Guin is simply seeking to make us think so that we will learn to act in ways that minimize the suffering of others. It is inconceivable that life will ever be Utopian, but it is not inconceivable that injustice and human suffering may be reduced.

Additional Topics for Critical Thinking and Writing

1. How convincing does the narrator think the picture of Omelas is? Why do you suppose that Le Guin did not offer details about the laws of the land? Does Omelas become more convincing when we learn about the child? Support your response with evidence.

2. What is the point of walking away from Omelas? Can the walker go to a better society? If not, is the story pointless? (Put another way, the story is a fantasy, but is it also escapist fiction?)

28
How Free Is the Will of the Individual within Society? (p. 809)

Plato

Crito (p. 810)

The headnote in the text gives a fairly full account of the context of *Crito*, both in Socrates' life and in Plato's dialogues. After decades of relative neglect, this dialogue, with its argument over the citizen's obligation to the state, has recently aroused interest among scholars, and several good books (among them those by A. D. Woozley and Richard Kraut) now are available to guide the interested reader through the intricacies of Plato's text.

The dialogue can be divided into three parts of unequal length and importance. In the brief first part (which ends when Crito says "Your death means a double calamity for me"), Plato does little more than set the stage. In the longer second part (which ends when Socrates offers the plea of "the Laws and Constitution of Athens"), Crito makes his feeble attempt to persuade Socrates to escape, and Socrates in rather leisurely fashion examines and rejects Crito's reasons. The final and longest part is also the most important because in it Socrates advances an early version of the social-contract argument for political obligation, later made famous and influential by Locke and Rousseau and revived in recent years in the sophisticated moral philosophy of John Rawls (see his *A Theory of Justice* [1971]). Socrates makes no attempt to rebut this long argument; the reader (along with Crito) is led to think that Socrates must, in all honesty, concede each step and so draw the conclusion the Laws want him to draw.

As for the adequacy of this argument (question 6), the notion of a "just agreement" between the individual citizen and the abstract state looks quite implausible if taken literally, even in the city-state of Athens. But if taken as a metaphor or as a model of an ideal relationship between the individual and the laws, then one has to answer this question: How can a hypothetical or ideal relation impose any actual or real obligation on anyone? The result is a classic dilemma for social-contract theorists, not easily resolved.

The dialogue can be effectively paired with Martin Luther King Jr.'s "Letter from Birmingham Jail" (p. 839). The most obvious difference between the positions of Socrates and King (questions 8 and 9) is that Socrates implies that the laws of Athens are just — though, unfortunately, wrongly applied to Socrates himself by his Athenian judges — whereas King asserts that the laws of Alabama are unjust and implies their application to him is unjust. In particular, Socrates implies that he gave his free and informed consent to the authority of Athens's laws, whereas King implies that black Americans never gave their free consent to segregation laws.

Samuel Johnson and James Boswell

Do We Have Free Will? (p. 823)

"Edwards of New England" is, of course, Jonathan Edwards, whose writings on free will and other philosophical-theological topics secure him a prominent place in the history of American philosophy. (For edifying diversion read his famous Calvinist sermon, "Sinners in the Hands of an Angry God.") The free-will controversy historically divides into two problems: (1) Can we reconcile divine foreknowledge (as James Boswell puts it, "universal prescience") of all events from eternity with human free will? and (2) Can we reconcile universal natural causality (scientific determinism) with human free will? Boswell alludes to the first problem but not to the second.

Johnson's blunt commonsensical defense of free will appeals to our certainty that one can "lift up [a] finger or not" as one pleases. Suppose (to reformulate the issue) I can do either *A* or *B*, and I decide to do *A* if a coin turns up heads or do *B* if it turns up tails. The coin is flipped and turns up heads. If I then do *A,* surely that *act* is "free." Of course, my *will* might not be free (did I decide to do *A* if the coin turns up heads out of some "necessity" of which I am unaware?).

Johnson moves the argument in another direction. He suggests it is certain that either he will go home that night or that he will not; this proposition is a tautology, of the form: *p* or *not-p*. Like all tautologies, it cannot be false. Johnson then rightly points out that the necessity of the truth of that proposition "does not prevent [his] freedom" in deciding whether to go home or not.

But Boswell, after agreeing with the above, insists that "if one of these events be certain now, you have no future power of volition. If it be certain you are to go home tonight, you must go home." Johnson dodges the point, but we won't. Boswell is just wrong. First, we have reason to believe the antecedent of his conditional ("one of these events be certain now") only if we believe that God has complete foreknowledge of all events. Edwards and other Calvinists did believe that, and probably Boswell did too, but did Johnson? Second, Boswell tries to infer a necessity in events ("you must go home") from a certainty in knowledge ("it be certain you are to go home tonight") of those events. But no such inference is valid. If I am certain that Whirlaway will win the Derby (I've bribed the other jockeys, doped the other horses, among other ploys), it doesn't follow that Whirlaway will necessarily win. Boswell's basic error, in short, is to try to infer a metaphysical necessity from an epistemological certainty. But knowledge, whether human or divine, does not control events; it does not make anything necessary or contingent. If anything, it is the other way around.

George Orwell

Shooting an Elephant (p. 825)

Orwell explicitly tells us that his experience as a police officer in Burma was "perplexing and upsetting" (para. 2). (One might compare this statement with the feelings of Thomas Hardy's soldier in "The Man He Killed," p. 868.) He characterizes himself as "young and ill-educated" at the time (clearly in the past), and he says he was caught between his hatred of imperialism and his rage against the Burmese. The essay's paradoxical opening sentence foreshadows its chief point (that imperialism destroys the freedom of both the oppressor and the oppressed), but Orwell devotes the rest of the first paragraph, with its ugly characterizations of the Burmese, to dramatizing his rage. Students unaware of Orwell's preoccupation with decency may fail to understand that the first two paragraphs do not contradict but reinforce each other. The racial slurs in the first paragraph and elsewhere in the essay are deliberate; they show the alienation from normal feelings, the violations of self that were, as Orwell goes on to show, the by-products of his role.

That he was playing a role — but a role that captured the player — is highlighted by the theatrical metaphors that accumulate as he is about to shoot the elephant: he sees himself as a "conjurer" with a "magical rifle," as an "actor," and as "an absurd puppet" (para. 7).

The essay's final paragraph, with its cold tone, its conflicting half-truths and rationalizations, again effectively dramatizes the deadening of feeling and loss of integrity Orwell experienced and that he believes all who turn tyrant experience.

Walter T. Stace

Is Determinism Inconsistent with Free Will? (p. 831)

The general position taken by Stace on the free-will controversy is owed — though Stace doesn't mention it — to the Scots philosopher David Hume. In his *Enquiry Concerning Human Understanding* (1748), Section VIII, "Of Liberty and Necessity," Hume argues that if acting of one's own free will means acting without external coercion or internal compulsion, and if "necessity" (or determinism) means that every event has a cause, then there is no incompatibility between the two. We reprint Stace's version of the solution to the free-will problem (a version of what is now called *compatibilism*) rather than Hume's because it is briefer and much more accessible to the modern reader.

The answer to question 1, stated as a formal deductive argument, goes like this:

1. If one acts without free will, then one cannot be held responsible for what one does.

2. If one cannot be held responsible for one's acts, then moral praise and blame — morality, in short — are impossible.

3. Therefore, if one acts without free will, then morality is impossible.

The argument as stated is surely valid. It has the form: if p then q, if q then r, therefore if p then r — a case of a hypothetical syllogism and a valid form of reasoning. Most philosophers think it is sound; whether it is, of course, depends on the truth of both premises. Of the two, premise 1 is likely to be the more controversial.

Now consider question 9. Here is a valid argument in the spirit of Stace's views in paragraph 28:

1. A person's acts must be the effects of her beliefs and decisions for her to be morally responsible for those acts.

2. A person's acts must be predetermined for those acts to be the effects of her beliefs and decisions.

3. Therefore, unless determinism is true at least as regards a person's acts, no one is morally responsible for anything.

Here, the more problematic premise is the second one.

Regarding question 2, a classic example of a purely verbal dispute is arguing whether a glass of water is half full or half empty or whether you are taller than I am or I am shorter than you are. Such disputes are absurd, since in truth neither party can be correct unless the other is also; what is at stake in the dispute is nothing but each disputant's preferred way of stating the facts. There is no dispute about any fact of the matter.

Stace's claim that the free-will controversy is "merely verbal" or is "a semantic problem" (para. 3) is slightly more complicated. The problem arises because the term *free will* has been incorrectly defined ("by learned men, especially philosophers," he says), with the result that nothing counts as action of one's own free will. This, Stace argues, is absurd because in the ordinary sense of the phrase "He did so-and-so of his own free will," it is perfectly clear that such an imputation has plenty of applications. So Stace in effect says the free-will controversy is "merely verbal" because whether we act with a free will turns entirely on how we define *free will*.

As a side note, Stace's strategy in this essay is reminiscent of the linguistic analytic philosophy that flourished in the 1950s and 1960s here and in Great Britain (though a reader of the book from which our excerpt is taken will find no other evidence of sympathy with that style of philosophy). He proposes to defend the compatibility of free will and determinism by relying on "common usage . . . in ordinary conversation" (para. 8) — that is, he will rely on the way ordinary people talk in deciding whether someone did or did not act of his or her own free will. We think his examples of conversation (paras. 9–10, 14) do reflect ordinary usage and show us how we do use the term *free will*. These snippets also show that people believe they can tell whether someone is acting out of a free will; Stace implies this is enough to show they are correct in this belief (and he does not seem to worry about addressing that issue directly).

Not one to have been overawed by professional academic philosophers (prior to a midcareer move into teaching and writing philosophy, Stace had rendered long years in the British foreign service and like many of his British academic contemporaries earlier in this century never pursued any postgraduate degrees in philosophy), Stace concocts an outrageous imaginary conversation between a philosopher and a jury foreman (para. 12). The philosopher's unforgivable error, Stace claims, is to think that a person can act of his or her own free will if and only if that act is *not* the effect of any causes. But as the earlier hypothetical dialogues showed not being the effect of any cause has nothing to do with the meaning of *free will* in ordinary discourse.

Stace does not point out that his pompous philosopher talks as if he had made a momentous discovery: "there is no such thing as free will." Compare that to "there is no such thing as a square circle" and "there is no such thing as a unicorn." Both these propositions are true, but only the latter is true as a matter of fact; the former is true by implicit definition of the terms. Has the philosopher who insists there is no such thing as free will made a discovery about any matter of fact? No. Has he drawn a necessary conclusion from the ordinary meaning of the terms being used? Again, no. (By the way, just what real, as opposed to imaginary, philosophers Stace may have in mind here is not clear to us. His discussion is none the worse if in fact no philosophers ever actually argued as in his example.) So the philosopher's rejection of the very possibility of anyone acting of free will can be entirely ignored.

The classic objection to compatibilism of the sort Stace defends is that it fails to guarantee that there are free *acts* because it fails to guarantee that these acts are the effects of a free *will*. The careful reader will note that the explicit definitions that Stace gives (para. 18) of free versus unfree *acts* are silent on the freedom or unfreedom of the *will*. Libertarians (in the metaphysical, not the political, sense of that term) argue, plausibly enough, that unless the will is free, the acts caused by that will cannot be free. And so one might well reject Stace's definition of "acts done freely" as acts where the "immediate causes are psychological states of the agent" because that is far too broad and too silent on the status of the agent's will. It is too broad because it all depends on just what kind of "psychological state" is in question. For surely a person who acts out of inner compulsion, posthypnotic trance, or an addiction would not be said to act freely. It is too silent because we need to know more about what constitutes the psychological states that do result in free acts. We do not have an adequate theory of free will until we have solved these problems.

For further reading in the spirit of the Hume-Stace approach to the problem of free will, we select from a whole library of books one that is unusually original, informative, and even entertaining, the volume titled *Elbow Room* (1984) by our colleague D. C. Dennett.

Martin Luther King Jr.

Letter from Birmingham Jail (p. 839)

King's letter was prompted by a letter (printed in the text) by eight Birmingham clergymen. His letter is unusually long ("Never before have I written so long a letter") because he was jailed at the time and thus was unable to speak to audiences face to face.

King here goes to some length to show that his work is thoroughly in the American (and Judeo-Christian) tradition. That is, although he rebuts the letter of the eight clergymen, he represents himself not as a radical or in any way un-American (and of course not as an opponent of the Judeo-Christian tradition), but as one who shares the culture of his audience. Thus, although he rejects the clergymen's view that he is impatient, he begins by acknowledging their decency. They are, he says, "men of genuine goodwill" — and in saying this King thereby implies that he too is a man of goodwill. Moreover, King's real audience is not only the eight clergymen but all readers of his letter, who are assumed to be decent folk. Notice, too, in his insistence that he is speaking on an issue that involves all Americans, his statement that "injustice anywhere is a threat to justice everywhere" (para. 4). But his chief strategy early in the letter is to identify himself with Paul (para. 3) and thus to guide his mainly Christian audience to see him as carrying on a tradition that they cherish. Notice also the references to Niebuhr, Buber (a Jew), and Jesus.

It is usual, and correct, to say that King is a master of the appeal to emotion. This essay reveals such mastery, as when he quotes a five-year-old boy: "Daddy, why do white people treat colored people so mean?" (para. 14). And because King is really addressing not so much the eight clergymen as a sympathetic audience that probably needs encouragement to persist rather than reasons to change their beliefs, an emotional (inspirational) appeal is appropriate. But the essay is also rich in lucid exposition and careful analysis, as in paragraph 6 (on the four steps of a nonviolent campaign) and paragraphs 15 and 16 (comparing just and unjust laws).

Additional Topics for Critical Thinking and Writing

1. Think of some injustice that you know something about, and jot down the facts as objectively as possible. Arrange them so that they form an outline. Then, using these facts as a framework, write an essay (possibly in the form of a letter to a specific audience) of about 500 words, presenting your case in a manner somewhat analogous to King's. For example, don't hesitate to make comparisons with biblical, literary, or recent historical material, to use personal experiences, or to use any other persuasive devices you wish, including appeals to the emotions. Hand in the objective list along with the essay.

2. If some example of nonviolent direct action has recently been in the news, such as actions by persons fearful of nuclear power plants, write an essay evaluating the tactics and their effectiveness in dealing with the issue.

3. Read Plato's *Crito,* and also Plato's *Apology* (in your library). Write an essay of 500 words explaining whether, as King says, "Socrates practiced civil disobedience."

Stanley Milgram

The Perils of Obedience (p. 855)

Milgram's chief finding ("adults [are willing] to go to almost any lengths on the command of an authority") is hardly cheering, especially when we realize that (1) this finding was based on experiments in a university laboratory and did not involve dire threats or coercion and (2) the experiments seemingly required one person to inflict severe pain on another person merely because (a) the person caused to suffer had failed a trivial memory test and (b) the experimenter insisted that the pain be inflicted no matter how anguished the response of the sufferer.

To be sure, not every subject complied; Milgram professed to be amazed that so few — only 40 percent — refused (para. 24). We take little consolation from the fact that in Munich, Germany, 85 percent of the subjects — the highest percent achieved anywhere the experiment was performed — were obedient to the end (para. 29).

Do the results of Milgram's experiments really reveal "the banality of evil" — that is, one need not be a sadist or otherwise pathological to be willing to do horrible things to others simply because one is under "superior orders" (para. 96)? An interesting project for students in connection with studying Milgram's essay would be to read Hannah Arendt's *Eichmann in Jerusalem* (1963) and write a 500-word report on the "banality of evil."

Doubts about Milgram's findings were raised in the *New York Times* by Christopher Lehmann-Haupt (Jan. 3, 1974, p. 39) in his review of Milgram's book, *Obedience to Authority: An Experimental View* (1974), from which our excerpt is taken. He pointed out that Milgram's subjects were hardly a true cross-section of society; most participated out of "curiosity about 'science'" and were paid a modest fee for their services.

Lehmann-Haupt also wondered just how despairing of ourselves the experimental results ought to leave us. If 40 percent of Milgram's "ordinary people" as subjects eventually refused to obey the seemingly cruel orders of the experimenter, perhaps we are not as mindless and inhumane as first appears.

Even before Milgram's book was published, his research provoked grave doubts about the ethical status of his experiments. In a brief essay in *American Psychologist* 19 (1964): 848–52), he replied to critics that there was nothing immoral about his research, even though it depended essentially on misrepresenting what was going on to the subjects involved and forcing them into a crisis of conscience. Little did they know their victims were in fact actors pretending to suffer agony and that the voltage generator was a fake. Is it a satisfactory response to say (as some of Milgram's defenders did) that psychologists constantly perform experiments that depend essentially on manipulating and misrepresenting the situation to their human subjects? (If you are interested in pursuing these issues further, read Steven C. Patten, "The Case that Milgram Makes," *Philosophical Review* 86 (1977): 350–64, and his "Milgram's Shocking Experiments," *Philosophy* 52 (1977): 425–40.)

Thomas Hardy

The Man He Killed (p. 868)

Almost every student will be able to report the occurrence of some action they took that seems just to have happened, unwilled and inexplicable. Or if they can explain it, the consequences nevertheless seem vastly disproportionate to the action. With such happenings in mind, one finds oneself murmuring that chance governs all or, if one is given to proverbs, "Man proposes, God disposes." Taking a long view of things, they may comment on how little each of us can actually control by our wills. After all, we did not will our own existence or the family that surrounds us, and it takes only a little thought to realize that, had a different person in the Admissions Office read our application, we might not have been admitted to the college where we now are taking classes and making friends. And yet most students will also report that they certainly *feel* free — that they can decide to come to class or to cut class, to take this course or that course, to major in this subject or that subject, and to enter this field or that field. Samuel Johnson, in a passage that we reprint in the text, sums up this contradictory state: "All theory is against the freedom of the will; all experience for it."

Hardy's speaker, presumably a fairly simple ordinary fellow (notice the diction, which includes such words as "'list" [for "enlist"] and "off-hand-like") who enlisted because he was out of work and had no money, found himself (given the date, probably in South Africa, during the Boer War) face to face with another man, who was, he had been told, his "foe," so he did what he was supposed to do: He shot his "foe." The experience has stayed in his mind, and the best *reason* he can offer for his action is to say that war is "quaint and curious." But the fact that he is repeating the story indicates that he himself is not fully satisfied with his own explanation. Presumably he thinks he acted freely, but he is somewhat puzzled by his action. We, with our superior view, can see that he was the victim of economic circumstances (he was unemployed) and the victim of an imperialistic government that used him for its own purposes.

In discussing the poem one may find oneself talking about the irony of fate, whereby a man who joined the army to keep himself alive finds that he has to kill another man who is pretty much like him. Almost surely students will see that there is a gap between their awareness and the speaker's unawareness, but they may also agree that all of us, no matter how clever we think we are, move in a world that is largely mysterious to us, a world that (in Hamlet's words) "shapes our ends, / Rough-hew them how we will."

T. S. Eliot

The Love Song of J. Alfred Prufrock (p. 869)

Few instructors in introductory courses will encounter students who have much familiarity with poetry, but you may find that some students have read Robert Browning's "My Last Duchess" and have been instructed in the ways of the dramatic monologue, usually defined as a poem with a speaker and a listener. It will be necessary to explain to these students that "Prufrock" is a different sort of monologue, an internal monologue. At least this is the way we take it; the "you" (as we say in this manual on p. 53) is the speaker's amorous self, addressed by his timorous self. In our view, the speaker does not actually make a visit — or at least may not — and does not speak aloud to anyone; rather, he imagines a visit, with all of its distressing episodes, and we hear an unspoken inner debate. In the words that John Stuart Mill used to characterize lyric poetry, we get "feeling confessing itself to itself."

(Again, we refer to this manual on p. 53, where, in a discussion of the relevance of the author's interpretation of a work, we quote T. S. Eliot himself, saying something different.)

"Prufrock" gives us a particularly inhibited protagonist, but we assume that all readers can empathize with his sense of paralysis. After all, the epigraph that opens the poem — in medieval Italian, a language that most of us do not know — is in itself almost enough to terrify the reader, to turn all of us into Prufrocks who dare not read another line lest we again reveal our inadequacies. Having said this, we want to assure instructors that the poem *can* be taught effectively, despite all of the footnotes. Students enjoy talking about the speaker's name (a combination of *prude* and *frock*, therefore suggesting what in politically incorrect days was called an *old maid*?), about the people at the cocktail party commenting on Michelangelo, about the comic rhyme of *crisis* and *ices*, about Prufrock momentarily gaining strength by the absurd expedient of thinking about his collar and his stickpin, and so forth. A good way to proceed is to ask a student to read the first stanza and then to invite comments on what the students like (or find especially interesting) about the passage. In our experience, with only a little assistance, they will comment on particularly memorable phrases and images. And so on, stanza by stanza; they may admit, for instance, that Prufrock's terrors (his fear that people will say, "How his arms and legs are thin") are not foreign to their own thoughts. Have they ever feared they would be judged absurd? (We have never gone so far as to ask if they have ever judged themselves absurd.) Do they dare to wear clothing not sanctioned by contemporary fashion?

Suggestion: In class make use of *T. S. Eliot Reading "The Love Song of J. Alfred Prufrock,"* a recording (one cassette) available through HarperAudio.

Susan Glaspell

Trifles (p. 874)

Some students may know Glaspell's other version of this work, a short story titled "A Jury of Her Peers." Class discussion can focus on the interchangeability of the titles. "Trifles" could have been called "A Jury of Her Peers," and vice versa. A peer, of course, is an equal, and the suggestion of the story's title is that Mrs. Wright is judged by a jury of her equals — Mrs. Hale and Mrs. Peters. A male jury would not consist of her equals because, at least in the context of the story and the play, males simply don't have the experiences of women and therefore can't judge them fairly.

Murder is the stuff of TV dramas, and this play concerns a murder, of course, but it's worth asking students how the play differs from a whodunnit. Discussion will soon establish that we learn, early in "Trifles," who performed the murder, and we even know, fairly early, *why* Minnie killed her husband. (The women know what is what because they correctly interpret "trifles," but the men are baffled, since they are looking for obvious signs of anger.) Once we know who performed the murder, the interest shifts to the question of whether the women will cover up for Minnie.

The distinction between what the men and the women look for is paralleled in the distinction between the morality of the men and the women. The men stand for law and order and for dominance (they condescend to the women, and the murdered Wright can almost be taken as a symbol of male dominance), whereas the women stand for mutual support or nurturing. Students might be invited to argue about *why* the women protect Minnie. Is it because women are nurturing? Or because they feel guilt for their earlier neglect of Minnie? Or because, being women, they know what her sufferings must have been like and feel that she acted justly? All of the above?

Mitsuye Yamada

To the Lady (p. 885)

First, some background: In 1942 the entire Japanese and Japanese American population on the Pacific coast — about 112,000 people — was incarcerated and relocated. More than two-thirds of the people moved were native-born citizens of the United States. (The 158,000 Japanese residents of the Territory of Hawaii were not affected.)

Immediately after the Japanese attack on Pearl Harbor, many journalists, the general public, Secretary of the Army Henry Stimson, and congressional delegations from California, Oregon, and Washington called for the internment. Although Attorney General Francis Biddle opposed it, on February 19, 1942, President Franklin D. Roosevelt signed Executive Order 9066, allowing military authorities "to prescribe military areas . . . from which any or all persons may be excluded." In practice, no persons of German or Italian heritage were disturbed, but the Japanese and Japanese Americans on the Pacific coast were rounded up (they were allowed to take with them "only that which can be carried") and relocated in camps. Congress, without a dissenting vote, passed legislation supporting the evacuation. A few Japanese Americans challenged the constitutionality of the proceeding but with no immediate success. (For two good short accounts, with suggestions for further readings, see the articles titled "Japanese Americans, wartime relocation of," in *Kodansha Encyclopedia of Japan* 4:17–18, and "War Relocation Authority" in *Kodansha Encyclopedia of Japan* 8:228. For a readable account of life in a camp, see Jeanne Wakatsuki Houston's *Farewell to Manzanar* [1973].)

It may be interesting to read Mitsuye Yamada's poem aloud in class, *without* having assigned it for prior reading, and to ask students for their responses at various stages — after lines 4, 21, and 36. Lines 1 to 4 pose a question that perhaps many of us (young and old, and whether of Japanese descent or not) have asked, at least to ourselves. The question, implying a criticism of the victims, shows an insufficient awareness of Japanese or Japanese American culture of the period. It also shows an insufficient awareness of American racism; by implying that protest by the victims *could* have been effective, it reveals ignorance of the terrific hostility of whites toward persons of Japanese descent.

The first part of the response shows one aspect of the absurdity of the lady's question. Japanese and Japanese Americans were brought up not to stand out in any way (certainly not to make a fuss) and to place the harmony of the group (whether the family or society as a whole) above individual expression. Further, there was nothing that these people could effectively do, even if they had shouted as loudly as Kitty Genovese did. For the most part they were poor, had no political clout, and were hated and despised as Asians. The absurdity of the view that they could have resisted effectively is comically stated in "should've pulled myself up from my / bra straps" (echoing the red-blooded American ideal of pulling oneself up by one's bootstraps), but of course the comedy is bitter.

Then the speaker turns to "YOU," nominally the "lady" of the title but in effect also the reader, and by ironically saying what we would have done points out what in fact we did not do. (The references to a march on Washington and letters to Congress are clear enough, but most students will not be aware of the tradition that the King of Denmark said that he would wear a Star of David [line 27] if Danish Jews were compelled by Nazis to wear the star.)

Thus far the speaker has put the blame entirely on the white community, especially since lines 5 to 21 strongly suggest that the Japanese Americans *couldn't* do anything except submit. Yet the poem ends with a confession that because Japanese Americans docilely subscribed to "law and order" — especially the outrageous Executive

Order 9066 — they were in fact partly responsible for the outrage committed against them. The last line of the poem, "All are punished," is exactly what Prince Escalus says at the end of *Romeo and Juliet.* Possibly the echo is accidental, though possibly the reader is meant to be reminded of a play, widely regarded as "a tragedy of fate," in which the innocent are victims of prejudice.

This poem can be the starting point for an argumentative research paper concerning the internment (or was it "relocation"?) of Japanese Americans during World War II. Was the internment justifiable, given the circumstances? Was it legal? Is the compensation voted by Congress in 1988 appropriate? (The law promised $20,000 to each of the 75,000 survivors of the camps.)

29
What Are the Grounds of Religious Faith?
(p. 887)

The graying authors of these notes were brought up to believe that one did not publicly discuss money or religion. So far as money goes, we can still see some merit to that position. But there really is no need to avoid the subject of religion, provided that we make it clear that discussion of these essays is not a discussion of the superiority of any one religion but essentially a discussion of *ways of arguing* — in this case about religion.

The Hebrew Bible

Psalm 19 (p. 887)

Modern Bibles with fairly brief but highly useful apparatus (for example, an introduction to the Psalms and helpful annotations) include *The HarperCollins Study Bible, The Oxford Study Bible,* and *The Jerusalem Bible.* The multivolume *Interpreter's Bible* (the Psalms are in vol. 4) has fuller apparatus, but it is somewhat dated; still, it is worth consulting if time is available, as is the one-volume *Interpreter's Bible Commentary,* edited by Charles M. Laymon. The entry on Psalms in *The Anchor Bible Dictionary* (vol. 5), running to about fourteen double-column pages, also provides an excellent survey, though it does not have commentary on each psalm.

C. S. Lewis, in his *Reflections on the Psalms* (1958), says that Psalm 19 is "The greatest poem in the Psalter and one of the greatest lyrics in the world" (63). Lewis, like many other commentators, calls attention to the structure, which he sees as "six verses about Nature, five about the law, and four of personal prayer." The usual academic view is that the psalm probably consists of two poems that at some point were joined, one (verses 1–6) (probably an adaptation of an ancient Canaanite hymn to the sun) celebrating the revelation of God in nature, and the other (verses 7–14) (probably later) praising the revelation of God's will in the Mosaic law. The argument of the poem as a whole is this: The firmament (the sky) reveals God's glory or creative power in nature; the Law — not a lifeless body of rules but a living expression of God's will — reveals God's presence in the history of the world, especially in the history of the people with whom he has made a covenant.

Lewis takes the psalm as a unified poem with transitions that only seem abrupt. He says of the author:

> First he thinks of the sky; how, day after day, the pageantry we see there shows us the splendor of its Creator. Then he thinks of the sun, the bridal joyousness of its rising, the unimaginable speed of its daily voyage from east to west. Finally, of its heat. . . . The key phrase on which the whole poem depends is "there is nothing hid from the heat thereof." It pierces everywhere with its strong, clean ardor. Then at once, in verse 7 he is talking of something else, which hardly seems to him something else because it is so like the all-piercing, all-detecting sunshine. The Law is "undefiled," the Law gives light, it is clean and everlasting, it is "sweet." No one can improve on this and nothing can more fully admit us to the old Jewish feeling about the Law; luminous, severe, disinfectant, exultant. One hardly needs to add that this poet is wholly free from self-righteousness and the last section is concerned with his "secret faults." As he has felt the sun, perhaps in the desert, searching him out in every

nook of shade where he attempted to hide from it, so he feels the Law searching out all the hiding-places of his soul. (63–64)

Two additional points:

1. The device called *synonymous parallelism* is nicely evident twice in the first verse, where *the heavens* is paralleled by *the firmament* and *the glory of God* is paralleled by *his handiwork.* The second verse, too, contains synonymous parallelism, in *uttereth speech* and *showeth knowledge,* but it also illustrates *antithetic parallelism,* since *day unto day* contrasts with *night unto night.*

2. In the King James Version, verse 3 runs thus: "There is no speech nor language, where their voice is not heard." Virtually all modern scholars agree that the addition of *where* is a mistake. The KJV loses the synonymous parallel of the original, which says that the glories of the heavens have "no speech nor language" and that "their voice is not heard." That is, the KJV gives us something consistent (the heavens speak, and they are heard wherever people speak), but it loses the parallelism of the original and it also loses the implied paradox of the original, which in effect says that the heavens are silent — but they nevertheless speak to us.

Paul

1 Corinthians 15 (p. 889)

The selection from Paul (1 Corinthians 15) is the most difficult piece in this chapter, partly because of the seventeenth-century language and partly because it has engendered an enormous body of commentary. Yet the main lines of Paul's argument are clear, and we have no hesitation in recommending the piece, not least because of the moving analogy in verses 37 to 48.

First, a brief bibliographic note. On New Testament ideas of resurrection see the long article in *The Interpreter's Dictionary of the Bible,* 4:43–53. For a short but useful article, see *Harper's Bible Dictionary,* edited by Paul J. Achtemeier et al. On our selection from Paul, most instructors will probably not have time to do more, at most, than to read the commentary in a one-volume work, such as *The Interpreter's One-Volume Commentary on the Bible,* edited by Charles M. Laymon, or *A New Catholic Commentary on Holy Scripture,* edited by Reginald C. Fuller et al. Those who manage to find time to give the epistle additional study may wish to look at volume 10 of *The Interpreter's Bible* or at (for an even more highly detailed line-by-line technical study) Hans Conzelmann's *1 Corinthians.*

Because the text is in some ways very dense, and because we have had more time to do homework than most instructors will have, we offer some tentative responses (based chiefly on our reading of the texts just cited) to the questions that we pose after the selection in the text.

1. Christ's Resurrection (which Paul bases not on the empty tomb — he doesn't even mention the tomb — but on appearances of Christ) proves that we are to believe in Christ's words. The post-Resurrection appearances of Jesus are the main evidence for the Resurrection. These, according to Paul, were witnessed by many (15:5–7), including Paul himself (15:8). (The Gospels agree that Jesus rose from the dead and appeared in bodily form several times to the disciples. See, for instance, Luke 24:16–43; John 20:24–29; Matthew 28:9. Paul's Epistle is earlier than any of the Gospels, but the writers are not thought to have borrowed the idea from Paul. Paul, writing circa A.D. 55, is quoting what he had spoken to the Corinthians a few years earlier, when he founded the community. But as verse 1 indicates, verses 3–7 were already a tradition that he had received from earlier Christians.) In Paul's view, believers in Christ rise with Christ. That is, the Resurrection is not simply a past event but

is of the present. Cf. Galatians 2:20: "For I am crucified with Christ: nevertheless I live; yet not I, but Christ liveth in me: and the life which I now live in the flesh, I live by the faith of the Son of God, who loved me and gave himself for me." (One might also think of Christ's words at the Last Supper, as given in John 6:55: "The man who eats my flesh and drinks my blood enjoys eternal life, and I will raise him up at the last day.")

2. Verses 12–18 argue that the denial of belief in the resurrection of the dead is a denial of belief in the Resurrection of Jesus. For Paul, the issue is pivotal to the Christian faith. If the dead cannot be resurrected, the Resurrection of Christ — who was a man — did not take place, and believers (including Paul and the recipients of his letter) are deluded sinners. If there is no resurrection, believers are in a more miserable situation (verse 19) than if they had no such delusory hope. But for Paul the Resurrection is evidence that Christ's teachings should be accepted. According to verses 20–28, the Resurrection of Christ is an anticipation of the general resurrection of the believers.

3. Those who are "in Adam" will die as a consequence of sin, but those who are "in Christ" (that is, who belong to Christ) will share His victory over death. (*Adam* is the Hebrew word for "man" and thus stands for the natural progenitor of the race. In Romans 5:12–21, Paul contrasts the disobedient, earthly Adam with Christ, who was "the second, the new, the heavenly Adam." Christ — the second or last Adam — gives human beings a higher life, a life-giving spirit. "The first man is earthy, of clay; the second Man is from Heaven.")

4. In verses 30–34 Paul assumes that human beings will not strive morally unless they have hope of personal survival. If death were victorious, Paul says, one would live only for the pleasures of the day. (The assumption may be questioned. Certainly some of the Hebrew prophets [for example, Amos], the Stoics, and many later figures have earnestly sought to live moral lives although they had no hope for survival. Still, one might ask students why one should try to live a moral life —and what *is* a moral life — if evil and death triumph.)

5. Paul uses the transformation of seeds into plants (verses 36–38) as an analogy to explain that the body that dies and the body that is resurrected are radically different and yet are continuous. Analogy seems to us not only the best but perhaps the only effective way of making the point. After all, Paul is dealing with something mysterious, something that cannot be clearly seen in this world, and so he compares it to something that *can* be seen but that nevertheless strikes one (if one thinks about it) with amazement. The point of 42–44 is that the spiritual body, though linked to the physical body as the plant is to the seed, is gloriously superior to the body that dies. The main point of similarity between the two things compared (seed and body) is that both are associated with the earth. And as the seed is transformed, so the body is transformed. By using the word *sown*, in reference to the birth of a human being, he links — even identifies — the two terms of his analogy, body and seed. In verse 45, the analogy having done its work, Paul uses the Adam-Christ contrast. But this contrast is connected with the analogy. Adam, we know from Genesis 2:7, was formed from dust. He is of the earth (like the seed, or the physical body); Christ, as the last Adam, is for Paul the beginning of a new creation that flourishes above the earth.

6. Because the body is resurrected, as is proved by the Resurrection of Christ (testified by various witnesses, including Paul), death is not triumphant. (For Paul, sin is death's weapon.) Teachers of argument will want to call attention to *therefore* in verse 58. Paul's point, apparently, is that awareness of the resurrection of the dead should encourage us that our steadfast devotion to "the work of the Lord" will not be "in vain." For Paul, the death of Christ on the cross obviously has no power to quench that which C. R. Dodd, in *The Meaning of Paul for Today* (1920; reprint of 1957) calls "the living activity of Jesus Christ," and we may see in this idea, Dodd

writes, "a pledge that the natural order itself is subordinate to the ends of the spiritual life" (105). Dodd's comment is worth quoting at some length:

> Putting it negatively, we might say: Suppose Christ, having lived as He did live and died as He did die, had then simply gone under. Suppose no one had henceforward had any sense of dealing with him. Suppose in particular that that great wave of spiritual experience had not passed over the primitive Christians, assuring them that their Lord was in their midst, and making a Church possible. Suppose all this to be true: It would not necessarily destroy the validity of what Christ stood for; but it might leave us asking whether perhaps he was a mere rebel against a universe which, on the whole, stood for something quite different. There are many who do think so. They are our allies in the great fight, but they are apt to be depressing allies. If, on the other hand, we hold the continued personal existence and activity of Jesus Christ to be an assured fact, then we know that what He wrought on our behalf is also wrought into the very fabric of the universe in which we live; and we are at home in it, even while we rebel against its wrongs. (106)

One other point: What the resurrected body will be like is not clear. Christ states that after the resurrection there will be no marrying or giving in marriage and that we shall be like angels in heaven. Dodd says that for Paul the resurrection of the body does not mean the resurrection of the bone, flesh, and blood that we call the body. A person's body today is different in most of its material particles from what it was a few years ago. According to Dodd, Paul is talking about the resurrection of "individual identity." Dodd goes so far as to say that Paul would have been horrified by the phrase "the resurrection of the flesh," in the Apostles' Creed, for Paul did not expect, or want, the "flesh" to rise again. He wanted the "body" to be emancipated from the "flesh."

Finally, some people argue that if (despite the testimony of Paul and of the writers of the Gospels) the evidence *for* the Resurrection is not overwhelming, there is not much evidence *against* it. To argue that we lack evidence demonstrating that anyone other than Christ has been resurrected bodily is, for some people, not much of an argument that Christ was not resurrected. On the other hand, this lack of evidence of other bodily resurrections is, for some, a strong inductive argument against the resurrection of Christ.

Bertrand Russell

Why I Am Not a Christian (p. 893)

Bertrand Russell's essay is relatively long, but it is easy reading. Here we offer a few comments on some of the questions that follow the selection in the text.

1. The audience — presumably most of them members of the National Secular Society, for that is the group Russell was talking to — was predisposed to Russell's point of view and doubtless enjoyed watching him toss Christians to the lions. The genial, almost wiseguy tone (for example, in the reference to the Indian's suggestion that "we change the subject," in para. 5; the reference to striking Prime Minister Baldwin on the cheek, in para. 14; and the reference to the person planting trees, in para. 17) presumes a thoroughly sympathetic audience.

3. What we say about question 1 is relevant here. Russell is being playful.

4. To Russell's charge that apparently an omnipotent creator "could produce nothing better than the Ku Klux Klan or the Fascists," believers in Christianity do not deny that human beings engage in evil.

5. We don't know why Russell ignores the argument that many Christians believe in God *because* Jesus believed in God. We can only conjecture that he thought Jesus' belief was an ill-founded bit of superstition, not worth the attention of a twentieth-century philosopher.

7. Russell's idea of a Christian (paras. 2–3) accords a primary role to certain beliefs — that is, a commitment to the truth of certain claims. He specifies belief "in God and immortality" as well as "some kind of belief about Christ" — at a minimum, that he was "the best and wisest of men." Russell recognizes that this is a pretty "elastic" definition, but it is hard to see how anything narrower will cover the Christian fundamentalists, Christian Scientists, Mormons, as well as more conventional Protestants and Catholics. Moreover, his definition seems consistent with that provided by at least one of our dictionaries (*American Heritage* says that a Christian is anyone who "professes belief in Jesus as the Christ or who follows the religion based on his teachings"). But notice the difference in emphasis: For Russell, it is metaphysical beliefs or doctrines about God and immortality that are crucial, whereas for the dictionary it is the holy life of Jesus that alone matters. It would take little effort to show the tension implicit in these two orientations to what it is to be a Christian.

Russell is not particularly interested in the teachings of Jesus as recorded in the Gospels, at least not until he has examined and disposed of (paras. 4–13) the classic arguments for the God of Christian theism. When he does turn to consider these teachings (para. 15), it seems only for the purpose of twitting the professing Christians of his day who, he implies (probably correctly enough), see no inconsistency between their claiming to be Christians, their daily practices and the social policies they endorse, and the literal precepts of Jesus. Russell leaves it for the reader to relish the irony here. His purpose (question 7) is not to show that these biblical teachings are wrong or that it is unreasonable to believe in Jesus as the Christ but that life in the modern world provides endless opportunities for self-deception and hypocrisy among avowed Christians (para. 16).

8. Speaking of the Gadarene swine (Matthew 8:28–34), Russell suggests (para. 21) that "it certainly was not very kind to the pigs to put the devils into them and make them rush down the hill to the sea. You must remember that He was omnipotent, and He could have made the devils simply go away." Again Russell probably is being mischievous; his feeling for the pigs is suspect, for he was not a vegetarian. (Yes, we are being mischievous too.) The biblical passage, in fact, is one that secularists long before Russell had regularly used to discomfort believers. Thomas Huxley, for example, had his fun with it several decades before Russell turned to it. In Charles Gore et al., *A New Commentary of Holy Scripture* (1928), the passage is recognized as one that contains "all possible difficulties," and a number of highly tentative solutions are put forth, followed by a more confident assertion that "the loss of the herd weighed as nothing in comparison with the rescue of one single human being." Probably, too, a reader should understand that swine were, for Jesus, unclean; transferring the evil spirits into the swine was a way of showing that the "men were purged, and that the spirits that had inhabited them were abominable." In any case, the real point of the story is Jesus' ability to overwhelm the forces of evil.

As for cursing the fig tree (Matthew 21:18–19), nearly all commentators on the text agree that the act is out of character for Jesus. They explain it by conjecturing some confusion in transforming a historical action (some sort of symbolic gesture) into a parable. Of course the passage is deeply troublesome if one believes in a literal interpretation of every line of the Bible, but surely Russell knew that most Christians of his day would grant that the Bible shows the influence (for example, in scribal errors) of the people who recorded it.

Additional Topic for Critical Thinking and Writing

Can it be effectively argued that Russell merely sets us a straw man — a childish version of Christianity — and makes it the object of his attack?

(text pp. 907–908)

Joseph Addison

Ode (p. 907)

In our biographical note and in question 2 in the text we mention the argument from design. For a good short discussion, see "Design Argument" in *Dictionary of the History of Ideas* (1973–74), edited by Philip Wiener. The following account is partly indebted to this source.

In brief, the argument from design is this: We see evidence of intelligent planning (design) in the world, so we may reasonably conclude that the world was created by an intelligence. This idea has a long history, and in one form or another it was held by such distinguished thinkers as Plato, Aquinas, and Newton. (Aristotle seems not to have held it, despite Addison's reference to him in the comment that we quote in the text. Addison was drawing on a quotation by Cicero, attributing the idea to Aristotle.) Newton, for instance, in a comment added in 1713 to his *Principia*, wrote: "This most beautiful system of the sun, planets, and comets, could only proceed from the counsel and dominion of an intelligent and powerful Being." In fact, Newton went further and deduced more than intelligence and power: "He is eternal and infinite, omnipotent and omniscient; that is, his duration reaches from eternity to eternity; his presence from infinity to infinity; he governs all things, and knows all things that are or can be done."

The argument from design reached what perhaps is its most memorable and most popular form in the writings of William Paley (1745–1805), an English theologian, especially in his *Natural Theology; or, Evidences of the Existence and Attributes of the Deity Collected from the Appearances of Nature* (1802). The gist is this: If we examine (for instance) a watch and a stone, we see a contrast. The watch has been designed, its parts all work together for some purpose, and the purpose is evident. Similarly, if we look at human anatomy, we see that every part is so cunningly constructed and so suited to a particular end (for example, the fingers for grasping, the eye for seeing) that it must have been created by "an intelligent designing mind." (Whereas Newton looked to astronomical phenomena, Paley looked chiefly to the biological world around him, though the passage that was most widely quoted concerned the watch.) If a "savage" found a watch, he (today we would say he or she) would infer the existence of a watchmaker. Well, Paley argued, we find a cunningly constructed universe, and so we must infer the existence of a universe-maker, God. And from our perception of this universe we can infer the characteristics of the creator. But he was more cautious than Newton; he denied that "omnipotence" and "omniscience" can be inferred from the creation.

Paley wrote, of course, in pre-Darwinian days and before Tennyson had told us that nature is "red in tooth and claw," but one wonders how he overlooked the violence evident in nature. Obviously he was able to conclude that the creator is benevolent not because he saw benevolence throughout the creation but because the Christianity of his day had taught him that God is benevolent.

Perhaps the strongest criticism of the argument from design was advanced (even before Paley wrote) by David Hume, in *Dialogues Concerning Natural Religion* (posthumously published in 1779). Hume pointed out that the argument is based on an analogy. Analogy is most reliable when the things being compared are closely related, but in this case we are comparing things created within the universe with the universe itself. The universe is *unique;* we have no experience of its origin, whereas we do have experience of the origin of watches.

A second reply to the argument from design points out that if we take the analogy seriously, we can ask, who created the intelligence that created the world? That is, if the analogy leads us to conclude that the world has a designer, it is legitimate for us to take the next step and to ask who designed the designer.

Hume also offers a third criticism. Why conclude from the evidence that the creator is intelligent, benevolent, and so on? Why not take notice of sickness and evil and conclude that the creator is malicious or stupid or incompetent? (In fact, if we argue from analogy, we probably will have to argue that the creator is *im*perfect, since all creators — for example, those of watches — are imperfect.)

Finally, a few words about Addison's poem. The third (final) stanza, which begins by referring to "Silence," is a response to the ancient, but by Addison's day discredited, idea of the music of the spheres. Pythagoras had argued that the planets move at different rates; that they must make sounds in their motion, according to their rates; and that (since in nature all things are harmonious) the combined sounds of the motions of the planets must be musical. Obviously Addison, a spokesman for "reason," could not go along with this as a matter of fact, but he could (and *did*) say that "In Reason's ear" the planets sing; that is, they don't literally sing but nevertheless our reason tells us that their very existence says something to us —and what it says is what the Christianity of Addison's day taught.

Emily Dickinson

Papa above! (p. 908)

First, a brief comment about Emily Dickinson and religion: She clearly was not fond of the patriarchal deity of the Hebrew Bible. "Burglar! Banker — Father," she wrote of this deity, and in a note to Thomas Wentworth Higginson she says that the members of her family, except for herself, "address an Eclipse every morning — whom they call their Father." She seems to have been amused by preachers. She said, of one, that "the subject of perdition seemed to please him somehow." Still, in the words of Charles R. Anderson, in *Emily Dickinson's Poetry* (1960), no reader can doubt that she "faced creation with a primal sense of awe" (17). And, as Anderson and everyone else points out, the Bible was "one of her chief sources of imagery" (18).

Now for the poem. At one extreme, we have encountered readers who find the poem a bitter protest masquerading as a prayer, a scathing attack on the anthropomorphic God of Judaism and Christianity; at the other extreme we have encountered readers who find nothing but piety in the poem, albeit piety in a very Dickinsonian idiom, a piety rooted in affection for God's creatures, even the mouse or rat. Our own view is somewhere in the middle; we hear genial — even affectionate — satire of anthropomorphism, and we also hear acceptance of the strange government of the world. Chiefly, we think, the poem expresses — again, in a characteristically Dickinsonian way — the "primal sense of awe" that Anderson commented on.

"Papa above!" begins with a domesticated version of the beginning of the Lord's Prayer (Matthew 6.9–13, "Our Father who art in heaven"; Luke 11.2–4, "Father"). In "Regard a Mouse / O'erpowered by the Cat" we hear a solemn (and perhaps a wondering) voice, although we grant that one might hear some comedy in the letdown. That is, a reader who expects, after the invocation of the deity, something like "Regard the sufferings of mortals," or some such thing, is surprised to find that the speaker calls attention to a mouse. Or if the reader expects something that continues the idea of the Lord's Prayer, the shift from the expected "Give us this day our daily bread" to a picture of a mouse overpowered by the claws or jaws of a cat is indeed shocking, first because of the implied violence and second because of the ironic contrasts between the meal Jesus spoke of and the meal Dickinson shows.

In the next two lines ("Reserve within thy kingdom / A 'Mansion' for the Rat!") we hear primarily a serious if not a solemn voice, though others hear mockery in the juxtaposition of "Mansion" and "Rat." In any case, there is surely a reference (as we point out in a footnote in the text) to the comforting words Jesus offered to his disciples (John 14.2) when he assured them of reunion in heaven: "In my Father's house are many mansions." But a heavenly mansion (dwelling place) for a rat? We are by no means convinced that Dickinson must have abhorred mice and rats, and that therefore "A 'Mansion' for the Rat" must be ironic. As we see it, the poem thus suggests that the mouse (or rat), destroyed at the moment, has its place in the enduring heavenly scheme. Again, some readers take this to be so evidently absurd or so disgusting that they believe Dickinson is satirizing the idea of a divinely governed universe; others find a tolerant pantheism.

The first two lines of the second stanza get us almost into a Walt Disney world of cute animals — here the mouse is "Snug" and is able to "nibble all the day" — but in the final two lines the camera draws sharply back from the domestic scene and gives us a world of immense space and time, a world indifferent to ("unsuspecting") the mouse (and by implication indifferent to all of us). If there is any satire here, we think it is of persons who believe the "Cycles" are concerned with their existence, but we do not take these lines to be the fierce condemnation of the Judeo-Christian God that some readers take them to be.

The poem raises enough difficulties in itself, but you may want to ask students to compare it with Frost's "Design," which appears later in the chapter in the text. Is Frost's "Design" a sort of restatement of Dickinson's "Papa above!"? Or is Frost's poem something of a reply?

Emily Dickinson

Those — dying, then (p. 909)

The gist of the idea is that belief engenders superior behavior. The faith of her ancestors is, she apparently feels, no longer possible, but it serves to enrich behavior. An *ignis fatuus* (a phosphorescent light — caused by gases emitted by rotting organic matter — that hovers over a swamp) presumably resembles, however weakly, the beautiful flames of heaven and the demonic flames of hell. It is only a will-o'-the-wisp, but at least it is *something*. The image of amputation is shocking, but it can be paralleled in the Bible, for example by "And if thy right eye offend thee, pluck it out, and cast it from thee. . . . And if thy right hand offend thee, cut it off, and cast it from thee" (Matthew 5:29–30).

Gerard Manley Hopkins

Thou Art Indeed Just, Lord (p. 909)

As we say in our brief introduction to the poem, it is hard to speak confidently about Gerard Manley Hopkins's state of mind, but we take the "terrible sonnets" to reveal not a lack of faith in God's existence but in Hopkins's relation to God. In this poem, following Jeremiah, he even dares — for a moment — to attribute injustice to God.

The "sir" in line 2 is worth comment. It is respectful but not affectionate, and it somehow seems to be less than worshipful. Lines 3 and 4 are redolent with injured pride. Lines 5 and 6, even in asserting that God is *not* his enemy, manage to raise the thought of the possibility that God *is* his enemy, and in the reference to the prosperity of "the sots and thralls of lust" there is again a touch of wounded pride. But in the middle of line 9 the protest takes an utterly unexpected turn, when Hopkins sees in "banks and brakes" and "fretty chervil" and "fresh wind" and "birds" a joyous activity or fulfillment that he himself lacks. From a logical, or (more relevant) a doctrinal point of view, this talk about the doings of nature would seem to have no connection with the initial moral and theological problem that the poem begins with, but imaginatively it is right; Hopkins sees himself as less flourishing, less productive, than even the vegetation and wildlife around him. The excited "See" in the middle of line 9 serves (almost without the poet knowing it) to introduce a breath of fresh air, a moment when he gets out of his dwelling on himself, and with "look" in line 10 he seems both to speak enthusiastically to himself and to invite God to share in his joyous perception of His thriving creation. But by the middle of line 12, when the delighted vision of the birds building causes him to contrast their activity with his own unproductiveness, he returns to his painful self-awareness. The bitterness of the image in which he characterizes his unproductive straining as that of a eunuch (lines 12–13) is almost unbearable, as is his self-denunciation (he says he is unable to "breed one work that wakes"), but then, having reached this depth, in the very last line we hear a renewed note in his description of God as "lord of life" and in the prayer in which he associates himself with the natural phenomena that he had earlier envied (the banks and brakes and fretty chervil), "send my roots rain."

In the text we call attention to the passage in which Hopkins compares himself unfavorably with natural phenomena. On one occasion a student expressed great displeasure with the idea of a priest berating himself because he seemed less productive than the natural phenomena around him — it is our recollection that the student objected to a comparison between a moral creature and a creature outside of the world of moral behavior — but we find nothing troubling in these lines. As we read the poem, Hopkins moves from distress that sinners seem to prosper to distress (but here there is a mingling of joy that the reader delights in) that God's lesser creatures are more productive than he. But the vision of a happy natural world, which has brought a moment of joy into the poem, turns painful by the contrast it implies ("birds build — but not I build"). Still, this vision of a flourishing nature is refreshing compared to the opening quatrain, with its assertion that sinners flourish ("sinners' ways prosper"), and it hardly seems objectionable to us that Hopkins speaks of himself as having "roots" (line 14).

Robert Frost

Design (p. 911)

On Robert Frost's "Design," see Randall Jarrell, *Poetry and the Age* (1953); Richard Poirier, *Robert Frost* (1977); Reuben A. Brower, *The Poetry of Robert Frost* (1963); Richard Ohmann, *College English* 28 (Feb. 1967): 359–67; *Frost: Centennial Essays* (1974); and Reginald Cook, *Robert Frost: A Living Voice* (1974), esp. pages 263–67. Brower is especially good on the shifting tones of voice — for example, from what he calls "the cheerfully observant walker on back country roads" who reports "I found a dimpled" — but then comes the surprising "spider, fat and white" — to the "self-questioning and increasingly serious" sextet. Here, for Brower, "the first question ('What had the flower to do . . .') sounds like ordinary annoyance at a fact that doesn't fit in." The next question brings in a new note, and irony in "kindred." For Brower, with the last question ironic puzzlement turns into vision: "What but design of darkness to appall?" And then Brower says that in the final line "the natural theologian pauses — he is only asking, not asserting — and takes a backward step." The title echoes the argument from design, the argument that the universe is designed (each creature fits perfectly into its environment: the whale is equipped for the sea; the camel for the desert), so there must be a designer, God.

The word *design* has two meanings: (1) pattern and (2) intention, plan. Frost certainly means us to have both meanings in mind: There seems to be a pattern and also an intention behind it, but this intention is quite different from the intention discerned by those who in the eighteenth and nineteenth centuries argued for the existence of a benevolent God from the argument from design.

"Design" was published in 1922; below is an early (1912) version of the poem, titled "In White":

A dented spider like a snow drop white
On a white Heal-all, holding up a moth
Like a white piece of lifeless satin cloth —
Saw ever curious eye so strange a sight? —
Portent in little, assorted death and blight
Like the ingredients of a witches' broth? —
The beady spider, the flower like a froth,
And the moth carried like a paper kite.

What had that flower to do with being white?
The blue prunella every child's delight.
What brought the kindred spider to that height?
(Make we no thesis of the miller's plight.)
What but design of darkness and of night?
Design, design! Do I use the word aright?

By the way, an ingenious student mentioned that the first stanza has eight lines, corresponding to the eight legs of a spider, and the second stanza has six, corresponding to the six legs of a moth. What to do? We tried to talk about the traditional structure of the sonnet, and about relevant and irrelevant conjectures, and about the broad overlapping area. Does the conjecture — about as good a criterion as any is — make the poem better?

Additional Topics for Critical Thinking and Writing

1. Do you find the spider, as described in line 1, cute or disgusting? Why?

2. What is the effect of "If" in the last line?

3. Is the revised version a better poem than "In White"? Support your answer with reasons.

Leslie Marmon Silko

The Man to Send Rain Clouds (p. 912)

The church — perhaps especially the Roman Catholic Church — has often adapted itself to the old way beliefs of new converts, sometimes by retaining the old holidays and holy places but adapting them and dedicating them to the new religion. For instance, although the date of birth of Jesus is not known, from the fourth century it was celebrated late in December, displacing pagan festivals of new birth (for example, the Roman Saturnalia, which celebrated the sowing of the crops on December 15 to 17, and the feast of the *Natalis Solis Invicti* (Winter Solstice), celebrating the renewal of the sun a week later).

Practices of this sort have facilitated conversion, but from the church's point of view the danger may be that the new believer retains too much faith in the old beliefs. In Leslie Marmon Silko's story the priest has every reason to doubt that his parishioners have fully accepted Christianity. The Native Americans paint the corpse, attach a feather to it, and ask it to send rain clouds (paras. 1–3); the old men carry medicine bags — that is, shamanistic appurtenances (para. 15); Louise sprinkles corn meal around the corpse (presumably a fertility rite). Father Paul — he is named only once, and for the most part he is just "the priest" or "the young priest," not anyone with a personal identity so far as the other characters are concerned — is kind and well-meaning, and he is even willing to bend the rules a bit, but he knows that he does not have the confidence of the people. He is wrong in suspecting that Teofilo (the name means "beloved of God," from the Greek *theos*, God, and *philos*, loving) is not in front of him, but he is right in suspecting that a "trick" is being played, since the reader knows that the holy water is wanted not to assist Teofilo to get to the Christian heaven but to bring rain for the crops. In Part One we hear Leon say, "Send us rain clouds, Grandfather"; in Part Three we hear Louise express the hope that the priest will sprinkle water so Teofilo "won't be thirsty"; and at the very end of the story we hear that Leon "felt good because it was finished; now the old man could send them big thunderclouds for sure."

We aren't quite sure what to make of the passage in which the water, disappearing as soon as it is sprinkled on the grave, "reminded" the priest of something, but the passage is given some emphasis and surely it is important. Our sense is that the priest vaguely intuits an archetypal mystery, something older and more inclusive than the Roman Catholic ritual he engages in.

Judith Ortiz Cofer

Latin Women Pray (p. 916)

The poem has a wry tone — how odd it is that "Latin women pray / . . . in Spanish to an Anglo God / With a Jewish heritage" — and yet it isn't really very odd, when one thinks about it. The Bible tells us that *all* of us are made in God's image, and we have only to look at our neighbors to see that we are a varied lot. Artists (responding to popular demands) have not hesitated to produce a wide range of images of Jesus, witness the very non-Jewish-looking Christs in painting and sculpture throughout the ages. Most students will be familiar with at least some of these images, possibly Byzantine icons and almost surely the rather sentimental-looking Christs of the nineteenth century that still adorn popular religious texts. A few may even be familiar with images that show an Asian-looking Christ or a black Christ. The images we have of Jesus are at least as varied as the conceptions we have of him, ranging from the Prince of Peace ("all who take the sword will perish by the sword," Matthew 26.52) to the militant figure who drove the money-changers out of the temple (Matthew 21.12–13).

In the United States the commonest image of Jesus shows a man with decidedly Anglo features (though with longer hair than would be respectable in most quarters today), and Judith Ortiz Cofer is moved by the thought that "brown daughters" pray in Spanish to this Anglo male (who seems "unmoved by their persistent prayers"). We take it, however, that the poem is not merely a joke. Probably all people who pray, including Anglos, find themselves "fervently hoping" that their prayers are heard, but they are aware that no matter how deep their faith, they can hardly be confident. Or, better, their prayers may be heard, but whether the prayers will be heeded is another matter, ultimately uncertain and mysterious.

Directory to Documentation Models in MLA Format